PUBLIC FINANCE IN THEORY AND PRACTICE

PUBLIC FINANCE IN THEORY AND PRACTICE

Third Edition

Richard A. Musgrave
H. H. Burbank Professor of Political Economy
Harvard University

Peggy B. Musgrave
Professor of Economics
University of California at Santa Cruz

McGraw-Hill Book Company

New York   St. Louis   San Francisco   Auckland   Bogotá   Hamburg
Johannesburg   London   Madrid   Mexico   Montreal   New Delhi
Panama   Paris   São Paulo   Singapore   Sydney   Tokyo   Toronto

Public Finance In Theory and Practice

Copyright © 1980, 1976, 1973 by McGraw-Hill, Inc. All rights reserved. Printed in the United States of America. No part of this publication may be reproduced, stored in a retrieval system, or transmitted, in any form or by any means, electronic, mechanical, photocopying, recording, or otherwise, without the prior written permission of the publisher.

4 5 6 7 8 9 0 FGRFGR 8 9 8 7 6 5 4 3 2

This book was set in Times Roman by Science Typographers, Inc.
The editors were Bonnie E. Lieberman and James B. Armstrong;
the production supervisor was Charles Hess.
New drawings were done by J & R Services, Inc.
The cover was designed by Robin Hessel.
Fairfield Graphics was printer and binder.

Library of Congress Cataloging in Publication Data

Musgrave, Richard Abel, date
    Public finance in theory and practice.

    Includes indexes.
    1. Finance, Public—United States. I. Musgrave,
Peggy B., joint author. II. Title.
HJ257.2.M87   1980   336.73   79-21473
ISBN 0-07-044122-7

to B. R. B.

Contents

Preface to the Third Edition

The fiscal system, like no other part of the economic picture, is in constant flux; and fiscal theory as well is heading in new directions. Our text, which is aimed at the integration of theory and practice, must keep up with the changing scene. To meet this need, and in response to the fine reception given to the second edition, we now present this third version.

In line with recent events, increased attention has been given to all aspects of inflation, including the effects of fiscal policies on inflation and the effects of inflation on the fiscal system. Recent changes in the tax law have been incorporated, and special attention has been given to the emergence of new issues in tax policy, such as the debate between income tax and consumption tax proponents. The new issues in social security finance, posed by an aging population, have been explored. Novel aspects of fiscal federalism have been examined, including the changing pattern of federal support, the improved position of state finances, and the emergence of regional problems.

In addition, all institutional material has been updated, and many revisions have been made in the treatment of particular topics. The discussion of social-goods theory has been restructured, as has that of cost-benefit analysis and of incidence. Following the suggestions of our readers, we have inserted a general introduction to incidence theory before the chapters on tax structure and have incorporated more specific incidence problems into those chapters. This should eliminate the need for moving back and forth which was occasioned by the earlier arrangement. The discussion of fiscal policy, especially in the context of inflation, has been revised and expanded. As before, the volume is organized to permit selection for and adaptation to courses of different length and difficulty.

Once more we are indebted to many of our colleagues and students for helpful suggestions and critiques. Benjamin Bridges, Robert Kirk, Selig Lesnoy, Carl Shapiro, James Medoff, Stephan Mehay, Richard Nathan, and Dave Terkla have been especially helpful with various parts of this edition. Finally, our thanks go to James Armstrong, who has been most helpful and efficient in seeing this volume through the editing and production process, and to Leslie Burkett for her especially fine editing work.

Richard A. Musgrave
Peggy B. Musgrave

Excerpt from the Preface to the First Edition

Choosing the title for a book is like naming a product. It must describe the basic service which it renders, yet one wishes to differentiate one's own brand. *Public Finance* does the former and *Theory and Practice* serves the latter purpose.

Public Finance is the term which has traditionally been applied to the package of those policy problems which involve the use of tax and expenditure measures. It is not a good term, since the basic problems are not financial but deal with the use of resources, the distribution of income, and the level of employment. Yet the term is familiar and it would be no less misleading to call this a study of public sector economics. While budgetary policy is an important part of that broader subject, it can hardly lay claim to the entire story. Important issues, such as antitrust and monetary policy, remain which fall outside the compass of this volume.

Theory and Practice is the flag under which this study is designed to sail. The subject matter derives its fascination precisely from the close interaction of theory and practice which it entails. On one side there is the vast array of fiscal institutions—tax systems, expenditure programs, budget procedures, stabilization instruments, debt issues, levels of government, Congress, the Executive, city halls, and the voters. On the other, there is the endless stream of issues arising in the operation of these institutions. How big a share of GNP should be included in the public sector and how should the choice of public expenditures be determined? What taxes are to be chosen and who really bears their burden? How should fiscal functions be divided among levels of government? How can a high level of employment be reconciled with stable prices? Pursuit of these issues leads from one end of economic analysis to the other. Thus the distinction between social and private goods lies at the heart of welfare economics while the incidence of taxation is one of the prime applications of microtheory. Public expenditure analysis leads into the nature of capital and how its returns should be measured. Fiscal relations among governmental units involve the rudiments of international economics. Stabilization policy has been central to the development of macro-analysis, and so forth.

Our study, therefore, must combine a thorough understanding of fiscal institutions with a careful analysis of the economic issues which underlie budget policy. There is no way of doing the one without the other. As a result, the institutional material presented here may go a bit further than the theoretically inclined reader may wish and the analytical tools drawn upon may demand a bit more than the institutionalist would like. Though both are needed to understand the subject, the reader may adjust the material to his interest. Road signs are put up where sections of a more technical nature may be passed over by readers who have less interest in pursuing these aspects.

As a study in public policy, this volume deals with many of the central economic and social issues of the 1970s. They are issues which call for resolution by public policy because, like it or not, they cannot be handled adequately through a decentralized market. The existence of externalities, concern for adjustments in the distribution of income and wealth, as well as the maintenance of high employment and price level stability all pose issues which require political processes for their resolution. A public sector is needed to make society work and the problem is how to do this in a framework of individual freedom and justice. Given the central role of the political process in fiscal decisions, the study of public finance thus reaches beyond the sphere of economics narrowly defined and into what might otherwise be considered matters of political science and philosophy. Recognizing the importance of these overlaps, we have not shied away from such problems but have tried to meet them where they arise. *Making the fiscal system work is, after all, a large part of making democracy function.*

An enterprise of this sort, especially a conjugal one, leaves the authors with many debts to colleagues and students who at one time or another have commented on or contributed to various parts of the material. Our thanks to all of them.

Richard A. Musgrave
Peggy B. Musgrave

PUBLIC FINANCE IN THEORY AND PRACTICE

Part One

Introduction

Chapter 1

Fiscal Functions:
An Overview*

A. Introduction: *Subject of Study; Modes of Analysis; Need for Public Sector; Major Functions.* **B. The Allocation Function:** *Social Goods and Market Failure; Public Provision for Social Goods; National and Local Social Goods; Public Provision versus Public Production.* **C. The Distribution Function:** *Determinants of Distribution; Optimal Distribution; Fiscal Instruments of Distribution Policy.* **D. The Stabilization Function:** *Need for Stabilization; Fiscal Instruments of Stabilization Policy; Monetary Instruments; Policy Mix.* **E. Coordination or Conflict of Functions:** *Coordination; Conflict.* **F. Interaction of Private and Public Sectors.** **G. Summary.**

A. INTRODUCTION

In the United States economy of today, over 20 percent of total output is purchased by government budgets and one-third of total income is collected in taxes. Though sizable, this government participation falls short of that in other developed economies, especially those in Western Europe, where the governmental share of economic activity is even larger. Beyond the budgetary

---

Reader's Guide to Chapter 1: This chapter is designed to give the general setting to the fiscal problem, thereby taking a sweeping view of the issues to be considered in detail later on. You may therefore be left with many questions. But don't worry. They will be cleared up (it is hoped) as you proceed.

function, public policy influences the course of economic activity through monetary, regulatory, and other devices. Public enterprise also plays a major role in most European countries, though it is of limited importance in the United States. The modern "capitalist" economy is thus a thoroughly mixed system in which public- and private-sector forces interact in an integral fashion. The economic system can be viewed as neither public nor private, but involves a mix of both sectors.

Subject of Study

This volume deals with the economics of the public sector, including not only its financing but its entire bearing on the level and allocation of resource use, as well as on the distribution of income among consumers. Although our subject matter is traditionally referred to as public finance, it thus deals with the real as well as the financial aspects of the problem. Moreover, it cannot be a matter of "public" economics only. Since the public sector operates in interaction with the private, both sectors enter the analysis. Not only do the effects of expenditure and tax policies depend upon the reaction of the private sector, but the need for fiscal measures is determined by how the private sector would perform in their absence.

Notwithstanding this broad view, we shall not deal with the entire range of economic policy but limit ourselves to that part which operates through the *revenue* and *expenditure* measures of the public budget. Other aspects, such as the regulation of competition through the courts, the operation of public enterprise, and the conduct of monetary policy, are only minor budget items, but of great importance as instruments of economic policy. Yet, we shall deal with them only where they are associated with the economics of budget policy. The term "public sector" as used here thus refers to the budgetary sector of public policy only.

Modes of Analysis

In an analysis of the public sector, various types of questions may be asked. They include the following:

   1. What criteria should be applied when one is judging the merit of various budget policies?
   2. What are the responses of the private sector to various fiscal measures, such as tax and expenditure changes?
   3. What are the social, political, and historical forces which have formed the shape of present fiscal institutions and which determine the formulation of contemporary fiscal policy?

Question 1 asks how the quality of fiscal institutions and policies can be evaluated and how their performance can be improved. The answer requires setting standards of "good" performance. Corresponding to the analysis of efficient behavior of households and firms in the private sector, this calls for a type of economics which, in professional jargon, is referred to as "welfare economics." Its application to the public sector is more difficult, however, because the objectives of fiscal policy are not given but must be determined through the political process. Moreover, objectives of efficiency in resource use must be supplemented by considerations of equity and distributional justice, thus enlarging the sphere of "normative" analysis.

Question 2 must be asked if the outcome of alternative policies is to be traced. If the merits of a corporation profits tax or of a sales tax are to be judged, one must know who will bear the final burden, the answer to which in turn depends on how the private sector responds to the imposition of such taxes. Or if aggregate demand is to be increased, one must know what the effects of the reduction in taxes or increase in public expenditures will be, effects which once more depend upon the magnitude and speed of responses by consumers and firms in the private sector. Analyzing the effects of fiscal measures thus involves what has been referred to as "positive" economics —i.e., the type of economic analysis which deals with predicting, on the basis of empirical analysis, how firms and consumers will respond to economic changes and with testing such predictions empirically.

Question 3 likewise involves a "positive" approach, asking in this case why the fiscal behavior of governments is what it is. This not only is a matter of economics but also includes a wide range of historical, political, and social factors. How do interest groups try to affect the fiscal process, and how do legislators respond to such pressures? How are the fiscal preferences of voters determined by their income and their social and demographic characteristics, and how does the political process, in fact, serve to reflect their preferences?

Need for Public Sector

From the normative view, why is it that a public sector is required? If one starts with the premises, generally accepted in our society, that (1) the composition of output should be in line with the preferences of individual consumers and that (2) there is a preference for decentralized decision making, why may not the entire economy be left to the private sector? Or, putting it differently, why is it that in a supposedly private enterprise economy, a substantial part of the economy is subject to some form of government direction, rather than left to the "invisible hand" of market forces?

In part, the prevalence of government may reflect the presence of political and social ideologies which depart from the premises of consumer choice and decentralized decision making. But this is only a minor part of the story. More important, there is the fact that the market mechanism alone cannot perform all economic functions. Public policy is needed to guide, correct, and supplement it in certain respects. It is important to realize this fact since it implies that the proper size of the public sector is, to a significant degree, a technical rather than an ideological issue. A variety of reasons explain why this is the case, including the following:

1. The claim that the market mechanism leads to efficient resource use (i.e., produces what consumers want most and does so in the cheapest way) is based on the condition of competitive factor and product markets. This means that there must be no obstacles to free entry and that consumers and producers must have full market knowledge. Government regulation or other measures are needed to secure these conditions.

2. They are needed also where, due to decreasing cost, competition is inefficient.

3. More generally, the contractual arrangements and exchanges needed for market operation cannot exist without the protection and enforcement of a governmentally provided legal structure.

4. Even if the legal structure were provided, and all barriers to competition were removed, the production or consumption characteristics of certain goods are such that these goods cannot be provided for through the market. Problems of "externalities" arise which lead to "market failure" and require solution through the public sector.

5. Social values may require adjustments in the distribution of income and wealth which results from the market system and from the transmission of property rights through inheritance.

6. The market system, especially in a highly developed financial economy, does not necessarily bring high employment, price level stability, and the socially desired rate of economic growth. Public policy is needed to secure these objectives.

7. The rate of discount used in the valuing of future (relative to present) consumption may differ as seen from a public and a private point of view.

As we shall see later on, items 3 through 7 are of particular importance from the viewpoint of budget policy.

To argue that these limitations of the market mechanism call for corrective or compensating measures of public policy does not prove, of course, that any policy measure which is undertaken will in fact improve the performance of the economic system. Public policy, no less than private policy, can err and be inefficient; and the basic purpose of our study of public finance is precisely that of exploring how the effectiveness of policy formulation and application can be improved.

Major Functions

Although particular tax or expenditure measures affect the economy in many ways and may be designed to serve a variety of purposes, several more or less distinct policy objectives may be set forth. They include:

1. The provision for social goods, or the process by which total resource use is divided between private and social goods and by which the mix of social goods is chosen. This provision may be termed the *allocation function* of budget policy. Regulatory policies, which may also be considered a part of the allocation function, are not included here because they are not primarily a problem of budget policy.

2. Adjustment of the distribution of income and wealth to assure conformance with what society considers a "fair" or "just" state of distribution, here referred to as the *distribution function.* DISTRIBUTION

3. The use of budget policy as a means of maintaining high employment, a reasonable degree of price level stability, and an appropriate rate of economic growth, with allowance for effects on trade and on the balance of payments. We refer to all these objectives as the *stabilization function.* STABILIZATION

B. THE ALLOCATION FUNCTION

We begin with the allocation function and the proposition that certain goods —referred to here as *social* as distinct from *private* goods—cannot be provided for through the market system, i.e., by transactions between individual consumers and producers. In some cases the market fails entirely, while in others it can function only in an inefficient way. Why is this the case?

Social Goods and Market Failure

The basic reason for market failure in the provision of social goods is not that the need for such goods is "felt" collectively, whereas that for private goods is felt individually. While people's preferences are influenced by their social environment, in the last resort wants and preferences are experienced by individuals and not by society as a whole. Moreover, both social and private goods are included in their preference maps. Just as I can rank my preferences among housing and backyard facilities, so I may also rank my preferences among my private yard and my use of public parks. Rather, the difference arises because the benefits to which social goods give rise are not limited to one particular consumer who purchases the good, as is the case for private goods, but become available to others as well.

If I consume a hamburger or wear a pair of shoes, these particular products will not be available to other individuals. My and their consumption stand in a rival relationship. This is the situation with private goods. But now consider measures to reduce air pollution. If a given air quality improvement EXTERNAL is obtained, the resulting gain will be available to all who breathe. In other VS words, consumption of such products by various individuals is "nonrival," in INTERNAL the sense that one person's partaking of benefits does not reduce the benefits available to others. To put it differently, the benefits derived by anyone's SOCIAL consuming a social good are "externalized" in that they become available to VS all others. This is the situation with social goods. In the case of private goods, PRIVATE the benefits of consumption are "internalized" with a particular consumer, GOODS whose consumption excludes consumption by others.

The market mechanism is well suited for the provision of private goods. It is based on exchange, and exchange can occur only where there is an exclusive title to the property which is to be exchanged. In fact, the market system may be viewed as a giant auction where consumers bid for products and producers sell to the highest bidders. Thus the market furnishes a signaling system whereby producers are guided by consumer demands. For goods such as hamburgers or pairs of shoes this is an efficient mechanism.

Nothing is lost and much is gained when consumers are excluded unless they pay. Application of the exclusion principle tends to be an efficient solution.

But not so in the case of social goods. For one thing, it would be inefficient to exclude any one consumer from partaking in the benefits, when such participation would not reduce consumption by anyone else. The application of exclusion would thus be undesirable, even if it were readily feasible. Furthermore, the application of exclusion is frequently impossible or prohibitively expensive. Gains from air-cleaning measures cannot readily be withheld from particular consumers, streetlights shine upon all who pass by, and so forth. Given these conditions, the benefits from social goods are not vested in the property rights of certain individuals, and the market cannot function. In other instances, such as provision of sewer lines, fees can be charged and the government can function on a market basis.

But where the benefits are available to all, consumers will not voluntarily offer payments to the suppliers of social goods. I will benefit as much from the consumption of others as from my own, and with thousands or millions of other consumers present, my payment is only an insignificant part of the total. Hence, no voluntary payment is made, especially where many consumers are involved. The linkage between producer and consumer is broken and the government must step in to provide for such goods.

Public Provision for Social Goods

The problem, then, is how the government should determine how much of such goods is to be provided. Refusal of voluntary payment is not the basic difficulty. The problem could be solved readily, at least from the theoretical point of view, if the task were merely one of sending the tax collector to those consumers to whom the benefits of social goods accrue. But matters are not this simple. The difficulty lies in deciding the type and quality of a social good that should be supplied to begin with and how much a particular consumer should be asked to pay. It may be reasonable to rule that the individual should pay for the benefits received, as in the case of private goods, but this does not solve the problem; the fundamental difficulty lies in how these benefits are valued by the recipient.

Just as individual consumers have no reason to offer voluntary payments to the private producer, so they have no reason to reveal to the government how highly they value the public service. If I am only one member in a large group of consumers, the total supply available to me is not affected significantly by my own contribution. Consumers have no reason to step forward and declare what the service is truly worth to them individually unless they are assured that others will do the same. Placing tax contributions on a voluntary basis would, therefore, be to no avail. People will prefer to enjoy as "free riders" what is provided by others. A different technique is needed by which the supply of social goods and the cost allocation thereof can be determined.

This is where the political process enters the picture as a substitute for the market mechanism. Voting by ballot must be resorted to in place of dollar voting. Since voters know that they will be subject to the voting decision (be it simple majority or some other voting rule), they will find it in their interest to vote so as to let the outcome fall closer to their own preferences. Thus decision making by voting becomes a substitute for preference revelation through the market. The results will not please everyone, but they will approximate an efficient solution. They will do so more or less perfectly, depending on the efficiency of the voting process and the homogeneity of the community's preferences in the matter.[1]

National and Local Social Goods

Although social goods are available equally to those concerned, their benefits may be spatially limited. Thus, the benefits from national defense accrue nationwide while those from streetlights are of concern only to local residents. This suggests that the nature of social goods has some interesting bearing on the issue of fiscal centralization. As we shall see in Chapter 24, a good case can be made for letting national public services be provided by national government and local public services by local government.

Public Provision versus Public Production

Before considering how such public provision is to be arranged, a clear distinction must be drawn between public *provision* for social goods, as the term is used here, and public *production*. These are two distinct and indeed unrelated concepts which should not be confused with each other.

Private goods may be produced and sold to private buyers either by private firms, as is normally done, or by public enterprises, such as public power and transportation authorities or the nationalized British coal industry. Social goods, such as spaceships or military hardware, similarly may be produced by private firms and sold to government; or they may be produced directly under public management, as are services rendered by civil servants or municipal enterprises. If we say that social goods are provided publicly, we mean that they are financed through the budget and made available free of direct charge. How they are produced does not matter.

This distinction is brought out in the estimates of Table 1-1, where the total product of the United States economy is broken down according to (1)

---

[1]This summary of the allocation function oversimplifies matters in various respects. Two major qualifications, to be noted in the later discussion, are:

(a) It is unrealistic to think of all goods as being divided into those which are private and those which are social. The existence of externalities and the social-goods problems to which they give rise are a matter of degree, and many goods carry both characteristics. Your education, for instance, will benefit not only you (we hope) but also others.

(b) In some instances, government decides to interfere with consumer preferences. Certain goods may be considered meritorious (milk), whereas others are considered harmful (liquor), so that one is subsidized while the other is taxed. This practice does not fit into the above framework and requires further explanation. See p. 84.

TABLE 1-1
Forms of Production and Types of Goods
(United States Data for 1977)

	Privately Purchased Goods (Private Goods) (I)	Goods Provided through Budgets (Social Goods) (II)	Total (III)
1. Public production, billions of dollars	25*	208†	233
2. Private production, billions of dollars	1468	186	1654
3. Total, billions of dollars	1493	394‡	1887§
4. Percentage publicly produced	1.7	52.8	12.4
5. Percentage privately produced	98.3	47.2	87.6
6. Percentage, both forms	100.0	100.0	100.0
7. Percentage of public production	10.7	89.3	100.0
8. Percentage of private production	88.8	11.2	100.0
9. Percentage of total production	79.5	20.5	100.0

Notes:
*Equals income originating in public enterprise. (*Survey*, table 1-14.)
†Equals income originating in government. (*Survey*, table 1-14.)
‡Equals government purchases. (*Survey*, table 1-1.)
§Equals GNP. (*Survey*, table 1-1.)
Other items are residuals.
Source: U.S. Department of Commerce, *Survey of Current Business*, July 1978.

whether the goods and services are purchased privately or provided through the budget (corresponding roughly to our distinction between private and social goods), and (2) whether they have been produced publicly or by private firms. We find that only 12.4 percent of total production is in the public sector (line 4, column III), while 20.5 percent of output is provided through the budget (line 9, column II). We also note that 52.8 percent of the social goods provided through the budget involves public production (line 4, column II), while this ratio is only 1.7 percent for private goods (line 4, column I). Finally, 89.3 percent of public production consists of social goods (line 7, column II) as against 11.2 percent of private production (line 8, column II). In short, production in the United States is undertaken almost entirely in the private sector, although social goods constitute a substantial part of total output; and such public production as exists is very largely for the provision of social goods. Public production for sale (public enterprise) plays only a very minor role.

A similar analysis for other countries[2] shows that the United States ranks low in the public production share, as does Canada. The share rises as we move to the United Kingdom and Sweden, where public enterprise is more important. It becomes much larger for the case of socialist economies such as the U.S.S.R., where the bulk of production is by public enterprise. But one also finds that the share of total output going into social goods differs much less. This is true even with regard to the U.S.S.R., provided that investment in

[2]See Richard A. Musgrave, *Fiscal Systems*, New Haven, Conn.: Yale, 1969, chap. 2.

public enterprise is excluded and that the comparison is limited to final goods. It is thus evident that the decision whether to allocate resources to social goods or to private goods is quite different from that whether to produce any good (private or social) in a public or a private enterprise. A socialist economy, in which most production is public, may produce largely private goods, while a capitalist economy, where all production is private, may produce a larger share of social goods. In fact, provision for social goods poses much the same problem in the capitalist (private firm) as in the socialist (public enterprise) setting. In both cases, it is difficult to determine how such goods are valued by consumers. At the same time, provision for social goods requires taxation, which may interfere with incentives. As explained later, this may be more damaging in the capitalist than in the socialist setting.[3]

C. THE DISTRIBUTION FUNCTION

The allocation function of securing an efficient provision of social goods poses the type of problem with which economic analysis has traditionally been concerned, but the problem of distribution is more difficult to handle. Yet, distribution issues are a major (frequently the major) point of controversy in the determination of public policy. In particular, they play a key role in determining tax and transfer policies.

Determinants of Distribution

In the absence of policy measures to adjust the prevailing state of distribution, the distribution of income and wealth depends first of all on the distribution of factor endowments. Earnings abilities differ, as does the ownership of inherited wealth. The distribution of income, based on this distribution of factor endowments, is then determined by the process of factor pricing, which, in a competitive market, sets factor returns equal to the value of the marginal product. The distribution of income among individuals thus depends on their factor supplies and the prices which they fetch in the market.

   This distribution of income may or may not be in line with what society considers fair or just. A distinction must be drawn between (1) the principle that efficient factor use requires factor inputs to be valued in line with competitive factor pricing, and (2) the proposition that the distribution of income among families should be fixed by the market process. Principle 1 is an economic rule that must be observed if there is to be efficient use of resources. But, proposition 2 is a different matter. For one thing, factor prices as determined in the market may not correspond with the competitive norm. But even if all factor prices, including wages and other returns to personal services, were determined competitively, the resulting pattern of distribution might not be acceptable. It involves a substantial degree of inequality,

[3]See p. 100.

especially in the distribution of capital income; and though views on distributive justice differ, most would agree that some adjustments are required.

Optimal Distribution

This being the case, one must consider what constitutes a fair or just state of distribution. Modern economic analysis has steered shy of this problem. The essence of modern welfare economics has been to define economic efficiency in terms which exclude distributional considerations. A change in economic conditions is said to be efficient (i.e., to improve welfare) if, and only if, the position of some person, say A, is improved without that of anyone else, including B and C, being worsened. This criterion, which may be qualified and amended in various ways, cannot be applied to a redistributional measure which by definition improves A's position at the expense of B's and C's. While the "someone gains, no one loses" rule has served well in assessing the efficiency of markets and of certain aspects of public policy, it contributes little to solving the basic social issues of distribution and redistribution.

The answer to the question of fair distribution involves considerations of social philosophy and value judgment. Philosophers have come up with a variety of answers, including the view that persons have the right to the fruits derived from their particular endowments, that distribution should be arranged so as to maximize total happiness or satisfaction, and that distribution should meet certain standards of equity, which, in a limiting case, may be egalitarian. The choice among these criteria is not simple, nor is it easy to translate any one criterion into the corresponding "correct" pattern of distribution. We shall encounter these difficulties when dealing with redistribution policy and again in interpreting the widely accepted proposition that people should be taxed in line with their "ability to pay."

There are two major problems involved in the translation of a justice rule into an actual state of income distribution. First, it is difficult or impossible to compare the levels of utility which various individuals derive from their income. There is no simple way of adding up utilities, so that criteria based on such comparisons are not operational. This limitation has led people to think in terms of social evaluation rather than subjective utility measurement. The other difficulty arises from the fact that the size of the pie which is available for distribution is not unrelated to how it is to be distributed. We shall find that redistribution policies may involve an efficiency cost which must be taken into account when one is deciding on the extent to which equity objectives should be pursued.

Notwithstanding these difficulties, however, distributional considerations have remained an important issue of public policy. Attention appears to be shifting from the traditional concern with relative income positions, with the overall state of equality, and with excessive income at the top of the scale, to adequacy of income at the lower end. Thus the current discussion emphasizes prevention of poverty, setting what is considered a tolerable cutoff line or floor at the lower end rather than putting a ceiling at the top, as was once the popular view.

Fair DISTRIBUTION

Fiscal Instruments of Distribution Policy

Among various fiscal devices, redistribution is implemented most directly by (1) a tax-transfer scheme, combining progressive income taxation of high-income households with a subsidy to low-income households.[4] Alternatively, redistribution may be implemented by (2) progressive income taxes used to finance public services, especially those such as public housing, which particularly benefit low-income households. Finally, redistribution may be achieved by (3) a combination of taxes on goods purchased largely by high-income consumers with subsidies to other goods which are used chiefly by low-income consumers.[5]

In choosing among alternative policy instruments, allowance must be made for resulting "deadweight losses" or efficiency costs, i.e., costs which arise as consumer or producer choices are interfered with. Redistribution via an income tax–transfer mechanism has the advantage that it does not interfere with particular consumption or production choices. However, even this mechanism is not without its "efficiency cost," since the choice between income and leisure remains affected. But chances are that the distortion will be less than with more selective measures, so that we shall think of the function of the distribution branch as being discharged by a set of direct income taxes and transfers, a process to be examined later under the heading of "Negative Income Tax."

Where redistribution involves an efficiency cost, this consequence by itself establishes no conclusive case against such policies. It merely tells us that (1) any given distributional change should be accomplished at least efficiency cost, and that (2) a need exists for balancing conflicting policy objectives. Efficiency in the broad sense, i.e., an optimally conducted policy, must allow for both concerns.

D. THE STABILIZATION FUNCTION

Having dealt with the bearing of budget policy on matters of allocation and distribution, we must now examine its role as an instrument of macroeconomic policy. Fiscal policy must be designed to maintain or achieve the goals of high employment, a reasonable degree of price level stability, soundness of foreign accounts, and an acceptable rate of economic growth.

Need for Stabilization

Fiscal policy is needed for stabilization, since full employment and price stability do not come about automatically in a market economy but require public policy guidance. Without it, the economy tends to be subject to

---

[4]A *progressive tax* is defined as one in which the ratio of tax to income rises with income.

[5]We disregard here other and nonfiscal approaches to distribution policy, such as manpower and education policies or policies designed to counteract discrimination. These measures, of course, also have an important part to play.

substantial fluctuations, and it may suffer from sustained periods of unemployment or inflation. To make matters worse, unemployment and inflation may exist at the same time. To hold that public policy is needed to deal with these contingencies does not preclude the possibility that public policy, if poorly conducted, may itself be a destabilizer. The purpose of our study, as noted before, is to see how policy can be shaped more effectively.

The overall level of employment and prices in the economy depends upon the level of aggregate demand, relative to potential or capacity output valued at prevailing prices. The level of demand is a function of the spending decisions of millions of consumers, corporate managers, financial investors, and unincorporated operators. These decisions in turn depend upon many factors, such as past and present income, wealth position, credit availability, and expectations. In any one period, the level of expenditures may be insufficient to secure full employment of labor and other resources. Because wages and prices are downward rigid and for other reasons, there is no ready mechanism by which such employment will restore itself automatically. Expansionary measures to raise aggregate demand are needed. At other times, expenditures may exceed the available output under conditions of high employment and thus may cause inflation. In such situations, restrictive conditions are needed to reduce demand. Furthermore, just as deficient demand may generate further deficiency, so may an increase in prices generate further expectations of price rise, leading to renewed inflation. In neither case is there an adjustment process by which the economy is automatically returned to high employment and stability.

A wide range of models may be constructed on the drawing boards of economic theory, some of which are explosively unstable, while others are characterized by dampened oscillations or continuous, limited fluctuations. As we know from the world around us, the actual behavior of the economy is fortunately not explosive. Built-in stabilizers exist which limit fluctuations. There remains, however, a band of instability which is sufficiently serious to require stabilizing action.

This task is complicated by the fact that economies do not operate in isolation but are linked to one another by trade and capital flows. Policies which affect the level of domestic income and prices also affect a country's exports, imports, and balance of payments. This in turn affects the economic position of other countries. Stabilization policy thus must be conducted in a way which involves the complex problems of international policy coordination.

Whereas, in the thirties and forties, the problem of stabilization was mainly seen as one of reaching full employment within a given level of potential output, developments since the fifties have shifted attention to the rate of growth of potential output and inflation. Given the rate of increase in population and/or productivity, the level of aggregate expenditures must be adjusted to rise accordingly, so as to permit demand to expand in line with potential output. This objective will require periodic adjustments in fiscal policy. Furthermore, public policy may not accept the rate of growth of potential output as determined by market forces, but may wish to influence this rate. Since growth depends, among other things, upon the rate of capital formation, the rate of saving and investment incentives become of strategic importance.[6]

Most recently, primary focus has been on inflation. After a high level of employment was reached in the mid-sixties, the problem became one of restraining inflation without losing the full-employment objective. As the experience of the seventies has shown, policy may have to fight inflation and unemployment at the same time. As we shall see, the appearance of "stagflation" has raised doubts regarding the effectiveness of traditional fiscal measures and has called for new approaches.

Fiscal Instruments of Stabilization Policy

The very existence of the fiscal system has an immediate and inevitable influence on the level and structure of demand. Even if fiscal policy was intended to be "neutral," it would be necessary to consider effects on aggregate demand to secure such neutrality. Moreover, changes in budget policy may be used as a positive means of obtaining or offsetting changes in demand.

① **Leverage Effects of a Given Budget** Government expenditures add to total (private plus public) demand, while taxes reduce it. This suggests that budgetary effects on demand will be the larger the higher is the level of expenditures and the lower that of tax revenue. Deficits are expansionary and surpluses are restrictive, but even a balanced budget has an expansionary effect.

② **Changes in Budget Policy** Discretionary policy measures may thus be taken to affect the level of aggregate demand. The government may raise its expenditures or reduce tax rates if demand is to be expanded and vice versa if it is to be contracted. Depending on the type of expenditure or tax adjustments made, consumption or investment in the private sector may be affected, and the promptness of the expenditure response may differ. The policy problem, therefore, is not only one of direction of change but also of selecting the proper type and magnitude of change.

③ **Built-in Responses** Not only may changes in the level of public expenditures or tax rates be used to affect the overall level of demand, but changes in the level of economic activity will also affect public expenditures and tax revenue. Thus, the level of expenditure under any given program may

---

[6]Since the choice of a desirable rate of growth is essentially a question of present versus future consumption, it may be argued that this is a problem of resource allocation rather than of stabilization, and that policy decisions to affect the rate of growth are in fact allocation decisions. There is much to be said for this point of view, but the close link to other aspects of stabilization policy renders it convenient to treat growth in this macropolicy context.

vary with economic activity, most obviously so in the case of unemployment benefits and welfare. More important, the revenue obtained from given tax rates will rise or fall with changes in the level of income or sales subject to tax. Thus, the fiscal system possesses a "built-in flexibility" which responds to changes in the economic scene, even though no changes in policy (changes in tax rates or expenditure legislation) are made. As we shall see later, these built-in responses are helpful under some, and harmful under other, circumstances.

Monetary Instruments

While the market mechanism, if it functions well, may be relied upon to determine the allocation of resources among private goods, economists agree that it cannot by itself regulate the proper money supply. As Walter Bagehot pointed out a century ago, "Money does not control itself." The banking system if left to its own devices will not generate just that money supply which is compatible with economic stability, but will—in response to the credit demands of the market—accentuate prevailing tendencies to fluctuation. Therefore, the money supply must be controlled by the central banking system and be adjusted to the needs of the economy in terms of both short-run stability and longer-run growth. Monetary policy—including the devices of reserve requirements, discount rates, open market policy, and selective credit controls—is thus an indispensable component of stabilization policy.

Policy Mix

Although monetary and fiscal measures supplement each other, they differ in their impact. By using them in proper combination, it is possible to achieve more objectives than would be possible with the use of one policy instrument alone. Thus, a mix of easy money (permitting high expenditures, particularly investment) and a tight budget (reducing the level of aggregate expenditures, particularly consumption) is favorable to economic growth. Given fixed exchange rates, we shall note that monetary policy has a special advantage (due to its effects on international capital movements) in securing balance-of-payments adjustments, while fiscal policy is more effective in dealing with domestic needs. Monetary and fiscal policies, therefore, are linked by the need for obtaining a policy mix which will permit the pursuit of multiple policy objectives.

Moreover, there is a mechanical link between fiscal and monetary measures. While budgetary imbalance (surplus or deficit, depending on the needs of the situation) is an important tool of fiscal policy, this means that the structure of claims, including money and public debt, is changed in the process. These "claim effects" are an inevitable by-product of budgetary imbalance, providing an important link between fiscal and monetary policy.

Fiscal and monetary policies thus interact and complement each other in important ways. But they also suffer from the same weakness. So long as the problems of unemployment and inflation are merely due to a deficiency or excess of aggregate demand, measures aimed at controlling aggregate demand are likely to be effective, but they become less so in dealing with stagflation, where structural maladjustments in various markets are at the root of the problem. As noted before, new uses of the old tools or indeed new tools may be needed to deal with these problems.

E. COORDINATION OR CONFLICT OF FUNCTIONS

It remains to consider how the three basic functions of fiscal policy—allocation, distribution, and stabilization—can be coordinated into an overall pattern of budget policy. Here in particular, our earlier distinction between a normative and a descriptive (or predictive) view of the fiscal process must be kept in mind. Although fully coordinated policy determination permits simultaneous achievement of the various objectives, actual practice gives rise to multiple conflicts.

Coordination

Consider first the coordinated approach as it would proceed under a normative or optimally conducted fiscal process. In dealing with the analysis of public policy, economists have shown that the number of available policy tools must match the number of policy targets. If the tools are insufficient, a conflict among targets must be accepted. Given our three targets—(1) provision for social goods, (2) adjustments in distribution, (3) stabilization—three policy instruments are needed to meet them. Let us think of them as three separate subbudgets or fiscal branches, each designed for the implementation of its particular objective.

The manager of the distribution-branch budget will design a tax-transfer plan to secure the desired adjustment in distribution. For this purpose a full-employment level of income will be assumed. The manager also assumes that the allocation branch provides for public services financed by taxes imposed in line with consumer evaluation thereof. The subbudget of the distribution branch, by its very nature, will be balanced. The manager of the allocation branch in turn will provide for social goods and finance them by taxes imposed in line with consumer evaluation thereof. In so doing, this manager will assume that the distribution branch has secured the "proper" state of income distribution and that the stabilization branch has secured full employment. Again, this will involve a balanced budget.[7] The manager of the stabilization branch, finally, will provide for the necessary adjustment in aggregate demand, again proceeding on the assumption that the other two branches have met their tasks. By its nature this final budget will consist of either taxes or transfers and thus usually be in imbalance. Taxes and transfers

---

[7]Subject, however, to the qualification given in connection with considerations of intergeneration equity. See p. 706.

used to accomplish the stabilization task may be designed so as not to interfere with the "proper" distribution as provided by the distribution branch, i.e., they will be proportional to the "proper" pattern of income distribution.

The reader may wonder how this can be done, since the respective plans of the three branches are closely interdependent. The answer is that the system may be solved by simultaneous determination.[8] When the three budgets have been determined in this fashion, it would then be cumbersome for administrative purposes to carry out each budget separately. Rather, it will be convenient to clear the taxes imposed by the allocation branch, the taxes and transfers of the distribution branch, and the taxes and transfers of the stabilization branch against each other and to implement only the resulting net transfers and taxes with regard to each consumer. In addition to these net taxes and transfers, government must undertake the purchases of products or resources needed to provide for the services of the allocation branch.

The combined or net budget may thus be viewed as a composite of the three subbudgets. It will have a deficit or surplus, depending on the position of the stabilization branch. Whether the net payment system will be progressive, proportional, or regressive is not obvious. The distribution branch component would tend to make it progressive, but it remains to be seen how the allocation component will look.[9]

This system has been spelled out not as a description of the actual budget process, but to show how the various objectives could be coordinated and pursued without interference with one another. We now turn to the real world of fiscal politics, where the situation is quite different.

Conflict

The distinction among the allocation, distribution, and stabilization aspects of fiscal policy is helpful not only in separating more or less distinct policy objectives but also as a guide to fiscal politics. In the real world setting, budget planning frequently does not permit evaluation of the various policy objectives on their own merits. Individual and group interests clash in their implementation so that achievement of one objective is frequently accomplished at the cost of another. The history of fiscal politics abounds with illustrations of this sort.

Allocation and Distribution   Consider first the relationship between allocation and redistribution measures. Although redistribution is accomplished most directly through tax-transfer schemes, it is achieved also by progressive tax finance of the provision for social goods. This is based on an

---

[8]For further discussion, see Richard A. Musgrave, *The Theory of Public Finance*, New York: McGraw-Hill, 1959, chap. 2.

[9]See p. 239.

"ability-to-pay approach," by which the distribution of the tax burden is determined by the ability of a taxpayer to sustain the sacrifice of income reduction, independent of the mix of social goods which is supplied and the benefits derived therefrom. Because of this, the degree of redistribution tends to depend on the levels of programs which are to be financed, thus associating extensive provision for social goods with extensive redistribution.

This approach furthered the cause of redistribution when budgets were small and the additional burden could be imposed on high-income recipients. But over time as budgets have increased relative to national income, additional finance had to be drawn more largely from the middle- and low-income groups, thus reversing this effect. In either case, the linkage between expenditure levels and redistribution does not make for efficiency from a normative point of view. People's attitudes toward redistribution need not coincide with their preferences for social goods. A person who wants public services should not have to oppose them because he or she dislikes redistribution, or vice versa. A better policy choice will be made, therefore, if each issue is taken up on its merits.

Allocation and Stabilization   Now take the relationship between considerations of allocation and stabilization. In times of unemployment, when an expansion of aggregate demand is needed, an increase in government expenditures is often proposed as a remedy. Similarly, at times of inflation, when demand is to be restricted, a case is made for a reduction in such expenditure.

While it is proper for social goods to share in a general expansion or restriction of expenditures, there is no reason why they should account for the entire or major part of the change. As we have seen, the stabilizing adjustment can also be made through increase or reduction in taxes, or reduction or increase in transfers, while leaving the provision for social goods (appropriate at full-employment income levels) unaffected.

Mixing the issues leads to an oversupply of social goods or to wasteful public expenditures when expansion is needed; and to a no less wasteful undersupply when restriction is called for. Moreover, mixing the issues leads to opposition to expansionary fiscal measures by those who oppose high provision for such goods and to opposition to restrictive measures by those who favor high provision of social goods. If the issues are separated, reasonable people may agree on the need for stabilizing action while differing, in line with their preferences, on the appropriate scale at which social goods are to be provided.

Distribution and Stabilization   Finally, consider the relationship between distribution and stabilization objectives. In the past it has been argued during periods of severe unemployment that lower-income groups should be given greater tax relief, since they are likely to spend more of their tax savings than higher-income recipients. The opposite case has been made in times of inflation, namely that taxes on low-income groups should be raised, since they are more potent in reducing demand than taxes on the higher incomes.

Again, proper stabilization action may be interfered with, or redistributional action may be biased, because the two objectives are linked. This is unnecessary since the stabilization adjustment can be made with distributionally neutral taxes—or, for that matter, any pattern of tax distribution—provided only that the overall level of taxation is raised or reduced by a sufficient amount.

Distribution and Growth   Similar problems arise if the growth objective is introduced. A higher rate of growth may call for a higher rate of capital formation, which calls for increased saving and investment. Since the marginal propensity to save is higher among high-income recipients than among low-income groups, and since high-income taxpayers undertake most investment, it would seem that the tax structure should be such as to concentrate on lower incomes. Again the conclusion need not follow if we permit the possibility of public saving which, for any given tax-burden distribution, may be achieved through higher tax rates. But, as we shall see, the conflict may not be resolved as easily if effects of taxation on investment incentives are considered. Unless larger reliance on public investment is introduced, a higher rate of growth may be in conflict with redistribution objectives.

As we view these potential conflicts, it becomes evident that the normative view of neatly attuned subbudgets is not a realistic description of the fiscal process. Rather, it must be understood as a standard against which actual performance may be measured and the quality of existing fiscal institutions may be assessed.

F. INTERACTION OF PRIVATE AND PUBLIC SECTORS

It will be evident from the preceding review that the functions of the public sector differ sharply from those pursued by private households or firms. At the same time, both sectors interact and are linked in the overall economic process. This interdependence is illustrated in Figure 1-1, which presents a highly simplified picture of the circular flow of income and expenditure in the economy. We disregard business saving and the foreign sector and assume that all tax revenue derives from the income tax.

Income and Expenditure Flows   The solid lines of Figure 1-1 show income and expenditure flows in the private sector; the broken lines show public sector flows. Suppose first that there is no public sector. Moving clockwise along the solid lines, we note how households obtain income through the sale of factors in the factor market (line 1), income which is then spent (line 4) or saved (line 5). Saving in turn finances investment expenditure (line 6).[10] Lines 4 and 6, combining in the purchase of products in the product

---

[10]For a discussion of what happens if people wish to invest more or less than others intend to save, see p. 593.

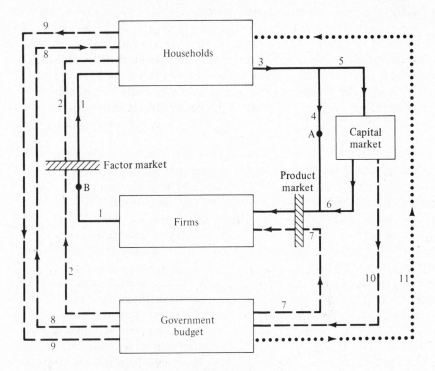

FIGURE 1-1   The Public Sector in the Economy.

market, give rise to the receipts of firms, which in turn are used for the purchase of factor services.

When the government is introduced, we note that factors are bought by the public sector (line 2) as well as by the private sector, and that output of private firms is purchased by government (line 7) as well as by private buyers. In addition to factor and product purchases, the government also makes transfer payments (line 8). Government revenue in turn is derived from taxes (line 9) and from borrowing (line 10).

As this diagram shows, the private and public sector flows are closely intertwined. Note especially that the public sector participates as a buyer in both the factor and the product markets. Its operations are thus an integral part of the pricing system. This is why it is necessary, in designing fiscal policies, to allow for how the private sector will respond. Imposition of a tax at one point in the system—for instance, at point A or point B—may lead to responses which will shift the burden to a quite different point. Moreover, the government not only diverts private income to public use, but through factor and product purchases also contributes to the income flow to households. It is thus misleading to think of the public sector as being "superimposed" on the private sector. Rather, they are both integral and interacting parts of what in fact is a mixed economic system.

Factor and Product Flows   Instead of viewing Figure 1-1 in terms of income and expenditure flows, it may also be interpreted as showing the real flows of factor inputs and product outputs. Reversing the arrows and moving now in a counterclockwise direction, lines 1 and 2 show the flow of factor inputs into the private and public sectors, respectively, while lines 4, 6, and 7 show the flow of firm outputs to private and government buyers, respectively.[11] We must now add dotted line 11 to show the flow of public goods and services which are provided free of direct charge to the consumer. This flow, which bypasses the product market, is financed not through sales proceeds but through taxation or through borrowing. Note also that the goods and services which government thus provides (line 11) are only in part produced by government (based on the factor inputs of line 2); the remainder is privately produced (and sold to government as shown in line 7).

G. SUMMARY

This chapter, being itself in the form of a summary, can hardly be summarized further. However, the main ideas presented are these:

   1.   Modern so-called capitalist economies are in fact "mixed" economies, with one-third or more of economic activity occurring in the public sector.
   2.   For purposes of this book, the term "public sector" is used to refer to those parts of governmental economic policy which find their expression in budgetary (expenditure and revenue) measures.
   3.   Three major types of budgetary activity are distinguished, namely, (1) the public provision of certain goods and services, referred to as "social goods"; (2) adjustments in the state of distribution of income and wealth; and (3) measures to stabilize the level of economic activity in the economy at large.
   4.   In discussing the provision of social goods (the allocation function), reference is made to payment for certain goods and services through budgetary finance. Whether the production of these goods is under public management, or whether the goods and services are purchased from private firms, is a different matter.
   5.   Provision for so-called social goods poses problems which differ from those which arise in connection with private goods. The main point of difference is that social goods tend to be nonrival in consumption and that consumer preferences with regard to such goods are not revealed by consumer bidding in the market. Therefore a political process is required.
   6.   The pattern of distribution which results from the existing pattern of factor endowments and from the sale of factor services in the market is not necessarily one which society considers as fair. Distributional adjustments may be called for, and tax and transfer policies offer an effective means of implementing them, thus calling for a distribution function in budget policy.
   7.   Tax and expenditure policies affect aggregate demand and the level of economic activity. They are also an important instrument in maintaining eco-

---

[11]Since public sector sales (the role of public enterprise) are quite small in the United States economy, this item has been omitted in Figure 1-1. We may think of government enterprises as included under private firms.

nomic stability, including high employment and control of inflation. Hence, the stabilization function enters as the third budgetary function.

8. Fiscal policies may be conducted in centralized or decentralized fashion, with different budgetary functions being more or less appropriate at various levels of governmental activity.

9. Theoretically, budget policies can be designed so that allocation, distribution, and stabilization objectives are accomplished without conflict. But in practice, conflicts are frequent and distortions arise.

10. Although the functions of the public and private sectors differ in important respects, the operations of both interact in the product and factor markets as well as in the income and expenditure flows of the economy.

FURTHER READINGS

Buchanan, J.: "Social Choice, Democracy and Free Markets," *Journal of Political Economy*, December 1954.

Colm, G.: *Essays in Public Finance and Fiscal Policy*, New York: Oxford University Press, 1955, chap. 1.

Houghton, R. W. (ed.): *Public Finance*, Baltimore: Penguin, 1970.

Musgrave, R. A.: *The Theory of Public Finance*, New York: McGraw-Hill, 1959, chaps. 1, 2.

Pigou, A. C.: *A Study in Public Fiance*, London: Macmillan, 1928, part I.

Stigler, George F.: *The Citizen and the State*, Chicago: University of Chicago Press, 1975, chaps. 1, 2, 5.

Chapter 2

Fiscal Institutions*

A. Survey of United States Fiscal Structure: *All Levels Combined; By Levels of Government; The Role of Intergovernmental Grants.* **B. The Constitutional Framework:** *Federal Powers and Limitations; State Powers under Federal Constitution; State Constitutions and Local Powers.* **C. Policy Implementation: (1) Expenditure Policy:** *History of Budget System; Budget Preparation; Form of Presentation; Budgeting Techniques; Congressional Budget Process; Presidential Approval; Execution of Program; Auditing.* **D. Policy Implementation: (2) Tax Policy:** *Executive Preparation; Legislation; Balance of Power; Administration; Reform Proposals for Tax Policy Mechanism.* **E. Overall Fiscal Policy. F. Trust Funds. G. Debt Management. H. Summary.**

The economic rationale for fiscal policy is one thing, and the existing set of fiscal institutions is another. These institutions, like other aspects of political and social organization, are the product of a multiplicity of historical forces, not necessarily well suited to perform the normative tasks set in the preceding discussion. Yet they must be drawn upon to do the job, and they must be adapted to its changing tasks.

* Reader's Guide to Chapter 2: Here we follow the preceding survey of fiscal issues with a similar sketch of fiscal institutions—federal, state, and local. The two chapters are equally important and provide the setting for what is to come.

A. SURVEY OF UNITED STATES FISCAL STRUCTURE

The fiscal structure of the United States for the fiscal year 1975–76 is set forth in Tables 2-1 to 2-3. Since that year, total expenditures and receipts have increased further but the basic pattern has remained unchanged, and this is what matters for our present discussion.

All Levels Combined

We begin with the entire public sector, in which all levels of government— federal, state, and local—are included.

Expenditures   As shown in Table 2-1, column IV, total expenditures to the public, including all levels of government (but leaving out intergovernmental transfers), amounted to $607 billion. Of the total, $100 billion went for national defense, or $120 billion if veterans' programs are included. Interest on public debt was $40 billion, leaving $447 billion for other purposes.[1]

[1]We are dealing here with the breakdown by expenditure functions, including in each function purchases as well as transfer payments. For a breakdown by national income categories, in which these two types of payment are distinguished, see p. 141.

TABLE 2-1
Expenditures to the Public by Function and Level of Government, Fiscal Year 1975–76
(In Billions of Dollars)

		Federal (I)	State (II)	Local (III)	Total (IV)
1.	Expenditure to the public, total	322.0	122.3	162.1	606.6
2.	National defense and international relations	100.4	—	—	100.4
3.	Veterans	19.3	—	—	19.3
4.	Interest	29.3	4.1	6.1	39.6
5.	General government	10.5	9.5	16.1	36.1
6.	Human resources	125.2	84.0	99.2	308.3
7.	Education	3.7	25.5	71.7	100.9
8.	Hospitals and health	3.4	9.9	10.8	24.1
9.	Housing and urban renewal	2.3	0.3	2.9	5.4
10.	Welfare	13.6	20.2	11.3	45.1
11.	Social insurance	102.2	28.1	2.5	132.8
12.	Development	33.3	19.0	11.7	64.0
13.	Natural resources and agriculture	12.3	3.6	1.0	17.0
14.	Transportation	3.6	15.4	10.7	29.7
15.	Postal Service	13.7	—	—	13.7
16.	Space research and technology	3.7	—	—	3.7
17.	Police and fire protection and correction	1.4	3.8	13.4	18.6
18.	Other	2.6	1.9	15.6	20.2

Notes: Since the figures record expenditures to the public, expenditures financed out of intergovernmental grants are included at the recipient level. Because of rounding, detail may not add to totals.
Line 3: Includes veterans' component of categories 7, 8, and 11.
Line 18: Utility and liquor store expenditures are excluded.
Source: U.S. Bureau of the Census, Governmental Finances in 1975–76, tables 5, 7, and 8.

TABLE 2-2
Revenues from the Public by Sources and Level of Government, Fiscal Year 1975–76
(In Billions of Dollars)

		Federal (I)	State (II)	Local (III)	Total (IV)
1.	Revenue from the public, total	323.5	140.5	108.6	572.6
2.	Property	—	2.1	54.9	57.0
3.	Individual income	131.6	21.4	3.1	156.2
4.	Corporation income	41.4	7.3	—	48.7
5.	Death and gift	5.2	1.5	—	6.7
6.	General sales	—	27.3	4.7	32.0
7.	Selective sales and excises	17.2	20.1	2.4	39.7
8.	Customs duties	4.5	—	—	4.5
9.	Other	1.5	9.6	2.4	13.4
10.	Subtotal	201.4	89.3	67.5	358.2
11.	Payroll	85.8	30.9	2.5	119.2
12.	Total taxes	287.2	120.2	70.0	477.4
13.	Charges and miscellaneous	36.3	20.3	38.6	95.3

Notes: Includes net surpluses of public enterprises (Postal Service, utilities, liquor stores). Because of rounding, detail may not add to totals.
Line 8: Includes motor vehicle and operator license revenue.
Line 11: Includes all insurance trust revenue.
Line 13: Includes miscellaneous charges, assessments, interest earnings, and surpluses of public enterprises.
Source: U.S. Bureau of the Census, Governmental Finances in 1975–76.

Of this, the lion's share of $308 billion went into human resources or "people-oriented" programs, including $101 billion for education and $133 billion for social insurance. Next in importance are various items pertaining to economic development. The leading item in this category is transportation with $30 billion, followed by natural-resources development (including agriculture and recreation facilities) with $17 billion. Next, $19 billion was expended for internal protection, while "general government" including other local services claimed $20 billion. Over half of total government expenditures thus went to human resource programs, while 17 percent went to national defense.

Revenues   Total revenue from the public as shown in Table 2-2, column IV, amounted to $573 billion. The difference between this figure and the preceding expenditure total of $607 billion was the public sector deficit for the year.

Total revenue was divided between $477 billion of taxes and $95 billion of charges of various types. Looking at the tax structure, we find that the individual income tax is the most important single source, accounting for one-third of tax revenue. Close behind comes the payroll tax, with 25 percent, followed at some distance by sales taxes (general and selective) at 15 percent, the property tax at 12 percent, and the corporation tax at 10 percent. Death and gift taxes, as well as customs duties, are of quite minor importance in the total revenue picture. The overall tax structure is thus heavily income tax–oriented, the combined yield of the individual and corporation income taxes contributing 43 percent of the total, with payroll taxes next (and rising) in importance.

By Levels of Government

While it is important to keep this overall picture in mind, we must now turn to the way in which expenditures and revenues are divided among the various levels of government. This apportionment is of crucial importance because the United States is a federal, not a unitary, system. As distinct from such countries as the Netherlands and the United Kingdom with their highly centralized system of government, the United States—for better or worse—is a federation with a correspondingly decentralized fiscal system. Moreover, various levels of government specialize in particular expenditure functions, so that the changing role of various functions has brought with it changes in the distribution of expenditures among levels. Since the various levels of government also specialize in different taxes, these changes have also affected the changing composition of the overall tax structure.

Expenditures   As shown in Table 2-1, the federal share in expenditures to the public (with intergovernmental transfers excluded) amounts to 53 percent of the total, with the local government share at 27 percent and the state share at 20 percent. If national defense is excluded and civilian programs only are considered, the federal share falls to 44 percent. If we go a step further and exclude social security benefits, the federal share becomes 32 percent. The direct role of the federal government as a spending agent in civilian programs other than social security is thus only one-third. Most of the business of providing for social goods is accounted for by the lower, and especially the local, level.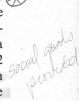

As we move down the columns, the table shows the two biggest items in the federal budget to be social insurance and national defense, claiming 32 and 31 percent, respectively. Other important items are interest, welfare, and natural-resource programs. The major items at the state level are education, welfare, and transportation (mostly highways), accounting for 21, 16, and 13 percent, respectively. By far the most important category at the local level is education with 44 percent, followed by protection with 8 percent. Moving across the lines, we note that the national defense function is all federal, that education is mainly local, and that transportation is largely a state function. Welfare, finally, is of major importance at the state and local level but less so at the federal level.

Revenue   As we turn to the revenue side of the picture, Table 2-2 gives the distribution of revenue from the public (which excludes grant receipts) by levels of government. Of the total, 57 percent went to the federal, 24 percent to the state, and 19 percent to the local level. As shown in column I, the individual income tax furnished 44 percent of federal revenue and the corporation tax another 13 percent, making the federal tax structure highly

TABLE 2-3
Role of Intergovernmental Grants, Fiscal Year 1975–76
(In Billions of Dollars)

	Federal (I)	State (II)	Local (III)	Total (IV)
Revenue				
1. Revenue from public	323.5	140.5	108.6	572.6
2. Grants from federal government	—	42.0	13.6	55.6
3. Grants from state governments	1.3	—	56.2	57.5
4. Grants from local governments	—	2.7	—	2.7
5. Total grants	1.3	44.7	69.8	115.8
6. Total revenue	324.8	185.2	178.4	688.4
Expenditures				
7. Expenditures to public	322.0	122.3	162.1	606.6
8. Grants to federal government	—	1.2	—	1.2
9. Grants to state governments	51.4	—	1.8	53.2
10. Grants to local governments	17.6	56.7	—	74.3
11. Total grants	69.1	57.8	1.8	128.7
12. Total expenditures	391.1	180.1	163.9	735.1

Notes:
Line 1: Includes payroll tax receipts.
Line 7: Includes trust fund expenditures.
Revenues from federal grants as shown in line 2 differ from federal expenditure on grants as shown in column 1, lines 9–11. The difference arises because the revenue figures relate to state and local fiscal years and accounting procedures, whereas the expenditure figures reflect federal practice. Federal grants to local government are direct, with pass-through included at the state level. Because of rounding, detail may not add to totals.
Source: U.S. Bureau of the Census, Governmental Finances in 1975–76.

income tax–intensive. Payroll taxes furnished 27 percent, while excises and customs duties contributed 6 percent.

At the state level, sales and excise taxes contributed 34 percent, with all income taxes together amounting to about 21 percent. At the local level, tax revenue remains dominated, as it always has been, by the property tax, which still contributes over 80 percent of tax revenue and over 50 percent of total revenue. The role of charges, finally, is unimportant at the federal level but more significant at the lower levels, especially for local government, where charges and miscellaneous sources contribute one-third of the total.

The Role of Intergovernmental Grants

The preceding discussion, by focusing on expenditures to and revenues from the public, has bypassed the important problem of intergovernmental transfers. While netting out for the public sector as a whole, they are of major importance regarding the fiscal structure by levels of government.

As shown in lines 1 through 6 of Table 2-3, the federal government does not receive substantial grants, but grants play an important role on the revenue side of the state and local accounts. The states receive 24 percent of their revenue from grants, while local governments receive 39 percent in this form. On the other side of the picture, shown in lines 7 through 12, grants comprise 18 percent of federal and 32 percent of state outlays, but they are not a significant feature at the local level. Grants received by the states originate at the federal level, while grants received by local governments come largely from the states. It is important to note, however, that local governments also receive a substantial amount of federal grants, with over 25 percent of federal grant money going directly to the local level. As we shall see later, this is one of the most important recent developments in our fiscal system.

Due to the importance of grants, the distribution of expenditures to the public by disbursing level as shown in line 7 of the table is less concentrated at the higher levels of government than is that of revenue from the public as given in line 1. The federal, state, and local shares in line 7 are 53, 20, and 27 percent, respectively, while in line 1 they are 56, 24, and 19 percent. As we shall see later, this is significant for two reasons. For one thing, the grant system permits taxes imposed by higher levels of government to be used in the financing of lower-level functions. Since the federal tax system is more progressive, this permits greater reliance on progressive taxation and lesser reliance on the local property tax. For another, the grant system permits a transfer of fiscal resources between jurisdictions so as to secure a better balance of fiscal needs and resources. All this will be considered in a later chapter.[2]

B. THE CONSTITUTIONAL FRAMEWORK

The fiscal framework of the United States is deeply embedded in the Federalist spirit of its Constitution. Whereas a unitary government need not have its taxing and spending powers specified in the constitution, a federation by necessity must have them so specified. Indeed, fiscal arrangements—the assignment of taxing and spending powers—are at the very core of the contract between the constituent governments (the states in the United States, the provinces in Canada, or the *Länder* in the German Federal Republic) which combine to form the federation. While the central government necessarily must have fiscal powers, the composing units retain a sovereign right to conduct fiscal transactions of their own.

This is the spirit in which the fiscal provisions of the U.S. Constitution were written. Prior to the adoption of the Constitution, the Continental Congress was without taxing powers; the Revolutionary War was financed by the taxes of the Colonies and by borrowing. In no small part the Constitutional Convention of 1787 was called to deal with the financial aftermath of

[2]See page 545.

the war. The war debt had to be serviced and financial resources were needed to conduct the business of the future federal government. Fiscal arrangements were thus a major problem confronting the Convention.

Federal Powers and Limitations

The fiscal powers of the federal government were laid down in a series of specific constitutional provisions which came to be further defined by judicial interpretations given to certain other provisions not exclusively aimed at fiscal matters. The major provisions which are specifically fiscal include:

1. The granting of taxing powers
2. The uniformity rule
3. The apportionment rule
4. The prohibition of export taxes

What has been the significance of these provisions, and how have they been modified since their inception?

Taxing Powers and Expenditure Functions   The general enabling statute for federal taxing powers is contained in Article 1, Section 8, of the Constitution, which provides that "the Congress shall have power to levy and collect Taxes, Duties, Imposts and Excises, to pay the Debts and provide for the Common Defense and General Welfare of the United States." By including the "general welfare" as a legitimate objective of federal finance, the Constitution refrains from setting specific limits to the federal government's expenditure function. Interpretation of the term "general welfare" was left to the Congress and the courts, and it has come to be interpreted in an extremely broad sense. The general welfare is understood to cover not only general objectives, such as national defense or the administration of justice, but also highly selective programs aimed at particular regions or population groups, such as aid to Appalachia, grants-in-aid, and transfer payments. Thus, taxation for the finance of almost any type of expenditure program seems to be within the powers of the federal government.

Should the general welfare be understood to justify the use of taxation for regulatory purposes as well as for the financing of expenditures? The courts at times have disallowed such use, but the later trend has been toward permitting regulatory objectives. In all, the taxation and expenditure powers granted by Article 1, Section 8, of the Constitution are broad and general, subject only to certain specific limitations and judicial constraints.

Uniformity Rule   The first specific limitation imposed by the Constitution is the uniformity rule of Article 1, Section 8. The rule requires that "all Duties, Imposts and Excises shall be uniform throughout the United States." Thus, excises on tobacco or automotive products must be applied at the same rate in all states; but if this condition is satisfied, they are permissible, even though their revenue impact will differ greatly among the states, depending on where particular industries are located.[3] Uniformity, in other words, means uniform application of the statute, not of the amount of revenue collected from each state.

The uniformity rule, therefore, has imposed no significant limitation on the development of the federal tax structure on a nationwide basis. On the contrary, it contributed to the development of an equitable system by requiring equal treatment of taxpayers in equal position, independent of their place of residence. Similarly, it is also in accord with the efficiency rule that arbitrary interference with the location of industry—such as would be caused by regionally differentiated taxes—should be avoided. Nor does the uniformity rule interfere with the use of taxes as a tool of general stabilization policy, since tax rates may be raised and lowered on a nationwide basis as required.

The only respect in which the uniformity rule may interfere with the freedom of fiscal policy is in the use of the taxing power to deal with regional problems of economic development. Thus, a lower rate of manufacturer's tax on automobiles produced in West Virginia or Mississippi might serve to encourage automobile production in these states and help develop these particular regions. This could not be done under the uniformity rule.

While the Constitution relates the uniformity rule to "Duties, Imposts and Excises," thereby excluding "direct taxes," this was not meant to invite the use of direct taxes for regulatory purposes on a regionally differentiated basis.[4] Indeed, the framers of the Constitution did not visualize federal use of direct taxes, which at that time were thought of primarily in terms of the property tax. Nor is it likely that the courts would permit a regionally differentiated use of the income taxes under the Sixteenth Amendment.

Apportionment Rule and the Sixteenth Amendment Whereas the uniformity rule proved to be a generally sound constraint in the development of a rational nationwide tax structure, the apportionment rule imposed a barrier which later on was to prove unacceptable. By demanding that "no capitation, or other direct tax shall be levied, unless in Proportion to the Census or Enumeration herein before directed to be taken," Section 9 of Article 1 in effect required all such taxes to be head taxes. Thus, tax rates would vary among states in inverse proportion to their per capita tax base. The rates of property tax, for instance, would have to be twice as high in state A as in state B if the per capita property tax base in A were one-half that in B. Adopted initially as a tradeoff which offered the wealthier states a tax assurance in return for their willingness to accept a smaller number of representatives in the Congress, the need for such assurance did not materialize for over a century, during which time federal revenue needs were met by the proceeds of indirect taxes, especially customs duties.

---

[3]Note we are speaking here of the initial impact or place of *collection*, and not of the place of *incidence*. Tobacco excises are collected in Virginia, and automotive excises in Michigan, while neither is collected in Nevada. Yet, the burden of both taxes will be spread among all three states, depending on their share in cigarette and automotive consumption.

[4]For a discussion of the economic distinction between direct and indirect taxes, see p. 775.

The apportionment clause did not bite until much later, when the federal government came to be confronted with the need for income taxation. The development of a national federal income tax was not possible if the apportionment rule were held by the courts to apply to such a tax. The rate schedule, even if proportional within states, would have had to differ between states, being higher for those states with lower per capita income. This would have been incompatible with the principle of equal treatment of taxpayers with equal capacity on a nationwide basis and would have imposed a regressive pattern of rates on an interstate basis. Under these conditions, a modern income tax could not have been developed, and though the original intent of the clause was to protect the wealthy against the poor *states*, its application in the modern setting would have been to prevent progressive (or even proportional) taxation at the federal level and thus to protect the wealthy against the poor *taxpayer*.

The question, therefore, was whether the income tax should be considered a "Duty, Impost or Excise" under the uniformity rule, or a "capitation or other direct tax" under the apportionment clause. When the first federal income tax was held valid in 1880, the court chose to interpret it as an excise, but the opposite view was taken in 1895, when the second attempt at income taxation was held unconstitutional as an unapportioned direct tax. While it seems evident, in economic terminology, that the income tax is a direct tax, it is less clear which interpretation was the correct one on constitutional grounds. However this may be, the die was cast in the 1895 decision. Given the rising revenue needs of the federal government, especially in response to the potential need for war finance, the problem was resolved in 1913 by the Sixteenth Amendment. It states that "Congress shall have power to levy and collect taxes on incomes, from whatever source derived, without apportionment among the several states, and without regard to census or enumeration," thus clearing the way for a uniform and nationwide income tax. Such a tax was introduced in 1913 and, as noted before, was destined to become the mainstay of the federal revenue structure.

But though federal *income* taxation has been totally freed from the shackles of the apportionment rule, the rule might retain some future significance were additional taxes, such as a federal net worth tax or property tax, to be considered. Such a tax could be held to be in the nature of an income tax and thus be validated under the Sixteenth Amendment, but until the matter is decided, the skeleton of the apportionment rule continues to haunt the tax lawyer's closet.

Export Taxes   Article 1 of the Constitution prohibits the levying of export taxes. Reflecting the desire of the Southern states to protect their interest in cotton exports, this limitation did not prove a major factor in later years. However, it is interesting to note, in connection with the potential use of tax policy to affect the balance of payments, that there is no corresponding prohibition of export subsidies.[5]

[5]See p. 775.

Judicial Constraints   In addition, certain other constitutional provisions have proved relevant to the federal taxing powers.

1.   The Supreme Court once interpreted the federal system, with its "dual sovereignty" of federal and state governments, to imply that the federal government must not tax the instrumentalities of the state and local governments. Accordingly, interest on securities issued by such governments was held exempt from federal income tax and sales to such governments were held not to be subject to federal excise taxes. Though originally exempted on similar grounds, salaries of state and local government employees are generally subject to federal income tax. While the income tax statute continues to exempt interest on state and municipal bonds, chances are that the powers granted by the Sixteenth Amendment would now be interpreted by the Court as overruling the immunity doctrine as applied to the income tax.

2.   Under the due process clause, provided in the Fifth Amendment to the Constitution, the federal government is constrained from depriving people of "life, liberty or property without due process of law." As applied to taxation, this means that taxes must not be arbitrary. While classification and differentiation are allowed, they must be "reasonable." The due process clause has not been interpreted, however, as placing an upper limit on permissible tax rates. At the same time, the taxpayer is protected by being given the right of judicial appeal.

Conclusion   As this brief survey suggests, it can hardly be said that the development of the federal tax structure has been hampered greatly by constitutional provisions. The uniformity rule has been a wholesome constraint and the apportionment rule has been effectively overruled by the Sixteenth Amendment; in addition it has become increasingly apparent that taxation can be used for regulatory purposes. However, constitutional constraints still limit the feasibility of using taxation as an instrument of regional policy.

State Powers under Federal Constitution

Whereas the federal government had to be granted basic taxing powers by the Constitution, the states did not need this provision. Taxing power of the states is vested in their sovereign rights as constituent members of the federation and retained by them under the residual power doctrine. The Constitution, however, imposes certain restrictions on the taxing power of the states, partly through specific provisions and partly again through judicial application of other clauses of the Constitution to tax matters.

General Limitations   Among various general limitations, the following three are of major importance:

1.   In Article I, Section 10, of the Constitution, the states are prohibited specifically from imposing taxes not only on exports (which prohibition also applies to the federal government) but on imports as well. The purpose, of course, was to place the regulation of foreign commerce exclusively under the authority of the federal government.

2. The immunity doctrine, which forbids federal taxation of state and local instrumentalities, also applies in reverse. States may not tax the instrumentalities of the federal government. Thus, interest on federal securities is exempted from state income taxes. State excises cannot be levied on sales to the federal government, and federally owned property cannot be subjected to property tax. Yet salaries paid by the federal government are subject to state income tax. As in the case of federal taxation, the question of what constitutes an "instrumentality" of state and local governments is not defined by the Constitution, and judicial interpretation remains in flux.

3. The due process clause of the Fourteenth Amendment has been interpreted to grant the taxpayer the right of appeal against arbitrary acts of state or local tax administration, similar to its application at the federal level.

4. The equal protection clause of the Fourteenth Amendment holds that a state must not "deny to any person within its jurisdiction the equal protection of the laws." This clause has been interpreted as a prohibition against "arbitrary" classification, and sets some limits (though loosely defined) on the extent to which states may discriminate among various categories of taxpayers.

Interstate Commerce   Most significant and interesting to the economist are the provisions relating to interstate commerce and to the nondiscriminatory treatment of residents of other states. These provisions dealt, almost 200 years earlier, with essentially the same problems currently faced in the debate on fiscal integration of the Common Market countries. Among various provisions which are relevant in this connection, the following should be noted:

1. The due process clause is interpreted to limit a state's taxing power to its own jurisdiction.

2. The equal protection clause is interpreted as prohibiting discrimination against out-of-state citizens. Residents and nonresidents must be treated equally. This nondiscrimination rule, however, does not apply to out-of-state corporations not subject to process within the state.

3. Article VI, Section 8, delegates to the federal government the power "to regulate commerce with foreign nations, and among the several states . . ." This clause has been interpreted as prohibiting states from using their taxing powers so as to interfere with the flow of foreign and interstate commerce. Imports from other states or exports to other states cannot be subject to discriminatory taxes. Thus, the character of the United States as a large area without internal trade barriers but common external tariffs is assured. At the same time, this does not assure neutrality of state taxation with regard to industrial location, as location may be influenced by differential rates of excise or profit taxes.[6]

4. The same clause is applied to regulate the taxation of businesses engaging in interstate commerce. Taxes on gross receipts or profits can be imposed by the various states involved, but the total tax base must be allocated among them on a reasonable basis. There has been considerable debate about what constitutes reasonable allocation, and the entire problem is currently under reconsideration by the Congress.[7]

[6]See p. 316.
[7]See p. 424.

Right to Education and School Finance   Although, in general, the states
have wide freedom in designing fiscal measures, a series of recent cases have
challenged the system for funding the public schools. The bulk of the funds
for public elementary and secondary education comes from the local property
tax. Since the property tax base varies among school districts, children in
low-base districts may be disadvantaged. Starting in 1971 with the decision of
California's Supreme Court in *Serrano v. Priest*,[8] a number of state courts and
lower federal courts found the existing scheme for funding the public schools
unconstitutional. The California Supreme Court in *Serrano v. Priest* held that
the "right to an education in public schools is a fundamental interest which
cannot be conditioned on wealth." Judicial opinions in these cases referred to
both the equal protection clause of the United States Constitution and to the
pertinent provisions of the relevant state constitution. However, primary
emphasis in most of these early cases was placed upon the federal, not the
state, constitution.

Those who hoped that the educational finance decisions would bring
immediate change to the system of local government finance were disap-
pointed by the United States Supreme Court's 1972 decision in *San Antonio
Independent School District v. Rodriguez*.[9] In a 5-to-4 decision, the Supreme
Court held that the Texas system for funding its public schools did not violate
the equal protection clause of the Fourteenth Amendment to the United
States Constitution. The basis of the Court's opinion seems sufficiently broad
to validate the existing financial systems of most, if not all, of the states.

The *Rodriguez* decision did not foreclose arguments that the system of
educational finance of a particular state violates the provisions of that state's
constitution. Since *Rodriguez*, the Supreme Court of New Jersey has held that
New Jersey's scheme of public school finance was unconstitutional under the
New Jersey constitution[10] and a number of states have followed, while
litigation continues in others.

Even though the United States Supreme Court has refused to lay down a
strict rule, state constitutions are interpreted increasingly as calling for equal
educational opportunity and independence of education finance from the
local property tax base. These rulings are implemented only slowly, but in
time they may give rise to a substantial restructuring of state-local finance
and the role of the property tax.

There remains the broader question whether these rulings as to education
might be extended to other expenditures of local government. If so, the line of
thought initiated by the educational finance cases could come to have a
substantial impact upon existing fiscal arrangements with regard to other
services as well. However, most legal experts do not expect such change in the
near future.[11]

[8]5 Cal. 3d 584 (1971).
[9]411 U.S. 1 (1972).
[10]62 N.J. 473 (1973).
[11]For further discussion, see O. Oldman and F. P. Schoettle, *State and Local Taxes and
Finance*, Mineola, N.Y.: The Foundation Press, 1974, pp. 944–1008.

Coordination   This new perspective aside, we conclude that the constitutional framework (as amended) leaves almost complete freedom for development of the fiscal structure. There is no assignment of particular expenditure functions to the various levels, nor is there a prescription (apart from customs duties on foreign imports) about what taxes should be used by the various levels of government.

Although little or no coordination among the fiscal systems of the various levels of government is provided for, the Constitution has been successful in barring direct interference of state taxation with the development and functioning of the United States economy over a large free-trade area. At the federal level, the uniformity rule prohibits regional discrimination for excise taxes. At the state level, interference with interstate trade through customs or export duties is prohibited.

In short, the constitutional framework assures the absence of trade barriers in the sense of internal import duties as well as uniform external duties; but it does not attempt to equalize the fiscal structures of the states, thereby precluding all tax-induced interference with internal commodity or capital flows. Since state and local tax rates have been relatively low, adverse effects on economic efficiency have not been serious and have received less attention than those encountered in the European Common Market, where the conflict is greater since it stems from much larger differentials in national tax structures. Yet, the basic problems are the same. While we shall find that fiscal decentralization has its attractions, it also has its efficiency costs.[12]

State Constitutions and Local Powers

State taxation operates under constraints imposed by state constitutions in addition to these federal constraints. These limitations differ in nature and in degree of detail. In some states, the tax structure is defined in detail, whereas in others, constitutional provisions deal with specific matters, such as debt limitations or prohibition of progressive tax rates. Currently various states are in the process of adopting constitutional amendments to limit the growth of state tax revenue in relation to the growth of state personal income or to other factors. Thereby, the power of the legislature to raise taxes by a simple majority is limited, as is the ability of the states to benefit from built-in, especially inflation-induced, revenue gains.

The fiscal powers of local government are granted by the states, since local government has no sovereign powers of its own. By the same token, the federal limitations on the taxing powers of the states also apply to the derived powers of the local governments. Moreover, led by the passage of Proposition 13 in California, state constitutional limitations are now being placed on the growth of local property tax revenue. Though formally creatures of the states, it can hardly be said that local governments are without political strength of their own. Their fiscal powers may only be "derived" in the constitutional sense, but in reality they have grown beyond this, and local governments,

[12]See p. 531.

especially those of the larger cities, have become full-fledged partners on the fiscal scene. The intergovernment problem of the United States, therefore, is very much a triangular, federal-state-local affair.

C. POLICY IMPLEMENTATION: (1) EXPENDITURE POLICY

We now turn to the governmental system by which the fiscal program is planned, legislated, and executed. Focus will be on the federal operation since it is much the largest, but more or less similar procedures are followed by states and localities. The three groups involved in the federal fiscal process are (1) the voters, (2) the President and the executive branch, and (3) the Congress. Our concern here is with the latter two, leaving the voters for later and more detailed consideration.[13]

The central instrument of expenditure policy is the budget. The four steps involved in the "budget cycle" are (1) formulation of the President's budget by the executive branch; (2) appraisal of the President's budget by Congress and budget legislation; (3) the execution of this legislation by the executive branch; and (4) the auditing by the General Accounting Office. In this chapter, we briefly consider these four functions as parts of the decision-making and administrative process.

History of Budget System

The modern United States budget begins with the Budget and Accounting Act of 1921, some 100 years after Great Britain instituted an annual budget. Based on the earlier (1912) recommendations of President Taft's Commission on Economy and Efficiency, this act charged the President with the preparation of a comprehensive annual executive budget and its presentation to the Congress. The Bureau of the Budget was established as an agency in the executive branch to assist the President in this task and to coordinate the budget requests of the various departments. Thus, presentation of a centrally coordinated program replaced the earlier practice, under which each department submitted direct requests to the appropriation committees of the Congress. Now called the Office of Management and Budget, the budget agency is subject to Presidential arrangement and has been modified and reorganized from one administration to another.

Given the great expansion of the executive departments and their programs over the previous fifty years, the creation of a centralized agency with an executive budget was imperative. Budgeting, by its very nature, requires that all expenditure items be weighed against one another. Consideration of departmental expenditure programs on an isolated basis is not enough. Preparation of the national budget calls for a large amount of coordinated staff work which cannot be done adequately in each department.

At the same time, it must be recognized that the struggle for a centralized and comprehensive budget, beginning with Alexander Hamilton's defeat in

---

[13]See p. 108.

this quest, was not just a drive for efficient budget planning. More important, it was a struggle between executive and congressional control over expenditure policy. With the creation of an executive budget, the President's powers were greatly increased, though less than had been proposed. Thus, the 1921 Act did not follow the recommendations of the Taft Commission to allow the executive a greater degree of policy flexibility, but required the submission of detailed expenditure estimates and appropriations. Moreover, Congress continues to deal directly with the individual departments (Commerce, Labor, Agriculture, and others) before, and again after, the budget has been submitted. The debate over the budget system continues and the historical conflict between executive planning and congressional control is still very much a part of the scene. The most recent development has been the Congressional Budget and Impoundment Control Act of 1974, designed to strengthen budget procedure and the weight of Congress in the budget process.

Budget Preparation

The fiscal year to which the 1981 budget applies runs from October 1, 1980, to September 30, 1981. The executive preparation for the 1981 budget begins in early 1979; the budget is submitted to Congress in January 1980; and legislation is to be completed by the beginning of the fiscal year on October 1. Budget preparation and enactment thus extend over a period of about twenty months.

This lengthiness of the budget process should not be surprising. The federal budget contains the government's detailed expenditure plans, now approaching $550 billion, and by its nature it is an enormously complex instrument. The central responsibility for its preparation rests with the Office of Management and Budget (OMB), prior to 1972 referred to as Bureau of the Budget. The function of the OMB is to coordinate the presentation of budget requests from the various governmental departments and agencies and to see that each department's plan is in line with the "President's Program." Thus, during the early months of 1979, each department is asked to present its budget for the fiscal year 1981, including requirements under existing programs as well as recommended program changes. After an initial review of these plans, the OMB formulates a tentative budget. All this work begins immediately after the fiscal 1980 budget has been submitted to Congress.

The tentative budget is then considered by the President, who studies it together with appraisals of the economic outlook and of revenue projections as presented by the Council of Economic Advisers, the Treasury Department, and other agencies. On the basis of this preliminary picture, the President establishes general fiscal policy and budgetary guidelines. For example, it might be decided that expenditure increases from new programs should be held to $10 billion, or that economies in existing programs should yield an expenditure reduction of $5 billion and that this move is to be combined with tax changes raising revenue by $5 billion. As a result of these deliberations, preliminary expenditure ceilings are set for the various departments and agencies, which are then asked to prepare a second round of expenditure plans.

Beginning in summer, the Office of Management and Budget undertakes an intensive review of these programs. The examination division of the office conducts hearings in which the various agencies are called upon to defend their proposals. In late fall, the revised programs are brought together and presented to the President for final approval. Remaining conflicts between departmental claims have to be resolved by the President. At the same time, revenue prospects and the economic outlook are reviewed and both revenue and expenditure recommendations are evaluated from the point of view of stabilization policy. The final budget message is then drafted for submission in January, within fifteen days after Congress convenes.

Budget preparation is simplified by the fact that budgeting is a continuing process. The government's entire expenditure program cannot be planned anew each year. Expenditures for any one year stem largely from programs which were legislated by Congress in earlier years. Budget planning is a marginal or incremental rather than a total process. This fact simplifies matters, but it also renders change more difficult. In all, the task of budget preparation is enormous, and the Office of Management and Budget plays the key role.

Whereas the various departments and agencies are expected to represent the interests of their particular program areas, it is the function of the OMB, acting for the President, to weigh conflicting claims and to produce an overall budget which is in line with his policy judgments. The ability of the office to perform this task depends upon the authority lent to it by the President. This power is of crucial importance, especially in dealing with the large departments, such as Defense, which traditionally have preferred to deal with Congress directly. While the executive budget process as now operating is reasonably efficient, there is a continuous search for new approaches and methodologies. During the sixties, much emphasis was placed on the development of program budgeting. The Carter administration has featured a zero-base approach. These devices will be noted presently and considered further when techniques of efficient expenditure planning are discussed.[14]

Form of Presentation

The form of budget presentation has changed over the years and is an important factor because it determines the level of understanding with which budgetary matters are discussed. As currently presented, the budget comprises three parts. The first part includes the President's budget message, in which the major policy outlines are set forth and the most important information is summarized. The second part includes a vast amount of detailed estimates, providing the basis for appraisal by the congressional appropriations committees. The third part includes special analyses of certain selected aspects of the total program. In all, the budget documents cover over 1,000

[14]See p. 219.

pages and deal with half a million items. Given the mass and detail of material to be evaluated, a clear and informative arrangement of the budget document is all-important. Basic requirements of good budgeting call for (1) comprehensiveness, (2) a meaningful presentation of the state of budgetary balance, and (3) an appropriate grouping of expenditure items.

Good Budgeting Requirements

① **Comprehensiveness**   Budgeting means the setting of expenditure priorities and the weighing of alternatives. For this purpose, it is essential that a comprehensive view of the government's expenditure programs be taken. Comprehensiveness is necessary also to assure congressional control and to assess the impact of budget operations upon economic activity. This objective has by now been fairly well accomplished. The transactions of trust accounts, which used to remain outside the budget, are now included and the scope for "backdoor financing" has been reduced. However, there still exist off-budget activities such as the Federal Financing Bank and certain other credit activities of the federal government.

② **Budgetary Balance**   In measuring the impact of the budget upon economic activity, the state of budgetary balance (the level of deficit or surplus) is of considerable importance. All expenditures and receipts must be included. Although some problems remain with regard to the treatment of lending and debt transactions, this objective is also met fairly well. Moreover, in recent years the state of budgetary balance has come to be presented in two ways, one being the estimated actual state of balance and the other being the so-called full-employment balance, i.e., the state of balance as it would be (with given expenditure programs and tax laws) if the economy were at full employment. More will be said about these various concepts later on when stabilization policy is examined.[15]

③ **Expenditure Categories**   The budget presents two sets of classifications, one by departments and agencies and the other by functions. The former grouping, as presented in the upper part of Table 2-4, is needed because the departments and agencies are the units to which congressional appropriations are made and which are responsible for the administration of expenditure programs. The functional classification in turn is needed to measure the costs and benefits of entire programs, even though more than one agency may participate therein. Although functional classification was already called for in the 1921 legislation, emphasis thereon is a relatively new development. It is related closely to the previously noted idea of "program and performance budgeting" and the application of cost-benefit analysis to the evaluation of expenditure programs. It will be given closer consideration when we examine program evaluation.[16]

[15]See p. 622.
[16]See p. 219.

TABLE 2-4
Budget Outlays by Agencies and Functions, Fiscal Year 1979
(In Billions of Dollars)

Budget Outlays by Agencies	
Health, Education, and Welfare	199.5
Defense	125.4
Treasury	69.9
Veterans' Administration	20.5
Agriculture	18.4
Transportation	15.8
Housing and Urban Development	10.6
Environmental Protection Agency	4.7
Commerce	3.3
Other	63.5
Total	531.6
Budget Outlays by Functions	
Income security	79.1
National defense	125.8
Interest	57.0
Health	53.4
Education, manpower, and social services	30.2
Veterans' benefits and services	19.3
Transportation	17.6
Natural resources, environment, and energy	19.4
Commerce	3.4
Other	34.7
Total	531.6

Source: *The Budget of the United States Government,* Fiscal Year 1980, pp. 523 and 524.

Time Horizon   Budget presentation has become increasingly geared to the need for considering the longer-run implications of expenditure programs. Thus the Carter administration has adopted the practice of presenting five-year projections, giving outlays for existing as well as recommended programs.

Budgeting Techniques

The task of budgeting involves a decision (1) of how much should be spent and (2) of how the total should be allocated among uses. Step 1 involves balancing the importance of alternative uses in the public and private sector. Step 2 involves balancing the importance of alternative public uses. As discussed in more detail later on, the economist's solution is to equate the marginal benefits derived from alternative uses. But this is easier said than done. As we shall see later, difficult technical problems arise in assessing the costs and benefits of alternative programs. The requirements of stabilization policy must be allowed for, and political pressures must be considered. The likely reception of the President's budget by Congress must be taken into account, and so forth. Given these complexities and the mass of detail that must be decided upon, it is not surprising that there has been a continuing search for systems and techniques which will contribute to a more efficient procedure.[17]

[17]For further discussion of these approaches, see p. 219.

BUDGETING TECHNIQUES

Controllability   Flexibility in budget planning is limited, since budgeting is an ongoing process. Most expenditures are made in line with statutes enacted in the past, so that many outlays are not controllable on a year-to-year basis. Thus the budget for 1980 lists outlays of $397 billion as "relatively uncontrollable," with only $135 billion rated as "relatively controllable." Of the former, $316 billion reflects fixed costs and outlays under open-end programs, while $88 billion reflects prior-year contracts and obligations. Given the fact that 75 percent of the budget is uncontrollable in the short run, the scope for prompt innovation is necessarily limited. The budget process is an incremental process only.

Of course, flexibility increases if a longer period is considered. In the longer run, legislative changes can be made, although even then certain past commitments—such as the obligation to pay interest on public debt or to pay social security benefits—must be honored. Nevertheless, a longer-time horizon permits greatly increased flexibility. This means that budgeting, if it is to meet its real purpose, must be placed on a longer-term basis. This has come to be recognized by recent administrations. As noted before, the 1979 budget contains five-year projections, showing the longer-run costs of existing and proposed programs.

Program Budgeting   Under Presidents Kennedy and Johnson, a new procedure, referred to as planning-programming-budgeting (PPB) was introduced. Emphasis was to be placed on evaluation of entire program areas, rather than on appropriations for particular departments of the government. Moreover, programs were to be analyzed and evaluated in terms of cost-benefit analysis, and a formal procedure was prescribed for this purpose. While fine in principle and feasible in certain settings, especially the Department of Defense, the scheme was applied on too ambitious a scale and thus bogged down in application. However, the principle of program analysis and of project evaluation has remained an important feature or, perhaps, ideal of budget planning.

Zero-Base Budgeting   A more recent approach, featured under the Carter administration, is that of zero-base budgeting. As the term suggests, the idea is to consider the budget as a whole, rather than to examine incremental change only. Each department is required to justify its budget request from the bottom up, evaluating alternative program packages and ranking programs so as to indicate what would be included and excluded at various budget levels. Once more, this is a helpful procedure but clearly impracticable in detailed application. A more realistic approach would be to apply the zero-base method to particular departments or programs on a rotating basis, thus subjecting each unit to detailed zero-base analysis, say, every five years.

Sunset Legislation   This spirit is reflected also in various bills proposing what has come to be referred to as "sunset" legislation. Such laws would terminate ongoing expenditure programs every five years or so and require fundamental reconsideration. Thereby it is hoped to combat the tendency for old expenditure programs to continue long after the circumstances which prompted them have disappeared. This approach is in line with zero-base budgeting on a rotating basis, thus calling for legislative-executive cooperation in its implementation.

Congressional Budget Process

Up to this point, the task of budget preparation is essentially similar to that under a parliamentary type of government. Indeed, it may be simpler since the various cabinet secretaries, in representing their departments, tend to have less independence than do ministers under the parliamentary system, as in the United Kingdom or in Canada. The situation is changed, however, when it comes to legislation. Under the parliamentary system, the government's budget is accepted as a whole without amendment. Thus a more or less unified budget plan is assured. Under the United States system, where executive and congressional powers are separated, Congress is free to change (add to, delete from, or substitute for) the President's budget proposals, and it may deal with them not as a whole but department by department. That Congress is not subject to the kind of party discipline which controls most other parliaments adds to the difficulty.

The Old System   Until recently, the congressional budget process was exceedingly cumbersome and lacking in coordination. After presentation, the President's budget message would be considered first in the House of Representatives. Examined initially by the Appropriations Committee, it would then be passed on to thirteen subcommittees dealing with appropriations for the various departments. After intensive hearings and consideration by these committees, the proposed bills would be returned to the Appropriations Committee which would report them to the floor of the House. After passage, they would then go to the Senate, where the entire procedure would be repeated by the Senate Appropriations Committee and its thirteen subcommittees. After being voted upon on the floor of the Senate, the House and Senate bills would be reconciled in conference, prior to receiving their final vote by both houses.

This procedure involved serious shortcomings. Insufficient coordination among the subcommittees led decisions on the budget to be made in a piecemeal fashion, without reference to a common budget total. Lack of coordination between the efforts of the two houses of Congress resulted in excessive duplication, and Congress did not have the staff support necessary to cope with the mass of detail and the technical problems involved. For these and other reasons, Congress increasingly felt that it had "lost control" over the budget.

Attempts had been made at various times to remedy these difficulties, but a concerted effort to improve matters was made only recently under the Congressional Budget and Impoundment Control Act of 1974, which is now in the process of implementation. This legislation introduced a new congressional budget calendar and proposed a number of major innovations.

A New Approach   A budget committee was established in each house in addition to the existing appropriations committees. In the House, the new committee includes members from the Appropriations and Ways and Means Committees, the other standing committees, and the leadership of both parties. The Senate committee has a somewhat narrower membership. The two committees follow a common schedule, beginning with the preparation of a "concurrent resolution" on the budget. Each committee must report its version of the resolution to its house by April 15. This resolution is to set the overall level of expenditures for the coming fiscal year as well as to provide a breakdown among major functional categories and to determine the required level of revenue. By May 15, the legislative process on the resolution must be completed, including the conference to reconcile the difference between the two resolutions. Then, trying to stay within the limits set by the budget resolution, the Congress acts on the appropriation bills, finishing shortly after Labor Day. In the time remaining before the start of the new fiscal year on October 1, the Congress must pass a second concurrent resolution on the budget in which it reaffirms its earlier decisions or revises them. In the latter case, a reconciliation bill that carries out the dictates of the resolution—including cuts in appropriation bills already enacted—must be passed before the start of the new fiscal year. To help Congress to follow this expeditious and exacting budget schedule, a congressional budget office was established to provide Congress with technical and staff assistance. The new approach is still at an experimental stage and it remains to be seen how successful it will be. So far it appears that the new approach, under the leadership of the Congressional Budget Committee and its staff, has been effective in focusing attention on the macro aspects of budget policy. At the same time, less progress appears to have been made in the basic budget function of securing an efficient allocation of outlays among alternative uses.

Authorizations and Appropriations   As we have seen, Congress does not legislate the budget as a whole, but deals with particular sections of it. The bills take two forms. First, Congress authorizes agencies to undertake particular programs, often with a limit on the amount that may be appropriated for the programs. This basic authorizing legislation may be for one or more years, or it may be unlimited. Subsequent to this basic authorizing legislation, Congress grants appropriations or authorizations to spend. From twelve to fifteen such appropriation bills are passed each year and these may be made on a year-to-year basis or for longer periods, with unused funds carried over to be used later for the originally determined purpose.

The legislative process thus involves both the determination of new programs and the financing of current outlays under previously determined programs. As we may well expect, there is no neat balance between new authority granted and outlays made. Unused authority granted in past years is drawn upon and the balance of unused authority is then carried over to the next year.

Presidential Approval

The President must sign or veto budget bills within ten days, but his hand may be forced. Congress may choose to include particular items in an appropriation bill which are unacceptable to the President even though the rest of the bill meets his approval, and passage cannot be postponed, because funds are needed for current operations. For this reason, budget experts have urged that the President be permitted to veto individual items, but the power to exercise such an item veto has not been granted by Congress.

Execution of Program

After an agency or department has received its appropriation or authorization to spend, it may proceed to do so, but the execution of the program remains under the supervision of the Office of Management and Budget to which periodic financial reports have to be made. The office apportions the amounts expendable in particular time periods and may establish reserves against appropriations.

While the basic task of the Executive is to administer the budget as legislated by the Congress, some flexibility remains. This is desirable, since changing circumstances may make it advisable to speed up or retard certain programs. At the same time, Congress has been concerned with limiting executive discretion in the matter. To forestall potential lack of congressional control because of executive use of previously authorized but unexpended funds, such funds may be rescinded by the Congress. Under the Nixon administration, Congress became concerned with the opposite contingency, that of assuring that legislated programs will in fact be carried out. Thus, the Congressional Budget and Impoundment Control Act of 1974 forestalled executive impoundment of appropriated funds by requiring the President to submit a rescission bill to Congress, without approval of which he must carry out the program. These difficulties arise because, under our executive system of government, the executive branch may not work in concert with Congress.

Auditing

The final stage in the budget cycle is the accounting and auditing function. According to the Budget and Accounting Act of 1921, this function is performed by the General Accounting Office, operating under the Comptroller General. This office is an independent agency, outside the Executive Office of the President and responsible directly to the Congress. Its task is to certify that funds have been expended for the purposes designated by Congress and to perform the auditor's function of certifying that the accounts truthfully reflect the underlying fiscal operations. Although many students of the budget process feel that the auditing function should be integrated with the Office of Management and Budget, Congress is not inclined to grant this request. The political issue is again one of congressional control over expenditure policy.

D. POLICY IMPLEMENTATION: (2) TAX POLICY

While expenditure legislation is required annually to provide appropriations, be it for new or existing programs, this need not be the case with tax policy. The existing tax structure provides a continuous if fluctuating flow of revenue, without further legislative action being taken. Action may be taken, however, to improve (or, for that matter, worsen) the equity of its burden distribution, to adjust overall revenue to changing expenditure requirements, and to adjust tax policy for stabilization purposes, where prompt measures to raise taxes (so as to curtail aggregate demand) or to reduce them (so as to increase demand) may be needed.

The major concern of tax reformers has been with the need to improve the equity of the tax structure so as to make it comply more nearly with prevailing views of what constitutes a fair distribution of the tax burden. Such standards change with the times and the political climate. Tax reform, therefore, is always a popular topic for discussion, but it tends to be handled in a discontinuous fashion. Major structural changes occur once or twice a decade, when political and other circumstances are ripe for "reform." Such changes occurred in 1954 and also in the periods 1962–64 and 1969–70. Typically, these were years following major changes in administration.

Executive Preparation

Tax policy proposals originate at both the executive and the congressional levels. At the executive level, a number of agencies are involved, depending on the nature of the proposal. Equity-oriented reforms of the tax structure are the primary responsibility of the Treasury Department. Administration proposals for such reform are prepared by the Office of Tax Analysis and the Office of the Tax Legislative Counsel. The work draws on a large staff of tax experts, economists, and lawyers, and it is a continuing process. Many tax economists, in and out of government, are consulted and participate in this work. Eventually, usually after a year or more of preparation, the program emerges and is presented to the President for consideration. After the Presidential decisions are made, the final program is formulated and presented to the Congress in a tax message.

Proposals dealing with the short-run stabilization aspects of tax policy involve a wider range of agencies, including the Treasury, the Council of Economic Advisers, the Federal Reserve, and the Office of Management and Budget. The Treasury, moreover, must implement such changes in tax rates as have been decided upon, including prompt adjustments in withholding rates.

Legislation

The President's tax message is initially presented to the Ways and Means Committee of the House, not to the Senate. This is done because, according to Article 1, Section 7, of the Constitution, "All bills for revenue raising shall originate in the House of Representatives." After receiving the administration's recommendations or (at other times) on its own initiative, the Ways and Means Committee holds hearings. These typically begin with a presentation by the Secretary of the Treasury, followed by testimony from outside groups, such as industry representatives, unions, and other organizations. Apart from the Treasury, which is to represent the national interest, the bulk of the testimony is given by interest groups, with only occasional presentations by experts or individuals representing the public interest at large. After the hearings are completed, the bill is formulated in executive session, sessions which are now open to the public. Frequently, the committee bills bear little resemblance to the original administration plan. The bill is then reported out and, after limited discussion, usually subject only to amendments which are approved by the Ways and Means Committee, it is passed by the House.

The bill is then sent to the Finance Committee of the Senate where the same procedures, including a Treasury response to the House bill and extensive hearings, are repeated. Although the Senate legislation is based on the House bill, the Finance Committee is free to make changes or substitute its own proposals. Indeed this committee has become of increasing importance in recent years. The bill is then considered on the Senate floor, where it is discussed extensively, without limitation on amendments. After being voted on by the Senate, the bill is sent to Conference Committee where differences between the House version and the Senate version are ironed out. The bill is then returned to both houses, passed, and sent to the President for signature.

Both the Ways and Means Committee and the Senate Finance Committee are assisted in their complex task by the staff of the Joint Committee on Taxation, as well as by the staff of the Treasury Department. Many committee members serve for lengthy periods and thus acquire considerable technical expertise. However, they are subject to a great deal of political pressure, and vested interests are built up which render action on reform exceedingly difficult to obtain.

Balance of Power

The President rarely vetoes a tax bill, and when vetoed, such bills have usually been sustained by a vote to override the veto. Indeed, the balance of power over tax policy lies very much on the congressional side. Congress may respond to administration recommendations or it may disregard the administration's wishes and substitute its own proposals. Moreover, the committees may act on their own, without administration initiative. Underlying a latent hostility between the Ways and Means Committee and the Treasury Department (independent of party lines) is the congressional feeling that revenue legislation is a constitutional prerogative of the Congress, and not really in the domain of the executive.

Administration

The tax laws, as defined by past revenue acts, are assembled in the Internal Revenue Code. This code is prepared by the legal staff of the Internal Revenue Service (IRS), and it interprets the revenue acts in their detailed application to a vast range of complex situations. Regulations are issued and codified on a continuous basis to guide both taxpayers and tax officials in the administration of the law. The IRS staff engaged in this task includes some 60,000 tax agents, operating in sixty district offices throughout the country. The 1980 budget for the IRS (excluding refunds) amounts to slightly over $2 billion, a lot of money but less than one-half of 1 percent of revenue collected.

Although tax payments in the United States are based on the taxpayer's own declaration rather than on official assessment, the returns (about 120 million in all) must nevertheless be checked and audited. Procedures involved in examining and auditing tax returns are currently being revolutionized by the use of computers, but a large and highly trained staff remains necessary to assess the additional information.

A final function in the taxing process is performed by the tax courts, to which the taxpayer may turn with complaints. The prosecution staff of the Internal Revenue Service in turn may enforce the tax law through criminal charges in the regular system of the federal courts.

Reform Proposals for Tax Policy Mechanism

Many suggestions have been made to improve the operation of the tax policy mechanism. They relate primarily (1) to matters of flexibility and timing, (2) to establishing a closer linkage between tax and expenditure policies, and (3) to obtaining a better representation of the public interest in the committee hearings.

(1) **Flexibility**   The tax-legislative process is too slow and cumbersome to permit flexible use of tax policy for purposes of stabilization. The time lapse between the President's request for a change and the passage of the legislation may range from a speed record of one month (the Excise Tax Reduction Act of 1965), over fourteen months (the 1968 surcharge), to a marathon eighteen months (the Revenue Act of 1962). However, the tax reduction of Spring 1975 was legislated in a period of three months.

This delay in tax action reflects the difficult technical problems which must be dealt with in tax legislation, as well as the heavy political pressures which are brought to bear. While careful and even lengthy discussion is appropriate with regard to structural reforms of the equity type, the resulting delay constitutes a severe handicap when it comes to tax increase or reduction as called for by economic stabilization. For this reason, ways should be found to separate structural reform from such short-run stabilization changes.

To meet this problem, it has been suggested that the President be given the authority to make changes in the level of tax rates as needed for stabilization purposes. To protect congressional control, the Congress could in advance prescribe the pattern of such changes (such as equal percentage changes in income tax liabilities, limited to 10 percent) and could retain the privilege of terminating them. However, such proposals, as advanced in various forms by President Kennedy in 1962 and 1963, and by President Johnson in 1964 and 1966, have as yet been unsuccessful. Congress is adamant in its desire to preserve its control over the purse strings and has not been persuaded as yet that cyclical flexibility may be introduced without endangering this basic prerogative.[18]

Coordinated Tax-Expenditure Policy   A closer linkage between tax and expenditure policies is desirable on two grounds. First, the net impact of fiscal policy on aggregate demand and economic activity depends on both the tax and the expenditure sides of the fiscal process. Thus, the proper levels of taxation and expenditures, as seen from the stabilization point of view, need be determined in relation to each other. As noted earlier, an attempt has been made in the Congressional Budget and Impoundment Control Act of 1974 to provide such a linkage.

Second, it is through decisions on tax policy that Congress is made aware of the cost of expenditure programs. The choice of expenditure programs must be traced in the last resort to the preferences of individual consumers, the taxing process being the instrument through which this tracing has to occur. By separating the two sides of the picture, the opportunity cost of public expenditures is obscured, thus inviting careless expenditure policy; at the same time, expenditure benefits come to be overlooked when tax decisions are made, thus establishing an undue presumption against taxes.

Third, tax and expenditure policy is linked by the role of the so-called tax expenditures.[19] If special tax benefits are given to, say, homeowners, these benefits may be viewed from the expenditure side as housing subsidies. The question then arises of who should have jurisdiction over such items.

Public Interest   Finally, provision should be made for a more balanced presentation at tax committee hearings, involving a more equitable distribution of time between industry and other interest-group representatives on the one side, and tax experts or general representatives of the public on the other. Although industry and other group representatives have much to contribute, especially with regard to technical issues applied to particular industries or firms, their testimony on general policy approaches tends to be biased and should be balanced by other views.

E. OVERALL FISCAL POLICY

The role of expenditure and tax policies as instruments of economic stabilization has been mentioned in various connections. The Executive was charged

[18]See also p. 623.
[19]See p. 367.

with the responsibility for stabilization policy under the Employment Act of 1946, which called upon the President to "promote maximum employment, production and purchasing power," and, as added by the amendment of 1953, to promote "a dollar of stable value," to develop the policies needed for these objectives, and to report thereon to the Congress annually in his Economic Report. In this connection, the act established the Council of Economic Advisers to the Executive and the Joint Economic Committee at the congressional level.

The Council of Economic Advisers, including three council members and a staff, is to assist the President in the preparation of his Economic Report. Designed to play a key role in formulating the broader economic guidelines for stabilization policy as well as to deal with other aspects of the government's economic program, the actual role and influence of the Council has differed with various administrations, each administration having, in the end, its own style of policy formulation.

At the congressional level, the Council of Economic Advisers is matched by the Joint Economic Committee. This committee receives the President's Economic Report submitted in late January, after the State of the Union Message and the Budget Message have been submitted. The report is discussed in hearings and evaluated by the committee. The creation of this committee and its work have been of great value in promulgating an intelligent approach to economic policy in fiscal and other areas and in raising the level of congressional economic policy discussion. However, the committee has declined in importance in recent years, with the Congressional Budget Committee taking its place.

F. TRUST FUNDS

While revenue and expenditure legislation are generally separated, with tax revenue accruing to the government's General Fund, they are linked in the case of trust funds, which therefore carry a special role in the fiscal system. Total trust fund receipts for fiscal year 1980 are estimated at $212 billion, or nearly one half of total budget receipts. Of this, $117 billion goes to the Old Age and Disability Insurance (OASDI) Fund, $20 billion to the Health Insurance (HI) Fund, and $16 billion to the Unemployment Insurance Fund, all financed by earmarked payroll tax contributions. Another major fund is the Highway Trust Fund, financed by $8 billion of gasoline tax receipts.[20]

The role of these trust funds and the merit of linking particular receipts and expenditures in this fashion will be considered later. Here we only need to note that trust fund expenditures are not subject to annual appropriations but are made by each trust fund according to the rules set by Congress for its operations.

[20]See *Budget of the United States Government*, Fiscal Year 1980, Special Analyses, p. 80.

G. DEBT MANAGEMENT

Finally, the role of debt management should be noted. The responsibility for debt management is vested in the Treasury Department although, as we shall see later, it is closely related to monetary policy as determined by the Federal Reserve System.[21]

One function of debt management is to carry out the debt transactions necessitated by a current budget deficit or surplus, involving either an increase or a decrease in the total debt. Even though the budget may be balanced over the fiscal year as a whole, the flow of tax receipts and expenditures is not synchronized on a monthly basis, so that intermediate debt financing is required. A further function, and much more important in volume, takes the form of vast refunding operations. They must be undertaken as maturing debt instruments are replaced by new issues of varying maturities and other characteristics. This operation is carried out by the Debt Management Division of the Treasury, with the assistance of the Federal Reserve Bank of New York.

The function of debt management is essentially an executive one and does not involve direct congressional participation. However, Congress has legislated certain restrictions with which debt managers must comply, including an interest ceiling and the provision that debt obligations may not be issued at a price below their maturing value. Also, Congress imposes a ceiling on the total debt which the Treasury is allowed to incur. This ceiling is used by Congress as an additional device to control the level of expenditures, even though expenditure programs have been authorized previously by congressional legislation. As will be seen later, this limitation has interfered with efficient conduct of public debt operations, but it is now being discarded.[22]

H. SUMMARY

This review of federal fiscal institutions, sketchy though it is, suffices to show that the fiscal machinery is highly complex and slow-moving. Many functions appear in triplicate, at the executive, House, and Senate levels, and coordinating them is cumbersome and not readily responsive to changing situations. Yet, much of this is the reflection of our executive system of government and of the bicameral organization of Congress. The expenditure and taxing process, which is at the heart of the governmental operation, can hardly be exempted from the constraints which this system imposes. At the same time, better coordination could be obtained and a higher degree of flexibility should be possible, without disturbing the basic balance provided by our constitutional system.

Regarding the federalist nature of our fiscal system, the major factors to

[21]See p. 697.
[22]See p. 701.

be kept in mind are these:

1. The United States fiscal structure is decentralized, with 53 percent of expenditures to the public made at the federal level, 20 percent at the state level, and 27 percent at the local level. Revenues from the public are more centralized, with shares of 56, 24 and 19 percent, respectively. The difference reflects the importance of grants from higher to lower levels of government.

2. The levels of government differ in their expenditure structures, with defense and transfer programs of major importance at the federal, highway expenditures at the state, and education expenditures at the local levels.

3. A similarly sharp difference exists in the composition of the revenue structure, with the federal level characterized by income, the state level by sales, and the local level by property taxes.

4. Transfers from the federal to the state and from the state to the local level have greatly increased in importance over the last decade. There has also been a significant increase in direct federal grants to local government.

Fiscal affairs are conducted within a framework provided by the United States Constitution. The major constitutional provisions are:

5. The Constitution requires federal taxes to be uniform in all states and originally called for direct taxes to be proportioned among states on a per capita basis. The uniformity requirement is still in effect but raises no problem with regard to national taxes; but the apportionment requirement has been largely eliminated by the Sixteenth, or Income Tax, Amendment.

6. The Constitution does not lay down explicit rules with regard to federal expenditure policy, but authorizes the government to provide "for the common defense and general welfare of the United States."

7. The Constitution prohibits states from imposing export taxes and requires state taxation to comply with its "due process" and "equal protection" clauses.

8. Recently it has been argued that the "equal protection" clause requires states to provide equal education services to all citizens, a requirement which would cut across local differentials and which is still in process of adjudication.

9. Localities are the creatures of the states and their fiscal powers derive from the state constitutions.

Implementation of expenditure policy has been examined for the federal level. Both the executive and legislative branches have an important role to play:

10. The primary responsibility for budget preparation rests with the executive. The budget (fiscal) year runs from October 1 to September 30. The budget is presented to the Congress in January and legislation thereon is to be completed by October 1.

11. In presenting the budget, expenditures are shown on both a departmental and a functional basis and the major rules of good budgeting (in particular, the requirement of comprehensiveness) are reasonably well observed.

12. Congressional legislation in 1974 has provided for a streamlined and coordinated congressional budget procedure which is designed to strengthen the role of the Congress in the budget process.

The implementation of tax policy follows a similar pattern:

13. Proposals for tax legislation are made by the Treasury and are submitted to the Ways and Means Committee of the House, where all tax legislation must originate. After a vote by the House, they are passed on to the Senate Finance Committee and, after a vote on the Senate floor, the two bills are reconciled in Conference Committee.

14. Shortcomings of the existing tax policy process include a lack of flexibility with regard to the use of tax adjustments for purposes of stabilization policy. Moreover, deliberation of the tax committees suffers from inadequate exposure to the general interest as distinct from presentations on behalf of particular interest groups.

FURTHER READINGS

The Budget of the United States Government, Fiscal Year 1980.

Burkhead, Jesse, and Jerry Miner: *Public Expenditure*, Chicago: Aldine-Atherton, 1971.

Economic Report of the President, latest year.

Governmental Finances in 1975–76, U.S. Department of Commerce, Bureau of the Census.

Groves, Harold M.: *Financing Government*, 6th ed., New York: Holt, 1965. See chap. 19, "The Power to Tax," for a discussion of the constitutional setting.

Pechman, Joseph A.: *Federal Tax Policy*, 3d ed., Washington: Brookings, 1977. See chap. 3.

Smithies, Arthur: *The Budgetary Process in the United States*, New York: McGraw-Hill, 1955.

Tax Foundation: *Facts and Figures on Government Finance*, New York, 1977.

Wildawsky, Aaron: *The Politics of the Budgetary Process*, Boston: Little, Brown, 1964.

Chapter 3

The Theory
of Social Goods*

A. Social Goods and Market Failure: *Market for Private Goods; Market Failure due to Nonrival Consumption; Market Failure due to Nonexcludability; Combined Cause of Market Failure; Summary.* **B. Provision for Social Goods:** *Comparison with Private Goods; Need for Budgetary Provision.* **C. Models of Efficient Allocation:** *Meaning of Efficiency; The General Model for Private Goods; The General Model for Social Goods; Social-Goods Allocation through the Budget.* **D. Summary.**

The theory of social goods provides a rationale for the allocation function of budget policy. Although difficult to resolve, it is of central importance to the economics of the public sector, just as the theories of the consumer household and of the firm are at the core of private sector economics.

* Reader's Guide to Chapter 3: This and the following chapter explore in some detail the complex problems underlying the theory of social goods. The central problem posed by the nature of "pure" social goods is discussed in sections A and B, which are essential to an understanding of the public sector problem. In section C we turn to a more rigorous statement of the theoretical issues, as viewed now in a general equilibrium setting. To show the similarities involved, efficient allocation for both private and public goods is considered. This discussion requires some acquaintance with intermediate microtheory. Though important for a more penetrating look at the problem, section C may be passed over by readers with less interest in theory.

Our task in this chapter is to extend the principles of efficient resource use to the public sector. Some believe this to be impossible and hold that the determination of budget policy is a matter of "politics" only and not amenable to economic analysis. This view is unduly pessimistic. While it may not be possible to find and implement the optimal solution, not all feasible policies are equally good. Efficiency of resource use, here as in the private sector, is a matter of degree, and economic analysis can help us in seeking the best answers. The task is to design a mechanism for the provision of social goods which, operating in a democratic setting, will be as efficient as feasible. The politics of fiscal policy, and the inefficiencies which may ensue, are considered in a later chapter.

A. SOCIAL GOODS AND MARKET FAILURE

The market economy, when certain conditions are met, serves to secure an efficient use of resources in providing for private goods. Consumers must bid for what they wish to buy, and they thus reveal their preferences to producers. Producers, in trying to maximize their profits, will produce what consumers want to buy and will do so at least cost. Competition will assure that the mix of goods produced corresponds to consumers' preferences. This view, of course, is a highly idealized picture of the market system. In reality, various difficulties arise. Markets may be imperfectly competitive, production may be subject to decreasing cost, consumers may lack sufficient information or be misled by advertising, and so forth. For these reasons, the market mechanism is not as ideal a provider of private goods as it might be. But even so, it does a good job and better than can be done otherwise.

At the same time, the market cannot solve the entire economic problem. First, and most important in the present context, it cannot function effectively if there are "externalities," by which we mean situations where consumption benefits cannot be limited and charged to a particular consumer or where economic activity results in social costs which need not be paid for by the producer or the consumer who causes them. Next, the market can respond only to the effective demand of consumers as determined by the prevailing state of income distribution, but society still must judge whether this is the distribution it wants. Finally, there is the problem of unemployment and inflation which does not take care of itself automatically. These are three of the major areas where budget policy comes into play. This chapter deals with the first, or allocation, aspect.

Market for Private Goods

The market can function only in a situation where the "exclusion principle" applies, i.e., where A's consumption is made contingent on A's paying the price, while B, who does not pay, is excluded. Exchange cannot occur without property rights, and property rights require exclusion. Given such exclusion, the market can function as an auction system. The consumer must bid for the product, thereby revealing preferences to the producer, and the producer, under the pressures of competition, is guided by such signals to produce what consumers want. At least, such is the outcome with a well-functioning market.

This process can function in a market for private goods—for food, clothing, housing, automobiles, and millions of other marketable private goods—because the benefits derived therefrom flow to the particular consumer who pays for them. Thus, benefits are internalized and consumption is *rival*. A hamburger eaten by A cannot be eaten by B. At the same time, the nature of the goods is such that exclusion is readily feasible. The goods are handed over when the price is paid, but not before. But budgetary provision is needed if consumption is nonrival and/or if exclusion cannot be applied.

Market Failure due to Nonrival Consumption

Social goods are goods the consumption of which is *nonrival*. That is, they are goods where A's partaking of the consumption benefits does not reduce the benefits derived by all others. The same benefits are available to all and without mutual interference. Therefore it would be inefficient to apply exclusion even if this could readily be done. Since A's partaking in the consumption benefits does not hurt B, the exclusion of A would be inefficient. Efficient resource use requires that price equal marginal cost, but in this case marginal cost (the cost of admitting an additional user) is zero, and so should be the price.

Consider, for example, the case of a bridge which is not crowded, so A's crossing will not interfere with that of B. Charging a toll would be quite feasible, but so long as the bridge is not heavily used, the charge would be inefficient since it would curtail use of the bridge, the marginal cost of which is zero. Or consider the case of a broadcast, which (by jamming devices) can be made available only to those listeners who rent clearing devices. Again, the jamming would be inefficient since A's reception does not interfere with B's. These are situations where exclusion *can* be applied but *should not* be because consumption is nonrival. Since the marginal cost to previous users of adding an additional consumer is zero, no admission price should be charged.

But though the marginal cost of admitting additional users is zero, the cost of providing the facility is not. This cost must be covered somehow, and it must be determined how large a facility should be provided. In the absence of exclusion (either because exclusion is not feasible, or because it is undesirable), this task cannot be performed through the usual market mode of sale to individual consumers. Provision through the market cannot function and a political process of budget determination becomes necessary.

Market Failure due to Nonexcludability

A second instance of market failure arises where consumption is rival but exclusion is not feasible. While most goods which are rival in consumption also lend themselves to exclusion, some rival goods may not do so. Consider, for example, travel on a crowded cross-Manhattan street during rush hours. The use of the available space is distinctly rival and exclusion (the auctioning off or sale of the available space) would be efficient and should be applied. The reason is that use of crowded space would then go to those who value it most and who are willing to offer the highest price. But such exclusion would be impossible or is too costly at this time.[1] We are dealing with a situation where exclusion should but cannot be applied. Here the difficulty of applying exclusion is *the* cause of market failure. Public provision is required until techniques can be found to apply exclusion.

Think once more of why nonexcludability causes market failure. If partaking in consumption is not made contingent on payment, people are not forced to reveal their preferences in bidding for social goods. Such, at least, is the case if the number of participants is large. Since the total level of provision will not be affected significantly by any one person, the individual consumer will find it in his or her interest to share as a "free rider" in the provision made by others. With all consumers acting in this fashion, there is no effective demand for the goods. The auction system of the market breaks down, and once more a different method of provision is needed.

Combined Cause of Market Failure

Although the features of nonrival consumption and nonexcludability need not go together, they frequently do. In these instances—for example, air purification, national defense, streetlights—exclusion both *cannot* and *should not* be applied. Since these are situations where both causes of market failure overlap, it may be futile to ask which is *the* basic cause. However, the nonrival nature of consumption might be considered as such, since it renders exclusion undesirable (inefficient) even if technically feasible.

Summary

The previous distinctions may be summarized as follows, classifying goods into four cases, according to their consumption and excludability characteristics:

CONSUMPTION	EXCLUSION	
	Feasible	Not Feasible
Rival	1	2
Nonrival	3	4

Characteristics of case 1 depict the clear-cut, private-good case, combining rival consumption with excludability. This is where provision through the market is both feasible and efficient. In all other cases, market failure occurs. For the setting reflected in case 2, market failure is due to nonexcludability or

---

[1]As suggested by Prof. William Vickrey of Columbia University, electronic devices may eventually be developed which record the passage of vehicles through intersections and permit the imposition of corresponding charges, adjusted to differ for rush hours and slack periods. Such charges may then be billed to the vehicle owner via a computer, and the costs of crowding city streets may thus be internalized.

high costs of exclusion, while for the setting of case 3 it is due to nonrival consumption. In the fourth case, both impediments are present. If we applied the term "social good" to all situations of market failure, cases 2, 3, and 4 would all be included. It is customary, however, to reserve the term for cases 3 and 4, i.e., situations of nonrival consumption. These situations, to be sure, are similar to case 2 in that provision is made without exclusion and hence a budgetary process is called for. But they differ from case 2 in that the existence of nonrival consumption changes the conditions of efficient resource use from those applicable where consumption is rival.

B. PROVISION FOR SOCIAL GOODS

The nonrival nature of social-good consumption thus has important bearing on (1) what constitutes efficient resource allocation, i.e., allocation of resources to produce at least cost what consumers want most, and (2) the procedure by which their provision is to be achieved.[2] These implications will now be examined more carefully.

Comparison with Private Goods

To explore problem 1, it is helpful to compare the familiar demand and supply diagram for private goods with a corresponding construction for social goods. The latter, as we shall see presently, is unrealistic, but it is nevertheless useful in noting essential differences between the two situations. The left side of Figure 3-1 shows the well-known market for a private good. D_A and D_B are A's and B's demand curves, based on a given distribution of income and prices for other goods. The aggregate market demand curve D_{A+B} is obtained by horizontal addition of D_A and D_B, adding the quantities which A and B purchase at any given price. SS is the supply schedule, and equilibrium is determined at E, the intersection of market demand and supply. Price equals OC and output OH, with OF purchased by A and OG by B where $OF + OG = OH$.

The right side of the figure shows a corresponding pattern for a social good. We assume for this purpose that consumers are willing to reveal their marginal evaluations of the social good—say, weather forecasting installations—it being understood that daily reports will be available free of charge. As before, D_A and D_B are A's and B's respective demand curves, subject to the same conditions of given incomes and prices for other goods. Since it is unrealistic to assume that consumers volunteer their preferences, such curves have been referred to as "pseudo-demand curves." But suppose for argument's sake that consumer preferences are revealed. The crucial difference from the private-good case then arises in that the market demand

---

[2]As noted previously, the term "provision" as used here refers to the choice and payment process rather than to whether the products or services are *produced* by government (such as the services of civil servants) or by private firms (such as private construction companies which are contracted to build public roads). See p. 9.

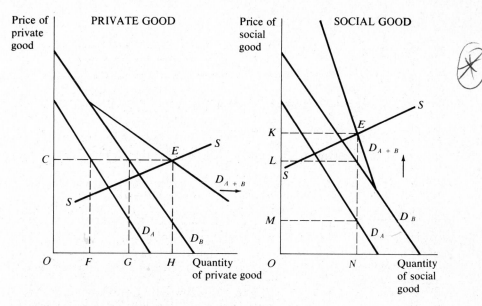

FIGURE 3-1   Demand for Private and Social Goods.

curve D_{A+B} is obtained by vertical addition of D_A and D_B, with D_{A+B} showing the sum of the prices which A and B are willing to pay for any given amount.[3] This follows because both consume the same amount and each is assumed to offer a price equal to his or her true evaluation of the marginal unit. The price available to cover the cost of the service equals the sum of prices paid by each. SS is again the supply schedule, showing marginal cost (chargeable to A and B combined) for various outputs of the social good. The level of output corresponding to equilibrium output OH in the private-good case now equals ON, which is the quantity consumed by both A and B. The combined price equals OK, but the price paid by A is OM while that paid by B is OL, where $OM + OL = OK$.

Returning to the case of the private good, we see that the vertical distance under each individual's demand curve reflects the marginal benefit which derives from its consumption. At equilibrium E, both the marginal benefit derived by A in consuming OF and the marginal benefit derived by B in consuming OG equals marginal cost HE. This is an efficient solution because marginal benefit equals marginal cost for each consumer. If output falls short of OH, marginal benefit for each individual exceeds marginal cost and each will be willing to pay more than is needed to cover cost. Net benefits will be gained by expanding output so long as the marginal benefit exceeds the marginal cost of so doing, and net benefits are maximized therefore by producing OH units, at which point marginal benefit equals

[3]This vertical addition of the demand curves for social goods was first presented by Howard R. Bowen in *Toward Social Economy*, New York: Rinehart, 1948, p. 177.

marginal cost. Welfare losses would occur were output expanded beyond *OH*,
for marginal cost would thereby exceed marginal benefits.

Now compare this solution with that for social goods. The vertical
distance under each individual's demand curve again reflects the marginal
benefits obtained. Since both share in the consumption of the same supply,
the marginal benefit generated by any given supply is obtained by vertical
addition. Thus the equilibrium point *E* now reflects the equality between the
sum of the marginal benefits and the marginal cost of the social good. If
output falls short of *ON*, it will again be advantageous to expand because the
sum of the marginal benefits exceeds cost, while an output in excess of *ON*
would imply welfare losses, since marginal costs outweigh the summed
marginal benefits.

Thus the two cases are analogous but with the important difference that
for the private good, efficiency requires equality of marginal benefit derived
by *each* individual with marginal cost, whereas, in the case of the social good,
the marginal benefits derived by the two consumers differ and it is the sum of
the marginal benefits (or marginal rates of substitution) that should equal
marginal cost. This is the rule established by Professor Samuelson in his
pathbreaking articles of the late 1950s and which is explored further in
section C of this chapter.[4]

[4]A somewhat different way of presenting the case of the social good, first used by the
Swedish economist Erik Lindahl, is as follows:

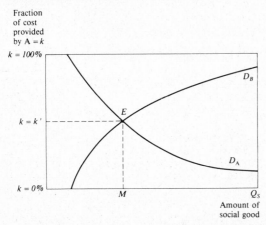

The vertical axis measures k or the fraction of unit cost contributed by A. Given the unit cost C
and assuming it to be constant, kC is the price paid by A and D_A is his demand schedule for the
social good S. Since B's price equals $(1-k)C$, and since both share the same quantity of S, B's
demand curve drawn with regard to k is given by D_B. Individual A may then look upon D_B as
showing the price at which various quantities of S are available to him, i.e., as a supply schedule
for the social good which confronts him. B similarly may regard D_A as his supply curve. The
fraction of the price which both are willing to pay (k for A and $(1-k)$ for B) adds to 1 at the
intersection of D_A and D_B, at output OM. See Erik Lindahl, "Just Taxation: A Positive
Solution," in Richard A. Musgrave and Alan Peacock (eds.), *Classics in the Theory of Public
Finance*, International Economic Association, London: Macmillan, 1958, pp. 168–177. See also
J. G. Head, " Lindahl's Theory of the Budget," *Finanzarchiv*, Band 23, Heft 3, October 1964, pp.
421–454.

Figure 3-1 also shows how, by applying the same pricing rule to both social and private goods—where the price payable by each consumer equals the individual's marginal benefit—different results are obtained in the two cases. Whereas in the private-good case, in which A and B pay the same price but purchase different amounts, in the social-good case, they purchase the same amount but pay different prices. Yet, in both cases, the same pricing rule is applied. Each consumer pays a single price for successive units of the good purchased, with the price equal to the marginal benefit the purchaser derives.

Need for Budgetary Provision

While the presentation of Figure 3-1 is helpful in bringing out the change in efficiency conditions, it is misleading if taken to suggest that the provision of social goods might be implemented by a market mechanism of demand and supply, with equilibrium at E as in the case of the private good. This interpretation implies that consumers will bid as they would for private goods and thus overlooks the crucial fact that social goods are provided without exclusion. Because of this, consumer preferences for such goods (the value which they assign to successive marginal units of consumption) will not be revealed voluntarily. Since the number of participants is usually large, any one contribution will make little difference in total provision. Knowing this, consumers will find it in their interest to act as free riders. The pseudo-demand curves of Figure 3-1 do not come into play and the market mechanism cannot function. Moreover, even if consumers were to bid, the competitive market could not yield the multiprice result arrived at in the preceding illustration.

To bypass this difficulty, economic theorists have defined efficient allocation for social goods in terms of a model which simply assumes that preferences are known, but this is not an operational approach. In practice, a political process must be used (1) to obtain revelation of preferences, i.e., to tell the government what social goods should be provided; and (2) to furnish it with the fiscal resources needed to pay for them. This is done through voting on tax and expenditure decisions. Individuals, knowing that they must comply with the majority decision, will find it in their best interest to vote for that solution which will move the outcome closer to their own desires, and in this way they will be induced to reveal their preferences. To serve as an efficient mechanism of preference revelation, the voting process should link tax and expenditure decisions. Voters are then confronted with a choice among budget proposals which carry a price tag in terms of their own tax contribution. This price tag will depend on the total cost for the community as a whole as well as on the share to be contributed by others. Voters' choices are thus contingent on their own knowledge that others must also contribute in line with the adopted tax plan. It is this mandatory nature of the budget decision which induces preference revelation and permits the determination of social-good provision.

As will be seen in Chapter 6, the political mechanism is imperfect and can only approximate what would be the optimal budget choice. But it is the best (or only) available technique and must be used as well as it can be.

C. MODELS OF EFFICIENT ALLOCATION

In Figure 3-1 we have compared efficient provision for social and for private goods. To simplify, this was done by comparing a market for private goods with a pseudo-market for social goods, each viewed in a separate, partial-equilibrium setting. We now allow for interdependence between the production and consumption of private and of social goods and reconsider the problem in general equilibrium terms. We begin with a brief look at what is meant by efficient resource use. This is followed by a parallel view of the problem as applied first to private, and then to social, goods. The present section requires some understanding of intermediate microtheory and may be passed over by the reader who is disinterested in these theoretical aspects.[5]

Meaning of Efficiency

Economics, as one learns in the first college class on the subject, deals with the efficient use of resources in best satisfying consumer wants. If the economy consisted of one consumer only, the meaning of efficiency would be quite simple. Robinson Crusoe would survey the resources available to him and the technologies at his disposal in transforming these resources into goods. Given his preferences among goods, he would then proceed to produce in such a way and such a mix of output as would maximize his satisfaction. In so doing, he would act efficiently. But the real world problem is more difficult. The economic process must serve not one but many consumers; and various outcomes will differ in their distributional implications. This calls for a more careful definition of what is meant by "efficient" resource use.

To separate the problem of efficient allocation from that of distribution, economists have come up with a narrower concept of efficiency. Named *Pareto efficiency* after the Italian economist who proposed it, the definition is as follows: A given economic arrangement is efficient if there can be no rearrangement which will leave someone better off without worsening the position of others. Thus, it is impossible in this situation to change the method of production, the mix of goods produced, or the size of the public sector which would help A without hurting B and C. If, on the other hand, such a change is possible, then the prevailing arrangement is inefficient and an efficiency gain can be had by making the change.[6] This definition, so far as it goes, is quite reasonable. Provided only that envy is ruled out or

[5]For a compact statement and literature references, see Francis M. Bator, "The Simple Analytics of Welfare Maximization," *American Economic Review*, March 1957, pp. 22–59.

Introductory expositions will also be found in microtheory texts, such as Jack Hirshleifer, *Price Theory and Applications*, Englewood Cliffs, N.J.: Prentice-Hall, 1976, chap. 7, and C. E. Ferguson and S. Charles Maurice, *Economic Analysis*, rev. ed., Homewood, Ill.: Irwin, 1974, chap. 12.

overlooked, most people would agree that a change which helps A without hurting B and C is efficient. Moreover, this approach permits one to separate the concept of efficient resource use from the more controversial problem of distribution, a topic to be dealt with in Chapter 5.

The General Model for Private Goods

In discussing efficient resource use, we shall begin with the more familiar case of private goods. This approach will also permit us to see just how the case of social goods differs. Suppose there exists an omniscient planner who has all the relevant information, including knowledge of the stock of available resources, the state of technology, and the preferences of consumers. The planner is then asked to determine how resources are to be used efficiently, allowing for all possible states of distribution.

Efficiency Rules   Economists have laid down certain conditions which must be met if the solution is to be efficient. To state the problem in simple terms, we shall consider an economy with two consumers, A and B, and two products, X and Y. These conditions must then be met:

1. Efficiency requires that any given amount of X should be produced in such a way as to permit the largest possible amount of Y to be produced at the same time and vice versa. The best available technology should be used. If one technique permits production of 100 units of X and 80 units of Y, and another permits 100 units of X combined with only 50 units of Y, the former method is obviously to be preferred.

2. The "marginal rate of substitution" in consumption between goods X and Y must be the same for consumers A and B. By this we mean that the rate at which A and B will be willing to trade the last unit of X for additional units of Y should be the same. If A is willing to give 1 unit of X for 3 units of Y, while B will give 4 units of Y for 1 unit of X, it will be to the advantage of both to exchange, with A increasing his consumption of Y and B consuming more of X until equality of the marginal rates of substitution is restored.[7]

3. The marginal rate of substitution of X for Y in consumption should be the same as their marginal rate of transformation in production. The latter is defined as the additional units of X that can be produced if production of Y is reduced by one unit. Thus, if the marginal rate of substitution in consumption is 3 X for 2 Y while the marginal rate of transformation in production is 3 X for 1 Y, it will be desirable to increase the output of Y and to reduce that of X until the two ratios are equalized.

---

[6]As always happens, this principle has come to be qualified and has been made subject to various interpretations. The discussion has turned especially around the topic of compensation. Some say that for an arrangement to be efficient, compensation must be made, while others say that it is enough to conclude that compensation could be made. Consider a rearrangement under which a gain to A is worth $100, while the loss to B is valued at $90. If A compensates B, B's position is unchanged, while there remains a gain to A of $10. For purposes of our discussion, we assume that B is compensated.

[7]The underlying reasoning is that a consumer's marginal rate of substitution of X for Y declines as more X and less Y are consumed. Putting it differently, consumption of both X and Y is subject to decreasing marginal utility.

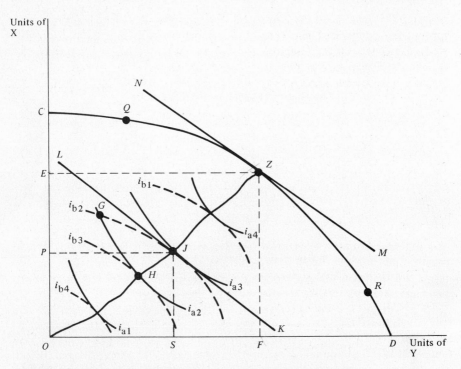

FIGURE 3-2   Efficient Output of Private Goods and Their Assignment.

If these conditions are met (as well as some others not specified here), resource allocation will be efficient in the Pareto sense.

Finding the Set of Efficient Solutions   The steps to be followed in tracing out the efficient solution may be summarized briefly. To facilitate matters, we consider again an economy with two private goods, X and Y, and two consumers, A and B. The first step is to construct the production possibility frontier *CD* in Figure 3-2. With output of private good X measured vertically and that of Y measured horizontally, *CD* shows the best possible combinations of both that can be produced. If all resources are put into X, the largest possible output of X equals *OC*; and if all resources are put into Y, the largest possible output equals *OD*. If *OE* of X is produced, the largest possible output of Y equals *OF* and so forth. As previously noted in condition 1, it is obviously desirable to produce any given output of X so as to supplement it by the largest possible output of Y, and vice versa. Just how this is done need not concern us here in detail, since this part of the problem is the same for both the private- and the social-good cases.[8]

The second step is to determine how the output at any one point on *CD* should be divided between A and B. Suppose that the output mix indicated

---

[8]Drawing the production possibility curve *CD* concave to the origin implies that both X and Y are produced under conditions of increasing cost.

by point Z is produced, involving OE of X and OF of Y. To show how this output may be divided between A and B, we consider the "box diagram" encompassed by $OEZF$. Beginning at O as origin, i_{a1}, i_{a2}, i_{a3}, etc., are consumer A's indifference curves, showing A's preferences for X and Y. The curves are constructed so that while moving down any one curve, A remains equally well off, with more of Y being traded for less of X. At the same time, A will be better off when moving from a lower to a higher i (indifference) curve, say from i_{a1} to i_{a2}.

We next draw a similar pattern of indifference curves for B, but now we choose Z as the origin. That is to say, B's take of Y is measured by moving left along ZE, and B's take of X is measured by moving down along ZF. Various successively higher indifference curves for B are shown as i_{b1}, i_{b2}, etc. It can now be shown that the best possible solutions all lie along the "contract curve" OZ, which traces out the tangency points of the two sets of indifference curves. If the initial position is at G, movement to J will improve A's position without hurting B, just as movement to H will improve B's position without hurting A. By landing somewhere between H and J, the gain will be divided between the two. By following the rule that a gain to A without a loss to B (and vice versa) is an improvement, the efficient solutions must fall along OZ. Since these are the points at which the two sets of indifference curves are tangent, and since the slope of the indifference curves equals the MRS (marginal rate of substitution in consumption), it also follows that at each point on OZ the MRSs for A and B are equal. This reflects condition 2 above.

The next problem is to choose among the various points on OZ. The answer is that among all these points, that particular point is the best solution at which the MRS of consumers, as indicated by the slope of the indifference curves, is equal to the MRT (marginal rate of transformation in production), thus meeting the previously noted condition 3. This is the case at J, where the tangent LK, whose slope measures the MRS of both consumers, is parallel to MN and thus equals MRT. Given this solution, A receives OP of X and OS of Y, while B receives EP of X and FS of Y. Having decided that the efficient assignment of output mix Z between A and B is given at J, the planner will now solve the same problem for all other mixes of output as shown as points on CD, such as Q and R.

Choice of Optimum   Having completed this job, our planner, acting as an omniscient technician, has derived the set of equally efficient solutions, but it remains for the policy makers to choose between these efficient alternatives. Each solution, corresponding to the various points on CD, specifies the division of X and Y among A and B and permits us to rank the resulting utility levels for each of them. Thus, point J in Figure 3-2 implies a utility level i_{a3} for A and of i_{b2} for B. Choosing among points on CD is a matter of judgment on distribution and, as noted earlier, cannot be made according to the efficiency rules by which Pareto optimality is defined. A tradeoff between the welfare levels of A and B is involved.

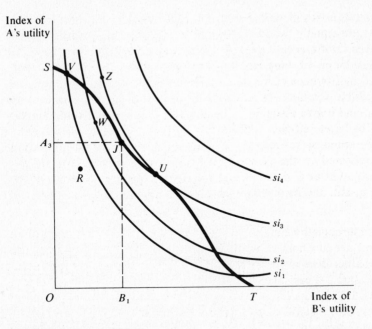

FIGURE 3-3   The Distribution Choice.

This is illustrated in Figure 3-3, where the vertical axis records a welfare or utility index for A while the horizontal axis does so for B. We now take the best solution for each output mix in Figure 3-2 and record the corresponding utility levels for A and B. Taking mix Z and the allocation given by J, we find A at utility index i_{a3} and B at index i_{b2}. These indices may be assumed to correspond to utility rankings OA_3 and OB_2 of point J in Figure 3-2. We may now trace out the utility positions of A and B for all other efficient solutions (corresponding to various product mixes along CD) of Figure 3-2 and in this way we obtain a "utility frontier" such as ST, which shows for each level of utility allowed to A the largest possible level of utility obtainable for B. Each of these solutions involves a particular pattern of resource use between private goods X and Y and their distribution between consumers A and B. The best possible points lie on this utility frontier, with points northeast thereof unobtainable and points southwest inferior. Note that this construction involves only utility rankings, not cardinal measurement. Moreover, so far no comparison of A's and B's utility levels is involved.

Although the rules of Pareto efficiency guide us to the frontier ST, the choice among the "best" points traced by this frontier involves a tradeoff between gains for A and losses for B, or vice versa. As we move from S to T, A's welfare declines and B's rises, and vice versa. The choice is one of distribution and must be made on the basis of a social welfare function, expressing an ordering by which society assigns relative values to levels of welfare experienced by A and B. Assuming these assignments to be known, they may be expressed by the social indifference curves si_1, si_2, etc., where each curve shows mixes of welfare derived by A and B that, from society's point of view, are equally "good." The gain to B which results when moving down any social indifference curve *si* is considered just offset by the resulting loss to A. The point of tangency of the utility frontier with the highest possible social indifference curve is at *U*. This is the so-called bliss point, the best of all possible solutions. It reflects a solution such as that indicated by output mix *Z* and goods assignment *J* in Figure 3-2; thus it meets both the requirements of Pareto efficiency as dealt with in Figure 3-2 and the broader equity considerations as reflected in Figure 3-3. Provided the social welfare function as reflected in the pattern of the *si* curves is also given to the planner, the solution at *U* thus involves a simultaneous determination of the efficient output mix and its distribution among consumers.

Allocation through the Market Having stated the problem in terms of an omniscient planner to whom all information is given, we must now recognize that such a planner does not exist. It is fortunate, therefore, that the efficient solutions of Figure 3-2 can also be obtained by the functioning of a competitive market system. Producers, guided by their desire to maximize profits, will adopt the least-cost method of production, thus meeting condition 1. Moreover, they will produce those products which consumers want most as indicated by the price which they fetch in the market. Consumers, in turn, will allocate their respective budgets among products so as to equate their marginal rates of substitution with their price ratios, thus meeting condition 2. Consumers will do so because, if the price of X is twice the price of Y while their level of satisfaction would be unchanged by replacing consumption of 1 unit of X by less than 2 units of Y, they will choose to purchase and consume more Y and less X until the marginal rate of substitution of Y for X is equal to the price ratio. The same prices are paid by all consumers but, depending on their tastes and incomes, they consume different amounts. Sellers, in trying to maximize profits, equate marginal cost with marginal revenue, which, under conditions of competition, also equates marginal cost with price or average revenue. Thus condition 3 is met as well. Without spelling out the details, we can thus see that the market mechanism, acting as an auctioning system and functioning through competitive pricing, secures an efficient use of resources. Even socialist planners (provided that they wish to adapt their output mix to consumer wants) will find it helpful to play the competitive game or to advise their computers to do so, in order to obtain efficient results.

Solving the problem through the instrument of a market mechanism has the great advantage of inducing consumers to reveal their preferences and of inducing producers to meet them, thus providing a solution without the use of a hypothetical and all-knowing planner. This is the magic of the "invisible hand," which as noted first by Adam Smith permits a decentralized and competitive market system to secure efficient allocation. However, for the market mechanism to operate, we must take a distribution of money income to be given. Returning to Figure 3-3, we note that each of the points on the utility frontier corresponds to the solution reached by the competitive market (and the pricing rule which it implies) on the basis of a given distribution of income. The quality of the solution, therefore, depends on the appropriateness of the prevailing distribution.

The General Model for Social Goods

We now reconsider the preceding problem in a situation where both social and private goods are produced. To simplify, we include only one social good S and one private good X. Proceding as before, we again begin with a general model in which an omniscient planner, to whom all the information is given, is charged with determining the efficient set of solutions. The solution, as first developed by Professor Samuelson, is quite analogous to that previously developed for the efficient allocation of private goods, yet it differs in important respects.[9]

Efficiency Rules   Returning to the efficiency rules previously stated in connection with private goods, we see no change with regard to condition 1. Construction of the production possibility frontier poses the same problem as before. But conditions 2 and 3 will change. Since consumers will now consume the same amount, their marginal rates of substitution of social for private goods may differ; and since they share in consuming the same units of social goods, efficiency now calls for equality between the marginal rate of transformation in production and the *sum* of their marginal rates of substitution in consumption. The solution may again be traced out in a number of steps.

Finding the Set of Efficient Solutions   This is shown in Figure 3-4. The production possibility curve *CD* in the upper part of the figure again records the mixes of X and S that may be produced with available resources. The middle section of the figure shows the amounts of X and S consumed by A and the lower part gives the corresponding picture for B. Since both consume the same amount of S, both will be at the same point on the horizontal axis; but they may consume different amounts of X and be at different points on the vertical axis. These points are related, however, by the condition that the amounts of X consumed by A and B must equal the total output of X. To illustrate, suppose that A is at *G* in the middle panel, consuming *OF* of S and *FG* of X. We know from the upper panel that the efficient output mix which includes *OF* of S also includes *FE* of X. Since *FG* is consumed by A, the amount left for B equals $FE - FG = FH$, placing B at point *H* in the lower panel of the figure.

We now choose a particular level of welfare for A, say, that indicated by A's indifference curve i_{a1} in the middle panel. We have seen that if A is at *G*, then B will be at *H* in the lower panel. Next, let us move along i_{a1} to such

[9]See Paul A. Samuelson, "The Pure Theory of Public Expenditures," *Review of Economics and Statistics*, November 1954, pp. 387–389, and "Diagrammatic Exposition of a Theory of Public Expenditures," *Review of Economics and Statistics*, November 1955, pp. 350–356.

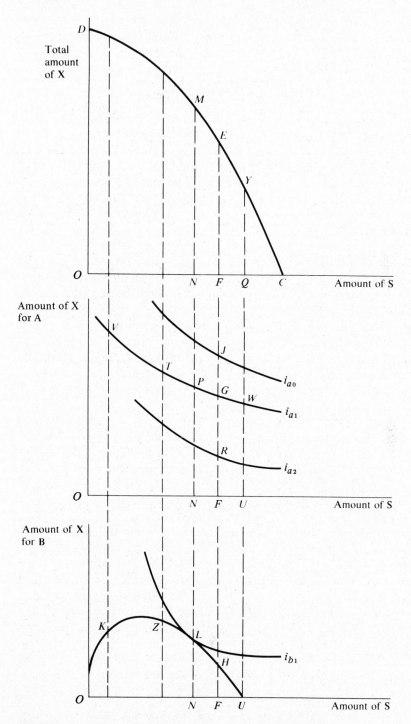

FIGURE 3-4   Social and Private Goods in General Equilibrium.

points as P, T, and V. Following the same reasoning, this places B at L, Z, and K. As A travels along i_{a1} from W to the left, B travels to the left along ULK. Since all points along i_{a1} are equally good for A, welfare is maximized by choosing that point which leaves B best off. This is at L, where ULK is tangent to B's highest indifference curve. If A is to be at indifference level i_{a1}, the best solution is thus that which leaves A and B at P and L, respectively, with total output including ON of S and NM of X, divided between A and B so that A receives NP and B receives NL.

We may now repeat the procedure for other utility levels for A, such as i_{a0} or i_{a2} in the middle panel. For each of these, we arrive at a new locus of B's position in the lower panel (corresponding to ULK) and a new optimum (corresponding to L). In this way, we arrive at a set of solutions corresponding to various levels of welfare for A and B. All these are efficient in the Pareto sense and meet the condition of equality between the sum of the marginal rates of substitution in consumption and the marginal rate of transformation in production.[10]

Looking back, we note that the steps involved in planning for efficient allocation have run parallel for the cases of private and of social goods. However, the efficiency conditions differ, due to the nonrival nature of social-goods consumption.

Choice of Optimum   The welfare levels achieved by A and B under the various efficient solutions may now again be recored on a utility frontier, as shown in Figure 3-3. Given the social welfare function (the pattern of si curves) which evaluates relative welfare positions, U emerges as the best of all possible solutions. Once more this solution simultaneously determines the output mix between S and X and the division of X among A and B. Since both consume the same amount of S, no further assignment is needed.

Social-Goods Allocation through the Budget

This general model integrates the properties of social goods into the theory of welfare economics, but it tells us little about how the solution is to be implemented. In the real world setting, there is no omniscient planner who can solve the problem for us. A mechanism is needed by which preferences are revealed and the corresponding allocations are made. For the case of private goods, this mechanism was provided through the use of a competitive pricing system which, based on a given distribution of income, serves to secure an efficient solution. For the case of social goods, a political process is needed, with consumers expressing their preferences through voting and on the basis of a given distribution of income.

Efficient Allocation   To provide a link to this process, social-goods allocation will now be restated in terms of a budget model, a system in which an initial distribution of income is taken to exist, and where the provision for

[10]See footnote 15 on p. 73.

social goods is decided upon in line with consumers' evaluations as based on their incomes. The cost of social goods is then covered by taxes, imposed in line with consumer evaluation, i.e., by a generalized system of benefit taxation. This moves the model in the direction of realism, but we retain for the time being the assumption that preferences are known to the planner.

More specifically, we assume that the tax prices are set for particular consumers such as to charge them for their consumption of social goods in accordance with a pricing rule similar to the one operating in the competitive market for private goods and implied in Figure 3-1 above. That is to say, for each consumer, all units of a good are to be sold at the same price (there is to be no higher price on intramarginal units), and the ratio of unit prices for X and S is to equal the consumer's marginal rate of substitution in consumption. A and B will pay the same unit price for X while consuming different amounts thereof; and they will pay different unit prices for S while consuming the same amount.

The solution is illustrated in Figure 3-5. The production possibility line CD in the upper figure shows various mixes of S (the social good) and X (the private good) that can be produced and that are available to the economy as a whole.[11] The middle figure shows the position of consumer A and the lower that of B. Suppose that income is divided between A and B so that A receives a share equal to OM/OC of potential private-good output OC, while B receives ON/OC, where $OM + ON = OC$. The broken line MV will then record the optimal allocation of A's income between X and S at varying price ratios. It traces the point of tangency of a set of price lines anchored at M with successive indifference curves. Given the price ratio OM/OP for instance, A's preferred position will be at Q where MP is tangent to the highest attainable indifference curve i_{a2}. The broken curve NW traces a similar price line for B.

Following A's positions along MV, we may trace out the corresponding positions available to B as shown by the broken curve NJ. At each pair of points, both must consume the same amount of S while B's consumption of X is obtained by deducting A's consumption (as recorded by MV) from the total supply of X (as recorded by CD). The NW curve in turn traces out the preferred positions for consumer B which would result if different price ratios were applied to B's purchases of social and private goods. The NJ and NW curves intersect at G, and the correct pricing and output solution is thus obtained where B is placed at G while A is positioned at F and total output is divided between private and social goods as shown by E. Both consume OH of S while private-good output OI is divided so that OK goes to A and OL to B where $OK + OL = OI$. This solution has the following characteristics:

---

[11]The assumption of a linear transformation schedule is necessary if the pricing rule here specified is to result in the necessary equality of tax revenue and cost. Allowing for increasing cost and a concave schedule, our pricing rule yields excess revenue. This is the case because intramarginal units of the social good can then be produced at a lower opportunity cost as measured in terms of private goods. Hence a more complex formula or a rebating of the excess revenue would be needed.

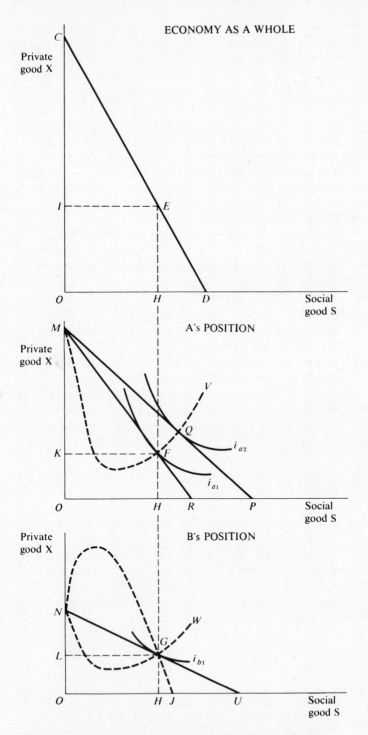

FIGURE 3-5   Social and Private Goods with Given Distribution.

   1. The solution conforms to the initial distribution of income, with A's share equal to OM/OC and B's share equal to ON/OC.
   2. A and B both pay a tax price such that each one's marginal rate of substitution of S for X in consumption is equal to each one's price ratio, so that our pricing rule is complied with.[12]
   3. The combined tax contribution of A and B equals the cost of S to the group as a whole.[13]
   4. The solution meets the efficiency criterion of the Samuelson model, i.e., that the sum of the marginal rates of substitution equals the marginal rate of transformation.[14] The solution E thus reflects a point on the utility frontier of Figure 3-3, it being that point which corresponds to a given income distribution and specified pricing rule.

Extension to Voting   This view of the fiscal problem takes one step toward reality, since an initial distribution of money income is assumed to exist and tax shares are determined. But it remains unsatisfactory in that it is still implemented through a planner to whom preferences are known. In the real world setting, there is no omniscient planner to whom the preference patterns of Figure 3-5 are revealed and who can derive an optimal solution therefrom. Nor is the case of realism helped by substituting an assumption of *voluntary* bidding. As was noted earlier in our discussion of Figure 3-1, this solution breaks down with a large number of voters, where the free-rider problem arises. To provide an operational view of the budget, the model must thus be extended to incorporate a theory of the voting process.
   More specifically, the task is to devise a voting system which is effective in securing preference revelation and an efficient system of tax-expenditure determination. The solution should approximate an efficient pricing rule, such as that shown in Figure 3-5.[15] Through the voting process, the pseudo-demand schedules of the earlier discussion tend to be revealed, the budget size determined, and the tax price applied. This is the best we can do, although as shown in Chapter 6, the voting process by its very nature cannot

---

   [12]The unit price for private good X or P_X is the same for both A and B, but the unit price for S differs. A's price ratio P_S^A/P_X as given by price line MR equals OM/OR (Figure 3-5). Since the price line is tangent to the indifference curve at F, the price ratio equals the marginal rate of substitution in consumption. The same holds for B's ratio P_S^B/P_X equal to ON/OU (Figure 3-5), with price line NU again tangent to the indifference curve bi_1 at G.
   [13]The amount of tax paid by A or T_A equals $P_S^A \cdot OH$. Given $P_S^A/P_X = OM/OR$ and setting $P_X = 1$, we have $P_S^A = OM/OR$ and $T_A = (OM/OR)OH$. Since $OM/OR = KM/KF = KM/OH$, we obtain $T_A = KM$. Arguing similarly for B, we obtain $T_B = LN$. Since $OM + ON = OC$ and by construction of NW we know that $OL + OK = OI$, it follows that $T_A + T_B = IC$.
   For the group as a whole, the price ratio is given by $P_S/P_X = OC/OD$. Setting $P_X = 1$, we have $P_S = OC/OD$, with the cost of supplying OH of S equal to $(OC/OD)OH$ which again reduces to IC. See, however, footnote 11 above.
   [14]This follows because $(OM/OR)+(ON/OU)=(KM/OH)+(LN/OH)=IC/OH$.
   [15]To be efficient, the pricing rule used to solicit preference revelation must equate each consumer's rate of substitution with *his* or *her* price ratio at the *margin*. But it is not required that the intramarginal units be sold at the same price. By charging higher prices for intramarginal units of the social good, "consumer surplus" will be taxed away. Thus more than one efficient pricing rule is available. Among them, that one should be used which best permits implementation through the voting process.

bring about a perfect result. Except for a society where preferences are so homogeneous as to permit unanimity, some voters will remain dissatisfied. Yet some procedures will do better than others and the task is to find the best approximation.

Setting the Distribution   Voting on the provision of social goods and assignment of their cost through taxes presumes the distribution of income to be given, just as did the solution of private-goods allocation through the market mechanism; and for the result to be optimal in the sense of Figure 3-3, this distribution must again be the correct one. The overall solution once more involves two steps—namely, (1) determining the proper distribution of money income, and (2) deriving the efficient allocation of resources based on that distribution. Although some eminent theorists hold that this is an artificial distinction, it is essential for constructing an operational bridge between the theoretical model of social-goods allocation and its application to the practice of budget determination.[16] This leaves open the question of how the optimal state of distribution is to be determined, a puzzling problem to which we turn in the next chapter.

D. SUMMARY

This chapter deals with the efficient use of resources, in particular where the provision of social goods is concerned. The three basic concepts used in this

[16]The case *against* separation of the two issues may be summarized as follows: Resource allocation, as determined by the budget model, is to be optimal. But the optimal distribution of money income cannot be determined without knowing relative prices and hence allocation. (This is so because the basic issue of distribution must be seen in terms of real, rather than of money, income.) It follows that the general model must be solved in any case, thus determining distribution and allocation simultaneously, involving the reasoning of both Figures 3-3 and 3-4. Nothing is gained, therefore, by the introduction of a distribution of money income and of tax shares.

This reasoning is valid and the introduction of money income distribution and of tax shares is redundant if the problem is to be solved by an omniscient planner to whom all preferences are known; but the separation of issues becomes useful in a more realistic setting where preferences are unknown and a mechanism must be provided to induce their revelation. This requires a distribution of money income on the basis of which consumers can express their evaluation, whether through bidding in the market—as in the case of private goods—or through voting—as in the case of social goods.

Since the "proper" state of distribution must in the end be defined in terms of welfare rather than of money income, the "proper" distribution of money income must be determined with the applicable pricing rule in mind. While more than one efficient rule can be devised, the choice is not an arbitrary one. In the case of private goods, the most convenient rule is that given by the competitive market (i.e., marginal cost pricing, with the same price charged to each consumer); in the case of social goods, it is that which can be implemented most effectively by the voting mechanism. In Figure 3-5, the rule was assumed to be one which, analogously to the private-good case, equates the price ratios with the consumer's marginal rate of substitution between social and private goods, but this may not be the only solution.

For a further discussion of the separability of allocation and distribution, see the contributions by Paul A. Samuelson and Richard A. Musgrave in J. Margolis and H. Guitton (eds.), *Public Economics*, New York: St. Martin's, 1969.

discussion are:

1. *The concept of efficiency.* Efficient resource use occurs when there is no possibility of making a change which helps one without hurting anyone else. There are many efficient solutions to the allocation problem, each reflecting a different state of distribution among consumers.

2. *Private goods.* These are goods which are rival in consumption, so that consumption by A renders consumption by B impossible. If a particular good is consumed by A, B will be excluded from the benefits.

3. *Social goods.* These are typically goods which are nonrival in consumption, so that the same benefits can be enjoyed by all members of the group. In this case, exclusion is undesirable and in many instances not feasible.

Given these definitions, certain conditions may be laid down which must be met if resources are to be used efficiently, and the mechanism that can lead to efficient use may be considered. Thus:

4. In the case of private goods, the marginal rates of substitution in consumption must be the same for all consumers, and equal to the marginal rate of transformation in production.

5. This result can be achieved through a competitive market where consumers reveal their preferences by bidding for goods.

6. In such a market, all consumers would pay the same price but consume different amounts, depending upon their income and their preferences. A market demand schedule is obtained by horizontal addition of individual demand schedules.

For the case of social goods, the solution to the problem differs for the following reasons:

7. Since such goods are nonrival in consumption, the same amount is consumed by all. Since consumers differ in incomes and tastes, the marginal rates of substitution are no longer the same and a pseudo-demand schedule is now obtained by vertical addition of individual schedules. The requirement now is that the *sum* of the marginal rates of substitution in consumption should equal the marginal rate of transformation in production.

8. An omniscient planner, to whom all preferences are known, can thus arrive at an allocation of resources to the production of private and of social goods and at a distribution of private goods among consumers which is optimal. Such a solution is optimal both in the sense of meeting the efficiency conditions of Pareto optimality and of satisfying the distributional norms of the given social welfare function.

9. This solution, however, is not operational. Since the benefits from social goods are available to all, consumers will not reveal their preferences by bidding in the market but will act as free riders. Hence, a political process or voting system, based on a given distribution of money income, is needed to induce the revelation of preferences. The voting process, it is hoped, approximates an efficient solution. But this solution, like that of a competitive market for the allocation of private goods, is optimal only if the underlying distribution of money income is also the correct one.

FURTHER READINGS

Arrow, K. J.: "Political and Economic Evaluation of Social Effects and Externalities," in J. Margolis (ed.), *The Analysis of Public Output*, National Bureau of Economic Research, New York: Columbia, 1970.

Bator, F. M.: "The Simple Analytics of Welfare Maximization," *American Economic Review*, March 1957, pp. 22–59.

Buchanan, J. M.: *The Demand and Supply of Public Goods*, Chicago: Rand McNally, 1968.

Head, J. G.: *Public Goods and Public Welfare*, Durham, N.C.: Duke, 1974, chap. 1.

Johansen, L.: *Public Economics*, Amsterdam: North-Holland, 1965, chap. 6.

Samuelson, Paul A.: "Pure Theory of Public Expenditures and Taxation," in J. Margolis and H. Guitton (eds.), *Public Economics*, New York: St. Martin's, 1969.

_____: "The Pure Theory of Public Expenditures," *Review of Economics and Statistics*, November 1954, pp. 386–389; and "Diagrammatic Exposition of a Theory of Public Expenditures," *Review of Economics and Statistics*, November 1955, pp. 350–356. Both articles reproduced in R. W. Houghton (ed.), *Public Finance*, Baltimore: Penguin, 1970.

Wicksell, K., and E. Lindahl: Excerpts of writings in R. A. Musgrave and A. Peacock (eds.), *Classics in the Theory of Public Finance*, New York: Macmillan, 1958.

Chapter 4

Social Goods,
Further Considered*

In the preceding chapter, we have dealt with pure social goods, i.e., goods which are wholly nonrival in consumption, and we have examined how they can be provided in a setting in which a large number of consumers are involved. In this chapter, we deal with some qualifications to this pure model, including (1) cases of "mixed goods," which fall in between the polar cases of purely private and purely social goods, and (2) situations where the number of consumers is limited so that bargaining can occur. We also (3) raise the issue of merit goods, dealing with situations where it may be questioned whether the basic premise of individual preferences offers an adequate framework for public sector analysis.

* Reader's Guide to Chapter 4: In this chapter we continue the discussion of social goods. Departing from the purist approach of Chapter 3, situations falling in between those of purely private and purely social goods are examined. Consideration is also given to collective as against individualistic evaluation of wants and the related problem of merit goods. This material is essential for an understanding of the policy problems posed by externalities and social goods.

A. MIXED GOODS

Throughout the preceding discussion, a sharp distinction was drawn between private goods, such as hamburgers, the benefits of which are wholly internalized (rival), and others, such as air purification, whose benefits are wholly external (nonrival). This polarized view was helpful in understanding the essential difference between private and social goods, but it is not realistic. In reality, mixed situations of various kinds arise.

Externalities from Private Activities

Problems of the social-good type arise not only in the budgetary context but wherever private consumption or production activities generate external benefits. Suppose, for instance, that A derives benefits from being inoculated against polio, but so do many others for whom the number of potential carriers, and hence the danger of infection, is reduced. Or, by getting educated, A not only derives personal benefits but also makes it possible for others to enjoy association with a more educated community. Since large numbers of other consumers may be affected, bargaining does not work and a budgetary process will again be needed to secure preference revelation. But the correct budgetary intervention in this case will not involve full budgetary provision; rather, it will take the form of subsidy to private purchases.

This is shown in Figure 4-1, where D_P represents the market demand schedule, obtained by *horizontal* addition of demands for the private benefits which individuals derive from being inoculated or from having their houses painted. Now let D_X be a supplementary schedule reflecting the evaluation (or, as noted above, pseudo-demand) by others for the external benefits generated by these activities, e.g., the reduced risk of contagion or pleasure of an improved neighborhood. The D_X schedule is obtained by *vertical* addition of individual demand curves for such benefits. Adding D_P and D_X vertically, D_S is obtained to reflect total benefits, including both the D_P and D_X components. Given this situation, the private market will result in equilibrium output OQ_P, since only the D_P schedule is backed by voluntary purchases. But this is inefficient since the optimal output is at Q_S, where external or social benefits are included.

In order to expand output from OQ_P to OQ_S, the government should pay a subsidy per unit equal to FC, the difference between D_S and D_P at output OQ_S. Such a subsidy raises the effective demand confronting the supplier to D^* and output will be extended to OQ_S. Consumers pay a net price of OR, with the subsidy contributing the difference RT. The total cost of the subsidy equals $RTCF$ and is paid for out of the budget, financed by taxes on A and B, imposed in line with the principles that were discussed in the preceding chapter.

All this would be simple enough if D_X and hence the required level of subsidy were known, but this is usually not the case. Thus, the evaluation of the external benefits—and the determination of the proper rate of subsidy—poses problems of preference revelation similar to those which arise

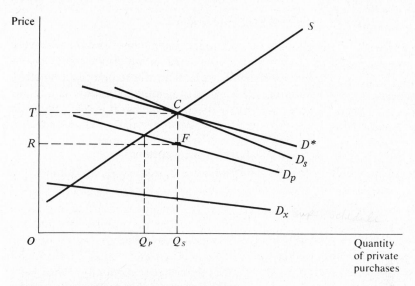

FIGURE 4-1   Adjustment for External Benefits.

with social goods. Resolution through the political process is again called for.

The polar case of social goods, examined earlier, may thus be extended into a band of cases involving goods in which internal benefits to the individual consumer are increasingly supplemented by external benefits. At the one extreme of the purely private good, the distance FC in Figure 4-1 becomes zero, as D_S is the same as D_P and no subsidy is needed. At the other extreme of the purely social good, D_S becomes equal to D_X and the subsidy pays the entire price, i.e., benefits are wholly external. The good becomes a pure social good and is entirely provided for through the budget. In between, we have the cases of mixed goods, to be financed by a mix of private payments and of subsidies. The tax-expenditure theory of the preceding chapter may thus be restated more generally as a tax-subsidy theory, with subsidies ranking from 0 to 100 percent. While the use of such subsidies is limited in practice, the frequent occurrence of external benefits suggests that a wider use might be in order.

The phenomenon of benefit externalities has its counterpart in external costs. Private consumption or production activities may generate costs which are not "internalized" and not paid for by consumers or producers. As a result, costs are imposed on society which are not accounted for, and the activity in question tends to be overextended. While the case of external benefits was shown to call for a subsidy, that of external cost calls for a penalty tax. This, of course, is the problem of how to deal with social "bads," such as pollution and environmental damage, a topic which will be considered at some length later on.[1]

[1]See Chap. 34, Sec. E.

Spatial Limitation of Benefits and Local Finance

When speaking of social goods as "being available to all," we do not mean that the world population, or even the entire population of one country, is to be included. The spatial benefit area is limited for most social goods and the members of the group are thus confined to the residents of that area. This restriction does not change the nature of the preceding argument. A group which is sufficiently large to require provision for social goods by political process need not be all-inclusive. At the same time, this feature of spatial limitation of benefits is central to the application of social-goods theory to local government. This being a major topic in its own right, consideration is postponed until the issues of fiscal federalism are examined.[2]

Congestion

Another case of mixed goods, also of special importance in relation to local finance, arises where goods, though consumed in equal amounts by all members of a particular group, are not truly nonrival in consumption. As more users are added, the quality of service received by all users from a given installation declines. Thus, the quality of instruction received by the individual student from a single teacher may decline as the size of the class increases. Demand schedules are still added vertically, but the marginal cost of adding an additional consumer is no longer zero. Thus, there is now the additional problem of determining how large the size of the group should be. Once more, we shall take up this problem later on when discussing local finance.[3]

Alternative Modes of Provision

Another obstacle to a clear-cut distinction between social and private goods arises because certain needs may be met in a variety of ways, some of which involve provision of private, and others provision of social goods. Thus, the need for protection may be met by private locks for each house or by police protection for the entire city block. If the first route is taken, provision may be left to the market, whereas in the second, budgetary provision is needed. In situations where this option exists, a choice must then be made between the two modes. Since the private mode has the advantage of permitting individuals to consume different amounts, the social-goods mode, to be preferred, must more than outweigh this advantage by offering a lower cost per user.[4]

B. BARGAINING IN THE SMALL GROUP

Our preceding argument has been that a political process is needed to provide for social goods because voluntary payments and preference revelation will

[2]See Chap. 24, Sec. E.
[3]See p. 521.
[4]See Carl S. Shoup and John Head, "Public Goods, Private Goods and Ambiguous Goods," *Economic Journal*, September 1969.

not be forthcoming in the absence of exclusion. The reason is that any one individual will not consider it worth his or her while to pay because, with large numbers involved, individual contributions will not significantly affect the total supply. Individuals find it in their interest to act as free riders. This difficulty is less of a problem when few people are involved. Individuals will now find it worthwhile to contribute and to bargain, since individual contributions now significantly affect their own position and that of others.

While the problem of social goods arises primarily in the large-number context, there are important situations in which the small-number conditions apply. Neighbors, for example, may get together in a mutual effort at tree spraying; municipalities may join in building a common garbage-disposal plant; or national governments may cooperate in undertaking joint ventures, such as NATO. Moreover, budgetary decisions are typically made not by referenda which involve a large number of voters but by bargaining among elected representatives. The small-number case is thus worth considering.

Figure 4-2 depicts a situation where two consumers share in the benefit of a social good.[5] The provision may be paid for by A or B, but the quantities provided are available equally to both. D_A and D_B are A's and B's demand schedules for the social good and SS is the supply schedule. D_{A+B} is the aggregate demand schedule, obtained by vertical addition of D_A and D_B. Up to output OQ_E, the maximum prices which A and B would be willing to offer, as shown by D_{A+B}, add to more than cost. This suggests that output will be bid up to OQ_E where D_{A+B} intersects SS at N. Both A and B pay a price equal to their marginal evaluation, i.e., $Q_E F$ and $Q_E G$, respectively. Another way of viewing the process is as follows: Since B's offers are given along D_B,

[5]For a diagram similar to Figure 4-2, see James M. Buchanan, *The Demand and Supply of Public Goods*, Chicago: Rand McNally, 1968.

FIGURE 4-2 The Small-Number Case.

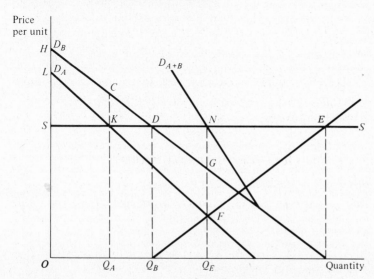

we may deduct D_B from SS so as to obtain $Q_B E$, which now reflects the supply schedule at which various levels of output are available to A. Moving along D_A to its intersection with $Q_B F$, A will then purchase output OQ_E, at price $Q_E F$. Thus equilibrium is established at quantity OQ_E, with A contributing $Q_E F$ and B contributing $Q_E G$.

This process leads to an efficient solution, but there is little reason to assume that our two consumers will behave in this fashion. Both parties may attempt to get a better deal by offering prices below the maximum shown by their respective demand schedules. Each will learn to allow for the effects of his/her actions on the other and follow strategic behavior. They may engage in "all-or-nothing" bargaining, rather than undertake marginal adjustments along their demand schedules. How then may we expect the bargaining to proceed? Consider B's position. If Mr. A were not present, Ms. B would purchase OQ_B. But she may not do so if she allows for A's reaction. Suppose that she expects A to purchase OQ_A if she purchases nothing, but to purchase nothing if she purchases OQ_B. Given these alternatives, she will decide to purchase nothing since her gain from A's purchase of OQ_A (measured by the area $OQ_A CH$) exceeds the gain from her own purchase of OQ_B (measured by the area of SHD).[6] Similarly, A will not be eager to purchase OQ_A since this may deter B from purchasing OQ_B, and his gain from his own pruchase of OQ_A (measured by SLK) falls short of his gain from her purchase of OQ_B (measured by $OLKQ_A$). Eventually, someone will move and there will be responses, but it is uncertain what the result will be. Output may reach OQ_B and proceed to OQ_E or may fall short thereof. The cost share in the final quantity may be divided (or, putting it differently, the gains in consumer surplus may be distributed) in different ways. While B stands to gain more from efficient provision if both contribute along their maximum offer (or demand) curves, it does not follow that she will push the bargain to OQ_E if she can get a lower price at some smaller output. The outcome will depend on the bargaining strength and skills of the two parties.[7]

Bargaining, be it over private or social goods, need not have an efficient outcome. Whereas increasing the number of participants leads to a competitive solution in the private-good case, such will not be the result where social goods are concerned. Although bargaining imperfections are reduced, individuals will have no further reason to reveal their preferences and make their contributions. One difficulty replaces another and a political process becomes necessary to solve the problem.

[6]B's gain from purchasing OQ_B at price OS is measured by her consumer surplus of SHD, arrived at by deducting her cost, or $OSDQ_B$, from $OHDQ_B$, the total utility which she derives from the consumption of OQ_B. Her gain in consumer surplus derived from A's provision of OQ_A equals $OHCQ_A$, since there is no cost to be deducted.

Note also that the result of $OHCQ_A > SHD$, while correct for Figure 4-2 as drawn, need not always hold. Thus, if D_B is shifted sufficiently far to the right, the triangle corresponding to SHD may come to exceed $OHCQ_A$ and B may find it worthwhile to purchase an output corresponding to OQ_B even if this deters A from making a purchase.

[7]This does not mean that anything can happen. Further analysis shows that there is a "bargaining area" into which the solution must fall. See H. Shibata, "A Bargaining Model of the Pure Theory of Public Expenditures," *Journal of Political Economy*, January 1971.

C. BASES OF WANTS AND MERIT GOODS

In concluding this survey of the social-good problem, we once more return to the basic nature of social goods, this time focusing on the way in which wants for such goods are generated and on the further problem of "merit goods."

The Premise of Individualistic Evaluation

Our distinction between private and social goods was based on certain technical characteristics of social goods, i.e., the nonrival nature of consumption and the inapplicability of exclusion. It did not depend on a difference in psychological attitudes, or in social philosophy regarding the two types of goods. Social as well as private goods are experienced by individuals and included in their preference systems. The same individualistic psychology was applied to both types of goods.

The premise that all wants (private or social) are experienced by individuals rather than group entities is quite compatible with the notion that individuals do not live in isolation, but in association with others. Therefore A's preferences will be affected by those of B and C. Dominant tastes and cultural values influence individual preferences and in turn are determined by them. Fashions are a pervasive factor in molding tastes and not only with regard to clothing. To say that wants are experienced individually, therefore, is not to deny the existence of social interaction. Nor can it be argued that social goods differ from private goods because they satisfy the more noble aims of life.

Furthermore, the proposition that wants are experienced individually does not exclude altruism. If A is a socially minded person, he will derive satisfaction not only from his own consumption but also from consumption by B; or B, who is selfish, may enjoy only her own consumption. Utilities are interdependent and this fact broadens the range over which the economics of social goods applies. But granting all this, what matters here is that satisfaction is experienced in the last resort by A and B individually and not by a mysterious third entity called A + B.

Finally, we recognize that the quality of wants may differ. Some are concerned with the more noble and others with the baser aspects of life. But this does not bear on the distinction between private and social goods. The wants to be satisfied may be noble or base in either case: social goods may carry high cultural or aesthetic values, such as music education or the protection of natural beauty, or they may relate to everyday needs, such as roads and fire protection. Similarly, private goods may satisfy cultural needs, such as harpsichord recordings, or everyday needs, such as bubblegum. Clearly, no distinction between private and social goods can be drawn on this basis.

Communal Wants

The premise of wants, based on the needs and preferences of individuals, appeals to widely held values of Western culture. It also permits one to

conduct the analysis of public provision within the usual economic framework shared by the analysis of private goods. The concept of communal
needs, on the other hand, is hard to interpret and does not fit such analysis.
Moreover, it carries the frightening implications of dictatorial abuse. Yet, the
concept of community also has its tradition in Western culture, from the
Greeks through the Middle Ages and to date, and should be given at least
brief consideration.

The central proposition to be examined is that there exists a community
interest as such, an interest which is attributable to the community as a whole
and which does not involve a "mere" addition, vertical or horizontal, of
individual interests. This community interest then gives rise to communal
wants, wants which are generated by and pertain to the welfare of the group
as a whole. This raises two basic questions: one is to whom and how the
community interest is revealed, and the other is over what range of needs the
communal concept should be applied.

Some would view the structure of communal wants as revealed through a
great teacher or political leader who, as was once believed in Maoist China,
transmits these insights to the people. The people, after an initial period of
compulsion, come to accept these values as their own, thus removing the
distinction between private and collective wants. This tenet is clearly incon-
sistent with our views of democracy, nor can it be defended by arguing that
"in the end" all preferences are socially conditioned. Social and environmental influences, to be sure, are pervasive, but there remains a considerable
degree of freedom (unless suppressed) in individual responses thereto.

A more attractive interpretation is that, by virtue of sustained association
and mutual sympathy, people come to develop common concerns. A group of
people, for instance, share an historical experience or cultural tradition with
which they identify, thereby establishing a common bond. An individual will
not only defend *his* home but join others in defending *our* territory or in
protecting *our* countryside. Such common interests and values may give rise
to common wants, i.e., wants which individuals feel obliged to support as
members of the community. These obligations may be recognized as falling
outside the freedom of choice which applies in deciding whether to drink tea
or coffee.

This interpretation of communal wants can hardly be rejected, and it
suggests that the individual preference approach does not tell the entire story.
Yet, recognition that common concerns or values exist does not lead one to
conclude that all resource allocation, or even the larger part thereof, should
be based on considerations of community interest, rather than on individual
preferences. No apology is needed, therefore, for having based our analysis of
public provision on the individualistic premise.

Merit Goods

At the same time, a realistic view of the fiscal scene cannot avoid noticing
many instances where policy seems to aim at interfering with rather than
responding to individual preferences. Some goods are considered "meritori-

ous" while others are held undesirable. For instance, low-cost housing is subsidized because decent housing is held to be desirable, while sumptuary taxes are imposed on liquor because drinking is held undesirable. Note, however, that the consumption choices which are supported or penalized may involve goods which are private (rival in consumption), as well as goods which are social (nonrival). The distinction between goods which are given a social stamp (favorable or unfavorable) and those which are considered neutral, therefore, must not be confused with that between private and social goods. The merit-good issue cuts across the latter distinction.

Policies to provide merit goods, or to deter the provision of de-merit goods, cannot be explained in terms of our earlier approach to social-goods theory. Although the approach called for the compulsory acceptance of the voting decision and involved some interference with minority views, such interference was but the unfortunate by-product of a procedure designed to meet individual preferences as well as possible. In the situations now considered, interference is not accidental but the very purpose of public policy.

The existence of merit goods thus defined may be taken to suggest that our society, which considers itself democratic, retains elements of autocracy which permit the elite (however defined) to impose their preferences. Or, it may be interpreted as adherence to community interests or values by which individual preferences are overridden. Either explanation contravenes free consumer choice, the otherwise accepted principle of resource use.

At the same time, certain practices which seem to involve imposition of preferences do not really do so when examined more closely. Consider, for instance, a situation where the government subsidizes products which generate external benefits. As shown above, such a policy serves to implement efficient resource use in line with individual preferences, rather than to interfere with them. Similarly, corrective action may be called for where consumer choice is distorted by inadequate information or misleading advertising. By way of temporary interference, consumers may be exposed to an educational process which will permit more intelligent choice later on. Or, interference may be directed at children or the mentally disabled, but again this occurs in a protective or remedial rather than interventionist spirit.

Moving closer to a genuine merit-good situation, consider the many instances where government provides special services to the poor, such as low-cost housing. If the purpose of such aid were merely redistributional, it could be better met by cash grants, leaving it to the recipient to decide how to spend the money. By making the grant in kind, the government imposes its own preferences. This may come about because a majority can be found for contributing to, say, the housing consumption of the poor, but not for adding to their income which may be spent on "frivolous" things. Such restrictions may be interpreted as interference with the recipient's choice, but they may also be viewed as conditional charity offered (but not imposed) by the donor.[8] However this may be, the appearance of merit goods is not confined

[8]See p. 103.

only to provision for the poor. Public subsidies to the arts, be they granted directly or via the charitable contribution provision of the income tax, are directed at the public at large and may be of special benefit to higher-income groups.

Where does this leave the concept of merit goods? Policies aimed at correcting for externalities or providing consumer information can still be fitted into the framework of traditional, individual-preference–based analysis. But not all practices can be explained in this way. Genuine merit-good situations aimed at interference exist, and they do not fit the traditional framework. In part this reflects elitist domination, but in part it also reflects the prevalence of communal interests. The fact that such interests are inconvenient to conventional analysis (What does not fit cannot be!) does not disprove their existence.

D. SUMMARY

Although the specific aspects of the social-goods problem are seen best by dealing with the polar cases of purely private and social goods, the actual nature of goods in many instances falls between these extremes. Among various mixed situations, the following have been considered:

   1. The consumption or production of primarily private goods can give rise to external benefits. Such benefits are not accounted for in the market. This leads to undersupply and a subsidy is required to correct this defect.
   2. Externalities may involve not only benefits or social goods, but also costs or social bads. An example is the problem of pollution. Again, market failure occurs since external costs are not allowed for by the offending firm or consumer. In this instance oversupply results and a tax is required to internalize such costs.
   3. The benefit incidence of social goods is frequently subject to spatial limitation.
   4. While available to all members of the group, the level of benefits obtained from a given amount of social-good provision may decline as the number of members in the group increases, thus causing a "congestion" problem.

Whereas the free-rider problem (and consequent market failure) arises in the case of large numbers, external benefits and costs may be accounted for through bargaining in the small-number case:

   5. With small numbers, bargaining may permit a more or less complete accounting for external benefits and costs, thus reducing the need for public policy intervention. However, the outcome of such bargaining may not be fully efficient.
   6. Whereas imperfections in the market for private goods decline as the number of participants is increased, moving from the small- to the large-number case in the social-good context only replaces one difficulty with another. Finally, consideration has been given to the nature of the wants underlying the provision of private and of social goods.

7. Our concepts of social and private goods do not differ with regard to how the underlying wants are experienced. The demands for private and for social goods are both integral parts of the preference systems of individuals. While each person's preferences interact with those of others, all wants are basically experienced by the individual consumer and not by the collective entity.

8. There remains, however, the fact that budgetary provision frequently involves goods which are rival in consumption. This suggests interference with individual choice and is here referred to as provision for "merit goods." Such provision may include private as well as social goods and cannot be accommodated within the context of the traditional theory of social goods.

FURTHER READINGS

Buchanan, J. M.: *The Demand and Supply of Public Goods*, Chicago: Rand McNally, 1968, chap. 4.

Mishan, E. J.: "The Postwar Literature on Externalities: An Interpretive Essay," *Journal of Economic Literature*, March 1971, pp. 1–35.

Oakland, W. H.: "Congestion, Public Goods and Welfare," *Journal of Public Economics*, November 1972.

Shibata, H.: "A Bargaining Model of the Pure Theory of Public Expenditures," *Journal of Political Economy*, January 1971.

Shoup, Carl S., and John Head: "Public Goods, Private Goods and Ambiguous Goods," *Economic Journal*, September 1969.

Chapter 5

Theory of Optimal
Distribution*

A. Does Equity Belong in Economics? *Determinants of Distribution; Distribution as a Policy Issue.* **B. Approaches to Distributive Justice:** *Alternative Views; Endowment-Based Criteria; Utilitarian Criteria; Equity Criteria; Choice among Criteria; Subjective versus Social Utility.* **C. The Size of the Pie:** *Limits to Redistribution; Efficiency Cost of Redistribution; Efficiency-Equity Tradeoff; An Ideal Solution?* **D. Further Issues:** *Voluntary Redistribution; Categorical Equity; Equity among Generations; Implementation Problems.* **E. Summary.**

Throughout the preceding chapter we have emphasized that the optimal use of scarce resources involves two basic issues. One is to secure efficiency and the other is to secure a state of just distribution. Defined in terms of Pareto efficiency, the proposition that there is a welfare gain when the position of any one individual can be improved without hurting that of another, the efficiency objective is noncontroversial. But, since there exists an efficient solution corresponding to each and every state of distribution, the question

Reader's Guide to Chapter 5: The theory of optimal distribution, considered in this chapter, poses problems not usually dealt with in the study of public finance. Yet the questions raised must be faced up to in designing budget policy. Moreover, criteria of distributive justice, though philosophically based, are constrained in application by economic considerations, so that the two perspectives must be joined.

remains: which state should be chosen as equitable or just? Here the concept of Pareto efficiency helps little, if at all. The problem of distribution is one of evaluating a change in which someone gains while someone else loses. It is one of choosing among the points on the utility frontier of Figure 3-3.

As shown in that connection, the choice of the best or just solution might be found by postulating a "social welfare function," i.e., a set of rankings in which social weights are given to gains by some and losses by others. Given such a function, technical economics can grind out the answer, as illustrated by the tangency solution of Figure 3-3. But there remains the more basic problem of what shape this set of values (or the social welfare function) should take. In the end, one cannot avoid the question of what should be considered a fair or just state of distribution.

A. DOES EQUITY BELONG IN ECONOMICS?

Economists, over the last fifty years, have increasingly held that a theory of just or equitable distribution is not within the purview of economics but should be left to philosophers, poets, and politicians. Indeed, when talking about the "theory of distribution," economists have traditionally referred to the theory of factor pricing and the division of national income among returns to land, labor, and capital. This theory of factor shares plays an essential role in economic analysis, but its significance lies mainly in the area of efficient allocation. For resource use to be efficient, factors of production must be applied so as to equate the value of their marginal product in all uses, a condition which holds in a socialist, as well as a capitalist, society. But the theory of efficient factor use by itself is not a theory of distributive justice. For one thing, the proposition that factor allocation should be based on efficient factor pricing does not require that the final distribution of income among individuals be set equal to the proceeds from sales of their factor services in the market. The two can be separated by intervention of the distribution branch of the budget. For another thing, the ultimate concern of justice in distribution is with distribution among individuals or families and not among groups of factors. Factor shares are only loosely related to the interfamily distribution of income. While it is true that capital income accrues more largely to high-income families and wage income more largely to low-income families, there are important exceptions to the rule. The problem of distribution among individuals or families must thus be addressed directly.

Determinants of Distribution

In the market economy, the distribution of income is determined by the sale of factor services. It thus depends upon the distribution of factor endowments. With regard to labor income, this distribution involves the distribution of abilities to earn such income, as well as the desire to do so. With regard to capital income, it involves the distribution of wealth as determined by inheritance, marriage patterns, and lifetime saving. The distribution of labor and capital endowments is linked by investment in education, which in turn affects the wage rate which a person can command.

Given the distribution of endowments, the distribution of income depends further on factor prices. In a competitive market, these prices equal the value of the factor's marginal product. As such, they depend upon a wide set of variables, including factor supplies, technology, and the preferences of consumers. In many instances, however, returns are determined in imperfect markets where institutional factors, such as conventional salary structures, family connections, social status, sex, race, and so forth, play a significant role. As a result, the returns to various jobs may differ in line with status considerations rather than marginal product, and who gets the job may depend upon connections rather than superior productivity.

The distribution of income, as generated by the above forces, shows a substantial degree of inequality. This may be seen by comparing the percentage of income which accrues to various percentages of households as ranked by their income. Thus, 5 percent of personal income in the United States accrues to the 20 percent of families with the lowest incomes, while the income share received by the successively higher quintiles of family groups is 12, 18, 24, and 42 percent, respectively. As among various forms of income, the distribution of capital income is less equal than that of wage and salary income. Thus, if capital income only is considered, the corresponding income shares may be estimated at 6, 7, 8, 18, and 62 percent.[1] How does this pattern, which is fairly similar in most advanced countries, relate to what might be considered a fair or just state of distribution?

Distribution as a Policy Issue

By posing this question, the focus shifts from distribution as a market outcome to distribution as a policy issue. However any one reader may view this issue, it is evident that distribution problems have been, are, and will continue to be a vital factor in politics and policy determination. Three aspects of the problem may be distinguished:

    1. Even where distributional objectives are not the primary policy target, the distributional implications of various policies must be taken into account in setting the overall policy package.

    2. If distributional changes are to be made, they should be designed so as to be least costly in terms of efficiency loss.

    3. To decide what distributional changes, if any, should be made, or to evaluate the distributional implications of various policies, there must be a basis for choosing among alternative distributions, i.e., a standard of distributive justice or fairness must be applied.

---

[1]For distribution of personal income, see U.S. Bureau of the Census, *Statistical Abstract of the United States*, 1978, p. 455 (data for 1977). Distribution of capital income is estimated on the basis of U.S. Treasury Department, *Individual Income Tax, Statistics of Income*, 1975, preliminary, p. 18.

Beginning with aspect 1, it is evident that almost all policy measures, even those not immediately concerned with distributional objectives, have distributional repercussions. Thus, an inflationary situation may call for a restrictive policy so as to reduce aggregate demand. Its distributional effects will differ, depending on whether the demand reduction is obtained by increasing sales taxes or income taxes, by reducing various types of public expenditure programs, or by applying monetary restriction. Policies aimed at increasing the flow of international trade will have different distributional implications, depending on which tariffs are reduced. Antitrust measures designed to render markets more efficient will affect the income of capital and labor in particular industries, as well as the real income of consumers of their products. Public investment programs, such as regional development or road construction, will affect the economic welfare of various population groups and hence the patterns of distribution. Public pricing policies, such as the pricing of publicly operated subways, similarly will affect the real income of subway riders, and so forth.[2]

When we turn to aspect 2, it is evident that such distributional changes as are to be made should be implemented in the most efficient manner. If a decision is reached to improve the position of low-income recipient L relative to that of high-income recipient H, this improvement should be designed so that for a given gain to L, H is hurt least; or that for any given loss to H, L will be benefited the most. This objective poses questions with regard to both sides of the transfer. Will it be more or less burdensome for H to pay a given amount through an excise tax on luxuries rather than a progressive income tax? As we shall see later, the burden may not be the same under alternative measures. Similarly, will the benefits to L be greater if given as a cash subsidy rather than as services in kind, such as subsidized public housing or subsidized private goods (for example, bread) which can then be purchased at a lower price?

Standard economic analysis may be utilized in providing guidance with regard to aspects 1 and 2, but it does not tell us how to resolve 3. It does not tell us what state of distribution should be our goal, i.e., what the criteria for distributional justice and fairness should be. Traditionally, this final question has been considered as out of bounds for economists, whose job is taken to end with answers to 1 and 2. But given the close bearing of distributional issues on questions of economic policy, economists who are concerned with public policy can hardly detach their thinking from equity issues. They can be required only to distinguish such issues from efficiency considerations. This is especially true for the application of economics to the problems of public finance, an integral part of which is the function of our "distribution branch." The efficiency-based analysis of the preceding chapter must therefore be followed by at least a brief consideration of what constitutes just or equitable

[2]While such distributional effects should be allowed for by the policy maker, they need not be a decisive factor in each policy decision. Instead, they may be allowed for in some other part of the overall policy package. See p. 183, where the use of distributional weights in cost-benefit analysis is discussed.

distribution. Otherwise, our normative view of public sector theory cannot be complete.

B. APPROACHES TO DISTRIBUTIVE JUSTICE

If a choice is to be made between alternative criteria for just distribution, their implications must be understood. We first view this problem on the assumption that the amount of goods or total income available for distribution is fixed. Effects of distribution policy on the size of the pie will be allowed for later on.

Alternative Views

Among possible criteria for what constitutes a just state of distribution, the following may be considered:

1. Endowment-based criteria
   a. Keep what you can earn in the market.
   b. Keep what you could earn in a competitive market.
   c. Keep labor (earned) income only.
   d. Keep what you could earn in a competitive market, given equal positions at start.
2. Utilitarian criteria
   a. Total welfare is maximized.
   b. Average welfare is maximized.
3. Equity criteria
   a. Welfare is equalized.
   b. Welfare floor is set with the endowment rule applicable above it.
   c. Welfare of the lowest group is maximized.

In choosing among these criteria, high-income persons will find 1(a) in their best interest, while having to be altruistic in supporting 3(a). Low-income persons are in the opposite position. This, however, is not the only way of considering this choice. An alternative is offered by the philosopher's view of the problem as one of social contract where people, placed in what philosophers call the "state of nature," consider what should govern the relationship among persons in a just society, including the distribution of economic welfare.[3] In this original state, people do not as yet know what their own position in society will be, so they can consider the problem in an impartial way. This assembly, moreover, should be viewed not as an initial historical occurrence but as a mental experiment to be made when examining such issues. You may place yourself in this position right now. Given such a setting, your choice between, say, 1(a) and 3(b) is not a matter of selfishness versus altruism, but of deciding, in a personally disinterested way, the moral principles upon which the just society should be founded.

 state of nature.

[3]See Ernest Barker (ed.), *The Social Contract*, London: Oxford, 1946.

Endowment-Based Criteria

Theorists of the social contract formulated the problem in terms of certain rights and duties to which all members of society are both entitled and committed, but they differed in their views on the content of the contract. Natural-law philosophers such as Hobbes and Locke, writing in the second half of the seventeenth century and following what are here referred to as endowment-based criteria, postulated a person's innate right to the fruits of his or her labor, thereby giving ethical support to distribution by factor endowment and the pricing of factors in the market.

This principle of entitlement may be accepted without qualification, as in 1(a), or it may be limited to such earnings as can be obtained in a competitive market, as in 1(b). Claims to monopoly profits would then not be legitimate, nor would claims to wage or salary incomes in excess of marginal product. Still another possibility, 1(c), is to apply the endowment principle only to earned (wage or salary) but not to capital income. This may be proper because, in line with Locke's thinking, natural resources are held "in common" or simply because it is held that earning wages involves disutility of work whereas drawing interest does not. Some such consideration was applied by the classical British economists when they argued that "unearned" or capital income should be taxed more heavily than wage income.

A modern version, 1(d), of the endowment approach sanctions only such inequality as would remain if all people were given an equal position at the start. This means acceptance of such inequalities as result from innate differences in earning ability, in preferences between income and leisure, and in thrift. In contrast, inequalities that arise from inheritance, different educational opportunities, or family status would not be acceptable. It might indeed be argued that this constraint on inequality is called for by the logic of a pure "enterprise" system.[4]

Utilitarian Criteria

As distinct from supporters of these endowment-based criteria, other social philosophers rejected innate inequality in ability as a legitimate source of differences in economic well-being. The existence of such inequalities is recognized, but they should not be permitted to determine the state of distribution. To be born with a high- or low-ability level is not due to the will or action of the particular individual. Like social status, this accident of birth is considered as lacking ethical sanction as a basis for distribution. According to this view, some other principle of assignment must be sought.

One answer was given by the utilitarians, such as Bentham, who would have income distributed so as to achieve the greatest sum total of happiness, an objective which they thought appealing to all "reasonable men." According to this criterion, A should be given more income than B if A's "utility

---

[4]For an eloquent expression of this spirit, see Henry Simons, "A Positive Program for Laissez-Faire: Some Proposals for a Liberal Economic Policy," in *Economic Policy for a Free Society*, Chicago: University of Chicago Press, 1967.

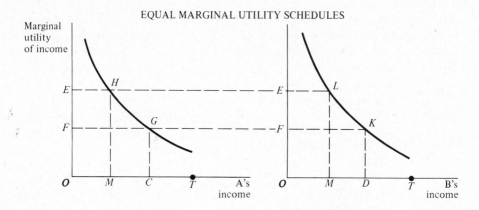

EQUAL MARGINAL UTILITY SCHEDULES

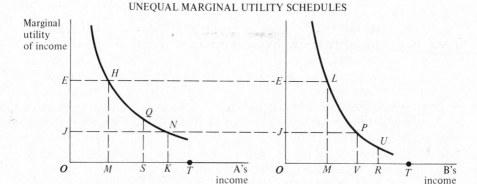

UNEQUAL MARGINAL UTILITY SCHEDULES

FIGURE 5-1   Patterns of Distribution.

level," or ability to derive happiness from personal income, is higher. Only if we assume that the marginal income utility schedules for all individuals are the same and are declining will an equal distribution of income be called for. The maximum satisfaction view, therefore, may or may not lead to an egalitarian solution.

This is illustrated in Figure 5-1. In each diagram, income is measured along the horizontal axis, while the vertical axis records the marginal utility of income, i.e., the increment in total utility which results as another dollar is added to income. The area under the curve thus measures the total utility derived at various income levels. To bypass the difficulty which arises because the utility of initial dollars may well be infinite, we consider the distribution of income above a certain minimum level OM. We assume, for the time being, that the utility of income can be measured in "utils" and that a utility comparison among various individuals is possible. The difficulties involved in these assumptions will be considered presently. We assume further that after providing each with OM, total income available for assignment between A and B is fixed at MT.

In the upper part of the figure, we postulate that two individuals, A and B, have the same marginal utility schedules. To maximize total satisfaction, this income will then be divided equally between A and B so that A receives MC while B receives MD, with $MC + MD = MT$. The marginal utilities of A and B are set equal at OF, as are their total utilities, reflected by $MCGH$ and $MDKL$, respectively.[5] In the lower part of the figure, we assume that A's marginal utility schedule, beyond the minimum income level OM, lies above B's. A, in other words, has a higher capacity to derive additional utility from income above OM. Assuming again a total income MT to be available for distribution, total utility is now maximized by assigning the larger amount MK to A and the smaller amount MV to B, where $MK + MV = MT$. Marginal utilities are equated at OJ, and A's total utility, or $MKNH$, now exceeds B's or $MVPL$. Having a higher-lying utility schedule, A is better off for two reasons: A not only derives greater utility from the same income but, in addition, receives a larger income share.

The "maximum total welfare" criterion presents certain difficulties if population changes are taken into consideration. As the size of population increases, total income rises. But, with other factors constant, per capita income may sooner or later be expected to decline because of diminishing returns. The increase in total welfare will thus be accompanied by a decline in average welfare. Maximizing total welfare then calls for a population increase until the addition to total welfare, due to the welfare of the additional workers, falls short of the loss in total welfare due to the reduction in the welfare of the "old" population. Since the marginal utility of income rises with declining per capita income, this point may be reached after the marginal product of the last worker has become negative. By then, the average level of welfare may be exceedingly low. To avoid this unreasonable result, the maximum satisfaction criterion may be restated in terms of average welfare. The criterion then points not only to a principle of distribution, but also to a principle of optimum population size. However, this is not of major importance in the present context, where the problem of distribution may be viewed in terms of a given population.

Equity Criteria

Viewing the problem in terms of maximum welfare (whether total or average) is a somewhat artificial construction. Society, after all, consists of individuals, not of a sum of individuals or of an average individual. This being so, why should "all reasonable men" assembled in the natural state agree to maximize total welfare? Is not the essential problem of distribution one of relative position *among* individuals? This is the focus of the equity-based formulations.

[5]It is easy to see that the sum of utilities is maximized by equating marginal utilities. As long as more income is assigned to A than to B, A's marginal utility will be lower. Total utility, therefore, is increased by transferring income from A to B until marginal utilities and (given the same utility schedules) incomes are equalized.

A first version [3(a)] postulates that equality of welfare is inherently desirable. Based on the humanistic view of the equal worth of each individual, this tenet underlines the egalitarian thought of such writers as Rousseau and Marx. It is also in accord with some current interpretations of Christian ethics, although in other times such ethics were interpreted more nearly in line with the endowment-based criteria, as reflected in the idea of the Protestant Ethic.[6] The implications of the equal-welfare rule for the distribution of income depend again on whether or not the utility schedules are the same. If they are, the upper part of Figure 5-1 applies and income is divided equally between A and B. The utilitarian (maximum total welfare) and egalitarian precepts both call for an equal distribution of income. But if utility levels differ, as assumed in the lower part of the figure, egalitarian distribution would assign MS to A and MR to B where $MS + MR = MT$ and $MSQH = MRUL$. The larger share of income now goes to the person whose utility scale is lower, and the pattern of income inequality becomes opposite to that achieved under the maximum total satisfaction rule.

It is doubtful, however, whether egalitarians such as Rousseau or Marx would have recognized differences in the level of utility schedules as legitimate reasons for income inequality. When Marx postulated, "From each according to his ability, to each according to his need,"[7] he evidently referred to differences in need due to objective factors, such as family size or health, and not to subjective differentials in the capacity to enjoy income. Although enjoyment capacities may differ, the egalitarian philosophers would have interpreted the "equal worth" doctrine as calling for society to proceed as if utility schedules were the same, thereby arriving at an egalitarian distribution, qualified only by allowance for objective differentials.

The variety of possible views is increased by combining equity- and endowment-based considerations. Thus, it may be held [criterion 3(b)] that equity calls for assuring that no one suffers poverty, but that an endowment-based approach may be applied once this objective is met. It would seem that among the various criteria so far noted, this compromise view (combined perhaps with some recognition of the equality-at-the-start interpretation of the endowment criteria) most nearly approximates emerging United States mores regarding the distribution problem. Thus it was argued in a recent Economic Report that "those who produce more should be rewarded more; and no individual or household should be forced to fall below some minimum standard of consumption regardless of production potential."[8]

Still another view [criterion 3(c)] is reflected in John Rawls's principle of "maximin."[9] According to this rule, a person is not entitled to the fruits of

[6]See Max Weber, *The Protestant Ethic and the Spirit of Capitalism* (trans., Talcott Parsons), New York: Scribner's, 1958.

[7]See Karl Marx, "Critique of the Gotha Program," in P. C. Tucker (ed.), *The Marx-Engels Reader*, New York: Norton, 1972, p. 388. In the same context Marx notes that incentive considerations do not permit application of this norm under socialism, it being attainable only in the final state of communism.

[8]*Economic Report of the President*, 1974, p. 137.

[9]Using the previously noted philosophical construct of an "original position" where individuals agree to consider the question of distribution in the abstract, Rawls concludes that

superior ability, but inequality is accepted to the extent that it serves to raise the position of the lowest person on the scale.

Choice among Criteria

Given this range of criteria to choose from, how is one to know which is the correct solution? Or, moving one step back, can it be argued that there *is* a correct solution? And if so, how can it be demonstrated to be correct? These, of course, are philosophical questions which cannot be resolved here, if at all. Some philosophers (from Plato on) have held that there exists a natural order of things in which a person's place in society is assigned by his or her station at birth. Others, such as Locke, have held that people may make use of their natural endowments. Still others, like Rousseau, believed that individuals are potentially equal and that their social relations must be derived from this premise. Thinkers like Kant and, more recently, Rawls have maintained that a set of moral imperatives points to a single rational solution, while according to others such principles are merely taken to prescribe the rules by which decisions are to be made. The basic question of whether the design of the good society can be derived by "reason" alone or whether "value judgment" is needed remains unresolved, a matter to be rethought as civilization proceeds.

Subjective versus Social Utility

Much of the reasoning underlying our equity criteria calls for a comparison between the utility levels enjoyed by various individuals. The difficulties involved in such a comparison, however, pose serious questions as to the meaningfulness of the entire procedure. What is to be the unit in which utility is measured? How can the level and slope of A's utility schedule be determined and, most difficult, how can it be compared with that of B? Economists have had little success in answering these questions.[10] Yet, it is evident that society does in fact engage in policies which involve interpersonal comparisons. People formulate opinions on how the tax burden should be distributed or who should receive transfers.[11] One way of cutting the Gordian knot is to suppose that society proceeds on the premises (1) that

---

the choice would call for (1) equality in the assignment of basic rights and duties, with (2) inequalities being "just only if they result in compensating benefits for everyone and in particular for the least advantaged members of society." Rational choice, he feels, calls for 2 because people do not wish to run the risk of being too badly off if caught at the bottom of the scale. In the economist's terms, they are taken to be extreme risk averters. See John Rawls, *A Theory of Justice*, Cambridge, Mass.: Harvard, 1972.

[10]Empirical studies may be made of the rate at which people are willing to trade income for leisure, but this does not solve our problem because their evaluation of leisure in terms of utility may differ. Similarly, studies may be made of the *slope* of people's income utility schedule by measuring their responses to risk taking, but this again does not tell us what are the absolute (and comparable) levels of utility which they derive from different levels of income. See Milton Friedman and L. J. Savage, "The Utility Analysis of Choices Involving Risk," *Journal of Political Economy*, August 1948, reprinted in G. Stigler and K. Boulding (eds.), *Readings in Price Theory*, American Economic Association, Homewood, Ill.: Irwin, 1954, pp. 57–96; and Armen A. Alchian, "The Meaning of Utility Measurement," *American Economic Review*, March 1953.

[11]See p. 254 for application to taxation and p. 182 for application to project evaluation.

marginal utility schedules are downward sloping and (2) that all individuals should be treated *as if* their schedules were identical, whether this is in fact the case or not. Given these assumptions, it readily follows that the utilitarian and equity criteria listed above all call for an egalitarian distribution, although of course this result does not hold for the endowment approach. Since policy in fact does not provide for an equal distribution, are we to conclude that the endowment principle prevails? Not necessarily so since, as we shall presently see, the outcomes of both utilitarian and equity rules are qualified once the effects of redistribution on the size of the pie are allowed for.

C. THE SIZE OF THE PIE

So far, we have discussed the problem of distribution under the simplifying assumption that the total available for distribution is given. But it is not. We must now allow for the fact that individuals can choose between income and leisure, so that the size of the pie may be affected by how it is distributed. This introduces two complications: (1) the feasibility of redistribution may be limited; and (2) redistribution imposes an efficiency cost that must be allowed for.

Limits to Redistribution

The fact that income redistribution will affect people's choices between income and leisure may limit the scope of feasible redistribution. Suppose that there are two individuals, H with high and L with low earnings capacity. To simplify, suppose L's earnings capacity is, in fact, zero. In the absence of intervention, H has a substantial positive income, while L has none. Now a tax is imposed on H and a transfer is paid to L. As a result of the tax, the net wage rate of H (the return in goods which H can obtain for selling leisure) is reduced. Initially H may respond by working more (H's labor supply schedule slopes backward over this high-wage-rate range), but thereafter a further increase in the tax rate will induce H to retain more leisure—that is, to work less.

As a result, the revenue obtainable from a given tax is not unlimited. As the tax rate is increased further, revenue will rise for some time until a point is reached beyond which further increases in the tax rate will result in declining revenue and hence reduced funds available for transfer to L. This point of diminishing revenue may be reached well before a 50 percent rate and full equalization applies, with further attempts at equalization resulting in income losses for L as well as H. Whereas the egalitarian solution calls for a rate of 50 percent, the maximin rule may fall short thereof.

This is illustrated by the accompanying schedule, showing H's response to various tax rates and assuming the hourly wage rate to be $10. As the tax is introduced, H increases working hours until a rate of 15 percent is reached and then reduces them. Tax revenue in this illustration reaches a maximum at

Tax Rate (Percentage) (I)	H's Hours Worked (II)	H's Pretax Income (Dollars) (III)	Tax Revenue (Dollars) (IV)	H's Posttax Income (Dollars) (V)	L's Income (Dollars) (VI)
A ⟶ 0	6.0	60.0	0	60.0	0 *Keep what you get*
B 15	7.0	70.0	10.5	59.5	10.5
C 30	5.0	50.0	15.0	35.0	15.0
D 50	2.5	25.0	12.5	12.5	12.5 *income equalized*
80	1.0	10.0	8.0	2.0	8.0
100	0	0	0	0	0

a rate of 30 percent.[12] Columns V and VI are plotted in Figure 5-2, where H's after-tax income is measured horizontally and L's transfer receipts are measured vertically. The 45° line OZ shows equal distribution. If H did not respond to the tax, the policy options would lie along AE, with both egalitarian and maximin solutions given at Z. Since H responds first by working more and then by working less, the set of options is given by curve $ABCDO$, showing the positions of H and L at various tax rates.

[12]See p. 468 for further discussion of the point of maximum yield.

FIGURE 5-2   Redistribution with Variable Income.

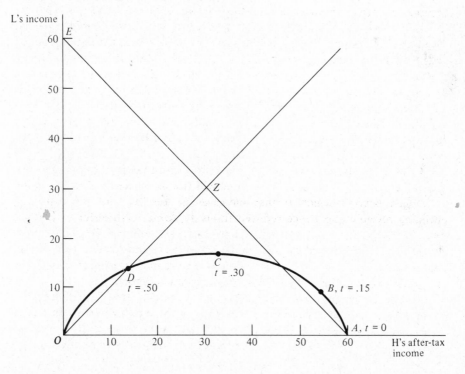

Which point on *ABCDO* should be chosen? Under the endowment rule, the tax rate is to be zero, with the solution at point *A*. If total income is to be maximized, a tax rate of .15 and point *B* are called for. If income is to be equalized, point *D* with a tax rate of 50 percent is chosen. This, however, leaves both H and L with lower incomes than they would have enjoyed at *C*, where the tax rate is 30 percent and L's income is maximized. An egalitarian who would choose *Z* in the absence of a resulting change in income must now decide whether to move as far as *D* or stop somewhere between *C* and *D*. No one except a sadist would want to go beyond *D*.

John Rawls, as noted before, would stop at *C* where L's income reaches a maximum. Others, whose dislike for inequality is greater, may wish to go further toward *D* and accept some decline in the lowest income in order to achieve a higher degree of equality. Still others, including perhaps most people, would want to stop short of *C*. Even though they are prepared to go beyond *B* in order to further improve L's position, they also want to allow for the cost of lost income which is involved in moving toward *C*.

Efficiency Cost of Redistribution

The nature of the distribution problem thus changes considerably, once we allow for the fact that the income total which is available for redistribution is itself a function of distribution policy. If taxed too heavily, H may work less, and less is available for distribution to L. In the absence of compulsory labor, H has a form of veto power.

This point is brought out clearly in Figure 5-2, but it does not tell the entire story. A person's welfare not only depends on the receipt of income but also on the retention of leisure. The tax interferes with H's choice between income and leisure and this entails an efficiency cost. As we shall discuss in detail later on, the burden imposed on H tends to exceed the amount of tax which the government collects. The existence of an efficiency cost, however, does not mean that no transfer should be made, since a dollar gain to L is considered more valuable, in terms of social utility, than a dollar loss to H. But this cost must be allowed for and be balanced against the social gain that is derived. Its presence limits the desirable degree of transfer. This is the problem of "optimal income taxation" which will be noted further at a later stage.[13]

 Since the efficiency cost of redistribution depends on economic responses, including responses in work effort, saving, investment, and risk taking, it also depends on the form of economic organization and on social institutions that prevail. Thus, the burden and disincentive effects imposed by the taxation of capital income may be of major importance under capitalism but carry little significance in a socialist setting, where savings and investment decisions are performed by the state. Such a regime may thus have more flexibility with regard to distribution than has our system. Both, however,

[13]See p. 315.

must allow for responses in work effort, provided of course that the socialist system calls for labor to be supplied on a voluntary basis.

Efficiency-Equity Tradeoff

The nature of the efficiency-equity tradeoff is illustrated best by returning to Figure 3-3 of Chapter 3. Suppose that with a given state of distribution of income and a efficient market system, a welfare position corresponding to point V is reached. Now it is desired to redistribute in favor of B by moving to point U. Since the tax-transfer system needed to redistribute imposes an efficiency cost (excess burden), this is not possible, the only available alternative being a move to, say, W. This move would be desirable even though it involves an efficiency loss (narrowly defined), i.e., a move to inside the utility frontier, because W lies on a higher social indifference (si) curve. If, however, the result is a move to R, the efficiency loss would outweigh the equity gain and the case would be against the adjustment. The choice thus depends on the magnitude of the efficiency cost and how society values it relative to equity gains.

While society may well accept some efficiency loss to obtain an equity gain, distributional adjustments should be made so as to minimize this efficiency loss. In our initial sketch of distribution policy, as given in Chapter 1, we have suggested that a combination of income taxes and income transfers provides the most plausible mechanism to expedite distributional adjustments. This, we said, would have the advantage of permitting decisions on distribution policy to be made independent of policies aimed at the provision of social goods. The use of a general income tax most likely would interfere less with individual choices (i.e., impose a smaller excess burden) than would selective taxes on consumption or other uses of income. Similarly, the use of a general income transfer would leave the recipient with a greater benefit than would services in kind or subsidies to particular forms of consumption that would distort the individual's preferred consumption pattern. These conclusions remain plausible, but it must be noted that even income taxes and transfers are not free of distortions, since they affect economic choices. We shall have to consider more carefully, later on, what combination of tax and expenditure measures will involve the least burden.[14]

An Ideal Solution?

The necessity for tradeoff, to repeat, arises because redistributive taxes and transfers have to be related to a person's income and its uses. The tax thus affects the rate at which H can trade leisure for goods (the cost of leisure is reduced) and substitution will result. If it were possible to assess H's *potential* income (or include leisure as well as goods in the base), tax liability would become independent of work effort. This would have two great advantages: (1) H would not be able to block redistribution by working less and (2) there

[14]See p. 314.

would be no efficiency cost involved. Moreover, (3) redistributional measures could then be undertaken without discriminating against A, whose potential income is high but who prefers goods to leisure, in favor of B, whose potential income is the same but who prefers leisure to goods.[15] Unfortunately, a tax on potential income is not a practical proposition, but it may be possible to develop techniques which move somewhat in that direction.[16]

D. FURTHER ISSUES

In recent years attention has been given to some further aspects of the distribution problem, including voluntary redistribution, the concept of categorical equity, and intertemporal distribution among generations.

Voluntary Redistribution

In the preceding section we have viewed redistribution as a budgetary process and have considered the resulting efficiency cost. Such costs do not arise if we deal with voluntary transfers, i.e., giving.

Basis for Giving   Gifts are made because utilities are interdependent. Humans, as noted before, are social beings and their satisfactions are not derived in isolation. Thus, A may derive utility not only from personal consumption but also from that of B and C. After A's own consumption has reached a relatively high level, A may derive greater satisfaction from giving income to B, whose consumption is low, than from adding to personal consumption. This will generate voluntary redistribution from A to B and offers a rationale for charitable giving.

Such voluntary redistribution may be analyzed with the same tools used to determine efficiency in allocation economics. Since gains are obtained by both donor and donee, adjustments in distribution now improve efficiency under the "someone gains, no one loses" rule. This aspect of redistribution may thus be handled in the context of Pareto optimality.[17] But note that giving and the resulting final state of distribution depends on that which prevailed prior to the adjustment. Secondary redistribution thus differs from the more basic question of how the prior state of primary distribution should be determined.[18]

Giving in Kind   Voluntary redistribution, moreover, may be of two kinds. A's preferences may be such that A derives utility from B's consump-

---

[15]The term "leisure" in this argument should be interpreted to mean all activity not aimed at earning income (e.g., taking a strenuous hike or studying Sanskrit) and not necessarily staying in bed.

[16]See p. 315.

[17]See H. H. Hochman and J. D. Rogers, "Pareto Optimal Redistribution," *American Economic Review*, September 1969.

[18]Pushing the argument back further, James Buchanan has noted that primary distribution might be defined in terms of entitlement to one's endowments, subject to reassignment by majority rule. See James Buchanan, "Before Public Choice," in Gordon Tullock (ed), *Explorations in the Theory of Anarchy*, Blacksburg, Va.: Center for the Study of Public Choice, 1972.

tion independent of what products B consumes. In this case, A will wish to make a transfer to B in terms of money income. Or A may derive more satisfaction from B's consumption of milk than of beer; A's giving will then take a paternalistic form and the transfer will be made in kind. The question was raised, in connection with our discussion of merit goods, whether such "paternalistic giving" should be viewed as interference with the recipient's choice.[19]

Distribution as a Social Good   Consider now a situation where the donor derives welfare not from adding to the well-being of the particular recipient but (proceeding in a more intellectual fashion) from reducing the overall degree of inequality in society at large. In this case, the potential donor would find individual giving of little use. The problem becomes similar to provision of social goods, as A will find it worthwhile to contribute only if B and C do the same; and since each may act as a free rider, taxes are needed just as they were with social goods.

In all, it is difficult to say to what extent the actual budgetary process of redistribution should be viewed in terms of voluntary giving and the social goods approach; or the extent to which it should be viewed as a process by which a majority succeeds in transferring income from an unwilling minority.

Categorical Equity

The distinction between grants in cash and grants in kind, just noted in connection with voluntary giving, may be applied also to the broader problem of distributive justice. Should the problem of just distribution, especially as related to the assurance of minimum levels, be defined in terms of income (free to use as the recipient wishes) or in terms of a specified basket of goods, e.g., essential items of food, clothing, and shelter?[19] This formulation, which has been referred to as "categorical equity," links the merit-good approach to that of distributive justice. As such, categorical equity involves all the difficulties inherent in the merit-good concept, but along with it helps to explain the prevalence of public policies aimed at in-kind support of low-income households, or at subsidizing products bought by them.

Equity among Generations

Those now living may affect the welfare of future generations in various ways. Thus, advances in science and technology made by this generation will be at the disposal of the next. Similarly, the capital stock accumulated by the present generation is bequeathed as a legacy to the next one. In many ways the present generation thus benefits the future one. On the other hand,

---

[19]This position differs from simply holding that the minimum income should suffice to buy such a basket. If the recipient is not required to make the purchase, the procedure differs little from a cash grant. The approach is a distinct one only if the grant is made in kind *and* the goods thus provided cannot be resold.

exploitation of irreplaceable natural resources and destruction of the environment place a burden upon the future. All these relationships—the asymmetri-
cal fact that the present can affect the future but not vice versa—pose
questions of "intergeneration equity" to which we shall return later when
discussing public debt and social security finance. Now we only note that
introduction of a time dimension further adds to the complexities of the
distribution problem.[20]

Implementation Problems

Having dealt with mainly theoretical issues of distribution policy, in this
concluding section we shall bring out some additional problems of implementation, problems which must be faced as specific tax and transfer
measures are applied.

1.   While dealing with the problem of distribution on an abstract level, it
is possible to think of it in general terms, referring to the distribution of welfare
at large. In practice, concern must be with a more concrete formulation involving
the question of whether the distribution issue should be viewed in terms of
income, consumption, or wealth. At a later point we shall have to consider this
question when evaluating the case for or against reliance on particular tax
bases.[21]

2.   Assuming income to be chosen as the preferred base, one must then
face the question of just how income should be defined for tax and transfer
purposes. As we shall see when we discuss the income tax in detail, this is a
thorny problem which reflects the complexities of economic and legal organization in modern society.

3.   Another important question is whether the problem of distribution
should be viewed in short- or long-run terms. Assuming again that distribution is
viewed in terms of income, should reference be to annual, more extended, or
even lifetime income? Obviously, short-run income positions are subject to the
impact of particular events and are less significant than are income positions over
the longer run. Yet, administration of the tax system on a lifetime basis would
hardly be feasible, and shorter-term positions have to be considered.

4.   A further issue relates to defining the units among which the distribution problem should be applied. These definitions involve choice between individual earners and family units as the appropriate base for distribution analysis.
If the family unit is chosen, further consideration has to be given to its definition,
including such questions as the treatment of various types of dependents.[22] As
one moves away from the broader philosophical issues of the distribution
problem to its practical application, these and related issues advance into the
foreground of the policy discussion. Yet the broader aspects must be kept in
mind. Here, as in other connections, the details of policy implementation cannot
be decided upon without knowing what the policy objectives are to be.

[20]See p. 706.
[21]See p. 243.
[22]See p. 385.

E. SUMMARY

The problem of just distribution, along with that of efficiency, is an essential part of the broader problem of optimal resource use:

    1. The theory of factor shares as determined in a competitive market is important for efficient resource use, but it is not a theory of distributive justice.

    2. The distribution of income as determined in the market depends on the distribution of factor endowments and the prices which the services of these factors will fetch.

    3. The resulting distribution is also affected by the presence of market imperfections.

    4. The distribution as determined by factor incomes need not coincide with what is considered socially desirable. The final distribution of income among families can be adjusted by fiscal measures.

Various approaches to distributive justice have been distinguished, and their implications for the distribution of income have been considered.

    5. Endowment-based views sanction the distribution of income as determined by factor ownership and returns.

    6. Utilitarian views call for a distribution of welfare so as to maximize total satisfaction. Here, an equal distribution of income is required only if the marginal utility schedules of all individuals are the same and are declining.

    7. Egalitarian views would distribute welfare so as to equalize the position of all individuals. They again call for an equal distribution of income only if utility schedules are similar or differences are disregarded.

In implementing these rules, some major difficulties arise:

    8. The reasoning underlying the utilitarian and some egalitarian approaches involves interpersonal utility comparisons which, in the opinion of most economists, are nonoperational.

    9. Instead, social utilities might be assigned to successive income increments and the resulting schedule be taken to apply to all individuals.

The problem is complicated further by the fact that individuals may choose between income and leisure:

    10. The higher income person, in response to being taxed, may substitute leisure for income, thus setting a limit to the feasible scope for income redistribution.

    11. Redistribution policies involve an efficiency cost which must be taken into account. A tradeoff between efficiency and equity has to be considered.

    12. The consumption of both income and leisure enters into a person's welfare, and both components should be evaluated in considering distributive justice.

    13. These difficulties would be met by taxes and transfers relating to potential rather than to actual income, an ideal but not an operational solution.

Among further aspects of the distribution problem, we have noted that:

14. Voluntary as distinct from mandatory redistribution will be undertaken where the donee's welfare appears in the donor's utility function.
15. Such redistribution may be in cash or in kind.
16. The state of equality viewed as a social good calls for budgetary implementation.
17. Rather than dealing with the distribution of income, distributional justice may concern itself with provision for a minimum basket of essential goods (categorical equity), thus combining the concept of merit goods with distributional considerations.
18. The problem of equity arises not only among individuals but also among generations.

FURTHER READINGS

Phelps, E. S. (ed.): *Economic Justice*, Baltimore: Penguin, 1973.
Rawls, John: *A Theory of Justice*, Cambridge, Mass.: Harvard, 1972, part 1.
Tobin, James: "On Limiting the Domain of Inequality," *Journal of Law and Economics*, October 1970; reprinted in Phelps, op. cit.

Chapter 6

Voting Rules and
Fiscal Politics*

A. **Voting Systems and Individual Choice:** *Voting Rules; Majority Rule and the Median Voter; Nonarbitrariness: (1) Voting Paradox; Nonarbitrariness: (2) Fiscal Choices; Representativeness of Outcome; Role of Strategy.* B. **The Theory of Representative Democracy:** *Vote Maximization; Platforms and Coalitions; Logrolling; Political Change; Imperfections in the Political Marketplace.* C. **The Government as Decision Maker:** *Politicians and Statesmen; Bureaucrats and Civil Servants.* D. **Classes and Interest Groups:** *The Marxist View; Interest Groups.* E. **Political Bias and the Size of the Public Sector.** F. **Estimating Budget Behavior:** *Regression Estimates; Median-Voter Model; Alternative Formulations.* G. **Summary.**

We have noted repeatedly that budget determination involves a political rather than a market process. The purpose of this chapter is to consider this political process more closely. How are the individual's views on fiscal

Reader's Guide to Chapter 6: Since the political process is at the heart of budget determination, fiscal theory must transgress the traditional bounds of economics and invade the adjacent domain of political theory. This is precisely what is done in this chapter, and some fascinating problems are encountered in the process. The more hidebound economics majors may skip this chapter. Others should enjoy it.

matters expressed and how are they translated into political action? How are fiscal decisions related to political decisions in other areas? What is the role of the party system, of Congress, and of the Executive? How do classes and interest groups enter, and what built-in biases are there in budgetary decisions? Although traditionally these matters have been classified as political science rather than economics, both disciplines must be drawn upon in dealing with budget determination.

A. VOTING SYSTEMS AND INDIVIDUAL CHOICE

Once more our story begins with the individual consumer who is the final beneficiary of public services and whose consumption of private goods is reduced when resources are transferred to the public sector. The key question is how preferences on the matter can be expressed and implemented. As we have seen, decisions may be reached in the small group by a process of negotiation and bargaining. Each individual's contribution is sufficiently important to the individual and to others for them to enter into a bargaining process. Negotiation among the parties may lead to an agreement on what supply of social goods should be provided and on who contributes how much. In the real world setting, this situation is approximated by the town meeting in a small village, or by compacts between nations, states, or municipalities designed to carry out common projects, be they a dump shared by various municipalities, the St. Lawrence Seaway undertaken jointly by the United States and Canada, or a peace-keeping mission financed by the United Nations. In these small-number cases, some bargaining solution will be reached, although, as noted before, the outcome may not be efficient.[1] But such bargaining solutions are not feasible for political units in which large numbers are involved. Here the contribution of any one individual acting alone is too small to make a difference, and numbers are so large as to make negotiation unmanageable. Individual preferences must now be translated into budgetary decision through a political process, involving the individual's preferences as recorded by voting and the response of those political parties or leaders to whom the voter delegates the final decision.

Leaving the issue of delegation until later, we begin with a simplified setting where fiscal decisions are made by direct referendum among individual voters. Voters know that the group decision reached by voting will be binding on them. Therefore, they will vote so as to move the decision in a direction more compatible with their own tastes.[2]

Voting Rules

The situation differs, depending on the voting rules which apply. They involve (1) the distribution of votes, and (2) the rules by which the winning vote is determined.

In the modern (post-eighteenth century) view of democracy, it is generally agreed that each person should be given one vote. As distinct from

[1]See p. 61.
[2]See, however, p. 80.

Plato's Republic, where decisions are made by the intellectual elite, the views of all citizens are to be given equal weight. Thus our mores combine a radically egalitarian standard of "one person, one vote" in politics with a nonegalitarian distribution of "dollar votes" in the economic sphere. But though the principle of uniform vote distribution is hardly debated, the specifics of voter eligibility are still in flux. Swiss women were allowed the right to vote for the Federal Assembly only recently, but some cantons still exclude them. Eighteen-year-olds are now eligible to vote in the United States, whereas previously they were not. In some countries extra voting rights are retained by special groups (e.g., British university representation up to 1948), and so forth.

Next, a particular voting rule must be chosen. The most commonly used rule is that of *simple majority*. Each individual has one vote, the yeas and nays are counted, and the simple majority wins. Where more than two alternatives are considered, they must be voted upon by successive elimination among surviving pairs. The United States Congress and other legislatures follow this rule of majority vote except in particular circumstances, such as a constitutional change or the overriding of a presidential veto or impeachment, where a *qualified majority* (usually two-thirds) is called for. Fiscal (tax and expenditure) decisions are generally made by simple majority vote.

Theoretically, many other voting systems may be designed. Under *plurality voting*, each voter ranks the issues in order of preference. If there are ten issues, one point is assigned to the top choice and ten points to the lowest-ranked choice, the choices are added across voters, and that issue wins which has received the lowest number of points. Or variants of this approach may be used, whereby the top-ranking contenders in the first round are then rematched in a runoff, and so forth. The outcome under the plurality rule is the same as under majority vote if there are only two issues, but it may well differ if more alternatives are involved.

Another possibility is a system of *point voting*. Here, the voter is given a number of points which may be allocated among the various alternatives as the voter wishes. Thus, one may give all points to a top choice, or distribute them among the alternatives. The alternative receiving the largest number of points wins. The result now depends on the intensity of feeling, and the outcome of point voting may well differ from that obtained under majority or plurality.

Majority Rule and the Median Voter

Voting under majority rule is illustrated in Figure 6-1. Suppose that there are three levels of budget activity to choose from—high (A), medium (B), and low (C). To simplify exposition, assume that there are three voters only, X, Y, and Z, the same reasoning being applicable to the large-number case. Finally, we assume that the cost will be spread equally among them.

Suppose, further, that X is a large-budget person who prefers A to B to C; Y is a small-budget person who prefers C to B to A; and Z is a moderate-budget person who prefers B to C to A. Z is the median voter, i.e., the voter who is at the midpoint of the size scale. This pattern is plotted as

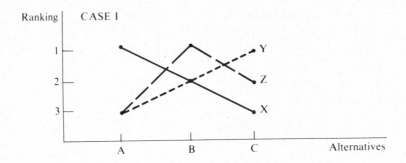

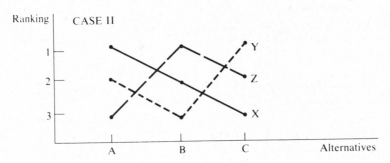

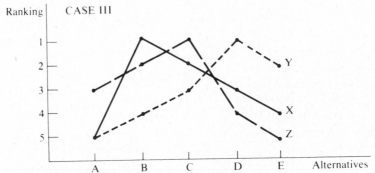

FIGURE 6-1   Preference Patterns and Majority Rule.
(Voters X, Y, and Z; Alternatives A, B, C, D, and E)

Case I in Figure 6-1, where 1 is the highest and 3 is the lowest rank. Since more than two issues are involved, successive pairs must be voted upon. Beginning with A versus B, we find that B wins; and matching B with C, B is again the winner. The same holds if we begin with A versus C followed by C versus B, or with C versus B followed by B versus A. In all instances B will win. As shown in the figure, all preferences, if plotted, show a single-peaked pattern, and the sequence of pairing does not matter. Voter Z, who prefers the median alternative and who is referred to as the "median voter," wins. As we shall see below, this simple voting model is the one typically used in designing empirical studies of fiscal decision making.[3]

[3]See p. 130.

Nonarbitrariness: (1) Voting Paradox

VOTING RULES

In considering the quality of various voting rules, a number of requirements may be noted. These include: (1) that the outcome should be nonarbitrary, (2) that it should be representative of voter preferences, and (3) that it should not be disturbed by strategic behavior. We begin with the requirement that the outcome not be arbitrary—i.e., it should not depend on the sequence in which pairs of issues are put to the vote. This problem arises especially under majority rule. As just noted, nonarbitrariness results if all patterns are single-peaked, as in Case I.

Preference structures such as those depicted in Case II must not occur. Single-peaked preferences may follow the pattern exhibited by X, Y, or Z in Case I, or all preferences may follow the cone patterns of Case III, with the peak reached at different points in the scale, and with the win going to the median peak.

But now suppose that Y has extreme tastes, and prefers C to A to B. That is to say, Y prefers both extremes to the middle solution. As plotted in Case II, Y's is a multiple-peaked pattern. The final result in this case depends on the sequence in which the issues are paired. Beginning with A versus B, we find that A wins over B, and in turn C wins over A; thus C is the winner. However, if we begin with B versus C, then A wins; and if we begin with A versus C, then B wins. This "voting paradox," explored by Professor Arrow, comes as a shock to one's faith in electoral democracy. Fortunately, the paradox does not imply that majority rule *cannot* work. Rather, the conclusion is that for majority rule to give nonarbitrary results, the preference structure of individuals must be typically single-peaked.[4]

Moreover, this possibility of arbitrariness does not occur in situations where plurality or point voting is used to determine the outcome. Since no pairing of issues is needed, the issue of voting sequence does not arise. Draws may still occur, but they narrow the choice and may be resolved by runoffs among the highest-ranking alternatives. But, as we shall see later, there are other disadvantages to plurality or point voting. It is useful, therefore, to inquire whether the voting paradox is likely to arise in majority decisions on fiscal issues.

Nonarbitrariness: (2) Fiscal Choices

The voting paradox of majority rule will not arise if preference patterns are single-peaked, i.e., if there is an absence of voters with "extremist" preference patterns. The question then is whether fiscal choices will tend to be of this single-peaked type.

[4]See Kenneth J. Arrow, *Social Choice and Individual Values*, New York: Wiley, 1951, where it is more generally argued that it is impossible to devise a social ordering which meets certain requirements of consistency. Among them Arrow includes the requirement that the outcome not be affected by the dropping out of a nonwinning alternative. This requirement is not met by plurality or point voting, but its validity for fiscal choices (as distinct from scoring athletic contests) is not evident. See also J. M. Buchanan and G. Tullock, *The Calculus of Consent*, Ann Arbor: University of Michigan Press, 1962, pp. 323–340.

Variable Size of Budget The answer depends on the type of choice under consideration. As the simplest case, suppose that the budget contains only one type of public expenditure, that successive units are provided at constant cost for the group,[5] and that the cost is to be spread equally among all. With three consumers, each bears a "head tax" equal to one-third of total cost. The problem is only to determine the desired amount.

In this situation, there is good reason to expect that preferences will be single-peaked and of the Case III variety. Provided the public good is useful to the consumer, he or she will prefer some budget size to both larger and smaller sizes. The principle is the same as with private goods. If apples cost 25 cents a pound, the consumer will choose to purchase a given number, say 5 pounds rather than 4 or 6.

This is shown in Figure 6-2, where private goods are measured on the horizontal axis and social goods on the vertical axis. Suppose that a certain consumer's intake of private goods in the absence of social goods equals OA. She is thus located at A on indifference curve i_1. Now the choice of a social good is offered, and the tax price charged to her is shown by the price line AB, the price ratio of social to private goods available to her being OA/OB. Her preferred point—the peak of her ranking schedule in Figure 6-1—will be at E on her highest feasible indifference curve i_4, with OC of social and OD of private goods being consumed. Further expansion of the budget size to OF, or reduction to OG, will place her at H or J on indifference curves i_3 and i_2, respectively, and will leave her in less satisfactory positions. Preference schedules being single-peaked, majority rule will lead to the same solution, independent of the sequence in which the issues are paired. The voting paradox does not arise.

Moreover, the budget size selected by majority vote will be that preferred by the median voter. Ranking voters in Case III of Figure 6-1 in terms of preferred budget size, Z is the median voter and his preferred budget (alternative C) wins. Above him is the high-budget group and below him the small-budget group, both of equal size. Standing in the middle, he can cast the decisive vote. Although the majority decision will thus please voters at the center of the preference scale, it does not follow that it is the best or most efficient choice. If intensity of feeling is allowed for, the large-budget people might gain more from substitution of a large budget than the middle- and small-budget people lose, or vice versa. In this simple case at least, majority rule does not allow for intensity of feeling, and this restriction is a major disadvantage. But, as shown below, intensity of feeling is not excluded as a determinant of the outcome under majority rule provided that the formation of coalitions and logrolling are taken into account.

Variable Tax Price Will preferences remain single-peaked if we replace the head tax by more realistic types of taxation? Suppose that finance is by

---

[5]The following reasoning remains unchanged if we assume that conditions of increasing cost prevail. Preference patterns will then peak at a smaller budget, but they will still be single-peaked.

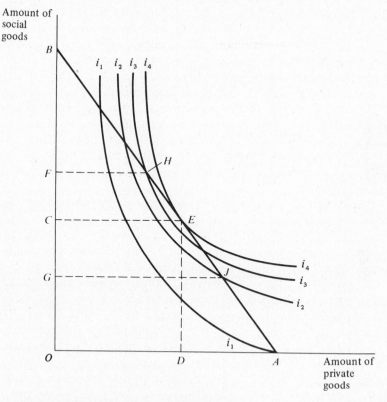

FIGURE 6-2   Choice of Private and Social Goods.

proportional income tax. Here, the price per unit of public service differs among consumers with different incomes. As the budget expands, the tax rate goes up, but the unit price of the public service to any one taxpayer remains unchanged.[6] The conclusion, therefore, is the same as under the head tax. Preferences remain single-peaked.

If the income tax is progressive, the answer depends on how rates are increased as the budget expands. If all liabilities are raised by the same percent (i.e., all bracket rates go up by the same percentage), the price per unit of public service again remains unchanged for the individual taxpayer. The earlier conclusion still holds. But suppose that bracket rates are raised by equal percentage points. This increase will make the rate structure less progressive. The share contributed by people with lower incomes will rise. A 10 percent increase in the budget or quantity of public services will raise their taxes by more than 10 percent, and they will now have to pay a higher price per unit of public service. The reverse will apply to people with high incomes. For low-income people, preferences among budget sizes will remain single-peaked, although the peak will be at a smaller budget. High-income people

[6]As before, we assume that the service is produced under constant cost. See the preceding footnote.

will prefer a larger budget, but the impact on their preference structure is more complex.

More important, no general conclusion can be drawn if the change in tax shares changes directions as the budget expands. For instance, a rising budget may first raise and then lower the share of high-income taxpayers. As a result, they find that their unit cost for public services is highest for a medium-sized budget. Consequently, a V-shaped or multiple-preference pattern may emerge similar to that of Y in Case II, thereby introducing the voting paradox and rendering majority rule arbitrary.

Variable Expenditure Mix   While the level of expenditures on identical parks may be ranked numerically, the choice between types of parks, or between parks and fire protection, is a different matter. If we think of projects A to C in Figure 6-1 as a lineup among alternative outlays of a given amount on parks (A), fire protection (B), and roads (C), no presumption for single-peakedness can be derived from the preference function of the individual consumer. There is no obvious ordering (such as holds for the case of budget size), and all depends on how the choices are lined up. Only if tastes among consumers are highly homogeneous will there be an ordering for which all preference rankings are single-peaked.

In all, the nature of fiscal choices—especially choices among various budget mixes—is not such that single-peaked preferences may be readily assumed to exist. However, the contingency of arbitrariness may be reduced by combining issues which, as a bundle, permit decisions to be reached, even though this may not be possible over single issues. As we shall see presently, it is the function of the politician to identify and present such bundles or political programs.

Representativeness of Outcome

Even if conditions are such that majority rule can be made to work without arbitrary results, it still remains necessary to evaluate the "quality" of the outcome under the various voting rules. By this we mean how close the resulting solution, including level and mix of goods provided for and the assignment of costs, comes to reflect the actual preferences of the voters. We have noted before that decision by vote is not an ideal solution, since mandatory application of the outcome (the resulting combination of services and tax prices) will leave some voters dissatisfied. Voters whose preferences diverge from that of the group may be left either with better terms than they would have been willing to accept or with worse terms. In the latter case, they must submit to a consumption pattern (mix of private and social goods) which is not to their liking. Nevertheless, not all solutions will be equally defective in these respects, and various voting rules must be compared from this point of view.

The obvious way to protect the minority, of course, would be to substitute the requirement of unanimous consent for majority rule. If only those expenditure-tax propositions are undertaken which command unanimous consent, no individual will be forced to accept projects which he or she does not value. But unanimity is not a realistic option, because the granting of a universal veto would tend to block provision for public goods entirely. It is unlikely that any of the proposed expenditure-tax packages would receive unanimous consent, the more so as it is not feasible to consider an infinite number of combinations. A voting rule (be it majority, plurality, or point voting) with mandatory enforcement of the outcome is needed, therefore, to induce the revelation of preferences[7]; and if some are hurt or benefit less while others benefit more in the process, this fact is a disadvantage which must be accepted. The more closely bunched are the peaks of the individual preference patterns, the closer will the result approximate a unanimous vote, and the less will be the disadvantage which the minority must suffer.

In comparing the quality of the various voting rules, let us assume first that all voters record their true preferences, without regard for the attitude of others. In other words, let us suppose that no "voting strategy" (a concept to which we shall presently return) is applied. In this case, it is readily seen that point voting is the best approach, followed by plurality and majority voting in that order. Under majority rule, voters (in the absence of coalitions and logrolling) can express only their rankings between pairs of issues as they come up; they cannot give expression to their strengths of preference, nor can they relate issues appearing in different pairs. Under the plurality rule, they can relate all issues to one another at the same time, but this relation can again be expressed in terms of ranking only. A voter may rank alternative B first, A second, and C third, but the difference between B and A may be large while that between A and C is small, or vice versa.

Intensity of preferences is directly allowed for only under point voting.[8] In the extreme case, a voter may give all points to B and none to A or C. Suppose, for instance, that each voter is allotted 10 points and that within the rankings of Case I above, the distribution of points is as follows:

Choice	VOTER X		VOTER Y		VOTER Z	
	Rank	Points	Rank	Points	Rank	Points
A	1	5	3	1	3	1
B	2	3	2	3	1	5
C	3	2	1	6	2	4

The majority rule would let B win. Under plurality, where the rankings are added, B receives the low score and is again the winner.[9] Under point voting,

---

[7]This necessity was recognized by Knut Wicksell, the great Swedish economist who first developed this approach. While the unanimity rule would be ideal, "approximate unanimity" or a qualified majority must do. For excerpts from Wicksell, see R. A. Musgrave and A. Peacock (eds.), *Classics in the Theory of Public Finance*, New York: Macmillan, 1958, p. 87.

[8]This conclusion will be amplified in the following discussion of coalitions.

[9]Where the majority rule yields a nonarbitrary result, its outcome will be the same as for the plurality rule.

the highest and winning score goes to C. This solution is more representative of how the voters feel and makes a case for some form of point voting.

Role of Strategy

Such is true, provided that voting strategy is not used. But in the real world, voting strategy *is* important. Because of this, B and C may not be the winners. Voters (like speculators in the stock market) will take into account how others will vote, and will not throw away their votes on issues which cannot win, even though they prefer them. They may rather settle for their second choice, so as to avoid ending up with the third. Voter X may thus overstate her preference for A, giving it all 10 points, thereby making A, which she prefers to C, the winner under point voting. Others may use similar strategies, and the outcome then comes to depend on political skills.

Attempts to deal with these problems in an analytical way have not been very successful, and the outcome is hard to predict.[10] What matters here is that the scope for strategy differs with the various voting rules. While the outcome depends on the particular preference structure, this dilemma results: The better the rule in the absence of strategy (i.e., the more sensitive the voting rule to intensities of preference), the greater tends to be the scope which it leaves for the use of strategy. Thus, a compromise must be drawn between these various aspects, and in the end a cruder system less open to manipulation, such as majority voting, may be the better choice. However, interesting work is now in process aimed at developing voting rules which offer an incentive to reveal true preferences.[11]

B. THE THEORY OF REPRESENTATIVE DEMOCRACY

Our discussion must now be made more realistic by discarding the assumption that individual voters participate directly in the decision process. While the degree of direct participation differs among countries, it is only at the local level that fiscal decisions are made in referendum style. Rather, they are delegated to members of Congress or other legislative representatives who seek election as nominees of political parties. How does this affect the decision-making process, and to what extent will the preferences of individual voters be reflected in the final decisions?

One explanation, which is of particular interest to the economist, draws an analogy between the firm's competition for consumers in the market and the politician's competition for voters in the political arena. Just as economic competition, under certain assumptions, guides producers to supply in line with preferences of consumers, so does political competition under certain assumptions guide representatives to act in line with the interests of the voters.

[10]The basic work in this area remains J. von Neumann and O. Morgenstern, *The Theory of Games and Economic Behavior*, Princeton, N.J.: Princeton, 1944.

[11]See G. Tullock and N. Tiedeman, "A New and Superior Principle of Public Choice," *Journal of Political Economy*, December 1976.

Vote Maximization

This model, as sketched by the famous economist Joseph Schumpeter and developed in detail by Anthony Downs, offers an intriguing interpretation of the democratic process.[12] In analogy to the economist's precept of "homo economicus," it is assumed that political action is rational, with both politicians and voters acting in their self-interest. The politician's objective is to maximize votes so as to stay in power. The voter's objective is to maximize the net benefits which he or she derives from the fiscal operation, i.e., the excess of benefits derived from government expenditures over the voter's tax costs. People will thus cast their votes for those who will best represent their interests, and politicians will offer programs and support legislation which best meet the interests of their constituents. Those politicians who come closest to so doing will receive most votes and hence gain or retain political power. In this way, the politician's competition for votes resembles the producer's competition for consumers and the preferences of voters are served in the process.

Platforms and Coalitions

Under majority rule, successful political leadership must take a position on combinations of issues so as to obtain a program which is acceptable to a majority. Except for referendum voting, issues are not considered in isolation, but are typically combined in packages or party platforms. Coalitions are formed which combine voters with congenial views on a set of issues. Policies which would lose if considered separately may win if considered in combination.

In forming winning coalitions, intensity of preferences comes to be accounted for, even though a majority rule applies. This is illustrated in Table 6-1. We assume that there are three voters and two issues presented as pairs of options. Issue 1 offers a choice between options A and B, while issue 2 offers a choice between options C and D. Decision is by majority vote, but to indicate the strength of consumer preferences, numbers are used to serve as an index of the relative value which the voter attributes to various options.[13] For issue 1, X considers option B ninety-nine times as valuable as option A; for issue 2, she considers option C slightly more desirable than D; and so forth.

Beginning with the preferences as recorded in Case I, suppose that a majority-vote choice is to be made with regard to issue 1. It follows from the assigned numbers that both Y and Z prefer A, which therefore wins. When

[12]Joseph A. Schumpeter, *Capitalism, Socialism and Democracy*, New York: Harper, 1950, p. 282; and Anthony Downs, *An Economic Theory of Democracy*, New York: Harper & Row, 1956, (see especially chaps. 4 and 10). See also H. Bowen, "The Interpretation of Voting in the Allocation of Resources," *Quarterly Journal of Economics*, 1943.

[13]In the illustration, the voter is given 100 points to allocate between A and B, and 100 points between C and D. The choice of 100 is arbitrary, as we are concerned with relative weights only. Moreover, the results would be the same if different point totals were given to different voters. The argument implies no interpersonal ranking or utility comparison between voters.

TABLE 6-1
Preferences and Party Platforms

	CASE I			CASE II		
	VOTER			VOTER		
	X	Y	Z	X	Y	Z
Issue 1						
Option A	1	51	60	1	51	60
Option B	99	49	40	99	49	40
Issue 2						
Option C	51	52	45	51	52	20
Option D	49	48	55	49	48	80
Combinations						
Winners: A and C	52	103	105	52	103	80
Losers: B and D	148	97	95	148	97	120
Preferred	B, D	A, C	A, C	B, D	A, C	B, D

voters turn to issue 2, option C emerges as the winner, with X and Y joining in the majority. This much can be concluded without recording the intensity of preferences—namely, that two out of three voters rank A ahead of B and C ahead of D. But now let us consider a vote between combinations of issues. For instance, let the winners (A and C) be combined into one platform and the losers (B and D) into another.[14] Combining the numbers assigned to the two options in each platform, we find that X prefers the B-D combination while Y and Z prefer A-C. The A-C combination thus wins as a platform, just as A and C won in the separate votes.

The result seems as one might expect, but, as shown in Case II, the outcome might easily be reversed. Case II differs from Case I in that voter Z has a much stronger preference for option D over option C than in Case I, assigning 80 percent of his points to D. We again find that A wins over B in issue 1 and C wins over D in issue 2 if the issues are considered separately. But now we find that the B-D combination is preferred by both X and Z and beats the A-C combination. The winning platform combines options which would lose if considered separately. This result comes about because, in Case II, the minority voter Z feels more strongly about his position on issue 2 than in Case I. Strength of preferences thus matters even under majority voting, if the voting is on platforms rather than on isolated pairs of issues.

The successful politicians (or statesmen) are thus those who can find winning combinations, and for this they must consider the intensity of preferences. As voters' preferences change, they must keep abreast of such changes and spot the development of new groupings which make for potential winners. It is this ability which, at the political level, may be compared with the sense for profit possibilities which guides the successful entrepreneur in

---

[14]Given the points assigned in Case I, the A-C combination also wins over the A-D and B-C combinations.

the economic sphere.[15] But here, as in the economic sphere, we shall find situations where such maximizing behavior does not lead to an efficient solution.

Logrolling

The same example also serves to illustrate the role of "logrolling." Returning to Case II, the winners, in the absence of communication between voters, will be option A in issue 1 and option C in issue 2. X will be displeased with the first outcome; Y will be pleased with both; and Z will be satisfied with issue 1 but not with issue 2. Suppose now that the voters know one another's preferences. X will then suggest to Z that she is prepared to vote for D on issue 2 if Z will vote for B on issue 1. This will involve a net gain for both X and Z and the bargain will be made. Y loses as a result, but for the values shown in Case II, the gain obtained by X and Z exceeds Y's loss. The outcome is the same as that achieved previously by the winning platform. As in that case, intensity of feeling comes to be allowed for and results in a more efficient choice.[16]

This illustration, of course, oversimplifies matters but it shows that logrolling in the sense of vote trading on issues is a constructive factor in decision making, to be distinguished from the shady practice of "pork-barrel" deals, which suggests a disregard of the voter interest.

The linking of positions on a variety of issues, far from being disreputable, is thus an essential and useful part of the political process. Moreover, those issues entering the combination need not be confined to the fiscal sphere. The winning combination may encompass fiscal issues, such as highway construction or income tax rates, along with other issues, such as school prayers and busing. The fact that some of these issues are fiscal while others are not does not exclude the possibility that they may be related systematically within preference patterns. Thus, progressive taxation, restriction of billboards, and abolition of the death penalty, for example, might be joined in a platform, even though they are technically unrelated issues. Through this linkage of preferences, fiscal decisions are related to public policy determination at large. Thereby the complexity of the problem is increased, but so also is the scope for choosing combinations of issues on which determinate decisions, and decisions commanding a substantial majority, can be reached.

[15]More specific models may be developed by stipulating further rules of the game, e.g., that the incumbent party offers a set of majority options, while the opposition counters with a minority coalition, and so forth. In this way, Downs (op. cit., chap. 4) develops a dynamic theory of government change.

[16]This, however, is not a necessary result. The loss on Y's part may outweigh the gains of X and Z. Only if logrolling could operate through side payments among voters would the outcome be assured by unanimous vote and thus be entirely efficient. This being impossible with large numbers, majority voting has to be used, with the result that some inefficiency remains. However, chances are that logrolling can improve the quality of the outcome.

Political Change

If this were the nature of the political process, why would there be more than one party, or one political program? If there is *a* most desired combination of positions on various issues, why is not this combination discovered and supported by all politicians, so that only one program is offered? A number of reasons may be offered to explain why competing parties arise and why governments may change in successive elections.

1. The party in power, even though it offers the winning program, may not do a good job in implementing it. Sooner or later, corruption and inefficiency set in and eventually they become apparent. The voting public then decides "to throw the rascals out" and to place their confidence in a new team. This, apart from policy differences, is a basic reason why more than one party is needed. It is also the rationale for the traditional view of the two-party system in the United States, in which both parties are needed even though they represent more or less similar cross-sections without deep ideological or program differences.

2. Preference patterns may be such that there is no single winning solution or combination of issues. The voting paradox may apply. The incumbent party may then lose to an opposition simply because of a change in the sequence in which issues are paired. The position is an inherently unstable one.

3. Politicians do not operate in a world of certainty, where voter preferences are known and getting voter support is only a matter of designing the proper program. The issues involved are highly complex, and even though governments tend to make only marginal changes in budget plans, there are many possible combinations. One party may guess better than another.

4. Uncertainty is the greater since voter preferences may change. The winning program this year may be the losing one next year. The political reward thus goes to the most skillful politician, just as the financial reward goes to the most skillful entrepreneur. Parties rise and fall, depending on the astuteness of their leadership.

5. The politician's skill, finally, is directed not only at responding to the voter preferences but also at generating new preferences which the politician considers desirable. Voter support is gained not only by response to existing preferences but also by creation of new preference patterns and loyal adherence thereto. Political leadership introduces a dynamic element into party structures, thus making for further change.

For these and other reasons, competition for votes does not lead to a single and irreversible solution. Governments come and go and programs change. At the same time, there is a tendency toward maintaining the status quo. Old expenditure programs and tax preferences once established build pressure groups in their support and a substantial change in leadership may be needed to introduce change. Public policies like private habits are subject to lethargy and change is hard to come by.

Imperfections in the Political Marketplace

The preceding model of the political process, like the economic model of markets, will achieve efficient results only if perfect competition prevails. Voters must have equal access and information, and all views must have an equal chance of being reflected. These conditions may not be met. While the principle of "one person, one vote" is accepted, the availability of registration and voting facilities may differ, thus affecting people's ability to exercise their voting rights. People *must* themselves go shopping for private goods and must decide what to buy, but they *may* or may not vote.[17] The assumption of competitive political markets involving many independent candidates vying for the voter's favor is also unrealistic. Candidates and representatives operate within the framework of parties and are subject to party discipline. Such discipline is relatively mild in the United States, more severe in Canada and the United Kingdom, and quite strict in most continental systems. Given this situation, representatives may be unable to reflect the preferences of their constituents, or it may even be difficult for unrepresented groups to gain representation.

In the absence of proportional representation or central candidates to whom splinter votes are credited, an absolute majority must be obtained within the election district, a difficult task for new or minority groups. In some cases, the rise of minority parties is complicated further by a minimum requirement being set (for instance, in the West German Constitution) in terms of total votes on a nationwide basis. This aids political stability, but also interferes with popular representation.

Moreover, political campaigning is costly, both in obtaining information about voter preferences and in seeking voter support for particular positions or platforms. Expenditures in the Presidential campaign of 1975–76 exceeded $200 million. The politician must obtain massive financial support and, in so doing, is likely to accept constraints on particular issues. Voters, in turn, may not be given the option to vote for representatives who will reflect their position, or (to put it in less extreme form) representatives with financially supported positions may be able to launch stronger campaigns. Incumbents, for obvious reasons, dispose over resources which put them at an advantage relative to the opposition, and so forth.

Furthermore, political (like economic) choice is frequently warped by inadequate information. The costs and benefits of public programs may be difficult to appraise, media bias may stand in the way of correct information, and candidates (a factor to be noted more closely in the next section) may find it in their interest to mislead the public. "Charismatic appeal" may replace judgment of programs. For these and other reasons, it would be surprising indeed if the voting outcome and decisions by representatives were fully to reflect the preferences of voters.

C. THE GOVERNMENT AS DECISION MAKER

It is thus unrealistic to view the political process simply as the implementation of voter preferences and government as an expediting force only, without

---

[17]Indeed, it has been argued that a rational person will not bother to vote, since the probability that any one vote will affect the result is negligible. This application of the free-rider principle is disturbing but, fortunately for the functioning of democracy, most people do not abide by this rule.

an influence or will of its own. Even in a democratic setting (where representatives must meet the test of periodic reelection), the preferences of voters are not the only determining force. The government apparatus itself also enters as a controlling factor.

Politicians and Statesmen

Candidates and representatives not only implement given preferences by building winning coalitions, but may direct the outcome in line with their own objectives.

To begin with, there is the popular view of "politicians" as seeking to serve their self-interest. As businesspeople maximize profits, so politicians maximize their public salaries or build connections which will be helpful after leaving office. Or, their concern may be with personal power and status rather than financial gain, leading to support of programs which will serve these ends rather than the public interest or the wishes of the voters. Having established entrenched positions, elected representatives may become insensitive to the voters' wishes. Sooner or later voters will fight back, whether by special referenda (witness California's recent Proposition 13) or by "throwing the rascals out" in the next election. Such are the eventual safeguards of democracy, but in the meantime the process of public choice may have been severely distorted.

At the other end of the scale there is the view of candidates or elected officials (call it "public leadership") as advocating policies which they consider in the "public" interest. They may support programs to provide what they consider merit goods, or to meet what they consider desirable distributional objectives. While hoping that public support will be forthcoming in response to their advocacy, representatives may follow this course at the cost of losing votes, and they may even accept the risk of losing reelection. Such political leadership, especially if combined with a charismatic personality, may be a powerful factor in shaping voter behavior. Depending on the quality of leadership, it may prove to be a constructive or destructive force. History provides ample illustration of both outcomes. While the powers of political leadership are constrained under a democratic system by the requirement of reelection, they are nevertheless an important factor.

In short, the political role is not confined to building coalitions which reflect existing voter preferences. Elected representatives come to exert an influence of their own, be it in pursuit of selfish gain or of what they considered to be the public interest. Diverse motivations enter and become a factor in policy determination.

Bureaucrats and Civil Servants

Nor are voters and their representatives the only actors on the stage. The role of public employees, administrators, and technicians must also be allowed for. Once more, quite different connotations can be ascribed to the same institution. On the one side, we have self-serving "bureaucrats," who seek to maximize their power and/or income, as determined by the size of their

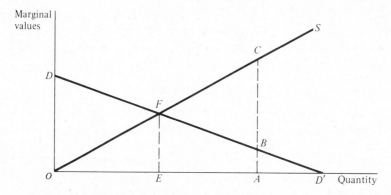

FIGURE 6-3   Maximizing Behavior of Bureaucrats.

bureaus. On the other, we have the dedicated "civil servant," who seeks to contribute to an efficient operation of the public sector and to the public interest.

Beginning with the former view, as reflected in the popular meaning of "bureaucracy," the officeholder's central objective is to maximize the size of his or her bureau. The empire-building bureaucrat will submit a budget request which (1) asks for more funds than needed to perform a given function, (2) overstates the benefits to be derived from a given level of services, and (3) inflates the total in anticipation of expected cutbacks. The granting agency may be duped by these tactics, but an excessive level of activity may result even if such cheating is ruled out. Thus it has been postulated that the "sponsor" of an activity, who decides on the budget request, will accept any proposal, provided only that "the project is worth the money" in the sense that total benefits do not fall short of total costs. The bureaucrat will then propose the largest budget compatible with this condition. As shown in Figure 6-3, this budget will be in excess of the efficient level.[18]

DD' in Figure 6-3 represents the sponsor's marginal evaluation of successive units of service, and *OS* gives the marginal costs of providing them. At output *OA*, the *total* benefit or area *ODBA* matches total costs or area *OCA*. For lower levels of outlay, benefits exceed costs, and for higher levels costs exceed benefits.[19] Service level *OA*, and the corresponding budget of *OCA*, is thus the largest which the sponsor will grant, and this is the budget which the bureau head will request. This budget, however, exceeds the

[18]For this approach and the argument given in Figure 6-3, see W. A. Niskanen, *Bureaucracy and Representative Government*, Chicago: Aldine, 1974, chap. 5.

[19]To derive point *A* we may redraw Figure 6-3 in terms of total benefit and total cost curves. They will both be upward-sloping, with the benefit curve initially above the cost curve and rising at a decreasing rate, while the cost curve rises at an increasing rate. The output corresponding to *OA* is reached where the benefit curve intersects the cost curve and total benefits begin to fall below total costs; and the output corresponding to *OE* is reached where the vertical distance between total benefits and total costs (the excess of benefits over costs) is largest.

efficient budget output *OE* and expenditure level *OFE*, the level at which *marginal* costs and benefits are equal. While budget additions involving quantities from *OE* to *OA* still appear worthwhile to the grantor since total benefits continue to exceed total costs, extension beyond *OE* is inefficient since the excess of total benefits over costs declines.

The question, then, is whether the sponsor will in fact follow such a faulty rule, thereby permitting the applicant bureau to overexpand? Such may be the case where sponsorship rests with an appropriations committee dealing with particular program areas such as water projects. But this faulty rule will not stand up under a rigorous budget procedure. As shown in Chapter 8, such a procedure calls not only for efficient cost-effectiveness analysis and marginal-benefit evaluation, but also for a balancing of *marginal* benefits to be derived from outlays on various programs. In short, much depends on the efficiency of the budgeting process and the extent to which congressional committees are guided thereby.

We now turn to the second or "civil service" perspective. Civil servants, in this view, play a central and constructive part in the governmental operation. They are needed (1) to provide technical expertise in the design of programs, so as to enable decision makers (the elected representatives) to make intelligent choices; and (2) to implement and operate programs once they are enacted. In this role, they provide an element of continuity to the governmental process and introduce a sense of rationality into its operation. Their services are crucial to the functioning of the modern state and to the design as well as implementation of public policy.[20]

At the same time, civil servants not only are aids to elected representatives, but they themselves affect the outcome. In the conduct of government, as anywhere else, knowledge is power. Public programs are complex and elected officials may have neither the time nor the expertise to analyze them. That branch of the government which is backed by technical experts is thus at a great advantage.[21] Moreover, in rendering advice, the technician can hardly avoid (and may not wish to avoid) introduction of his or her own policy judgments.[22] Similar considerations apply when it comes to the role of

---

[20]Arguing along these lines, the great sociologist Max Weber viewed the growth of civil service as crucial to the development of the modern state and the spreading of a rationally rather than traditionally based mode of political action. See H. H. Gerth and C. Wright Mills, *From Max Weber*, New York: Oxford University Press, 1972, chap. 8, pp. 196–245. The role of the civil servant as trustee of the public interest, with special application to budget policy, was stressed by Gerhard Colm, *Essays in Public Finance and Fiscal Policy*, New York: Oxford University Press, 1955.

[21]One of the most interesting developments in recent years has been the growth of technical staff at the service of Congress, thus counterbalancing the technical assistance previously available only on the executive side. As a result, the ability of Congress to deal critically with executive proposals has been greatly enhanced and Presidential power has been reduced. See p. 44.

[22]Anyone testifying before a congressional committee knows that the impression given by a chart (showing, say, the change in money supply or unemployment) will depend greatly on the scales chosen; or, at a more sophisticated level, that econometric results will depend on how the

the civil servant in implementing policies after their enactment. Legislation is typically passed in more or less general terms, and its application to specific cases requires interpretation. Thus, regulations must be developed, as illustrated by the Internal Revenue Code which spells out the tax laws. The design of such regulations and their detailed application tends to be in the hands of civil servants, who thereby function as secondary legislators. They again become a positive and not only an accommodating force in the political process.

Once more, we arrive at the conclusion that both these perspectives have some merit. Bureaucracy tends to interfere with efficiency by aiming to maximize its own size and scope. But the same institutions, acting in the spirit of civil servants, are needed to conduct governmental operations in an efficient way and to provide the expertise by which such abuses can be avoided. Both features must be allowed for. Along with voters and representatives, bureaucrats and civil servants enter as a third force in the process of fiscal decision making.

D. CLASSES AND INTEREST GROUPS

Finally, allowance must be made for the fact that voter preferences and interests do not operate atomistically. There exists a structure of classes or interest groups which share common concerns and which help to determine the fiscal process.

The Marxist View

This is in line with the Marxist view, where the state (prior to the revolution) is to be seen as an instrument by which the ruling (capitalist) class exploits the subjugated (working) class. Actions of the state must be interpreted as part of the class struggle, which transcends the political as well as the individual sphere of social relations.

Fiscal history may be seen in this perspective.[23] In the Middle Ages, the feudal lord extracted payments in cash or kind from his serfs to sustain his rule and the military establishment needed to maintain or improve his position. Thus it was in the interests of the ruling class to have as strong a state and as rich a state treasury as possible. With the rise of democratic government, the ruling class lost its tight control over the state, and power went increasingly to popular majorities who shifted the costs of maintaining the state to the hitherto ruling class. As a result, the ruling class changed its view of the state. Its interests were now served better by a weak state, and it

---

model is designed. The interaction between technical analysis and policy direction is recognized in the United States setting by having top-level technicians serve under political appointment and for the duration of the administration only, rather than as permanent civil servants as is the British or Canadian practice.

[23]See Rudolf Goldscheid, "A Sociological Approach to Public Finance" (translated from the German, 1925), in Richard A. Musgrave and Alan Peacock (eds.), *Classics in the Theory of Public Finance*, New York: Macmillan, 1958.

thus came to favor small budgets, low taxes, and general noninterference with the private sector. Marx in turn advocated a highly progressive income tax, listed in the *Communist Manifesto* as one of the means to hasten the breakdown of the capitalist system.[24]

In recent years, Marxist writers have emphasized the interdependence between "monopoly capital" and the fiscal state. The need to absorb surplus output is said to call for expanding public outlays, especially on defense; and a rising level of transfer payments is seen necessary to maintain social peace. At the same time, monopoly capital is said to object to the necessary financing, thus creating a fiscal crisis of the state.[25]

This view of fiscal politics reflects the Marxist framework in which the social process is seen in terms of class struggle. It is not surprising then, that tax and expenditure decisions will be a major instrument thereof. Dissatisfaction with taxation has indeed been a major factor in the history of revolutions and redistributive fiscal measures have to a degree expropriated the "capitalist class." But, by the same token, the role of budgetary activity may change from a means of struggle to a tool of social accommodation, once a less divisive view of society is taken. Budget policy then becomes an instrument of gradual reform and cooperation. Looking back at the history of the last century, there can be little doubt that fiscal action played a key role in this growth of social cohesion. Indeed, the rise of the modern welfare state, with its emphasis on transfers and progressive taxation, has placed the public budget at the hub of the social system. The recent growth of political attitudes which are critical of the welfare state in turn focuses on a critique of its fiscal arrangements.

Interest Groups

While the fiscal process as an instrument of class struggle is too partial a view, fiscal interest groups are nevertheless a powerful factor cutting across the Marxist categories of class. Capital and labor in the construction industry will combine to promote highway programs, while capital and labor in the defense industry will combine in favor of defense. Consumers receiving both wage and capital income will combine to support programs the benefits of which they value highly. Thus, the actual interest structure is much more complex than a simple division into capital and labor would suggest.

A similar picture may be drawn with respect to taxation. Various taxpayer groups organize to represent their interests, and the congressional tax committees, as previously noted,[26] are under great pressure from such groups, whether it be the oil industry arguing for depletion allowances, the real estate lobby wanting faster depreciation, governors advocating exemption of interest, or university representatives calling for deductibility of tuition payments. Consumers of product X will combine in opposing its taxation,

---

[24]See *A Handbook of Marxism*, New York: International Publishers, 1935, p. 46.
[25]See James O'Connor, *The Fiscal Crisis of the State*, New York: St. Martin's, 1973.
[26]See p. 47.

whether their income is derived from capital or from labor; and they will be joined by both workers and capitalists deriving their income from the production of X. The distinction between capital and labor income becomes relevant, however, when it comes to the treatment of the two income sources under the income tax. But even here alignment by income level, independent of source, is as or more important.

In all, a realistic view of the fiscal system cannot deny the important role of interest groups. By offering a well-organized reflection of voter concerns, they can make a constructive contribution to the fiscal process. Indeed, John R. Commons and his school have argued that such groups are more representative of the interests of their members than territorially selected delegates and that, in fact, it would be better to have a parliament which is selected by representatives of such groups.[27] The same view is found in the theory of the corporate state and is rooted in the social philosophy of the Roman Catholic Church.[28] But the outcome depends on the extent to which interest groups provide for a balanced representation. Group interests are not represented with equal effectiveness in all cases, and the automatic development of a neatly balanced structure of countervailing powers cannot be relied upon. This imbalance is not only a matter of lethargy on the one side or of diabolical purpose on the other. For collective action to be undertaken, individuals must be assured that others will participate, since otherwise their action is not worthwhile; and mutual support can be developed more readily in some groups than in others.[29] Thus, effective organization of individuals into consumer and taxpayer groups is more difficult than is the organization of industry or union interests. There has been a huge expansion in lobbying activities in recent years. To secure better balance, public policy should assist consumer and taxpayer groups in attaining effective representation.

E. POLITICAL BIAS AND THE SIZE OF THE PUBLIC SECTOR

Given the imperfections and difficulties of the process by which individual preferences are translated into political decisions, the final outcome will only approximate these preferences, and sizable distortions of one type or another may well occur. Various writers have gone further and argued that there will be a systematic bias leading to underexpansion or overexpansion of the public sector.

To begin with, it is readily agreed that social goods, or goods the benefits of which are largely external, will be in undersupply unless public provision is made. The only question is whether the scope of public provision will be deficient or excessive. We take this to mean whether it is above or below what

---

[27]See John R. Commons, *Economics of Collective Action*, New York: Macmillan, 1940; and the discussion of group action in Mancur Olson, Jr., *The Logic of Collective Action*, Cambridge, Mass.: Harvard, 1965, especially chap. 5.

[28]Such views, going back to scholastic philosophers such as Thomas Aquinas, were developed in the encyclical *Rerum Novarum*, issued by Pope Leo XIII, May 15, 1891.

[29]See Olson, op. cit., chap. 1.

would be provided with unanimous vote under a true system of benefit taxation.

James M. Buchanan and Gordon Tullock have argued that majority voting, by its very nature, will result in oversupply.[30] The reason is that 51 percent of the voters may join in legislating a particular program which meets their interest, while the tax cost is borne by all members of the group. Assuming finance by a head tax, the cost to the majority will be only 51 percent of the total and they will disregard the 49 percent borne by the others who have no interest in the project. Oversupply thus results because the majority will consider only that part of the cost which *it* must bear. But one may also construct a counterexample, where a majority will keep a project from being adopted, even though what the majority gains thereby falls short of the minority loss.

Whether majority voting results in oversupply or undersupply depends on the circumstances of the particular case. There is no inherent bias in one or the other direction. However, proponents of a particular project may be in a better position to organize or, feeling strongly about the project, may find it worth their while to spend more effort in building a coalition to secure a majority vote. In such cases there results a tendency to oversupply, but the solution does not lie in granting a veto to the minority. If a unanimity rule was enforced, few or no public services would be provided, and the resulting undersupply would involve an even greater departure from the efficient solution. The best that can be done is to render the voting procedure as efficient as possible, so that for most decisions majority gains will outweigh minority losses.

Presenting the opposite hypothesis of undersupply, John Kenneth Galbraith has argued that the political process leaves a deficiency in the provision for social goods because the consumer-voter is subject to intensive advertising pressure from the producers of private goods, without corresponding praise for the attractions of social goods.[31] Thus, the voters' choices are distorted away from their true preference patterns. While this argument has merit, it should not be overlooked that the producers (if not the consumers) of social goods are also capable of making themselves heard. Such is clearly the case with defense industries, highway lobbies, or (we are forced to add) teachers' associations. These efforts, as noted before, will be supported by "bureaucrats" involved in the particular programs.

Advertising aside, people may be biased in favor of private purchases because these are subject to their own control and provide a visible link between outlays and benefits received. Taxation is paid into a general fund without clear linkage to benefits. If I want my shoes repaired, I must pay the

---

[30]See James M. Buchanan and Gordon Tullock, *The Calculus of Consent*, Ann Arbor: University of Michigan Press, 1962, chap. 10.

[31]See John Kenneth Galbraith, *The Affluent Society*, Boston: Houghton Mifflin, 1958, p. 261.

cobbler; but more sophistication is needed to understand that taxes must be paid if public services are to be provided.

But this very argument may also be reversed. Voters may favor expenditure legislation without being fully aware that an opportunity cost is involved, or they may assume that the cost will be borne by someone else. This will be the tendency particularly if taxes are invisible. Thus, an increase in property or income tax is felt more directly and therefore meets more opposition than does an increase in indirect taxes, especially if such taxes are added to cost at earlier stages of production, rather than appear as an addition on the retail bill. The less visible the taxes, the more likely it is that expenditures will be considered costless and that overexpansion will result. Under conditions of deficit finance in particular, an increase in expenditures seems costless.[32]

Similar considerations apply when tax revenue rises due not to a legislated rate hike but to an automatic increase. Such built-in revenue gain may come about due to economic growth and inflation and may permit additional outlays which might not have been agreed to if a tax increase had to be enacted.[33] Putting these various aspects together, we leave it to the reader to decide whether public provision is undersupplied or oversupplied on balance. This question, of course, must be distinguished from the quite different one of whether, based on one's own preferences, provision should be higher or lower!

F. ESTIMATING BUDGET BEHAVIOR

Theorizing about the budget behavior of jurisdictions has been followed by empirical work aimed at predicting and explaining actual budget patterns. We conclude our discussion of fiscal politics with a brief survey of this interesting work.[34]

Regression Estimates

The basic task is to estimate demand equations for public service outputs. The general idea is similar to that of consumer-demand analysis, except that the demander in this case is not an individual but a jurisdiction. Assuming that the political process somehow reflects voter preferences, the quantity demanded should depend on cost and relevant characteristics of the voters, such as their income. If applied to the federal level, the observations upon which the analysis is based must be obtained from various points in time, i.e., a time-series analysis must be used. But if applied to the state or local level, the behavior of many different jurisdictions may be compared and a cross-section approach can be used. Given the econometric advantages of

[32]See p. 622.
[33]See p. 618.
[34]For a comprehensive review of the literature, see Robert P. Inman, "The Fiscal Performance of Local Governments: An Interpretative Review," in P. Mieszkowski and M. Straszheim (eds.), *Issues in Urban Economics, II*, Baltimore: Johns Hopkins, 1978.

cross-section models, and the much richer data base, most empirical analyses of budget behavior deal with the local level.[35]

In the early stages of such investigation, the approach was simply to relate expenditures, as the dependent variable, to certain likely determinants of fiscal behavior such as income, federal or state aid, and some social characteristics of the resident population. To permit inclusion of different-size jurisdictions in the sample, income, aid, and other characteristics are standardized by being placed on a per capita basis. We then have a regression equation such as

$$E = \beta_0 + \beta_1 Y + \beta_2 A + \beta_3 S + u \qquad (1)$$

where E is per capita expenditures, Y is per capita income in the jurisdiction, A is per capita aid from higher-level governments, S reflects social characteristics such as age, religion, or other features of the community, and u is a normally distributed error term. E may include total expenditures or be estimated for particular functions. Depending on the function under investigation, specific need factors might be added to the predetermined variables. Thus, if E is expenditures on elementary education, the ratio of elementary school–age children to population would be relevant. If E stands for expenditures on fire protection, density and type of structures might be included.

Using such regressions on a cross-section basis, the income coefficient β_1 typically ranges from .01 to .09, so that an additional dollar of per capita income generates from 1 to 9 cents of local spending. The aid coefficient β_2 typically exceeds 1.0, so that a dollar of federal or state aid generates more than a dollar of additional spending. This reflects the combined role of nonmatching and matching grants, a distinction to which we shall presently return. With the help of such cross-section regressions, researchers were able to explain over 50 percent of the variation in behavior, with a substantially higher explanatory value obtained from time-series analysis.[36]

Median-Voter Model

Later work has taken a more systematic approach to designing the estimating equation, based on a specified model of economic behavior and more careful consideration of how fiscal variables are to be entered. Most of these models rest on the previously discussed proposition that under majority voting, and given a single-peaked preference distribution, the median voter wins. In most cases, the median voter is defined simply as the resident with median income, a point to which we shall presently return.

[35]Studies of political behavior at the federal level have mostly dealt with the effect of economic conditions and macropolicies on Presidential elections. See Ray C. Fair, "The Effect of Economic Events on Votes for President," *Review of Economics and Statistics*, May 1978; and Bruno S. Frey and Friedrich Schneider, "An Empirical Study of Politico-Economic Interaction in the United States," *Review of Economics and Statistics*, May 1978.

[36]For a review of this literature, see E. Gramlich, "State and Local Governments and Their Budget Constraints," *International Economic Review*, June 1969.

The Model   Having reduced the problem to one of median-voter preference, the analysis then proceeds along the usual lines of consumer-demand
studies. The median voter, in determining his demand for public services, acts
as he does in determining his demand for private goods. Operating within his
budget constraint, he tries to maximize his utility to be derived from his
outlays. Returning to Figure 6-2 above, his income in terms of private goods
equals OA. With the price ratio of private to social goods, P_p/P_s^m, equal to
OA/OB, he will consume OD of private and OC of social goods. Note that
P_s^m is the price per unit of social good payable by the median voter. We thus
have $P_s^m = sC_u$, where C_u is the unit cost of the social good to the community
as a whole and s is the share which the median voter must contribute. In the
case of a head tax, s would be equal to $1/N$ where N is the number of
taxpayers.

The equation expressing the budget constraint for the median voter is
thus $Y = sC_uQ + D$, where Y is his income and Q is the quantity of social
goods. With sC_u his tax price per unit of social good, sC_uQ is his tax payment.
D, finally, is his disposable or after-tax income available for the purchase of
private goods. Allowing further for government grants, the equation is written
as follows:

$$Y + sR = sC_u(1 - m)Q + d \tag{2}$$

where R stands for nonmatching grants of the revenue-sharing type and m is
the matching rate provided by matching grants. Note that R increases the
income of the median voter by his share, or sR, while the matching grants
reduce the tax price from sC_u to $(1 - m)sC_u$. Given the taxpayer's preferences
between private and social goods and his budget constraint, utility maximization then leads to the median voter's demand function for social goods as
given by

$$Q = \beta_1 + \beta_2 sC_u(1 - m) + \beta_3 sR + \beta_4 Y + u \tag{3}$$

Note that in this formulation the individual's demand for public service is
independent of the number of people serviced thereby. The amount or quality
of service received per individual is independent of numbers, i.e., the service
is a pure social good.[37]

Simultaneous estimation of equations 2 and 3, usually rewritten in
log-linear form, then permits determination of Q, with the jurisdiction's
expenditures equal to $QC_u(1 - m)$. These values may be estimated for budget
expenditures as a whole or for particular types of expenditures. The main
difference from the simple regression of equation 1 is that grants are dealt
with more explicitly and that income and price effects are distinguished.

---

[37]Further allowance may be made for the recoupment of local taxes through resulting
reduction in state or federal taxes. We replace $sC_u(1 - m)$ as our expression for the tax price by
$(1 - f)sC_u(1 - m)$, where f is the fraction of the local tax which is recovered because the
higher-level tax is reduced.

Results   The results of various studies differ considerably as the sample of included jurisdictions and the specification of the model vary. However, it appears that price elasticities of demand for various public services as given by β_2 in the log-linear form of equation 3 are generally less than unity. A decline in price raises quantity, but by a smaller percentage so that expenditures decline. Income elasticities, given by β_3, are positive but typically less than 1, ranging from .5 to 1.0. Local public services, it appears, are in the nature of necessities. Expenditure responses to nonmatching grants are low, while responses to measures such as deductibility against state and federal taxable income are substantial.

Difficulties with Median-Voter Model   Even if the general premise of ballot democracy underlying the median-voter model is accepted, a number of difficulties arise:

1. In our earlier discussion of majority voting, choosing the size of the budget with a single expenditure item was used as illustration. The median voter was defined as the one who, when all voters are ranked by their preference for budget size, occupies the median position. But Jones, who is the median voter when it comes to appropriations for nuclear energy, may not be the median voter for appropriations on clean-air legislation. The identity of the median voter may differ with the issue. Furthermore, on any one issue, the median voter may not be the one with median income. Thus, if we deal with school expenditures, the median voter might be defined better in terms of number of school children in the family rather than in terms of median income. Other characteristics become relevant for other expenditure categories, so that there is no uniquely appropriate definition of the median voter.

2. The tax price payable by median-income voters depends on s, and thus on the tax structure. In the case of the property tax, for instance, which is the typical source of local revenue, it will depend on the share in the property tax base held by the median-income voter. If the cross-section includes jurisdictions with different tax structures, the values of s, and hence tax prices, will differ among jurisdictions.

3. Taking the typical case of property tax finance, allowance has to be made for the fact that the tax base includes commercial as well as residential property. But commercial property does not vote, so that the median voter is concerned with the tax on his or her residential property only. Thus the value of sC_u which concerns the voter has to be reduced by the fraction of the cost borne by commercial property. If the tax rate is uniform, this will equal the share of such property in assessed value. This, however, is too extreme a statement of the matter. While business property does not vote, it can leave the jurisdiction—a risk the median voter should allow for. Nevertheless, a high ratio of commercial to residential property reduces the tax price payable by the median voter, so that the two base components should be distinguished.[38]

---

[38]For a distinction between the two components of the tax base, see Helen F. Ladd, "Local Education Expenditures, Fiscal Capacity and the Composition of the Tax Base," *National Tax Journal*, June 1975.

4. Further difficulties arise where programs are loan-financed. While the median voter should consider his or her future share in the cost of debt service, residency might not overlap the amortization period.

5. The nature of local public goods frequently makes it difficult to measure output in physical units. One hour of instruction may differ greatly depending on the teacher's qualifications. Yet output Q must be measured for a proper formulation of the demand function.

6. A final complication relates to the way in which the model can be adjusted to deal with mixed goods.[39] In the formulation of equation 3 it was implicitly assumed that the public service is in the nature of a pure social good. The median voter's demand was taken to be independent of the number of other consumers, this number entering only in affecting s and hence the tax price. But, as noted before, local goods and services are frequently of the mixed type with some degree of congestion present. Because of this, the quality of output as well as the tax price may be affected by N.[40]

Alternative Formulations

The median-voter model refines the earlier regression studies and yields interesting results, but still falls considerably short of a realistic interpretation of the political process. Thus alternative models are being explored. A "dominant-party model" has been used to describe a situation where individual voters have limited control and budget decisions are made by the bosses of dominant parties. In one version, the controlling party boss is assumed to maximize personal income, with such income a function of the level of expenditures (the larger the outlays, the larger the kickbacks) and the after-tax income of voters (if you will support me, I will tax you less). The level of expenditures is then determined by maximizing the bosses' income subject to the budget constraint of the average voter. In another, less cynical version, politicians are budget maximizers with the budget level chosen by infrequent referenda. With limited options given to the voters, a budget larger than the median-voter choice may be agreed on by the voters.

These are interesting beginnings but still far from doing justice to the full complexity of the political process. The needed model is not so much one of depraved politicians or helpless voters but one which allows for institutional

---

[39]See p. 78.

[40]The demand function given in equation 3 expressed the demand of an individual voter for quantity Q of a public service. To allow for the congestion factor, we define the congestion coefficient such that $Q_i = Q/N^\gamma$, where Q_i is the quantity of service per individual, a quantity which now depends on the number of participants, N. If $\gamma = 0$ we have $Q_i = Q$ and a pure social good. If $\gamma = 1$ we have $Q_i = Q/N$ and a pure private good. Equation 3 then becomes

$$Q_i/N^\gamma = \beta_1 + \beta_2 s(1-m)C_u + \beta_3(sR+Y) + u$$

or

$$Q_i = [\beta_1 + \beta_2 s(1-m)C_u + \beta_3(sR+Y) + u]N^\gamma$$

In estimating this equation, the observed value of γ appears to be close to 1, thus suggesting a high degree of congestion. However, this result has to be interpreted carefully, because γ thus measured reflects not only congestion but also technical economies of scale in relation to city size. See R. P. Inman, op. cit. Also see T. C. Borcherding and R. R. Goodman, "Private Demand for Public Goods," *American Economic Review*, June 1973.

arrangements such as the role of the city manager, control over the budget process by city council and school board, and prevailing tax systems. Moreover, the outcome is affected by coalitions reflecting the particular community structures. Given these complexities, it is an oversimplification to deduce fiscal behavior of the community from the preference function of one particular actor, whether the median voter, the mean voter, or the party boss. As work proceeds, more complex but more satisfactory models will emerge.

G. SUMMARY

Because preferences for social goods are not revealed except in the small-number case, budgetary determination based on a voting process is needed:

1. Majority voting may lead to arbitrary decisions, which will depend on the sequence in which issues are paired.

2. This outcome, however, is less likely if preferences are homogeneous.

3. As applied to various fiscal choices, the voting process is simplest when deciding the size of the budget for a single social good and with a fixed tax assignment. The problem becomes more difficult if budget composition and tax structure are allowed to vary.

4. Plurality and point voting lead to more representative outcomes, as intensity of preferences comes to be reflected. But use of voting strategy may interfere with efficient outcomes.

A system of representative democracy has been examined, and these features have been noted:

5. Politicians may be thought of as maximizing votes by providing popular options.

6. By combining issues and platforms, majority voting may come to reflect intensity of preferences.

7. Similar considerations apply to logrolling, which may therefore be a constructive feature.

8. Delegation of decision making to elected representatives introduces small-number bargaining at the final level of decision making.

9. Voting outcomes may be imperfect due to factors such as uneven voter participation, differences in campaign financing, and lack of information.

While voters have the final say, there are other agents of decision making:

10. Candidates and elected representatives not only reflect the preferences of their constituents, but also their own. Acting as "politicians," they may be guided by their personal self-interests; acting as "statesmen," by their views of the public good.

11. Bureaucrats and civil servants similarly affect the outcome, be it in their role as experts or administrators. Empire building by bureaucrats may be supported by their sponsors, especially if unchecked through proper budgeting procedures.

Classes and interest groups, as well as individual voters, enter into fiscal decision making:

12. According to the Marxist view, the main division is between capital and labor, and the struggle over fiscal issues may be seen as reflecting class struggle.

13. On closer consideration, however, we find the structure of fiscal interest groups to be multidimensional, including income groups, industry groups, and other groupings, as well as and frequently cutting across capital and labor.

The political process, by not precisely reflecting the preferences of voters, may introduce biases into the size and composition of the budget:

14. Since individual voters do not allow for that part of the cost which is paid for by others, the size of the budget as decided by majority vote tends to be larger than it would be under true benefit taxation. But equipping the minority with veto would lead to undersupply.

15. Redistribution through giving in kind further adds to the provision of public services.

16. Since provision of social goods is not supported by consumer advertising and since the benefits are more remote, the size of the budget may be too small. But other factors, including the availability of built-in revenue, push in the other direction.

Empirical studies of budget behavior have emphasized local finance where cross-section data can be used:

17. In conducting such studies, it is typically assumed that the budget reflects the demand of the median voter.

18. The estimating model includes two equations, one giving the median voter's budget constraint and the other the tax price.

19. Both price and income elasticities of demand for public services are less than 1.

FURTHER READINGS

Arrow, Kenneth: *Social Choice and Individual Values*, 2d. ed., New York: Wiley, 1951.

Black, Duncan: *The Theory of Committees and Elections*, Cambridge, England: Cambridge University Press, 1958.

Buchanan, James M.: *The Limits of Liberty*, Chicago: University of Chicago Press, 1975, chap. 9.

Inman, Robert P.: "The Fiscal Performance of Local Governments: An Interpretive Review," in P. Mieszkowski and M. Straszheim (eds.), *Issues in Urban Economics, II*, Baltimore: Johns Hopkins, 1978.

Musgrave, Richard A.: "Marxist and Other Theories of Fiscal Crisis," in H. J. Aaron and M. J. Boskin (eds.), *The Economics of Taxation*, Washington: Brookings, 1979.

O'Connor, James: *The Fiscal Crisis of the State*, New York: St. Martin's Press, 1973.

Part Two

Expenditure Structure

Chapter 7

Public Expenditures: Structure and Growth*

A. Size of the Public Sector: *United States Public Sector Share; Comparison with Other Countries.* **B. Growth and Status of Public Expenditure Structure:** *Absolute Expenditure Growth; Expenditure Growth in Relation to GNP; Expenditure Elasticity; Inflation-Adjusted Ratios; Changing Composition of Civilian Expenditures.* **C. A Cross-Sectional View. D. The Causes of Expenditure Growth:** *Growth of Per Capita Income and Product Mix; Other Causes of Rising Share; Changing Scope of Transfers; Availability of Tax Handles; Threshold Effects and War Finance; Political and Social Factors.* **E. Summary. Appendix: Public Sector in the National Income Accounts:** *Public Sector in GNP; Public Sector in National Income; Public Sector in Personal Income; Public Sector in Disposable Income.*

We now turn to a series of chapters dealing with public expenditure structure and the policy issues involved in designing expenditure programs. To set the stage, this chapter examines the size of the public sector in the United States economy and surveys its growth. The concept of the public sector, as we have

---

Reader's Guide to Chapter 7: This chapter provides the background for the subsequent study of expenditure policy. We examine the size of the public sector as viewed from various perspectives and survey the United States expenditure structure at various government levels. This exploration is followed by a study of expenditure growth and its causes—easy reading, but important for an understanding of where the public sector has been and where it is going. An appendix on the place of budget items in the national income accounts is added for those who wish to pursue this aspect further.

seen previously, may be interpreted in various ways. It may be conceived as reflecting budgetary transactions, public enterprise, public regulation, and similar concerns. All these policies are of significance, but our focus here is on budgetary activity.

A. SIZE OF THE PUBLIC SECTOR

Even if this narrower view is taken, the size of the public sector may be measured in different ways. Various ratios may be devised, relating budgetary activities to different components of the national income accounts, such as gross national product, national income, and personal income. The more precise relation of budget items to these accounts is considered in the appendix to this chapter, but the major ratios are examined here.

United States Public Sector Share

These ratios offer a convenient way of examining the relative importance of the public sector in the structure of the United States economy.

Relation to GNP The most comprehensive measure is given by the ratio of total government expenditures to GNP. This ratio, which stood at 32.5 percent in 1978, is, however, not a wholly satisfactory measure. Government expenditures which go into the numerator include transfer payments, while GNP in the denominator includes expenditures for the purchase of goods and services only. If government expenditures are to be related to GNP, it would be more meaningful, therefore, to exclude transfer payments from government expenditures. This ratio, amounting to 20.6 percent in 1978, shows the share of total output which is purchased by government. As noted earlier, it reflects in a rough way the weight of social goods in total output.

Consideration of a global ratio is less objectionable if we deal with the ratio of tax revenue to GNP. This ratio, at 32.4 percent in 1978, is close to the overall expenditure ratio, the only difference being that nontax receipts and public borrowing are excluded. It measures the country's tax effort, or the share of gross income which is diverted from the private income stream into the public budget.

Relation to National Income National income measures the sum total of factor incomes (wages, profits, rent, interest, and so on) earned during a given period. In 1978, 13 percent of this total originated in general government, being dispensed in the form of wage and salary payments. Viewing the role of earnings from government in a somewhat different way, we may also note that 17.9 percent of total nonagricultural employment was provided by the public sector.

Relation to Personal Income Personal income includes income received by households, and it contains three government components. One consists of transfer payments, which in 1978 amounted to 13.2 percent of personal income; another is made up of wage and salary earnings from public employment, accounting for 12.6 percent; and a third is composed of interest receipts, which amounted to 3.5 percent. The government thus contributed over 29 percent of total personal income. Of this contribution, 53 percent was returned to the public budget in the form of personal taxes.

Comparison with Other Countries

In short, the public sector in the United States diverted 32 percent of GNP as tax revenue, purchased slightly over 20 percent of total output, and paid out some 13 percent of national income. Its contribution to personal income amounted to 27 percent, while personal taxes drew back 15 percent. How do these magnitudes compare with those of other countries?

A comparison for 1975 is given in Table 7-1, with the ratios based on gross domestic rather than gross national product. This results in somewhat higher ratios but does not greatly affect the comparative pattern. Lines 1 and 2 show that the 1975 ratio of both expenditures and taxes is lower for the United States than for Canada, substantially lower than for the United Kingdom and other European countries, and very much below that for Sweden, where the public sector is largest. If social security taxes are excluded in the comparison, the United States tax ratio as shown in line 3 exceeds that of France, comes close to that of Germany, but remains substantially below that of the other countries. As shown in line 4, the United States ratio of government purchases to GNP is on a par with that of the other countries, with transfer payments being the main reason for the lower level shown in line 1. It appears that, although the welfare state has been advancing in the United States, it has not moved as far as it has in other countries.

TABLE 7-1
Relative Size of Public Sector in the United States and Other Countries, 1975*
(All Levels of Government Included)

	United States	Canada	United Kingdom	France	Germany	Sweden
1. Total expenditures as percentage of GDP	35.1	38.0	45.9	43.0	43.6	53.9
2. Tax receipts as percentage of GDP	30.0	31.7	36.1	38.5	38.9	50.8
3. Tax receipts excluding payroll tax as percentage of GDP	22.7	28.1	29.5	16.0	25.0	39.0
4. Government purchases as percentage of GDP	21.0	21.4	26.2	17.7	22.9	29.4
5. Transfers to persons as percentage of personal income	12.6	13.1	13.9	21.3	16.7	17.7

All ratios are derived from data presented in *National Accounts of OECD Countries*, 1976, vol. II, Paris: OECD Department of Economics and Statistics, 1978. Since this source reports GDP (gross domestic product) rather than GNP (gross national product), GDP is used in the denominators.

B. GROWTH AND STATUS OF PUBLIC EXPENDITURE STRUCTURE

Writing in the 1880s, the German economist Adolph Wagner advanced his "law of rising public expenditures." He felt, perhaps in anticipation of trends to be realized fifty to a hundred years later, that the development of modern industrial society would give rise to increasing political "pressure for social progress" and call for increased allowance for "social considerations" in the conduct of industry. In consequence, continuous expansion in the public sector should be expected.[1] Has this law been borne out over the years, and just how should it be defined?

Absolute Expenditure Growth

Obviously, public expenditures have risen in absolute terms. As shown in Table 7-2, line 1, expenditures (including all levels of government) have increased 600-fold in the United States over the last ninety years. But this is not a meaningful way of looking at expenditure growth. Prices over the same period (line 10) rose nearly sevenfold, so that the multiple in terms of constant dollars (line 2) was cut to above 100. Also, population (line 9) more than tripled, so that the multiple, measured on a per capita basis (line 3), falls to 30.[2]

Expenditure Growth in Relation to GNP

These are obvious corrections, but they are not enough. One must also note that there has been a vast increase in productivity over the period, leading to a nearly sixfold rise in per capita income in constant dollars. There is every reason to expect that part of this gain should have been spent on the goods and services provided by the public sector. In other words, focus should be on the share of government in total expenditures, and the law of rising public expenditures should be defined in terms of a rising public sector *share.*

Total Expenditures   Beginning with the most global measure, we find that the ratio of public expenditures (all forms of government) to GNP rose from 7 to 32 percent over our nearly ninety-year period, a nearly fivefold increase in the relative size of the public sector.[3] This leaves us with a substantial increase, but by no means so drastic a rise as is suggested by the record of growth in absolute expenditures.

[1]See the relevant passages from A. Wagner in Richard A. Musgrave and Alan Peacock (eds.), *Classics in the Theory of Public Finance*, New York: Macmillan, 1958, pp. 1–16. Also see chap. 3 in Richard A. Musgrave, *Fiscal Systems*, New Haven, Conn.: Yale, 1969.

[2]The nature of social goods poses an interesting problem in the interpretation of growth in GNP as a measure of rising welfare. Regarding private goods, growth in welfare is approximated by the growth in per capita income. With regard to social goods, focus on rising per capita income understates the welfare gain. If consumption is truly nonrival, an increase in numbers (with GNP constant) should not reduce per capita income.

[3]By omitting price level adjustments, we assume that the same price index can be applied to both public and private expenditures. If, as has been argued, productivity gains for publicly provided goods lag behind those of private goods, failure to distinguish price changes in the two sectors will overstate the growth of the public sector share. See p. 147.

The path of overall expenditure growth, as measured by the ratio of total public expenditures to GNP, is shown in line 4 of Table 7-2 and is further plotted in Figure 7-1, where comparable ratios for the United Kingdom and Germany are included as well. With years selected so as to avoid wartime peaks, we note a one percentage point growth in the United States ratio from 1890 to 1902, little change from 1902 to 1913, and a rise of 4.8 points from 1913 to 1922. This was followed by a decline in the 1920s and a sharp 7.2 point increase in the 1930s. The rise continued in the subsequent decades but at a declining rate, 5.5 points for the 1940s, 3.9 points for the 1950s, 5.2 points for the 1960s, and only 0.3 percent for 1970–77. However one may interpret

TABLE 7-2
Growth of Government Expenditures in the United States—Absolutes and Relatives

	1890	1902	1913	1922	1929	1940	1950	1960	1970	1978
Total Expenditures										
1. Current dollars (billions)	0.8	1.5	3.2	9.3	10.7	17.6	65.9	136.1	313.6	684.2
2. 1958 dollars (billions)	2.8	4.6	8.6	17.9	21.1	40.0	82.4	132.1	232.2	298.6
3. Per capita, 1958 dollars	45	58	89	163	173	303	542	730	1,133	1,336
4. As percentage of GNP	6.5	7.3	7.8	12.6	10.4	17.6	23.1	27.0	32.2	32.5
Civilian Expenditures										
5. Current dollars (billions)	0.7	1.2	2.8	7.9	9.5	15.5	42.2	84.4	225.1	554.0
6. 1958 dollars (billions)	2.3	3.6	7.6	15.2	18.6	35.2	52.8	81.9	166.7	235.8
7. Per capita, 1958 dollars	36	46	78	138	152	267	347	453	813	1,082
8. As percentage of GNP	5.0	5.8	6.8	10.7	9.2	15.5	14.8	16.7	23.1	25.6
Related Statistics										
9. Population (millions)	63	79	97	110	122	132	152	181	205	218
10. Price index (1958 = 100)	30	32	37	52	51	44	80	103	135	229
11. GNP, current dollars (billions)	13	20	41	74	103	100	285	504	974	2,107

Sources:
Lines 1 and 5: 1890–1929: Richard A. Musgrave and J. M. Culbertson, "The Growth of Public Expenditures in the United States," *National Tax Journal*, June 1953. 1940–1950: U.S. Bureau of the Census, *Historical Statistics of the United States*, 1960, pp. 719, 723. 1960: U.S. Department of Commerce, *Survey of Current Business*, July 1974, and *National Income Accounts*, 1929–1965. 1970: *Survey of Current Business*, March 1978. 1978: *Economic Report of the President*, 1979.
Line 9: 1890–1940: *Historical Statistics of the United States*, 1960. Later years: *Economic Report of the President*, January 1979.
Line 10: 1890 and 1922 estimated by carrying implicit price deflator for GNP for 1929 back in line with the Bureau of Labor Statistics wholesale price index given in *Historical Statistics of the United States*, 1960, p. 116. For 1929–1978: *Economic Report of the President*, 1974 and 1979.

the precise pattern by subperiods, it is evident that Wagner's law of rising public expenditures is borne out for the past ninety-year period. As shown in Figure 7-1, much the same picture holds for the United Kingdom and Germany, although their ratios have been higher throughout these years than those in the United States.

Defense versus Civilian Expenditures   The reader will wonder whether this evidence of expenditure growth is to be explained in terms of expenditures for defense, or whether it applies to civilian expenditures as well. The ratio of civilian expenditures to GNP is shown in line 8 of Table 7-2 and both ratios are plotted in Figure 7-2. The figure shows that for the ninety-year period the defense expenditure ratio has increased somewhat faster than the civilian ratio, but both have risen substantially. However, the pattern by

FIGURE 7-1   Public Expenditures as Percentage of GNP.

Notes: Includes all levels of government. GNP at factor cost. *Sources:* Up to 1958: *Fiscal Systems,* op. cit., p. 100. For the United States, 1958–1970: *Survey of Current Business,* July 1971. For Germany and the United Kingdom: *National Accounts of OECD Countries,* 1953–1969, OECD, 1971 and 1976.

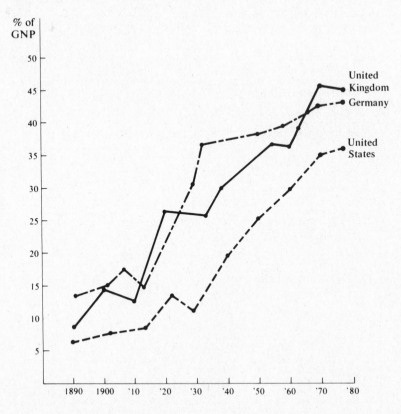

subperiods differs sharply. The increase in the defense ratio occurred primarily from 1940 to 1950, while the rise in the civilian ratio explained almost the entire increase for the 1890–1940 and 1950–1970 periods. From 1970 to 1978, finally, civilian expenditures (especially at the state and local levels) rose sharply while defense expenditures rose but slightly in absolute terms and continued to decline as percentage of GNP. Although such comparisons have their shortcomings, it is evident that expenditure growth has not only been a matter of rising defense expenditures.[4] Viewed over the longer run, the civilian expenditure ratio has risen at a substantial rate. As against a ratio of 9 percent in the pre-Depression year 1929, it stood at about 23 percent of GNP in 1970 and had risen to 25.6 percent by 1978.

Purchases versus Transfer Payments   Figure 7-3 shows a further breakdown of United States expenditure growth, this time between purchases and transfers (including interest). Since national defense expenditures are almost entirely purchases, the comparison is limited to civilian expenditures only. We find that both purchases and transfers have contributed to the rising expenditure share, but that the transfer share has been of increasing importance since the 1930s. Reflecting the rise of social security and the growing importance of welfare payments, transfer payments have accounted for over one-half the growth in the civilian expenditure ratio since that time.

[4]One element of arbitrariness lies in the choice of the particular years which are taken for comparison and another rests with the definition of defense expenditures. Our choice of years was made such as to avoid wartime peaks, while the underlying definition of defense expenditures is comprehensive, including not only military expenditures, but military aid and all veteran outlays as well.

FIGURE 7-2   United States Civilian and Defense Expenditures as Percentage of GNP.

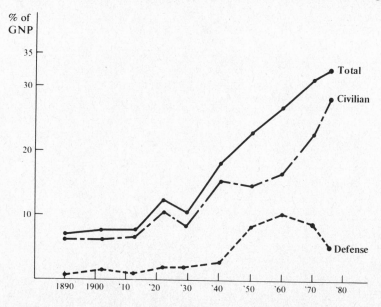

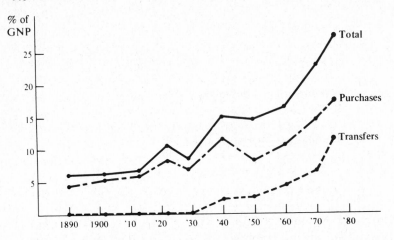

FIGURE 7-3   United States Civilian and Defense Expenditures as Percentage of GNP.

Notes: Defense includes veterans' benefits. Civilian transfers exclude veterans' benefits.
Sources: 1890–1922: U.S. Bureau of the Census, *Historical Statistics of the United States,*
1929–1977: U.S. Department of Commerce, *The National Income and Product Accounts of the
United States, Survey of Current Business.*

Expenditure Elasticity

Another view of the same development is taken in Table 7-3 where the data
of Table 7-2 are recast in terms of expenditure elasticities. The table shows
the GNP elasticity of total and civilian expenditures over selected years. We
note that both elasticities were substantially above unity throughout, reflecting the rising expenditure-GNP ratios. The table also shows the economy's
marginal propensity to spend in the public sector. Defined as the increase in
public expenditures as a percentage of the increase in GNP, the marginal
propensity for public spending has moved up with regard to both total and
civilian outlays.

TABLE 7-3
Expenditure Elasticities and Propensities
(All Levels of Government)

	GNP ELASTICITY*		MARGINAL PROPENSITY†	
	Total	*Civilian*	*Total*	*Civilian*
1890–1929	1.7	1.8	10.9	9.0
1929–1950	2.9	2.2	30.4	18.4
1950–1970	1.6	1.8	35.9	26.5
1970–1978	1.1	1.1	32.9	33.9
1890–1978	5.3	5.2	28.0	29.3

*Ratio of percentage rise in public expenditures to percentage rise in
GNP.
†Increase in public expenditures as percentage of increase in GNP.
Sources: Same as Table 7-2.

Inflation-Adjusted Ratios

It remains to consider how the preceding indices of expenditure growth have been affected by inflation. Since we have been dealing with ratios, it might appear that inflation is not relevant since rising prices will affect both the level of expenditures in the numerator and the level of GNP in the denominator of our ratios. This is correct if all prices change at the same rate, but in fact they do not. The index (1972 = 100) for deflating GNP rose from 69 in 1960 to 151 in 1978, while that for government purchases rose from 58 to 158. While general prices rose by 119 percent, the prices of goods and services purchased by government rose by 172 percent. Because of this differential a revised ratio with numerator and denominator deflated by their respective indices shows a lesser increase than does the unadjusted ratio.

This is shown in Table 7-4, where columns I and II repeat the unadjusted *purchase* ratios while columns III and IV give the adjusted ratios. Beginning with the longer view, we note (line 5) that the increase in the adjusted ratio from 1929 to 1978 was only one-third that of the unadjusted ratio. We also note (line 6) that the unadjusted ratio rose during 1960–70, whereas the adjusted ratio fell. Finally, both ratios dropped during 1970–78, but the adjusted ratio fell more sharply. In columns II and IV the same procedure is applied to the *total* expenditure ratio, with transfer expenditures deflated by the index of consumer prices. We now find that the overall expenditure ratio for 1978 is slightly below that for 1960. The image of a precipitously rising public expenditure share during the last two decades has disappeared.

It is not obvious which of the two approaches—the adjusted or the unadjusted ratio—is the more meaningful one. They reflect different facts

TABLE 7-4
Inflation-Adjusted Expenditure–GNP Ratios*
(In Percentages)

		CURRENT PRICES		1972 PRICES	
		Purchases (I)	Total (II)	Purchases (III)	Total (IV)
1.	1929	8.5	10.0	13.0	13.9
2.	1960	19.8	27.0	23.5	35.4
3.	1970	22.3	31.7	23.3	34.1
4.	1978	20.6	32.5	19.9	34.5
			CHANGE IN RATIO		
5.	1929–1978	142.4	225.0	56.1	148.2
6.	1960–1970	12.5	17.7	−0.1	−3.7
7.	1970–1978	−7.7	2.2	−14.6	1.2
8.	1960–1978	4.0	20.4	−14.3	−2.5

*Economic Report of the President, 1979, pp. 257, 258, 259, 313, 342. Transfers, equal to total expenditures minus purchases, are deflated by the consumer price index and added to deflated government purchases to obtain total deflated expenditures. For similar data, see M. Beck, "The Expanding Public Sector, Some Contrary Evidence," *National Tax Journal*, March 1976, and E. Durbin, "Comments," ibid, March 1977.

TABLE 7-5
Development of Government Expenditures in the United States
(All Levels of Government)

		1902	1927	1940	1950	1960	1970	1977
As Percentage of Total Expenditures								
1.	Defense-related	20.8	11.8	11.8	36.0	38.0	28.2	20.5
2.	Civilian	79.2	88.2	88.2	64.0	62.0	71.8	79.5
3.	Total	100.0	100.0	100.0	100.0	100.0	100.0	100.0
As Percentage of Civilian *Expenditures*								
4.	Social welfare	9.0	7.5	16.3	16.3	29.1	34.7	43.5
5.	Education	22.4	25.5	18.2	22.9	22.3	24.8	22.3
6.	Civil safety	14.7	10.9	6.4	5.9	7.6	7.2	4.1
7.	Economic development	18.9	26.3	34.2	23.9	19.6	14.8	13.2
8.	Transportation	17.1	23.6	16.5	10.7	11.7	8.1	5.9
9.	Other	1.8	2.7	17.7	13.2	7.9	6.7	7.3
10.	General government	15.2	6.0	4.8	3.7	8.9	9.5	11.7
11.	Interest	8.4	15.3	10.0	11.5	8.9	6.6	4.6
12.	Foreign relations and aid	0.3	0.2	0.1	10.0	2.6	1.2	1.0
13.	Miscellaneous	11.1	8.3	9.8	5.9	0.9	1.2	1.7
14.	Total	100.0	100.0	100.0	100.0	100.0	100.0	100.0
As Percentage of GNP								
15.	Defense-related	1.5	1.2	2.1	8.3	10.3	9.1	6.7
16.	Civilian	5.8	9.2	15.5	14.8	16.7	23.1	26.2
17.	Social welfare	0.5	0.7	2.5	2.4	4.9	8.0	11.4
18.	Education	1.3	2.3	2.8	3.4	3.7	5.7	5.9
19.	Civil safety	0.9	1.0	1.0	0.9	1.3	1.7	1.0
20.	Economic development	1.0	2.4	5.4	3.5	3.3	3.5	3.4
21.	Transportation	1.0	2.2	2.6	1.6	2.0	1.9	1.6
22.	Other	0.1	0.2	2.8	1.9	1.3	1.6	1.8
23.	General government	0.9	0.5	0.7	0.5	1.5	2.2	3.1
24.	Interest	0.5	1.4	1.6	1.7	1.5	1.5	0.6
25.	Foreign relations and aid	*	*	*	1.5	0.4	0.3	0.3
26.	Miscellaneous	0.6	0.8	1.5	0.9	*	0.3	0.4
27.	Total	7.3	10.4	17.6	23.1	27.0	32.2	32.9

*Less than 0.05.
Notes: Includes general and trust fund expenditures. Detail may not add to total because of rounding.
Defense-related: Includes military assistance abroad and veterans' benefits and services.
Social welfare: Includes social security and welfare, health and hospitals, unemployment insurance, housing and community development.
Civil safety: Includes sanitation, fire and police, and recreation.
Transportation: For 1902–1950 excludes state and local nonhighway transportation which is included in miscellaneous.
Other economic development: Includes space, natural resources, agriculture, and net subsidy to Postal Service.
General government: For 1902–1950 this item is classified as "General Control."
Foreign relations and aid: Excludes military assistance which is included in "Defense-related."
Sources:
1902–1950: U.S. Bureau of the Census, *Historical Statistics of the United States*, Calendar years, p. 723.
1960: U.S. Department of Commerce, *National Income Accounts*, 1929–1965.
1970 and 1977: U.S. Department of Commerce, *Survey of Current Business*, July 1974 and July 1978.

and both are of interest. The adjusted ratio, especially as applied to purchases, gives a better measure of the changing public sector claim on the economy's real resources; whereas the unadjusted ratio gives a better picture of the public sector share in the value of total output, and of the share of private income which has to be paid into the public sector through taxation.

Changing Composition of Civilian Expenditures

We now turn from the overall expenditure-GNP ratios to changes in the composition of expenditures and the growth of particular functions. We continue to combine all levels of government for purposes of this discussion. While changes in the composition of expenditures had important bearing on the division of total expenditures among the levels of government, their effect will be considered at a later point. The broad outlines of this development are shown in Table 7-5. Lines 1 and 2 show the composition of total expenditures between defense-related and civilian outlays. As noted before, the rise in total expenditures (except for the 1940s) was fueled by the civilian component, leading to a rising share of civilian expenditures in the expenditure total up to 1940, a sharply declining share in the 1940s, and once more a rising share in the 1960s, with a sharp upturn in recent years.

Turning now to the changing composition of the civilian expenditure structure, we note that the most striking feature is the rising trend in the share of social welfare expenditures (line 4) and particularly the dramatic upturn in the 1950s and 1960s. Primarily, this reflects the expansion of social security but also includes other welfare payments. The share of education in total civilian expenditures (line 5) has remained more or less constant, with a temporary decline in the 1940s. The transportation share (line 8) showed a sharp rise in the 1920s, when the development of the automobile had its major impact on highway needs, but followed a downward trend since then. Development expenditures other than transportation (line 9) show a decline since 1940 but are not a very meaningful category since widely differing items such as farm support and the space program are included. Other categories, shown in lines 10 to 13, follow a fluctuating pattern.

The same picture is repeated in lines 15 to 26, giving this time the expenditure-GNP ratios for the various functions. Since the ratio of total civilian expenditures to GNP rose sharply (line 16), the expenditure–GNP ratio for particular functions (such as education) which maintained a constant expenditure share also showed a substantial increase relative to GNP.

C. A CROSS-SECTIONAL VIEW

The historical picture, as presented in Figure 7-1, shows a steady rise of the public expenditure share over time for the United States, the United Kingdom, and Germany. During the same period, these countries also experienced a substantial increase in per capita income. Putting the two developments together suggests an association between rise in per capita income and a rising share of public expenditures in GNP. But the rise in per capita income was only one among many factors of change during the period. The rising expenditure share may also have been due to changing social and political forces, so that it is difficult to isolate the influence of per capita income in the historical process.

As an alternative way of looking at the role of per capita income in explaining the rising share of the public sector, we now compare the shares for countries with varying levels of per capita GNP but at the same point of time. Again, this approach does not neatly isolate the influence of per capita income, since low-income countries may operate under different social and political conditions than do high-income countries, but it should throw some light on the matter.

Such a comparison is shown in Figure 7-4. For lack of adequate expenditure data, the comparison is in terms of a tax–GNP ratio, but the results are essentially the same. A group of countries at widely differing levels of development are compared.[5] We find that if all are included, the ratio is related positively to per capita income, in line with the rising-share hypothesis.[6] This relationship, however, is largely a reflection of the fact that the countries are grouped in two clusters, with the ratio much lower for the low per capita income group than for the high-income group. Taking the low-income countries by themselves, we find no significant relationship, and for high-income countries the relationship appears to be negative. The good linear fit obtained for the sample as a whole may thus be misleading, hiding a more complex relationship between the public sector share and per capita income. The experience reflected over the last seventy years by particular

[5]The data are averages for 1969–71. See R. J. Chelliah, H. J. Baas, and M. R. Kelly, "Tax Ratios and Tax Effort in Developing Countries, 1969–71," *IMF Staff Papers*, International Monetary Fund, 1975. See also p. 800.

[6]Writing T for tax revenue and GNP_{pc} for per capita income, the regression equation (based on fifty-three countries) is

$$T/GNP = 14.64 + .006GNP_{pc}$$

$$(11.3) \quad (8.6)$$

where the figures in parentheses are the ratios of intercept and regression coefficient to their respective standard errors and the R^2 is 0.59.

If social security taxes are excluded, the equation (based on sixty-three countries) becomes

$$T/GNP = 14.11 + .004GNP_{pc}$$

$$(15.2) \quad (6.7)$$

with an R^2 of 0.41. Thus, per capita income has a high explanatory value in both cases and a good fit is obtained. This picture, however, deteriorates if developing and developed countries are grouped separately. Excluding social security, the equation for forty-seven developing countries is

$$T/GNP = 13.69 + .004GNP_{pc}$$

$$(10.5) \quad (1.3)$$

and that for sixteen developed countries is

$$T/GNP = 23.36 + .001GNP_{pc}$$

$$(4.7) \quad (0.5)$$

with R^2 values of 0.040 and 0.024, respectively. (For source, see preceding footnote.)

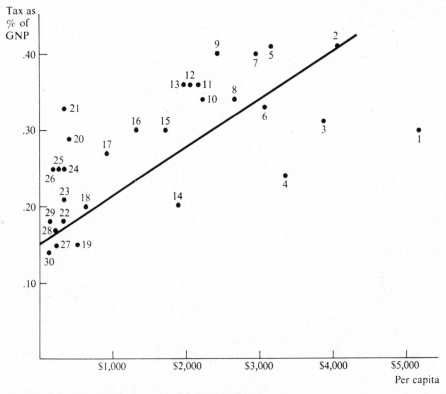

FIGURE 7-4   Tax–GNP Ratio and Per Capita Income.

Identification of Numbers

1.	U.S.A.	11.	United Kingdom	21.	Zambia
2.	Sweden	12.	Austria	22.	Turkey
3.	Canada	13.	France	23.	Malaysia
4.	Switzerland	14.	Japan	24.	Guyana
5.	Denmark	15.	Italy	25.	Ecuador
6.	Germany	16.	Ireland	26.	Tunisia
7.	Norway	17.	Chile	27.	South Korea
8.	Belgium	18.	Jamaica	28.	Ghana
9.	Netherlands	19.	Costa Rica	29.	Sri Lanka
10.	Finland	20.	Brazil	30.	Kenya

developed countries (see Figure 7-1), moreover, may not be applicable to the case of countries which now exhibit very low income levels. Nevertheless, the evidence of Figure 7-4 is at least generally in line with the rising-share hypothesis.

D. THE CAUSES OF EXPENDITURE GROWTH

The preceding survey shows that the law of public expenditure growth (defined in share terms) has been in operation in the United States at least over the last half-century or so. Some of the causes have already been noted, including increased needs for transportation and education, the introduction of welfare programs, and finally, the rise of defense expenditures. Yet, it is interesting to pause and consider what may be said more systematically about the underlying causes of expenditure growth, not only in the United States but in a more general framework.

Growth of Per Capita Income and Product Mix

In dealing with the underlying causes of expenditure growth, consider first the proposition that the efficient product mix between private and social goods changes as per capita income rises, and that this change involves a rising share of social goods. If so, this would suggest that efficient budget policy calls for a rising ratio of government *purchases* (and civilian purchases in particular) to GNP, as noted in Figure 7-2.

The rise in per capita income, seen in the historical context, records the development of the economy from an agricultural and low-income state to an industrial and high-income state. It would be surprising if, in the course of this development, the output of social goods (assuming it to be determined efficiently) should remain constant. To put it differently, the demand for such goods can hardly be expected to have an income elasticity of zero. At the same time, there is no particular reason to expect that this elasticity should be just unity, thereby leaving the public purchase share unchanged as per capita income rises. As we have seen, this share has increased considerably. Including government purchases for civilian purposes only, the United States elasticity (ratio of percentage increase in per capita expenditures to percentage increase in per capita GNP) has been 1.4 for the period from 1890 to 1929 and 1.8 for the period from 1929 to 1969.

Consumer Goods and Services In trying to explain this result, it is well to distinguish between consumer goods and capital goods. We shall begin with the former. The German economist Ernst Engel pointed out over a century ago that the composition of the consumer budget changes as family income increases.[7] A smaller share comes to be spent on certain goods, such as work clothing, and a larger share on others, such as fur coats. As average income increases, similar changes in the consumption pattern for the economy as a whole may be expected to occur. Is there any reason to foresee that, in the dynamics of consumer budgeting, social consumer goods will exhibit a higher income elasticity than do private goods?

At first sight, the opposite may be expected. One thinks of government services as related to basic needs, such as safety, elementary education, and basic sanitation, which seem more like necessities than luxuries. Further consideration suggests, however, that there are other public services, such as higher education or improved health services, which move within reach as income rises above poverty levels. Also, there are items, such as parks,

---

[7]His finding, which came to be known as Engel's Law, referred to the declining portion of outlays on food.

marinas, high-speed highways, and space exploration, which (at present levels of income) are of the luxury type. Some of these reflect the rising tendency for government to render services which are complementary to luxury-type private goods. In all, speculation on the point does not lead to any clear-cut hypothesis about what might be expected: the government share in consumption may well rise and fall over successive phases of income growth.

Capital Goods   The relationship is more discernible with regard to public provision for capital goods. In the earlier stages of economic development, a particular need exists for the creation of overhead capital, such as roads, harbors, and power installations. Many of these items are such that the benefits are largely external, or they require large amounts of capital the returns on which are spread over a long time, and thus do not lend themselves readily to private provision. Hence, there is reason to expect that the public share in the provision for capital goods should be larger at the earlier stages of development. As these basic facilities are built up and capital markets are developed, the path is cleared for capital formation of the manufacturing type to go into place and for industrial development in the private sector to occur. Accordingly, one would expect the public share in capital formation to decline over time.

The law of expenditure growth thus seems to be reversed. But again there are countervailing trends. Industrial development generates problems of its own, such as urban blight and congestion, which then call for a rising level of public investment. Such investment, being of a more or less remedial sort, aims at meeting social diseconomies generated by the private sector. Moreover, as income rises, an increasing share of investment is directed at "human investment" and the finance of education has been primarily a public function. On balance, it is again difficult to forecast what the trend should be, and chances are that periods of rising and of declining share may alternate.

Other Causes of Rising Share

While rising per capita income is of major importance, it is by no means the only factor to be considered.

Technical Change   Certain other elements, such as technological or population change, may also alter the share of social goods in an efficient product mix. Technological change in particular has a major bearing on the development of the expenditure share. As technology changes, so do the processes of production and the product mix which it is efficient to produce. These changes in technology may be such that they increase or decrease the relative importance of goods whose benefits are largely external, and which must therefore be provided by government.

Consider the invention of the internal combustion engine and the resulting rise of the automobile industry. This development generated a vast increase in the demand for travel and for highways, making for a larger public sector operation than was called for in the horse-and-buggy and steam-engine eras. As we noted already, the consequence has been especially burdensome for state finances. Changes in weapons technology, similarly, greatly increased the cost of military outlays, an equipment-intensive military establishment being more costly than a manpower-intensive one, especially if soldiers are conscripted rather than paid going wages. Moreover, as obsolescence is speeded up by technological change, the cost of replacement increases.

Future technological changes are difficult to predict, but chances are that the course of space technology—e.g., whether space stations will prove to be social or private goods—will be among the most important factors in determining the share of public purchases over the next century.

Population Change Population changes may also be a major determinant of the public expenditure share. Changes in the rate of population growth generate changes in age distribution, and this trend is reflected in expenditures for education as well as care for the aged. The baby boom of the postwar period has resulted in a vastly higher school and college enrollment, thus placing a major burden on state and local finances. If the more recent population trends continue, education needs will give way to demands for housing facilities; and as the population bulge moves up further in the age scale, the major fiscal problem forty or fifty years hence may well be that of support for the aged.

In addition to these conditions, the need for public services is influenced by factors such as population mobility, leading to the growth of new cities and resulting in demands for additional municipal facilities.

Relative Costs of Public Services Another cause of a rising expenditure share may be found in the rising relative costs of public services. This may reflect differential rates of inflation. As was shown in Table 7-4, the more rapid rate of inflation in the price of inputs or goods purchased by the public sector resulted in an increase in the nominal expenditure–GNP ratio well ahead of that recorded by the deflated ratio. But inflation in the general level of prices is not the only factor. Over the longer run, the nature of publicly provided goods and services may be such as to render these components of GNP less receptive to technological progress than is the case for private goods. For this reason alone, some increase in the expenditure–GNP ratio may be expected.[8]

Changing Scope of Transfers

The preceding discussion has related to the share of public purchases or the role of social goods in the efficient product mix. It remains to consider the role of transfers. While transfers were relatively unimportant up to the

[8]See D. F. Bradford, R. A. Malt, and W. E. Oates, "The Rising Cost of Local Public Services: Some Evidence and Reflections," *National Tax Journal*, June 1969, pp. 185–202; and W. Baumol, "Macroeconomics of Unbalanced Growth: The Anatomy of Urban Crisis," *American Economic Review*, June 1967, pp. 415–426.

thirties, since then about one-half the rise in the share of civilian expenditures in GNP has been due to the growth of transfers. The major factor in this development has been the rise of old-age insurance. This program developed, initially at least, not as a means of adjusting the distribution of income but rather as a means of providing old-age security on a self-financing basis. Since then, the system has moved away from this principle and now involves a considerable degree of redistribution. In addition, there are transfer programs—such as welfare payments—which are pointed directly at equalizing the size distribution of income. Moreover, distributional measures do not appear only in the transfer section of the expenditure budget but also are present in purchase programs aimed at the provision for social goods and services to low-income groups.

Nevertheless, is there reason to expect the role of redistributive transfers to increase with rising per capita income? As the level of per capita income rises, the need for, and scope of, redistributional measures may be affected in two ways.

1) For one thing, the need for redistribution (given society's views on the desirability of equality) depends on the prevailing state of distribution prior to adjustment. If income inequality decreases as per capita income rises, less extensive redistribution measures are needed. Actually, this change has not occurred to any considerable degree. The size distribution of income has been surprisingly stable over the years, with only a slight tendency toward greater equality.

2) For another thing, the case for redistribution may change as income rises, depending on how the objective of redistribution policy is defined. If the objective is to adjust family incomes so as to achieve a given relative income distribution, an increase in the average level of income leaves the need for redistribution unchanged. The situation differs if the objective is to set a tolerable minimum level determined in absolute terms, such as the cost of meeting minimum nutrition requirements. In this case, the need for redistribution falls as average income rises. But again, if the minimum level is defined as a function of average income, say one-third thereof, the need for redistribution once more remains unchanged as income rises. A reading of United States social philosophy would suggest that concern is with minimum levels, rather than a generalized state of relative shares, but it also appears that the minimum is set in relation to the average, rather than in absolute terms. Hence, one might expect the scope of redistribution (income transfers as a percentage of GNP) to remain constant.

This is illustrated in Table 7-6 for a simple three-family case. Policy I is to give an income to A (the poor family) equal to 50 percent of the average, to B (the middle family) equal to the average, and to leave C (the rich family) with 150 percent of the average. Policy II is to give A a minimum income of $2,500 as defined in absolute terms, while leaving the relative positions of B and C unchanged. Policy III provides A with an income equal to 50 percent of the average but again avoids redistribution between B and C. Thus the tax on B and C in policies II and III is assessed on a proportional basis. In the

TABLE 7-6
Redistribution Policies

	FAMILY			TRANSFER BUDGET	
	A	B	C	Total	As Percentage of Earnings
Low Level					
Earnings	1,000	4,000	10,000		
Transfers (+) and taxes (−)					
Policy I	+1,500	+1,000	−2,500	2,500	16.6
Policy II	+1,500	−428	−1,072	1,500	10.0
Policy III	+1,500	−428	−1,072	1,500	10.0
High Level					
Earnings	3,000	12,000	30,000		
Transfers (+) and taxes (−)					
Policy I	+4,500	+3,000	−7,500	7,500	16.6
Policy II	0	0	0	0	
Policy III	+4,500	−1,284	−3,216	4,500	10.0

Note: For explanation, see text.

lower part of the table, the same policies are repeated for a higher level of earnings. We see that the scope of redistribution (the level of transfers in relation to the level of total earnings) does not change for policies I and III but declines for II as we move from the low-income to the high-income case.

A further change in the appropriate scope of redistribution may result from demographic factors. A declining rate of population growth is reflected in an aging population, thus calling for increased provision for the aged. But, though the growth of old-age security payments (OASI) in the United States began in a phase of aging population, it was followed by two decades of accelerated population growth. Now that the rate of population growth is on the decline, the turn of the twentieth century will bring a sharp increase in the ratio of retired to working-age population and, with it, a rise in the ratio of old-age benefit payments to GNP.

Although these factors are of interest, they do not adequately explain the phenomenon of sharply rising welfare and transfer payments both in the United States and in other countries. This development, it appears, must be explained primarily in terms of social and political change, including growing political pressures for "forced" redistribution ("taking") as well as use of the budgetary mechanism in providing for voluntary or semivoluntary redistributional measures ("giving").[9]

Availability of Tax Handles

So far, we have looked primarily at changing needs for public expenditures as the economy develops. Parallel to that, we also find a changing ability to

[9]See p. 102.

finance such expenditures. In the typical low-income economy, it is much more difficult to impose and collect taxes than in the advanced economy. Not only are the skills and facilities of tax administration less developed, but the structure of the economy is such that it affords fewer and less adequate "handles" on which to attach taxes. The features of economic organization which lend themselves to income taxation are absent. Income is typically derived from self-employment and such wage income as exists is typically paid by small establishments. This makes income taxation much more difficult than in the modern economy, where earned income is largely in the form of wages and salaries and people work in large-scale establishments which readily permit the withholding of income taxes. To make matters worse for the less developed countries (and this is relevant for profit as well as income taxation), accounting practices are not adequately developed to permit effective determination of taxable income and efficient auditing procedures.

Nor are matters much better with regard to sales taxation. Retail taxes are made difficult by the existence of small and nonpermanent retail outlets, and even excises at the producer level are not readily applied in a situation where the market is divided among many small suppliers. One feasible source of revenue collection is imports and exports, explaining why the tax and expenditure ratio to GNP among low-income economies with high trade involvement is usually larger than in economies which do not have this convenient tax handle.[10]

These difficulties do not exist, or exist to a much smaller degree, in highly developed countries, where effective income, profit, and sales taxation is feasible. In spite of the fact that taxation in highly developed countries must adapt itself to an extremely complex financial and industrial structure, these complications can usually be solved, provided there is the necessary political determination to deal with them. The relative absence of adequate tax handles in low-income countries, therefore, is a major factor in explaining why their tax–GNP ratios are lower, and this quite apart from sociological or cultural characteristics which are said to create an aversion to tax collection in low-income countries.

Threshold Effects and War Finance

A further hypothesis regarding the rising ratio of expenditures to GNP runs as follows: Voters have a basic resistance to raising taxes, but after taxes have been increased, they grow to accept them and do not insist on reducing them to their former level. National emergencies, particularly war, may cause a temporary but compelling increase in the need for public expenditures, for which voters are willing to overcome the old "tax threshold" and to accept an increase in the level of taxation which they otherwise would resist. After the emergency has passed, they are willing to retain the new level of taxation, or in any case a level substantially above that tolerated previously. Hence, new

[10]See Musgrave, op. cit.

TABLE 7-7
United States Public Expenditures in War Years
(As Percentage of GNP; All Levels of Government)

	Fiscal Year	Total	Defense-related	Civilian
	1913	8.0	1.1	6.9
World War I	1919	29.4	17.7	11.7
	1922	12.1	1.9	10.2
	1938	19.1	1.8	17.3
World War II	1945	46.1	39.2	6.9
	1948	22.3	7.4	14.9
Korean war	1953	30.9	15.4	15.5
	1955	29.1	11.9	17.2
	1965	27.6	8.5	19.1
Vietnam war	1969	34.3	9.9	24.4
	1971	33.1	8.1	25.0
	1978	32.5	6.9	25.6

Notes: Military includes defense expenditures and veterans' benefits and services. Figures are based on budget and census rather than national income accounts data.
Sources:
1913–1969: Facts and Figures on Government Finance, 16th ed., New York: Tax Foundation, 1971.
1971: Based on *Budget of the United States Government,* Fiscal Year 1974.
1978: See Table 7-2.

civilian public expenditures can be accommodated which otherwise would not have been provided for.

This fact is of particular importance in connection with war finance. War expenditures first displace private outlays and then are displaced by non-emergency public outlays. Since the aftermath of war is typically accompanied by social upheaval and change, the revenue windfall coincides with a change in preferences and political powers which raise the effectively desired level of civilian public expenditures. The resulting increase is thus attributable to both social and political change on one side and the availability of excess revenue at prevailing rates of tax on the other.[11]

Testing this theory for the United States, we find the pattern shown in Table 7-7. We note that the overall expenditure ratio rose sharply during both world wars, and fell off sharply thereafter. We also note that the ratio for defense-related expenditures remains above prewar levels. All these facts are in line with the threshold hypothesis. However, the pattern of civilian expenditures may also be taken to reflect the normal rise of the expenditure ratio—as shown in Figure 7-1—interrupted only by war periods. The threshold theory, while interesting, cannot be taken to give a conclusive explanation of the growth of the public expenditure ratio, at least in the

[11]This approach is developed in Alan T. Peacock and Jack Wiseman, *The Growth of Public Expenditures in the United Kingdom*, National Bureau of Economic Research, Princeton, N.J.: Princeton, 1961.

United States. The table also shows that the Vietnam war did not result in a sharp increase in the expenditure ratio comparable to that of previous wars. Moreover, it was followed by a sharply declining ratio of defense expenditures to GNP during the seventies.

Political and Social Factors

It remains to note the importance of political and social change as determinants of expenditure growth. Over the last century, there have occurred vast changes in social philosophy, as well as shifts in the balance of political power among various sectors of the population. They all have had a deep effect not only on what individuals consider to be the desirable size of the public sector, but also on the force with which the views of various groups make themselves felt in the political decision process.

Quite possibly, the effect of these developments—particularly the rise of transfer payments as a by-product of the incipient welfare state—outweighed the economic and structural factors noted in the preceding discussion. But more likely, they combined with these factors in shaping the actual course of events. Whatever the influence of these particular forces, it is evident that their combined result was a substantial rise in the share of the public sector in GNP.

E. SUMMARY

The size of the public sector may be defined in relation to the major totals in the national income accounts, such as gross national product (GNP), national income, and personal income. The following ratios were noted:

1. Total public expenditures are somewhat over 31 percent of GNP, with the ratio of tax revenue to GNP generally slightly lower.

2. Government purchases are about 21 percent of GNP.

3. Income originating in the public sector is about 14 percent of national income.

4. Transfer payments from government are about 11 percent of personal income, and all receipts from government (including transfers, wages, and interest) constitute about 26 percent.

The public sector share in total economic activity has risen over the years:

5. Total expenditures as a percentage of GNP have shown a more or less steady upward trend since the end of the nineteenth century, and especially over the last forty years.

6. This process applies not only to public expenditures as a whole but also to the defense and nondefense components separately.

7. The increase in the civilian expenditure share has been fueled largely by the rise of social security and welfare programs.

8. The pattern of the rising expenditures share which may be observed historically on a time-series basis also holds for a cross-section comparison between high- and low-income countries.

Turning to the causes of the rising public sector share, various factors may have been of importance:

9. Consumer demand for public services may be income-elastic, so that public services are in the nature of luxury goods, claiming a rising proportion of expenditures as per capita income increases.

10. Depending on the stage of a country's economic development, the structure of capital formation may be such as to require more or less public investment.

11. Changing attitudes, social structures, and political forces may have been behind the rising share of transfers and redistribution-oriented programs.

12. The occurrence of periods of war finance, with a sharp rise in the budget share for war purposes, may have served to raise the threshold of what are considered acceptable levels of taxation and subsequent civilian outlays.

FURTHER READINGS

Federal Expenditure Policy for Economic Growth and Stability, Joint Economic Committee, U.S. Congress, Nov. 5, 1957, part I: Arnold M. Soloway, "Growth of Government over the Past 50 Years," and Paul B. Trescott, "Some Historical Aspects of Federal Fiscal Policy."

Kendrick, M. Slade: *A Century and a Half of Federal Expenditures*, Occasional Paper 48, New York: National Bureau of Economic Research, 1955.

Musgrave, Richard A.: *Fiscal Systems*, New Haven, Conn.: Yale, 1970, chaps. 3 and 4.

Peacock, Alan T., and Jack Wiseman: *The Growth of Public Expenditures in the United Kingdom*, National Bureau of Economic Research, Princeton, N.J.: Princeton, 1961, chap. 2.

Wagner, Adolph: "Three Extracts on Public Finance," in Richard A. Musgrave and Alan Peacock (eds.), *Classics in the Theory of Public Finance*, New York: Macmillan, 1958, pp. 1–16.

APPENDIX: PUBLIC SECTOR IN THE NATIONAL INCOME ACCOUNTS

Since the national income accounts offer the most comprehensive frame of reference in which to view the economy, it is helpful to understand the role of government items in these accounts. This is shown in Table 7-A1 for 1977 data. For this purpose, federal, state, and local governments are combined into one public sector.

PUBLIC SECTOR IN GNP

The gross national product may be looked upon as the aggregate of expenditures on currently produced output. Government contributes to these expenditures through its purchases of goods and services.

TABLE 7-A1
Composition and Uses of United States Gross National Product for 1977
(In Billions of Dollars)

	Major Items	
1.	Personal consumption expenditures	1,206
2.	Gross private domestic investment	298
3.	Net exports	−11
4.	GOVERNMENT PURCHASES	394
5.	Gross national product	1,887
6.	− Capital consumption allowances	196
7.	Net national product	1,691
8.	− INDIRECT BUSINESS TAXES	165
9.	+ SUBSIDIES LESS SURPLUS OF GOVERNMENT	
	ENTERPRISE	13
10.	− Business transfer payments	10
11.	− Statistical discrepancy	5
12.	National income	1,515
13.	− CORPORATION PROFITS TAX	72
14.	− Retained earnings, etc.	29
15.	− CONTRIBUTIONS TO SOCIAL INSURANCE	140
16.	+ GOVERNMENT TRANSFERS TO PERSONS	199
17.	+ INTEREST FROM GOVERNMENT	43
18.	+ Business transfers payments	10
19.	Personal income	1,529
20.	− PERSONAL TAX PAYMENTS	226
21.	Disposable personal income	1,303
22.	− Outlays for consumption	1,236
23.	Personal saving	67

Note: Government items are shown in capital letters.
Source: U.S. Department of Commerce, *Survey of Current Business,* July 1978.
Line 14 includes inventory and capital consumption adjustment. Line 15 includes $61 billion of personal and $79 billion of employer contribution.

Total Share

As shown in item 4 of Table 7-A1, such purchases are a major component of GNP, with 27 percent of total output purchased by government. Looked at from the other end, 27 percent of goods and services when received by users are not paid for directly but are provided free of direct charge and paid for indirectly through the government budget. While not all these goods can be strictly classified as "social goods" as defined in Chapter 3, we may nevertheless record the fact that over one-quarter of total output is based on budgetary provision.

In examining how this provision fits into the economic structure, we now inquire how government purchases are divided between (1) purchases of factors and purchases of products; (2) provision for consumption and provision for investment; and (3) provision to consumers and provision to firms.

Purchase of Factors versus Purchase of Products

The first distinction does not appear directly in the national income accounts, but it can be approximated by equating governmental factor purchases with public sector wage payments. Not shown in the table, such compensation amounted to 53 percent of total government purchases, the remainder being the purchases of products from private firms. Thus government assumes the role of producer for about one-half the goods and services which it provides through the budget.

Provision for Consumption versus Investment

The second distinction is between consumption and capital formation. While the private component of GNP is broken down by consumption and gross capital formation, no such distinction is drawn in the recording of government purchases. If structures only are included, the share of government purchases going into capital formation is about 10 percent of total purchases. But if we define capital formation by government as similar to that in the private sector, new structures, all durable equipment, and additions to inventory should be included. On this basis, well over 20 percent of government purchases of goods and services go into capital formation. This is above the corresponding private sector ratio of 18 percent (private investment as a percentage of private purchases) for the same year.

It may be argued, moreover, that the concept of investment should be defined more broadly so as to include investment in human resources. This is especially important for the government sector. Here, expenditures for such functions as research, education, and health might be included. Using such a broad concept of capital formation, capital expenditures of the public sector come to comprise a much larger share of public purchases. According to this approach, about two-thirds of civilian government purchases (excluding defense) are of the capital formation type, thus raising the ratio of capital formation to consumption substantially above that in the private sector. Such remains true even if we apply an equally broad concept of investment to the latter. Capital formation, it appears, is a major function of the public sector, a fact to be kept in mind in our later discussion of fiscal policy effects on growth.

Provision to Consumers versus Provision to Firms

The division of publicly provided goods and services between final goods supplied to consumers and "intermediate goods" supplied to firms does not lend itself readily to statistical determination. A substantial part of highway expenditures, of municipal services, and of developmental outlays are in the intermediate good category, i.e., they are grants which reduce the cost of production for private firms rather than go directly to the private consumer.[12]

---

[12]See p. 174, for a further discussion of this distinction.

At least part of education outlays also belong in this category. Some intermediate goods are of the current service type (police protection for plants), whereas others are of the investment type (roads). Excluding defense, it may well be that one-third or more of total purchases are of the intermediate type.

PUBLIC SECTOR IN NATIONAL INCOME

In moving from GNP to *net national product*, depreciation or capital consumption allowances are deducted. These include (or should include) depreciation on government assets.[13] Moving on to *national income*, we deduct indirect business taxes (item 8 of Table 7-A1).[14] Indirect business taxes, such as sales taxes, are deducted because they reduce the amount available for disbursement to factors, with national income defined as the sum of factor incomes.

For similar reasons, subsidies to business firms are added, the impact being the same as that of negative taxes (item 9). Moreover, profits of public enterprise are deducted. If government enterprises make profits, such profits, unlike business profits, do not become available as income to the private sector. Similarly, if they record losses, factor earnings by the private sector exceed the value of the product as recorded in GNP. Therefore, the surplus must be deducted and the deficit must be added when moving from net national product to national income.[15]

Since national income reflects the total of private factor earnings, it may be broken down into income derived from, or "originating in," the government and the private sector. The bulk of income originating in government is in the form of wages and salaries paid by government; i.e., it is equal to the share of government purchases which are used for factor rather than product purchases. For 1977, such payments equaled 13 percent of national income.

PUBLIC SECTOR IN PERSONAL INCOME

Moving from national to personal income, we again encounter a number of government items, of which some divert from, and others add to, income available at the personal level.

---

[13]To obtain a proper figure of net output, depreciation on government as well as on privately held assets should be deducted, but in fact the national income accounts do not allow for this.

[14]There are two difficulties with this treatment:

1. In the United States national income accounts as prepared by the Department of Commerce, indirect business taxes include property tax receipts, about half of which are derived from owner-occupied residences and should not be included in this part of the accounts. Rather, these taxes should be deducted along with income tax when moving from personal to disposable income.

2. While it is customary in the United States accounts to think of factor shares as shares in national income, it may be preferable to focus on net national product, thus including indirect taxes as part of gross factor earnings.

[15]Other items included in the transition from net national product to national income do not involve government. They are business transfer payments and the statistical discrepancy, which reconciles the estimation of the accounts from the product and the income sides.

First, the corporation profits tax (item 13 of Table 7-A1) is deducted,[16] followed by social security contributions (item 15), including contributions by both employers and employees.[17] Government transfer payments are then added. They largely involve social security payments (somewhat in excess of contributions), while veterans' benefits and public assistance are the next most important items.

Finally, government interest payments to persons are added. This is necessary because interest paid by government is not included in GNP or in national income. The reason is that interest paid on government debt must be distinguished from earnings imputed to government-owned assets. Such imputation clearly should be a part of GNP, but interest on public debt cannot serve as proxy for it. This is evident when one considers that the bulk of public debt has been incurred in the cause of war finance, rather than in acquiring government assets. The service which is rendered by the bond-holders, and for which they must be paid, is significant for stabilization policy,[18] but it does not enter into current output. Debt issued by private business, on the other hand, goes to finance capital used in the process of production, and interest on such debt reflects the factor earnings which accrue to the capital which this debt finances. It is thus included in the value of total output (GNP) as in the factor payments which comprise national income.[19]

Personal income, finally, may again be broken down into the part received from payments by government, and the part received from private disbursements. For 1976, the government share (including earnings, net transfers, and interest) was 28 percent. Reflecting the important role of transfer payments, this is a substantially larger share than that of national income originating in the public sector.

PUBLIC SECTOR IN DISPOSABLE INCOME

In moving to disposable income, personal tax payments (item 20 of Table 7-A1) must be deducted. These amount to 15 percent of personal income. Of this, 10 percent is accounted for by the federal individual income tax and 4 percent by other taxes.

Proceeding to the uses of disposable income (item 22), no further budget items appear since all taxes have been deducted in advance and since public enterprise sales to consumers are included in consumption, along with private

[16]There is some question why indirect business taxes should be deducted when moving from net national product to national income, while the corporation profits tax is deducted when moving from the latter to personal income. See Richard A. Musgrave, *The Theory of Public Finance*, New York: McGraw-Hill, 1959, p. 198.

[17]It might be argued that the employee contribution part of the payroll tax should be included in personal income and be deducted (along with the income tax) only when moving from personal to disposable income.

[18]See p. 699.

[19]The exclusion of government interest from GNP is analogous, however, to the treatment of interest on consumer debt in the private sector, which is excluded for similar reasons.

sales. Disposable income as defined in the accounts, however, falls short of a person's real income. In addition to the cash earnings that are reflected in an individual's disposable income, real income also includes the free provision of public services by government; and if such real income were included on the income side, public services would become an important item of income use.

Chapter 8

Expenditure Evaluation: Principles*

A. Introduction: *Divisible Projects; Lumpy Projects; Summary.* **B. Project Benefit and Consumer Surplus. C. Types of Benefits and Costs:** *Real versus Pecuniary; Types of Real Benefits.* **D. Measurement of Benefits and Costs:** *Valuation of Intangible Items; Shadow Pricing of Market Items.* **E. Assigning Weights in Project Selection:** *Objective Function; Multiple Objectives; Distributional Weights.* **F. Discounting and the Cost of Capital:** *Importance of Discounting; Choice of Discount Rate: (1) Private Rate; Choice of Discount Rate: (2) Social Rate; Opportunity Cost of Capital; Further Problems; Current Practice.* **G. Risk and Economic Change:** *Risk; Dynamic Aspects.* **H. Summary.**

In our earlier discussion of social goods, we examined how provision for such goods may be determined, how it might be related to consumer choice, and how the political process enters in solving the problem. We now turn to a more limited, if more practical, view of expenditure determination.

Sound expenditure decisions, whether made by the legislator or the executive, require detailed information regarding the merits of alternative

*Reader's Guide to Chapter 8: Here we present the analytical framework of cost-benefit analysis, an aspect of public finance on which there has been much lively discussion since the sixties. Eminently practical in application, it nevertheless involves some knotty theoretical problems. As discussed in section F, they arise especially in connection with discounting.

projects. The technician can perform an important service in providing this information. Our task is to explore the general methodology which has been developed to deal with this problem.

In recent years this analysis has become one of the most lively branches of fiscal economics at both the practical and the analytical levels. Actually, it has a long history, beginning with the evaluation of federal expenditures in the field of navigation undertaken by the Corps of Engineers. The Flood Control Act of 1936 lent further impetus to cost-benefit analysis in the realm of water resource projects, and in 1950 general principles and rules were set out by an interagency committee concerned with the evaluation of various river basin projects.[1] Following a period of rapidly developing interest and research in cost-benefit analysis, in 1965 a planning-programming-budgeting (PPB) system was introduced by executive order to apply to all federal departments. While this early enthusiasm has since abated, these procedures remain of importance. Along with applications of cost-benefit analysis to particular situations, they will be examined in the next chapter. First, the underlying principles will be considered.

A. INTRODUCTION

Project evaluation, like all issues in allocation economics, involves determination of the ways in which the most efficient use can be made of scarce resources. In its simplest form, the issue is how to determine the *composition* of the budget of a given size or how to allocate a total of given funds among alternative projects. There is also the more complex question of determining the appropriate *size* of the budget. Further complications arise when various types of benefits and benefit mixes may be generated by one project and tradeoffs must be made among them. In taking a first look at these various situations, we assume that benefits and costs are known. The identification and measurement of costs and benefits are considered in the following sections.

Divisible Projects

We begin with a setting in which all projects are finely divisible, i.e., may be increased or decreased by small amounts. As will be noted later, this is not a very realistic assumption, but it permits us to bring out the basic rationale of project selection.

Budget Size Fixed Suppose the budget director is to advise the legislature—be it Congress or a city council—how best to allocate a given sum, say $1 billion, between two expenditure projects, X and Y. The problem may be likened to that of the head of a consumer household who has to allocate the family budget. First, the director must determine the cost C involved in providing each service and the benefit B to be derived therefrom. Then

---

[1]Inter-Agency River Basin Committee (Subcommittee on Costs and Budgets), *Proposed Practices for Economic Analysis of River Basin Projects*, Government Printing Office, 1950.

outlays must be allocated between X and Y so as to derive the greatest total benefit from the budget, i.e., to maximize net benefits (ΣNB) or the excess of total benefits (ΣB) over costs (ΣC). With ΣC given by the size of the budget, the task is simply to maximize ΣB.

This is shown in Figure 8-1, where the M_x and M_y schedules show the value of the marginal benefit (additions to total benefits) derived from spending successive dollars on X and Y. The opportunity cost of spending a dollar on X is the loss of benefits due to not spending it on Y. Total expenditures should therefore be distributed between X and Y so that the benefit derived from spending the last dollar on X will equate that derived from spending the last dollar on Y. Thus OA is spent on X and OB on Y such that $AC = BD$ and $OA + OB$ equals total permissible outlays. By equating the benefits derived from the marginal dollars on X and Y, the sum of total benefits derived from X (as measured by the area $OACF$) and from Y (as measured by the area $OBDG$) will be maximized.

Budget Size Variable   Taking a more global view of budgeting, the problem is not simply one of dividing up a budget of given size, but also one of determining the size of the budget itself. Thereby, the government must decide how resources are to be divided between private and public use. We must therefore drop the assumption of a fixed budget and reconsider project choices along with determination of total budget outlays. Within the fixed budget, the opportunity cost of pursuing one public project consists of the benefit lost by not pursuing another public project. But in the open budget the opportunity cost of public projects must be redefined as the lost benefits from private projects which are forgone because resources are transferred to public use.

FIGURE 8-1   Expenditure Allocation with Fixed Budget.

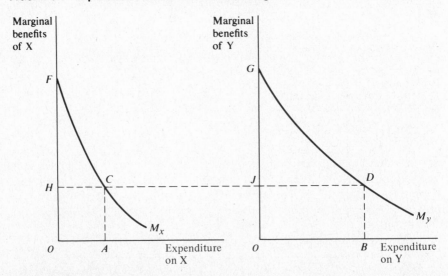

The task now is to maximize $\Sigma B - \Sigma C$, including benefits and costs of both public and private projects. This condition is met by equating marginal benefits for the last dollar spent on alternative public and private projects. Public projects are expanded and private projects are restricted until the benefit from the last dollar spent in either sector is the same. Interpreting X as "the" public project and Y as "the" private project, the solution of Figure 8-1 again applies. Given perfect markets, the marginal benefit from spending $1 in the private sector or BD equals $1, and the same must hold on the public side. Thus public expenditures are extended until the last dollar spent yields a dollar's worth of benefits.

Lumpy Projects

We have assumed so far that expenditures may be divided finely between projects X and Y, so that benefits may be equated for the marginal dollar spent on each. Where we deal with the allocation of funds between broad expenditure categories, this marginal approach is more or less applicable. But when it comes to specific allocation within departments, choices must be made among particular projects which are indivisible, involve lump-sum amounts, or are not smoothly expandable. If a choice has to be made between a road connecting cities X and Y and another connecting X and Z, where the X to Y distance is twice the X to Z distance, no marginal adjustment is possible.[2]

Budget Size Fixed We begin once more with the fixed budget case. Suppose that we have $700,000 to spend, say, on alternative highway projects, and that we may choose among projects I to VII, as shown in Table 8-1. The cost of each project is measured by the dollar amount required. The benefit valuation gives the total benefit for each project. Returning to Figure 8-1, the total benefit for a project, involving cost OA, corresponds to the area $OACF$.

[2]This situation contrasts with one involving the building of, say, a penetration road into an undeveloped area, which may be expanded by small increments.

TABLE 8-1
Project Choice with Fixed Budget

Project	Costs C	Benefits B	Net Benefits $B-C$	B/C	B/C Ranking
I	200	400	200	2.0	2
II	145	175	30	1.2	5
III	80	104	24	1.3	4
IV	50	125	75	2.5	1
V	300	420	120	1.4	3
VI	125	125	0	1.0	6
VII	300	270	−30	0.9	7

To choose among projects I to VII, we must compare their relative merits. The selection should be such that, within the constraint set by the budget size, total benefits are maximized. To find the best package, we try all combinations that are feasible within this constraint and see which package yields the highest total net benefit. It turns out in the above illustration that the best choice is to include projects I, II, IV, and V, with total cost of $695,000, benefits of $1,120,000, and net benefits of $425,000.

This somewhat cumbersome approach is needed, because an accurate result cannot be obtained simply by ranking the projects from the top down and choosing accordingly. Ranking by absolute net benefits would be meaningless since different costs are involved. Ranking by benefit/cost (B/C) ratios would avoid this difficulty but would also be misleading. In the above illustration, such ranking would call for inclusion of project III rather than II, with the result that net benefits would be reduced to $419,000. Moreover, evaluating projects in terms of B/C ratios has the disadvantage that it is frequently difficult to decide whether undesirable indirect effects of a project should be considered as costs (and included in the denominator) or as negative benefits (and subtracted from the numerator), or whether certain benefits should be entered as benefits or be deducted as negative costs. There is also the question of whether recurring costs should be included with the initial capital cost in the denominator or subtracted from the benefit numerator. The B/C measure greatly depends on how these questions are resolved, whereas this does not matter under the net benefit or $B - C$ approach. For this reason, the latter should be used where possible. But unfortunately it cannot be applied to choose among projects of different costs.

Budget Size Variable   If there is no fixed limit to the budget size, the problem is once more one of weighing public against private uses or resources. Since we are now dealing with lumpy projects, this can no longer be done by balancing the benefits derived from marginal outlays on both uses. We now proceed by the rule that a public project is worth undertaking so long as the benefits derived therefrom exceed its costs. The justification for the rule is that the cost of spending n dollars in the public sector is the loss of n dollars of benefits, a loss which results from not spending n dollars in the private sector. The rule may be stated by saying that a project should be undertaken so long as $B - C \geqslant 0$.

Summary

The principle of project selection, in the case of *divisible* projects, simply calls for the equating of marginal benefits. If the budget size is fixed, this involves equating between public projects only. If the budget size is variable, the process has to be extended to include outlays in the private sector. If projects are *lumpy*, no such neat marginal analysis applies. In the case of the fixed budget, projects must be chosen so as to maximize the sum of net benefits within the budget constraint. If the budget is variable, projects are to be accepted if their benefits exceed their costs. In practice, the combination of lumpy projects and limited budgets is the most typical setting, but policy decisions tend to be made without comparative examination of all possible projects.

B. PROJECT BENEFIT AND CONSUMER SURPLUS

Marginal project benefits, as measured on the vertical axis of Figure 8-1, are the additional benefits that are provided as outlays on the project are increased. Their measurement and relation to consumer surplus is shown in Figure 8-2.[3]

Suppose that the demand schedule for the services provided by a road is known and given by JK. The services in question may be the number of trips to be taken. If taking trips is costless, the consumer would take OK trips and the consumer surplus would be OJK. But trips are costly, with costs including gasoline, car wear, and time lost. Suppose that with the given road facility, the user cost per trip equals OG. In this case, GS is the cost or supply schedule per trip. OB trips will be taken. The total benefits derived equal $OJAB$ and the cost to the user equals $OGAB$. The difference, or GJA, is the "consumer surplus." It is the difference between what the consumer would have been willing to pay (or $OJAB$) and what the consumer must pay (or $OGAB$).

Now we assume that the facility is expanded at the cost of X dollars. The road having been widened and the surface improved, user cost falls to OF. FS' is the new cost schedule and the number of trips rises to OD. With total benefits equal to $OJCD$ and costs equal to $OFCD$, consumer surplus has risen to FJC. The increase in consumer surplus, or $FGAC$, is the "marginal benefit" derived from expansion of the facility. This is the item which must equal or

---

[3]Note that Fig. 8-2 differs from Fig. 8-1. Whereas Fig. 8-1 related marginal product benefits to expenditures, we now relate price (or marginal benefits) to quantity bought.

FIGURE 8-2 Measuring Benefits as Gain in Consumer Surplus.

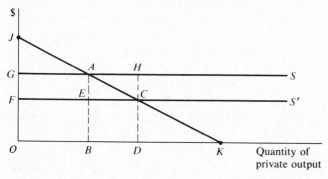

exceed the cost of project installation (X dollars) if the expansion is to be undertaken.[4]

C. TYPES OF BENEFITS AND COSTS

In dealing with various types of benefits and costs, these major categories may be distinguished:

Benefits and costs may be real or pecuniary
Real benefits and costs may be:
    direct or indirect
    tangible or intangible
    final or intermediate
    inside or outside

Illustrations of various types of benefits and costs are given in Table 8-2.

Real versus Pecuniary

The most important distinction is that between real and pecuniary aspects. Real benefits are the benefits derived by the final consumers of the public project. They reflect an addition to the community's welfare, to be balanced against the real cost of resource withdrawal from other uses. Pecuniary benefits and costs come about because of changes in relative prices which occur as the economy adjusts itself to the provision of the public service. As a result, gains or losses accrue to some individuals but are offset by losses or gains which are experienced by others. They do not reflect net gains or costs to society as a whole.

As labor is hired and a road is constructed, the wage rates for construction workers may rise because the relative scarcity of their skills is increased. This result is a gain to them, but it is offset by a decline in (relative) wage rates in some other employment where demand is reduced because of higher income taxes needed to finance the project. Or, the construction of the road may lead to increased demand for tents (if it is an access road to camping grounds) or for trucks (if it is a trucking highway) with increased earnings for their producers. These increased earnings are gains to people occupied in these particular industries, but they do not reflect a net gain to society. They are offset by costs to the consumers of other products who must pay higher prices because resources are transferred into the production of tents or trucks. Still another illustration would be rising land values of adjoining parcels which enrich the owner but do not add to the real wealth of society. Rising earnings of roadside restaurants similarly would be a gain to their operators, but this gain would be offset by reduced food purchases somewhere else.

---

[4]For a fuller discussion of this illustration, see the next chapter, p. 200.

TABLE 8-2
Illustrations of Project Benefits and Costs*

		Benefits	*Costs*
		IRRIGATION PROJECT	
Real			
Direct	tangible	Increased farm output	Cost of pipes
	intangible	Beautification of area	Loss of wilderness
Indirect	tangible	Reduced soil erosion	Diversion of water
	intangible	Preservation of rural society	Destruction of wildlife
Pecuniary		Relative improvement in position of farm equipment industry	
		MOON SHOT PROJECT	
Real			
Direct	tangible	As yet unknown	Cost of inputs
	intangible	Joy of exploration	Pollution of universe
Indirect	tangible	Technical progress generated	
	intangible	Gain in world prestige	
Pecuniary		Relative increase in land values at Cape Kennedy	
		EDUCATION PROJECT	
Real			
Direct	tangible	Increased future earnings	Loss of students' earnings, teachers' salaries, cost of buildings and books
	intangible	Enriched life	Foregone leisure time
Indirect	tangible	Reduced costs of crime prevention	
	intangible	More intelligent electorate	
Pecuniary		Relative increase in teachers' incomes	

*The benefits and costs noted in the table are merely illustrative for each project and not intended to be comprehensive.

These pecuniary changes do not reflect net gains to society and hence must be distinguished from real costs and benefits which do. The latter must always be allowed for, while pecuniary changes should not enter into the evaluation. Such at least is the case unless distributional weights are to be attached to the particular gains or losses which accrue to various individuals. If such weights are assigned, pecuniary costs and benefits have to be considered since they are no longer likely to be offsetting.

Types of Real Benefits

As noted before, all real benefits should be allowed for in cost-benefit analysis, but various types of benefits may be distinguished.

Direct versus Indirect   Real benefits and costs may be direct or indirect or, which is the same, primary or secondary. Direct benefits and costs are those related closely to the main project objective, while indirect benefits are in the nature of by-products. This distinction has a common-sense meaning but cannot be defined rigorously. The most useful interpretation is in terms of legislative intent. Thus, a river development program may have flood control as its immediate objective but may also have important bearing on the supply of power, on irrigation, or on soil erosion in adjacent areas. Development of defense technology, while aimed primarily at increased defense capacity, may have important side effects on improving technology in the private sector. The space program may be undertaken primarily to explore the moon, but it may also lead to gains in defense technology or technological improvements in the automobile industry. An education program may be directed primarily at raising the earning power of the student but it may also reduce the need to combat delinquency. In all these cases, indirect or secondary results may be distinguished from the direct or primary objective. Obviously, the former should be included along with the latter in assessing project benefits. Tracing of the more indirect benefits may be difficult, but they should be included.

Tangible versus Intangible   The term "tangible" is applied to benefits and costs which can be valued in the market, whereas others which cannot are referred to as "intangible." Social goods and social costs, as shown in Chapter 3, fall into the category of intangible. Thus, the beautification of an area which may result from an irrigation project is an intangible benefit, whereas the increased farm output is tangible. Moreover, intangible features may arise with regard to certain benefits or costs, such as health or loss of life which are private in nature but which cannot be readily assessed in money terms. While intangible costs and benefits are more difficult to measure, they should nevertheless be included in the analysis.

Intermediate versus Final   Another significant distinction is between those projects which furnish benefits to consumers directly (since they involve the provision of final goods), and those which enter into the production of other goods and are thus of an intermediate type. A particular project may in fact provide for both types of goods. Thus weather forecasts may be considered as a consumer good for those who plan an outing, as well as an intermediate good in servicing aviation.

Inside versus Outside   A final distinction is between benefits and costs which accrue inside the jurisdiction in which the project is undertaken and others which accrue outside. Thus, flood-control measures undertaken on the Connecticut River by Vermont may not only be helpful in Vermont but also prevent floods farther down in the state of Connecticut. The former benefits are internal and the latter are external. They constitute a "spillover" from one jurisdiction to another. Both benefits should be included in assessing the project, but interstate cooperation is needed to do so. This is a matter which we shall pursue further when dealing with the economics of fiscal federalism.[5]

D. MEASUREMENT OF BENEFITS AND COSTS

In Section A the principle of project selection was introduced, based on the simplifying assumption that the dollar value of benefits and costs is known. We must now take a more careful look at the problem of measurement. We consider for the time being the valuation of costs and benefits "when they occur,"[6] leaving the question of time profile and discounting for later consideration. The question of measurement would be simple if all values could be observed in terms of market prices. But such is not the case. Costs and benefits are frequently in intangible form, and even where market prices are observable these may be in need of adjustment because markets are not perfect and distortions must be allowed for.

Valuation of Intangible Items

We begin with the valuation of intangible (nonmarket) items, a problem which has to be solved for many public projects before cost-benefit analysis can be applied to them.

Social Benefits and Costs   Project benefits may be essentially intangible as with the case of national defense, or both tangible and intangible benefits may result. Thus, education yields intangible benefits via cultural enrichment and improved functioning of the democratic process. At the same time, there is a tangible benefit of increased earning power. Similarly, costs may be partly tangible (e.g., the cost of the resource input into the construction of a superhighway) and partly intangible (e.g., the resulting damage to the beauty of a wilderness area).

Wherever intangible benefits and costs are involved, measurement takes us back to the central problem of social-good evaluation. The value of such benefits and costs cannot be derived readily from market prices, and a political process is needed to determine them. Voters must decide how much they value clean air or water, or the protection afforded by an addition to national defense. Cost-benefit analysis is no substitute for this process; it is only a way of choosing among projects *after* the value of a benefit has been determined. Thus it is most easily applied in those areas where benefits are tangible and there is least need for public provision to begin with.

Intangible Private Benefits or Costs   Related problems arise in connection with benefits and costs which are private in nature (the problem not being one of externalities) but which do not lend themselves to market evaluation. If the government undertakes a cancer research project with resulting reduction in suffering, how can the benefits be valued? How should one evaluate the cost of death and injury which result from highway accidents? What about the benefits of crime prevention? The benefits and costs of some of the most important public projects may encounter these more or less insoluble difficulties of evaluation. Yet they must be faced before the mechanism of benefit-cost analysis can be applied.

In certain cases, indirect valuation methods of a more or less satisfactory nature may be applied to these intangible items. For instance, the personal value of time may be derived by observation of the differential prices paid for modes of transportation involving different speeds of travel.[7] The value of life has variously been held equal to the present value of future expected earnings had death not occurred or to life insurance values.

Cost-Effectiveness But even though evaluation of benefits may be difficult, analysts may be helpful in two respects. First, they can point out just what benefits (gains in literacy, increases in offensive or defensive capability, reduction in number of accidents, and so on) or costs will result from particular projects. This at least shows what end results should be valued in dollar terms. In some cases, as will be noted in the later discussion of park benefits, indirect methods of evaluation may be developed. But even where benefits and costs cannot be measured indirectly, analysts may examine how the desired effect can be maximized for a given cost or how a given result may be obtained at least cost. Thus, the analyst may compare the effectiveness in strengthening military capability or in reducing the rate of school dropouts by spending a given amount, say, $1 billion, in alternative ways. This more modest approach, referred to as "cost-effectiveness" analysis, is helpful even though the valuation of the end product may be difficult.

Benefits from Intermediate Goods The task of benefit evaluation is facilitated where the public facilities are in the nature of intermediate rather than final goods. In the case of final goods such as parks, the social-good aspect must be faced head on. Since evaluation through toll pricing would require the inefficient device of exclusion, some other approach is needed. But in the case of a trucking road, the benefits of the road may be evaluated in terms of the reduction in trucking cost to industry. Even though the road

---

[7]Let the cost per trip by the faster mode of transportation, A, be $C_A = a_A + bT_A + M_A$, and for the slower mode, B, be $C_B = a_B + bT_B + M_B$, where a is the inherent pleasure (displeasure) of travel, T is the time per trip, b the value of time, and M other travel costs per trip. Then the cost differential between the two modes is $\Delta C = (a_A - a_B) + b\Delta T + \Delta M$.

It is further postulated that the relative probability P_A of using the A rather than the B mode is a function of the cost differential, or

$$\frac{P_A}{1 - P_A} = f(\Delta C) = f(a + b\Delta T + \Delta M)$$

Since P_A, ΔT, and ΔM are all observable, the equation may be estimated either in a linear or nonlinear regression form and a value for the parameter b (the value of time) thereby derived.

itself may be a social good (if we assume absence of crowding), it enters as an intermediate good into the production of a final output which is a private good (the transported product ready for sale), the value of which can be assessed in market terms. Flood control, irrigation, and many other projects may be evaluated in these terms. Even though irrigation water is not sold to individual farmers, its value may be computed as the value of the increased output of farm products minus the cost of the other inputs which the farmer needs to secure the increased output.

Referring back to Figure 8-2, we may think of JK as the demand schedule for a private good and GS its supply schedule. Output equals OB, price equals OG, and consumer surplus equals GJA. Now a public facility is provided which reduces private cost, such as a road improvement which cuts transportation costs. The private cost schedule thus falls to FS', price drops to OF, output rises to OD, and consumer surplus rises to FJC. The point to be noted is that the gain in consumer surplus, $FGAC$, can be measured by reference to observed changes in output and price.

Cost Saving Another situation which facilitates the task of benefit evaluation arises where provision of the public service relieves society of other costs which now become unnecessary. Thus, benefits of a program to reduce school dropouts may be measured in terms of savings in outlays on correctional institutions, for example, or public health measures may be evaluated in terms of reduced hospital costs. The estimation of benefits in terms of costs saved provides an approximation by which to determine project selections.

Shadow Pricing of Market Items

We now turn to costs and benefits which are recorded in market prices.

Valuation of tangible costs and benefits is simple if we deal with competitive markets. In this case, the tangible benefit is measured by the price which the public service fetches in the market, or the price at which a similar service is purchased by consumers from private suppliers. The cost, similarly, is measured by the price which the government must pay for the product (if the government purchases it from private firms) or by the cost which it must incur (the factor prices which it must pay) if it undertakes the production itself. The costs thus determined will measure the opportunity cost incurred in forgoing the alternative private use of resources.

Monopoly Matters are more difficult, however, in the case of imperfect markets. Here market prices and costs do not reflect true social valuations and adjustments are needed. Such adjusted values are referred to as "shadow prices." Thus, rental incomes or monopoly profits should not be counted. Suppose that the market cost of a given product is $1 million, but that in a competitive market it would have cost only $900,000. The opportunity cost in this case is $900,000, not $1 million, even though the government pays the higher price. The profit of $100,000 is a pecuniary gain to the monopolist, but not a real cost to society.[8]

A problem of shadow pricing may also arise in competitive markets where the transfer of a factor to public use raises its price in private use, and the question arises as to the price (before or after reduction in private activity) at which the opportunity cost should be measured. A midway value offers a reasonable approximation to the proper result.

Taxes   A similar problem arises in connection with taxes. If the government purchases inputs needed in the construction of a project, the market price may include sales or excise taxes. This price component does not reflect a social cost (being merely a transfer from purchasers to the government) and should therefore be disallowed in computing the cost of the project. Another major tax-related problem arises in determining the social opportunity cost of capital and, as we shall see in the discussion of discounting, the appropriate treatment of taxes on capital income. Once more, shadow pricing is needed to correct for the tax.[9]

Unemployed Resources   Another aspect of shadow pricing relates to the costing of otherwise unemployed resources. The cost to be accounted for in public resource use is the lost opportunity for putting these resources to alternative uses, be they other public projects (in the fixed budget context) or private projects (in the open budget setting). This reasoning breaks down if the resources are otherwise unemployed and the opportunity cost is zero. Thus, it might be argued that public works are costless in a period of unemployment, or may even be beneficial beyond their own value in that they create additional employment via multiplier effects.

This argument is correct as far as it goes. Using unemployed resources poorly may indeed be better than not using them at all. But it is not as good as using them for a superior purpose. Unless there are political constraints which permit only one use, cost-benefit analysis should apply the concept of opportunity cost even where resources are otherwise unemployed. This applies with regard both to choices among rival public works projects and to choosing between higher public outlays and increased private spending through tax reduction.

But though unemployment is no excuse for failing to evaluate the merits of alternative uses, employment effects of particular projects become relevant to benefit evaluation if alternative policies to deal with unemployment are not

[8]More precisely, the adjusted price should be applied only to the *addition* to output which results in response to the government purchase. To the extent that private purchases are displaced by the public purchase, units are valued properly in terms of their market price as this reflects consumer evaluation. See following note.

[9]Again the shadow price should be applied only to the extent that the project purchase results in increased output, but not to the extent that it reflects a diversion from private use. In the former case, the tax does not reflect a social cost. In the latter, the social opportunity cost is measured properly by the gross price (including tax) which consumers pay. More precisely, the tax should be disallowed where the government purchase results in an addition to output, while the gross price should be charged where a replacement of output is involved.

available. The resulting gain in employment is then an additional benefit, or the opportunity cost of labor is zero. Project A may be preferred to project B even though its intrinsic merit is less, provided that the superior effect on unemployment outweighs the latter shortfall. Thus, building a road in location X may be superior to doing so in location Y if X has a high unemployment rate while Y does not, even though benefit calculus in the absence of employment effects would point to Y. Such is the case provided that alternative ways of dealing with unemployment in X are not available. This may be so because unemployment is of a regional nature and not amenable to reduction by stabilization policy on a national scale. If alternative approaches, such as relocation, are available, cost-benefit analysis should compare policy packages, e.g., road construction in Y plus relocation of manpower from X, with road construction in X. To put it differently, efficient policy planning has to be on a comprehensive basis and cannot be limited to an isolated consideration of specific policy tools or projects.

Developing Economies   The problem of shadow pricing assumes particular importance in developing economies where government investment and project evaluation frequently play a major role.[10] Consider the pricing of labor in a labor-surplus economy. While labor is typically unemployed or underemployed in the traditional sector of the economy, labor costs in the developed sector may be subject to forces which push them well above the true social cost of labor. In such a situation, it becomes desirable in project evaluation to use a shadow price for labor substantially below its market price.

Another aspect of shadow pricing which is frequently of importance in developing countries relates to the exchange rate. If the local currency is overvalued, as is frequently the case, both imports and exports will be undervalued relative to that of domestic goods. One of the implications is that imported capital goods are cheap relative to domestic inputs, especially where labor is overvalued. In consequence, an excessively capital-intensive method of production is encouraged. Once more, proper project evaluation will apply a corrected or shadow price for the market rate of exchange, reflecting its value in the absence of measures to support it.

E. ASSIGNING WEIGHTS IN PROJECT SELECTION

Projects frequently do not generate just one type of benefit or cost. Various benefits and costs may result, and it may be desirable to assign them different weights. Moreover, the benefit mix may differ depending on how the project is designed, and the design may affect the way in which similar benefits are divided among various sectors of the economy, or among income groups. All these alternatives have to be considered in designing the project so as to maximize total benefits.

[10]See p. 812.

Objective Function

Stated most generally, budget planners may base this process of project selection on an "objective function" which defines the social welfare, W_s, that is to be maximized. This may take the form

$$W_s = \sum_{i=1}^{z} \sum_{j=1}^{n} G_{ij} - \sum_{i=1}^{z} \sum_{k=1}^{m} L_{ik}$$

where the first term expresses the real welfare gains of the jth type accruing to the ith group summed for all j's and i's, and the second term expresses the real welfare losses of the kth type accruing to the ith group again summed for all k's and i's, the losses resulting as resources are withdrawn from their best alternative uses. If all gains and losses, of whatever type and to whomever accruing, are given equal weight, the objective function calls for maximizing the aggregate net gain as defined by

$$W_s = \sum_{j=1}^{n} G_j - \sum_{k=1}^{m} L_k$$

But the government may wish to assign different weights to different types of gains and losses, G_j and L_k, or it may wish to give different weights to benefits and losses accruing to various groups of individuals or sectors of the economy. In the latter case, the objective function which is to be maximized becomes

$$W_s = \alpha \sum_{i=1}^{m} (G_i - L_i) + \beta \sum_{i=n}^{z} (G_i - L_i)$$

where gains of individuals 1 to m are given weight α, while those of individuals n to z are given weight β. The choice of groupings may refer to income brackets, regions, or whatever characteristics are relevant to the government's objective function.

Multiple Objectives

Frequently, an expenditure project does not yield one single type of benefit but serves a number of objectives. For instance, a particular weapon system may have various defensive and offensive uses, expenditures on education may serve both to reduce illiteracy and to stimulate scientific progress, projects differ in their distributional implications, and so forth. In redesigning the project, one or the other objective may be emphasized. In such cases, a comparison among projects involves attributing relative weights to the various benefits which result.

Suppose, for instance, that $3 billion is to be spent on schools and to be distributed between elementary and higher education. Also suppose that for each $1 billion spent, outlays on elementary education contribute more to literacy than do outlays on secondary education, but their contribution to advancing technology is less than that of higher education. For this purpose, we may think of literacy units as measured by the number of students receiving a given test score and of technology units as the number of science majors that result. Using alternative expenditure allocations, we then have these options:

Expenditure Pattern	EXPENDITURES ON Elementary Education	Higher Education (In Billions of Dollars)	UNIT GAINS IN Literacy	Technology
I	3	0	12	3
II	2	1	10	8
III	1	2	7	12
IV	0	3	3	15

The figures showing unit gains in the literacy column tell us that expenditure pattern I yields a gain 4 times as large as pattern IV, and so forth, without expressing absolute values of these gains in dollar terms.[11] The same holds for the column showing gains in technology, where pattern I is one-fifth as effective as pattern IV. If a choice is to be made, a common measure of valuation for the two types of unit gains is needed. This may be in terms of resulting increase in GNP, or it may involve other considerations. For example, the gains in education may be valued on cultural grounds, quite apart from the resulting addition to GNP as measured by the official statistics, and a dollar value may be put on this gain.

When moving from pattern I toward pattern II, 2 technology units are gained for each literacy unit lost, while moving from pattern II to III, the substitution ratio is $1\frac{1}{3}$ technology units for each literacy unit lost. Finally, movement from pattern III to IV results in a gain of only $\frac{3}{4}$ technology unit for each literacy unit given up. If 1 literacy unit is valued at 2 technology units or more, pattern I will be chosen; if at between $1\frac{1}{3}$ and 2 technology units, pattern II will be chosen. If 1 literacy unit is valued at $\frac{3}{4}$ to 1 technology unit, pattern III would be chosen, while if valued at less than $\frac{3}{4}$ technology unit, pattern IV would be the chosen education program mix. This is shown in Figure 8-3, where the dotted lines i_1, i_2, i_3, etc., are the social indifference curves pertaining to literacy and technology. The tradeoff between literacy and technology units in production gives us a convex "project transformation" frontier as illustrated by points I to IV in the figure. As shown, II is now the preferred pattern, since it places us on the highest

[11]For a similar presentation, see Arthur Smithies, "Programs, Objectives and Decision Making," in H. Hinrichs and G. T. Taylor (eds.), *Program Budgeting and Benefit-Cost Analysis*, Pacific Palisades, Calif.: Goodyear Publishing, 1969, p. 181.

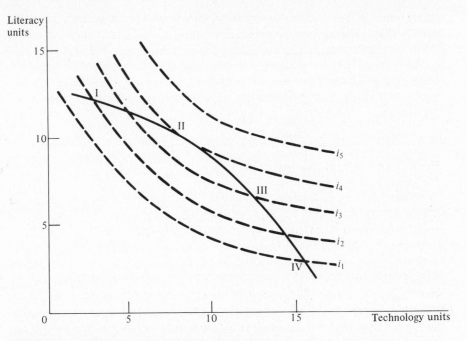

FIGURE 8-3   Multiple Objectives and Program Selection.

possible social indifference curve i_4. At this point the marginal rate of substitution of technology units for literacy units as a matter of social valuation (the slope of indifference curve i_4 at the point of tangency II) equals the marginal rate of transformation of the educational output (the slope of the project transformation curve at the point of tangency II).

Distributional Weights

As noted before, the benefits of various projects are likely to differ in their distributional implications.[12] Thus the benefits from one project may accrue primarily to people in low-income groups, while those of another may accrue to higher-income consumers. Moreover, distributional differences may come about because factor payments made in the course of construction accrue primarily to high- or low-income earners. These differences may matter greatly once distributional weights are attached to costs and benefits.

Choosing Weights   If distributional weights are to be introduced, their values (i.e., coefficients α and β in the objective function) must be specified. How these specifications are to be determined once more raises the problem

[12]See Burton Weisbrod, "Income Redistribution Effects and Benefit-Cost Analysis," in S. B. Chase (ed.), *Problems in Public Expenditure Analysis*, Washington: Brookings, 1968; and "Collective Action and the Distribution of Income: A Conceptual Approach," in *The Analysis and Evaluation of Public Expenditures*, Joint Economic Committee, 91st Cong., 1969.

encountered in our earlier discussion of the social welfare function. A table such as the following may be specified as an illustration:

Income	Social Weights
Under $ 2,000	10
$2,000–$ 5,000	5
$5,000–$10,000	2
Over $10,000	1

Benefits and costs of the project may be weighted accordingly, depending on the group on which they fall.

The difficulty is how to determine the proper set of weights. Short of returning to the philosophical issues discussed in Chapter 5, attempts have been made to derive such weights from the evidence provided by past behavior. Thus a clue might be obtained by comparing past project decisions with what they would have been if based purely on an efficiency analysis without distributional weights. Or, weights might be derived by analyzing the income tax, based on the assumption that when setting the rates, Congress intended to distribute the income tax burden in line with a rule of equal sacrifice.[13] One may then compute the marginal income utility schedule which is implicit in the prevailing tax-liability distribution.

Results such as these are of interest but assume that past congressional action was in fact based on rigorous application of a social utility rule, which is hardly a realistic assumption. But though it is difficult to derive a social income utility function, it may well be desirable for the government to state explicitly what function it proposes to use. This would permit consistency in the use of distributional weights in cost-benefit analysis, as well as in dealing with the distribution of the tax burden. Also, inclusion of such a function in the party platform might be a helpful piece of information for the voter!

Should Distributional Weights Be Applied?   Assuming the weights to have been determined, there remains the more general question of whether the use of distributional weights is appropriate for cost-benefit analysis. To illustrate, suppose that a project planner is to consider the location of a park facility in L or in H, where L is a low-income town and H is a high-income town. Suppose also that the same facility costs less in H and that the number of residents is the same in both places. In the absence of distributional considerations, cost-benefit analysis calls for installation in H, but allowance for distributional considerations may tip the scale in favor of L, where the benefits become available to a lower-income group. Or suppose that the question is whether to locate a shipyard in H or L. Suppose that H has better port facilities, so that without distributional considerations, H is chosen. But location in L will give additional employment to lower-income residents, with

---

[13]See p. 251 for a discussion of this approach.

distributional considerations once more tipping the balance toward L. What then is the correct solution?

The case for using distributional weights in the cost-benefit calculus depends on whether alternative measures for distributional adjustments—such as tax and transfer policies—are available. If so, project selection does not have to serve this function and H can be chosen. Cost-benefit analysis should be seen as one of a number of policy instruments, rather than be made to implement all objectives. This view is called for by the functional approach taken in Chapter 1, where it was argued that policy objectives can be reconciled by applying an appropriate combination of fiscal instruments.[14] This, however, may not be readily feasible in practice. The public works department, in which the project is planned, may have no influence on tax-transfer policy, and there may be no coordinated policy which aligns the two departments. Consequently, use of distributional weights and the choice of location L may be called for as a second-best solution.

Moreover, as we shall note later, alternative distributional adjustments, even if feasible, may involve an efficiency cost or excess burden which must be weighed against the cost saving otherwise derived from location in H.[15] Only if this saving is larger is there a clear case for choosing H. If the efficiency cost of alternative redistribution policies is larger, L may be the best choice.[16] The appropriateness of using distributional weights in cost-benefit analysis thus depends on the circumstances of the particular case. While there is a presumption in favor of locating projects where the cost is least or the benefits are largest, situations arise where distributional weights are in order. The same holds for public purchases in general. While the rule should be to buy where the cost is least, exceptions based on distributional considerations may at times be appropriate.

F. DISCOUNTING AND THE COST OF CAPITAL

So far we have disregarded the fact that benefits and costs do not accrue instantaneously, but over time. This situation must now be addressed. Some expenditures, such as current salaries for firefighters, yield immediate benefits, while others, such as investments in fire trucks, river basin developments, or turnpikes, yield a benefit stream over many years. To evaluate such benefit streams, future proceeds (or costs) must be translated into present values. They must be discounted, to allow for the fact that future benefits are less valuable than present ones. The same applies to the evaluation of costs. The opportunity cost of resources withdrawn from the private sector should now be measured in terms of the present value of private consumption forgone, where future consumption losses (due to forgone investments) are similarly discounted to their present value.

---

[14]See p. 17.

[15]For a discussion of excess burden, see Chap. 14.

[16]Note, however, that distributional adjustments can also be made by taxing certain private goods while subsidizing others. If distributional adjustments are to be made by interfering with resource allocation, it is arbitrary to limit this option to *public* projects.

TABLE 8-3
Present Value and Discount Rates

Projects	X	Y	Z
Cost ($)	10,380	10,380	10,380
Number of years	5	15	25
Annual benefits ($)	2,397	1,000	736
Interest Rate (%)	PRESENT VALUE OF BENEFIT STREAM IN DOLLARS		
3	10,978	11,938	12,816
5	10,380	10,380	10,380
8	9,571	8,559	7,857
	PRESENT VALUE OF BENEFIT-COST DIFFERENTIAL (B−C) IN DOLLARS		
3	598	1,558	2,436
5	0	0	0
8	−809	−1,821	−2,523
	BENEFIT-COST RATIO (B/C)		
3	1.057	1.150	1.235
5	1.000	1.000	1.000
8	0.922	0.825	0.757

Importance of Discounting

The evaluation of projects and their ranking is highly sensitive to the discount rate which is used. This is illustrated in Table 8-3, where the present values of benefits and benefit-cost ratios for various investments are compared.[17]

We consider three investments X, Y, and Z with equal cost and income flows extending over 5, 15, and 25 years, respectively. The annual incomes are chosen such that present values of benefits are the same at a 5 percent rate of

---

[17]The present value P of a sum R due in n years, discounted at the rate of interest i, is

$$P = \frac{R}{(1+i)^n}$$

The present value of an income stream $R_1, R_2, \ldots, R_n$ for n years equals

$$P = \frac{R_1}{1+i} + \frac{R_2}{(1+i)^2} + \frac{R_3}{(1+i)^3} + \cdots + \frac{R_n}{(1+i)^n}$$

For a case where the R's are constant, the above expression reduces to

$$P = R\frac{1-(1+i)^{-n}}{i}$$

and can conveniently be obtained from annuity tables. For the case of a perpetual constant R (annuity), the above expression becomes

$$P = \frac{R}{i}$$

discount. As we move from a 5 percent to a 3 percent rate, Z becomes the best and X the poorest choice. Reducing the discount rate will raise present value more if the period over which income accrues is longer. Moving to an 8 percent rate has the opposite effect. Project X now becomes most attractive and Z least. Raising the rate of discount favors the relatively short investment. While the present value of all investments rises as the discount rate is reduced and falls as it is raised, the ranking of the various investments changes in the process.

Based on these present value figures, we obtain the corresponding benefit-cost differentials $(B - C)$ and the corresponding benefit-cost ratios (B/C). With the initial cost of building the project assumed to be \$10,380, the annual returns are chosen so that with a discount rate of 5 percent the net benefit $(B - C)$ equals zero or the benefit-cost ratio (B/C) equals 1 for all investments.[18] The present value of benefits equals that of costs, and whether to invest or not is a matter of indifference. At the 3 percent rate, all three investments are profitable with net benefits positive, but Z does best and X comes last.[19] At the 8 percent rate, none of the three investments pays its way, but X is now best while Z has become last. As will be seen from this illustration, the ranking of various investments and their acceptability depends greatly on which discount rate is used. The lengths of the income stream dealt with in public projects cover a wide range so that finding the "proper" rate is of major importance.

Choice of Discount Rate: (1) Private Rate

In choosing the discount rate, government may proceed on the premise that it is desirable to use a rate equal to the time preference of private consumers; or, it may substitute a social discount rate of its own. We begin with the former view. The rationale for using the private rate of discount is that it reflects consumer choice between present and future consumption. Just as public policy accepts the valuation of oranges and apples by the prices which they fetch in the market, so should it honor the individual's valuation of future relative to present consumption. Assuming perfectly competitive capital markets and absence of risk, all consumers will borrow and lend at the same rate. Moreover, with perfect markets, this rate equals the marginal efficiency of investment. Thus there exists an equality between the marginal rate of substitution of present for future consumption and their marginal rate of transformation in production. The rate of interest, like other competitive prices, is at its efficient level. In practice, this seemingly simple solution is complicated by various factors, including market imperfections, uncertainty, risk, and taxes on capital income.

---

[18] We assume for the time being that all costs are incurred in the first year, overlooking additional considerations which arise when costs are spread out over longer periods.

[19] Since all investments involve the same cost, ranking may be in terms of net benefits $(B - C)$ or, for that matter, in terms of B only.

Imperfect Markets The assumption of perfectly competitive capital markets is unrealistic. Due to market imperfections, such as differential access to credit and investment institutions, different individuals may be confronted with different costs and returns to their borrowing and lending. Since there no longer is a single rate which reflects the time preference of consumers, some average must be used.[20]

Uncertainty Since the future level of interest rates is uncertain, short- and long-term rates in the capital market differ. Once more, the question arises as to which rate should be used in discounting. Should it be the rate on one-, two-, or five-year deposits? Should the yield on short- or long-term bonds be used? Since the term structure of market yields may be taken to reflect the probable cost of capital in future years, a case can be made for choosing a yield which corresponds to the period over which the benefit stream of the public investment will extend.

Risk Since some investments are more risky than others, gross rates of return differ by the amount of risk premiums. To have the discount rate reflect "pure" time preference, one should use the yield on a "safe" invest- ment, i.e., an investment which has little or no default risk, such as federal government bonds.[21]

Income Tax Lenders must pay income tax on their capital income. The proper measure of their time preference, therefore, is the *net* or after-tax rate of return and not the gross or market rate. If the consumer lends at rate i, his or her net return or i_n equals $(1-t)i$, where t is the consumer's personal tax rate. Since different consumers are in different marginal tax brackets, net rates will differ among individuals. Again, the best that can be done is to use an average rate. If the gross rate is, say, 8 percent and the marginal tax rate on the average is 30 percent, the net rate would be 5.6 percent.

Macro Policy A more general difficulty arises from the very existence of a macroeconomic system which generates unemployment and inflation. The case for application of the market rate rests on the proposition that this rate can be taken to secure an efficient allocation of consumption over time. This rationale involves a model of national income determination such that planned saving is always matched by investment, with neither unemployment nor inflation occurring. This is hardly the case in the real world setting. Rather, conditions are typically such that stabilization measures are needed to maintain macrobalance, i.e., full employment and stability of the price level. These measures may be taken in various combinations of monetary and

---

[20]It has been suggested that in choosing this average, weights should be used which reflect the position of taxpayers who contribute to the finance of the project. In this case, the correct discount rate depends on how the project is financed. See Otto Eckstein, "A Survey of the Theory of Public Expenditure Criteria," in James Buchanan (ed.), *Public Finances: Needs, Sources and Utilization*, Princeton, N.J.: Princeton, 1961.

[21]For a discussion of the risk involved in the public investment itself, see p. 195.

fiscal restraint or expansion, all of which result in different levels of interest. Given the fact that stabilization policies are needed in the modern market economy, the market does not reveal a unique "correct" level of interest rate by which "true" consumer time preference is reflected.[22]

Conclusion   In the presence of these complications, it is evident that the seemingly simple idea of using "the" private rate meets with considerable practical difficulties. Instead, some average or approximate rate has to be used.

Choice of Discount Rate: (2) Social Rate

So far we have proceeded on the assumption that the rate of discount used in project evaluation should equal the time preference of consumers in the private sector, provided that this may be derived from observed market rates. There are also reasons for not using the time preference rate of private consumers, but instead substituting a "social" rate:

1.   Individuals are said to suffer from "myopia," so that, in arranging their private affairs, they underestimate the importance of saving and overestimate that of present consumption. Such may be the case especially in low-income countries where the advantage of higher income levels has not been experienced and where aspiration levels are low. Hence, the consumers' time discount is too high and government should correct this error by applying a lower rate.

2.   Next come several arguments related to the welfare of future generations. One argument is that people are too greedy and do not care sufficiently about the welfare of those who follow them. If they did, they would save more so as to leave future generations with a larger capital stock and hence higher level of income. The government, as guardian of future generations, can offset this by using a lower rate of discount and investing more. This may be a decision faced by the planning board of a developing country, which must choose between more rapid development and an early increase in the level of consumption.[23]

3.   Alternatively, it is held that people do in fact care about future generations and that they would derive pleasure from contributing to their welfare. But any one person acting alone cannot contribute enough to make a difference, even though he or she would be willing to save more if others contributed as well. As in all cases of benefit externality, the private market results in undersupply. Once more the government can remedy this by using a lower rate of discount, thereby increasing the range of eligible public investment.

4.   The concern with future generations may not simply be one of benevolence but may reflect a broadened application of just distribution rules so as to include intergeneration equity.[24] For instance, the goal may be to equalize per capita consumption over time. Under this criterion, the requirement for current saving and capital formation (or, more precisely, for passing capital stock to the future) will depend on factors such as population growth, availability of exhaust-

[22]Similar considerations apply regarding determination of the optimal rate of growth. See p. 686.
[23]See p. 791.
[24]See p. 103.

ible resources, and, above all, technical progress. With technical progress raising future productivity, the capital stock needed to sustain the consumption standard may fall, calling for a higher discount rate.

All but the last point suggests that the social rate should be set below the private rate so that use of the social rate calls for a higher level of investment. Using the social rate rather than the private rate in product selection will then give a higher present value of the benefit stream, passing projects which might be excluded by the use of the private rate.[25] Moreover, use of the social rate will result in the choice of longer-lived projects. Once more, this is an important instance of shadow pricing.

Opportunity Cost of Capital

The choice of discount rate is important, but it is only part of the problem. The other part is to measure the social cost involved in withdrawing resources from private use. This "social opportunity cost" equals the loss of consumption, current or future, which results as these resources are withdrawn.

Resource Withdrawal from Consumption Suppose the government undertakes a project at cost C of $1 million in material, labor, and equipment. Assume further that this resource withdrawal is financed in such a way (e.g., by a consumption tax) that private consumption falls by $1 million. This is by how much consumers value the lost consumption and hence its social value. Such at least is the case unless market imperfections as discussed previously call for corrections in the form of shadow prices.

Resource Withdrawal from Investment Suppose next that the resource withdrawal is reflected in reduced private investment and capital formation. The loss now takes the form of a future consumption stream, corresponding to the income stream that is forgone. To determine the present value of this income stream, it must again be discounted at the market rate. Assuming a perfectly competitive market, this discounted value equals C. Such must be the case, since in a competitive market there exists a unique rate of interest and investors will invest up to the point where their costs are covered by the present value of the return as discounted by the market rate. Thus, the social opportunity cost of capital (a term not to be confused with "social rate of discount") is properly measured by the private cost of investment. Once more, C is the proper measure of social cost.

If markets are imperfect, different investments in the private sector may yield different returns, so that the income stream which is lost by diverting resources from private investment may depend on just which investment is reduced. This is impossible to determine, so the analysis has to proceed by choosing an average return.

---

[25]This conclusion must be qualified. As we shall see presently, use of a lower discount rate also increases the opportunity cost of capital. Depending on the timing involved, this may more than offset the increased present value of benefits.

A further complication, and one which can be dealt with more effectively, results because capital income is subject to tax. This is shown in Figure 8-4, where II is the investment schedule, showing the returns that may be obtained at various levels of investment, and SS is the savings schedule, showing the levels of saving forthcoming at various rates of interest or return on savings. In equilibrium E, savers save and lend OA to investors who then invest that amount. The rate of return obtained by investors on their marginal investment equals i, which is also the return which the savers receive.

Now let a corporation tax be imposed. As a result, the investment schedule will swivel down, with $I'I'$ showing the reduced levels of investment that will now be undertaken at various gross (before corporate tax) rates of return. As an individual income tax is added, the savings schedule shifts to the left, with $S'S'$ now showing the higher gross (before personal tax) rates of return which borrowers must pay the savers to generate given amounts of saving. The new equilibrium is at E', the intersection of the $I'I'$ and $S'S'$ schedules, with OB the level of saving and investment. The gross (before corporate tax) rate of return on investment now equals i_g, while the net return to the investor (also called the market rate) equals i_m. In the equilibrium position, i_m also equals the gross rate of return before personal tax obtained by the saver. The net (after personal tax) rate of return to the saver, finally, is given by i_n, which also reflects the saver's rate of time preference. Provided that a private rate approach is to be followed, i_n is now the correct rate of discount to use in determining the present value of the income stream which is derived from the public project.

FIGURE 8-4   Income Taxes and Discounting.

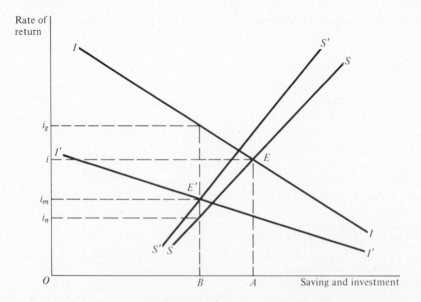

Returning to our previous illustration, we now find that the opportunity cost of capital exceeds the dollar value of reduced private investment, i.e., the market cost of the project or $1 million. To see why, note that this private investment cost, C_p, as recorded by the market, equals the discounted value of the investment income *net* of corporation tax, with the market rate or i_m used as rate of discount. This reflects the behavior of the investor who will invest up to the margin where his or her cost is covered. In contrast, the income stream to be discounted in determining the social opportunity cost of capital, C_s, is the rate of return *before* corporation tax or i_g. While the investor obtains only a return net of tax or i_m, this does not matter since the tax is a transfer from investor to government and not a social loss. Moreover, the rate of discount to be used in obtaining the present value of the gross income stream is not i_m but the consumer's rate of prime preference i_n.[26] We thus discount a larger income stream at a lower rate, and for both these reasons arrive at a higher present value. Thus C_s exceeds C_p.[27]

Conclusion   Summarizing the preceding discussion and using the simplifying assumption of constant and perpetual returns, the present value of the net benefit (PVNB) of a project may be defined as follows:

$$\text{PVNB} = \frac{B}{i_n} - \left[\gamma C + \frac{(1-\gamma)i_g C}{i_n} \right]$$

where the first term on the right measures the present value of its annual benefits B, discounted by i_n, and the second term measures the opportunity cost of resource withdrawal.[28] With the fraction γ thereof withdrawn from private consumption, the first component shows the opportunity cost of this

---

[26]If, instead, a social rate is to be used, i_s is substituted for i_n.

[27]Assuming a perpetual income stream, the cost of the investment to the private investor C_p thus equals

$$C_p = \frac{(1-t_c)i_g C_p}{i_m} \tag{1}$$

while the social cost equals

$$C_s = \frac{i_g C_p}{i_n} \tag{2}$$

Thus $C_s > C_p$ for two reasons: in (2) the numerator is larger and the denominator is smaller than in (1).

[28]These simplifying assumptions may be qualified readily to allow for the more realistic case of finite investments with uneven income streams. Further complications arise (1) because the loss of private capital income due to the reduction in investment does not fully reflect the resulting decline in national income, except for the case of the marginal investment dollar, and (2) because the outcome may be affected by the extent to which the loss of income in the private sector would have been saved and invested, as well as by the extent to which the gained public income stream is so used. See Martin Feldstein, "Net Social Benefit Calculation and the Public Investment Decision," *Oxford Economic Papers*, March 1964, vol. 16, no. 1, pp. 114–131.

part of the resource withdrawal, where C is again the market price of the resource inputs. The second component shows the opportunity cost of resource withdrawal from private investment, equal to the forgone gross income stream $(1 - \gamma)i_g C$, discounted again at the net rate i_n. If a social rather than a private rate approach is taken, the above formula is simply adjusted by substituting i_s for i_n.

The value of γ will depend on how the investment is financed. In the case of income tax finance, it will equal the taxpayers' marginal propensity to consume. Some taxes, such as sales taxes, fall most heavily on consumption, while others, such as estate duties, fall more heavily on saving.[29] Furthermore, loan finance will tend to have a heavier displacement effect on savings and on capital formation than will tax finance.[30] The way in which a project is financed thus affects its eligibility under cost-benefit analysis. Finance which draws on saving involves a higher opportunity cost and leaves fewer projects eligible than does finance which draws on consumption. This tends to correct for the fact that taxes on capital income leave private investment short of its efficient level.

Further Problems

Before we turn to actual practice in the use of discount rates and determination of opportunity cost, three further aspects of the discounting problem will be noted.

Internal Rate   The preceding discussion was based on the assumption that project evaluation is to be carried out by discounting at a uniform rate of discount, private or social. But this is not the only possible procedure. Instead of determining the profitability of a project by measuring the present value of the net income stream, we may turn the table and ask what discount rate would be needed to equate the present value of the benefit stream with the cost of the asset? Thus, by setting the present value of benefits equal to the present value of costs, we get the expression

$$\sum_{j=0}^{n} \frac{B_j - C_j}{(1+i)^j} = 0$$

[29]Note that tax aspects have threefold importance for project analysis. First, the value of γ will be determined by the way in which the project is financed, i.e., by the choice between taxation and borrowing and between various types of tax. Second, income taxation enters in determining the net rate of return which the lender can receive in the market, and hence the proper rate of discount. Third, taxation enters because the corporation tax drives a wedge between the gross and net rate of return received by the investor, and hence the social opportunity cost of capital.

[30]Such at least is the case in the shorter run. In the longer run, it might be argued that the difference disappears due to tax finance of debt service. See Martin Feldstein, "Financing in the Evaluation of Public Expenditures," in W. Smith and J. Culbertson (eds.), *Public Finance and Stabilization Policy: Essays in Honour of Richard A. Musgrave*, Amsterdam: North-Holland, 1974.

and solve for i, the internal rate of return.[31] In ranking two projects, preference is then given to the one which has the higher internal rate. This approach has the advantage of bypassing the thorny question of what rate of discount to use in determining present values. However, it also has some serious shortcomings.

Closer analysis shows that if the net benefit stream fluctuates and becomes negative at some time (as might happen if future benefits or costs are bunched in one period), there is more than one internal rate which will satisfy the above equation. Moreover, ranking by internal rate of return may differ from ranking obtained by discounting with a common rate. Thus, two investments of different maturity may have the same internal rate, but their ranking will differ if benefits are discounted with a market rate. If the market rate is above the internal rate, the shorter investment now ranks first, and vice versa if the market rate is lower. For these and other reasons, the internal rate approach is not commonly used, although it may be drawn upon to provide additional evidence on project rating. This is the case especially for very long term investments, where it is difficult to predict future levels of interest rates and hence the appropriate private rate of dicount.

Outside Borrowing The preceding discussion applied to project evaluation by a national government, drawing on resources within its own economy. Actually, project evaluation is frequently undertaken by local governments which draw on outside capital markets or by national governments of developing countries which obtain funds from New York or the World Bank.

This would not greatly change the problem if all capital markets were perfect, with interest rates being the same in all locations and for all transactors. But such is not the case. A local government may be able to borrow at rates in the New York market quite different from those available at local banks and to local savers. Or the government of a developing country may borrow from the World Bank at 5 percent while domestic rates are 20 percent. Given such market imperfections, it cannot be argued that benefits should be discounted at the time preference rate of local residents. Rather, project evaluation should discount benefits at the borrowing rate and undertake the project if positive net benefits are recorded. Where international borrowing is involved, allowance must be made, however, for future debt service and effects on the balance of payments.

Inflation Since the rate of inflation tends to be reflected in the nominal interest rate, the latter rises with inflation. But a higher rate of discount means a lower present value, thus affecting project eligibility. This effect of inflation may be neutralized in two ways. One is to use the nominal rate of interest (including its inflation premium) for discounting, while applying it to the nominal (inflated) value of the benefit stream. The other is to adjust the

---

[31]Returning to the second equation in footnote 17, we may substitute the asset cost C for P, enter the income stream $R_1, \ldots, R_n$, and with the help of annuity tables, solve for i.

nominal rate of interest for inflation, discounting with the real rate component only, while measuring the benefit stream in real terms. In either case, distorting effects of inflation are avoided.

Current Practice

Actual practice falls considerably short of these sophisticated considerations. Current practice in the federal government is to apply a 10 percent discount rate to the benefit stream of the project and to compare this with the dollar cost of its construction.[32] No attempt is made to adjust for the social opportunity cost of capital. A special rate applies to water projects where, as legislated by Congress, a rate equal to the yield of long-term United States bonds is to be used. This yield can, however, be changed each year by one-quarter of 1 percent only and now stands at about 7 percent.[33]

No explicit rationale is given for these rules. Use of the bond rate for discounting may be rationalized by taking it to reflect consumer time preference, although as noted above, a further reduction to adjust for individual income tax would then be in order. The 10 percent rate, in turn, may be taken to reflect the bond rate grossed up by the corporation tax rate, thus approximating the gross yield on private investment. A popular, if fallacious, justification for this is that the government should recover its entire project cost, defined to include the cost of borrowing plus the loss of corporation tax revenue, because taxable income in the private sector is reduced. This line of reasoning confuses private and social profitability. The purpose of the government is to maximize social welfare and not profits as calculated by the private firm.

The grossed up bond yield is useful, however, as an indicator of the gross income stream displaced as private investment is reduced. Following the proposition that government should undertake an investment only if it matches the social yield of the private investment forgone,[34] the forgone income stream is properly measured as income gross of corporation tax. This rule has the advantage of simplicity, but to be correct both the private and public investment streams should then be discounted by the proper rate of discount. Assuming a private rate approach is followed, this proper rate is given by i_n, the consumer's lending rate net of income tax, and not by the gross rate of return on private investment. The latter should enter in computing the opportunity cost of capital but not in selecting the discount rate.

---

[32]See Office of Management and Budget, Circular No. A-94, Revised, Mar. 27, 1972.

[33]Water Resources Development, Public Law 93-251, 93d Cong., Mar. 7, 1974. Also see Water Resources Council, *Water and Related Land Resources, Establishment of Principles and Studies for Planning (Federal Register*, Sept. 10, 1973, vol. 38, no. 174, part III), p. 9 in final section on "Final Environmental Statement."

[34]See A. C. Harberger, "The Opportunity Cost of Public Investment Financed by Borrowing," in R. Layard (ed.), *Cost-Benefit Analysis*, Baltimore: Penguin, 1972, chap. 12. Harberger qualifies this approach by calling for a discount rate reflecting a weighted average of i_n and i_g, as defined above. The weights depend on the elasticities of the saving and investment schedules.

G. RISK AND ECONOMIC CHANGE

It remains to consider some further aspects which can be of major importance in cost-benefit analysis, including the treatment of risk and dynamic change.

Risk

Project benefits may not be readily predictable at the outset, since public project planning, no less than private investment, proceeds under uncertainty. Thus, highway planning involves forecasting population growth in the area, a weapons program involves forecasts regarding future weapons technology or strategic developments, and so forth. Such risk and uncertainty regarding future benefits reduces their present value and must be allowed for in investment planning. While it may be argued that in certain situations the social risk is less than the private risk involved in particular activities, it does not follow that risk is a minor matter in public project planning.[35]

Allowance can be made for risky outcomes by weighting the various possible outcomes by their probabilities, with the sum of the probabilities equal to 1. The sum of these appropriately weighted outcomes will then be used in the analysis as the expected value of the benefits, $E(B)$. Thus,

$$E(B) = p_1 B_1 + p_2 B_2 + \cdots + p_n B_n \qquad \text{where } p_1 + p_2 + \cdots + p_n = 1$$

In cases where numerical probabilities are unknown, the analyst may resort to various techniques derived from game theory to aid in the selection process, but this takes us beyond the scope of this book.[36]

It may also be assumed that the expected value of benefits as obtained above exceeds its "certainty equivalent" because of a prevailing aversion to risk. There is considerable evidence that people would derive greater utility from receiving, for instance, the certainty of $10 than from receiving a 50 percent chance of $15 together with a 50 percent chance of $5, the expected value of which would be $10 [$= .5(15) + .5(5)$]. The degree of risk attached to a range of possible outcomes may be expressed as the standard deviation of the probability distribution. It has therefore been suggested that a risk premium be added to the discount rate used for public project discounting purposes, the premium designed to reflect the magnitude of this standard deviation.

Dynamic Aspects

The evaluation of costs and benefits, finally, is complicated by the fact that both benefits and costs occur over time. This is evident with regard to benefits which flow from an investment project, the economic life of which may extend far into the future. But it also holds for costs. While capital costs

[35]For a discussion of the pros and cons of allowance for risk in project evaluation, see ibid., pp. 53–57.
[36]See R. Dorfman, "Decision Rules under Uncertainty," in ibid., chap. 15.

are typically incurred at the outset, substantial operating costs may have to be undertaken in future years. One major implication of this time dimension of benefits and costs is the need for discounting, a problem discussed in an earlier section. Another aspect is that the valuation of benefits and costs may change over time. Project evaluation must therefore allow for the dynamics of economic development. This is of particular importance for developing countries. Not only may relative prices change, but so may the extent of price distortions. The case for setting a shadow price of labor much below its market price, for instance, may disappear over time as previously unemployed and underemployed labor comes to be drawn into the modern sector and wages move more nearly in line with the social opportunity cost of labor. Allowing for such structural changes will have considerable significance for projects which have a long time horizon.

Brief mention should also be made of a further problem which is presented by changes which are associated with the passage of time (as distinct from the age of the project). The profile of benefits and costs over time may be such as to suggest that postponement of the project may be in order. For instance, if future demand for the output of the project is expected to increase, while costs of production due to improved technologies will decrease, the benefit-cost analysis should be made under alternative starting times. The effects of one year's postponement will be the change in the present value (today) of future benefits, minus the change in the present value of costs. The project should be delayed until this net change (if favorable) is maximized.[37]

H. SUMMARY

In developing some basic concepts of project evaluation, we have distinguished between divisible and lumpy projects:

1. Where projects are freely divisible, the best solution is reached by equating the marginal benefits from the last dollar on each project (where the budget is fixed) and on public and private projects (where the budget total is open).

2. Lumpy projects in a fixed budget should be chosen so as to maximize the sum of net benefits. In an open budget such projects should be adopted as long as total benefits exceed costs.

In measuring the social benefits and social costs of public projects, certain rules have to be followed:

3. Only real costs and benefits should be included, while pecuniary costs and benefits should be excluded.

4. Both direct and indirect costs and benefits should be included.

---

[37]See S. Marglin, *Approaches to Dynamic Investment Planning*, Amsterdam: North-Holland, 1963.

5. Valuation of intangible benefits and costs is more difficult and poses similar problems as does the valuation of social goods.

6. Intermediate-type benefits can be valued more readily than benefits of the final type.

7. Even if intangible benefits cannot be valued readily, cost-effectiveness analysis may be helpful.

8. This includes adjustment for distortions introduced by monopoly, taxes, and unemployed resources.

9. Shadow pricing is of special importance in developing countries where labor tends to be overvalued and foreign exchange undervalued.

In selecting the particular projects to be undertaken, allowance must be made for the fact that multiple objectives may be involved.

10. Where alternative projects differ in their relative capacity to serve one or another objective, the two objectives must be valued so as to permit comparison.

11. Where the distributional implications of alternative projects differ, such differences may be allowed for by the introduction of distributional weights. The appropriateness of applying such weights depends on the availability of alternative means of securing distributional adjustments and on the efficiency cost of using them.

Where the benefit stream from a public project accrues over future years, present value must be determined by discounting. The same discounting procedure must be applied in determining the cost of resource withdrawal where such withdrawal is from private investment.

12. In choosing the discount rate, government may aim at a rate which corresponds to that used in the private sector or it may wish to apply a social rate of discount.

13. In the former case, the proper rate of return is given by the rate of return on capital net of corporation and individual income tax, as this reflects the time preference of consumers.

14. This rationale applies to competitive markets but is complicated by risk differentials, market imperfections, and taxes on capital income. The rate typically used is the long-term bond rate, grossed up by the rate of corporation tax.

15. Choice of a social rate usually rests on the proposition that the private sector tends to underestimate the social value of future consumption and capital formation, thus calling for the use of a lower rate by the public sector.

16. As distinct from the issue of discount rate, correct procedure calls for careful determination of the social opportunity cost of capital. This issue arises where resource withdrawal from the private sector is from private capital formation rather than from consumption. The social opportunity cost of capital equals the discounted value of the gross (before-tax) income stream, and this exceeds the actual dollar cost (or discounted value of the net income stream) of the private investment forgone.

17. Current federal practice is to use a 10 percent rate of discount in all cases except for water projects, where a rate equal to the long-term bond yield is used.

FURTHER READINGS

Dasgupta, P., S. A. Marglin, and A. K. Sen: *Guidelines for Project Evaluation*, New York: United Nations Industrial Development Organization, 1972.

Eckstein, Otto: "A Survey of the Theory of Public Expenditure Criteria," in James Buchanan (ed.), *Public Finances: Needs, Sources and Utilization*, Princeton, N.J.: Princeton, 1961.

Feldstein, M.: "Financing in the Evaluation of Public Expenditures," in W. Smith and J. Culbertson (eds.), *Public Finance and Stabilization Policy: Essays in Honour of Richard A. Musgrave*, Amsterdam: North Holland, 1974; excerpts in Layard (see below), chap. 13.

_____: "The Social Time Preference Rate," *Economic Journal*, June 1964; also in Layard (see below).

Harberger, A. C.: *Project Evaluation*, London: Macmillan, 1972.

Layard, Richard (ed.): *Cost-Benefit Analysis, Selected Readings*, Baltimore: Penguin, 1972. An excellent summary of the major arguments is given in his introduction.

Little, I. M. D., and J. A. Mirrlees: *Project Appraisal and Planning for Developing Countries*, New York: Basic Books, 1974.

Mishan, E. J.: *Cost-Benefit Analysis*, New York: Praeger, 1976.

Musgrave, R. A.: "Cost-Benefit Analysis and the Theory of Public Finance," *Journal of Economic Literature*, September 1969.

Prest, A. R., and R. Turvey: "Cost-Benefit Analysis: A Survey," *Economic Journal*, December 1965.

Roemer, M., and J. J. Stern: *The Appraisal of Development Projects*, New York: Praeger, 1975.

Chapter 9

Expenditure Evaluation:
Case Studies*

A. Highway Construction: *Rationale of Project Evaluation; An Illustration; Further Problems.* **B. Outdoor Recreation:** *Measuring Benefits to Users; Other Benefits.* **C. Education:** *Benefit-Cost Evaluation Based on Earnings; Benefits Other than Earnings.* **D. Sectoral Allocation of Police. E. Project Analysis and Budget Procedures:** *The Planning-Programming-Budgeting System; Zero-Base Budgeting and Sunset Legislation.* **F. Summary.**

Application of the principles set forth in the preceding chapter is now being actively promoted in various areas of expenditure planning, and beyond this, attempts are being made to build such analysis systematically into the budget process. The problems and difficulties encountered differ with the type of expenditure, and ingenious approaches have been developed to deal with some of them. The purpose of this chapter is to illustrate these problems by considering a number of case studies.

---

*Reader's Guide to Chapter 9: This chapter provides a set of illustrations examining the application of cost-benefit analysis to various areas of project evaluation. The discussion should be of particular interest to practically inclined readers. They may apply the analysis of section C to their returns on the purchase of this book.

A. HIGHWAY CONSTRUCTION

Highway expenditure in 1976 amounted to $27 billion, $14 billion of which went for capital outlays, $7 billion for maintenance, and the remainder for interest and administrative services. About half of the total went into state highways, one-quarter into local roads, and the rest into unclassified roads.[1] Combining all levels of government, highways and roads are the fourth most important civilian expenditure function, surpassed in magnitude only by education, welfare, and health. While highway expenditures enter at the federal level only as intergovernmental transfers, they are a dominant factor in state budgets.

Looked at from a broader point of view, planning of highway investment is part of the general problem of designing an efficient transport system. For distant transport, highways compete with rail and air facilities. In the metropolitan area, they compete with mass transit facilities such as commuter trains. The product to be furnished is transport and the most efficient facility should be chosen. This broader setting of the transportation problem is important, but will be excluded here. To illustrate the essential aspects of cost-benefit analysis, let us consider a quite specific and limited problem, i.e., the evaluation of a particular highway project.

Rationale of Project Evaluation

Our problem is that of a state highway department which must decide whether to improve highway facilities between two cities. Is such an investment worthwhile, and how extensive should the new facility be?[2]

To answer the question, we must evaluate the benefits and costs involved. Benefits are measured in terms of reduced travel cost to the user. This approach is possible because travel is an "intermediate good," entering into the final product, which is "being at the point of destination." Reduction in travel cost is a reduction in the price at which this final product can be purchased.[3] The better the available facilities, the lower will be the cost per trip for any given volume of traffic. Also, the greater the volume of traffic, the higher will be the cost per trip.

---

[1] See Tax Foundation, *Facts and Figures on Government Finance*, New York: 1977, p. 162.

[2] The economics of highway investment has received considerable attention by economists. See, for instance:

Hans A. Adler, "Economic Evaluation of Transport Projects," in G. Fromm (ed.), *Transport Investment and Economic Development*, Washington: Brookings, 1965, pp. 170–194.

Robert W. Harbeson, "Some Allocation Problems in Highway Finance," in *Transportation Economics*, National Bureau of Economic Research, New York: Columbia, 1965, pp. 139–169.

Herbert Mohring, "Urban Highway Investments," in R. Dorfman (ed.), *Measuring Benefits of Government Investments*, Washington: Brookings, 1965, pp. 231–291.

James R. Nelson, "Policy Analysis in Transportation Programs," in *The Analysis and Evaluation of Public Expenditures: The PPB System*, A Compendium of Papers, Joint Economic Committee, 91st Cong., 1969, vol. 3, pp. 1102–1127.

[3] By the same token, this calculus does not apply to the pleasure driver, where the trip itself is the product. Benefit estimation in this case is more difficult, as shown in the following section on recreational facilities.

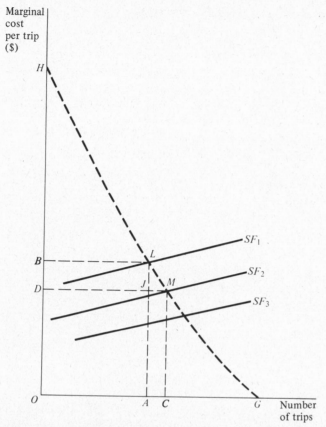

FIGURE 9-1   Highway User Demand at Various Levels of Facility.

This is shown in Figure 9-1. The total number of trips is measured along the horizontal axis, and dollar costs and prices per trip are measured on the vertical axis. Schedule SF_1 shows the marginal cost per trip to the road user at which various traffic volumes can be accommodated with a given level of highway facilities F_1, while SF_2 and SF_3 show the same for expanded levels of facilities F_2 and F_3. We may think of the subscripts as reflecting the number of lanes in the highway. With any given facility, the cost per trip rises with increasing traffic volume or number of trips, mainly owing to crowding and longer driving time. The SF schedules thus represent travel supply schedules to the users, where their own travel cost is the "price" which they must pay to make a trip in terms of travel time, accident cost, automotive expenses, and so on. Their demand schedules are not known, but we observe point L which shows that with existing facility F_1, the number of trips equals OA, with an average user cost per trip of OB. We estimate that if costs are reduced by expanding facilities from F_1 to F_2, users will move from L to M. The number of trips will increase to OC with a user cost of OD. This estimate may be based on observing the effects of expanding facilities in other locations. LM

may then be regarded as the estimated demand curve over the relevant range. It is extended here to G and H to develop the subsequent analysis.

The gain from increasing the facility level from F_1 to F_2 may be measured as the area DHM minus BHL, or as $DBLM$. $DBLM$ is the gain in consumer surplus which results from introduction of the new facility. Of this, $DBLJ$ reflects the cost saving on the old number of trips OA, while JLM reflects the gain on the additional trips AC. This latter gain on the new trips equals JLM, not $ALMC$, because $AJMC$ is offset by the additional user cost which results as the number of trips is expanded.

Turning now to Figure 9-2, we see that levels of highway facility (measured again in terms of lanes) are measured on the horizontal axis. The demand schedule DD reflects the marginal benefit which consumers derive from various facility levels, assuming the optimum use (as defined in Figure 9-1) for each level. Thus, at facility level F_2, the marginal benefit (obtained by moving from F_1 to F_2) equals OP as shown in Figure 9-2, where OP equals the area $DBLM$ in Figure 9-1. These marginal benefits must then be assessed against the costs to the highway department of securing the expansion of facilities. The marginal costs of expansion are shown in Figure 9-2 by the supply schedule SS, which represents the resource costs of supplying additional lanes.[4] To allow for economies of scale in construction, the marginal costs of adding lanes is assumed to decline with the scope of expansion. Thus the marginal cost of moving from facility level F_1 to level F_2 equals OR, that of moving from F_2 to F_3 equals OV, and so forth. If facilities were divisible, facility level F^*, where marginal cost equals marginal benefit, would be best. But facilities are lumpy, so that only certain points on the supply schedule, corresponding to F_1, F_2, and F_3, are possible. Choice of F^*, the intersection of DD and SS, is not feasible. The best solution, therefore, is to choose level F_2, because in moving from F_2 to F_3 additional benefits (or F_2UWF_3) would be outweighed by additional costs (or F_2NTF_3). Marginal user benefits OP still exceed marginal costs OR, but expansion to the next feasible facility level F_3 would result in higher marginal costs than benefits.

An Illustration

This is the principle which underlies the typical cost-benefit calculation for highways such as is shown in Table 9-1. Column I gives the situation at facility level F_1, column II after expansion to F_2, and column III after expansion to F_3.

Calculation of Net Benefits to Users   Benefits, as noted previously, are to be measured in terms of savings in reduced travel time and other transport costs to the user. The first step, therefore, is to determine the reduction in travel cost which results from the expansion of facilities. Column I shows the computation of travel cost prior to project expansion. The first item is the cost of travel time. If we assume that the average trip takes thirty minutes

[4]See also Fig. 8-2.

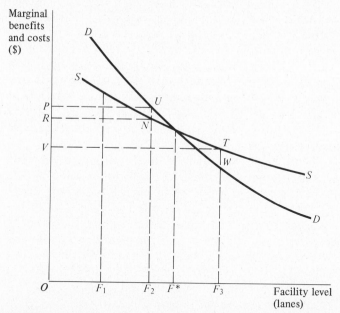

FIGURE 9-2 Highway User Demand for Various Levels of Facility.

(line 1) and that the average cost of travel time is $4 per hour, the money cost of travel time per trip prior to expansion is $2 (line 2, column I).

Figuring the average cost of travel time is far from simple. The required time, here assumed at thirty minutes, depends on the type of road as well as on traffic conditions. As any commuter well knows, travel time differs greatly between peak and slack hours, so that the average time requirement must be determined. Furthermore, the opportunity cost of time spent in travel, here assumed at $4 an hour, varies according to the type of traveler. Again the average cost must be found. In the case of a truck driver, the cost of travel time may be measured readily by wage rate, but the estimate is difficult for the commuter, who could either sleep longer or get to work sooner. The cost of travel time per trip is thus a complex figure to estimate.[5]

Next, certain other user costs must be allowed for. These are fuel costs (including taxes)[6] and wear of car, as well as accident costs. All these costs in turn depend on the type of road as well as on the type of vehicle used. These additional costs are shown in line 3. Setting them at an average 15 cents per mile for the preexpansion case and taking our road to be 11.7 miles long, we find that such costs equal $1.75 (line 3).[7] We thus arrive at the total variable

---

[5]To simplify, we may assume that all costs are capital costs incurred in the initial year of construction and that the highway department incurs no variable costs, such as increased maintenance or traffic control.

[6]The proper treatment of gasoline taxes depends on the governmental unit involved. Thus a state should not count its tax as a part of gasoline cost, while a locality which does not receive the revenue may include it.

[7]Cost estimates for various types of vehicles and roads are given in Marshall F. Reed, Jr., *The Economic Cost of Commuting*, Technical Study Memorandum 13, Washington: Highway Users Foundation, 1975; also see *Road User Benefit Analysis for Highway Improvements*, Washington: American Association for State Highway Officials, 1977.

TABLE 9-1
Profitability of Highway Construction

	Preexpansion Level F_1 (I)	After Expansion to F_2 (II)	After Expansion to F_3 (III)
Estimation of Benefits to Users			
1. Time per trip (minutes)	30	18	16
2. Time cost of trip ($4 per hour)	$2.00	$1.20	$1.07
3. Other cost per trip	$1.75	$1.90	$1.95
4. Total variable cost per trip	$3.75	$3.10	$3.02
5. Number of trips per year	1,000,000	1,500,000	1,600,000
6. Total variable costs per year	$3,750,000	$4,650,000	$4,832,000
7. Cost savings per trip	—	$0.65	$0.08
8. Cost savings on previous number of trips	—	$650,000	$120,000
9. Cost savings on additional trips	—	$162,500	$4,000
10. Total benefits per year	—	$812,500	$124,000
11. Present value of benefits (8%, 25 years)	—	$8,673,438	$1,323,700
Estimation of Project Cost			
12. Capital cost	—	$4,000,000	$2,000,000
13. Annual maintenance cost	$50,000	$60,000	$68,000
14. Increase in maintenance cost	—	$10,000	$8,000
15. Present value of increased maintenance cost (8%, 25 years)	—	$106,750	$85,400
16. Total project cost, present value	—	$4,106,750	$2,085,400
Evaluation			
17. Benefit-cost ratio (line 11 ÷ line 16)		2.11	0.63
18. Present value of net benefits (line 11−line 16)		$4,566,688	−$761,700
19. Internal rate of return (%)		20	3

user cost per trip of $3.75 (line 4). Assuming 1,000,000 trips to be made on the old facility, total variable costs are $3,750,000 (line 6). Assuming our preexpansion road to correspond to facility level 1 in Figure 9-1, we see that this total corresponds to area *OBLA* in Figure 9-1.[8] Total benefits from the existing facility level are not shown. To determine them, the entire demand schedule for the service (i.e., area *OHLA* in Figure 9-1) would have to be known. We assume that operation of the existing facility F_1 is worthwhile, which is the case if benefits exceed user and maintenance costs. The cost of the original construction need not be considered, since it is a sunk cost.[9]

Now an expansion is considered. The project is lumpy, so expansion has to take the form of adding successive lanes. Expansion from facility level F_1

[8]More precisely, the references to Fig. 9-1 should be in terms of discounted values of benefits and costs.
[9]Since an expansion is considered, we may infer that the original investment providing for facility level 1 was worthwhile, i.e., the benefits exceed the combined costs including that of original construction.

to F_2 involves addition of one lane, costing $4 million and corresponding to OR in Figure 9-2. Expansion from F_2 to F_3 adds a second lane and costs $2 million, corresponding to OV in Figure 9-2. Column II shows the situation after expansion to F_2. We note that the time per trip has gone down to 18 minutes, while other costs per trip have increased slightly to $1.90. More gasoline is used at the higher speed and wear is increased. On balance, the total variable cost per trip has fallen by 65 cents. The number of trips has increased to 1,500,000 and total annual travel cost has gone up to $4,650,000. This corresponds to area $ODMC$ in Figure 9-1.

We are now ready to compute the net user benefits from project expansion as reflected in the net savings in user cost. As shown in line 7 of the table, expansion to facility level F_2 reduces travel cost per trip from $3.75 to $3.10, or by 65 cents. Applying this to the old number of trips, we obtain a saving of $650,000 (line 8), corresponding to area $DBLJ$ in Figure 9-1. Regarding the 500,000 additional trips, we count only one-half the saving, or 32.5 cents, thus obtaining a further gain of $162,500 (line 9), corresponding to the triangular area JLM in the figure.[10] Total benefits, corresponding to the area $DBLM$ in the figure, thus amount to the combined annual cost savings of $812,500 (line 10).

Since the benefits (cost savings) will occur in the future, the present value of the future stream of benefits must be obtained by discounting. Suppose that the planning horizon extends twenty-five years ahead and that a discount rate of 8 percent is applicable. As shown in line 11, this gives us a present value of $8,673,438 for the benefit stream generated by expanding facilities to F_2.

The same procedure is followed in column III of the table for raising facilities from F_2 to F_3. Travel time is reduced further and other costs rise slightly. The total saving in user cost is 8 cents per trip and the number of trips rises slightly to 1,600,000. Following the same procedure as before, the present value of anticipated benefits (or cost savings to users) equals $1,323,700.

Calculation of Costs Turning now to the costs involved in the expansion of facilities, the main items to be considered are construction costs, site costs, and maintenance costs.

Construction costs are measured in terms of market price and need no further explanation. Site acquisition is by eminent domain and involves evaluation of the taken property, but this may again be based on fair market value, reflecting the opportunity cost of the land in alternative uses. As shown in line 12, total construction costs are assumed to be $4 million for the F_2 expansion and $2 million for further expansion to F_3. These capital costs are undertaken at the outset, so that no discounting is needed.

---

[10]Counting half the savings, or 32.5 cents, is a rough-and-ready procedure for measuring the gain in consumer surplus which results, since it assumes a linear demand schedule between traffic volumes A and C in Fig. 9-1. In the absence of better information, this is the best that can be done. For an explanation of this technique, see p. 171.

Road maintenance costs are partly dependent on traffic volume and type and are partly independent thereof. The estimation of maintenance cost thus involves some of the same considerations which arise in estimating the savings in user cost. Maintenance costs are assumed to increase by $10,000 per year in raising the facility level from F_1 to F_2 and by a further $8,000 in going from F_2 to F_3. The present values of these maintenance-cost streams, accruing over a twenty-five year period, are shown in line 15, and total costs (both construction and operating) in present-value terms are shown in line 16. These costs correspond to OR and OV for the F_2 and F_3 expansions, respectively, in the supply schedule of Figure 9-2.

Comparison of Costs and Benefits   We are now ready to compare the present value of costs and benefits.[11] For raising facilities from F_1 to F_2, benefits exceed costs by $4,566,688 (line 18) and, as shown in line 17, the benefit-cost ratio is 2.11. The internal rate of return on the F_2 expansion is 20 percent. For raising facilities from F_2 to F_3, costs exceed benefits at the chosen 8 percent rate of discount by $761,700, the benefit-cost ratio is only 0.63, and the internal rate of return falls to 3 percent. It follows that expansion to F_2 is profitable, while expansion to F_3 is not.[12] The high return to expansion to F_2 also suggests that a modified extension beyond it, but less ambitious than F_3, would be desirable. If projects can be carried out in small units and the budget is flexible, additional expansion to F^* in Figure 9-2 would indeed be desirable until the incremental benefits and costs are the same and the benefit-cost ratio becomes 1 for the last unit of expanded facilities. But given the lumpiness of the project, expansion to F_2 is the best that can be done.

Alternative Choices   The question posed here was whether and how far road facilities between two particular cities should be expanded. The same question, obviously, can be asked for facilities between any other pair of cities. If there is no budget constraint, all such facilities that are profitable

---

[11]Our procedure has been to reduce both cost and benefit streams to their present value. An alternative procedure is to compare the undiscounted annual benefit with a corresponding annual cost, defined to include amortization of capital as well as maintenance cost. If the amortization period is the same as the number of years over which benefits are estimated, and the annual benefits and costs accrue at constant rates, the two procedures give the same result.

In practice the alternative procedure is usually followed and the amortization period is estimated independently of the benefit period. The amortization period, estimated in accordance with the physical life of the asset, differs for various components of the project, such as surface and grading. The average amortization period for the project thus determined frequently exceeds the number of years over which benefits can be estimated. The analysis (see *Road User Benefit Analysis*, op. cit.) is then based on the shorter benefit period, comparing the annual benefits with the present-value annual cost computed to include only that part of amortization that occurs during this shorter period.

[12]Note that the analysis should not proceed by considering the benefit-cost ratio obtainable by immediate expansion from F_1 to F_3 without considering the partial expansion from F_1 to F_2. Although expansion from F_1 to F_3 appears profitable with a benefit-cost ratio of 1.6, the incremental expansion from F_2 to F_3 is unprofitable. Since an incremental approach is possible, the expansion should stop at the expansion to F_2.

(i.e., have a present value of net benefits above zero) should be undertaken. Provided the proper rate of discount is used and the social opportunity cost of capital is correctly calculated, this resource use would then be more profitable than would have been the private use that is displaced.

Typically, budget choices are not made in this fashion, but within a given budget constraint. The highway budget is fixed and the question is where the funds should be spent. The problem, then, is to compare the return obtained by expanding facilities between alternative pairs of cities. If the projects are indivisible, the various benefits and costs are computed, following the above procedure in each case, and the best mix is chosen. If the improvements can be made in small amounts, a number of facilities may be improved in varying degrees, such that the net benefits for the marginal expenditure will be the same in all cases.

Further Problems

The preceding illustration oversimplifies matters in various respects, some of which may be noted briefly.

Changing Environment   We have noted that estimation of benefits involves considerable difficulties, even in a static setting, such as determining the value of travel time. But the complexities are increased greatly once economic change is allowed for. Highways have a long life span, say forty years, and the traffic volume is difficult to predict over such a period. Cost estimation should not be based on a comparison of user's cost before and after project expansion while holding "other factors" constant, but should make full allowance for changes in such factors. Thus, traffic volume will be affected by changes in population and per capita incomes, and by the pattern of regional development. Moreover, the project itself may have an important effect on these variables. All these factors must be allowed for in estimating cost savings and in calculating benefits on that basis. Thus a sizable task of economic forecasting is involved.

Project versus System Analysis   As noted before, the individual transportation project is part of a broader transportation system and cannot be evaluated properly if considered in isolation. Expanding the direct road from town X to town Y may reduce traffic previously routed via Z, or expanding road facilities may divert traffic from other modes of transportation. Intelligent transport planning must thus relate to the entire transport system, linking individual highways with the road system, and the road system with the transport system at large. The profitability of expanding highway facilities in the metropolitan area in particular must be assessed in relation to that of other transport facilities, such as buses or commuter trains. As just noted, availability of transport facilities is itself an important factor in economic development, and transport systems no less than individual projects must be planned in that context.

Moreover, transport facilities by their very nature provide a linkage between regions and hence require cooperation between various governmental units, such as states and municipalities. This is an aspect to which we will return later, when problems of fiscal federalism are considered.[13]

Indirect Benefits and Costs Benefit measurement in the preceding illustration has allowed for benefits to direct highway users only. These "direct" benefits are relatively easy to measure, owing to the nature of transportation as an "intermediate" good. But in a fuller analysis, other benefits or costs must be considered as well.

Important indirect benefits may result from the repercussions of transport expansion on economic development. Thus expansion of facilities between two cities may generate economic development of the region and permit a better division of labor between the two locations. The resulting benefit will exceed the gain as measured above since factor earnings in both locations will increase. In developing countries in particular, the opening of communication brings heretofore unutilized resources into use and establishes communication with the market. The early development of canals, the growth of the United States railroad system in the middle of the nineteenth century, or today's highway construction in Latin America are cases in point. The developmental gains to the economy resulting from such growth in transport facilities are more difficult to predict and cannot be formulated simply in terms of reduced travel cost.

On the cost side, social cost may exceed the direct construction cost in a variety of ways. Dwellings may have to be destroyed and their replacement cost must be included as an indirect though tangible cost. Beyond this, a throughway may disrupt established communities and force relocation, introducing a further indirect and, this time, intangible cost. The true social cost may, in fact, greatly exceed the replacement cost of housing. Moreover, the pecuniary losses and gains which result may have important distributional implications. The destruction of low-cost housing may not hurt the landlord, who is compensated, but nevertheless places a burden on the tenants if the supply of low-cost housing is reduced in the process.[14]

B. OUTDOOR RECREATION

As our next case, we consider the evaluation of projects for outdoor recreation, say, a public park. The benefits which accrue include (1) benefits to the users, (2) benefits to the surrounding community, and (3) certain other benefits, such as preservation of the natural beauty of the environment, which are of a more or less intangible sort. As before, we focus first on user benefits, which are considered the major component of the benefit calculation.

In contrast to highways, we now deal with a social good which is in the nature of a final or consumer good, rather than of an intermediate good. The

---

[13]See p. 528.

[14]The present discussion has dealt with evaluating the profitability of alternative projects, not with how they are to be financed. For a discussion of toll finance and gasoline taxes as benefit taxation, see p. 241.

problem is to evaluate the benefits, such as reduced congestion, which are derived from the park itself or its expansion and not, as in the case of roads, from the reduced cost of obtaining other benefits, such as those of getting to a destination. The question "What is a visit to the park worth?" must be faced. Given the answer, we can then compare the present value of costs and benefits along much the same lines as in the preceding illustration.

Measuring Benefits to Users

Various techniques of benefit measurement have been suggested and used. They include direct pricing through user charges, estimation of willingness to pay hypothetical user charges, use of prices paid for similar private facilities, costs undertaken in using the facilities, and the construction of indices such as merit-weighted user days.

User Charges Let us assume our park to be such that "exclusion" can be readily applied, i.e., that the administrative cost of limiting admission to those who pay the price is insignificant. We have seen that, in the absence of crowding, exclusion is incompatible with efficient use of the particular park since consumption is nonrival.[15] However, individual parks are not planned in isolation. A park agency will be confronted with providing parks in different locations, and the experience gained from A may be used for planning the location of B. A case can thus be made for testing the profitability of park construction by charging fees in one initial park, even if attendance cost is zero, so as to obtain a measuring rod for further park construction.[16] If the present value of prospective fees from park A exceeds the project cost, similar facilities will be called for in other locations where demand conditions are expected to be similar. The inefficiency which results from underutilizing park A (or from having constructed a park which proves unprofitable) may be more than offset by the increased efficiency in planning other park construction made possible by the information gained.

Hypothetical User Charges Instead of experimenting with actual user charges, market survey techniques may be used in an attempt to obtain the same information. Potential users may be asked how much they would be willing to pay for various facilities, or how much use they would make of given facilities at various prices. By this means, an attempt can be made to construct a simulated demand schedule and to evaluate benefits without the inefficiency of exclusion. But the difficulty is that the respondents are not likely to tell the truth: they will give too high an evaluation if they wish to encourage the construction of the facility and too low a figure if they wish to discourage it. Nevertheless, this approach has proved to be of some use and has been strongly advocated by several experts.[17]

---

[15]See p. 56. Of course, charging of fees is appropriate to cover maintenance costs or where crowding occurs.

[16]For further discussion of pricing schemes, see p. 744.

[17]See Jack L. Knetsch and Robert R. Davis, "Comparison of Methods for Recreation Evaluation," in A. V. Kneese and S. C. Smith (eds.), *Water Research*, Washington: Resources for the Future, 1965, pp. 125–143.

Prices for Private Facilities In some instances it may be possible to draw a parallel to prices paid for more or less similar private facilities. Thus, fees paid for membership in a private club providing similar facilities may be indicative of the consumption value obtained by the use of the public park. There are two weaknesses to this approach. First, it may well be that the price paid for the private facility is depressed because another public facility is available free of direct charge. Thus, use of the price paid for admission to the private facility understates the value of the additional public park. Second, a factor working in the opposite direction is that the price paid for the private facility may include a premium for "exclusiveness" generated by membership in the private facility. Thus, the value of the public park would be overstated. For the method to be reliable, it would be necessary for the two facilities to be fairly comparable, a condition that will rarely be found.

Costs Incurred Approaching the estimation of the dollar value of recreation benefits indirectly, some studies have made use of the personal costs incurred by users in securing their outdoor recreation. The first question is how this cost should be estimated; the second is whether the procedure of using costs as a proxy for benefits is valid.

Pursuing this approach, it has been estimated that the average expenditure per person for all outdoor recreation in 1962 was $74.90, including travel cost and other outlays. It was also estimated that people spent an average of 258 hours for recreational purposes. This finding suggested an expenditure of roughly 30 cents for each hour spent in outdoor recreation, and the conclusion was drawn from this that, on the average, the value of services provided by recreation facilities was roughly 30 cents per hour.[18] Thus the benefit stream of a given park may be obtained by valuing visiting hours at 30 cents. The present value of this stream is then compared with the construction and maintenance costs of the facility. The same magic figure of 30 cents is obtained if one divides the widely used figure of a price of $2 per visit by an assumed average stay of six or seven hours.[19]

Allowing for price rise since 1962, the figure of 30 cents might now be raised to, say, 60 cents, but this is not the main problem. The entire procedure

[18]See Ruth P. Mack and Summer Myers, "Outdoor Recreation," in Robert Dorfman (ed.), *Measuring Benefits of Government Investment*, Washington: Brookings, 1965, p. 87.

[19]In guidelines proposed by the federal government, the per-person value of a recreation day for the use of general facilities has been set at 50 cents to $1.50, while the value of specialized facilities is rated from $2 to $6. (See *Evaluation Standards for Primary Outdoor Recreation Benefits*, supplement no. 1, Washington: Ad Hoc Water Resources Council, June 4, 1964, p. 4.) Although the document does not give the basis on which these figures are reached, the reasoning was presumably similar to that given in the text. A point system by which to choose the appropriate value in the indicated range of 50 cents to $1.50 is given in *Methodology for Determining General Recreation Values*, Senate Doc. No. 97, Pacific Southwest Inter-Agency Committee, July 1969.

For further discussion of program evaluation, see also *Policies, Standards, and Procedures in the Formulation, Evaluation and Revenue of Plans for Use and Development of Water and Related Land Resources*, Senate Doc. No. 97, May 29, 1962; and Inter-Agency Committee on Water Resources, Subcommittee on Evaluation Standards, *Report of the Panel on Recreational Values on a Proposed Interim Schedule of Values for Recreational Aspects of Fish and Wildlife*, May 24, 1960.

of estimating benefits from user costs is open to serious objection. At best, the recreationist's travel cost measures the marginal benefit derived from his or her last visit to the park. The product of travel cost and number of visits falls short of total benefits by the consumer surplus obtained from acquiring the earlier visits at the same cost. Yet, it is precisely this consumer surplus which constitutes the benefit that should be matched with the cost of providing the facility.[20] But to estimate consumer surplus we would have to know the demand curve over various levels of usage and cost, and not only a single point. Various attempts have been made to derive such points by reference to the comparative use made of recreation areas by different communities at varying distances from such areas and therefore at varying user cost.[21]

A more meaningful role of travel cost is to consider the saving in cost which results as a new and closer facility is opened. This saving offers an approximation to the gain from the additional facility.[22] But, except in this context, travel cost is a poor basis on which to estimate benefits. Not only does it fail to estimate consumer surplus but it also constitutes a poor measure of total cost to the consumer. To determine the latter, the opportunity cost of time spent in the park should also be allowed for. The importance of travel cost in total user cost thus defined varies widely, depending on the travel time involved, and parks with little or no travel cost may be at least as useful as those with high travel cost. A park which involves no user cost except the opportunity cost of the time spent should be used up to the point where this opportunity cost comes to exceed the benefit derived. The gain as measured in terms of consumer surplus is increased, rather than reduced, by the absence of travel cost.

---

[20]Let OA be the cost per trip and OB the observed number of trips, so that C is the observed point on the demand schedule. The product of cost and number of trips, or $OBCA$, falls short of total benefits, or $OBCD$, by consumer surplus, or ACD. Since benefit component $OBCA$ is paid for by travel cost, it is the ACD component which must be matched against the cost of the facility.

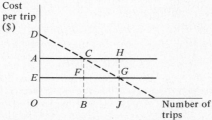

Instead of matching the benefit stream as measured by ACD with the facility cost, total benefits as measured by $OBCD$ may be matched with facility plus travel cost. In maximizing the excess of benefits over cost or expanding output to the point where the two are equal, both procedures give the same result. However, different cost-benefit ratios are recorded, depending on which method is used, unless the ratios are equal to 1. This shows a certain arbitrariness of the ratio approach. See p. 170.

[21]See R. Layard (ed.), *Cost-Benefit Analysis*, Baltimore: Penguin, 1972, pp. 211–218.

[22]Referring back to the figure in footnote 20, let provision of the new facility reduce travel cost from OA to OE. The gain is then given by area $EGCA$ or, assuming a linear demand schedule by $EFCA + \frac{1}{2} FGHC$, the formula used in our earlier discussion of the highway case. This use of travel cost was pointed out to us by N. A. Back, Director, Center for Economic Studies, Institute for Water Resources, Corps of Engineers, Department of the Army.

Merit-weighted User Days   As an alternative procedure to estimating the value of user days, it has been proposed that certain weights be assigned to various user characteristics.[23] Thus, user days may be weighted according to the user's income, residence, age, or other characteristics. The weights are to be determined in terms of specified policy objectives, such as income redistribution or regional development, thus permitting the comparison of various projects where more than one policy objective is to be taken into account. The spirit is essentially that of cost-effectiveness studies, where comparison is made between the efficiency of alternative uses of given funds in achieving a desired set of objectives and where the value weights to be attributed to these objectives are given in advance.

Other Benefits

So far, only benefits accruing to and valued by users have been allowed for. In addition, other benefits may enter. Outdoor recreation projects are frequently part of broader programs aimed at multiple objectives, e.g., water resource or regional development projects. Thus, a dam may be built to generate power, to control floods, to serve irrigation, *and* to yield recreational facilities. The benefits from the various products must then be evaluated in conjunction with one another so as to obtain the best product mix.

Outdoor recreation, moreover, may be considered a merit good, so that social valuation exceeds the value attributed by private users, resulting in a writing-up of their benefit evaluation similar to a subsidy to private-type merit goods. Similar considerations arise with regard to objectives such as conservation of natural beauty or of wildlife. These objectives involve social values which cannot be measured readily by market tests and thus tend to be set aside. Possible conflicts between social and private time preference are also involved, relating in this instance to the interests of future versus present generations. In recreation as elsewhere, it is natural for economic analysis to focus on those aspects of the problem which permit analogy to market pricing and which are therefore more feasible to deal with. These are by no means the only, or even in some cases the most important, aspects.

C. EDUCATION

The analysis of education expenditures has received a great deal of attention by economists in recent years.[24] Viewed as "investment in human resources," returns to education expenditures have been computed and the profitability of "human" investment relative to "plant and equipment" investment has been assessed.[25] By concentrating exclusively on the earnings-generating effects of education while disregarding other aspects, this approach does less

---

[23]See Mack and Myers, op. cit.

[24]We are here dealing with the cost-benefit aspects of education only. Other questions, such as how education should be financed and whether it should be public or private, are considered in a later chapter. See p. 577.

[25]For the basic work, see Gary S. Becker, *Human Capital*, New York: Columbia, 1964.

than justice to the role of education. These other aspects will be noted later on, but for the time being we address ourselves to the more tangible and readily measured earnings feature.

The importance of education in public sector policy is enormous. As seen in Table 9-2, public expenditures on education amounted to $106 billion in fiscal 1976. Accounting for nearly 30 percent of total public expenditures other than defense, education is by far the most important single civilian item. About 70 percent of the expenditures were at the local level, directed at the provision of elementary and secondary education. Higher education is primarily financed at the state level, but federal money plays an increasingly important role. Evaluation of education programs is thus a vital factor at all levels of government.

Benefit-Cost Evaluation Based on Earnings

As noted before, the approach typically followed in evaluating expenditures focuses on gains in earnings. The methodology may be illustrated by considering the major steps in estimating the returns to college education.

Benefits   Benefit evaluation has concentrated on the increase in the student's lifetime earnings that is due to education. This gain in earnings has been estimated by observing earnings differentials among people with various levels of education and attributing these differentials to the influence of education. The earning increment is then projected over the student's working life and discounted to obtain a present value. The process is complicated by adjusting for such factors as productivity changes and lifetime earnings profiles. However, a rough estimate is shown in Table 9-3 on the next page.

Lines 1 and 2 give estimated annual lifetime earnings for male workers with high school and college education and line 3 shows the differential. Line 4 gives the total gain in earnings over an estimated working life of 41 years (age 24 to 65). Lines 5 and 6 show the present value of these gains using a discount rate of 8 and 4 percent, respectively. To simplify, it is assumed that annual earnings are constant. Since earnings of college graduates typically

TABLE 9-2
Direct Public Expenditures on Education, Fiscal 1975–76
(In Billions of Dollars)

	Federal	State	Local	All
Elementary and secondary	—	0.6	67.1	67.7
Higher	—	19.7	4.6	24.3
Other	9.0	5.3	—	14.3
Total	9.0	25.6	71.7	106.3

Source: U.S. Bureau of the Census, *Governmental Finances in 1975–76*, p. 22. The table shows expenditures to the public, with grant-financed expenditures included at the recipient level.

TABLE 9-3
Benefit-Cost Estimates for College Education, 1975

Average Value of Education to Student	
1. Mean annual earnings, high school graduates	$10,500
2. Mean annual earnings, college graduates	15,800
3. Gain in annual earnings	5,300
4. Total (41 years)	217,300
5. Present value, 8% discount	46,600
6. Present value, 4% discount	90,600
Average Cost per Student	
7. Running of colleges (4 years)	$11,600
8. Forgone earnings (4 years)	21,900
9. Other incidental costs (4 years)	6,000
10. Total (4 years)	39,500
11. Present value, 8% discount	32,707
12. Present value, 4% discount	35,845
Net Gain	
13. Benefits minus cost, 8% discount	$13,893
14. Benefits minus cost, 4% discount	$54,795
15. Benefit-cost ratio, 8% discount	1.42%
16. Benefit-cost ratio, 4% discount	2.53%
17. Internal rate of return	11.2%

Lines 1 and 2: See U.S. Bureau of the Census, *Current Population Reports,* series P-60, no. 105, "Money Income in 1975 of Families and Persons in the United States," 1977, p. 205.

Lines 5 and 6: Earnings assumed to begin after graduation and to be constant at average level.

Line 7: See U.S. Department of Health, Education and Welfare, *The Condition of Education*, 1978, p. 72, table 2.11, and p. 226, table 5.10. Figures are for 1976 levels, deflated to 1975 dollars.

Line 8: Earnings of high school graduates in 18–24 age group. Same source as for lines 1 and 2.

rise with age, this overstates the present value of the gain as insufficient discounting is applied. Note that the present value of the gain from college education depends greatly on the discount rate used. This is so because investment from education has a very long payoff period.

Costs   Turning to the cost side, we include (1) the capital and operating cost of running schools, and (2) the costs incurred by the student. The latter include the opportunity cost of earnings forgone and outlays incurred, such as books, travel, and additional (not total!) living costs. These costs differ widely by type of school and region of the country, but, on the average, they may be estimated as shown in lines 8 and 9. As there shown, the cost of forgone earnings accounts for over half of the total cost.

Net Benefits   We may now put the two sides together and obtain the various measures of net benefit shown in lines 13 to 17. The outcome, be it in absolute (lines 13 and 14) or ratio (lines 15 and 16) terms, again depends greatly on the rate of discount. Given a long-term market rate of interest of about 8 percent, lines 13 and 15 give the more realistic picture. If this market rate is taken to reflect the return on investment in physical assets, the conclusion is that investment in college education does slightly better. Another view of the matter is given in line 17, which shows the internal rate of discount on investment in college education. This rate, which is slightly above the market rate, again suggests that, from the social point of view, there is a slight degree of underinvestment in college education. This, however, may only reflect a tendency for our estimate to be on the high side.[26]

Problems of Measurement Various difficulties arise in the measurement of earnings benefits, including the following:

1. Measuring the returns to education in terms of observed average earnings differentials of people with varying levels of education assumes that these differentials are caused entirely by education. Other factors may be present as well. Thus, differences in earnings may reflect differences in innate earnings capacity, whether due to differences in intelligence, drive, pecuniary motivation, or what not. Since innate earning ability may be positively related to the length of education, part of the difference in average earnings by education levels may be due to ability rather than training differentials. Attempts have been made to correct for this by comparing earnings of people with equal ability (as measured by test scores, IQ, etc.) but different schooling, but this is a much more difficult task.

2. Further overestimation of the social return to education may arise where wage rates are not closely related to the worker's marginal product, but higher-paying jobs are reserved for people with higher ranking in the educational hierarchy. "Prestige hiring" is not an unknown feature, and not all personal services are valued in a competitive market. In such cases, training differentials are relevant from the private point of view but resulting differentials in earnings reflect pecuniary rather than real benefits and therefore should not be allowed for in measuring social gains.

3. Use of averages is misleading if applied to subgroups or individuals. Thus, it has been shown that rates of return to education differ by social groups since the fruits of education are not always competitively priced. Furthermore, educational investment opportunities may be restricted rather than freely available.

Social versus Private Benefits In Table 9-3 we have considered earnings gains and costs to society and thus have derived a *social* benefit-cost ratio for college education of 1.42. This ratio, however, is not the same as the one which confronts the individual student who is concerned with *private* benefits and costs only.

While benefits from a college education were estimated at $46,600 (present value), the net gains to the individual will be less because taxes must be paid thereon. Assuming an average tax rate of 25 percent, discounted benefits are reduced to $34,950.[27]

---

[26]As noted above, the bias results from our assumption of level earnings. Since earnings profiles are actually rising with age, this suggests that our estimates involve insufficient discounting.

[27]A further aspect of the tax treatment should be noted here. Earnings from private investment in education are taxed on a gross basis without provision for depreciation or expensing of capital cost, as applies to plant and equipment investment. This may be expected to lead to private underinvestment in education, a factor which tends to be compensated for by public investment therein. See p. 682.

On the cost side, private costs fall short of the total because the operating cost of schools is only partly sustained by tuition. Assuming one-third of the operating cost to be tuition financed, the private cost is reduced to $36,600. Allowing for some recoupment of lost earnings through tax savings, suppose that private cost equals $25,000. With private benefits of $34,950, the net gain is reduced to $9,450, the benefit-cost ratio falls to 1.37, and the internal rate of return is cut to 10.9. The average college student, it appears, received a private rate of return which is somewhat below the social. The difference accrues to the general public as a net gain in tax revenue, shared in with or without benefit of college education.

Benefits Other than Earnings

The preceding analysis, following common practice, has viewed the benefits from education in terms of enhanced earnings. It remains to note that this is too limited a view. Earnings are important, but so is the contribution to fuller life which education (hopefully) renders. Investment in education, therefore, should not be viewed purely as the creation of an income-earning asset, where income is defined as factor earnings in the market. It should also be viewed as an investment in a durable consumer good which generates a psychic income stream to the student throughout life.[28] Suppose, for instance, that the cost of educational inputs is divided equally between earnings and psychic income-generating investment. Assuming further that both yield equal returns, the income stream (monetary and imputed) would be doubled and the internal rate of return would be twice that shown in the table.

A further source of underestimation of benefits arises because the earnings differential records only those gains which are internalized in the student's earnings prospects. It does not capture external benefits which others may derive from the student's education. As noted earlier, education is a mixed good which generates both private and social gains.[29] The latter may be tangible gains which arise because the labor force can sustain a more advanced technology, or because of increased productivity stemming from innovations; or, they may be intangible benefits in the form of a more intelligent political process, or a culturally more rewarding environment.

Finally, education policy has a profound bearing on income distribution and social stratification. It can thus be a vital instrument of social policy. Inequalities in the distribution of income are strongly related to inequalities in educational investment. Unequal education thus perpetuates unequal income, while more equal distribution of education inputs helps to reduce inequality. Investment in education thus opens an opportunity for policy measures which are both efficient in the output-oriented sense of the economist and which serve desirable social ends of reduced inequality. By extending human investment where it has been held back artificially through discrimination, rigidities, and inability to obtain the necessary funds, both

---

[28]In addition, there are consumption aspects to the very process of going to college.
[29]See p. 78.

these purposes are served. Moreover, where earnings are low because of discrimination, they are not the proper prices to be used in assessing social gain. Rather, use should be made of shadow prices which account for the return receivable without discrimination. Beyond this, some degree of overinvestment in education of underprivileged groups may be desirable as a superior form of distributional adjustment. Preferable on social grounds to transfer payments, it may offer a better chance for permanent escape from poverty.

Considerations such as these suggest that preoccupation with the earnings aspect has led to too narrow a view and distorts the choice between types of education. A broader approach to benefit evaluation is needed.

D. SECTORAL ALLOCATION OF POLICE

Another illustration is given by the problem of allocating police forces among sections of a city.[30] Suppose there is an uptown precinct X and a downtown precinct Y. Population size is the same in both but the crime rate is higher in Y. Assume further that crime prevention is subject to increasing cost in both districts. The question is how a given police budget shall be allocated between X and Y. Among various targets, the following may be considered:

    1. Equal number of crimes prevented in each sector
    2. Equal protection, or equal number of crimes still committed in each sector
    3. Maximum crime reduction for both sectors combined
    4. Equality of the marginal rate of transformation between crime reduction in the two districts and the marginal rate of substitution of utilities derived from crime reduction in the two districts

Which of these goals is preferable on equity and/or efficiency grounds?

The alternative solutions to the problem are illustrated in Figure 9-3, where the crime level in sector X is measured on the vertical axis and that in Y on the horizontal axis. AB is a transformation schedule showing what combinations of remaining crime levels can be obtained with a given budget.[31] If the entire police force is used in X, crime levels will be shown by B; if it is all allocated to Y, crime levels will be as shown by point A. If there is no protection for either, the location is at C.

To implement goal 1, the appropriate solution is at D, obtained by drawing a line through C at a 45° angle with the axes and taking its intersection with the transformation curve. Crime in X will fall by CL and in

---

[30]See Carl S. Shoup, "Standards for Distributing a Free Government Service: Crime Prevention," *Public Finance*, 1964, pp. 393–394; and Douglas Dosser's comment, ibid., pp. 395–401.

[31]The slope of AB reflects the assumption of increasing cost of crime prevention in each sector. The function is concave from above rather than convex, since we plot "crime remaining" rather than "crime prevented." To simplify matters, we also assume equal population size for the two sectors and disregard spillover effects between them. On the latter point, see p. 527.

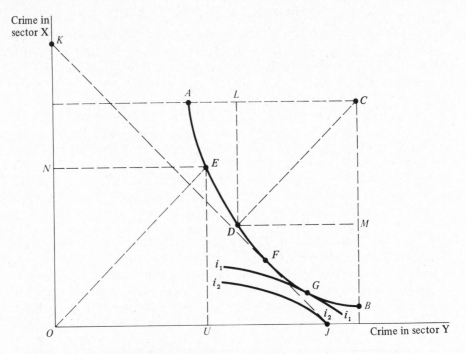

FIGURE 9-3   Police Allocation among Sectors of City.

Y by CM, where $CL = CM$. To implement goal 2, the solution is at E, obtained by drawing a 45° line through the origin and again taking its intersection with AB. Remaining crime will equal ON in X and OU in Y with $ON = OU$. To implement goal 3, the marginal cost of crime prevention must be equal in both sectors. The solution is at F where the slope of the transformation function equals -1, it being tangent to the line JK where $OK = OJ$. Goals 1 to 3 cannot be ranked without involving some distributional judgment, which judgment is made explicit in goal 4.

Goal 4 calls for a social welfare function which values crime prevention in X and Y as expressed by indifference curves $i_1 i_1$ and $i_2 i_2$. The optimal solution is given at G where AB is tangent to the highest possible indifference curve.[32] This is where the marginal rate of transformation of crime reduction in X into crime reduction in Y equals the marginal rate of substitution of the social value assigned to crime reduction in Y for that in X. The analyst thus recommends assignment in line with G which, given the indifference curves as expressed by the policy maker, is the efficient solution. As drawn here, the policy maker considers crime in sector X to be more harmful than in Y, since with equal weights, the point of tangency would be at D.

[32]The indifference curves are convex from above because we plot remaining crime rather than absence of crime.

E. PROJECT ANALYSIS AND BUDGET PROCEDURES

Over the years, various attempts have been made to incorporate cost-benefit analysis more or less formally into budget procedures. The link is obvious, since the essence of effective budgeting is (or should be) to weigh the social net benefits of alternative uses of public funds.

During the 1960s increasing efforts were made to expand the application of principles of cost-benefit analysis to government expenditure decisions. These efforts began with the application of cost-effectiveness analysis in the Defense Department and later centered on the introduction of the so-called planning-programming-budgeting (PPB) system to the entire federal government as well as to a number of state and local governments. At the same time, this development may be looked upon as the extension of long-standing efforts to improve the formulation of expenditure policy at the executive level. At the time the Bureau of the Budget was created in the Treasury Department by the Accounting Act of 1921, the emphasis was on operational control over expenditure programs.[33] When the bureau was separated from the Treasury and placed in the President's office in 1939, emphasis shifted to managerial efficiency. This tendency was supported by the report of the Hoover Commission in 1949 which called for the introduction of "performance budgeting." Improvements in accounting and cost data were introduced by the 1950 Budget and Accounting Act. As noted, a broader and more systematic approach to expenditure planning was developed in the Department of Defense in the early 1960s, and the extension of this methodology was pushed by various executive directives, beginning in 1965. More recently, related techniques have been advanced under the labels of "zero-base budgeting" and "sunset legislation."

The Planning-Programming-Budgeting System

The planning-programming-budgeting system, also referred to as PPBS, is the most systematic attempt at introducing cost-benefit analysis into budgeting.

Objectives and Procedures   Three basic ideas underlie the concept of PPBS:

> 1. Although, for purposes of legislative control, appropriations must be made to agencies, expenditure programs may overlap agencies, and there is need to look at the program and planning unit as a whole.
>
> 2. A proper evaluation of an expenditure program requires scrutiny of more than one time period.

[33]Prior to that time, each department submitted its own appropriation requests directly to the Congress, but as early as 1912, President Taft had submitted to the Congress a model budget, involving classifications by functions and activity as well as by organization. For a discussion of this history, see Allen Schick, "The Road to PPB: The Stages of Budget Reform," *Public Administration Review*, December 1966, p. 243; and Charles Schultze, *The Politics and Economics of Public Spending*, Washington: Brookings, 1968.

3. In the interests of applying standards of efficiency to the budget, cost-benefit analysis should be applied where feasible and expenditure programs should be evaluated in these terms.

Thus the objective of the PPBS has been described as "an approach to decision making designed to help make as explicit as possible the costs and consequences of major choices and to encourage the use of this information systematically in the making of public policy."[34] This approach involves the use of new tools of analysis, e.g., cost-benefit techniques, and, beyond this, an effort to assure the use of these tools in a systematic fashion.

The main responsibility for implementing the new approach was to rest with the various governmental departments and agencies, but the central responsibility for coordination and guidance remained with the Office of Management and Budget. As one of the major innovations, program structures were prescribed to secure the grouping of activities into objective-oriented classifications. The purpose was to obtain a view of the total costs and benefits involved in a program, components of which may appear in different parts of the organization and may be included in different appropriation categories. Given such total program evaluation, a better basis is provided for analyzing the comparative merits of alternative programs and the possible tradeoffs among them.

The budget for the fiscal year 1970 for the first time included a presentation of agency budgets by program as well as by appropriation categories and this approach has been expanded in subsequent budgets. The presentation for the Department of Health, Education, and Welfare, for instance, includes major program categories such as health, social and rehabilitation services, and income security. The education program category is divided into subcategories such as development of basic, occupational, and academic skills, etc., grouping together in each subcategory a number of program elements, such as education of the disadvantaged and the physically handicapped, otherwise included in separate appropriation categories. In recent years, the budget presentation has given increasing attention to presenting budget outlays by function as well as by agencies.

The PPB system as introduced in 1965 also prescribed various procedures by which to integrate the approach into step-by-step budget planning. Thus, the Office of Management and Budget, in negotiation with each agency, was to submit an "issue letter" to the agency, defining the major issues which should be analyzed in each budget cycle. The agencies were to prepare, along with the budget submission, brief program memoranda for selected major program categories. These were to incorporate the results of

[34]See J. Carlson, "The Current Status of the Planning-Programming-Budgeting System," in *The Analysis and Evaluation of Public Expenditures: The PPB System*, Joint Economic Committee, 91st Cong., 1st Sess., 1969, vol. 2, p. 613; Jesse Burkhead and Jerry Miner, *Public Expenditure*, Chicago: Aldine-Atherton, 1971, chap. 6. See also David Novick (ed.), *Current Practice in Program Budgeting (PPBS); Analysis and Case Studies Covering Government and Business*, New York: Crane, Russak, 1973.

the underlying analysis, identify alternatives, and then serve as evidence in the program evaluation. As a final component of the PPB system, the agency was to submit a current program and financial plan covering the preceding two and the coming five years. This plan was to show the funds committed to various program areas by past decisions, as well as projected program outputs for the same period. It would then serve as a guide in relating annual budget allocations to longer-term plans and priorities.

Evaluation and Shortcomings The objectives of the PPB system were clearly desirable, but the details proved too cumbersome and most of the specific requirements imposed upon the agencies were subsequently reduced or withdrawn. Some of the major difficulties were as follows:

1. The PPB system placed the major responsibility for program evaluation on departments and agencies. This is unsatisfactory since programs are frequently interdepartmental, so that comprehensive program evaluation must also be interdepartmental, or components must be transferred out of present departments into new units.

A similar difficulty arises from the fact that federal programs in many instances operate through grants to state and local governments. Program evaluation therefore requires a joint effort, an effort that is not provided for in the federal budget process.

2. While program evaluation and planning along PPB lines is important, the budget must also function as a framework for congressional appropriation and control, and as a tool of executive management.[35] For these purposes, expenditures have continued to be classified by departments, bureaus, and divisions within departments. In time, congressional appropriation categories should be made to coincide with planning (program) categories, thus eliminating the complex system of "crosswalk" required by the present practice.

3. PPB has been criticized for tying the implementation of expenditure analysis too closely into the budget process. The budget process, so this argument goes, must be directed essentially at preparing appropriations requests for Congress. In this task there is neither time nor the analytical frame of mind which is needed to apply rigorous program evaluation. Thus, it is suggested that the task of program evaluation be taken out of the Office of Management and Budget and put into a new executive agency. Similarly, there is the question of how intensively the Congressional Budget Office should also engage in such analysis.

4. Finally, the efforts made in the late 1960s to introduce a comprehensive PPB system have been criticized for requiring too much too soon and for transplanting the Defense Department system, where cost-benefit analysis proved most readily applicable, to civilian agencies where it is less feasible. Weapons systems are easier to evaluate by cost-effectiveness analysis than are many civilian programs, where less readily measurable results must be identified and the required expert staff is not available. Sham figures may be reported to pacify the OMB. Indeed, so this criticism goes, project analysis should be decentralized and left to the initiative of the individual departments.

[35]See p. 41.

5. The task of project analysis has been broadened and complicated in recent years by the requirement to include an environmental impact evaluation. It appears that the latter involves requirements which are so broad and difficult to meet that conclusive project analysis is impeded.

These criticisms have some merit and future experience will undoubtedly bring new developments in this area. These will include not only modifications in PPBS and the governmental structure involved in its application, but perhaps more drastic departures from traditional practice.

Zero-Base Budgeting and Sunset Legislation

The two approaches most recently in the news are zero-base budgeting and sunset legislation, the former aiming at the executive and the latter at the legislative role in the budget process.

Zero-Base Budgeting   The congressional budget process is essentially one of first setting the expenditure total and then allocating it among its uses. The idea of zero-base budgeting takes the opposite track: all possible projects are appraised and judged on their merits, with the budget total the end result of this micro process.[36] The former pattern corresponds to what in the preceding chapter was described as the fixed budget case, while the latter corresponds to the variable budget setting. Seen from the economist's viewpoint, the variable budget approach is what matters: the opportunity cost of public project A is not simply that of forgoing public project B; it is equally important to consider the loss of private project C which would have been undertaken had neither A nor B been chosen. From a theoretical point of view, the idea of zero-base budgeting is thus the correct one and cost-benefit analysis may be seen as its instrument, i.e., the technique by which alternative budgets are appraised.

Putting it differently, cost-benefit analysis tends to stress a detailed project-by-project approach, rather than a broad balancing of projects against each other. The difficulty, of course, is that it is totally impossible in any one year (if indeed, ever) to weigh all project yields against each other. Project analysis is tedious, costly, and difficult, so that at best it can be applied annually to only a small part of the budget. The term "zero-base budgeting" (as used by the Carter administration) is thus overly ambitious and in a sense misleading. At the same time, it contains what may be a useful shift in emphasis from overly detailed analysis of single projects under PPBS to primary concern with balancing out the merits (if only roughly assessed) of alternative programs.

For this purpose, the Carter program for zero-base budgeting requires each agency to set up "decision packages" and to rank their importance.[37]

[36]See Aaron Wildawsky, "Ask Not What Budgeting Does to Society, but What Society Does to Budgeting," *The Federal Budget Process*, National Journal Reprint Series, 1977–78, p. 4.
[37]See *Zero Base Budgeting*, Office of Management and Budget, Bulletin No. 77–9, Apr. 19, 1977.

For any given program area, the agency sets the minimum outlay needed to continue the essential program function, as well as a somewhat higher level and one which permits substantial program extension. Working up through various layers of decision making within the agency, the agency executives (a term used to emphasize the "businesslike" nature of the approach) then rank the importance of various project packages, thereby revealing what functions can be performed over a range of budget levels. These sets of budget requests, in turn, are to permit OMB to choose between packages across agencies and to determine the needed budget total.

As with all such schemes, it remains to be seen how helpful it will be in practice. Obviously, it will be difficult to restrain agencies from overstating their needs and to deal with all the aspects of gamesmanship which this procedure invites.[38] Similarly, it will be impossible to apply the concept in great detail. Yet the approach may prove helpful in forcing agencies to think in terms of alternative choices which, after all, is the essential task of budgeting. And it may also be useful in compelling agencies and departments to show their hand in revealing what would happen if their budgets were to be reduced or expanded.

Sunset Legislation A more pinpointed approach to zero-base budgeting is contained in various legislative proposals (the so-called sunset legislation) to limit the life of most federal programs to five years unless thoroughly reviewed and approved by both House and Senate committees. This legislation should help to block the tendency for old programs to continue in existence after the original need has disappeared. Similar reviews would be required by governmental agencies. OMB, in presenting its budget, would include a thorough zero-base review of particular segments of the budget such that each department would be reviewed carefully over a five-year cycle. Detailed zero-base budgeting, if it is to be practicable, will clearly have to be given such a framework and proceed on a rotating basis. It thus differs from the broader-based but inevitably more sketchy procedures suggested by the Carter approach.

F. SUMMARY

The application of cost-benefit analysis to the evaluation of highway projects was examined, with the following conclusions:

> **1.** The measure of benefits involved the cost of travel time saved as well as other reductions in travel costs. The analysis involved determination of incremental cost savings from successive expansion of facilities.

[38]The OMB directive is careful not to set a fixed percentage of last year's budget which should be considered as the "minimum level," although it appears that a range of 70 to 80 percent is used. Given such a floor, departments will have an incentive to exclude the most essential or popular programs from the "minimum budget" so as to have a better chance for being granted a larger appropriation.

2. On the cost side, construction costs, site costs, and maintenance costs were considered.

3. In addition, indirect benefits and costs were allowed for.

In dealing with outdoor recreation, the major difficulty was how to value the resulting benefits to users:

4. Benefits may be measured by user charges, but this method interferes with efficient utilization.

5. Market surveys may be used to measure potential demand.

6. Benefits may be measured in analogy to charges for comparable private facilities.

7. The personal cost incurred by users may be taken to measure their evaluation.

8. In computing merit-weighted user days, various weights might be attached to different users.

Consideration was given to an application of cost-benefit analysis to education and to estimating a rate of return on investment in education:

9. Benefits were estimated as the discounted value of the resulting increase in expected earnings.

10. In estimating costs, the student's forgone earnings were included as well as the cost of operating schools.

11. Various qualifications were introduced and a distinction was drawn between the social and the private return to education.

Finally, various techniques of budget planning were considered, including the planning-programming-budgeting system (PPBS) and some more recent techniques:

12. PPBS calls for a comprehensive application of cost-benefit analysis to detailed expenditure projects applied to functional expenditure categories.

13. Zero-base budgeting calls for a total review of the entire budget each year, with emphasis on a ranking of alternative projects rather than a detailed item-by-item analysis.

14. Sunset legislation would require periodic reconsideration and reenactment of major expenditure programs on a rotating basis.

FURTHER READINGS

The Analysis and Evaluation of Public Expenditures: The PPB System, Joint Economic Committee, 91st Cong., 1969.

Chase, S. B. (ed.): *Problems in Public Expenditure Analysis,* Washington: Brookings, 1968.

Dorfman, R. (ed.): *Measuring Benefits of Government Investments,* Washington: Brookings, 1965.

Harberger, Arnold C.: *Project Evaluation,* London: Macmillan, 1972.

Hinrichs, Harley H., and G. M. Taylor: *Program Budgeting and Benefit-Cost Analysis,* Pacific Palisades, Calif.: Goodyear Publishing, 1969.

————: *Systematic Analysis: A Primer on Benefit-Cost Analysis and Program Evaluation,* Pacific Palisades, Calif.: Goodyear Publishing, 1972.

Roemer, M., and J. J. Stern: *The Appraisal of Development Projects,* New York: Praeger, 1975.

Rider, Kenneth L.: "The Economics of the Distribution of Municipal Fire Protection Services," *The Review of Economics and Statistics,* vol. 61, May 1979, p. 2.

Schultze, Charles: *The Politics and Economics of Public Spending,* Washington: Brookings, 1968.

Part Three

Principles of Taxation

Chapter 10

Introduction to Taxation*

A. **Categories of Revenue:** *Taxes, Charges, and Borrowing; Taxes in the Circular Flow; Taxes on Holding and Transfer of Wealth; Personal versus In Rem Taxes; Direct versus Indirect Taxes.* B. **Requirements for a "Good" Tax Structure. C. Summary.**

We now leave the expenditure side of budget policy and consider the revenue side. While good economic analysis calls for joint consideration of both aspects, the practice is to deal with them as more or less separate issues. In this and the following chapters we examine the principles, economic and otherwise, of tax policy and the requirements for a good tax system. After this foundation has been laid, we proceed in Part Four to deal with the more specific aspects of the United States tax structure.

A. CATEGORIES OF REVENUE

Government derives receipts to finance expenditures, whether transfers or purchases, or to pay off public debt. These receipts may take the form of taxes, charges, or borrowing. We begin with a brief look at the various forms

Readers' Guide to Chapter 10: Taxes are grouped in line with their impact in the circular flow of income and expenditures, as well as with regard to other important kinds of characteristics. The requirements for a "good" tax structure are outlined.

of receipts, considering how they may be distinguished and what their characteristics are.

Taxes, Charges, and Borrowing

Taxes and charges are withdrawn from the private sector without leaving the government with a liability to the payee. Borrowing involves a withdrawal made in return for the government's promise to repay at a future date and to pay interest in the interim. Taxes are compulsory imposts, whereas charges and borrowing involve voluntary transactions. As shown in Table 10-1, taxes provide much the larger part of receipts. More will be said about the distinction between charges and taxes when discussing benefit taxation in the next chapter and the economics of borrowing are examined in a later part of the volume.

Taxes in the Circular Flow

One helpful way of distinguishing among types of taxes is to consider their point of impact in the circular flow of income and expenditures in the economy.

Impact Points   Figure 10-1 presents a simplified picture of the circular flow of income and expenditures in the private sector, together with the major points at which the various taxes are inserted. The monetary flow of income and expenditures shown in the figure proceeds in a clockwise direction, while

TABLE 10-1
Sources of Receipts, Fiscal 1975
(In Billions of Dollars)

	Federal	State	Local	All
Taxes*	271	100[†]	75[†]	446
Charges*	32	17	16	65
Borrowing	45[‡]	7[§]	8[§]	60
Total	348	124	99	571
*Types of Tax**				
Property	—	1	50	51
Individual income	122	19	3	144
Corporation income	40	7	¶	47
Sales	23	52[†]	20[†]	95
Motor vehicle and operators' licenses	—	4	¶	4
Death and gift	5	1	¶	6
Payroll	81	17	2	100
Total	271	100	75	446

*See Tax Foundation, *Facts and Figures*, New York: 1977, p. 19. Note that the table shows receipts from the public, with intergovernmental transfers disregarded.
[†]Includes receipts from liquor stores.
[‡]*Economic Report of the President*, 1978, p. 344.
[§]ACIR, *Significant Features of Fiscal Federalism*, 1976–77, p. 72.
¶Small amount, included elsewhere.

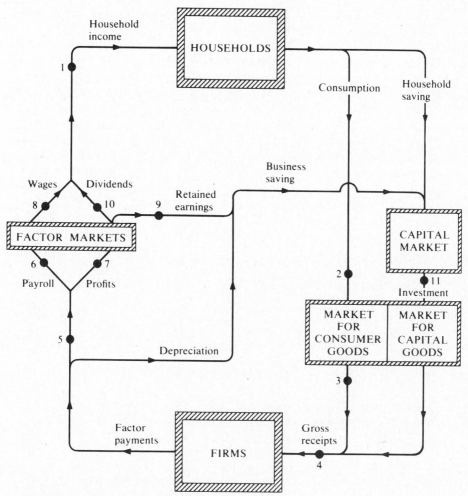

FIGURE 10-1   Points of Tax Impact in Circular Flow.

the real flow of factor inputs and product outputs (not shown) moves in a counterclockwise direction. Thus, income is received by households and divided into consumer expenditures and household savings. Consumer expenditures flow into the market for consumer goods and become receipts of firms selling such goods. Savings are channeled into investment, become expenditures in the market for capital goods, and turn into receipts of firms producing such goods. Part of business receipts is set aside to cover depreciation and the remainder goes to purchase the services of labor, capital, and other inputs in the factor market, representing various factor shares in national income. These shares are paid out to suppliers of factors—in the form of wages, dividends, interest, rent, and so on—and become income of households. Some profits, however, are withheld as retained earnings rather than paid out as dividends. Retained earnings, together with depreciation allowances, comprise business savings and combine with household savings to finance investment or the purchase of capital goods. Thus the circular flow of income and expenditures is closed.[1]

We may now locate the impact points of various taxes as shown in Figure 10-1. Taxes may be imposed on household income at point 1, on consumer expenditures at 2, on business receipts from retail sales at 3, on total gross receipts of business at 4, on business receipts net of depreciation at 5, on payrolls at 6, on profits at 7, on wage receipts at 8, on retained earnings at 9, or on dividends at 10.[2] The major taxes in the United States system are readily identified with these various points of impact. The personal income tax is imposed at 1, the corporation income tax at 7, retail sales taxes at 3, the employer contribution to the payroll tax at 6, and the employee contribution to the payroll tax at 8. Taxes imposed at 2 and 5 do not exist in our tax structure, but are potential candidates for tax reform and will be discussed later under the headings of the expenditure tax (2) and value-added tax of the income type (5).[3]

Classification of Taxes   Referring again to Figure 10-1, the various taxes may be classified as follows:

1. They may be imposed in the product or in the factor market.
2. They may be imposed on the seller's or the buyer's side of the market.
3. They may be imposed on households or firms.
4. They may enter on the uses or sources side of the taxpayer's account.

Classifying our major taxes along these lines leaves us with the picture shown in Table 10-2. This classification will prove useful at a later point when the incidence of various taxes is examined.

Equivalence between Taxes   At this point we need only observe that there are certain pairs of taxes which may look different but which are in fact equivalent.[4]

1. In a competitive market, it makes no difference on which side of the counter the tax is imposed. In the product market, a tax of 10 percent on the seller and imposed on the net price of, say, $100, raises gross price to $110 and gives precisely the same result (i.e., revenue, gross price, and output) as a purchase tax upon the buyer imposed at the same rate on the net price. This holds whether we deal with a selective tax or with a tax on the sale or purchase of all consumer goods.

2. The same holds for the factor market where a tax on the employer imposed on his payroll at 10 percent gives the same result as a (equal revenue)

---

[1]Since the national income accounts take and ex post view, saving an investment must be equal as a matter of accounting identity. For a further discussion of this, see pp. 600 and 678.

[2]Note that the circular flow as shown in Fig. 10-1 pictures private sector flows only. For a more complete picture, including private and public sector flows, see Fig. 1-1, p. 21.

[3]See pp. 455 and 458.

[4]See p. 288.

TABLE 10-2
Classification of Taxes*

Taxes Imposed	ON FIRM		ON HOUSEHOLD	
	As Seller	As Buyer	As Seller (Sources)	As Buyer (Uses)
In Product Market All products	Retail sales tax Value added (consumption type) (3)	—	—	Expenditure tax (2)
Some products	Cigarette tax (3)	—	—	Gasoline tax (2)
In Factor Market All factors, all employments	—	Value added (income type) (5)	Income tax (1)	—
Some factors, all employments	—	Employer's payroll tax (6)	Employee's payroll tax (8) Tax on wages or capital income (8), (10)	—
Some factors, some employments	—	Corporate profits tax Local property tax		—

*Numbers in parentheses refer to impact points shown in Fig. 10-1.

10 percent tax imposed on the income of the wage earner. Similarly, a general tax on factor purchases is equivalent to a general tax on factor sales, i.e., an income tax.

3. Finally, in an economy without saving, there would be a further equivalence between a general tax on factor purchases, a general tax on factor income, a general tax on product purchases, and a general tax on product sales. This chain of equivalence among taxes does not apply, however, once we allow for savings, since a tax on factor sales (income tax) now ceases to be equivalent to one on product purchases.

Keeping in mind these identities and how various taxes fit into the national income accounts will be helpful in analyzing similarities or differences among them and in tracing taxpayer responses in our later discussion of incidence and effects of taxation.

Taxes on Holding and Transfer of Wealth

Taxes may be imposed on the holding of wealth or stocks, rather than on transactions or flows generated in current production. The principal example is the property tax. If interpreted as a tax on capital income, it might be incorporated in Figure 10-1, but other wealth taxes, such as those imposed on the transfer of wealth by inheritance or gift, cannot be so included.

Personal versus In Rem Taxes

Cutting across the above categories, we distinguish between personal taxes and in rem taxes. Personal taxes are taxes which are adjusted to the taxpayer's personal ability to pay, while in rem taxes (taxes on "things") are imposed on activities or objects as such, i.e., on purchases, sales, or the holding of property, independently of the characteristics of the transactor or the owner.

In rem taxes may be imposed on either the household or the firm side. But personal taxes, by their very nature, *must* be imposed on the household side of the transaction. Thus, if proceeds from the sale of factors of production are to be taxed in a personal fashion, the tax must be imposed on households as a personal income tax. Taxes imposed on factor payments of firms cannot distinguish the taxpaying ability of particular income recipients. While family size can be allowed for in the withholding schedule, the final settlement must be with the individual employee. Similarly, if consumption is to be taxed in a personal fashion, the tax must be placed on the household in the form of a personal expenditure tax. A sales tax imposed on firms is not responsive to the particular consumer, but gives the same treatment to all households which undertake the taxed transaction. The same again holds for the taxation of wealth under the property tax, as against a net worth tax relating to the entire wealth position of the individual owner.

As we shall see later, the distinction between personal and in rem taxes is of crucial importance when it comes to the equity of the tax system. Equity must be evaluated in terms of the resulting burden distribution among people. Since the burden of all taxes, including those imposed on "things," must ultimately be borne by persons, their equity must be evaluated by the resulting burden distribution among persons. As such, in rem taxes are inferior to well-designed personal taxes imposed directly so as to allow for the particular taxpayer's ability to pay. Since personal taxes must be assessed on the household side, such taxes tend to be generally superior in equity to those imposed on the firm side.

Direct versus Indirect Taxes

Finally, brief attention should be given to the frequently used distinction between "direct" and "indirect" taxes. While this distinction is ambiguous, most writers define direct taxes as those which are imposed initially on the individual or household that is meant to bear the burden. Indirect taxes are taxes which are imposed at some other point in the system but are meant to be shifted (a concept which will be examined presently) to whomever is supposed to be the final bearer of the burden.

Personal taxes, such as the individual income tax, are thus "direct," and most in rem taxes, such as the sales tax, are "indirect." At the same time, the distinction between direct and indirect taxes does not always coincide with that between personal and in rem taxes. Thus the employee contribution to the payroll tax may be considered direct, yet it is not a personal tax since no allowance is made for the owner's ability to pay. Rather, it is an in rem tax, assessed on wage receipt as a transaction. Similarly, the property tax on owner-occupied residences is direct, but it is an in rem tax (being imposed on ownership as such) rather than a personal tax which would allow for the owner's individual circumstances.

The term "excise," finally, refers to a subcategory of indirect taxes and is applied to certain selective sales taxes imposed at the manufacturer level. A legal, rather than economic, category in nature, it appears in the constitutional provision that direct taxes must be imposed on a population basis, while others, such as "duties, imposts, and excises," need not be.[5]

B. REQUIREMENTS FOR A "GOOD" TAX STRUCTURE

The United States tax system, like that of any other country, has developed in response to many influences—economic, political, and social. It has not been constructed by a master architect in line with the optimal requirements for a "good" tax structure. Yet, ideas as to what constitutes a "good" tax system have had their influence. Economists and social philosophers, from Adam Smith on, have propounded what such requirements should be. Among them, the following are of major importance, although they are not meant to be all-inclusive.

   1. The distribution of the tax burden should be equitable. Everyone should be made to pay his or her "fair share."

   2. Taxes should be chosen so as to minimize interference with economic decisions in otherwise efficient markets. Such interferences impose "excess burdens" which should be minimized.

   3. Where tax policy is used to achieve other objectives, such as to grant investment incentives, this should be done so as to minimize interference with the equity of the system.

   4. The tax structure should facilitate the use of fiscal policy for stabilization and growth objectives. (MACROECONOMICS)

   5. The tax system should permit fair and nonarbitrary administration and it should be understandable to the taxpayer.

   6. Administration and compliance cost should be as low as is compatible with the other objectives.

These and other requirements may be used as criteria to appraise the quality of a tax structure. The various objectives are not necessarily in agreement, and where they conflict, tradeoffs between them are needed. Thus, equity may require administrative complexity and may interfere with neutrality, corrective use of tax policy may interfere with equity, and so forth. These conflicts will be considered as we proceed.

[5]See p. 30.

C. SUMMARY

In considering the impact point of various taxes in the circular flow of income and expenditures in the economy we noted that:

    1. Taxes may be imposed in the factor or in the product markets.
    2. Taxes may be imposed on the buyer's or the seller's side of the market.
    3. Certain taxes, though different in appearance, are equivalent to each other.

Examining the requirements for a good tax system, we noted that:

    4. Personal taxes are superior to in rem taxes.
    5. The good tax system should be designed so as to meet the requirements of equity, efficiency, and ease of administration.

Chapter 11

Approaches to Tax Equity*

A. Application of Benefit Principle: *A General Benefit Tax; Specific Benefit Taxes; Taxes in Lieu of Charges; A Note on Earmarking.* **B. Ability to Pay and Choice of Tax Base:** *Horizontal and Vertical Equity; Income versus Consumption as Tax Base; Wealth as Tax Base; Implementation.* **C. Ability to Pay and Vertical Equity:** *Equal Sacrifice Rules; Social Utility Approach.* **D. Summary.**

We begin with the equity objective. While not always controlling, it is a basic criterion for tax-structure design. Everyone agrees that the tax system should be equitable, i.e., that each taxpayer should contribute his or her "fair share" to the cost of government. But there is no such agreement about how the term "fair share" should be defined. As noted in our earlier discussion of

Reader's Guide to Chapter 11: All are agreed that the tax system should be fair and equitable, but there is less agreement on how to interpret this requirement. In this chapter we examine the principles of benefit and ability-to-pay taxation. In connection with the latter we take a careful look at how ability to pay should be measured and whether income or consumption offer the superior index. Next we consider how the tax burden should be distributed among people with unequal ability to pay. The problems here examined are basic to an understanding of tax policy.

distributive justice, a variety of approaches may be taken. In particular, two strands of thought may be distinguished.

One approach rests on the so-called benefit principle. According to this theory, dating back to Adam Smith and earlier writers, an equitable tax system is one under which each taxpayer contributes in line with the benefits which he or she receives from public services. According to this principle, the truly equitable tax system will differ, depending on the expenditure structure. The benefit criterion, therefore, is not one of tax policy only, but of tax-expenditure policy. This is in line with our approach in Chapter 3 where we viewed the economics of the public sector as involving a simultaneous solution to both its revenue and its expenditure aspects.

The other strand, also of distinguished ancestry, rests on the "ability-to-pay" principle. Under this approach, the tax problem is viewed by itself, independent of expenditure determination. A given total revenue is needed and each taxpayer is asked to contribute in line with his or her ability to pay.[1] This approach leaves the expenditure side of the public sector dangling, and is thus less satisfactory from the economist's point of view. Yet actual tax policy is largely determined independently of the expenditure side and an equity rule is needed to provide guidance. The ability-to-pay principle is widely accepted as this guide.

Neither approach is easy to interpret or implement. For the benefit principle to be operational, expenditure benefits for particular taxpayers must be known. For the ability-to-pay approach to be applicable, we must know just how this ability is to be measured. These are formidable difficulties and neither approach wins on practicality grounds. Moreover, neither approach can be said to deal with the entire function of tax policy.

The benefit approach, ideally, will allocate that part of the tax bill which defrays the cost of public services, but it cannot handle taxes needed to finance transfer payments and serve redistributional objectives. For benefit taxation to be equitable, it must be assumed that a "proper" state of distribution exists to begin with. This is a serious shortcoming since, in practice, there is no separation between the taxes used to finance public services and the taxes used to redistribute income. The ability-to-pay approach better meets the redistribution problem but it leaves the provision for public services undetermined.

---

[1]Historically, the benefit principle of taxation derives from the contract theory of the state as understood by the political theorists of the seventeenth century, such as Locke and Hobbes. Subsequently it was woven into the greatest-happiness principle of the utilitarians, such as Bentham. It appeared early in classical economics in Adam Smith's first canon of taxation, which in one sentence combines both the benefit and the ability-to-pay approaches: "The subjects of every state ought to contribute towards the support of the government as nearly as possible in proportion to their respective abilities; that is, in proportion to the revenue which they respectively enjoy under the protection of the state." (Adam Smith, *The Wealth of Nations*, vol. 2, edited by E. Cannan, New York: Putnam, 1904, p. 310). Benefits are here viewed in terms of protection received and are thus related to income which, in turn, is also a measure of ability to pay.

Notwithstanding these shortcomings, both principles have important, if limited, application in designing an equitable tax structure, one which is acceptable to most people and preferable to alternative arrangements.

A. APPLICATION OF BENEFIT PRINCIPLE

As we have seen in Chapters 3 and 6, the political process involves determination of both tax and expenditure policy and, in a democratic framework, tends to approximate application of the benefit rule. People, or some majority thereof, would not be willing to sustain a fiscal program if, on balance, they did not benefit therefrom. We have also noted that, by relating particular tax to particular expenditure decisions, a more rational decision process may be achieved. Let us now see how the benefit principle may be applied as a guide to tax-structure design.

A General Benefit Tax

Under a strict regime of benefit taxation, each taxpayer would be taxed in line with his or her demand for public services. Since preferences differ, no general tax formula could be applied to all people. Each taxpayer would be taxed in line with his or her evaluation. Still, some pattern might be expected to emerge. The typical mix of private goods purchased is known to vary with the income level of the consumer household, and similar patterns may be expected to prevail for social goods. But instead of noting how quantities bought (at the same price) will vary with income, we now ask how much various consumers are willing to pay for the same amount. Unless the social good in question is what economists call an "inferior" good, consumer valuation may be expected to rise with income. To simplify, suppose that taxpayers have the same structure of tastes (i.e., pattern of indifference curves) so that persons with the same income value the same amount equally. People with incomes of $10,000 value a given level of public services at, say, $1,000. With 1,000 units of the service supplied, they would be willing to pay $1 per unit. Making the usual assumption that marginal utility of income falls with rising income, others with incomes of $20,000 would be willing to pay a higher unit price of, say, $2. In this case, a proportional rate schedule will apply. If they are not willing to pay as much as $2 but only, say, $1.50, the appropriate rate schedule will be regressive. If they will pay more, a progressive schedule will be in order.[2]

The appropriate tax formula thus depends upon the preference patterns. More specifically, it depends upon the income and price elasticity of demand for social goods. If income elasticity is high, the appropriate tax prices will rise rapidly with income; but if price elasticity is high, the increase will be

---

[2]Returning to Fig. 3-5 (p. 72), we noted that the taxes paid by A and B for OH units of social goods equal KM and LN, respectively. If $KM/OM = LN/ON$, a proportional tax rate is required. Since $OM > ON$, a situation where $KM/OM > LN/ON$ calls for a progressive rate structure, while one where $KM/OM < LN/ON$ calls for regression.

dampened. More specifically, the required rate structure will be proportional, progressive, or regressive, depending on whether income elasticity equals, exceeds, or falls short of price elasticity.[3]

This finding is interesting, but it does not permit easy implementation. The relevant price and income elasticities are not known or readily derived from market observation as in the case of private goods. Moreover, they will differ among various types of public services. It is not at all obvious which elasticity (income or price) will be larger and by how much, especially if the entire budget is considered. The question of rate structure thus remains open. Nevertheless, this line of reasoning points up the fact that the rationale for or against progressive taxation may be discussed in terms of benefit taxation as well as in the usual ability-to-pay context. Even if the latter points to progression, the former need not do so.[4]

Specific Benefit Taxes

Whereas the general benefit tax is of interest mainly as a theoretical concept, practical applications of benefit taxation may be found in specific instances where particular services are provided on a benefit basis. This may be the case where direct financing is made via fees, user charges, or tolls. Or certain taxes may be applied indirectly in lieu of charges, as is done in the taxation of gasoline and other automotive products for purposes of highway finance.

Under what conditions is this technique feasible and desirable? The case for finance by direct charges to the user is clear-cut where the goods or services provided by government are in the nature of private goods, i.e., where consumption is wholly rival. Benefits can be imputed to a particular user who can be asked to pay. The issuance of licenses, the financing of municipal transportation, and the provision of airport facilities are more or less in this category. Where benefits are internalized, the government may act in a capacity similar to that of a private firm and the same principles of pricing are appropriate. As has been pointed out in recent years, a considerable range of public services might be placed on this basis, thereby easing the pressure on general revenue finance. By using a market mechanism, a more efficient determination of the appropriate level of supply becomes possible.[5]

---

[3]This relationship may be specified as follows: Let P be the appropriate unit price of public services to a taxpayer with income Y. Now suppose that the person's income rises. The required tax rate will be proportional, progressive, or regressive, depending on whether $(\Delta P/P)/(\Delta Y/Y)$ equals, exceeds, or falls short of 1. Since income elasticity $E_y = (\Delta Q/Q)/(\Delta Y/Y)$ and price elasticity $E_p = (\Delta Q/Q)/(\Delta P/P)$, we have $(\Delta P/P)/(\Delta Y/Y) = E_y/E_p$. Thus, the tax will be proportional, progressive, or regressive according to whether E_y is equal to, greater than, or less than E_p. See James M. Buchanan, "Fiscal Institutions and Collective Outlay," *American Economic Review*, May 1964, pp. 227–235.

[4]Since the price chargeable under the benefit rule will vary with the taxpayer's income, it may be said to reflect ability to pay. The two rules are thus not quite unrelated. Nevertheless, they remain different in that the ability-to-pay approach does not consider taxpayer preferences between various goods.

[5]Other situations may be such that direct charges are technically possible (exclusion can be applied at a relatively low cost) but would not be an efficient mode of finance. For a fuller discussion of public enterprise pricing and user charges, see Chap. 34.

Taxes In Lieu of Charges

In other instances, where imposition of direct charges is desirable but too costly, a tax on a complementary product may be used in lieu of charges. Gasoline or automobile taxes may be viewed in this light. The yield of automotive taxes (on gasoline and cars) in the United States, including all levels of government, roughly matches the cost of highway expenditures. In the case of the federal highway program, gasoline tax proceeds are earmarked for the Highway Trust Fund, and the income of the fund is used to defray the cost of a federal highway network. In the instance of state and local financing, such direct earmarking does not always exist, but proceeds from highway user taxes nevertheless go largely into road finance.

How effective an approach to benefit taxation does this offer? Although it may be true that such taxes place the total cost of highways on all drivers as a group, it is questionable whether the equity objective of benefit taxation for the individual driver is met. While gasoline use depends on distances driven, not each mile driven results in the same variable cost, nor does it require the same capital outlay in providing new road facilities. Driver X, using road A, may be called upon to support road B, used by driver Y. Gasoline taxes, therefore, are only a rough approximation to the benefit rule in highway finance. Nor will such taxes effectively enter into the determination of demand for new highway construction. Expenditure decisions are made for specific outlays, while taxes are paid independently of particular highways used, so that there is no direct linkage between the two at a disaggregated level. Moreover, there has been increasing support in recent years for legislation which will permit diversion of Highway Trust Fund receipts into the financing of mass transportation. This is justified as a way of internalizing the external costs of highway use.

Another illustration is given by certain uses of the property tax. Special assessments may be used to charge dwellings in a certain block for the cost of improvements which service their particular location. At a more general level, the property tax has traditionally been viewed as a charge for services rendered by local government, it being assumed that the benefits which result are roughly proportional to property values. How well founded this belief is remains to be seen.[6]

Social security taxes may provide another instance of benefit taxation. Payroll tax contributions by the employee may be considered a strict benefit tax, provided that the later benefit payments stand in direct relation to the contribution and that the benefit formula is not redistributive.[7] The same cannot be said for the employer contributions unless they are passed on to the employee.

A Note on Earmarking

Finally, a word on earmarking in relation to benefit taxation. Fiscal experts have argued that earmarking is poor budgeting procedure, since it introduces

---

[6]See p. 470.

[7]As noted in Chap. 33, these assumptions do not hold for the present United States system.

rigidities and does not permit proper allocation of general revenue among competing uses. Thus, it is inefficient to freeze, say, 50 percent of sales tax revenue as the state contribution to the cost of elementary education. The appropriate allotment may be larger or smaller than this amount. Moreover, it may be desirable to use the sales tax for other purposes.

At the same time, other uses of earmarking may be appropriate and in line with the benefit approach. First, particular taxes may be linked to particular expenditures because tax payments are equivalent to (or are held to approximate) charges imposed on the consumer. As just noted, this holds to some extent for gasoline taxes. Such linkage may be both efficient (in charging for variable costs) and equitable (in distributing costs in line with benefits received). Second, linkage of voting on particular taxes with specified expenditure votes may be helpful in inducing preference revelation and thus contribute to better expenditure decisions. Depending on how it is used, earmarking may thus be an arbitrary procedure leading to budgetary rigidity, or it may be a helpful device for approximating benefit taxation.[8]

B. ABILITY TO PAY AND CHOICE OF TAX BASE

While the benefit principle may be applied directly to the finance of certain governmental functions, it does not solve the general problem of tax-structure design. The range of expenditures to which specific benefit taxes may be applied is relatively limited and the bulk of tax revenue is not derived (nor derivable) on a specific benefit basis. While tax legislation should be related to expenditure legislation, application of the benefit rule in this broader sense does not obviate the need for tax formulas and a rule by which they are designed. Moreover, we have noted that benefit taxation, even at its best, can relate only to the financing of public services and not to the redistributive function of the tax-transfer process.

Thus an alternative principle of equitable taxation must be applied. This is the rule that people should contribute to the cost of government in line with their "ability to pay".[9] Under this approach, the tax problem is viewed by itself, independent of expenditure determination. A given total revenue is needed and each taxpayer is asked to contribute in line with his or her ability to pay. This approach has the advantage that it can encompass the redistributive tax-transfer function; but it has the disadvantage that it leaves the determination of public services out of the picture.

Horizontal and Vertical Equity

Taxation according to ability to pay calls for people with equal capacity to pay the same, while people with greater ability should pay more. The former

---

[8]See Chap. 3, and James M. Buchanan, "The Economics of Earmarked Taxes," *Journal of Political Economy*, October 1963.

[9]The origin of the ability-to-pay principle predates the benefit rule. It dates back to the sixteenth century and has found prominent supporters ever since. They include a wide range of thinkers such as Rousseau, Say, and John Stuart Mill. In the twentieth century, ability to pay has been emphasized primarily by redistribution-oriented writers.

is referred to as horizontal and the latter as vertical equity. The horizontal equity rule merely applies the basic principle of equality under the law. Under the income tax, for instance, people with the same income should pay the same tax. The vertical equity rule is also in line with equal treatment, but proceeds on the premise that different amounts of tax should be paid by people with different ability if they are to experience equal burdens. Taking ability to be measured by income, person A, whose income is higher, should pay more than B. In this sense, both equity rules follow from the same principle of equal treatment and neither is more basic.

Moreover, implementation of either rule requires a quantitative measure of ability to pay. Ideally, this measure would reflect the entire welfare which a person can derive from all the options available to him or her, including consumption (present and future), holding of wealth, and the enjoyment of leisure. Unfortunately, such a comprehensive measure is not practicable. The value of leisure, in particular, cannot be measured, so that some second-best but observable measures must do. Given this constraint, what is the best index to use: is it income, consumption, or wealth?

Income versus Consumption as Tax Base

Income has been the most widely accepted measure of ability to pay, but others hold that consumption would be a superior choice. To be sure, income has served as *the* base of personal taxation under the income tax, whereas the consumption base has been used in the impersonal or in rem form of sales and excise taxes. Thus, use of the income base has been more equitable than use of the consumption base. But it does not follow that the income base remains superior if the consumption base is used in the form of a personalized expenditure tax, with allowance made for family size and expenditure taxed at progressive rates.[10] This is the premise on which our present comparison will be based.

In drawing this comparison, a number of questions may be asked: (1) What are the merits of the two bases, assuming that each tax is properly implemented? (2) What are the technical difficulties of correctly implementing each type of tax? (3) What are the chances that special preferences will be created by political pressure groups under the two approaches? All three questions are relevant, but our present concern is with the first question.

Comprehensiveness of Bases   Both income- and consumption-base advocates agree that the respective bases should be defined comprehensively.

For the *income base* this means that income (looked at from the *sources* side of the household account) should be thought of as a person's entire accretion to his or her wealth, including all forms thereof. As we shall examine in detail later on, a person's economic capacity and hence ability to pay is increased whether income accrues in the form of money income (such as wages, salaries, interest, or dividends), as imputed income (such as imputed

[10]For examination of such a tax, see p. 455.

rent from owner-occupied housing), or as an appreciation (whether realized or not) in the value of assets.[11] The same requirement of comprehensiveness can be stated if we look at income from the uses side of the household account. Income then equals increase in net worth (or saving) plus consumption during the period. The two formulations amount to the same, provided that increase in net worth and consumption are also given a comprehensive definition.

For the *consumption base*, the requirement of comprehensiveness calls for inclusion of all forms of consumption, whether this takes the form of cash purchases or whether the consumption stream is derived in imputed form. Since income equals increase in net worth (or saving) plus consumption, whereas the consumption base includes consumption only, the consumption tax differs from the income tax by excluding income which is saved.

Which is the Better Base?   Assuming that both bases are defined comprehensively, which is the better choice? This has become a lively topic of debate in recent years and should therefore be considered in some detail. To begin with, it must be recognized that the issue has been approached from a number of different perspectives:

1. Dating back to Hobbes, it has been argued that a person should pay tax on what he or she uses and not on the fruits of labor which are saved and thereby (it is implied) left to be used by others.[12] On this basis, there is no case for taxing savings, as consumption is on moral grounds considered the only "proper" source of taxation. Apart from whether it is desirable to define the tax base in terms of virtue, it seems questionable to view savings as a service to others, rather than as undertaken for compensation and in line with one's own plans. Moreover, work as well as saving has beneficial externalities, so that exclusion of the one also justifies exclusion of the other.

2. As we shall see in our discussion of excess burden, the income tax distorts the choice between present and future consumption, while the consumption tax does not. It may thus be concluded, under certain assumptions, that the consumption tax is more efficient.[13]

3. The consumption tax, by being more favorable to saving and economic growth, recommends itself where public policy wishes to accelerate growth. As we shall see later, this is of particular interest to fiscal policy in developing countries.[14]

4. The choice between the two bases may be made on equity grounds, i.e., by examining which offers the better measure of ability to pay.

All these diverse considerations will enter into the final choice between the income and consumption approaches, but our immediate concern is with the equity aspect only.

---

[11]For discussion of income definition, see Chap. 16, Sec. C.
[12]See John Hobbes, *Leviathan*, part 2, Baltimore: Pelican, Chap. 30, p. 386.
[13]See p. 311.
[14]See p. 807.

The Equity Issue   Assuming that both bases are defined properly, which offers the better index of ability to pay? Since economic activity is undertaken to permit consumption, our criterion is that ability to pay be measured in terms of potential consumption. Therefore, the base should be such as to impose equal taxes on people with the same *potential* to consume. With this criterion in mind, compare A, B, and C during a single period, say, a year (Table 11-1).

Under a 10 percent income tax, the respective liabilities are $10, $10, and $8. Raising the same total revenue of $28 under a consumption tax, a rate of 15.6 percent is needed, leaving liabilities of $15.6, 0, and $12.4, respectively. Thus A and C will prefer the income tax while B will prefer the consumption tax, but who is right? Consider first the burden distribution under the income tax. A and B must pay more than C and they may object to this. But they have no valid basis for complaint. They both have a greater potential for consumption than C and hence should pay more. Nor can B object, on grounds of lower consumption, to paying as much as A. Such complaint would be without basis since B had the same option to consume as did A. In short, the burden distribution under the income tax is fair. Now consider that under the consumption tax, A must pay more than B and has good reason to object. Since B had the same potential to consume, B is not worse off and should pay as much. The same holds a fortiori in comparing C with B. In short, the burden distribution under the consumption tax is unfair. Using our criterion of equal tax for equal potential consumption, the income tax wins the day.

This reasoning is valid as long as the analysis is limited to only one time period. But this is hardly satisfactory. After all, saving is undertaken to permit future consumption, the benefits of which should not be overlooked. We should thus redefine equal option in terms of the potential consumption stream over a longer period. Although A and B choose different consumption patterns over time, they are still in equal position since they can generate the same consumption stream. They should thus bear equal burdens. But now this is no longer the case under the income tax. Table 11-2, which extends the earlier case to a second period, shows why.

Consider first the income tax. We note that A pays in period I only, while B pays in both periods. After paying the same tax as A in period I, B

TABLE 11-1
Comparison of Income and Consumption Taxes during a Single Period
(In Dollars)

	Income (Dollars)	Consumption (Dollars)	Saving (Dollars)	Income Tax (Dollars)	Consumption Tax (Dollars)
A	100	100	—	10	15.6
B	100	—	100	10	—
C	80	80	—	8	12.5

TABLE 11-2
Comparison of Income and Consumption Taxes during Two Periods
(In Dollars)

	Income Tax (I)		Consumption Tax (II)		Tax on Wage Income (III)	
	A	B	A	B	A	B
Period I						
Wage income	100	100	100	100	100	100
Tax	10	10	10	—	10	10
Consumption	90	—	90	—	90	—
Saving	—	90	—	100	—	90
Period II						
Interest	—	9.00	—	10	—	9
Tax	—	.90	—	11	—	—
Consumption	—	98.10	—	99	—	99
Saving	—	—	—	—	—	—
Total tax	10	10.90	10	11	10	10
Present value	10	10.82	10	10	10	10

pays a further tax on interest income in period II. B's tax for both periods thus equals $10.90 as against A's tax of $10. Under the consumption tax, A pays tax in period I while B pays in period II. B's tax is again higher, but it is also payable later. Since a tax postponement is a gain to the taxpayer (after all, the money can be invested at interest in the interim), it is reasonable to compare the discounted value of the tax burdens. As shown in the last line of the table, this value is the same for both A and B under the consumption tax, but B pays more under the income tax. Seen in this context, the consumption-tax approach gives the fair solution since it places the same burden on people with equal (potential consumption) options. Thus the equal-option criterion now leads to the consumption base, in contrast to the one-period model where it led to the income base.

As between the two approaches, there is much to be said for the longer view. Practical difficulties aside, the ideal solution may be to take the date of birth as departure and impose lifetime taxes of equal present value on people with equal present value incomes or consumption (which is the same). But the elegance of the argument becomes shaky once a more realistic setting is considered:

1. The proposition that individuals with equal present value lifetime incomes are in equal position assumes that this value is known at the outset so as to permit optimal disposition. Since the income stream is in fact uncertain, the position is inferior where uncertainty is greater.
2. The proposition that individuals with incomes of equal present value are in the same position, independent of when the income accrues, assumes further that there are perfect capital markets, allowing all taxpayers to borrow and invest at the same rate. This is an unrealistic assumption. Lower-income consumers

having less access would be disadvantaged, with the consumption tax especially burdensome during those periods of the life cycle when high outlays are needed.

3. Since no one can say what future income will be, the tax would have to be recomputed (under progressive rates) as time passes. A complex system of cumulative averaging would be called for.[15]

4. This would be complicated by the fact that tax rates change over time. By the nature of the lifetime approach, tax burdens should not be affected by whether income is earned during high- or low-rate periods, so that rate changes would have to be allowed for in the averaging process.[16]

5. Most important, note that our two-period model of Table 11-2 was drawn up so as to let all income be consumed within the two-period span. If, instead, B does not consume in period II but leaves savings as bequests, B will never be taxed. If B's heirs continue to save, no tax will ever be paid, which contradicts our requirement that equal burdens should be imposed on A and B. If B's heirs dissave and consume, a tax will be paid later on, but not by B. To argue that this makes no difference is to hold that the taxpaying unit should be defined dynastically, so as to include B, B's heirs, and heirs of heirs. This being unreasonable, we conclude that the equal-options rule calls for inclusion of bequests and gifts in the donor's consumption base. Options must be redefined so as to include present consumption, future consumption, and leaving bequests. Exclusion of bequests would benefit those who choose this option and would tend to be of special importance for taxpayers with high lifetime incomes.[17]

Given these complications, it is evident that a perfect lifetime approach would be impracticable. This being the case, the comparison between the income and consumption bases must be drawn in a realistic rather than idealized setting; and here the traditional income-base approach may well be the better solution. Note, moreover, that our comparison so far has been based on the assumption that both income and consumption bases are defined comprehensively. In practice, comprehensive definition encounters technical and political obstacles, which must be allowed for as well in choosing between the two approaches.[18]

Relation to Tax on Wage Income   Before leaving the choice between the income and consumption bases, it is interesting to observe that the expenditure tax may be likened not only to an income tax which excludes savings from its base, but also to an income tax which excludes capital income while only taxing wages.[19] Returning to case III of our two-period illustration, a tax on wage income alone would tax both A and B in only the first period and would be similar to the consumption tax in that both bear the same burden.

---

[15]See p. 375.

[16]See p. 375.

[17]For relation of this to the estate tax, see p. 496.

[18]For a discussion of these difficulties under the income tax, see Chap. 16. For a discussion of the expenditure-tax base, see Chap. 20, Sec. D.

[19]Such at least is the case under the simplifying assumptions of our two-period model, especially that the two taxes are introduced at the outset of a person's working life rather than in midstream.

This way of comparing the taxes is of interest because some observers who find it reasonable to exempt saving from tax might be startled by the idea of exempting capital income. Exemption of capital income runs counter to the traditional thought from Adam Smith on, which states that if there is to be any discrimination, it should be in favor of wage ("earned") rather than capital ("unearned") income.

Wealth as Tax Base

Instead of measuring taxable capacity in terms of flows, such as income or consumption, can a case also be made for using stocks in the form of wealth as a capacity measure?

Taxpaying capacity inherent in the holding of wealth may be viewed as the capacity to receive capital income therefrom. If the yield of capital is 10 percent, the income derived from a $1,000 asset is $100. A 1 percent tax on this asset is thus equivalent to a 10 percent tax on its income. For a tax on an asset worth X dollars to yield the same revenue as an income tax on iX dollars (where i is the rate of interest or asset yield), we must have $t_a X = t_y iX$, or $t_a = it_y$, where t_a and t_y are the respective rates of tax. Given this simplified formulation, the form in which revenue is collected becomes a matter of indifference. A tax on wealth may be viewed simply as a tax on income therefrom. But if capital income is already taxed under a comprehensive income tax, why should such a supplementary income tax on capital income be applied?[20] As we shall see in the next chapter, income is income whether derived from labor or capital services, and it should be treated equally as part of the global income tax base.

Now it might be argued that the ownership of wealth carries with it beneficial attributes other than the income derived therefrom. Is not A, who owns $100,000 of property and receives $10,000 of interest therefrom in a better position than B, who receives $10,000 of wage income? Certainly A can fall back on property and dissave while B cannot. But provided that an income tax was applied initially when the property accrued, this does not justify an additional tax on its holding. In short, taxable capacity as seen in the income tax context is measured adequately by taxing interest, independent of whether saving is undertaken to finance future consumption or to enjoy the pleasures of holding wealth.

But though a taxation of wealth is not needed if accretion is taxed correctly, there might well be a place for a wealth tax if the imperfections of actual tax practice are allowed for. To begin with, not all forms of accretion are subject to income tax, especially not accretion in the form of receiving gifts or bequests. Moreover, a wealth tax might be useful in providing a more feasible way of reaching certain forms of capital income than does the income tax. For one thing, wealth is more visible than capital income and hence can

---

[20]If the earnings of labor could be capitalized, then a general tax on wealth would be similar to a general tax on income. The asymmetry arises because labor income cannot (should not?) be capitalized.

be detected more readily by the tax assessor, a factor of special importance in developing countries. For another, wealth taxation can be applied to non-income-earning assets such as paintings or cash balances, imputed income from which cannot be reached readily under the income tax.

Further Considerations   Finally, a case may be made for the taxation of wealth involving considerations other than ability to pay. Thus society may be concerned with the effects of concentrated wealth holdings on the distribution of political power. Where this is the case, the tax base might be defined properly in terms of a person's gross wealth, as distinct from the ability-to-pay approach where wealth would have to be defined in terms of net worth, i.e., assets minus indebtedness.[21]

Moreover, society's concern with inequality or vertical equity may be related not only to income but also to the uses to which it is put, i.e., to the distribution of consumption or of wealth. Regarding consumption, concern might be with minimum consumption standards or with the unpleasantness of conspicuous consumption. Regarding wealth, concern might be with inequalities in social and political power which result from inequalities in wealth. What is considered an acceptable degree of inequality may differ for the two cases. If so, more than one tax with varying degrees of progression may be needed to accomplish both distributional objectives. Such a system would be in conflict with horizontal equity but might be found desirable on other grounds.

Implementation

In the last resort, the choice of tax base cannot be made in a theoretical vacuum. It depends on the structure of the economy in which the taxation occurs and the "tax handles" which this structure provides. In an agricultural society where most income is derived and consumed on farms, the income tax approach would be extremely difficult to apply. A tax on property or cattle, as in Colonial America, would offer a more feasible way of approximating taxable capacity. Similarly, developing countries find it difficult to reach capital income under the income tax. In such situations, a tax on real property, which can be readily detected, offers a useful supplement. Nor do these difficulties apply to developing countries only. The individual income tax, as applied in the United States, is far from comprehensive and it is even less so in most other nations. As we shall see in Chapters 16–18, some forms of capital income are excluded from the tax base and others are given preferential treatment. For these reasons, a supplementary tax on wealth may be called for, if only as the second-best means of approximating taxation under a comprehensive income tax.

Moreover, though choosing the proper index of economic capacity is important, it is only a first step in designing an equitable tax structure. The second step is to apply this index—be it income, comsumption, or wealth—to

[21]See p. 489.

the complexity of economic and legal institutions. In this process, a host of highly technical and difficult problems arise. How should corporations be taxed, how should capital gains be treated, how should depreciation be timed, how should the particular problems of financial institutions be dealt with, and so on? Since the economy itself is complex and the tax law must be tailored thereto, no single concept of tax base can be implemented to perfection. Moreover, an equitable tax system cannot be simple. An excessively complex tax structure, on the other hand, leads to lawful tax avoidance (some taxpayers adapt their activities to minimize liabilities) as well as illegal evasion, which in turn undermines equity. Tax policy, therefore, is an art no less than a science; and equity is to be sought as a matter of degree, rather than as an absolute norm.

C. ABILITY TO PAY AND VERTICAL EQUITY

We now leave the question of how ability to pay is to be measured and take it to be in terms of income. People with equal income should then pay the same tax. The question to be considered now is how the taxes payable by people with different incomes should differ. How should the problem of vertical equity be resolved? In posing this question, we return to some of the issues dealt with in our earlier discussion of just distribution.

Equal Sacrifice Rules

Since John Stuart Mill, vertical equity has been viewed in terms of an equal-sacrifice prescription. Taxpayers are said to be treated equally if their tax payments involve an equal sacrifice or loss of welfare.[22] The loss of welfare in turn is related to the loss of income. If the level of welfare as a function of income (i.e., the marginal utility of income schedule) is the same for all taxpayers, the equal-sacrifice rule calls for people with equal income (or ability to pay) to contribute equal amounts of tax. Further, people with different incomes should pay different amounts. The more difficult question is how these amounts should differ. To answer it, one must know the shape of the marginal utility of income schedule, and even then the answer differs, depending on how the term "equal" is interpreted. In particular, does equal sacrifice call for a progressive tax?

Alternative Rules   The answer depends on both the shape of the income utility schedule and by what rule "equality of sacrifice" is defined. It may be interpreted to mean equal *absolute*, equal *proportional*, or equal *marginal* (least total) sacrifice. These concepts may be explained with the help of Figure 11-1, where the left diagram pertains to low-income taxpayer L and the right to high-income taxpayer H. MU_L and MU_H are the respective marginal utility of income schedules which are identical and assumed to decline at a decreasing

[22]See John Stuart Mill, *Principles of Political Economy*, edited by W. J. Ashley, London: Longmans, 1921, p. 804.

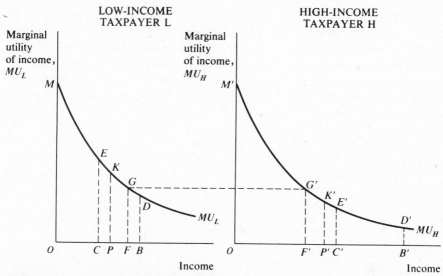

LOW-INCOME
TAXPAYER L

HIGH-INCOME
TAXPAYER H

FIGURE 11-1 Measures of Equal Sacrifice.

rate. L's income before tax is OB while that for H is OB'. The total utilities derived by L and H are $OBDM$ and $OB'D'M'$, respectively. If a given revenue T is to be drawn from the two, how will it be allocated under the three rules?

Absolute Sacrifice Beginning with the equal absolute sacrifice rule, L, with income OB, pays CB, while H, with income OB', pays $C'B'$, where $CB + C'B'$ is the needed revenue T. The loss of utility or sacrifice incurred by L equals $CBDE$ while the loss to H equals $C'B'D'E'$, and T is distributed such that $CBDE = C'B'D'E'$.

If marginal utility were constant (MU parallel to the horizontal axis), equal absolute sacrifice would require tax liabilities to be the same for all incomes. Equal sacrifice would call for a head tax. But with a declining MU schedule, tax liability must rise with income. This much is clear, but it does not follow that a progressive tax will be called for. As may be shown mathematically, the required tax distribution will be progressive, proportional, or regressive, depending on whether the elasticity of the marginal income utility with respect to income is greater than, equal to, or less than unity.[23] While it seems reasonable to assume that the MU schedule falls, there is no intuitive answer about its rate of decline. Thus, there is no ready basis on which to conclude whether equal absolute sacrifice calls for progression, not to speak of the proper degree of progression.

Proportional Sacrifice If the tax burden is distributed in line with equal proportional sacrifice, L will pay PB and H will pay $P'B'$, with $PB + P'B'$

[23]See Paul A. Samuelson, *Foundations of Economic Analysis*, Cambridge, Mass.: Harvard, 1947, p. 227.

again equal to T. The tax is divided between the two so that the fraction of pretax utility lost for L (or $PBDK/OBDM$) is the same as that for H (or $P'B'D'K'/O'B'D'M'$). Under this rule, it is evident that a constant MU schedule will call for proportional taxation. It can also be seen that a declining but straight-line MU schedule calls for progression, but generalizations become difficult if the MU schedule falls at a decreasing rate, as is usually assumed. The result in any particular case depends on the level and slope of the MU schedule, as well as on the initial distribution of income and the amount of revenue that is to be raised.

Marginal Sacrifice Under the equal marginal sacrifice rule, L pays FB and H pays $F'B'$, where $FB + F'B'$ is the required revenue T. The marginal sacrifice is the same, since $FG = F'G'$. At the same time, the total sacrifice for both (or $FBDG + F'B'D'G'$) is minimized. After-tax incomes are equalized at $OF = O'F'$.

If the marginal utility of income were constant, the distribution of the tax bill under *equal marginal* sacrifice would be indeterminate. Any distribution drawing at least some small amount from all taxpayers would meet the requirement. Given a declining MU schedule, equal marginal sacrifice calls for "maximum progression"; i.e., the leveling down of income from the top until the required revenue is obtained. The rate of decline does not matter in this case.

The principle of equal marginal sacrifice as applied in Figure 11-1 leaves both taxpayers with the same income. It also results in *least total* sacrifice (equal to $FBDG + F'B'D'G'$) for both H and L combined. The same result is obtained whether we use an equal marginal, or a least total, sacrifice rule. But suppose now that the revenue requirement is less than the excess of H's over L's income. Here, equal marginal sacrifice cannot be achieved and the result must be stated in terms of least total sacrifice. To achieve least total sacrifice, the tax is applied so as to lop off incomes from the top down, leaving all those who pay tax with equal marginal sacrifice, but not necessarily including all individuals in the tax-paying group.

The equal marginal sacrifice rule may thus be viewed as an efficiency rule (calling for total sacrifice to be at a minimum) rather than as an equity rule; and once this step is taken, the argument is readily extended beyond the amount of revenue that happens to be required. Instead of saying that the sacrifice due to taxation should be minimized, we can also say that the welfare derived from what is left over should be maximized, thus leading us to the previously examined utilitarian view of a just distribution.[24] After all, if maximum satisfaction from private income is called for, the adjustment should not be limited to the amount of revenue needed to finance public services.

Conclusion Comparing the results for H and L, we see that the marginal rule is worst for H and best for L. This will always be the situation so long

[24]See p. 93.

as the utility schedule declines. Given the schedule as drawn in Figure 11-1, H also does better under the absolute than under the proportional rule, but this need not be so in all situations.

With the exception of equal marginal sacrifice, the case for progression (or the degree thereof) is thus quite inconclusive, and this is true even if the underlying assumptions of declining and identical utility schedules are accepted. Even with equal absolute sacrifice, which some consider the most reasonable of the three formulas, all that follows for sure is that tax liabilities should rise with income. Beyond this, there is no intuitive conclusion about whether progression is called for and, if so, what degree of progression should apply. Matters are even less predictable under the equal proportional sacrifice rule. In all, the ability-to-pay rule is doubly inconclusive as the answer depends on (1) what formulation of equal sacrifice is chosen, and (2) the precise shape of the *MU* schedules.

Social Utility Approach

As it was noted in our earlier discussion of justice criteria, there are serious difficulties with this entire approach. While the assumption of a declining marginal utility schedule seems to be reasonable, the precise slope of the schedule is not known and schedules may differ among individuals. More basically, the entire proposition of interpersonal utility comparison is questionable.[25]

Social Utility of Income   It is more realistic, therefore, to view the problem in terms of a social utility schedule based on society's evaluation of successive units of income, rather than of one based on a measure of subjective utilities as actually experienced by each individual.

Approaching the problem in this way, suppose that the income tax structure as enacted by Congress does in fact reflect its intention to implement a given sacrifice rule. Postulating a declining *MU* schedule, we know that the intent could not have been to implement equal marginal sacrifice. Although progression applies, it falls far short of leveling down incomes from the top. But suppose that the intent was to implement equal absolute sacrifice. One may then compute the social marginal income utility schedule which is implicit in the prevailing tax-liability distribution. If we set the marginal income utility at an income of $3,000 as equal to 1, the schedule shown in Table 11-3 emerges for a single person; and corresponding schedules may be derived for larger family units.

These results are based on the rather heroic assumption that the rate schedule reflects a rigorous application of congressional intent to apply an equal sacrifice rule. Nevertheless, this interpretation illustrates a potentially useful approach. As noted previously, Congress or the executive branch might stipulate an explicit social income utility schedule and then proceed to formulate its tax and expenditure policies accordingly.[26]

[25]See p. 97.
[26] See our earlier discussion of income weights in cost-benefit analysis, p. 182.

TABLE 11-3
Index for Marginal Utility of Money Income Derived from
Income Tax Schedule

Income (Dollars)	Marginal Utility Index	Income (Dollars)	Marginal Utility Index
1,000	8.51	20,000	0.05
2,000	1.83	30,000	0.03
3,000	1.00	50,000	0.01
4,000	0.64	70,000	0.009
5,000	0.45	100,000	0.007
10,000	0.15	200,000	0.003

Notes: The index is derived from liabilities computed by applying 1965 rates and standard deductions to adjusted gross income. An alternative computation based on reported tax liabilities gives a much lower degree of effective progression (see p. 374) and hence implies a less rapidly falling marginal income utility schedule. It should also be noted that the income levels shown in the table refer to 1965 dollars. With prices now 100 percent higher, and assuming corresponding adjustments in the rate schedule through legislative changes, the income amounts in a revised estimation would be doubled.

Source: From Koichi Mera, "Experimental Determination of Relative Marginal Utilities," *Quarterly Journal of Economics*, August 1969, pp. 464–477.

D. SUMMARY

Two traditions in the analysis of equity criteria were distinguished, including the benefit and ability-to-pay approaches.

1. The benefit principle has the advantage of linking the expenditure and tax sides of budget policy, but it is not readily implemented, since consumer evaluation of public services is not known to tax authorities but must be revealed through the political process. However, in some instances, benefit taxation can be applied.

2. The benefit principle has the disadvantage of excluding redistributional considerations.

3. The ability-to-pay principle calls for a distribution of the tax burden in line with the economic capacity of the taxpayer. It has the advantage of permitting inclusion of distributional considerations but the disadvantage of dealing with the tax problem in isolation, the provision of social goods being left out of the picture.

4. The ability-to-pay principle calls for a distribution of the tax burden in line with horizontal and vertical equity. To obtain horizontal equity, taxpayers with equal ability to pay should contribute equally. To secure vertical equity, taxpayers with unequal capacity should contribute correspondingly different amounts.

Implementation of equitable taxation in line with ability to pay requires the definition of a specific index by which ability to pay is to be measured.

5. Ideally, this index would encompass all forms in which economic welfare is derived, including leisure as well as present and future consumption. Unfortunately, such a comprehensive index is not feasible, the value of leisure in particular not being measurable.

6. Income is the most widely used general measure of economic capacity. Used for this purpose, income should be defined broadly, so as to include all forms of accretion, independent of the sources from which it is derived and the uses to which it is put.

7. An alternative measure of capacity is in the form of consumption. The merits of the two bases, from the point of view of horizontal equity, may be appraised in terms of an "equal potential consumption" rule.

8. Applied as an expenditure tax, the consumption base may be made the basis for personal and progressive taxation.

9. Given the framework of an idealized system of lifetime taxation, the consumption base is preferable, on grounds of horizontal equity, to the income base. This advantage becomes questionable, however, once a more realistic framework is considered.

10. Taxation of wealth is not necessary if all income has already been subject to a comprehensive income tax; but since this condition is in practice not met, supplementary taxes on consumption and wealth may be called for on ability-to-pay grounds.

Determination of the proper distribution of the tax burden among unequals involves complex considerations of vertical equity.

11. The principle of vertical equity may be formulated so as to call for equality of sacrifice. This may or may not require progressive taxation, depending on how "equal sacrifice" is defined and on the slope of the marginal utility of income schedules.

12. Since it is debatable whether and how such schedules can be measured and compared, implementation of the ability-to-pay principle has to make use of a socially determined income utility approach.

13. Separate taxes on income, consumption, and wealth may be called for if society takes different views of how each should be distributed.

FURTHER READINGS

Blum, Walter J., and Harry Kalven, Jr.: *The Uneasy Case for Progressive Taxation,* Chicago: University of Chicago Press, 1953.

Goode, Richard: *The Individual Income Tax,* rev. ed., Washington: Brookings, 1976, chap. 2.

Kaldor, N.: *An Expenditure Tax,* London: G. Allen, 1955, chap. 1 and appendix.

Pigou, A. C.: *A Study in Public Finance,* 3d ed., London: Macmillan, 1951, part 2.

Thurow, Lester C.: *The Impact of Taxes in the American Economy,* New York: Praeger, 1971, chap. 7.

Chapter 12

Tax and Expenditure Incidence: An Overview*

A. Nature of Tax Burden: *Tax Burden and Resource Transfer; Magnitude of Burden.* **B.** **Concepts of Incidence:** *Statutory Incidence, Economic Incidence, and Tax Shifting; Alternative Concepts of Incidence.* **C. Measuring Incidence:** *Burden Distribution among Whom? Burden Impact from Sources and Uses Side; Measuring Changes in Distribution.* **D. Incidence of the United States Fiscal Structure:** *Distribution of the Tax Burden; Distribution of Expenditure Benefits; Net Residue; Scope of Redistribution; Conclusion.* **E. Summary.**

We now turn from the preceding analysis of fiscal structure to a closer view of its economic effects. These include micro effects on the distribution of income and the efficiency of resource use as well as macro effects on the level of capacity output, employment, prices, and growth. All these effects interact. Thus, the distributional effects (or incidence) of particular budget measures depend on their effects on capacity output and employment just as the latter

---

* Readers' Guide to Chapter 12: The determination of tax and expenditure incidence poses complex issues to be considered in subsequent chapters. In this chapter we deal with the general formulation of the problem, and in the concluding section, we give a quantitative picture of the incidence of the United States fiscal structure, including tax burdens, expenditure benefits, and net positions. This chapter presents a basic introduction to the incidence problem, important for the general reader who may wish to bypass the more detailed analysis of Chapter 13.

depend on concurrent changes in distribution. Nevertheless, each type of effect is of interest in itself and must be considered as such in policy formulation. One policy may be superior with regard to distributional results but inferior with regard to efficiency, growth, or employment effects. Tradeoffs must then be made. Moreover, as a matter of exposition, not all aspects can be dealt with at once. Keeping in mind the general fact of interdependence, we begin with the effects of budget policy on the state of distribution. Such effects are key features, especially in the determination of tax and transfer policy. It is these effects which we have in mind when talking about the "incidence" of tax or expenditure policies.

A. NATURE OF TAX BURDEN

Before considering who bears the tax burden, we must examine what the concept of burden implies. Here a distinction must be drawn between budget operations which involve a resource transfer to the public sector and others which do not.

Tax Burden and Resource Transfer

In the first case, the government imposes taxes to finance the purchase of goods and to pay public employees needed to provide social goods and services. Suppose that the government collects $1 billion and spends it on highway facilities. As a result, the resources available for private use are reduced by a like amount. This is the opportunity cost of the highway services, the gross burden which their provision imposes on the private sector as a whole. Tax incidence refers to the way in which this gross burden is shared among individual households. This burden in turn is accompanied by the benefits of highway services which must be allowed for to derive the net gain or burden (or to determine the net incidence) of the entire transaction. If the program is worthwhile, the benefits should outweigh the costs.

When budget operations do not involve resource transfers to the public, the government simply collects taxes from the private sector and returns transfers to that sector. There is no shift of resources to public use and no opportunity cost in reduced private resource availability. Some may gain while others will lose, but taxes being equal to transfers, there will be no net change in income available for private use. The problem of incidence is now merely one of tracing the redistribution of privately available income among households.

Magnitude of Burden

Implicit in the preceding argument is the simplifying assumption that the tax burden is equal to the revenue collected. On this basis, the opportunity cost of $1 billion of public resource use equals the $1 billion of revenue that is needed to pay for it. By the same token, obtaining $1 billion in taxes and spending it on transfers leaves private income unchanged and involves no resource cost. This view of tax burden oversimplifies matters and must now be reconsidered.

Excess Burden   The total burden may exceed the revenue collected because an efficiency loss or "excess burden" results. To illustrate, suppose that $1 billion revenue is collected from a tax on automobiles. The sum total of tax collections from various consumers equals $1 billion, but the burden imposed on the private sector will be larger. This is so because the tax interferes with consumer choice. Thus, some people may forgo a car purchase because of the tax payable. They pay no tax but their budget choice is less satisfactory than it was before and they therefore suffer a burden which is not reflected in total revenue. Others may buy a cheaper car and pay a tax on the reduced amount. In both cases the consumer's expenditure pattern has been distorted by the tax and each suffers a burden which is greater than that which would have applied if they had paid the same amount as a flat charge. Because of this, the overall burden suffered by the private sector tends to exceed the amount of revenue obtained. An additional burden—referred to by economists as "excess burden"—results. The nature of this burden will be examined further in Chapter 14.

Input Effects   There is another reason why tax revenue and total burden as measured by the loss of income available for private use may differ. Imposition of the tax may lead to a change in factor supply and hence in total output. We may illustrate this case by supposing that the same revenue as in the previous examples was collected under a progressive income tax. As a result, workers may work more or less because the tax is imposed. Let us suppose that they work less and, as a result, their earnings fall. If this decline in earnings is counted as part of the burden, the total burden once more exceeds tax revenue; and the opposite is true if people work harder so that their earnings rise as a result of the tax. Similarly, tax policy may lead to a change in the rate of savings and investment and hence in the rate of output growth. These changes will again be reflected in the level of pretax income, once more causing the change in income to differ from the amount of revenue.

Employment Effects   Furthermore, changes in output may result, not because of adjustments in factor inputs in response to changes in after-tax factor rewards, but because of resulting changes in the level of aggregate demand and unemployment. Introduction of a tax may reduce the level of employment, or an increase in expenditures may raise it. This once more complicates the problem of observing the effects of taxation on the distribution of income. As is evident from these considerations, the concept of tax burden is more complex than suggested by the simple formulation in which revenue and burden are set equal to each other. However, this assumption remains a useful approximation when dealing with the problem of burden distribution in an operational way. We shall accept it for purposes of this chapter.

B. CONCEPTS OF INCIDENCE

In a discussion of tax incidence, certain concepts and issues must be clarified if confusion is to be avoided. Quite apart from the difficulties of measurement, one ought to be clear on just what it is that one wishes to measure.

Statutory Incidence, Economic Incidence, and Tax Shifting

Taxes, according to Justice Holmes, are the price of civilization, but the question is, who pays? As we saw earlier, taxes are not voluntary purchase payments but mandatory impositions, payable in line with whatever tax statute has been legislated. Although these statutes in the end are a reflection (more or less imperfect) of voters' preferences, once legislated they become mandatory levies, imposing burdens which the individual taxpayer will try to avoid or to pass on to others. To determine who pays, we must thus look beyond the tax statutes and the pattern of statutory incidence, i.e., beyond those on whom the legal liability for payment rests. This involves two considerations. First, it must be recognized that in the end, the entire tax burden must be borne by individuals. Though taxes may be collected from business firms, their ultimate burden must be traced to individual households in their capacity as owners of the firms, as employees, or as consumers of their products. Second, the final burden distribution may differ from that of statutory liabilities, whether the tax is imposed on individuals or on firms. Individuals as well as firms may adjust their sales and purchases, thus affecting the position of others.

Suppose first that Mr. Jones is called upon to pay a given amount, say, $100 of tax, independently of what he does. Such a tax, referred to as a lump-sum tax, cannot be escaped. Yet, Jones will adjust himself to this loss by cutting back his purchases or savings, or by increasing his work effort. Although he cannot escape payment of the tax, his adjustment thereto will affect the people with whom he transacts and thus will have further repercussions. Moreover, taxes are rarely imposed in lump-sum form. The tax law typically expresses liabilities as a function of some aspect of economic behavior, such as earning income, making sales, or making a purchase. Since such taxes are imposed on economic transactions and since transactions involve more than one party, the transactors on whom the statutory liability rests may avoid tax payments by cutting back on their taxable activity; or they may attempt to pass on the burden to others by changing the terms under which they are willing to trade. Their ability to do so will depend upon the structure of the markets in which they deal and the way in which prices are determined.

Thus, imposition of an income tax may lead to reduced hours of work, thereby driving up the gross wage rate and burdening the consumer. Or, an automobile excise levied on the sellers may cause them to raise their prices, hoping to pass the burden of tax to the buyers, who in turn will attempt to avoid it by substituting other purchases. A tax on the use of capital may lead a firm to substitute labor, and so forth. In each case, the taxpayer's ability to make such adjustments will depend on the willingness of the other transactor to go along. If the seller raises the price, the buyer will fight back by purchasing less, so that the outcome will depend on the response of the two parties. Nevertheless, the resulting chain of adjustments—the process of "*shifting* the tax burden"—may lead to a final distribution of the burden or *economic* incidence, which differs greatly from the initial distribution of liabilities or *statutory* incidence.

Legislators are quite aware of this. When imposing a manufacturer's tax on automobiles, they do not intend this burden to fall on the manufacturer. If they wished it to do so, they would impose a tax on the manufacturer's profits. Manufacturers merely serve as convenient collection points and are meant to pass the tax forward to the consumer in the form of higher automobile prices. Determining the actual distribution of the tax burden therefore requires an analysis of the economic adjustment process, or the transmission of the burden from its impact point (the place of statutory incidence) to its final resting point (the place of economic incidence). This process is generally referred to as "shifting."

As a matter of ultimate policy concern, it is obviously the distribution of the burden *after* shifting that counts. If this distribution is to be as intended, legislators must choose tax formulas which give the desired result in terms not of statutory incidence but of the economic incidence which ensues after the system has adjusted to the imposition of the tax. This, to say the least, is no simple task, even for the economist who must be called upon to advise what the final incidence of particular taxes will be. As we shall see later, especially tough problems arise with regard to the corporation profits tax and the property tax.

Alternative Concepts of Incidence

Although the expenditure side of the budget should be allowed for, concern with incidence has traditionally focused on the tax side of the picture. There are three ways in which the narrower problem of tax incidence may be viewed, namely as "absolute," "differential," or "budget" incidence.

Absolute Tax Incidence   One way is to examine the distributional effects of imposing a particular tax while holding public expenditures constant. Suppose that income taxes are increased without there being a corresponding change in expenditures or an offsetting change in other taxes. In determining the distributional consequences of such a change, one can hardly overlook the macro effects which follow from the resulting decline in aggregate demand. Assuming public policy to pursue a stabilizing course, there will be no burden on consumers as a group, but the question is how the distributional implications of alternative stabilization policies will differ. If no offsetting measures are taken, the tax change, depending upon the state of the economy, may lead to unemployment, a decline in price level, or a reduced rate of inflation.[1] Each result will have its distributional implications which cannot be separated from those of the tax change itself. Any attempt to consider the absolute incidence of a particular tax thus leads one to a much broader set of considerations. The approach is not a satisfactory one.

Differential Tax Incidence   To avoid this difficulty, one might examine the distributional changes which result if one tax is substituted for another while total revenue and expenditures are held constant. Thus, the government may replace $1 billion of income tax revenue with a cigarette excise yielding an equivalent amount.[2] This policy change involves no resource transfer to public use and (disregarding the issue of excess burden for the time being) imposes no net burden on the private sector. It merely involves a redistribution among households. Households whose income tax is reduced will gain, while others with high cigarette purchases will lose. Going beyond this, tobacco growers and cigarette workers will lose, while others producing the output purchased by former income taxpayers stand to gain. The resulting total change in the state of distribution is referred to as "differential incidence."

The concept of differential incidence also applies when we compare alternative ways of raising or lowering revenue. This view of tax incidence is particularly useful because actual tax policy decisions usually involve such issues.

Budget Incidence   Still another way of looking at the problem is to consider the changes in household positions which result if the combined effects of tax and expenditure changes are considered. The income available to particular households for private use will now be affected not only by tax but also by expenditure measures. In the case of transfer programs, private incomes are added to, just as they are reduced by, taxes. In the case of provision for public services, the necessary purchases (whether of the services of civil servants or products) affect the distribution of private income through their effects on earnings. Thus, the expenditure side of the budget has its effects on private incomes as do taxes; and since tax and expenditure effects occur simultaneously, they cannot be separated in this case.

The overall effect of the budget transaction now consists of four parts:

1. Earnings from production for private use are reduced.
2. Earnings from production for public use are increased.

[1] A similar problem arises if we consider an increase in public services without a corresponding change in revenue. Deficit finance, no less than tax finance, has its incidence.

[2] As a first approximation, the "equivalent amount" may be defined as the same amount of dollars. But this may be too simple a view. Allowing for changes in relative prices and hence possible changes in the cost of goods bought by government, the equivalent amount is that which permits government to make the same real purchases. Moreover, the equivalent amount should be such as to maintain the same level of aggregate demand. For the latter aspect, see p. 601.

3. Disposable income from earnings is reduced by taxation.

4. Benefits from public services are received free of direct charge, while benefits from private purchases are reduced.

The dollar value of item 1 equals that of 2, as public purchases are substituted for private purchases. Similarly, the dollar value of item 3 will equal that of benefits under 4 if the latter are measured at cost. While each of the three incidence concepts may be used, the differential approach offers the most helpful tool for tax policy analysis.

C. MEASURING INCIDENCE

Since incidence deals with how the tax burden is distributed, what are the relevant groupings and how is the burden distribution to be measured? To begin with, it must be clearly understood that the entire tax burden is in the end borne by individuals. Legal persons such as corporations are owned by individuals and taxes levied on such enterprises must be traced to their owners, customers, or employees.

Burden Distribution among Whom?

In studying the distribution of the tax burden, our concern is therefore with its incidence among individuals or households. This differs from the approach taken by the classical economists (David Ricardo, for instance) who viewed the incidence problem in terms of the impact of tax burdens on the suppliers of capital, labor, and land. For them, incidence theory was primarily an aspect of the theory of factor shares or factor pricing. This was also useful from the point of view of public policy since, in their time, industry, labor, and agriculture did in fact reflect the major social groups. Today the pattern is more mixed, and primary concern—from the viewpoint of social policy—has moved to the size distribution of income. A person receiving only a small amount of capital income and unable to work is poor, whereas a person receiving a large salary is well off. This is also in line with the global income tax approach, where our concern is with the person's level of *total* income, independent of the particular source from which it is derived.

If one wishes to analyze a practical incidence problem—e.g., the distributional changes which result if the corporation tax is replaced by a value-added tax, or if a sales tax is substituted for a property tax—it is not feasible to determine what happens to each of the over 50 million households in the economy. To make the task manageable, households must be grouped by categories. For this purpose, our primary concern is with the distribution of the burden among households grouped by income classes. At the same time, other groupings, such as age or type of family, are also of interest.

Burden Impact from Sources and Uses Side

Substitution of one tax for another will improve the position of some households and worsen that of others. Changes in the position of any one household may be measured in terms of the resulting change in its real income. Real income may change because disposable income changes or because there is a change in the price of the products which are purchased. Taking a somewhat simplified view of the matter, we note that the disposable real income (DRY) of a household may be defined as

$$\mathrm{DRY} = \frac{E - T_y}{P + T_s} = \frac{DY}{GP}$$

where E is earnings, T_y is income tax, P is the price (at factor cost) of products bought, and T_s is the sales tax addition thereto. DY is disposable or after-tax money income, and GP is the gross (or market) price. We can now see how DRY is subject to both direct and indirect tax effects.

Primary effects of tax changes which operate on the earnings or *sources* side of the household account will change T_y, while primary effects which operate on the expenditure or *uses* side of its account will change T_s. Thus an increase in income tax lowers DRY via an increase in T_y and hence a fall in DY. An increase in sales tax lowers DRY via an increase in T_s and hence in GP.

In addition, the general adjustment process may result in secondary changes from the sources side, or in E, and in secondary changes from the uses side, or in P. While such secondary effects may be of great importance to particular households, chances are that they will not result in a systematic offset to such changes in the size distribution of DRY as have resulted in line with the primary effects.[3] As we shall see later for taxes on earnings such as the individual income tax, distributional results tend to be dominated by effects from the sources side, whereas in other cases, such as selective excise taxes, changes on the uses side are of primary importance.

While households differ widely in their sources and uses patterns, there are generally applicable relationships between the level of income and the pattern of sources as well as the level of income and the pattern of uses. This will prove to be a strategic feature of our incidence analysis. Since the share of capital income rises as we move up the income scale,[4] a tax on capital income tends to be more progressive than a general income tax, while a tax

---

[3] Measuring changes in real income raises considerable difficulties which we are overlooking for the time being.

Thus, the above formulation does not distinguish between changes in E due to changes in the wage rate with hours of work unchanged, and changes in E due to changes in hours worked. In the latter case, the formulation overlooks the gains or losses from resulting change in leisure.

In measuring the implications of price change, there is the problem posed by choice of the proper index. Consider, for instance, the imposition of a tax on product X which raises its price, while the amount purchased declines from Q_1 to Q_2. If the burden is measured by $\Delta P Q_1$, true cost will be overstated, while if measured by $\Delta P Q_2$, it will be understated. The true burden, as we shall see later, would be measured by the lump-sum amount which the taxpayer would be willing to pay instead. These problems and the related issues of excess burden are considered in Chap. 14.

[4] Such at least is the case except at the bottom end of the scale where pensions play a major part.

on wage income only tends to be regressive. Similarly, a tax on luxury products, such as champagne, tends to be progressive, whereas a tax on mass-consumption items—say, beer—tends to be regressive. These relationships, as we shall presently see, play a key role in dealing with the incidence of various taxes.

Measuring Changes in Distribution

A comprehensive measure of incidence may be obtained by comparing the state of distribution before and after a particular tax change. Such a comparison is illustrated in Figure 12-1. Measuring the cumulative percentage of disposable income on the vertical axis and the cumulative percentage of households (ranked from the lowest to the highest) on the horizontal axis, the curve OAB shows the percentage of income received by the lowest 10, 20, 30, etc., percent of households. Thus the lowest 20 percent of households receives 6 percent of income and the lowest 80 percent receives 60 percent, leaving 40 percent for the highest 20 percent.[5] If distribution were equal, curve OAB would coincide with the straight line OB. Given a state of unequal distribution, the ratio of the two areas $OABC/OBC$ may be taken as the index of equality. It will equal 1 if the distribution of income is totally equal.

Suppose now that the distributional pattern with the existing tax system is as indicated by OAB but that, due to a tax change, it becomes $OA'B$. This means that distribution has become more equal—since $OA'BC/OBC > OABC/OBC$—and in this sense the effect of the tax change has been progressive.[6] Note, however, that this change may have come about in two ways. Thus, the distribution of the initial tax burden might have changed, e.g., the rates of the income tax may have been made more progressive while holding total revenue constant. Alternatively, yield may have been increased without changing the progressivity of the rate structure, e.g., by raising all liabilities by the same percentage.

The total effect on distribution, therefore, depends not only on how progressive particular taxes are (i.e., how fast the effective rate or ratio of liability to income rises as we move up the income scale), but also on the overall level of taxation and on the underlying distribution of income.[7] A high but moderately progressive level of taxation may have a greater impact upon the distribution of income than does a low-level but sharply progressive system.

---

[5] To obtain the complete picture and allow for changes from the sources side as well, disposable income would have to be expressed in real terms, i.e., be deflated by the relevant index of consumer prices. The figures here refer to money income.

[6] $OA'B$ need not lie inside OAB throughout but the two curves may intersect. If so, distribution may become more equal over part of the range and less so over another. Social policy, of course, must be concerned not only with the overall state of distribution but also with distribution over particular income ranges. Thus more partial measures of incidence may be devised.

[7] For this concept of tax rate progression, see p. 376.

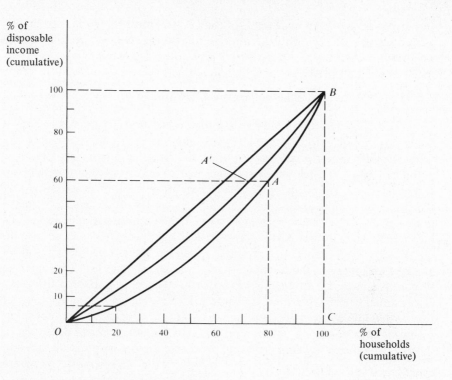

FIGURE 12-1   Measure of Income Equality.

Notes: Total taxes, federal taxes, and state and local taxes are derived from Table 12-1, lines 17, 6, and 15, respectively.

D. INCIDENCE OF THE UNITED STATES FISCAL STRUCTURE

In the following chapter, we shall examine carefully the economics of shifting and incidence as applied to the major taxes in our system. But before doing so, it will be useful to gain an overview of the distributional implications of the United States fiscal structure. The estimates presented here are the result of somewhat heroic estimating procedures and are based on data for 1968, as well as tax laws then prevailing.[8] Since that time, per capita income has more than doubled in money terms, so that a better picture of the current pattern of effective rates might be obtained by doubling the dollar value of the bracket limits which are shown in the tables. In addition, the pattern has undergone some changes owing to new legislation and the impact of inflation, both of which tend to make the system somewhat more progressive. Unfortunately, corresponding estimates for current levels of income, expenditures,

---

[8]See R. A. Musgrave, Karl E. Case, and Herman B. Leonard, "The Distribution of Fiscal Burdens and Benefits," *Public Finance Quarterly*, July 1974.

and tax revenue are not available[9]; but since there has been no drastic change in the overall pattern of distribution, the following estimates are still instructive.

Distribution of the Tax Burden

The distribution of the tax burden is estimated first. The estimates shown in Table 12-1 involve three stages. (1) Assumptions are made regarding the incidence of various taxes, leaving it to the next chapter to explore their rationale. Thus, it may be postulated that the corporation tax falls on shareholders, on recipients of capital income in general, on wage earners in the corporate sector, or on consumers. (2) On the basis of whatever assumption is made, the revenue from each tax is assigned to households in various income brackets, using for this purpose such distributive series as are available. If the corporation tax is assumed to fall on the shareholder, it will be assigned according to the distribution of dividend income; if it is assumed to be passed on to the consumer, it will be assigned according to the distribution of consumer expenditures, and so forth. (3) The effective or average rates of tax are determined by expressing the tax allocation to each income bracket as a percentage of income in the bracket. For this purpose, a broad definition of income, including total corporate-source income (before corporation tax) and imputed income (such as rental income of owner-occupiers), is more appropriate.

Standard Assumptions   Table 12-1 shows the results under a set of "benchmark" assumptions. According to these, the various taxes are allocated

[9]Preliminary estimates for 1978 by Joseph Pechman show a somewhat more progressive pattern than the Pechman-Okner estimates for 1966. The comparison is as follows:

TOTAL TAX AS PERCENTAGE OF INCOME

Adjusted Family Income (In Thousands of Dollars)	1966 Estimate (I)	1978 Estimate (II)
5–10	22.6	16.7
20–25	24.0	22.8
50–100	31.5	27.0
500–1,000	48.8	59.1

Note: The ratios for 1966 shown in col. I are below those shown in our text table due to a broader definition of the income base.
Source: For 1966 estimates, see Joseph A. Pechman and Benjamin A. Okner, *Who Bears the Tax Burden?* Washington: Brookings, 1974. For 1978 estimates, see Joseph A. Pechman, "Taxation in the United Kingdom," in a forthcoming volume on the British economy, Washington: Brookings.

TABLE 12-1

Estimated Distribution of Tax Burdens by Income Brackets, 1968

(Taxes as Percentage of Total Family Income)

Taxes	INCOME BRACKETS*										
	Under $4,000	$4,000–$5,700	$5,700–$7,900	$7,900–$10,400	$10,400–$12,500	$12,500–$17,500	$17,500–$22,600	$22,600–$35,500	$35,500–$92,000	$92,000 and over	All Brackets
Federal Taxes											
1. Individual income tax	2.0	2.8	5.9	7.1	7.9	10.1	10.6	12.7	14.8	18.5	9.9
2. Estate and gift tax	—	—	—	—	—	—	—	0.6	2.0	2.7	0.4
3. Corporation income tax	5.1	6.1	5.0	4.0	4.3	4.6	4.8	5.1	5.3	6.6	5.0
4. Excises and customs	2.5	2.8	3.1	3.0	2.9	2.7	2.1	1.1	0.9	0.6	2.3
5. Payroll tax	5.5	6.3	7.0	6.9	6.7	6.1	5.2	4.2	1.5	0.6	5.2
6. Total	15.2	17.9	20.8	21.6	21.6	23.4	22.6	23.8	24.5	29.1	22.7
7. Total excluding line 5	9.7	11.6	13.9	14.7	14.9	17.3	17.4	19.6	23.0	28.5	17.5
State and Local Taxes											
8. Individual income tax	—	0.1	0.3	0.6	0.7	1.1	1.4	2.3	1.6	1.3	1.0
9. Inheritance tax	—	—	—	—	—	—	—	0.2	0.6	0.8	0.1
10. Corporation income tax	0.4	0.5	0.4	0.4	0.3	0.4	0.4	0.4	0.4	0.5	0.4
11. General excise tax	3.4	2.8	2.5	2.3	2.2	2.0	1.7	1.0	0.5	0.3	1.8
12. Excises†	2.7	3.0	3.3	3.0	2.9	2.5	1.9	1.0	0.8	0.6	2.1
13. Property tax	6.7	5.7	4.7	4.3	4.0	3.7	3.3	3.0	2.9	3.3	3.9
14. Payroll tax	0.2	0.5	0.8	1.0	1.0	1.0	1.1	1.2	0.2	0.1	0.8
15. Total	13.4	12.5	11.9	11.6	11.1	10.6	9.7	9.1	7.1	6.9	10.3
16. Total excluding line 14	13.2	12.1	11.1	10.6	10.1	9.6	8.6	7.9	6.9	6.8	9.5
All Levels											
17. Total	28.5	30.5	32.8	33.1	32.8	33.9	32.4	32.9	31.6	35.9	33.0
18. Total excluding lines 5 and 14	22.9	23.7	25.0	25.3	25.0	26.9	26.0	27.5	29.9	35.3	27.0

*As noted in the text, these estimates pertain to 1968 levels of income and revenue. Since personal income (per capita, in nominal terms) has doubled since then, the current pattern of effective rates may be approximated by doubling the income brackets accordingly.

Notes:

†Includes motor vehicle licenses, excises, and miscellaneous revenue.

For brief explanation of estimates, see text.

Uneven bracket limits are used for computational reasons.

Items may not add to totals because of rounding.

as follows:

Tax	Incidence Assumptions	Allocated according to
Individual income tax	Stays put	Tax payments
Corporation income tax	One-half on consumption	Consumption
	One-half on capital income	Capital income
Excises and sales taxes	Consumption	Type of consumption
Estate and gift taxes	Donors	Capital income above $25,000
Property tax		
Residences	Homeowners	Ownership
Rental housing	Tenants	Rental payments
Business	One-half consumption	Consumption
	One-half capital income	Capital income
Payroll tax		
Employer	Consumers	Consumption
Employee	Employees	Covered earnings

The validity of these assumptions will be explored further in the following chapters. Proceeding on this basis, we obtain the results shown in Table 12-1. We find that the federal income tax (line 1) is a distinctly progressive component. The corporation tax (line 3) is regressive at the lower end of the scale and mildly progressive thereafter.[10] The estate tax (line 2) is highly progressive but carries little weight in the total picture. Excises (line 4) are regressive, as is the payroll tax (line 5) for all but the bottom end of the scale.[11] The federal system as a whole (line 6 and Figure 12-2) is mildly progressive over most of the range, flanked by sharper progression at both ends of the scale. If the payroll taxes are excluded (line 7), the pattern becomes progressive throughout.

The state and local picture shows a less progressive pattern for the income tax, which in fact turns regressive at the upper end.[12] The regressivity of the general sales tax (line 11) exceeds that of excises, and the property tax distribution (line 13) is mildly regressive under the assumptions used here.

The combined pattern, including federal, state, and local taxes (line 17 and Figure 12-2), is the most interesting part of the picture. We find the overall burden distribution to be more or less proportional over a wide middle range—from, say, $5,000 to $30,000—which includes the great bulk of

[10]These results correspond to the gross burden concept of Table 18-2, line 19. Regressivity at the lower end reflects the weight of dividends in retirement income.

[11]The progressive payroll tax burden at the lower end reflects a low share of covered wages in low-bracket incomes, a feature not reflected in the pattern of Table 23-2.

[12]Since bracket rates level off at a moderate level, the increasing share of income subject to preferential treatment results in a decline in the average rate as computed on a full-income base.

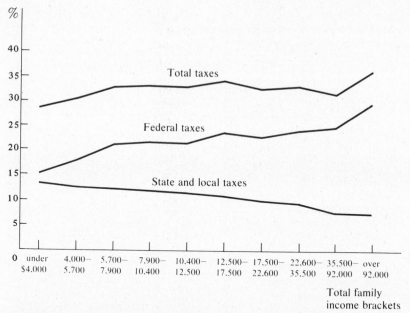

FIGURE 12-2   Total Taxes as a Percentage of Total Family Income.

all families. Again we find mild progression at both ends of the scale. If payroll taxes are excluded (line 18), lower-end progression is increased.

Alternative Assumptions   We have noted that the choice of the incidence assumptions is the most crucial element in determining the resulting pattern of burden distribution. This is shown in Table 12-2, where the significance of alternative incidence assumptions is explored. The results are shown for selected income brackets only.

Lines 1 to 5 show a wide variation in the pattern of corporation income tax incidence. Total assignment of the burden to shareholders (line 2) greatly increases upper-end progression as compared with our benchmark of line 1. Total assignment to capital income (line 3) increases progressivity at the lower and reduces it at the upper end. Total assignment to consumption (line 4) would render the tax regressive. In line 5, finally, the consumption component of the benchmark assumption is divided between wage earners and consumers, but we find that this variation does not greatly change the result.

Lines 6 to 10 show alternative assumptions for the property tax. Compared with the benchmark assumption (line 6), imputation of the entire burden to recipients of capital income (line 7) sharply changes the picture and renders the tax progressive throughout the range. This result is not affected greatly if the tax on owner-occupied residences is left with the owner (line 8). Assignment of the entire tax on business property to capital income (line 9) raises progression, and assignment to the consumer (line 10) results in regression.

TABLE 12-2
Significance of Alternative Incidence Assumptions
(Tax as Percentage of Total Family Income)

	SELECTED INCOME BRACKETS*			
	$4,000– $5,700	$12,500– $17,500	$35,500– $92,000	$92,000 and over
Corporation Tax				
1. One-half capital income, one-half consumption	6.6	5.0	5.7	7.2
2. Dividend income	4.7	2.6	8.8	28.2
3. Capital income	6.1	3.7	10.0	13.7
4. Consumption	7.1	6.3	1.4	0.6
5. One-half capital income, one-fourth consumption, one-fourth wages	6.0	5.0	5.8	7.3
Property Tax†				
6. OR on owner; R on tenant; B—one-half capital income, one-half consumption	5.7	3.7	2.9	3.3
7. All on capital income	4.4	2.7	7.2	9.9
8. OR on owner, R and B on capital income	4.4	3.3	5.4	7.1
9. OR on owner, R on tenant, B on capital income	5.3	3.3	4.5	5.8
10. OR on owner, R on tenant, B on consumption	6.1	4.1	1.2	0.8
Payroll Tax				
11. Employer tax on consumption, employee tax on wages	6.8	7.1	1.7	0.6
12. All on wages	5.6	7.4	1.7	0.4
Total, All Levels of Government				
13. Line 17, Table 12-1‡	30.5	33.9	31.6	35.9
14. Substituting lines 2 for 1, 7 for 6, 12 for 11	26.1	30.8	39.0	63.2
15. Substituting lines 4 for 1, 10 for 6	31.4	35.6	25.6	26.9

*See note to Table 12-1.
†OR stands for owner-occupied residences; R stands for rental property; B stands for
other business property.
‡Includes the payroll tax.

Lines 11 and 12 compare the benchmark assumption for the payroll tax (line 11) with one which assigns the entire burden to the wage earner (line 12). It appears that the difference is of minor importance only.

In the final part of the table, we compare the overall pattern of the benchmark case (line 13) with corresponding patterns which result if the most progressive (line 14) and least progressive (line 15) assumptions are used. After having gone over the incidence analysis of the following four chapters, readers may wish to construct what they themselves take to be the most likely combination.

Limitations   Before leaving this survey of tax-burden distribution, some of its shortcomings should be noted:

1. We find that for some taxes the distributional conclusions depend crucially on what incidence hypothesis is chosen.

2. The precise distribution series needed to implement the particular hypothesis may not be available. Thus, the distribution of corporate-source income (which includes retained earnings) must be approximated by the distribution of dividend income.

3. The argument rests on the simplifying assumption that the distribution of earnings before tax will be the same with different taxes. In fact, the distribution of earnings may change in response to changes in the tax structure.[13]

4. The analysis as pictured in Table 12-1 views the problem in terms of absolute incidence and overlooks the difficulties which we have shown to underlie this approach.[14] This difficulty, however, is less serious in Table 12-4, where net benefits or burdens are considered and the problem is viewed in terms of budget incidence.

Having noted these difficulties, it nevertheless remains useful to attempt an estimate of burden distribution. The issue being of such interest and importance to policy makers, the economists can hardly plead complete ignorance in the matter. While the incidence problem is exceedingly complex, as will appear in the following chapters, some hypotheses are more reasonable than others, and even an informed guess at the resulting burden distribution is of some value. In the course of time, it may be hoped that estimating procedures and econometric models will become capable of giving more definite answers.

Distribution of Expenditure Benefits

Estimating the distribution of expenditure benefits is similar in some respects to estimating the distribution of tax burdens, but it is more difficult in other respects.[15]

Types of Expenditures   In allocating expenditure benefits, we distinguish among (1) goods and service expenditures which permit direct allocation, (2) transfer payments which by their nature lend themselves to allocation, and (3) goods and services expenditures which do not permit direct allocation. It appears that at the the federal level, about 40 percent of total expenditures for

---

[13]For a critique along these lines, see A. P. Prest, "Statistical Calculations of Tax Burdens," *Economica*, August 1955.

[14]The data provided in Table 12-1 will permit the reader to restate the results in terms of differential incidence, where the prevailing system is compared with the burden distribution under a proportional income tax. As indicated in line 17 of the table, the burden under a proportional tax equals 33 percent in each bracket, i.e., the ratio applicable to the group as a whole. The differential rate for each bracket is then obtained as the recorded rate in line 17 minus 33.0. We find the differential rate slightly negative at the bottom, around zero over the middle range, and positive at the upper end, in line with the previously recorded pattern of effective rates.

[15]Note that we consider only the distribution of benefits from the provision of public services, but not the changes in earnings which may result as production for public use is substituted for production for private use.

1968 lend themselves to direct allocation, with national defense the major item in the other group. At the state and local levels, the share is over 70 percent, and for all levels combined, it equals somewhat less than 50 percent.

Specific Benefits Estimated benefit allocations for certain expenditure categories are shown in lines 1 to 7 of Table 12-3 for the federal level and in lines 9 to 13 for the state and local levels. In making these allocations, it has been assumed that costs incurred on behalf of various groups reflect the value of benefits received.[16] Thus, benefits from education are allocated among households by the distribution of students. In the case of highways, expenditures are divided in line with consumer and business use of facilities. The former are allocated according to household expenditures on automotive products, while the latter, by reducing business costs, are assumed to be passed forward to the consumer. Interest payments are imputed to the holders of public debt with payments to banks imputed to holders of bank shares. Transfers are treated as negative taxes and are assumed to stay put with the recipients.

As shown in lines 6 and 13, the benefit rate from allocated expenditure categories (except for the extreme brackets) falls as income rises, this being so at both the federal and the state and local levels. In the case of transfer payments (lines 7 and 14), much of the highest benefit rate applies in the lowest bracket; then it drops off sharply to the second bracket and continues to decline thereafter. This of course reflects the fact that such payments are largely composed of old-age pensions and welfare payments. Lines 16 to 18 show the picture for all levels combined. Once more the pattern is heavily pro–low income. Indeed, the low-income advantage is much more pronounced in the pattern of benefit distribution than was previously noted for the relative position of low incomes in the tax-burden distribution.

Total Benefits Unfortunately, not all expenditures lend themselves to an attempt at specific allocation. Defense in particular is in this category, but expenditures going to sustain the general cost of government are also difficult to impute. To complete the picture (and to permit an estimation of net benefits as considered in the next section), lines 19 to 21 show distributions of total benefits, but under three alternative assumptions. Variant A postulates that such general benefits are distributed in line with total family income; variant B allocates such benefits in line with tax burdens; and variant C uses a per capita distribution. The latter, of course, results in the most favorable pattern for the low-income groups. However, in all cases the overall benefit rate declines as we move up the income scale. We also note that the benefit rate in the bottom brackets is substantially above 100 percent, meaning that benefits from public expenditures are considerably larger than are earnings.

---

[16] A complete analysis of expenditure incidence would have to allow for such changes as well. We are thus not attempting to measure the true value received by any one group, e.g., we do not measure the rate of return which various students will receive from their education, nor do we allow for differences in education costs among locations.

TABLE 12-3
Distribution of Expenditure Benefits
(Benefits as Percentage of Total Family Income)

			SELECTED INCOME BRACKETS*					
		Under $4,000	$4,000–$5,700	$5,700–$7,900	$7,900–$10,400	$12,500–$17,500	$35,500–$92,000	All
I. SPECIFIC BENEFIT ALLOCATIONS								
Federal								
1. Purchases:	Education	0.6	1.1	1.1	1.0	0.6	0.2	0.6
2.	Interest	2.1	2.0	1.2	0.6	0.8	2.3	1.5
3.	Highways	0.6	0.8	0.9	0.8	0.7	0.2	0.6
4.	Agriculture	†	0.2	0.3	0.4	0.4	2.6	0.7
5.	Medical	1.9	1.8	1.0	0.5	0.2	†	0.4
6.	Total	5.2	5.9	4.5	3.3	2.6	5.3	3.8
7. Transfers		78.3	19.8	8.8	4.3	2.1	0.2	6.2
8. Total		83.5	25.7	13.3	7.6	4.7	5.5	10.0
State and Local								
9. Purchases:	Education	5.5	9.9	10.4	8.7	5.4	1.5	5.2
10.	Interest	0.1	0.1	†	†	†	0.1	†
11.	Highways	1.2	1.6	1.9	1.8	1.5	0.5	1.3
12.	Medical	5.7	5.6	2.9	1.5	0.5	0.1	1.1
13.	Total	12.5	17.2	15.2	12.0	7.4	2.2	7.7
14. Transfers		14.5	1.6	0.6	0.2	†	†	0.7
15. Total		27.1	18.7	15.8	12.2	7.4	2.2	8.4
All Levels								
16. Purchases		17.8	23.0	19.7	15.3	10.0	7.5	11.5
17. Transfers		92.8	21.4	9.4	4.5	2.1	0.2	6.9
18. Total		110.6	44.4	29.1	19.8	12.1	7.7	18.4
II. TOTAL BENEFIT ALLOCATION								
All Levels								
19. Variant A		127.3	61.1	45.8	36.5	28.8	24.4	35.1
20. Variant B		123.7	58.9	45.2	36.3	29.2	24.5	35.1
21. Variant C		180.4	77.0	57.9	40.8	26.2	12.3	35.1

*See note to Table 12-1.
†Less than 0.05 percent.
Notes:
Lines 2 and 10: Interest is included here under purchases although, according to national income accounts, it should appear as a separate category.
Lines 19, 20, 21: For explanation, see text.

Benefit Evaluation   In the preceding illustration, benefits have been distributed in line with estimated expenditures made or costs undertaken on behalf of various income groups. Alternatively, benefits might be measured in line with the value at which public services are assessed by the recipient, i.e., for what he or she would be willing to pay for them. Since the marginal utility of income is lower at higher levels of income, recipients with higher incomes would be willing to pay more. Estimating benefits on this basis, the resulting benefit distribution becomes more favorable to higher income groups than shown in our estimates.[17] However, this reasoning applies to public services only and not to transfers. It thus leaves unaffected the expenditure component which is responsible for the heavy concentration of benefits at the lower end of the income scale.

Net Residue

We may now put the two sides together and consider the fiscal residue or net benefit (or burden) which the entire fiscal system imposes at various points in the family income scale. This gives an approximate picture of budget incidence as applied to the entire budget. In proceeding to this final stage, one is confronted with this dilemma: If we limit the netting-out to the more meaningful part of the benefit analysis, which covers only those expenditures for which specific benefit allocations are feasible, an arbitrary judgment must be made in deciding just what part of the total tax bill should be charged against these particular expenditures. Yet, if the entire tax bill is to be used, total expenditures (including those for which benefits must be allocated more or less arbitrarily) must be included.[18] Neither choice is satisfactory, yet it *is* of interest to obtain an impression of the overall distributional impact of the fiscal structure.

The residues shown in lines 1, 4, and 7 of Table 12-4 are based on the assumption that each expenditure dollar for programs subject to specific allocation is financed by an average tax dollar. The allocation of general benefits shown in lines 2, 5, and 8 corresponds to variant A in Table 12-3, it being assumed that such benefits accrue in proportion to income. The picture, also repeated in Figure 12-3, shows a positive net residue at the lower end of the income scale. Moving up the scale, the net residue falls sharply and becomes negative. For the 1968 data, the breakeven point at the federal level occurs around $8,000, while that for the state and local level is somewhat higher, placing that for the system as a whole at around $10,000. As noted before, the nominal levels of revenue expenditures and per capita income have about doubled since then, so that the current breakeven points might be about twice these amounts. It may be noted that the breakeven point falls close to the midpoint of the income scale, a finding which fits nicely into our earlier discussion of fiscal politics and the median voter.[19]

Scope of Redistribution

Another way of viewing the overall aspect of fiscal redistribution is in terms of Table 12-5, which shows the estimated distribution of income among families before and after fiscal intervention. Line 1 gives the distribution of

[17]See H. Aaron and M. McGuire, "Public Goods and Income Distribution," *Econometrica*, April 1970.

[18]Another difficulty arises in the case of deficit finance. However, for the year examined here (1968), budgets were approximately in balance.

[19]For other comparisons of income distribution before tax with distributions after federal individual income tax (but not allowing for other taxes), see E. C. Budd, *Inequality and Poverty*, New York: Norton, 1967. For annual comparisons up to 1964, see U.S. Department of Commerce, *Survey of Current Business*, April 1964, p. 98.

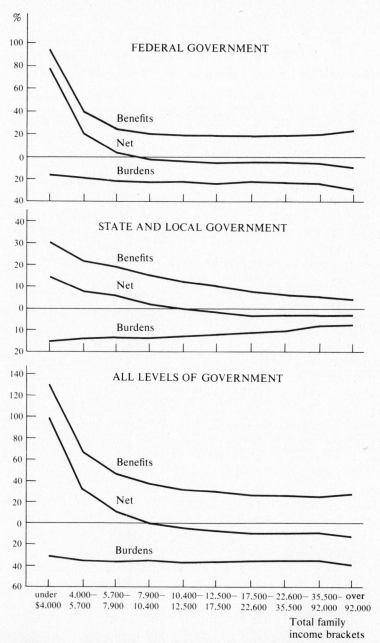

FIGURE 12-3 Tax Burdens and Expenditure Benefits as a Percentage of Total Family Income.

Notes: For *federal* pattern, burdens are based on line 6, Table 12-1; net curve is based on line 3, Table 12-4; and benefits equal line 3, Table 12-4, minus line 6, Table 12-1. For *state and local* pattern, burdens are based on line 15, Table 12-1; net curve is based on line 6, Table 12-4; and benefits equal line 6, Table 12-4, minus line 15, Table 12-1. For *all levels* of government, burdens are based on line 17, Table 12-1; benefits are based on line 19, Table 12-3; and net curve equals line 19, Table 12-3, minus line 17, Table 12-1.

TABLE 12-4
Distribution of Net Benefits and Burdens
(Net as Percentage of Total Family Income)

					INCOME BRACKETS*					
	Under $4,000	$4,000–$5,700	$5,700–$7,900	$7,900–$10,400	$10,400–$12,500	$12,500–$17,500	$17,500–$22,600	$22,600–$35,500	$35,500–$92,000	$92,000 and over
Federal										
1. Specific allocation	76.7	17.7	4.1	−1.9	−4.2	−5.6	−5.6	−5.1	−5.1	−5.1
2. General, variant A	4.3	2.7	1.0	0.7	0.6	−0.4	−0.1	−0.6	−1.0	−3.6
3. Total	81.0	20.5	5.1	−1.3	−3.6	−6.0	−5.6	−5.7	−6.1	−8.7
State and Local										
4. Specific allocation	15.7	8.2	5.9	2.7	0.2	−1.4	−3.2	−3.7	−3.4	−4.4
5. General, variant A	−1.1	−0.8	−0.6	−0.5	−0.3	−0.1	0.2	0.4	1.1	1.2
6. Total	14.6	7.4	5.4	2.2	−0.1	−1.5	−3.0	−3.2	−2.3	−3.2
All Levels										
7. Specific allocation	92.4	25.9	10.0	0.8	−4.0	−7.0	−8.8	−8.7	−8.5	−9.5
8. General, variant A	3.2	1.9	0.4	0.2	0.3	−0.5	0.1	−0.2	0.1	−2.4
9. Total	95.6	27.9	10.5	0.9	−3.7	−7.4	−8.6	−8.9	−8.4	−11.9

*See note to Table 12-1
Note:
Lines 2, 5, and 8: General expenditures are allocated in proportion to family income levels and tax distributions, as in Table 12-1.

TABLE 12-5
Distributional Aspects of Fiscal System, 1968

	QUARTILES RANKED BY INCOME				
	Lowest 25%	Next 25%	Next 25%	Highest 25%	All
1. Income including transfers	6.4	14.9	26.2	52.5	100
2. Taxes	5.8	14.7	26.5	53.0	100
3. Income minus taxes	6.6	15.4	26.0	52.0	100
4. Transfers	56.2	21.0	11.8	11.0	100
5. Income minus transfers	1.9	15.1	28.0	55.0	100

Note: All taxes and levels of government are included.
Source: See Tables 12-1 and 12-3 and the discussions thereof in the text.

income (including government transfers) before tax. Line 2 shows the distribution of tax liabilities (including all taxes), and line 3 gives the resulting distribution of family income minus taxes. The higher quartiles pay a larger share of taxes but also receive a larger share of income, and comparison shows the distribution of tax burdens to be quite similar to that of income, reflecting the essentially proportional nature of the tax structure. It is not surprising, therefore, that the distribution of after-tax income (line 3) is only very slightly more equal than that of income before tax (line 1).[20] Measuring the resulting changes in distribution in line with Figure 12-1, we find the coefficient of inequality to be changed only very slightly.[21]

A comparison of lines 1 and 3 is not, however, a sufficient basis on which to evaluate the significance of fiscal redistribution. To obtain a more complete picture, the expenditure side must also be considered; and as we have just noted, the expenditure distribution is more pro-poor than the tax distribution is anti-rich. For this purpose, we compare the actual (postfiscal) distribution of line 3 with the distribution of income before fiscal transactions. The latter distribution is obtained by reducing family income by transfer payments. Since the distribution of transfer payments (line 4) is highly pro-poor, the distribution of income net of transfer payments (line 5) is more unequal than that of total income (line 1). Comparison of lines 3 and 5 is the most significant one to consider. It shows the operation of the fiscal system to result in a sharp increase in the share received by the lowest quartile and some decrease in that of the top quartile, but there is little change in the rest of the distribution. This reflects a previously noted view of the distribution problem which focuses on the position of the lower end of the scale rather than on the pattern of distribution in general.[22]

[20]See p. 267.
[21]In similar estimates by Joseph A. Pechman and Benjamin A. Okner, inequality as measured by the pretax ratio of areas $OABO/OBC$ in Fig. 12-1 equals 0.43, while the after-tax ratio $OA'BO/OBC$ equals about 0.42. See Joseph A. Pechman and Benjamin A. Okner, *Who Bears the Tax Burden?* Washington: Brookings, 1974, p. 56.
[22]See p. 96.

Conclusion

It is evident that the difficulties involved in estimating the distribution of tax burdens and expenditure benefits are very great and that the results shown here must not be taken as the final truth. The difficulties in allocating burdens and benefits by income brackets must be kept in mind. Moreover, there is some question of how meaningful it is to consider a burden pattern which in fact compares an average taxpayer in one income bracket with an average taxpayer in another. There are few average people and the position of individuals within each bracket is dispersed. This problem is serious enough if one takes a separate view of burdens and benefits, with benefits in particular tending to accrue in line with certain characteristics (such as age, employment, and location), not all of which can be shared by the "average" household. The difficulty is greatly compounded if both sides are combined and net benefits are considered. Low-income households which pay payroll tax are typically not recipients of welfare payments or retirement pensions, while others which receive such payments do not pay tax. Thus, the first group may incur a heavy net burden, while the second receives benefits at a rate much in excess of that shown to apply for the average household in the bracket. For these reasons, a more disaggregated approach, in which consideration is given to the position of various subgroups in each bracket, may be in order; or it may be desirable to consider the net pattern for a longer period than a year, say, a lifetime. The problem is obviously a complex one in both conceptual and empirical terms. Yet the need for a global view of the distributional impact of the fiscal system is also evident. Consideration of the tax side only, such as has been the traditional approach, leaves us with a biased picture. In the end, it is fiscal rather than tax equity that matters, and both sides of the budget must be accounted for.

E. SUMMARY

Various concepts of incidence were considered and the following distinctions were drawn:

    1. Statutory incidence differs from economic incidence, and it is the latter that matters.

    2. The opportunity cost of resource transfer to public use, associated with an increase in public services, imposes a burden on consumers as a group as resources are withdrawn from private use. This transfer is to be distinguished from redistribution among consumers which arises in the case of tax-financed transfers or tax substitutions.

    3. Owing to efficiency costs, employment, and output effects, the tax burden may exceed the revenue gain.

    4. Budget incidence allows for distributional effects of both tax and expenditure policies.

    5. In formulating the problem of tax incidence, the differential approach is most useful.

The problem of incidence deals with the effects of fiscal operations on the distribution of real income among households:

6. This problem involves taxation effects on both the sources and uses side of the household account.

7. Distributional changes which result are viewed primarily in terms of distribution among income brackets, but other groupings may also be considered.

8. An overall measure of incidence may be derived by observing the resulting change in the coefficient of inequality.

9. Taxes may be grouped as direct or indirect, and as *in rem* or personal. The latter distinction is most important.

A survey of the estimated distribution of tax burdens and expenditure benefits in the United States fiscal structure shows the following:

10. The income tax is the major progressive element in the tax structure, just as the payroll tax is the major regressive element. Sales taxes tend to be regressive. The roles of the corporation income tax and of the property tax greatly depend on the shifting assumption which is applied.

11. The distribution of the federal tax burden is progressive, while that of state and local taxes tends to be regressive.

12. Burden distribution for the tax system as a whole is proportional over the larger part of the income range.

13. The distribution of benefits is strongly pro-poor, owing to the role of transfer payments, especially at the federal level.

14. The resulting distribution of net benefits is distinctly pro-poor, but more or less proportional over the remainder of the income range.

FURTHER READINGS

Hansen, Bent: *The Economic Theory of Fiscal Policy*, London: G. Allen, 1958, chap. 5.

Hicks, Ursula K.: "The Terminology of Tax Analysis," *Economic Journal*, March 1956.

Musgrave, Richard A.: *The Theory of Public Finance*, New York: McGraw-Hill, 1959, chap. 10.

Pechman, J. A., and B. A. Okner: *Who Bears the Tax Burden?* Washington: Brookings, 1974.

Chapter 13

Principles of Tax Incidence*

A. Partial Equilibrium View of Product Taxes: *Responses to Unit and Ad Valorem Tax; Role of Demand and Supply Elasticities; Division of Burden; Coverage and Time Period; Adjustment under Monopoly; Tax on Seller versus Tax on Buyer.* **B. Partial Equilibrium View of Factor Taxes:** *Adjustments in Price and Quantity; Demand and Supply Elasticities; Burden Distribution; Adjustments in Imperfect Markets.* **C. Incidence in General Equilibrium:** *Product Taxes; Factor Taxes; Selective Taxes on Capital Income; Adjustments in Imperfect Markets.* **D. Summary.**

The incidence or burden distribution of a tax will depend on how it is imposed, what rate structure is used, how the base is defined, and how general is its coverage. All this determines statutory incidence, but it is only the beginning. In the end, economic incidence will depend on how the economy responds. This response depends on conditions of demand and supply, the structure of markets, and the time period allowed for adjustments to occur. Adjustments to a tax will cause factor and product prices to change,

Readers' Guide to Chapter 13: This chapter lays out the principles of tax incidence. Sections A and B give a partial equilibrium view of product and factor taxes, while section C considers incidence in a general equilibrium setting. For most of the discussion, we assume perfectly competitive markets to prevail. Further discussion of incidence will be found in the tax chapters of Part Four.

and these changes will affect households from both the sources and uses sides of their accounts, thus determining the burden distribution among them. The final outcome depends on the interaction of these changes in a general equilibrium system. The task of incidence theory, as of any economic theory, is to cut through these complex forces and to identify the strategic elements in each case. We begin with a partial equilibrium view and consider the responses of sellers and buyers in the particular market in which the tax is imposed. Thereafter we turn to a more complex general equilibrium setting where repercussions in other product and factor markets are taken into account.

A. PARTIAL EQUILIBRIUM VIEW OF PRODUCT TAXES

A product tax may be imposed per unit of product, in which case it is referred to as a "unit tax." State taxes on gasoline, cigarettes, and liquor and the federal tax of 49 cents per barrel of beer illustrate this type. Alternatively, the product tax may be imposed as a percentage of price, in which case it is referred to as an "ad valorem tax." The federal tax on firearms, imposed at 10 percent of manufacturer's price, illustrates this type. General product or "sales taxes" are necessarily of the ad valorem form, with a uniform rate applied to a wide range of products.

Responses to Unit and Ad Valorem Tax

Figure 13-1 shows introduction of a tax into a competitive product market. *SS* is the supply schedule prior to tax and *DD* is the demand schedule. Price equals *OB* and output equals *OC*.

Unit Tax   Beginning with Case I, a tax of u per unit is imposed. The tax enters as a wedge between the market price which sellers get and the net price

FIGURE 13-1   Adjustment to Unit and Ad Valorem Tax.

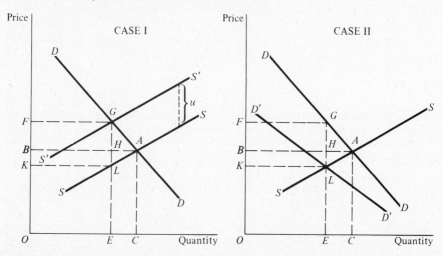

which they keep. Since sellers are interested in the net price, they must now charge a higher market price to cover their cost. The supply schedule which confronts buyers therefore rises from SS to $S'S'$, the vertical distance between the two schedules being equal to u. Buyers purchase less and quantity falls to OE, given by the intersection of DD with $S'S'$. Market price rises to OF and the net price to sellers falls to OK. Since in this example the product is produced under conditions of increasing cost, the net price falls as quantity declines. Because of this, the market price rises by less than the tax. Thus, at the new quantity OE, the market price has risen by BF whereas the tax per unit of output equals KF.

Ad Valorem Tax   Imposition of an ad valorem tax is shown in Case II of Figure 13-1. The tax again forms a wedge between the gross or market price paid by the buyer and the net price received by the seller. As seen by the seller, the tax results in a downward shift of the demand schedule. Unlike the parallel shift of the unit tax case, the shift now takes the form of a swivel from DD to $D'D'$, with the amount of tax per unit falling as the quantity sold rises.[1] The rate of ad valorem tax, commonly expressed as the ratio of tax to net price kept by the seller, equals GL/EL.[2] The new equilibrium is at the intersection of SS and $D'D'$, the price paid by the buyer equals GE, and the net price received by the seller is LE. The amount of tax per unit is GL and revenue equals $KFGL$.

Note that the ad valorem rate in Case II is chosen so as to give the same yield as a unit tax of GL. For a given unit tax u, there is always an ad valorem rate t such that both give the same revenue. The relationship between the two rates, as may be seen from the diagram, depends on the supply and demand schedules.

Role of Demand and Supply Elasticities

As a tax is imposed on a particular item, its price will rise and the quantity bought or sold will decline. The magnitude of these changes will depend on the elasticities of supply and demand. Understanding of this rule is the first step in incidence analysis. The importance of demand and supply elasticities is shown in Figure 13-2, with a unit tax used for purposes of illustration. All cases begin in the same position and involve the same unit tax, but elasticities and hence the outcomes differ.

---

[1]Note that the unit tax in Case I of the figure was shown as a parallel shift in the supply schedule. This follows the usual form of presentation, but we might as well have recorded the tax as a parallel drop in the demand schedule. In the case of the ad valorem tax, the tax is a function of price and should therefore be recorded as affecting the demand schedule. Moreover, since the tax is now imposed as a *percent* of net price, the adjustment is reflected in a swivel rather than a parallel shift.

[2]See George P. Lephardt and T. Norman Van Cott, "Ad Valorem Tax Analysis versus Ad Valorem Tax," *Public Finance Quarterly*, April 1979. Alternatively, the ad valorem rate might be defined as GL/EG. The difference is a formal one only, since the net rate $t_n = GL/EL$ and the gross rate $t_g = GL/EG$ are related by $t_g = t_n/1 + t_n$.

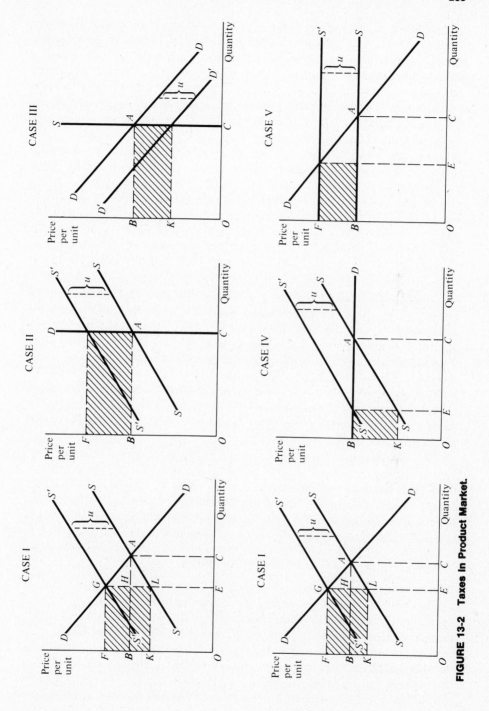

FIGURE 13-2 Taxes In Product Market.

Changes in Output and Price   Case I, with both demand and supply schedules elastic, shows price to rise less than the tax. In Case II, we assume a wholly inelastic demand schedule. As the supply schedule shifts up, quantity remains unchanged but the increase in market price by BF now equals the full amount of tax. In Case III, we take supply to be wholly inelastic. As a result, output and market price remain unchanged, but the net price falls by BK, the full amount of tax. In the lower row of diagrams, we begin again with Case I and then consider situations of infinitely elastic demand (Case IV) and infinitely elastic supply (Case V). With demand infinitely elastic, market price remains unchanged but quantity drops sharply to OE, with the net price falling to OK, i.e., by the amount of tax. In Case V, we once more have a situation where market price rises by the amount of tax, combined now with a fall in output to OE. We conclude (1) that the increase in price will be the larger, the less elastic is the demand and the more elastic the supply schedule; and (2) that the decrease in quantity will be the larger, the more elastic are both schedules.[3]

Revenue Response   Returning to Case I of Figure 13-2, we see that the revenue which the government obtains equals the product of unit tax $u = KF$ and quantity KL, or the shaded area $KFGL$. The magnitude of this revenue gain also depends on the elasticities of demand and supply. Moving from Case I to Cases II and III of the diagram shows that revenue increases as the DD and SS schedules become less elastic. Moving from Case I to Cases IV and V shows revenue to fall as the schedules become more elastic. This stands to reason since, with demand less elastic, it is more difficult for the buyer to avoid the tax by switching to other products, just as a less elastic supply makes this more difficult for the seller.

An increase in u thus pushes revenue in two directions. The effect is (1) to increase the amount of tax per unit sold and (2) to reduce the number of units sold. Revenue will increase as long as effect 1 outweighs effect 2. But sooner or later a point will be reached where effect 2 outweighs effect 1. If u is pushed beyond this point, revenue will decline. The level of u at which revenue is maximized again depends on the elasticity of demand and supply.[4]

Division of Burden

Returning to Case I of Figure 13-2, we may think of the tax burden $KFGL$ as divided between buyers and sellers, such that the buyer pays $BFGH$ and the seller contributes $KBHL$. The former reflects the additional amount which the buyers must pay for quantity OE, compared with what they would have paid at the old price. The latter, similarly, reflects the smaller amount which the sellers receive in net income for the sale of OE, compared with what they would have received before. As we shall see later, this is not a wholly satisfactory way of looking at tax burden and its division, since it disregards

---

[3]For further analysis of these relationships, see the appendix to Chap. 20.
[4]See pp. 99 and 468.

the problems of excess burden.[5] But it nevertheless suggests an interesting rule—namely, that the burden of the tax is divided between buyer and seller as the ratio of elasticity of supply to elasticity of demand in the relevant range of the demand and supply schedules.[6] Therefore, if you bought a product which now becomes subject to tax, you will be in a better position to avoid the tax and leave the seller with a larger part if your demand is elastic while the seller's supply is inelastic.

The burden borne by buyers affects households from the uses side of their accounts. The burden distribution will be progressive if the income elasticity of demand exceeds 1, i.e., if expenditure on the product as a percent of income rises when moving up the income scale. Taxes on luxuries will thus be progressive while those on necessities will be regressive. A general sales tax on all products will be regressive since consumption as a percentage of income falls when moving up the income scale.

To the extent that the burden falls on the seller, factor earnings are reduced and households are affected from the sources side of their accounts. Whether the tax will be progressive or regressive now depends on whether factor earnings generated in the production of the taxed product rise or fall as a percentage of income when moving up the scale. Thus, if the product requires highly skilled workers, the decline in earnings will be distributed progressively, whereas the opposite holds if unskilled labor is involved.

The net effect of a product tax involves both aspects, but the impact on the uses side is likely to be the key factor. This is the case since there is no systematic relation between the distribution in consumption of any particular product and the distribution of the factor earnings which it generates. Pending specific evidence to the contrary, it may thus be concluded that the burden distribution is dominated from the uses side, so that the burden of a tax on luxuries is distributed progressively while that of a tax on necessities is distributed regressively.

Coverage and Time Period

We have seen that a product tax tends to fall on the consumer if demand is inelastic while supply is elastic, and on the producer when the opposite holds. What determines which set of conditions applies?

Consumer economics tells us that the price elasticity of demand for a particular product depends on consumer preferences, i.e., their willingness to give up the consumption of a particular product for that of another. If a particular product is essential and if only a small part of the budget is spent

---

[5]See p. 303.

[6]By rotating DD and SS around A in Figure 13-2, Case I, it may be seen that the buyer's share in the burden increases as demand becomes less and supply becomes more elastic, i.e., the demand schedule steepens and the supply schedule flattens.

It may be shown that $B_b/B_s = E_s/E_d$, where B_b and B_s are the buyer's and seller's shares of the burden, respectively, E_s is the elasticity of supply, and E_d is the elasticity of demand. Thus, referring to Case I of Fig. 13-2, E_d over the relevant range equals $(EC/OC)(OB/BF)$, while E_s equals $(EC/OC)(OB/KB)$. We thus obtain E_s/E_d equal to BF/BK, where BF is the buyer's share and BK the seller's share.

thereon, price elasticity will be low. A tax on salt is likely to be borne by the consumer. Moreover, the price elasticity for a group of products (such as cars in general) will tend to be lower than for a particular item in that group (such as blue Pintos with air conditioning). The reason, of course, is that substitution is easier in the latter case. Selective taxes thus leave the consumer in a better position to avoid payment than do broad-based taxes.

A tax on Pintos can be avoided by buying some other car; a tax on cars in general can be avoided, if less conveniently, by taking buses or by flying; but a general sales tax can be avoided only by consuming less and saving. Another important feature is that elasticity increases with the length of the response period. Budget adjustments take time, since consumption habits do not change readily. The price elasticity of demand, therefore, will be higher and the consumer will be in a better position to avoid the tax in the long run than in the short run.

Parallel considerations apply to the elasticity of supply. Once more, supply can be changed more readily if only a minor change in product is involved. The production line can be retooled to produce Mustangs rather than Pintos, while it would be very difficult to shift to airplanes. Thus suppliers as well as buyers will find their ability to avoid tax to be greater if coverage is limited. The time factor similarly reappears on the supply side. Indeed, it is even more important here than for demand. Supply cannot readily be changed in the short run, unless inventories are available, since retooling may be needed and new machinery may have to be acquired. But substantial changes can be made over time.

Since both demand and supply become more elastic as the tax base is narrowed and more adjustment time is allowed, we cannot generalize who (sellers or buyers) will gain in the process.

Adjustment under Monopoly

Figures 13-1 and 13-2 have depicted competitive markets. Figure 13-3 shows the response to a product tax under monopoly using a unit tax for the purpose.[7] AR and MR are the average and marginal revenue schedules before tax, respectively, and MC is the marginal cost schedule. Output is at the intersection of MC and MR and equals OA, while price equals OB. As the unit tax of amount u is imposed, the MC schedule shifts up to MC'. Output falls to OC and the price rise BD falls short of the unit tax EH. Tax revenue equals $EHGF$. As in the competitive case, the resulting changes in output, price, and revenue depend on the elasticities of demand and supply. The adjustment differs, however, and it may be shown that output declines by less than under competition.[8]

Tax on Seller versus Tax on Buyer

Sales taxes are typically collected on the seller's side of the market, but given a competitive setting it is a matter of indifference which side of the counter is chosen.

---

[7]For the more complex case of the ad valorem tax, see p. 465.
[8]See p. 466.

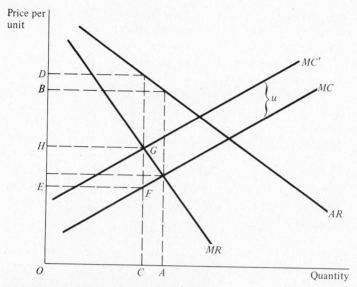

FIGURE 13-3   Unit Tax under Monopoly.

This is readily seen in the case of the unit tax. If the tax is fixed at 20 cents per gallon of gasoline, it is a matter of indifference if the seller, after charging 60 cents to the customer, passes 20 cents to the government; or if the buyer, after paying 40 cents to the seller, must pay an additional 20 cents in tax. This is shown in Figure 13-4 where the charge against the seller may be depicted as a shift of the gross supply schedule from SS to $S'S'$, whereas the charge against the buyer may be depicted as a shift in the net demand schedule from DD to $D'D'$. In both cases, equilibrium moves from E to E', market price rises from OB to OC, net price falls from OB to OD, and revenue equals $DCE'A$.[9]

The same holds for the case of an ad valorem tax. Since the tax is expressed as a percent of net price, it appears as a swivel in the demand schedule whether imposed on the buyer's or the seller's side of the market. Moreover, it will be a matter of indifference whether the tax is paid by the seller as a deduction from gross price or by the buyer as an addition to net price.[10]

B. PARTIAL EQUILIBRIUM VIEW OF FACTOR TAXES

Taxes imposed in the factor market typically apply to the sale of factor services, i.e., to the income which the factor service yields.[11] They take the

---

[9]See note 1, page 282.

[10]More specifically, the outcome will be the same if the same tax rate is applied to either the net supply price (i.e., seller's price before tax) or the net demand price (i.e., the buyer's price net of tax.).

[11]Instead of being imposed on income generated by selling the services of the factor, a tax may be applied to a sale of the factor itself. Thus, capital assets or land (though not workers!) may be sold. This, however, leaves the analysis essentially unchanged. See p. 481 for discussion of tax capitalization.

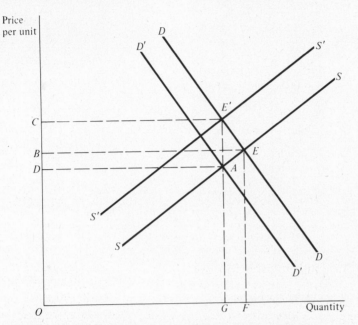

FIGURE 13-4 Equivalence of Tax on Seller and Tax on Buyer.

form of a percentage charge against such income and thus belong to the ad valorem family. As distinct from the case of product taxes, the tax rate is defined typically as a percentage charge against the gross (before-tax) income of the factor. As seen by factor suppliers, the factor tax appears as a downward swivel of the demand schedule for their services.[12]

Adjustments in Price and Quantity

The analysis is quite similar to that for product taxes.

Tax on Wage Income Case I of Figure 13-5 shows a tax on wage income in a competitive labor market. Quantity (hours worked) and price (wage rate) equal OC and OB, respectively. As a tax at rate LG/EG is imposed on wage income, the worker's net wage rate falls, thus swiveling the net demand schedule from DD to DD'. Since it is the net schedule that matters to the worker, the new equilibrium is at L, the intersection of DD' with the supply schedule SS. Hours worked fall from OC to OE, the gross wage rate rises from OB to OF, and the decline in the net wage or BK falls short of the tax per work-hour or KF.

Tax on Capital Income Figure 13-5 may also be interpreted as applying to other factor earnings, such as a tax on capital income. For this purpose, we need merely substitute the rate of return to capital for the wage rate, and capital employed for hours worked. The rest of the argument is the same.

---

[12]Once more the same result may be obtained by an equivalent rate tax imposed on the buyer. We then have a factor purchase tax.

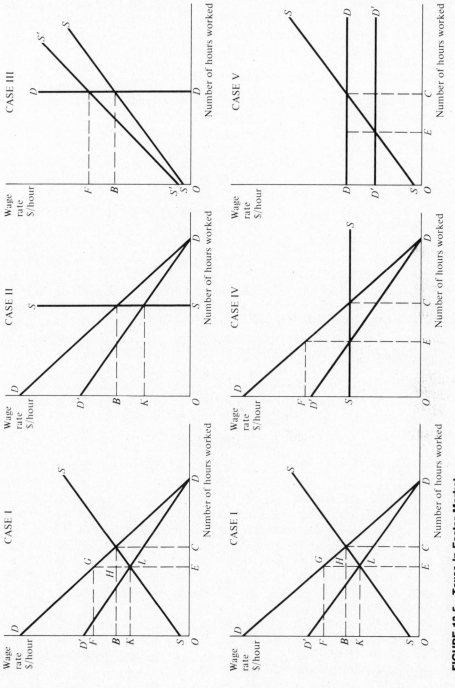

FIGURE 13-5   Taxes In Factor Market.

Tax on Rent of Land   A tax on income from land is pictured in Case II, where supply is fixed. With supply totally inelastic, income derived from land depends on demand only and is thus in the nature of economic rent. The entire burden of the tax therefore falls on the owner.

Demand and Supply Elasticities

As before, the outcome hinges on the elasticities of demand and supply, and similar rules apply. The seller (now the worker or investor) is in a better position to avoid the tax if supply is elastic while demand is inelastic, and the opposite holds for the buyer (now the employer or firm).

Supply and demand elasticities will again be larger if the tax is selective than if it is general. The personal income tax is a general tax, aimed at income from all employments of factors.[13] A worker cannot escape tax by moving from one employment to another, nor can investors by changing their investment. The burden, therefore, is likely to stay put with the payee. But the situation differs with the corporation tax, which applies to capital earnings in the corporate sector only. As we shall see presently, investors may avoid the tax by moving into a tax-free sector.

As in the case of the factor tax, adjustments cannot be made at once but take time. This is especially important with regard to the demand for capital. After a firm has acquired a plant or has put equipment in place, nothing can be done if income derived therefrom is taxed. Demand is wholly inelastic. The income from a sunk investment is in the nature of a "quasi-rent" and the firm must bear the tax. But as time passes, adjustments may be made. Outworn capital may not be replaced and previously planned expansions may be canceled. The supply of investment funds likewise is more flexible over the longer run as savings habits are sticky within a short period.

Burden Distribution

The primary impact of a tax on factor earnings is from the sources side of the household account. A flat-rate tax will thus impose a progressive burden distribution if earnings from the taxed factor rise as a percentage of income when moving up the income scale; and it will be regressive if the opposite holds. This tends to render a tax on wage income regressive, just as it tends to render a tax on capital income progressive. Such is the case because the wage share in income falls and the capital share rises when moving up the income scale. There is, however, an exception to this rule at the lower end of the scale, where capital earnings of the elderly and pensioners comprise a relatively large share of income.

Turning to the uses side, we see that a tax on factor earnings raises the prices of products which draw heavily on the taxed factor. This impact from the uses side will be progressive or regressive depending on whether these products are of the luxury or necessity variety. Such effects from the uses side may cushion or run counter to the burden impact from the sources side. A tax

---

[13]As we shall see later, the actual income tax is not as general as it should be. See Chap. 17, Sec. A.

on capital earnings, for instance, will be progressive from the sources side; but some capital-intensive products such as housing take up a larger share of low-income budgets, which may render the tax regressive from the uses side. Such offsets may occur, but barring special evidence to the contrary, it is reasonable once more to expect that there will be no systematic relationship between the distribution of earnings from a particular factor and the distribution of expenditures on the products into which the factor enters. This being the case, we may expect the impact from the sources side to be controlling.

Adjustments in Imperfect Markets

As with product taxes, the response to factor taxes differs, depending on the structure of the market in which the taxpayer operates. Given imperfect markets, our simple rule of burden division (related to elasticities of demand and supply) may no longer apply.

Tax on Wage Income   In a competitive labor market, wage rates are set by the intersection of the demand schedule (recording the marginal value product of labor) and the supply schedule (showing the minimum price at which various quantities of labor are forthcoming). With labor supply rather inelastic, a tax on wage income tends to be absorbed by labor. But matters become more complex if a realistic view is taken.

Wages in the modern economy are not determined in highly competitive markets. A large part of the wage structure is set by collective bargaining, and even wages in nonunionized sectors are influenced by wage rates in the unionized sectors. The question then arises whether the income tax on wage income may not enter into the bargaining decision. Will not the union be able to shift an increase in income tax by demanding higher pay, and will not the employer be able to pass on the cost of higher wages to the consumer?

Much as unions would like to react this way, the question is whether they can do so. The answer is "no" if all parties to the bargain behaved as maximizers prior to tax. Under these rules, unions and employers have already struck the best bargain which they were able to obtain, and imposition of the tax does not change this position. To alter the conclusion, one would have to assume that, prior to tax, unions had asked for less than they were able to obtain. If they had done so, union leaders, under pressure to protect take-home pay, might demand greater wage increases if tax and withholding rates were to rise. This does not seem to have been a major factor in the United States where unions traditionally respond to changes in the cost of living but not to tax-induced changes in take-home pay. Yet, such a response is not impossible. This is shown by countries such as Sweden, which engage in highly centralized collective bargaining and set wage rates as part of a general incomes policy. With income levels viewed in terms of after-tax wages, the income tax comes to be part of the overall wage settlement. Similarly, in the United Kingdom policy has recently traded income tax reduction against a promise of wage restraint, and comparable policies were proposed for consideration in the United States. Labor is to be encouraged to moderate wage demands by the promise of tax relief if wages lag behind prices.

Turning to the upper end of the income scale, we find the compensation of executives to be determined in a highly administered market. Both the general level of executive compensation and the salaries paid to executives at particular points in the business hierarchy are set in a market where the supply of, and demand for, such services are hard to distinguish and their contribution to output is not readily measured. The compensation pattern for executives depends upon custom and general status considerations rather than upon the precisely measured marginal productivity of their services. In such a market, tax changes may well be reflected in changes in compensation designed to maintain desired patterns of after-tax remuneration. While empirical evidence is difficult to interpret (owing in part to the tax-induced complexity of forms in which executive compensation is given), it would not be surprising to find that the spread of before-tax compensation has widened as tax rates have become more progressive.

Similar considerations hold for fees charged by professionals. At low levels of taxation, lawyers or surgeons may find it prudent to charge less than what the market will bear. But as tax rates are raised, they may compensate by making upward adjustments to their fees.

Payroll Tax Given perfect markets, we saw that it is a matter of indifference whether a tax is imposed on the buyer's or seller's side of the counter. This rule holds for taxes in the factor as well as in the product market. Given a perfectly competitive labor market, the division of the payroll tax between employer and employee contributions is thus a fiction, the outcome being precisely the same on whichever side of the market the tax is applied. Yet, as a matter of legislative intent, this sharing provision was introduced to "divide" the burden. While this leaves open the question of whether the employer's half was "meant" to fall on profits or on consumers, the intention was clearly to saddle employees with only one-half the contribution. Was this statutory division of rates mere stupidity or, as is frequently the fact when there are differences between theory and practice, are there other aspects to the problem which the preceding argument overlooks?

Raising the question is to point to the answer: Markets need not operate in a competitive fashion and real world responses may differ from the above model. If payroll taxes are increased, unions may accept an increase in the employer contribution without demanding a wage increase, but they will hardly agree to a reduction in their wage rate in order to offset an increase in the employer contribution. Firms, in turn, will not absorb the increase in *their* contribution in reduced profits, but will make it an occasion to raise prices. As a result, the employer contribution tends to be translated into a product tax with most of the burden falling on the consumer.[14]

[14]For further discussion, see p. 507.

Profits Tax   Finally, consider the case of a tax on capital income. In a competitive market, incidence will depend on the elasticities of demand and supply for capital services. How is the outcome changed if the services of capital are priced in an imperfectly competitive market?

At first sight, one would expect a firm which occupies a monopoly position in the product market to be better able to shift a tax on profit income than a firm which operates under competitive conditions. The competitor, after all, is a price taker, while the monopolist is a price setter. But closer consideration shows that the monopolist must absorb the tax. The reason is that the pure monopolist will have maximized profits prior to tax and hence can do no better after the tax is imposed. Since the tax is imposed so as to equal x percent of profits, the firm will remain best off by having the largest possible gross profits. With a tax rate of 46 percent, 54 percent of $100 million is better than 54 percent of $80 million. Therefore, the output and price which give maximum profits without tax will still be the best position after the tax is imposed. In other words, the monopolist finds the corporation's profits reduced by the tax and cannot pass it on to the consumer via higher prices and still remain a profit maximizer.[15]

But profit maximization of this type may not be a realistic interpretation of how firms behave. They may choose to exercise market power in different ways or follow different pricing rules.[16] As we shall see later, corporations may aim to maximize sales rather than output, or a combination of the two. Alternatively, potential monopolists may exercise restraint in setting price, aiming at a target rate of return rather than maximizing profits. Firms operating in an oligopolistic market may take a tax increase as a signal to raise price. Wage demands under collective bargaining may be made with reference to after-tax profits and thus be moderated by an increase in profits tax. In cases such as these, part of the tax may be passed on to consumers or wage earners rather than be absorbed by capital, with the adjustment process differing from that in the competitive setting.

C. INCIDENCE IN GENERAL EQUILIBRIUM

The preceding discussion makes a good start on incidence analysis, but it does not tell the entire story. The reason is that the analysis was limited to what happens in the particular market of the taxed item, and is therefore

---

[15]If TR is total revenue and TC is total cost, then profits, P, equal $TR - TC$. Profits are maximized at a level of output where $dP/dQ = 0$, i.e., where

$$[d(TR)]/dQ - [d(TC)]/dQ = 0, \text{ or MR} = \text{MC}$$

After imposition of a profits tax at rate t, the monopolist seeks to maximize $(1-t)(TR - TC)$. Differentiating this with respect to Q and setting equal to zero gives us

$$(1-t)\frac{d(TR)}{dQ} - (1-t)\frac{d(TC)}{dQ} = 0$$

Dividing by $(1-t)$ again leaves us with MR = MC. See also p. 427.

[16]For further discussion, see p. 428.

partial in nature. But the economy is an interdependent system in which all prices are related to each other. Changes in the price and quantity of one product or factor affect those of others. Households not directly involved in the taxed market may lose or gain, and those which are directly involved may become subject to further indirect effects.

Product Taxes

Returning to the case of perfectly competitive markets, we saw how imposition of a product tax leads to a rise in the price of the taxed product and to a decline in its quantity. Thereby consumers of the taxed product are burdened from the uses side, and suppliers from the sources side. Turning now to repercussions in other markets, we see that two further chains of adjustment result:

    1. As consumers buy less of the taxed product, the demand for other products is increased. Assuming production to be subject to increasing cost, this will raise their price, while lowering that of the taxed product. Thus, the burden from the uses side will be spread to consumers of other products.

    2. As the output mix changes, so does the demand for various factors of production. Suppose that the taxed product is highly capital-intensive, while products which are substituted for it are labor-intensive. Such substitution leads to an increase in the return to labor and a decrease in the return to capital. As a result, further effects from the earnings side come about.

Indeed, as the impact of the tax works its way through the general adjustment process, a chain of effects on both the uses and sources sides of household accounts will result, and there is no a priori way of predicting the end result. Nor do we, at the present state of the art, have econometric models which are sufficiently precise to predict the outcome. Must we then conclude that nothing can be said about incidence? Hopefully not. Reasoning in the partial equilibrium setting, we concluded with a strong presumption that the uses effect of product taxes is controlling, so that substitution of a tax on luxuries for a tax on necessities will render the tax structure more progressive, and vice versa. We argued that, unless there is specific evidence to the contrary, the burden pattern on the uses side will not be canceled out by indirect effects on the sources or earnings side. Allowing for the general equilibrium setting, it now has to be assumed further that secondary adjustments in other product and factor markets, being broadly diffused, will follow a more or less neutral pattern.

Factor Taxes

Similar considerations apply to factor taxes. The initial effect in the partial equilibrium setting was to reduce the net return to the taxed factor, thus burdening its suppliers from the sources side; and to raise the price of products into which the factor enters, thus burdening the consumers of these products from the uses side. Allowing now for repercussions in other factor and product markets, we see that these further adjustments occur:

1.   As the supply of the taxed factor falls off, the relative scarcity of other factors declines. As a result, their rates of return will fall. Thus, the impact on the earnings side, initially centered on the taxed factor, comes to be shared to some extent by other factors. An especially important aspect of this mechanism arises with the effects of capital taxes on capital accumulation, an aspect of tax incidence which we shall consider further later on.[17]

2.   As the prices of products which draw heavily upon the taxed factor rise, consumers will tend to substitute other products. Given conditions of increasing cost, the prices of such products will rise, thus spreading the burden impact from the uses side among a broader group of consumers.

Once more, these adjustments continue until they have worked themselves through the system and a new equilibrium is reached. As in the case of the product tax, there is no a priori way of predicting the precise outcome, but once more some hypotheses can be advanced. Reasoning in the partial equilibrium setting, we concluded that substitution of a tax on capital for a tax on labor income, or steepening the schedule of income tax rates, will render the burden distribution more progressive. The initial impact from the earnings side was not likely to be offset by changes from the uses side. Expanding this hypothesis to the general equilibrium setting, it may be assumed further that subsequent adjustments in other factor or product markets will not reverse this initial pattern.

Selective Taxes on Capital Income

We have noted that the elasticity of factor supply is higher if the tax is limited to selective uses of a factor, rather than applied generally to all its uses. There are two important instances of this in the United States tax system. One pertains to the corporation tax, which applies to the use of capital in the corporate sector only; the other involves the property tax, which is imposed at differential rates in various local jurisdictions.

Corporation Profits Tax   To simplify matters, we assume that the supply of capital to the economy as a whole is fixed, so that a national profits tax, applicable to all capital, would have to be absorbed by the recipients of capital income. But the corporation tax applies to capital invested in the corporate sector only, and this creates additional problems.

In the short run, the supply of capital to the corporate sector is fixed, and the burden falls on the owners of corporate shares. This is the case even though they may wish to sell the asset and transfer the investment to a tax-free industry. This conclusion follows since the owners cannot sell without accepting a lower price for the taxed asset, thereby bearing the full cost of the tax. Whatever they choose to do, the loss has been capitalized and is borne by the owner of the asset at the time the tax is imposed.

[17]See p. 687.

To illustrate tax capitalization, suppose that prior to tax, capital assets in sectors X and Y both yield an income stream of $10 per year. With an interest rate of 10 percent, both have a capital value of $100. Now let capital income originating in X be subject to a tax of 50 percent. The X assets will fall in value to $50 and their owners, if wishing to sell, will have to accept this reduced price. This is the case because the potential buyer will not invest in the taxed asset unless the rate of return net of tax matches that which can be obtained by purchasing a tax-free asset.

In the longer run, the flow of capital to the corporate sector is elastic. Since the tax applies to the corporate sector only, capital will move from the corporate to other sectors where the tax does not apply. As a result, output in the corporate sector will fall, and the *gross* rate of return on the remaining capital in the corporate sector will increase. The opposite development will take place in the tax-free sectors, with output increased and the rate of return to capital decreased. Assuming perfect capital markets with no obstruction to the movement of capital, this capital flow will continue until the net (after-tax) rate of return in the corporate sector equals the untaxed rate of return in the other sectors. The tax burden on corporate profits is thus spread to capital invested in the untaxed sectors. In the longer run, the burden is thereby shifted in part to capital invested in the untaxed sectors.

This is shown in Figure 13-6, where the two panels depict the two sectors respectively. Before the tax is imposed, schedule *CD* on the left-hand panel represents the marginal efficiency of capital in the corporate sector. It shows the various rates of return attached to different sizes of the capital stock invested in that sector. A similar schedule, *FG*, is shown on the right-hand panel for the other sector. Before tax, total capital is divided between the two sectors, with *OH* invested in X (the corporate sector) and *OM* invested in Y (the unincorporated sector), where *OH* plus *OM* equals the total capital stock. In this way, the return to capital in both sectors is equated at the margin and equals *OI*.

Now a tax on capital income originating in the corporate sector is imposed. The net return per unit of capital to investors in this sector now equals $(1-t)r$ where r is the gross rate of return and t the rate of tax. This schedule of net returns is represented by *ED* in the left panel. As a result, capital will move out of the taxed and into the tax-free sector where the rate of return to the investor is higher. This reallocation of capital continues until investment in the corporate sector falls to *OK*, where the net rate of return is *OP*. At the same time, investment in the unincorporated sector rises to *OL* and the rate of return falls to *OP*. Thus the *net* rates of return to the investor are equalized in both sectors. It is therefore evident that the tax burden on capital in the long run will be shared by investors in both the taxed and untaxed sectors. After an initial period during which the burden on capital falls on the owner of capital in the taxed sector only, this burden will eventually come to be shared by the owners of capital in both sectors.

Beyond this, the adjustment process may involve further changes from both the uses and sources sides. On the sources side, the shift in output from the corporate to the unincorporated sector may affect returns to labor as well

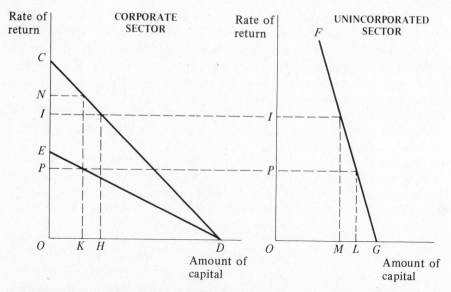

FIGURE 13-6   Tax on Capital Income from One Sector.

as to capital. Thus, if the output of the unincorporated sector is more labor-intensive, the return to labor will rise in the process and the burden on capital will be increased further.[18] On the uses side, consumers of products produced in the corporate sector will be burdened, since prices rise with falling supply. At the same time, consumers of products produced in the unincorporated sector will benefit, since such products will experience a relative decline in price. These subsequent effects, however, are not likely to overrule the progressive nature of the tax as reflected in its initial impact on the net return to capital.

Local Property Tax   Another illustration of a factor tax on selected uses only is given by the local property tax.[19] As we shall see later on, a tax on property may be viewed as analogous to a tax on the capital income which it

---

[18]See Arnold C. Harberger, "The Incidence of the Corporation Income Tax," *Journal of Political Economy*, June 1962; reprinted in Arnold C. Harberger, *Taxation and Welfare*, Boston: Little, Brown, 1974, pp. 135–162.

The problem is straightforward if production relationships in both sectors are such that substitution between capital and labor leaves factor shares unchanged, i.e., that the elasticity of substitution is unitary throughout. This is the widely used assumption made in the so-called Cobb-Douglas production function. The flow of capital from the taxed to the tax-free sector then leaves factor shares unchanged. Labor's net income is unaffected and the entire tax falls on capital. Harberger considers this to come fairly close to the actual situation.

Matters are more complex if the elasticities of substitution are other than unity. The burden on capital will then tend to be the greater (and that on labor the smaller), the lower is the elasticity of substitution between labor and capital in X as compared with that in Y. The burden on capital will also tend to be the larger, the lower is the elasticity of substitution in consumption of the two goods. These, however, are tendencies only. The various relationships are interwoven in a complex fashion and no simple conclusion emerges. Moreover, Harberger's analysis holds total factor supplies constant and, as noted in the text, the outcome changes further if factor supplies to the economy as a whole change.

[19]See p. 482.

generates. This is the case because the value of property reflects the capital-ized value of the income stream which is derived therefrom.[20] The property tax in the United States, however, is not imposed nationally but locally, and the rates of tax differ by jurisdictions. If jurisdiction X taxes at a rate of 2 percent while Y taxes at 4 percent, the differential of 2 percent reflects the extra tax imposed on earnings from capital in Y. As a result, capital will leave Y and move to X. Such movement will push up the gross (before-tax) rate of return in Y and lower that in X, with movement continuing until net rates of return are equated in both sectors. Note, however, that this applies only to mobile capital and not to land, since the latter cannot move. Thus, the part of the differential tax which applies to capital comes to be generalized in reducing returns to capital in both X and Y, whereas the part falling on land stays put with the owners of land in the high-tax jurisdiction.

Adjustments in Imperfect Markets

The preceding discussion of price and quantity adjustments in the general equilibrium setting has been based on the assumption of perfect markets. This assumption permits one to predict the nature of the adjustment process. Thus we can expect factors to move until net rates of return in all uses are equalized, we can expect factor prices to be in line with the value of their marginal products, and so forth. In the absence of perfect markets, mobility may be limited, returns may not be equalized, pricing may involve monopoly profits, and so on. Under such conditions, it is no longer possible to apply general rules of adjustment which permit one to predict the outcome. The assumption, therefore, tends to be made that although markets are not perfectly competitive, the adjustment process will generally push in the direction of the competitive model.

But though it is difficult to allow for market imperfections in dealing with the general adjustment process, such imperfections can be allowed for in assessing the initial response in the market where the tax applies, a response which will determine the direction of the general equilibrium adjustment that follows. Take the case of a profits tax as illustration: If the initial effect of the tax is to reduce the net rate of return, the general equilibrium response will operate through adjustments in saving and investment as it does with a tax on profit income. If the initial response is to pass the tax on to consumers in higher prices, the general equilibrium response will be through adjustments in consumption, as it will be with a sales tax.

D. SUMMARY

The task of incidence theory is to trace the final burden distribution of a tax. Beginning with the point of statutory impact, we first consider the responses of buyers and sellers in the particular market in which the tax is imposed and then trace its repercussions in other markets until the entire economy has

[20]See p. 481.

adjusted itself. This is a complex process, but certain general rules and conclusions can be reached.

Beginning with a product tax imposed in a competitive market, we concluded as follows:

1. Imposition of the tax raises price and lowers quantity.

2. A unit tax enters through a parallel upward shift in the supply schedule. An ad valorem tax enters through a downward swivel of the demand schedule.

3. The magnitudes of price and quantity changes depend on the elasticities of demand and supply.

4. The burden will be distributed between sellers and buyers in the ratio of elasticity of demand to that of supply.

5. Both schedules are more elastic for a selective than for a general tax, and both become more elastic if a longer period of adjustment is allowed for.

6. If the tax rate is raised beyond a certain point, revenue may decline.

7. Given a pair of equivalent rates, it does not matter on which side of the market the tax is imposed.

8. The distributional impact of a product tax (i.e., whether it is progressive or regressive) involves both the uses and sources sides of the household account. The former is likely to be decisive, leaving a tax on luxuries progressive and a tax on necessities regressive.

9. The resulting price increase will be dampened if the tax is imposed in a monopolistic market.

Turning now to taxes in factor markets, the tax typically applies to the sale of factor services and takes the form of an ad valorem tax.

10. The tax raises the gross rate of return to the factor, while reducing factor supply and lowering the net rate of return.

11. The magnitude of adjustment and distribution of the burden between sellers and buyers again depends on the elasticities of demand and supply.

12. Once more, households are affected from both the uses and the sources sides of their accounts, but the sources side now tends to be decisive.

13. A tax on capital income tends to be progressive, whereas a tax on wage income tends to be regressive.

14. The outcome may differ depending upon the structure of the market in which the tax applies. Incidence of a tax on wage income may be affected by collective bargaining. A tax on executive or professional incomes may be shifted to consumers due to administered pricing. While a profit-maximizing monopolist cannot shift a profits tax, shifting may occur under other forms of market behavior.

The preceding conclusions have been directed at responses in the immediate market to which the tax is applied. Allowing for broader repercussions in a general equilibrium setting, these additional effects arise:

15. As product X is taxed, its price rises and consumers tend to substitute purchases of product Y. As a result, the return to factors strategic to the

production of X will fall while that of other factors strategic to Y will rise. Thus effects from the earnings side are broadened into other markets. Similarly, increased demand for Y will tend to raise the price of Y, thus broadening the impact on the uses side to consumers of Y.

16. Similar considerations apply to a factor tax. A tax on factor X will tend to reduce its supply, which in turn will lower the returns obtained by factor Y, thus broadening effects from the earnings side.

17. Where a factor tax is limited to earnings in certain uses only, employment of the factor will tend to move to tax-free sectors until net rates of return are equalized. Thus the burden of the corporation profits tax is spread to capital employed outside the corporate sector. Similar considerations apply to local property tax differentials.

FURTHER READINGS

Break, George F.: "The Incidence and Effects of Taxation" in A. A. Blinder and R. M. Solow (eds.), *The Economics of Public Finance*, Washington: Brookings, 1976, pp. 112–129.

McLure, Charles E., Jr., and Wayne R. Thirsk: "A Simplified Exposition of the Harberger Model," *National Tax Journal*, March 1975.

Mieszkowski, Peter M.: "Tax Incidence Theory: The Effects of Taxes on the Distribution of Income," *Journal of Economic Literature*, December 1969, pp. 1105–1124.

For further references, see Chapters 16–23.

Chapter 14

Excess Burden and Efficiency*

A. Administration and Compliance Cost: *Administration Cost; Compliance Cost.* **B. Tax Distortions in Household Choices, Partial Equilibrium View:** *Choice among Products; Choice between Goods and Leisure; Choice between Present and Future Consumption; Maximum Yield and Efficiency Cost.* **C. Tax Distortions in Household Choices, General Equilibrium View:** *Conditions for Economic Efficiency; Choice among Products; Choice between Present and Future Consumption; Choice between Goods and Leisure.* **D. Efficiency Ranking of Taxes under Single and Multiple Choice. E. Optimal Income Tax Rates. F. Tax Distortions in Production:** *Partial Tax on Corporate Sector; Inter-jurisdictional Differentials.* **G. Magnitude of Excess Burdens. H. Further Aspects of Efficiency:** *Neutralizing Private Sector Distortions; Efficiency Aspects of Expenditure Policy.* **I. Tradeoff between Equity and Efficiency:** *Horizontal Equity; Vertical Equity.* **J. Summary.**

Having examined equity and the distribution of the tax burden, we now turn to our second requirement for a good tax structure, namely that the taxing

---

* Readers' Guide to Chapter 14: This chapter deals with the unpleasant proposition that the taxing process is costly. The burden placed on the economy exceeds what the government gets in revenue. In section A the straightforward problems of administration and compliance cost are considered. In section B we give an introduction to the more subtle problem of excess burden or efficiency cost. In sections C to E, excess burden is dealt with further. These sections will be of special interest to the theoretically inclined reader. Others may wish to proceed directly to section F.

process should be efficient. Tax administration should not be wasteful and compliance cost for the taxpayer should not be unnecessarily large. Moreover —and this is a more subtle point—the "excess burden" of taxation should be minimized. These two aspects will be considered in turn.

A. ADMINISTRATION AND COMPLIANCE COST

Economists have given little attention to the problem of administration and compliance costs, but they are an important issue in the operation of the fiscal system.

Administration Cost

Assessment and collection of taxes require personnel and equipment. This activity provides an important public service, and, like all public services, it should be provided efficiently. The desired quality of service should be offered at minimum cost. The cost of federal tax administration for the fiscal year 1979 was about $2 billion, or 1/2 cent per dollar of federal revenue. Obviously, this cost is subject to large economies of scale. Overhead costs can be spread among taxpayers and higher rates yield higher revenue without greatly adding to costs. At the same time, the cost of administration per dollar of revenue rises with the complexity of the tax law. Thus, income tax administration is more costly than that of the payroll tax. A head tax would be cheapest. Here, as elsewhere, quality is expensive. In setting criteria for efficient administration, these issues arise:

1. First, there is the choice of appropriate technologies and administrative procedures. In recent years, the Internal Revenue system has been increasingly computerized, which reduces cost and provides more detailed information. Nevertheless, it is impossible to check all returns in detail. Only a limited number of returns are audited carefully (in fact, less than 10 percent) and they have to be chosen so as to make enforcement most effective.

2. The question therefore is how far auditing and enforcement should be carried. Should it be carried to the point where at the margin an additional dollar of cost brings in less than a dollar of revenue? Hardly so, since the resource cost of administration is a social cost, whereas the revenue-expenditure process is a transfer between alternative resource uses. The marginal dollar of administration cost, therefore, has to be balanced against the value of more equitable administration.

3. As in all matters of legal rules, better compliance can be secured either by threatening a higher penalty if the offender is caught, or by spending more on enforcement so as to increase the probability of being caught. The former is cheaper than the latter, but is less acceptable on equity grounds.

4. Next, there is the question of how complex the tax structure should be. A head tax is cheaper to administer than a sales tax, and a sales tax is cheaper than an income tax. A tax on gross income is cheaper than one which attempts to determine net income, and so forth. As will become apparent in Part Four, an equitable tax system for a highly complex economy is itself inevitably complex. Yet such complexity increases administration and compliance costs. Once more a tradeoff is needed.

5.   Finally, it is evident that tax administration in a federal system is more costly than in a highly centralized system, since much of the administrative apparatus must be duplicated many times.

As this brief discussion suggests, tax administration and enforcement offer interesting problems in policy design and tradeoffs, not only for the administrator but also for the economist.

Compliance Cost

Compliance cost is substantially larger than administration cost. Of the 82 million income tax returns in 1975, 26 million used itemized deductions. Suppose that the average time spent on such returns is one to two days. Valued on the average at, say, $75, we arrive at a total of about $2 billion. For the 56 million returns which do not itemize, let us assume a cost of $25 per return or $1.4 billion. To be sure, the cost will be less for some and more for other taxpayers, especially if the costs of tax lawyers and advisers are allowed for. Compliance costs for the 2 million corporation tax returns may well add another $1 billion. In all, income tax compliance cost will surely be in excess of $5 billion. This is a significant amount and substantially above administration cost, but once more it must be evaluated in terms of what it buys. Our income tax system, as noted below, is based on declarations submitted by the taxpayer, in the hope that this will lead to more complete recording and a fairer base on which to determine tax liability. This procedure is costly for the taxpayer, but socially worthwhile if justified by a more equitable outcome. Policy once more must choose between equity considerations which may call for a more complex law, and the saving in compliance cost which goes with simplification.

B. TAX DISTORTIONS IN HOUSEHOLD CHOICES, PARTIAL EQUILIBRIUM VIEW

We now examine a second and more sophisticated aspect of tax efficiency. If you pay $1,000 in tax, the burden which this imposes on you may well be in excess of this amount. Unless imposed in the form of a lump-sum tax (i.e., a tax, such as a head tax, which is unrelated to economic activity), a tax interferes with economic decisions and distorts efficient choice. This distortion is burdensome to you, while being of no help to the Treasury. Efficient policy, therefore, should minimize this burden, referred to variously as excess burden, deadweight loss, or efficiency cost.

The most obvious way of avoiding this cost, of course, would be to obtain all revenue from a head tax, with everyone paying the same amount. This would avoid all excess burdens, but it would clearly be unacceptable on equity grounds. If taxes are to be related to ability to pay, they must be based on economic indices such as income, consumption, or wealth.[1] Equitable taxation, therefore, must be based on economic activity and as such inevit-

[1]See p. 242 for a discussion of such bases.

ably interferes with economic choices, thereby causing an excess burden. The task of tax policy, as we shall see shortly, is to reach a compromise solution which allows for both criteria. Among equally equitable taxes, the more efficient one should clearly be used; but a less efficient one may be preferable if the tradeoff between equity and efficiency so indicates.

Choice among Products

Taxes may affect household choices among various consumer goods, between present and future consumption (or saving), and between leisure and income (or goods). The problem is simpler and the efficiency implications of particular taxes can be seen more clearly if we assume that taxpayers are limited to one type of choice, while holding the others fixed. This assumption is, therefore, a good point of departure. Moreover, we look for the time being at the taxed item only, while disregarding other markets. We begin with distortions in the choice between two consumer products, X and Z, caused by a tax on X only, while assuming the division of income between present and future consumption and time allocation between work and leisure to be fixed. We return for this purpose to the concept of consumer surplus as applied in our earlier discussion of cost-benefit analysis.[2]

Figure 14-1 is a partial-equilibrium market demand and supply diagram for product X. The demand schedule for product X is shown as DD', while SS is the supply schedule. To simplify, we assume constant costs.[3] Beginning with Case I in Figure 14-1, the pretax equilibrium is at A, the price being OS and the quantity OC. Now a sales tax at rate $t = SS'/OS$ is imposed. The supply schedule rises to $S'S'$ and the new equilibrium is at G. The gross price (inclusive of tax) rises to OS' while output falls to OE and tax revenue equals $SS'GF$. Since we are dealing with a case of constant cost, consumers (in line with our earlier argument) bear the entire burden, defined as $SS'GF$ and equal to revenue. Whereas, prior to tax, they would have paid $OSFE$ for the amount OE, they must now pay $OS'GE$, the additional amount being $SS'GF$, or tax revenue.

This, however, is not a complete description of the consumer burden. Prior to tax, consumers paid $OSAC$ for amount OC, but would have been willing to pay $ODAC$.[4] Since, under competitive pricing, all units are priced at their marginal value, consumers received a "consumer surplus" equal to the difference between actual and potential payment, or SDA. Under the tax, their consumer surplus has been reduced to $S'DG$. They have thus suffered a loss of surplus equal to $SS'GA$. Of this, $SS'GF$ is offset by the government's revenue gain but the triangle FGA remains as a net loss or "excess burden" to the economy.

---

[2]See p. 171.

[3]See p. 464, where variable costs are allowed for.

[4]Under certain assumptions regarding the utility function, the demand schedule may be taken to measure the marginal value of consumption applicable to successive quantities. Adding the vertical blocks under the demand curve from O to C, we obtain the total utility derived from the consumption of OC or $ODAC$. The necessary assumption is that the marginal utility of income remains constant or changes by the same amount for an additional dollar of income change at any point on the income scale.

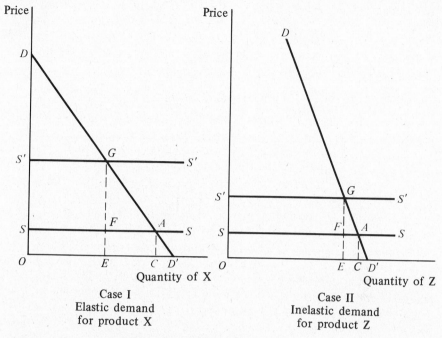

FIGURE 14-1   Excess Burden of an Excise Tax.

What determines the magnitude of this excess burden? For the constant cost case, the area of the triangle is approximated by $1/2(Et^2PQ)$, where P and Q are the pretax quantity and price respectively, E is the price elasticity of demand, and t is the ad valorem rate of tax.[5] As may be seen by rotating DD' around point A as pivot, the triangle FGA will become smaller as demand becomes less elastic (the DD' schedule becomes steeper) at point A (i.e., at any given initial P and Q). If demand is wholly inelastic, consumers do not adjust their purchases to price, and the tax cannot interfere with consumer choice. There will be no excess burden.

We may now compare the excess burden which results if the revenue is obtained from product X, the demand for which is elastic in the initial equilibrium, and from product Z (as in Case II), the demand schedule for which is inelastic. Pretax quantity and price are the same in both cases, but the tax rate SS'/OS needed to obtain revenue $SS'GF$ is less for Z than for X. We note that for Z, where demand is less elastic, the excess burden FGA is smaller. If the choice is between taxing X or Z, Z should therefore be chosen on efficiency grounds. More generally, the quality of a tax may be measured by the ratio of excess burden to revenue. For the constant cost case this equals $FGA/SFGS'$ in Case I of Figure 14-1 and may be expressed as

---

[5]The triangle FGA equals $1/2(\Delta P \Delta Q)$ where $\Delta P = FG$ and $\Delta Q = FA$. Given $t = \Delta P/P$ and $E = \Delta Q/Q \cdot P/\Delta P$, we substitute and obtain $1/2(Et^2PQ)$. Using a unit tax u, we obtain the measure $1/2(u^2E \cdot Q/P)$ where, in equilibrium, $u = tP$. See Arnold C. Harberger, *Taxation and Welfare*, Boston: Little, Brown, 1974, p. 35.

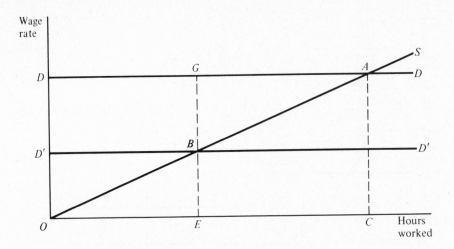

FIGURE 14-2   Excess Burden of Tax on Wage Income.

$\frac{1}{2}[tE/2(1-tE)]$. The quality of the tax thus depends on the elasticity of demand.[6] The larger that elasticity, the larger the excess burden and the poorer the quality of the tax.

Choice between Goods and Leisure

A similar analysis applies to the choice between goods and leisure. To focus on this aspect, we now assume that there is only one consumer good (a composite of goods X and Z) and once more take the choice between present and future consumption as fixed.

The resulting excess burden is now shown in Figure 14-2. Let OS be the supply schedule of labor and DD be the demand schedule. Pretax equilibrium is at A, while hours worked are OC and the wage rate is equal to OD. To simplify, we assume an infinitely elastic demand for labor, corresponding to Case V in Figure 13-5 in the previous chapter. As a tax on wage income is imposed at a rate $D'D/OD$, the net demand schedule drops down to $D'D'$. The new equilibrium is at B, with hours worked falling to OE and the net wage to OD'. Tax revenue equals $D'DGB$ and the entire burden is borne by workers.

Once more, this is not the entire story. Prior to imposition of the tax, hours OC were worked at a wage OD and total wages paid were $ODAC$. But workers would have been willing to offer their labor at a wage bill equal to OAC. ODA was thus a rent or supplier surplus. After tax, this surplus declines to $OD'B$. The decline in surplus thus equals $D'DAB$. Of this, $D'DGB$ is offset by the gain in revenue, leaving the triangle BGA as the net loss or excess burden. This burden will now be smaller, the less elastic is the supply schedule.

---

[6]With revenue equal to $tP(Q-\Delta Q)$ and excess burden equal to $\frac{1}{2}(Et^2PQ)$, the above result follows.

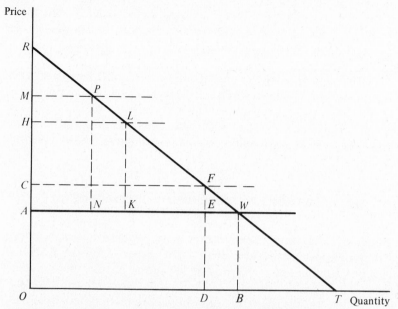

FIGURE 14-3   Maximum Tax Revenue under a Unit Sales Tax.

Choice between Present and Future Consumption

The argument may be repeated once more for the choice between present and future consumption. For this purpose, we now hold the choice between work and leisure fixed and deal with one product only. Returning to Figure 14-2, we relabel the horizontal axis to measure saving and the vertical axis to measure the rate of interest. Proceeding as before, the rectangle BGA reflects the excess of loss of saver's surplus over the revenue gain to the Treasury.

Maximum Yield and Efficiency Cost

As the rate of taxation is increased, the efficiency cost or excess burden also rises. But revenue may not follow suit. It must not be assumed that by setting a higher rate, we can increase revenue indefinitely. Rather, there is a rate level at which yield is at a maximum, so that a further increase in rates would be counterproductive.

This is shown in Figure 14-3 for the simple case of a unit tax imposed on a good produced at constant cost OA, although a similar argument applies to other taxes such as a tax on wage income. In the absence of tax, OA is the price and output is at OB. With a unit tax equal to AC, output equals OD, the price rises to OC, and tax revenue equals $ACFE$. As the tax is increased to AH, revenue changes to $AHLK$, and with a further increase in tax to AM, revenue equals $AMPN$. Tax revenue will be greatest where the excess of consumer expenditures over cost is at a maximum. This holds for unit tax AH and revenue equal to $AHLK$.[7] Moreover, as the tax is raised from AC to AH,

[7]See p. 468 where it was shown that (assuming constant cost) for revenue to be at the maximum, we must have $u=(a-c)/2$, where a is the intercept of the demand and c that of the supply schedule. Applied to Fig. 14-3, we obtain $u=(OR-OH)/2$, so that $u=AR/2=AH$.

the magnitude of the efficiency cost rises from *EFW* to *KLW*, but this is accompanied by the advantage of revenue gain. Pushing the tax beyond *AH* adds to efficiency cost while reducing revenue. It is therefore clearly a perverse policy.

Nor does it follow that the tax rate should be raised that far. An efficient tax system is one which obtains the needed revenue with a combination of taxes such that the marginal dollar derived from each tax imposes the same efficiency cost. Depending on the elasticities involved, this will leave the optimal rates of various taxes falling short of maximum yield to varying degrees.[8]

C. TAX DISTORTIONS IN HOUSEHOLD CHOICES, GENERAL EQUILIBRIUM VIEW

In the preceding discussion, the measure of excess burden was viewed in terms of loss of consumer surplus or of "rent" received by the worker or saver. This is a helpful way of looking at the problem, since the "triangle" which represents the excess burden lends itself to measurement.[9] We shall return to this later. But the preceding exposition once more suffers from being a partial equilibrium approach. A second and more general view of the problem will thus be helpful.

Conditions for Economic Efficiency

To understand how excess burdens arise, we return briefly to the conditions which must be met if resource allocation is to be efficient.

Economists consider an arrangement efficient if resources are used in a way which does not leave a possibility of alternative arrangements under which somebody could be better off without anyone being worse off. As discussed in Chapter 3, economic efficiency involves various requirements, including these conditions relating to choices between (1) alternative products, (2) income and leisure, and (3) present and future consumption:[10]

   1. The marginal rate of substitution (MRS) of any two products in consumption should be equal to their marginal rate of transformation (MRT) in production. Such will be the case in a competitive market where both rates are equal to the price ratio for the two products.[11] Thus,

$$\text{MRS of X for Z} = \text{MRT of X for Z} = P_x / P_z$$

where X and Z are two products.

---

[8]See the discussion of optimal taxation, p. 314.
[9]See also p. 204.
[10]See also p. 63.
[11]The MRS of X for Z is defined as the amount of Z which the consumer is willing to surrender for an additional amount of X. The MRT of X for Z is the amount by which the output of Z must be cut to produce an additional unit of X.

2. The marginal rate of substitution of leisure for goods (as expressing workers' preferences) should be equal to the marginal rate of transformation of leisure into goods (via work effort), with both rates in a competitive system equal to the wage rate. Thus,

$$\text{MRS of } L \text{ for } Y = \text{MRT of } L \text{ for } Y = w$$

where L is leisure, Y is income (or goods in general), and w is the price of leisure or the wage rate.

3. The marginal rate of substitution of future for present consumption (as valued by consumers or savers) should be equal to the marginal rate of transformation of present into future goods in production with both equal to $1/(1+i)$, where i is the rate of interest. Thus,

$$\text{MRS of } C_f \text{ for } C_p = \text{MRT of } C_f \text{ for } C_p = 1(1+i)$$

where C_f and C_p are future and present consumption and i is the return paid for postponing consumption or the rate of interest.

Whenever any of these conditions is not met, economic welfare can be improved by rearrangement designed to move toward it.[12]

The cause of excess burden may now be viewed in terms of interference with the cited efficiency conditions. Selective excises interfere with condition 1, a general consumption tax with condition 2, and a general income tax with both conditions 2 and 3.

Choice among Products

Distortions in product choice arising from a selective product tax are now shown in Figure 14-4, where the horizontal axis measures units of product X and the vertical axis measures units of product Z. AB is the price line, and the ratio of prices P_x/P_z equals OB/OA. Consider a consumer with income sufficient to purchase OB of good Z. The consumer can then allocate consumption between X and Z along the price line AB which is the opportunity locus. Given the consumer's preference pattern as expressed by indifference curves i_1, i_2, i_3, the choice will be combination E' since this places the

---

[12]This may be illustrated with regard to divergence from condition 1 as follows: Consumers will adjust their budget mix so that their marginal rate of substitution in consumption equals the price ratio. Let the price of good X equal $6 while that of good Z equals $3. The rate at which consumers are willing to substitute good X for good Z is therefore 2 (i.e., two units of Z for each unit of X), being equal to the ratio of the price of X to that of Z. Suppose, however, that the rate of transformation of X for Z in production is 3 (i.e., three units of Z must be given up to produce one additional unit of X). In this case, it will be efficient to produce and consume more of good Z and less of good X. This will be so because one additional unit of Z (worth 1/2 of X to the consumer) may be gained by giving up only 1/3 unit of X in production. The satisfaction derived from the additional units of Z exceeds that lost through the reduction in X. Hence, there will be a welfare gain. As more Z and less X are consumed, the marginal utility of Z falls while that of X increases, thus raising the marginal rate of substitution of X for Z in consumption. However, as production shifts toward Z, the marginal rate of transformation of X for Z in production tends to fall, thus contributing to the equalization process. The final result will yield a MRS, MRT, and price ratio all equal to somewhere between 2 and 3. This is the best possible position. See also the references given in footnote 5 p. 62.

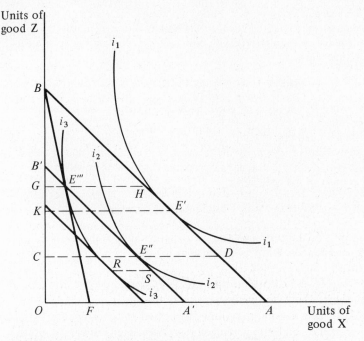

FIGURE 14-4   Adjustment to Selective and General Taxes.

consumer on the highest possible indifference curve i_1. At this point, the marginal rate of transformation in production, as given by the slope of the price line, equals the marginal rate of substitution in consumption, as given by the slope of the indifference curve.[13]

Now let a tax be imposed. Suppose first that the government uses a *head* or *lump-sum* tax, such that the liability is the same whatever the consumer's economic characteristics and response. As a result, the price line will shift to the left parallel to AB. Since relative prices are not affected, the slope of the price line remains unchanged. If tax equals AA' in terms of X or BB' in terms of Z, the consumer's new price line (opportunity locus) will be $A'B'$ and the new equilibrium will be at E''. The consumer now retains OC of Z, surrendering BC to obtain CE'' of X. $E''D$ is the government's revenue in terms of product X. As before, the equality of the marginal rate of substitution, the marginal rate of transformation, and the price ratio is maintained. Resources are allocated efficiently and there is no excess burden.[14]

Now suppose that the government obtains revenue $E''D$ by imposing a *general* tax on consumption. Applied at the same rate to X and Z, the tax

---

[13]For an explanation of indifference curves, see Jack Hirshleifer, *Price Theory and Applications*, Englewood Cliffs, N.J.: Prentice-Hall, 1976, chap. 3.

[14]The illustration of Fig. 14-4 is helpful but oversimplifies matters by disregarding the possibility that a change in output mix may result in a change in the slope of the original price line AB. This implies that government purchases the identical products which are released from the private sector and/or that the transformation schedule for X and Z is linear, i.e., that the MRT and therefore the price ratio are constant.

inserts the same wedge between the gross and net prices of both. The price line again moves to $A'B'$, being parallel to AB, with the tax rate equal to AA'/OA' or BB'/OB'. Equilibrium is once more at E''. The producer remains in equilibrium with the ratio of net prices equal to the marginal rate of transformation while the consumer's marginal rate of substitution equals the ratio of gross prices. Since the tax applies equally to both X and Z, the net and gross price ratios are the same and MRS = MRT.

The situation differs, however, with a *selective* tax, imposed on one product, say, X only. The tax now enters as a wedge between the net and the gross price of X, with no such wedge for Z. To be efficient, the ratio of the *net* price of X to the price of Z available to the producer must equal the MRT of X for Z in production, while the ratio of the *gross* prices of Z and X to the consumer must equal the MRS of X for Z in consumption. The two ratios are rendered unequal. Condition 1 is not met and inefficient allocation results.

Returning to Figure 14-4, the government, in order to obtain the same revenue $E''D$ from a tax on X only, must apply a rate equal to FA/OF.[15] The consumer now finds that P_x has risen relative to P_z so that $P_x/P_z = OB/OF$. The price line or opportunity locus swivels from BA to BF and the consumer now purchases less of X than he or she did under the general tax. The new equilibrium is at E'''. It will be seen that at E''' the slope of BF, or the MRS, exceeds that of $B'A'$ or the MRT. The consumer now surrenders BG of Z to purchase GE''' of X, while retaining OG of Z. Whereas E'' falls on i_2, E''' falls on the lower curve i_3.[16] The burden imposed on the taxpayer by a selective consumption tax is thus greater than that which would have resulted under a lump-sum tax providing equal revenue. It is the movement from i_2 to i_3 that reflects the excess burden.

To put the matter differently, the general tax has an "income effect" only, involving reduced purchases of both X and Z and a shift from E' to E''. The selective tax has in addition a "substitution effect," or replacement of X by Z because of the relative price change resulting in a shift from E'' to E'''. The burden reflected in the move from i_1 to i_2, as caused by the shift from E' to E'', is inevitable if revenue $A'A$ is to be raised. The further burden, referred to as "excess burden" (reflected in the move from i_2 to i_3), is caused by the shift from E'' to E''' and occurs with the selective tax only.

Choice between Present and Future Consumption

We now turn to tax effects on the choice between consumption and saving, while holding the other two choices (among consumer goods and between goods and leisure) constant.

---

[15]We know that the new equilibrium must fall on $B'A'$ since the government is to obtain the same revenue of $A'A$. To find the new price line BF, we therefore draw a line through B such that it is tangent to an indifference curve at its point of intersection with $B'A'$.

[16]This follows because (1) E''' lies northwest of E'', and (2) indifference curves cannot intersect. Point (1) holds because at E''', the marginal rate of substitution of X for Z in consumption must exceed the marginal rate of transformation in production, due to the tax wedge.

To consider this case, we relabel the horizontal axis of Figure 14-4 to show future consumption C_f and the vertical axis to measure present consumption C_p. OB equals present consumption available if all income is consumed, and OA equals future consumption available if all income is saved. Thus, OA equals $(1+i)OB$ where i is the rate of interest. BA thus represents all possible combinations of present and future consumption available to the individual, given his or her current income. Pretax equilibrium is at E'.

If a general consumption tax, applicable alike to C_p and C_f and yielding a revenue of AA', is imposed, the price line once more shifts, paralleling BA to $B'A'$, and the new equilibrium is at E''. Since both C_p and C_f are reduced at the same rate, relative prices are unchanged, the MRT and MRS of present for future consumption remain equal, and no excess burden results. The general consumption tax is now neutral and equivalent in its excess-burden aspects to a lump-sum tax.

An income tax, however, reduces the ratio C_f/C_p, since the net interest rate is reduced by the tax and less is gained by postponing consumption.[17] As noted already in our discussion of tax equity, it discriminates against the saver and in favor of the consumer.[18] The price line swivels to BF and equilibrium moves to E'''. An excess burden (equal to the loss of welfare in moving from i_2 to i_3) results. This is the case because the tax now destroys the equality between the MRT of present into future consumption as seen by the producer (equal to $1+i_g$, where i_g is the gross rate of return to capital) and the MRS as seen by the consumer (equal to $1+i_n$, where i_n is the net after-tax return). While people may differ regarding the superiority of the consumption base on equity grounds, there does exist a difference in efficiency cost in the above formulation.

Choice between Goods and Leisure

The same argument may be repeated, finally, for a tax on wage income. For this purpose, we measure leisure on the vertical axis and income or consumption on the horizontal axis.[19] Since the tax applies to goods only and not to leisure, the price or wage line swivels to BF, and equilibrium shifts to E'''. Once more the taxpayer moves from the higher indifference curve i_2 to the lower curve i_3. The tax inserts a wedge between the gross wage rate paid by the employer and the net wage rate received by the worker. The MRT and MRS for goods and leisure are no longer equal to each other. Condition 2 is

---

[17]Prior to tax, consumers may enjoy their entire income Y in the form of current consumption C. Or they may save it, earn an income equal to iY, and enjoy a future consumption of $(1+i)C$. The ratio between present and future consumption is thus: $C/[(1+i)C]$. With a general consumption tax, present consumption equals $(1-t)C$ and future consumption equals $(1-t)(1+i)C$, with the ratio of the two remaining unchanged at $C/(1+i)C$.

With an income tax, present consumption is $(1-t)C$, but future consumption equals $(1-t)C+(1-t)(1-t)iC$, so that the ratio becomes $C/[1+i(1-t)]C$.

[18]See p. 244.

[19]To simplify we assume all income to be consumed currently, so that the horizontal axis may be taken to reflect either income or consumption. A consumption tax, no less than an income tax, discriminates against leisure.

not met and an inefficiency results. To avoid this outcome, it would be necessary to redefine taxable income so as to include leisure in the base. This would be an ideal solution not only with regard to efficiency but also on equity grounds.[20] Unfortunately, however, such a solution is impracticable, since it is difficult to measure a person's potential (rather than actual) earnings.

D. EFFICIENCY RANKING OF TAXES UNDER SINGLE AND MULTIPLE CHOICE

In the preceding discussion, we have examined excess burdens which may arise in the choice between consumer goods, between present consumption and future consumption, and between income and leisure. To simplify matters, we assumed in each case that only one of these choice sets is open, while the others are fixed. This must now be compared with a setting in which multiple choices are allowed for.

Single Choices   For the single-choice setting, certain conclusions were reached which may be summarized as follows:

	Choice Fixed between	Choice Variable between	Taxes without Excess Burden	Taxes with Excess Burden
1.	L and Y; C_p and C_f	X and Z	Lump-sum tax Income tax General con- sumption tax	Selective con- sumption tax
2.	X and Z; L and Y	C_p and C_f	Lump-sum tax General con- sumption tax Selective con- sumption tax	Income tax
3.	X and Z; C_p and C_f	L and Y	Lump-sum tax	Income tax Selective con- sumption tax General con- sumption tax
4.	None	All	Lump-sum tax	All other

X and Z in the table stand for two consumer goods respectively, C_p is present and C_f is future consumption, Y is income and L is leisure. As shown in part 1, we find that a selective product tax distorts the choice between X and Z and is therefore inferior to a general sales tax, applicable at the same rate on

[20]See p. 101.

both X and Z, which does not involve such distortion. Similarly, we see in part 2 that a tax on income distorts the choice between present and future consumption and is therefore inferior to a tax on consumption which does not. Finally, we note in part 3 that a tax on income distorts the choice between goods and leisure and is therefore inferior to a hypothetical factor income tax which would apply to potential income.

Multiple Choices These are interesting conclusions, but their significance is lessened by the restrictive nature of the underlying assumptions. To arrive at a more realistic view, we must allow for various choices to be open at the same time. Consider a situation where there is a choice between both (1) X and Z and (2) income (or combinations of X and Z) and leisure. Can it still be argued that an equal-rate tax on X and Z is preferable to a tax on X and Z only, or for that matter, to some combination of unequal rates on both?

The answer is "no." The threat of potential distortion now becomes triangular: the tax may distort the choice between X and Z, X and L, and Z and L. Let the initial tax apply equally to both X and Z. Thus there is no distortion between X and Z, but the choices between X and L and Z and L are both biased in favor of L. Suppose now that the rate on Z is reduced while that on X is raised. This introduces a distortion between X and Z and increases that between X and L. But it reduces the distortion between Z and L. If X is a boat the enjoyment of which is complementary to leisure, while Z is work clothing the consumption of which is rival to leisure, a higher rate of tax on X and a lower rate of tax on Z may be desirable so as to correct for the defect which arises because leisure cannot be taxed. Thus the a priori case in favor of a general, equal-rate tax on X and Z breaks down once flexibility in the leisure-income choice is introduced.

Similar reasoning shows that there is no longer an a priori case for ranking a general consumption tax ahead of the income tax. The consumption tax, to be sure, is neutral as between C_p and C_f, whereas the income tax discriminates against C_f, but both discriminate between C_p and L as well as between C_f and L. Since the tax base is smaller under the consumption tax, a higher rate is needed to obtain the same revenue as under the income tax. Thus, discrimination in favor of leisure is increased, and this may more than offset the gain from avoiding discrimination between present and future consumption.

In all, we conclude that no hard and fast rules can be drawn. The "optimal mix" of commodity taxes, defined as that which minimizes excess burden, would comprise a complex set of taxes and rates;[21] and even then the outcome would be second best to a hypothetical tax under which leisure could be included in the base.

---

[21]In deriving a set of optimal commodity taxes, economists have distinguished between three situations: case 1, where there is substitution among various products only, but not between products and leisure; case 2, where there is substitution between products and leisure but not among products; and case 3, where both substitutions may occur.

Progressive Rates and Substitution Effect   In tracing the excess burden of a tax, we may distinguish between its substitution effect and its income effect. As an income tax is imposed, the cost of goods in terms of leisure is increased. The taxpayer, therefore, will substitute leisure for goods—the so-called substitution effect. But he or she is also left poorer. This will cause the taxpayer to work more so as to spread the loss between reduced consumption of both goods and leisure—the so-called income effect. As the two effects work in opposite directions, the net effect may be to lower or raise hours worked, but what matters for purposes of excess burden is the distortion caused by the substitution effect only.

It may be concluded further that the level of work effort will be lower and the excess burden higher if Ms. Jones is asked to pay $1,000 under a progressive tax than under a proportional tax. This is the case because the income effect will be the same in both cases, whereas the substitution effect (which depends on the *marginal* rate of tax) will be higher under the progressive schedule.

E. OPTIMAL INCOME TAX RATES

Economists have recently addressed themselves to the problem of designing a schedule of "optimal" income tax rates. If the government must collect a given amount of revenue, it may withdraw the sum from taxpayers at various points in the income scale. A more progressive distribution will have the disadvantage of calling for higher marginal rates of tax, thereby imposing a heavier excess burden; and it will have the advantage, in line with our earlier discussion of ability to pay, of leaving income where society considers its marginal utility to be higher.[22] The problem of constructing an optimal rate schedule essentially is to balance these two factors at the margin, thereby minimizing the total burden. To put it more generally, the problem may be viewed as one of designing a set of negative and positive income tax rates which will secure an optimal solution, allowing for both equity and efficiency aspects.

The solution to the problem of setting the optimal rate schedule depends on a number of considerations, including (1) the distribution of earnings capacities in the population, and (2) the behavior pattern of workers, telling us how much they will work at various net wage rates available to them. In addition, the solution relates to (3) the social welfare function which society wishes to apply. Depending on this function, the objective may be to

---

Assuming a given revenue to be obtained, the set of optimal tax rates for case 1 should be such as to equalize the resulting percentage change in price for all products, i.e., an across-the-board, equal-rate ad valorem tax is called for. The set of tax rates for case 2 should be such that the resulting percentage changes in prices will be inversely proportional to the own elasticity of demand for the various products. The solution for case 3 involves both types of elasticities of substitution (between products and between products and leisure) and is of more complex form. See W. J. Baumol and David E. Bradford, "Optimal Departures from Marginal Cost Pricing," *American Economic Review*, June 1970, pp. 165–283; and David F. Bradford and Harvey S. Rosen, "The Optimal Taxation of Commodities and Income," *Compilation of OTA Papers*, vol. 1, U.S. Department of the Treasury, Washington, 1978.

[22]See p. 250.

maximize an unweighted sum of utilities experienced by various individuals, or to maximize a sum of utilities weighted in line with a declining social marginal utility function. Finally, the goal may be to maximize the utility of individuals at the bottom of the scale. This type of analysis, which is still in its early stages, presents a more sophisticated restatement of some of the problems with which we were concerned in Chapter 5. Here, as there, the crux of the problem is to determine the choice of the social welfare function from which the set of optimal rates can be derived.[23]

F. TAX DISTORTIONS IN PRODUCTION

The preceding discussion dealt with distortions in household choices defined broadly to include alternative forms of current consumption, present and future consumption, and goods and leisure. Another requirement for efficient resource use is that whatever is produced should be produced in the least costly way. Taxes may be a further cause of inefficiency by interfering with this requirement. Illustrations of tax-induced production inefficiencies are easily found.

Partial Tax on Corporate Sector

In the context of the corporation tax, production distortions may arise in a variety of ways, including the following:

1.   The corporation tax is a tax on capital income originating in a particular sector of industry only. As such, it leads to a reallocation of capital from the taxed to tax-free industries. We have seen that this flow continues (assuming flexible markets) until *net* rates of return in the two sectors are equalized. In the process, output in the taxed sector is reduced while that in the tax-free sectors is increased, giving rise to the previously discussed type of consumption distortion.

In addition, however, production in the taxed industries will have become less capital-intensive while production in the tax-free industries will have become more capital-intensive than before, thus introducing a distortion in the method of production and a resulting efficiency loss which adds to that imposed by changing the output mix. Thus, if both capital and labor employed in a particular industry were taxed equally, that further distortion in production methods would be avoided.

2.   Depreciation rules for the determination of taxable income may interfere with the choice between short- and long-lived capital assets. A neutral policy would apply so-called economic depreciation, where the amount of depreciation allowed each year equals the reduction in the present value of the future income stream during the year. If depreciation is faster, the present value of the tax is reduced. This reduction is greater for long-lived assets, so that rapid depreciation favors the acquisition of such assets relative to short-lived ones. As a result, there

---

[23]Among a growing literature in the field, see A. B. Atkinson, "How Progressive Should Income Tax Be?" in E. S. Phelps (ed.), *Economic Justice*, Baltimore: Penguin, 1973. For an application to United States data and further literature references, see Robert Cooter and Elhanan Helpman, "Optimal Taxation for Transfer Payments under Different Social Welfare Criteria," *Quarterly Journal of Economics*, November 1974.

will be a bias in technology toward the use of such assets in lieu of assets with shorter lives.

3. Special treatment given to extractive industries in the form of depletion allowances lowers the tax burden on such industries relative to that imposed on others. It thus tends to induce overinvestment therein.

4. Preferential treatment of capital gains offers an inducement for investment in those assets the income from which may be obtained in the form of capital gains.

5. Determination of taxable income permits deduction of interest payments on business debt as a cost of doing business. Yet, no deduction for imputed interest is permitted for the case of equity finance. As a result, the corporation tax gives an incentive to use debt rather than equity finance, which may impose an efficiency cost.

6. Deductibility of expense accounts may distort business expenditures. Entertainment outlays are chargeable as costs to the corporation but are not counted as income to the management on its income tax. Thereby, such expenses are encouraged and various (though unsuccessful) attempts have been made at limiting their deductibility under the corporation tax.

Interjurisdictional Differentials

Another aspect of production distortion arises from the effects of tax differentials on product and factor movements between tax jurisdictions.

Effects on Product Flows   Suppose that, before tax, jurisdiction A has a comparative advantage in producing product X while jurisdiction Y has an advantage in producing product Z. As a result, A will produce X and export it to B, while B will produce Z and export it to A. Now let A impose a tax which increases the cost of producing X. As a result, its comparative advantage may be blocked. B may find it no longer worthwhile to import from A, and trade flows will be distorted. Thus, tax policy, much like tariffs, may interfere with international specialization and, as a result, efficiency suffers. This effect has been of central concern to Common Market policy and will be considered more closely at a later point.[24] Similar problems arise among jurisdictions within one nation, but they are usually less severe, since product tax rate differentials applicable at the state and local levels are not very large.[25]

Effects on Factor Flows   Differentials in the rate of income or capital taxation induce labor and capital flows among jurisdictions and divert resources from their most efficient regional pattern.

On the domestic scene, the problem involves differentials in corporation tax rates among states and in property tax rates among localities. The latter are of primary importance since corporation tax rates at the state level have remained relatively low, with rate differentials of two or three percentage points hardly a major factor in location decisions. Property tax differentials

[24]See p. 776.
[25]See p. 443.

have been more important and the lure of tax preferences is used by municipalities as a device for attracting investment. However, tax differentials are only part of the picture. Differentials in fiscal positions may arise not only from the tax side of the budget operation but also from the expenditure side. Thus a business firm may be attracted by good schools, roads, and other public services as well as repelled by high tax rates. What matters are the *net* differentials in fiscal burdens or benefits. Nevertheless, net differentials remain and, as we shall see later on, are a cost of fiscal pluralism to be weighed against the disadvantages of a highly centralized structure.[26]

As with product taxes, rate differentials in income and profits taxes are again larger if viewed in the international context. Capital flows in particular are sensitive to international rate differentials; and unless appropriate measures are taken to avoid such effects, the worldwide allocation of capital will be diverted from its efficient pattern. Again, this is a major concern for international tax integration, which will be dealt with further in a later chapter.[27]

G. MAGNITUDE OF EXCESS BURDENS

Although it is easy to argue that under certain conditions one tax will have an excess burden while another will not, this is not sufficient. Excess burden characteristics are only one aspect in the choice of taxes and must be weighed against other (including equity) considerations. For this purpose, ranking according to excess burden is not enough. A quantitative and operational measure of burden is needed. Estimates of the excess burden for various parts of the United States tax structure have been attempted, based on the "triangle" technique and econometric studies of the relevant demand and supply elasticities.[28]

Estimates of excess burden are still in a rudimentary and controversial stage. On one end of the scale, the excess burden of capital income taxation (resulting from penalizing saving) has been estimated at an annual cost of $50 billion, based on a high interest elasticity of saving of 0.40 percent.[29] Other estimates, using a lower elasticity and more limited concept of saving, have resulted in substantially smaller amounts of excess burden. Corresponding estimates of the excess burden of wage income taxation (resulting from favoring leisure) show a lower level of losses due to the postulated lower elasticity of labor supply with regard to the net wage rate.[30] However this

---

[26]See p. 531.

[27]See p. 771.

[28]This approach has been pioneered by Prof. A. C. Harberger. See Harberger, op. cit., chaps. 1, 2, and 8.

[29]See M. J. Boskin, "Taxation, Saving and the Rate of Interest," *Journal of Political Economy*, vol. 86, no. 32, part 2. For further discussion, see *Conference on Expenditure Tax*, Washington: Brookings, forthcoming.

[30]See Marvin Kosters, "Effects of an Income Tax on Labor Supply," in A. C. Harberger and M. J. Bailey (eds.), *The Taxation of Income from Capital*, Washington: Brookings, 1969, pp. 302–325. Kosters does not offer a quantitative measure, but the conclusion appears to be that the wage elasticity of labor supply is generally low.

may be, the more relevant estimate relates to the change in excess burden which would result if the present system were replaced by an alternative way of raising the same revenue. This alternative would hardly take the form of a lump-sum tax, free of excess burden. Addressing this problem of differential excess burden, it has been estimated that the reduction in burden, to be gained by replacing the tax on wage income with a tax on capital income, would be in the order of magnitude of from $15 to $25 billion.[31] The efficiency gain in replacing the corporation tax by a general tax on capital income has been estimated at $7 billion.[32]

In all, these magnitudes are not insignificant as they reflect annual rates of gain, but they should be seen in proper perspective. An overall efficiency loss of $50 billion would be below 1 percent of GNP. It may well be surpassed by other inefficiencies in the economy, including imperfect markets and, above all, losses which result from failure to maintain full employment.

H. FURTHER ASPECTS OF EFFICIENCY

It remains to note two further aspects of efficiency, including (1) the use of taxes to offset inefficiencies in the private sector, and (2) expenditure efficiency.

Neutralizing Private Sector Distortions

In considering the distorting effects of various taxes, the implicit assumption has been that such taxes are introduced into an otherwise efficient market. If market imperfections already exist, as of course they do, the evaluation of particular taxes becomes more difficult. Rather than introducing an inefficiency, taxes might then act as correctives to other nontax inefficiencies. Illustrations for this may be readily supplied:

  1. Consider two substitute products, X and Z, with X produced by a monopolist and Z in a competitive market. As a result, production of X will be too small relative to that of Z when compared with an efficient solution. This result might then be remedied by imposing a selective tax on Z even though, in a competitive market, taxing both X and Z equally would have been preferable.
  2. Or, suppose that in an otherwise perfect market, there already exists a tax on X but not on Z. The excess burden might then be reduced if additional revenue were obtained from a tax on Z rather than from a general tax on both products.
  3. Next, selective taxes (or subsidies) may correct for inefficiencies where production or consumption in the private sector involves external costs (or

---

[31]See Martin Feldstein, "The Welfare Cost of Capital Income Taxation," *Journal of Political Economy*, vol. 86, pp. 529-551; and Jerry R. Green and Eytan Sheshinski, "Approximating the Efficiency Gain of Tax Reforms," *Journal of Public Economics*, vol. 11, no. 2 (April 1979).

[32]See Don Fullerton, John B. Shoven, and John Whalley, "A General Equilibrium Appraisal of U.S. Corporate and Personal Tax Integration," in R. Haveman and K. Hollbeck (eds.), *Macreconomic Simulation*, Institute for Research on Poverty, Madison, Wis., 1979. Also see David J. Ott and F. Attiat Ott, "The Effects of Non-neutral Taxation on the Use of Capital by Sector," *Journal of Political Economy*, July 1973, pp. 972–981.

benefits) which are not accounted for by the market. As will be shown later, such is the case with effluent charges imposed to internalize the cost of pollution.[33]

For these and other reasons, potential inefficiencies introduced by particular taxes must be evaluated in relation to other inefficiencies which already exist in the system. This evaluation may reduce the resulting excess burden and efficiency may in fact be increased.

All this, of course, assumes that efficient allocation is in line with individual preferences. Selective excises may be desirable where it is the explicit purpose of public policy to correct consumer preferences, i.e., in connection with "demerit" goods, or selective subsidies in turn may be desirable where "merit" goods are involved. This presumably is the rationale for heavy taxation of liquor and tobacco. In this case, the usual efficiency argument based on free consumer choice is inapplicable and social preference is substituted for private choice.[34]

Efficiency Aspects of Expenditure Policy

Efficiency problems arise on the expenditure side as well as on the tax side of budget policy. The political process by which public expenditures are determined can only approximate true consumer preferences and may do so but poorly. Less subtly, the execution of public expenditures may involve inefficiencies in that public goods are not provided at least cost. Finally, and of major interest in the present context, reasoning similar to that involved in the excess burden of taxation also applies to expenditure policy. Expenditure, like tax policy, may interfere with the efficiency of choice in the private sector.

Choice among Products   The same reasoning which suggests that a general consumption tax tends to be less burdensome than a selective tax also shows that a general consumption subsidy will be more beneficial than a selective subsidy which reduces the price of a particular product only.[35] This may be shown by repeating the arguments of Figure 14-4 in reverse.[36] A selective subsidy cannot leave the recipient better off than an equal-cost general subsidy, but it may well leave the person in a worse position. The tax concept of excess burden here finds its parallel in that of "deficient benefit."

Rather than subsidize the purchase of particular products, the government may provide them free of charge, e.g., school lunches or medical services. Such provision will not cause an efficiency cost if the amount

[33]See p. 759.
[34]See p. 81.
[35]The subsidy may be given to the consumer in cash, with prescribed use; or it may be given indirectly through intermediate expenditures of government which reduce the cost of production for the private firm, such as an access road to its plant.
[36]In line with Fig. 14-4, suppose the consumer is initially positioned at E'' on price line $B'A'$. After a general subsidy of amount $A'A$ is granted, the price line shifts parallel to the right and the new equilibrium is at E'. Now let an equal cost subsidy on X only be applied. The price line remains anchored at B' but swivels around to the right. The new equilibrium is at its intersection with BA, at a point where the new price line is tangent to an indifference curve below i_1.

supplied falls short of what consumers would have purchased privately, but an efficiency cost arises (or a benefit is lost) if public supply is larger.[37] The fact that relief measures so frequently take the form of payments in kind rather than in cash is therefore in need of explanation. As noted before, possible causes may be found in merit-good considerations or the fact that voluntary giving is made more acceptable to the donor if the recipient must use the funds in line with the donor's own preferences.[38]

Choice between Income and Leisure   Income tax effects on the choice between income and leisure are paralleled (in reverse) by transfer payments, where the amount of transfers is related positively to earnings. This will be the case with a wage subsidy. Such a subsidy imposes an efficiency cost (or benefit shortfall) as does an income tax, although the substitution effect now works in the opposite direction. As the price of leisure is raised (by the increase in the wage rate), workers substitute work (goods) for leisure. The larger the increase in work effort, the higher will the efficiency cost now be.

More important for practical purposes are transfer payments which are related inversely to earnings, as, for example, are relief payments. Such payments result in a negative substitution effect similar to that of an income tax, as we shall see in our later discussion of income maintenance programs.[39] Since the marginal rates implicit in a welfare formula are high, this poses a central problem in the design of income maintenance plans.

I. TRADEOFF BETWEEN EQUITY AND EFFICIENCY

Suppose that the federal government, in collecting some $400 billion in revenue, imposes an excess burden of $50 billion, incurs an administrative cost of $2 billion, and causes compliance costs of $5 billion. Total costs would then amount to $57 billion, or 13 percent of revenue. If the entire revenue were collected in the form of a head tax, these costs might be reduced to, say, $100 million. Is the difference, or 56.9 billion, worth paying for? Or, to put it differently, what is it that the public gets for this payment?

The benefit to be obtained is a more equitable tax structure. There are few who would maintain that a head-tax system is a tolerable way of raising revenue, even if there would be a saving of nearly $57 billion. But like all matters of economic choice, the intelligent decision is not made on an all-or-nothing basis but at the margin. The tradeoff between equity and cost considerations should be pushed to the point where the gain is matched by the price of increased administrative, compliance, and efficiency cost. At the same time, any given level of equity should be purchased at the least cost. Among equally equitable taxes, those should be chosen which carry the least efficiency, administrative, and compliance cost.

---

[37]This reasoning is explained in the context of intergovernmental grants, where earmarked and bloc grants are compared. See p. 535.

[38]See p. 102.

[39]See p. 721.

Horizontal Equity

Horizontal equity, so we have argued, calls for equal treatment of people in equal position, which in the case of the income tax, means a broad-based tax including income from all sources and independent of its use. This broad definition of the income base is mostly in line with efficiency considerations and avoidance of excess burden. Failure to define income comprehensively usually offends efficiency as well as equity considerations. But this is not always the case. The supply of some services, e.g., those of opera stars, is less elastic than the supply of services with easily acquired skills. Or, the labor supply of second earners in the family, mostly women, tends to be more elastic than that of men. This suggests that opera stars and male workers should be taxed more heavily than clerks and female workers, if the criterion is to minimize excess burden. Yet, such a solution would be offensive to horizontal equity. Once more, a balancing of conflicting considerations is called for. The task, therefore, is to find a set of taxes which would go at least part way in meeting both the efficiency and equity objectives. Recent efforts to derive an "optimal" system have been oriented towards efficiency. They would combine taxes on products with inelastic demand (i.e., cigarettes or basic foodstuffs) so as to reduce the substitution effect, with taxes on goods which are complementary to leisure (such as skis or pleasure boats) so that leisure would be included in the tax base by indirection. Such a combination of taxes would be attractive on efficiency grounds, and less objectionable in terms of equity than a head tax. But horizontal equity would still be offended, as the weight of such taxes in the budgets of households at any given income level might vary widely. A broad-based and uniform tax, such as the comprehensive income or consumption tax, may well continue to offer the best compromise, even though it falls short of perfection.

Vertical Equity

The problem of vertical equity is how to implement a given, presumably progressive, distribution of the tax bill with a minimum of excess burden. Here the conflict must be met head on. We have seen that for any one person, the excess burden involved in paying a given amount of tax will be larger if this amount is paid under a progressive, rather than under a flat rate, schedule. Yet the use of a progressive schedule (with marginal or bracket rates in excess of average rates) is unavoidable if tax liability is to rise as a percentage of income when moving up the income scale. The question then is, up to what point will the equity gain from such taxation be worth the efficiency cost inherent in the higher marginal rates? This is the problem noted previously under the heading of "Optimal Income Taxation."

Posed somewhat differently, the problem is how to secure a given distributional correction with a minimum of excess burden. With labor supply relatively inelastic, chances are that an income tax–transfer approach (as outlined earlier for our distribution branch) remains the best technique. It might be supported by commodity taxes (on the products consumed primarily by high-income taxpayers) and subsidies (to the products consumed primarily by low-income recipients). But even with the best of tax designs, an efficiency cost remains which must be weighed against equity objectives. Neither consideration should be permitted to dominate tax policy, and neither should be neglected.

J. SUMMARY

Operation of the tax system is costly in that the burden exceeds what the government gets in revenue. This involves costs of tax administration and compliance, as well as an excess burden which arises as conditions of efficient resource use are interfered with:

1. The cost of tax administration is small relative to the revenue obtained. Nevertheless, interesting problems arise with regard to how intensively tax administration should be conducted.

2. Compliance costs by taxpayers are substantially larger than administration costs.

Regarding the imposition of excess burden, various taxes were compared and the following conclusions were reached:

3. A selective consumption tax interferes with the choice between products, whereas a general consumption tax does not.

4. An income tax interferes with the choice between present and future consumption, whereas a general consumption tax does not.

5. An income tax and a general consumption tax both interfere with the choice between goods and leisure.

6. When all choices are permitted to be flexible, it can no longer be concluded that a general sales tax must be superior on efficiency grounds to a selective product tax, or that a general consumption (sales) tax must be superior to an income tax.

7. Only a head tax imposes no excess burden, but it is unacceptable on equity grounds, since it is wholly unrelated to economic capacity.

8. As the rate of a tax is increased, efficiency cost rises, but revenue reaches a maximum and then decreases.

9. Theoretically, a set of taxes may be devised which minimize excess burden, but such minimization is difficult to accomplish in practice and may not be acceptable on equity grounds.

10. The excess burden imposed by a progressive income tax exceeds that of a proportional tax, as the excess burden depends upon the marginal or bracket rate. The problem of optimal income taxation, therefore, is one of weighing the equity gains of progressive taxation against its efficiency cost.

Among other aspects of the efficiency cost of taxation, the following considerations were noted:

11. Efficiency in production may be interfered with if the use of capital or labor is subject to tax in one particular sector only.

12. Similar distortions may arise between jurisdictions, as the location of production may be affected by differentials in tax rates.

13. Empirical measurement of the magnitude of efficiency costs is difficult, with estimates varying widely with underlying assumptions.

14. The proposition that taxes should be neutral so as to avoid excess burden is based on the hypothesis that taxes are introduced into an otherwise efficient market. The case for neutrality does not apply where taxes are used to correct for market imperfections in the private sector.

Efficiency costs may result from the expenditure side as well as the tax side of budget policy:

15. There is an assumption that a policy of cash subsidy to households is superior on efficiency grounds to providing free services in kind, or to applying selective product subsidies.

16. Potential interference with the choice between income and leisure poses a major consideration in the design of income maintenance schemes.

FURTHER READINGS

Atkinson, A. B.: "How Progressive Should Income Tax Be?" in E. S. Phelps (ed.), *Economic Justice*, Baltimore: Penguin, 1973.

Baumol, W. J., and D. F. Bradford: "Optimal Departure from Marginal Cost Pricing," *American Economic Review*, June 1970, pp. 265–283.

Harberger, A.: *Taxation and Welfare*, Boston: Little, Brown, 1974, chaps. 1–3 and 8.

Sandmo, A.: "Optimal Taxation—An Introduction to the Literature," *Journal of Public Economics*, July-August 1976.

Part Four

Tax Structure

Chapter 15

Development
and Composition of
United States Tax Structure*

A. Development of United States Tax Structure: *Federal Level; State Level; Local Level; All Levels.* **B. Comparison with Other Countries. C. Summary.**

Economic analysis has much to contribute to our understanding of how taxation works and how it affects the economy. As we have seen in the preceding chapters, some important conclusions may be drawn regarding the incidence or burden of various major types of taxes. But much depends on how particular taxes are designed in detail and on how the tax structure is fitted into the highly complex set of economic institutions in which it must operate. Concern with this question is the subject matter of Part Four of our study.

A. DEVELOPMENT OF UNITED STATES TAX STRUCTURE

Paralleling the growth in public expenditures, the overall level of taxation as shown in Table 15-1 has risen substantially in recent decades. The picture

Readers' Guide to Chapter 15: A brief survey of how the United States tax structure has developed since the beginning of the century.

TABLE 15-1
Development of United States Tax Structure

	1902	1913	1922	1927	1940	1950	1960	1970	1975
			I. TAX REVENUE AS PERCENT OF GNP						
1. Federal	2.3	1.7	4.6	3.6	5.7	13.6	18.2	19.8	17.7
2. State	0.7	0.8	1.4	1.8	4.4	3.4	4.5	6.0	6.4
3. Local	3.2	3.3	4.2	4.7	4.5	2.9	3.8	4.2	4.0
4. Total	6.2	5.8	10.2	10.1	14.5	19.9	26.5	30.0	28.1
			II. PERCENTAGE COMPOSITION OF TAX REVENUE						
Federal									
5. Individual income tax	—	—	} 56.8	25.6	16.9	40.7	45.4	48.1	45.2
6. Corporation income tax	—	5.3 }		36.6	19.8	27.1	24.0	17.5	15.0
7. Sales and excises	47.6	45.6	24.4	14.6	31.6	19.2	12.8	8.4	6.5
8. Customs duties	47.4	46.8	9.3	17.0	5.8	1.1	1.2	1.3	1.6
9. Death and gift	1.0	—	4.1	2.6	6.3	1.8	1.8	1.9	1.7
10. Payroll	—	—	1.2	2.1	14.2	9.0	14.2	22.3	29.7
11. Other	4.1	2.3	4.2	1.4	5.5	1.1	0.7	0.5	0.1
12. Total	100.0	100.0	100.0	100.0	100.0	100.0	100.0	100.0	100.0
State									
13. Individual income tax	—	—	4.1	4.0	4.7	7.4	9.9	16.0	19.2
14. Corporation income tax	—	—	5.5	5.3	3.5	6.0	5.3	6.5	6.7
15. Sales and excises	17.9	19.9	27.2	42.8	51.0	55.6	54.0	52.2	48.3
16. Property tax	52.6	46.5	33.0	21.2	5.9	3.1	2.7	1.9	1.6
17. Payroll	—	—	10.1	7.9	24.5	18.8	19.4	16.4	18.3
18. Death and gift	29.5	33.6	20.1	18.9	10.3	9.1	1.9	1.7	1.5
19. Other	—	—	—	—	—	—	6.9	5.2	4.6
20. Total	100.0	100.0	100.0	100.0	100.0	100.0	100.0	100.0	100.0
Local									
21. Individual income tax	—	—	—	—	} 0.4	0.8 }	} 1.3	} 4.1	} 4.3
22. Corporation income tax	—	—	—	—		0.1 }			
23. Sales and excises	—	0.2	0.6	0.6	2.8	5.9	7.7	8.1	10.6
24. Property		91.0	96.4	96.8	91.3	86.2	85.0	82.1	81.6
25. Payroll	—	0.2	0.5	0.6	1.5	2.3	2.9	3.2	3.6
26. Other	11.4	8.6	2.5	2.1	3.9	4.7	3.0	2.5	1.0
27. Total	100.0	100.0	100.0	100.0	100.0	100.0	100.0	100.0	100.0

TABLE 15-1 (*Continued*)

		1902	1913	1922	1927	1940	1950	1960	1970	1975
All Levels										
28.	Individual income tax	—	—	}27.0	9.8	8.1	29.3	33.0	35.4	33.4
29.	Corporation income tax	—	1.5		13.9	8.7	19.6	17.3	12.8	11.0
30.	Sales and excises	19.8	16.1	15.1	13.2	28.5	23.6	19.1	17.2	16.6
31.	Customs duties	17.7	13.6	4.2	6.0	2.3	0.7	0.8	0.9	1.0
32.	Property	51.4	58.6	44.0	48.8	30.3	13.0	12.7	11.9	12.0
33.	Payroll	—	0.1	2.1	2.4	13.3	9.7	13.4	18.5	23.4
34.	Death and gift	11.1	10.1	7.5	5.8	8.9	4.2	1.5	1.6	1.4
35.	Other	—	—	—	—	—	—	2.1	1.7	1.1
36.	Total	100.0	100.0	100.0	100.0	100.0	100.0	100.0	100.0	100.0
	III. LEVELS AS PERCENT OF TOTAL									
37.	Federal	37.4	29.1	45.2	35.5	38.8	68.3	68.5	65.8	62.9
38.	State	11.4	13.2	13.9	18.0	30.0	17.3	17.1	20.1	22.8
39.	Local	51.3	57.6	40.9	46.5	31.2	14.4	14.5	14.1	14.3
40.	Total	100.0	100.0	100.0	100.0	100.0	100.0	100.0	100.0	100.0

Notes:
Calendar years through 1950, fiscal years 1960, 1970, and 1975.
Detail may not add to total due to rounding.
Local motor vehicle and operator's licenses included in "other" to 1950 and in sales taxes thereafter.
Sources:
1902–1950: U.S. Bureau of the Census, *Historical Statistics for the United States; Colonial Times to 1957*, pp. 724, 727, 729.
1960, 1970, and 1975: U.S. Bureau of the Census, *Governmental Finances*, 1959–60, 1969–70, and 1974–75.

(see line 4 of the table) is similar to that of Table 7-2, where expenditure growth was shown. As with expenditures, the growth of tax revenue must be seen in relation to that of GNP and not in absolute terms. Omitting the temporary wartime peaks, the ratio of tax revenue to GNP hovered around 6 percent in the first two decades of the century and around 10 percent during the twenties. By 1940, the level had risen to nearly 15 percent. In each of the following three decades the ratio was to rise by 5 percentage points, reaching 20 percent in 1950, 26 percent by 1960, 30 percent by 1970, but falling back to 28 percent by 1975. The causes of increase are similar to those underlying the development of the expenditure side and need not be restated. Instead, we now focus on the major changes in the composition of the tax structure which accompanied this overall growth. For this purpose, it is useful to begin with a separate view of the various levels of government before proceeding to the overall picture.

Federal Level

Beginning with the federal component (lines 5 to 12 of Table 15-1), we find an almost exclusive reliance on indirect taxes up to World War I, with revenue about equally divided between receipts from customs duties and domestic excises. The introduction of the Sixteenth Amendment in 1913 opened the way for income taxation, and by the early twenties income taxes had come to supply nearly 60 percent of federal revenue. Excises had declined in relative importance, and customs duties had become but a minor item. The increase in the ratio of total federal revenue to GNP (line 1) was met largely by the introduction of federal income taxes, with the corporation tax leading the individual income tax.

The relative importance of the income taxes continued to rise during the twenties while the excise tax share declined. This trend was reversed in the Depression years of the thirties, when excise rates were raised in a futile attempt to balance the budget, and revenue from the income taxes suffered from the decline in national income. The late thirties also brought the advent of payroll taxes associated with the creation of the social security system.

World War II finance brought the second major expansion of income taxation and of the individual income tax in particular. Over the decade of the 1940s, the individual income tax share rose from 17 to 49 percent of federal revenue, while the corporation income tax share increased from 20 to 27 percent. The ratio of federal tax revenue to GNP doubled in this period, and the ratio of individual income tax to GNP rose from 1 to 6 percent. In the process, this tax was transformed from a tax on the rich, paid by a small fraction of high-income recipients, to a mass tax paid by almost all income earners. The number of income taxpayers rose from 7 million in 1939 to 50 million in 1945. The very process which produced this extensive shift from indirect to direct taxation at the same time served to render the income tax a less progressive instrument.[1] The number of income tax returns is now close to 85 million, including 98 percent of all those employed.

The fifties brought a further sharp rise in the ratio of federal tax to GNP. Accounted for largely by increased payroll taxation, it resulted in a declining share of revenue from other taxes, with only the individual income tax showing further gain. The sixties, finally, saw the overall tax to GNP ratio rise a further 3 to 4 percentage points, accompanied by a further sharp increase in the payroll tax share. The payroll tax by this time had become the second most important tax in the system, while the corporation income tax declined sharply and excises fell moderately. Notwithstanding these changes, the individual income tax has remained much the largest component, contributing 45 percent of the 1975 total. Payroll taxes are next with 30 percent, followed by the corporation income tax with 15 percent. Indirect taxes provide only 7 percent. This highly income and payroll tax–intensive revenue

---

[1]A tax is said to be regressive, proportional, or progressive, depending on whether the ratio of tax revenue to income falls, remains constant, or rises as we move up the income scale. See p. 376.

structure stands in sharp contrast to the earlier federal tax structure, which included indirect taxes only.

While the income tax has become a mass tax, now paid by over 75 percent of earners, it is still the most progressive major component of the tax structure. This remains the case even though the tax, as we shall see presently, falls far short of completely covering the entire base. It is not surprising, then, that the predominance of the individual income tax continues to render income tax reform one of the most lively aspects of federal tax policy.

The second major feature of change, especially over the last two decades, has been the growth of payroll taxation. Taken by itself, this tax is regressive over the middle- to upper-income ranges, so that its increased weight has provided an offset to the progressive income tax. It should be noted, however, that the rise of this tax has been accompanied by a similar increase of social security benefits. As we shall see later, this raises the question of whether the burden of this tax should be considered by itself or be related to the benefits which it finances.

State Level

At the state level, the major development over the first half of the century (see lines 13 to 20 of Table 15-1) was the dwindling of the property tax share from 53 to 3 percent, and a rise in the importance of sales and gross receipts taxes, particularly retail sales and gasoline taxes. Owing to the preponderance of these taxes, state taxation, as was noted earlier, is less progressive and may even be regressive in its distributional impact.[2] Although the data record a rise in the individual income tax share in recent decades, this increase has not been sufficient to change the highly sales tax–intensive nature of state taxation. The overall ratio of state tax revenue to GNP (line 2) rose slowly during the twenties but increased more sharply during the thirties and sixties. It has now leveled out at about 6 percent.

Local Level

The local tax structure has always been, and continues to be, almost entirely a property tax system. As shown in lines 21 to 27 of Table 15-1, the property tax has provided over 80 percent of local revenue throughout the period. The use of sales and income taxes has increased in recent decades but remains a relatively minor factor. Since the distributional impact of the property tax is not assessed as readily as that of income or sales taxes, judgment on the incidence of local taxation is postponed to a later point.[3] The overall level of local taxation (total revenue as a percentage of GNP) has remained fairly stable, ranging between 3 and 5 percent from the beginning of the century to World War II (line 3). The ratio declined during the forties, making room for war finance, and recovered the 4 percent level during the fifties. The ratio continued to rise slowly during the sixties, but its level is not above what it

[2]See p. 267.
[3]See p. 481.

was half a century ago, in contrast to the state and federal ratios which rose to several times their earlier levels.[4]

All Levels

The changing composition of the combined tax structure—which is what matters for overall tax policy—reflects both changes at each level and their changing weights in the total picture. As shown in lines 37 to 40 of Table 15-1, the federal share was relatively stable at 30 to 40 percent of the total from 1900 to 1940, but rose sharply during the forties, reaching 68 percent in 1950. It showed little change during the 1950s but by 1975 had turned down and fallen to 63 percent. For the first half of the century, the state share rose slowly, while the local share declined sharply; but thereafter, both shares evened out during the fifties and sixties. Whereas state and local taxation accounted for over two-thirds of the total prior to World War II, by 1960 it had dropped to little more than 30 percent. The overall picture was thus one of increasing centralization, with the federal share rising primarily at the cost of the local. Recent years, however, have shown a reversal of this trend, with the state-local tax share rising to 37 percent in 1975.[5]

The historical trend toward revenue centralization made for heavier reliance on income taxation in the overall tax structure (lines 28 to 36). Whereas income taxes (individual and corporate) provided only 17 percent of total revenue in 1940, they now furnish 44 percent. Over the same period the share of sales taxation fell from 31 to 17 percent, that of payroll taxes rose from 13 to 23 percent, and that of property taxes declined from 30 to 12 percent. These changes have left the United States with an overall tax structure which is highly income and payroll tax–intensive.

B. COMPARISON WITH OTHER COUNTRIES

As shown in Table 15-2, the United States tax structure is in line with the general pattern present in other advanced industrial countries. The overall level of United States taxation as viewed by the ratio of revenue to GDP is distinctly at the lower end of the scale (line 3).[6] This continues to be the case, although to a lesser degree, if payroll taxes are excluded (line 1). The pattern remains similar for the personal income tax (line 4), although the United States ranks with the higher countries with regard to the corporate tax (line 5).

The composition of the tax structure, shown in lines 7 to 12, reveals the United States to be relatively low in taxes on goods and services, a category which includes selective as well as general taxes such as retail sales and value-added taxes. These differences in part reflect the structure of the

---

[4]See p. 27.

[5]The reasons for this, as noted earlier, are to be found on the expenditure side and need not be repeated here. See p. 142.

[6]The denominator in these ratios is gross domestic product, or GDP, rather than gross national product, or GNP, as used in Table 15-1. GDP includes domestic output only, while excluding earnings from abroad.

TABLE 15-2
International Comparison of Tax Structures, 1975*
(All Levels of Government)

As Percentage of Total	Netherlands	Sweden	Norway	France	United Kingdom	Germany	Canada	United States	Australia	Japan
Taxes as Percentage of GDP										
1. Excluding payroll tax	28.9	37.1	36.4	22.2	30.1	23.2	30.8	22.9	30.1	15.1
2. Payroll tax	18.0	8.4	8.3	14.7	6.7	12.0	3.2	7.4	—	5.1
3. Total	46.9	45.5	44.7	36.9	36.8	35.2	34.0	30.3	30.1	20.2
Income Taxes as Percentage of GDP										
4. Personal income tax	12.7	21.2	17.1	4.6	14.3	10.6	11.3	10.0	13.1	5.1
5. Corporate income tax	3.6	2.0	1.3	2.9	1.9	1.6	4.7	3.3	3.7	3.4
6. Total income taxes	16.3	23.2	18.4	7.5	16.2	12.2	16.0	13.3	16.8	8.5
As Percentage of Total Tax Revenue										
7. Personal income tax	27.0	46.0	38.2	12.4	38.9	30.1	33.3	33.0	21.3	25.0
8. Corporation income tax	7.7	2.0	2.9	5.4	5.2	4.4	13.6	10.8	12.3	17.0
9. Property tax	3.2	1.1	2.3	3.4	12.4	3.1	9.2	13.6	9.3	9.6
10. Payroll tax	18.0	8.4	8.3	14.7	6.7	12.0	3.0	7.4	—	5.1
11. Product taxes†	22.0	18.4	36.7	32.8	23.3	25.1	26.1	16.1	25.4	15.8
12. Other	20.1	24.1	11.6	31.3	23.5	25.3	14.3	19.1	31.7	27.5
13. Total	100.0	100.0	100.0	100.0	100.0	100.0	100.0	100.0	100.0	100.0

**Revenue Statistics of OECD Member Countries, 1965–75*, tables 1–29.
†Includes both general and selective taxes.

various economies, e.g., the importance of the corporate sector in the United States, but they also reflect differences in tax policy and attitudes.

C. SUMMARY

The United States structure has undergone major changes over the years, especially at the federal level:

1.   Prior to World War I, the federal tax system relied entirely on indirect taxes, with heavy emphasis on tariffs. Now the latter contribute only a very minor share of total revenue.

2. With World War II, the income tax became the major federal revenue source.

3. More recently, the payroll tax has come to contribute an important and increasing share of federal revenue.

4. State revenue, prior to the thirties, relied heavily on the property tax, but this tax then came to be reserved almost entirely for local use. Primary reliance of the states came to be on sales taxation, both general and selective. Since the sixties, income taxation also has come to play a major role.

5. Local taxation always has relied and still does rely very largely on the property tax.

6. The increase in the federal share in total tax revenue has been a major factor in increasing the importance of income taxation.

A comparison of the United States tax system with that of major other countries shows that:

7. The overall level of taxation in the United States is comparatively low.

8. The United States system relies more on income and less on indirect taxes.

Chapter 16

Individual Income Tax: Defining Taxable Income*

A. Major Provisions: *Determining Taxable Income; Application of Rates; Declaration, Payments, and Withholding; Audit.* **B. Structure of the Tax Base:** *From GNP to Taxable Income; Size Distribution of Tax Base; Distribution of Tax Base by Income Source.* **C. Principles of Income Definition:** *Gross Income versus Net Income; Capital Income versus Labor Income; Real Income versus Nominal Income; Accrued Income versus Realized Income; Imputed Income; Earnings versus Transfers; Regular versus Irregular Income.* **D. Practice of Income Definition: (1) Exclusions:** *Tax-Exempt Interest; Capital Gains; Dividend Exclusion; Pensions.* **E. Practice of Income Definition: (2) Deductions:** *Types of Deductions; Rationale for Itemized Deductions; Evaluation of Itemized Deductions; Standard Deduction; Conclusion.* **F. Summary.**

The individual income tax is much the most important single tax and the kingpin of the federal, if not the entire United States, tax structure. It is

*Reader's Guide to Chapter 16: This is the first in a series of chapters dealing with the particulars of various taxes. The practically inclined reader will find these chapters of particular interest. The theorist in turn is urged to take them seriously, since little good can come of theorizing about the principles of taxation and its economic effects unless one knows the statutes and how they work. While studying the structure of the income tax, students are urged to examine the Individual Income Tax Return, Form 1040, and its major subschedules, and practice filling one out.

therefore the first tax to be considered and one to be dealt with at greater length. While our concern is primarily with the federal tax, brief attention is also given to state and local income taxes.

A. MAJOR PROVISIONS

The basic principle of the United States individual income tax is that the taxpayer's income from all sources be combined into a single or "global" measure of income. Total income is then reduced by certain deductions and exemptions to arrive at taxable income. This is the base to which tax rates are applied in computing the tax.

Determining Taxable Income

The derivation of taxable income begins with adjusted gross income (AGI), the base which is then reduced by deductions and personal exemptions. The provisions here given are those applicable under the Revenue Act of 1978.

Adjusted Gross Income Income from all sources is combined to determine AGI. This includes wages, interest, dividends, rent, royalties, profits from unincorporated business operations, and so forth. Although the resulting total is referred to as adjusted *gross* income, this is misleading since, in the economist's language, it reflects a *net* income concept, i.e., income net of costs incurred in earning that income. Unincorporated business income is included in AGI on a net basis, and adjustments are made for certain personal costs incurred in earning income (such as moving expenses and certain employee business expenses) before arriving at AGI. While AGI is meant to give a comprehensive measure of the taxpayer's income position, we shall find that in practice it is not as comprehensive as it should be. Noncash income (such as imputed rent and unrealized capital gains) is omitted and certain forms of cash income or parts thereof are specifically excluded.

Personal Exemptions AGI thus determined is then reduced by the allowable amount of personal exemptions. These equal $1,000 per taxpayer, spouse, and each dependent. The exemption for a single person thus equals $1,000, for spouses filing joint returns, $2,000, for a family of four, $4,000, and so forth, rising with the number of dependents. Certain groups, including the blind and aged, are allowed an additional exemption.

Deductions The remainder is then given the benefit of a further amount of tax-free income, also referred to as zero-rate bracket or standard deduction. This amount equals $2,300 for single and $3,400 for joint returns, but there is no allowance for dependents. Instead of claiming this amount, taxpayers may choose to itemize their deductions. Among allowed itemized deductions, the most important are interest paid on mortgages and other consumer loans, certain state and local taxes, and charitable contributions. Other deductible items include unusually high medical expenses and casualty losses. However, usually only higher-income taxpayers choose to itemize.

About 70 percent of returns choose the standard deduction, as it ordinarily exceeds what would be the itemized amount.

Application of Rates

Next, the tax is computed by application of the rate schedule. This schedule is legislated in the form of marginal or bracket rates, applicable to successive slabs of income. Table 16-1 shows the rate schedule for joint returns. The first $3,400 is taxed at a zero rate, this being the previously noted amount of standard deduction. The next slab of $2,100 is taxed at a rate of 14 percent, the next $2,100 at 16 percent, and so forth, until income in excess of $215,400 is reached, where a rate of 70 percent applies. Note that the amounts of income shown in the table refer to AGI minus personal exemptions and minus the excess of itemized over standard deductions, with the standard deduction of $3,400 already being accounted for by the zero-rate bracket. To allow for the difference in tax-free amount and for other reasons, different rate schedules apply for single and certain other returns.

As noted in detail later on, application of the rate schedule is qualified by a number of other provisions, principally the following:

1. So-called earned income (defined as income from wages, salaries, and

TABLE 16-1
Tax Rate Schedule for Married Taxpayers Filing Joint Returns*

Amount of Income† (Dollars)	Tax on Lower Limit (Dollars)	Rate of Tax on Excess (Percentages)
0– 3,400	—	0.0
3,400– 5,500	—	14.0
5,500– 7,600	294	16.0
7,600– 11,900	630	18.0
11,900– 16,000	1,404	21.0
16,000– 20,200	2,265	24.0
20,200– 24,600	3,273	28.0
24,600– 29,900	4,505	32.0
29,900– 35,200	6,201	37.0
35,200– 45,800	8,162	41.0
45,800– 60,000	12,508	49.0
60,000– 85,600	19,466	54.0
85,600–109,400	33,290	59.0
109,400–162,400	47,332	64.0
162,400–215,400	81,252	68.0
Over 215,400	117,292	70.0

*Revenue Act of 1978, applicable to 1978 income and later years.

†To determine the income to which these rates apply, the taxpayer will reduce AGI by (1) personal exemptions and (2) the excess of itemized over standard deductions. The standard deduction amount is already reflected in the zero-rate bracket.

professions) is subject to a top bracket rate of 50 percent only, with rates in excess of that amount limited to other forms of income.

2. Special relief is given to low-income earners in the form of an "earned income credit." This provision allows a credit against tax of 10 percent of earnings up to earnings of $5,000. As AGI rises above this amount, the credit is reduced by 10 percent of the excess, thus falling to zero as an AGI of $10,000 is reached. Where the credit thus computed exceeds tax liability, a refund or "negative tax" is due. The provision applies only to taxpayers with dependents.

3. Long-term capital gains are given preferential treatment, as only 40 percent of such gains are subject to tax.

4. High-income taxpayers are subject to a so-called minimum tax, payable in addition to their regular tax.

Declaration, Payments, and Withholding

Taxes are paid on a pay-as-you-earn basis, with payments during the tax year based on an estimated return. Quarterly payments are made during the year to allow for the excess of estimated liabilities over withholding. A final return is filed by April 16 of the following year, at which time the final payment is made or a refund is claimed.

Over 90 percent of the tax liability is collected through withholding. This system was introduced in World War II and has great advantages. By linking tax payments to the current level of income, rather than by having them lag behind one year, the responsiveness of tax payments to changes in the level of personal income is greatly increased. This responsiveness is of vital importance for the effectiveness of stabilization policy. The withholding system also assures fuller compliance since the declaration of income is not left entirely to the recipient. Indeed, certain forms of income (such as interest and dividends) which are not subject to withholding are subject to the requirement that the payer must file an information return.

At the same time, the withholding system has its costs. Taxpayers who underpay on the basis of their estimated returns must make a final payment and the Treasury must make refunds to those who overpaid. For the taxable year 1975, about 75 percent of returns were overwithheld and received refunds, with overpayments equal to about one-third of liabilities.

Audit

The basic system underlying the United States income tax is one of self-assessment. Each taxpayer is responsible for declaring income and computing income tax thereon. While the Bureau of Internal Revenue checks the arithmetic of tax computations, it cannot carefully audit over 80 million returns. The cost of doing so would be excessive. However, spot checks are made to keep taxpayers on their toes. Returns with unusual features (e.g., very high deductions or unusual sources of income) may be audited, and at various times particular groups of taxpayers, such as doctors or cattle ranchers, are singled out for special attention. Nevertheless, the extent of audit is relatively limited. This may change in time, when increasingly sophisticated use of computer facilities (involving not-as-yet feasible cross-checking between returns) should greatly extend the range of practicable audit and cross-checking.

B. STRUCTURE OF THE TAX BASE

Having surveyed the major provisions of the income tax, we now turn to the size, composition, and distribution of its base.

From GNP to Taxable Income

As shown in Table 16-2, taxable income for 1977 amounted to $705 billion (line 25) as against a gross national product of $1,890 billion (line 1). Thus only 37 percent of GNP appeared in taxable income. For a tax which is reputed to be the most comprehensive measure of ability to pay, this may seem a rather poor performance. Closer consideration, however, shows that, say, two-thirds of the difference reflects justifiable adjustments. Nevertheless, this leaves a substantial shortfall of taxable income below what would be included under a full income concept.

GNP to AGI In moving from GNP to AGI, these major additions and subtractions are made:

1. Capital consumption or depreciation (line 2) is deducted. This is clearly appropriate since the income tax is to be a tax on net income.

2. Indirect business taxes (line 3) are deducted. Collected from business, they are not part of net earnings and they reduce business receipts available for income payments. We shall question, however, whether all such taxes should remain outside the base, especially those which are in fact paid by consumers of government services and which therefore may be viewed as benefit charges.

3. Interest payments by government which are not part of GNP are included when moving to personal income (line 8), and they properly remain in the tax base. However, interest paid by state and local governments is not taxable and is taken out subsequently (item 14). This exclusion is one of the least justifiable omissions.

4. Both corporation tax and retained earnings drop out when moving on to personal income (lines 4 and 5). As we shall see later, a good case can be made for including retained earnings in the base.

5. Government transfer payments are added to GNP when moving to personal income (line 7), but they are excluded when arriving at AGI (line 11). Like all other sources of income, they should be included in a comprehensive base.

6. To the extent that such transfer payments are in the nature of social security benefits, however, it may be argued that they should be excluded, provided that insurance contributions are not deductible. This provision is in effect with regard to employee contributions which, after being deducted in line 6, are added back in line 15, but not with regard to employer contributions, which appear in line 6 only.[1]

7. Elements of income in kind and imputed income (line 13) which are

---

[1]See p. 355.

TABLE16-2
Taxable Income In Relation to GNP, Estimate for 1977
(In Billions of Dollars)

1. Gross national product			1,890
2.	Deduct:	Capital consumption allowances	197
3.		Indirect business taxes	163
4.		Corporation income tax	69
5.		Retained earnings of corporations	61
6.		Social security contributions	139
7.	Add:	Government transfers to persons	198
8.		Interest paid by government	42
9.		Other, net	35
10. Personal income			1,536
11.	Deduct:	Transfer payments	198
12.		Other labor income	89
13.		Imputed income	45
14.		Other exclusions	50
15.	Add:	Social security contributions, employee	51
16.		Net gain from sale of capital assets	25
17.		Other	20
18. AGI estimated from personal income			1,260
19.	Deduct:	Nonreported AGI	80
20.		AGI on tax returns	1,180
21.	Deduct:	AGI on nontaxable returns	50
22.		AGI on taxable returns	1,130
23.	Deduct:	Exemptions on taxable returns	175
24.		Deductions on taxable returns	250
25. Income subject to tax			705

Notes:
Line 12: Includes fringe benefits, employer pension contributions, etc.
Line 13: Of the total of 45 billion, over $20 billion is accounted for by imputed rent.
Line 14: Includes sick pay, business expenses of employees, moving expenses, contributions to self-employed retirement plans, tax-exempt military pay, tax-exempt interest, and excluded dividends.
Line 19: A residual equal to line 18 minus line 20.
Sources:
Lines 1–13 and 15: See U.S. Department of Commerce, *Survey of Current Business*, March 1978.
Lines 16 and 18–25: Estimates based on U.S. Treasury Department, *Individual Income Tax Returns, Preliminary Statistics of Income for 1975*, 1977.
Lines 14, 16, and 17: Estimated on basis of past levels. See also J. A. Pechman, *Federal Tax Policy*, 3d ed., Washington: Brookings, 1977.

included in the Department of Commerce concept of personal income are not included in AGI, thereby causing a substantial deficiency in the tax base. As shown below, this is significant especially with regard to imputed rent of owner-occupied residences.

8. Capital gains which are not included in the Department of Commerce concept of personal income, on the other hand, enter the tax base (line 16). But, as we shall see later, they do so only to a partial degree, thus posing the most important and controversial problem of income tax reform.

After these and other adjustments, an estimated AGI of $1,260 billion (line 18) is arrived at. This compares with an estimated AGI recorded on tax returns of $1,180 billion. The difference of $80 billion (which compares with a recent Treasury estimate for 1976 of $100 billion) includes small incomes not subject to filing. This factor might account for, say, $30 billion. The remainder of $50 billion is missing and reflects failure to declare income. A recent Treasury estimate, arrived at directly rather than as residual, showed a 1976 gap of $75–$100 billion. This margin is surprisingly small since it seems unlikely that 90 percent or more of the true total is in fact reached. Our low residual may well reflect understatement of personal income in the national income accounts.

From AGI to Income Subject to Tax   Moving on from the reported AGI of $1,260 billion, a loss of $50 billion reflects nontaxable returns, $175 billion personal exemptions, and $250 billion deductions, leaving income subject to tax of $705 billion. Together, these items reduce reported AGI by 40 percent and are major determinants of the final level of taxable income. Income subject to tax as finally determined is somewhat below 40 percent of GNP.

Size Distribution of Tax Base

The distribution of the tax base by adjusted gross income brackets, shown in Table 16-3, is of great importance for tax policy because it shows where the money comes from.[2] The data are not readily summarized, but they suggest these conclusions:

1.   The lowest 40 percent of returns (with AGI below $10,000) received 17 percent of AGI and contributed 10 percent of revenue. Since the share of the tax base received by this lower sector is relatively small (even though the number of returns is large), providing relief to this group will not greatly impair revenue.

2.   The next 40 percent (with AGI between $10,000 and $20,000), which we may think of as including the lower-middle income range, received 20 percent of AGI and contributed 32 percent of revenue. Thus this range covers a substantial part of the total and is a major contributor to revenue.

3.   The next 18 percent, which we may think of as the middle-upper range (with AGI from $20,000 to $50,000), received 33 percent of AGI and contributed 37 percent of the revenue. Clearly, this covers a major part of the tax base and revenue source.

4.   The top 2 percent finally (with AGI in excess of $50,000) received 19 percent of AGI while contributing 20 percent of revenue. Although the ratio of contribution to base is high, the base is a relatively small part of the total. Since the number of rich people is relatively small, the tax base provided by this group is limited.

In all, we conclude that the bulk of the revenue must be drawn from the broad middle-income ranges, with heavy taxation of the bottom 40 percent

---

[2]Note that the figures given in Table 16-3 are for 1975, the latest available year, but the general pattern is not changed significantly for later years. For a rough adjustment to 1980 levels, you may raise the dollar levels as given in the table by, say, 60 percent.

TABLE 16-3
Distribution of Income Tax Base, 1975
(Taxable Returns Only)

Adjusted Gross Income (Dollars)	Number of Returns* (Millions)	AGI (Billions of Dollars)	Taxable Income (Billions of Dollars)	Tax (Billions of Dollars)
Under 5,000	7.3	27.4	9.5	1.3
5,000– 10,000	17.4	130.8	70.5	10.7
10,000– 15,000	14.8	182.8	113.0	19.1
15,000– 20,000	10.3	177.4	116.9	21.2
20,000– 50,000	11.0	297.4	215.0	46.6
50,000–100,000	0.8	51.2	40.1	13.4
Over 100,000	0.2	32.6	25.9	12.4
Total	61.8	899.7	590.9	124.8
AS PERCENTAGE OF TOTAL				
Under 5,000	11.8	3.0	1.6	1.0
5,000– 10,000	28.2	14.5	11.9	8.6
10,000– 15,000	23.9	20.3	19.1	15.3
15,000– 20,000	16.7	19.7	19.8	17.0
20,000– 50,000	17.8	33.1	36.4	37.3
50,000–100,000	1.3	5.7	6.8	10.7
Over 100,000	0.3	3.6	4.4	9.9
Total	100.0	100.0	100.0	100.0

Note: Details may not add to totals due to rounding.
Source: U.S. Treasury Department, *Individual Income Tax Returns, Preliminary Statistics of Income for 1975,* 1977, table 2.
*If nontaxable returns are included, the total is 82 million.

not essential. The additional revenue share is obtained from the rich, who pay high tax rates but contribute only a small part of the total requirement.

The distribution of the tax base in turn determines the addition to total yield obtained from successive bracket rates. The initial rate of 14 percent applies to the entire base. In 1975 it contributed $0.14 \times \$591$ billion = $83 billion, or 66 percent of the revenue total. It is estimated further that bracket rates up to 25 percent yield 85 percent of total revenue while bracket rates up to 50 percent yield 98 percent of the total from present rates.[3] Thus, using 50 percent as the top marginal rate for all sources of income, the revenue loss would only be 2 percent.[4]

In evaluating this result, one must keep in mind that the tax base itself reflects the statutory definition of taxable income with all its imperfections. A more comprehensive definition of taxable income would raise the revenue potential of the higher brackets and thus increase their liabilities under present rates. But even if all preferences were to be eliminated, AGI in the

[3]Revenue includes that obtained from all income "slabs" subject to rates up to 25 percent, including the share paid by taxpayers with higher incomes.
[4]Estimates furnished by the Department of the Treasury, Division of Tax Analysis.

brackets above, say, $100,000 would still be far from dominating the revenue picture. Thus, even if liabilities in these brackets were doubled (as might be the case if all preferences were removed), their share in total revenue would be raised to only 20 percent. Moreover, adoption of a comprehensive base would also raise taxable income at the lower end of the scale. Our previous conclusion regarding the dominating importance of the base provided by the middle-income brackets would not be greatly changed.

To put it differently, the case for steeply rising marginal rates must be made on equity rather than revenue grounds. It is a fact of life that for a high-yield income tax, the bulk of revenue must be derived from the middle ranges since this is where most taxable income is received. Only if yield requirements are low relative to national income, can "soaking the rich" (as it was referred to in the New Deal years of the thirties) be a major revenue consideration. By the same token, tax relief at the bottom (if given so as to accrue entirely to low-income taxpayers) is relatively inexpensive.

Distribution of Tax Base by Income Source

If the income tax were a truly global tax, the distribution of income by source would not affect the burden distribution. But even though our income tax is meant to be global rather than schedular, elements of differential treatment among income sources remain. The distribution by income source is thus of considerable interest.

As shown in the upper half of Table 16-4, the composition of AGI by source changes greatly as we move up the income scale. As shown in column III, the share of capital income in total income forms a U-shaped pattern, falling first and then rising sharply, with the importance of capital income at the bottom of the scale reflecting mainly pension receipts of retirees. High-bracket income is largely in the form of capital income. Of special importance for our subsequent discussion is the sharp rise in the capital gains share at the high-income levels. But, though capital income is much more important as a share of total income in the high-income brackets than in the lower-income brackets, it does not follow that the bulk of capital income accrues to the very rich. As shown in the lower part of the table, this is not so. About 43 percent of dividend, interest, rent, and royalty income goes to returns below $20,000 and over 70 percent goes to returns below $50,000. The below-$20,000 group similarly receives about 27 percent of capital gains income. In all, capital income weighs much more heavily in the upper-income groups, but a substantial share of total capital income also goes to the middle- and lower-income ranges. The importance of this distribution for income tax policy will become apparent as we move along.

C. PRINCIPLES OF INCOME DEFINITION

The basic income concept upon which the determination of income tax liability in practice rests is AGI, or adjusted gross income. How satisfactory a concept is AGI? Or, more precisely, how good a measure of taxable capacity does it furnish? In our earlier discussion of tax bases we concluded that

TABLE 16-4
Distribution of Tax Base by Type of Income, 1978
(Taxable Returns Only)

Adjusted Gross Income (Dollars)	Wages and Salaries (I)	Business Professions, Farms, Partnerships (II)	Dividends, Interest, Rent, Royalties (III)	Sale of Capital Assets (IV)	All Other (V)	All Sources (VI)
PERCENTAGE OF AGI DERIVED FROM EACH SOURCE						
Under 5,000	84.8	1.1	9.0	1.1	4.0	100.0
5,000– 10,000	84.3	3.1	6.9	0.8	5.0	100.0
10,000– 20,000	89.2	3.3	4.3	0.6	2.5	100.0
20,000– 50,000	82.4	7.8	6.5	1.2	2.2	100.0
50,000– 100,000	54.5	23.5	15.7	3.8	2.5	100.0
100,000– 500,000	43.5	20.5	25.1	8.1	2.8	100.0
500,000–1,000,000	17.4	17.4	43.5	21.7	*	100.0
Over 1,000,000	8.3	12.5	45.8	33.3	*	100.0
Total	82.3	6.4	7.1	1.3	2.9	100.0
PERCENTAGE OF EACH SOURCE GOING TO VARIOUS BRACKETS OF AGI						
Under 5,000	3.1	0.5	3.9	2.4	4.3	3.0
5,000– 10,000	14.7	7.0	14.2	7.9	25.7	14.5
10,000– 20,000	43.4	20.6	24.5	17.5	35.8	40.0
20,000– 50,000	33.1	39.8	30.3	27.8	26.1	33.1
50,000– 100,000	3.8	20.9	12.7	15.9	5.1	5.7
100,000– 500,000	1.6	9.9	11.0	18.3	3.1	3.1
500,000–1,000,000	0.1	0.7	1.5	4.0	*	0.3
Over 1,000,000	*	0.5	1.7	6.3	*	0.3
Total[†]	100.0	100.0	100.0	100.0	100.0	100.0

*Less than 0.05 percent.
[†]Ratios may not add to total due to rounding.
  Notes: Column I equals column 4 in *Statistics of Income*, table 4; column II includes columns 6, 8, 10, 12, 14, and 16; column III includes columns 24, 26, 30, 32, and 34; column IV includes columns 18 and 20; column V includes columns 22, 28, 36, 38, and 40.
  Source: U.S. Treasury Department, *Individual Income Tax Returns, Preliminary Statistics of Income for 1975*, 1977.

income and consumption are the prime candidates for a broadly based personal tax, and we need not here review their comparative merits.[5] Given the choice of income as tax base, it is evident that income, as an index of taxpaying capacity, should be defined broadly as total accretion to a person's wealth. All accretion should be included, whether it be regular or fluctuating, expected or unexpected, realized or unrealized. No consideration should be given to how the income is used, i.e., whether it is saved or consumed.

Moreover, income from all sources thus defined should be treated uniformly and be combined in a global income total to which tax rates are applied. Without globality, the application of a progressive rate schedule cannot serve its purpose of adapting the tax to the taxpayer's ability to pay.

[5]See p. 243.

This view of the income tax, as expounded by Henry Simons, has been widely accepted by students of taxation.[6] Appealing and clear enough in principle, the accretion concept must now be considered more closely for what it implies in practice and how well it is satisfied by the AGI definition.

Gross Income versus Net Income

Income under the accretion approach should be measured in terms of net income, i.e., income after the costs of earning it are deducted. As noted before, the tax law attempts to define adjusted gross income as a net income concept, since costs incurred in earning income are usually, though not always, deducted. Thus, income from business activity is taxed on a net basis, i.e., after deducting costs incurred. The law also permits deduction of certain work-related expenses, such as membership fees in professional associations. Tax-free recovery of costs of investment in education, on the other hand, is not allowed. In other instances, items which are more nearly income are treated as costs, e.g., entertainment expenses charged on expense accounts. As shown below, there is also a question of what interest deductions should be allowed. But these are exceptions rather than the rule; AGI, as defined by the statute, is generally in line with the principle of *net* income.

Another principle in defining net income is that losses should be allowed for fully. Since accretion is designed to measure consumption plus increase in *net* worth, operating losses should be deducted in arriving at the net income of a business. Losses reduce net worth just as gains increase it, and the government should be a partner in both cases. While the law does not go so far as to grant a refund in case of net losses, it does make substantial provision for the spreading of losses over an eleven-year period, including three years past and seven years ahead. As will be seen later, adequate allowance for losses is of key importance for the investment effects of an income tax.[7]

Capital Income versus Labor Income

According to the accretion concept it does not matter from what source income has been derived. Yet writers on taxation have traditionally distinguished between "earned" (or wage) and "unearned" (or capital) income, implying that the former should be taxed less heavily. This may be rationalized as allowing for disutility of work, or as a convenient device to grant low-income relief. Neither argument is convincing. If disutility of work had to be allowed for, it would surely be necessary to distinguish among types of jobs; and if relief is to be granted to low incomes, it should be made available also to low-income families with capital (e.g., retirement) income.

Notwithstanding these considerations, the income tax favors earned income in two respects. At the lower end of the scale, the Tax Reduction Act of 1975 provided for the previously noted earned-income tax credit, while at

[6]See Henry Simons, *Personal Income Taxation*, Chicago: University of Chicago Press, 1950.
[7]See p. 674.

the upper end of the scale the Revenue Act of 1969 limited the top-bracket rate applicable to earned income to 50 percent but continued a top rate of 70 percent for other income. Note that both these measures lean in the direction of favoring earned income. They thus move in the opposite direction of what would be the practice if consumption rather than income was chosen as tax base.[8]

Real Income versus Nominal Income

If income is to serve as a measure of ability to pay, it should be defined in real terms. An increase in money income which is matched by a rise in prices does not constitute a gain in real income. Hence tax liability in real terms should not be affected. This consideration has become of major importance during the inflationary climate of recent years and more will be said about it later on, especially in connection with the treatment of capital gains.

Accrued Income versus Realized Income

Given our definition of income as based on accretion to wealth, it should be a matter of indifference whether gains (1) have been realized in terms of cash, as is the case with wages or the sale of assets which have appreciated in value, or (2) have been permitted to accrue by way of raising the value of assets which continue to be held. Whether or not a realization occurs is a matter of portfolio choice for the investor and should not affect income as measured for purposes of taxation. As we shall see presently, this has important bearing on the controversial topic of capital gains taxation.

Imputed Income

Some people hold earning assets that bring cash income; others hold durable consumer goods that earn imputed income. The most important example is the owner-occupied residence. The resident obtains an "imputed rent" equal to the return he or she could obtain by letting the house. Since accretion is defined as increase in net worth plus consumption, such imputed consumption values should be included in the tax base. AGI, by adhering to a cash income concept, does not include imputed income. This omission, as we shall find later on, causes inequities in the tax treatment of houseowners and renters.

Income received in kind, such as food grown on farms, the services of company cars, or gains from fringe benefits, are similarly omitted in AGI but should be in the income concept. This is especially important where payments in kind may be substituted for cash payments to avoid income tax. At the same time, the inclusion of imputed income becomes unworkable if carried too far. Thus, a good case could be made conceptually for imputing earnings to housewives for the services which they render to the family. If this were done, the tax base might well be raised by, say, $250 billion, but part of this

[8]See p. 247.

might be lost by allowance for increased personal exemptions. An even more puzzling problem is posed by leisure. If a person chooses leisure, this is evidence (arguing in analogy to unrealized capital gains) that he or she values it by the income equivalent lost in not working. The pure logic of accretion would suggest that consumption in the form of leisure be included in the tax base, but implementation of such a rule, as noted earlier in our discussion of distributive justice, seems to be impracticable More will be said about this when discussing the definition of the taxpaying unit.[9]

Earnings versus Transfers

From the economist's point of view, national income is the sum of factor earnings during the period, reflecting in turn the value of output which the factors have produced. Transfers received from government or private sources (such as gifts or bequests) are not components of income in the national income sense. But it does not follow that they should be excluded from taxable income. Choosing a suitable definition of taxable income is an issue in tax equity, not in national income accounting. A person's taxable income need not be the same as his or her share in national income; nor need total taxable income equal total national income.

Transfer receipts from government, such as welfare and veterans' benefits, are excluded from AGI, but there is no good reason for this exclusion. Indeed, $1,000 received in benefits adds no less to a person's economic capacity than does $1,000 received in wages. While the transfer recipient's income will frequently be too low to justify its taxation, this situation should be taken care of by devices such as exemptions and the low-income allowance, devices which apply equally to all sources of low earnings. The treatment of social security benefits poses a special problem, to be discussed later in this chapter.

Private transfers, such as bequests and gifts, also remain outside the income tax. Such transfers are neither deducted by the donor, nor included by the donee. In terms of the accretion concept, the receipt of bequests or gifts constitutes an addition to economic capacity just as does accretion from other sources. Although such transfers are taxed separately under the estate and gift taxes, a good argument can be made for including them in the income tax base of the recipient.

Regular versus Irregular Income

The argument is sometimes made that irregular and unexpected income should not be included for tax purposes. While there is an advantage to certainty, even uncertain accretion adds to the recipient's wealth. After all, why should wages be taxed but gambling gains be exempted? The only special problem to be recognized in this connection is that progressive rates tend to discriminate against fluctuating income. This, however, calls for averaging provisions and not for the exclusion of such gains.

[9]See p. 381.

D. PRACTICE OF INCOME DEFINITION: (1) EXCLUSIONS

Examination of the tax law shows considerable departures from these principles. Some items which should be included are in fact excluded from AGI, or are deducted from AGI in arriving at taxable income. We begin with exclusions.

Tax-Exempt Interest

Interest on state and local securities is not taxable under the federal income tax. Although this exclusion was originally based on the constitutional provision that any one level of government should not tax the instrumentalities of another, most legal opinion now holds that the inclusion of such interest would be permissible under the Sixteenth Amendment. Inclusion can no longer be ruled out on constitutional grounds. On its merits, exclusion is undesirable because it undermines the equity of the income tax. Moreover, tax exemption is an inefficient means of supporting state and local government borrowing.

Beginning with equity aspects, exclusion gives the greatest advantage to high-income taxpayers with capital income. The gains from exemption rise with the investor's tax bracket. For an investor whose marginal rate is 50 percent, a tax-exempt security yielding 5 percent is equivalent in net yield to a taxable issue yielding 10 percent. For an investor whose marginal rate is 60 percent, the equivalent yield on a taxable issue is 12.5 percent, while for an investor with a bracket rate of 20 percent, it is only 6.25 percent. This explains why the great bulk of tax-exempts held outside banks are held by wealthy individuals. Of the $6 billion of estimated revenue loss from interest exemption (fiscal year 1979), over $2 billion involved individual returns, with over 80 percent of the benefits going to taxpayers with AGI above $100,000. The remainder, accruing to trust accounts and financial intermediaries, also largely benefits upper-income groups. While these tax savings are much less than those from the capital gains preference, they are nevertheless a major reason why so little tax is paid by many high-income taxpayers. Moreover, they are another major cause of horizontal inequity among upper-bracket taxpayers.

Apart from being inequitable, the exemption is an *inefficient* way of subsidizing state and local governments. More aid could be given at the same cost if the federal government were to subsidize state and local interest payments directly. Because interest on state and local securities is tax-exempt, such securities are worth more to investors. Therefore they will pay a higher price or, what amounts to the same, accept a lower before-tax yield. Because of this, the governments can issue securities at a lower interest cost. However, less than the entire revenue loss is passed on to state and local governments in the form of lower borrowing costs.

Consider the following situation: Mr. H, who pays a high-bracket tax rate of 60 percent, has $800 to invest, while Ms. L, who pays a lower rate of 40 percent, invests $200. Both can invest in federal securities at 10 percent, giving them a net yield of 4 and 6 percent, respectively. Neglecting risk differentials, they will purchase state and local securities yielding below this level. If $1000 of such securities are to be placed, the yield must be at least 6 percent so that both will participate. The state and local governments then save $40 in interest cost since they now lend at 6 rather than 10 percent. The federal government loses income tax revenue of $56, which it would have obtained had H and L invested in taxable 10 percent issues. The net loss to governments of $16 accrues to Mr. H, whose earnings are $48 as against after-tax earnings (in the absence of the exclusion provision) of $32. Ms. L has $12 left, the same as from investing in taxable 10 percent issues.

In practice, matters are more complicated, but our illustration shows why the device is inefficient: the subsidy must be set sufficiently high to attract the marginal investor, while investors with higher-bracket rates could have been attracted for less. The same aid could be given to state and local governments through a direct subsidy of $40, leaving them with the same net interest cost of $60. Or, by giving a direct subsidy of $56, that gain could be raised by nearly 30 percent and damage to tax equity would be avoided. Moreover, by raising the yield, the market for state and local securities would be broadened as investment by savings institutions would be attracted.

Administration proposals to provide for a direct subsidy for tax exemption on new issues have been advanced, most recently in 1977, but have been rejected by Congress. State and local governments, like other groups, prefer their subsidies in hidden form, and they fear that a direct subsidy would be less permanent in nature. For these reasons, the combined opposition of governors, mayors, and high-bracket taxpayers has, to date, been too strong to permit a sensible reform. On the contrary, the range of tax-exempt issues has been widened by the inclusion of industrial development bonds (sponsored by state or municipal governments but in effect raising capital for private firms) under this privilege. Most recently, mortgage bonds have been issued, the interest on which is tax exempt, with the proceeds made available to private homeowners as mortgage loans.

Capital Gains

Turning now to the treatment of capital gains, we arrive at perhaps the most important and controversial issue in income definition.

Present Status   Under current law, realized gains are taxed on a preferential basis while unrealized gains are not taxed at all. Realized capital gains are defined as gains which result from the sale of assets other than those held in the ordinary conduct of business. Inventory gains made by a department store and gains from appreciation in the value of securities held by a security dealer or of houses held by a real estate firm are treated as ordinary income. But gains from the sale of securities held by an investor or of a house by a homeowner are given capital gains treatment. While short-term gains (or gains from the sale of assets held for less than twelve months) are treated as ordinary income and included in AGI in full, long-term gains (from the sale of assets held over one year) are included only at 40 percent. The top rate on long-term gains is thus 40 percent of 70 percent, or 28 percent.[10]

The partial taxation of capital gains is matched by a limited allowance for capital losses. One-half of net long-term losses may be charged against short-term gains, but the charging of losses (short- or long-term) against other income is limited to $1000.

Implications for Equity   Quite apart from the possibility of total tax avoidance through nonrealization, this preferential treatment of realized gains gives a strong incentive to receive capital income in the form of capital gains rather than as operating profits, dividends, or interest. This incentive rises with the taxpayer's bracket rate. It is not surprising, therefore, that the share of capital gains in AGI rises sharply as we move up the income scale. As was shown in Table 16-3, capital gains in 1975 rose from about 3 percent of AGI at the $50,000 level to around 7 percent at $100,000, and to 33 percent at the $1 million level.[11]

The damage to tax equity is evident. Horizontal equity is damaged because of resulting differentials in tax liabilities at given levels of income; and vertical equity is interfered with because the capital gains preference goes far in offsetting the bite of progressive taxation on capital income. As will be seen in the next chapter, the capital gains issue dwarfs the importance of all other tax preferences for high incomes, so that full taxation of capital gains at ordinary rates would result in a much more progressive tax. But full taxation of capital gains could be accompanied by a reduction in bracket rates, in which case the major result would be an improvement in horizontal equity.

Are Capital Gains Income?   The case for full taxation of capital gains is based on the hypothesis that capital gains are part of accretion and should be treated accordingly. Is this a valid assumption?

No case can be made on equity grounds for giving preferential treatment to realized gains as compared to, say, operating profits. Income is received in both cases and there is no basis on which to distinguish the two. While a special problem arises in that capital gains are discontinuous and volatile, so that they would pay more under progressive rates than would an equal amount of income received in a steady flow, this difficulty can be met through adequate averaging provisions. Nor can it be argued convincingly that capital gains should be given special treatment because they frequently are not expected or "regular" income, but are windfalls which happen to accrue without intention. This may be the case for some gains though not for others; and even where gains are unexpected, they nevertheless add to the recipient's taxable capacity. There seems little doubt, on equity grounds, that realized capital gains should be treated as ordinary income.

---

[10]To this is added a "special minimum tax" at rates of 10 to 25 percent on the exempt portion of gains, which may raise the total to a maximum of 29 percent.

[11]Of course, the capital gains share in total income varies with stock market behavior and in good years has been substantially higher than here shown for 1975.

But what about the treatment of unrealized gains? Since AGI is defined in cash terms and includes cash income only, unrealized gains are not taxed. This is clearly in contravention of the accretion principle. According to this principle, income as an index of taxpaying ability should be measured as accretion to wealth. All increments should be included, whether realized (turned into cash) or not. If Mr. Jones holds corporate shares which have appreciated in value by $100,000, this is the amount by which his net worth has risen and which he would have been able to turn into cash if he had so chosen. The fact that he has retained this particular asset shows that he preferred continued holding over the available alternatives, e.g., sale with consumption or reinvestment in some other asset. Whether the gain is realized or not is irrelevant to whether or not there has been an increase in economic capacity. Provided that realization is possible, the decision whether or not to realize is a problem in portfolio (asset) management and not in the creation of income. Postponement of the tax until realization gives an unfair advantage to such income. The Treasury in effect grants an interest-free loan on the amount of the postponed liability. If no realization occurs, this gain will in fact last forever, as no tax becomes due.

Nevertheless, these conclusions have been subject to continuous debate, as shown by the following arguments:

1. "Unrealized gains should not be taxed because the owner has refrained from consumption."

While there has been no consumption, this is not relevant in defining the base of an *income* tax. Here the principle is that all income should be taxed, independently of how it is used; and even under a consumption tax, the distinction between realized and unrealized gains is not the decisive issue.[12]

2. "Unrealized gains should not be taxed because in the absence of realization we do not know whether they really exist."

Thus, in the early origins of bookkeeping the Venetian merchant was well advised not to count his proceeds until his captain had returned to home port and delivered the treasure chest. Prudent accounting would call for "realization" in cash (or gold) before income was said to exist. But institutions change and the analogy is quite inappropriate for, say, a holder of AT&T shares which can be sold at once. As will be noted later, measurement of unrealized gains may be difficult, but this is not an insuperable obstacle.

3. "Taxation of unrealized gains requires the owner to pay a tax even though he or she has not obtained cash with which to pay it."

The observation is correct, but does it matter? As would be necessary with other debts that may come due, it is not unreasonable to ask the taxpayer to liquidate part of his or her assets to make the tax payment if needed. For situations in which partial liquidation is not possible (e.g., a family business), adequate time must be granted.

4. Finally, the following argument is occasionally made: For income to be

---

[12]Under a consumption tax, unrealized gains would be excluded and realized gains would be included *only if consumed*. Realized gains which are not consumed but are reinvested or held as cash would be excluded. On the other hand, consumption financed by drawing down balances would be subject to tax.

received, it must be "separated" from the asset. This view, which had much legal support in the earlier stages of the income tax discussion, is hard to fathom from the economist's point of view. Separation is a matter of investment choice, whereas income accrues when the asset value is increased.

It may be fairly concluded that, on equity grounds, unrealized gains should be considered taxable and included along with income from all other sources.

Implementation Problems   Suppose that this was to be done. Is there a feasible way of reaching unrealized gains? Full taxation of realized gains can be implemented without technical difficulties, but the situation is more difficult for unrealized gains. Taxation of unrealized gains on a current basis is not feasible owing to the impracticality of annual valuation of all assets. Some assets, such as traded securities, could be valued and taxed periodically, say, every five years, but other assets (e.g., paintings or farms) may be more difficult to value. It has therefore been proposed that accrued gains be taxed at death or transfer (by gift) as if realized at that time. Referred to as "constructive realization," this would reduce the need for valuation to a single time, thus reducing this task to manageable proportions. By permitting averaging and the spreading of payments over a period of time, inequities which would arise from forced liquidation of assets may be avoided. Under such a procedure, all gains would be eventually taxed, thus reducing the lock-in effect. A constructive realization provision has recently been enacted in Canada[13] and has been repeatedly proposed in the United States, but has not as yet been accepted by the Congress.[14]

While constructive realization would move unrealized gains into the tax base, it would still leave capital gains with some advantage. Whereas other income is taxed on a current basis, the tax on unrealized gains would be delayed until death, thus leaving the taxpayer with the possibility of earning income thereon in the meantime. Tax delay is equivalent to receiving an interest-free loan, the value of which may be substantial, especially for young investors.[15]

---

[13]Under the Canadian legislation of 1971, unrealized gains are taxed at death but gains accrued prior to enactment of the new provision are excluded. The earlier proposal for periodic taxation of accrued gains on shares was not enacted. See *Proposals for Tax Reform*, Ottawa: Queen's Printer, 1969, p. 36.

[14]Constructive realization was proposed by the Kennedy administration in 1964 but was rejected out of hand by Congress. A more modest substitute was introduced in 1976. This relates to the computation of gains by the heir who sells an asset acquired from an estate. Under previous provision, the heir could use the written-up asset value at the time of the estate as base, rather than the original cost incurred by the deceased. Thus, even realized gains escaped taxation if the asset was passed through an estate. Under the new law, the heir is required to use the original cost as the base when computing capital gains upon future realization. However, this was to apply only to appreciation in value subsequent to 1976, which date has now been postponed to 1980. It is doubtful whether the change will be applied even then.

[15]This consideration, it may be noted, runs directly counter to frequent proposals for reducing the inclusion rate of long-term gains with the length of the holding period.

Inflationary Gains   The equity case for full taxation of capital gains is tempered, however, by the impact of inflation. If capital gains are a reflection of an inflationary increase in nominal values only, they should not be taxed. To produce a meaningful index of taxable capacity, it is evident that income should be defined in real terms, i.e., that changes in the price level should be allowed for in determining taxable income. This is of special importance with regard to changes in asset value. A rise in the money value of an asset which is matched by an increase in price level is an illusory capital gain and should not be considered income. In fact, a substantial fraction of gains in recent years has been of this sort.

The case for adjusting capital gains for inflation is evident, but the question arises whether the same principle should not be extended also to allow for the real losses suffered by holders of claims, such as cash, savings bonds, or mortgages, and for real gains made by debtors of these instruments. Granted that an across-the-board adjustment would be best, it may be arguable whether a partial adjustment (for capital gains only) would be an equitable solution. More will be said about this at a later point.[16]

Economic Effects of Full Taxation   While equity considerations on the whole point to the taxation of capital gains as regular income, albeit with inflation adjustment, the potential effects of full taxation on capital markets and economic growth must also be considered:

1. Taxation of realized gains is detrimental to the mobility of the capital market. Since transfers of assets (selling and reinvesting) occasion a tax, such shifts are discouraged. The tax tends to lock in investments, especially where the investor is subject to a high bracket rate.[17] Thus, application of a lower (preferential) rate is considered desirable. While this is a valid argument, its force would be greatly reduced if unrealized gains were taxed at death, since this would lower the tax savings from postponing realization.

2. It is argued that full taxation of realized gains, and especially the inclusion of unrealized gains into the tax base, would be detrimental to economic growth.[18] By the same token, further liberalization is proposed to stimulate investment and to attract equity capital. Evaluation of this argument not only involves the effectiveness of reduced capital gains taxation as an investment

---

[16]See p. 388.

[17]Suppose the investor has an asset with a market value M and a yield y, which gives an income $I = yM$. If the asset was purchased at original cost C this income after sale and reinvestment equals $I^* = y^*[M - t(M - C)]$, where y^* is the yield of the new asset and t is the investor's marginal rate of tax. Now let $(M - C)/M = \alpha$, the capital gain as a fraction of M. By substitution, $I^* = y^*M(1 - t\alpha)$. If the switch is to be worthwhile, we must have $I^* > I$ or $y^* > y/(1 - t\alpha)$. Thus, if the yield on the old asset was 10 percent, α is 60 percent and t is 50 percent, the yield on the new investment would have to be over 14.3 percent. The level of y^* required to make the asset switch profitable will be the higher, the larger are t and α.

If the asset was held for over 12 months, t in the above formula is replaced by $0.4t$, and the required yield on the new investment becomes 11.4 percent.

[18]A case for the importance of saving to economic growth is made in C. Lowell Harriss, *Innovations in Tax Policy and Other Essays*, Hartford: John C. Lincoln Institute, 1972, p. 277.

incentive but also a comparison of its merits with those of other investment incentives. More will be said about this at a later point.[19]

Considerations such as these have weighed heavily in the congressional move to further liberalize capital gains taxation under the Revenue Act of 1978, when the excluded fraction was raised from 50 to 60 percent and the minimum tax was liberalized, thus reversing the legislative trend of the preceding decades.

Conclusion   It appears that the preferential treatment of capital gains as provided for under present law is unsatisfactory on equity grounds. It severely damages horizontal equity and to a substantial degree negates the progressive rate schedule. As a matter of tax equity, full taxation of gains, combined perhaps with a leveling of progressive rates, would be preferable. It also appears that techniques may be devised which permit full taxation of realized gains and inclusion at death or transfer of unrealized gains. Combined with an inflation adjustment, this would provide for equitable treatment of gains. It remains necessary, however, to balance the resulting improvement in equity against the loss of beneficial economic effects which may result from preferential treatment. In the meantime, it should be noted that preferential treatment of gains is not confined to the United States. In fact, most countries exclude unrealized gains, and in most instances realized gains as well are given preferential treatment.

Dividend Exclusion

The first $100 of dividends are excluded from AGI. Looked at from the point of view of the income tax alone, there is no justification for permitting a supplementary exemption on this particular form of income. Evaluation of this exclusion must, however, be made in a broader framework, involving the interaction of corporation and income tax liabilities. Since the $100 limit makes the provision insignificant for high-income taxpayers, it may be considered as a rough (but only a very rough) offset to the higher incremental burden which the corporation income tax imposes upon dividends received by shareholders at the lower end of the income scale.[20]

Pensions

Contributory pension plans involve the setting aside of current income for future use. Proper tax treatment would disallow deduction of employee contributions when made and exclude benefits when received later on, except for such part thereof as reflects interest earnings on earlier contributions. An alternative, allowing for deduction of contributions when made with full taxation of subsequent benefits, would not be so satisfactory since it would leave the taxpayer with two advantages not enjoyed by other savers. Since tax

[19]See p. 439.
[20]See p. 428.

TABLE 16-5
Tax Treatment of Pension Plans

Type	Contributions or Premiums	Benefits	Interest
OASI			
Employee	Not deductible	Not taxed	Not taxed
Employer	Deductible	Not taxed	Not taxed
Private Retirement Plans			
Employee	Not deductible	Not taxed	Taxed
Employer	Deductible	Taxed	Taxed
*Self-Employed**	Deductible	Taxed	Taxed
Life Insurance	Not deductible	Not taxed	Not taxed[†]

*Limited to 10 percent of AGI with annual ceiling of $2,500.
[†]If distribution made prior to death, interest component is taxed.

payments are postponed, the taxpayer would receive an interest gain. Moreover, as his or her future income is likely to be smaller, a lower bracket rate would apply. As shown in Table 16-5, the actual treatment of pension and insurance plans varies and usually falls short of the proper solution.

Social Insurance Beginning with old age and survivors' insurance (OASI), note that employee contributions are not deducted from AGI but employer contributions are deducted. Benefits in turn are tax-free. Viewing OASI as a contributory system, the proper procedures would be to (1) disallow deduction of all contributions while including only such part of the benefits as reflect interest earnings, or (2) permit deduction of all contributions while fully taxing benefit receipts. Present procedure thus involves a somewhat preferential treatment with regard to the employee contribution and a highly preferential treatment regarding the employer-financed part where the insured remains entirely tax-free.

The situation differs if, as is increasingly the case, OASI is viewed in noninsurance terms. The proper solution would then be to treat benefits like other income and to tax them accordingly. Since the federal income tax does not allow for deduction of other federal taxes, the present treatment of the employee contribution as nondeductible would remain unchanged.

Private Retirement Plan The treatment of private retirement plans comes closer to inclusion of the full tax base. While treatment of contributions is the same as for OASI, benefits based on the employer contribution are now taxable. Employee contributions may be deducted and the entire benefits thereon become taxable at disbursement.

More important, however, is the tax advantage which results because the deferred payment mechanism of pension plans works as an averaging device. Since averaging is generally desirable on equity grounds, this is not necessarily objectionable, except that the option to postpone is not always available. It has been of special importance for highly paid executives and has led to extensive use of various deferred-payment arrangements. Similar but more limited provisions are now available for self-employed persons.

Life Insurance Similar rules apply to the savings component of life insurance. Premiums are not deducted and benefits are not taxed, thus permitting interest on premiums to escape. However, interest is taxable if distribution is made prior to death. Forms of insurance which carry no savings component (such as term insurance) yield no interest earnings. Benefits are properly exempted, without allowing a deduction of premiums.

E. PRACTICE OF INCOME DEFINITION: (2) DEDUCTIONS

Deductions may be used to make taxable income a better measure of economic capacity; but inappropriate use may again give rise to preferences and distortions.

Types of Deductions

In 1975, the latest year for which detailed data on deductions is available, the standard deduction was taken by 60 percent of taxable returns and accounted for 38 percent of total deductions. Only 40 percent of taxable returns itemized. Since then, the standard deduction has been raised substantially, so that at present levels ($2,300 for single and $3,400 for joint returns) the share of itemizers has fallen further and for 1979 may be close to 30 percent. However, the general pattern of itemizing has not changed greatly, so that it remains useful to look at the 1975 picture.

As shown in column II of Table 16-6, low-bracket returns typically use the standard deduction, but the percentage of itemizers rises sharply when we move up the income scale. Thus the percentage of itemizers rose from below 5 percent in the under-$5,000 bracket to nearly 100 percent at the top.

Table 16-6 also shows various deductions as a percentage of AGI. As shown in column III, the standard deduction as percentage of AGI falls when we move up the income scale. The ratio of total itemized deductions to AGI of itemizers (column IX) is highest at the bottom, reflecting the fact that such returns will use itemizing only in unusual cases, such as heavy medical expenses. The ratio then settles at around 18 percent over the $30,000 to $200,000 range but rises again for top income.

Particular items vary in importance by income levels. Medical deductions are of primary significance at the lower end of the income scale, with interest deductions (reflecting mortgage interest) most important in the low-middle range. Charitable contributions are most vital at the upper end, with deduction of state and local taxes of importance throughout the income scale.

Rationale for Itemized Deductions

The principle of income taxation calls for a comprehensive tax base, including all forms of accretion. This approach establishes a prima facie case against deductions, yet some deductions may be justified.

TABLE 16-6
Deductions as Percentage of AGI, 1975
(Taxable Returns Only)

AGI CLASS (Dollars)	PERCENTAGE OF RETURNS BY TYPE OF DEDUCTION		DEDUCTIONS AS PERCENTAGE OF AGI						
	Standard (I)	Itemized (II)	Standard Deduction (III)	Itemized Deductions					
				Taxes (IV)	Interest (V)	Contributions (VI)	Medical Expenses (VII)	Other (VIII)	All (IX)
4,000– 5,000	95.2	4.8	35.6	14.1	7.4	7.5	11.7	4.2	45.0
5,000– 10,000	82.9	17.1	18.3	8.9	10.0	3.6	5.2	3.3	30.9
10,000– 15,000	59.3	40.7	16.2	8.4	9.0	2.9	3.3	3.0	26.6
15,000– 20,000	44.9	55.1	14.7	8.2	8.2	2.5	2.0	2.6	23.5
30,000– 50,000	10.8	89.2	7.2	8.1	5.7	2.5	0.9	1.7	18.8
50,000–100,000	5.4	94.6	4.1	7.9	4.7	2.9	0.6	1.8	18.1
100,000–200,000	2.6	97.4	2.1	7.5	4.4	3.9	0.4	1.9	18.1
Over 1,000,000	0.9	99.1	*	6.2	3.7	13.7	*	2.6	26.2
Total	60.3	39.7	17.6	8.1	6.9	2.8	1.7	2.3	21.8

*Less than 0.05 percent.

Notes: Standard deduction includes low-income allowance and percentage deduction and is shown as percent of AGI of returns using standard deduction. Itemized deductions are shown as percent of AGI of returns using itemized deductions.

Source: U.S. Treasury Department, Individual Income Tax Returns, Preliminary Statistics of Income for 1975, 1977, tables 4 and 5.

Equity Aspects   Equal income may not imply equal ability to pay if taxpayers are in otherwise different positions. This is recognized with regard to family size, but may apply also in other respects. Taxpayers with heavy emergency expenses, such as large medical bills, may be said to have less taxable capacity than others with equal income but no such emergencies. It is also reasonable to suggest that such situations will be of special importance for low-income taxpayers. This principle is reflected in the allowance for medical expenses which may be deducted if in excess of 3 percent of AGI. A similar argument can be made regarding casualty losses and losses from theft, such losses now being allowed above $100. If designed properly, emergency deductions are not objectionable and may indeed be helpful in securing a more equitable tax base.[21] The objective, after all, is not to maximize the tax base but to secure a fair measure of taxable capacity.

A further case for deductions is based on the proposition that certain components of income are not available to the taxpayer for his or her own free use. This argument is usually made to support the deduction of state and local taxes but, as we shall see presently, is more appropriate for some such taxes than for others.

This rationale does, however, raise the question of whether allowance should be made as a deduction from AGI in arriving at taxable income or as a credit against tax. In the former case, the value of the benefit (in terms of tax reduction) rises with the bracket rate and hence with income, whereas in the latter case it is constant for all taxpayers. If allowance for emergency needs is viewed as a matter of income definition, the deduction approach is in order, but if considered in the nature of hardship relief, a credit (granted if total hardship items exceed a certain percentage of AGI) seems more appropriate.

Incentive Aspects   Deductions may be viewed as a way of providing an incentive to use income in a "meritorious" form or to encourage expenditures on items which generate external benefits. The deduction here acts as a matching grant by which the government reduces the cost of certain activities for the taxpayer, thereby inducing the individual to spend more on this activity. If the particular activity merits support and if tax deduction is the best technique of giving it, the resulting gain may outweigh the damage to tax equity. There is no law of nature which says that taxation must not be used for purposes other than revenue collection. Rather, the question is whether the supported activity merits a subsidy, and if so, whether the subsidy should be given in this form. More will be said about this when we consider charitable contributions.

Evaluation of Itemized Deductions

The single most important itemized deduction is that for state and local taxes. In 1975, this accounted for a loss in taxable income of $44 billion. Next came

---

[21]Similar considerations arise in connection with extra exemptions for the blind. To the extent that being blind calls for extra expenses, the equal treatment principle justifies an extra allowance. The same case cannot be made, however, with regard to the extra exemption for aged.

interest deductions, with $38 billion, and charitable contributions, with $15 billion. Together, these accounted for 83 percent of total itemized deductions of $122 billion.

State and Local Taxes   Deduction of taxes is clearly appropriate where they enter as a cost of doing business, and such deduction is permitted for both federal and lower-level taxes. In addition, the law permits deduction of income, property, and of all general sales taxes imposed by state and local governments even where they are nonbusiness taxes paid by households and consumers.

Here the case hinges on whether such tax payments are viewed as uses of income similar to other private uses, or whether they should be considered a forced reduction in the taxpayer's own income. In the first case, deduction is inappropriate, while in the second, it is proper. It follows from this that the case for deductibility is weakest where taxes are in the nature of benefit charges, such as gasoline taxes which may be considered payment for high-way services. In line with this, gasoline tax deductibility was repealed in the Revenue Act of 1978. By the same token, the case for deduction is strengthened with income taxes. Such taxes are general charges which reduce the taxpayer's disposable income, and the relationship of the person's own contribution to benefits received is less direct. Although the taxpayer receives the benefit of public services, the situation differs from that of private uses of his or her income. Taxpayers must pay the tax, and while they have a vote, they do not have a veto. For these reasons, deductibility of state and local income taxes is generally counted as valid.

With regard to other taxes, the case remains controversial. While dis-allowance of the sales tax deduction has been argued on the grounds that the consumer is not forced to buy (so that tax payment is optional), this is hardly convincing, especially where the tax is general. Nor can disallowance of the property tax be justified simply by looking at the tax as a benefit tax, since most of property tax revenue is used to finance more or less general outlays. From a theoretical point of view, the best approach might be to allow the deduction of all taxes (including, for that matter, federal taxes) while includ-ing benefits from public services in the tax base, but this would not be a feasible procedure. Short of this approach, there does not appear to be a clear-cut solution.

Mortgage Interest and Housing   Next in importance are deductions for interest payments. Such deductions comprise 32 percent of total itemized deductions, with mortgage interest accounting for the larger part thereof. As with taxes, a distinction must be drawn between interest paid as a cost of doing business and interest paid on consumer debt. Deductibility of business interest is clearly appropriate for the simple reason that taxable income should be defined as net income. But deductibility of interest on consumer debt, such as mortgages, is a different matter. While both types of interest are cost payments or negative income streams, the treatment of the correspond-ing benefit streams differs. In the case of business borrowing, the benefit

stream is normally included as taxable business income, while in the instance
of mortgage or consumer debt, the benefit stream (in the form of imputed
rent or other services) is not treated as part of the resident's taxable income.

Consider three people, each with $30,000 to invest and wishing to live in
a $30,000 house. Also assume that the return on all capital is 5 percent. Mr. R
decides to rent and invest his funds in shares. As shown in the table, he
receives $1,500 in dividends. On this he pays a tax of 30 percent, or $450. Mr.
O decides to own his house outright and pays $30,000 in cash. He buys no
shares and receives no dividend income, but benefits from imputed rent of
$1,500. Since this is not counted as taxable income, he pays no tax. Ms. M
purchases a $30,000 residence by taking up a mortgage, while using her
$30,000 to purchase shares. She derives $1,500 in dividends but pays $1,500 in
interest. Since the latter can be deducted, she is again left without taxable
income. Now compare the three as in line 5. They all have the same net worth
and live in similar houses, but R pays $450 in tax while O and M are tax-free.

		Renter R	Equity Owner O	Mortgage Owner M
1.	Owner's imputed rent	0	$1,500	$1,500
2.	Interest paid	0	0	$1,500
3.	Dividends	$1,500	0	$1,500
4.	Taxable, present law	$1,500	0	0
5.	Tax, present law	$ 450	0	0
6.	Variant 1 tax	$ 450	0	$ 450
7.	Variant 2 tax	$ 450	$ 450	$ 450
8.	Variant 3 tax	0	0	0

How can the three be placed in an equal position? Removal of the
interest deduction (variant 1) will not do. While M would lose her advantage
and be placed in the same position as R, O would remain free of tax. In order
to treat all alike, we must either make imputed rent taxable while continuing
to allow deduction of interest (variant 2), or disregard imputed rent and
deduct interest, but make rent payments deductible as well (variant 3). With
variant 2, O and M must both pay the same tax as R, while with variant 3,
R's liability is removed and no one pays. Both solutions are neutral as
between the various types of housing arrangements, but variant 2 shows no
preference for housing while 3 makes all housing expenditures tax-exempt.
From the point of view of a global income tax, variant 2 is clearly the
preferred solution. Equal treatment should apply not only among people who
consume housing in different form, but also among those who consume
housing and others who consume different items.[22]

[22]The question may be raised whether—from the point of view of the tax structure as a
whole—preferential treatment of housing under the income tax might be considered an offset to
the extra burden imposed on housing under the property tax, provided that its proceeds are used
to finance general (rather than housing-oriented) expenditures. See p. 489.

The case for preferential treatment would thus have to be made on incentive grounds. The question then is whether the incentive should be given to ownership in particular or to housing expenditure in general. The present procedure, which gives preferential treatment to ownership, is difficult to defend, especially since low-income housing is more largely in rental form. But even generalized tax relief for housing (ownership or rental) is of dubious validity. Support for low-cost housing in particular may be desirable, calling for limitation of the tax preference to rental payments and interest deduction on such housing. But for this purpose, tax preferences are hardly the appropriate solution. Taxes paid by truly low-income families are too low (if the family is taxable at all) to make a substantial difference. Rental subsidies and direct provision for low-cost housing offer superior approaches.

However strong the case for inclusion of imputed rent may be in principle, it is politically unpopular and not in the cards.[23] Given this situation, would removal of the interest deduction (variant 1) be desirable as a second-best solution? As noted before, this would equalize the position between R and M, but leave O in a preferred position. Moreover, it would differentiate the treatment of O and M, who are now in similar positions. Nevertheless, there would be an equity gain in such a change. The Rs and Ms are more numerous than the Os, so that horizontal equity would be improved by equalizing their treatment.[24]

Similar reasoning applies to interest on other types of consumer debt such as automobile loans. Again interest is deductible but the imputed income derived from the car is not taxed. Here, renting is of only limited (though growing) importance, but the difference between outright purchases and debt finance remains. With low-income families in this case typically in the debtor position, the vertical equity aspect of the interest deduction is modified, the deduction now being beneficial at lower levels of income.

Business Interest   Interest on funds borrowed for business purposes is appropriately deducted in arriving at net income. However, to avoid abuse, such deduction is now permissible only against investment income.

Charitable Contributions   Charitable contributions in 1975 accounted for 12 percent of itemized deductions. Taxpayers may deduct contributions to a wide range of nonprofit institutions up to 50 percent of AGI. Prior to the Tax Reform Act of 1969, taxpayers whose charitable contributions and tax liability together exceeded 90 percent of AGI were allowed to deduct without limit. This provision, which resulted in about 100 of the wealthiest taxpayers paying little or no tax, was repealed in 1969. Under the same act, exemption

---

[23]Great Britain, which has traditionally included imputed rent, has discontinued the practice in recent years. Other countries, including Scandinavian countries and Germany, do, however, include it.

[24]For further discussion of the tax treatment of housing, see H. Aaron, "Income Taxes and Housing," *American Economic Review*, December 1970.

For a study of horizontal inequity in the tax treatment of housing, see M. White and A. White, "Horizontal Inequality in the Federal Income Tax Treatment of Homeowners and Tenants," *National Tax Journal*, September 1965.

from capital gains tax of gifts of appreciated property was limited to 30 percent of total contributions.

Since the revenue cost of deductions for charitable contributions is around $7 billion, Congress, in effect, allocates this amount as a public contribution to eleemosynary institutions. These contributions, however, are made as matching grants to private donors, leaving it to them to select the recipient. The matching rate equals the donor's marginal tax rate. A donor in the 70 percent bracket must put up only 30 cents to make a gift of $1, while a donor in the 20 percent bracket must put up 80 cents. A philosopher-economist might observe that the opportunity cost of virtue falls as one moves up the income scale.

The merit of charitable deductions is not easy to judge. On the pro side it is evident that, without the pincer effect of high marginal rates and deductibility, charitable contributions would be considerably less. Taking charitable giving as a whole, it has been estimated that charities gain about what the Treasury loses in revenue.[25] The incentive is no bargain, but neither is there a significant leakage.[26] It is argued that without such deductions, charities would suffer a severe loss and some might not survive. Congress would hardly be willing to spend corresponding amounts for such purposes. Moreover, there may be an advantage in decentralizing the choice of supported projects. On the con side, it is argued that some of the functions now supported by charity should be the responsibility of the state and that allocations made from public funds (whether as a direct appropriation or via special tax provision) should be subject to public direction and scrutiny. The issue carries broad social and cultural implications which go much beyond the purely fiscal aspects of tax policy.

The question is not only whether an incentive should be given, but how this should be done. Thus it has been suggested that deductibility be replaced by a credit against tax. If a 30 percent credit was given, everybody would be granted the same matching rate and the net cost of a dollar of charity would be 70 cents throughout.[27] This seems fair enough, but what would be the implications? Recent empirical work has yielded two interesting results. First, it has been estimated that substitution of a credit with the same revenue cost would have little effect on total giving. The cost of giving would rise for high- and fall for low-income taxpayers, but there would be little change in the total.[28] Second, it has been shown that there would be a very substantial change in the composition of giving. Contributions to churches, which figure

[25]See M. Feldstein, "Income Tax Charitable Contributions, Part I," *National Tax Journal,* March 1975.

[26]The incentive (deduction or credit) might be more effective by limiting it to giving in excess of a set floor, such as 3 percent of income. A much higher credit or deduction could then be given at the same revenue cost.

[27]With deducted contributions of $15 billion and a revenue loss of $4.5 billion (1975), a 30 percent credit could be granted instead.

[28]The conclusion that *total* giving would be unaffected is based on the finding that the price elasticity of giving (including giving to all charities) is close to unity and varies little with income. See Feldstein, op. cit.

heavily in low-income giving, would increase, while there would be a sharp drop in giving to educational institutions and other charities which are preferred by high-income donors.[29] It appears that, in designing the incentive, public policy can hardly be neutral regarding the way in which charitable donations come to be distributed among types of charities.

Child Care Credit A new item, which has received considerable attention in recent years in line with general concern for women's rights, is the child care credit.[30] Treated previously as an exclusion from AGI, the allowance is now given in the form of a credit, equal to 20 percent of eligible expenses, with a maximum credit of $500 for one child and $800 for two or more.

Education Costs Many proposals have been advanced to grant tax relief for expenditures on education, including a deduction from AGI and—as in more recent proposals—a credit against tax. The distributional results differ and the previously noted issues in the choice between credit and deduction again arise. Against such tax incentives, it is argued that assistance to education can be granted more equitably and efficiently through subsidies.

Yet, there is one form of tax relief for education which would have particular merit as a tax device. Expenditures on education may, at least in substantial part, be considered as a form of investment in human resources undertaken to increase earnings in later life.[31] These earnings will be taxed, although they constitute a net income only to the extent that they exceed the capital cost. Therefore, the taxpayer should be allowed to recover his or her cost in computing net income; in other words, depreciation should be permitted against human as well as against physical investment. The appropriate solution—in line with charging depreciation over asset life—would be to allow such charges against the student's income after the investment is made, rather than as a current deduction from parents' income while education costs are incurred.[32]

Standard Deduction

Given these options to itemize, why should the taxpayer be granted the alternative of a standard deduction? Since the rationale for deductions is to

---

[29]See M. Feldstein, "Income Tax Charitable Contributions, Part II," *National Tax Journal*, June 1975. This conclusion is based on the finding that the price elasticity of giving for educational institutions and other high-income charities is considerably above unity, while that for churches and other low-income charities is substantially below unity.

[30]While the adjustment removes a disadvantage otherwise imposed on the working spouse, it does so in a rough fashion. The theoretically correct (though hardly practical) solution would be to include imputed income of housewives in the tax base, while granting an individual exemption (whether parents work or not) sufficiently large to compensate for child care. There would thus not only be an imputation of income of stay-at-home spouses but also a recognition of costs included in child care. See p. 385.

[31]See p. 213.

[32]For such a proposal, see Richard Goode, *The Individual Income Tax*, rev. ed., Washington: Brookings, 1975, chap. 5.

deal with special circumstances, it makes little sense to grant them on an across-the-board basis. What, then, has been the thrust behind the repeated increase in the standard deduction over recent years?

A first reason is that itemizing is cumbersome for both the taxpayer and the Internal Revenue Service. Use of the standard deduction in lieu of itemizing simplifies matters for the taxpayer and permits the use of tax tables. A second reason is that some of the itemized deductions are of dubious merit. Since they cannot be repealed, they might be voided by making the resulting tax benefits available generally, as done via the standard deduction. Third, there is the fact that increasing the standard deduction has served as a means of giving tax relief to the lower end of the income scale.[33] Since high-income taxpayers tend to itemize, they are not likely to benefit from an increase in the standard deduction.

Conclusion

The principle of accretion may be stated without too much difficulty, but implementation is troublesome and the actual definitions of AGI and of taxable income fall far short of full implementation. In some instances, this reflects the technical difficulties which permit only approximation to the correct solution. In others, however, the deficiencies reflect policy intent of granting preferential treatment. But, though implementation is imperfect, it remains crucial that the specific issues of income definition, as they arise in practice, be measured against the yardstick of an income concept which provides a meaningful and consistent criterion of equity. In the absence of such a norm, technical issues of taxable income definition applicable to particular cases cannot be settled in a consistent and equitable fashion and the ever-present pressures for loophole snatching cannot be resisted.

F. SUMMARY

Among the basic features of the income tax law by which liabilities are determined, we have noted the following:

1. Adjusted gross income (AGI) minus personal exemptions minus deductions equals income subject to tax.
2. Though referred to as adjusted "gross" income, reference is to a net concept, i.e., income after deducting the cost of doing business.
3. Deductions may be itemized or a flat standard deduction may be used.
4. The tax is computed by applying bracket or marginal rates.
5. Bracket rates in excess of 50 percent apply to "earned income" only.
6. The regular tax may be supplemented by certain minimum tax provisions.

[33]This was the case especially with the so-called low-income allowance, permitted prior to 1977 as an alternative form of standard deduction. The benefit of the low-income allowance was limited to low-income groups, with middle-income groups making use of the so-called percentage standard deduction. Both these devices were replaced in 1977 by a flat standard deduction.

Regarding the size and structure of the tax base, our findings were these:

7.   Total AGI amounts to about two-thirds of GNP. It differs from GNP by some items which are added in and others which are excluded.

8.   The bulk of income tax returns and of taxable income fall in the AGI range from $10,000 to $50,000.

9.   Wage income is most important for low-income brackets, and capital income for high-income brackets.

The ideal definition of AGI is given by a broad-based or accretion concept of income. However, numerous difficulties arise in implementing it:

10.   Costs of doing business should be excluded in arriving at net income, but they are not always easily defined.

11.   Under present practice, 60 percent of realized "long-term" capital gains are excluded from the tax base, and unrealized gains are fully excluded. Fuller taxation of gains is desirable as a matter of tax equity, and techniques can be developed to achieve this, including constructive realization and inflation adjustment.

12.   The merits of preferential treatment of capital gains as an incentive device are examined later on.

13.   Equitable treatment of homeowners calls for inclusion of imputed rent in the tax base.

14.   Transfer income should be included in the tax base, with special problems arising in the treatment of social security and private pension plans.

15.   Exclusion of interest from state and local securities is inequitable and an inefficient form of assistance to these governments.

16.   Losses should be adequately allowed for.

After AGI is determined, certain deductions are made in moving to taxable income:

17.   About 70 percent of all returns now use the standard deduction, with only 30 percent itemizing.

18.   The extent to which various itemizable deductions may be justified differs. Among the most important items are state and local taxes, mortgage interest, and charitable contributions.

19.   The granting of a standard deduction is difficult to justify in principle. However, it is an expedient way of reducing compliance and administrative cost and may be used to give relief to low-income taxpayers.

FURTHER READINGS

See references at end of Chapter 17.

Chapter 17

Individual Income Tax: Further Problems*

A. Tax Preferences: *Tax Preferences and Tax Expenditures; Revenue Loss; Implications for Equity; Minimum-Tax Provisions.* **B. Rate Structure:** *Marginal and Average Rates; Effective Rates; How Progressive Should Rates Be? Maximum Rate; Averaging; Measuring Progression.* **C. Treatment of Low Incomes:** *Level of Tax-Free Minimum; Effect on Progression; Alternative Techniques; Earned-Income Tax Credit.* **D. Choice of Taxable Unit:** *Family-Unit Approach; Earnings-Unit Approach; Efficiency Aspects; Dependents and Stay-at-Home Spouses.* **E. Inflation Aspects:** *Rate Escalation; Base Adjustment.* **F. State and Local Income Taxes:** *State Income Taxes; Local Income Taxes.* **G. Appraisal of Income Tax. H. Summary.**

A. TAX PREFERENCES

We have seen that the statutory definition of taxable income, after allowing for exclusions and deductions, is by no means identical with the theoretical concept of accretion. Substantial differences exist and, in most cases, result in a taxable income below that called for by the accretion concept.

* Reader's Guide to Chapter 17: This chapter presents more on the structure and workings of the individual income tax, including the implications of tax preferences and tax expenditures, rate structure, definition of the taxable unit, as well as the effects of inflation and adjustments thereto. All this material is crucial to an understanding of how our income tax works.

Tax Preferences and Tax Expenditures

Tax preferences (the polite term for loopholes) arise from the exclusion of certain items which should be included and the deduction of others which should not be deducted. Both have important implications for revenue yield and the distribution of the tax burden. Since it is not always obvious what constitutes a "tax preference," careful evaluation of particular provisions is needed. The same applies with regard to a "tax penalty" which results where the definition of taxable income is unduly inclusive. Seen from a different perspective, tax preferences may be viewed as subsidy payments to preferred taxpayers. Such implicit payments have come to be referred to as "tax expenditures" and the Budget Act of 1974 requires that they be listed in the budget. To illustrate, there is no basic difference between making outright expenditures for a low-cost housing program and forgoing revenue because of accelerated depreciation on such housing. The objective in both cases is to increase the supply of low-cost housing. Exclusion of interest from state-local securities, similarly, gives a subsidy to state and local borrowing; deduction of mortgage interest subsidizes mortgage-financed house ownership; charitable deductions give a budgetary subsidy to churches and educational institutions, and so forth. In all these cases, an expenditure program (subsidy or matching grant) can be constructed which is equivalent to the tax device.

Where such provisions are not needed to secure a better measure of taxable capacity, the basic issues are (1) whether the particular expenditure objective merits support and, if so, (2) whether this support is best given by tax relief or by outright subsidies. Point 1 should not be viewed as an issue in tax policy, but as a general matter of setting budget priorities. Even if the tax relief route is to be used, efficient program planning requires that the policy objectives be faced explicitly; and program budgeting calls for the inclusion of such outlays under their respective program headings. Chances are that expenditure planning will be more efficient if subsidy programs are voted on by the relevant appropriation committees rather than by the tax committees which have no particular expertise in specific expenditure areas and which should concentrate on designing an equitable tax system based on a comprehensive measure of ability to pay.

An attempt is made in the budget to classify tax expenditures in line with the functional classification of budget outlays, so as to indicate the program areas into which they belong. While this is of interest, it must not be concluded that all or most tax expenditures reflect a genuine program intent. As likely as not, they are simply the result of circumstances which permit some groups of taxpayers to pay less than their full share of the tax bill. Nevertheless, the concept of tax expenditures is intriguing and has done much to dramatize the existence of tax preferences. But it is only a derived concept. Tax expenditures only reflect the tax preferences which exist because the base of taxable income falls short of what it would be under a comprehensive approach. To decide whether some item constitutes a tax expenditure, one has to determine whether it offends against the comprehensive-base criteria.

Revenue Loss

While it is debatable just which provisions constitute tax preferences, it is evident that the revenue cost of existing preferences is very substantial. The major items and their revenue implications for 1979 are listed in Table 17-1. Using a very broad definition of tax expenditure, the combined revenue loss, for 1979 is estimated at about $102 billion for the individual income tax.[1] With an estimated yield of $190 billion, this means a loss of over one-third from the potential yield of $292 billion. Or putting it differently, the same revenue could be obtained from the comprehensive base while cutting rates across the board by one-third. As shown in the table, the revenue losses from preferential treatment of capital gains, homeowner preferences, private pension plans, deduction of state and local taxes, and transfer-payment exclusions are among the most important items. Corresponding losses for the corporation tax are estimated at $34 billion or over 20 percent of the potential yield.

Implications for Equity

The existence of preferences would be of little concern if base reductions due to tax preferences were a fixed proportion of the "full" base for all taxpayers. In this event, they could be readily neutralized by correspondingly higher rates. But in fact, the incidence of preferences varies considerably. Preferences are important, not so much because they narrow the base and because they reduce tax yield with given rates—as is sometimes suggested—but because they are distributed unequally and thereby affect the distribution of liabilities.

Preferences cause the distribution of liabilities to differ from that intended by the pattern of tax rates, with resulting horizontal and vertical inequities. While the equity implications of the major preferences listed in Table 17-1 have already been noted in Chapter 16, their joint impact on vertical and horizontal equity of the income tax is here considered in quantitative terms.

Vertical Equity   Table 17-2 shows the distribution of tax expenditures (or tax savings due to preferences) by "expanded income" class.[2] As shown in line 9, tax preferences are by no means a high-income privilege. Tax savings due to preferences are especially high at both ends of the scale, reflecting primarily preferential treatment of transfers such as the exclusion of social insurance benefits (line 7) at the lower end and of capital gains (line 1) and

---

[1]These totals are here obtained by aggregating the revenue effects of the various preferences as estimated in the United States budget. This procedure is questionable because the budget estimates for each item assume that only this particular preference is repealed. Since revenue effects are interdependent, simple aggregation will involve some error and may well overstate the total.

Also see U.S. Bureau of the Census, *Special Analysis, The Budget of the United States Government, Fiscal Year 1979*, p. 155.

[2]Expanded income equals AGI plus the untaxed half of capital gains and certain other preference items.

TABLE 17-1
Tax Expenditures, 1979
Estimated Revenue Loss from Removal of Major Tax Preferences
(In Billions of Dollars)

		Individuals	Corporations
1.	Capital gains	18.5	0.8
2.	Tax-exempt interest	7.7	4.4
3.	Investment credit	2.7	12.3
4.	Other investment incentives	2.4	11.2
5.	Mortgage interest	5.5	—
6.	Property tax on owner-occupied homes	5.2	—
7.	Deductibility of state and local nonbusiness tax	10.3	—
8.	Charitable contributions	6.5	0.8
9.	Private pension plans	14.2	—
10.	Employer contributions for medical insurance	7.3	—
11.	Income maintenance	9.1	—
12.	Veterans' benefits	1.0	—
13.	Medical deductions	2.7	—
14.	Elderly provisions	1.2	—
15.	Educational provisions	1.1	—
16.	Child care	0.6	—
17.	Other	6.2	4.8
18.	Total	102.2	34.3

Notes:
The total is divided about equally between preferential treatment of realized and unrealized gains.
Of the total, $6.3 billion is accounted for by OASI benefits. The remainder includes unemployment insurance, public assistance, etc.
Source: Based on U.S. Bureau of the Census, Special Analysis, The Budget of the United States Government, Fiscal Year 1979, pp. 158–160.

tax-exempts (line 2) at the upper end of the scale. However, they are substantial also in the middle range, where benefits from tax preferences are expressed as a percentage of tax. Line 18 shows tax preferences as a percent of liabilities. The ratio follows a U-shaped pattern, very high at the bottom, then falling and again rising at the high-income levels. This broad-based sharing in the spoils of tax preferences explains why tax reformers have been so unsuccessful in dealing with the problem. It is always easy to establish a coalition to oppose this or that correction, or to open this or that additional set of loopholes.

Horizontal Equity   The impact of tax preferences upon the vertical distribution of the tax burden causes the true burden pattern to differ from that suggested by the nominal rate schedule; and it could be compensated for simply by adjusting that schedule. But preferences pose a further and more fundamental problem. This results because different individual taxpayers,

TABLE 17-2
Distribution of Tax Expenditures, 1977

Item	EXPANDED INCOME CLASS (Thousands of Dollars)*				
	$0–5	$10–15	$30–50	$200+	All Brackets
AS PERCENTAGE OF EXPANDED INCOME					
1. Capital gains	0.1	0.2	1.8	20.4	1.3
2. State-local interest	†	†	0.1	3.0	0.2
3. Homeowner items	†	0.4	1.9	0.8	0.9
4. Charitable contributions	†	0.1	0.8	4.7	0.5
5. State-local taxes	†	0.2	1.5	3.0	0.8
6. Medical	†	0.2	0.3	0.2	0.2
7. Transfers	3.7	0.7	0.5	†	0.8
8. All other	2.3	2.0	4.3	5.9	3.0
9. Total	6.2	3.8	11.2	38.1	7.7
AS PERCENTAGE OF TAX LIABILITY					
10. Capital gains	40.4	2.2	10.4	68.2	10.8
11. State-local interest	†	†	0.7	9.9	1.4
12. Homeowner items	12.8	4.4	10.5	2.6	7.2
13. Charitable contributions	1.4	1.3	4.4	15.8	3.9
14. State-local taxes	3.5	2.4	8.8	9.9	6.2
15. Medical	6.4	1.7	1.9	0.8	1.6
16. Transfers	1,512.1	7.7	2.6	0.1	6.5
17. All others	946.8	22.6	24.5	19.7	24.6
18. Total	2,523.4	42.3	63.7	126.9	62.1

*Expanded income equals AGI plus the untaxed half of capital gains and certain other preference items.
†Less than 0.1 percent.
Line 1: Excludes deferral of capital gain on home sales, which is included in line 2.
Line 2: Includes deduction for mortgage interest and real estate taxes, the credit for new home purchase, and deferral of capital gain on home sales.
Line 3: Includes deductibility of state gasoline taxes and other state and local taxes.
Line 4: Includes charitable contributions for health and education as well as all other.
Line 5: Includes exclusion of interest on state and local pollution control bonds, industrial development bonds, and general debt.
Line 6: Mainly OASDI benefit payments, but including also unemployment, railroad retirement, workers' compensation, public assistance, and veterans' pension and disability payments.
Line 7: By including total OASI benefits, it is implied that the social security system should be viewed as a pure transfer system. See p. 732.
Source: U.S. Treasury Department and Tax Notes, March 13 and July 17, 1978.

even though they may have equal levels of income, do not share equally in the benefits which the preferences bestow. Thus individual taxpayers who receive the same income and therefore should pay the same tax may in fact pay at very different rates. Preferences therefore offend against the principle of horizontal equity.

This is shown in Table 17-3 for 1976 taxes. The table demonstrates how preferences result in a wide dispersion of average or effective rates as

TABLE 17-3
Distribution of Tax Returns by Effective Rate, 1976

Effective Rate of Tax* (Percentage)	ADJUSTED GROSS INCOME (Thousands of Dollars)					
	0–10	10–20	40–50	100–200	200+	All
No tax	45.4	1.1	0.4	0.3	0.2	23.9
0– 5	20.1	5.8	0.6	0.6	0.4	12.3
5–10	23.9	39.4	7.3	1.2	0.9	24.0
10–15	10.6	49.3	7.1	1.3	1.5	27.8
15–20	†	9.1	34.9	2.8	2.1	9.1
20–25	†	0.2	47.4	4.6	3.2	1.8
25–30	†	†	10.1	10.4	4.6	0.5
30–40	†	†	2.1	55.3	24.1	0.4
40–50	†	†	†	21.5	38.4	0.1
50 and over	†	†	†	2.0	24.6	†
All	100.0	100.0	100.0	100.0	100.0	100.0

Source: U.S. Treasury Department, Office of Tax Analysis, based on *Statistics of Income* for 1976. Also see U.S. Treasury Department, Office of Tax Analysis, *High Income Tax Returns, 1975 and 1976,* August 1978, p. 25.
*Tax as percent of AGI.
†Below 0.1 percent.

applicable at similar AGI levels. Moreover, the table shows how this dispersion widens as AGI increases. It is thus evident that the system results in a high degree of horizontal inequity, especially at high-income levels.

Conclusion The conclusion to be drawn from this brief survey are that tax preferences or tax expenditures have had these effects:

1. They have resulted in a substantial revenue loss, such that adoption of a full base would permit an average rate reduction by one-third or more while holding revenue constant.
2. With regard to vertical equity, they have resulted in sharp reductions in liabilities at both ends of the income scale, with more or less constant proportional reduction over a wide middle range.
3. They have given rise to substantial horizontal inequities over the entire scale, but mostly at the upper end.

Adoption of a broader base would thus permit improvement in horizontal equity as well as a reduction in bracket rates over the entire scale. At the lower end, it may be expected that substantial rate reductions would be applied to offset the increase in liabilities which would otherwise result from expansion of base. Similarly, upper-end liabilities would hardly be permitted to rise to levels resulting from application of present bracket rates to a full income base. But some increase in liabilities would remain even if the top marginal rate on full income were reduced to, say, 50 percent. Over the middle range, rate reductions of 10 to 15 percent would be possible to offset base expansion, the major result being a redistribution of liabilities between homeowners and others. In all, the gain would be primarily in improved horizontal equity and lessened distorting effects on taxpayer behavior. From the point of view of vertical equity, the major gain would be in the curtailment of tax avoidance in the high-income ranges.

Minimum-Tax Provisions

The preceding survey of exclusions and deductions makes it amply evident that deficiencies in the definition of taxable income lead to a substantial difference between the apparent and the actual level of tax rates. The efforts of tax reformers over the last forty years at improving the tax base by plugging specific loopholes (or eliminating specific preferences) have not been very successful. While students of taxation are widely agreed that it would be desirable to trade reduced rates for a fuller tax base, not much has been accomplished to date. Gains have been made on some fronts (most recently by elimination of gasoline tax deductibility in 1978), but setbacks have been suffered on others (e.g., the increase in capital gains exclusion in the same act). This lack of progress had led to the view that reform might be achieved more effectively by a more generalized approach to preference limitation, second-best though it may be in nature, than it would be via item-by-item reform.

The minimum tax introduced by the Tax Reform Act of 1969 and tightened in 1976 was such an innovation. This provision was designed to assure that at least some tax is paid by people who benefit heavily from the variety of available tax preferences, especially capital gains. The Revenue Act of 1978 has amended this provision and made it less stringent. The new law provides for two minimum taxes, one directed at capital gains and the other at other forms of preference income. The so-called special minimum tax applies to the excluded 60 percent of capital gains plus "excess deductions," defined as deductions in excess of 60 percent of AGI. The rate ranges from 10 to 25 percent, and the tax is applied as an alternative to the regular tax if above it. It is designed to deal with a compounding of preferences derived from capital gains and excess deductions. The ordinary minimum tax of 15 percent is applied to certain other types of preference income and is added to the regular tax.[3] In all, the minimum tax provisions help to ensure that some tax is paid at high levels of income, but these provisions fall far short of resolving the tax preference problem.

B. RATE STRUCTURE

Determination of taxable income is the first step; setting the schedule of tax rates is the second step which must be undertaken in the determining of tax burdens.

---

[3]Interest on state and local securities and certain other items such as medical deductions are not included.

Marginal and Average Rates

The rate structure is legislated in the form of marginal or bracket rates, applicable to successive slabs of income. These rates were shown in Table 16-1 and are plotted in Figure 17-1. The resulting tax liabilities may then be expressed as a percentage of income subject to tax, thus giving the set of average rates also shown in the figure. It is the average-rate schedule that matters, but use of bracket rates is a convenient way to determine it. Alternatively, Congress could legislate a set of average tax rates, but this would require a complex formula (of parabolic form) which would be difficult for taxpayers and legislators to interpret. As shown in the figure, the marginal rates lie above and pull up the average rates, until the latter approach the former at the top marginal rate of 70 percent.

Effective Rates

The average rates in Figure 17-1 and in column IV of Table 17-4 give ratios of tax to taxable income. But taxable income is only part of AGI, as personal exemptions and deductions are subtracted to arrive at it. A better view of tax-burden distribution is thus obtained by considering tax liabilities as a percentage of AGI. Such ratios, referred to as "effective rates," are shown in column III of Table 17-4. When one examines the degree of income tax progression, this is the schedule which should be considered, with the impact of exemptions and deductions as well as bracket rates allowed for. The distinction between columns IV and V is of special importance at the lower end of the income scale, where exemptions and deductions are the primary factor in making for a rising ratio of tax to AGI.

FIGURE 17-1   Marginal and Average Rates (Joint Return).

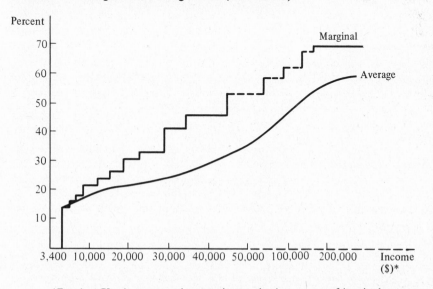

*Equals AGI minus personal exemptions and minus excess of itemized over standard deduction, with the standard deduction reflected in the zero-rate bracket.

TABLE 17-4
Effective Rates of Tax
(Joint Return without Dependents)

AGI (Dollars) (I)	Taxable Income (Dollars) (II)	Tax (Dollars) (III)	Tax as Percentage of Taxable Income (IV)	Tax as Percentage of AGI (V)
5,400	—	—	—	—
10,000	4,600	702	15.3	7.0
20,000	14,600	2,457	16.8	12.3
30,000	21,100	4,477	21.2	14.9
50,000	37,500	10,089	26.9	20.2
100,000	75,000	29,402	39.2	29.4
200,000	152,000	76,772	50.5	38.4

Notes: Based on provisions applicable to 1979 income. The standard deduction of $3,400 applies up to $20,000, beyond which itemized deductions assumed equal to 23 percent of AGI are applied. For the $100,000 and $200,000 levels, the rates applicable to unearned income are used. The earned-income credit is not allowed for, since there are no dependents.

This analysis may be extended by broadening the denominator of the tax–income ratio even further. Rather than using AGI as base, we may use a concept of "economic income," which includes total capital gains (realized or not) as well as certain other tax preference items which remain outside AGI. The resulting set of effective rates would be substantially lower than that shown in Table 17-4, and progressivity at the upper end of the scale would be considerably reduced.[4]

How Progressive Should Rates Be?

As we have seen in our earlier discussion of distributive justice and equal sacrifice, no absolute statement about the desirable degree of rate progression can be made. While the economic effects of alternative patterns must be examined and allowed for, the final answer is essentially one of social value judgment.[5] However, the following points may be noted:

1. The present system, under which some income recipients are subject to high marginal rates while others (with the same total income) pay much less, is unsatisfactory and in urgent need of revision. The principle should be that of defining taxable income comprehensively, taxing it globally at the same scale, and then limiting bracket rates to such level as is considered appropriate and enforceable. This, clearly, would be much superior to the past practice of enacting highly progressive bracket rates which are then made ineffective by a deficient income definition.

[4]In recent presentations, the Treasury has made use of a concept of "expanded income," which includes the excluded 60 percent of realized gains as well as certain other tax preference items. It falls short, however, of our concept of economic income, which includes unrealized gains as well as interest on state and local securities.

[5]The literature on "optimal taxation" does not dispose of this necessity. See p. 316.

and after-tax income on a log chart. The coefficient again equals 1 for a proportional tax but progression is now indicated by a coefficient of less than 1. Progression under all indicators tends to decline as we move up the income scale, but may rise over particular income spans.

Coefficients for tax to AGI ratios are shown in Table 17-5 as they apply to various income spans. We note that the degree of progression as measured by the various coefficients differs considerably, as does the change in the level of progression over various income spans. Not even the direction of change need be the same. As we move up the income scale, the coefficient for average-rate progression falls, indicating declining progressivity. The coefficient of liability progression also decreases throughout as we move up the scale, once more indicating falling progressivity. But for residual income progression the trend is reversed, i.e., progressivity rises, this being reflected now in a declining coefficient. Although all these measures describe the same set of liabilities, that of residual income progression is perhaps the most interesting. Concern with the progressivity of the tax structure, after all, is not only with the way in which the tax burden is distributed but also, and perhaps primarily, with the way in which the distribution of after-tax income is affected. The latter is reflected in residual income progression. Thus, if a new piece of legislation brings an increase in residual income progression (reduction in our coefficient), this signals that the distribution of residual income has become more equal.[11]

To avoid confusion in comparing progression over different income ranges or for different tax structures, it is necessary to specify just what measure is used. This is of special importance in considering what happens to progression when tax rates are changed. When rates are to be increased or reduced, Congress may consider it desirable to do so in a "neutral" fashion, calling for an "across-the-board" change. But what is meant by "neutrality"?

Suppose that taxes are to be increased. If average-rate progression is held constant, all liabilities are increased by an equal percentage. Bracket rates are increased by a rising number of percentage points as we move up the scale. If liability progression is held constant, all bracket rates are increased by the same number of percentage points. If residual income progression is held constant, bracket rates are increased by a falling number of percentage points as we move up the scale. Representatives of low-income groups will thus be inclined to interpret neutrality in the sense of average-rate progression, with liability progression next and residual income progression last. Representatives of high-income groups will be inclined to take the opposite view. Amusingly, the orders of preference are reversed when it comes to a tax reduction. Thus, theoretical concepts may carry their political implications.

---

[11]Note that the degree of residual income progression depends upon the level as well as the slope of the effective-rate curve, while the other measures depend on its slope only. Residual income progression is thus similar in nature to our earlier and more comprehensive approach of "effective progression," where changes in the equality of the entire residual income distribution were measured. See p. 264. For further discussion, see Ulf Jacobson, "On the Measurement of the Degree of Progression," *Journal of Public Economics*, January–February 1976, p. 161–68.

TABLE 17-5
Measures of Progression
(Joint Return without Dependents)

AGI (Dollars)	Liability (Dollars)[†] (I)	Average Rate (II)	Average-Rate Progression (III)	Liability Progression (IV)	Residual Income Progression (V)
	TAX		**DEGREE OF PROGRESSION[*]**		
10,000	702	7.0			
			0.53	1.75	0.94
20,000	2,457	12.3			
			0.26	1.64	0.91
50,000	10,089	20.2			
			0.18	1.45	0.90
100,000	29,402	29.4			
			0.09	1.31	0.87
200,000	76,772	38.4			
Coefficient for proportional tax			0	1	1
Coefficient for progressive tax			>0	>1	<1
Coefficient for regressive tax			<0	<1	>1

[*]Values computed from formulas in footnote 10, p. 376, reflecting progression over specified AGI ranges.
[†]See Table 17-4.

C. TREATMENT OF LOW INCOMES

The problem of progressivity in the income tax is not only a matter of how heavily high-income taxpayers should be taxed. It is also and perhaps more importantly a question of how little those with low incomes should pay.

Level of Tax-Free Minimum

There is fairly general agreement that an initial slice of income should not be taxed. Taxable income should be defined as AGI minus this basic allowance. In defining this allowance, we might use the level below which the taxpayer is considered to be "in poverty." Since the poverty level differs with size of family, the level at which the tax begins differs accordingly.

In our tax structure, the starting point for tax liability depends on various factors. First, there is the personal exemption of $1,000 per taxpayer, spouse, and each child. Family size is allowed for, but the assumption seems to be that family needs are not subject to economies of scale. Next, the beginning level depends on the standard deduction, equal to $2,300 per single and $3,400 per joint return, without any allowance for children. Finally, the floor is affected by the earned-income credit, which we shall consider shortly.

Allowing for all these factors, the relationship between family size, tax-free income, and the poverty-line income is shown in Table 17-6. As may be seen from the table, the minimum income at which a positive tax begins to apply increases with family size. For taxpayers with dependents, moreover, it is substantially higher for returns with earned as against unearned income. Also, the tax-free limit is slightly below the poverty line for taxpayers without dependents, but above it for taxpayers with dependents.

TABLE 17-6
Levels of Tax-Free Income*
(Applicable to 1979 Income, in Dollars)

Taxpaying Unit	LEVEL OF AGI ABOVE WHICH TAX LIABILITY BECOMES POSITIVE		Poverty Line Income† 1979
	Earned Income	Unearned Income	
Single	3,300	3,300	3,585
Married	5,400	5,400	4,600
Married, one dependent	7,900‡	6,400	5,630
Married, two dependents	8,483‡	7,400	7,210
Married, four dependents	9,650‡	9,400	8,530

*Allows for personal exemptions, zero-rate bracket or standard deduction, and earned-income credit.
†Office of Research and Statistics, Social Security Administration.
‡Tax becomes negative below these levels of AGI.

Effect on Progression

The tax-free limit, moreover, is important not only in setting the floor for tax liability but also dominates the pattern of progression over the lower-middle income scale. The effective rate of tax just above the tax-free amount (exemptions and standard deduction) is very low, simply because the tax-free amount is a very large fraction of AGI.[12] As AGI rises, the tax-free amount falls relative to AGI, so that the effective rate rises. Putting it differently, the tax-free amount may be viewed as a zero-rate bracket and is thus an integral part of the rate structure.

By permitting a progressive distribution of the tax burden at the lower end of the income scale, the income tax is superior to other forms of low income taxation—such as the sales tax—which tend to be regressive. There is nothing to be gained for low-income families if the tax-free amount under the income tax is set too high and the resulting loss of revenue is then made up by use of regressive taxes.

Alternative Techniques

A tax-free income range may be established in various ways, including personal exemptions, standard deductions, or credits.

The personal exemption and standard deduction devices are similar in that the tax saving which results from a $100 increase depends on the taxpayer's marginal bracket rate. Thus the value is $14 for a low-income and up to $70 for a high-income taxpayer. To avoid this effect, it has been proposed that the allowance be given in the form of a credit against tax rather than as a deduction from AGI. A credit of $250 is estimated to involve the

[12]Note that in Table 16-1 the standard deduction but not the exemption is included in the zero-rate bracket.

same revenue cost of about $24 billion (1978 level) as the exemption of $1,000, but the resulting benefits would be distributed more toward the lower end, and especially toward large low-income families. For this reason, substitution of a credit has been proposed at various times, but it has not been acceptable to Congress.[13]

While the exemption and deduction approaches are similar in that they are deductions from taxable income, they differ in other respects. For instance, the standard deduction of $2,300 for single and $3,400 for joint returns does not increase with the number of dependents, whereas the personal exemption does.

Another difference arises because the standard deduction is not used by taxpayers who itemize. Because of this, an increase in the standard deduction is of value primarily over the lower-middle income range. The same effect would be obtained by using a "vanishing" exemption, i.e., by letting the personal exemption decline as AGI rises.

Earned-Income Tax Credit

A major change in the treatment of low incomes was made in the form of the earned-income tax credit. Introduced in the Tax Reduction Act of 1975, this credit applies to earned income only, with capital income excluded. Equal now to 10 percent of earned income up to $5,000, the credit is reduced by 10 percent of AGI in excess of $5,000 so that it is wiped out at an AGI of $10,000. The credit applies only to returns with dependents and, most important, is refundable in the form of a "negative tax," to the extent that it is in excess of the tax liability.

Thus, a taxpayer filing a joint return and claiming two dependents would, in the absence of this credit, pay a zero tax up to an AGI of $7,400 and pay positive tax thereafter. Under the credit, the same taxpayer enjoys a negative tax (receives a refund) up to an AGI of $8,483, since up to that level, the credit exceeds the taxpayer's liability. A positive tax becomes due only above the $8,483 level. This pattern of negative and positive taxes is shown in Table 17-7.

Introduction of the earned-income credit may be viewed as a first step toward a negative income tax. There is good reason to argue that the principle of progressive taxation calls for a downward extension of the income tax below the zero-rate point into a negative range, and such proposals have been made in the context of welfare reform, a matter to be considered in a later chapter.[14] For now it should only be noted that the earned-income credit falls short of a full negative income tax approach because it is limited to earners and to returns with dependents only. As a result, the tax liability for returns with dependents is substantially lower at the

---

[13]A small credit of $35 per return, introduced in 1975, was repealed in 1978. Another aspect of the choice between the credit and exemption approach is considered below, in the discussion of the treatment of the family unit. See p. 381.

[14]See p. 724.

TABLE 17-7
Positive and Negative Taxes on Earned Income
(In Dollars)

AGI	Single (I)	Joint (II)	Joint, Two Dependents (III)	Joint, Four Dependents (IV)
2,000	—	—	−200	−200
3,000	—	—	−300	−300
4,000	98	—	−400	−400
5,000	250	—	−500	−500
6,000	422	84	−400	−400
7,000	602	224	−300	−300
8,000	787	374	−116	−200
9,000	977	534	124	−100
10,000	1177	702	374	84

Notes:
Column I: Tax begins at AGI of $3,300.
Column II: Tax begins at AGI of $5,400.
Column III: Tax begins at AGI of $8,483.
Column IV: Tax begins at AGI of $9,650.

bottom of the scale than for returns without dependents. Similarly, low-income recipients whose income comes from other sources, such as pensions, do not benefit.

D. CHOICE OF TAXABLE UNIT

Proper treatment of the taxpaying unit under a progressive income tax is a controversial matter to which there may be no satisfactory solution. It is also a problem which has been complicated by two recent socioeconomic trends, one being the increased participation of women in the labor force and the other being the increasing frequency of cohabitation without marriage.

Family-Unit Approach

We begin with the hypothesis which traditionally has applied to most income-tax discussion, that the tax-paying unit and the measurement of ability-to-pay should refer to the family unit. We will then consider an alternative which defines the tax-paying unit in terms of the individual earner.

Equity Aspects   Looking at the matter from the point of view of taxation by ability to pay, equity calls for compliance with these three rules:

   1.   Units with the same income and the same numbers should pay the same tax.
   2.   Among units with the same income, the unit with the smaller number should pay more.

3. Given a progressive rate schedule, the tax (as a percentage of income) for equal number units should rise with income.

Rule 1 requires no explanation as it simply represents the requirement that equals should be treated equally. It need only be noted that it is a matter of indifference, for gauging ability to pay in the family-unit context, whether the given income is contributed by a single earner or by multiple earners. Rule 2 reflects the proposition that a single person living at, say, $15,000 is better off than a couple with the same amount. While certain consumption items (e.g., the light in the living room) serve two persons as well as one, others (e.g., chairs to sit on) are more costly for two. Thus, it is only fair for the tax on singles to be somewhat higher than the tax on marrieds with the same income, so that such a differential (if at the appropriate level) should not be viewed as a discriminatory "singles" tax. Rule 3, finally, follows directly from the principle of progression, and no further explanation is needed. A system complying with these equity rules may be approximated by granting a higher exemption to the joint than to the single return[15] while taxing both under the same progressive rate schedule.

Effects on Decision to Marry   These equity rules are an important part of the problem, but they are not the entire concern. Rather, legislators have been equally, or even more, concerned with the effects of the tax system on the institution of marriage. Here the focus is on the change in liabilities due to marriage and how this is affected by progressive rates.[16] Assuming the same progressive schedule of rates to apply to both single and joint returns, how will liabilities be affected by marriage? If the marriage is between a single earner and a nonearner, tax liability falls slightly due to the second exemption. But if two earners marry, the combined liability will increase. This must be the case because the combined earnings will fall into a higher rate bracket then did the single earnings. Thus, marriage among earners is discouraged by a "marriage tax." The situation is complicated by the fact that the increase in combined tax due to marriage will vary with the distribution of earnings between the two partners. The more even the distribution of earnings, the larger the increase in tax.[17]

[15]The question arises whether this additional exemption should be the same for all levels of combined income, as is now the case, or should vary. If taxpaying ability of singles and marrieds is to be compared in terms of income in excess of necessities, the constant addition is appropriate. If comparison is in terms of outlays needed to sustain whatever living is customary at the designated level of income, the additional exemption should rise with income. Two people need more bread than one (the relevant considerations at low-income levels), but they also need a larger yacht (which becomes relevant at high levels).

[16]See James W. Wetzler, "Marriage and the Federal Income Tax," unpublished manuscript. Also see J. A. Pechman, "Income Tax Treatment of Two-Earner Married Couples," in Joint Economic Committee, *Economic Problems of Women*, 93rd Congress, 1st Session, July 24–26, 1973, and Aline Quester, "Women's Behavior and the Tax Code," *Social Science Quarterly*, vol. 59, no. 4 (March 1979).

[17]The point is explained best by beginning with the fact that the tax after marriage will be independent of the earnings split. But the more even the split, the smaller the combined singles taxes before marriage. Therefore, the more even the split, the larger the increase.

Worried about detrimental effects on the institution of marriage, legislators have provided a lower rate schedule to be applied to joint returns. In so doing, policy has sought an uneasy balance between avoiding a disincentive to marriage (the "marriage tax") and imposing an excessive extra tax on singles. As shown in Table 17-8, this has resulted in a rather arbitrary mix of losses and gains from marriage, depending on the way in which earnings are distributed among the partners and their income levels.

Moving across lines 3, 11, and 19, we observe the tax changes with marriage for partners with similar earnings-splits but different levels of combined income. Moving down the columns, and again focusing on lines 3, 9, and 11, we note how the change is affected as earnings become split more evenly while holding combined earnings constant. We find that the absolute change in tax rises with income and that the change turns from decrease to increase as the distribution of earnings becomes more even. Combining both aspects, we find that the tax increases with marriage where earnings are high

TABLE 17-8
Income Tax Liabilities for Single and Joint Returns*
(1979 Levels)

	COMBINED AGI		
	$10,000	*$50,000*	*$100,000*
Single Earner			
1. Tax, single	1,177	12,559	31,325
2. Tax, joint	702	10,183	28,630
3. Difference (2−1)	−475	−2,376	−2,695
4. (3÷1)	−.40	−.23	−.08
Two Earners: 3/4 to 1/4			
5. AGI of A	7,500	37,500	75,000
6. AGI of B	2,500	12,500	25,000
7. Singles tax on A	692	8,040	21,860
8. Singles tax on B	—	1,585	4,364
9. (7+8)	692	9,625	26,224
10. Joint tax	702	10,183	28,630
11. (10−9)	+10	+558	+2,406
12. (11÷9)	+.01	+.06	+.09
Two Earners: 1/2 to 1/2			
13. AGI of A	5,000	25,000	50,000
14. AGI of B	5,000	25,000	50,000
15. Singles tax on A	250	4,364	12,118
16. Singles tax on B	250	4,364	12,118
17. (15+16)	500	8,728	24,236
18. Joint tax	702	10,183	28,878
19. (18−17)	+202	+1,455	+4,642
20. (19÷17)	+.40	+.17	+.16

*No dependents and earned income only. For AGI under $20,000, the standard deduction is used. Above this level, a deduction equal to 23 percent of AGI is assumed.

and evenly split (the southeast corner of the table), while it falls where earnings are low and unevenly split (the northwest corner). Either outcome is nonneutral, inducing love without marriage in the first and marriage without love in the second case. Nor is the result satisfactory on equity grounds. Tax reduction by marriage leaves singles overtaxed, and the earnings split (which should not enter) becomes a major factor.[18] Combining focus on the family unit with progressive rates renders the combination of marriage neutrality and equity an unachievable goal.

Earnings-Unit Approach

This difficulty disappears if the taxpaying unit is defined in terms of the single earner independent of the family or spending unit to which the earner may belong.[19] Under this approach, which is followed by many European countries, all returns are granted the same exemption and standard deduction and are subject to the same rate schedule. Double earners would no longer find their tax increased when joining in marriage. The tax would be rendered neutral with regard to marriage decisions.

While the tax would be inequitable if evaluated in terms of family unit–based ability to pay, it might be argued that this is no longer the proper criterion. But even if the ability to pay is considered separately for each earner, it is hard to overlook the fact that married persons benefit from at least part of the outlays of their spouses (e.g., the previously mentioned living room light), and are better off than two singles with equal earnings. Moreover, the single-earner approach poses the problem of assigning earnings to each spouse. While this is done easily for wage and salary income, the assignment of capital earnings can be manipulated so as to minimize the combined tax.

Efficiency Aspects

Though wobbly on equity grounds, the single-earner approach gains when efficiency considerations are introduced. Under the family-unit approach, the marginal tax rate of the secondary earner (whose earnings are typically below those of the primary earner) is substantially higher than it would be under an earner approach. Yet labor supply studies have shown that labor supply of secondary earners is more elastic with respect to the net wage rate. Because of this, the earner approach tends to result in a lower efficiency loss or excess burden than does the family-unit approach.[20]

---

[18]Note that when considering *incentive* effects on marriage, we compare (a) the combined tax paid by both single earners before marriage with the tax when married. For purposes of *equity* we compare (b) the tax of a single person earning a given amount with that paid by a couple earning the same amount. Comparison (a) is not relevant for equity purposes under the family-unit approach.

[19]For further discussion of this approach, see Alicia Munnell, "The Couple vs. the Individual under the Federal Personal Income Tax," in H. J. Aaron and J. J. Boskin (eds.), *The Economics of Taxation*, Washington: Brookings, 1979.

[20]See p. 312 and Harvey Rosen, "A Methodology for Evaluating Tax Reform Proposals," *Journal of Public Economics*, July-August 1978.

Dependents and Stay-at-Home Spouses

A number of further issues arise, only two of which will be noted here.

Allowance for Dependents   In measuring the ability to pay of a family unit, the number of dependents should obviously be allowed for. A large family with a given AGI has a lower ability to pay than a small family with the same AGI. The question is only who should be considered a dependent and how the allowance should be made. The first question involves issues such as the treatment of children living away from home and earning some income. The second involves the question of whether the allowance should be given as deduction from AGI, as is now the case, or as a credit. If the cost of an additional child is to be measured in terms of a standard (say, average) expenditure per child, the credit approach is appropriate; but if the cost is to be measured in terms of what the particular taxpayer undertakes, the deduction approach becomes preferable. Since a taxpayer with a higher income spends more per child, it would then be appropriate to give a larger tax benefit. If the former interpretation were chosen, a substitution of a credit for the additional exemption now granted would be in order.

Another aspect of the tax treatment of dependents involves the standard deduction. As the latter has increasingly taken on the nature of an additional exemption (rather than an approximation of what otherwise would be itemized deductions), a good case can be made for permitting it to rise not only with a move from a single to a joint return but also with the number of dependents.

Stay-at-Home Spouses   Finally, there is the question of how to deal with spouses who do not earn outside income but stay at home, whether to keep house, to tend children, or to enjoy leisure. Consider a family of two spouses A_1 and A_2 where A_1 earns outside income while A_2 does not; and compare them with another family of two spouses B_1 and B_2 both of whom have outside jobs. Assume that the wages of A_1 and B_1 are the same and that A_2 has the same earnings potential as B_2. Under present law the B family pays more than the A's. Yet, our equal option rule tells us that both should pay the same, as does our earlier conclusion that imputed income should be considered part of accretion.[21]

Given that this procedure involves some unfairness toward the B's, the law permits B_2 a credit for child care expenses, but it does not provide a remedy where B_2 is without children. To meet this situation, a $600 credit for the second earning spouse was proposed in 1978 but was not enacted. But these are second-best solutions only. In principle it appears that imputed earnings (in terms of wages forgone) of stay-at-home spouses should be included in the tax base, in which case there would be no need for a child care or second-earner allowance. Moreover, in principle, the same procedure

[21]See p. 346.

would have to be applied to stay-at-home singles or, for that matter, to earners who work part time. This would in fact call for a tax on potential income, which would be the ideal (if impracticable) solution on both efficiency and equity grounds.[22]

A less ambitious solution might be to impute to the nonearning spouse A_2 an income equal to the standard cost of housework and child care (the cost which would be incurred if this work were done by outside help) without attempting to estimate the potential wages of A_2. Such an approach would be more practicable and the imputation would be increased with the number of children.

E. INFLATION ASPECTS

The inflationary setting of the United States economy in recent years has had a major impact on the income tax and has created a new set of problems. Two issues may be distinguished. The first is that as nominal incomes rise with inflation, taxpayers are pushed into higher rate brackets, even though their real income has not changed. The second relates to nominal gains or losses which result from changes in the price of assets, or in the real value of fixed claims. A still further aspect, bearing on the role of the income tax in stabilization policy, is considered in a later chapter.[23]

Rate Escalation

As prices rise in the course of inflation, so does the level of money incomes. For families whose money income rises at the same rate as prices, real income remains unchanged. If the income tax were imposed without exemptions and at a proportional rate, disposable or after-tax income would also rise at the same rate as prices and there would be no change in its real value. Under a progressive tax the situation differs because the tax rate rises with money income. Thus, a household with constant real income finds itself sliding up the rate brackets and must pay a higher tax. This is an arbitrary and unintended tax increase, the magnitude of which depends on the slope of the effective rate schedule over the range of increase in money income. If rate brackets were fixed in terms of real rather than money income, this increase would not occur. The dollar value of bracket limits would be inflated with prices so that the tax rate applicable at a given level of money income would fall as prices rise, holding it constant for any given level of real income.

Table 17-9 shows how tax liabilities have changed under the impact of inflation during the seventies. Column I shows levels of AGI for 1970, while column II shows the money value of corresponding levels of real income for 1979. With prices having risen by about 90 percent over the period, a 90 percent increase in money income is needed to retain the same real value. We assume that the money income of our five taxpayers has increased with

[22]See p. 101.
[23]See p. 617.

TABLE 17-9
Change In Tax Burden with Inflation, 1970–1979
(Joint Return without Dependents)

AGI (DOLLARS)		TAX ON 1970 INCOME, UNDER 1970 LAW		TAX ON 1979 INCOME			
				UNDER 1970 LAW		UNDER 1979 LAW	
1970 (I)	1979 (II)	In Dollars (III)	As Percentage of AGI (IV)	In Dollars (V)	As Percentage of AGI (VI)	In Dollars (VII)	As Percentage of AGI (VIII)
5,000	9,500	489	9.8	1,258	13.2	614	6.5
10,000	19,000	1,328	13.3	2,605	13.7	2,390	12.6
25,000	47,500	3,820	15.3	10,056	21.2	9,355	19.7
50,000	95,000	10,902	21.8	28,374	29.9	27,535	29.0
100,000	190,000	30,882	30.9	73,713	38.3	72,056	37.9

Notes: 1979 level of AGI equals 190 percent of 1970 level. Assumes deductions of 23 percent of AGI when in excess of standard deduction. Liabilities do not allow for 50 percent maximum rate.

inflation, so that their income has remained constant in real terms. Columns III and IV show the tax paid in 1970 on 1970 levels of income. Columns V and VI show what the tax would have been under 1970 law if applied to the corresponding levels of money income in 1979. Comparison of columns III and V shows the sharp increase in tax liabilities which would have resulted for given levels of real income if the tax law had remained unchanged. Comparison of columns IV and VI shows the corresponding increase in effective rates. This increase reflects the movement into higher rate brackets experienced by a constant real income as inflation pushes up the level of nominal income.[24]

But in fact tax laws did not remain unchanged. Exemptions and deductions were raised repeatedly and bracket rates were reduced somewhat, with 1979 liabilities as shown in columns VII and VIII. Comparing columns IV and VIII, we find that over the lower half of the income scale, effective rates at given levels of real income declined from 1970 to 1979, while over the upper half of the range they increased. While for the group as a whole, statutory changes largely offset the built-in revenue gain,[25] the adjustments were such as to render the income tax more progressive. This shift might not have taken place, or might have differed in pattern, if rate brackets had been indexed, so that changes in burden distribution would have called for explicit legislative action.

To avoid arbitrary rate change due to inflation, various countries are now giving consideration to linking bracket limits to price change. This approach has been used for some time in various Latin American countries, where much sharper inflation rates have been experienced. Canada has recently adopted such indexation, as have some Western European countries. The possibility of applying a similar procedure has been discussed in the United States, but Congress has not as yet taken such action, preferring rather to make periodic adjustments in the rate structure. This may serve to cancel the resulting gain in revenue or increase in the average taxpayer's real burden, but it may not neutralize (and over the past decade distinctly has not neutralized) the effects of inflation on the distribution of the tax burden. In fact, it appears that much of the discontent with taxation (the so-called tax revolt of the late seventies) has been due to the arbitrary impact of inflation on the level and structure of tax liabilities.

Base Adjustment

The inflation distortion discussed in the preceding section arises because the income tax is progressive. As a result, taxpayers with fixed nominal but

---

[24]A similar argument also applies to taxpayers whose income has remained constant. Since rate brackets are defined in nominal terms, such taxpayers continue to pay the same rate of tax although their real income has fallen. If bracket limits were defined in real terms, the rate of tax for such taxpayers would be reduced.

[25]See p. 165. See also Emil M. Sunley and Joseph A. Pechman, "Inflation Adjustment for the Individual Income Tax," in H. G. Aaron (ed.), *Inflation and the Income Tax*, Washington: Brookings, 1976.

falling real income do not find their rate reduced, while others with rising nominal but constant real income find their rate increased. This, of course, would not happen if the rate were proportional. But there is a further problem which would result even under a proportional tax. As prices rise, the nominal value of real assets tends to increase as well. Thus there results a capital gain in nominal but not in real terms. Since taxable capacity or accretion should be measured in real terms, such gains should not be taxed. Moreover, a rise in the price level lowers the real value of claims which are fixed in money terms. This results in a real gain to the debtor, just as it imposes a real loss on the creditor. How should such changes in the real value of assets or debts be allowed for?

In a well-adjusted tax system, it appears that (1) capital gains and losses should be adjusted for inflation so as to allow for real gains and losses only; (2) debtors should be taxed on the gain which they derive as the real value of their indebtedness is reduced; and (3) creditors should be allowed a loss as the real value of their claims has fallen. The question is how far the adjustment can be carried in practice. With regard to item 1, there is a strong case for adjustment. Such allowance should be included in a capital gains reform package provided, however, that gains are then treated as ordinary income. Short of this, it has been argued that failure to deflate such gains is a rough compensation for failure to tax them as ordinary income.[26]

The case is more difficult with regard to items 2 and 3. To begin with, a distinction may be drawn between anticipated and unanticipated inflation. If inflation is anticipated, lenders will ask for a higher rate of interest to offset the decrease in the real value of their claims. This being the case, does the latter constitute a loss which need be allowed for? Also, would it be fair to render the addition to the rate of interest, which constitutes no real gain, subject to tax? The answer is that the adjustment can be made either by allowing for the loss in the real value of the claim, or by exempting the inflationary component of the interest rate, but not both. However this may be, much of the inflation process is unanticipated, so that allowance for real losses offers the better approach. While revenue effects of allowing for losses to the creditor and gains to the debtor would tend to wash out, such allowance would have a substantial effect on burden distribution.

In all, adjustment for all claims, including private debt, public debt, and money holdings, would be too difficult a task to undertake. The more realistic question, therefore, is whether an inflation adjustment should be applied to capital gains without going all the way. The answer seems to be in the affirmative, although such adjustment has to be viewed as part of the broader problem of capital gains treatment. Certain other aspects of the inflation problem, including the treatment of depreciation and balance sheet adjustments, are considered in connection with the corporation tax.[27]

[26]See Roger E. Brinner, "Inflation and the Definition of Taxable Personal Income," in Aaron, op. cit.
[27]See p. 419.

F. STATE AND LOCAL INCOME TAXES

As noted before, the income tax is primarily a federal tax. In 1975, 89 percent of individual income tax revenue went to the federal government, 9 percent to the states, and 2 percent to local governments. As a percent of their general revenue, the three levels of government derived 54, 19, and 3 percent from this source, respectively. Nevertheless, the income tax is used by forty-one states and in recent years has also become increasingly important at the local level.

State Income Taxes

Structure of State Taxes   Of the forty-one states which use a general income tax (applicable to both earned and unearned income), thirty-two make use of AGI as defined under the federal income tax. Where the federal base is used, certain adjustments are made, with interest on federal securities and frequently capital gains excluded.[28] Most states permit a 10 percent standard deduction. Personal exemptions are typically at the federal level or somewhat higher, with a few states using a credit in lieu of an exemption. Rates in all but four states are progressive, ranging typically from 2 to about 8 percent, but in some states reaching as high as 15 percent. While rate progression is moderate, the effective rate (even in states using a flat rate schedule) is strongly progressive, especially over the lower-income ranges, owing to generally high exemptions. Three states (Vermont, Nebraska, and Alaska) determine liability under the state tax as a percentage of federal tax. Some states tax capital income at a higher rate while others exempt wage income. Most states permit income tax paid to other states as a credit against their tax. We thus find considerable variety among the state income taxes, but the typical pattern is one of approximating federal AGI and exemptions and of progressive rates from 2 to 8 percent.

Deductibility   State income taxes are deducted in computing taxable income under the federal income tax, and the federal income tax is deducted in some (though a decreasing number of) states in computing taxable income for purposes of the state tax. The deductibility provisions are important because they determine the *net* addition to the tax burden which results from the state tax.

Suppose first that only the federal government permits deductibility and that a 10 percent state tax is imposed. The net cost (increase in combined state and local tax) per dollar of state tax depends on the taxpayer's federal rate bracket. If this bracket is 70 percent, the net cost of each dollar of state tax equals 30 cents, with 70 cents recouped through the reduction in federal tax. If the bracket is 14 percent, the net cost equals 86 cents, since only 14 cents is recaptured in reduced federal tax. The incremental tax caused by a flat-rate state tax is thus regressive. As shown in column III of Table 17-10,

---

[28]For these and other relevant facts, see Advisory Commission on Intergovernmental Relations, *State and Local Finances, Significant Features*, Washington: 1976–77, p. 206.

TABLE 17-10
Effects of Tax Deductibility

Taxable Income (Dollars)	Federal Marginal Rate (Percentages) (I)	INCREMENTAL BURDEN FROM 10 PERCENT STATE TAX (Percentages of taxable income)		
		No Deductibility (II)	Deductibility of State Tax at Federal Level (III)	Mutual Deductibility (IV)
100	14.0	10.0	8.6	7.5
20,000	32.0	10.0	6.8	4.8
44,000	50.0	10.0	5.0	2.6
200,000	70.0	10.0	3.0	1.0

the incremental effective rate imposed by a 10 percent state tax falls from 8.6 percent at the bottom to 3 percent at the top of the income scale. Taking the state of California as an illustration, liabilities under the state income tax rise from 1 percent to 3.6, 7.0, and 10.1 percent of taxable incomes of $100, $20,000, $44,000, and $200,000, respectively. The corresponding net rates, after allowing for deduction at the federal level, however, are only 0.86, 2.4, 3.5, and 1.5 percent, respectively, rendering the net tax regressive at the upper end of the scale. Some might argue that this is not relevant, since the state should consider the liability which it imposes, without allowing for repercussions at the federal level.[29] Yet, to overlook repercussions is unrealistic since, in fact, a substantial part of the state tax is financed by recoupment of federal tax.

The situation becomes more complex if the state also allows deductibility of the federal tax.[30] As shown in column IV of Table 17-10, this deduction further reduces the liability at the state level and adds to the regressivity of the net state tax. Furthermore, closer consideration shows that the net gain to the taxpayer from deducting the federal tax is but slight, while the revenue loss to the state is very substantial.[31] It is inadvisable, therefore, for states to permit deduction of the federal tax.

[29]The relationship is similar to that which will be observed in the next chapter when the interaction of corporation and individual income taxes at the federal level is considered.

[30]To apply mutual deductibility on a current basis, the taxpayer would have to be adept in solving simultaneous equations; and the process would be difficult because the appropriate rate brackets would be unknown. In practice, the problem is solved, however, by deducting last year's tax.

[31]Let the federal and state statutory tax rates be f and s. With federal deductibility, the effective federal rate becomes $f(1-s)$ and the combined rate is $f(1-s)+s$. With mutual deductibility, the effective federal rate is $f(1-s)/(1-fs)$ and the net state rate is $s(1-f)/(1-fs)$, the combined rate being $[f(1-s)+s(1-f)]/(1-fs)$.

Assuming $s=0.10$ and $f=0.7$, the combined rate prior to deduction of the federal tax at the state level is 0.73. With mutual deductibility, it becomes 0.71, giving a reduction in the net tax of 2 cents per dollar of income. At the same time, state revenue falls from 10 to 3 cents per dollar of income.

Limitations It is not a matter of accident that state income tax rates are relatively modest, as compared with federal rates. This reflects the fact that at higher rate levels, interstate rate differentials would come to have significant effects on economic location. Moreover, in dealing with capital income, the difficulties inherent in the treatment of income earned outside the jurisdiction would become substantial. Unless all jurisdictions were to use the same rate structure, the role of distributional adjustments through progressive taxation at the state and local level is quite limited; but with uniform rates, policy would in fact be a national one. The function of redistribution, as we shall see later, must be largely centralized.[32]

Local Income Taxes

While income taxes at the local level are relatively unimportant in overall magnitude, they are of considerable importance in some of the larger cities. New York City, for instance, derives 20 percent of its municipal tax collections from this source. Some form of income tax is now imposed by about 4,000 local governments, including cities, counties, and over 1,000 school districts. The rate is typically at 1 percent and in most cases no exemptions are granted. Local earnings by nonresidents are included in the tax base, which in some cases is limited to wage and salary income. As we shall see in a later chapter, local income taxation of earnings by nonresidents may come to play a major role in restructuring urban finances.[33]

G. APPRAISAL OF INCOME TAX

The individual income tax has the great advantage of relating tax liability to a comprehensive measure of ability to pay and of permitting adaptation to the personal circumstances of the taxpayer. Among existing taxes, it is the personal tax *par excellence*, and, at its best, it is superior to all other taxes (except perhaps a personalized expenditure tax) in implementing horizontal and vertical equity.

Since it is a comprehensive tax, the taxpayer cannot avoid it by changing employment or investment from one occupation or industry to another. Such, at least, is the case for the federal tax; and, since factor supplies to the economy as a whole are relatively inelastic, we have seen that the tax burden tends to remain with the taxpayer. However, we have noted settings of imperfect markets where part of the burden is passed on to consumers, as well as potentially burdensome efficiency effects of high marginal rates.[34]

As shown in our earlier discussion of the incidence of the United States tax structure (see Table 12-1, line 1), the individual income tax, owing to the use of exemptions and progressive rates, is by far the most important contributor to progressive taxation in the overall tax structure. This is so even

[32]See p. 524.
[33]See p. 573.
[34]See p. 291.

though the degree of progression, especially over the upper-income ranges, is much less than observation of the bracket rates would suggest. The debate over the role of the income tax in the tax structure, therefore, to a considerable degree reflects debate over the desirability of progressive taxation.

But whatever the virtues of the income tax may be in principle, it must also be recognized that its implementation involves many difficulties and that the existing United States income tax is far from perfect. The definition of taxable income as accretion (i.e., increase in net worth plus consumption) provides us with a norm by which to resolve a host of specific problems pertaining to various forms of income and the institutional arrangements under which it is earned. Without such a norm, resolution of these problems would be impossible; yet application of the norm is frequently difficult. The existing income tax base falls far short of what it should be, with tax preferences of various kinds resulting in a substantial impairment of horizontal, as well as vertical, equity standards.

Moreover, in recent years the effects of inflation have interfered severely with the equity of the income tax. There remains much scope for improvement, and income tax reform continues to provide the most lively topic in tax policy discussions. Yet, when all is said and done, the income tax is still the best instrument of taxation that is available, and the United States income tax structure compares favorably with that of most other countries.

H. SUMMARY

Tax preferences result in a deficient definition of taxable income and thereby weaken the equity of the income tax in both its horizontal and vertical aspects.

1.   Preferences result in a loss of one-third of the revenue which would be obtained under a full tax base.

2.   Preferences are especially important at the lower and upper ends of the income scale. Owing mostly to the preferential treatment of capital gains, the effective rate flattens out at slightly above 30 percent, much below the level suggested by the nominal bracket rates.

3.   Horizontal inequities result because the benefit of tax preferences is distributed unequally among taxpayers with the same income.

4.   By using a "minimum tax" approach, a modest attempt has been made to remedy the preference situation at the upper end of the income scale.

The rate structure is defined in terms of bracket rates which, together with exemptions and deductions, determine the average or effective rates.

5.   The present law is characterized by highly progressive bracket rates of up to 70 percent which, because of deficient definition of taxable income, are not reflected in a corresponding set of average or effective rates.

6.   Earned income, however, is subject to a top rate of 50 percent only.

7. Progressive rates discriminate against fluctuating incomes unless adequate allowance is made for income averaging.

The level of personal exemptions and other low-income provisions is important, both in obtaining progression at the lower end of the income scale (where such allowances may be viewed as a zero bracket rate) and in differentiating among taxpayers by family size.

8. The levels of tax-free income as provided by personal exemptions and deductions lie somewhat above the so-called poverty line.

9. In addition to the personal exemption, the taxpayer may deduct a flat standard deduction in lieu of itemizing. This option is widely used except at the upper end of the income scale.

10. The earned-income credit, being refundable if in excess of tax liability, results in a limited form of negative income tax, but it applies to taxpayers with dependents only.

Definition of the taxable unit involves the differential treatment of single versus joint returns and the treatment of single versus multiple earners within the taxpaying unit.

11. Taking the family-unit approach, ability-to-pay considerations suggest that a single return with a given income should pay a higher tax than a joint return with the same income. This is achieved by giving the joint return higher exemptions.

12. Under progressive rates, marriage between two single earners will increase the combined liability unless a lower rate schedule is applied to the joint return.

13. The combination of a lower rate schedule and higher exemptions under present law results in a tax bonus at marriage for low-income earners with evenly divided incomes and a tax increase for high-income earners with unevenly divided income.

14. This difficulty would disappear if, instead, the taxable unit were defined as the earner, and all would file a single return with a uniform rate schedule applicable thereto.

Over the last decade the advent of inflation has added new complications to income taxation:

15. Inflation raises money incomes, thereby pushing taxpayers into higher rate brackets and causing an arbitrary increase in tax liabilities at given levels of real income. The difficulty may be corrected by indexing the bracket limits.

16. Inflation creates nominal gains in the value of real assets which do not reflect real gains. Moreover, it changes the real value of claims, which does result in real gains and losses to debtors and creditors. The problem may be met by indexing the tax base, but there is a question of how far this adjustment can be carried.

While the individual income tax is primarily a federal revenue source, most states also impose such a tax, and over the past decade it has gained in importance in municipal finance:

    17.   State income taxes may be simplified greatly by using the same income concept as applies under the federal tax.

    18.   State income taxes are deducted from taxable income under the federal tax so that the net tax becomes less progressive.

FURTHER READINGS

Aaron, Henry J. (ed.): *Inflation and the Income Tax*, Washington: Brookings, 1976.

Goode, Richard: *The Individual Income Tax*, Washington: Brookings, 1964.

Pechman, J. A. (ed.): *Comprehensive Income Taxation*, Washington: Brookings, 1977.

Simons, Henry: *Personal Income Taxation*, Chicago: University of Chicago Press, 1938; and *Federal Tax Reform*, Chicago: University of Chicago Press, 1950.

Surrey, Stanley: *Pathways to Tax Reform*, Cambridge, Mass.: Harvard, 1973.

U.S. Treasury Department, *Blueprints for Basic Tax Reform*, 1977, chap. 3.

_____: Joint Publication, Committee on Ways and Means and Committee on Finance, *Tax Reform Studies and Proposals*, part 1, Feb. 5, 1969.

Chapter 18

Corporation Income Tax: (1) Structure and Integration*

A. Structure of Federal Corporation Income Tax: *Determination of Taxable Income; Derivation of Tax Base; Structure of Tax Base; Incentive Provisions.* **B. Should There Be a Corporation Tax?** *The Integrationist View; The Absolutist View; Other Reasons for Corporation Tax.* **C. Distribution of Burden among Shareholders:** *Gross Burden Distribution; Net Burden Distribution; Extra Burden Distribution.* **D. Techniques of Integration:** *Full Integration; Dividend Integration Only; Revenue Cost of Integration; Conclusion.* **E. Income Definition:** *Timing of Depreciation; Depletion; Inventory Accounting; Interest; Capital Gains; Real Estate Tax Shelters; Expense Accounts.*
F. Inflation Adjustment. G. Progression and Small-Business Relief: *Should Rates Be Progressive? Aid to Small Business.* **H. Organizations Subject to Special Treatment:** *Financial Institutions; Cooperatives; Nonprofit Institutions.* **I. State Corporation Taxes.**
J. Summary.

* Readers' Guide to Chapter 18: The purpose of this chapter is to appraise the role of the corporation tax and its burden distribution. The central question is whether there should be an "absolute" corporation tax or whether it should be integrated with the individual income tax. If so, how should such integration be accomplished? In addition to these problems, we consider questions of income definition and, once more, inflation adjustments. Given the complex structure of the modern corporation, the tax law needed to determine taxable income is equally complex and only a few of the major issues can be examined here.

The corporation income tax, like the individual income tax, is primarily a federal tax. Over 90 percent of total revenue from this source accrues at the federal level, where it now contributes 15 percent of total revenue, only about one-half its share of two decades ago. The corporation tax is also used by most states, though at much lower rates than at the federal level.

A. STRUCTURE OF FEDERAL CORPORATION INCOME TAX

The federal corporation tax is imposed at rates of 17, 20, 30, and 40 percent on the first four slabs of $25,000 of net income, with a rate of 46 percent on profits in excess thereof. While nearly 80 percent of all corporations are taxed at the lower rates only, over 90 percent of all profits are subject to the highest rate of tax. This reflects the fact that large corporations furnish the bulk of the tax base, the size distribution of corporate profits by profit brackets being much more unequal than that of personal income by personal income brackets.

Determination of Taxable Income

The basic principle in determining taxable income is simple enough. Gross income of the corporation is reduced by costs incurred in doing business, and the rest is net income subject to tax. Certain problems posed by exclusions and deductions under the individual income tax again arise, such as capital gains, tax-exempt securities, and charitable contributions. Other issues are added, further complicating the design of an equitable corporation tax. This involves determining just what items should be deductible as business costs and what the timing of such charges should be. Different industries present different problems and it is difficult to design a uniform tax treatment for such divergent industries as, for instance, manufacturing and banking. Given the legal complexities of corporations and their interrelationships, it is evident that a fair corporation tax cannot be a simple tax.

Derivation of Tax Base

Whereas the individual income tax is a general tax (or at least aims at being so), the profits tax applies to capital income only. Moreover, it is limited to capital income which (1) accrues in the form of profits, and (2) originates in the corporate sector. Corporate profits as reported in the national income accounts for 1977 may be estimated to account for over 70 percent of total profit income and for nearly 50 percent of total capital income.[1] Thus the

[1] Based on the following figures for 1977:

		In Billions of Dollars
1.	Corporation profits	164.3
2.	Profits of unincorporated enterprise	65.0
3.	Rental income of persons	22.5
4.	Net interest	95.4
	Total	347.2

See U.S. Department of Commerce, *Survey of Current Business*, July 1978. Item 1 is before inventory valuation adjustment. Item 2 is estimated by assuming that the ratio of profits to depreciation in the unincorporated sector is the same as that in the corporate sector.

corporate tax is rather general if viewed as a tax on profits, but less so if viewed as a tax on capital income.

Taxable corporate profits differ from profits as defined in the national income accounts in that inventory valuation gains (or losses), foreign income, and one-half realized capital gains are included. Certain other items such as depletion allowances and state income taxes are deducted. These items, however, are relatively minor, and the difference between taxable profits and profits as defined in the national income accounts is less than that between personal income and taxable income under the individual income tax. There is no counterpart to personal exemptions, although exclusions due to tax preferences again enter. Moreover, tax credits such as the investment credit play a more important role in arriving at the final tax.

Structure of Tax Base

The structure of the corporation tax base, as shown in Table 18-1, differs strikingly from that of the individual income tax. The total number of returns is much smaller and there is a much heavier concentration of returns at the lower end of the scale. In 1975, 48 percent of the returns were from corporations with assets of less than $100,000, and 83 percent had assets of less than $500,000. Yet, these returns contribute only 8 percent of net income and 4 percent of tax. Turning to the other end of the scale, corporations with assets of over $250 million comprise less than one-tenth of 1 percent of returns but contribute nearly 60 percent of total net income and 65 percent of tax paid. This simply reflects the predominating importance of large enterprises in the corporate sector. From the revenue point of view, then, only the large and giant corporations matter.

Incentive Provisions

Since almost all plant and equipment investment originates in the corporate sector, the effects of the corporation tax on the level of investment is a major policy concern. This has led to a number of incentive provisions, including allowance for accelerated depreciation and the investment credit. Allowance for loss carryover is also of major importance in this connection. In addition, the law provides for a small employment credit, aimed at creating employment for targeted groups in the labor force. These aspects will be considered in the next chapter.

B. SHOULD THERE BE A CORPORATION TAX?

The role of the corporation tax in a good tax system is by no means obvious and requires careful examination. Some view the tax as a mere device for integrating corporate-source income with the individual income tax base; others see it as an additional, "absolute" tax applied to corporate-source income independent of that imposed under the individual income tax.

TABLE 18-1
Corporation Tax Returns by Size Groups
(Returns with Net Income, 1975)

Size of Total Assets (Thousands of Dollars)	RETURNS		NET INCOME		TAX	
	Number (Thousands)	As Percentage of Total	In Billions of Dollars	As Percentage of Total	In Billions of Dollars	As Percentage of Total
Under 100	568	48	3.8	2	0.4	1
100– 250	265	22	4.9	3	0.8	1
250– 500	152	13	5.4	3	1.1	2
500– 1,000	94	8	6.4	4	1.6	2
1,000– 25,000	98	8	29.5	18	10.5	16
25,000–100,000	7	1	12.1	7	4.5	7
100,000–250,000	2	*	10.7	6	4.1	6
Over 250,000	1	*	95.5	57	42.2	65
Total	1,187	100	168.3	100	66.2	100

*Less than 0.05 percent.
Notes: Components may not add to total because of rounding. Corporations with assets of zero or unreported are excluded.
Source: U.S. Treasury Department, *Corporation Income Tax Returns, Preliminary Statistics of Income for 1975,* 1977, table 4.

The Integrationist View

Those who take the integrationist position view the problem of taxation at the corporate level merely as a way of including all corporate-source income in the individual income tax base. Their basic proposition is that, in the end, all taxes must be borne by people, and that the concept of equitable taxation can be applied to people only. Moreover, they hold that income should be taxed as a whole under a global income concept, independently of its source. Proceeding on the assumption that the corporation income tax falls on profits, they criticize such a tax because (1) profits, if distributed, are taxed twice—first at the corporation level under the corporation tax and then at the personal level as dividends under the individual income tax; and (2) retained profits are taxed at the corporate rate, a rate which usually differs from that which would apply under the shareholder's individual income tax at the personal level. Thus, if a person has corporate-source income of $100, such income is first subject to a 46 percent corporation tax. If one-half of profits after tax is distributed, dividends equal $27. Suppose that the marginal rate under the individual income tax is 40 percent. The shareholder then pays a further $10.40 in income tax. The total tax equals $58.80. If the personal income tax had applied to the entire profit income, it would have equaled $40. Thus the shareholder pays an "extra tax" of $116.10. "Integration" means adjustment of the system in such a manner that profits are taxed at the personal rate, neither higher nor lower, whether they are retained by the firm or distributed to the shareholder.

The integrationist's position can be brought out most clearly by asking this question: What would be your view on corporate taxation if in fact corporations made it a practice to distribute all profits as dividends and to retain no earnings? The integrationist would answer that, in this case, no corporation tax would be called for. All that would be needed would be source withholding of individual income tax on dividend income, just as is done with wages paid out by the corporation.

But in reality not all profit income is distributed as dividends. During the sixties, approximately 60 percent of corporate profits after taxes were paid out, while the remainder was retained. The corporation tax thus serves the useful purpose of bringing retained earnings into the tax base. Although the corporation tax does not do this at the proper rate (low-income shareholders in particular are overtaxed), it nevertheless plugs what would otherwise be an intolerable tax loophole. Integrationists, therefore, must find a way by which, in the absence of the corporation tax, this part can be included in taxable income under the individual income tax, just as they must find a way to avoid imposing an "extra tax" on such corporate income as is, in fact, distributed. The integrationists thus find the present arrangement unsatisfactory because it does not do a proper job of taxing retained earnings and because it imposes an extra tax on dividends. As shown below, they are prepared to suggest procedures by which a correct solution can be found, i.e., all corporate-source income can be taxed similarly to other income under the individual income tax. In the absence of a correct solution, they may find that the corporation tax as it stands does more good in reaching retained earnings than it does harm in imposing an extra tax on dividends, but they will accept it as a second-best solution only.

This view, of course, is based on the assumption that the tax on corporate profits will in fact be reflected in reduced corporate profits and, hence, in reduced corporate-source income of shareholders. As we saw earlier, this is not necessarily the case. Part of the burden may well be passed on to consumers in higher prices or to wage earners in reduced wages, thus cushioning the impact of the tax on net profits.[2] To the extent that this is done, the tax neither imposes an extra tax on dividends nor acts as a proxy for income taxation on retained earnings. The implications of this for the integration problem will be noted later on.

The Absolutist View

Those who take an opposing position believe that the integrationist approach rests on an unrealistic view of the corporation. The large, widely held corporation — which accounts for the great bulk of corporation tax revenue — is not a mere conduit for personal income. It is a legal entity with an existence of its own, a powerful factor in economic and social decision making, operated by a professional management subject to little control by

[2]See p. 428.

the individual shareholder. From this it is concluded that, being a separate entity, the corporation also has a separate taxable capacity which is properly subject to a separate and absolute tax. Whether profits after tax are distributed or retained is irrelevant in this context.

This "absolute" or "classical" view of the tax is hardly tenable. Corporations do indeed act as distinct decision-making units, only more or less vaguely related to the wishes of the shareholders, thus calling for a regulatory policy at the corporate rather than the shareholder level. Moreover, tax devices may be useful under certain circumstances for such regulatory purposes. However, this is quite a different matter from proposing that a corporation has an ability to pay of its own and should be subject to a distinct tax.[3] Obviously, all taxes must in the end fall on somebody, i.e., on natural persons. Corporate profits are part of the income of the shareholders and, in the spirit of the accretion approach to the income tax, should be taxed as part of their income. There is no reason why they should either bear an extra tax or be given preferred treatment.

Once more, note that this view of the corporation tax rests on the assumption that the tax falls on profits and is not passed on to consumers or wage earners. To the extent that such shifting occurs, the intent of the absolutists to impose an extra tax on corporate source income is thwarted. The tax, in this case, becomes an inferior and arbitrary sales or wages tax, without a rational place in an equitable tax structure.[4]

Other Reasons for Corporation Tax

While there is no valid argument for an absolute corporation tax on ability-to-pay grounds, a number of other considerations might justify such a tax. However, it would hardly be of the same order of magnitude or structure as the federal profits tax.

Benefit Consideration Corporations may be called upon to pay a benefit tax. Government renders many services which benefit business operations by reducing costs, broadening markets, facilitating financial transactions, and so forth. Most of these services, however, do not accrue solely to corporations but to other forms of business organization as well. The rationale would therefore be for a general tax on business operations, rather than for a tax on corporations only. While there are certain governmental costs incurred in connection with corporations in particular, these costs are a minor factor and hardly justify a tax.[5] The privilege of operation under limited liability is, of course, of tremendous value to corporations, but the institution of limited

---

[3]One may, of course, speak of the ability of a corporation to pay a certain tax without going bankrupt or without curtailing its operations. The concept of capacity to pay as used in this sense, however, relates to the economic effects of the tax rather than to ability to pay as used in the context of equity considerations.

[4]It is inferior because the implicit rates of sales or payroll taxation will vary arbitrarily with the profit-sales ratio (margin) or the profits-wage bill ratio of particular corporations.

[5]The combined costs of the Securities and Exchange Commission and of the Justice Department's Antitrust Division for fiscal year 1980 are estimated at $114 million, or 1.6 percent of corporation tax revenue of $71 billion.

liability as such is practically costless to society and hence does not justify imposition of a benefit tax. The purpose of benefit taxes is to allocate the cost of public services rendered, not to charge for costless benefits.

To the extent that a benefit tax is appropriate, two further questions arise. One relates to the level at which such a tax should be imposed. Since most public services which accrue as benefits to business are rendered at the state and local levels, it is evident that such a tax would not be primarily a federal matter. The other relates to the appropriate tax base. This will differ with the service rendered, but in most cases it will not be profits. Thus, real property would best reflect the value of fire protection; employment would reflect the input of school expenditures; transportation would reflect road services; and so forth. If a general proxy is to be used, total costs incurred in the state or locality might be the best overall measure, with value added (which includes profits as well as other factor costs) a second possibility.

Regulatory Objectives   A different case for an absolute corporation tax may be made if the tax is viewed as an instrument of control over corporate behavior. The appropriate form of corporation tax then depends on the particular policy objective that is to be accomplished.

> **1.** The control of monopoly has been traditionally undertaken through regulatory devices, but a tax approach might be used. This, however, would not call for a general tax on profits, which would not be effective in correcting monopolistic behavior. Rather, it would call for a more complex tax, related to the degree of monopolistic restriction.
>
> **2.** If it were desired to restrict the absolute size of firms or bigness (which is not the same as restricting monopoly or market shares), a tax might again be used for this purpose. Here, a progressive business tax would be called for. The reason for progression, however, would not be ability to pay, as in the individual income tax. Large firms might be owned by small investors and small firms might be owned by wealthy investors. Rather, progression would be used to discriminate against the large firm and curtail what are considered to be undesirable social effects of bigness. The question then arises whether such a tax should not be on asset size or sales, rather than on profits. Even if bigness is held undesirable, it is not a reason for penalizing the profitable big firm in particular.
>
> While we have no full-fledged experience with such an approach (a progressive corporation tax was recommended by the Roosevelt administration in 1936 but rejected), a limited application is found in the four-rate schedule which applies various lower rates to small firms. This is a subject to which we shall return later on.[6]
>
> **3.** An excess profits tax may be imposed in periods of emergency (such as wars) when direct controls over wages and prices are needed. Wage constraints under such conditions cannot be applied effectively without corresponding profit constraints, and a tax on excess profits is a helpful tool in this connection. The United States imposed such a tax in both world wars as well as during the Korean war. While sound in principle, the excess profits tax is difficult to administer since excess profits are not readily defined. Such profits may be

[6]See p. 420.

measured by comparison with a base period, but inequities may result from differences in initial position; or, a standard rate of return may be used, in which case risk differentials can hardly be overlooked, thus posing the difficult problem of what rates are appropriate for what industries.

A different type of situation in which a selective excess profits tax may be called for is created by the current oil crisis and the removal of price controls on oil.

4. As a stimulus to capital formation and growth, it may be desirable to encourage corporate saving and to discourage dividend distribution. This objective may be accomplished by imposing a tax on dividends paid out while exempting earnings retained. Alternatively, it may be held desirable to encourage corporate distributions and to discourage retentions in order to improve the functioning of the capital market or to increase consumption expenditures. This goal may be achieved by imposing a tax on undistributed profits while exempting profits which are paid out as dividends. Such a tax was imposed in the late thirties with the intention of stimulating consumer spending.

5. Finally, the corporation tax may be used to provide incentives or disincentives to investment, as distinct from corporate savings. Devices like the investment credit or accelerated depreciation may be used for this purpose, and they may be applied on a cyclical or a secular basis. The effectiveness of such measures will be considered in more detail later on, but it should be noted here that such incentives are better given directly—i.e., in the form of investment subsidies or penalties—rather than as relief under the profits tax.

In all, these considerations suggest that tax instruments may be helpful devices in controlling corporate behavior but, in most cases, a form of taxation would be required which differs from the profits tax.

C. DISTRIBUTION OF BURDEN AMONG SHAREHOLDERS

In assessing the burden of the corporation profits tax, much depends on whether the tax falls on corporate profits, whether it is shared by other capital income, or whether it is passed on to consumers or wage earners, a question to be discussed later.[7] Unless otherwise indicated, we assume for the time being that it falls on corporate profits, i.e., on shareholders. On this basis, how is the burden distributed among income groups? The answer depends on how the burden concept is defined. Here a distinction will be drawn between *gross burden*, *net burden*, and a third concept which we shall refer to as *extra burden*. Derivation of various burden concepts and their pattern of distribution is shown in Table 18-2.

Gross Burden Distribution

In the table, we compare the position of low-income shareholder A, whose marginal rate under the individual income tax is 20 percent, with that of high-income shareholder B, whose rate is 70 percent. Their respective levels of AGI and corporate-source income are shown in lines 16 and 17, with the ratio

[7]See p. 269, and also the next chapter.

TABLE 18-2
Alternative Concepts of Corporate Tax Burden

Marginal Income Tax Rates (Percentage)	SHAREHOLDER A (20)			SHAREHOLDER B (70)		
Dividend Payout Ratio (Percentage)	100 (I)	50 (II)	0 (III)	100 (IV)	50 (V)	0 (VI)
I. TAX PER $100 OF CORPORATE SOURCE INCOME						
Gross Corporation Tax						
1. Corporate source income	100	100	100	100	100	100
2. Corporation tax	46	46	46	46	46	46
Net Corporation Tax						
3. Corporate income after tax (1 − 2)	54	54	54	54	54	54
4. Dividends	54	27	—	54	27	—
5. Personal tax on (4)	10.8	5.4	—	37.8	18.9	—
6. Combined tax (2 + 5)	56.8	51.4	46.0	83.8	64.9	46.0
7. Dividends without corporate tax	100	50	—	100	50	—
8. Personal tax on (7)	20	10	—	70	35	—
9. Net corporation tax (6 − 8)	36.8	41.4	46.0	13.8	29.8	46.0
Integrated Tax						
10. Advanced by corporation	46	46	46	46	46	46
11. Dividends	54	27	—	54	27	—
12. Taxable personal income	100	100	100	100	100	100
13. Personal tax on (10)	20	20	20	70	70	70
14. Payment (−) or refund (+)	26	26	26	−24	−24	−24
15. Extra burden (6 − 13)	36.8	31.4	26	13.8	−5.1	−24
II. EFFECTIVE BURDEN RATIOS						
16. AGI	20,000	20,000	20,000	250,000	250,000	250,000
17. Corporate source income	1,000	1,000	1,000	100,000	100,000	100,000
18. AGI*	20,460	20,730	21,100	296,000	323,000	350,000
19. Gross burden ratio (2 ÷ 18)	2.25	2.22	2.18	15.54	14.24	13.14
20. Net burden ratio (9 ÷ 18)	1.80	2.00	2.18	4.66	9.23	13.14
21. Extra burden ratio (15 ÷ 18)	1.80	1.51	1.23	4.66	−1.58	−6.86

Notes:
To simplify, this table does not allow for capital gains taxes on sale of assets whose value has increased due to retention of earnings.

Line 18: AGI* is defined to include the shareholder's entire corporate source income —not only dividends (as in AGI) but also his or her share in corporation tax and retained earnings. Per $100 of corporate source income, this additional amount equals line 1 minus line 4. For column I this is equal to $46, so that AGI*, as shown in line 18, exceeds AGI as shown in line 16 by $460.

For a table similar to lines 1 − 15, see Charles McLure, Jr., *Must Corporation Income Be Taxed Twice?* Washington: Brookings, 1979, p. 6.

of corporate-source income to AGI substantially higher for B. Our procedure involves two steps. Step I, shown in part I of the table, is to determine the tax burden per $100 of corporate-source income. Step II, shown in part II of the table, is to translate this tax into effective burden ratios (tax rates) allowing for the applicable shares of corporate-source income in AGI.

In determining the "gross-burden," we simply divide the corporation tax between shareholders in line with their share in corporate equity. Step I is shown in lines 1 and 2 of the table. The corporation tax per $100 of corporate-source income equals $46 throughout, independent of the shareholders' marginal tax rates or the corporation's retention ratio. Turning to step II, we apply this gross tax per $100 of corporate-source income to the shareholder's entire holdings and then express the total as a percent of AGI or, more precisely, of AGI*, which allows for inclusion of retained earnings and corporation tax in the base.[8] The resulting pattern of effective rates is shown in line 19. We note that the incidence of the gross burden is sharply progressive. For the 50 percent distribution, the low income taxpayer has a rate of 2.2 percent while the high-income taxpayer pays 14.2 percent. This simply reflects the rising ratio of corporate-source income to AGI while moving up the scale.

Net Burden Distribution

This way of looking at the matter is misleading, however, and overstates the true progressivity of the corporation tax. The reason is that we have disregarded the effects on individual income tax liability which result as the corporation tax is introduced. These effects are allowed for in our concept of "net burden."

For this purpose, we compare the shareholders' combined corporate and individual income tax with what their income tax would have been without a corporation tax. The difference between the two is the net, or incremental, burden of the corporation tax.[9] This net tax consists of two parts. One is the additional tax imposed by the corporation tax. The other is a tax saving which results because dividends and, hence, individual income tax on dividend income will be less if a corporation tax applies. This tax saving per dollar of dividends will be greater for high-income shareholders whose bracket rate under the individual income tax is higher. Therefore, the extra tax per dollar of dividends will be less for the high-income shareholder.

---

[8]Because of this, the effective rate varies somewhat with the distribution assumption.

[9]The net tax T_n equals the joint tax T_j, minus the personal income tax T_p, which would apply if there were no corporation tax. We thus have

$$T_j = t_c P + t_p d(1 - t_c)P$$

$$T_p = t_p dP$$

$$T_n = T_j - T_p = t_c(1 - dt_p)P$$

where t_c is the corporate rate, t_p is the applicable personal bracket rate, d is the percentage of after-corporation-tax profits which is paid out, and P is the taxpayer's share in before-tax profits.

If allowance is made for the capital gains tax on increases in the share value at the time of realization, the net tax becomes

$$T_n = t_c(1 - dt_p)P - gt_p(1 - d)t_c P$$

where g is the fraction of gains that comes to be included in the tax base.

Determination of the net tax per $100 of corporate source income (step I) is illustrated in lines 3 to 9 of the table. Line 3 gives corporate source income after corporation tax. Line 4 gives dividends, per $100 of corporate source income, varying with the three rates of dividend distribution. Line 5 shows the personal tax on dividend income, varying with the applicable rate of income tax. Line 6 gives the combined corporation and personal tax. We next consider what the personal tax would have been in absence of corporation tax. Line 7 gives the new and higher level of dividends which would then apply, while line 8 shows the increased level of personal tax. By deducting line 8 from line 6, we obtain the net increase in the shareholder's total tax which results from the introduction of the corporation tax. We see that the additional tax per dollar of dividends falls as we move up the income scale. For a low-income shareholder with a marginal income tax rate of 20 percent, the tax, per $100 of dividend income (assuming full distribution), is increased by $36.80, whereas for a high-income shareholder with a marginal rate of 70 percent, the increase is only $13.80. We also find that the net burden rises sharply as the payout ratio falls. This stands to reason, since in the absence of distribution there can be no offsetting reduction in personal tax.

In line with step II, we again apply this net tax to total corporate source income and, dividing by AGI, arrive at the net burden ratios of line 20. We find that the burden pattern remains progressive but (as we expect) very much less so than the gross burden ratio. While the gross burden ratio (using line 19, columns I and IV as illustration) rose from 2.2 to 15.5 percent, the increase now (line 20) is from 1.8 to 4.6 percent only. The net burden distribution is only mildly progressive.

Extra Burden Distribution

Under the present system there are two reasons why corporate-source income is taxed differently from other income. Distributed profits are subject to both the corporation tax and the personal tax, while retained profits are subject to the corporation tax only and escape the personal tax. As a result, the tax burden on corporate profit income differs from that on the other income. How important is this difference, and how does it relate to the shareholder's income level?

To measure the difference, or "extra tax," we compare the present combined tax (including corporation tax and individual income tax on dividends) with what the tax would be under an integrated system, i.e., a system without corporation tax but with application of individual income tax to retained as well as distributed earnings.[10]

---

[10]The extra tax T_e equals the joint tax T_j minus the tax under integration T_i. Using the notations as in the preceding note, we have

$$T_j = t_c P + t_p d(1 - t_c) P$$
$$T_i = t_p P$$
$$T_e = T_j - T_i = [t_c + t_p d(1 - t_c) - t_p] P$$

It is thus seen that $T_e = T_n - t_p(1 - d)P$.

The extra tax thus contains two components. One is the net burden of the corporation tax and the other is the tax savings which arise because, under the present system, retained earnings are not subject to personal income tax. The net burden, as we just saw, is mildly progressive, at least for the 50-percent distribution case; but tax savings rise with AGI, not only because the ratio of retained earnings to AGI rises but also because a higher marginal rate comes to apply. The extra rate should thus be lower and less progressive than the net rate.

The extra tax per $100 of corporate-source income is derived in lines 10 to 15 of the table. Line 10 shows the amount of tax paid by the corporation. Line 11 shows the level of dividends, while line 12 shows the corresponding (grossed-up) amount on which personal tax is paid. Dividends of $54 reflect a corporate source income of $100 (assuming no retention) because $46 was already paid by the corporation on the shareholder's behalf. Line 13 shows the new personal tax, while line 14 gives the personal payment or refund due. Line 15, finally, shows the difference between line 6 (the combined burden under the present arrangement) and line 13 (the tax payable under an integrated arrangement). Line 15 thus measures the extra burden which the present arrangement imposes over and above that in an integrated system. We find that the extra burden equals the net burden in the case of full distribution but falls below it as the distribution ratio drops.

Moving to step II, we obtain the extra burden ratios of line 21. We find that the extra burden remains progressive if distribution ratios are high. As the distribution ratio declines, the extra burden ratio turns negative for high-income taxpayers and the burden distribution becomes regressive. High-income taxpayers, investing in high-retention corporations, fare better under the present system (the corporation becomes a tax shelter) because tax savings on retained earnings more than offset the additional tax on dividends.[11]

In choosing among these concepts of tax burden, one must decide what question is to be answered. Given the fact that the personal income tax is the centerpiece of the federal tax structure, it would seem that the contribution of the corporation tax to the progressivity of the tax structure should allow for its effects on personal income tax liabilities and thus be viewed in net, rather than in gross, terms. If, instead, the corporate tax burden is viewed by comparison with a horizontally equitable system, the extra burden concept is

---

[11]The shelter situation arises if

$$t_p > t_c + t_p d(1 - t_c)$$

or

$$t_p > \frac{t_c}{1 - d(1 - t_c)}$$

With t_c equal to 0.46 and d equal to 0, 0.3, 0.5, and 1.0 respectively, the levels of t_p at which T_e becomes negative are 46, 54, 63, and 100 percent respectively.

what matters. Seen this way, the corporation tax is not progressive, and at very high incomes it becomes regressive. Integration, therefore, would increase the progressivity of the tax structure at the top of the scale.

D. TECHNIQUES OF INTEGRATION

As noted before, there is much to be said for viewing the corporation as a conduit of income accruing to the individual shareholder and for integrating corporate-source income with the individual income tax. What adjustments in the tax structure would be called for to accomplish this objective?

Full Integration

To secure complete integration, the adjustment must integrate the tax treatment for both retained earnings and dividend distributions. This may be accomplished either via the partnership method or through full taxation of capital gains.

Partnership Method This solution is to impute total profits to the shareholders and to tax them under the individual income tax. Where earnings are retained, the corporation would inform its shareholders that a specified amount has been retained on their behalf and added to their equity; the shareholders would then include this amount in computing their taxable income.

At the same time, it would still be highly desirable to apply source withholding to profit income. Just as the corporation acts as a withholding agent for the individual income tax on the wage income of its employees, so it will act as withholding agent for the profit income of shareholders. Suppose a certain shareholder receives a profit share of $1,000 and is notified accordingly. It does not matter for tax purposes whether cash dividends are paid out or the profits are retained. The corporation withholds at a rate of, say, 25 percent, leaving the shareholder a net income of $750, and pays $250 to the Treasury. The shareholder then "grosses up" his net share by the tax paid on his behalf, thus including the full $1,000 of profits in his taxable income. Suppose that his marginal tax rate is 40 percent, so that he owes a tax of $400. The amount of $250 withheld for him by the corporation is then credited against this liability, reducing the additional amount due to $150. By using this grossing-up procedure, the taxpayer will pay at his proper marginal rate. If the withholding rate exceeds his personal rate, a refund will be due to him.

Shareholders, in other words, are treated for tax purposes as if they were partners in an unincorporated business. Since their tax is paid when the profits accrue, capital gains which reflect an increase in share value caused by retention of profits must then be excluded from subsequent capital gains taxation. This is done by permitting shareholders to write up the base (add to the purchase cost of their shares) by an amount equal to their share in retentions.

This procedure seems eminently fair, and it has been among the standard proposals made by tax reformers for a long time. However, certain difficulties with the method have been pointed out. Thus, it has been argued that the taxpayer should not be required to pay a tax on income which has not been "received." Hence, it is "unfair" to impute retained earnings to the person's taxable income. This objection is essentially the same as that raised against the taxation of unrealized gains. It is not convincing. For one thing, a substantial part of the tax will be paid by source withholding, thus imposing no liquidity problem on the shareholder. The remainder, payable where the individual's marginal rate exceeds the withholding rate, may be financed by a sale of shares. This may not be possible in the case of closely held corporations which are not traded, but here shareholders may obtain the necessary cash by raising their payout ratios.

It is also argued that the partnership approach, while feasible for small and closely held corporations, would not be practicable for large and widely held firms.[12] Since shareholders move in and out of the securities market, it might be difficult to allocate profit shares among them. Moreover, difficulties arise in connection with incentive measures, such as the investment credit. Management, which typically makes the investment decision, might not respond to a credit the benefits of which are passed through to the shareholder, and the pass-through process itself invites technical difficulties. Nevertheless, these problems should not prove beyond solution if a serious effort at integration were made.

However this may be, it should be noted that integration by the partnership method does not in any way bypass the problems involved in determining taxable income of corporations. This determination remains as important as it is under the absolute corporation tax. Integration by the partnership method does not simplify tax administration but places new demands upon it.

Capital Gains Method   Alternatively, full integration might be secured through full taxation of all (including unrealized) capital gains, combined with a repeal of the profits tax. The distributed part would then appear in the shareholder's income as dividends, while the retained part would appear as capital gains.[13] No determination of taxable profits would be needed. Under this approach, periodic (say quintennial) taxation of unrealized gains on traded shares might be combined with taxation at death or transfer of other assets. However, in the absence of taxation at the corporate level, investment incentives such as the investment credit would now have to be granted at the shareholder level, or be given as a direct subsidy to the corporation.

Dividend Integration Only

A more limited approach would remove the differential tax for dividends only, while leaving an absolute tax on retained earnings. This may be done in two ways.

---

[12]For an analysis of the technical problems involved, see Charles McLure, Jr., op. cit.

[13]As an objection to this approach, it is argued that retained earnings may not be reflected properly in share values. The adherent of the accretion principle must respond that if they are not thus reflected, no income has accrued.

Dividends-Received Credit   One procedure is to apply the corporate rate to all profits, but to consider the part imputed to dividends as source withholding on the shareholder's individual income tax. As under the partnership method, the shareholder is then required to gross up. Shareholders will raise their dividends by the amount withheld thereon, compute their individual income tax on the grossed-up basis, and then credit the amount withheld against their tax.[14] Under this arrangement, called the withholding method or "dividends-received credit," differential treatment is eliminated for dividends but continues for retained earnings. Shareholders whose marginal rate exceeds the corporate rate benefit, while those whose marginal rate is less, lose. The credit rate might be set so as to eliminate fully the corporation tax on dividends, or only some fraction thereof might be credited.

In either case, the question arises of what corporate rate should be used. Should it be the statutory rate of 46 percent, or should it be the actual effective rate at which the particular company has paid? As a matter of fact, many corporations, due to investment credits and other provisions of the law, pay at a much lower rate, say, 30 percent. If the benefits of such provisions are to be passed through to the shareholder, the dividends-received credit should be allowed at the full corporate rate of 46 percent. But if the benefits are to be canceled upon distribution, then this credit should be at the effective rate of tax that actually applies. In the latter case, the applicable credit would differ among corporations, thus greatly complicating procedures at the shareholder level.

Dividends-Paid Credit   An alternative approach, known as the "dividends-paid credit," is to exclude dividends paid from the corporation tax base, i.e., to apply the corporation tax to retained earnings only. Assuming no effects on payout ratios, the two methods give identical results, but they differ in their implications for the handling of the pass-through problem. For various reasons, the dividends-paid credit approach has found little favor with the business community. The reason, perhaps, is that dividend exclusion may be seen as leaving business with a tax on undistributed profits which, if memories prove that long, was an unpopular feature of New Deal tax experimentation in the late 1930s.

Revenue Cost of Integration

The revenue cost of integration would be substantial. To illustrate, take 1976 taxable corporation profits of $176 billion, corporation tax revenue of $50 billion, and dividends of $32 billion. Of these, only $24 billion are taxable under the individual income tax, with 24 percent estimated to go to tax-exempt organizations. Assuming an average rate of 30 percent, income tax revenue on dividend income is $7 billion. Total revenue from corporate

---

[14]The grossing up is an essential part of proper withholding. The 4 percent dividend credit, enacted in 1954 and repealed in 1964, did not provide for grossing up and was therefore highly inequitable. Since all shareholders received the same gain per dollar of dividends, the differential tax was cut by a larger percentage for the high-bracket shareholder. See J. A. Pechman, *Federal Tax Policy*, 3d ed., Washington: Brookings, 1977, p. 172.

source income is thus $57 billion. To obtain the base for an integrated tax, we reduce the total of $176 billion by foreign-source income of $48 billion. Since such income is subject to foreign tax it would presumably not be included in the domestic base.[15] Deducting further state and local property taxes of $7 billion, we arrive at the remainder of $121 billion. From this, we exclude again the estimated 24 percent accruing to tax-exempt organizations, thus obtaining a base of $92 billion. Applying now a somewhat higher rate of 40 percent, we obtain a revenue total of $37 billion. The loss from integration thus equals $57 billion minus $37 billion, or $20 billion. While the benefits from integration itself would mirror the "extra burden" distribution shown above, the net distributional effect would depend on how this revenue loss is made up, or what alternative tax reductions are forgone. Note, however, that if the corporation tax on corporate-source income of tax-exempt organizations is retained, this loss could be cut to about $8 billion.

Conclusion

The case for integration involves both equity and efficiency considerations.

Equity Gain   Integration, by granting relief to shareholders, would not remove the inequity (differential taxation of corporate-source income) which was imposed when the corporation tax was originally introduced. The reason is that the additional tax has long been "capitalized" and has come to be reflected in reduced share prices.[16] Assets have changed hands since imposition of the corporation tax, and most present shareholders bought at the lower price. Hence they have suffered no loss, and removal of the differential tax, by leading to a rise in share prices, would leave them with an unjustified capital gain. Original sin, once committed, lingers on. The equity gain from integration, therefore, centers on removal of differential treatment of capital as against labor income rather than of differential treatment among types of capital income.

Efficiency Gain   The efficiency gain from integration would result from removing the distortion brought about because investment in the corporate sector is taxed at a higher rate than is investment in other sectors of the economy. As shown below, this results in a flow of capital from the corporate to the unincorporated sector, so as to leave net rates of return the same in both sectors.[17] The economy is left with too little capital in the corporate and too much in the unincorporated sector, which causes an efficiency loss.

[15]This foreign tax is now credited against the United States corporation tax. If the same procedure was followed after integration, with the foreign tax credit passed through to the shareholder, foreign profits would be included in the tax base, but United States revenue would not be increased thereby. See p. 772.

[16]Before application of taxes and with an interest rate of 5 percent, asset A, bringing an annual income stream of $10,000 will sell for $200,000, while B bringing an income stream of $20,000 will sell for $400,000. Now let income from asset A be taxed at 50 percent while B is exempted. Net income from A falls to $5,000 and the capitalized value falls to $100,000. The next owner of the asset buys it at $100,000 only and receives the same return obtained by the holders of the tax-free asset B.

[17]See p. 295.

Implications of Shifting The preceding discussion of integration was based on the assumption that the corporation tax falls on corporate profits and is borne by the shareholder. What happens to the argument if shifting does occur?

The case for integration is not affected if we assume the burden of the tax to be spread to all capital income.[18] Full integration will simply annul the corporate tax and lead to an increase in the net return on all capital assets. But the situation differs if the tax is shifted (in the sense of being charged to the consumer or wage earner) so that net profits are not reduced. In this case, dividends pay no additional tax. The corporation tax comes to be in the nature of a sales tax and its crediting to the dividend recipient would be inappropriate, as this would result in deficient taxation of profit income under the individual income tax. If the tax is shifted in part, only partial crediting (for the nonshifted part) is in order.[19]

Moreover, the possibility of shifting bears on the problem of how retained earnings are best integrated into the income tax. If corporate management shifts an absolute tax, how will it react to source withholding of the shareholder's personal income tax? Given the possibility that shifting may apply to a source-withholding type of tax, the better part of wisdom would be either to approach integration via full taxation of capital gains or to collect the tax at the shareholder level. In the latter case, the corporation would be required to file information returns on the profits accruing to shareholders in order to prevent tax evasion. By the same token, if integration is to be partial and apply to dividends only, exclusion of dividends from corporation tax will be preferable to collection from the corporation with crediting at the shareholder level.

Prospects As in most problems of tax reform, the issue of integration does not lend itself to a clear-cut answer. On grounds of horizontal equity, there is no reason why capital income should be taxed more heavily than labor income. On efficiency grounds, the singling out of capital income from the corporate sector distorts capital allocation. Moreover, the overall level of investment may be affected detrimentally. For these reasons, a strong case can be made for full integration. Integration applied to dividend income only is easier to manage but leaves the problem of retained earnings unresolved, resulting in overtaxation in some cases and tax avoidance in others. Finally, the integration issue is closely linked to the treatment of capital gains. As long as gains are given preferential treatment, the "double taxation of dividends" may be viewed as a partial offset thereto.

However this may be, the trend is toward partial integration. Thus, Canada, the United Kingdom, France, and Germany have all moved in this direction, and this will put pressure on the United States to follow suit.[20]

---

[18]For a discussion of corporation tax shifting, see p. 295.

[19]Suppose that prior to tax, the profits of a firm equal $100,000. After a 50 percent tax is imposed, gross profits rise to $150,000 while net profits fall to $75,000. The amount of tax borne by the shareholder thus equals $25,000, or one-third of the total tax of $75,000. Thus, two-thirds of the tax is shifted and only one-third of the tax (or $25,000) should be credited.

[20]For a review of foreign practices, see Charles McLure, Jr., op. cit.

E. INCOME DEFINITION

Whether one thinks in terms of an absolute corporation tax or of partnership-type integration, taxable income must be defined and the countless difficulties which this poses must be faced. It is bypassed only if integration takes the form of full taxation of capital gains.

Timing of Depreciation

Since the corporation tax is a tax on *net* income, recovery of the capital outlay must be permitted in computing taxable income. The question is how this recovery is to be timed.[21]

Certain outlays, like those for research and development, are expensed (i.e., are deducted in full as incurred) even though they are in the nature of capital formation. Physical capital assets used in the production process (i.e., plant and equipment) cannot be expensed but may be charged over a prescribed period of time. The timing of the recovery of capital cost is important because the present value of tax liability is reduced when depreciation is charged. Deduction of capital costs gives rise to tax savings to the investor, and these are the greater the earlier the capital costs are deducted. This is so because a time discount must be applied to future tax savings. The present value of the tax paid over the life of the investment may be thought of as containing two parts. One is the present value of the tax as it would be without depreciation. The other, which is subtracted, is the tax savings which are due to deducting depreciation.[22] Thus the reduction in earnings, brought about by a tax, depends not only on the tax rate, but also on the timing of depreciation deductions. These factors involve both the time span over which depreciation is charged and the speed at which it proceeds within this interval.

The time span is in practice set in line with the "useful service life" of the asset. The Internal Revenue Service has set "guideline" lives ranging from three years for automobiles to ten years for machinery and forty to sixty years

---

[21]Under conditions of inflation there is the further question of how the depreciable base should be defined. See p. 419.

[22]Consider an investment giving a constant annual income stream R for n years. Prior to tax, the investor equates the cost of the investment with the present value of its income stream so that

$$C = R_n A_n$$

where C is the cost of the investment and A_n is the present value of an annuity of $1 for n years, discounted at the market rate of interest.

After tax, we have

$$C = R_n A_n - t(R_n A_n) + t\frac{C}{d}A_d$$

where t is the tax rate and d (assuming straight-line depreciation) is the number of years over which depreciation is spread. A_d accordingly is the present value of an annuity of $1 over d years. The second term on the right-hand side of the equation is the present value of gross tax, and the third term is the present value of the tax saving due to the depreciation allowance.

The present value of the net tax equals

$$t\left[RA_n - \frac{C}{d}A_d\right]$$

for structures. These guidelines relate to about eighty fairly broadly defined classes of assets. The Revenue Act of 1971 introduced the so-called asset depreciation range (ADR) system, permitting the taxpayer to raise or lower the service lives by 20 percent.[23]

The rate of depreciation over this time span depends on which of several write-off methods are applied. Three methods are distinguished. Under the *straight-line* method, the same amount of C/n is written off each year, where C is the asset cost and n is the asset life. Thus, for a $100,000 asset with a life of ten years, $10,000 is deducted each year. Under the *double-declining balance method*, twice the straight-line percentage is deducted in the first year and this same percentage is then applied to the as yet undepreciated amount in each successive year. Thus, $20,000 is deducted the first year, $16,000 in the second year, and so forth.[24] Under the *sum-of-years-digits method*, the fraction deducted each year equals the ratio of remaining years to the sum of the years over the service life. Thus, for a $100,000 asset with a ten-year useful life, the sum of the years is $10+9+8+\cdots+1=55$. The charge for the first year is $10/55$ of $100,000 = $18,111$; for the second year the charge is $9/55$ of $100,000 = $16,374$; and so forth.

As shown in Table 18-3, the present value of depreciation is higher under the double-declining balance than under the straight-line method, and the difference increases with the length of service life. The same holds if we compare the sum-of-years-digits method with the straight-line method. As between declining balance and sum-of-years digits, we note that the former is preferable for short, and the latter for long, investments.

The straight-line method is available for all depreciable assets, but various categories may be depreciated at a faster rate. Thus, depreciable property other than real estate with a useful life of over three years, if newly acquired, may be depreciated at double-declining balance, years-digits, or other "consistent" methods. In the case of used property, the declining-balance method may be used but not at a rate exceeding 150 percent of the straight-line method. Special provisions apply for real estate. New real estate may be depreciated at 150 percent declining balance, except in the case of rental property where double-declining balance or years-digits may be applied. A 125 percent declining-balance method is available for used rental property, and rehabilitation outlays for low-cost housing may be depreciated over a five-year period. Certain pollution-control facilities, finally, may be depreciated over a thirty-month period. Depreciation schedules, once agreed upon, must be adhered to thereafter and cannot be changed without agreement from the Internal Revenue Service.

---

[23]This act also repealed the so-called reserve-ratio test, introduced in 1965 and designed to hold service lives for tax purposes in line with the actual depreciation practice used by the firm. Unfortunately, the period of application was too short to give this method a fair test.

[24]The taxpayer is also permitted to switch to straight-line when the amount deductible under straight-line becomes larger than that deductible under double-declining balance. Thereby, the total amount is depreciated within ten years. If double-declining balance is retained, a salvage value remains which is accounted for in the last year.

TABLE 18-3
Present Value of Depreciation
(In Dollars, Asset Cost $100,000)

Service Life (Years) (I)	Straight Line (II)	Double-Declining Balance (III)	Sum-of-Years-Digits (IV)
6 PERCENT DISCOUNT			
5	86,750	87,811	87,515
10	75,787	78,716	79,997
20	59,055	64,661	67,680
50	32,460	40,935	44,756
10 PERCENT DISCOUNT			
5	79,534	81,100	80,614
10	64,469	68,528	70,099
20	44,663	51,539	54,697
50	20,806	28,829	31,439

Source: Harold Bierman, Jr., and Seymour Smidt, *The Capital Budgeting Decision,* 2d ed., New York: Macmillan, 1966.

Given the advantage of more rapid depreciation, it is surprising that most corporations still use the straight-line method.[25] However, more than 50 percent of total depreciation is now taken under double-declining balance, which is coming into increasing use. The use of rapid depreciation rates for tax purposes (in order to reduce taxable profits) and slow depreciation for book purposes (in order to appear more profitable to the shareholder) is not looked upon with favor by the tax authorities, but is nevertheless often the practice.

There remains the basic question of what constitutes the "proper" rate of depreciation. If rapid write-offs are advantageous to the taxpayer, they are costly to the Treasury. With regard to any one investment, the same burden —defined as present value of tax—may be imposed by various combinations of tax rate and depreciation rate. A lower tax rate and slower depreciation rate will give the same present value of tax as a higher tax rate and a more rapid depreciation rate. If all investments were the same, it would make little difference which combination were chosen to provide the Treasury with a given revenue stream. The difficulty arises because investments differ in length and profitability and thus fare differently under the various policies. Yet they should be treated equally, as a matter of both equity (investors with the same income should pay the same tax) and neutrality (taxation should not distort the pattern of investment). What depreciation pattern is required to secure an equitable and neutral income definition?

[25]For an investment of $100,000 (fifty-year life), the present value of depreciation under years-digits exceeds that under straight-line by $12,326. At a 46 percent tax rate, the present value of the tax saving equals $5,328.

The depreciable asset, as noted before, may be looked upon as generating two income streams. One is a positive income stream of earnings, arising from the use of the asset. The other is the negative income stream, or diminution of capital, which results as the asset is worn out and declines in value because of obsolescence. Netting out, the asset gives rise to a net income stream, the present value of which is the value of the asset. Assets with equal present value of net income streams should carry an equal burden as defined by the present value of the tax.

This might be done by charging depreciation in line with the actual diminution in asset value, thus taxing the true net income stream as it is received each year. If the current value at any one time equals the capitalized value of the future income stream generated by the asset, the decline in value equals the capitalized value of the reduction in the remaining income stream. This then is the capital cost which should be charged along with other costs in computing net income. This is the approach which, in line with the accretion concept, gives the correct definition of net income. But, though the principle is clear, it is not easily applied. Modern capital equipment does not wear out evenly and it frequently becomes obsolete before it has been "used up." Obsolescence rates will differ and cannot be predicted. Thus, the best that can be done is to gear service lives to actual business practice while relying on the assumption that the latter will tend to reflect the "true" service life and time path of the income stream. With this as the standard, more rapid rates of depreciation may be referred to as "accelerated" depreciation. Such depreciation has been used as an instrument to provide investment incentives, and its effectiveness for this purpose will be considered later on.[26]

Depletion

A related problem arises in the case of the extractive industries. Such industries have been given preferential treatment in two respects. First, investors were permitted to expense (rather than depreciate) outlays for exploration cost. Second, they were permitted a percentage depletion allowance. This is a deduction over and above recovery of actual costs equal to a set percentage of gross receipts.

The depletion allowance was granted initially because it was difficult to assess the original cost of developed wells when the tax was introduced, and depletion was to serve as a proxy for previously undertaken but not as yet depreciated costs. Later it came to be looked at as an allowance, justified in its own right, for the "using up" of the stock of mineral resources and the resulting reduction in asset value. At first sight, this seems a proper procedure, since the drawing out of oil resources reduces the remaining deposit and renders it less valuable. Such diminution of value would appear to be deductible under the accretion concept. But this is only one side of the coin. The other is that the accretion or gain involved at discovery should be

[26]See p. 436.

included in taxable income. Since this gain is in fact not included, its subsequent loss should also not be allowed for as a deduction. In short, deduction for actual cost (exploration and drilling) is appropriate, and expensing (rather than gradual deduction) of such costs may be an acceptable concession, since exploration costs are frequently undertaken in vain. But without initial taxation of the gain, there is no justification on equity or neutrality grounds for depletion allowances.

While the justification of percentage depletion as compensation for loss of asset value has come to be recognized as untenable, the defense has shifted to other grounds. One viewpoint is that since investment in natural resources is said to be especially risky, a lower rate of taxation is called for. Again, this is not a convincing argument. Another is that extractive industries may be of special importance to national policy, be it for purposes of defense or to assure the interests of future generations. There is no reason to believe, however, that the granting of depletion allowances serves the purposes of development and more efficient resource management over time. On the contrary, it tends to encourage more rapid exploitation, whether by attracting additional capital through offering a tax shelter or by increasing sales through lowering prices to consumers.

The Tax Reform Act of 1969 reduced the depletion allowance from 27.5 to 22 percent for oil and by 1 percentage point for other natural resources previously enjoying depletion allowances of 23 and 15 percent. The Tax Reduction Act of 1975 moved farther in this direction with elimination of percentage depletion on oil and gas industries, except for the small producers for whom depletion is to be gradually reduced to 15 percent.

Inventory Accounting

Increases in the value of inventories (i.e., stock-in-trade held as a normal part of conducting business over the taxable year) are included in the firm's operating profits. These changes may be measured on either a LIFO (last-in, first-out) or a FIFO (first-in, first-out) basis which, once selected, must continue to be used by the firm.[27] LIFO gives smaller profits in periods of rising prices and smaller losses when prices fall. It thus makes for a more stable tax base over the business cycle than does FIFO. Being used by most corporations, LIFO also makes for a continuously smaller tax base under conditions of sustained inflation, automatically excluding inflation gains from the tax. Moreover, the treatment of inventory profits and losses is an interesting application of taxing unrealized capital gains, just as depreciation is a case of allowing for unrealized capital losses.

---

[27]Suppose that at the end of 1979 an automobile dealer had a stock of ten cars, acquired at $5,000 each. In 1980 twenty additional cars are acquired at $6,000, while ten cars are sold at $7,000 each. Stock at the end of 1980 is twenty cars. Under the LIFO method, profits are $10 \times (\$7,000 - \$6,000)$, or $10,000. Under the FIFO method, profits equal $10 \times (\$7,000 - \$5,000)$, or $20,000. Since prices have risen, FIFO profits are larger.

Interest

Interest paid by corporations is properly deducted in computing taxable income. It is a cost of doing business, just as are wage payments. Since earnings derived from the investment of borrowed funds are included, the equity issue posed by the deduction of mortgage interest does not occur.

A problem does arise, however, because interest on borrowed funds may be deducted while deduction of imputed interest on equity capital is not permitted. This may bias management toward use of debt finance. To secure neutrality in the choice between debt and equity finance, corporations would have to be allowed to deduct imputed interest on invested capital. This deduction in turn would call for inclusion of such income in the shareholder's tax base, i.e., for integrated treatment under the partnership method. However this may be, the share of equity finance (mainly from internal sources) has increased rather than decreased in recent decades, and there is little evidence that the differential tax treatment has been a significant factor in retarding this increase.

Capital Gains

The corporation tax, like the individual income tax, gives preferential treatment to capital gains in the form of realized gains from the sale of assets which are not stock-in-trade. While such gains are included fully, an alternative rate of 28 percent may be applied.

Real Estate Tax Shelters

Finally, we should take note of certain tax advantages which may arise from the interaction of depreciation and capital gains provisions. If accelerated depreciation is permitted, the early years of asset life may result in depreciation charges in excess of income, thus recording a loss for tax purposes. By offsetting this loss against other income, taxpayers will reduce their liability thereon. A loss of $100 is worth $46 of tax reduction. When a given taxpayer decides to sell the asset, the remaining cost base is less because more depreciation was charged under the accelerated schedule. Thus, for each additional $100 of depreciation that was taken, the gain will be increased by $100. But the capital gains tax, paid at the maximum rate, will be only $28. Thus leaving the taxpayer with a net saving in tax of $18. In other words, income which otherwise would have been taxed at an ordinary rate of 46 percent is transferred into capital gains income taxable at 28 percent only. As a result, the net return on the investment subject to accelerated depreciation is greatly increased. This advantage, moreover, can be magnified if a relatively small amount of equity is given the leverage of a large amount of borrowed capital.[28] In this case the investor may find that his or her total tax

---

[28]This is of special importance where borrowed funds are obtained on terms which do not leave the borrower with full liability. Deductibility of losses for certain taxpayers (especially real estate investors) is limited to the amount of capital which the investor has at risk.

liability is reduced rather than increased by making an additional investment, so that the implicit rate of tax on the latter is negative.

Such was the mechanism which in the fifties and sixties led to the development of the so-called real estate tax shelter, when real estate investment was permitted to depreciate at a double-declining balance. Since then, the preference has been greatly curtailed, partly by limiting accelerated depreciation and partly through the so-called recapture clause. Under the latter, such part of capital gains as reflects depreciation in excess of the straight-line depreciation must be taxed as ordinary income, i.e., at the full rate. However, accelerated depreciation without the recapture clause continues to apply for rental housing. Support of such housing by a tax subsidy which bestows a large windfall on the developers (provided they subsequently sell) is hardly the best way of accomplishing this incentive objective. Similar problems arise in connection with depreciation rules for leasing of equipment.

Expense Accounts

Expense accounts and "expense-account living" have been a much discussed topic. When entertainment expenses are treated as deductible business costs, the net cost of such outlays is reduced by nearly one-half and activities which hardly deserve public subsidy are encouraged. Moreover, by making payments in kind rather than in cash, the corporation may help its employees to reduce their personal income tax. Thus, if a $4,000 car is furnished to the executive, the cost to the corporation is the same as if his or her salary were raised by this amount. But a salary gain would increase the individual's tax liability, whereas the car services may not.

This avenue of individual income tax avoidance may be closed either by including income in kind in the individual's taxable income, or by disallowing deduction of such costs at the corporation level. A modest effort was made in the Revenue Act of 1964 and again in that of 1978 to limit deductibility and to reduce expense-account allowances. But though the "three martini lunch" has been a key feature in the recent tax reform debate, efforts to limit expense accounts have met with heavy opposition and have not been very successful. Since making detailed distinctions between deductible and nondeductible items would cause serious administrative difficulties, the British practice of disallowing almost all entertainment expenses is perhaps the only feasible alternative, but hardly one which the Congress will entertain.

F. INFLATION ADJUSTMENT

As in the case of the individual income tax, inflation poses serious problems of tax adjustment. But since the corporate rate is proportional, except for small companies, the resulting problems relate primarily to the matter of base adjustment.

The law sets the depreciation base equal to original cost, but it is argued that, in times of inflation, original-cost depreciation is insufficient to enable the firm to replace the asset, replacement-cost depreciation being needed for this purpose. When we look at the problem in equity terms, we are returned to the previously noted distinction between nominal and real income. As the price level rises, the services of the asset generate a higher income in money terms, and the investor must pay tax thereon. But the tax savings from depreciation (if based on original cost) do not rise accordingly. Investors thus find the real value of their after-tax return reduced. In order to define income in real terms, the depreciable base should be adjusted upward for inflation. It has been estimated that this would reduce taxable income by about 15 percent, i.e., corresponding to a reduction in the corporate rate by 7 percentage points.[29]

There is merit to this argument, but it tells only part of the inflation story. The question is whether the adjustment should be limited to depreciation, or whether the entire balance sheet should not be adjusted. For companies with net indebtedness, this would call for an addition to income as the real value of indebtedness falls with rising prices. For the corporate sector as a whole, the resulting addition to net income would on balance offset or outweigh the reduction in net income due to increase in the depreciation base. Some sectors, such as public utilities, would actually experience an increase in tax liability.

G. PROGRESSION AND SMALL-BUSINESS RELIEF

There are now five corporate tax rates: 17, 20, 22, and 40 percent on the first four slabs of $25,000 of income, and 46 percent on the remainder. As noted before, 80 percent of corporations pay at the lower rate only, but 90 percent of taxable income is received by large corporations and subject to the 46 percent rate. The revenue cost of applying the lower rates is about $3 billion, or 6 percent of total profits tax revenue in 1975.

Should Rates Be Progressive?

The rationale underlying progressive rates for the individual income tax cannot be applied to the corporate sector. The corporation does not have a taxpaying ability of its own in the sense in which individuals do, and all tax burdens are ultimately borne by individuals. Nor can it be said that progressive taxation of firms is a means to progressive taxation of shareholders. There is no positive relationship between the size of the corporation and the net income of its owners. Many small corporations are owned by high-income individuals and a substantial share of dividends (the bulk of which are paid by large corporations) are received by middle-income individuals.

If a case is to be made for a progressive rate structure, it must be based on other grounds, such as a desire to restrain "bigness" and to support small firms. As noted before, restraining bigness differs from restraining monopoly. The latter is a matter of market shares, the former of absolute size. If bigness

[29]See Sidney Davidson and Roman W. Weil, "Inflation Accounting: Explanation of the FASB Proposal," in H. J. Aaron (ed.), *Inflation and the Income Tax*, Washington: Brookings, 1976.

is to be restrained, this may be done through a progressive tax, but such a tax would be related more appropriately to asset size than to profits. If it is bigness that is held undesirable, there is no reason to favor big firms that are unprofitable. The economic case for restraining bigness is, however, of questionable value. Middle-sized and large firms tend to be more efficient than small firms, although there is little evidence that giant size is needed to achieve efficiency. However this may be, the Jeffersonian ideal is not a viable alternative for modern society, and chances are that balance between large units is the more reasonable solution.

Nevertheless, tax relief for small firms has always been and continues to be a popular political cause. Partly, this may be justified to balance the superior ability of large firms to operate in imperfect capital markets and to benefit from restrictive practices. More important, however, is the persistent view that the maintenance of a small-business class is socially desirable even though it may be inefficient.

Aid to Small Business

For this and other reasons, preferential treatment of small business is an ever-present topic of tax reform. Assuming that such aid is to be given, the question is how it may be done most efficiently.

Partnership Option   The law now permits corporations with no more than ten shareholders to elect taxation on a partnership basis. This option is especially advantageous to corporations with small shareholders who pay a low-bracket rate on dividends and plan to operate with a high payout ratio. This choice typically benefits small firms. Large corporations which are closely held are usually owned by wealthy people for whom corporate tax treatment is an advantage since they are subject to a high marginal personal tax rate which may be avoided by a low payout ratio. The partnership option is thus an effective method of relieving the corporate tax burden of small firms with low-income owners, without depriving them of the advantage of limited liability.

Low Initial Rate   The benefits of lower rates of tax on the first $100,000 of income primarily accrue to small corporations. The effect of these lower rates on the liability of large corporations is not very significant. The trouble with the low initial rate is that it can readily serve as a shelter from individual income tax. In effect, it increases the range over which the "extra" corporation tax is negative. With a corporate rate of only 17 percent and a shareholder individual income tax rate of 50 percent, the differential rate is negative (incorporation gives a tax advantage) provided the payout ratio is below 80 percent! This result might be avoided by disallowing the lower corporation rate to small but closely held corporations if the marginal rates of their shareholders are, on the average, above a certain level.

A further difficulty arises because larger corporations are induced to split up into multiple units (to spin off), so as to benefit from a number of surtax exemptions. Prior to 1969, corporations were permitted to split into a group of "controlled corporations" using multiple surtax exemptions at the penalty of an additional tax of only 6 percent. This practice was terminated under the Tax Reform Act of 1969, which largely eliminated the availability of multiple surtax exemptions by 1974.

Other Approaches Small firms especially benefit from certain other tax privileges, such as the additional first-year depreciation bonus on machinery and equipment of 20 percent up to a cost base of $10,000. This type of concession may well be preferable to the lower-rate technique since it lends itself less readily to tax-shelter abuse. Moreover, provisions may be designed which are of special value to new and expanding firms rather than based exclusively on the size criteria.

H. ORGANIZATIONS SUBJECT TO SPECIAL TREATMENT

Differences in the structure and function of various types of corporations pose special problems of tax treatment. The previously noted problem of depreciation is a case in point. Some others are as follows.

Financial Institutions

The assets on the balance sheet of manufacturing corporations are largely in the form of plant and equipment. Those of financial institutions are largely in the form of claims and securities. Given the nature of their assets, good accounting practice for such institutions requires that a "bad-debt" reserve be set aside. Charges to such a reserve are a legitimate cost of doing business and are appropriately allowed for as deductions under the tax law. The question is how high such charges should be. In the past, very high charges unrelated to actual bad-debt experience were permitted, but these have been cut back by the Tax Reform Act of 1969.

Since this act, additions to bad-debt reserves by commercial banks have been reduced from 2.4 to 1.2 percent of outstanding loans, or they may be computed on the basis of actual bad-debt experience. This percentage will be reduced gradually over the years until such reserves will be based entirely on actual experience, using a six-year moving average.

Mutual savings banks and savings and loan associations previously were permitted to deduct 3 percent of real property loans or 60 percent of taxable income. The former method, which once resulted in complete tax exemption for most of such institutuions, was repealed in 1969, and the permissible percentage deduction has been reduced sharply since.

Cooperatives

Farmers' or consumers' cooperatives may qualify for tax exemption. Such cooperatives are allowed deduction of patronage dividends, but the patron in turn is taxable thereon. Retained income is considered paid out for tax purposes by distribution of retention certificates. In effect, cooperatives are treated in line with a completely integrated system. The same principle applies to mutual savings banks and mutual insurance companies.

Nonprofit Institutions

Up to the 1950s, nonprofit organizations such as churches, educational institutions, and foundations, though organized as corporations, were exempt from corporation tax. Since then, such corporations have become taxable on income obtained from the operation of an "unrelated business." In addition, a 4 percent tax is now imposed on their net investment income.[30] Moreover, various provisions were enacted to limit abuses of their tax-exempt status, such as profitable arrangements between foundation and donors ("self-dealing") and leaseback arrangements. Finally, foundations must now distribute 6 percent of their assets annually or pay a penalty tax of 15 percent on deficient distributions.

I. STATE CORPORATION TAXES

The role of the corporation tax, like that of the individual income tax, is of primary importance at the federal level. Even though a corporation tax is imposed by forty-seven states, it provided only 7 percent of state tax revenue in 1975. Its contribution to local tax revenue is below 1 percent. State corporation tax rates range from 3 to 12 percent, with most states applying lower rates to small corporations. Allowing for deductibility from profits taxable under the federal tax, net rates range from 1.6 to 6.5 percent. In some cases, alternative bases are provided and the highest tax is chosen. Thus, the New York 10 percent tax on net income is linked with two alternative taxes: (1) a 1.78-mill tax on invested capital, and (2) a 10 percent tax on 30 percent of net income plus compensation paid to officers.

The rates of state corporation taxes are low compared to federal rates because capital is mobile and sharp rate differentials might cause capital to flow from high- to low-rate states. Even though slight rate differentials may be relatively unimportant as compared with other factors in location decisions, states tend to consider them a major factor and therefore engage in low-rate competition to attract capital. All these considerations produce a built-in tendency toward modest rates and a fair degree of uniformity.

Interesting problems arise in determining how the tax base of corporations engaging in interstate trade should be divided among the different states. Any one state may tax a corporation doing business within its jurisdiction, and various state laws use different formulas to determine what share of profits they should tax. Typically, this involves an apportionment formula, including property, payrolls, and sales within the state, with equal weight to the three factors under the so-called Massachusetts formula. It is now widely believed that a uniform set of rules should be adopted, subject to

[30]Taxable corporations are permitted to deduct 85 percent of dividends received from other taxable corporations, and in the case of affiliates, 100 percent deduction is allowed. With a 46 percent corporate rate, the 95 percent deduction leaves a net tax of 2.3 percent.

the supervision of the Treasury, and that sales should be eliminated from the formula.[31]

Choice of the appropriate formula depends on the philosophy of base allocation. If benefit considerations are controlling, the ideal solution would be to charge in accordance with the cost of public services rendered to the firm in its various locations. As a first approximation, it might be argued that all costs are reduced equally by the provision of public services, in which case an allocation by costs incurred would be appropriate. At the same time, it would not be very meaningful to allocate profits on this basis. The benefit approach, as noted before, calls not for a profits tax but for an ad valorem charge on costs incurred.

If the philosophy of an absolute profits tax is applied, the appropriate method of apportionment should be according to the source of profits. If we assume that the firm's return on capital is the same in all locations, profits should be allocated in line with the location of capital use. Sales would enter the formula, but only to the extent of capital invested in sales operations and not in the form of gross sales. The payroll factor would enter in line with the average capital requirement for payroll finance, but not total wages paid. Under such an approach, the sales and payroll factors would be weighted less heavily than in the conventional three-factor formula, while immovable capital would be included at its full value.

Until recently, it was felt that the inclusion of sales in the profits apportionment formula would be strongly in the interest of low-income states, while that of capital and payroll would be in the interest of high-income, manufacturing states. The Report of the Judiciary Committee, however, showed that the role of the sales factor had been misjudged.[32] The states which do most of the producing also offer the biggest markets and do most of the buying. While inclusion of the sales factor will affect the states to which a particular firm must pay its revenue, the effect on overall revenue allocation is but minor. Since the inclusion of the sales factor causes high compliance costs—to assure proper administration, a firm would have to file returns in all the states to which it sells—the Judiciary Committee's recommendation for a two-factor formula, including capital and payroll only, is justified on both pragmatic and theoretical grounds.

J. SUMMARY

The corporation tax remains an important source of federal revenue, but is of lesser significance at the state level:

   1. Corporate profits account for over 90 percent of total profits and nearly 40 percent of all capital income.

---

[31]See *State Taxation of Interstate Commerce, Report of the Special Subcommittee on State Taxation of the Committee on the Judiciary*, 88th Cong., 2d Sess., House Report No. 1480, 1964. See also C. Lowell Harriss, "State-Local Taxation of Interstate Commerce: Progress and Problems," *Innovations in Tax Policy*, Hartford: John C. Lincoln Institute, 1972.

[32]See ibid., vol. I, chap. 16. Also see p. 775.

2. Unlike the personal income tax base, the bulk of taxable profits is received by a small number of very large corporations.

In assessing the role of the corporation tax in the good tax structure, we have distinguished between a view of this tax as an "absolute tax" on corporations as such and its role in "integrating" the taxation of corporate-source income under the individual income tax. As a basis for an absolute corporation tax, it might be argued that:

3. Corporations should be charged for benefits received from public services. Such a tax, however, would be smaller in amount than the present corporation tax and also different in form.

4. Various regulatory uses of taxation with regard to controlling size or monopoly power might be made but would also call for different forms of taxes.

The case for corporate taxation as a major revenue source has to be based on its role as an ability-to-pay tax. Here we have drawn these conclusions:

5. The equity of the corporation tax must be assessed in terms of its burden impact among individuals, not firms. Provided that the corporation tax is not to be passed on to consumers or wage earners, its burden must be attributed to shareholders or recipients of capital income at large.

6. Since all sources of income should be treated equally, this calls for integration of corporate-source income into the personal income tax.

7. Imputing the burden of the corporation tax to the shareholder, its burden distribution differs, depending on how the burden ratio is defined:
  a. The *gross burden* is strongly progressive.
  b. The *net burden* distribution is less progressive.
  c. The distribution of the *extra burden* is not progressive and becomes regressive at the upper end of the income scale.

Various techniques of integration were examined, including both full and partial integration:

8. Full integration may be obtained by the partnership or the capital gains method.

9. Implementation of either approach involves administrative difficulties, but these should not prove insoluble.

10. Partial integration may be obtained by the exclusion of dividends from corporation tax or by granting a dividend credit at the shareholder level.

Numerous problems arise in the appropriate definition of taxable income, among which the following were noted:

11. Proper treatment of depreciation should set the rate of depreciation so as to correspond to the flow of "economic" income.

12. Depletion allowances involve preferential treatment for natural-resource industries.

13. Other items covered included the treatment of losses, inventory profits, tax shelters, and expense accounts.

14. Under conditions of inflation, a good case can be made for replacement-cost depreciation. However, a similar case can be made for taxing real income gains due to net indebtedness.

In dealing with the role of the corporation tax at the state and local level, we noted that mobility of capital requires rates to be moderate.

FURTHER READINGS

Break, George F., and Joseph A. Pechman: *Federal Tax Reform*, Washington: Brookings, 1975, chap. 4.

McLure, Charles, Jr. (ed): *Must Corporation Income Be Taxed Twice?* Washington: Brookings, 1979.

Pechman, Joseph A.: *Federal Tax Policy*, 2d ed., Washington: Brookings, 1971, chap. 5.

Report of the Royal Commission on Taxation, vol. 4, *Taxation of Income*, part B, "Taxation of Income Flowing through Intermediaries," Ottawa: Queen's Printer, 1969.

U.S. Treasury Department, *Blueprints for Basic Tax Reform*, 1977, pp. 68–75.

Chapter 19

Corporation Income Tax: (2) Incidence and Investment Incentives*

A. **Incidence:** *Competitive Markets; Imperfect Markets; Historical Patterns; Econometric Evidence.* B. **Investment Incentives:** *Accelerated Depreciation; Investment Tax Credit; Capital Gains Preference; Evaluation of Alternative Measures.* C. **Summary.**

Given the central place of the corporate sector in the United States economy, the incidence and effects of the corporation tax occupy a strategic role in tax policy. The present chapter addresses these issues.

A. INCIDENCE

As was shown in Tables 12-1 and 12-2, the distribution of the corporate tax burden will differ greatly, depending on what shifting hypotheses one applies.[1] Depending on what market structure and firm behavior are assumed,

---

*Readers' Guide to Chapter 19: In this chapter we consider corporation tax incidence in some detail, with allowance for the effects of market imperfections. Next, the merits of various types of investment incentives are evaluated. A further discussion of taxation effects on saving, investment, and capital formation is found in Chapter 30.

[1]See pp. 267 and 270.

the corporation tax may prove a highly progressive or regressive part of the tax system. Which is the correct view remains a matter of controversy and constitutes one of the major unknowns of tax policy.

Competitive Markets

The incidence of the corporation tax in a competitive setting was considered previously and can be restated briefly here.[2] The competitive firm cannot affect price as it is confronted with a horizontal demand schedule. As the tax is imposed, the firm's response in the short run will be to continue production on the same scale, as long as price exceeds variable cost, thus absorbing the tax in a reduced return to previously invested capital. But in the longer run, the capital invested in the corporate sector will be reduced. Capital will flow out until the *net* rate of return in corporate and other sectors is equalized. In this way the burden of the corporation tax is spread among all capital income, whether invested in the corporate sector or not. Since capital income rises as a percentage of total income when we move up the income scale (with the exception of the lower end), incidence is generally progressive.

Imperfect Markets

The situation differs in imperfect markets. Here it may be possible for corporations to respond by raising prices or lowering wages, thus recouping part of the tax without requiring an outflow of capital as called for in the competitive model. As a result, the tax may be similar in nature to an excise or wages tax on the corporate sector. We now explore under what conditions such results may come about.

Incidence with Monopoly   We begin with a situation where firms enjoy a monopolistic position in the product market. Though different from the competitive case in important respects, the situation is similar in that pure monopolists cannot recover their tax by adjusting price or output policy. The reason simply is that if profits are maximized before the tax is introduced, after-tax profits (even at a 99 percent rate) will still be greatest by maximizing pretax profits.

This result is illustrated in Figure 19-1, giving the familiar diagram for profit maximization of the monopolist. Before tax, profits are maximized at output OA, where marginal revenue (MR) equals marginal cost (MC). Price equals OB and profits are $CDEB$. As a tax of one-third is imposed, the MR and MC curves remain unchanged but net profits are cut to $CDFG$.[3]

The same is shown in the lower part of the figure where OPQ gives total profits at various levels of output, with profits peaking at output OA. After the tax is imposed, net profits are reduced by one-third and are given by

---

[2]See p. 295.

[3]We may also think of monopolists as including their *marginal* tax in marginal cost. This tax is given by VAW, as shown in the lower part of the figure. When added to MC in the upper figure, we obtain MC′, which intersects MR at precisely the same point as did MC. The reason of course is that the marginal tax cost is zero where total profits reach their maximum.

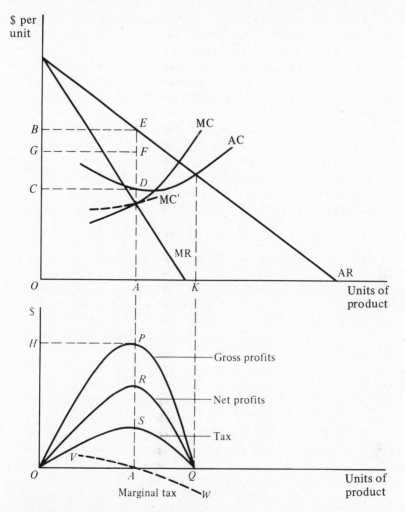

FIGURE 19-1   Profits Tax under Monopoly.

ORQ with *OSQ* showing the amount of tax. Net profits, like gross profits, peak at output *OA* which, therefore, is optimal in both cases.

In the short run at least, the tax is again absorbed by profits in the taxed sector. Moreover, such may remain true even in the longer run. If firms in the taxed sector enjoy monopoly profits, it may be to their advantage, even after their profits are reduced by the tax, to remain where they are rather than to shift to the untaxed sector where they would enjoy a less sheltered position. The earlier conclusion that the tax is shared equally by capital in all sectors must then be qualified.

Restrained Profit Maximization   Another possibility is that firms exercise restraint in profit maximization. A firm whose market position is such that monopoly profits can be obtained may choose not to exploit its situation to the fullest. That is to say, it will operate at a larger output and sell at a lower price than it would if profit maximization were its only goal. It may be satisfied with obtaining a target rate of return, say 15 percent, on invested capital. A higher rate of return may be considered "gouging" and socially improper; management may feel that a prudent profit target may help to maintain profits in the long run; or it may fear that excessive returns would invite antitrust action.

As a tax is imposed, the firm finds that its net rate of return has fallen below the target level. It will then be driven to exploit its monopolistic position, to restrict output and raise price in order to restore its net profit position. As it does so, it moves closer to the maximum profit position at output OA in Figure 19-1. In this way the burden will be passed to the consumer. Whether the entire burden can be passed on in this fashion will depend on the rate of tax relative to the pretax profit slack. The basic point is that the tax may induce the firm to make fuller use of its monopoly power; and to the extent that it does so, the burden is passed on.

Oligopoly Behavior   Another possibility of price adjustment arises in an oligopoly situation. Here prices and output are not set in the traditional profit-maximizing manner. The price tends to be established by the price leader in the industry and no one firm will wish to depart from it for fear of losing its sales if it raises price or of having its competitors follow suit if it tries to undercut the price. In such a situation, an increase in the tax rate may act as a signal to firms to raise price in concert. Since each firm has reason to expect that the others will act similarly, it can raise price without concern for its competitive position.

Sales Maximization   In recent years, various writers have criticized the classical assumption of profit maximization. While granting that firms will maximize something, they hold that profits may not be the only, or even the primary, objective of maximization. Rather, a firm may wish to maximize its sales or market share.

Since the profits tax does not change total sales as a function of price, simple sales maximization would again lead to the conclusion that the tax does not change output and price. The impact, therefore, would still be on profits. But a firm is not likely to maximize sales while disregarding profits altogether. Sales maximization may well be an objective, but it must be tempered by a minimum profit constraint. Defining the latter as net profits, we then have a behavior pattern which may well lead to shifting.

This is shown in Figure 19-2, where the curve OCB gives total sales receipts at various levels of output, while curve OD shows total cost.[4] The corresponding levels of profits or receipts minus costs are given by OEF. Under profit maximization, output is at OG with profits at GE. As a 50

---

[4]See W. Baumol, *Economic Theory and Operational Analysis*, 3d ed., Englewood Cliffs, N. J.: Prentice-Hall, 1973, p. 326. We are indebted to Tapas Kumar Sen for helpful suggestions regarding this presentation.

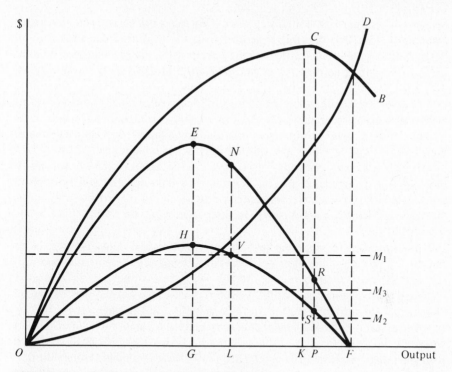

FIGURE 19-2   Profits Tax under Sales Maximization.

percent tax is imposed, the level of net profits is given by OHF. Net profits are still maximized at OG but fall to GH. No shifting occurs. Under sales maximization, the output prior to tax depends on the profit constraint. With required minimum profits given by M_1, the firm prior to tax will produce at OK, or somewhat short of the point of maximum sales OP. As the tax is imposed, output is cut to OL. Net profits remain at their original level and the tax is fully shifted, with gross profits rising from LV to LN or by the amount of tax. Next, suppose that the profit minimum is set much lower, say, at M_2. Output before tax will now be at OP, since sales maximization leaves profits PR above the desired minimum. Moreover, sales continue to be maximized even after tax, since net profits PS will still meet the minimum requirement. Output remains unchanged at OP, the tax is absorbed in reduced profits, and there will be no shifting. A situation of partial shifting, finally, is indicated where minimum profits are set at M_3. The degree of shifting, therefore, depends on the required level of profits and the relationship between output, costs, and sales receipts.

Other Pricing Rules   Economists like to think of business behavior as being rational in the sense of following a maximizing rule. But business executives may not act rationally. They may base their pricing rules upon certain customary criteria which need not follow this pattern.

One criterion is the practice of markup or margin pricing. Under this rule, costs are "marked up" to allow for a customary ratio of profits to costs, or price is set such as to leave profits (i.e., sales minus cost) a customary fraction of sales. Whether this approach gives rise to shifting depends on how costs and margins are defined. Shifting occurs if the tax is included as a cost, or if the margin is defined net of tax. The tax now assumes the nature of an excise tax.[5]

Another approach is that of average or full-cost pricing. Prices are set to yield a stream of receipts which will recover full cost (including overhead as well as variable costs) within a given period. Since the tax reduces this stream, higher prices will be asked and shifting may occur once more.

Both these rules may thus lead to a pricing behavior which *intends* to pass the tax on in higher prices. Whether the firm actually succeeds in so doing is a different matter. The outcome depends on the extent to which it already exercised its market power in the pretax situation.

Imperfections in Labor Market   So far, we have considered the possibility that firms operating under various forms of administered pricing may attempt to raise product price to recoup profits. As a result, the burden is passed "forward" to consumers. Another possibility is that the burden will be passed "backward" to the wage earner through reduction in the wage rate.

Once more, such adjustments cannot occur in a competitive labor market where the wage earner is paid the value of his or her marginal product and is paid the same return by firms which are profitable as by others which are not. If labor markets are imperfect, the situation may differ. If labor is weak and employers are in a monopsonistic position, the wage rate may be set below the value of labor's marginal product. The situation may then be similar to that of restrained monopoly pricing in the product market. Employers in the pretax setting may not fully exploit their position, but the tax may lead them to utilize their market powers more fully, with the result that part of the tax burden is passed to labor.

A similar outcome may result in a quite different setting where labor is in a strong position. Wage rates are set under collective bargaining, but unions in making wage demands may (and frequently do) allow for the profitability of the firm. They may aim to divert a share of monopoly profits to the wage earner while leaving the firm in what they consider an adequate profit position. Since this position depends on corporate profits *after* tax, an increase in the profits tax rate may reduce wage demands. In this way, part of the increase in tax may again be passed "backward" to the wage earner.

Faulty Definition of Tax Base   A final factor which may account for forward shifting into higher prices is based on imperfections in the definition of the tax base. The profits tax base may diverge from profits as defined in

---

[5]Since the profit margin (ratio of profits to sales) differs between industries and firms, the implicit rate of sales tax (ratio of price increase to pretax price) will also differ. Thus, the required price change will differ among industries. See Carl S. Shoup, "Incidence of the Corporation Income Tax: Capital Structure and Turnover Rates," *National Tax Journal*, March 1948; reprinted in R. A. Musgrave and C. S. Shoup (eds.), *Readings in the Economics of Taxation*, Homewood, Ill.: Irwin, 1959.

economic theory and include items which in fact are part of a firm's cost. Thus, profits as defined under the tax law do not allow for deduction of imputed interest on equity-financed working capital. Since such interest is a cost of doing business, the tax base is overstated. Part of the tax becomes an addition to cost and may be reflected in output and price. This possibility, however, is not likely to be very important since most deductions from taxable profits are liberally defined.

Who Pays?   We have noted a variety of situations where the corporation may be able to recoup part of the tax by raising prices or reducing wages, thus passing on the burden to their consumers or their employees. The nature of the corporation tax then becomes more like that of an excise or wages tax. Once more this initial impact will be followed by a general equilibrium adjustment; but the nature of this adjustment and its outcome now resemble that of an excise or wages tax. If the burden is passed on to consumers, the primary determination of incidence will occur from the uses side; if it is passed on to employees, primary determination will be from the sources side. The burden distribution in the two cases may not differ very sharply, but both will differ (and be less progressive) from that which results in the competitive case.

Historical Patterns

While most economists view the burden of the corporation tax as falling on capital in line with the competitive model, business people frequently view the tax as a cost which is passed on. The former view is correct if one assumes that all markets operate in profit-maximizing fashion. But if firms operate as restrained monopolists, if sales rather than profits are maximized, or if other pricing rules apply, firms may well attempt to pass on the tax in higher prices. Moreover, if labor markets are imperfect, higher taxes may be reflected in more limited demands in collective bargaining and thus be passed on to labor.

The outcome, therefore, depends on existing market structures and behavior. The structure of American industry—and especially the larger manufacturing corporations from which the bulk of the corporation tax is derived—is such that administered pricing is likely to occur. Shifting due to administered price adjustments (as distinct from shifting due to factor movements and changing factor supplies in the competitive market) cannot be ruled out on a priori grounds. The same holds for the highly organized labor markets in which these firms operate. Theoretical analysis is inconclusive in such a setting and further empirical investigation is needed to settle the problem.

There have been repeated attempts in recent years to provide such evidence. The first question is what one should look for. If corporate tax rates differed between industries, the problem would be fairly simple. Insights might be gained from examining resulting price changes and comparing the relative positions of various sectors before and after the tax change. This cannot be done, however, since the tax applies to all incorporated firms at more or less the same effective rate. Nor is a comparison of rates of return on investment in incorporated and unincorporated firms feasible since no adequate data are available for the latter. The remaining possibility is to examine the experience of the corporate sector without the benefit of comparison with tax-free sectors and to explore how various elements of the corporate sector responded to the tax, including such features as rates of return on corporate equity, the share of corporate profits in 'value added by (i.e., income originating in) the corporate sector, or corporate profit margins. Even this approach is not too instructive, because major changes in the rate of corporation tax have been infrequent.

We begin by taking a bird's-eye view of the relevant historical statistics. Some of the key variables are given in Table 19-1. Since the major increases in tax rates occurred during World War II, and since both the thirties and forties were highly unusual periods—one being dominated by the Great Depression and the other by a major war—the best that can be done is to compare the twenties and the decades following World War II.

Comparison of the statutory tax rates and *after-tax* rates of return (columns I and II) for the earlier period with those for the later period at first

TABLE 19-1
Corporate Tax Rates and Profits Share
(In Percentages)

Years	Statutory Corporation Income Tax Rate (I)	MANUFACTURING CORPORATIONS		ALL CORPORATIONS Profit Share in Income Originating in Corporate Sector (Before Tax) (IV)
		After-Tax Rate of Return (II)	After-Tax Profit Margin (III)	
1927–1929	11–13.5	8.0	5.9	21.8
1936–1939	15–19	6.3	4.6	14.8
1955–1959	52	10.9	4.9	22.4
1960–1963	52	9.5	4.5	20.6
1964	50	11.6	5.2	21.9
1965–1967	48	12.7	5.4	22.1
1968–1969	52.8	11.7	4.9	19.8
1974–1977	48	13.6	4.9	17.5

Notes:
Column I: 1968–1969 and 1970 statutory rates include surcharge.
Column II: Profits after tax (excluding inventory valuation adjustment) of manufacturing corporations as percentage of stockholder's equity.
Column III: Profits after tax (as in column II) as percentage of net sales by manufacturing corporations.
Column IV: Profits before tax (excluding inventory valuation adjustment) of all corporations as percentage of all income originating in the corporate sector.
Sources:
Columns I to IV, 1927–1929 and 1936–1939: M. Krzyzaniak and R. A. Musgrave, *The Shifting of the Corporation Income Tax*, Baltimore: Johns Hopkins, 1963, pp. 15, 17.
Columns I to III, 1955–1959 and on: *Economic Report of the President*, January 1978, p. 356.
Column IV, 1955–1959 to 1969: U.S. Department of Commerce, *Survey of Current Business* and *National Income and Products Accounts*, table 1.14; 1974–1977: *Survey of Current Business*, July 1978, table 1.14.

sight supports the shifting hypothesis. In the absence of shifting and assuming no other influences, the 8 percent return of the later twenties should have fallen to below 5 percent as the tax rose from 12 to 52 percent in the fifties. Actually, no such decline occurred. Instead, the net rate of return rose by nearly 40 percent. To put it differently, the gross rate of return rose by more than was needed to secure full shifting.[6] Similar support for the shifting hypothesis is presented by the more or less constant *after*-tax profit margin, shown in column III. With after-tax margins constant, gross margins rose to reflect the tax. Column IV, however, gives a different picture. Gross profits or profits *before* tax as a share in total income originating in the corporate sector were much the same in the post-World War II decades and in the twenties. This runs counter to the shifting hypothesis. If the tax had been passed on to consumers or wage earners to recoup profits, the share of gross profits in national income should have risen accordingly.

The evidence derived from a comparison of the twenties with the postwar decades is thus conflicting and is consistent with both the shifting and the no-shifting hypotheses. Nor should one expect this simpleminded appraisal to be very helpful. Many nontax factors were at work over this tumultuous period, so that it is not legitimate to ascribe the entire changes in the profit picture to the tax factor. This is also brought out in the later period when substantial fluctuations in the profit picture occurred even though no drastic tax rate changes took place.[7] A more sophisticated approach is needed to permit separating out the effects of the tax changes from those of other changes which came to pass during the period.

Econometric Evidence

An empirical measure of shifting thus calls for an econometric approach, designed to isolate the effects of the corporation tax. Various studies of this sort have appeared in recent years, but the issue remains controversial. One type of study has expressed the corporate rate of return as a function of various predetermined variables, such as the level of consumer demand, capacity utilization, government expenditures, and corporation tax rates. By including corporate tax rates, analysts hoped to use the regression coefficient pertaining to this variable to measure the effects of rate changes on the rate of return. Some of these studies have indicated a high degree of shifting, lending more support to a full-shifting, rather than to a zero-shifting, hypothesis. The evidence, furthermore, pointed to fairly rapid responses to tax

---

[6]Since these data cover the corporate sector only, it may be noted that some increase in the rate of return might have been expected to result from the flow of capital into the unincorporated sector, being matched by a decline in the rate of return in the unincorporated sector. An increase in the corporate rate of return caused by this adjustment would be compatible with the no-shifting hypothesis, but would have fallen far short of the increase shown in the table.

[7]The relative levels of effective tax rates in the later period were, however, lower than indicated in the table since the investment credit and accelerated depreciation are not reflected in the statutory rate.

rate changes, thus suggesting the tax to be shifted via administered price adjustments rather than via capital movement to other sectors.[8]

These studies were criticized by other analysts, who held that the case for such shifting has not been made or that the evidence is against it.[9] Since tax rate changes typically coincide with changes in government expenditures, the effects of the two variables are difficult to isolate. Moreover, tax rate changes typically occur in periods of general economic change. Rate increases are associated with economic expansion and decreases with contraction. The tax variable in these regressions may therefore reflect changes in current economic conditions, so that its coefficient cannot be interpreted as indicating the degree of shifting only. Addition of a variable measuring the current degree of "economic pressure" (such as unemployment or shortfall of actual below potential GNP) reduces the tax coefficient. Moreover, the experiment shows that the results are sensitive to just how the model is formulated. Participants in the debate should agree that results reached so far cannot be considered definitive. Improved data and econometric techniques, combined with the use of less aggregative analysis, should produce better answers in time, but until then, a considerable degree of uncertainty regarding the incidence of the corporation tax remains. This uncertainty is unfortunate because the incidence issue is of crucial policy importance in assessing the implications of the corporate profits tax.

B. INVESTMENT INCENTIVES

A perpetual concern of tax policy has been with the design of tax incentives so as to increase investment.[10] The simplest approach, of course, would be to reduce the taxation of capital income, but this would also be the most costly in terms of revenue. The search therefore has been for more selective measures which would be effective in stimulating investment, while avoiding an excessive revenue loss. The "bang for the buck" should be made as big as possible.

Accelerated Depreciation

One approach, favored most strongly by the business community, has been that of accelerated depreciation. The effective rate of tax, as noted before, depends upon both the statutory tax rate (e.g., 46 percent under the corpora-

---

[8]Marion Krzyzaniak and Richard A. Musgrave, *The Shifting of the Corporation Income Tax*, Baltimore: Johns Hopkins, 1963.

[9]Richard Goode, "Rates of Return, Income Shares and Corporate Tax Incidence," in M. Krzyzaniak (ed.), *Effects of Corporation Income Tax*, Detroit: Wayne State University Press, 1966; J. Cragg, A. Harberger, and P. Mieszkowski, "Empirical Evidence of the Incidence of the Corporation Income Tax," *Journal of Political Economy*, December 1967; M. Krzyzaniak and Richard A. Musgrave, "Corporation Tax Shifting: A Response," and J. Cragg, A. Harberger, and P. Mieszkowski, "Corporation Tax Shifting: A Rejoinder," *Journal of Political Economy*, July-August 1970. These papers are reprinted in A. Harberger, *Taxation and Welfare*, Boston: Little, Brown, 1974. Also see R. J. Gordon, "The Incidence of the Corporation Income Tax in U.S. Manufacturing," *American Economic Review*, September 1967, and response by Krzyzaniak, Musgrave, and Gordon in *American Economic Review*, August 1968.

[10]For further discussion of investment effects, see p. 672.

tion income tax) and the rate at which depreciation is permitted.[11] The faster the depreciation rate, the lower is the effective rate of tax.

When considering an investment, the investor weighs the present value of its net income stream against the cost of the asset. This present value equals the present value of the income stream before tax minus the present value of tax payments thereon. The latter in turn may be viewed as equal to the present value of the gross tax (as it would be if no depreciation were allowed) minus the present value of the tax savings due to depreciation. This negative component will be the larger and the net tax will be the lower, the more rapidly depreciation may be taken. This is so because the present value of the tax savings will be the higher the sooner they are realized. Speeding up depreciation thus reduces the effective rate of tax by postponing the due date of the tax liability. It is equivalent, from the investor's point of view, to an interest-free loan, with the present value of interest savings thereon equal to the present value of the resulting tax saving.

If we consider a single investment, accelerated depreciation does not reduce the total amount of tax that will be paid. The liability is reduced in the earlier years and increased in the later years. The gain results from a once-and-for-all tax postponement, with the Treasury losing revenue in the earlier years and recouping it thereafter. If the case of a continuing invest- ment is considered (i.e., if the asset is replaced as it wears out so as to keep the depreciable base unchanged), the gain from postponement rises over the early years and then levels off. After a while, the loss of revenue ceases but there is no recoupment of the initial loss so long as continuous reinvestment takes place. Recoupment takes place only after reinvestment ceases. Finally, there is the case of a firm with continuing expansion of depreciable assets. If depreciation is sufficiently fast and expansion sufficiently sharp, such a firm may be able to postpone tax payment indefinitely. All payment is avoided and no ultimate recoupment occurs.

It is evident, therefore, that rapid depreciation is helpful to the investor and especially to the investor in long-lived assets. This is evident since the gain from early deduction (or the length of tax postponement gained) is the greater, the longer the waiting period that otherwise would have applied. While we have seen that the standard set by "economic" depreciation is neutral with regard to length of asset life, accelerated depreciation dis- criminates in favor of long-lived assets and thereby interferes with investment choice. This is a disadvantage of this particular type of investment incentive.

Depreciation rates now permitted on machinery tend to be faster than economic depreciation, and in certain cases (e.g., rehabilitation of low-cost housing) explicit acceleration is allowed. On the whole, however, United States tax depreciation is still geared to the length of asset life and what is considered "good business practice." Some other countries have gone much further in speeding up tax depreciation. The United Kingdom, for instance, permits full depreciation to be charged in the first year, thus greatly reducing the burden of and revenue derived from the corporation tax. A combination

[11]See p. 413.

of instantaneous write-off with perfect loss offset would in fact mean that there is no tax.[12] With a 50 percent tax rate, investment of $100 would yield an immediate refund of $50 which, if reinvested, would yield a refund of $25, and so forth until a total refund of $100 was obtained. The investor would thus combine the initial investment of $100 with an additional $100 advanced by the Treasury, and resulting earnings on $200 net of the 50 percent tax would be the same as the earnings on $100 without tax.

Investment Tax Credit

In recent years emphasis in United States incentive policy has been on the investment credit. Such a credit is currently provided in the form of a 10 percent allowance on the cost of qualified investments and is taken as an offset against tax. The credit is limited to 90 percent of tax liability in excess of $25,000. Qualified investments are investments in new depreciable assets (other than buildings) which are used in production and with useful lives of at least three years.[13] For firms with taxes sufficient to permit the credit to be offset at once, the investment credit is similar to a cash grant made at the time of investment, and thus reduces the cost of an asset by 10 percent; for others, the credit may be carried over against future taxes.

An asset costing $100 thus involves a net cost of $90 only, with the gross cost of $100 recoverable through depreciation in subsequent years. As distinct from accelerated depreciation, the investment credit involves not merely a tax postponement, but an outright tax reduction. For any particular investment, with a specified length of useful life, it is possible to devise a pair of accelerated depreciation and credit provisions which will yield the same present value to the investor. But the two approaches differ among investments. Whereas accelerated depreciation favors the long investment, the credit works to the advantage of the short-lived asset. The shorter asset can be replaced more frequently, thus permitting more frequent use of the credit. For this reason, the tax law reduces the investment credit if the useful life of the asset falls short of seven years and grants no credit for assets with lives below three years.

In addition to the investment credit, the law provides for a job credit designed to encourage employment of certain sectors in the labor force which have been subject to structural unemployment. This provision, however, is limited in scope and not to be interpreted as a general economic incentive.[14]

Capital Gains Preference

Preferential treatment of capital gains offers a further (and currently much advocated) approach to the incentive problem. Undoubtedly, the preferential treatment of realized gains and the exemption of unrealized gains has been a major factor in reducing the impact of taxation on property income, espe-

---

[12]For further discussion of loss offset, see p. 674.

[13]In addition investment in used property up to $100,000 is eligible, as is investment to rehabilitate industrial and commercial buildings which have been in use for at least twenty years.

[14]See p. 811 for the potentially more important role of such a credit in less developed countries.

cially of high-bracket rates under the individual income tax.[15] But it has also been a costly approach.

A blanket preference for capital gains is not an efficient criterion by which to decide which types of investments should and should not be given relief. Not all investments yielding capital gains are worthy of particular support, since such gains may be derived from gilt-edged securities and real estate speculation as well as from risk investments in new products and processes which are essential to economic growth. At the same time, it may be desirable to encourage investments the profits from which cannot be realized readily in the form of capital gains, but accrue as ordinary income. The investment credit, which may be limited to investment in productive assets and the benefits from which are independent of how the income is derived, does not share this defect.

Evaluation of Alternative Measures

What can be said about the merits of the various approaches, including (1) rate reduction, (2) accelerated depreciation, and (3) the investment tax credit?

Investment Stimulus per Dollar of Revenue Loss   One basis of comparison is in terms of investment gained per dollar of revenue loss. Here accelerated depreciation and the investment credit are superior to rate reduction, since they may readily be limited to new investment (or some part thereof), whereas rate reduction has to be applied to profits from all investments, whether new or old. Since it is the profitability of *new* investment that matters for incentive purposes, accelerated depreciation and the investment credit can give a more powerful stimulus than can rate reduction.

Comparison between accelerated depreciation and the investment credit is more complex. The outcome depends on how long a view is taken and on how the level of investment behaves. If we consider the revenue cost for the first year of the new policy only, it is obvious that a credit involving a revenue loss of $1 billion will buy the Treasury more incentive than will accelerated depreciation in the form of an initial first-year allowance costing the same amount. Current tax liabilities will be reduced $1 billion in both cases, but the credit is an outright gain to the investor, whereas the initial allowance is a loan only. Hence the investor's net rate of return is increased more under the credit. But the situation becomes more favorable to the initial allowance if a longer view is taken. Under the allowance, the Treasury will recoup revenue later as depreciation charges become less than they would normally have been. There is no such recoupment with an investment credit. Allowing for revenue costs over a longer period, the initial allowance may therefore come to be preferable.

The comparative results, moreover, depend on what happens to the capital stock. If the economy expands, the advantage of subsequent revenue recoupment which goes with accelerated depreciation comes to be postponed and the investment credit approach remains superior even in the long run.

[15]See p. 349.

Moreover, the effectiveness of the investment credit per dollar of revenue loss could be increased greatly by limiting it to incremental investment, such as the excess of investment over some past base or investment in excess of depreciation charges.[16] Such a limitation is more difficult to apply to accelerated depreciation.

Neutrality   We have seen that both accelerated depreciation and the investment credit fail the neutrality test. Rate reduction is preferable on these grounds. A measure may be designed, however, which applies to new capital only while avoiding discrimination by length of asset life. This would be an initial allowance (where some fraction, say 25 percent, of the asset cost is depreciated in the first year), with depreciation of the remainder in line with the economic life of the asset.[17]

Flexibility   Advocates of the investment credit approach hold that depreciation rates should be set so as to obtain an equitable definition of income, while investment incentives are better given in the more explicit form of an investment credit or an outright investment grant. They also point out that the investment credit performs better as a flexible tool of stabilization policy. Proponents of accelerated depreciation, on the other hand, have preferred the faster write-off method since they have viewed it as a more permanent and stable form of relief.

Equity   Finally, the effects of investment incentives on the equity of the tax structure must be considered. If preferences are to be granted to achieve special policy objectives (in this case, increase in investment), they should be designed so as to interfere least with the equity of the tax system. By the nature of the investment process and the structure of our economy, investment decisions are made largely by taxpayers in high-income brackets, whether as owners or managers, and investable funds also flow largely from such sources. This readily creates a situation where tax incentives to investment double as tax relief to high incomes. The politics of growth policy thus become intertwined with distributional issues. Pending the creation of growth incentives which are distributionally neutral, more targeted measures such as the investment credit or an initial allowance involve a lesser conflict with tax equity than do blanket devices such as the capital gains preference.

C. SUMMARY

The analysis of corporation tax incidence leads to different conclusions depending on whether competitive or imperfect markets are assumed.

---

[16]For further analysis, see E. Cary Brown, "Tax Incentives for Investment," *American Economic Review*, May 1962; and S. B. Chase, "Tax Incentives for Investment and Spending," *National Tax Journal*, March 1962.

[17]See Arnold C. Harberger, "Tax Neutrality in Investment Incentives," in H. J. Aaron and M. J. Boskin (eds.), *The Economics of Taxation*, Washington: Brookings, 1979.

1. Assuming competitive markets, the tax falls on corporate profits, leading capital to flow out of the corporate sector until net rates of return are equalized and the burden is spread among all capital income.

2. A profit-maximizing monopolist must absorb the tax.

3. Shifting to consumers may occur where other pricing rules apply.

4. Imperfect labor markets may result in partial shifting of the tax to employees.

The issue cannot be resolved in purely theoretical terms and calls for empirical investigation:

5. Historical evidence shows the net rate of return to have remained more or less unchanged after introduction of a high-rate corporation tax. This evidence is consistent with the hypothesis of shifting.

6. However, many other changes occurred over the same period. Econometric attempts to isolate the tax effects have led to conflicting conclusions, leaving the matter one of continuing controversy.

The role of investment incentives has been one of the most controversial aspects of tax policy:

7. Accelerated depreciation raises the rate of return but discriminates in favor of long-lived assets.

8. The investment credit carries the opposite bias, but is preferable on other grounds.

9. Preferential treatment of capital gains is not an efficient technique of granting investment incentives.

10. Tax incentives should be designed so as to minimize interference with tax equity.

FURTHER READINGS

Brown, E. Cary: "Business Income Taxation and Investment Incentives," in *Income, Employment and Public Policy: Essays in Honor of Alvin Hansen*, New York: Norton, 1948.

———: "Tax Incentives of Investment," *American Economic Review*, Supplement, May 1962.

Harberger, Arnold C.: "Tax Neutrality in Investment Incentives," in H. Aaron and M. Boskin (eds.), *The Economics of Taxation*, Washington: Brookings, 1979.

For further references, see Chap. 30.

Chapter 20

Sales Taxes*

A. Sales Taxes in the United States Tax Structure: *Federal Taxes; State Taxes; Local Taxes.* **B. Types of Sales Taxation:** *Sales Tax Alternatives; Choice of Base; Stage of Imposition; Ad Valorem versus Unit Tax.* **C. Incidence of Sales Taxes:** *Selective Taxes; General Sales Tax.* **D. Personal Expenditure Tax:** *Determining Taxable Consumption; Evaluation.* **E. Value-Added Tax:** *Final Value as Aggregate of Value Added; Types of Value-Added Taxes; Features of Consumption-Type Value-Added Tax.* **F. Summary.** **Appendix: Incidence of Unit and Ad Valorem Taxes.**

Sales taxes are like income taxes in that they are imposed on flows generated in the production of current output. But income taxes are imposed on the sellers' side of *factor* transactions (i.e., on the income received by households) or point 1 in Figure 10-1, whereas sales taxes are imposed on the sellers' side of *product* transactions (i.e., on the sales of business firms) or point 3. Sales taxes on consumer goods, moreover, may be considered equivalent to taxes

---

* Reader's Guide to Chapter 20: In this chapter we discuss the conventional forms of sales taxation as well as some novel approaches to the taxation of consumption, including the value-added tax, which has received much attention in recent years, and a personalized approach referred to as the expenditure tax. Consumption taxation in these various forms promises to be an active area of tax reform discussion in the future.

imposed on household purchases, i.e., to taxes imposed at point 2.[1] While income taxes are based on the sources side of the household account, sales taxes are based on the uses side. For a general tax on consumer goods, all uses except saving are included.

Finally, and most important, sales taxes differ from the income tax in that they are *in rem* rather than *personal* taxes. As such, they do not allow for the personal circumstances of consumers as does the individual income tax with its exemptions, deductions, and progressive rates. Sales taxes are thus inferior on both horizontal and vertical equity grounds. But even though consumption taxes usually take this form, it is not a necessary feature of consumption taxation. As we shall see presently, a personal consumption or expenditure tax may be constructed which is not open to this objection.

A. SALES TAXES IN THE UNITED STATES TAX STRUCTURE

We begin with a brief look at the role of sales taxes in the United States tax structure. As was shown in Table 15-1, sales taxes are of only limited importance at the federal and local level, where they produce 10 percent of total revenue; but they are the major source of revenue at the state level, where over 50 percent of the total is derived from this source. Charges and special assessments, though related to sales taxes in nature, are dealt with at a later point. It will be seen that they are of special and growing importance at the local level.

Federal Taxes

Federal sales taxes, also referred to as excises, are all of the selective type, being imposed on specific products.[2] As may be seen in Table 20-1, the bulk of the revenue comes from a small group of products, including alcohol, tobacco, gasoline, and telephone services. Customs duties which once were very important are now a negligible factor in the overall revenue picture of the federal government. Federal sales taxes are imposed largely at the manufacturer level, the major exceptions being telephone services and air transportation, which are, in effect, charged at retail. Most federal sales taxes (including those on alcohol, tobacco, gasoline, and tires) are levied on a unit basis, while others (including telephone taxes) are of the ad valorem type.

State Taxes

At the state level, the retail sales tax holds the center of the stage. Being a tax on retail sales, it corresponds to a more or less general tax on consumer expenditures. Such a tax is now imposed by all but four states. Rates range from 2 to over 6 percent, and the comprehensiveness of base varies. Moreover, the states also make substantial use of selective taxes. As shown in

---

[1]See p. 231.

[2]The term "excise," as used in the U.S. Constitution (Art. 1, sec. 8), was to distinguish such levies from "capitation and other direct taxes" dealt with in section 9. General as well as selective sales taxes would be "excises" in this sense. See p. 30.

TABLE 20-1
Sales Taxes in the United States Tax System
(Fiscal Year 1975–76; in Billions of Dollars)

	Federal	State	Local	Total
General	—	27.3	4.7	32.0
Selective				
Motor fuel	4.6	8.7	0.1	13.4
Alcoholic beverages	5.4	2.1	0.1	7.6
Tobacco products	2.5	3.5	0.1	6.1
Public utilities*	2.7	2.1	1.6	6.4
Other	2.0	3.8	0.6	6.4
Total	17.2	47.5	7.2	71.9
Motor vehicle and				
operator's licenses†	—	4.4	0.3	4.7
Liquor stores‡	—	2.2	0.4	2.6
Total domestic	17.2	54.1	7.9	79.2
Customs duties	4.5	—	—	4.5
Total	21.7	54.1	7.9	83.7

*Taxes paid by public utilities. Does not include net revenue from publicly owned utilites.
†Classified by Census as tax revenue rather than as charges.
‡Net revenue from government-owned liquor stores, included here even though not classified as tax revenue by Census.
Source: U.S. Bureau of the Census, *Governmental Finances in 1975–76,* 1977.

Table 20-1, the primary objects of selective taxation are again gasoline, liquor, and tobacco. These and most other selective sales taxes are imposed on a unit basis, although ad valorem taxes are also used. The general sales tax is imposed at the retail level, as are most selective taxes. However, manufacturers' taxes are used as well. As noted later, the choice between taxation at the retail level (involving taxation at destination of the product) and taxation at the manufacturer level (involving taxation at the origin) has important bearing on the size of the tax base available to any jurisdiction as well as the distribution of the tax burden between jurisdictions.[3]

Local Taxes

Sales taxes in 1975 provided 10 percent of local tax revenue. Two-thirds came from general sales taxes, now imposed by thousands of municipalities, usually as a surcharge to the state tax and at rates ranging up to 3 percent. Selective sales taxes are of minor importance at this level.

B. TYPES OF SALES TAXATION

As is apparent from the preceding view of sales taxation at the various levels, sales taxes may take a variety of forms. In some cases they reflect varying policy objectives, while in others they reflect differing administrative devices to accomplish the same objective.

[3]See p. 779.

Sales Tax Alternatives

Such taxes may differ with regard to scope of coverage or base, to points of collection, and to assessment on unit or ad valorem base. Leaving aside the latter distinction for the time being, the various approaches may be summarized as shown in Table 20-2.

Horizontally, Table 20-2 shows the distinction among various sales tax bases. These include a comprehensive consumption base (column I), a selective consumption base (column II), and a base in which both consumer and capital goods are included (column III). Whereas the base covered in I equals the consumption component of GNP, that covered in III equals total GNP. In column IV, the base is defined not in terms of final output (as in columns I through III) but includes all sales, thus covering a unit of output more than once as it moves through successive stages of production and trade.[4]

Vertically, the table shows the various stages at which the tax may be collected. Among single-stage taxes, these include retail, wholesale, or manufacturers' taxes. Under the multiple-stage group, we have the value-added tax, which, as we shall see below, differs from the single-stage approach only in matters of administration, as well as the turnover tax which is basically different in nature.

The various sales taxes may now be classified readily in terms of Table 20-2. The retail sales taxes imposed at the state level correspond to case 1, although they fall short of being truly general. Gasoline taxes illustrate case 5, while federal taxes on liquor illustrate case 7. The value-added taxes now imposed in European countries correspond to 4, while the turnover taxes which they replaced corresponded to 13.

Choice of Base

The choice of base is the crucial policy issue in sales tax design. Assuming that the tax is to be general, the question is whether it should include consumption only (type I), consumption plus investment or GNP (type III), or all turnover (type IV).

Inferiority of Total Transactions Base   To begin with, the turnover tax which applies to the total of transactions may be eliminated as least desirable. Under this tax, a product is taxed repeatedly as it moves through the stages of production. Thus, the sale of iron ore is taxed when it moves from mine to steel mill; the sale of steel is taxed when it moves from the mill to a rolling plant; sheet metal is taxed when it is sold to an automobile body plant, and so on until the final tax is imposed on the retail sale of the car. As a result, the tax base is a multiple of GNP and high yields can be obtained at very low rates. With a GNP of $2,000 billion, a comprehensive 1 percent turnover tax could yield $70 billion, or nearly one-half the yield of the income tax. This

---

[4]The base will thus be larger even though included transactions are limited to those involved in the production of current output as it moves from one stage of production to another. Beyond this, the base may be made to include "secondhand" transactions among final users and even financial assets.

TABLE 20-2
Types of Sales Taxes

Stage	Consumer Goods General (I)	Consumer Goods Selective (II)	Consumer and Capital Goods (III)	Total Transactions (IV)
Single				
Retail	1	5	9	—
Wholesale	2	6	10	—
Manufacturer	3	7	11	—
Multiple				
Value-added	4	8	12	—
Turnover	—	—	—	13

has political appeal, and inclusion of total transactions would do no harm if each product went through the same number of transactions, so that the combined turnover tax liabilities as a percentage of value at final sale would be the same. But they are not. A turnover tax, therefore, imposes arbitrary discrimination against products which involve many stages of production and distribution. Moreover, in order to avoid tax, firms will attempt to join with their suppliers, thus encouraging vertical integration and reducing competition. Further inequities are introduced as the tax is "pyramided" from stage to stage, by entering into the base of each successive stage. For these reasons, the turnover tax is considered an inferior form of taxation, and the recent replacement of the turnover tax by the value-added tax in European countries reflects a belated recognition of this fact. The United States, fortunately, has never suffered from a turnover tax.

GNP Base versus Consumption Base   Granted that such double-counting should be avoided, there remains a choice between a tax based on gross national product, net national product, or consumption. Most general sales taxes are, or at least aim to be, of the consumption-based type.

The GNP type would impose a sales tax on both consumer and capital goods. Thus, its base would be equivalent to that of a tax on gross income, i.e., an income tax which does not allow for depreciation. Such a tax would be objectionable on both equity and efficiency grounds. With regard to equity, it would offend the basic dictum of income taxation which says that income from all sources should be taxed fully, but on a net basis. With regard to efficiency, it would compound the discrimination against saving which even a tax on net income involves.[5]

These objections do not apply if the tax is limited to a base which in fact equals net national product, or GNP minus depreciation. Such a tax would be similar in base to a general income tax and (as will be noted a little later) may

[5]See p. 311.

TABLE 20-3
Estimated Base of National Retail Sales Tax, 1976

	Billions of Dollars
Consumer expenditures	1,093.9
Items generally excluded:	
Housing*	167.9
Domestic services	6.4
Food furnished employees	3.3
Medical supplies	10.7
Insurance premiums	23.0
Foreign travel	9.4
Other personal business	55.6
= Remaining base	817.6
As percentage of total consumption	75
Items frequently excluded:	
Home-consumed food	165.6
Other medical expenses	106.4
Household utilities	50.7
Tobacco and gasoline	57.6
Private education	16.9
Miscellaneous	40.0
= Remaining base	380.4
As percentage of total consumption	35

*Includes rental payments and imputed rent of owner-occupied housing.
Source: U.S. Department of Commerce, *Survey of Current Business,* July 1977, p.

be implemented via an income type of value-added tax.[6] Since the income base is already available under the income tax, this leaves the consumption base under which consumer goods only are subject to tax. This approach is the one most generally used and must now be considered more closely.

Comprehensive versus Narrow-Based Consumption Tax   The so-called general or retail sales tax, as imposed by the states, aims at a comprehensive coverage of consumption. Nevertheless, all these taxes exclude certain items, thereby reducing the base to one-half or one-third of the total available under a truly general consumption tax.

This is shown in Table 20-3. We note than even a broadly defined base, estimated at $818 billion for 1976, falls 25 percent short of total consumer expenditures of $1,094 billion. The main single item of slippage is rent (imputed and rental payments), which accounts for over one-half of the loss.

[6]Imposed in single-stage form, this would call for a tax both on consumer and on capital goods, with the base defined as sales value minus the depreciation component of cost. Since the retailer does not have this information, such a tax would be impractical. For the value-added type of income tax, see p. 459.

Most states exclude further items such as food grown and consumed on farms, private education, prescription drugs, and foreign travel. Other states use a much narrower base and exclude additional items, with food purchased for home consumption accounting for the largest base loss. Exclusion of products subject to selective excise taxes and utilities comes next in importance. Allowance for such items reduced the 1976 sales tax base to about $380 billion or two-thirds of total consumption as measured in the national product accounts.

It is evident, therefore, that adoption of a narrow base requires a substantially higher tax rate if the same revenue is to be obtained. This requirement is not objectionable in itself if the base is improved thereby, but unless there are specific reasons for excluding certain items, the inclination is in favor of a broad-based tax. One reason for excluding items such as imputed rent and certain services may be that inclusion would be administratively difficult. Exclusion of such items as rent or home-consumed food may be designed to reduce the regressivity of the tax, although—as we shall note presently—other and more effective ways of doing this are available. Finally, still other items, such as prescription drugs, may be excluded because their consumption is to be encouraged as a merit good, their exclusion from the general sales tax being equivalent to a subsidy in the absence of tax.[7] But, as with the income tax, the admission of certain exclusions readily spreads and erodes the tax base.

Selective Sales Taxes   As distinct from the more or less general type of sales tax, selective sales taxation is applied to particular products. This may be done for various reasons.

1.   Selective sales taxes may be rationalized as substitutes for service charges. Thus, the gasoline tax may be considered an approximation, if an imperfect one, to a service charge for the use of roads.

2.   Selective sales taxes may be imposed to implement progressivity. Thus, taxation of products which weigh heavily in high-income budgets results in a progressive burden distribution. In situations where a progressive income tax is difficult to implement—as is typically a problem in developing countries—selective excises on luxury goods, supported by corresponding taxes on imports, may offer a feasible substitute.[8]

3.   Particular products may be chosen for taxation in situations where tax administration is difficult, because such taxes are easier to collect. This approach is again useful in developing countries where products produced by a small number of manufacturing establishments may offer a readily available tax handle. The same advantage applies to the taxation of imports.

4.   Selective taxes may be imposed to discourage the consumption of "demerit" goods. This approach explains why, honoring the spirit of Carrie Nation, alcoholic beverages and tobacco account for nearly one-half of federal sales taxes. Such taxes, though they tend to be highly regressive, are supported on

[7]See p. 89.
[8]See p. 807.

"sumptuary" grounds, because the consumption of such products is considered
to be immoral or unhealthy. Society decides to interfere with consumer choice,
and to treat such items as demerit goods. Whatever the desirability of such
interference, there is the further question of effectiveness. Consumption will be
reduced only to the extent that demand is elastic. Since the demand for cigarettes
and liquor is relatively inelastic, these taxes are not likely to have a major effect
on consumption, as evidenced by the very fact that they produce such a large
yield. For regulatory taxes to be effective, the activity in question must be greatly
curtailed, resulting in little or no tax revenue.

   5.   A further use of regulatory taxes, likely to be expanded in the future, is
as a deterrent to pollution.[9] Imposed to internalize the external costs generated
by certain production or consumption activities, excises may be used to correct
for inefficiencies in resource use.

   6.   Still another type of control objective underlies a set of federal taxes
officially designated as regulatory taxes. Such taxes, including those on narcotics,
adulterated butter, and wagers, are imposed to facilitate enforcement of other
regulations or other taxes without a direct revenue objective.

Stage of Imposition

We now turn to the stage at which the tax is to be imposed. This decision
involves the choice of the best stage for single-stage taxes, as well as the
choice between a single- and a multiple-stage approach. Whereas setting the
scope of coverage is a substantive issue in determining what kind of tax is to
be applied, the choice of the appropriate stage or stages is essentially a matter
of administrative efficiency in implementing a tax on the chosen base.

   Manufacturing versus Retail Level   In dealing with single-stage taxes, the
question is whether the tax should be imposed at the manufacturing, the
wholesaler, or the retail level.

   If the tax is to be general, the retail base is preferable because it permits
the imposition of a uniform ad valorem rate. Equal-rate ad valorem taxes
imposed on various products at the manufacturing level result in dissimilar
equivalent rates at the retail level. This occurs because the ratio of retail to
manufacturer's prices differs among products. Imposition of differential rates
to allow for this diversity would be a difficult and clumsy way to approximate
what can be done better with a uniform tax at the retail level.

   If the tax is to be selective, the answer is less evident. If the product is
identified at the manufacturing stage, e.g., low- or high-priced cars or television sets, it will be advantageous to tax at that level, since selective retail
taxation may be more difficult. In other situations (e.g., fabrics which may be
made into low- or high-priced garments), this may not be possible. Differentiation here may have to be related to the nature of the final product at
retail. Nevertheless, the general presumption in favor of retail, applicable to
the case of the general tax, does not hold for the selective case.

   In developing countries in particular, a good argument can be made for
taxing at the manufacturing level. This approach reduces the number of

[9]See p. 759.

taxpayers from whom the tax has to be collected and thus facilitates administration. Moreover, manufacturing establishments tend to be larger than retail establishments, more permanent, and conducted on a more sophisticated basis, with better bookkeeping methods. These characteristics improve their quality for assessment purposes. Developing countries may do better with a set of manufacturers' taxes, where the number of collection points is smaller, even though this may result in differentials in the implicit retail rates.

Another aspect of the stages problem arises where goods are traded between jurisdictions. Taxation at the retail stage (the so-called destination principle) permits the inclusion of imported goods, thus making it possible for states to tax the use of gasoline and automobiles even though they do not produce these items. On the other hand, taxation at the manufacturing level (the so-called origin principle) permits inclusion of exported goods which are consumed abroad. Thus, the state of Michigan may find it beneficial to tax automobiles at the manufacturer level rather than at the retail level. But, as we shall see later, this may not be desirable from an interstate (or, seen more broadly, from an international) point of view. Resulting effects on trade and the division of revenue between governments must then be allowed for. In the international context, effects on the balance of payments also enter the picture.[10]

Retail Level versus Value Added   The other question is whether the tax should be collected in one swoop and at the final point of sale only, or whether it should be collected in slabs as under the value-added procedure. With this approach, the value of the product is divided into slices or slabs (the value added at each stage) to which the tax is applied at successive stages in the production process. Notwithstanding this difference in technique, the base of a value-added tax of the consumption type is the same as that of a retail sales tax; only the method of collection differs. A choice between the two, therefore, has to be made in terms of administrative convenience.

Use of the multiple-stage approach in the value-added context must be distinguished sharply from its previously noted use in connection with the turnover tax. Since the value-added tax has come to be the basic instrument of tax coordination among Common Market countries, where it has replaced widespread use of turnover taxes, it has also received increasing attention in the United States. The old debate over whether there should be a federal retail sales tax has been revised in this form. A more detailed examination of the value-added approach is presented in the concluding section of this chapter.

Ad Valorem versus Unit Tax

It remains to note the form in which the sales tax is imposed. It may be assessed as a percentage of net (before tax) price, when it is referred to as an

[10]See p. 778.

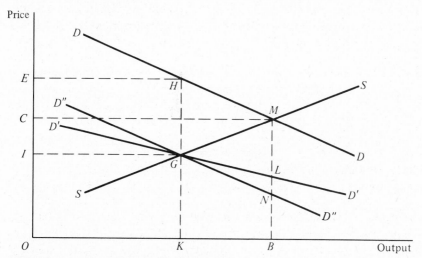

FIGURE 20-1   Ad Valorem and Unit Sales Tax.

ad valorem tax. Or, it may be assessed as a given amount per unit of product, in which case it is referred to as a *unit* tax. The one is a tax on the value of sales, while the other is a tax on the quantity of sales.

The two taxes are compared in Figure 20-1. *DD* is the market demand schedule for product X, *SS* is the supply schedule, equilibrium before tax is at *M*, output equals *OB*, and price equals *OC*. Now an ad valorem tax at rate $t = GH/KG$ is imposed. The demand schedule swivels to *D'D'*. The new equilibrium is at *H*, output falls to *OK*, the gross price rises to *OE*, and the net price falls to *OI*. Revenue equals *IEHG*.

To obtain the same amount of revenue, a unit tax in the amount $u = GH$ is needed. This is shown here as a parallel downward shift in the demand schedule to *D"D"*.[11] Output is set where *D"D"* intersects *SS*, with gross price again equal to *OE*, net price equal to *OI*, and revenue equal to *IGHE*. The same revenue is obtained with the same increase in price.[12] Also observe that the ratio of unit tax *u* to net price at the equilibrium output must equal the ad valorem rate *t*.[12] At the same time, the ratio of unit tax to initial price exceeds *t*.

Under competitive conditions, the outcome is thus the same for unit and ad valorem taxes of equal revenue. The ad valorem approach, however, has the advantage that it permits the same rate to be applied to various products, which renders it superior on efficiency grounds.[13] Finally, the unit tax reduces the built-in revenue flexibility of the tax system with regard to inflation, since

[11]Alternatively, the unit tax may be presented as a parallel upward shift in the supply schedule by distance *GH*, showing that sellers suffer a corresponding increase in cost. In the case of the ad valorem tax, however, the tax is expressed as a function of price and thus is shown as a swivel in the demand schedule.

[12]This is not the case for monopoly, where it may be shown that the price will be higher under the unit tax than under an ad valorem tax yielding equal revenue.

[13]See p. 314.

the tax per unit remains constant as prices rise. For these and other reasons, there is a strong case for transforming the existing unit taxes to an ad valorem basis.

C. INCIDENCE OF SALES TAXES

We now turn to a brief evaluation of sales taxes in the revenue system at both the federal and lower levels of government.

Selective Taxes

In our earlier discussion of sales tax incidence, resulting changes in output and price were shown to depend on the elasticities of supply and demand, a proposition which is explored further in the appendix to this chapter.[14] We also concluded that the burden distribution by income groups is dominated from the uses side, i.e., by the pattern of consumer expenditures on the taxed product. The incidence of a tax on necessities will thus tend to be regressive, while that of a tax on luxuries tends to be progressive. The bulk of selective sales taxes being derived from items of mass consumption such as liquor, tobacco, and gasoline, incidence tends to be regressive. Moreover, by falling on selected items of consumption, such taxes tend to involve a higher efficiency cost than a more general tax.

Given these disadvantages, why are selective sales or excise taxes in continuing use? The question is answered by considering the kind of products that are taxed. As shown in Table 20-1, nearly 50 percent of selective sales or excise taxes come from motor fuel or other automotive taxes, 25 percent come from liquor, and 15 percent from tobacco products. The fuel and automotive taxes may be considered as in lieu of highway user charges and (more recently) as part of an energy conservation policy. The latter reflect a view of tobacco and liquor as "demerit goods," be it because of detrimental externalities, a desire to protect consumers against self-inflicted damage, or for "moral" reasons.

General Sales Tax

As distinct from selective sales or excise taxes, the general sales tax is still a major component of the tax structure at the state level. As concluded earlier, its incidence is determined again primarily from the uses side of the household account, a general retail sales tax on consumer goods being similar in this respect to a flat-rate tax on consumer expenditures. Seen from the point of view of *horizontal* equity, a general sales tax is equitable if the index of equality is defined in terms of consumption but inequitable if the index is defined in terms of income. Families with similar incomes may have differing consumption (or saving) rates due to age or other factors. Such families will pay different amounts of tax, thus violating horizontal equity in terms of income.

[14]See p. 464.

Viewed in terms of *vertical* equity, a general sales tax is proportional as related to consumption but regressive as related to income. This is so because consumption as a percentage of income declines (savings as a percentage of income rises) as we move up the income scale. As was shown in line 11 of Table 12-1, the sales tax is a major regressive element in the tax structure.[15] The same is shown in Table 20-4. Column I shows the burden distribution of $40 billion raised by income tax, while column II shows the estimated distribution for a broadly based 5 percent sales tax yielding a similar amount. We note that the effective rate (ratio of tax to income) of the income tax rises as we move up the income scale, while that of the sales tax falls. We should, however, qualify this conclusion in two ways.

Cross-Section versus Lifetime Pattern   To begin with, our finding that a sales tax on consumer goods is regressive rests on evidence from cross-section data which shows that in any particular year, low-income families will on the average consume a higher fraction of their income than will high-income families.[16] The average propensity to consume declines when moving up the income scale. By allocating the sales tax burden in line with this distribution of consumption among income classes, the regressive incidence shown in line 11 of Table 12-1 is obtained.

The appropriateness of evidence drawn from a cross-section for any single year may be questioned.[17] Evidence of a falling consumption-income ratio for *any one year* is consistent with a wide range of hypotheses regarding the consumption-income ratios at particular income levels over a *longer period*. Households in any given income bracket will include those whose income is permanently in that bracket as well as others who occupy it only temporarily. In the low brackets, this temporary group will typically consist of units whose income is normally higher. If such households tend to maintain past consumption patterns, they will consume more than do households with permanently low incomes.[18] Because of this, the consumption rates for

---

[15]See p. 267.

[16]No such data have been available for recent years, but the Bureau of Labor Statistics Survey for 1961 clearly brought out this fact. See U.S. Bureau of Labor Statistics, *Survey of Consumer Expenditures, 1960–61*, Report 237-93, May 1966.

[17]See also the similar argument in relation to the property tax, p. 485.

[18]The hypothesis is that an individual's consumption for any one year depends not only on his or her income for that year but also on what the person expects to be his or her more "permanent" (or even lifetime) income. People will thus attempt to maintain consumption at customary levels in any one year, whether their income is normal, unusually high, or low. As a result, their consumption-income ratio will be high in low-income years and low in high-income years. Applying this to the cross-section picture, we should expect that the lower end of the income scale includes a larger proportion of people whose incomes are temporarily high. Reasoning along these lines helps to explain why the consumption ratio falls as we move up the scale.

The consumption functions used in current econometric models generally make use of lagged, as well as current, income as determinants of current consumption. If past income is interpreted as an indicator of future income, this evidence may be read as supporting the hypothesis that consumption in any one year is a function of expected *lifetime* income. (For a discussion of this issue, see M. Friedman, *A Theory of the Consumption Function*, Princeton, N.J.: Princeton, 1957.) Alternatively, the evidence may be interpreted merely as showing current consumption to depend on past income. In either case, use of cross-section data overstates regressivity of the sales tax as related to more permanent income.

TABLE 20-4
Comparison of Estimated Tax Rates under
Various Methods of Raising $40 Billion
(1977 Levels)

Adjusted Gross Income (Dollars)	TAX AS PERCENTAGE OF AGI			
	Income Tax (I)	Sales Tax		
		Broad Base 5% (II)	Food Excluded 6% (III)	With Credit 7% (IV)
5,000–10,000	0.6	3.4	3.2	2.6
15,000–20,000	3.3	3.2	3.2	3.7
20,000–25,000	3.8	3.0	3.0	3.5
30,000–50,000	4.3	2.4	2.5	2.9

Notes:
Column I: 25 percent of 1977 income tax liabilities, to yield $40 billion.
Column II: 5 percent tax rate. Distribution from J. A. Pechman, *Federal Tax Policy,* 3d ed., Washington: Brookings, 1977, p. 168. Estimated yield of 5 percent tax on 1977 base is $40 billion.
Column III: See Pechman, op. cit. Rates are raised to 6 percent level to maintain yield while exempting food.
Column IV: A credit of $150 is given (equivalent at 7% rate to $2,142 of tax-free consumption), but the credit is assumed to decline by $25 for each $1,000 of AGI above $5,000.

households in the bottom group (which in the cross-section data includes households whose income is only temporarily low) will be higher than those for households with permanently low incomes. As a result, use of such cross-section data overstates the decline in the average propensity to consume when moving up the income scale and, with it, the regressivity of a sales tax as applied to the more permanent income position of households.

Indeed, if all income were consumed over a person's lifetime, the consumption tax would be proportional in relation to lifetime income.[19] But in fact, not all income is consumed and estates are left; and, though no adequate data are available, it seems likely that the ratio of estates to lifetime income rises when moving up the scale of lifetime income. With bequests allowed for, the sales tax thus remains regressive even in relation to lifetime income.

Exclusions and Credits   Next, we note that the regressive nature of the general sales tax is reduced substantially if home-consumed food is exempted. Two-thirds of the sales-tax states provide such exemptions. Since this practice results in a substantial reduction in tax base, the rate as shown in column III must be raised from 5 to 6 percent to maintain the yield. The tax now

---

[19]The present value of lifetime consumption taxes at the beginning of a person's working life would still depend on his or her lifetime income and consumption profile. If a larger share of lifetime consumption occurred earlier for low-income (lifetime) families, the distribution of lifetime burden would still be regressive, and in the opposite case it would be progressive.

becomes more or less proportional over the lower and middle range, remaining regressive over the top end of the scale only.

A more direct way of dealing with regressivity is to permit a tax-free amount of expenditure. In the absence of an outright expenditure tax, to be discussed presently, this may be done by permitting the taxpayer a corresponding credit against income tax. Such a credit is now used by six states. In some states, the credit is given as a flat amount, while in others it is limited to taxpayers below a certain income level. In yet others, the credit declines as income rises. A credit of $4 given in Massachusetts, for example, capitalized at a tax rate of 5 percent implies a tax-free expenditure of $80. As the credit is given per person, it allows for the number of dependents. Thus it reduces not only regressivity for a given family size, but also the burden for large, as against small, families.

The potentialities of a credit arrangement are shown in column IV of Table 20-4, where it is assumed that a similar amount of $40 billion is obtained while adding a substantial credit to column III. To make up for the resulting revenue loss, a 7 percent rate is applied. We now find that the rate pattern becomes progressive over a substantial part of the income scale covering well over one-half of all taxpayers. To hold down the revenue cost of the credit (here set at $150 for a family of four), we assume that the credit is to decline for levels of AGI above $5,000 and to disappear when $11,000 is reached.

As shown in the table, it is thus possible, by use of a credit, to remove regressivity and render the sales tax progressive over a large part of the income range. At the same time, two important qualifications remain: (1) The credit can be administered readily over the income ranges which are subject to income tax, but cash refunds are needed at the lower end of the scale where no income tax applies. Cash refunds, especially to low-income households, are difficult to administer effectively. (2) The credit device does not lend itself to achieving progressivity over the upper end of the income scale. There one must either rely on the income tax, or, if a consumption base is to be used, apply a personal expenditure tax.

D. PERSONAL EXPENDITURE TAX

It is not surprising, therefore, that in the historical development, income taxation has been identified with progressive taxation and sales taxes with regressive taxation. Accordingly, the political support for income taxation has tended to come from proponents of progression, while that for consumption taxation has tended to come from its opponents. But there is nothing in the logic of the two tax bases which makes this necessarily so. This situation has arisen because the income tax has developed in the framework of *personal* taxation, while consumption taxes have been locked into the vise of the impersonal or in rem approach of sales taxation. Resort to a personal type of expenditure tax would break this bondage and permit the taxation of consumption to be based on a personal and progressive basis. Such a tax was proposed by the U.S. Treasury during World War II but was given little consideration. While it has been tried briefly in Sri Lanka and India, actual experience with such a tax under modern conditions has been absent to date. It is still a new and exciting idea.[20] We will not reconsider here the basic question whether ability to pay is measured better in income or in consumption terms, as this was examined in detail at an earlier point.[21] However, it remains to explore some of the technical problems involved in applying an expenditure tax.

Determining Taxable Consumption

When consumption is taken as the index of taxpaying ability, all that has been said previously about the desirability of a global definition of the income tax base again applies.[22] All consumption should be included in the base and people's tax liabilities should be independent of the particular pattern of their consumption outlays. In analogy to the income tax, the taxpayer would determine his or her consumption for the year, subtract whatever personal exemptions or deductions were allowed, and apply a progressive rate schedule to the remaining amount of taxable consumption.

The idea sounds simple, but it remains to be seen how taxable consumption is to be determined. Addition of individual consumption items would not be feasible. One possibility would be to begin with income and deduct savings. To arrive at consumption, savings would have to be defined as *net* saving (saving minus dissaving) or increase in net worth. This would be a formidable task. The best and most feasible procedure would be to determine the taxpayer's annual consumption in line with the following schedule:

1. Bank balance at the beginning of the year
2. + receipts
3. + net borrowing (borrowing minus debt repayment or lending)
4. − net investment (costs of assets purchased minus proceeds from assets sold)
5. − bank balances at end of year
6. = consumption during the year

Consumption in this way would be derived from the change in bank balances and the flow of receipts and nonconsumption payments during the year. The tax return would call upon the taxpayer to declare the listed items (broken down in more detail) just as income is shown under the income tax.

The concept of receipts as used in the above schedule equals income as

---

[20]Like most new ideas, it also has a long history behind it. A personalized expenditure tax was put forth as an ideal by Alfred Marshall and proposed in detail by Irving Fisher (*Constructive Income Taxation*, New York: Harper, 1942), who felt (going back to John Stuart Mill) that income taxation is unfair because it discriminates against the saver. In modern form, the case for a personal expenditure tax has been made by N. Kaldor, *An Expenditure Tax*, London: G. Allen, 1955. Kaldor recommends such a tax as a supplement to an imperfectly functioning income tax, especially because of ineffective progression at high-income levels.

[21]See p. 243.
[22]See p. 243.

defined under the income tax, adjusted to exclude capital gains but to include imputed rent of owner-occupied housing as well as all bequests and gifts received. Net investment would be defined to include net purchases of all assets, including owner-occupied residences, but excluding other durable consumer goods. While housing consumption would be included via the imputed rent component of income, purchases of durable consumer goods, such as cars, would be treated as current consumption, with averaging permitted to avoid inequities.

In some respects, the approach would be simpler than under the income tax. The dilemma of how to deal with unrealized capital gains would disappear. If assets were sold, the proceeds would enter into the tax base unless offset by purchases of other assets or an increase in balances. Unrealized changes in the value of capital assets would be irrelevant. Also, there would be no need to determine corporate profits. Dividends would appear as receipts, and unrealized capital gains, obtained through retention of profits or otherwise, would be irrelevant until realization occurred and the proceeds were channeled into consumption. The difficult problem of depreciation accounting, similarly, would disappear. Adjustment to inflation would call only for indexing of rate brackets, as the more troublesome problem of adjusting for changes in nominal values would not arise.

But an expenditure tax would also pose new difficulties. Source withholding would have to be dropped or be based on a presumed income-consumption relationship. Next it would be crucial that there be a complete recording of cash balances at the outset. Otherwise, tax-free consumption might be financed later by withdrawing such balances. To assure that borrowing is accounted for, lenders would have to be required to file information returns on loans made. More cross-checking would be needed. Similarly, it must be assured that all sales of assets would in fact be declared. For this purpose it might well be necessary to require a balance sheet statement or at least a full listing of asset holdings in the tax return.

Other problems would arise in dealing with long-lived consumer goods such as housing. These might be taxed either as imputed consumption over their useful life, or at the time of initial outlay, with appropriate averaging permitted. A further difficulty would arise in drawing a line between consumption and investment. Certain investments (such as purchase of shares in a country club or a pleasure farm) carry consumption benefits and would be difficult to classify. Outlays on education would pose a similar problem, as they again involve both consumption and investment aspects. Inclusion of imputed consumption—e.g., housing and homegrown food—would be needed to obtain a meaningful tax base, especially at the lower end of the scale. The expense-account problem, difficult enough under the income tax, would assume larger proportions. Finally, the proper definition of the taxable unit would pose new problems. Unless a strict definition applied, high-consumption taxpayers might commission low-consumption taxpayers (under the guise of a gift or otherwise) to make purchases for them. Extensive provision for averaging would be called for, new international aspects of taxation would have to be dealt with, and so forth.

In addition to these continuing considerations, serious problems would arise in the transition stage from an income to an expenditure tax. Taxpayers who have saved in the past when the income tax regime applied and are now about to dissave would be hurt by the change, as compared to others who are at an earlier stage in their cycle and will do their saving in the future. Transition provisions would be needed to avoid such hardship. On balance it is hard to say whether the administrative difficulties of an expenditure tax would be less than those now encountered with the income tax.[23] Only practical experience would give an answer to this question.

Evaluation

Though the difficulties might be considerable, use of a personal expenditure tax would greatly raise the quality of consumption taxation, transforming it into a genuine personal rather than in rem tax. At the federal level, an expenditure might be used in partial substitution for the income tax as a component of a progressive tax system, leaving it with a dual approach to personal taxation. This would remove the traditional objection to sales taxation, although it would leave the basic question as to whether income or consumption offers the better base. As noted in our earlier discussion of "equal options," this question cannot be resolved without allowing for the problem of bequests.[24] If all income were consumed during the recipient's lifetime, the difference between the two bases would be one of timing only. But such is not the case. Income may be left in the form of bequests or be passed on as gifts. Unless such transfers are included in the base of a consumption tax, no tax would be paid in the lifetime of the bequeathing individual and indefinite postponement might result.

E. VALUE-ADDED TAX

As noted before, a sales tax may be imposed in either single- or multiple-stage form. If the latter is implemented in the value-added (rather than the turnover) sense, it is equivalent, from the economists' point of view, to a corresponding single-stage tax. Unlike the expenditure tax, the value-added tax is not a genuinely new form of taxation, but merely a sales tax which is administered in a different form. Nevertheless, the value-added approach has received repeated notice, most recently as a possible substitute for part of the payroll tax, and therefore deserves our attention.

Final Value as Aggregate of Value Added

Consider a finished product, such as shoes. Tracing it through the various stages of production, we begin with the rancher selling the hides to the tanner, the tanner selling the leather to the shoe manufacturer, the manufacturer

---

[23]For a discussion of expenditure-tax implementation, including the transition problem, see U.S. Treasury Department, *Blueprints for Basic Tax Reform*, 1976, and John J. Minarik (ed.), *What to Tax, Income or Expenditure?*, Washington: Brookings, 1979.

[24]But is not the problem of bequests taken care of by estate and inheritance taxes? We prefer to think of this as a separate issue. See p. 496.

selling the shoes to the wholesaler, the wholesaler selling them to the retailer, who finally sells to the customer. At each stage the value of the product is increased and the sales price rises accordingly. Each increment in price reflects the value added at that stage, with the value or price of the final product equal to the sum of the increments or values added at the various stages. A tax imposed on the increments is thus identical in its base to a tax imposed on the final value of the product.

Types of Value-Added Taxes

Three major types of value-added taxes (corresponding to the gross national product, net national product, and consumption bases) may be distinguished, although only the consumption type is up for practical consideration.

GNP Type   Suppose now that *all* final goods and services produced and sold during a given period, i.e., the entire gross national product, were subject to a general sales tax. This tax would be applicable to both consumer and capital goods. It would be paid by the seller when the product was sold to its last purchaser, be it a consumer, a firm which adds to its inventory, or a firm which purchases capital goods. With a GNP of $2 trillion, an all-inclusive 5 percent tax would yield $100 billion. The same would be accomplished by using the value-added approach, taxing each seller at a rate of 5 percent on value added, i.e., gross receipts minus the cost of purchasing intermediate goods from prior producers in the production line. The tax base at each stage would thus equal depreciation, wages, interest, profits, and rent. This would be the most comprehensive form of value-added tax, and may be referred to as a value-added tax of the GNP type. As noted before, it is equivalent to a sales tax applicable to both consumer and capital goods, with its impact point (in terms of Figure 10-1) at 11 or, which is the same, at 4.

Income Type   The value-added approach, as previously noted, may also be used to implement a sales tax on *net* product. Suppose that the intent is to tax net national product, equal to GNP minus capital consumption allowances or depreciation. Such a tax may be imposed in multiple-stage form by taxing the *net* value added by each firm, with net value added defined as gross receipts minus purchases of intermediate goods and depreciation.[25] The same result may also be accomplished by a general income tax, since the bases of a net product and an income tax are in fact the same. The value-added tax of the income type thus differs from that of the consumption type in that the former permits the firm to deduct depreciation while the latter permits it to deduct gross investment, i.e., purchase of capital goods.[26]

---

[25]Such a tax could not be imposed as a tax on the total *net* value of the product when the last sale is made, since this procedure would require the recording of depreciation costs incurred by all producers further down the line. Thus, only the value-added approach is feasible if a sales tax is to be imposed on net product.

[26]The base of the income-type tax therefore exceeds that of the consumption-type tax by the difference between gross investment I_g and depreciation D, i.e., by net investment I_n. Disregarding governmental purchases, indirect business taxes, and net exports, this relationship is

Consumption Type   Next, consider a tax which is to be imposed on consumption only. This may be accomplished in any of three ways, namely, a flat-rate consumer expenditure tax inserted at point 2 in Figure 10-1; a retail sales tax inserted at point 3; or a tax on the incremental value added in the production of consumer goods. The last method is referred to as the consumption type of value-added tax.

The base of the value-added tax is now defined as the firm's gross receipts minus the value of all its purchases of intermediate products (materials and goods in process) as well as its capital expenditures on plant and equipment. By permitting each firm to deduct its capital expenditures, we are left with the value of consumer goods output only. Such a tax, therefore, is equivalent to a general retail sales tax on consumer goods, the two differing in administrative procedure only.

Features of Consumption-Type Value-Added Tax

As noted earlier in this chapter, there is nothing to be said for a value-added tax of the GNP type. The choice between the income and the consumption bases is less evident and, as we have pointed out, involves both efficiency and equity considerations. However, income is already taxed under the income tax which, as a personal tax, is superior to an income-type but in rem value-added tax. A good case can be made, therefore, for relating a possible value-added tax to the consumption base as is, in fact, done in the current European usage of this tax.

Size of Base   The size of the tax base for a consumption-type value-added tax is similar to that of a retail-type sales tax on consumer goods. As was shown in Table 20-3, the base depends greatly on the breadth of coverage, ranging from $818 billion for a broad-based tax (1976 data) to $380 billion for a narrowly defined base. Thus, the former falls short of consumer expenditures by one-quarter, while the latter falls short by 65 percent. Although the retail sales and value-added taxes tend to be thought of as general taxes, in reality they are far below this goal of complete generality.

An Illustration   An illustrative computation of the various types of value-added tax is given in Table 20-5.

---

brought out by the following identities:

$$GNP = I_g + C$$
$$I_g = D + I_n$$
$$NNP = I_n + C$$
$$NY = NNP$$

where NNP is net national product, NY is national income, I_g is gross investment, I_n is net investment, D is depreciation, and C is consumption. Note that $GNP - D$, equal to NNP or NY, is the base of the income-type value-added tax; and that $GNP - I_g$, or $GNP - (I_n + D) = C$, is the base of the consumption-type value-added tax.

TABLE 20-5
Illustration of Value-Added Tax Bases

	FIRMS			
	A	B	C	Economy
Current Receipts				
1. Sale of consumer goods	—	70	151	221
2. Sale of intermediate goods	120	45	—	165
3. Sale of capital goods	—	100	—	100
4. Total	120	215	151	
Current Costs				
5. Wages, interest, profits, etc.	100	80	90	270
6. Purchase of intermediate goods	—	120	45	165
7. Depreciation	20	15	16	51
8. Total	120	215	151	
Capital Costs				
9. Purchase of capital goods	—	—	100	100
Tax Bases				
10. Consumption base (line 4 minus line 6 minus line 9)	120	95	6	221
11. Income base (line 4 minus line 6 minus line 7)	100	80	90	270
12. GNP base	120	95	106	321
National Accounts				
13. Consumption				221
14. Plus investment				100
15. GNP				321
16. Minus depreciation				51
17. National net product (NNP) or national income (NY)				270

The consumption base, shown in line 10, is computed for each firm by taking total sales receipts (line 4) and deducting the purchase of intermediate and capital goods (lines 6 and 9).[27] The income base, shown in line 11, is computed for each firm as sales (line 4) minus the cost of intermediate goods and depreciation (lines 6 and 7). The GNP base, shown in line 12, finally equals total sales (line 4) minus the purchase of intermediate goods (line 6). Adding the bases for the three firms, we obtain the base for the entire economy. As shown in the last column, the total bases in turn equal the values of consumption, national income, and GNP as defined in the national income accounts.

---

[27]The text shows derivation of the three bases in line with the so-called deduction method. Alternatively, an "addition method" may be used. For the income base, this simply involves the addition of various factor payments included in line 5. The GNP base is determined by adding factor payments and depreciation (lines 5 and 7). The consumption base is determined by adding factor payments and depreciation (lines 5 and 7) while deducting the purchase of capital goods (line 9). Thus, the addition method is readily applicable to the income type but clumsy for the consumption type of value-added tax.

Collection Method   Taking the consumption type of value-added tax, we have seen that each firm computes its tax base as sales minus purchases of intermediate and capital goods. When it has done so, there are two possibilities for collecting the tax. One, the so-called accounts method, is to ask each firm to pay its tax on the base thus determined. Another, the so-called invoice method, is to have the firm compute its gross tax by applying the tax rate to total sales, and then to credit against this tax an amount equal to the tax already paid by the suppliers from which the firm has purchased intermediate and capital goods.[28] By making the tax credit for each firm contingent on presentation of the tax receipt made out to the preceding supplier, the invoice method includes a self-enforcing element as each buyer will demand copy of such receipt. The invoice method is used generally in European countries and constitutes an advantage of the value-added approach, especially in countries where tax compliance is otherwise poor.

Retail Sales versus Value-Added Tax   We have seen that the value-added tax of the consumption type has the same base as a retail sales tax with corresponding coverage. This being so, why should there be such a strong difference of opinion regarding which of the two taxes is preferable?

One difference relates to the politics of the matter. Proponents of the value-added tax feel that it "looks" different and thus may not share the traditional disrepute of a retail sales tax. This may or may not be the case. If the retailer's gross tax is shown as a separate part of the consumer's price, the consumer should be equally aware of his or her tax under either approach. Beyond this political consideration, there are some technical differences in implementation which are of importance.

Under the retail tax, the number of taxpayers is less than under the value-added tax. This facilitates administration provided that retailers can be reached effectively. In the United States setting, this would be feasible, but in other countries (especially in developing countries where retail establishments are small), it might not be. Under the value-added tax, on the other hand, exclusion of capital goods may be accomplished more effectively than under the retail sales tax, where it is difficult to trace the use of items purchased from the retailer. Furthermore, under the invoice method of collection, the value-added tax has an element of self-enforcement which the retail sales tax lacks.

These and other points may be cited in favor of one or the other approach, but most important is the question of how a federal consumption tax, if it were to be introduced, would relate to the existing consumption taxes at the state level. Since these taxes are in retail form, their integration with a federal consumption tax would be much easier if the latter were also imposed at the retail level. In this case, state taxes could be levied as supplements to

---

[28]See section on value-added tax in R. A. Musgrave (ed.), *Broad Based Taxes: New Options and Sources*, A Supplementary Paper of the Committee for Economic Development, Baltimore: Johns Hopkins, 1973, especially the contributions by John F. Due, Charles E. McLure, Jr., and Carl S. Shoup.

the federal tax and the duplicative administrative costs of a federal value-added tax could be avoided. Just as, in the income tax field, we are now in the process of using the federal income tax as a base for state income tax collection, so an integrated system of consumption taxation would be preferable to a set of separate tax administrations. Since it would be exceedingly difficult to integrate a federal value-added tax with retail taxes at the state level, the conclusion is that a federal consumption tax, if it were to be imposed, should also take the retail form.

F. SUMMARY

The role of sales taxation in the United States tax structure is characterized as follows:

1. About 60 percent of sales tax revenue accrues to the states and most of the remainder to the federal government.

2. About one-third of the total comes from general retail sales taxes imposed at the state level. The remainder comes from selective taxes, with nearly one-half thereof drawn from the taxation of tobacco, liquor, and gasoline.

There are various ways in which sales taxes may be imposed and administered. These are the major differences:

3. General sales taxes may be GNP- or consumption-based.

4. Consumption-based taxes may be comprehensive or more narrowly defined.

5. Selective taxes may be designed to serve as benefit taxes, to discriminate against demerit goods, or simply to be imposed on readily available transactions.

6. Sales taxes may be single- or multiple-stage.

7. Single-stage taxes may be imposed at the manufacturing, wholesale, or retail level.

8. Multiple-stage taxes may be of the turnover or value-added variety. Whereas the former is undesirable, the latter may serve as a helpful way of administering what, in its final result, is similar to a single-stage tax at the retail level.

Sales taxes have generally been considered as regressive, and have thus been contrasted with the progressive income tax:

9. The regressive nature of the sales tax arises because it falls on consumption, and consumption as a percentage of income declines when moving up the income scale.

10. Regressivity may be reduced considerably by the exemption of certain mass-consumption items or by the granting of a credit against income tax.

11. The linkage between regressivity and consumption taxation could be broken by the use of a personalized expenditure tax.

12. Such a tax would avoid some of the major difficulties of the income tax but it would also give rise to new ones.

While a personalized and progressive expenditure tax would be a genuinely new form of taxation, the value-added tax is simply a sales tax which is administered in a multiple-stage form:

13. Value-added taxes may be of the consumption or income type.

14. A consumption-type value-added tax is equivalent to a retail sales tax on consumer goods.

15. The value-added approach offers administrative advantages as well as disadvantages.

FURTHER READINGS

Due, John F.: *State and Local Sales Taxation*, Chicago: Public Administration Service, 1971.

Kaldor, N.: *An Expenditure Tax*, London: G. Allen, 1955.

Minarik, John J. (ed.): *What to Tax; Income or Expenditure?* Washington: Brookings, 1979.

Pechman, Joseph A.: *Federal Tax Policy*, 3d ed., Washington: Brookings, 1977, chap. 6 and references, p. 384.

Shoup, Carl S.: *Public Finance*, Chicago: Aldine, 1969, chap. 9 on value-added tax.

APPENDIX: Incidence of Unit and Ad Valorem Taxes

I. PRICE AND OUTPUT EFFECTS OF A UNIT AND AN AD VALOREM TAX UNDER COMPETITION

Given a linear demand schedule for product X relating average revenue (AR) or price to quantity sold (Q),

$$AR = a - bQ$$

and a linear market supply schedule relating averge unit cost (AC) to Q,

$$AC = c + dQ$$

the industry is in equilibrium where demand and supply intersect at a quantity Q_0 such that $AR = AC$ or $a - bQ_0 = c + dQ_0$ and

$$Q_0 = \frac{a - c}{b + d}$$

with

$$P_0 = a - b\left(\frac{a - c}{b + d}\right)$$

Unit Tax

After a unit tax u is imposed, the average net revenue schedule AR_n becomes

$$AR_n = a - bQ - u$$

and the gross price P_t is

$$P_t = a - b\left(\frac{a - c - u}{b + d}\right)$$

The change in the gross price $(P_t - P_0)$ then is

$$\Delta P = \frac{bu}{b + d}$$

Under conditions of constant cost, $d = 0$ and the change in price reduces to $\Delta P = u$.

Ad Valorem Tax

For the case of an ad valorem tax, it is convenient to define the tax rate t_g as applying to gross or market price, such that tax per unit $T = t_g P_g$ rather than as t_n where $T = t_n P_n$. While the t_n version is used in the tax statutes, use of the t_g version simplifies the algebraic statement. Since $t_g = t_n/(1 + t_n)$, the results may be adapted by substituting t_n thus defined for the t_g in our equations. For the case of an ad valorem tax imposed at rate $t = t_g$, the average net revenue schedule then becomes

$$AR_n = (1 - t)(a - bQ)$$

and the gross price becomes

$$P_t = a - b\left(\frac{a - ta - c}{b - tb + d}\right)$$

The change in price, therefore, is given by

$$\Delta P = bt\left[\frac{ab + bc}{(b + d)^2 - tb(b + d)}\right]$$

For the case of constant cost, this reduces to

$$\Delta P = \frac{ct}{1 - t}$$

We note that for the case of the unit tax, the change in price is a function of the slopes of the demand and supply schedules only, while for the ad valorem tax the intercepts of the two functions also enter as determinants of the price change. Given the value of u or of t, the resulting change in gross price from either tax will be the greater the larger is b (the slope of the demand function) and the smaller is d (the slope of the supply function).

II. PRICE AND OUTPUT EFFECTS OF UNIT AND AD
VALOREM TAXES UNDER MONOPOLY

In the case of a linear demand schedule, it may be shown that the increase in price under conditions of monopoly is one-half that of the competitive case. The average revenue schedule AR again is

$$AR = a - bQ$$

while the total revenue schedule TR is

$$TR = AR \cdot Q = aQ - bQ^2$$

Marginal revenue MR is thus

$$MR = \frac{dTR}{dQ} = a - 2bQ$$

The average cost schedule is again

$$AC = c + dQ$$

with total cost TC equal to

$$TC = cQ + dQ^2$$

and marginal cost MC equal to

$$MC = \frac{dTC}{dQ} = c + 2dQ$$

Setting MR equal to MC, we obtain

$$a - 2bQ_0 = c + 2dQ_0$$

or

$$Q_0 = \frac{a - c}{2(b + d)}$$

and the pretax price is

$$P_0 = a - b\left(\frac{a - c}{2(b + d)}\right)$$

Unit Tax

After imposition of a unit tax u, the net marginal revenue schedule becomes

$$MR_n = a - 2bQ - u$$

and the new quantity Q_t is obtained by setting $MR_n = MC$, so that

$$Q_t = \frac{a - c - u}{2(b + d)}$$

Thus, the gross price after tax (P_t) equals

$$P_t = a - b\left(\frac{a - c - u}{2(b + d)}\right)$$

and the change in price becomes

$$\Delta P = \frac{bu}{2(b + d)}$$

which equals one-half the change in the competitive price. For the constant cost case, where $d = 0$,

$$\Delta P = \frac{1}{2}u$$

Ad Valorem Tax

With imposition of an ad valorem tax at rate t, the net marginal revenue schedule now becomes

$$MR_n = (1 - t)(a - 2bQ)$$

and the new quantity where $MR_n = MC$ equals

$$Q_t = \frac{(1 - t)a - c}{2[(1 - t)b + d]}$$

and the gross posttax price then becomes

$$P_t = a - \frac{b}{2}\left(\frac{(1 - t)a - c}{(1 - t)b + d}\right)$$

Thus, the change in price resulting from the tax equals

$$\Delta P = \frac{bt}{2}\left(\frac{ad + bc}{(b + d)^2 - tb(b + d)}\right)$$

again one-half that for the competitive case.

III. MAXIMIZATION OF REVENUE UNDER A UNIT TAX

For a competitive industry and using linear schedules, let the demand schedule be defined by

$$P = a - bQ$$

and the supply schedule by

$$AC = c + dQ$$

After imposition of a unit tax (u), the net demand schedule becomes

$$P_n = a - bQ - u$$

with output equal to

$$Q_t = \frac{a - c - u}{b + d}$$

Tax revenue then equals

$$R = uQ_t = u\frac{(a - c - u)}{b + d}$$

Differentiating this expression, we obtain

$$\frac{dR}{du} = \frac{a - c - 2u}{b + d}$$

To maximize tax revenue, we set $dR/du = 0$ and obtain

$$u = \frac{a - c}{2}$$

Given the intercepts of the demand and supply functions, the rate of tax giving the maximum yield is thus independent of the slopes of the schedules.

Chapter 21

Property and Wealth Taxes*

A. Rationale for Wealth Taxation: *Benefit Considerations; Ability-to-Pay Considerations; Social Control; Taxation of Land; Conclusions.* **B. Composition and Distribution of Wealth:** *Stock of Wealth; Distribution of Wealth Holdings.* **C. Structure and Base of Property Tax:** *History; Tax Base; Nominal Rates, Assessment Ratios, and Effective Rates; Market Value versus Income as Assessment Base; Land versus Improvement Components of Base.* **D. Burden Distribution of Property Tax:** *Property Tax as Tax on Capital Income; Alternative View; Circuit Breaker.* **E. Appraisal and Outlook for Property Tax. F. Net Worth Tax:** *Foreign Experience; Structure and Base; Role of Intangibles.* **G. Capital Levy. H. Summary.**

Having considered the taxation of income and expenditure *flows*, we now turn to that of *stocks*, i.e., of wealth. Such taxes may be imposed on pieces of property (payable by the owner) and thus be of the impersonal, in rem type; or they may be imposed on the combined property holdings of a person, or on his net worth, thus being in the nature of a personal tax.

---

* Readers' Guide to Chapter 21: This chapter examines the role of wealth taxation in the tax system. The property tax, though the oldest tax in the United States tax structure, has always been controversial and is currently again in the center of tax debate. Both its weight in the overall tax structure and its role in local government finance are discussed.

In the United States the term "property tax" is applied to an in rem tax on pieces of real property. As previously noted in Table 10-1, this tax was the most important single source in the United States tax structure up to the 1930s. Thereafter, its relative importance declined sharply because of the rise of income taxation. The property tax, nevertheless, continued to dominate the local tax scene and still furnishes over 80 percent of revenue at that level. Indeed, property taxation in recent decades has been almost entirely local, as the United States has no federal property tax and the property tax lost its former importance for state revenue prior to World War II.

A. RATIONALE FOR WEALTH TAXATION

Some argument for wealth taxation may be made on both benefit and ability-to-pay grounds, but neither suggests a tax such as the existing property tax, imposed more or less uniformly on real property only. Benefit considerations point to a set of in rem–type property taxes on real assets while ability-to-pay considerations point to a personal tax on net worth.

Benefit Considerations

The benefit rationale for wealth taxation is that public services increase the value of real properties and should therefore be paid for by the owners. In its most general form, the supporting argument may be derived from Locke's theory of the state as a protector of property, expounded toward the close of the seventeenth century. One of the basic functions of the state, as seen by the natural-law theorists, is the protection of property; and property owners should therefore pay for the state's expenses. Whatever the merits of the premise as a theory of state, its logic points to a comprehensive tax, including a person's entire property (intangible as well as real property) in the base. Better still, the base would be defined in terms of *net* worth, i.e., the taxpayer's property minus his or her liabilities. Also, in the spirit of this approach, revenue from this tax would be limited to cover the cost incurred in rendering protection services, such as the cost of law enforcement, legislation, and judicial administration. While the range of includable costs is debatable, certainly not all governmental functions would be covered. Use of the property tax for education finance, for instance, cannot be rationalized in this way.

A more specific application of the benefit rule, pertinent especially at the local level, suggests that property owners should pay for particular services which go to raise property values. Building a sidewalk, for instance, increases the values of adjoining homes, as does the rendering of police protection in the precinct. In some cases, the specific benefit share derived by any one property may be measured by indices such as the length of its road frontage or its location. In others, benefit shares may have to be approximated by relative property values. This line of reasoning, however, does not point to a general tax on real property. Rather, it indicates special charges or assessments, imposed to finance particular services. Such assessments, which are a special form of user charge or of public pricing, are especially made use of in local finance, but so far remain of only minor importance in the overall picture. As noted above, a good case can be made for wider use of such charges.[1]

To make a benefit case for the general property tax as now applied, one would have to maintain that all real property benefits equally from local public services and that the value of such benefits equals the property tax yield. Neither proposition holds. The bulk of property tax revenue goes to provide general public services such as education, the benefits from which need not be distributed in line with property ownership. A general tax on real property, therefore, is a poor instrument for charging for services rendered. A classified tax, with differential rates by type of property (grouped in line with benefits received) might do better, but other indicators would be superior. Thus income or family size might be a better proxy than value of residences for general benefits received by individuals, and value added might be a better proxy than business structures for benefits to firms.

A more subtle benefit argument in support of a local property tax arises from differential service levels among communities. If the level of public services is higher in community A than in community B, this difference will be reflected in higher house values in A. Such will be the case provided that residence in A is prerequisite to the enjoyment of this higher service level. Thus, homeowners in A may be said to benefit, even though the services are not directly housing-related. A benefit link is established, via the capitalization of service benefits, between ownership and the service level. However, this link is a tenuous one and applies only to the extent that service levels in A exceed those in B. The argument does not give benefit-taxation status to the total property tax but only to the differential. If the service level were the same in both A and B (in other words, if the same services were rendered to capital everywhere), there would be no reason for its being reflected in the value of assets. Moreover, if pursued carefully the analysis points to a tax on ground rent rather than a tax on total property values. The reason is that capital will move, thus equalizing net (after-tax) returns, whereas land cannot move between jurisdictions.

Ability-to-Pay Considerations

Consider now the case for wealth taxation from the point of view of ability to pay. As noted previously, there is no single tax base which is best under all circumstances. In the Colonial period, real estate and personal property (such as cattle) were the most convenient index of "faculty," or ability to pay. A significant share of income was received in kind, so that money income as it is now defined would have been a misleading index. But under modern conditions, income is received largely in money form and wealth is more difficult to measure than income. Under these circumstances, can property taxation still be justified on ability-to-pay grounds and, if so, in what form?

[1] See p. 240.

When considering the use of wealth as a measure of taxpaying ability, we concluded that a tax on wealth, being a supplementary tax on capital income, is not called for if capital income is already taxed under a comprehensive income tax.[2] But we also noted that a wealth tax may be useful in supplementing incomplete coverage of capital income under the income tax. While it may be difficult to reach capital income in developing countries, real property is readily visible to the tax collector and a real property tax, though only a crude substitute, may be used effectively where the income tax fails. Even where the income tax works fairly well, the base of wealth taxation is broader in some respects, as nonearning as well as earning assets are included. However, if wealth is to be taxed on ability-to-pay grounds, what is called for is not an in rem tax on real property but a personal tax on net worth.[3]

This has important implications. First of all, the tax should be imposed on individuals only, with business property being imputed to its owners. Second, the tax should be imposed on an individual's net worth, rather than on the gross value of his or her assets. Both sides of the balance sheet should be considered. Just as a determination of net income involves deduction of interest paid on business debt, so should a person's net worth be determined by deducting his or her liabilities from assets. Third, the tax should be imposed uniformly rather than through differential charges against particular pieces of property. All assets (tangible and intangible) should be included and all debts should be deducted. The principle of global assessment should apply as under the income tax, with exemptions and progressive rates related to the taxpayer's total net worth.

Social Control

Alternatively, the taxation of wealth may be approached not as a matter of charging for benefits received or of ability to pay, but as a form of social control. The social consequences of inequality in the distribution of wealth, as is easily seen, differ from those in the distribution of consumption, so that society may wish to deal with them separately. For this purpose, a progressive tax on wealth, rather than on income, is the proper instrument. As under the ability-to-pay approach, the indication is again for a personal tax and a global wealth definition.[4] But it might now be argued that the base should be defined in terms of gross rather than net wealth, since it is the former which determines the scope of economic control which the owner derives.

Taxation of Land

The singling out of land (as distinct from taxable property in general) has been advocated on both efficiency and equity grounds. Since the return to land is in the nature of economic rent (being a return to a factor of

---

[2]See p. 248.

[3]For a development of this view and a plea for a net worth tax, see Lester C. Thurow, "Net Worth Taxes," *National Tax Journal*, September 1972; and Thurow, *The Impact of Taxes on the American Economy*, New York: Praeger, 1971, chap. 7.

[4]See p. 249.

production in inelastic supply), it may be taxed without giving rise to an "excess burden." Indeed, land taxation may be used, especially in developing countries, to encourage more intensive utilization. Moreover, gains derived from increases in land values may be considered unjust enrichment, as initially argued by Henry George.[5]

Conclusions

Wealth taxation may be advocated on various grounds, each calling for a different type of tax. While the benefit view points to differentiated taxes or charges on particular items of real property, the ability-to-pay approach points to a global and personal tax on net worth. The rationale for a uniform property tax based largely upon realty, as reflected in the existing property tax, is more difficult to establish. However, we should note that it is a convenient means of local taxation and one which is not likely to be dispensed with in the foreseeable future.

B. COMPOSITION AND DISTRIBUTION OF WEALTH

While ample data on the distribution of income are available, statistics on the composition and distribution of wealth are very imperfect. Nevertheless, some picture of the scope and nature of the tax base may be derived and is needed to assess the potential of wealth taxation.

Stock of Wealth

The composition of privately held wealth in the United States for 1975 is given in Table 21-1. Privately held real wealth is estimated at about $4.4 trillion. With a GNP of $1.5 trillion in that year, wealth holdings are about 3 times GNP. The major categories are housing, business plant and equipment, and consumer durables. Financial assets held by the private sector (including public debt and outside money) add nearly another $500 million.[6] The resulting total of $4.8 trillion equals the combined net worth of the private sector. It falls short of national wealth because wealth owned by government is excluded. As shown below, it substantially exceeds assessed value under the property tax.

Distribution of Wealth Holdings

While there is much data available on the distribution of income, that on the distribution of wealth is very scarce. However, there is ample evidence that the distribution of wealth among wealth holders is substantially more unequal than that of income among income recipients. This may be seen in Table 21-2.

[5]Henry George, *Progress and Poverty*, New York: Appleton, 1882.

[6]Private debt is excluded because it enters as both an asset into the balance sheet of the creditor and as a liability into that of the debtor. The same holds for deposits or inside money which, though an asset to the holder, is canceled by debt owed to banks. Outside money (Federal Reserve credit and currency in circulation) is not offset by private debt and hence is included.

TABLE 21-1
Composition of Privately Held Wealth, 1975

	Billions of Dollars
Real Assets	
Structures	
1. Residential, owner-occupied	953
2. Residential, rented	351
3. Nonresidential, nonfarm	710
4. Farm structures	21
Land	
5. Nonfarm	706
6. Farm	36
Other	
7. Business equipment	500
8. Inventories	600
9. Consumer durables	497
10. Total, real assets	4,374
Financial Assets, Net	
11. Public debt, privately held	303
12. Outside money	174
13. Total, financial assets	477
14. All privately held wealth	4,851

Notes:
Line 7: We assume that out of total equipment of $544 billion, $44 billion is publicly owned.
Line 12: Includes Federal Reserve credit and currency in circulation.
Sources:
Lines 1–10: U.S. Bureau of the Census, *Statistical Abstract of the United States,* 1976, p. 428.
Lines 11 and 12: *Economic Report of the President,* January 1978, pp. 330 and 347.

TABLE 21-2
Distribution of Income and Wealth

Groups	Percentage of Income Received by Percentage of Income Recipients		Percentage of Wealth Owned by Percentage of Wealth Owners
	All Income	Capital Income*	
Lowest 20 percent	5†	2	—
Top 20 percent	41†	74	75‡
Top 1 percent	5*	12	24§

*Based on U.S. Treasury Department, *Individual Income Tax Returns, Preliminary Statistics of Income for 1975,* 1977.
†See U.S. Bureau of the Census, *Statistical Abstract of the United States,* 1976, p. 406.
‡Based on Dorothy S. Projector, "Survey of Changes in Consumer Finances," Board of Governors of the Federal Reserve System, 1968, pp. 318, 320.
§See U.S. Bureau of the Census, *Statistical Abstract of the United States,* 1976, p. 427. Ratio is for 1972.

Whereas the top 1 percent of wealth owners hold an estimated 24 percent of personal wealth, the top 1 percent of income recipients receive 5 percent of all income. The top 20 percent of wealth holders own 75 percent of wealth, as against 41 percent of income accruing to the top 20 percent of income recipients. The lowest 20 percent of wealth holders are without significant holdings, while the lowest 20 percent of income recipients receive 5 percent of all income. The distribution of wealth holding as shown in the table is rather more similar to the distribution of capital income, although even here the distribution of wealth shows a somewhat higher degree of inequality.[7]

C. STRUCTURE AND BASE OF PROPERTY TAX

We now take a closer look at the local property tax, which is *the* major representative of wealth taxation in our tax system. As previously noted, it is still the third most important tax in the United States and practically the sole source of local finance.

History

The American property tax has its origins in early American history. Initially, it was assessed on selected items of property such as land and cattle, with different rates imposed on various categories. This "classified" property tax was the main source of revenue to the Colonies. During the eighteenth and nineteenth centuries, a greater variety of property emerged, making it difficult to maintain such differentiation. Thus, the tax developed into a general and uniform-rate tax. This uniform tax was applied to property independent of form, with total property viewed as a general measure of taxable capacity. Subsequently, this approach gave way under the increasing complexity of property forms. The growing importance of intangible property, in particular, made it increasingly difficult to apply a general tax on a comprehensive base. By the end of the century, the general property tax had been supplanted by a much narrower approach. It became a selective tax on real estate and business personalty (i.e., equipment and inventory) and has remained so ever since. Tangible property, other than real estate, held by persons now largely escapes tax, and no attempt is made to reach intangible property. While the share of the property tax in total tax revenue (including all levels) has declined from over 50 percent at the beginning of the century to around 10 percent at present, property tax revenue as a percentage of privately held wealth or as a percentage of GNP has not changed greatly over the last century. It is estimated that the revenue-wealth ratio has remained at about 1 percent.

---

[7]The above pattern is qualified if the capitalized value of social security benefits is included in the wealth distribution, in which case the share of the top 1 percent might drop to 19 percent. See Martin Feldstein, "Social Security and the Distribution of Wealth," *Journal of the American Statistical Association*, December 1976. The question arises as to whether such inclusion should not be matched by allowing for negative wealth corresponding to the capitalized value of future payroll contributions.

The property tax in the United States originated as a local tax and has continued as such. In 1975 it accounted for 82 percent of local tax revenue, its importance being greatest for school districts (98 percent), followed by townships (92 percent) and counties (82 percent). The share was lower, however, for municipalities (61 percent) which are increasingly developing additional revenue sources.[8] Not only does property tax revenue accrue almost entirely to local government but the tax is imposed locally. It thus differs greatly between localities in both rates and administrative procedure. While some guidance is provided by state legislation and certain types of property (such as railroads and utilities) are assessed by the state, assessment is still far from equalized. The United States property tax differs sharply in this respect from that of other countries, such as the United Kingdom, where the system of "rates" is administered as a national tax although revenue goes to local governments. Among the larger countries, only Canada has a decentralized property tax of the United States type.

Tax Base

The distribution of property tax revenue by type of tax base is shown in Table 21-3 for 1975. The revenue was divided about equally between nonbusiness and business property. In the nonbusiness sector, almost the entire amount came from residential realty, with farm realty, vacant lots, and personalty (i.e., personal property other than real estate) contributing only 8 percent. In the business category, over one-half came from realty and one-quarter from personalty (including, in this case, inventory and part of business machinery).

Turning to the underlying tax base, we find that the total assessed value for 1976 was reported at $1,216 billion. Of this, $982 billion was in the form of locally assessed real property.[9] The market value of included property, however, was substantially larger since property for tax purposes is assessed below market value. Using an average assessment ratio of one-third, the market value of assessed property for 1976 was about $3.6 trillion. If we estimate the 1976 value of all eligible real property at $4.5 trillion, it appears that about 80 percent thereof was accounted for by the property tax base, with a good part of the remainder reflecting tax-exempt institutions whose holdings do not appear on the assessment rolls. The breakdown of the tax base among types of property again shows residential real estate as the major component. Census data for 1976 show 50 percent of assessed values to have been from single-family houses, 10 percent from other residential property, 16 percent from vacant lots and acreage, and 24 percent from commercial and industrial property.[10]

---

[8]See U.S. Bureau of the Census, *Governmental Finances in 1975–76,* 1977, p. 29.
[9]U.S. Bureau of the Census, *Assessed Valuations for Local General Property Taxation,* 1977 Census of Governments, Preliminary Report No. 2, November 1977, p. 3.
[10]Ibid., p. 3.

TABLE 21-3
Property Tax Revenue by Type of Base, 1975
(In Millions of Dollars)

Nonbusiness	
Nonfarm residential realty	23,680
Farm realty	1,017
Vacant lots	398
Personalty	959
Total	26,053
Business	
Farm realty	2,315
Vacant lots	597
Other realty	11,415
Personalty	5,901
Public utilities	3,758
Total	23,987
Total	50,040

Source: See Advisory Commission on Intergovernmental Relations, *Federal-State-Local Finances: Significant Features of Fiscal Federalism,* Washington: 1976–77, p. 106.

Nominal Rates, Assessment Ratios, and Effective Rates

In judging the level of property taxation, it is important to distinguish between the nominal and the effective rate, the latter being the product of nominal rate and assessment ratio.[11] With an assessed value of $1.2 trillion and estimated market value of $3.6 trillion, the 1976 revenue of $57 billion gives an effective rate of 1.6 percent and a nominal rate of 5 percent. Applied to a base of $1,000, this gives a "mill rate" of $50.

Since it is the effective rate that matters, it would seem to make little difference whether properties are assessed at full market value or less. Depending on the required revenue, a lower assessment ratio simply means that the nominal rate has to be correspondingly higher. Such indeed would be the case if all properties were subject to the same assessment ratio. Actually, assessment ratios differ between jurisdictions, and within any one jurisdiction among types of property, a condition that causes inequities to arise.

Differentials between Jurisdictions   In comparing levels of property tax rates between jurisdictions, differences in nominal rates must not be taken to stand for differences in effective rates. Jurisdictions with high nominal rates tend to have low assessment ratios, and those with low nominal rates tend to have high assessment ratios. As a result, the dispersion of nominal rates is significantly greater than that of effective rates. Thus, in 1971 nominal rates ranged from over 15 percent for the highest 10 percent to under 5 percent for

---

[11] We have $T = t_n AV$ and $AV = rMV$, where T is the tax, t_n is the nominal rate, AV is the assessed value, r is the assessment ratio, and MV is the market value. Also, we have $t_e = T/MV$ where t_e is the effective rate. Thus we obtain $t_e = t_n r$.

the lowest 20 percent of cities. The corresponding range for effective rates was only from 3.7 percent to below 1.7 percent.[12]

Failure to apply a uniform assessment ratio across jurisdictions becomes exceedingly important when assessed values are used as a measure of fiscal capacity and considered in allocating state aid among local jurisdictions. To avoid this difficulty, an increasing number of states have introduced measures to secure uniform statewide assessment practices. Short of transferring the assessment function to the state level, full uniformity is difficult to bring about.

But even if assessment ratios were equalized, nominal rates and hence effective rates would still differ among jurisdictions. As a result, location decisions, whether by business or residents, may be affected by tax differentials, leading to inefficient location choices. This influence will be modified where higher rates of property taxation are indicative of higher service levels (rather than higher costs), so that tax differentials are offset by benefit differentials. However, such is not always the case. Resulting inefficiencies are a cost of fiscal decentralization which can be eliminated only by equalizing effective rates, at least across neighboring jurisdictions, such as units within a metropolitan area. This equalization, however, involves moving toward a more centralized revenue system, with the likely result of reduced variety on the expenditure side.

Differentials within Jurisdictions   While the same nominal rate applies to different types of property in any one jurisdiction, assessment ratios may differ. Thus it is estimated that the 1971 average assessment ratio for the United States as a whole was 33 percent for residential real estate, 34 percent for commercial and industrial real estate, 28 percent for vacant lots, and 22 percent for acreage.[13] In some jurisdictions, these differentials are substantially larger. There is a tendency, in large cities in particular, for business property to be assessed at a higher rate than residential housing, and for multiunit houses to be assessed at a higher rate than single-unit residences. These differentials are not accidental but reflect a desire to impose the property tax at differential rates. Under most state constitutions this is not permitted, but in six states, with Massachusetts the most recent addition, the constitution permits classification, with different assessment ratios applied to different groups of property. This ranges from 22 separate classes in Minnesota to the more customary scheme of distinguishing between residential, commercial, and industrial properties only.

As distinct from differentiating between types of property, which may meet a legitimate policy objective, actual practice also results in substantial and unjustifiable differentiation between specific properties within the same general category. In a census study for 1971, for example, 49 percent of the

---

[12]Approximate ratios, based on U.S. Bureau of the Census, *Taxable Property Values*, 1972 Census of Governments, vol. 2, p. 19.

[13]Ibid., p. 9.

covered sample areas showed coefficients of dispersion in the assessment ratio for nonfarm houses of below 20 percent, 30 percent had ratios from 20 to 30 percent, and the remainder had ratios above 30 percent.[14] Or, to offer another illustration, effective rates of tax on single-family houses within the city of Boston ranged from 3.6 percent in the lowest rate quartile to 5.1 percent in the third quartile, with a median ratio of 4.2 percent.[15] These are substantial divergencies, introducing a capricious element of differentiation into the property tax. Although complete conformity in effective rates is difficult to obtain, experts argue that the coefficient of dispersion for single-family houses should not exceed 20 percent.

For all these reasons, sound property tax administration calls for a uniform assessment at 100 percent of value. Unless this is done, it is unlikely that uniform effective rates can be obtained. If there is to be deliberate differentiation between classes of property, i.e., if the property tax is to be classified, this should be provided for explicitly by varying nominal rates and not assessment ratios.

Market Value versus Income as Assessment Base

In addition to the need for equalized assessment, there is the more basic question of how property values should be measured. Should property be assessed on sales or rental income values and should use be made of actual or potential values? The United States approach has been in terms of sales or market value, while the British tradition has been to assess on the basis of actual rental income derived from the asset. Assuming perfect markets and optimal utilization, this difference disappears since the sales value of property equals the capitalized value of actual income and the latter is equal to its income-earning potential. But under realistic conditions, this equality does not hold.

If property is underutilized, assessment on the income base yields a lower value. Such assessment, therefore, discriminates in favor of underutilization. This has adverse incentive effects, especially in developing countries. Little or no income may be received as land is held idle for speculative purposes or as potentially productive farmland is used for grazing only. In other instances, real estate, such as vacation homes, may be left idle or rented at nominal charges for part of the year. If assessment is based on market value, such understatement of assessed value is less likely to arise since market values are likely to reflect alternative and more profitable uses. However, where markets are imperfect, recorded sales values may also fall short of the potential. To assure full assessment, determination of potential income or market value is required. This is feasible only if up-to-date and accurate cadastral surveys are available, a precondition which is usually not met in developing countries. As an alternative, it has been proposed that the determination of full value be

---

[14]Ibid., p. 55. The coefficient measures the average deviation from the median assessment ratio.
[15]Ibid., p. 127.

obtained through a system of self-assessment, under which the property owner would be required to sell the property at a price equal to his or her declared value. This is an ingenious proposal, but its implementation would be difficult if at all feasible.[16]

Another difference between the market value and income approaches stems from differences in risk. One property with an annual income of $100,000 may have a market value of $500,000, while another property with the same income may have twice that market value. Incomes are capitalized at different rates of interest or, to put it differently, at gross rates which add different risk premiums to the market rate on safe investment. This is the case with regard to properties in urban slums which have high yields of income relative to market values. Such properties do better under the market value approach than under the income base of assessment. Where such differences exist, the market value offers the better base since the income base should be corrected to allow for differences in risk.

Short of a major effort to determine potential as distinct from actual income, market value is the preferable approach. At the same time, even the determination of true market value poses a difficult problem, especially in developing countries.

Land versus Improvement Components of Base

The property tax is imposed on the market value of a given piece of real estate without a distinction being drawn between its land and improvement components. Yet, from an economic point of view, this is an important distinction; it will be examined when we deal with the incidence of this tax.

Since the supply of land is given, taxing the rent of land or imposing a tax on the value of land (reflecting the capitalized value of its rent) has long been recognized as a form of taxation which is least likely to deter incentives to invest in improvements.[17] Moreover, the windfalls which arise from rising land values due to population and income growth might be considered as socially unwarranted gains. This indeed was the main theme of Henry George's *Progress and Poverty*, which swept the United States in the 1890s and gave rise to the single-tax movement, calling for exclusive reliance on land taxation.[18] Unfortunately, the exaggerated claims on behalf of the single tax have interfered with a continuing and strong case for taxing site values at a higher rate.

In fact, actual practice frequently does the very opposite. As will be noted later, urban property tax, by placing a tax burden on improvements, has discouraged such investment, especially in low-income housing. A heavier tax on land value, combined with a lighter tax on improvement, would have slowed rather than accelerated urban decay.[19]

---

[16]See John D. Strasma, "Market-Enforced Self-Assessment for Real Estate Taxes," *Bulletin for International Fiscal Documentation*, September and October 1965.

[17]Land being fixed in supply, no excess burden results from its taxation. See p. 290.

[18]Henry George, op. cit.

[19]See Dick Netzer, "The Local Property Tax," in G. E. Peterson (ed.), *Property Tax Reform*, Washington: The Urban Institute, 1973, p. 23 and p. 571.

D. BURDEN DISTRIBUTION OF PROPERTY TAX

The incidence of the property tax is controversial. One view takes it to be a tax on capital income, imposed in competitive markets; another differentiates by type of assessed base and places more weight on the consequences of market imperfections.

Property Tax as Tax on Capital Income

We begin with the former view, which has gained increasing acceptance among economists in recent years.

National Tax Suppose first that there existed a truly national tax on all capital assets. As noted in our earlier discussion of incidence, a tax on capital assets may then be viewed as a tax on capital income. Given perfect capital markets and assessment procedures, a 5 percent tax imposed on the value of an asset may readily be translated into an income tax on the income derived from the asset. Suppose that an asset worth $1,000 yields an annual income of $100, in line with a 10 percent market rate of interest. The liability under a 5 percent tax on the asset value is $50. Expressed as a percentage of the asset's income, it equals 50 percent. The 5 percent tax on the asset value (or property tax) is thus equivalent to a 50 percent tax on the property income (or income tax). Putting it more generally, the value of an asset in a perfect capital market is given by $Y = iV$, so that $V = Y/i$ where V is its value, Y is its annual income, and i is the market rate of interest obtainable on other investments.[20] If the same yield is to be obtained from a property tax at rate t_p and a tax on income therefrom at rate t_y, we must have $t_p Y/i = t_y Y$ or $t_p = it_y$.

In a market where capital yields a 10 percent return, the incidence of a general tax on the value of capital assets imposed at a rate of $5 per $100 of asset value is thus the same as that of a 50 percent tax on capital income. This being so, all that has been said above about the incidence of a general tax on capital income again applies. With incidence determined primarily from the sources side, such a tax reduces the net return to capital and is absorbed by the recipients of capital income. With the exception of the bottom end, such income rises as a share of total income when we move up the income scale, so that incidence is progressive. In the longer run, the reduction in the net return to capital may depress the capital stock, thereby reducing future productivity of labor, so that it may come to share the burden. While this may qualify the outcome, the pattern of burden incidence set by the short-run effect is likely to be dominant. The resulting pattern of incidence is generally progressive, as was shown in line 7 of Table 12-2.[21]

---

[20]This capitalization formula holds for a perpetual income stream. The value of a finite annuity is given by

$$V = Y \frac{1 - (1+i)^{-n}}{i}$$

where n is the number of years over which the annual payments extend.

[21]See p. 270.

Local Tax   These conclusions are qualified though not basically changed by the fact that our property tax is not imposed at a uniform national rate but at widely varying local rates. If all local jurisdictions were to impose a tax at the same rate, the result would be similar to that of a national tax. But we have seen that they do not. Effective rates vary widely, whether the variation is due to differences in statutory rates or in assessment ratios. To understand how this affects incidence, suppose that a single jurisdiction raises its rate above the national level. What will happen?

In the *short run*, capital invested in the high-rate jurisdiction is immobile and its owners must bear whatever higher rates are imposed. As noted before for the corporation tax, the burden of partial taxes on capital income is capitalized and reduces the value of the property. This goes for improvements and sites alike. Short-run incidence is on the owners of the local property subject to the higher tax. Moreover, the burden is on the owners who held the property at the time the tax was raised. They cannot shake off the burden by selling the taxed asset.

To illustrate this, we assume again that the rate of return on capital before tax is 10 percent, so that an asset yielding $100 per year is worth $1,000. Now let a particular jurisdiction impose a property tax of $50 per $1,000 of property value. As noted before, this is equivalent to a 50 percent income tax. Net income is reduced to $50 which, capitalized at 10 percent, lowers the property value to $500. If the initial owner of the asset wishes to sell it, he or she must absorb the tax loss, since the buyer will want to obtain a net return of 10 percent, similar to that available from an investment elsewhere. The burden of the tax thus falls on the initial property owner, i.e., the owner of the property prior to the imposition of tax. Subsequent owners who purchase the old asset will do so at a lower price only and are not burdened by the tax. The loss has been capitalized and stays with the initial owner.

In the *long run*, that part of the tax which reflects land or site values remains fixed. Land cannot move, so that the original owners of land in the high-tax jurisdiction will thus suffer a permanent loss equal to their share in the tax. There is no difference in this case between the short-run and the long-run adjustment. Since income from the ownership of land is more important to high-income than to low-income groups, incidence is progressive.

The situation differs with regard to capital. Capital invested in improvements is not caught permanently. In the longer run, it will flee the high-tax jurisdiction and move to a jurisdiction where rates are lower. Maintenance expenditures on old assets will be reduced, and new investment in the high-rate jurisdiction will decline. As the capital stock in the higher-rate jurisdiction falls while that in the low-rate jurisdiction rises, the gross rate of return on capital in the former goes up while the rate of return in the latter declines. This movement continues until the *net* rate of return from investment in the high-tax jurisdiction equals the rate of return outside. The process ceases when net returns in various jurisdictions are equalized. As was the situation with the corporation tax, a tax imposed upon capital in one sector of the economy comes to be shared by the owners of capital at large.

The extent of capital outflow from the high-rate jurisdiction will depend on the outward mobility of labor. If labor can leave readily, it must be paid what it receives elsewhere and the capital outflow will have to be larger. If labor is locked in, the tax may be reflected in wage reduction, thus maintaining the earnings of capital without forcing it to leave. Since unskilled labor is less mobile than skilled labor, this introduces a regressive effect. But while labor in high-tax jurisdictions stands to lose, labor in low-tax jurisdictions (which, as a result of the adjustment, comes to have a more ample capital stock) will tend to gain.[22] Similarly, landlords and owners in the high-tax jurisdiction stand to lose from capital outflow, while their counterparts in the low-tax jurisdiction stand to gain from capital inflow. These effects may be of major importance if viewed from the perspective of a particular jurisdiction, although they may not greatly affect the overall or national burden distribution.

Inside versus Outside Burden A further distinction between the national and local tax is that the local jurisdiction will be concerned only with that part of the burden which is borne by its residents and not with that part which is borne by others.

Thus, suppose that real property located in jurisdiction A is owned by residents of jurisdiction B. As a result, the short-run burden will be borne by outside individuals while local residents may enjoy a free ride. But they may not fare as well in the longer run when capital can move out. Now local residents find their rents increased and wages reduced while outsiders have gained. The greater the outflow of capital, the less will be the revenue obtained and the greater will be the rise in rents and reduction in income suffered by the residents of the high-tax jurisdiction. Not only are local residents unable to export the burden of such taxes as are collected, but they lose to the outside because less capital is available to them. It is not surprising, therefore, if a particular community is hesitant to raise its tax rate much beyond that imposed by rival jurisdictions. Indeed, a community might be tempted to derive net benefits from lowering its tax below that applicable in rival jurisdictions.

Local tax policy thus involves a difficult choice between (1) the gain to be derived by shifting tax burdens to the outside through the taxation of capital owned by "foreigners," and (2) the danger of loss to the local economy from the flight of "foreign" capital. This condition, moreover, does not apply to local finance only. We shall meet it again and on an enlarged scale when examining the coordination of tax policy at the international level.

Benefit Differentials The preceding discussion has been one-sided in that it has considered the tax side of the picture only, without allowance for

[22]Since the gain will be spread more widely than the loss, it will be less noticeable.

the benefits from public services which the revenue may provide. Yet, they must be taken into account when examining the overall effects of an increase in a local property tax.

Just as an increase in property tax rates may reduce property values and induce capital outflows, so may the provision of additional public services raise values and attract capital inflow. Better schools or municipal services may render the town a more attractive place in which to reside or to operate a business. The improvement raises the demand for housing and structures, leading to higher property values, and thus counteracts the effects of increased property tax rates. Thus, expenditure benefits may be capitalized no less than tax burdens, so that the combined tax and expenditure effects may leave housing values reduced, increased, or unaffected, depending on how the revenue is obtained and what it is used for.

If all property taxes were imposed in strict conformity with the benefit principle, the two effects should wash out with property values independent of tax rates. Actually, such is not the case. The property tax is used as a general revenue source and goes to finance expenditure benefits not always in close alignment with tax contributions. Nevertheless, empirical investigations show that property values respond to expenditure as well as tax differentials, thus pointing to the importance of considering both aspects.[23]

Allowance for Income Tax   Since the major complaint over the property tax has come from homeowners, it is interesting to compare their position as investors in housing services with that of investors in corporate shares, allowing in both cases not only for the property tax but also for the personal income and corporation tax. Although the investor in housing services is likely to pay more in property tax, the overall tax burden remains substantially less if all three taxes are combined.[24] This is partly due to the additional burden borne by the shareholder under the corporation income tax, and partly to the favorable treatment of the homeowner under the personal income tax.

[23]See W. Oates, "The Effects of Property Taxes and Local Public Spending on Property Values: An Empirical Study of Tax Capitalization and the Tiebout Hypothesis," *Journal of Political Economy*, vol. 77, November–December 1969.

[24]Consider a homeowner with a house valued at $35,000. Applying an average property tax rate of 1.8 percent of market value, the property tax is $630. Assuming a 40 percent mortgage at 5 percent, the interest payment will be $700, giving a total deduction from taxable income under the individual income tax of $1,330. With, say, a marginal tax rate of 23 percent, the savings in personal income tax equal $306 (23 percent of $1,330), and the net tax will be $324 ($630 minus $306). Assuming the rate of return on capital to be 5 percent (net of property tax), the imputed rent is $2,074 (5 percent of $35,000 plus $324), and the tax rate thereon is 16 percent ($324 as a percentage of $2,074).

Turning now to the corporate investor, let us assume that this individual's property tax equals 15 percent of profits. The net corporate tax equals $.48(1-.15)=.41$, or 41 percent. The personal tax, assuming a 50 percent dividend distribution, equals $.23 \times .5(1-.15-.41)=.05$, or 5 percent. The overall tax burden in turn is $.15+.41+.05=.61$, or 61 percent. This is nearly 4 times that paid by the investor in housing services.

For further discussion, see Helen F. Ladd, "The Role of the Property Tax: A Reassessment," in R. A. Musgrave (ed.), *Broad Based Taxes, New and Old*, Committee for Economic Development, Baltimore: Johns Hopkins, 1973.

Alternative View

An alternative view, now referred to as the "traditional approach" and yielding a less progressive burden distribution, was reflected in line 13 of Table 12-1. Here incidence assumptions differ depending on the components of the tax base, and more attention is given to market imperfections. The discussion here returns to the case of a national tax.

Burden Distribution   A distinction is drawn between the parts of the tax which are assessed on land and those assessed on improvements, with the latter divided further between the tax on business plant and equipment and the tax on residential construction. The tax on land is taken to fall on the landlord, as land is inelastic in supply. Burden distribution is progressive. The tax on business improvements is taken to fall on capital income and hence is progressive; or, depending on market structures, to be shifted in part to consumers or employees with a less progressive or regressive burden distribution. The component assessed on residential housing is distributed in line with the consumption of housing services and regressive. Line 13 of Table 12-1, specified further in line 6 of Table 12-2, is based on such a composite hypothesis. The resulting distribution of the combined burden is regressive at the lower end of the income scale and is slightly progressive at the upper end. It thus differs considerably from the progressive distribution shown in line 7.

Tax on Housing   This view is in line with the perception held by the general public and politicians that the property tax on residential housing is regressive. Since housing expenditures as a percent of income fall when moving up the income scale, so does the tax burden relative to income. This burden distribution is shown in Table 21-4. Column I shows the tax on real estate as a percentage of family income to decline sharply when we move up the income scale; and though the table applies to homeowners only, the burden of the property tax on rental housing (if imputed to tenants) may be expected to show a similar pattern. As with our earlier analysis of the sales tax, this picture is based on cross-section data showing the relationship between family income and property tax payment for a particular year. The degree of regressivity may be reduced and the tax might even turn progressive if, instead, the comparison could be based on a lifetime pattern of expenditures.[25] This hypothesis, however, seems contradicted by the fact that, as shown in columns III and V of the table, the regressive pattern holds for the nonelderly as well as for the entire group.

---

[25]The issue turns on the income elasticity of housing expenditures with respect to "permanent," as against current, income. Estimates of income elasticity with regard to permanent income range from well above 1 percent, which would make for a progressive burden distribution (see Frank de Leeuw, "The Demand for Housing: A Review of Cross-Sectional Evidence," *Review of Economics and Statistics*, February 1971, p. 1) to much below 1 percent, which sustains regressivity (see Geoffrey Carliner, "Income Elasticity of Housing Demand," Institute for Research in Poverty, University of Wisconsin Discussion Paper 144–172, November 1972). For a similar point in connection with sales taxation, see p. 453. Note, however, that this view is not supported by columns II and III of Table 21-4, which show similar patterns for elderly and nonelderly homeowners.

TABLE 21-4
Burden of Real Estate Tax on Low-Income Households
and Elderly Single-Family Homeowners, 1970

Family Income* (Dollars)	REAL ESTATE TAX AS PERCENTAGE OF FAMILY INCOME			PERCENTAGE OF HOMEOWNERS	
	All (I)	Elderly† (II)	Nonelderly (III)	Elderly† (IV)	Nonelderly (V)
Less than 2,000	16.6	15.8	18.9	74.5	25.5
2,000– 2,999	9.7	9.5	10.1	70.3	29.7
5,000– 5,999	5.5	6.2	5.1	32.0	68.0
10,000–14,999	3.7	3.9	3.7	6.4	93.6
Over 25,000	2.9	2.7	2.9	9.8	90.2
All groups	4.9	8.1	4.1	20.2	79.8

*Census definition of income, which excludes imputed rent.
†Age sixty-five and over.
Source: Advisory Commission on Intergovernmental Relations, *Federal-State-Local Finances: Significant Features of Fiscal Federalism,* Washington: 1976–77, pp. 143–144.

Reconciliation   The focus of controversy between the two approaches lies in how the tax on residential property should be interpreted. Is it progressive, as the analogy to a tax on capital income suggests, or is it regressive, as appears to be the case if treated as a tax on the consumption of housing services?

Regarding the case of owner-occupied residences, it should not be overlooked that investment in housing is a consumption as well as an investment choice. Because of this, the owner-occupier may be willing to accept a lower imputed rent on housing than on other investment. Part of the tax will be absorbed in this ownership-rent and thereby be distributed in line with consumption, rather than be shared with all capital income.

This does not hold for rental property, where owners are concerned only with an investment choice. If markets are competitive, capital invested in rental housing will command the same net return as other capital, with the burden distribution in line with capital income. But the outcome may differ if, as is frequently the case, rental markets are imperfect. The tax may then lead to an increase in rent ceilings or to relaxation of previously constrained monopoly pricing. Moreover, not all property is taxed at the same rates. Effective property tax rates tend to be especially high in low-income neighborhoods, partly because property tax rates in central cities are high in general and partly because residential properties in low-income neighborhoods are often assessed at a higher rate than are higher-income surroundings.[26] The resulting additional tax on rental property may well be borne by the tenant.

[26]See George E. Peterson,"The Property Tax in Low-Income Housing Markets," in Peterson, op. cit., p. 110. Peterson also notes that owing to higher risk, the ratio of market value to rent is lower in low-income neighborhoods, so that the tax per dollar of rent is less, thereby providing an offset to the higher assessment ratio.

The outcome for both residential and rental housing will thus be a combination of the capital income and housing expenditure approaches, with the precise incidence pattern in considerable doubt.

Circuit Breaker

The property tax on residential housing is considered especially burdensome for the aged. As shown in the last two columns of Table 21-4, a large number of low-income homeowners are elderly, so that the problem does pertain especially to this group. For this reason, measures have been developed in recent years to provide property tax relief for the aged and low-income families. Given mostly in the form of a credit against state income tax, practically all states now apply some such relief provisions, referred to as "circuit breakers." Various techniques are used to limit the credit to low-income families.[27] Most, but not all, states limit the relief to the aged, and all states extend it to renters by stipulating a presumptive property tax. Since vanishing or otherwise limited credits go primarily to low-income families and since exemptions under state income taxes are relatively high, most claimants are without income tax liabilities and the credits must consequently be paid as cash refunds. As in the case of sales tax credits, this provision raises the question of whether such refunds will in fact be claimed by low-income taxpayers.

E. APPRAISAL AND OUTLOOK FOR PROPERTY TAX

The property tax, as a percentage of state-local tax revenue, has declined over the past two decades, falling from 45 percent in 1957 to 36 percent in 1977, but the corresponding drop as a share of local revenue has been from 87 to 82 percent only. The property tax has remained the predominant source of local tax revenue. The easy visibility and relative immobility of real property renders it a ready object of local taxation, and the benefits which such property derives from local public services justify its taxation. However, the property tax has come in for increasing criticism. Indeed, it ranks as the least popular type of tax, and complaints over it have been at the core of the recent tax revolt.

The problem is not that the property tax has risen much more rapidly over the years than have other taxes. Property tax revenue rose by 256 percent over the period from 1960 to 1977, as against 462 percent for other state and local taxes and 266 percent for federal taxes. Indeed, the average effective rate of property tax on single-family homes declined from 1.98 percent in 1971 to 1.89 percent in 1975.[28] Since the mid-seventies, and under

---

[27]For a discussion of such credits, see Advisory Commission on Intergovernmental Relations, *Significant Features of Fiscal Federalism*, vol. 2, Washington: 1976–77, p. 117. For a critique of these provisions, especially their failure to allow for the taxpayer's wealth position, see Henry Aaron, "What Do Circuit-Breaker Laws Accomplish?" in Peterson, op. cit., p. 53.

[28]See Advisory Commission on Intergovernmental Relations, op. cit., p. 107.

the impact of the inflationary rise in property values, liabilities have risen sharply in absolute terms, but the effective rate may well have fallen further.

A major factor explaining the unpopularity of the property tax is that, among all major taxes, it is the only one which is subject to direct annual or semiannual payments. The property tax comes due in large chunks and is highly visible to the taxpayer. It thus differs sharply from the other major taxes, including the income tax which for most taxpayers is taken care of by withholding, and the sales tax, which is largely invisible and paid in small installments. Next, there is the fact that taxpayers may compare their own assessed values with that of their neighbors and, finding them to differ, become irritated by the inequities, real or imagined, in the assessment process.

In recent years, these irritations have been compounded by the impact of inflation. As prices rise, so do house values. Sooner or later this becomes reflected in higher assessed values. Assuming tax rates unchanged, taxes rise in dollar terms. This angers the taxpayer, who feels that "the same old house" is being taxed "more," while overlooking the fact that the nominal value of the house has risen and that the tax in real terms has not changed.

But the problem is not entirely one of money illusion. For one thing, not everybody's income rises with inflation. Elderly people living on fixed incomes can no longer afford to stay in the same house. The economist might respond somewhat callously that this is too bad but no different from the fact that fixed-income people at a time of inflation cannot afford to buy as much of other products either. There is, however, a difference in that housing is not adjusted as easily as are other consumption patterns. Elderly people resist having to change their neighborhoods. This difficulty has led some states to permit tax postponement for the elderly, with payments only at sale or death.

Matters are made worse in situations such as that of California, where the value of houses in recent years has risen much more rapidly than the general price level. This has increased tax liabilities relative to income, while providing local governments with a revenue windfall, a gain in revenue over and above that needed to maintain a constant level of public services at rising prices. Failure to pass back this windfall by rate reduction has added to taxpayer dissatisfaction. It was one of the most important factors in California's tax revolt of 1978 and in the passage of Proposition 13.

Looking ahead, how much continued reliance will be placed on this tax? Notwithstanding the current wave of complaint, it will surely continue as a major source of revenue at the state-local level. But there is the further question of who will collect it, and how its revenue will be used. In the past, the property tax has been *the* source of local finance and its use has been largely for education. This practice has become subject to criticism as giving rise to unequal educational opportunities.[29] Consequently, a partial transfer of the property tax to the state level is a distinct possibility, thereby breaking the traditional link with local school finance.

[29]See p. 577.

F. NET WORTH TAX

In discussing the rationale for property and wealth taxation, we have distinguished between a benefit argument pointing toward differential user charges on real property imposed on an *in rem* basis and an ability-to-pay argument pointing toward a tax on net wealth, imposed on a *personal* basis. The existing property tax—which applies more or less uniformly as an in rem tax to all real property within the jurisdiction—follows neither pattern. We now turn to a brief consideration of its theoretically more attractive though less widely used cousin, the net worth tax.

Foreign Experience

A net worth tax is used in about seventeen countries, including the Netherlands, West Germany, the Scandinavian countries, and Switzerland. India and various Latin American countries also make use of this tax. In most countries the tax is imposed on natural persons only, though in some (including West Germany and India), corporations are also taxable. The definition of taxable assets usually includes intangibles as well as tangibles, and in most cases, all debt obligations are deductible. However, some countries disallow obligations not related to the acquisition of taxable assets. Natural persons are granted exemptions and rates are either proportional (typically 1 percent or less) or progressive (ranging up to 2.5 percent).

　　The net worth tax, except in the Swiss cantons, is imposed at the central level. Countries making use of this tax usually impose it in addition to the ordinary property tax, with net worth tax revenue typically only a small fraction (below 5 percent) of total revenue. Nevertheless, as noted at the outset of this chapter, a net worth tax is a potentially important component of the tax structure. Recent discussion has noted it as a supplement to a possible expenditure tax.

Structure and Base

Some of the problems and difficulties posed by the implementation of a net worth tax may be noted briefly.

　　Tax Base　 The net worth tax relates to ability to pay. Hence it should be imposed on individuals and not on corporations. Corresponding to the partnership view of the corporation profits tax, the net worth of the corporation should be imputed to the owners. Similar to the case of the income tax, the base should be defined globally, so as to give equal treatment to all components of net worth. Moreover, the principle of uniformity should be applied to both the asset and the liability side of the balance sheet. Intangible as well as tangible and nonearning as well as earning assets should be included. Similarly, all debt obligations should be deductible.

　　Rates and Exemptions　 As always, imposition of a personal tax raises the question of exemptions and rate structure. If exemptions and progressive bracket rates are applied under the income tax, they would also seem in order

for the surcharge on capital income implicit in a net worth tax. As noted
before, the basic question is whether and why such a surcharge is called for.
One use of the net worth tax (especially important for developing countries) is
as substitute for ineffective taxation of capital income under the income tax.
In the case of real property, at least, the property itself may be located more
readily than the income derived therefrom, and the taxes in combination may
be administered more effectively than either tax by itself can be.

Measuring Net Worth   Administration of the net worth tax calls for
identification of the taxable assets and for verification of debts claimed. In
short, it calls for tax returns which include an annual balance sheet in which
the taxpayer's assets and liabilities are listed.

With regard to accounting for assets, authorities must be assured that all
assets have in fact been declared. Moreover, there is a problem of asset
valuation. Difficulties inherent in current valuation of all assets have already
been discussed in connection with capital gains taxation. Here, as there,
approximations must be used. Thus, assets subject to property tax (especially
if assessment is equalized) may be valued on that basis, while others, such as
traded securities, may be valued by market quotation. For the remainder,
rough approximations (such as cost of acquisition minus depreciation) have
to be used. Similar difficulties arise with deductible debts. The difficulties of
administering a bona fide net worth tax are considerable. It is not surprising,
therefore, that in many instances it degenerates into a tax on real estate only.
However, they are not insurmountable, especially if administration is integrated closely with that of the income tax. In the age of computerized tax
administration, cross-checking between the net worth and income tax returns
should permit the identification of most income-earning assets and allowable
liabilities.

Role of Intangibles

Suppose that the property tax base was expanded to include all real assets.
How would it then differ from a net worth tax which adds intangibles, be
they assets or liabilities, to the base?

Private Claims   Consider first a setting in which there is no public debt
or government-issued money. All debt instruments are between private persons. Suppose that there are two individuals, A and B, whose wealth positions
are as follows:

	A	B	A+B
Real property	$100	$50	$150
Debt owed	10	—	
Debt claims	—	10	—
Net worth	90	60	150

As shown in the illustration, the total base for a tax on real property and a net worth tax is the same at $150. But they differ otherwise. If we collect $15 from a 10 percent tax on all real property, A pays $10 while B pays $5. If we collect a similar amount from a tax on net worth—i.e., a tax which includes debts claimed and deducts debts owed—A pays $9 while B pays $6. At first sight this suggests that A prefers the net worth tax and B the property tax. But the market will adjust accordingly. As the tax on real property is imposed, borrowers will not be willing to pay the same rate of interest as they did before, since the net earnings from their investment in real property is reduced. Lenders will have to be satisfied with a lower rate of interest, so that part of the burden is passed from A to B. In the end, the burden distribution will be the same as it would have been under a net worth tax, i.e., in line with distribution of net worth. Assuming a proportional rate to apply, the choice between the two taxes is thus a matter of indifference.

But they differ if the tax is imposed at progressive rates. Returning to our illustration, the burden distribution of a progressive rate tax on real property (where A's base is twice B's) will obviously differ from that assessed on the net worth base (where A's base exceeds B's by only 50 percent). Since a personal tax calls for assessment in line with ability to pay, the net worth tax is the superior form of wealth taxation.

Claims against Government   A further difference arises if we allow for claims against government, whether such claims are in the form of public debt or money backed by Federal Reserve credit and the Treasury. Such claims add to the wealth of one private holder without reducing that of another. Unlike private debt, they are thus an addition to the net worth base for the group as a whole, so that the base of the net worth tax exceeds that of the tax on real property. Suppose that the above illustration is expanded as follows:

	A	B	A+B
Net worth from above	$ 90	$60	$150
Claims against government	70	20	90
Net worth, total	160	80	240

In this case, collection of $15 under a flat-rate net worth tax will call for a rate of 6.2 percent, drawing $9.88 from A and $5.12 from B. To obtain the same revenue from a tax on real property, a 10 percent rate is needed, with payments of $10 and $5 respectively. The market once more will compensate for the reduced net return on real property, but A's burden will remain higher under the net worth tax than under that on real property.[30]

[30]It may be argued that since public debt must be serviced, taxpayers will capitalize the increased tax liabilities which they must bear in the future. In this case a liability would be added, canceling entry of public debt into aggregate net worth. But even if this liability were allowed for in the net worth base, public debt would not simply drop out of the picture, as the distribution of debt holding would most likely differ from that of increased tax liabilities.

G. CAPITAL LEVY

Still another type of wealth taxation takes the form of a capital levy. Imposed on a once-and-for-all basis, such levies have been used by various countries in emergency situations such as monetary reforms to terminate postwar infla- tions, but there is no record of such levies in United States fiscal history. If truly in the nature of a once-and-for-all tax, which is neither anticipated nor expected to be repeated, such a levy differs from other forms of wealth taxation because it has no disturbing effects on economic behavior. This adds to its attraction as an instrument of redistributional taxation, but the underly- ing assumption of unique application and nonanticipation is not easily met.

H. SUMMARY

The role of wealth taxation in the tax structure may be based on either benefit or ability-to-pay considerations, but neither points to the present type of real property tax:

1. Wealth may be taxed on an in rem basis as under the property tax, or on a personal basis as under the net worth tax. The latter is superior on ability-to-pay grounds.

2. The net worth tax may be used as a corrective to imperfect taxation of capital income under the income tax.

3. The local property tax serves as a rough approximation to ability-to- pay taxation, but other and superior indices of benefits received could be devised.

Regarding the composition and structure of wealth holdings in the United States, we have observed that:

4. The value of privately held wealth is about $5 trillion.

5. Residential housing accounts for about 30 percent of privately held real property.

6. The distribution of wealth is more unequal than that of income.

The major form of wealth taxation in the United States is the local property tax. As the major source of local tax finance, it remains one of the crucial concerns of tax policy:

7. The United States property tax is largely a tax on real estate.

8. About one-half of property tax revenue is derived from residential property and one-half from business property.

9. A large part of real property is covered by the property tax. However, the property tax base or assessed value is typically only one-third of market value.

10. A distinction must be drawn between nominal and effective rates.

11. Effective rates vary widely among jurisdictions within a state, due partly to wide variations in assessment ratios.

12.   Equalizing assessments within a state is important for the distribution of state aid.

13.   A "circuit breaker" provision is used to reduce the tax burden on elderly property owners with low income.

In considering the incidence of the property tax, it is helpful to begin with the hypothetical case of a uniform, national tax on all real property:

14.   Under competitive conditions, such a tax is equivalent to a tax on all capital income. As such its burden distribution is progressive, except for the lower end of the income scale.

15.   If the supply of capital is elastic, the longer-run adjustment to the tax may involve sharing of the burden by wage earners and consumers of capital-intensive products such as housing.

16.   The part of the tax which is imposed on residential property may be viewed as a tax on housing consumption. This suggests a regressive burden distribution.

17.   For owner-occupied residences, part of the tax is absorbed in imputed rent. For rental housing, imperfect markets may place part of the burden on tenants.

The pattern is complicated further if local differentials in the United States property tax are allowed for:

18.   If one jurisdiction raises its effective rate above the average, short-run incidence of the differential will be on the owners of property in the high-tax jurisdiction.

19.   In the longer run, the burden of the tax on mobile capital (but not land) comes to be shared by all capital, including that located outside the taxing jurisdiction. In addition, two-way shifts may occur between various groups of workers and consumers inside and outside the taxing jurisdiction.

20.   From the point of view of the taxing jurisdiction, an important distinction arises between those parts of the burden which are borne inside and others which are borne outside.

21.   To the extent that the tax-burden differentials between jurisdictions are matched by benefit differentials from public services, house values will remain unaffected and capital will not move.

22.   Firms selling in local markets are in a better position to shift the tax to consumers than are the firms selling outside the taxing jurisdiction.

As an alternative form of wealth taxation, the tax may be imposed in personal form and be applied to net worth only:

23.   Such a tax may be applied on a person's global net worth with exemptions and progressive rates similar in spirit to the income tax.

24.   As distinct from the property tax, the base would include all assets, intangible as well as tangible, but liabilities would be deducted.

25.   Equity in corporations would be treated on an integrated basis.

26.   To be effectively implemented, such a tax would have to be national rather than local in scope.

FURTHER READINGS

Aaron, Henry J.: *Who Pays the Property Tax?* Washington: Brookings, 1975.

_____ et al.: "The Property Tax: Progressive or Regressive?" *American Economic Review*, May 1974.

Advisory Commission on Intergovernmental Relations: *The Property Tax in a Changing Environment*, Washington: 1974.

McLure, Charles E.: "The 'New View' of the Property Tax: A Caveat," *National Tax Journal*, March 1977.

Netzer, Dick: *Economics of the Property Tax*, Washington: Brookings, 1966.

Peterson, George E. (ed.): *Property Tax Reform*, Washington: John C. Lincoln Institute and Urban Institute, 1973.

Tait, Alan A.: *The Taxation of Personal Wealth*, Urbana: University of Illinois Press, 1967.

Thurow, Lester: *The Impact of Taxes on the American Economy*, New York: Praeger, 1971, chap. 7.

Chapter 22

Death Duties*

A. Rationale for Death Duties. B. The Federal Estate Tax: *Structure; Estate Tax Issues; Rates, Exemptions, and Revenue Potential.* **C. Federal Gift Tax. D. State Inheritance Taxes. E. Summary.**

We turn now to the taxation of wealth, not on an annual basis but at the time of transfer by bequest or gift. Taxation of bequests is much the more important item. It may be in the form of taxes imposed on the estate under the federal type of estate tax or of inheritance taxes imposed on the heir by the states. As was shown in Table 10-1, these taxes are not of major revenue importance and, even if expanded substantially, could not become such. But they are of considerable interest as a matter of social philosophy and as a policy instrument in adjusting the distribution of wealth. For this reason they are an important element of the tax structure.

---

* Reader's Guide to Chapter 22: Death duties, though of minor revenue significance, are of potentially great importance as an instrument of distribution policy, applied in this case to wealth and its transfer. Difficult technical problems arise in implementing death duties and in making them effective.

A. RATIONALE FOR DEATH DUTIES

Death taxes may be imposed in various forms and for various reasons. Disregarding gifts for the time being, let us suppose that all transfers are made at death. The tax may then be imposed either on the estate as a whole (referred to as estate tax) or on each inheritance to which the estate gives rise (referred to as inheritance tax) with or without allowance for family ties between testator and donee. The distinction is not so much whether the tax is imposed on the donor or donee but also, and more importantly, on what is chosen as base. Which is to be considered the proper approach depends on the objectives that are to be achieved. Various objectives and types of taxes may be distinguished.

1. Society may wish to limit a person's right to dispose of his or her property at death. Society says to individuals that they may use their property during their lifetime, but that their title ceases or is curtailed at death. In this case, an estate tax of the federal type is the appropriate approach. If society wishes to allow free bequests up to a certain amount, an exemption is in order. If it wishes to confiscate estates in excess of a certain limit, a 100 percent rate above that limit would apply.

2. Society may wish to limit a person's right to pass on wealth more severely as subsequent generations are reached. In this case, the level of applicable rates may rise as the property passes through successive bequests, an approach initially suggested by the Italian economist Eugenio Rignano.[1]

3. Society may wish to limit a person's right to acquire wealth by way of bequests, i.e., without his or her "own effort."[2] This objective is served by an inheritance tax, imposed on the heir. Again, society may wish to differentiate between small and large acquisitions, thus calling for progressive rates. Given this objective, it would in fact be more sensible to combine such accessions from all sources, i.e., to relate progression to total accessions from bequests over lifetime, rather than to each specific inheritance. This is referred to as an "accessions tax."

4. Society may have the more general objective of achieving a more equal distribution of wealth. The institution of inheritance is one of the major factors making for concentration of wealth, with inherited wealth accounting for half or more of the net worth of every wealthy man and for most of the net worth of equally wealthy women.[3] Therefore an inheritance tax or, better, an accessions duty is one of the most effective approaches to this problem. The logic of this approach, however, would call for rate progression relating to the heir's total net worth (including the bequest and his or her prebequest wealth) rather than on the size of the bequest only. Moreover, a supplementary measure might be a concentration-of-wealth tax, applicable to the combination of wealth through marriage.

---

[1]See Eugenio Rignano, *The Significance of Death Duties*, London: L. Douglas, 1928.
[2]See p. 92.
[3]See John A. Brittain, *Inheritance and the Inequality of Material Wealth*, Washington: Brookings, 1978.

5. Finally, the objective may be not to impose a separate tax on transfers at death, but simply to correct the income tax and fully implement the accretion view of income by including the receipt of bequests as part of the taxpayer's income under the income tax. This objective was previously noted as a possible rationale for a wealth tax. If implemented as a death duty instead, it would call for imposition of the tax on the heir, but the rates in this case would depend on the heir's other income. This approach would call for liberal averaging allowances so as to avoid the penalty of bunching under progressive income tax rates.

There is no reason, of course, why these five objectives should be mutually exclusive. Society may wish to integrate bequests into the income tax as suggested under 5, while at the same time pursuing both objectives 1 and 3. Thus, it may wish to impose both an estate tax, thereby limiting the testator's right to dispose, and an inheritance tax designed to limit the heir's right to receive and/or to compensate for noninclusion of bequests into taxable income. Choice among these objectives and selection of the appropriate tax device, it should be noted, is an issue which should be distinguished from the further question of how high rates should be and how far equalization should be pushed.

Moreover, the design of death duties must again address itself to the proper definition of the taxpaying unit, involving society's view of the family.[4] While people may agree that there should be some limit to the leaving or receiving of bequests, most people feel that this limitation should be less strict if the recipient is in a close family relationship to the deceased. This principle is reflected under the federal estate tax which exempts up to one-half of the estate if left to the spouse. However, an inheritance tax approach is needed if finer differentiation is to be applied. This is done under the state inheritance taxes which apply differential rate structures depending on the closeness of the family relationship.

B. THE FEDERAL ESTATE TAX

We now turn to the federal estate tax and some of its problems. From a technical point of view, this tax and the closely related problem of gift taxation have been one of the most complex areas of the tax law.

Structure

The filing requirement is set at gross estates of $60,000 or above. The gross estate includes all the property owned by the decedent and is reduced by debts owed to arrive at the economic estate. Prior to 1978, the first $120,000 was exempt from tax, which exemption has now been replaced by a credit of $34,000. This credit is equivalent to an exemption of $134,000.[5] In addition

[4]See also p. 381.
[5]The credit will rise to $47,000 by 1981, corresponding to an exemption of $175,625.

the taxpayer is permitted a marital deduction, equal to one-half of the estate if left to the spouse. Assuming the marital deduction to be fully applicable, estates thus become taxable above $270,000 only. In addition the taxable estate may be reduced by granting charitable contributions.

According to Table 22-1, only 41 percent of estates declared in 1973 came to be included in the tax base, with most of the loss due to the marital and personal exemptions. The taxable estate is then subject to progressive rates ranging from 18 percent on the first $10,000 to 30 percent on $100,000 to $150,000, 49 percent on $2 to $2.5 million, and 70 percent for estates above $5 million. As we shall note later, a limited credit for state inheritance taxes is permitted.

The number of estate tax returns filed in 1973 was 174,000, which corresponds to about 9 percent of the number of deaths. The 1973 distribution of returns is shown in Table 22-2. We note that the largest 9 percent of all taxable estates contributed 45 percent of the tax base and 68 percent of estate tax revenue. The estate tax in this respect has remained much like the income tax prior to World War II, when it was applied to a small fraction of the highest recipients only. We also note that a large share of the smaller estates (those up to $500,000) are not subject to tax and that even some of the largest estates escape without tax liability. This points to the importance of exemptions, deductions, and related aspects, to which we now turn.

Estate Tax Issues

Estate tax design raises a host of technical issues, only some of which are noted here.

Capital Gains Assets for purposes of estate tax are valued by their market value at the time of the owner's death. In the past this same base was used also for purposes of capital gains taxation at the time of sale of such assets by the heir. Thus only appreciation from the time of death was counted, leaving appreciation prior to death untaxed. Under 1976 legislation, the heir is to carry over the original base of the testator, so as to apply the heir's capital gains tax to the full appreciation of the assets when the gain is realized. Application of this provision, however, was postponed, to become effective in 1981, and it may well be postponed again.

Marital Deduction To begin with, there is the problem of intrafamily bequests. As noted before, the estate tax permits one-half of the estate to be transferred to the spouse tax-free. Mr. D leaves an estate of $300,000 to his wife after expenses are allowed for and debts and charitable bequests are deducted. Of this, he leaves $150,000 to his wife tax-free, leaving a taxable estate of $150,000. Of this $134,000 remains in effect tax-free due to the $34,000 credit, leaving a taxable amount of only $16,000, with a tax of $3,000. Mrs. D keeps the estate intact and leaves $297,000. Once more the estate receives the benefit of the credit, so that in effect only $163,000 is taxable, with a tax of $42,960. The marital deduction has two consequences. If Mrs. D

TABLE 22-1
Reported Federal Estate Tax, 1973
(In Millions of Dollars)

Tax Base	
Total estate	38,868
− debts	2,188
Economic estate	36,680
− expenses	120
− charitable bequests	1,998
− marital deductions	7,526
− exemptions	10,494
Taxable estate	15,850
Tax	
Tax before credit	4,729
− credits	576
Tax after credit	4,153

Note: Items may not add to totals due to rounding.
Source: U.S. Treasury Department, *Estate Tax Returns, Statistics of Income for 1974*, 1977.

decides to consume her bequest during her lifetime, her ability to do so is substantially increased by the marital deduction. But if she maintains the estate intact, the allowable credit has, in fact, been doubled from $34,000 to $68,000.

Alternative approaches to correct for this might be (1) to disallow the initial marital deduction, thus treating the spouse like any other heir, or (2) to disallow the second $34,000 credit, in which case the surviving spouse would be treated preferentially only for purposes of consumption of the estate.

TABLE 22-2
Federal Estate Tax Returns, 1973

Income (Dollars)	NUMBER OF RETURNS		Gross Estates* (Millions of Dollars)	Estate Tax after Credits (Millions of Dollars)	TAX RATES (Percentages)	
	Taxable (I)	Nontaxable (II)	(III)	(IV)	Marginal[†] (V)	Effective (VI)
0– 100	30,588	34,376	2,848	234	18	8.2
100– 500	79,150	19,467	14,976	1,331	30	8.9
500– 1,000	7,083	203	4,816	1,354	37	28.1
1,000– 2,000	2,569	⎰ 93	3,503	620	41	17.7
2,000–10,000	1,277	⎱	4,607	680	49	14.7
Over 10,000	89		1,899	426	70	22.4
Total	120,761	54,138	33,293	4,153	n.a.	12.5

*Gross estates of taxable returns only.
[†]Rate applicable to income exceeding lower end of bracket.
Note: Items may not add to totals due to rounding.
Source: U.S. Department of the Treasury, *Estate Tax Returns, Statistics of Income for 1974*, 1977, pp. 12, 15.

Which of these policies is preferable depends on how one sees the role of inheritance and the family in society. Most people would agree that the right to leave or receive inherited wealth is more clear-cut in the case of close relatives than in the case of strangers or distant relatives. On the basis of this argument, some such allowance as now applies to the spouse might in fact be extended to estates left to children. As we shall see presently, this principle is applied extensively under the inheritance taxes of the states. Evidently, these are issues linked closely to those encountered previously when discussing the taxable unit under the income tax.

Generation Skipping   Next, there is the use of trusts as a device of estate tax avoidance. The deceased may leave half his or her property to the surviving spouse tax-free, while leaving the other half not outright (in which case it is taxable) but in *trust*, provided (1) that the spouse receive the income therefrom during his or her lifetime (i.e., establishing the spouse as a life tenant), (2) that children of the deceased become life tenants after the death of the spouse, and (3) that at the death of the children, the estate becomes the property of a third person (the remainderman). An estate tax is paid initially when the estate is placed in trust, but the trust arrangement permits the skipping of the estate tax when the property passes from the surviving spouse to the children.[6] If the property had been left to the surviving spouse outright, such a tax would have been due at the time of the spouse's death.

Given these tax implications, trust arrangements are advantageous to wealthy decedents and wide use is made of them. While there is nothing wrong with trust arrangements as a way of designing bequests, the tax implications of such arrangements should be neutralized. Although the revenue loss due to generation skipping is not very large, the equity implications are unfortunate. This was recognized in the 1976 legislation which limited such trust to $250,000 for each child. Under a more drastic correction, the trust would be made taxable as received by the successive tenants.[7]

Charitable Contributions   Charitable contributions are of no less importance under the estate than under the income tax. Generally speaking there is no limit to the deduction of charitable contributions under the estate tax. In 1973, such contributions amounted to nearly $2 billion or 13 percent of taxable estates. Frequently, such contributions go to establish foundations, the Rockefeller, Carnegie, and Ford Foundations having been created in this fashion. Also, bequests are a major source of support for private universities.

---

[6]The permissible chain of life tenants is not unlimited, such limitations as apply being a matter of state law. According to the law of most states, the trust must terminate (the property must accrue to the remainderman) not later than twenty-one years after the death of the last life tenant living when the trust is established. This effectively limits the trust arrangement to a hundred years or so.

[7]Under British law, the trust is included in the estate of the first life tenant and the estate tax is allocated between the property and the trust. Several objections have been raised to this procedure, but it would seem to be the most feasible.

High estate tax rates make such contributions more or less costless to donors with large estates and thus encourage them to use their funds in this fashion.

The role of charitable contributions under the estate tax, as under the income tax, poses cultural, social, and political issues which go much beyond the realm of tax policy and which cannot be pursued here. Following the pattern of high income donations under the income tax, charitable bequests are of primary importance to universities, foundations, and similar institutions. Such organizations serve many useful purposes which would not be forthcoming from the public budget, but tax deductibility also permits a high degree of private control in the use of what are essentially public funds. To deal with these issues, the Tax Reform Act of 1969 placed certain restrictions on the use of such funds, especially for political purposes.

In addition, it is necessary to assure that the setting up of tax-free foundations is not used to accomplish essentially private purposes. Thus, a foundation may be set up to maintain family control over a particular business. If the estate tax had to be paid, the business would have to be sold and control would go to the public. If a foundation is established which owns the business, continued control may be maintained via control over the foundation. The Tax Reform Act of 1969 tried to deal with this problem by requiring the broadening of control over time. It also imposed certain restrictions, including a requirement to file tax returns, to pay a 4 percent tax on investment earnings, and to dispose of all earnings.

Rates, Exemptions, and Revenue Potential

As shown in column V of Table 21-2, marginal estate tax rates begin at modest but rise to high levels. At the same time, as shown in column VI, effective rates (ratio of tax to gross estates) are much more modest. The distinctly progressive pattern at the lower end of the scale reflects the importance of the basic credit and the marital deduction, while with the higher ranges charitable contributions become a decisive factor so that rates cease to be progressive.

An attempt to increase the importance of the estate tax as a revenue source would have to focus on base-broadening rather than on raising bracket rates. It is thus important to know the potential size of the tax base. Unfortunately, the data needed for answering this question are hard to come by. While estate tax returns for 1973 numbered 175,000 (and taxable returns 121,000), deaths numbered 2 million. The total number of estates associated therewith may be estimated at 1 million.[8] Thus, filed and taxable returns were about 9 and 6 percent of total estates respectively. Only a very small fraction of estates was covered. Since the covered estates included the larger estates, this does not, however, tell us what fraction of the potential base was included.

---

[8]For estimating procedure, see John C. Bowen, "Transfer Tax Yield," *National Tax Journal*, March 1959.

The potential base is given by the amount of wealth which passes through estates each year. While there are no reliable data by which to estimate this amount, some speculation may be helpful to suggest the order of magnitude. The value of privately held wealth (net worth) in 1975 was estimated at $4.8 trillion in Table 21-1. A corresponding figure for 1973 might have been $4 trillion. Assuming that about 3 percent of the total passes through estates each year, we estimate the potential base at about $120 billion.[9] This compares with the amount of $39 billion actually recorded in tax returns. On the basis of these figures, it thus appears that the value of estates recorded on returns accounts for only one-third of the total and that the actual tax base (after allowing for exemptions and deductions) accounts for only 10 percent thereof. A very substantial expansion in the base could thus be obtained by reducing the tax-free limit of bequests. Nevertheless even drastic efforts in this direction would hardly render the estate tax a major revenue producer relative to other sources, such as the income, property, or sales tax. The trouble simply is that death is too infrequent an event. The major role of death duties in the tax structure is not so much one of revenue but as an instrument by which to moderate the distribution of inherited wealth.

C. FEDERAL GIFT TAX

As noted at the outset, estate taxation and gift taxation are inherently linked. Prior to 1977 the Federal gift tax was imposed independently of the estate tax and at somewhat lower rates. Since then, the two taxes have been combined into a uniform system, with the same credit and rates applicable in both cases and to a combined base. Thus the estate tax liability is determined by applying the uniform rate schedule to the total of estate and cumulative gifts made previously, with prior gift tax payments deducted from the estate tax. The gift tax liability in turn is determined by applying the uniform rate schedule to cumulative gifts previously made, with prior gift tax payments again deducted. Certain transition provisions apply with regard to gifts made prior to 1977.

D. STATE INHERITANCE TAXES

Death duties at the state level take various forms. They are applied most commonly in the form of inheritance taxes, imposed on the heir. Such taxes are used in thirty-two states. Different exemptions and rate schedules apply, depending on the heir's family relationship to the deceased. This approach is illustrated by the following pattern, used under the Minnesota law.[10]

---

[9]Based on Bowen, op. cit., who derives the 3 percent estimate from available data on distribution of wealth holdings by age groups and application of mortality rates thereto.

[10]See Advisory Commission on Intergovernmental Relations, *Significant Features of Fiscal Federalism*, vol. 2, Washington: 1976–77, p. 231.

	Rates	Exemption
Spouse	1.5–10%	$30,000
Adult or child	1.5–10%	$6,000
Brother or sister	6–25%	$1,500
Other than relative	8–30%	$ 500

Ten states use not inheritance taxes but estate taxes, with rates from 8 to 21 percent and exemptions substantially below those at the federal level. Sixteen states also impose a gift tax.

Under a law passed in 1926, state estate taxes may be credited against the federal estate tax, up to 80 percent of the federal liability. The purpose of this law was to coordinate estate taxes among states and to avoid unfair competition for wealthy residents. This provision is still in effect, but has lost its significance since it relates to federal liabilities under 1926 rates only. Nevertheless, it enables states to gain revenue through estate taxes for at least this amount. Accordingly, all states, including those which impose inheritance taxes, have a minimal estate tax to pick up this credit.

E. SUMMARY

The structure of death duties in the United States tax system is dominated by the federal estate tax, but also includes inheritance taxes in most states. Neither type of tax plays a major role in the tax system.

The federal tax base is exceedingly narrow due to high credits and deductions, and a good case can be made for a broader base. Moreover, exclusive reliance on the estate tax approach appears undesirable, since it does not make allowance for the family relationship between testator and heirs, nor does it allow for the wealth of the recipient. Reform in this area should therefore go beyond revision of the estate tax and consider a broader approach to the entire issue of federal death duties. Since passage of wealth through bequests is one of the major causes of concentration of wealth holding, the design of death duties is of strategic importance for the country's social structure. Moreover, it might be argued that the disincentive effects of death duties on capital accumulation will tend to be less than those of comparable taxes on capital income.

FURTHER READINGS

Brittain, John A.: *Inheritance and the Inequality of Wealth*, Washington: Brookings, 1978.

Kurtz, Jerome, and Stanley S. Surrey: "Reform of Death and Gift Taxes: The 1969 Treasury Proposals, Their Criticism and a Rebuttal," *Columbia Law Review*, December 1970.

Shoup, Carl S.: *Federal Estate and Gift Taxes*, Washington: Brookings, 1967.

Chapter 23

Payroll Tax*

A. Development. B. Coverage. C. Administration. D. Distribution of Burden: *Incidence of Payroll Tax; Relation to Benefits.*

It remains to consider the payroll tax. Imposed as *the* source of finance for social insurance, this tax has increased greatly over the last decade. In 1960, it contributed 18 percent of federal tax receipts. By 1970, this share had risen to 26 percent and the payroll tax had become the second most important federal revenue source. By 1978, the payroll tax contribution had come to account for over one-third of the total. Payroll taxes as a percentage of personal income rose from 4 to 8 percent over the same period. Payroll taxation is also being used at the local level as an approximation to a local income tax, but our present focus is on the social security tax. Since the payroll tax is an intrinsic part of the social security system, it cannot be properly evaluated without reference to the transfer payments to which it gives rise. Consideration of these broader issues of social security, however, is postponed until later, leaving present concern with the tax side only.[1]

---

* Reader's Guide to Chapter 23: This chapter deals with payroll taxes from the point of view of tax structure only. An evaluation of the payroll tax as an instrument of social security finance follows in Chap. 33, and an introduction to its incidence was given in Chap. 13.

[1] See p. 726.

A. DEVELOPMENT

Old-age and survivors insurance (OASI) was introduced in 1935. Designed to provide retirement payments for the aged, it was to be financed by a payroll tax. Revenue from this tax was to suffice to accumulate reserves and to put the system on a self-financing basis. For this purpose, gradual increases in tax rates were provided for. The initial rate of tax was 1 percent, payable by employees and employers alike and applied to the employee's first $3,000 of wage income. The range of covered employments to which the tax applied was relatively limited. Since then, there have been repeated increases in benefit levels and in payroll tax rates, as well as in the amount of wage earnings subject to tax and in the range of covered employment. Disability insurance was added in 1956. The combined (OASDI) rate for 1980 is 5.08 percent for employer and employee each and applies to the first $29,700 of earnings. The tax rate is scheduled to rise to 6.2 percent in 1990, while the ceiling is scheduled to rise to $29,700 in 1982 and to move automatically with the wage level thereafter.[2] The most recent addition to the system is hospital insurance (Medicare), which was introduced in 1962. Hospital insurance is financed by a contribution of 1.05 percent from employer and employee each. The combined social security payroll tax (OASDHI) for employer and employee each as of 1980 is thus 6.13 percent, and it is scheduled to rise to 7.65 percent in 1990.

The social insurance legislation of 1935 also provided for a system of unemployment insurance. Unemployment insurance is provided under state law and varies slightly among states. However, it is financed by a federally administered payroll tax of 3.2 percent applicable to the employer only, and in most states it covers the first $4,200 of earnings.

Combining the OASDHI and unemployment parts of the payroll tax, the total (for both employee and employer contributions) now equals 12.26 + 3.2, or 15.46 percent. If social insurance is expanded in the medical area, a substantial further increase may occur. This would move the United States toward the pattern of European countries, where payroll tax rates typically are above 25 percent.

As we shall see later, the entire system of social security finance—and with it the future of the payroll tax—is in a state of flux, and major policy changes may take place over the next few years. These include the possibility of partial substitution of general budget revenue or of a value-added tax for payroll tax finance.

B. COVERAGE

The coverage of the initial social security legislation was relatively limited, but it has expanded greatly since then. Since 1956 the system has covered practically all employees other than some groups, such as federal employees and railroad workers, who are covered by separate systems. Similarly, almost

[2] As provided for by the Social Security Amendment of 1977.

TABLE 23-1
OASDI Tax Base, 1978
(In Billions of Dollars)

1. Personal income	1,529.0
2. — sources other than wages and salaries	545.4
3. Total wages and salaries	983.6
4. — noncovered wages and salaries	33.6
5. Wages and salaries in covered employment	953.0
6. Not reported taxable	63.2
7. Reported taxable	886.8

Note: Lines 4 and 6 are residuals.
Sources:
Lines 1–3: U.S. Department of Commerce, Survey of Current Business, July 1978.
Lines 5 and 7: Estimated at 20 percent above 1976 levels as given in U.S. Department of Health, Education, and Welfare, Social Security Bulletin, September 1978, pp. 78 and 80.

all self-employed workers are included.[3] At the same time, the OASDI tax base falls considerably short of total personal income. This is shown in Table 23-1. The major loss of base (line 2) reflects noninclusion of capital income. Further base loss due to noncovered employment (line 4) is relatively small, but the exclusion of earnings above the ceiling (line 6) accounts for a further substantial reduction.

C. ADMINISTRATION

The payroll tax is collected from the employer, including the contributions of both employer and employee, the latter's being withheld at the source. Since the tax is on gross earnings and no allowance is made for exemptions, the employee need not be required to file a return. The self-employed, of course, must file a return since there can be no source withholding.

As an in rem tax, imposed on wage income and readily subject to withholding, the payroll tax is an ideal tax from the administrative point of view. It brings in a large amount of revenue while involving a minimum of complexity and compliance cost. Even in the case of the self-employed, compliance can be relied upon since it is in the taxpayer's interest to contribute in order to obtain the resulting benefit claims. No serious difficulty arises where covered income is received from more than one source. While both are subject to withholding, the upper limit of taxable wages remains set on a global basis because overwithholding may be credited against individual income tax. Moreover, if more than one member of a family is in covered employment and subject to tax, the secondary earner may choose between his or her separate claim and the benefits due him or her under the spouse's claim.

[3]Self-employed persons pay a combined (OASDHI) rate of 8.1 percent (1978).

TABLE 23-2
Distribution of OASDI Payroll Tax Burden among Hypothetical Income Recipients

1. Wage and salary income, $	3,000	5,000	9,000	15,000	50,000	100,000
2. Other income, $	100	250	900	3,000	15,000	30,000
3. Total income, $	3,100	5,250	9,900	18,000	65,000	130,000
4. Tax base, $	3,000	5,000	9,000	13,200	17,700	17,700
5. Tax at 10.16%, $	305	508	914	1,524	3,017	3,017
6. Average rate on wage income, %	10.16	10.16	10.16	10.16	6.0	3.0
7. Average rate on total income, %	9.8	9.6	9.2	8.5	4.6	2.3

Notes: Rates and ceiling applicable in 1980.
Line 2: Hypothetical levels of capital income are used for purposes of comparison.
Line 5: Both employer and employee contributions are assumed to be borne by the wage earner.
Line 6: Equals line 5 as percentage of line 1.
Line 7: Equals line 5 as percentage of line 3.

D. DISTRIBUTION OF BURDEN

Given the dramatic increase in the payroll tax in recent years, its incidence has become a major factor in the distribution of the tax burden. Moreover, special problems arise in interpreting its role, due to the additional if tenuous linkage of the payroll tax to social security benefits.

Incidence of Payroll Tax

As in all incidence analysis, the outcome differs depending on the market structure in which the tax is imposed.

Competitive Markets   The payroll tax is a tax on wage income. The resulting burden distribution, as shown in our earlier discussion of factor taxes, will depend on the elasticities of demand and supply in the labor market.[4] Since the tax is general and labor supply on the whole is fairly inelastic, the burden may be taken to fall largely on labor, i.e., be reflected in reduced net wages. However, the tax applies to wage income up to a certain ceiling level only. Although the rate is proportional, the incidence of the tax is thus regressive above that level. The ceiling in fact inverts the principle of income tax exemption by allowing such an exemption at the top rather than at the bottom of the scale. This is shown in Table 23-2 where line 6 gives the tax as a percentage of wage income. The tax is seen to be proportional up to the ceiling and then becomes sharply regressive. Such is the case if the tax is related to wage income. If the tax is related to total (including capital) income, regressivity is increased, as the share of wage to total income falls when one moves up the income scale, as shown in line 7.

Employer versus Employee Contribution   As noted before, the payroll tax involves two parts, with equal-rate taxes applied on both the employer

[4]See p. 288.

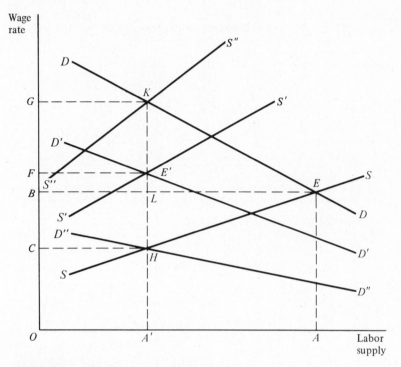

FIGURE 23-1 Incidence of Payroll Tax.

and employee sides of the market. Congress in making this distinction evidently intended to spread the burden, but it is readily seen that given perfectly competitive markets, the burden pattern is the same, on whichever side of the market the tax is collected.

This is shown in Figure 23-1, with DD the demand schedule for labor and SS its supply schedule. Initial equilibrium is at E, with supply of OA and a wage rate of OB. Introduction of the employee tax at rate CF/OF raises the supply schedule facing the employer from SS to $S'S'$, the difference between SS and $S'S'$ being the employee's tax.[5] At the same time, introduction of the employer tax at rate FG/OF, set so as to equal CF/OF, reduces the net demand schedule facing the workers from DD to $D'D'$. With both taxes in place, equilibrium shifts to E', the gross wage rate rises to OG, the net (after both taxes) wage falls to OC, and labor supply is reduced to OA'. The total tax equals $CGKH$, with $CFE'H$ collected from the employee and $FGKE'$ from the employer.[6] Exactly the same result would have been obtained had the entire revenue been collected as an employee tax at rate

---

[5]Note that both contributions are made at the same rate and applied to the same base, equal to OF, which is net of tax for the employer and gross of tax for the employee. (See p. 727.)

[6]The fact that $GKE'F$ is collected from the employer and $CFE'H$ from the employee tax must not be confused with the division of the burden between the demand and supply side of the labor market where (see p. 284) it might be argued that $BGKL$ is borne by the former and $CBLH$ by the latter. This division would remain the same if the entire tax was collected from either side.

CG/OC thereby raising SS to $S''S''$, or by an employer tax also at rate CG/OC thereby dropping DD to $D''D''$. Gross price, net wage, and revenue remain the same in all three cases. Given a competitive market, the differentiation between employer and employee contribution is therefore a fiction.

Imperfect Markets   This reasoning, though correct in the competitive model, stands in contrast to attitudes taken in the political debate over payroll tax policy. There, the distinction between employer and employee contribution is considered to be important, mainly because the employer tax is taken to be less burdensome to labor than the employee contribution. Moreover, an increase in the employer contribution is considered more likely to add to prices and thus be inflationary.

Economists would be ill-advised to write off these views as economic illiteracy. In the short run, a change in the employer contribution will not be reflected in the wage rate simply because wage contracts extend over several years or for other reasons of adjustment lag. This may prove an important difference for purposes of stabilization policy. But even in the longer run, the competitive market outcome may not apply where market imperfections prevail. Unions may be unwilling to accept a wage cut because the employer contribution is increased, while being willing to absorb an increase in the employee contribution without demanding a wage hike. Employers may find an increase in their tax an occasion for raising administered prices. Given such responses, the burden of the employer tax may well be passed on to consumers or, to a lesser extent, be absorbed by profits. If passed on to consumers, the impact will be from the uses rather than the sources side of the household account. Since a general consumption tax also tends to be regressive, the resulting pattern of burden distribution, however, may not differ greatly from that of the competitive case.[7]

Relation to Benefits

Viewed as part of the tax structure (rather than as a component of the social security system), the payroll tax has a low ranking on equity grounds. It imposes an additional tax on wage income only while excluding capital income entirely. Moreover, the ceiling renders the tax proportional up to a certain point and regressive thereafter. On all accounts it hardly seems a tax which is worthy of so major a role in the tax system.

The question remains, however, whether the payroll tax should be viewed as just one among other taxes. Payroll taxes, when introduced in 1935, were thought of as contributions for the purchase of insurance benefits, i.e., retirement income and unemployment compensation. The equity of the system was thus viewed in terms of *net* benefits received, rather than in terms of the tax burden only. Assuming an assignment of individual benefits in line with individual contributions and considering the net impact on lifetime

---

[7]See Table 12-2, lines 11 and 12, p. 270.

incomes, the distributional results of the scheme would be neutral. Use of a quid pro quo benefit formula, however, did not wholly apply even at the beginning. Redistributional elements were already present in the original benefit formula, resulting in a higher benefit-to-contribution ratio for low-income contributors. Over the years, this element has expanded and has rendered the system increasingly redistributive. This development has led many observers to the view that social security benefits should not be considered in insurance terms, but as an expenditure program forming part of an overall policy of income maintenance, to be provided for (like other expenditures) out of general tax revenue. Looked at in this way, the payroll tax may be judged like any other tax, independent of the benefit side of the social security system.

Whether this is the proper view of the matter we shall consider later, when the problems of social security finance are examined.[8] But if this view of social security *is* taken, the rising share of the payroll tax in the federal tax structure has involved a serious deterioration in its quality. For this reason, recent proposals have suggested introduction of a low-income allowance or exemption calling for possible administrative linkage between payroll and income tax, as well as continuing upward extension of the ceiling as provided for by the 1977 legislation. In this fashion the payroll tax could be made progressive over the larger part of the income range, even though a flat rate was retained. This change, however, would involve a further departure from the quid pro quo principle in social security finance; and if this step is taken, the question arises whether it would not be preferable to discard the payroll tax altogether and to substitute increased reliance on the income tax. This again is a question to which we shall return when the general issue of social security finance is examined.

FURTHER READINGS

Brittain, John A.: *The Payroll Tax for Social Security*, Washington: Brookings, 1972.
Pechman, Joseph A.: *Federal Tax Policy*, 3d ed., Washington: Brookings, 1970, chap. 7.
Also see readings for Chap. 33.

[8]See p. 726.

Part Five

Fiscal Federalism

Chapter 24

Principles of Multiunit
Finance*

A. Allocation Aspects: *Benefit Regions; Optimal Community Size; A Simplified Model; Local Finance and "Voting by Feet"; Differences in Income; Mixed National-Local Goods; Congested Goods; Economies of Scale; Protection of Minority Preferences; Other Aspects of Decentralization.* **B. Distributional Aspects:** *Redistribution as a Central Function; Local Aspects of Redistribution; Intercommunity versus Interindividual Redistribution; Regional Development.* **C. Stabilization Aspects. D. Intergovernmental Fiscal Relations:** *Benefit Spillovers; Local Services as Central Merit Goods; Equalization of Fiscal Position; Fiscal Differentials and Distortions in Location; Equity Advantages of Central Taxes.* **E. The Theory of Grants:** *Appropriate Grants; Matching versus Nonmatching Grants; General versus Selective Grants.* **F. Summary.**

So far, most of our discussion has been in terms of a fiscal system involving a unitary form of government. We must now consider the more realistic situation of a multilevel system with fiscal responsibilities vested in both

* Readers' Guide to Chapter 24: The principles of multiunit finance which we consider in this chapter may be viewed as an extension of our discussion of social goods in Chapter 3. The general reader will find the implication of spatial benefit limitation explained in pp. 513–516 and may wish to pass over the more technical discussion of pp. 516–520. The analysis of matching versus nonmatching grants in section E traces the response of jurisdictions to grants, in line with the principles of consumer behavior. The general framework offered in this chapter will be helpful in tackling the more institutional and current policy issues which are to be examined in Chapters 25 and 26.

central and lower-level governments (in the United States—federal, state, and local).

The problems of a decentralized fiscal system, or "fiscal federalism," as it is called, have received much attention in the public finance literature of the past decade. In part, this has been due to an extension of the theory of social goods, initially conceived in terms of national governments, to the problem of state and local governments. It has also reflected certain developments in the United States fiscal structure, including an imbalance in the distribution of resources and needs among jurisdictions, which have called for a reconsideration of the fiscal roles to be performed by various levels of government and of their relations to one another. In this chapter we explore the more theoretical aspects of the problem, leaving the empirical discussion of federal-state-local fiscal relationships for the following chapters.

While the concrete problems of fiscal federalism are embedded in their historical setting, it is helpful to begin with a normative view. For this purpose, we assume that only national boundaries are given and that political subdivisions may be designed *de novo* so as to secure the most efficient performance of governmental fiscal functions. Considering the basic fiscal functions—allocation, distribution and stabilization—we inquire whether each function properly belongs to a central government, to lower-level jurisdictions, or to both.

A. ALLOCATION ASPECTS

The allocation function is most directly related to the federal problem and poses the most difficult issues: Should social goods and services be provided on a centralized or a decentralized basis? If the latter, what spatial arrangement of fiscal organization is most efficient in rendering such public services? To begin with and to link up with our earlier discussion of the theory of social goods,[1] we will assume that all publicly provided goods and services are pure social goods, i.e., they conform with the characteristic of nonrival consumption. Let us then ask why the efficient provision of such goods might call for a multiunit system of government.

Benefit Regions

The crucial feature which was noted only briefly in our discussion of social goods is that of spatial limitation of benefit incidence.[2] Some social goods are such that the incidence of their benefits is nationwide (e.g., national defense, space exploration, cancer research, the Supreme Court) while others are geographically limited (e.g., a local fire engine or streetlight). Therefore, the members of the "group" who share in the benefits are limited to the residents of a particular geographic region.

Allocation theory as applied to the public sector has led us to the conclusion that public services should be provided and their costs shared in

[1]See p. 56.
[2]See p. 80.

line with the preferences of the residents of the relevant benefit region. Moreover, given the fact that a political process is needed to secure preference revelation, it follows that particular services should be voted on and paid for by the residents of this region. In other words, services which are nationwide in their benefit incidence (such as national defense) should be provided for nationally, services with local benefits (e.g., streetlights) should be provided for by local units, still others (such as highways) should be provided for on a regional basis. Given the spatial characteristics of social goods, there is thus an a priori case for multiple jurisdictions. Each jurisdiction should provide services the benefits of which accrue within its boundaries, and it should use only such sources of finance as will internalize the costs. The spatially limited nature of benefit incidence thus calls for a fiscal structure composed of multiple service units, each covering a different-sized region within which the supply of a particular service is determined and financed. While some services call for nationwide, others for statewide, and still others for metropolitan-area–wide or local units, the argument so far does not call for an ordering of "higher-level" and "lower-level" governments. Rather, we are faced with coordinate units covering regions of different sizes.

Optimal Community Size

The theory of multiunit finance must provide an answer to the question of what constitutes the optimum number of fiscal communities and the number of people within each community. To deal with this complex problem, we begin with a simple model which allows for one public service only, the benefit incidence of which is limited to all within a given geographical area but vanishes beyond it.[3] To simplify, we also assume that consumers have identical tastes and incomes, so that they agree on the desirability of social-goods provision. The crux of the problem is that the cost to each consumer will be less, the larger the number of consumers who partake of the benefits. Since we postulate a pure social good so that the quality of service received per person is not affected by the number of participants, this means that the efficient solution calls for all consumers to congregate in the same benefit area. The presence of savings from cost sharing due to large numbers leads to a single benefit area and, in fact, to a unitary structure of fiscal provision.

There are, however, other considerations which may pull in an opposite direction, toward a multiunit solution. For instance, one must allow for the fact that people may dislike crowding. Even the number of angels that can dance on the head of a pin is limited. Moreover, as we shall see, the services provided may not wholly meet the definition of pure social goods, so that the quality of service received (from one given overall service level) by any one member deteriorates as numbers rise. The problem, dealt with later in the

---

[3]Instead of assuming that benefits are uniformly distributed within a specific area, it may also be postulated that the intensity of benefits tapers off as one moves away from the location of the service facility. This would be the situation, for instance, with the quality of television reception. Residents would have a tendency to move toward the center, a tendency which would be restrained only by dislike of crowding.

section called "Congested Goods," is disregarded for the time being. But crowding must be allowed for, and this condition limits the optimal community size.

A Simplified Model

To bring out the nature of the problem, it will be helpful to consider a simplified model in which all individuals are assumed to have the same tastes and incomes.[4] The argument involves three steps.

Step I   The first step involving the choice of *optimum size for a given service level* is shown in Figure 24-1. We assume that a given level of social goods is provided, the total cost of which (the cost to the group as a whole) equals Z dollars. Let us suppose further that each member pays a price equal to the marginal benefit received, which (given equal tastes and incomes) means that the cost is split equally among them. The AA curve then shows the per capita service cost (measured on the vertical axis) for various community sizes (measured on the horizontal axis). This cost decreases as numbers, N, increase. Since the total cost remains equal to Z throughout, the curve AA is a rectangular hyperbola with per capita cost equal to Z/N. It reflects a form of "decreasing per capita cost" with increasing numbers of consumers in the group.[5] The $A_m A_m$ curve, which is derived from the AA curve, shows the marginal saving of (or reduction in) per capita service cost that results as the group number is increased.[6] If this were all there was to be considered, the optimal group size would be such as to include the entire community. The community would be expanded so long as $A_m A_m$ is positive (i.e., AA is downward sloping), no matter how large the group becomes.

The situation changes if the cost of crowding is allowed for. Let OB trace the per capita cost or disutility of crowding for various sizes of the group while OB_m shows the marginal per capita crowding cost. The optimal size of the community will then be given by ON_2 where OB_m is equated with $A_m A_m$, calling for N_2 members in this case. The community will be expanded in numbers so long as the extra per capita savings from cost sharing within a larger group exceeds the incremental per capita costs of crowding. Beyond this point, further expansion of the group would reduce total welfare and is therefore not undertaken. Various governmental units of size ON_2 will thus be established with per capita costs for each unit set at OC. With a total population P and given total service cost Z in each community, there will be P/N_2 jurisdictions with per capita costs of N_2/Z.

---

[4]The less technically inclined reader may wish to bypass this section, based on James M. Buchanan, "An Economic Theory of Clubs," *Economica*, February 1965.

[5]The curve is similar in form to that of decreasing average fixed cost with increasing output as drawn in the usual cost-curve diagram for the individual firm.

[6]Mathematically, $A_m A_m$, the marginal saving in per capita service cost, is equal to

$$d(Z/N)/dN = Z/N^2$$

i.e., the negative of the slope of the AA curve.

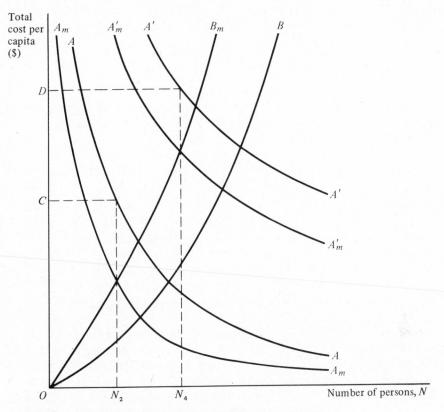

FIGURE 24-1   Choice of Optimum Size for Given Service Level.

AA curve: Per capita service cost or ZIN
$A_m A_m$ curve: Marginal savings in per capita service cost
OB curve: Per capita crowding cost
OB curve: Marginal per capita crowding cost

Such is the solution for a service level with total cost Z, but we can readily see from Figure 24-1 what happens if the service level increases. The AA and $A_m A_m$ curves shift up and the optimum size of the group increases. Thus, for a higher service level involving cost Z', the per capita service cost curve rises to $A'A'$ and the marginal curve to $A'_m A'_m$, with the optimal group size increasing to ON_4 at a per capita service cost of OD and with group enlarged to N_4 members.[7]

Step II   We now turn to step II, which is to determine the *optimal service level for any given group size.* This is shown in Figure 24-2, where various

---

[7]Two features of this presentation should be noted: (1) Up to a certain community size, crowding costs may be negative, i.e., additional numbers may be considered a gain (e.g., from increased social contacts) rather than a disutility; (2) since we are here dealing with a pure social good, we assume the OB curve to be independent of the service level. If the "congestion phenomenon" is allowed for (i.e., a decline in service quality with rising numbers), the OB curve will swivel down to the right as service levels are increased. In this case, the increase in group size when moving from level Z to level Z' will be greater than shown in Figure 24-1.

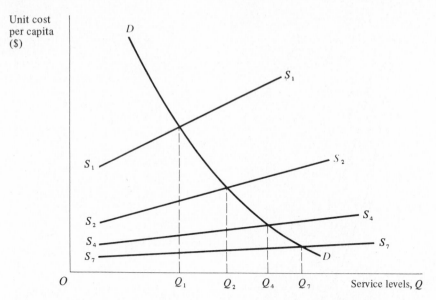

FIGURE 24-2   Choice of Optimum Service Level for Given Community Size.

service levels are measured along the horizontal axis and per capita unit service cost on the vertical. DD is an individual's demand schedule for the service, and since tastes and income levels are identical for all, it is representative for all members of the community. S_1S_1 is the cost schedule for the service showing cost to the community as a whole. The unit cost of the facility is here shown to rise with the service level, the slope of S_1S_1 depending on the nature of the facility and its production function.[8] S_2S_2 is the supply schedule which presents itself to the individual if the community contains N_2 members, S_4S_4 reflects the supply schedule in an N_4-member community, and so forth. The vertical level of S_2S_2 is one-half of S_1S_1, that of S_4S_4 is one-quarter of S_1S_1, and so on. Assuming a tax structure which divides total cost equally, all face the same SS schedule. Since the same quantity is available to each member of the community, the service level purchased by various sizes of communities will be determined at the intersection of the DD curve with the supply curve pertaining to the particular community size. Thus, the service level purchased with N_1 members will be that corresponding to the intersection of S_1S_1 with DD, namely OQ_1; the level purchased by N_2 members will be OQ_2 and the level desired by an N_4-member community will be OQ_4, as shown on the diagram.[9]

Step III   In the final step, the *two considerations are combined* in Figure 24-3, with community size N measured on the horizontal axis and service levels Q on the vertical axis. Returning to Figure 24-1, we find that a service

[8]See the section on economies of scale, p. 522.

[9]Alternatively, the same solution might be obtained by taking S_1S_1 to reflect the supply schedule for the group and by picking its intersection with successive vertical additions of demand schedules as the size of the group is increased. See also p. 59.

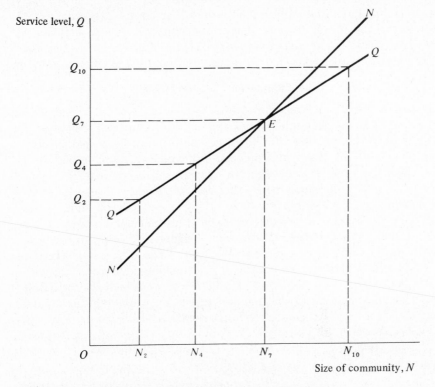

FIGURE 24-3 Combination of Optimum Size and Service Level.

NN line: Optimal community size at various service levels
QQ line: Optimal service level at various community sizes

level involving a total cost Z calls for a community size N_2, that a higher level involving cost Z' calls for size N_4 and so forth. This relationship is traced in line NN of Figure 24-3, which shows the optimal community size at each service level (measured in quantity terms), as corresponds to the various cost levels $(Z, Z',$ etc.) of Figure 24-1. Turning to Figure 24-2, we find that community size N_1 calls for service level Q_1, size N_2 calls for Q_2, and so forth. This relationship is traced in line QQ of Figure 24-3, showing the optimum service levels for various community sizes. The overall optimal solution is at E, where the two lines intersect, the optimal service level being OQ_7, and the optimal group size N_7.

Outcome Our model thus calls for a fiscal system which involves multiple units, with the number of units depending on the size of the population as well as on the strength of the crowding and congestion factors. If we assume all tastes to be the same, all these units will be similar, but they are not. Since different people will differ in their preferences for public services, the efficient solution will call for people with similar tastes to be grouped together. Thus, the system will contain multiple units, some similar and some different with regard to both size and composition of the public sector. At the same time, splitting up into smaller units will be at a cost. As the number of people in any one jurisdiction is reduced, some of the advantage from larger numbers (in terms of reduced per capita cost) is lost, a factor which must be taken into account in arriving at the efficient solution.

Local Finance and "Voting by Feet"

The preceding discussion has shown what the efficient solution would be like. As with our earlier discussion of social goods, this is only half the battle. The other is to consider how this solution may be reached. In the earlier discussion, the conclusion was that a process of majority voting is needed to gain preference revelation, even though this can only yield a second-best solution. We now find that there may be another way out, namely "voting by feet." If we stipulate that each community is to defray its own cost of public services, individuals will find it in their interest to choose such communities as will suit their particular preferences.[10] Those who like sports will want to reside with others who are willing to contribute to playgrounds. Those who like music will join with others who will participate in building a concert hall, and so forth. Each community will do its own thing and everybody will be happy.[11] Of course, this mechanism will function only to the extent that fiscal considerations are a decisive factor in location choice, as distinct from job opportunities or housing. This weakens the "voting by feet" hypothesis, but leaves it of some importance, especially in the metropolitan setting where location in alternative suburbs may be compatible with any given job choice.

Differences in Income

Differences in income remain to be taken into account. To assess their role, let us assume first that taxes are imposed on a benefit basis and then allow for redistributional taxation.

Benefit Taxation   Given a system of benefit taxation, two considerations arise. First, preferences with regards to social goods will differ by income groups. Demand will be more income-elastic for some services than for others. As a result, residents are more likely to be dissatisfied with the budget vote if their income varies greatly from the average for the community. Because of this, people with equal income will want to join in the same community.

Second, the price which people are willing to pay for a given supply of social goods will be higher if their incomes are larger. As a result, the gain from association with others is not merely a function of numbers but now

---

[10]It is interesting to observe that this is another respect in which the social-goods and private-goods cases differ. With regard to social goods, since costs are shared it is in a person's interest to associate with others whose tastes are similar. The opposite tends to hold for private goods, where a person with unusual tastes (provided that production is subject to increasing costs) will benefit from lower (relative) prices.

[11]The proposition that optimal local budget patterns will result from location choices of individuals was first developed in Charles M. Tiebout, "A Pure Theory of Local Government Expenditures," *Journal of Political Economy*, October 1956.

assumes an additional dimension. The gain in consumer surplus from the provision of public services will be larger for particular individuals if others with whom they associate have higher incomes and hence carry a larger share of the cost. By the same token, it will be less advantageous to associate with others whose incomes are lower, since they will be willing to contribute only a small share of the cost. This again creates a tendency for the wealthy to congregate, but it is now matched by a tendency for the poor to follow the wealthy, and for the wealthy to exclude the poor via zoning.

Redistributive Taxation   The tendency for the wealthy to flee the poor and for the poor to follow the wealthy is accentuated once we allow for the fact that taxation as set by the political process tends to be redistributive. Low-income voters may impose a higher share of the tax burden on high-income voters than is the case under benefit taxation. Moreover, they may vote transfers from the rich to the poor. Thus high-income residents have an additional reason for segregating and using zoning devices to keep out the poor. This is the dynamics which explains the flight of high-income residents to the suburbs, with consequent loss of tax base in the central city.[12] Chances are that this redistributive (or antiredistributive) aspect of "voting by feet" is a good deal more important than that based on the desire to associate with others whose public service preferences are similar. This poses the further question whether redistributive policies can be applied at the local level, a matter to which we shall return presently.

Mixed National-Local Goods

While we have so far assumed that the benefits of certain goods are strictly confined to a particular area, they may not be in reality. Some services may yield benefits which are nationwide but which apply with different intensity in various regions. Thus, antimissile defenses are part of a national defense system and therefore are properly provided for on a national basis, but their location on the East or West Coast will result in regional benefit differences. In this sense, such installations are rival in consumption, at least insofar as regional benefit differentials are concerned. The previously noted principle of aligning contributions with benefit areas will then call for regionally differentiated contributions to central finance. Our constitutional provisions which exclude geographic discrimination in federal taxation introduce an inefficiency in this respect.

Congested Goods

Up to this point, we have viewed the problem of multiple jurisdictions in terms of pure social goods, i.e., goods the consumption of which is truly nonrival although limited to the residents of a particular geographic area. We must now allow for the important fact that such goods are frequently—or even typically—not of this type. Consider a fire station, a school of given size,

---

[12]See p. 568.

a network of city streets, or a sewage disposal plant. They are all goods provided by the municipal government, yet they do not meet the precise criterion of "nonrival" consumption. Rather, the addition of one extra consumer (at least after a certain point is reached) will dilute the quality of service obtained from the given size of operation by the old set of consumers. In other words, there exists a congestion cost to previous users.

Under these conditions, the publicly provided good is no longer nonrival in consumption. But if this is so, should we not consider it a private good and leave it to be provided through the market? The answer is "no," because, unlike the private-good case, there is still the limitation that the same amount must be consumed by all members of the group. Formally, this may be depicted in the same way as was done previously for crowding costs in Figure 24-1. Thus, the OB_m curve may now be interpreted as plotting the marginal cost arising from quality deterioration as additional numbers are added to the group.[13] For any given service level, the problem is again one of balancing the gain from reduced per capita cost as numbers are increased against the resulting disadvantage. Thus, members will be added to the group until the old residents find that the marginal cost of quality deterioration equals the marginal saving (both on a per capita basis) in the form of reduced tax costs needed to finance the service.

Economies of Scale

The determination of efficient jurisdictions for the provision of social services is complicated further by the fact that various cost components of a given service may well call for differential scales of operation. Thus, the optimal size for individual schools may be 500 students; the optimal size for the services of a school superintendent may be 5 schools involving 2,500 students; and the optimal size for food purchases to be served in the school cafeterias may be 100 schools involving 50,000 students. Thus, efficient management may call for the combination of various service units to cover particular inputs, making for superstructures of various sizes. This, of course, is a prime factor in efficient arrangement of fiscal administration in the metropolitan area.

Moreover, it is treacherous in this context to speak of "increasing cost" or "decreasing cost" without defining clearly what is meant. In particular, a distinction should be drawn among the following three ways in which problems of scale may enter:

1. Economies of numbers which arise with a pure social good if numbers are increased while holding the facility level and its quality constant.

2. Economies or diseconomies of scale which arise with a pure social good if the facility level is increased while numbers are held constant.

---

[13]As noted before, an increase in service level now not only raises the AA or per capita service cost curve in Figure 24-1, but also swings the OB or congestion cost curve to the right. See footnote 7. A composite OB curve may be constructed which allows for both crowding and congestion costs.

3. Changes in facility quality which arise (due to crowding or congestion) from changes in numbers while holding the service level constant.

Whereas type 1 refers to the slope of AA in Figure 24-1 and type 2 to the slope of S_1S_1 in Figure 24-2, type 3 involves the slope of OB in Figure 24-1 and differs greatly for various types of services.

Protection of Minority Preferences

It is one thing to view the problem of multiunit finance in normative terms, assuming the provision for social goods within each community to be determined in line with the preferences of its members and costs allocated accordingly, a solution involving the idealized assumptions of an all-knowing referee; but it is another matter to allow for the fact that budget decisions must be made by majority vote and that differing tax formulas may be applied.

It is this fact which previously led us to the conclusion that the provision for social goods involves an inevitable dilemma: since preferences are not revealed without the pressure of a mandatory voting rule, such a rule is needed; yet, preferences of minority voters are inevitably offended thereby, and this violation involves an efficiency loss. The question here is whether this dilemma can be reduced in severity by resort to decentralized finance, providing for a relatively large number of small units. If the jurisdiction is small enough to include only one voter, no one can be in the minority. At the same time, all the economies of cost sharing are lost. Might it then be argued that numbers in the group should be increased up to a point where marginal gains from cost sharing just offset marginal losses from violation of minority wishes?

The argument holds if resort to smaller communities (decentralization) results in a situation in which preferences among members of each jurisdiction become more homogeneous. This may be the case because preferences of residents of different subregions within any existing jurisdiction differ (calling for larger jurisdictions to be divided up accordingly) or because the availability of multiple jurisdictions allows people with similar tastes to move together. When these conditions do not apply, the assumption in favor of small jurisdictions may not hold. Indeed, minority preferences may be violated more rather than less if we deal with two jurisdictions of four voters each rather than with one jurisdiction of eight voters. A related aspect of the voting problem is that fragmentation into single service districts (e.g., for water or electricity) may render it more difficult to obtain consensus since it will not be possible to form coalitions involving various budget mixes.[14]

Other Aspects of Decentralization

Other arguments on behalf of decentralization hinge on less tangible propositions, such as greater social integration through citizen involvement in local self-determination, the potential danger to individual liberty of centralized

[14]See Julius Margolis, in National Bureau of Economic Research, *Public Finances: Needs, Sources and Utilization*, Princeton, N.J.: Princeton, 1961, and p. 117.

power, and the gain from diversity and experimentation which results from decentralization. All these points have merit but so have the propositions that centralized government involves economies of scale and coordination and that a nation, though made up of diverse elements, is also served by a common sense of national purpose and concern. Nor can one discard the fact that, historically speaking, public policy and administrative initiatives have been generated largely at the central level.

B. DISTRIBUTIONAL ASPECTS

Next we consider how the distribution function is to be performed in the Federalist system.

Redistribution as a Central Function

Policies to adjust the distribution of income among individuals must be conducted largely on a nationwide basis. Unless such adjustments are very minor, regional differentiation will affect the choice of location for both individuals and businesses and will result in locational inefficiencies. Moreover, regional measures for redistribution are self-defeating, since the rich will leave and the poor will move to the more egalitarian-minded jurisdictions. The flight of high-income residents from the central cities to the suburbs illustrates the problem. Moreover, the present large differentials in public assistance among states have contributed to the migration of welfare recipients from the low-benefit rural areas to high-benefit urban locations.

To be effective, fiscal redistribution—both progressive income taxation applied to the upper end of the income scale and transfers granted to the lower end—must be uniform within an area over which there is a high degree of capital, labor, and residence mobility. It has to be a function of the national government. As we shall see later, failure to meet this condition in the United States is responsible for much of the fiscal distress experienced by certain local governments in recent years. There is thus a natural link between central finance and redistributive finance, and much of the political debate over fiscal centralization and decentralization must be understood in these terms.

Local Aspects of Redistribution

The reader at this point should recall our earlier distinction between mandatory and voluntary redistribution. While mandatory redistribution is not feasible on a local basis as losing residents can readily escape, a case for redistribution as a local function has been made in terms of the voluntary approach.[15] People are more likely to derive utility from giving to their neighbors than to faraway strangers. They will thus be more willing to vote for redistributive schemes which benefit their local community than for those

---

[15]See Mark V. Pauly, "Income Redistribution as a Local Public Good," *Journal of Public Economics*, February 1973.

which apply on a national scale. International redistribution in turn will be even more remote. This, however, assumes that low-income outsiders will not be attracted to in-migrate so as to benefit from the local redistribution. In the absence of stringent zoning this is hardly a realistic assumption. The case for redistribution as a local function is thus an interesting idea but not a very practicable one. The flight of high-income residents into the suburbs and away from their low-income central city neighbors is ample evidence for this. At the same time, the "neighborhood" argument explains why voters are unwilling to provide for welfare payments, while willing to contribute to Community Fund activities.

Intercommunity versus Interindividual Redistribution

While it is evident that major redistributional measures can be carried out only at the national level, should national concern be only with adjustments between rich and poor *individuals* or should it also be with adjustments between rich and poor *communities*?

The distribution of income as an issue in social policy relates to its distribution among individuals within or across communities, but not to distribution among average incomes by communities. The proper policy instrument therefore is a direct and nationally based transfer scheme from high- to low-income individuals, referred to later as a negative income tax, and not a transfer between jurisdictions. Where this objective is not met adequately by national policy, interjurisdictional redistribution may strengthen the ability of low-income jurisdictions to grant supplementary support to their low-income residents, but this is a second-best solution only.

Average levels of income by jurisdiction are relevant, however, in that they affect the price at which social goods are available to individuals in various communities. Central policy may serve to equalize these prices through a system of matching grants to jurisdictions. Moreover, the central government may view social goods which are provided at the local level as being in the nature of merit goods. Taking a view of distribution previously referred to as "categorical equity," it may wish to assure that all individuals, independent of their locations, enjoy a minimum level of local social goods.[16] Once more, interjurisdictional transfers are in order to accomplish this.

Regional Development

Another aspect of interregional redistribution relates to economic development and growth. While the responsibility for overall growth policy belongs to the central government, implementation of this policy may involve a regional orientation. Economically backward regions may persist where there are barriers to labor and capital mobility. One solution would be to remove such barriers and to let resources move. Yet this may be politically difficult, or national policy may hold it desirable to support traditionally important

[16]See p. 102.

regions or to maintain a broader population distribution. At the same time, excessive regional income differentials may be held undesirable, so that redistribution among regions may be called for.

C. STABILIZATION ASPECTS

It is readily seen that the use of fiscal policy for stabilization purposes has to be at the national (central) level. Lower levels of government cannot successfully carry on stabilization policy on their own for a number of reasons. This holds for fiscal no less than for monetary policies.

Since each subunit exists as a completely "open" economy within the national market area, local fiscal measures will meet with large import leakages.[17] While increased public expenditures can be directed at local resources, gains from further respending will be diluted by import leakages, thus resulting in little or no "multiplier effect." Therefore spending and taxing measures by lower levels of government, whether in an expansionary or restrictive direction, would be largely nullified by trade leakages. These leakages do not arise, or are substantially smaller, if such fiscal measures are undertaken at the national level.

Moreover, stabilizing fiscal policy requires periodic budgetary deficits or surpluses with corresponding borrowing and debt repayment. These pose a more serious problem for local governments, which have less ready access to the national capital markets and no control over supporting monetary policy should it be needed. The implications of local government debt, moreover, are different from those associated with national debt. Local debt is largely held by creditors outside the jurisdiction, and the use of debt finance at the local level should be geared to secure an equitable burden distribution among generations.

Whereas decentralized fiscal policy for stabilization purposes is largely ruled out by the foregoing considerations, the use of monetary policy by lower levels of government is even less acceptable. Central banking policy is inherently a national function. Not only would decentralized monetary policy be seriously blunted in its effectiveness by the openness of the regional economy, but the power to print money would invite monetary irresponsibility at the state or local level.

In sum, the necessary degree of fiscal coordination is not likely to emerge in a decentralized setting, so central responsibility for stabilization action is required. This is not to say, however, that central government responsibility for stabilization policy need not account for the needs of state and local governments. Thus, levels of spending and taxing at the lower levels of government (in line with their service-providing roles) may be influenced by the central government's stabilization policy. Central banking policy affects the availability and cost of credit for state and local governments, and grants to lower-level units may be varied depending on cyclical conditions.

[17]See p. 780.

Just as full employment of resources must be the concern of stabilizing measures at the central level, so must aims of economic growth be implemented by central government policies. The additional resources (such as investment in physical and human capital) required for more rapid economic growth are best generated through policies applied uniformly over the national area. Further, such resources should be put to most effective use without the kinds of distortion which arise from a pluralistic system. As noted before, development policy may be linked to regional problems and may thus call for equalizing resource transfers; but even where this condition exists, such transfers must again be a function of the central government.

D. INTERGOVERNMENTAL FISCAL RELATIONS

In the previous sections we have discussed the design of an efficient fiscal structure in which the stabilization and distribution functions belong with the central government and the allocation function is performed by jurisdictions defined as "benefit areas," which may be local, regional, or national in scope. In such a normative system, each jurisdiction would carry out and finance (from taxes paid within its borders) its appropriate allocative functions without reference to the fiscal activities of others. Any one resident would be within the boundaries of various jurisdictions (or "service clubs") and contribute to their respective activities.

Would such a scheme leave any place for "intergovernmental fiscal relations," that is, fiscal transactions and coordinating arrangements among the various communities? The answer is "yes," for various reasons:

1. Intervention by a higher level of government may be needed to correct for spillover of benefits.
2. The central government may consider local public services as merit goods and wish to subsidize them.
3. The philosophy of fiscal federalism may call for some degree of equalization in the fiscal position of lower-level jurisdictions.
4. Fiscal differentials among jurisdictions may result in inefficiencies in location which need to be moderated.
5. Advantages of central government taxation may lead central government revenue to be substituted for lower-level revenue.

Benefit Spillovers

One major reason for coordinating adjustments among jurisdictions is that existing jurisdictions do not neatly correspond to benefit and tax cost areas. Spillovers result and may be due to a number of factors.

Causes   A first cause arises from the complexities of benefit areas. While the spatial model of fiscal structure, which we have examined earlier, has its attractions, it oversimplifies matters unduly. Since spatial patterns differ for various types of public services, the model would call for different but overlapping jurisdictions for each service. A person residing in any one location would be a member of various "service clubs." For some services, the individual would join with close neighbors only, while for others the neighborhood concept would be extended to involve a radius of 10, 100, or 1,000 miles. This system would be exceedingly complex, especially where benefits are not uniform within a region but where extensive spatial "tapering off" of benefits occurs. Moreover, complete separation of services into separate service clubs, as noted before, would render the decision process more difficult, as the bargaining feature of changing budget mix would be lost. The administrative and political costs speak for a more consolidated and simplified system with governmental units performing a variety of functions and departing considerably from our principle of equivalence between taxing and benefit areas.

A further source of nonequivalence may arise because people and businesses are mobile. As a result, public expenditure benefits in one jurisdiction may be carried over to another. For example, benefits from education expenditures embodied in the form of "human capital" get transferred to other jurisdictions with the out-migration of the educated. Other benefits (such as city streets, police, and fire protection) may be currently consumed by suburban residents who commute to the city but have no part in deciding on, and paying for, the services in question.

Finally, and most important, existing jurisdictions are historically given. They were not created on the basis of fiscal rationality alone. State or city boundaries do not neatly coincide with benefit limits; and once established, they are not readily adjusted for purely fiscal reasons. For all these reasons, benefit and cost spillovers from one jurisdiction to another occur.

Interjurisdictional Bargaining with Small Numbers As in other cases of benefit externalities, spillovers must be accounted for and internalized if public service levels are to be efficiently determined. Unless the nonresident recipients of the benefit spillovers pay compensation to the community from which they emanate, there will be an undersupply of the public good in question. In some cases, it may be practicable to redraw boundaries or reassign spending responsibilities. Thus, in recent years there has been a trend in the United States toward the creation of special service districts to carry out certain functions the benefits of which extend across local and state boundaries. Examples are water-pollution abatement programs, sanitation districts, and metropolitan transit systems. In other, and indeed most, instances, intergovernmental cooperation will be needed. In some cases, direct negotiation between jurisdictions may be feasible.

The problem is quite similar in principle to that dealt with in our earlier discussion of benefit externalities from personal consumption. In particular, it resembles the small-number case of that discussion.[18] If jurisdiction A provides for service X, it may yield not only benefits in consumption for the residents of A but also spillover benefits which are consumed by the residents

---

[18]See p. 80.

of jurisdiction B. The latter are not accounted for by A, but should be internalized to yield efficient provision. This may be achieved through bargaining, as jurisdiction B may benefit by paying A for increasing its level of provision and by substituting this for B's own provision. Thus, negotiation tends to lead to some degree of internalization, but, as we concluded before, there is no assurance that an efficient solution will be reached. Nevertheless, bargaining does occur, and interjurisdictional agreements pertaining to such matters as garbage disposal or fire protection are a frequent and useful feature of intergovernmental cooperation.[19]

Federal Intervention with Large Numbers   Frequently, the number of interested parties may be sufficiently large to make a bargaining solution difficult. A higher level of government is then called upon to act as a referee or intermediary, so as to expedite cooperation and to secure both efficient and equitable solutions. With even larger numbers, a matching-grant system again becomes necessary to provide the called-for correction, with a subsidy paid to the benefit-generating lower-level government in line with the value of the benefit to the receiving governmental unit. As a matter of equity, such grants should be financed by charges imposed on the receiving jurisdictions to match the benefit spill-ins.[20]

The significance of such compensatory grants depends on the extent of interjurisdictional spillover and thus on the degree of decentralization. The larger the jurisdictions, the fewer the spillovers. But this fact does not make a decisive argument for centralization, since a highly centralized structure allows little opportunity for differences in expenditure patterns. If community preferences differ widely, it may be better to have more decentralization in public expenditure decisions and to accommodate to the larger spillovers rather than to do the reverse.

Local Services as Central Merit Goods

Quite apart from spillovers, the central government may wish to influence the fiscal behavior of lower-level governments in order to raise the level of local public services. To put it differently, the central government may view local public services as merit goods. This concern may be directed at local expenditures in general or at selective categories only; and financial support may be given to raise public services without limit or it may be restricted to assure minimum levels.

In principle, there is no difference between the central government's subsidizing expenditures on social goods by the lower levels of government and its subsidizing private goods purchased by individual consumers. As we have emphasized before, the merit-good characteristic is independent of the

---

[19]For the role of such agreements at the international level, see p. 783.

[20]If S_i is a grant or subsidy paid to the ith state, $S_i = \alpha_i X_i - \beta_i X_j$ where α_i is the rate of benefit spill-*out* expressed as a proportion of X_i or public expenditures undertaken by the ith state, while β_i is the rate of benefit spill-*in* to the ith state from expenditures X_j undertaken by the jth state, summed over all states. The matching rates α_i and β_i are weighted averages for various types of public expenditures and thus would vary for each state.

distinction between social and private goods.[21] In both cases, the purpose is to redirect consumption patterns, and both fall under the heading of "merit goods." There may, however, be a special argument for interference with consumer (or voter) choice in the provision of social goods at the local level. Where majority decision provides for only a substandard level of public services, the central government may wish to protect the interests of the minority in receiving a minimum level.

Once more, these corrections call for matching grants to reduce the price ratio of public services to private goods, thereby encouraging the local electorate to increase their own taxes and to spend more on public goods. Depending on how general the support is to be, the matching rates will be related to total expenditures or be earmarked for particular uses.

Equalization of Fiscal Position

The desire of central government to give support to local public services may be combined with objectives of fiscal equalization. Some jurisdictions—state or local—enjoy a high taxable capacity (the tax rate needed to obtain a given level of revenue is low) and have a relatively low level of need (the amount required to provide certain service levels is small). They are thus in a fiscally strong position, as measured by the ratio of capacity to need. Others are in the reverse position. The central government may then wish to equalize fiscal positions and it may do so in various ways:

> **1.** The central government may wish to equalize actual service levels and for this purpose impose such matching grants (where needed to raise levels) or taxes (where needed to lower levels) as are required to secure full equalization.
> **2.** The central government may wish only to secure common minimum levels and adjust its grant policy to secure this objective.
> **3.** The central government may wish to equalize the cost—in terms of tax effort or tax rate required—of providing public services in various jurisdictions, while leaving it to the local jurisdiction to decide what service level it wishes to provide. This approach, referred to below as "power equalization," calls for matching grants to jurisdictions which are fiscally weak, i.e., which have low taxable capacity and large needs; and these grants would be financed by taxes on the expenditures of strong jurisdictions, i.e., which have a high taxable capacity and low needs.
> **4.** As distinct from equalizing cost in terms of tax effort, the central government may wish to eliminate differences in service level which result from differences in income or wealth. As shown below, this calls for a more complex type of grant structure.

As noted before, these policies do not aim at correcting the distribution of income, or general wellbeing among individuals, but rather at equalizing the terms at which local social goods are provided. This implies a view of

[21]See p. 84.

distribution in line with categorical equity, as well as a recognition of local public services as merit goods.

Fiscal Differentials and Distortions in Location

A case for fiscal coordination arises where fiscal advantages or disadvantages of particular jurisdictions distort location decisions. A particular taxpayer, whether a corporation or an individual, may find jurisdiction A preferable to jurisdiction B because A's tax structure will result in a lower tax bill and/or because the structure of public services is more beneficial. Such differentials affect both product and factor flows and thereby interfere with efficient production.[22]

This gives a further rationale for measures of type 1 above, but the argument goes further. The purpose now is not just to equalize the tax costs which an individual faces in various jurisdictions. What matters here is the net differential or fiscal residue, whether it is the excess of benefits over costs or that of costs over benefits. As we shall develop more fully later, the need for coordination is of particular importance at the international level where fiscal differentials are large; but, to a limited degree, they also arise within a single country such as the United States. Coordination of business taxation at the state level, for instance, has been a subject of congressional concern.[23]

Equity Advantages of Central Taxes

Central taxes have the advantage of avoiding distortions in location, but they may also be preferred on grounds of equity. By drawing on the entire economy, the tax base can be defined more comprehensively, as can be done especially with the corporation profits tax. Moreover, progressive taxation cannot be applied effectively by lower-level jurisdictions. This leaves the function of progressive taxation largely at the federal level. Since the burden distribution of the overall tax system is the weighted average of taxes applicable at the federal, state, and local levels, overall progressivity depends upon their respective shares in the revenue total. In the absence of grants, these in turn are determined by the respective levels of expenditures at each level of government.

This relationship can be short-circuited, however, by the use of grants from the federal to the state and local levels. In making grants for this purpose, the federal government would share its revenue (presumably revenue from the income tax) with the state at which the revenue originated. At the same time, this transfer of the taxing function to the higher level would interfere with the requirement, noted earlier in the chapter, that each jurisdiction should determine and pay for those services whose benefits are limited to

---

[22]If all taxes in all jurisdictions were imposed on a benefit basis, such differentials would not exist and fiscal factors would not distort location decision. More precisely, this situation would exist only if "benefit taxation" were interpreted to call for setting taxes equal to total rather than marginal benefits. Since location choices are all-or-nothing propositions, it is the total benefit that matters.

[23]See p. 423.

that jurisdiction. This is one of the dilemmas which have to be faced in order to reconcile the advantages of fiscal decentralization with the disadvantages of resulting distortions in location decisions.

E. THE THEORY OF GRANTS

We have seen in the preceding section that grants may be used to accomplish various intergovernmental objectives. In this section, further consideration is given to the choice of the appropriate grant instrument and to the incentive effects of various types of grants.

Appropriate Grants

For this purpose, it is helpful to distinguish among various types of grants. The main distinctions are: (1) whether the grant is general (also referred to as block grant) or whether it is selective (also referred to as restricted or categorical grant); (2) whether the grant is nonmatching or matching; and (3) whether it is, or is not, related to the fiscal need of the receiving unit. Grouping grants in line with these three criteria, we have the following classification:

		Not Need-Related	Need-Related
General:	Nonmatching	1	5
	Matching	2	6
Selective:	Nonmatching	3	7
	Matching	4	8

Among these grants, the objective of spillover correction is served best by type 4, with the subsidy rate equal to the ratio of external to internal levels of benefits. The objective of support of merit goods will be best served by type 2 or type 4, depending on whether there is to be general support for all local social goods or whether the subsidy is to be selective. Equalization objectives in turn call for grants of type 5, provided the choice between public and social goods at the lower level is not to be affected, or type 6, if it is. A policy combining merit-good and equalization objectives will make use of type 8. A policy aimed at avoiding distortions and efficiency costs which arise from tax structure differentials among lower-level jurisdictions, finally, might call for uniform central taxes while returning revenue to jurisdiction-of-origin in line with type 1 grants. Type 1 is appropriate also for the purpose of substituting central taxes for revenue obtained at the lower levels.

Matching versus Nonmatching Grants

Leaving an examination of actual grant policy to the next chapter, we now take a more careful look at why some types of grants are more effective than others, i.e., accomplish the desired policy objective at a lower cost to the government. We begin with grants which are general in the sense that they do not distinguish among types of public services but may be matching or nonmatching.

Nonmatching Grants   The case of a nonmatching grant is shown in Figure 24-4. Social goods are measured on the horizontal axis and private goods on the vertical axis. AB is the community budget line, showing various combinations of private and social goods which are available to it. The curves i_1i_1, i_2i_2, etc., are indifference curves recording the community's preferences between the two. The initial equilibrium is at E, where the budget line is tangent to the highest possible indifference line. Consumption of private goods equals OC, and the consumption of social goods equals OD. To obtain OD of social goods, CA of private goods must be surrendered so that the tax rate equals CA/OA, where OA is income measured in terms of private goods.

Now a nonmatching grant equal to AF (measured again in private goods) is given to the community's treasury. As a result, the budget line shifts to FG and the new equilibrium is at E'. The community now obtains OH of private goods and OK of social goods. Private-good consumption has risen by CH and social-good consumption has increased by DK. Part of the grant has leaked into increased consumption of private goods rather than into increased provision of social goods. This is as may be expected. Since use of the grant is not tied in any way, it is equivalent to a general income subsidy. Hence, there

FIGURE 24-4   Response to a Nonmatching Grant.

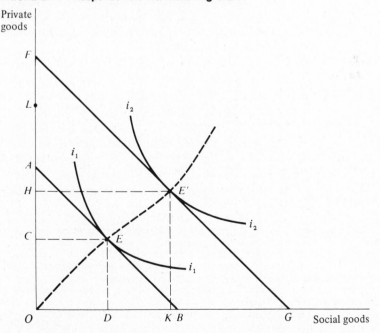

is only an income effect which normally may be assumed to be positive and to increase outlays on both social and private goods.

But how can it be said that the grant is equivalent to an increase in income, since it is given to the government rather than to consumers and the government buys social goods only? The answer, of course, is that part of the grant may be made available for private consumption through tax reduction.[24] Consider what happens in Figure 24-4. Since the consumption of private goods rises from OC to OH, the amount paid in tax falls from CA to HA. The tax rate, therefore, declines from CA/OA to HA/OA.[25] Tax reduction equals HC. With the cost of the grant to the government equal to AF (all measured in terms of private goods), $LF = HC$ passes into tax reduction and only AL is added to expenditures on social goods.

The dotted curve OEE' finally shows an income consumption path along which the equilibrium position of the jurisdiction moves as the grant is increased, with the leakage into private goods increasing and decreasing with the slope of this line.

Matching Grants   The case of a matching grant is shown in Figure 24-5. The initial equilibrium is again at E, with private-good consumption equal to OC and social-good consumption equal to OD. Introduction of a matching grant now swivels the budget line to AM, as the net price of social goods to the community has fallen relative to that of private goods. Equilibrium moves to E', with the consumption of private goods increased to ON and that of social goods increased to OP. The cost to the government now equals $E'S$, the additional amount of private goods which consumers would have to surrender to obtain OP of social goods. The tax reduction equals CN, with the tax rate reduced from CA/OA to NA/OA, CN being the part of the subsidy cost which leaks into private consumption.

Although the position of E' in Figure 24-5 shows that in this instance consumption of both private and social goods has increased, this is not necessarily the case. As distinct from the nonmatching grant where only an income effect was present, we now have a substitution effect as well. Since the price of social goods has fallen relative to that of private goods, the consumption of private goods might decline. The negative substitution effect might outweigh the positive income effect. In Figure 24-5, the dotted curve AQR shows the path along which E will travel as the price of social goods declines, with the movement from A to R being caused by increasing matching rates.

[24]Indeed, the text argument implies that it makes no difference whether the money is given to the government or to the consumers directly. If given to the government, part is used for private goods via tax reduction. If given to consumers, part of it is used for public expenditures via increased taxes. The outcome is the same in both cases. In a realistic setting, the two procedures may well lead to different results, i.e., voting a tax reduction and not voting an expenditure increase may not be symmetrical procedures. See Wallace E. Oates, *Fiscal Federalism*, New York: Harcourt Brace, 1972, chap. 3, app. A.

[25]Note that the tax rate is measured as the ratio of tax to earnings, thus excluding the subsidy to the treasury. If the leakage into private consumption is sufficiently large, taxes may be reduced to zero and a transfer payment (negative tax) may be needed.

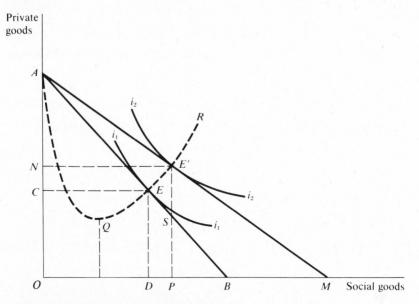

FIGURE 24-5   Response to a Matching Grant.

Up to Q, this results in a decline in the purchase of private goods, and beyond Q in an increase, with the purchase of social goods rising throughout. In a situation where both E and E' lie to the left of Q, there would be no leakage of grant money, but voters would in fact support the government's effort by voting a tax increase.

Comparison of Grants   The two types of grants are compared in Figure 24-6. E is again the initial equilibrium, and E_m is the new equilibrium with a matching grant. E_n is the new equilibrium with a nonmatching grant designed so that both grants secure the same provision for social goods, or OP. As before, the cost to the government under the matching grant equals $E_m S$ and that under the nonmatching grant equals $E_n S$. The same objective of securing a social-goods supply of OP can thus be secured at a lower cost with the matching grant, the difference being $E_m E_n$.[26] This is not surprising, since a matching grant is in fact a selective grant which supports provision of social goods only, whereas the nonmatching grant is general, since it may be used to support the purchase of additional private goods by way of tax reduction.

General versus Selective Grants

We now turn to grants earmarked for specific public outlays. If the government wishes to increase expenditures on a particular social good X, a selective grant earmarked for the use of X will be at least as effective in securing

---

[26]E_n must lie above E_m because the slope of successive indifference curves rises when moving up a vertical line, i.e., the marginal rate of substitution of private for social goods must increase.

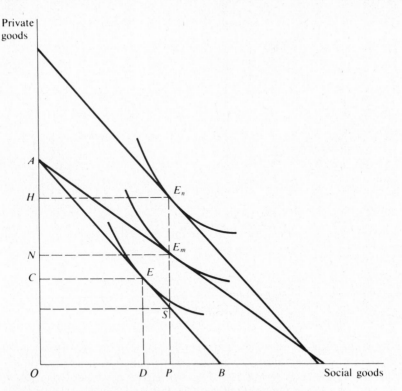

FIGURE 24-6 Comparison of Matching and Nonmatching Grants.

increased expenditures on X as will be an equal-cost general grant, and it may well be more efficient.

This is shown in Figure 24-7 for the nonmatching case. Measuring now social good Y on the vertical axis and social good X on the horizontal axis, let AB be the community's opportunity line prior to the grant with equilibrium at E. Now a general grant is given, moving the budget line to DC. Equilibrium shifts to E', provision of X increases to OG, and the cost to government is BC.[27] If the government gives a grant of equal amount but earmarked for the use of X, only section RC of the new budget line will be available to the recipient, but equilibrium is again at E'.[28] Both types of grants secure the same increase in the provision of X. This conclusion still holds if the government wishes to raise the provision of X to OK. This calls for a general

[27]Note that cost is measured here in terms of X. Alternatively, it may be measured in terms of Y and then equals AD.

[28]A selective grant earmarked for provision of X and costing BC may be pictured as moving the origin to the right from O to V, where $OV = BC$. VR then becomes the new vertical axis, and the effective opportunity budget line is given by RC.

The presentation of Figure 24-7 oversimplifies matters because it shows a choice between two social goods only. We may visualize a third axis showing private goods, in which case a selective grant on one social good is subject to a double leakage.

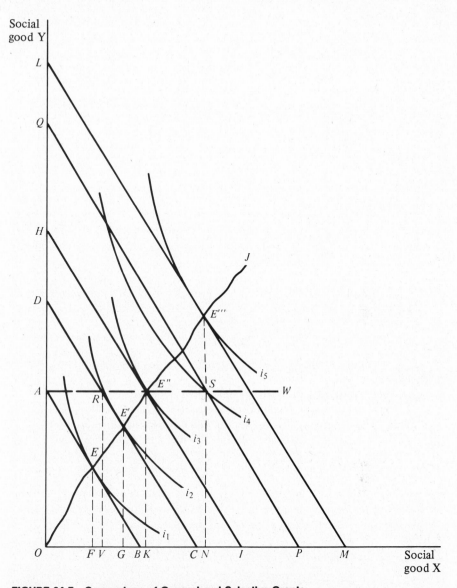

FIGURE 24-7   Comparison of General and Selective Grants.

grant so as to shift the budget line to *HI*, the new equilibrium is at *E″*, and
the cost equals *BI*. If use of the grant is limited to X, only the *E″I* section of
the raised budget line is available to the recipient, but equilibrium remains at
E″. The situation changes, however, if the government wishes to go further,
raising the provision of X to, say, *ON*. Now the general grant calls for the
budget line to be shifted to *LM*, with equilibrium at *E‴* and cost of *BM*. If
the selective approach is used, the budget line need only be shifted to *QP*.
With only section *SP* available to the recipient, point *S* will be chosen, with

the cost of the grant reduced to BP.[29] The selective-grant approach becomes cheaper once the provision for X is to be pushed beyond OK, where the income-consumption line OJ intersects AW and provision of Y comes to equal what it would have been if, without a grant, all resources had been spent on Y.

The conclusion that a selective grant becomes more efficient may now be combined with our earlier finding that a matching grant is superior.[30] Budget cost is minimized if the desired increase in a particular public service is secured by way of a matching and selective grant.

F. SUMMARY

In dealing with the principles of multiunit finance, we have inquired how the allocation, distribution, and stabilization functions of budget policy should be divided among the various levels of government. Beginning with the allocation function, we noted the following:

1. Since the benefit incidence of various social goods is subject to spatial limitation, each service should be decided upon and paid for within the confines of the jurisdiction to which the benefits accrue.

2. This principle of "benefit region" leads to the concept of optimal community size.

3. With pure social goods, it would be desirable to have the number of residents as large as possible, thus reducing per capita cost. At the same time, the cost of crowding enters to limit the optimal community size.

4. Allowing for differences in tastes, it further follows that people with similar tastes regarding social goods will join the same jurisdiction.

5. There is also a tendency for people with higher incomes to move away from people with lower incomes, and for the latter to follow the former.

6. The case for limiting the size of the optimal community is strengthened in the case of mixed goods, where congestion arises.

Turning to the assignment of the other budgetary functions among levels of governments, the situation is more straightforward:

7. The distribution function has to be performed largely at the central level.

8. Redistribution among communities is only a second-best approach to interindividual adjustments in distribution.

9. The stabilization function has to be central because of leakages at the local level.

---

[29] While S does as well as E''' in raising the provision of X to ON, the receiving jurisdiction will be better off at E''' since S lies on a lower indifference curve.

[30] When saying that the selective approach is more efficient, the term is used in the sense of permitting the government to achieve its objective of raising the provision of X to ON at a lesser cost. Using the term in the usual sense of Pareto optimality, E''' is a tangency point and hence efficient, whereas S is not. This consideration, however, does not apply in this context since by promoting X the government wishes to interfere with the recipient's choice. See p. 85.

While these principles suggest a division of the allocation function among levels and placement of the distribution and stabilization function at the central level, they nevertheless leave a place for intergovernmental fiscal relations:

10.   Existing jurisdictions are not neatly fitted to benefit areas, so that benefits generated in one area spill over into others. Federal intervention to internalize such benefits may be called for.

11.   The central government may consider local public services as merit goods and may wish to subsidize them.

12.   The central government may wish to take steps toward equalizing fiscal capacities among lower-level governments.

13.   The central government may wish to reduce the distorting effects of fiscal differentials on location decisions.

14.   It may desire to substitute central government tax revenue for that obtained at lower levels because central taxes are considered superior.

Consideration was given, finally, to the theory of grants. Here the following conclusions were drawn:

15.   Various types of grants may be distinguished and related to various policy targets.

16.   For most purposes, matching grants are more effective than are nonmatching grants.

17.   If the objective is to encourage particular public services, a selective grant is likely to be more effective than a general grant.

18.   Nevertheless, even with selective and matching grants, the revenue gain to the receiving jurisdiction may be partially diverted into other uses.

FURTHER READINGS

Buchanan, James M.: "An Economic Theory of Clubs," *Economica*, February 1965. "Federalism," *International Encyclopedia of Social Sciences*, vol. 5, New York: Macmillan, 1968, p. 360.

Musgrave, Richard A.: "Approaches to a Fiscal Theory of Political Federalism," with discussion, in National Bureau of Economic Research, *Public Finances, Needs, Sources and Utilization*, Princeton, N.J.: Princeton, 1961.

Oakland, W. H.: "Congestion, Public Goods, and Welfare," *Journal of Public Economics*, November 1972.

Oates, Wallace E.: *Fiscal Federalism*, New York: Harcourt Brace, 1972.

Tiebout, Charles M.: "A Pure Theory of Local Expenditures," *Journal of Political Economy*, October 1956.

Wagner, Richard E.: *The Fiscal Organization of American Federalism*, Chicago: Markham, 1971.

Wilde, James: "The Expenditure Effects of Grant-in-Aid Programs," *National Tax Journal*, September 1968.

Chapter 25

The Structure of
Fiscal Federalism
in the United States *

A. Structure of Fiscal Federalism in the United States: *Centralization by Level of Government; Differentials within States.* **B. Fiscal Position: Capacity, Need, Effort, and Performance:** *Defining Fiscal Position; Interstate Differentials; Intrastate Differentials; Differentials in Performance and Need; Local Governmental Units.* **C. The Grant System:** *Growth of System; Structure of Federal Grants; Categorical Grants; Bloc Grants; General Revenue Sharing; Recent Grant Developments; Evaluation.* **D. Summary.**

Having examined the general principles of multiunit finance, we now turn to the development of fiscal federalism in the United States and the urgent problems which currently face it.

A. STRUCTURE OF FISCAL FEDERALISM IN THE UNITED STATES

The United States is a federation consisting of a central (federal) government, fifty states, and the District of Columbia. Each state in turn shares its fiscal

*Reader's Guide to Chapter 25: Beginning with a brief sketch of the history and current status of fiscal federalism in the United States, this chapter examines the patterns of fiscal centralization and decentralization between levels of government and within states. This is followed by an analysis of fiscal capacity and needs, and of the structure of the rapidly expanding grant system. In the process, the complexity and diversity of the United States fiscal system becomes apparent.

tasks with local governments of various types, including cities, townships, counties, school districts, and other special service districts, 80,000 in all. Compared with that of most other countries, the fiscal structure of the United States has developed along relatively decentralized lines. At the same time, it has shown flexibility toward changing needs, as evidenced by the expanding role of intergovernmental transfers and the reassignment of fiscal responsibilities.

Centralization by Level of Government

A look back at the development of fiscal federalism in the United States is needed to understand its current position and trends. The fiscal structure of the original confederation was designed to protect the position of the states and to assure the fiscal weakness of the federal government, with the financing of national expenditures left to contributions by the states. But this structure was short-lived, as the Constitution of 1788 strengthened the fiscal position of the federal government and a viable system of federal finances based on customs duties and excises was established. At the same time, the Constitution set the framework for a decentralized system, without, however, determining specifically what the division of fiscal responsibilities was to be.[1] Nothing was said about the assignment of expenditure functions; and though federal taxing powers were limited by the uniformity and apportionment rules, these rules did not impose severe restrictions and eventually were relaxed further by the Sixteenth Amendment. The taxing powers of the states, similarly, were limited only by the strictures against the imposition of import duties and export taxes. Finally, nothing was said in the federal Constitution about the fiscal role of local governments, leaving its determination for the states to control.

The structure of fiscal federalism was thus left to develop in a flexible constitutional framework, and the relative strengths of the various levels of government have changed over the years. The nineteenth century opened with a great debate between the Jeffersonian view that the function of central government should be minimized and the Federalist position which assigned it a stronger function. Over time, the latter was to win out and the trend of development over the century was toward a stronger federal government. Proceeding slowly at first, this trend toward a stronger federal budget accelerated in the later part of the nineteenth century, driven by the needs of westward expansion and the conduct and aftermath of the Civil War. Federal revenues were dominated by customs proceeds up to the Civil War period, such receipts providing 90 percent or more of total revenue. By the close of the century, however, the contribution of customs duties had fallen below 50 percent. State and local revenues throughout were dominated by the property tax.

Expenditures by Origin of Funds   The distribution of expenditures by level of government may be viewed in two ways: (1) according to the origin

[1]See p. 30.

of funds, where grants are included at the level of the grantor, or (2) according to where expenditures to the public are made, in which case grants are included at the recipient's level. We begin with the former view.

At the beginning of the twentieth century, the share of local governments in public expenditures was 52 percent, that of the states 11 percent, and that of the federal government 36 percent. (See Table 25-1, lines 1 to 3.) With the exception of World War I, there was little change in this pattern until the 1930s, when the needs of the Great Depression brought the first major increase in the federal share. State and especially local governments were unable to meet these needs as their tax revenue dwindled with a falling level of national income, and the federal government was called upon to move into a wide range of new programs such as welfare, public works, and farm supports. The late thirties also saw the development of the social security program. As a result, the federal share in public expenditures rose from 33 percent at the close of the 1920s to 53 percent by 1940. This increase was

TABLE 25-1
Expenditures by Levels of Government
(As Percentage of Total)

	1902	1927	1940	1950	1960	1975
A. WITH GRANTS INCLUDED AT LEVEL OF ORIGIN						
Total Expenditures						
1. Federal	36.4	33.0	53.0	66.5	64.6	62.0
2. State	11.3	17.7	22.5	17.8	16.4	22.3
3. Local	52.4	49.3	24.5	15.6	19.0	15.7
Total	100.0	100.0	100.0	100.0	100.0	100.0
Civilian Expenditures						
4. Federal	21.2	24.7	47.3	48.4	48.5	54.5
5. State	13.9	19.8	25.2	27.5	23.8	26.7
6. Local	64.9	55.4	27.5	24.1	27.7	18.8
Total	100.0	100.0	100.0	100.0	100.0	100.0
B. WITH GRANTS INCLUDED AT LEVEL OF RECIPIENT						
Total Expenditures						
7. Federal	35.9	31.9	48.0	62.8	59.6	53.2
8. State	8.5	13.6	17.6	15.2	14.7	20.1
9. Local	55.5	54.5	34.4	22.0	25.7	26.7
Total	100.0	100.0	100.0	100.0	100.0	100.0
Civilian Expenditures						
10. Federal	20.6	23.5	41.7	42.7	41.2	44.6
11. State	10.6	15.2	19.7	23.4	21.5	28.9
12. Local	68.8	61.2	38.6	33.9	37.3	26.5
Total	100.0	100.0	100.0	100.0	100.0	100.0

Sources:
1902–1950: Data based on U.S. Bureau of the Census, *Historical Statistics of the United States,* 1960, pp. 725, 728, 330.
1960: Based on U.S. Bureau of the Census, *Government Finances in 1960,* p. 17.
1975: U.S. Bureau of the Census, *Governmental Finances in 1975–76.*

largely at the cost of the local share, which fell from 49 percent to 24 percent. At the same time, total public expenditures rose sharply relative to GNP, climbing from 10.4 percent in 1929 to 17.6 percent in 1940.

After 1940 the rising weight of defense expenditures brought about a second major increase in the total expenditure ratio and in the federal share. Whereas, prior to the 1940s, defense had accounted for 12 percent of total expenditures at all levels of government, this ratio shot up to 90 percent during World War II and settled at around one-third during the fifties and sixties.[2] With defense expenditures almost entirely at the federal level, this led to a further sharp increase in the federal share. Thus, federal expenditures by 1950 had come to account for 66 percent of the total. But the share has declined since then, with the 1975 level at 62 percent. At the same time, the federal share in civilian expenditures (see lines 4 to 6 of Table 25-1) showed little change from 1940 to 1960, but has risen significantly since then, standing now at 55 percent.

Expenditures to the Public   This picture of increasing expenditure centralization is arrived at by including grants at the level of the donor. The picture differs if, as shown in lines 7 to 12 of the table, intergovernmental grants are included at the level of the recipient. Distribution between levels is then in line with outlays to the public. As a result, the importance of the higher-level shares is reduced. The 1975 federal share in total expenditures drops from 62 to 53 percent and shows a substantial decline since 1950. That in civilian expenditures drops to 45 percent, leaving it only slightly above the 1950 level.

Both ways of looking at the matter are of interest. If concern is with revenue requirements, inclusion of grants at the level of origin is appropriate.[3] If interest lies with what levels control expenditures to the public, inclusion at the recipient level may be preferable. This is clearly the case if control over grants rests with the recipient, but must be qualified for categorical grants, the use of which is at least partly controlled by the donor. Nevertheless, assessment of fiscal centralization differs, depending on whether concern is with the tax or the expenditure side of the picture. Revenue centralization, as indicated by lines 1 to 3, has been more marked than has expenditure centralization, as measured by lines 7 to 9.

Differentials within States

Turning to a more disaggregated view, we now consider the pattern of fiscal centralization within states. The pattern varies greatly.

---

[2]The reader should view the changing pattern of shares by level of government in conjunction with the earlier discussion of overall expenditure levels in Chap. 7, especially Tables 7-3 and 7-5.

[3]The distribution of expenditures given in lines 1 to 3 generally resembles that of revenue (taxes and charges), with revenue shares of 56.5, 24.5, and 19.0 percent, respectively. Expenditure concentration, however, somewhat exceeds revenue concentration due to a deficit at the federal level and surplus at the state-local level.

State Share in Finance   This is apparent in Table 25-2, where the states' 1975 share in financing state and local expenditures from own sources is given. As shown in column I, the state share in total financing ranges from 72 percent for the most centralized quartile of states to 49 percent for the least centralized. We also observe that the degree of centralization differs greatly among functions (columns II to V), with welfare and highway expenditures the most centralized, and school expenditures the least. At the same time (not shown in the table), there is no distinct relationship between the degree of expenditure centralization and the overall composition of the state-local expenditure structure.

Effect on Tax Structure   The situation differs with regard to tax structure. As shown in Table 25-3, the composition of state tax structures varies widely. Thus, the 1975 share of total state-local tax revenue which is derived from property taxes ranges from 60 percent in the highest state (New Hampshire) to 13 percent in the lowest (Alaska), while the share derived from income taxes varies from 37 percent (Maryland) to 0 percent (Washington, Nevada, Texas, and Wyoming). Table 25-4 shows the relationship of these differences to the degree of tax centralization. We note (column I of Table 25-4) that the state share in total state-local tax revenue ranges from 76 percent in the most tax-centralized quartile of states to 40 percent in the least centralized quartile. Keeping the same rankings as in column I, columns II to V show the percentage of state-local revenue which is derived from various sources. We now note that the property tax share rises as the degree of centralization falls (column II), whereas the sales tax share declines (column III). Highly decentralized states, such as New Hampshire, tend to derive a large share of their revenue from the property tax, whereas centralized states, such as Alaska, Louisiana, and Delaware, derive a relatively small share from

TABLE 25-2
Percentage of State and Local Expenditures Financed by States, 1974–75*

Rankings[†]	Total (I)	Local Schools (II)	Highways (III)	Public Welfare (IV)	Health and Hospitals (V)
1. Highest quartile	71.7	72.8	87.2	99.7	89.3
2. Second quartile	62.1	56.5	76.8	94.7	60.2
3. Third quartile	55.6	43.0	65.4	87.7	49.1
4. Lowest quartile	48.7	29.1	53.8	56.9	36.6
5. Highest state	78.5	96.7	100.0	100.0	99.3
6. Average state	59.2	49.8	70.4	84.3	58.2
7. Lowest state	44.0	7.4	43.0	31.5	22.9

*Expenditures financed by state grants are included at the state level; expenditures financed by federal grants are excluded.
†States are ranked differently in each column, in line with the state share in expenditures on the particular function.
Source: Advisory Commission on Intergovernmental Relations, *Significant Features of Fiscal Federalism,* vol. 3, *Expenditures,* Washington: 1976–77, p. 18, table 9.

TABLE 25-3
Composition of State and Local Tax Structures, 1975

	PERCENTAGE OF REVENUE FROM			
	Property Tax	Income Tax*	General Sales Tax	Selective Sales Taxes
1. Highest state	60.0	36.8	38.9	28.9
2. Average state	33.4	18.4	21.4	16.4
3. Lowest state	12.7	0.0	0.0	9.2

*Includes individual and corporation tax.
Source: Advisory Commission on Intergovernmental Relations, *Significant Features of Fiscal Federalism*, vol. 2, *Revenue and Debt*, Washington: 1976–77, p. 32.

this source. However, this pattern is not uniform. Colorado and New York, for instance, are below the average in centralization but nevertheless have a relatively low property tax share. The reason for New York is that New York City places substantial reliance on city sales and income taxes.

B. FISCAL POSITION: CAPACITY, NEED, EFFORT, AND PERFORMANCE

Another aspect of fiscal diversity is reflected in the differentials in fiscal position of various jurisdictions.

Defining Fiscal Position

We begin by defining some of the concepts related to fiscal position. The ability of a jurisdiction to carry out its fiscal tasks (its fiscal position) depends

TABLE 25-4
Relationship of Tax Structure to Tax Centralization

State Share in State and Local Tax Revenue	State Taxes as Percentage of State-Local Taxes (I)	PERCENTAGE OF STATE-LOCAL TAX REVENUE FROM SELECTED TAXES			
		Property Tax (II)	Income Tax* (III)	General Sales Tax (IV)	Selective Sales Taxes (V)
1. Highest quartile	75.7	20.0	21.2	26.6	19.1
2. Second quartile	65.1	30.3	19.2	24.4	15.9
3. Third quartile	58.0	38.7	17.1	18.2	16.3
4. Lowest quartile	48.8	45.6	16.2	16.4	14.0
5. Highest state	82.7	17.5	11.9	34.8	16.5
6. Average state	61.6	34.0	18.4	21.2	16.3
7. Lowest state	40.1	60.0	8.1	—	22.9

*Includes individual and corporate income taxes
Source: Advisory Commission on Intergovernmental Relations, *Significant Features of Fiscal Federalism*, vol. 2, *Revenue and Debt*, Washington: 1976–77, p. 25, table 12, and p. 30, table 16.

on its tax base (its capacity) relative to the outlay required for rendering public services (its need). When jurisdictions with relatively high capacity are faced with low needs, their fiscal position is strong. A standard level of services can be provided with a low ratio of tax revenue to tax base (a low-tax effort); or, putting it alternatively, a standard level of tax effort will generate a high service level relative to need (high fiscal performance). Where the opposite holds, a high effort may be needed to provide only a substandard performance level. More precisely, the various concepts are related to each other as follows:

We define the *fiscal capacity* of jurisdictions j or C_j as

$$C_j = t_s B_j \tag{1}$$

where B_j is the tax base in j and t_s is a standard tax rate.[4] C_j thus measures the revenue which j would obtain by applying that rate to its base.

We also define the *fiscal need* of jurisdiction j or N_j as

$$N_j = n_s Z_j \tag{2}$$

where Z_j is the target population, such as number of school-age children, while n_s is the cost of providing a standard service level per unit of Z, such as instruction per child.[5] N_j thus measures the outlay in j required to secure a standard level of performance or service.

We can now measure the *fiscal position* of j or P_j as

$$P_j = C_j / N_j = t_s B_j / n_s Z_j \tag{3}$$

Fiscal position thus equals the ratio of capacity to need. Setting P for jurisdictions on the average equal to 1, a value of $P_j > 1$ implies a strong fiscal position and a value of $P_j < 1$ a weak fiscal position. The value of P, properly defined, is the index to which distributional weights in grant formulas should be linked. Next, we may define jurisdiction j's *tax effort* E_j as

$$E_j = t_j B_j / t_s B_j = t_j / t_s \tag{4}$$

or the ratio of actual revenue in j obtained by applying j's tax rate t_j to what would be raised by applying t_s. Finally, we define the performance level M as

$$M_j = n_j Z_j / n_s Z_j = n_j / n_s \tag{5}$$

---

[4]To simplify, we assume that there is one tax rate and one tax base only. Actually, there are different bases, such as sales, property, and income, calling for application of a standard tax structure rather than a single rate.

[5]Our presentation again oversimplifies as it allows for one service Z only rather than for a mix of services, the importance of which will vary among jurisdictions. Moreover, a more detailed analysis would have to allow for variations in n, such as school teachers' salaries.

or the ratio of actual outlay obtained by applying j's outlay rate n_j to that required to meet the standard level at rate n_s.

Assuming a balanced budget, we have

$$t_j B_j = n_j Z_j \tag{6}$$

By substituting from (6) into (3) we obtain an alternative definition of fiscal position:

$$P_j = \frac{n_j}{n_s} \bigg/ \frac{t_j}{t_s} \tag{7}$$

Fiscal position may thus be defined as the ratio of capacity to need as in (3) or as the ratio of performance to tax effort as in (7). These concepts and problems—which arise in comparing fiscal positions both among states and among jurisdictions within states—pose one of the principal issues in fiscal reform. They are of concern both to the federal government, called upon to reduce excessive differentials among states, and to state governments, called upon to deal with excessive differentials among local jurisdictions. Moreover, the federal government has in recent years become directly involved in the fiscal position of the cities.

Interstate Differentials

Comparison across states shows substantial differences in fiscal capacity and effort.

Capacity   A first approximation to fiscal capacity is given by per capita income. This figure provides a comprehensive measure of ability to pay but does not allow for the fact that the income tax plays only a minor role in state tax structures and as yet hardly any at the local level. Retail sales and assessed property value might be preferable indicators in this respect, or capacity might be measured by combining the various bases with appropriate weights. The latter may be done by applying a "standard tax structure" and may be measured in terms of the per capita yield of that structure.

Table 25-5 shows the range of differentials in fiscal capacity among selected states. Column I shows per capita income as percentage of average, while column II shows fiscal capacity as measured by the per capita yield of an average tax structure in any one state relative to the yield of that structure imposed in a hypothetical average-base state. Both state and local revenue is included. Using the per capita income measure, the range is from over 130 percent of the average at the high end of the scale to 69 percent at the bottom. Using the standard tax system, the range is somewhat narrower. As one would expect, the urban states show up better with the income index, and the natural-resource states do better under the standard yield measures which include the property base. The capacity measure ranges from 70 to 80 percent below average in the South to more than 110 percent above average in the wealthier states. The capacity of urban areas is typically around the average.

TABLE 25-5
Interstate Differentials in Tax Capacity and Effort, 1975

	CAPACITY MEASURES		EFFORT MEASURES	
	Per Capita Income as Percentage of Average (I)	Taxable Capacity as Percentage of Average* (II)	Tax Revenue as Percentage of Income (III)	Tax Revenue as Percentage of Standard (IV)
United States	100.0	100.0	100.0	100.0
High				
District of Columbia	130.3	126	92	101
Connecticut	119.5	112	93	106
New Jersey	117.7	112	101	113
New York	116.9	106	146	171
California	111.7	112	125	132
Middle				
Indiana	96.6	97	95	101
Colorado	100.9	106	99	100
Minnesota	95.8	97	121	127
Wisconsin	94.8	95	119	126
Low				
West Virginia	78.8	81	102	106
Alabama	76.2	76	84	90
Arkansas	73.1	81	82	79
Mississippi	69.1	71	102	106
Selected Urban Areas				
New York	116.9	106	146	171
Massachusetts	109.3	98	125	146
Pennsylvania	99.9	95	100	112
Maryland	109.3	101	105	121
New Jersey	117.7	112	101	113

*Revenue derived from tax base in particular state by application of average tax rate, as percentage of revenue which these rates yield on average base.
†Ratio of actual revenue of state to revenue which average rates would provide in that state.
Source: Advisory Commission on Intergovernmental Relations, *Measuring the Fiscal "Blood Pressure" of States*, Washington: February 1977.

Effort   The simplest measure of tax effort is given by the ratio of revenue to some broad index of tax base such as personal income. This is shown in column III, while column IV shows the ratio of actual yield to that obtained by a standard tax system. We find that effort measures vary more widely than do capacity measures and that there is no close relationship between the two. The low-income states exhibit an about-average effort ratio, while among other states there frequently exists a negative relationship between effort and capacity. Urban states show a well above average effort ratio, especially New York, which combines only average capacity with a very high effort ratio.

Intrastate Differentials

Comparison among municipalities is more difficult. Jurisdictions differ and fewer data are available. However, a comparison may be drawn in terms of differentials in property tax rates. This is shown in Table 25-6 for the New England states. Based on data for the late sixties, with later compilations not available, we note that assessed property value per pupil varies sharply across local jurisdictions. Thus, in Maine, the bottom 10 percent of jurisdictions showed an assessed value of $3,600 per pupil as against $25,000 in the highest decile. The variability among jurisdictions within states in most cases is substantially greater than that among states. As also shown in column V, the level of the property tax rate—or index of local effort—is related inversely to the level of tax base per pupil. As we move down column II, the valuation per pupil rises, while the tax rate, as shown in column IV, falls.

Differentials in Performance and Need

Given sharp differentials in fiscal capacities and revenue effort among states, it is not surprising to find equally sharp differentials in performance levels. As shown in Table 25-7, total per capita expenditures vary from below 80 to over 120 percent of the average. The differences are even wider with regard to certain categories such as local schools. While there is some positive relationship between per capita income and expenditures as measured across states, especially with regard to schools and welfare, there are also frequent exceptions to this rule.

Although comparison between average expenditure levels is instructive, these reflect differentials in real service levels (relative to an average standard) only to the extent that per capita needs (or costs of standard service

TABLE 25-6
Differentials in Tax Base and Effort within States
(Distribution across Jurisdictions)

	EQUALIZED VALUATION PER PUPIL (In Thousands of Dollars)			SCHOOL TAX RATE	
	Lowest Decile (I)	Median Decile (II)	Highest Decile (III)	Median (IV)	Simple Correlation of Tax Rate and Base (V)
Maine	3.6	7.8	25.6	28.9	−.81
Massachusetts	15.5	27.3	45.2	22.4	−.82
Vermont	16.0	25.9	57.4	12.3	−.71
New Hampshire	13.7	22.6	56.2	18.8	−.88
Rhode Island	23.1	28.9	42.5	17.8	−.73
Connecticut	19.3	29.5	46.8	14.0	−.75

Source: Steven J. Weiss and Robert W. Eisenmenger, "The Problem of Redistribution of Federal and State Funds," in *Financing State and Local Governments,* Boston: Federal Reserve Bank of Boston, 1970, p. 67.

TABLE 25-7

Per Capita State and Local Expenditures as Percentage of Average, 1975–76

Selected States Grouped by Per Capita Income	Local Schools	Highways	Public Welfare	Health	Sewerage	Total
High						
Connecticut	98	75	89	64	126	88
Illinois	104	114	112	75	96	103
California	115	70	146	111	100	117
Hawaii	90	156	126	122	174	106
Middle						
Ohio	96	83	82	87	81	92
Minnesota	118	139	125	96	158	121
Oregon	115	120	91	74	142	121
Texas	93	85	59	89	72	94
Low						
Vermont	97	150	118	71	40	110
Tennessee	70	115	62	102	92	78
New Mexico	105	131	56	93	50	109
Mississippi	72	147	60	108	35	80
Selected Urban States						
New York	121	75	192	184	148	114
Massachusetts	111	76	142	95	75	96
Pennsylvania	95	103	117	73	67	90
New Jersey	108	77	103	65	112	97

Source: U.S. Bureau of the Census, *Governmental Finances in 1975–76*, table 22, p. 64.

levels as measured in dollar terms) are the same in each state. As we have seen, this is not the case. Taking school expenditures as an illustration, correction should be made for cost differentials, differentials in the ratio of total to school-age population, and the share of enrollment in parochial schools. With regard to highways, comparison of per capita expenditures fails to reflect cost differentials of highway services due to density and climate. Welfare expenditures need to be translated into outlay per eligible recipient and so forth. While capacity can be measured without too much difficulty, measuring aggregate need levels poses a more complex and as yet unresolved task.[6] Nevertheless, the per capita data of Table 25-7, though crude, points to the existence of substantial differentials.

[6]To obtain a comprehensive measure of need, it is necessary to postulate a set of service levels—involving such items as education, roads, welfare, health, and municipal services—and to determine what it would cost to provide them in various jurisdictions. To do this, it is necessary to define service levels in "objective terms" and to allow for cost differentials. The definition of service levels in particular is a difficult task. Should service levels be measured in terms of inputs (e.g., teacher hours per grade school child) or in terms of output (e.g., reading proficiency requirements)? How can a meaningful comparison be drawn between the service levels provided by rural and city roads? After these difficulties are met, there is the further problem of costing any particular service, with allowance for the interdependence of costs and service levels. For reference to recent work on need indices for cities, see p. 568.

TABLE 25-8
Structure of Local Government Finance

	Number 1977 (I)	REVENUE, 1975 (Billions of Dollars)			
		General (II)	Intergovernmental (III)	Charges and Miscellaneous (IV)	Total (V)
Counties	3,042	18.1	14.7	5.5	38.3
Cities	18,856	30.2	19.6	5.5	55.3
Townships	16,822	3.9	1.7	0.5	6.1
School districts	15,260	26.8	26.1	4.0	56.9
Special districts	26,140	5.3	3.1	4.0	12.4
Total	80,120	84.4	65.2	19.5	169.0*

*Total is reduced to $160 billion if intralocal grants are netted out.
Sources:
Column I: See U.S. Bureau of the Census, *Governmental Units in 1977*, Preliminary Report No. 1, 1977 Census of Governments.
Column II: See Tax Foundation, *Facts and Figures in Government Finance*, New York: 1977, p. 246. General revenue includes *own* revenue from taxes, fees and charges but excludes grants.

Local Governmental Units

The preceding discussion has been in terms of federal, state, and local levels of government, but a word needs to be said about the large array of governmental units at the local level. In addition to one federal and fifty state governments, there are over 80,000 further governmental units, all of which are included under the rubric of local government. The number of local government units and their estimated role in the fiscal picture are shown in Table 25-8.

Townships, school districts, and municipalities rank about equal in number, with special districts more numerous and counties much less numerous. There is a great deal of variety in the pattern of local government among the different states. Thus, counties are of major importance in the South, school districts abound in South Dakota, Texas, and Nebraska, and townships are of special importance in the Northeastern states. Municipalities (i.e., cities) rank much ahead of the other units in fiscal importance, with school districts and counties next in line. Special districts and townships, though more numerous, are less significant in terms of the amounts of revenue or expenditures involved.

Two significant recent trends show (1) a decline in the number of school districts due to economies of scale in larger schools, and (2) increased use of special districts for particular functions such as mass transit, parks, police and environmental expenditures.

C. THE GRANT SYSTEM

In recent years, the growth of the grant system has been the most dynamic factor in the development of United States fiscal federalism.

Growth of System

As shown in Table 25-9, the recent growth of the grant system has proceeded at both the federal and the state levels, but the growth of federal grants has been most spectacular. These grants have grown from $7 billion in 1960 to $85 billion in 1979, with nearly half the growth having occurred since the mid-seventies. In the process, grants have risen from 8 to 17 percent of federal expenditures and, over the last decade, have accounted for over 20 percent of federal expenditure growth. This development has produced major structural changes in the fiscal pattern. One of these changes has been the rising importance of direct federal grants to local governments. Another is the growing importance of cities as recipients of grants, a development the importance of which will be considered when we deal with urban finance.

The growth of state grants to local government, as shown in Table 25-10, has proceeded steadily over the last decade, with grants to education the major growth item and total grants now over four times their level of the mid-sixties.

The growth of federal grants has had a major impact on state-local revenue. As shown in Table 25-11, the importance of grants in the state and local revenue structure has risen throughout the century and has increased

TABLE 25-9
Growth of Federal Grants
(In Billions of Dollars)

		1965	1970	1976	1979*
1.	Total	11.0	21.9	55.6	85.0
2.	Aid to state governments[†]	9.8	19.3	42.0	57.0
3.	Direct federal aid to local governments	1.2	2.6	13.6	28.0
4.	Direct federal aid to city governments	0.4	1.2	5.8	n.a.
	Ratios				
5.	(3) as percentage of (1)	10.5	11.9	24.4	35.0
6.	(4) as percentage of (1)	3.7	5.5	13.4	n.a.
7.	(4) as percentage of (3)	35.2	44.4	42.6	n.a.

*Estimated.
[†]Includes amounts to be passed through to local governments.
Source: For 1965 to 1976 data, see *City Needs and the Responsiveness of Federal Grant Programs,* Subcommittee on the City of the Committee on Banking, Finance, and Urban Affairs, House of Representatives, 95th Congress, Washington: April 1978, p. 42. For estimates for 1979, see Richard P. Mason, "The Outlook for Federal Cities," in Roy Bahl (ed.), *The Fiscal Outlook for Cities,* Syracuse, N.Y.: Syracuse University Press, 1978.

TABLE 25-10
Growth of State Aid
(Dollar Amounts in Billions)

	1964	1970	1976
Education	7.7	17.1	34.0
Public welfare	2.1	5.0	8.3
Other uses	3.2	6.8	14.4
Total	13.0	28.9	56.7
Aid as percentage of local revenue from own-sources	42.9	56.2	60.8

Source: Advisory Commission on Intergovernmental Relations, *Significant Features of Fiscal Federalism,* vol. 3, *Expenditures,* Washington: 1967–77, p. 9.

rapidly over the last fifteen years. With federal grants traditionally going almost entirely to the states, and state grants to local governments, federal grants in 1960 provided 19 percent of state revenue, and state grants provided 28 percent of local revenue. By 1975 these ratios had risen to 25 and 32 percent. In addition federal grants have become a significant factor in local revenue, with state and local governments by 1979 receiving about 20 percent of their total revenue from grant sources. The rising importance of direct federal grants to localities has been linked closely to federal aid to cities. As noted below such aid has come to exceed 50 percent of own-revenue in some of the major cities.

Since expenditure and revenue structures differ at various levels of government, the growth of grants has had important bearing on the composi-

TABLE 25-11
Intergovernmental Revenue as Percentage of Total Revenue*

Year	FEDERAL GRANTS AS PERCENTAGE OF			State Grants as Percentage of Total Local Revenue
	Total State Revenue	Total Local Revenue[†]	Total State and Local Revenue[‡]	
1902	1.6	0.1	0.7	6.1
1932	8.7	2.0	3.1	10.4
1940	11.6	3.0	8.8	23.6
1948	13.9	1.3	9.7	28.5
1960	19.4	1.5	12.6	28.4
1975	24.5	6.8	15.1	32.1
1979	n.a.	n.a.	20.0[§]	n.a.

*Total revenue includes own-revenue plus grants.
[†]Excludes revenue from utility and liquor stores.
[‡]Duplicate transactions between state and local governments are excluded in arriving at total state and local revenue.
[§]Estimated.
Sources: U.S. Bureau of the Census, *Census of Governments,* vol. VI, no. 4, 1962, pp. 38–46; Tax Foundation, *Facts and Figures in Government Finance,* New York: 1977, pp. 19 and 243.

tion of the overall fiscal system. On the one hand, it has strengthened the capacity of state and local governments to meet their expenditure functions, including transportation, education, and welfare. On the other hand, it has increased reliance on the federal individual income tax while relieving pressures on state and local taxes, especially the property tax.

Structure of Federal Grants

The federal grant structure is highly complex, containing a wide range of program areas and types of grants.

Program Areas   As shown in Table 25-12, the largest grant categories are the education, employment, and social service grants made by the Department of Health, Education, and Welfare (HEW), including the recently emerging federal grants to cities. Next in importance are income security and health. Grants in all these areas have grown rapidly in recent years, but the growth of grants directed at providing fiscal relief to the cities is especially noteworthy. Federal grants in 1976 paid for about 10 percent of state-local expenditures on education, 23 percent of expenditures on highways, and nearly 50 percent of expenditures on welfare.[7]

Types of Grants   Apart from distinguishing federal grants by program functions, we may also group them by type of grant. This is shown in Table 25-13. The most general type of grant is revenue sharing, under which grants are made with practically no strings attached. Next come general purpose or bloc grants, made in support of broad expenditure categories and leaving it largely to the receiving jurisdiction to decide how to spend the funds. Finally, there are categorical grant programs where the grant is earmarked for more narrowly defined purposes.

As shown in the table, the grant system until the early seventies was almost entirely in the form of categorical grants, but since then increased use has been made of general purpose and bloc grants. This has reflected dissatisfaction with a large number of highly specified categorical programs, and the desire to leave more discretion to the recipient governments, thereby decentralizing the decision process. However, this movement has slowed down, with about 75 percent of total grant funds still dispensed in categorical form. As noted below, the categorical grant approach appears to be regaining favor, not because stricter control is desired, but because it offers a politically feasible way of targeting funds into high-need jurisdictions.

Categorical Grants

Critics of categorical grants have pointed to the maze of over 1,000 such programs, although in reality 450 is a better estimate.[8] Among them, public assistance and Medicaid are the most important and account for over one-half of the total.

---

[7]Based on U.S. Bureau of the Census, *Governmental Finances in 1975–76*, p. 21.
[8]See Advisory Commission on Intergovernmental Relations, *Categorical Grants, Their Role and Design*, Washington: 1977, p. 92.

TABLE 25-12
Federal Grants by Program Area
(In Billions of Dollars)

		1960	1968	1975	1979*
1.	Education, training, employment, and social services	0.9	4.7	11.2	22.4
2.	Health	0.1	0.8	8.8	14.1
3.	Income security	2.1	5.4	9.3	14.8
4.	Transportation	2.9	4.3	5.6	10.4
5.	Community and regional development	—	—	3.4	6.3
6.	Natural resources and environment	2.0	3.2	2.4	5.6
7.	Other	—	—	9.6	11.4
8.	Total	8.0	18.5	50.3	85.0

*Estimated.
Sources: Data for 1960 and 1968, Advisory Commission on Intergovernmental Relations, *Significant Features of Fiscal Federalism,* vol. 1, Washington: 1976–77, p. 56. Data for 1975, Tax Foundation, *Facts and Figures in Government Finance,* New York: 1977, p. 85. Data for 1979,   Special Analysis, The Budget of the United States Government, Fiscal Year 1979, p. 187.

Types Categorical grants may be "formula-based" or they may be "project" grants.[9] Formula grants, which account for about 70 percent of the categorical grant funds, become available automatically to eligible recipients, with distribution among jurisdictions determined by the applicable formula. Project grants are made upon application by the grantee and their distribution is not based on such a formula. Since there are also in-between types of grants, neat classification is not always possible.

The formulas used differ widely among grants. Some grants begin with a flat per capita amount for each state; others set a cap on the total. The factors used in the formulas typically include population and per capita income as measures of need, but in some cases more specific indices are added. Thus, the distribution formula for the state boating-safety program allocates one-third of the funds in line with the number of registered vessels. In most cases, the resulting formulas may be viewed as a compromise between the principles (1) that each state is entitled to its "fair" share, (2) that the allocation should reflect "need" for the particular service, and (3) that "capacity" or ability to meet such needs from own-resources should be allowed for.

Another important feature of categorical grants is the matching requirement. This applies to both formula and project grants. About 60 percent of categorical grants require matching, with matching rates from 5 to 50 percent or more. However, most matching requirements are well below 50 percent. Matching rates may be uniform for the entire grant or they may vary by amount and by characteristics of the receiving jurisdiction, such as the level of per capita income.

[9]See ibid.

TABLE 25-13
Federal Grants by Type
(In Billions of Dollars)

		1960	1968	1975	1979
1.	General purpose aid			6.1	6.9
2.	General revenue sharing	—	—		
3.	Other	—	0.4	0.9	2.7
4.	Total	—	0.4	7.0	9.6
5.	Broad-based aid	—	0.1	5.4	10.8
6.	Categorical grants	7.0	18.2	37.6	64.6
7.	Total	7.0	18.6	49.7	85.0

Sources: See notes to Table 25-12.

HEW Grants   Most of the categorical grant programs are administered by the Department of Health, Education, and Welfare (HEW). While conditional in nature, the tightness of the strings and other aspects of grant design differ for various grants. Since the programs are categorical, they are linked to a particular need or target population, such as school children. But they differ in that some are capacity-related whereas others are not, and in that some require matching whereas others do not. Where capacity is allowed for, this is done by varying the allotment inversely to capacity or by adjusting the matching rate. Another possibility is to set a ceiling on the matching amount and let it relate inversely to the recipient's capacity. Allowing for these differences and in line with our earlier tabulation of grants, HEW grants may be grouped as follows:[10]

	Nonmatching	MATCHING	
Capacity		Uniform	Variable
Not allowed for	1	3	5
Allowed for	2	4	6

Group 1 typically takes the form

$$A_i = a_0 + a_1 \frac{P_i}{P_t}$$

with A_i the allotment to the ith state, P_i the size of the "target" population group in the ith state (such as elementary school pupils or welfare recipients), and P_t the total target population for the nation as a whole. The constant a_0 is introduced to allow for overhead administrative costs but is of minor weight. The distribution is thus essentially on a population basis. Though used in the majority of HEW grants, this formula makes no allowance for differentials in capacity and implies a very crude measure of need

[10]See p. 555.

since it fails to allow for cost differentials and other factors. In other instances, further allowance for need is introduced by relating the grant to average expenditures in the area, but once more, existing expenditure levels may be a misleading indicator of actual needs. Moving on to group 2, allowance for capacity may be introduced by letting the size of the allotment vary not only with target population but also inversely to capacity. Or it may be linked to the matching rate.

Most HEW grants which call for matching do so with a uniform matching rate. Such rates differ among programs and vary from 33 to 90 percent. Usually, a uniform matching rate is combined with a population-based allotment (group 3), but in some programs the allotment (the maximum available amount of matching monies) falls with per capita income (group 4).[11]

In other cases, a variable matching rate is combined with an allotment which does not allow for capacity (group 5). In still others, allowance for per capita income is made in both the allotment and the matching rate (group 6). An illustration is given by the Hill-Burton hospital facilities grant where the allotment is based on the above formula while the matching rate, made a function of per capita income Y, equals

$$F_i = 1.0 - 0.5\ Y_i / Y_t$$

The result is an increased redistributive effect when the allotment is in fact used up.

Without delving further into the details of various grant formulas,[12] we may note the significance of variability in the allotment and matching rate components of the formulas:

1. In the absence of matching, allowance for per capita income in the allotment formulas introduces a need component and renders the grant more equalizing.

2. Introduction of a matching requirement has a substitution effect making for increased own-expenditures.

3. Relating matching requirements inversely to per capita income exerts a stronger substitution effect on the low-capacity state, thus making for a tendency to equalize service levels.

[11]This is illustrated by the formula

$$A_i = a_1 \frac{P_i(1.0 - 0.5\,Y_i/Y_t)^2}{\Sigma P_j(1.0 - 0.5\,Y_j/Y_t)^2}$$

as used in allotments under the vocational rehabilitation grants. A_i is the basic allotment to the ith state and a_1 is a constant given by the appropriation. In the numerator, P_i is the population and Y_i the per capita income of the ith state, and Y_t is the average per capita income for the United States. In the denominator, the expression is summed for all fifty states and the District of Columbia. The basic allotment thus determined sets the maximum amount which can be obtained by a state, subject to compliance with a flat matching rate.

[12]For a description of these grant systems, see Selma J. Mushkin and John F. Cotton, *Functional Federalism*, Washington: George Washington University, 1968, chap. 4.

4. The combination of a variable allotment with a variable matching rate further increases the tendency to equalize service levels.

Recent Developments   Recent grant developments have included the emergence of a new type of grant, mostly categorical in nature but targeted more specifically than had been the case before to low-income residents and distressed jurisdictions. We shall deal with these grants when we examine the position of cities.

Bloc Grants

Bloc grants, also referred to as "broad-based aid," involve less central control and are easier to administer.[13] For both these reasons, the Nixon administration, in 1971, introduced plans for "special revenue sharing" under which the principle of bloc grants was to be broadened and the proliferation of categorical grants to be consolidated into a smaller number of grant packages. Six major grant areas were to be defined, with over 100 categorical grants folded into six special revenue-sharing programs.[14] The grants made under each program were to be earmarked for use in one of the six areas, but without strings as to their specific application and without matching requirements.

Congress responded slowly to these suggestions, but various pieces of legislation have taken some steps toward grant consolidation and increased flexibility for the recipient. Thus, the urban renewal and model cities program has been combined with five other programs to form a "community development" grant, and other such consolidations are pending. Nevertheless, as was shown in Table 25-13, broad-based or bloc grants still provide only 13 percent of the total.

While the bloc grant approach meets a need for simplification and is naturally favored by governors and mayors, it also has its disadvantages. Increased use of bloc grants reduces the ability of the federal government to meet particular expenditure needs which are of primary national concern. Moreover, the growth of bloc grants has been associated with reduced emphasis on matching, as a result of which the grant system is rendered less efficient in raising the level of public services. Finally, categorical grants may be pointed at programs which are of particular importance to fiscally distressed areas or low-income residents and may thus be used for purposes of fiscal equalization.

General Revenue Sharing

After lengthy debate, a new type of federal aid was enacted in 1972. Referred to as "general revenue sharing," it extended the bloc grant approach even

---

[13]See Advisory Commission on Intergovernmental Relations, *Bloc Grants: A Comparative Analysis*, Washington: 1977.

[14]The six areas are (1) education, (2) law enforcement, (3) manpower, (4) rural development, (5) transportation, and (6) urban development.

further and provided for a new system of unrestricted and nonmatching grants to the states and, via a pass-through provision, to local governments.

Enacted with strong bipartisan support in 1972 and for an initial five-year period, the legislation, known as the State and Local Fiscal Assistance Act of 1972, was extended in 1976 to continue through 1980. The major provisions of the revenue-sharing program are these:

1.   Revenue-sharing grants amounted to $6.9 billion in 1979.
2.   The grants are administered through a trust fund, financed by payments from the Treasury and without requiring annual appropriations or budgetary reconsideration.[15]
3.   The total is to be distributed among the states on the basis of:
   a.   A three-factor formula, involving population, tax effort, and inverse of per capita income; or
   b.   A five-factor formula, adding urban population and income tax revenue. In computing each state's share, the formula yielding the higher allotment applies.
4.   One-third of the allotment is retained by the state, with the remainder to be passed through to local governments.
5.   Distribution among local units includes all units of general government, i.e., counties, cities, and townships, while excluding school districts and certain special-purpose districts.
6.   Distribution among local units is based on a three-factor formula similar to that given in 3(a).
7.   Recipients must account for the use of their proceeds and comply with certain administrative provisions, but there are no major restrictions regarding the use to which the funds are put.

While initially this program was heralded as the pathway to a "new federalism," the enthusiasm has cooled since then. The fiscal position of states and localities on the whole has strengthened since the program was first adopted, and the allocation of funds has not been satisfactory. It is doubtful whether the program will be extended in 1980, even in reduced form.

Recent Grant Developments

Grant developments in the mid-seventies have led to the introduction of new types of grants aimed primarily at providing assistance to local jurisdictions with high rates of unemployment and in fiscal distress. These grants have greatly increased direct federal assistance to local governments as well as strengthened the redistributional impact of the federal grant system. They will be dealt with in the following chapter, where the fiscal crisis of the cities is considered.

---

[15]Under the original Heller-Pechman plan, revenue sharing was to be financed by a share in income tax revenue equal to 2 percent of net taxable income under the federal individual income tax. This would have permitted the allotment to grow with the tax base independent of tax rates. Congress, instead, limited the program to a five-year trial period and stipulated the amounts for each year roughly in line with the original proposal.

Evaluation

In order to evaluate the federal grant program, it is necessary to decide what purpose or purposes it is designed to serve. In line with our earlier discussion, a distinction may be drawn between these objectives:

1.   Substitution of federal for state-local revenue, thus relieving the burden imposed on property and sales taxes
2.   Stimulation of expenditures on public services in general or of particular public services, be it to correct for spillovers or to promote merit goods
3.   Fiscal equalization by transfer of funds from fiscally strong to fiscally weak jurisdictions

We consider now how these objectives may be met by choosing the appropriate type of grants.

Substitution of Federal Revenue   It may be argued that the federal income tax is superior as a revenue source to most state and local taxes. Thus a case may be made for financing a larger part of state and local expenditures by drawing on this source.[16] Grants are needed for this purpose and most appropriately would be of the general revenue-sharing type. To be distributionally neutral, revenue might be returned by origin of federal receipts, as is done, for instance, in the German revenue-sharing system, rather than by a per capita or weighted need formula as followed under the United States revenue-sharing policy.

Stimulation of State-Local Expenditures   Traditional emphasis on categorical grants reflects the desire of Congress to support state and local expenditures rather than to substitute federal revenue sources. Given the intent to stimulate public expenditures at the recipient level, a matching grant is clearly more efficient than a nonmatching one. By matching, the own-cost of public services is reduced, and this will induce increased outlay of own-funds.

If the intent is to stimulate expenditures in general, the appropriate matching base is the own-revenue of the recipient. Much the same is accomplished by permitting state or local taxes to be deducted from the federal income tax base or to be credited against federal tax.[17] Inclusion of a tax effort variable into grant formulas as with general revenue sharing also works in the same direction.

If the intent is to stimulate particular activities, the recipient's own-financed outlays on that activity are the appropriate matching base. While we have seen that even such grants involve leakages, they are more effective in encouraging a particular activity than are broad-based and nonmatching grants. Depending on the matching formula used, estimates of expenditure

---

[16]It appears that the introduction of general revenue sharing has been used largely to reduce state-local taxes (or to dampen their increase) rather than to stimulate new programs. See Richard P. Nathan and Charles F. Adams, Jr., *Revenue Sharing: The Second Round*, Washington: Brookings, 1977.

[17]See p. 390.

responses to matching grants typically show that per dollar of grant, expenditures are raised by \$1.20 or so, thus recording a modest stimulating effect. For the case of nonmatching grants, the response tends to be around 80 to 90 cents, thus showing a significant degree of leakage.[18]

Fiscal Equalization   It remains to consider the objective of fiscal equalization or "targeting," i.e., the channeling of funds to jurisdictions which are most in need of support.

As a first approximation, this might be interpreted as redistributing fiscal resources from high- to low-income states. Table 25-14 shows how the interstate distribution of aid relates to state per capita income. States are ranked by per capita income from the lowest up (column I), and their rank order by per capita grant received under various distribution formulas is given in columns II to IV. Column II shows the ranking for a hypothetical grant distribution with population weighted inversely by per capita income.[19] Column III shows the ranking for the actual distribution of total categorical grants in 1975, while column IV records the rankings under general revenue sharing. An overall comparison is given at the bottom of the table, where the average rankings for the ten states at the bottom, middle, and top of the scale are shown.

The income-weighted population formula, of course, favors the low-income states, but there is little relationship between the ranking by per capita income and that of columns III and IV. The ranking of grants under the categorical programs shows little or no relationship to per capita income, while ranking under revenue sharing registers a slight negative relationship.[20]

---

[18]For a survey of empirical work on responses to grants, see Advisory Commission on Intergovernmental Relations, *Federal Grants: Their Effects on State-Local Expenditures, Employment Levels and Wage Rates*, Washington: February 1977.

[19]Payments to the ith state equal

$$\frac{P_i \cdot P_i / Y_i}{\Sigma P_j \cdot \Sigma P_j / \Sigma Y_j} \cdot B$$

where P is population, Y is personal income, and B is the total amount to be distributed. Per capita payments, underlying the ranking in column II, accordingly equal

$$\frac{P_i / Y_i}{\Sigma P_j / \Sigma Y_j} \cdot B$$

[20]As noted above, revenue sharing is based on two formulas, with the higher-yielding one to be applied (see p. 559). The first formula (originally advanced by the Senate), assigns one-third of the weight each to population, to the inverse of per capita income, and to tax effort. The population weight in itself is somewhat redistributive since equal per capita grants result in a higher grant-income ratio for states with low per capita income. Moreover, this base helps the densely populated urban states. The use of an inverse income variable—defined as the ratio of per capita income for the United States to that in the particular state—is more redistributive since it directs additional funds to the low-income states. The tax effort variable, finally, is more or less neutral since there is no strong relationship between per capita income and tax effort. The additional urban population variable in the second formula (advanced by the House of Representatives) is designed to recognize particular urban needs while the income tax weight is added as an incentive to increased use of income taxation.

Given the nature of these weights, it is understandable that the urban Eastern states were primarily concerned with the population and urban weights, whereas the low-income and less populous states favored the income variable as a major factor. The final legislation which permits each state to choose between the two formulas is a compromise solution resulting in a rather ill-defined and not very meaningful pattern.

TABLE 25-14
Ranking of States by Per Capita Income and Aid under Alternative Grant Distributions

State	Per Capita Income (1975) (I)	GRANTS PER CAPITA DISTRIBUTED BY			
		Population Weighted by Inverse of Per Capita Income (II)	Categorical Grants-in-Aid (III)	Revenue Sharing Act of 1972 (IV)	Column IV, Net of Taxes (V)
Mississippi	51	1	16	1	1
Arkansas	50	2	24	18	9
New Mexico	49	3	4	9	6
South Carolina	48	4	41	19	11
Alabama	47	5	29	30	13
Kentucky	46	6	18	24	12
Louisiana	45	7	31	5	8
Tennessee	44	8	34	28	15
Maine	43	9	11	7	4
North Carolina	42	10	46	26	16
West Virginia	41	11	9	10	5
Utah	40	12	20	20	14
Vermont	39	13	5	6	3
Georgia	38	14	21	35	22
South Dakota	37	15	8	2	2
Idaho	36	16	17	23	23
Oklahoma	35	17	13	38	27
New Hampshire	34	18	35	45	25
Arizona	33	19	36	31	19
Texas	32	20	47	47	35
Missouri	31	21	43	44	45
Montana	30	22	7	13	10
Florida	29	23	49	51	31
Indiana	28	24	50	46	41
Oregon	27	25	14	34	29
Wisconsin	26	26	44	11	17
Virginia	25	27	38	43	26
Minnesota	24	28	30	15	36
Colorado	23	29	23	37	51
North Dakota	22	30	15	8	7
Pennsylvania	21	31	27	32	38
Ohio	20	32	47	48	46
Iowa	19	33	45	21	20
Rhode Island	18	34	12	22	32
Wyoming	17	35	3	27	18
Kansas	16	36	42	40	30
Massachusetts	15	37	19	12	24
Nebraska	14	38	33	33	33
Washington	13	39	28	41	34
Michigan	12	40	26	29	44

TABLE 25-14 (*Continued*)

| | | GRANTS PER CAPITA DISTRIBUTED BY | | | |
State	Per Capita Income (1975) (I)	Population Weighted by Inverse of Per Capita Income (II)	Categorical Grants-in-Aid (III)	Revenue Sharing Act of 1972 (IV)	Column IV, Net of Taxes (V)
Hawaii	11	41	10	16	23
Maryland	10	42	25	25	43
Nevada	9	43	22	50	37
California	8	44	51	17	28
New York	7	45	6	3	39
New Jersey	6	46	37	36	40
Illinois	5	47	40	42	49
Delaware	4	48	39	14	50
Connecticut	3	49	32	39	47
District of Columbia	2	50	1	4	42
Alaska	1	51	2	48	48
Average Rank					
Lowest 10 states	47	6	25	17	11
Middle 10 states	27	27	31	30	29
Highest 10 states	6	47	26	28	42
Simple Correlation Coefficients					
With column I	+1.00	−1.00	−.05	−.25	−.77
With column III	−.05	+.05	+1.00	+.49	n.a.

Sources:

Columns I and II: U.S. Bureau of the Census, *Statistical Abstract of the United States: 1976,* 97th ed., p. 402.

Column III: Ibid., p. 263. Derived as total federal aid less general revenue sharing.
Column IV: Ibid.

Column V: The cost of revenue sharing is allocated among states in proportion to their contribution to federal income tax revenue. By deducting this from their receipts under revenue sharing, the net figures are obtained. See *Statistical Abstract of the United States,* op. cit., p. 238.

It follows that general revenue sharing is slightly equalizing, while categorical grants do not contribute thereto. The general lack of correlation between grant distribution and per capita income also appears if particular grant categories are considered. Per capita grants are frequently largest to high-income states, this being the case even if the more traditional redistribution-oriented grant categories are examined.[21] While general revenue sharing has done somewhat better, its equalizing effect is much less than it might have been under alternative formulas which would have given more weight to the low-income states. One technique of doing so, as proposed by Senator Jacob Javits, would have been to assign a certain share of the total to the lowest-ranking states.

[21]See Advisory Commission on Intergovernmental Relations, *Categorical Grants*, p. 218.

The question remains whether a stronger tendency to redistribution toward lower-income states will not emerge if we consider grants on a *net* rather than gross basis. To test this, we assume revenue-sharing grants to be financed by income tax, so that the cost is taken to be distributed among states in line with their contribution to the federal individual income tax. The ranking of 1 is given to the state with the highest per capita net receipts, and that of 51 is given to the state (the District of Columbia is here considered a state) with the highest net payment. As shown in column V of Table 25-14, we find that 33 states are net gainers while 18 are net losers.[22] As may be expected, the *net* distribution shows a much higher (inverse) relation to per capita income than does the *gross* distribution of column IV, since residents of high-income states pay more income tax. Whereas we found that expenditure patterns are the decisive factor in interindividual redistribution, the revenue side plays the decisive role when we consider interjurisdictional redistribution.

Short of a formula which distributes benefits in line with income tax collection, there must be losing as well as gaining states. This, of course, is what makes redistributional measures so difficult to accomplish. With congressional representatives concerned with obtaining a "fair share" for their particular jurisdictions, and detailed results of alternative formulas readily provided by computers, explicit use of redistributional formulas has become increasingly difficult. More about this when considering regional aspects of Federal aid.

But even if this difficulty could be overcome, assigning increased weight to per capita income by states would not accomplish very much. High-income states may have even higher needs, thus ending up with a ratio of capacity to need below that of lower-income states. If concern is with programs which benefit low-income individuals, one must recognize the fact that high-income states typically contain large low-income pockets. This explains why there exists practically no correlation between the per capita distribution of traditional HEW grants and the percentage distribution of poor families.[23] Indeed, high-income states typically direct a larger share of their outlays into low-income–oriented programs than do lower-income states, so that discrimination against high-income states may hurt rather than help low-income programs.[24] In order to redirect fiscal redistribution toward low-income services, it is necessary either (1) to distinguish between high- and low-income jurisdictions within states, where differences are much larger than between states, and to make direct grants to such lower-level jurisdictions; or (2) to make categorical grants in support of particular programs which will benefit low-income residents. The new programs developed since the mid-1970s in support of distressed cities partake of both these characteristics.

[22]The biggest gainers are Mississippi with $31 per capita and South Dakota with $23 per capita, while the biggest losers are Delaware and Colorado with $15 per capita each.

[23]See Advisory Commission on Intergovernmental Relations, *Categorical Grants*, p. 218.

[24]See C. Brown and J. Medoff, "Revenue Sharing and the Share of the Poor," *Public Policy*, Spring 1974.

D. SUMMARY

The United States fiscal structure involves three major layers—federal, state, and local—with a great variety of patterns between states and among state-local relationships within states.

1. The federal share in total expenditures, while one-third at the beginning of the century, is now about two-thirds. Over the same period the state share rose from 11 to 20 percent while the local share declined from 52 to 16 percent. The overall trend has thus been toward expenditure centralization.

2. This tendency is somewhat less pronounced if civilian expenditures only are considered.

3. Expenditure concentration is reduced if intergovernmental grants are included at the level of recipient rather than of origin.

4. The degree of centralization at the state level varies widely between states.

5. Highly centralized states derive a larger share of state-local revenue from the sales tax and a smaller share from the property tax.

6. States differ widely in their fiscal capacity and need, leading to substantial differences in expenditure performance.

7. The United States fiscal system contains over 80,000 local fiscal jurisdictions.

The growth of the federal grant system has been the most dynamic feature of fiscal federalism in recent decades.

8. Federal grants have grown from $11 billion in 1965 to $22 billion in 1970 and $85 billion in 1979.

9. Of this total, $57 billion goes to states and $28 billion flows in direct grants to local governments. The latter figure was only $2.6 billion in 1970, with the growth of direct federal grants to local government the outstanding development of recent years.

10. Local governments now receive over 40 percent of their total revenue from grants, including over 30 percent from state grants and about 10 percent from the federal level. Combined grants now amount to nearly two-thirds of local own-revenue.

The structure of federal grants includes a wide variety of grant designs, based on different allocation formulas and grant objectives.

11. The largest program areas covered by grants are education, employment, social service, income security, and health.

12. Two-thirds of federal grants are of the categorical type, but bloc grants or "broad-based aid" has gained in importance, as has general revenue sharing.

13. Many technical problems enter into the design of various categorical grant formulas, most of which are of the matching type and are earmarked for specific program areas.

14. Bloc grants have been designed to combine specific categorical grants so as to avoid complexities and to leave more discretion to recipient governments.

15. General revenue sharing, introduced in 1972, provides largely unrestricted funds and is distributed on the basis of two formulas, involving population, the inverse of per capita income, urban population, and other factors as weights.

16. Over the last four years, new grants aimed at aid to distressed cities have been developed; these are considered further in the next chapter.

In evaluating the grant system, a distinction has to be drawn between the various objectives that are to be achieved.

17. General revenue sharing is an effective means of transferring tax burden from the state-local to the federal revenue system, but it has not been of major importance in equalizing fiscal capacity and need.

18. Categorical grants, characterized by earmarking and matching, are effective means of stimulating state and local expenditures in designated program areas, but traditional categorical grants have not been effective as a means of fiscal equalization.

19. One reason is that per capita income has been only one of the weights in formula allocation. More important, grant distribution in relation to state per capita income is not an effective approach. High-income states frequently have low-income jurisdictions, and intrastate differentials in fiscal capacity and need are much greater than are interstate differentials.

20. Fiscal equalization, to be effective, must take the form of either direct grants to needy local jurisdictions or of categorical aid aimed at the support of programs meeting the needs of low-income residents. Both these factors have been recognized in the recent development of grants to cities.

FURTHER READINGS

Advisory Commission on Intergovernmental Relations, *Significant Features of Fiscal Federalism*, 1978–79 edition, Washington, D.C., 1979. Also see other publications by the A.C.I.R. which provide an invaluable source of information on current developments in this area.

Break, G. F.: *Intergovernmental Fiscal Relations in the United States*, rev. ed., Washington: Brookings, 1980.

Hirsch, W. Z.: *The Economics of State and Local Government*, New York: McGraw-Hill, 1970.

Revenue Sharing and Its Alternatives, Joint Economic Committee, U.S. Congress, July 1967.

Chapter 26

Current Problems in
Fiscal Federalism*

A. The Fiscal Crisis of the Cities: *Causes of Fiscal Distress; The Federal Role; The Outlook.* **B. Regional Impact of Federal Finances:** *Types of Impact; Sunbelt versus Snowbelt.* **C. School Finance. D. Policy Options:** *Reassignment of Expenditure Functions? Reassignment of Revenue Sources? Redrawing of Jurisdictions? The Role of Grants.* **E. Summary.**

Among the most discussed issues of fiscal federalism over the last decade have been the urban fiscal crisis, the regional impact of federal finances, and the finance of education.

A. THE FISCAL CRISIS OF THE CITIES

The most critical area of local finance in recent years has been the fiscal plight of many of the large cities. While the near-bankruptcy of New York City has claimed most attention, the problem is more widespread. The economic malaise of many of the large cities, especially those of the Northeast, will be enduring, and so will be the fiscal strain to which it gives rise.

---

*Reader's Guide to Chapter 26: A survey of three of the most lively issues in fiscal federalism, as well as an appraisal of future policy options.

While the problem has been relieved temporarily by a spectacular increase in federal aid to the cities, the urban issue will be of major concern for a long time to come.

Causes of Fiscal Distress

The fiscal crisis of the cities is above all a result of their changing economic position. As shown in Table 26-1, large cities, especially in the Northeast and Midwest, where most of the distressed jurisdictions are located, have a lower per capita income than do smaller cities. They also have a higher percentage of poor families and a higher unemployment rate. Large cities, with the exception of those in the South, have suffered a population loss, while small cities, with the exception of those in the Northeast, have gained. As an additional indicator of weak economic base, the housing stock of the large cities is substantially older. While there are major exceptions—especially among Western and Southern cities such as San Diego, Houston, and Atlanta, the overall picture for large cities has been increasingly dismal.

Table 26-2 shows a similar pattern, involving now a comparison between the central city and its suburban ring. Although an increasing share of the United States population, now exceeding 70 percent, has come to live in

TABLE 26-1
Social and Economic Indicators for Large and Small Cities*

Region	Per Capita Income (Dollars) 1974 (I)	Percentage Poor 1969 (II)	Unemployment Rate (Percentages) 1976 (III)	Percentage Population Change 1970–75 (IV)	Percentage Old Housing† 1975 (V)	Tax Effort‡ 1975 (VI)
Northeast						
Small	4,524	10.1	9.2	−3.3	65.8	0.020
Large	4,463	15.0	9.4	−6.1	70.8	0.047
South						
Small	4,196	19.8	6.8	4.9	31.4	0.013
Large	4,627	18.3	7.2	1.5	32.7	0.037
Midwest						
Small	4,824	8.6	6.1	0.3	43.1	0.016
Large	4,659	14.0	8.1	−8.6	57.6	0.024
West						
Small	5,091	9.1	7.4	9.1	19.1	0.010
Large	5,439	12.1	9.6	−1.7	36.8	0.015
All Cities	4,724	12.2	7.6	1.6	39.8	0.017

*"Small" cities are cities with 75,000 to 100,000 population. "Large" cities are cities with population above 500,000.
†Percentage of housing stock built up before 1940.
‡Taxes for purposes other than education as percentage of property tax base.
Source: Tables 1, 3, and 7 in *City Needs and the Responsiveness of Federal Grant Programs,* Subcommittee on the City of the Committee on Banking, Finance, and Urban Affairs, House of Representatives, 95th Congress, Washington: April 1978.

TABLE 26-2
Unemployment and Income in Central Cities

	MEDIAN FAMILY INCOME* (Dollars)		UNEMPLOYMENT RATES (Percentages)	
	1970	*1976*	*1973*	*1977*
Total United States	9,867	14,958	4.9	7.0
Central city	9,900	13,700	5.9	8.7
Central city, poverty areas	n.a.	n.a.	9.8	14.9
Suburbs	12,425	18,419	4.6	6.3
Nonmetropolitan	8,348	12,831	4.4	6.6

*For SMSAs of over one million.
Source: Robert D. Reischauer, "The Economy, the Federal Budget and Prospects for Urban Aid," in Roy Bahl (ed.), *The Fiscal Outlook for Cities*, Syracuse, N.Y.: Syracuse University Press, 1978, pp. 95 and 96.

metropolitan areas, population in central cities has declined while that in the suburban rings has increased. There has been a widening income gap between central city and the ring, with suburban incomes nearly one-third above those of the central city. The rate of unemployment in the central cities, moreover, is substantially higher than in the suburbs, as central cities have lost their attraction as industrial centers. Central cities in declining regions have suffered especially severely from this decline. In addition, they have been caught in a pincer movement involving the influx of low-skilled and high-need residents on the one side and on the other the loss of high-income residents and businesses to the suburbs. While these factors of decline are of a structural and longer-term nature, involving social as well as economic issues, they were accentuated by the problems of recession (1974–1975) and inflation, with revenues lagging behind rising service costs.[1]

The decline in the economic base of central cities in turn has been reflected in growing fiscal distress. Expenditure requirements have risen faster than the revenue base, calling for higher rates of taxation, as shown in column VI of Table 26-1. This, in turn, has accentuated the outflow of high-income taxpayers and employment locations to the suburbs, thus setting into motion a spiral of fiscal decline. The fiscal decline in some cities has been worsened further by political factors such as aggressive demands by municipal employee unions, which have pushed compensation rates and employment beyond sustainable levels. But though this has been a contributing factor, the underlying forces of economic decline (compounded especially in the Northeast by regional troubles) could hardly have failed to result in a worsening of the fiscal position of cities.

[1]See Roy Bahl, Bernard Jump, and Larry Schroeder, "The Outlook for City Fiscal Performance in Declining Regions," in Roy Bahl (ed.), *The Fiscal Outlook for Cities*, Syracuse, N.Y.: Syracuse University Press, 1978, p. 14.

Various attempts have been made to prepare indices by which to compare the severity of the position in which various cities find themselves. For this purpose, measures of economic, social, and fiscal need have been distinguished, and cities have been ranked with regard to each. It appears that Newark and St. Louis are in the high-need group for each of these three indices; that Boston, New York, Jersey City, and Philadelphia are high in fiscal and economic need; that Detroit, Baltimore, and Birmingham rank high with regard to fiscal and social need; and that Buffalo and Cleveland are high in social and economic need.[2]

The Federal Role

Federal policy has had important bearing on the cities' position, helpful via grants-in-aid and harmful via tax policy.

Federal Aid   The deepening of the fiscal crisis of cities was met and temporarily relieved by a spectacular expansion of federal grants, targeted toward support of city needs. As was shown earlier in Table 25-9, these grants, largely taking the form of direct assistance to cities, have accounted for half or more of grant expansion since the mid-1970s. Direct federal aid to cities now is 15 times what it was in 1970, and federal aid has come to account for 50 percent or more of revenue in some of the major cities. The most important programs under which this aid is granted are given in Table 26-3.

General revenue sharing benefits cities through the pass-through provision, leaving cities of over 50,000 population with some 25 percent of the total by way of direct pass-through and 40 percent if benefits from pass-through to other units are included. But though population, inverse of per capita income, and urban weights in the distribution formula are helpful, there is no direct targeting in relation to city need. All the other programs included in Table 26-3 provide for such targeting. Thus 80 percent of CDGB grants go to metropolitan areas with such factors as poverty population, housing age, overcrowding, and population growth lag included in the formula. The ARFA program, now in the process of being tapered off, targeted funds at jurisdictions with high unemployment rates. Distribution of CETA grants, under the various titles of the Comprehensive Employment and Training Act, is also based on formulas in which heavy weight is given to unemployment, thus giving primary benefit to high-need jurisdictions. Much the same holds, finally, for allocations under the LPW program, which provides assistance for the completion of local public works.[3]

---

[2]See *City Need and the Responsiveness of Federal Grants Programs*, Subcommittee on the City of the Committee on Banking, Finance and Urban Affairs, House of Representatives, Washington: August 1978, p. 52. See also Richard P. Nathan and Charles Adams, "Understanding Central City Hardship," *Political Science Quarterly*, Spring 1976, pp. 47–62.

While it is of interest to construct separate measures of fiscal, social, and economic need, we would prefer a concept of fiscal need which, by allowing for own capacity and expenditure requirements, reflects the net effects of economic and social considerations.

[3]For a description and evaluation of the various programs, see *City Need and the Responsiveness of Federal Grant Programs*, op. cit., pp. 54–57.

TABLE 26-3
Major Programs Including Direct Federal Aid to Cities
(Fiscal 1979, in Billions of Dollars)

General Revenue Sharing (GRS)	7.2
Community Development Bloc Grant (CDGB)	3.5
Employment and Training (CETA)	10.0
Local Public Works (LPW)	4.0
Anti-Recession Fiscal Assistance (ARFA)	1.0

Source: President Carter's Urban Program, p. 117, in Roy Bahl (ed.), The Fiscal Outlook for Cities, Syracuse, N.Y.: Syracuse University Press, 1978.

The targeted aid provided by these programs has been a major factor in permitting cities to weather the 1974–1976 recession and in maintaining fiscal solvency throughout this period. Taking the forty-seven largest cities, federal aid as a percentage of local own-source revenue reached 50 percent in 1978, a factor without which the fiscal position of the cities would have become untenable on a large scale.

Tax Policy While being benefited by federal grants, cities have been hurt by federal tax policy.[4] Some special benefits have been given to the cities through accelerated write-offs for low-income housing rehabilitation, but this has been more than offset by other aspects of the tax law which have been to the advantage of suburban construction. The law in various ways has tended to favor new construction rather than rehabilitation of old structures. While some of these preferences have been reduced in magnitude, the bias still prevails. New rental housing construction benefits from highly accelerated depreciation, rising land values associated with suburban construction are given favorable capital gains treatment, and the use of tax-exempt bonds for the financing of utility investment has favored suburban locations.

Another and no less important factor has been the preferential treatment of owner-occupied housing under the income tax.[5] This has greatly encouraged the construction of single-family housing, thereby directing housing investment from the cities to the suburbs. Students of the problem have argued that removal of these general preferences would do more in helping the cities than would the addition of new tax preferences directed especially at city locations.

The Outlook

Most observers of the urban problem are agreed that the decline of the economic base of many of our larger cities—especially those in relatively declining regions such as the Northeast—will pose a continuing and perhaps worsening problem. This is the case if implementation of anti-inflation

---

[4]See George E. Peterson, "Federal Tax Policy and Urban Development," Tax Notes, January 1, 1979; and statement in Federal Tax Policy and Urban Development, Hearing before the Subcommittee on the City, Committee on Banking, Finance, and Urban Affairs, House of Representatives, 95th Cong., June 16, 1977.

[5]See p. 359.

programs calls for a recession or at least a slowdown in economic growth. The design of an urban strategy, and especially of urban fiscal strategy, may well be the number one problem for United States fiscal federalism in the 1980s. President Carter's Urban Program, announced on March 27, 1978, marks a beginning in recognizing the problem, but as yet fails to define a specific strategy to meet it.[6]

Objectives   There are several views on how to deal with the matter. A first approach, aimed at "saving the cities," would attempt to reconstruct their economic base by encouraging commercial development, the return of higher-income residents, townhouse neighborhoods, downtown plazas, and other amenities which in the past have rendered city life attractive. Given changing preferences, transport techniques, employment location for skilled workers, and the dynamics of income segregation,[7] this goal may not be achievable. But even if it is, the trickle-down gains to the low-income central city population may be slow or minor. Moreover, the question can be raised whether cities are in fact worth saving if alternative solutions are available. As urban economists have pointed out, reconstructing the decaying infrastructure of old cities may be more expensive than the construction of new facilities.

According to a second view, the primary objective is not to save the cities but to provide employment and improved living conditions for the inner-city poor.[8] As most urban economists see it, it would be exceedingly difficult and inefficient to reconstruct an economic base in the inner city, be it in manufacturing or trade, that could solve the employment problem. More likely, such employment can be created better in the suburbs to which inner-city residents can commute for work; and the longer-run solution may call for training programs, combined with out-migration of the inner-city labor force. All this, however, will not do much to improve the fiscal position of the cities, which must therefore continue to receive large-scale fiscal support until sufficient out-migration has occurred. With the employment picture improving only slowly, this support should be aimed at programs in aid of low-income residents. Until out-migration solves the problem over the years, cities will have to be placed on welfare, as are now their residents.

Neither of these approaches offers a satisfactory solution. The first gives inadequate consideration to the needs of the low-income population, and the second accepts a long-term welfare status for both cities and residents. Given the fact that only a small percentage of the inner-city population will find outside jobs within the foreseeable future, steps seem to be needed to create employment opportunities within the city, even if this involves some efficiency cost. To achieve this objective, aid to employment of inner-city residents, schooling aid, and attraction of manufacturing opportunities seem imperative, without placing entire reliance on a long-term solution through outside employment.

[6]See Bahl, op. cit., p. 111.
[7]See p. 524.
[8]For a strong advocacy of this approach, see Bahl, op. cit.

Sources of Finance   Apart from the question of how programs should be targeted, there is a further problem of who will provide the necessary fiscal resources. As noted before, the primary source to date has been in the form of federal grants. As these grants were developed in considerable part in the context of antirecession policies, their future may be endangered by emphasis on anti-inflation measures and cutbacks in the federal budget. But it seems inevitable that direct federal grants to cities continue to play a major and perhaps increasing role.

A second source of finance is through increased state aid, or state assumption of expenditure responsibilities such as school finance. In support of increased reliance on state aid, it is argued that state budgets as a whole have developed a sizable surplus (amounting to over $30 billion for state and local governments by the end of 1977) whereas the federal budget runs a heavy deficit.[9] It does not follow, however, that the very states which have a substantial surplus also contain the jurisdictions which are in greatest fiscal distress; and even if this were the case, it may well be argued that city distress is a consequence of national rather than state policies so that remedies should be viewed as primarily a national responsibility. Nevertheless, coordination of federal and state aid to cities is urgently called for. Moreover, increased federal aid to states—e.g., full federal assumption of welfare costs—may be conditioned on increased state aid to cities.

A third approach to fiscal relief is by restructuring the boundaries of jurisdictions. If the tax bases of the suburbs could be joined with that of the cities—creating a metropolitan area–wide jurisdiction—past outflow of capital and high-income residents could be recouped and further outflow could be stemmed, thereby strengthening the fiscal position of the city. While this would be a desirable objective, the legal and political obstacles in the way of such reform are most formidable. While metropolitan area–wide fiscal units have been discussed at great length, little progress has been made. With some exceptions, such as Indianapolis, developments have been limited to the design of special districts to perform specific policy functions, such as mass transit or the provision of parks.

Moreover, there is once more the question whether adjoining suburbs should carry particular responsibility for relieving city distress, over and above the gains which they in turn derive from inner-city services. Increased federal or state responsibility for welfare and other social services may indeed be a precondition for rendering a metropolitan area–wide jurisdiction acceptable to the suburbs.

B. REGIONAL IMPACT OF FEDERAL FINANCES

Another novel aspect of fiscal federalism which has received increased attention in recent years is the regional impact of federal finances. Concern here is with the impact of federal finances as a whole—including purchases as well as transfers, grants, and taxes—on the regional economies of the

[9] Ibid., p. 4.

country. This concern, which is not unrelated to the urban problem, has been linked to the shift in economic growth from the leadership of the Northeastern and North Central states to that of the "Sunbelt" states of the South and Southwest.

Types of Impact

There is no single way by which to measure the impact of federal finance upon lower-level jurisdictions. This may be shown by the following illustration. Suppose we have three jurisdictions, states, or regions (A, B, and C), which are affected as in Table 26-4. Lines 1 to 5 record monetary flows of federal purchases, grants, transfers, and taxes as they might appear in a balance of payments account. Line 6 records the regional incidence of federal taxes after allowing for interregional shifting, while line 7 shows the benefit incidence of public services by regions. For the group as a whole, line 7 equals line 1 as benefits are valued at cost.

Lines 8 to 10 reflect various ways of striking a balance, with B doing best in line 8, A doing best in line 9, and C doing best in line 10. Which is the correct formulation? Line 8 may be viewed as recording a balance of payments surplus or deficit, but it is not of major interest since there is no

TABLE 26-4
Per Capita Gains and Losses by Region
(Illustrative figures, in dollars)

	REGION			
	A	B	C	Total
Monetary Flows				
Credits				
1. Federal purchases in jurisdiction	28	31	25	84
2. Federal transfers to individuals and firms in jurisdiction	5	6	3	14
3. Federal aid to governments of jurisdiction	6	8	2	16
4. Total	39	45	30	114
Debits				
5. Federal tax withdrawals from jurisdiction	37	41	36	114
6. Federal tax incidence in jurisdiction	21	55	38	114
Service Flows				
7. Benefits from public services in jurisdiction	14	20	50	84
Types of Balance				
8. $(1)+(2)+(3)-(5)$	+ 2	+ 4	− 6	0
9. $(2)+(3)-(5)$	−26	−27	−31	−84
10. $(2)+(3)+(7)-(6)$	+ 4	−21	+17	0

exchange rate problem within the confines of a common currency area. Line 9, equal to aid plus transfers minus taxes, excludes purchases and thus reflects a first approximation to a fiscal balance. But with benefits from public services omitted, all regions suffer a loss equal in the aggregate to line 1. Line 9, therefore, falls short of our earlier measure of net benefits as applied to incidence among households.[10] A corresponding measure of regional net benefits or fiscal balance is given by line 10, in which benefits from public services are included. Moreover, we now enter the distribution of tax burdens among regions with shifting allowed for as given in line 6, rather than the regional tax collections of line 5.

Notwithstanding our case for line 10, public interest in the discussion of regional balance has focused on line 8. Public purchases are included, combined with a tendency to overlook benefits from public services. Why then are public purchases included? Clearly, they do not reflect a net gain, as do transfers to households, or aid to governmental units. While payments are received, resources or output must be surrendered in turn. Such, at least, is the case in a full-employment economy where the same resources might have been used to produce for the private sector instead.

Yet, inclusion of purchases is not entirely a fallacy. Resources may not be fully employed, so that government purchases (strengthened by a multiplier effect) will increase regional employment. Moreover, such purchases may improve the terms of trade at which a region exchanges its goods, and they may be an important factor in the context of regional development. Western states, for instance, have benefited greatly in their development from the growth of defense industries and electronics. For these reasons purchase patterns should be considered along with the concept of fiscal balance given in line 10.[11]

Sunbelt versus Snowbelt

In line with these considerations, the changing pattern of public purchases has been blamed for contributing to the relative decline of the Northeastern states.

Table 26-5 shows the above-average growth rate of per capita personal income in the East South Central and West South Central states and the below-average growth rate in the New England and Middle Atlantic states. While the absolute level of per capita income still remains higher in the latter states, the difference has been reduced.

Turning to the flow of federal funds, we find that the Eastern states have

---

[10]See p. 274.

[11]To simplify matters our illustration assumes a balanced federal budget. If borrowing is allowed for, lending regions will have an additional debit item, while regions which receive debt service will have an additional credit item in their balance of payments. Such items differ from tax payments and receipt of transfers in that they involve voluntary transactions; but disregarding them results in a net gain for the group as a whole equal to the central deficit.

In resolving the problem, it may be hypothesized that debt service will be financed by the prevailing tax structure. The balance may then be closed by allocating total net lending among the regions in line with their tax payments, rather than by the source of lending.

TABLE 26-5
Federal Aid by Regions, Per Capita

	PER CAPITA PERSONAL INCOME		PER CAPITA FEDERAL AID		PER CAPITA NET AID	
	1975	69–75,% Change	1975	69–75,% Change	1975	1969
New England	$6,098	53	$246	146	$ 8	$ −17
Middle Atlantic	6,398	53	265	177	16	−21
East North Central	6,121	56	192	156	−53	−36
West North Central	5,785	66	212	175	− 7	10
South Atlantic	5,510	67	222	141	13	17
East South Central	4,676	72	237	90	71	63
West South Central	5,346	71	206	94	− 4	30
Mountain	5,495	68	256	87	49	57
Pacific	6,520	58	243	113	− 7	7
U.S.	5,902	60	228	132	—	—

Source: See *Changing Patterns of Federal Aid to State and Local Governments, 1969–75,* U.S. General Accounting Office, December 1977. Net aid is estimated as the difference between aid received and tax payments contributed, where the latter equals the cost of total aid as distributed in line with federal income tax payments by regions.

benefited from a more not less, rapid growth of per capita aid, reflecting primarily their higher welfare load and hence larger share in public assistance. This situation differs, however, if per capita *net* aid is considered, where net aid is defined as the excess of aid received over taxes contributed to their finance. It thus corresponds to line 3 minus line 5 of Table 26-4, with total tax revenue reduced to the amount of aid. We now find that the East South Central states and the Mountain states have been the major gainers in the process, with the East North Central region the primary loser. New England, which appears as a loser in the 1969 balance, records a slight gain in 1975.

As shown in Table 26-6, inclusion of federal purchases leads to a much more drastic differentiation in the position of various regions. The Great Lake states, the North Atlantic states, and the New England states become massive losers, while the South Central, South Atlantic, Mountain and Pacific states are gainers. The outcome places the frostbelt states squarely in the losing column, thereby accentuating their difficulties as the slow growth sector of the country. The negative balance of these regions results in part because their tax shares are still relatively high, reflecting the as yet superior level of per capita income. At the same time, their favorable position with regard to expenditure receipts reflects in considerable part support for higher welfare needs. The sunbelt states, on the other hand, benefit from as yet relatively low tax shares, while enjoying substantial proceeds from purchases. The West in turn benefits from high defense outlays.

As will be seen by examining the role of various expenditure programs in this regional pattern, the overall result is not so much brought about by design as the accidental outcome of the program mix. As a result of these developments, new regional (cross-party) coalitions have made their appearance in Congress and influence the design of allocation formulas in

TABLE 26-6
Expenditure and Revenue Flows by Regions, 1976
(Per Capita, in Dollars)

	EXPENDITURES						
	Total	Defense	Welfare	Pensions	Other	Taxes	Net
New England	1,453	454	136	472	411	1,676	− 223
North Atlantic	1,405	226	139	455	585	1,718	− 313
Great Lakes	1,142	151	101	407	497	1,633	− 491
Great Plains	1,438	339	91	451	557	1,401	+ 37
South Atlantic	1,577	405	106	491	575	1,427	+ 150
South Central	1,447	333	127	429	658	1,227	+ 220
Mountain	1,701	384	83	443	791	1,372	+ 329
Pacific	1,904	628	142	453	741	1,650	+ 314
United States	1,524	346	119	449	616	1,524	—

Source: National Journal, July 2, 1977.

various grant programs. It is questionable, of course, whether from the national point of view primary concern should be with relative growth rates, in which case the Eastern states would deserve particular consideration; or whether primary concern should not be with relative levels of per capita income, in which case the current shift is desirable since the South and Sunbelt are still the weaker parts of the country.

C. SCHOOL FINANCE

Another critical area in the development of fiscal federalism—this time involving the relationship between states and local jurisdictions—has been the growing debate over school finance. Expenditures for elementary and secondary schools are made almost entirely at the local level, with only Hawaii as a notable exception. However, the financing of these expenditures has become increasingly a matter of state concern. Through the mechanism of state aid, state governments now provide nearly 50 percent of total education finance, and in over half the states the share is well over 50 percent. This reflects weakness of the property tax as a revenue source, as well as the fact that fiscal capacities among local units differ widely. Since local finance is very largely derived from the property tax, equal tax efforts would result in widely differing expenditures per student; or (which is the same), widely differing degrees of tax effort would be needed to finance similar expenditure levels. As noted before, low-tax-base jurisdictions do in fact have high tax rates.[12] The need for equalizing state aid thus arose from the desire to avoid both excessive differentials in educational opportunities and excessive differentials in tax efforts needed to provide them.

Constitutional Entitlements   Interest in the state role in educational finance was heightened in the early seventies by rulings of state supreme courts that local finance of education is unconstitutional under the equal

[12]See p. 548.

protection clause, since it deprives children in low-tax-base communities of an adequate education. While the United States Supreme Court failed to endorse this position, these decisions mirror and reinforce prevailing tendencies toward increased state concern with school finance. But given the principle of equal right to educational opportunity, it still remains to be seen how its fiscal implications are to be interpreted. The courts have been hesitant to set down the rules and the legislative search for an answer continues.[13]

Types of State Aid State aid to equalize expenditures per pupil has taken various forms, with some approaches more equalizing than others. *Flat grants*, involving fixed payments per pupil, were widely used at the outset; but since they were small, they provided only a modest degree of equalization. Subsequently, the so-called *foundation grants* became popular and are most widely used today. More recently, so-called *power* or *percentage equalization grants* have gained in attention.

The purpose of foundation grants is to equalize the tax rate which is required for providing a set minimum level of school services among jurisdictions. Thus, the grant S_i received by the ith unit equals

$$S_i = E^* P_i - t^* B_i$$

where E^* is the stipulated minimum level of per pupil expenditures, P_i is the number of pupils, B_i is the equalized assessed property tax base, and t^* is the tax rate which would be required in a jurisdiction with a standard or average base per student. The state will make up for the amount by which the cost of providing the minimum expenditure per pupil exceeds the revenue obtained from the average required tax rate. The formula may be modified by introducing weights which allow for wage rate differentials, grade-level compositions, and other factors determining the cost of providing a set minimum level of services[14]; and to this may be added a more complex measure of fiscal capacity in which per capita income as well as property values is allowed for. In addition, requirements for public services other than education might be taken into account.

But even with these adjustments, the foundation approach has become subject to an increasing amount of criticism. The support level is frequently set very low, so that substantial differentials in tax effort remain necessary to support what the communities consider to be adequate standards. Moreover, the foundation formula is not designed to impose negative grants (or tax payments to the state) for high-capacity communities, so that the budgetary cost which the states must carry increases rapidly as the foundation level is raised.

[13]See p. 35.
[14]There remains the more subtle question of how "equal levels" should be measured. Students with different backgrounds may require different inputs to achieve similar outputs, with the responsiveness of "educational achievement" and its measurement a subject of acute controversy. See, for instance, S. Bowles, "Schooling and Inequality from Generation to Generation," *Journal of Political Economy*, May–June 1972.

In recent years, interest has developed in so-called percentage equalization grants, also referred to as power equalization. Under this approach, no minimum level is set. The state participates in local education expenditures at whatever level of spending the local jurisdiction wishes to undertake, but the matching rate is again set so as to render the revenue per student the same, whatever the tax base of the particular jurisdiction. We then have

$$S_i = t_i(B_a - B_i)$$

where S_i is the subsidy to jurisdiction i, B_a and B_i are the average equalized values per student in the average and ith jurisdiction respectively, and t_i is i's tax rate. We can also express the subsidy as

$$S_i = mt_i B_i$$

where m is the subsidy rate, equal to $t_i(B_a - B_i)/t_i B_i$. Further, by setting $B_i = \alpha B_a$ and combining the two expressions, we get

$$m = \frac{1-\alpha}{\alpha}$$

so that as α rises from 0.25 to 0.5, 0.75, and 1.0, m falls from 3 to 1, 0.33, and 0. In practice, the matching rate is typically set not at the full value of m but a fraction thereof, so that equalization is only at a partial level. As against the foundation approach, it offers support to the education-minded low-capacity unit beyond a more or less arbitrarily set minimum level.[15]

Recently, it has been pointed out that power equalization does not fully assure independence of educational outlays from the level of assessed property.[16] Power equalization merely affects the cost or tax price at which education can be purchased in terms of own-resources. Thus, if the full cost per unit of the service equals C, matching at rate m reduces it to $(1-m)C$. Low property jurisdictions are thus enabled to buy school services more cheaply and are encouraged to spend more.

But, the outcome still depends on the relationship between the price and wealth elasticities of demand for education. With m defined as $(1-\alpha)/\alpha$, the net price in community X is half that in Y if the per capita base in X is half that in Y. Therefore, power equalization, which uses this definition of m, will eliminate all correlation between assessed value and per student expenditure only if the wealth and price elasticities of demand for education happen to be the same in absolute value. Otherwise, a more complex formula is needed to achieve this objective.

[15]In considering the problem of school finance, a distinction might be drawn among the social interest, the freedom of parents to choose how much they wish to spend on schooling, and children's right to adequate education. The foundation approach may be taken to emphasize children's rights by assuring a minimum level of education, whereas the equal power equalization adds emphasis to parental choice by the matching grant approach.

[16]See Martin S. Feldstein, "Wealth Neutrality and Local Choice in Public Education," *American Economic Review*, March 1975.

Another complication arises because jurisdictions with low assessed value per student are not necessarily jurisdictions with low per capita income. This being the case, the question arises whether equalization should be related to income or to property as the base. Given the administrative and political difficulties of legislating a grant system which would achieve a high degree of equalization (not only in tax effort but also in actual levels of education), the Advisory Commission on Intergovernmental Relations has suggested that the states assume the entire cost of education, excepting only the federal share.[17] This is clearly the best approach if total equalization of education within the state is desired. But it is unsatisfactory to those who favor adequate minimum levels while leaving local communities the option of going further.

Which objective is to be preferred poses a major issue in social and educational philosophy. However, it is evident that the problems of grant design will remain even in the case of total state finance. If local autonomy over the expenditure side of school finance is to be maintained, as seems to be generally agreed, it will still be necessary to decide how state funds are to be allocated among communities, i.e., how relative levels of need are to be measured.

Increased use of state finance, moreover, raises the question of what is to be done with the property tax. With 70 percent of local property tax revenue going into education finance, state assumption of this fiscal responsibility would permit local government largely to relinquish this revenue source. If so, would it be desirable to let the property tax drop out of the system while substituting traditional sources of state tax revenue such as increased reliance on state income or sales tax, or would it be best to transfer the property tax to the state level and continue it as a major part of the tax system? Growing dissatisfaction with the property tax and the "Proposition 13" climate suggest reduced reliance on the property tax, although its disappearance is hardly in the cards.

D. POLICY OPTIONS

One lesson to be learned from the experience of the past decade is that securing a balanced structure of fiscal federalism is not simply a matter of relating the federal position to that of the states as a whole or to that of local jurisdictions as a group. Rather the crucial problems relate to differences among states and, even more important, among local jurisdictions within states. During the 1960s, the outlook for state and local jurisdictions as a whole was bleak. Notwithstanding repeated increases in tax rates, rapidly rising expenditures moved ahead of revenue, with an increasing number of jurisdictions going into a deficit position. This trend pointed to a need for the federal government to take blanket steps to relieve the fiscal distress at lower

---

[17]See Advisory Commission on Intergovernmental Relations, *State Aid to Local Governments*, Washington: 1969, p. 16, and *Improving Urban America*, 1976, p. 45. In a recent report, *The States and Intergovernmental Aid*, 1977, the Commission further recommends use of unrestricted grants of the general revenue-sharing type to equalize local fiscal capacities.

levels of government. Revenue sharing was a response to this situation. Since then, the general outlook has changed considerably. State and local governments as a whole now show a substantial surplus, while the federal government runs a sizable deficit. One of the factors contributing to this change in pattern was the rise in federal aid. Another was that the rising trend of education expenditures during the sixties has leveled off. Most important, tax revenue has responded strongly to inflation, especially in the case of state income taxes. It is no longer evident therefore that an imbalance exists between the fiscal position of the federal government and that of state and local governments as a whole, but severe differentials remain between the fiscal positions of various state and local governments. The problem of imbalance, with regard to the cities in particular, has worsened, but it is a horizontal rather than a vertical one.

In considering available policy options, we return to the principles of fiscal federalism as considered in Chapter 24 and ask these questions:

1. Does there now exist a proper distribution of expenditure responsibilities?
2. Does there now exist a proper distribution of revenue sources?
3. Are existing jurisdictions properly drawn?
4. Is the present system of grants satisfactory?

Reassignment of Expenditure Functions?

In dealing with the general principles of multiunit finance, we argued that public services should be provided by the jurisdiction within which the benefits accrue.

How does this rule apply to the financing of education? In an earlier stage of United States history, local-source finance was appropriate since mobility was relatively low. Now the degree of mobility has become much greater, with but few people spending their working lives in the jurisdiction in which they received their public schooling. This offers an additional reason for increased centralization of school finance at the state level, quite apart from the previously noted case for equal educational opportunities. Moreover, the importance of external benefits at the national level justifies federal participation in the financing of education and especially higher education.

Another conclusion drawn in our earlier discussion was that the responsibility for distributional adjustments should be at the federal level, including centralization of welfare finance. The alleviation of poverty is a national problem, the burden of which cannot be left to neighborhood charity nor be placed on those who happen to live in jurisdictions with heavy welfare needs, or for that matter in metropolitan areas which encompass such jurisdictions. Developments of recent years have, in fact, moved in this direction, with the federal contribution to the total welfare cost now amounting to over one-half of the total. With states contributing about 40 percent, only 10 percent has to be paid for at the local level. A still further shift toward complete federal assumption of welfare finance is called for. States might then be required to redirect their present contributions to welfare into other city grants, such as partial assumption of school costs. This should greatly relieve fiscal pressures on the cities, take part of the burden off local property taxes, and contribute to equalizing educational opportunities. At the same time, local government should remain responsible for the finance and provision of specifically local services, such as police, fire protection, and sanitation. Given this reduced range of responsibility, resorting to metropolitan area–wide finance should then become more feasible.

Reassignment of Revenue Sources?

In determining whether a particular tax is appropriate to a particular jurisdiction, we have applied the criterion that benefits should be paid for where they accrue and that the burden should be borne within the jurisdiction. Efficient resource use requires that the electorate be confronted with the opportunity cost involved in public services. Moreover, it would be unfair for the residents of jurisdiction A to tax those of jurisdiction B.

From this point of view, taxes on residential property are a fair approximation to benefit taxation. Taxes on commercial and industrial property are appropriate as well, although other bases such as value added may be a better measure of benefits received. A highly appropriate form of local revenue is the service charge, and increased use of such charges may be a major direction of local fiscal reform.

What, then, should be the role of income taxation at the lower levels of government? Use of the personal income tax is appropriate in that it meets the requirement of placing the burden on residents of the jurisdiction, but its use at the subnational level is subject to the constraint that rates can only be slightly progressive, and that interjurisdictional differentials cannot become too large. Otherwise, higher-income taxpayers will tend to leave the jurisdiction and a loss of tax base will result. Moreover, it is difficult for a small jurisdiction to make the tax apply to all income sources of its residents. It is more feasible, however, to limit the tax to income (especially wage and salary income) originating within the jurisdiction.

Similar limitations apply to the corporation tax. As noted before, profit taxation at the state level poses substantial difficulties of interstate competition. We have also observed that the taxation of corporations on a benefit basis—such as would be especially appropriate at the local level—points to a value-added, rather than a profits or property, tax. State participation in royalties from natural resources, on the other hand, is appropriate and of considerable importance in some states.

Combining these considerations, it appears that the present state of tax assignments by levels, though not perfect, is reasonably in line with our indicated requirements. Whether this approach adds up to a desirable distribution of the overall revenue structure depends on how progressive one wishes the tax structure to be. As noted before, revenue centralization permits a more progressive tax system to be applied; and if combined with increased use of grants, it need not involve increased expenditure centralization.

Redrawing of Jurisdictions?

The existing structure of fiscal jurisdictions is the outcome of complex political forces and leaves sharp discrepancies between fiscal needs and resources. State boundaries in their historically determined form do not correspond to natural economic or fiscal units, but nothing can be done to change this disparity. The states and cities are here to stay, although increasing use can be made of fiscal cooperation among jurisdictions in financing mutually beneficial services. Illustrations range from interstate cooperation in port and transportation facilities to intermunicipal compacts in water supply, fire protection, and garbage disposal. Recent progress along these lines has been encouraged by the federal grant system, especially in the area of environmental services.

By far the most important aspect of jurisdictional reform, however, arises in connection with metropolitan areas. By expanding the fiscal jurisdiction to include both central city and ring, the tax flight into the suburbs would be halted and a better balance between needs and resources could be achieved. Unfortunately this course of action is unlikely since the legal structure of city charters, as determined many years ago, poses a formidable barrier. However, assuming federal assumption of welfare and state participation in school finance, the city problem might be eased sufficiently to reduce suburban resistance to metropolitan finance and to permit the sharing of certain tax bases as well as services. But as noted before, this valid case for a metropolitan area–wide tax base relates to the finance of city services which are of value to both groups of residents, rather than to the financing of welfare and other low-income services within the city. These functions should be recognized as a national responsibility, to be met out of nationwide fiscal resources.

The Role of Grants

Given such reforms, especially the assumption of federal responsibility for welfare and greater state responsibility for school finance, what remaining need would there be for grants-in-aid?

1. The importance of state aid would be increased. While the bulk of school expenditures would be financed out of state revenues, schools would continue to be locally operated, thus calling for increased state grants to local units. Concern with proper grant design would be increased.
2. Federal finance of the welfare system, unless combined with outright federal administration, would continue to call for large grants.
3. With state assumption of most school finance added to federal assumption of welfare, the fiscal position of municipalities would be greatly improved, but there would remain a need for equalizing grants targeted especially at high-need cities.
4. In addition, matching categorical grants for particular functions—designed to adjust for spillover effects and merit-good considerations—would continue. In designing these grants, a reasonable compromise between avoidance of excessive proliferation and earmarking for selective use would be required.

The role of grants, as reflected in these objectives, would continue to involve substantial and indeed increased interjurisdictional transfers. These transfers would be tied to particular uses, such as welfare, education, and correction for spillovers, rather than be of a general revenue sharing type. In some cases, such as welfare, the state or local role would be largely one of administering a federally set program. In others, such as education, the states' concern would be mainly with equalization and setting of minimum standards, while leaving the program content to local discretion. Where appropriate, increased use would be made of direct federal grants to local jurisdictions, such as the larger cities. Moving along these lines, a flexible balance would be struck between increased reliance on central taxation and the preservation of decentralized expenditure control. This would be accomplished without requiring the residents of one jurisdiction to finance uncontrolled uses of funds in others, and without permitting the receiving units to neglect their own fiscal responsibility.

E. SUMMARY

This chapter surveys three current issues of fiscal federalism, including (1) the issue of the cities, (2) the regional impact of federal finances, and (3) school finance.

In examining the fiscal crisis of the cities, we considered the causes of distress, the role of federal aid, and alternative strategies for future policy.

> **1.** The primary causes of fiscal distress have been loss of economic base, especially in the larger cities of the Northeast and Midwest.
>
> **2.** This general trend has been accentuated by the loss of high-income residents to the inner city.
>
> **3.** Since the mid-1970s, a new set of federal grants has been developed which, targeted at distressed cities, has greatly relieved the severity of the problem.
>
> **4.** Looking toward the future, the basic question is whether the economic base of cities can be reconstituted so as to make them viable, self-sustaining units, or whether the problem is essentially one of relief operations aimed at improving the position of low-income residents. Federal grants have a major role in both strategies, but their form would differ.
>
> **5.** Broadening the fiscal base by incorporating inner city and suburbs into metropolitan area–wide fiscal units is a further possibility. While the prospects for accomplishing this are not good, they may be improved by central and state assumption of responsibility for city social services.

Regional shifts in the structure of the United States economy have brought about a relative decline in the growth rate of the Northeast and parts of the Midwest, while speeding up economic development of the South and the Southwest.

> **6.** The question has been raised to what extent this changing pattern may be traced to a shifting regional impact of federal funds.

7. Fiscal impact in this context has not been defined as the net benefits or losses from grants, transfers, and taxes. Rather, federal purchases are included in measuring fiscal impact.

8. While the distribution of per capita federal grants favors the Northeast, that of per capita net aid (grants minus taxes) shows the Northeast a substantial loser.

9. This pattern—with Northeastern and Great Lakes states losers and Pacific, Mountain, and Southern states gainers—is accentuated greatly if government purchases are included in the comparison.

While provision for elementary and secondary education has remained a local function, state aid has assumed major importance in school finance.

10. With tax bases per student varying sharply between jurisdictions, state aid is necessary to provide more equal educational opportunities for children across jurisdictions.

11. In recent years the supreme courts of various states have held school finance by local property tax to be unconstitutional under the equal protection clause.

12. This has led to expansion and reconsideration of state aid. Traditional types of school aid grants have taken the form of flat per capita grants and foundation grants, which equalize the tax rate required to provide a minimum level of services.

13. These grants have been followed by power-equalization grants which permit the jurisdiction to set its own tax rate, but provide it with such revenue as this tax rate would yield with an average per student assessment base.

14. While power-equalization greatly reduces the dependency of per student expenditure on the tax base of the particular jurisdiction, a more complex formula would be needed to secure complete wealth neutrality.

15 As more emphasis comes to be placed on state support for education finance, the property tax as a revenue source may come to be transferred from local to state use.

FURTHER READINGS

Bahl, Roy (ed.): *The Fiscal Outlook for Cities*, Syracuse, N.Y.: Syracuse University Press, 1978.

Cuciti, Peggy: *City Needs and the Responsiveness of Federal Grant Programs*, Subcommittee on the City of the Committee on Banking, Finance, and Urban Affairs, House of Representatives, Washington: April 1978.

Downs, Anthony: "Creating a National Urban Policy," in Joseph E. Pechman (ed.), *Setting National Priorities, The 1979 Budget*, Washington: Brookings, 1978.

Feldstein, Martin S.: "Wealth Neutrality and Local Choice in Public Education," *American Economic Review*, March 1975, and literature on school finance there referred to.

Nathan, Richard P., and Charles Adams: "Understanding Central City Hardship," *Political Science Quarterly*, Spring 1976.

Oakland, William H.: "Central Cities, Fiscal Plight and Prospects for Reform," in Peter Mieszkowski and Mahlon Straszheim (eds.), *Current Issues in Urban Economics*, Baltimore: Johns Hopkins Press, 1970.

Part Six

Fiscal Stabilization

Chapter 27

Fiscal Effects on Aggregate Demand and Employment

A. Policy Targets and the Role of Aggregate Demand: *Policy Targets; Demand, Output, and Prices.* **B. Multiplier Models with Investment Fixed:** *Income Determination and Budget Policy; Fiscal Leverage.* **C. Multiplier Models with Investment Variable:** *Diagrammatic Presentation; Algebraic Presentation; Money Multiplier with Fiscal Sector.* **D. Comparing Fiscal and Monetary Policy. E. Summary.**

We now turn to the third function of budget policy, that is, economic stabilization. Under this rubric we include the effects of tax and expenditure policies upon the level of employment, the rate of inflation, and economic

* Reader's Guide to Chapter 27: The effects of fiscal policy upon aggregate demand have been at the heart of Keynesian macrotheory. This and the following two chapters address themselves to the role of fiscal policy in controlling aggregate demand. Section A gives the setting of stabilization policy and its concern with both unemployment and inflation. Thereafter, price level problems are disregarded in this chapter, with changes in the level of demand reflected in changing output and employment. The problem of inflation will be treated in Chapter 29. In section B we examine the effects of expenditures and taxes in a simple system of income determination with only consumption variable. The central argument is given in pages 593–600. In section C the system is expanded to allow for a variable level of investment and the role of money. Section D offers an analysis of the factors which determine the effectiveness of fiscal and of monetary policy.

growth. Whereas the preceding sections of this volume dealt with issues of microeconomics, we must now consider budget policy as part of the macroeconomic system.[1]

A. POLICY TARGETS AND THE ROLE OF AGGREGATE DEMAND

Leaving effects on capacity growth for later consideration, the primary objectives of stabilization policy are the assurance of capacity output and price level stability.

Policy Targets

Full utilization of economic capacity is obviously desirable, as underutilization involves waste and inequities. This full utilization includes utilization both of the capital stock and of the labor force. With regard to labor, the objective has come to be described as "full employment." But the level of employment, or rate of unemployment, that implies full employment is not obvious. Economists have defined a situation of full employment as one where all people who wish to work at the going wage rate in the labor market will in fact be able to find a job. But the concept is not easy to interpret in practice. To begin with, labor force participation varies, so that for a given adult population the size of the labor force is, in itself, a problematic concept. Moreover, not all those seeking employment will be employed at any one time because, in a changing economy, some persons will always be between jobs or seeking new employment. Retraining may be needed as the structure of employment changes. Cutting across these difficulties, the custom had developed during the sixties to define the full-employment target as a situation where unemployment does not exceed 4 percent of the labor force. But in more recent years the 4 percent line has been questioned. With changes in the structure of the labor force, including a larger proportion of females and young people, it is argued that the full-employment target should be adjusted to permit a somewhat higher rate of unemployment, say, 5 or even 5.5 percent. Moreover, as we shall see later on, recent economic analysis has introduced the concept of a "natural" rate of unemployment, meaning thereby the level of unemployment which results because people are in transitory positions between jobs.

The target of price level stability is more easily defined. Obviously, it does not imply that there should be no changes in *relative* prices. Rather, concern is with the *average* level of prices as measured by the cost of living or some other price index. In the modern economy, prices tend to be rigid in the

---

[1]The tools of analysis used in this and the following chapters are those of basic macrotheory. For a presentation of the basics, see Paul A. Samuelson, *Economics*, 10th ed., New York: McGraw-Hill, 1976, chaps. 11 and 12. Among macro texts, see Robert J. Gordon, *Macroeconomics*, Boston: Little, Brown, 1978; Rudiger Dornbusch and Stanley Fischer, *Macroeconomics*, New York: McGraw-Hill, 1978; and Gardner Ackley, *Macroeconomic Theory*, rev. ed., New York: Macmillan, 1979.

downward direction, owing to the behavior of money wage rates and other costs. The problem of price level change, therefore, is in practice one of increase or inflation. Inflation is undesirable because it introduces uncertainty and inequities into the economic system. These defects develop because the future rate of inflation is not foreseen and because not all prices (whether of products or factors) rise at the same rate. Moreover, the real value of claims (whether money or debt obligations) declines as prices rise, thus resulting in a loss to the creditor and a gain to the debtor. While few would define the policy target as one of absolute price level stability, an increase in excess of, say, 3 percent per annum is generally considered undesirable. Certainly, recent inflation rates of 6–10 percent or more are excessive. As we shall see later, simultaneous achievement of the two targets—full employment and reasonable price level stability—may be difficult, so a tradeoff between the two has to be considered.

Demand, Output, and Prices

We begin with a very simplified view of the relationship between output, employment, and prices. Total expenditures in the economy equal output times price. Thus we have

$$E = Q \cdot P$$

where E is total expenditures or GNP in money terms, Q is the amount of goods produced, and P is the price per unit of output.[2] In Figure 27-1, where the price level is measured vertically and output horizontally, this relationship is plotted as a rectangular hyperbola, such as E_1. Successively higher levels of expenditures or aggregate demand are reflected by E_2, E_3, and so forth. The upward-sloping curve AB is the supply schedule for total output. The intersections of the E curves with AB show how output (or employment) and prices respond to an increase in the level of expenditures.[3] Let the initial expenditure level be at E_1, with output OC and price level OD. As expenditures rise from E_1 to E_2, output rises from C to E and prices rise from D to G. With OF indicating the full-employment level of output, an increase in expenditures becomes reflected increasingly in rising prices as OF is approached. To reach output OF, expenditures must be raised to E_4 and prices be allowed to climb to OH. Thus raising output and employment is associated with an increase in prices.

When these problems were first discussed in the depression years of the 1930s there was heavy unemployment and it was reasonable to assume that

---

[2]The equation would be self-evident if output contained one product only. Since many different products are involved, Q must be thought of as an index of physical output and P as an index of prices.

[3]A more careful analysis would have to distinguish between the levels of output and employment, since labor productivity falls as employment is increased. According to a relationship referred to as "Okun's Law" a 1 percentage point growth in real output above 4 percent results in a one-third of a percentage point cut in unemployment. To simplify our exposition this relationship is here disregarded.

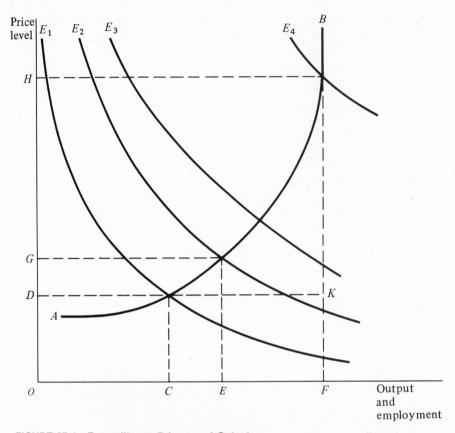

FIGURE 27-1   Expenditures, Prices, and Output.

the supply schedule would be horizontal or follow a rectangular path such as indicated by DKB. In this case, an increase in expenditures up to E_3 would move supply along the horizontal line DK and would permit the economy to reach full-employment output OF without experiencing any price inflation. Concern would be with raising employment only, and the inflation problem would not arise. After World War II, emphasis shifted to problems of excess demand and inflation. The supply schedule came to be viewed as following the upward-sloping AB pattern. Indeed, the nature of the aggregate supply schedule, as we shall see later, proved much more complicated than it was thought to be initially.

The most difficult issue, as economists now see it, is not how to avoid extreme swings in aggregate demand in either direction, but how to deal with "stagflation" and how to steer the economy along a continuous and stable path of high employment with an acceptable degree of price level stability. In pursuing these problems, it would be desirable to deal from the outset with a realistic model of income determination which combines the two contingencies of unemployment and inflation. But this would be too difficult a task. Following the usual pattern of macroanalysis, we therefore begin with a setting in which changes in aggregate demand result in a movement along a flat supply schedule such as *DK*, being reflected in changing output and employment while leaving prices unchanged. The more difficult problem of inflation will be considered in Chapter 29.

B. MULTIPLIER MODELS WITH INVESTMENT FIXED

Consider first a simple setting in which consumption is a function of income only and investment is given at a fixed level. We further assume that money wages are downward rigid so that the price level cannot fall, and that there is substantial unemployment of resources so that an increase in aggregate demand will raise real output (income) and employment rather than the price level. Given these assumptions (which will be relaxed later on), we need not concern ourselves with whether the variables under consideration are measured in monetary or in real terms since, without price level change, the two are equivalent.

Income Determination and Budget Policy

We now consider how the equilibrium level of income is determined, first without, and then with, a budget.

Income Determination without Government Income determination, in its simplest form, is shown in Figure 27-2, where income is measured on the horizontal axis and expenditures are measured on the vertical axis.[4] *CC* is the consumption function, showing consumption expenditures to be a rising function of the level of income. Investment expenditures, shown as *II*, are assumed constant and independent of the level of income. By adding *II* to *CC* vertically, we obtain the total expenditure line *C + I*. Equilibrium income is determined where the income received in any one period gives rise to expenditures of an equal amount which, in turn, become the income of the following period. Thus equilibrium income is shown on the diagram where the total expenditure line *C + I* intersects the 45° line along which expenditures equal income. This point of intersection is at *M*, the equilibrium income level being *OK*, with expenditures equal to *OJ* and *OK = OJ*. At equilibrium income *OK*, consumption equals *KN* and saving (or income minus consumption) equals *NM*. The latter in turn equals investment *KL*.

In equilibrium, expenditures must equal income so that saving (or income less consumption) must be offset or matched by investment spending. If the level of output (and thus of income) should exceed the level *OK*, total expenditures will be insufficient to purchase that level of output (i.e., the line *C + I* lies *below* the 45° line), and output and income will accordingly be reduced to *OK*. If, on the other hand, the level of output or income should be below *OK*, total expenditures will exceed the level of current output (i.e.,

---

[4]To simplify, we assume a closed economy so that trade effects can be disregarded. For an open economy multiplier, see p. 786.

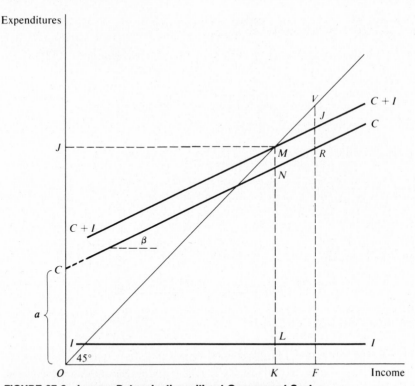

FIGURE 27-2   Income Determination without Government Sector.

$C + I$ lies *above* the 45° line), with the result that the level of output and income will be increased to OK.

The same story is told in Table 27-1. Equation 1 shows total income to equal the sum of consumption and investment, while equation 2 defines the consumption function. The constant term a is the intercept of the CC line in Figure 27-2 with the vertical axis, while the marginal propensity to consume c gives its slope, or tan β. The system is summarized in equation 3 where equilibrium income is obtained by substituting equation 2 into equation 1. The fraction $1/(1-c)$ is the so-called multiplier, and the sum of the constants $(a+I)$ is the multiplicand. If $c=0.8$, the multiplier is 5, and with a equal to $50 billion and I equal to $100 billion, income Y would be equal to $750 billion.

Returning to Figure 27-2, the resulting equilibrium income OK may be such that at prevailing prices a full-employment output is produced, but this need not be the case. Suppose instead that full-employment income equals OF. If the amount of saving RV which people wish to undertake at this level of income exceeds the given level of planned investment RJ, income must fall until saving is reduced to RJ. Income thus returns to its equilibrium level OK. There is no automatic mechanism in this system which assures that full-employment income is reached and maintained.

TABLE 27-1
Income Determination and Fiscal Multipliers
(With Investment Fixed)

	Equation No.
System without Government	
$Y = C + I$	(1)
$C = a + cY$	(2)
$Y = \dfrac{1}{1-c}(a+I)$	(3)
System with Government Purchases	
$Y = C + I + G$	(4)
$C = a + cY$	(5)
$Y = \dfrac{1}{1-c}(a+I+G)$	(6)
$\Delta Y = \dfrac{1}{1-c}\Delta G$	(7)
System with Lump-Sum Tax	
$Y = C + I$	(8)
$C = a + c(Y-T)$	(9)
$Y = \dfrac{1}{1-c}(a+I-cT)$	(10)
$\Delta Y = -\dfrac{c}{1-c}\Delta T$	(11)
System with Income Tax	
$Y = C + I$	(12)
$C = a + c(1-t)Y$	(13)
$Y = \dfrac{1}{1-c(1-t)}(a+I)$	(14)
System with Government Purchases and Income Tax	
$Y = C + I + G$	(15)
$C = a + c(1-t)Y$	(16)
$Y = \dfrac{1}{1-c(1-t)}(a+I+G)$	(17)
$\Delta Y = \dfrac{1}{1-c(1-t)}\Delta G$	(18)

Allowing for Government Expenditures   We may now introduce government purchases G into our system. As shown in Figure 27-3, these are added to the consumption function along with investment to obtain the total expenditure line $C + I + G$. Introduction of government expenditures thus raises output from OA to OB. An increase in government expenditures, by raising the total expenditure line, may thus be used to raise income. If income is below the level required for full employment, government expenditures may be used to move it there. This is also shown in equations 4 to 7 of Table 27-1. Equations 4 and 5 restate the basic equations, and 6 gives the new income level. Government purchases G become part of the multiplicand. Equation 7, obtained by putting equation 6 in differences form, shows the

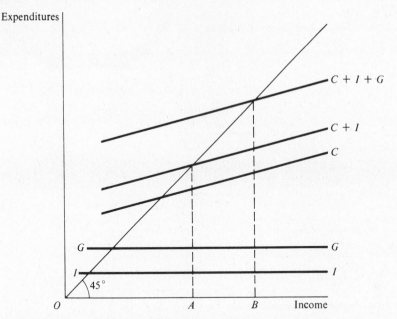

FIGURE 27-3   **Income Determination with Government Expenditures.**

resulting increase in income. With c equal to 0.8, an increase in G of $1 billion raises equilibrium income by $5 billion. This increase will be the larger, the greater is the multiplier. The same holds with reversed signs for a decrease in government purchases.

Allowing for Lump-Sum Taxes   Next, consider the role of taxes. As shown in Figure 27-4, taxation is first introduced in the form of a lump-sum tax, i.e., a tax of fixed amount, independent of income. Adding II and CC, we obtain $C + I$ and income level OA. Now a tax of revenue BR is introduced. As a result, the consumption function drops from CC to $C'C'$, with the horizontal distance between them equal to BR.[5] Consumption at any level of income falls by the vertical distance between the two. The intersection of the new expenditure line $C'C' + I$ with the 45° line moves down and income falls from OA to OB. A subsequent tax reduction, by shifting the $C'C'$ line up to the left, raises the total expenditure line and increases income. Thus taxation, as well as expenditure changes, may be used to adjust the total level of expenditures, and thereby the income and employment levels as well.

The same is also shown in equations 8 to 11 of Table 27-1. In equation 9, the tax is introduced into the consumption function with the marginal propensity to consume c pertaining to disposable income, or income after tax. In equation 10, we see how the tax reduces the multiplicand. In equation 11,

[5]A consumer receiving income OR, after paying BR in tax, has a disposable income equal to OB. Consumption thus equals BD. The new consumption function $C'C'$ is given by $C' = a + c(Y - T)$. While it shows consumption out of before-tax income, it allows for the fact that disposable income is reduced because of tax.

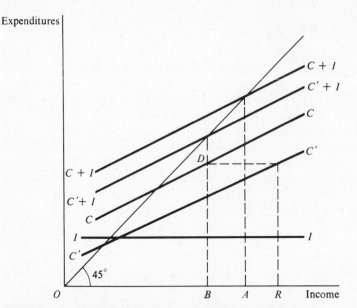

FIGURE 27-4 Income Determination with Fixed Tax Revenue.

obtained by putting equation 10 in differences form and solving for ΔT, we see how the tax relates to income. Note, however, that the income gain due to a tax cut is less per dollar of tax than was that from an increase in government purchases. While the lump-sum tax does not affect the multiplier, it reduces the multiplicand. Since the initial change in consumption equals $c\Delta T$ only, part of the tax reduction is neutralized by its reflection in increased saving rather than in increased consumption. The same argument holds for the effects of a tax increase, which now reduces the level of expenditures less than a corresponding reduction in purchases.

Role of Transfers Transfer payments, as distinct from government purchases G, may, for purposes of this analysis, be viewed as negative taxes. Thus, transfer payments R may be substituted for T in equation 11 but with the sign reversed, showing an increase in R to be expansionary. However, the resulting change in income is again less than for an increase in G. The reason once more is that part of the increase in disposable income due to the transfer payment will be reflected in increased saving rather than in increased consumption expenditures.

System with Income Tax We must now turn to the more realistic case where revenue is obtained from an income tax rather than a lump-sum tax. Introduction of such a tax does not shift the consumption function in a parallel fashion, as occurred with the lump-sum tax, but causes it to swivel downward around its point of intercept. This is so because the tax, equal to the horizontal distance between CC and $C'C'$, increases with income. As a result, the slope of the consumption function, rather than its intercept, is reduced. Expansionary action now calls for a reduction in t.[6] This is shown in Figure 27-5 where CC' is the consumption function before, and CC'' that after tax reduction, with income rising from OP to OF.

This process is shown in equations 12 through 18 of Table 27-1. Note that the way in which the tax enters into the consumption function in equation 13 differs from the case of the lump-sum tax in equation 9, with the result that introduction of the tax now reduces the marginal propensity to consume out of income before tax, and thereby also the multiplier.[7] This result is as one would expect, since tax revenue T now equals tY and is a function of Y. As income rises, so does tax revenue. This depresses disposable income and C, hence checking the overall expansionary effect of an increase in G. Thus, with $c = 0.8$, a tax rate of $t = 0.3$ reduces the multiplier from 5 to 2.27. As shown in equation 18, increasing G by \$1 billion now raises Y by only \$2.27 billion. The built-in response of tax yield thus dampens the effectiveness of an expenditure increase.

Balanced Budget Increase   Having noted that an increase in expenditures is expansionary while a tax increase is restrictive, we must now consider a balanced budget change such that $\Delta G = \Delta T$. In this case, the gain in income equals $[1/(1 - c)]\Delta G$, the expansionary effect of increased government purchases, while the decline in income equals $-[c/(1 - c)]\Delta T$, the restrictive effect of ΔT. The combined effect is $[1/(1 - c)]\Delta G - [c/(1 - c)]\Delta G = \Delta G$. The level of income thus rises by just the increase in government purchases and the so-called balanced-budget multiplier may be said to equal 1.0. A balanced increase in the level of the budget operation has an expansionary effect, but on a one-to-one basis only. The enlarging effect of the multiplier is absent in this case.[8]

Fiscal Leverage

Having seen how the level of aggregate demand may be affected by expenditure and tax policy, we may now measure the combined effect of the budget, or its overall leverage.

Level of Leverage   In measuring the extent to which the presence of the public sector affects the level of income, we compare the level of income Y_p which prevails with a public sector, with the level of income Y which would

---

[6]The formula for a change in t corresponding to equation 11 is

$$\Delta Y = -\frac{cY_0}{1 - c(1 - t_1)}\Delta t$$

where Y_0 is the initial level of income and t_1 is the new tax rate.

[7]The relationship between consumption and income as expressed in the consumption function relates to disposable income. With an income tax, disposable income rises by less than before-tax income. As a result, the ratio of incremental consumption to incremental before-tax income is reduced—i.e., the marginal propensity to consume out of income before tax declines.

[8]More detailed analysis will show that this proposition holds only under simplifying assumptions. For instance, the balanced-budget multiplier will be above 1 if the marginal propensity to consume of taxpayers is below that of other income recipients.

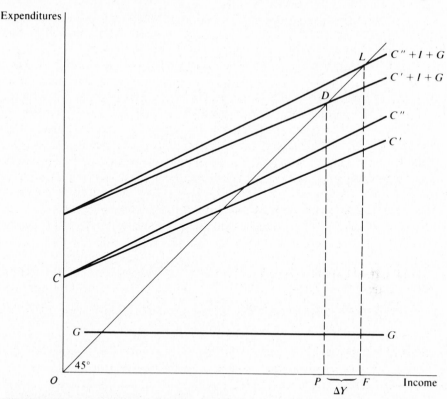

FIGURE 27-5   Tax Reduction with Income Tax.

prevail without it. The difference, to which we refer as "fiscal leverage," thus equals

$$L = Y_p - Y \tag{19}$$

Substituting for Y_p and Y from equations 3, 6, 10 in Table 27-1, we have

$$L = \frac{1}{1-c}(a + I + G - cT) - \frac{1}{1-c}(a + I) \tag{20}$$

so that

$$L = \frac{1}{1-c}(G - cT) \tag{21}$$

If we think of Y_p as the full-employment level of income, then L is the level of leverage required to be at full employment, or to close the full-employment gap. A corresponding definition of leverage may be given for a system with income tax.[9]

[9]See equation 14, p. 595.

To see how the budgetary deficit and surplus enter the picture, we note that

$$D = G - T \tag{22}$$

and, by substituting equation 22 into equation 21, that

$$L = G + \frac{c}{1-c} D \tag{23}$$

Leverage thus consists of two parts, the first corresponding to the balanced-budget multiplier and the second being added because part of G is deficit-financed.[10]

Returning to equation 21, we note that to obtain any given leverage, the appropriate levels of G and T are interrelated. Thus, if G is set, T follows. Moreover, once G and T are given, D follows. Thus, out of all three fiscal variables, G, T, and D, only one can be chosen to satisfy a given level of L and the other two will follow.

Alternative Policy Mixes with Equal Leverage   This relationship is illustrated in the table on the following page. Based on

$$Y = \frac{1}{1-c}(I + G - cT) \tag{24}$$

it shows alternative combinations of G, T, and D which are designed to maintain income Y at 100 while assuming $c = 0.75$ and $I = 10$. Since without budget $Y = 40$, the required value of leverage L is 60. If we want to specify a system in which the required revenue T is obtained from an income tax, we can substitute $T = tY$, so that both T and t are recorded in the table.[11]

---

[10]The concept of deficit as here defined is the deficit in the total budget and thus differs from the subsequently discussed balance in the current budget. See p. 678. This deficit (or surplus) in turn equals the excess of saving over investment (or investment over saving) in the private sector. Thus

$$Y = C + I + G$$
$$Y = C + T + S$$

so that

$$T - G = I - S$$

The equality of $T - G$ and $I - S$ may be interpreted in two ways. One view is to see it as an identity which follows from the nature of the national income accounts, while the other (used here) views it as an equilibrium condition. In the latter case, for any given level of income to be maintained, the budget deficit (surplus) must equal the excess (shortfall) of saving out of that level of income over (below) the level of planned investment in the private sector.

[11]In this case, the table may be derived from

$$Y = \frac{1}{1 - c(1 - t)}(I + G)$$

with T derived from $T = tY$.

	ALTERNATIVE BUDGETS FOR FULL EMPLOYMENT				
	(I)	*(II)*	*(III)*	*(IV)*	*(V)*
C	75	70	60	50	30
I	10	10	10	10	10
G	**15**	**20**	**30**	**40**	**60**
Y	100	100	100	100	100
T	**0**	**6.7**	**20**	**33.3**	**60**
D	15	13.3	10	6.7	0
c	0.75	0.75	0.75	0.75	0.75
t	**0**	**0.067**	**0.20**	**0.33**	**0.60**

In column I, we begin with a zero T or t, with total government purchases of 15 being deficit-financed. As we move to the right, G is raised with the necessary T or t increasing (if you wish, T or t is raised with the necessary G also rising), while the deficit D declines. In the last column, government purchases have increased to 60 and are totally tax-financed, with the deficit down to zero, thus showing the operation of the "balanced-budget multiplier."

This view of alternative policy mixes may be broadened by allowing for the fact that not all taxpayers have the same propensity to consume. Equation 24 may then be rewritten as

$$Y = \frac{1}{1 - c_w}(I + G - c'T' - c''T'') \tag{25}$$

where c_w is the marginal propensity to consume for income recipients as a whole, while c' and c'', refer to particular groups of taxpayers, paying T' and T'', respectively.[12] Variations in policy mix may then involve shifts between the mix of taxes or T'/T'' and the level of taxation or $T = T' + T''$. Thus the value of c for payroll taxes will be higher than for a progressive income tax so that a substitution of the former for the latter will permit a reduction in overall tax revenue.

Change In Leverage   A more realistic view of the same problem may be taken by considering changes in fiscal leverage, rather than the absolute level of leverage which attaches to the total budget. Thus, if Y is the initial level of income with given values of G and T, while Y' is the desired income level, the change in leverage required to reach Y' or

$$\Delta L_r = Y' - Y \tag{26}$$

is obtained by rewriting equation 21 in terms of change, so that for a system with lump-sum tax

$$\Delta L_r = \frac{1}{1 - c}(\Delta G - c\Delta T) \tag{27}$$

[12]More precisely, c_w is the weighted average of the marginal propensities to consume of all income recipients.

As before, in order to obtain ΔL_r, the policy maker can set either ΔG or ΔT, but not both. Thus, for a given value of ΔT, we have to set the change in government expenditures so that

$$\Delta G_r = (1 - c) L_r + c \overline{\Delta T} \tag{28}$$

and with a given value of ΔG, the required change in tax revenue is

$$\Delta T_r = \frac{\overline{\Delta G} - (1 - c) \Delta L_r}{c} \tag{29}$$

A similar analysis may be developed for the more complicated problem of measuring change in leverage in a system with income tax.

C. MULTIPLIER MODELS WITH INVESTMENT VARIABLE

The next step toward a more realistic view of income determination is to make private investment I an endogenous variable, i.e., determined within the system rather than given from outside. Following the standard Keynesian model, income determination now involves three behavioral relationships: the consumption, investment, and liquidity preference functions.

Diagrammatic Presentation

Such a system is presented in Figure 27-6. The consumption function remains the same as in the preceding section, but it is convenient for purposes of this particular diagram to draw it in the form of a savings function, where $S = Y - C$. This is shown by SS in the southwest quadrant of the figure, where saving is measured horizontally and income is measured vertically.[13]

Income Determination The investment function II shows investment as dependent upon the rate of return or interest. It is drawn in the northwest quadrant where the rate of return i is measured vertically and the annual amount of investment expenditures is measured on the horizontal axis. The schedule II may be taken to reflect the marginal efficiency of investment as investment proceeds at various annual rates.

In the northeast quadrant of the figure, the liquidity preference function LL is shown, with the interest rate i measured on the vertical axis and the amount of money available for holding as an asset, M_a, measured on the horizontal axis. LL expresses the amount of money which people are willing to hold over and above transaction needs as an alternative to other assets, such as equity and bonds at various levels of interest. The higher the rate of interest or return from investment, the greater is the opportunity cost of holding money balances and the less people will wish to hold. The schedule $M_a M_a$ in the southeast quadrant, finally, shows the amount of money which is available for such purposes at various levels of income and a given money supply M. This total M may be divided between M_t, or money needed for

---

[13]With the consumption function written as $C = a + cY$ and since $S = Y - C$, we have $S = (1 - c) Y - a$.

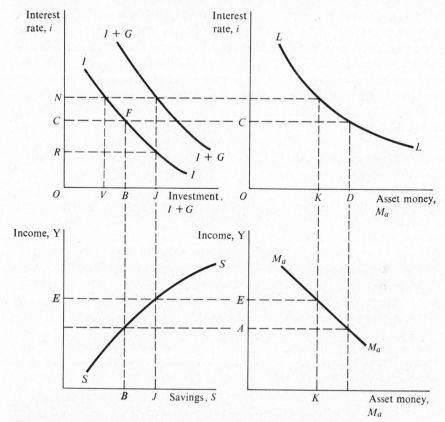

FIGURE 27-6   Income Determination with Investment Endogeneous.

transactions purposes, and M_a, or money held as an asset to maintain liquidity in the portfolio. Since the need for transactions money M_t rises with the level of money income, the amount left over for M_a declines.

Given these relationships, the equilibrium level of income (here equal to OA) is such that the amount of saving forthcoming from that income, or OB, just equals the level of investment which is made at an interest rate OC. This interest rate, in turn, is such that people wish to hold an amount of asset money OD which just equals the amount available at income level OA and a given money supply M. As before, equilibrium income OA may fall short of what is needed to purchase the full-employment output at prevailing prices.[14] If this output equals, for instance, OE, fiscal measures to raise output and income by an amount AE are called for.

---

[14]As explained in the sources given in footnote 1, p. 590, the failure of the system to adjust to a full-employment level of income may be due to various reasons, including (1) an inelastic investment function, (2) a highly elastic liquidity preference function, or (3) failure of the *II* and *SS* schedules to intersect at a positive rate of interest. Another reason frequently cited is (4) downward rigidity of costs and prices which keep the price level from falling, thereby forestalling a possible upward shift in the consumption function which (provided a wealth term is added to the consumption function) might otherwise result as the real value of money balances rises.

We again introduce fiscal variables into the system to see how this can be done. Introduction of government purchases G equal to FH, when added horizontally to the II schedule gives us $I + G$ and permits a higher level of income. Savings rise to OJ and income to OE, while M_a falls to OK and the rate of interest rises to ON. The expansion in income in response to government purchases will now be less than it was in the absence of monetary variables. The reason is that the increased need for transactions funds M_t (due to a higher Y) reduces M_a, thus raising the interest rate i and depressing I. The transaction drain acts as a brake on expansion, as VB of private investment is "crowded out."

The IS-LM Version The presentation of Figure 27-6 may be translated readily into the familiar *IS-LM* version, where points on *IS* reflect equilibrium in the product market while points on *ML* reflect equilibrium in the money market. The economy, as shown in Figure 27-7, is in equilibrium at Z where the *IS* and *LM* schedules intersect, with $Y = OA$ and $i = OC$.

The *IS* schedule shown in Figure 27-7 gives equilibrium combinations of i and Y such that $S = I$ and may be derived from the left side of Figure 27-6. Thus at income OA in the southwest quadrant of that figure, saving equals OB. In equilibrium this calls for investment OB in the northwest quadrant and hence (leaving out government) for $i = OC$. At the higher income OE, saving equals OJ, thus requiring investment OJ with $i = ON$. We thus arrive at points Z and H on the *IS* schedule in Figure 27-7. Similarly, the *LM* schedule drawn for a given money supply $\overline{M}$ may be derived from the right side of Figure 27-6. It gives equilibrium values of i and Y such that the demand for and supply of M_a are equated. It thus reflects equilibrium in the money market. At income OA, M_a equals OD and i equals OC. At the higher income OE, M_a equals OK and i equals ON, thus giving us points Z and K on the *LM* schedule. The equilibrium level of income again equals OA, as in Figure 27-6, and is now determined by the intersection of the *IS* and the *LM* schedules at F. An increase in G or c or a fall in t will cause the *IS* schedule to shift upward to the right, thereby increasing income. Similarly income may be increased by raising M, thus shifting the *LM* schedule down to the right. Similarly Y may be reduced by the inverse adjustments as private investment is depressed.

Algebraic Presentation

The matter may again be stated in algebraic form. Once more using linear functions, and expanding the earlier model of Table 27-1, we now have:

$$Y = C + I + G \tag{30}$$
$$C = a + c(1 - t)Y \tag{31}$$
$$I = d - ei \tag{32}$$
$$M_a = f - hi \tag{33}$$
$$M_a = M - M_t \tag{34}$$
$$M_t = kY \tag{35}$$

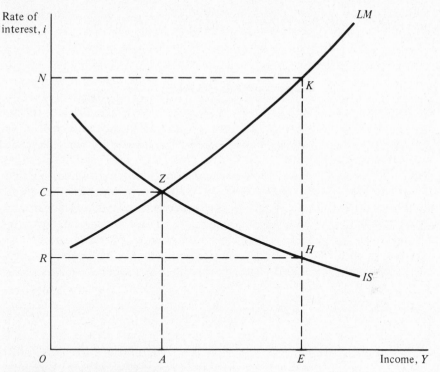

FIGURE 27-7   IS-LM Equilibrium.

(Note: Scale differs from that of Figure 27-6.)

Equations 30 and 31 are familiar from Table 27-1. Equation 32 is the investment function, showing I as a function of the rate of interest i. Equation 33 is the liquidity preference function, showing the demand for asset money M_a as a function of i. Equation 34 shows the total money supply M to be divided into transactions funds M_t and asset money M_a, while equation 35 defines M_t as a fraction of income. Together, equations 34 and 35 give the relationship between M_a and Y shown in the southeast quadrant of Figure 27-6. Given M, G, t and the parameters a, c, d, e, h, and k, the system determines the values of Y, C, I, i, M_a, and M_t.

By substitution, the system may again be reduced to multiplier formulas with income defined by

$$Y = \frac{1}{1 - c(1-t) + ek/h}\left(a + d - \frac{ef}{h} + \frac{eM}{h} + G\right) \qquad (36)$$

The change in income due to a change in government purchases G is then given by

$$\Delta Y = \frac{1}{1 - c(1-t) + ek/h}\Delta G \qquad (37)$$

We note that the multiplier in equation 37 is smaller than in equation 18 of Table 27-1. A large k reduces the multiplier because it makes for a heavy transaction drain as income rises, leading to a fall in M_a, a rise in the interest rate, and hence a "crowding out" of private investment. As will be noted later, this crowding-out effect tends to be accentuated as public debt is issued in financing the deficit.[15]

Money Multiplier with Fiscal Sector

By allowing for the role of money, the revised system also offers a further instrument of stabilization policy, i.e., changes in money supply, or ΔM. Returning to Figure 27-6, an increase in M will shift the M_a schedule in the southeast quadrant to the right. At any given level of Y and transactions demand for money, there will now be more money available for asset holding. At income level OA, more M_a becomes available, so that the interest rate declines in line with the liquidity preference schedule LL. This in turn increases investment and hence the sustainable level of income, i.e., that level at which a correspondingly higher amount of saving is forthcoming.

Returning to equation 36, we may derive a "money multiplier" showing the increase in income with a given increase in money supply. We thus obtain

$$\Delta Y = \frac{e/h}{1 - c(1 - t) + ek/h} \Delta M \qquad (38)$$

along with the expenditure multiplier given in equation 37. Monetary and fiscal measures thus offer alternative approaches to aggregate demand control.

As we shall see in the next chapter, the role of money is, in fact, considerably broader than this model allows for. Changes in money supply not only enter via their effect on the rate of interest and investment but also affect consumption expenditures. Moreover, the role of money cannot be appreciated fully until changes in price level and expectations are allowed for.

D. COMPARING FISCAL AND MONETARY POLICY

In concluding the discussion of this chapter, we may now compare the effectiveness of fiscal and monetary policy.

Effectiveness As follows from Figure 27-6, monetary policy is highly effective if the LL schedule in the northeast quadrant is inelastic. A small increase in money supply and upward shift of the M_a schedule then results in a sharp fall in the rate of interest. Moreover it is highly effective if the I schedule in the northwest quadrant is elastic, so that a small change in i results in a big change in I. On the other hand monetary policy is relatively ineffective if the L schedule is elastic while the I schedule is inelastic. This hypothesis, which was advanced in the Great Depression of the thirties, was a characteristic feature of early Keynesian economics. It is more likely to hold

[15]See p. 699.

in a depressed than a buoyant economy. With regard to fiscal policy, the reverse conditions hold. A change in G is most effective if the transaction drain is small, the L schedule is elastic, and the I schedule is inelastic, so that "crowding out" of private investment is of minor importance. These considerations again explain why the Keynesian approach to full-employment policy during the 1930s emphasized the fiscal instrument, as that period was characterized by an inelastic I and elastic L schedule, while the 1960s and 1970s brought increased emphasis on monetary policy.

The same story may be told by reference to the IS-LM schedule of Figure 27-7. Expansionary monetary policy causes the LM schedule to shift to the right; and for any given increase in money supply, the gain in output (moving along the IS schedule) will be the larger, the more elastic is the IS schedule. Including G along with I, we may think of fiscal expansion as reflected in an upward shift of the IS schedule. The output gain will now be the larger, the more elastic is the LM schedule.

Finally, the argument may be put in terms of equations 37 and 38, where a high value of e and a low value of h (indicating an elastic I and an inelastic L schedule) are favorable to monetary policy, just as a high value of h and a low value of e are favorable to fiscal policy.

Policy Mix   In practice, both policies are used in combination. Fiscal expansion may be combined with an accommodating monetary policy which provides for an expansion of M so as to hold i constant and thereby eliminate the crowding-out effect on I. Or, monetary policy may play an active role, thereby reducing the degree of fiscal expansion needed to achieve a given leverage effect. Depending on the particular phase in the business cycle, one or the other may be more effective. Moreover, the choice between alternative mixes of fiscal and monetary policy is important because it affects the rate of economic growth. This will be examined further when we deal with the growth effects of stabilization policy.[16]

E. SUMMARY

In considering the general setting of stabilization policy, we have examined its objectives and the key role of aggregate demand.

> **1.** The objectives of full employment and price level stability are readily understood even though some difficulties arise in defining the policy targets precisely.
> **2.** At any given level of prices, a certain overall level of expenditures is needed to secure full-employment output with price stability. An expenditure deficiency results in unemployment while an excess causes inflation.

In order to examine the effects of fiscal policy upon the level of aggregate demand, we begin with a situation of substantial unemployment,

[16]See p. 683.

where changes in overall expenditures are reflected in changes in real output rather than in prices.

3. Considering first a system in which the level of investment is given and in which there is no government, equilibrium income is determined at a level such that savings which people wish to undertake out of that income equal the given level of investment.

4. Introducing government expenditures and taxes into the system, various multiplier formulas were developed, showing that an increase in expenditures is expansionary, whereas a tax increase is restrictive.

5. Taxes (and in particular, the income tax), the revenue of which moves with income, generate automatic changes in revenue which reduce the multiplier and the expansionary effects of an increase in expenditures.

6. Allowing for differences in the marginal propensities to consume of various taxpayers, the expansionary effect of various tax changes will differ, depending on which taxes are adjusted.

The role of fiscal policy was then reconsidered in a setting where the level of investment is itself determined within the system.

7. Fiscal multipliers were shown to be reduced by the monetary transaction drain, as private investment is "crowded out" by the resulting rise in interest rates.

8. Changes in money supply were shown to offer a further instrument of stabilization policy.

9. Monetary policy, by accommodating fiscal policy, may forestall the "crowding-out" effect.

10. The effectiveness of monetary policy is enhanced by an elastic investment and inelastic liquidity preference schedule, whereas the opposite holds for the effectiveness of fiscal policy.

FURTHER READINGS

Hansen, Alvin: *Fiscal Policy and Business Cycles*, New York: Norton, 1941.

_____: *Monetary Theory and Fiscal Policy*, New York: McGraw-Hill, 1949.

Samuelson, Paul A.: "The Simple Analytics of Income Determination," in *Income, Employment and Public Policy*, *Essays in Honor of Alvin Hansen*, New York: Norton, 1948.

Smith, Warren L., and Ronald T. Teigen (eds.): *Readings in Money*, *National Income and Stabilization Policy*, Homewood, Ill.: Irwin, 1970, sec. 4.

Chapter 28

Applications of Stabilization Policy*

A. Timing of Multiplier Effects: *Multiplier Time Path; Accelerator; Fiscal Multipliers in Econometric Models; Policy Lags.* **B. The Role of Built-in Flexibility:** *Parameter Change versus Built-in Response; Cushioning Effect of Built-in Changes; Is Built-in Flexibility Desirable? Effects of Fiscal Expansion on Deficit; When is Policy Expansionary?* **C. Rules versus Discretion:** *Critique of Flexible Policy; Full-Employment Balance as Policy Rule; Formula Flexibility; Built-in Politics.* **D. The Fiscal Policy Mix:** *Tax versus Expenditure Changes; Tax Policy Alternatives; Fiscal-Monetary Mix.* **E. Summary.**

In this chapter we examine a variety of issues which arise in the application of fiscal policy, including the problem of timing, the role of built-in flexibility, and the choice among alternative policy instruments.

A. TIMING OF MULTIPLIER EFFECTS

In the preceding chapter we have traced the effects of fiscal changes upon the level of income by comparing the initial (prechange) level of income with the

*Reader's Guide to Chapter 28: The framework of fiscal policy analysis developed in the preceding chapter is expanded here to allow for timing, and the role of built-in flexibility. In the process, various current policy issues, such as the requirement for a balanced budget, are considered. Through most of the discussion the assumption of price level stability is retained, with a frontal attack on inflation postponed to the next chapter.

final (postchange) level. This method of "comparative statics" offers a convenient framework in which to analyze the variables involved, but the actual adjustment process takes time and policy is concerned with how long it takes. If the desired effects come about too slowly, economic conditions may have changed in the meantime and the initial policy may no longer be appropriate. Moreover, depending on lags in the responses of consumers and firms, a fiscal change may give rise to continuous movement rather than lead to a new equilibrium position.

Multiplier Time Path

To illustrate the time path of adjustment, we return to the simplest multiplier model of equations 4 to 7 in Table 27-1. In equation 7, we saw that an increase in the annual rate of government purchases ΔG raises equilibrium income by $[1/(1-c)]\Delta G$. Letting consumption in any one period be a function of income received in the preceding period,[1] we may trace the emergence of this result over successive periods:

Period	Increase in Income above Initial Level
1	ΔG
2	$\Delta G + c\Delta G = (1+c)\Delta G$
3	$\Delta G + c\Delta G + c^2\Delta G = (1+c+c^2)\Delta G$
n	$\Delta G + c\Delta G + c^2\Delta G + \cdots + c^{n-1}\Delta G$
	As n increases, this expression approaches
	$\dfrac{1}{1-c}\Delta G$

In period 1, income rises by ΔG only, since consumers have not as yet had time to respend their additional income. In period 2, such respending occurs and adds $c\Delta G$ to the initial increase. In period 3, the additional income received by persons from respending during the second period is also subject to respending so that a further amount equal to $c \cdot c\Delta G = c^2\Delta G$ is added and so forth. Note that the addition becomes less and less as only a fraction c of the additional earnings is respent with $(1-c)$ being saved, thereby becoming a "leakage" from the income stream. Finally, the addition approaches zero and the total gains approach $[1/(1-c)]\Delta G$, as previously shown. In other words, the level of income rises each period as a lengthening

---

[1]The income determination system may now be rewritten with time subscripts so that (in the absence of taxes)

$$C_t = a + cY_{t-1}$$
$$Y_t = a + cY_{t-1} + I_t + G_t$$

In equilibrium,

$$Y_t = Y_{t-1}$$
$$Y = \frac{1}{1-c}(a+I+G)$$

chain of respendings from past periods adds to earnings. But as time proceeds, the spillovers from earlier periods peter out and a higher level of equilibrium income is reached and maintained, provided, of course, that G continues at its increased annual rate.

Policy makers need to know how long this multiplier process takes or what fraction of the total gain is realized within, say, a six- or twelve-month period. This depends on the length of the time lags involved. In our simplified model, the only lag considered is that between income receipt and consumption expenditure by the household. In a more complete model, a variety of lags enter, including the lag between receipts and payments by the firm, drawing down and replacing inventory, and so forth. As we shall see presently, the adjustment turns out to be fairly rapid, with a substantial part of the total increase achieved in the first year.

Accelerator

The dynamic nature of the adjustment process was first brought out in connection with the investment function.[2] Whereas in the preceding section investment was shown as a function of the rate of interest, empirical observation has led many observers to depict investment as a function of past changes in income. This is the so-called accelerator type of investment function with investment defined as

$$I_t = b + \beta(Y_{t-1} - Y_{t-2})$$

where t is the time subscript. One interpretation of this formulation views β as a technical coefficient. An increase in GNP or Y calls for increased capacity to produce it, which requires investment.[3] Another interpretation views β as reflecting expectations. Investors take the rise in GNP from one year to the next as an indication of future markets and profit prospects and respond accordingly. Adding this accelerator type of investment function to equations 4 and 5 in Table 27-1, we obtain a dynamic system of income change.[4] Not only does an increase in government purchases result in a rise in income due to the operation of the multiplier effects (as derived from the consumption function), but such income increase generates further changes in

---

[2]This relationship was first analyzed in a famous article by Paul A. Samuelson, "Interactions between the Multiplier Analysis and the Principle of Acceleration," *Review of Economics and Statistics*, May 1939.

[3]The need for expansion depends upon the size of the existing capital stock and its degree of utilization. Thus a term measuring capacity utilization is frequently added to the investment function.

[4]The model of income determination now reads

$$Y_t = a + cY_{t-1} + b + \beta(Y_{t-1} - Y_{t-2}) + G_t$$

Depending on the magnitudes of c and β, the accelerator coefficient, the system when disturbed by an increase in G will return to a stable equilibrium, generate a continuing wavelike movement, or become explosive. With $c < 1$ and a small value of β, a change in G produces a fluctuation which tapers off, leading to a new equilibrium level of Y. This is most in line with what actual behavior of the real economy suggests.

investment which in turn are subject to the multiplier, giving rise to new consumption and income changes, and so forth. Depending on the values of the marginal propensity to consume and of the accelerator coefficient β, relating investment to income change, the system will move toward a new equilibrium, follow a steady cyclical pattern, or be explosive.

The lag structure is crucial for the behavior of income as determined by this model, and there is no theoretical intuition which tells us just what it should be. This is why theorizing becomes difficult once the dynamic nature of the system is allowed for, and empirical evidence must take over. However, observation tells us that the macroeconomic behavior of the economy is not explosive. Built-in stabilizers exist and income changes tend to level off.

Fiscal Multipliers in Econometric Models

To estimate the actual time path of the multiplier effect, an econometric model is needed. A change in policy variable may be introduced into such a model and the effects of these changes may be traced over subsequent periods. Such a simulation for the Department of Commerce quarterly econometric model is shown in Table 28-1.

Column I of the table shows the resulting change in GNP as a multiple of the assumed increase in the annual rate of government purchases, with the higher level maintained thereafter. We note that the multiplier reaches about two-thirds of its peak within three quarters and peaks at the end of the second year. Thereafter fluctuations result, reflecting the complex lag structures and interactions of the model. The tax reduction multipliers are somewhat smaller and rise more slowly, whereas the multiplier based on change in money-supply responds with a longer lag. These particular multipliers, it should be noted, relate to changes in *nominal* GNP and thus reflect changes in real output as well as in prices, a matter to be examined in detail in the next chapter. The lower is the initial level of unemployment, the lower will be the output and the larger will be the price component in the resulting change in nominal GNP. Moreover, these particular multiplier values reflect the economic conditions of the base period (here 1971–1975) over which the results were simulated. Nevertheless, most analyses assume a multipler of from 2 to 2.5, with full effectiveness largely reached by the end of one year.

Policy Lags

All fiscal adjustments take time and may be outdated by changing economic conditions before they become effective. This places a great premium on policy measures which minimize the lag involved, including (1) the lag between the time at which the need for action arises and the time at which it is recognized (recognition lag); (2) the lag between the decision to act and the introduction of the actual policy change (implementation lag); and (3) the lag between the introduction of the change and its becoming effective (response lag).[5]

---

[5]See Milton Friedman, "A Monetary and Fiscal Framework for Economic Stability," in *Essays in Positive Economics*, 2d ed., Chicago: University of Chicago Press, 1959.

TABLE 28-1
Magnitude and Time Path of GNP Multiplier,
Bureau of Economic Analysis Quarterly Econometric Model

Quarter Following Change	SIZE OF MULTIPLIER			
	Government Purchases (I)	Personal Taxes (II)	Corporation Profits Tax (III)	Nonborrowed Reserves (IV)
1	1.0	0.3	0.2	0.3
2	1.7	0.6	0.4	0.9
3	2.1	0.8	0.6	1.8
4	2.4	0.9	0.7	2.7
5	2.6	1.1	0.7	3.2
8	3.1	1.4	1.0	4.3
12	3.0	1.7	1.4	5.7
16	2.4	1.5	1.3	5.3
20	2.5	1.7	1.4	5.3

Notes: Column I assumes $5 billion increase in government purchases other than payments to employees. Column II assumes a $5 billion reduction in income tax revenue, sustained at that level thereafter. Column III assumes the same for corporation tax. Column IV assumes a $5 billion change in nonborrowed reserves. Simulations are based on quarterly data for 1971–1975 period. The multiplier coefficients show the resulting increase in nominal GNP reached in the various quarters as a multiple of the postulated increase in government purchases, decrease in tax revenue, or increase in money supply.
Source: See U.S. Department of Commerce, *Survey of Current Business*, June 1977, p. 64.

Recognition Lag Early recognition of the need for policy change is essential whether the policy to be undertaken is of a fiscal or a monetary variety. Hence, progress in the art of econometric model building and forecasting is of crucial importance to the success of fiscal policy and the maintenance of stability in a decentralized economic system.

Implementation Lag This lag involves both administrative and legislative delays. On expenditure policy, the President has limited discretion in adjusting the rate at which appropriated funds may be expended, but the available range may be inadequate. Moreover, changes in the rate of program expansion are not easily applied and require substantial advance planning. On the tax side, the executive branch has no (or very little) control.[6] Tax rate changes, as we saw earlier, must move through a lengthy congressional procedure before legislation can emerge.[7] This takes time, especially where tax increases are concerned. Unhappily, it is difficult to separate rate changes for purposes of stabilization policy from the more controversial issues of tax reform (as in 1975) or (as in 1963–1964 and in 1968) from disagreements over expenditure policy.

[6]Minor influences may be exerted via administrative measures which change withholding rates or provide for speedups in tax collection. But these are, at best, poor substitutes for a more flexible policy of rate change.
[7]See p. 46.

To reduce these delays and to enable the President to better meet the responsibilities assigned to him under the Employment Act,[8] it has been suggested (and recommendations have been made to the Congress by various Presidents) that discretionary authority to change income tax rates be given to the President. To protect the authority of Congress, such changes would be made within limits and patterns prescribed by Congress, e.g., flat percentage increases or decreases in existing liabilities within a 10 percent range. To give further reassurance to Congress, such changes might be made subject to congressional recall and automatic expiration after, say, six months. Congress, however, has been unwilling to grant such authority, holding that it would dilute its constitutional responsibility for control over the government's purse strings. Some solution to the dilemma must be found if fiscal policy is to be given the necessary degree of flexibility. As it stands, such flexibility is available only to monetary policy.

Response Lag   The third lag is related to the rate at which changes become effective after they have been introduced. In the case of adjustments in the level of government purchases, the initial impact is when the additional purchases are made or orders are given. Beyond this, effects on output and employment will differ, depending on whether purchases are made out of inventory and how suppliers respond.[9] In the case of income tax changes, the initial impact is when the taxpayer adjusts his or her outlays. As noted below, this adjustment may lag several quarters behind the change in disposable income. The change in income, in turn, lags behind the change in tax rates. This lag, however, is greatly reduced by source withholding of tax liabilities.

Lags In Monetary Policy   Policy lags arise not only with fiscal but also with monetary policy. The Federal Reserve Board, through decisions made by the Open Market Committee, can act promptly in affecting money market conditions, whether through adjustments in open market policy, changes in discount rates, or reserve requirements. The implementation lag is thus minimal, but the response lag remains and may well exceed that of fiscal measures. A substantial time period is required for changes in monetary policy to work themselves through the money markets and then to affect actual investment expenditures which typically are budgeted and planned well in advance. A similar delay occurs in response to changes in profits tax.

B. THE ROLE OF BUILT-IN FLEXIBILITY

In dealing with changes in the values of government purchases G and tax revenue T, an important distinction must be drawn between (1) changes in G and T which reflect changes in expenditure programs or tax rates, i.e.,

---

[8]See p. 50.

[9]For an empirical discussion of policy lags, see Albert Ando and E. Cary Brown, "Lags in Fiscal Policy," in Commission on Money and Credit, *Stabilization Policies*, Englewood Cliffs, N.J.: Prentice-Hall, 1963.

changes in "fiscal parameters" and (2) changes in G and T which are due to built-in flexibility, i.e., automatic responses to changes in the private sector. Changes in the level of income Y, resulting from a private sector change such as a change in investment I, will depend on these responses in G and T. As we shall presently see, the distinction between parameter changes and built-in changes is important in interpreting changes in the budget picture during any given period.

Parameter Change versus Built-in Response

On the expenditure side, an expansionary *parameter* change, also referred to as a "discretionary" change, is illustrated by the introduction of a new expenditure program or the expansion of an old program. Thus, a new public works program may be instituted or the weekly benefit level of unemployment insurance may be raised. On the revenue side, a parameter change may involve the removal of an old tax or a reduction in tax rates. Corresponding illustrations of restrictive parameter changes include discontinuation of expenditure programs or increases in tax rates. As distinct from these adjustments, a *built-in* change on the expenditure side is illustrated by a change in the level of benefit payments due to a rise in the number of unemployed or a change in farm prices.

While built-in expenditure changes occur, such responses are of primary importance on the revenue side where tax yield changes automatically with changes in the tax base. Thus, income tax revenue rises or falls (at given levels of tax rates) with changes in personal income; profits tax revenue rises or falls with changes in corporation profits, and so forth.

Another way of putting the matter is that parameter changes are "exogenous" to the system of income determination, since they change the fiscal variables such as the level of purchases G or tax rates t in the system of expenditure equations by which income is determined. They are thus an initiating source of change in the overall level of expenditures or demand. Built-in changes on the other hand are "endogenous." They do not initiate changes in the economy, but because of their existence the system will respond differently to a change in, say, the level of investment than it would in their absence. Fiscal parameters are not part of the response system. They are exogenous and call forth a response by the system.

Cushioning Effect of Built-in Changes

Built-in flexibility or automatic responsiveness of the fiscal system increases the stability of the economy without calling for discretionary action. Thus the very existence of a large public sector is a stabilizing factor since (1) a substantial block of expenditures is rendered more or less independent of changes in GNP or, as with unemployment benefits, may move counter to such changes; and (2) the built-in response of tax revenue cushions the repercussions of initial changes in private spending levels. Such, at least, will be the case provided that public expenditures do not move with changing revenue.

Index of Built-In Stabilization Dampening effects of the fiscal system upon changes originating in the private sector may be measured by comparing the actually resulting change in income with that which would result if there had been no automatic budget response. To illustrate, we return to the simple model given in equations 12 to 14 of Table 27-1. Comparing ΔY^* (the change in income in response to a change in I with T fixed) with ΔY (the change in income with $T = tY$), we obtain

$$\alpha = \frac{\Delta Y^* - \Delta Y}{\Delta Y^*} = \frac{ct}{1 - c(1 - t)} \tag{1}$$

where α is an index of "built-in stabilization," measuring the percentage of income change which is prevented due to the cushioning effect of rising tax revenues or the built-in response of the fiscal system.[10] If $c = 0.6$ and $t = 0.3$, α will be equal to 0.43, this order of magnitude being about what may be expected in the United States economy. Thus, about 40 percent of the expansionary effects of raising aggregate expenditures is choked off by the built-in increase in tax leakages.

The magnitude of built-in stabilization as shown in equation 1 depends on the propensity to consume c and the tax rate t. The larger is the public sector and hence the higher is t, the more powerful the effect of built-in stabilization. These simple relationships are complicated, of course, if built-in flexibility is restated in the context of a fuller model of income determination, as given in equations 30 to 35 of the preceding chapter. Additional factors, such as the response of private investment, then enter, but the general principle remains the same.

Flexibility of Major Taxes The automatic flexibility of proportional rate taxes is determined simply by the responsiveness of the tax base to changes in GNP. The built-in elasticity of revenue equals the elasticity of the tax base. For taxes with progressive rates, an additional factor enters. This is the responsiveness of the average tax rate (or ratio of revenue to base) to changes in the tax base. In combination these two factors (the GNP elasticity of the tax base and the base elasticity of the tax rate) make for substantial differences in the revenue elasticity of various taxes.[11]

[10]We have

$$\Delta Y^* = \frac{1}{1 - c} \Delta I \quad \text{and} \quad \Delta Y = \frac{1}{1 - c(1 - t)} \Delta I$$

from which we obtain equation 1.

[11]Given the revenue elasticity

$$E_{Ry} = \frac{dR}{R} \cdot \frac{Y}{dY}$$

rate elasticity

$$E_{tB} = \frac{dt}{t} \cdot \frac{B}{uB}$$

and base elasticity

$$E_{BY} = \frac{uB}{B} \cdot \frac{Y}{dY}$$

we obtain for small changes

$$E_{RY} = E_{BY}(1 + E_{tB})$$

If we look at built-in flexibility over the business cycle, the corporation profits tax ranks highest. This is the case because the base fluctuates more sharply than does GNP. Personal income and sales on the other hand fluctuate in line with GNP or at a somewhat lower level, so that their elasticity tends to be close to or below unity. The property tax, with assessments lagging, tends to have a very low elasticity. Note, however, that built-in flexibility exists provided that the elasticity is positive. The requirement is not that it be in excess of 1.

Over the longer run, proportional-rate taxes tend to have an elasticity coefficient of about 1, as factor shares and output components do not greatly change. The personal income tax, due to its progressive rate structure, however, has a higher elasticity. As real incomes rise due to rising productivity, people move into higher rate brackets so that revenue increases more rapidly than the base. The same happens, even more rapidly, in the process of inflation, unless rate brackets are indexed to be adjusted to rising prices.[12] In the absence thereof, the revenue elasticity of our income tax over the inflationary decade of the 1970s has been very high, at a value of about 1.5. Thus for every 10 percent increase in GNP, tax revenue rises by 15 percent. As will be noted presently, this "inflation dividend" has become a subject of considerable controversy.

Is Built-in Flexibility Desirable?

In assessing the role of built-in flexibility, we distinguish between short- and long-run aspects.

Short-Run Aspects   Built-in flexibility is helpful in that it cushions the amplitude of fluctuations in economic activity. Thus the need for discretionary measures or changes in fiscal parameters is reduced. If the level of expenditures in the private sector falls off and a recession sets in, the decline is dampened automatically. Built-in flexibility is also desirable in an economy which exhibits an inflationary bias. By the same token, however, the built-in response becomes perverse and undesirable if we begin with a position of unemployment. Automatic response now interferes with recovery to full employment and hence increases the burden on discretionary action. Indeed, the magnitude of the required action (e.g., of an increase in government expenditures) is increased because the built-in response dampens the leverage exerted by a given change.[13]

---

[12]See p. 386.

[13]If the desired income change equals ΔY, we have

$$\Delta Y = \frac{1}{1-c} \Delta G = \frac{1}{1-c(1-t)} \Delta G'$$

and

$$\Delta G' = \frac{1-c(1-t)}{1-c} \Delta G$$

where ΔG is the required change in G without built-in flexibility, and $\Delta G'$ the required change in G with built-in flexibility. Thus $\Delta G' > \Delta G$ for any positive tax rate t.

Furthermore, the stabilizing advantages of built-in flexibility pertain to the stabilization aspect of federal finance only. The situation differs at the state and local levels. Such governments do not have control over monetary and debt policy, so that revenue fluctuations can only interfere with continuity of expenditure policy. If revenues are high in the upswing and low in the downswing, expenditures tend to fluctuate in a way which will accentuate the cycle, making for "perverse" fiscal behavior. Moreover, expenditures will be concentrated in high-cost periods. Responsiveness of state-local revenue to cyclical fluctuations is thus undesirable not only from the point of view of state and local government, but also from the point of view of stability in the national economy.

Longer-Run Aspects: Fiscal Drag and Dividend   Turning now to the longer-run aspects of built-in response in a growing economy, we find that the need for discretionary action is increased rather than reduced. Given a passive policy which holds tax rates and expenditure programs unchanged, a built-in increase in revenue leads to a rising surplus at a full-employment level of income, thereby exerting a drag on the economy. The slowdown of the economy in the late 1950s and early 1960s was attributed to this development. A do-nothing policy, which leaves expenditure levels and tax rates unchanged, is in fact a policy of restriction as the economy grows. For policy to be neutral in a growing economy, expansion of demand is needed.

Economic growth may thus be said to yield a fiscal dividend, a concept which played a key role in the "New Economics" of the sixties.[14] This dividend may be used to reduce tax rates, or it may be used to expand public services without having to raise rates. The latter is a tempting option for the administration in office and may lead to the adoption of programs which would not have stood the test of having to meet the additional cost through increased taxation. Moreover, the burden distribution of built-in revenue growth may well differ from that which would have applied with explicit tax adjustments. Built-in revenue growth, therefore, is not an unmitigated blessing.

Inflation   As distinct from growth of real output, built-in revenue growth may reflect rising nominal income due to inflation. Provided that expenditures are not affected by revenue growth, the built-in response will reduce the deficit and be helpful in checking inflation. This is not the case, however, if increased availability of revenue induces an increased level of expenditures. Given such fiscal behavior, built-in revenue gains will not check inflation. Assuming revenue to rise at the same rate as money income and prices, the budget may be considered neutral as government outlays must rise in nominal terms so as to remain constant in real terms. But with progressive rates of income tax, revenue rises faster than nominal income and prices. If reflected in a corresponding increase in expenditures, this will tend to accelerate

---

[14]See W. Heller, *New Dimensions of Political Economy*, New York: Norton, 1967.

inflation. Given such a response, indexing income tax rate brackets may restrain inflation. Looking back over the last decade we find, however, that Congress, by undertaking periodic tax reductions, has removed most of the inflationary revenue gain, the ratio of income tax revenue to personal income having remained fairly constant. The main effect, as noted before, has been a change in burden distribution and not in the average rate of tax.[15]

Effects of Fiscal Expansion on Deficit

In the absence of an automatic revenue response, fiscal expansion (be it through raising G or reducing T) will reduce the budget surplus or increase deficit, and inversely for restrictive action. While this follows from the formulations of the preceding chapter, the outcome may differ if automatic responses are allowed for. Expansionary changes in fiscal parameters, whether involving an increase in expenditures or a cut in tax rates, still raise the level of deficit (or reduce the surplus) at the *initial* level of income. If tax revenue were independent of income, i.e., if a lump-sum tax were used, this would also hold for the future level. But given the fact that revenue rises with income, it does not follow that the *actual* deficit will go up, since income and hence tax yield will rise as well. Thus the deficit-*increasing* effect of the expenditure increase must be combined with the deficit-*reducing* effect of the resulting rise in tax yield. What then will determine the *net* effect of expansionary action on the budgetary deficit or surplus?

Taking the case of an expenditure increase and using equation 14 of Table 27-1 once more, it may be shown that the deficit at the new and higher level of income will be larger than before the expenditure increase so long as the marginal propensity to consume is less than 1.[16] While the resulting increase in tax yield cushions the rise in deficit, some increase in deficit must occur. We also find that with $c = 1$, the deficit remains unchanged, while for c in excess of 1 the deficit declines or a surplus is generated.

---

[15]See p. 388.

[16]Writing D' for the deficit in the initial period and D'' for the deficit in the subsequent period, we have

$$D' = G' - tY' \quad \text{and} \quad D'' = G' + \Delta G - tY''$$

and obtain

$$\Delta D = D'' - D'$$
$$\Delta D = \Delta G - t\Delta Y$$

and since

$$\Delta Y = \frac{1}{1 - c(1 - t)}\Delta G$$

$$\Delta D = \left(1 - \frac{t}{1 - c(1 - t)}\right)\Delta G$$

the deficit will increase (ΔD will be positive) with an increase in G so long as

$$\frac{t}{1 - c(1 - t)} < 1$$

which will be the case if $c < 1$. But the deficit will remain unchanged ($\Delta D = 0$) if $c = 1$. Finally, the deficit will be reduced ($\Delta D < 0$) if $c > 1$. Note also that a value of $c > 1$ is still compatible with stability (a finite value of the multiplier) provided that $c(1 - t) < 1$. By similar reasoning, it follows that D falls with a reduction in t if $c > 1$.

While the data show that the average value of c (ratio of consumption to disposable income) for any one year falls short of 1, it is quite possible, for limited periods at least, that the marginal c should exceed 1. Consumers, in anticipation of rising incomes, may take up consumer credit or draw down their balances. Thus a reduction rather than an increase in the deficit may come about even in the simple model in which the effects of expansionary fiscal policy on private investment are omitted. If responses of investment to changes in GNP are introduced and the system is viewed in dynamic terms, the possibility of expansionary fiscal policy leading to a decrease in the budgetary deficit is further enhanced. This is illustrated, as we shall see, by the experience of the late 1950s when restrictive fiscal action operated to increase the actual deficit; and that of 1964 when expansionary measures served to reduce the actual deficit because of an induced increase in investment. It also appears in the multiplier simulations given in Table 28-1.[17]

When Is Policy Expansionary?

In the absence of built-in flexibility, with revenue drawn from a lump sum tax, the effects of fiscal action on the level of income can be readily measured. This was shown in equation 21 of the preceding chapter. If the change in fiscal parameters (i.e., in G or T) occurs without an independent change in I, ΔL will equal ΔY, the entire change in income being due to the change in fiscal measures. If the change in G or T is made while there are concurrent changes in I, the change in leverage or ΔL may still be measured readily since it is independent of ΔI.

With built-in flexibility allowed for, measuring the magnitude and direction of fiscal policy change becomes more complex. Our measure of ΔL, when redefined for a system with income tax, no longer singles out changes in fiscal parameters but includes changes in T due to changes in I and Y.[18] How, then, can the effects of the fiscal policy change be separated? Clearly,

---

[17]Assuming an increase in the level of government purchases of $5 billion, the initial increase in deficit by that amount falls to almost zero in the course of two years. See p. 613.

[18]To allow for the role of built-in flexibility, we restate our measure of leverage (given in equation 21 of Chap. 27 with regard to a lump-sum tax) for a setting with income tax. To simplify, we continue to assume I to be given independently of Y. With leverage again defined as the difference between the level of income as ensues with the prevailing budget and the level which would result in the absence of a budget, we now have

$$L = \frac{1}{1 - c(1 - t)}(I'' + G) - \frac{1}{1 - c}I'$$

As will be seen from this equation, L again rises with expansionary fiscal action, i.e., an increase in G or a decrease in t. But L now also responds to a change in I. If policy changes in G and t are accompanied by independent changes in I, the resulting change in L will be a reflection of both sets of changes.

As will be seen from the equation, L declines as I increases. The reason is that an increase in I, by pushing up Y, also results in a built-in increase in T, since $T = tY$. Thereby the dampening component of the budget (i.e., the level of T) is increased, while the expansionary component (i.e., G) is unchanged. If we wish to measure the direction and potency of changes in fiscal parameters in their effect on Y, such effects must be isolated from those of changes in I.

they are not given by the observed change in the level of income or in the actual budget deficit. Y may remain unchanged or even decline while expansionary fiscal action (an increase in G or a cut in t) occurs, if such action is matched or outweighed by a fall in I. Similarly, the actual deficit D may reflect changes in I rather than in fiscal parameters. A sharp decline in I, such as results in a depression, typically increases D even though G and t are unchanged.[19]

Effects of changes in I may be excluded and those of changes in fiscal parameters be singled out if we focus on changes in the level of deficit or surplus at a fixed level of income, say the full-employment level. An increase in G or a reduction in t will raise the full-employment deficit, thus recording expansionary action and vice versa for restriction, quite independent of any concurrent changes in I and their effects on Y. At the same time, changes in the full-employment deficit or surplus still fall short of providing us with a satisfactory measure of the direction and magnitude of fiscal policy change. The reason is that they fail to record effects of balanced changes in the level of G and T. The "balanced-budget multiplier" effect is left out and should be added to obtain a comprehensive measure.

C. RULES VERSUS DISCRETION

The discussion of the preceding pages calls for a flexible fiscal policy, making use of built-in responses and adding such adjustments in fiscal parameters (tax rates or expenditures) as may be necessary to secure the targets of stabilization.

Critique of Flexible Policy

It remains to consider certain arguments which would constrain such flexible policy use:

1. At the extreme end of the scale there is the proposition that prudent budget policy calls for an annual balancing of the budget. The government, like any householder, should pay its bills lest disaster strike.
2. Unbalanced budgets may interfere with the efficiency of expenditure policy. If deficits are permitted, the discipline imposed by taxation (which tells the voter that public services involve an opportunity cost) is lost sight of.
3. Finally, the effectiveness of discretionary fiscal policy has been questioned because decision makers are held incapable of prescribing the right policy. If decision makers lack the necessary information and understanding of the economy, discretionary attempts at stabilization may do more harm than good.

The first of these arguments may be rejected as failing to take into account the nature of the public sector. The public budget differs from that of

---

[19]Even if I remains unchanged, the direction of change in the actual deficit or surplus may no longer indicate the direction of fiscal policy action. An expansionary policy, such as an increase in G, will raise the deficit with $T = tY$ measured at the *old* level of Y. But Y increases and so does T. The deficit, as was explained in footnote 16, may fall rather than rise.

the individual household and the same rules of the game do not apply. More will be said about this later when the nature of public debt is examined.[20] Strict adherence to annual balance rules out fiscal stabilization and indeed calls for perverse adjustments, raising taxes and cutting spending in the depression while doing the opposite in the boom.

The second point has merit. Expansionary policy, if undertaken in the form of increased expenditures rather than reduced taxes, may result in an excessive level of public outlays. Similarly, restrictive policy, if undertaken by expenditure cutbacks (rather than tax increases), may lead to deficient provision of public services. As noted in our introductory discussion of policy conflicts, such distortions are not a necessary result of stabilization policy, but they may well come about.

The third point, applicable equally to fiscal and monetary policy, appears excessively pessimistic. Past experience includes policy successes as well as failures. Substantial advances in econometric analysis and in ability to predict have been made and will continue to be made. Indeed, it would seem essential for the future of market economies that the art of stabilization be mastered.

Full-Employment Balance as Policy Rule

These considerations have led to a search for fiscal policy rules which seek a compromise solution. As a midstation between the positions of annual balance and total flexibility, it has been proposed that the budget should be balanced at the "full-employment" level of income. That is to say, tax rates should be such that revenue at this level of income matches outlays. First advanced by the Committee for Economic Development in 1947,[21] this rule is still under discussion.

Viewed purely as a matter of stabilization policy, the rule of full-employment balance is defective. Over sustained periods, conditions may be such that a deficit at full employment is needed for full employment to be reached in the average year; or conditions may be such that a surplus is called for to check inflation. Similarly, the amplitude of built-in flexibility around the average economic position may not be of the correct magnitude. It may overadjust or underadjust in either phase of the cycle. Discretionary policy changes remain necessary to offset such errors.

Viewed as a device to maintain fiscal discipline, the balanced budget rule is helpful, as it will call for changes in tax rates whenever expenditures are increased or decreased. This same advantage, however, may also be obtained by requiring the full-employment budget to be balanced at the margin, while permitting a full-employment surplus or deficit for a base level of expenditures.

One's view of full-employment balance as a rule of fiscal conduct depends on the weight given to policy flexibility on the one side, and to

---

[20]See p. 706.

[21]See Committee for Economic Development, *Taxes and the Budget: A Program for Prosperity in a Free Economy*, New York: 1947. See also Milton Friedman, op. cit.

maintaining fiscal discipline on the other. Current policy discussion places primary stress on the latter factor, as reflected in calls for a constitutional amendment which would require the federal budget to be balanced. This would not only preclude adjustments in expenditure levels and tax rates but would also eliminate such stabilizing effects as result from the built-in flexibility of the system. Alternative proposals call for an expenditure ceiling, expressed as a percent of GNP and designed to retard expenditure growth. The latter would be less constraining with regard to stabilization policy, as it would preserve built-in flexibility and would allow adjustment of tax rates, but it precludes free determination of the public sector share through the democratic process.[22]

Formula Flexibility

Another approach, again related to distrust of discretionary measures, is to increase the scope of automatic change by resorting to so-called formula flexibility. For example, legislation might instruct the Internal Revenue Service to lower income tax rates by, say, 10 percent if the unemployment rate exceeds 6 percent for two quarters; and to increase tax rates by 10 percent if the annual rate of price increase exceeds 6 percent for such a period. Thus, changes in tax rates would be removed from discretionary policy and be made part of an automatic system.

The basic question regarding reliance on built-in stabilizers, therefore, is not whether automatic revenue changes as now generated by existing taxes are sufficiently large, but whether formulas can be devised which will be superior to discretionary policies in securing appropriate changes in tax rates. One must be skeptical about the superiority of such formulas. The information needed to apply formula flexibility is also available to those in charge of discretionary measures and it appears doubtful whether the sources of instability in the economy are sufficiently unchanging to permit a once-and-for-all solution to the problem by devising a correct set of formulas. The responsibility for discretionary change—and the need to improve its performance—cannot be avoided. Some readers will like this challenge while others will prefer a setting which permits reliance on automatic measures.[23] As happens frequently in economic controversy, technical disputes are but the tip of ideological icebergs.

---

[22]See p. 108.

[23]See Don Juan's eloquent dialogue with the devil in G. B. Shaw's "Man and Superman," *Nine Plays*, New York: Dodd, Mead, 1945, p. 646, quoted with permission of The Society of Authors, on behalf of the Bernard Shaw Estate, London:

The Devil: What is the use of knowing?

Don Juan: Why, to be able to choose the line of greatest advantage instead of yielding in the direction of the least resistance. Does a ship sail to its destination no better than a log drifts nowhither? The philosopher is Nature's pilot. And there you have our difference: to be in hell is to drift: to be in heaven is to steer.

The Devil: On the rocks, most likely.

Don Juan: Pooh! which ship goes oftenest on the rocks or to the bottom? the drifting ship or the ship with a pilot on board?

Built-in Politics

It remains to note a second and different perspective on built-in change, allowing for the political gains to be derived from restrictive or expansionary measures. Thus it is hypothesized that political leadership will engage in expansionary policies prior to election time, while undertaking restrictive measures only if elections are distant and the administration disposes over a surplus of voter popularity which can be risked. It is argued that such behavior generates a "political business cycle," using what should be instruments of stabilization in a way which causes economic instability.

The hypothesis is an interesting one and not entirely without empirical foundation.[24] From the perspective of the social scientist, taking a positive view of why policy is conducted the way it is (as distinct from how it "should" be conducted) is clearly a desirable undertaking. Changes in tax rates, expenditure levels, and the money supply might then be predicted by reaction functions of policy makers, including reactions to political as well as economic variables. This would permit variables in the model which are now treated as exogenous (such as changes in tax rates and expenditure levels) to be transformed into endogenous parts of the socioeconomic system. The structural relations may, however, change with political attitudes. Thus anticipation of election time by expanding the level of income may be expected to occur in a setting where unemployment is the major concern of the electorate; but the opposite may come to hold in a situation where inflation is rapidly becoming the dominant issue.

D. THE FISCAL POLICY MIX

Throughout this discussion we have viewed expenditure and tax adjustments as alternative instruments of fiscal stabilization. It remains to consider which instrument is most appropriate and under what conditions.

Tax versus Expenditure Changes

The logic of our discussion in Chapter 1 suggested that the most appropriate instrument for implementing the stabilization function was provided by increases or reductions in the level of taxation. As was noted there, fiscal policy should be conducted so as to satisfy potentially conflicting policy objectives. Efficient expenditure policy or resource allocation among private and public uses was to be based on a full-employment level of output while leaving it to the stabilization branch—acting through tax and transfer measures—to assure that this level of output is provided. In the case of recession, this will avoid calling for additional expenditures to generate a higher level of employment, if such use of resources would be undesirable at full employment.[25] Under inflationary conditions, it will avoid cutbacks in

---

[24]See footnote 35, p. 130.

[25]Make-work spending was referred to in the thirties as "ditch digging" or "leaf raking." While better than no action, it is inefficient, since the beneficial employment effects could have been obtained also by choosing a more useful initial outlay, including increased private spending induced through tax reduction.

programs merely to restrain demand. While the public sector should contribute its share when expansion or restraint in the total level of expenditures is needed, there is no good reason why the entire adjustment should be in that sector. Priority therefore goes to the tax adjustment route.

This pairing of the tax instrument with the stabilization and the expenditure instrument with the allocation target has much merit in principle but needs to be qualified in practice. The cyclical sensitivity of various industries differs and the level of unemployment varies regionally. Use of expenditure policy may be desirable because it can be focused locally where unemployment exists, rather than diffused nationally, as is done with tax reduction. Another reason is that tax reduction, by its very nature, can benefit those who receive income but not the unemployed who are not subject to tax. Such at least is so in the absence of a negative income tax or separate transfer programs. There is something to be said for action on both fronts although, in principle, tax rate and transfer adjustments should be given priority over changes in purchase programs.

Tax Policy Alternatives

The appropriate type of tax adjustment will depend on whether the intention is to influence consumption, investment, or both. In the short-run context, this objective will depend on the prevailing degree of capacity utilization and other structural factors. For the longer view, it will depend on the targets of growth policy.

Consumption Effects Under the present tax structure, changes in income tax rates are the best way of affecting the level of consumption, although it is less obvious just how rates are to be changed. Expeditious legislative response will be easier if the change is "across the board" or "neutral," but it remains debatable how neutrality is to be defined, e.g., whether it entails equal percentage changes in liabilities or equal point changes in bracket rates.[26] For the case of a tax increase, the former is preferable to lower-income taxpayers, while for a decrease, the latter is more advantageous, and vice versa for higher incomes. In the temporary tax-change legislation of 1964 and 1969, equal percentage changes (reductions and increases) in liabilities were applied, but the 1975 tax reduction was directed more heavily at low-income taxpayers while that of 1978 paid more attention to middle and higher levels.

Next, there is a question of how effective changes in income tax will be in affecting consumption. As noted before, resulting changes in disposable income may be reflected either in changes in consumption or in saving. Consumption effects will be slight if people adjust their consumption to what they consider their more permanent (as distinct from temporary) level of disposable income, especially if the tax change itself is expected to be temporary. Or adjustments will be delayed if current consumption depends

---

[26]The two concepts of neutrality correspond to alternative measures of progression. See p. 376.

on *past* disposable income. In either case, the response is weakened and the lag in response to changes in the tax rate is increased.[27]

Temporary tax rate changes tend to be more effective if applied to a consumption tax. The reason is that a temporary increase in consumption tax will provide a substitution effect and a strong incentive for temporary saving, i.e., for postponement of purchases until rates are reduced. Thus a 10 percent consumption tax, expected to be effective for six months, would imply a return of 20 percent (annual basis) on saving over this period. Some observers have advanced this as an argument in favor of a broad-based federal consumption tax. Since postponement of consumption is most feasible with regard to outlays on durables, the objective might be achieved more effectively, however, by a durables tax, including such items as automobiles and appliances. Also note that the superior effectiveness of the consumption tax will depend largely on rate changes being recognized as temporary and on consumers having a firm expectation of early reversals.

Investment Effects The level of investment may be affected by varying the rate of profits taxation, by accelerating depreciation, or most conveniently through the use of a flexible investment credit. Use of such a flexible device has been widely advocated, but the credit as first introduced in 1962 was meant to be permanent. Since then, the credit has been suspended, reintroduced, or increased several times, most recently in 1975 and 1978, and it has now been made a permanent feature of the corporation tax. Other countries, such as the United Kingdom and Sweden, have also been using devices of this sort and have applied them on a more flexible basis.

Fiscal-Monetary Mix

Apart from choosing among various fiscal instruments, a choice must be made of the appropriate mix of fiscal and monetary policies. Either measure may be used to control the level of aggregate demand, but they differ in other respects.

Monetary policy bears primarily upon business investment and on housing, while fiscal measures affect demand on a wider front, including government purchases, consumption, and investment. The appropriate combination of policies thus depends on the structural position of the economy. The two policies also differ in timing, and both have their limits. Excessive monetary restriction may destabilize the money market, or monetary ease may be of limited value in a severe recession when the demand for credit is slack. Other limitations apply to fiscal measures, so that a proper balance between the two has to be reached.

Moreover, there are direct links between the two approaches. As noted in the preceding chapter, the effectiveness of fiscal leverage depends on whether or not it is accompanied by a supportive monetary policy, just as fiscal

---

[27]For a discussion of these issues as related to the 1964 tax reduction, see Arthur Okun, "Measuring the Impact of the 1964 Tax Reduction," in W. W. Heller, (ed.), *Perspectives on Economic Growth*, New York: Random House, 1968. In relation to the tax increase of 1968, see R. Eisner, "What Went Wrong?" *Journal of Political Economy*, May/June 1971.

restriction is reduced in effectiveness by maintaining monetary ease. Since
deficit or surplus policies involve changes in the level of public debt, the
resulting debt transactions have a direct bearing on the liquidity structure and
on money supply and are hence closely related to the sphere of monetary
policy. Finally, the proper fiscal-monetary mix is affected by long-run considerations of economic growth as well as by concern with the economy's
external payments position, two aspects which will be considered later on.[28]

E. SUMMARY

The response of the economy to changes in fiscal parameters occurs over
time, and the time dimension becomes an important aspect of fiscal policy:

1. As the rate of expenditures is increased, the level of income rises over
successive periods, gradually approaching the full multiplier effect.
2. With investment a function of change in income, the resulting increase
in income is subject to an accelerator effect. Depending on the lag structure, a
stable level of income may be reached, or fluctuations may continue.
3. The adjustment process may be traced with the help of econometric
models. Typically the GNP multiplier for an increase in public expenditure
equals about 2 and full effectiveness is largely reached within one year.
4. Various policy lags are distinguished, including a recognition lag, an
implementation lag, and a response lag.

A distinction is drawn between discretionary changes in fiscal policy
parameters, such as changes in the level of tax rates or expenditure legislation, and built-in or automatic responses of expenditures or revenue to
changes in the level of income.

5. The built-in responses, mainly of revenue, exert a cushioning effect on
economic fluctuations.
6. The magnitude of the stabilizing effect depends on the level of tax
rates and the elasticity of revenue with regard to GNP.
7. Revenue elasticity depends on the elasticity of the tax base with regard
to GNP and the elasticity of the effective tax rate with regard to the tax base.
8. Over the cycle the corporation tax shows the highest elasticity, whereas
in the longer run the individual income tax elasticity is greatest. This has been
the case especially in recent years when nominal personal income has risen
sharply as the result of inflation.
9. Built-in flexibility is desirable when cushioning the movement of the
economy into a recession or when stemming pressures for inflation.
10. This conclusion, however, depends on the assumption that public
expenditures are independent of and do not move in response to changes in
revenue.
11. Built-in flexibility in periods of rising income or inflation produces a
"fiscal dividend" which may be used for either expenditure increase or tax rate
reduction.

[28]See p. 686 and p. 781.

12. Because of the built-in revenue response, an increase in expenditures or a reduction in tax rates may lower rather than raise the deficit.

13. The expansionary or restrictive nature of fiscal policy is best measured by observing the resulting changes in the full-employment (rather than actual) deficit or surplus.

For several years there has been an ongoing debate of whether fiscal policy should rely on rules or on discretionary changes:

14. The issues involved are (*a*) whether discretionary deficit policy tends to weaken fiscal discipline and (*b*) whether discretionary measures can be designed with sufficient accuracy.

15. As a compromise, it has been suggested that policy should follow a rule of balancing the budget not annually but at the full-employment level of income.

16. As an alternative, it has been suggested that the principle of built-in flexibility be extended to allow for "formula flexibility."

17. An attempt has been made to treat changes in fiscal parameters as endogenous parts of the model, suggesting a policy behavior which generates a "political business cycle."

Consideration of the desirable mix of fiscal policy measures involves these two issues:

18. In affecting aggregate demand, primary use should be made of tax policy. Expenditures as a general rule (though subject to some exceptions) should be set at the level which is appropriate for a full-employment income.

19. In choosing between alternative tax measures, different adjustments are appropriate, depending on whether consumption or investment is to be affected.

20. The effectiveness of changes in income tax is weakened if consumption is a function of permanent income and consumers view the tax change as temporary.

FURTHER READINGS

Blinder, A., and R. Solow: "Analytical Foundations of Fiscal Policy," in A. Blinder et al., *The Economics of Public Finance*, Washington: Brookings, 1974.

Friedman, M.: "A Monetary and Fiscal Framework for Economic Stability," in *Essays in Positive Economics*, 2d ed., Chicago: University of Chicago Press, 1959.

Heller, W.: *New Dimensions of Political Economy*, New York: Norton, 1967.

Stein, H.: *The Fiscal Revolution in America*, Chicago: University of Chicago Press, 1969.

Tobin, J.: *The New Economics One Decade Older*, Princeton, N.J.: Princeton University Press, 1974.

For an ongoing survey of current issues and policies, also see *Economic Report of the President*, recent volumes.

Chapter 29

Output, Employment, and Inflation*

A. The Equilibrium Level of Output and Prices: *Model Restated; Policy Adjustments.*
B. Dynamics with Demand Pull and Cost Push: *Demand Pull with Budget Inflation; A Simple Model of Cost-Push Inflation.* **C. Equilibrium Rates of Inflation:** *Conditions of Equilibrium; Full Employment or Stagflation? Critique of Equilibrium Models; The Phillips Curve.* **D. Structural Uses of Fiscal Policy:** *Cost-Reducing Measures; Measures to Slow Escalation.* **E. Summary.**

Throughout Chapter 27 and for most of Chapter 28 we have assumed the price level to remain constant, so that changes in aggregate demand or expenditures were taken to be reflected in a change in output or real income and employment. This simplified framework served to analyze some im-

Reader's Guide to Chapter 29: The analysis of stabilization policy in relation to inflation, and especially the problem of stagflation, is more complex than the framework of the preceding chapters, where prices were held fixed and only output effects were dealt with. In section A of this chapter, we introduce price level determination into the preceding model, while continuing within the framework of comparative statics. The introduction of inflation dynamics in section B takes the form of a simple model of budget inflation, with emphasis on the importance of response lags. In section C the difficult and as yet not well understood problem of stagflation is considered. Section D finally examines structural uses of fiscal policy. Students not familiar with intermediate macrotheory may wish to pass over sections A to C and proceed directly to section D.

portant relationships between aggregate demand and employment and to examine the bearing of fiscal variables thereon. But we must now allow for the fact that changes in aggregate demand may result in changes in price level rather than in real output. In particular, an increase in demand may raise the price level, i.e., cause inflation rather than raise output and employment. We can no longer assume that the aggregate supply schedule in our earlier Figure 27-1 takes the rectangular form DKB; we must allow for the sloped schedule AB. Moreover, the problem is not only one of upward shifting expenditure levels. In addition, an inflationary rise in prices may be initiated by factors originating on the cost rather than the demand side of the system; and demand-induced changes may be reinforced by cost responses. This limits the powers of aggregate demand management to deal with the inflation problem. Stabilization policy, if it is to be effective, must assume new forms.

A. THE EQUILIBRIUM LEVEL OF OUTPUT AND PRICES

As we shall see presently, inflation is essentially a problem of disequilibrium and dynamic change, so that the methodology of comparative statics which was employed in the income determination models of Chapter 27 is no longer adequate.[1] Nevertheless, it will be helpful to begin by introducing a price level variable into our preceding equilibrium analysis.

Model Restated

To do so, we rewrite the system given in equations 30 to 35 of Chapter 27 (to simplify again in linear form) as follows:

$$Y = C + I + G \tag{1}$$

$$C = a + c(1-t)Y + j\left(\frac{M}{P} + W\right) \tag{2}$$

$$I = d - ei \tag{3}$$

$$\frac{M_a}{P} = f - hi \tag{4}$$

$$M_a = M - M_t \tag{5}$$

$$M_t = kY_m \tag{6}$$

$$P = u + nY \tag{7}$$

$$Y_m = PY \tag{8}$$

Income, consumption, investment, and government purchases as reflected in Y, C, I, and G are now defined in real terms, while Y_m is income in money terms. The money variables M, M_a, and M_t are also in nominal terms and must be divided by price level P to be translated into real terms. This distinction was not needed in the two preceding chapters, where the price

---

[1]Under "comparative statics" we begin with an initial equilibrium position and compare it with a new position which emerges as the result of a policy change or of a change in private sector behavior.

level was held constant, but it now becomes of central importance. Equation 1, which is definitional, remains unchanged. Equation 2 now shows consumption as measured in real terms as a function of real disposable income, assuming thereby that consumers have no "money illusion."[2] Furthermore, consumption is now related positively to wealth. The reason is that consumers find it less necessary to save if they have already accumulated a reserve. This wealth includes tangible wealth W as well as the real value of money balances or M/P. Thus if prices fall, the real value of balances rises. Consumers, feeling wealthier, find it less necessary to save so that consumption out of a given level of income rises. Equations 3 and 4 are unchanged, but note that in 4 the demand for asset money M_a is now defined in real terms. If prices fall, investors find that their holding of balances has risen in real terms. Hence the rate of interest declines, and investment rises, the effect being similar to that of an increase in nominal balances at constant prices. Equation 6 remains unchanged, but note that the demand for transaction money M_t remains a function of income in money terms.

Equation 7 is the important new part of the system. Whereas the models in Chapter 27 included a demand side only,[3] we now add a supply function for total output, showing the price level to be related positively to output or real income, corresponding to AB in our earlier Figure 27-1. We shall presently have to consider more closely why the supply schedule is upward sloping. For the time being, we simply assume that as output and employment increase, the labor market and availability of other resources tightens, so that prices are bid up by competing firms. Output, however, can increase only up to full employment, at which point the supply function becomes vertical.[4] Equation 8, finally, defines the relationship between real and money income. Having added two equations, we may now determine the two additional variables Y and P, to be arrived at for given values of our policy variables G, t, and M.

The new model no longer lends itself to a simple multiplier solution,[5] but the resulting equilibrium position is shown diagrammatically in part I of Figure 29-1. The vertical axis measures price level, while the horizontal measures output and employment.[6] DD, which must not be confused with the constant expenditure curves of Figure 27-1, shows the aggregate demand for output or Y in real terms, which will come about for given levels of the policy

---

[2]If nominal income rises with prices while leaving real income unchanged, consumers will continue to consume the same fraction of their income as before.

[3]We can readily reconcile the two models by setting n in equation 7 equal to zero, in which case the price level is fixed and the whole system may be written in money terms. With n equal to zero, the aggregate supply schedule becomes horizontal as was assumed in DK of Figure 27-1, so that an increase in aggregate demand up to K is reflected fully in increased output.

[4]We define full employment as the level at which all workers willing to accept the value of their marginal product can find work. This leaves room for some level of "normal unemployment," reflecting workers in transition between jobs.

[5]Our linear version of equation 7 now results in a quadratic solution. The reader may wish to rewrite the system in more general form.

[6]This equating of supply and output again oversimplifies matters, as the two are related by the production function. See footnote 3, p. 591.

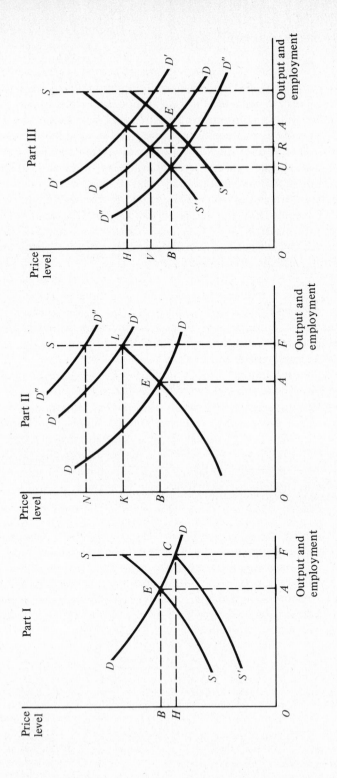

FIGURE 29-1 Equilibrium Levels of Output and Prices.

variables G, t, and M. Aggregate demand in real terms rises as prices fall because the fall in price level increases the real value of money balances, leading to increased demand for consumption (equation 2) and investment (equations 3 and 4). The aggregate supply function SS in turn shows the relationship between price level and output from the supply side. As noted in equation 7, the price level rises as higher levels of output and employment are reached. Given the DD and SS schedules, the equilibrium is reached at E, with output OA and price level OB.

But does E reflect a long-run equilibrium position? With full-employment output given at OF, and assuming a wholly flexible economy, we would expect the excess supply in the labor market to result in a bidding down of prices. This in turn would cause the supply schedule to shift down to the right, leading to falling prices and increasing employment. When the schedule drops to $S'CS$, full-employment equilibrium would be reached, with the price level at OH. But this automatic adjustment to full employment will occur *only if we assume* a wholly flexible labor market. Given a more realistic interpretation of modern economies, this assumption hardly holds. At best the adjustment process is a slow one, and the economy may well become stuck at a position of unemployment such as E.[7]

Policy Adjustments

We may now introduce fiscal and monetary adjustments into this expanded model.

Raising Employment   Beginning with a position of unemployment such as E in part II of Figure 29-1, stabilization policy may increase output and employment by raising aggregate demand. Thus full employment can be reached at L by raising the DD schedule to $D'D'$. This may be accomplished either by raising G, lowering t, or increasing M. Depending on which approach is taken, the mix of output between private and public purchases as well as between consumption and investment will be affected. Note, however, that this gain in employment is achieved at the cost of raising prices from OB to OK. A tradeoff has to be made between maintaining price level stability and reaching higher employment, but since the price rise (in this model) involves a once-and-for-all adjustment only, the conflict may be readily resolved in favor of higher employment.

Preventing Inflation   Suppose now that the economy is in equilibrium at L in part II of the figure, and that private investment expands, thereby shifting the demand schedule to $D''D''$. The result is a price rise from OK to

---

[7]Even if wage rates are downward flexible, there is no guarantee that full employment will be reached. This will be the case only if investment in real terms matches saving out of full-employment income. Note, however, that declining prices, by raising the value of money balances in real terms, will raise the consumption to income ratio, thus contributing to securing full employment. This is the so-called "Pigou effect," named after the British economist A. C. Pigou.

ON without a further gain in employment. This development may be blocked by restrictive fiscal or monetary measures which will hold the aggregate demand schedule at $D'D'$.

Meeting Cost Push   Or suppose that with the economy at E in part III of the figure, there is a "cost-push" disturbance from the supply side. Prices rise or higher wage demands move the supply schedule from SS to $S'S$. If policy holds aggregate demand at DD, output falls to OR and prices rise to OV. If policy chooses to validate the increase in cost by raising demand to $D'D'$, output is maintained at OA but prices rise further to OH. If policy wishes to hold prices at OB, restrictive measures may be undertaken which reduce demand to $D''D''$, but only at the cost of reducing output further to OU. Once more a choice must be made, but given the context of the present model, the price change is a once-and-for-all move only, so that high employment may be again given priority.

B. DYNAMICS WITH DEMAND PULL AND COST PUSH

In reality the choice is more painful, as inflation is a dynamic process and one price rise tends to lead to another. The inflation-employment tradeoff now involves a continuing price rise, be it at a constant or even an accelerating rate. The social costs of high employment thus become more severe and cannot be taken lightly.

The essential element which must now be added to the picture is interdependence between changes in costs and prices. An initial increase in the price level due to some form of demand-pull (originating in the private or the public sector) will lead to demands for higher wages and thus be reflected in increased costs. This in turn will lead to higher prices, calling forth renewed cost responses and so forth. Similarly, an initial increase in cost due to, say, a poor harvest not only will lead to an initial price increase but, if sustained by policies to raise demand so as to maintain employment, will once more generate a wage-price-wage spiral. In such a setting, it becomes difficult to determine whether an ongoing inflation process is of the cost-push or demand-pull variety. Nevertheless, it remains useful, for this discussion, to distinguish between inflation processes which are generated initially by disturbances from one or the other side.

Demand Pull with Budget Inflation

To illustrate the dynamic nature of the inflation process, we begin with the case of demand-pull inflation, assuming wages and other costs to respond promptly to rising prices. We take demand-pull to be initiated by budgetary expansion. To show what happens, we return to our simplest model of income determination (equations 12 to 14 of Chapter 27). We further assume that $I = 0$ and $c = 1$, with the entire disposable income spent on consumption.[8] We

---

[8]See p. 595.

now restate that model in dynamic terms and for this purpose identify the time periods in which expenditures are made or income is received. We begin with a situation of full-employment equilibrium, where the budget is balanced. We then assume that the government raises expenditures to increase its share in output and does so without raising its tax rate, with the additional outlays deficit-financed. We assume the economy to be in full employment to begin with, so that the entire increase in aggregate expenditures is reflected in rising prices. The resulting inflation process is shown in Table 29-1.

The model is described in column I, lines 3 to 7. As shown in line 3, income available in period t equals expenditures made and hence earnings received in period t_{-1}. Monday's expenditures equal Monday's earnings. They are paid out in the evening and become available for expenditure Tuesday morning. However, as shown in line 4, income available for spending is reduced by the tax rate r, so that consumption C_t equals $(1-r)Y_t$. Line 5 shows the level of government spending, defined as "percent" g of total expenditures E_t. In line 6 we add up the two types of expenditures to obtain E_t, and in line 7 we measure the inflation rate or percentage change in prices $\dot{P}$. With constant output, $\dot{P}$ equals the percentage change in total expenditures.

Substituting into line 6 we have

$$E_t = (1-r)E_{t-1} + gE_t$$

so that $E_t = E_{t-1}$ if $g = r$. The government takes out of the income stream what it puts back; and with a private sector propensity to spend out of income of 1, total income and expenditures remain stable. Thus the economy is stable, moving from period 1 to 2 with both g and r equal to 0.2.

The disturbance arises in period 3 when the government raises g to 30 percent while holding r at 20 percent. As shown in the numerical illustration, expenditures in period 3 rise over those of period 2 by 14.3 percent. Assuming the economy to be at full employment at the outset, this generates an equal

TABLE 29-1 Budget Inflation

I. ITEMS	II. TIME PERIODS							
	1	2	3	4	5	6	7	8
Policy Variables								
1. r, percentage	20	20	20	20	20	20	20	20
2. g, percentage	20	20	30	30	30	30	30	30
Model								
3. $Y_t = E_{t-1}$	100	100	100	114.3	130.6	149.3	170.6	195.6
4. $C_t = (1-r)Y_t$	80	80	80	91.4	104.5	119.4	136.5	155.9
5. $G_t = gE_t$	20	20	34.3	39.2	44.8	51.2	58.5	66.8
6. $E_t = C_t + G_t$	100	100	114.3	130.6	147.3	170.6	195.6	222.8
7. $\dot{P} = \dfrac{E_t - E_{t-1}}{E_{t-1}}$	0	0	0.143	0.143	0.143	0.143	0.143	0.143

percentage rise in prices. Moreover, as shown in the numerical illustration, expenditures, income, and prices continue to rise at the same rate in each successive period.[9] The government imposes a continuing "inflation tax" of 14.3 percent, a tax which reduces the real value of a dollar of money income by 14.3 percent in each period. To stop this inflation process, the government would have to reduce g to its original level of 20 percent, or raise r to 30 percent, thus shifting from an inflation to an outright tax. Given a progressive income tax, this development may come about automatically, thus making inflation self-terminating without further legislative action.[10]

This particular outcome depends on the underlying lag structure. While the model of Table 29-1 generates a steady rate of inflation, alternative and no less reasonable assumptions could be made regarding the responses of C or G which would bring about fluctuating, explosive, or declining inflation rates.[11] Moreover the adjustment of wages, and hence income, to rising prices may not be instantaneous as here assumed. Wage adjustments lag due to longer-term union contracts, thus slowing down the inflation process. Anticipation of rising inflation rates on the other hand may accelerate it. Since the applicable lag structure for the various variables is an empirical question, pure theorizing about the dynamics of inflation becomes unproductive.

Our illustration has been oversimplified also by making use of so minimal a model of income determination. To obtain a fuller picture, a model such as that given in equations 1 to 8 earlier in this chapter would have to be put into dynamic terms. As expenditures rise ahead of tax revenus, the deficit widens and must be financed. This finance may be through borrowing from the banks, so that the money supply will rise along with the deficit. Indeed, such expansion is necessary if the inflation process is to be sustained. Unless the money supply increases at the rate of prices, money supply in real terms

---

[9]Solving equations 3 to 6 of Table 29-1 for E_t we get

$$E_t = (1-r)E_{t-1} + gE_t$$

or

$$E_t = \frac{1-r}{1-g} E_{t-1}$$

Hence

$$\dot{P}_t = \frac{E_t - E_{t-1}}{E_{t-1}} = \frac{g-r}{1-g}$$

With $t = 0.2$ and $g = 0.3$, we have $\dot{P}_t = 0.143$. As g rises or r falls, $\dot{P}$ increases.

[10]See p. 388.

[11]Suppose consumer expenditures lag two periods, so that

$$E_t = (1-t)E_{t-2} + gE_t$$

We then have

$$E_t = \frac{1-r}{1-g} E_{t-2}$$

With $g = r$ we again have a constant level of E. But as g rises to g', there now results an inflation cycle with the inflation rate fluctuating between 0 and $(g'-g)/(1-g')$. Other assumptions regarding lags may be made which lead to a rising rate of inflation. See also our earlier discussion of the interaction of accelerator and multiplier. See p. 611.

will decline, and this will act as a break on the level of expenditures. As the full system of income determination is allowed for, additional lags are introduced, involving the response of changes in i to changes in M, of changes in I to changes in i, of changes in C to changes in Y, and so forth. All this will affect the actual path of the inflation process, and it becomes difficult to generalize about the outcome.

The story of demand-pull inflation, as recounted here, began with a change in the expenditure share claimed by government outlays. Precisely the same development might occur with a shift in private sector demand, such as an increase in investment or an upward shift in the consumption function. Inflationary processes similar to those shown in Table 29-1 may result. Policy once more must choose between sustaining or restraining the resulting rise in prices.

A Simple Model of Cost-Push Inflation

So far we have considered a situation where the disturbance begins with an increase in demand, public or private. This increase leads to a rise in prices and is followed by an escalation of costs (wage rates) so as to keep up with rising prices. We now consider a situation where the initial disturbance takes the form of a cost shock, such as the one provided by the increase in oil prices in 1974 or one that may result from a poor harvest. This initial cost shock, if sustained by demand expansion, once more leads to price rise and subsequent escalation into higher wages (needed to keep up with prices), generating once more a continuing inflation.

Such a process is illustrated in Table 29-2. We assume an initial shock to occur in period 3, which is at once sustained by expansionary policy, permitting expenditures to rise, so that the same real output can be purchased at the higher cost. This then leads to wage escalation and a further cost increase which must be sustained and so forth. We have $E_t = C_{t-1} + C_{s,t-1} + C_{e,t-1}$, where E is expenditures, C is cost, C_s is additional cost due to cost shock, and C_e is additional cost due to escalation. We also assume that $C_{e,t} = C_{t-1} - C_{t-2}$.

As shown in this example, an initial cost shock of $10 or 10 percent in period 3 comes to be translated into an inflation rate of 10 percent, as the

TABLE 29-2
Inflation Response to Cost Shock

	PERIOD				
	1	2	3	4	5
C_s (in $)	—	—	107	—	—
C_e (in $)	—	—	—	107	12
C (in $)	100	100	110	120	132
E (in $)	100	100	110	120	132
Units of output	100	110	100	100	100
Price per unit (in $)	1	1	1.10	1.20	1.32

initial shock leads to wage escalation and public policy expands the level of demand so as to maintain output unchanged and permit it to be purchased at rising prices. Once more, the continuing expansion of demand requires an expansion of money supply in order to be sustained. Again, the example is oversimplified by failing to allow for the variety of response lags which enter as the full system of income determination is introduced. As noted before, the outcome need not be a constant rate of inflation.

C. EQUILIBRIUM RATES OF INFLATION

Although the very concept of a stable rate of inflation seems incongruous, it is of interest to consider the conditions under which an equilibrium rate of inflation may come about and whether it can coexist with unemployment to create a situation of stagflation.

Conditions of Equilibrium

We define an inflation equilibrium as a situation where the price level rises at a constant annual rate, while the level of output and employment remain unchanged. For such a state to prevail, the level of expenditures on output or aggregate demand must grow at the same rate as the cost of output or the value of aggregate supply. Thus we must have $O\dot{P} = O\dot{C}$, where O is output, P is price level, C is cost, and the dot indicates rate of increase. To simplify, we assume that only wage costs are involved, so that the condition becomes $\dot{P} = \dot{W}$, where W is the wage rate.

Consider now how $\dot{P}$ is determined. With O constant, $\dot{P}$ equals the rate of increase in aggregate expenditures. As was shown in equations (1) to (8) above, the level of expenditures depends on behavioral relationships as well as on fiscal and monetary policy parameters. For purposes of exposition, let us hold fiscal policy in a neutral position by assuming that the level of government expenditures and tax revenue grow at the same rate as P. The rate of increase in the level of expenditures will then be related positively to M, the rate of increase in money supply. In equilibrium, any given rate of inflation can only be sustained if matched by an equal rate increase in money supply. Monetary policy, by setting $\dot{M}$, thus sets the rate of inflation, with $\dot{M} = \dot{P}$.

Turning to the determination of W, we must introduce assumptions about wage behavior. Suppose that workers demand wage increases or a level of $\dot{W}$ such that their real wage remains constant. They thus set the demanded $\dot{W}$ equal to the expected rate of inflation or $\dot{P}_e$. Assuming further that this expected rate is based on past experience and noting that in equilibrium the inflation rate is constant, it follows that in equilibrium $\dot{W} = \dot{P}$.

The inflation equilibrium is thus a situation where the rate of increase in money supply equals the inflation rate and the expected rate of inflation equals the actual rate. We then have $\dot{P} = \dot{P}_e = \dot{W} = \dot{M}$. The level of real balances, of real demand and of output, remains constant. The only change is in nominal values, all of which rise at the same rate.

Full Employment or Stagflation?

Having considered the nature of the equilibrium, it remains to enquire whether or not it will be combined with full employment. Both outcomes are possible, depending on the behavioral assumptions.

Full Employment Consider first inflation equilibrium in a full-employment model, i.e., a position in which there exists transitional unemployment only.[12] For this purpose, we assume that wage demands depend on the level of employment. We assume that workers, under conditions of unemployment, are willing to accept a rate of increase in wages, or $\dot{W}$, which falls short of the expected rate of inflation, $\dot{P}_e$. They are willing to incur a decline in their real wage rate in order to find jobs. Suppose now we begin in a position of less than full employment, but $\dot{P} = \dot{M}$, so that the inflation rate is in equilibrium. This position cannot continue because workers will set their demand for $\dot{W}$ below $\dot{P}$. As a result, cost escalation is reduced, slowing the rate of inflation generated by $\dot{M}$. This will cause the value of real balances to rise, which, in line with our earlier system of equations, leads to increased real expenditures, output, and employment. This process will continue until full employment is reached. At this point, workers cease to accept a further fall in real wages. The demanded $\dot{W}$ is restored to equal $\dot{P}$. The system will then be returned to an equilibrium rate of inflation equal to $\dot{M}$, now combined with full employment.

Full-employment equilibrium with a constant rate of inflation is shown in Figure 29-2. We now measure $\dot{P}$, or the rate of inflation, on the vertical axis as against P or the level of prices in Figure 29-1. $D'ED'$ is the demand for output in real terms. It is drawn for a given level of $\dot{M}$ equal to, say, r_1. With a given $\dot{M}$, real demand will be larger the lower is $\dot{P}$ and hence the higher the level of real balances. This is why the demand schedule is downward sloping. $S'E$ measures the demanded increase in money wages $\dot{W}$ as a function of output or employment. The schedule is drawn for an expected inflation rate $\dot{P}_e$ also equal to r_1.[13] For output below full employment, or N_f, the demanded $\dot{W}$ falls short of r_1 but reaches r_1 at full employment. Equilibrium is reached at E, the intersection of the demand and supply schedules with full-employment output and inflation rate $\dot{P} = r_1$.

Stagflation But this adjustment to full employment may not come about. Suppose that wage earners accept a lag in $\dot{W}$ behind $\dot{P}$ only so long as unemployment is severe and that they return to a demand for full escalation before full employment is reached. In this case, the adjustment mechanism leading to increased employment will fall short of the full-employment

---

[12]The presentation here given draws on (although in some respects differs from) Rudiger Dornbusch and Stanley Fischer, *Macroeconomics*, New York: McGraw-Hill, 1978, especially chap. 13.

[13]The $S'E$ schedule should be interpreted as reflecting the demanded rate of wage escalation in equilibrium, when $P_e = r_1 = P$. In moving toward the equilibrium, the schedule has shifted down from the left.

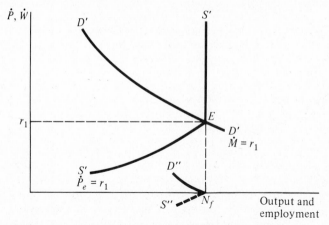

FIGURE 29-2   Inflation Equilibrium with Full Employment.

position. The economy becomes locked into a state of stagflation where less than full employment is combined with an equilibrium rate of inflation.

Such a stagflation equilibrium is shown in Figure 29-3. As before, the demand schedule $D'ED'$ is drawn for $\dot{M}=r_1$ and the supply schedule $S'ES'$ for $\dot{P}=r_1$. The supply now reaches $\dot{W}=\dot{P}_e$ at employment level N_u, which falls short of full employment N_f. Equilibrium is again reached at E, but with $\dot{W}=\dot{P}$ at employment N_u there is no inducement to move to N_f. The economy is now stuck in a stagflation position.

Policy Adjustment   Given the nature of these models, there is no reason why inflation should be permitted to continue. A reduction in $\dot{M}$ will shift the DD schedule down to the left. The resulting reduction in $\dot{P}$ will lower inflation expectations and shift the SS schedule down to the right. With $\dot{P}$ and $\dot{W}$ falling equally, real output and employment remain unaffected. This process continues until equilibrium in Figure 29-2 is reestablished at N_f, with the demand schedule $D''D''$ drawn for $\dot{M}=0$ and the supply schedule S'' drawn for $\dot{P}_e=0$. In Figure 29-2 an equilibrium involving full employment without inflation is achieved, while in Figure 29-3 employment remains at N_u and hence below full employment.

Critique of Equilibrium Models

Neither of the above models stands up well if a more realistic view of the economic process is taken. Among others, these qualifications should be noted:

1.   Adjustments in wage rates, prices, and the level of demand do not occur instantaneously, nor do the supporting changes in the rate of monetary and fiscal expansion. A complex structure of lags is involved. Because of this, the adjustment process may not follow a smooth path towards equilibrium. Rather, the outcome may be one of continuing instability.

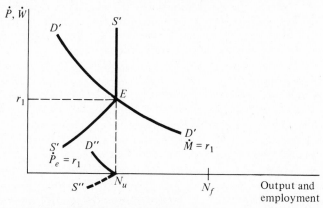

FIGURE 29-3 Stagflation Equilibrium.

2. The assumption that the economy will move towards full employment if only wages fall or lag behind prices assumes a high responsiveness of the system to the resulting increase in the value of real balances. Moreover, it disregards the possibility of detrimental effects of declining prices (or smaller increases thereof) on business expectations.

3. Similarly, wage demands may move ahead of the current rate of inflation if a cumulative inflationary development is expected.

4. Inflation expectations enter not only with regard to wage demands as implied in the above models. The escalation mechanism, in addition to wage demands, may involve marking up of prices in administered markets.

5. The rate of increase in money wages which unions demand may not be limited to keeping step with inflation but shoot ahead of the expected inflation rate, hoping thereby to increase their share in total output.

6. Inflation expectations also enter from the demand side as purchases are speeded up in anticipation of rising prices.

7. Outside shocks will recur and generate renewed inflationary impulses, transmitted from one sector of the economy to another, even before a past disturbance has been overcome.

For these and other reasons, policy makers take a severe risk if they rely on the equilibrating adjustments of the above models to run their course, hoping that this will terminate inflation and reestablish full employment. The idea of equilibrium inflation has merit in that the role of expectations ceases to be destabilizing if all relevant variables rise at the same rate, but this applies only after equilibrium is established. In the meantime, the important lessons to be learned are that inflation is an ongoing process and that disturbances, once built into the system, cannot be worked off easily.

The Phillips Curve

Since the mid-fifties, economists have been concerned with the proposition that the rate of inflation is related inversely to the rate of unemployment. This relationship, shown in AA of Figure 29-4, is referred to as the "Phillips

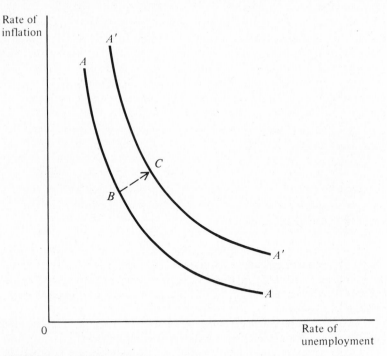

FIGURE 29-4   Phillips Curve.

curve," after the British economist who first observed it in an historical analysis of the British economy.[14]

Moving up the AA schedule from the right to the left, the inflation rate increases as unemployment falls. The underlying considerations are similar to those encountered previously in connection with the upward sloping supply schedule of Figure 29-1. Costs may rise due to a rising ratio of labor to capital as the economy moves towards full employment. Less-skilled labor may be drawn into production, and the approach to full employment may result in a variety of bottlenecks which are cost-increasing. Union demands, in line with our previous assumptions about wage behavior, may become more aggressive.

For these and other reasons, it would not be surprising to find strong empirical support for the Phillips curve hypothesis. But as shown in Figure 29-5, this does not seem to be the case for the United States economy. If we plot annual rates of inflation against those of unemployment for the years from 1950 to 1977, no clear relationship emerges. Note, however, that the postulated negative relationship tends to emerge if the points for the fifties

[14]See A. W. H. Phillips, "The Relation between Unemployment and the Rate of Change in Money Wage Rates in the United Kingdom, 1861–1907," *Economica*, November 1958, pp. 283–299.

For an evaluation of the applicability of the Phillips curve hypothesis to the United States economy, see G. L. Perry, "Slowing the Wage-Price Spiral: The Macroeconomic View," chap. 23 in Arthur M. Okun and George L. Perry (eds.), *Curing Chronic Inflation*, Washington: Brookings, 1978, pp. 23–65.

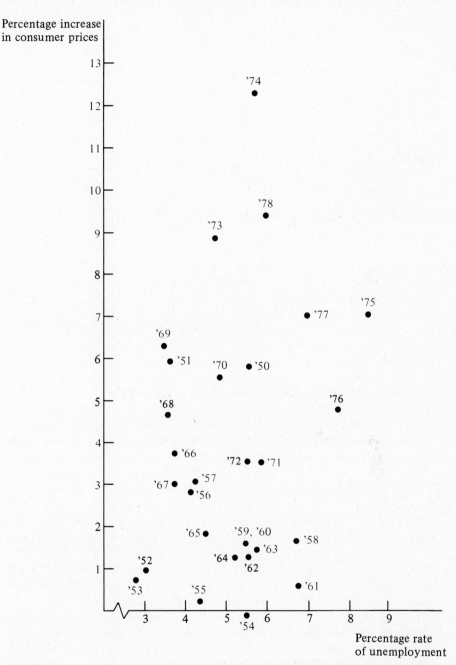

FIGURE 29-5   Inflation and Unemployment in the United States Economy, 1950–1978.

and sixties are considered in one group and those for the seventies in another, with the latter pattern lying to the right of that for the earlier years.

This suggests that the *AA* schedule of Figure 29-4 should be thought of as relating to a given level of expectations regarding the future rate of inflation. Once more this is in line with our earlier assumptions about wage behavior. As inflation expectations increase, the demanded rate of wage increase will rise for any given level of unemployment. The short-run Phillips curve, drawn for a given state of inflation expectations, will shift upward to the right, say, from *AA* to *A'A'*. Because of this, the observed relationship between the rate of inflation and unemployment may appear positive. For instance, we may observe points *B* and *C* in Figure 29-4, even though the relationship for any given level of expectations is negative. This in fact appears to have happened from the 1960s to the 1970s, when actual and expected rates of inflation increased, thus causing the Phillips curve to shift out.

It has been argued further that while the short-run Phillips curve is downward sloping, the long-run Phillips curve is vertical. Moreover, it is said to be vertical at full employment. This proposition derives directly from the adjustment mechanism of the full-employment model, where, in long-run equilibrium, full employment is established and changes in the rate of monetary or fiscal expansion can affect the rate of inflation only—not that of employment.

As noted before, the realism of this proposition, as that of the underlying adjustment model, is doubtful. Allowing for the various qualifications listed above, it is more likely that the adjustment process will fall short of equilibrium and that the changes in the nominal level of expenditures will continue to affect output and employment as well as prices. The tradeoff between inflation and employment thus remains a relevant policy issue.

D. STRUCTURAL USES OF FISCAL POLICY

The problems of stagflation, as suggested by the preceding discussion, render aggregate demand management incapable of achieving both price level stability and high employment. This raises the question whether other policy tools can be developed to solve the problem. These other tools primarily involve labor market policies, including training and improved mobility, which will reduce the slope of the aggregate supply schedule, fit available skills to job openings, and cut the level of transitional unemployment (the natural rate) which remains when "full employment" is reached. Analysis of these policies lies outside our range of study, but we will consider whether fiscal instruments can be used for the purpose.

Cost-Reducing Measures

Suppose first that the problem is one of halting a price-wage-price spiral set into motion by a once-and-for-all cost shock, such as the inflationary finance of the late sixties, or the oil price rise of 1974. What can fiscal policy do to deal with such a situation?

While a general demand-restricting tax increase is no longer appropriate, as it was with demand-pull inflation, attention must now be given to the impact of tax changes on cost as well as on demand. If taxes *are* to be raised, those which raise cost less will be preferable. Moreover, we cannot be sure that the net effects of a tax increase will be helpful. In the absence of wage escalation, the net effect of, say, a sales tax increase is deflationary. Notwithstanding an initial price increase, this once-and-for-all effect will be outweighed by continuing reduction in demand. But with wage escalation in the picture, the wage-price spiral induced from the cost side may more than outweigh the deflationary demand effect. Stagflation may in fact worsen. By the same token, the beneficial cost-reducing effects of a tax decrease may more than offset the inflation-aggravating effects of the resulting demand increase. To say the least, the situation will be improved by combining a cost-reducing tax decrease at one point in the system with a non–cost-increasing tax increase somewhere else.

This points to a new perspective on the quality of various tax changes. Whereas the traditional concern was with their differential demand effect, some being more potent per dollar of initial revenue loss than others, there is now the further concern with differential effects on costs. If restrictive action is called for, an increase in income tax will be preferable to one in sales tax; and if tax reduction is called for in dealing with stagflation, a sales tax cut will be more helpful. Since sales taxes are imposed mostly at the state level, an arrangement might be considered by which the federal government, instead of reducing its income tax, would compensate states for revenue loss from reduction in their sales tax rates.[15] Reduction in the payroll tax, especially of the employer contribution, is another alternative. By the same token, raising payroll taxes becomes an especially unsuitable way of dealing with the inflation side of stagflation.

Measures to Slow Escalation

Another way in which tax policy might be used to dampen inflationary pressures from the supply side is to intercept the continuing transmission of cost increases by offering tax reduction as a bribe for good (i.e., noninflationary) behavior. This practice has been followed in national wage-setting policies in countries such as Sweden, where the wage level is set net of tax. Tax reduction increases disposable real income without being cost-increasing, and, depending on the tax reduction chosen, costs may even be reduced in the process. A similar approach was used by Great Britain, which in 1976 adopted a "social contract," whereby tax reduction was traded for wage restraint.

As another variant of this theme, tax policy may be used to encourage compliance with wage-price guidelines. President Carter in 1978 proposed a scheme offering tax rebates to employees who, after agreeing to limit wage

---

[15]For this and related suggestions, see G. L. Perry, "Stabilization Policy and Inflation," in H. Owen and C. Schultze, *Setting National Priorities, The Next Ten Years*, Washington: Brookings, 1976, pp. 273–286; and also Okun and Perry, op. cit.

increases to guideline levels, fall behind the actual inflation rate. This "real-wage insurance" has not been enacted by the Congress.[16] Moreover, the administration proposed to redirect its purchase policies so as to reward companies which comply with price guidelines while penalizing others which do not.

While tax adjustments may be helpful, the progressive income tax may accentuate the wage-price spiral. This is the case where wage demands in response to rising prices will call for holding constant or raising real *after*-(rather than before-) tax wages. The reason is that inflation pushes taxpayers into higher brackets. With a proportional rate, the percentage increase in before-tax income needed to hold after-tax income constant in real terms equals the price rise. But if the taxpayer moves into a higher rate bracket, the required percentage increase in before-tax income comes to exceed the price rise. Thus, if the taxpayers' initial rate is 20 percent and their marginal rate is 30 percent, a 10 percent increase in prices calls for a 11.4 percent increase in money wages. If the marginal rate is 40 percent, the needed wage increase is 13.3 percent and so forth.[17] Thus the dynamics of cost-push inflation come to be magnified by failure to index the income tax schedule so as to neutralize it against inflation. This might not have been a major factor in the United States to date, since it is doubtful whether wage bargaining allows for after-tax income, and since the gradation of bracket rates over the relevant range is relatively modest. But it is a factor which has been given intensive consideration in the Swedish discussion.[18]

Finally, transfer policies may be used to subsidize firms, permitting higher costs to be absorbed without price increase, and thereby without subsequent wage escalation. Such policies have been used in Great Britain to cushion the impact of rising import prices. They may be of temporary help, especially where aimed at particular parts of the price structure. But the subsidies can become costly, and in the end they must be financed by additional taxes, thus reducing real incomes from the other side of the household account. They therefore do not offer a lasting solution.

---

[16]For a further discussion of these proposals, see Okun and Perry, op. cit.

[17]To maintain after-tax wages constant in real terms, we must have

$$\frac{M_1(1-t_1)}{P_1} = \frac{M_1(1-t_1) + \Delta M(1-t_m)}{P_2}$$

where M_1 is the initial money income, P_1 and P_2 are the price indices for the two periods, t_1 is the average tax rate applicable to M_1, and t_m is the marginal tax rate applicable to the required increase in money income. It follows that

$$\dot{M} = \dot{P} x \frac{(1-t_1)}{(1-t_m)}$$

where $\dot{M}$ is the required percentage increase in money income and $\dot{P}$ is the percentage increase in price level.

[18]See Lars Mathiessen and E. Lundberg, *Business Cycles and Economic Policy*, London: Allen and Unwin, 1957.

E. SUMMARY

As a first step toward dealing with inflation, the earlier model of income determination must be restated by introducing the price level.

    1. This calls for adjustments in the consumption function and in the demand for money.
    2. It also calls for the introduction of an aggregate supply schedule, showing a positive relationship between output or employment and the level of prices.
    3. As before, expansionary policy may be used to raise the level of aggregate demand, thereby increasing output and employment. But this is now achieved at the cost of raising prices.
    4. If wage behavior is such that excess supply in the labor market leads to a bidding down of wage rates, full employment will be reached automatically. This, however, is hardly a realistic assumption.

Turning to inflation as a dynamic process, attention must be given to the interdependence of costs and prices as well as emphasis on the response lags between the receipt of income and expenditure.

    5. A simple model of budget inflation is used to illustrate demand-pull and to show the time path of the inflation process. This path depends on the structure of response lags, which may be such as to cause inflation to taper off, rise, or fluctuate.
    6. A similar model is used to show the response of inflation to an initial cost shock.

Finally, we explored the nature of equilibrium rates of inflation and employment, using for this purpose a more complex model with emphasis on the role of inflation expectations.

    7. The rate of inflation is determined as a function of aggregate demand and supply schedules. With a given rate of increase in money supply, the level of real output demanded declines as the rate of inflation increases. On the supply side, the rate of increase in wages depends upon inflation expectations and the level of employment.
    8. Such a model yields an equilibrium rate of inflation equal to the rate of increase in money supply. This may coincide with full or less-than-full employment, depending on how supply behavior is defined.
    9. The concept of an equilibrium rate of inflation is questionable and may well be incompatible with the actual structure of response lags.

In recent years much attention has been given to the so-called Phillips curve, depicting a negative relationship between inflation and the level of unemployment.

    10. Observation of United States data for 1950–1978 does not seem to bear out this hypothesis, but a negative relationship does appear if the data for the 1950s and 1960s are separated from those of the 1970s.

11. An increase in inflation expectations causes the Phillips curve to shift up.

12. As distinct from the sloping short-run Phillips curve, the long-run Phillips curve is taken to be vertical.

Given a stagflation setting, policies of aggregate demand control, fiscal or monetary, are inadequate and must be supplemented by structural measures.

13. This calls primarily for labor market policies aimed at training and mobility, with the role of fiscal measures of secondary importance.

14. Nevertheless, structural aspects of fiscal policy may be used. Thus, tax adjustments may be made with allowance for their effects on costs, and tax policy may be used to encourage compliance with wage-price guidelines.

FURTHER READINGS

Dornbusch, Rudiger, and Stanley Fischer: *Macroeconomics*, New York: McGraw-Hill, 1978, part III.

Gordon, Robert J.: *Macroeconomics*, Boston: Little, Brown, 1978, part III.

Okun, Arthur M., and George W. Perry (eds.): *Curing Chronic Inflation*, Washington: Brookings, 1978.

Chapter 30

Fiscal Policy Experience*

A. **Early Record:** *The Thirties; World War II; 1946–1960.* B. **The Sixties and Seventies:** *Fiscal Indices; The Sixties; The Seventies; Key Features.* C. **Summary.**

In this chapter, we complete the discussion of fiscal policy with a brief look at our actual fiscal policy experience. Some of the concepts developed in the preceding chapters will prove helpful in interpreting what has occurred.

A. EARLY RECORD

In surveying United States experience with fiscal policy, we pass quickly over the earlier stages, then take a more careful look at the 1960s and 1970s.

The Thirties

The fiscal policy discussion in the United States dates back to the Great Depression of the 1930s when unemployment rose to the disastrous rate of over 25 percent (1933). While there was much talk about fiscal measures to

---

* Reader's Guide to Chapter 30: A brief survey of the successes and failures of United States fiscal policy in the Great Depression, World War II, and the recent decades, up to the new problems posed by operating fiscal policy in a setting of "stagflation."

"prime the pump," the principles of fiscal policy were not as yet properly understood, and they certainly had not penetrated to the policy level. While expenditures were increased to provide emergency relief and employment programs such as PWA and WPA, tax rates were raised as well, leaving only a slight net expansionary effect to the economy. Such modest recovery as had been realized by the onset of World War II had been largely a reflection of recovery in the private sector.[1]

World War II

The economic expansion of World War II brought a vast change and provided a powerful demonstration of what massive fiscal policy can accomplish. As federal government purchases increased from $6 billion to $89 billion (1940 to 1944) while the deficit rose from $1 to $52 billion, unemployment rapidly disappeared and GNP climbed from $100 to $210 billion. After allowing for price rise, real output increased by 60 percent. The resulting increase was so large that, even though the war effort came to absorb 40 percent of GNP, an increased output remained available for civilian use. Although wartime conditions differ from those of peace and general price controls permitted a level of deficit finance which otherwise would have resulted in sharp price rise, the experience nevertheless offered an overwhelming testimony to the expansionary potential of fiscal policy.[2]

1946–1960

There was widespread expectation in the councils of economists during the mid-forties that the dismantling of the war budget would reproduce the condition of economic stagnation that had prevailed during the thirties, calling for continued and sustained reliance on a high level of fiscal expansion. This prognosis, however, did not materialize. For one thing, the economic vigor of the private sector proved much greater than had been expected. For another, the responsiveness of the economy to monetary policy measures proved much stronger than it had been during the prewar years. Not only did the need for expansionary action prove more limited, but monetary policy was raised from its state of impotence to become a full-fledged partner of stabilization policy in the postwar period.

To be sure, the share of government in GNP continued at a substantially higher level than had been maintained in the prewar economy. This in itself contributed to the higher level of economic activity. After a drastic cut in defense spending in the immediate postwar years, defense spending again rose and the ratio of total federal expenditures to GNP remained about 20 percent, or twice the pre-World War II level. The unemployment rate, which had risen in the immediate postwar years, declined and remained in the 4 to 5 percent range for the first half of the decade of the 1950s.

---

[1]See E. Cary Brown, "Fiscal Policy in the Thirties: A Reappraisal," *American Economic Review*, December 1956.

[2]The inflationary aftereffects caused by large accumulations of liquid assets credited in the course of wartime deficits came to be felt in the late forties. Nevertheless, heavy reliance on deficit finance during the war period was appropriate, since it fueled economic expansion.

   The second half of the fifties brought the emergence of rising prices combined with resource slack, a forerunner of the conflict between high employment and price level stability which became such a significant factor in the policy setting of the late 1960s and 1970s. The first serious recession occurred in 1958, with unemployment rising to 7 percent. In the ensuing recovery, a sharp increase in full-employment surplus was permitted to develop and contribute to choking off a short-lived recovery. It was this increase in full-employment surplus that became the basis for concern with fiscal drag and played a role in changing policy attitudes during the 1960s.

B. THE SIXTIES AND SEVENTIES

The sixties and seventies witnessed both triumph and defeat of fiscal stabilization.

Fiscal Indices

To trace this development and appraise the role of fiscal variables, various relevant data are presented in Table 30-1 and in Figure 30-1. Lines 1 to 3 of the table show expenditures, receipts, and surplus or deficit in the actual budget. Given the sharp growth in the nominal level of GNP in the seventies (line 29) due to inflation (line 32), focus on absolute budget levels is misleading. For this reason, the position of the budget as percentage of GNP is shown in lines 4 to 6. To trace the pattern of fiscal policy, we also consider yearly changes as given in lines 7 to 12.

   As we have seen in the preceding chapters, it is helpful to distinguish between actual levels of expenditures, receipts, and budget surplus or deficit, and those which obtain at a high-employment level of GNP. This "high-employment" level is now estimated to correspond to a 5.1 percent rate of unemployment. In order to identify the role of discretionary changes in fiscal policy, changes in the high-employment position of the budget should be considered. The reason is that changes in the actual budget reflect the influence of built-in responses as well as of discretionary policy changes. For this reason, lines 13 to 28 repeat the previous items, measured now for high-employment levels of GNP. We also add a crude measure of fiscal leverage (lines 16 and 20), designed to show the overall contribution to aggregate demand which results from the federal budget.[3] The concluding part of the table shows certain other items, pertaining to the overall position of the economy and the role of monetary policy.

[3]Following equation 23, p. 600, we have

$$L_f = G + \frac{c}{1-c} D_f$$

Assuming that all transfer payments are fully spent, that 80 percent of the average tax dollar is reflected in reduced consumption, and that the marginal propensity to consume for all income recipients (including corporations) equals 0.67, we use 0.8 for the value of c in the numerator and 0.67 in the denominator. We thus obtain

$$L_f = G + 2.4 D_f$$

TABLE 30-1
Fiscal Policy Indices, 1960–1978*

	1960	1965†	1966	1967	1968	1969	1970	1971	1972	1973	1974	1975	1976	1977	1978
I. Actual Budget															
Billions of dollars															
1. Expenditures	93	124	143	164	181	189	204	221	245	264	299	357	386	423	461
2. Receipts	97	125	143	151	175	197	192	199	227	259	291	287	332	374	432
3. Surplus	4	1	—	-12	-6	8	-12	-22	-18	-6	-8	-70	-54	-50	-29
As percentage of GNP															
4. Expenditures	18.6	18.1	19.1	20.0	20.9	20.0	20.9	20.9	21.1	20.4	21.4	23.4	22.6	22.4	21.9
5. Receipts	19.4	18.2	19.1	19.0	20.2	21.2	19.6	18.9	19.7	20.1	20.8	21.7	19.4	19.8	20.5
6. Surplus	6.8	0.1	—	-1.0	-0.7	+1.2	-1.3	-2.0	-1.4	-0.3	-0.6	-1.7	-3.2	-2.6	-1.4
Changes from previous year															
7. In line 1		+31	+19	+21	+17	+8	+15	+17	+24	+19	+35	+58	+29	+37	+38
8. In line 2		+28	+18	+8	+24	+12	-5	+7	+28	+32	+32	-4	+45	+42	+58
9. In line 3		-3	-1	-12	+7	+14	-20	-10	+4	+12	-2	-62	+16	+5	+21
10. In line 4		-0.5	+1.0	+0.9	+0.9	-0.9	+0.9	-0.7	+0.2	-0.7	+1.0	+2.0	-0.8	-0.2	-0.5
11. In line 5		-0.2	+0.9	-0.1	+1.2	+1.0	-1.6	-0.7	+0.8	+0.4	+0.7	+0.9	-2.3	+0.4	+0.7
12. In line 6		+0.2	-0.1	-1.0	+0.3	+1.9	-2.5	-0.7	+0.6	+1.1	-0.3	-1.1	-1.5	+0.6	+1.2
II. High-Employment Budget															
Billions of dollars															
13. Expenditures	101	123	143	164	182	190	203	218	243	263	297	350	381	420	460
14. Receipts	111	126	139	152	174	198	207	216	232	266	320	321	357	394	447
15. Surplus	11	3	-4	-12	-8	9	4	-2	-10	3	23	-30	-23	-25	-13
16. Leverage	74	116	153	193	201	168	193	273	267	256	242	382	436	480	491
As percentage of high-employment GNP															
17. Expenditures	17.5	19.8	19.3	20.9	21.6	19.4	18.7	17.9	19.4	19.5	18.0	21.2	21.1	21.4	21.3
18. Receipts	19.4	20.4	18.7	19.3	20.7	20.3	19.1	17.7	18.7	19.6	19.4	19.4	19.9	20.1	20.7
19. Surplus	1.9	0.5	-0.5	-1.6	-0.9	0.9	0.4	-0.2	-0.7	0.1	1.4	-1.8	-1.3	-1.3	-0.6
20. Leverage	12.9	18.7	20.6	24.5	23.8	17.1	17.8	19.0	21.2	19.4	15.1	23.1	24.3	24.5	23.3

Changes from previous year

21. In line 13	+23	+20	+21	+18	+8	+13	+15	+25	+20	+34	+53	+31	+39	+40
22. In line 14	+15	+13	+13	+22	+24	+9	+10	+16	+34	+54	+1	+36	+37	+53
23. In line 15	−8	−7	−8	+4	+17	−5	−6	−8	+13	+20	−53	+7	−2	+12
24. In line 16	+42	+37	+40	+8	−33	+25	+36	+34	−11	−14	+140	+54	+44	+11
25. In line 17	+2.3	−0.5	+1.6	+0.7	−2.2	−0.7	−0.9	+1.5	+0.1	−1.5	+3.2	−0.1	+0.3	−0.1
26. In line 18	+1.0	−1.7	+0.6	+1.4	−0.4	−1.2	−1.4	+1.0	+0.9	−0.2	—	+0.5	+0.2	+0.6
27. In line 19	−1.3	—	−1.1	+6.7	+1.8	+0.6	−0.5	−0.5	+0.8	−1.7	−3.8	+0.5	—	+0.7
28. In line 20	+5.8	+1.9	+3.9	−0.7	−6.7	+0.7	+1.2	+1.2	−1.8	−4.3	+3.5	+1.2	+0.2	−1.2

III. Other Data

29. GNP, billions of dollars	520	685	750	794	864	930	977	1,055	1,155	1,288	1,397	1,529	1,706	1,887	2,106
30. High-employment GNP, billions of dollars	570	620	740	785	844	980	1,085	1,170	1,260	1,317	1,510	1,653	1,797	1,961	2,163
31. Unemployment rate, percentage	6.7	4.5	3.8	3.6	3.5	4.9	5.9	5.6	4.9	5.6	8.5	7.7	7.0	6.0	
32. Price rise, percentage	0.7	1.9	3.4	3.0	4.7	6.1	5.5	3.4	3.4	8.7	6.7	9.1	5.8	6.5	9.5
33. Change in money supply, percentage	7.0	8.6	4.7	9.8	8.3	2.3	7.9	3.4	13.1	8.7	10.7	11.4	13.7	11.1	8.8

*A decrease in surplus or increase in deficit is shown as − . An increase in surplus or decrease in deficit is shown as + .

†Change from 1960 to 1965 throughout this column.

Note: Items may not add to total due to rounding.

Sources:

Lines 1 to 3: *Economic Report of the President,* 1975 and 1979.

Lines 13 to 15: For years preceding 1969, see Arthur M. Okun and Nancy H. Teeters, "The Full Employment Surplus Revisited," *Brookings Papers on Economic Activity,* vol. 1, Washington: Brookings, p. 104. For years from 1971 to 1975, see *Economic Report of the President,* 1974, p. 80, and 1975, p. 64. For years from 1975 on, see *Economic Report of the President,* 1979, p. 46.

Line 16: Computed such that leverage equals high-employment expenditures minus 3×0.8 of high-employment surplus.

Line 30: See Okun and Teeters, op. cit., for years preceding 1969; figures for 1973 and 1974, unpublished estimates by E. Gramlich, Brookings Institution. For 1975 on, see *Economic Report of the President,* 1979, p. 75.

Line 32: Percentage change in consumer prices, December to December, *Economic Report of the President,* 1979.

Line 33: *Economic Report of the President,* 1979, p. 310. Reference is to M_3.

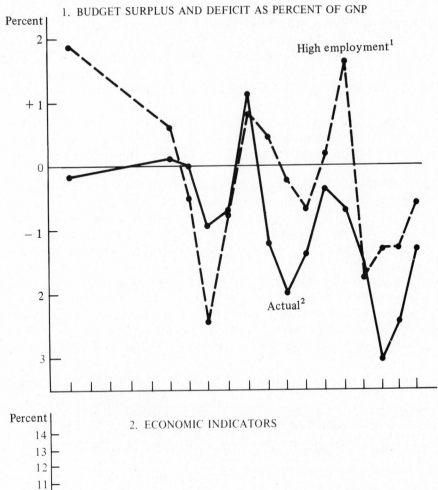

1. BUDGET SURPLUS AND DEFICIT AS PERCENT OF GNP

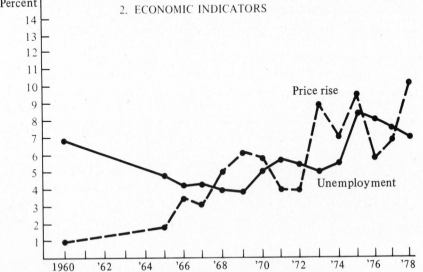

FIGURE 30-1   Fiscal Leverage and Economic Conditions, 1960–1978.

[1]High-employment surplus or deficit as percent of high-employment GNP.
[2]Actual surplus or deficit as percent of actual GNP.

In short, lines 25 to 28 are the most significant indicators for an analysis of discretionary policy, with the change in the leverage ratio (line 28) perhaps the single most significant item. Next, lines 10 to 12 are most interesting in appraising the entire role of the budget, including the influences of built-in flexibility. Clearly, these data offer a better insight into what happens than would a simple tracing of the absolute budget items given in lines 1 through 3.

The Sixties

The decade of the 1960s was of unusual interest to the student of fiscal policy, with the first half a resounding success and the second a painful failure.[4]

1960–1966   The Kennedy administration had come into office on a platform of fiscal expansion, and various measures were taken to implement it. During the earlier part of the period, this implementation primarily took the form of expenditure expansion (largely for national defense) supported by moderate tax reduction in 1962, which was followed by a more massive tax cutback in 1964. As a result, unemployment declined fairly continuously between 1961 and 1966, covering the longest period of sustained expansion on record. At the same time, the rate of price increase remained modest. Expansionary fiscal measures resulted in a sharp increase in leverage and a decline in full-employment surplus, while the expanding economy (and with it, built-in revenue growth) turned the actual balance from a deficit to a surplus position.

The expansionary role of fiscal policy in the first half of the sixties involved an increase in expenditures of $23 billion and a decline in full-employment surplus of $8 billion. Our measure of fiscal leverage (line 16) rose by over $40 billion, or from 13 to 19 percent of full-employment GNP (line 20). Operating in an economy as yet substantially below full employment, the result was to raise output and reduce unemployment, and to do so while maintaining a high degree of price level stability (lines 31 and 32).

One of the most dramatic events during this period was the tax reduction of 1964. Even though the actual budget was in deficit, the administration requested, and Congress granted, a cut in tax rates (mostly in the individual income tax) of about $10 billion, undertaken with the explicit purpose of stimulating employment. While risking a sharp increase in the actual budget deficit, the reduction in full-employment surplus, by generating expansion, in fact improved the actual budget position, the deficit of 1964 turning to a surplus in 1965. Fiscal policy, supported by an increased rate of growth in money supply (line 33), had proven highly successful in stimulating expansion. This was the high point of the "new economics" but, alas, also the end of its success story.

---

[4]For further discussion, see Walter W. Heller, *New Dimensions of Political Economy*, New York: Norton, 1967; Arthur M. Okun, *Political Economy of Prosperity*, New York: Norton, 1970; Herbert Stein, *The Fiscal Revolution in America*, Chicago: University of Chicago Press, 1969; and Charles E. McClure, Jr., *Fiscal Failure, Lessons of the Sixties*, Washington: Enterprise Institute, 1972.

1966–1968 Forebodings of trouble to come arose in the second half of 1965. After the level of unemployment had been sharply reduced and the "interim goal" of unemployment not in excess of 4 percent had been reached, the upswing continued to proceed at a rapid pace. Driven by an investment boom reflecting the stimulating effects of the investment credit of 1962, a rising level of consumption, and sustained increase in government expenditures, the rate of expansion came to exceed a level which could be sustained without inflation. While the speed of price increase still remained modest, proper policy would have called for slowing down the rate of expansion at this point, but a recommendation for tax increase—said to have been advanced by the Council of Economic Advisers late in 1965—went unheeded. Federal Reserve authorities, in trying to go it alone, produced a sharp slowdown in the rate of increase in money supply in 1966, leading to a painful "credit crunch."

Fiscal policies similarly added to, rather than checked, the rising level of excess demand. Expenditures continued to rise sharply from 1966 to 1968, including civilian as well as military programs, and repeated requests by President Johnson for a tax increase were not met by Congress until 1968. In the process, the full-employment surplus turned into a deficit and leverage was nearly doubled. Expansionary fiscal policies in 1967 and 1968 were supplemented by a rapid increase in money supply (line 33). With unemployment having reached a record low by 1966, the accelerated growth in aggregate demand turned into price increases, a first forerunner of the inflationary decade to come.

Who was to blame for the delay in restrictive fiscal action? Among various factors, the unpredictability of defense outlays offers the best excuse, but it is not a sufficient explanation. While federal expenditures rose sharply from 1966 to 1967, less than half the increase was for national defense. Political hesitation to urge increased tax rates on the part of the White House was another factor, and a rather tardy support for restrictive action by economists did not help matters. The most important single cause, however, was congressional delay in meeting the President's request for a tax increase. However this may be, the drastic rise in fiscal leverage from 1965 to 1968 was not primarily a matter of rising deficit. With tax receipts responding to the rising level of GNP, there was only a modest increase in deficit, leaving the major expansionary thrust to the expenditure side of the budget and the effects of balanced-budget expansion, reflecting the "Great Society" programs of the Johnson administration and the cost of the Vietnam war.

A marked turn in policy, including a sharply reduced rate of monetary expansion and decline in fiscal leverage, did not come until 1969. The latter reflected introduction of the income tax surcharge and suspension of the investment credit in 1969, as well as a decline in the rate of expenditure growth. As a result, both the actual and the high-employment budgets recorded a sharp turnaround from deficit to surplus and a decline in our measure of leverage. This shift served to halt the expansion but also turned the economy into a recession. Fiscal restriction had been postponed for too long, and it was now applied with excessive force.

The Seventies

With unemployment rising in 1970 and 1971 and the inflation rate declining, policy turned once more toward expansion. Fiscal leverage increased, reflecting both tax reduction (including suspension of the surcharge, reinstitution of the investment credit in the Revenue Act of 1971, and other tax relief) and a sharp increase in expenditures for civilian programs. In consequence, the full-employment surplus declined, with the actual budget moving sharply into deficit under the impact of a sluggish economy. This shift toward fiscal expansion was accompanied by a sharply expansionary turn in monetary policy. Together, these measures succeeded in retarding the rising rate of unemployment but were less successful with regard to inflation. They were accompanied in late 1971 by a direct attack on the inflation problem through a temporary price and wage freeze. With continued fiscal and monetary expansion in 1972, unemployment leveled off, as did the price rise.

Nineteen-seventy-three brought the dismantling of direct controls, combined with a more restrictive policy stance. The rate of monetary expansion was reduced sharply, with fiscal policy also on the restrictive side. Leverage declined as high-employment tax receipts (due largely to an increase in payroll tax rates and coverage) outpaced the increase in full-employment expenditure. As a result, the full-employment budget returned to a surplus position, while the deficit in the actual budget declined. With a strengthened private sector, the unemployment rate declined but the inflation rate took a sharp upturn. This was but the prelude to the unhappy developments of 1974 when a two-digit rate of price increase combined with a renewed rise of unemployment.

The course of fiscal policy in 1974 demonstrates what may happen to fiscal leverage under conditions of stagflation. GNP, which must rise in real terms to prevent an increase in the rate of unemployment, did in fact decline. Yet prices rose sufficiently to bring about an increase in GNP in money terms. Tax revenue consequently rose, with the gain about matching the increase in expenditures so as to leave the actual budget with a modest and only slightly increased level of deficit. At the same time, inflation made for a sharp increase in full-employment revenue. This gain far outpaced the expenditure increase, resulting in a sharp rise in full-employment surplus and decline in leverage. The role of fiscal policy as measured by our indices became severely restrictive, with full-employment leverage declining by over 20 percent. Unfortunately, the effect was to contribute to a deepening of the recession rather than a retardation of inflation.

By the end of 1974, the danger of deepening recession had displaced inflation as the primary concern. With unemployment about 8 percent and rising toward the two-digit level, fiscal policy shifted toward a sharply expansionary position. The budget message of January 1975 called for tax reduction. Congress, this time, reacted promptly, providing for a tax cut of $18 billion. Combined with a sharp rise in expenditures, this resulted in a 50 percent increase in fiscal leverage and a drastic swing of high-employment surplus into deficit. Notwithstanding the expansionary push, unemployment remained at a high level. The actual deficit, responding to the expenditure increase and tax reduction, shot up to $70 billion. This was a peacetime high, not only in absolute terms but also as a percentage of GNP.

Following the expansionary move of 1975, expenditures continued to rise but were outpaced by rising tax revenue. The rising level of GNP, due in part to economic recovery, but mostly due to price inflation, resulted in sharp automatic revenue gains so that the deficit declined rapidly during 1976. Once more, this reflected the close dependence of budgetary fortunes on the position of the economy. The high-employment deficit also declined, but at a lesser rate.

Fiscal policy during 1977 remained in a neutral position. There was no significant change in either actual or full-employment deficit. In 1978, however, there was a slight shift towards contraction. Once more, a buoyant economy led to sharp built-in revenue gains which, outpassing the expenditure growth, resulted in a sharp reduction in the actual deficit. The full-employment deficit also declined, as did full-employment leverage relative to GNP. But while the recovery had pulled out of the recession, the inflation rate also took a renewed upturn. Earlier plans for substantial tax reduction, designed to offset part of the built-in revenue gain of the preceding two years, thus had to be scaled down. While income and corporation profits taxes were cut back in late 1978, involving a 1979 revenue loss of nearly $20 billion, this was offset in large part by increased social security taxes. With renewed emphasis on fiscal constraint, the administration set the goal to reduce the level of expenditures to 21 percent of GNP, thus extending the downturn in this ratio which had started in 1976.

Key Features

If we look at the sixties and seventies as a whole, the data shown in Table 30-1 indicate certain characteristics of fiscal change which are of interest in relation to our earlier discussion of fiscal theory. Among them, the following may be noted:

1. Comparison of lines 12 and 31 shows a tendency for the actual deficit to increase in years of declining employment (mainly from 1970 to 1971 and from 1974 to 1975) and to fall in periods of rising employment (such as from 1960 to 1965 and from 1976 to 1978). This reflects built-in responses of the budget to economic change, as well as discretionary policy measures designed to dampen swings in economic activity.

2. Comparison of lines 12 and 23 shows that the actual and high-employment deficit or surplus moved in the same direction for all but three of our fourteen periods, with swings in the actual balance substantially larger. At first sight this seems to contradict our earlier analysis, which suggests that the actual balance should vary less.[5] The outcome, however, is explained by the fact that discretionary policy changes are made in the setting of an economy which itself is

[5]Restrictive action will raise the high-employment surplus and reduce the level of economic activity, thereby curtailing revenue and hence resulting in a lesser rise in the actual surplus. Restrictive action similarly will raise the high-employment surplus and reduce income and hence tax revenue, thus raising the actual surplus by less.

in motion. Thus, during the 1974–1975 period, sharp expansionary action was taken which reduced the high-employment surplus by $38 billion. But notwithstanding this action, economic activity declined and actual GNP fell substantially below its high-employment level. As a result, actual revenue fell below high-employment revenue, thereby increasing the actual budget deficit.[6]

Moreover, interpreting the relationship between changes in high employment and in actual surplus is complicated by the presence of lags. Whereas a change in expenditure or tax rate levels comes to be reflected immediately in the state of high-employment balance, its effects on economic activity and hence on the actual budget follow with a lag. It is not surprising, therefore, that if we compare changes in the actual budget with changes in the high-employment budget one year lagged, we now find that both moved in similar directions for only nine out of the fourteen years.

3.   Comparing lines 23 and 24, we find changes in the high-employment balance and in leverage to move usually in opposite directions. This is as expected, since a rise in the high-employment surplus will reduce leverage just as a decrease will raise it. In some instances, however, the two move in opposite directions. The restrictive effect of an increased surplus is outweighed in these cases by the expansionary effect of rising expenditures.

4.   Comparison of lines 23 and 24 also shows that changes in leverage are typically larger than those in high-employment surplus. This is as expected, since leverage rises with an increase in the level of both expenditures and deficit. Moreover, it reflects the fact that discretionary fiscal action relied more largely on changes in expenditures than on changes in the level of tax rates. Thus changes in leverage reflected to an important extent "balanced budget" effects.

5.   As shown by lines 1 to 3 and 13 to 16, the dollar value of fiscal magnitudes greatly increased over the sixties and seventies. But it does not follow that fiscal policy became more powerful. Since the level of nominal GNP, especially during the seventies, rose rapidly with inflation, the increase in fiscal magnitudes relative to GNP was much less. Turning to lines 4 to 6 and 17 to 20, we find that expenditures and receipts relative to GNP showed only a modest increase. We also note a decline in the second half of the seventies.

6.   While changes in fiscal leverage in response to discretionary policy action were substantial in absolute terms (line 16), they were rather small if viewed in relation to high-employment GNP (line 20). With actual GNP in the seventies typically 10 percent below the high-employment level (lines 29 and 30), stronger expansionary action might have been needed to close the gap; and with inflation moving at a two-digit rate, sharper curtailment might have been needed to have a substantial effect. Such at least might be concluded if the complicating forces of stagflation are disregarded; but given these forces, stronger expansion might have added to inflation without effectively raising employment, just as stronger restriction might have depressed employment without checking inflation.

C. SUMMARY

The record of fiscal policy, with the exception of the early sixties, has not been highly successful. Excessive expansion in the second half of the sixties

---

[6]Interpretation of the data is complicated further by the fact that restrictive policy, while pushing GNP below its high-employment level, did not reduce the nominal level of GNP. Due to inflation, the latter (and with it tax revenue) continued to rise.

was the beginning of the trouble, and abrupt and poorly timed policy swings thereafter reduced the effectiveness of fiscal policy in dealing with instability. Thus restrictive action when it came in 1969 was excessive and contributed to the recession of 1970–71. Sharp expansion in 1975 helped to stall the recession but contributed to the resumption of rapid inflation, even though unemployment remained high. It remains to be seen whether it will prove possible in the late seventies to deescalate inflation without inducing a severe recession.

This will not be an easy task, given the complex set of relationships by which current economic changes depend on how employment, prices, and wages have behaved in the past. Because of this structure of lags and expectations, the system, once derailed (as happened in the late 1960s), is difficult to return to a stable, full-employment path. Deescalation has to move at a slow rate. Thereafter, the hope is that more judicious policy decisions at an earlier stage can avoid renewed disruption and do so without placing too heavy a burden on "fine tuning." It may be noted also that policy during the last decade has been burdened by a heavy coincidence of outside shocks, such as the oil crisis, raw material shortages, and poor harvests—shocks which, it is hoped, will be less severe in the future.

But this may well be too optimistic a view. For one thing, the age of energy shortage may well bring an increased threat of outside shocks. Given rigidities which keep prices from falling, these shocks come to be reflected in inflationary pressures, magnified, and passed on through a cost-push process. For another, a continuing internal source of instability may be provided by the intent and (given imperfect market structures) ability of various groups to demand shares in output which aggregrate to more than the total. Barring willingness to accept high unemployment, policies of aggregate demand management (fiscal or monetary) will not sufice to deal with these problems. While such measures continue to play an important role in overall policy, they will have to be supplmented by other, structurally oriented policy tools.

FURTHER READINGS

Brookings Institution: *Setting National Priorities, The 1980 Budget,* and volumes for earlier years, Washington.

Economic Report of the President. Current discussions of fiscal policy issues may be found in each of the annual economic reports.

Heller, Walter: *New Dimensions of Political Economy*, New York: Norton, 1967.

McClure, Charles E., Jr.: *Fiscal Failure, Lessons of the Sixties*, Washington: American Enterprise Institute, 1972.

Stein, Herbert: *The Fiscal Revolution in America*, Chicago: University of Chicago Press, 1969.

Chapter 31

Fiscal Effects on
Capacity Output*

A. Effects on Work Effort: *Tax Effects; Expenditure Effects; Why Do Effects on Work Effort Matter?* **B. Effects on Private Sector Saving:** *Household Saving; Business Saving.* **C. Effects on Private Investment:** *Nature of Investment Function; Profitability Effects; Loss Offset and the Return to Risk; Research and Development.* **D. Saving and Investment in the Public Sector:** *Public Saving; Capital versus Current Budget; Tax versus Loan Finance; Public Investment; Technological Advance.* **E. Fiscal Policy and the Rate of Growth:** *Function of Saving; The Equilibrium Rate of Growth; Growth Options; Growth and Policy Mix; Growth Effects and Tax Incidence.* **F. Summary.**

The preceding analysis, especially that of Chapter 27, dealt with the effects of budget policy on the level of resource utilization and employment. We now turn to the effects on the supply of resources and the level of capacity output, i.e., the level of output or GNP which may be reached under conditions of full employment of labor and full utilization of capital stock. We assume for

* *Reader's Guide to Chapter 31:* In this chapter we deal with the effects of fiscal policy on capacity output and growth, including both the private and the public sectors. These effects have moved increasingly to the center of discussion in contrast to the earlier and most recent focus on stabilization policy. In assessing fiscal effects on growth, we consider effects on factor inputs and the bearing of such effects on the growth of output, as well as effects on the rate of equilibrium growth.

this purpose that the level of full-employment output is maintained automatically, i.e., that aggregate demand neither falls short of nor exceeds the value of this output as measured at prevailing prices. By the same token it is assumed further that demand expands in line with capacity output. Problems which arise if demand is deficient or excessive (thus creating unemployment or inflation) were considered in the preceding chapters.

The level of capacity output, or the size of total GNP, is of some interest in itself, but what matters for economic welfare is the level of output or income per person. With any given population size, total capacity output determines the feasible level of per capita income, so that output must grow if the standard of living is to rise. Over the years, per capita output has increased greatly, growing at an annual rate (corrected for price change) of about 2.5 percent during this century. Reflecting the powers of compound interest, output per head (again corrected for price change) is now about 5 times what it was in 1900. In addition, hours of work are substantially shorter, so that the total welfare gain has been even larger. While the merits of economic growth have come under scrutiny, this skepticism is based on the perspective of an already affluent society.[1] Economic growth remains the only hope for escape from misery for the majority of the world's population in the less developed countries; and if adequate aid from high-income countries is to be forthcoming (as it should be and under the pressure of events will have to be), so must economic growth in the developed countries be maintained.

The major determinants of capacity output are the level of factor inputs —including natural resources, labor, and capital—and the state of technology or productivity with which resources are used. Since the supply of natural resources is more or less given by nature, the major determinants of GNP growth are the rates of growth of labor input and of the capital stock, and the speed of technical improvement. We begin with the effects of fiscal policy upon these variables in the private sector.

A. EFFECTS ON WORK EFFORT

The effects of labor supply on economic growth are twofold. An increase in population results in an increase in output; but unless output rises at the same percentage rate as population, per capita income will fall. Population growth,

---

[1]This criticism involves a number of propositions which are frequently confused and need to be separated to appraise the case for or against growth:

1. A first proposition is that an affluent society should spend more time on creative use of leisure than on increased output of goods. This may well be true but is not an argument against growth properly defined. A proper measure of growth should include both increased leisure time and increased goods.

2. A second proposition is that growth generates cost externalities such as pollution. This again is an argument not against growth but for a proper measure of growth in which external costs and benefits are accounted for. If growth is to occur, output must rise net of external costs.

3. A third and more difficult proposition is that mankind is not up to living comfortably but needs the discipline of poverty to keep out of trouble, i.e., paradise lost cannot be regained. Judge for yourself.

therefore, may depress, rather than increase, per capita output. This outcome, of course, was the dismal fate which Thomas Malthus predicted some 175 years ago. While economic development in the industrial countries has managed to combine rising per capita income with rising population, the Malthusian specter still darkens the prospects of economic development in the less developed countries.

However this may be, fiscal instruments are not a major factor in population policy. Personal exemptions under the income tax, though related to family size, are hardly sufficient to enter into family planning, and expenditure programs for birth control are hardly within the realm of fiscal economics. Fiscal policy, however, enters the picture via effects on labor input with a given population. Changes in labor input—whether in hours worked or labor force participation—are positively related to the level of both total and per capita output.

Tax Effects

We begin with the effects of taxation on labor supply.

Income Tax   The effects of income taxation on work effort have been dealt with already in our earlier discussion of tax incidence and excess burden.[2] We saw that imposition of an income tax reduces the net wage rate, thereby generating an income effect which increases work effort and a substitution effect which reduces it. There is no a priori basis on which to judge the direction in which the net effect will go, although it is reasonable to assume (as we did in our earlier discussion of redistribution)[3] that effort will decline.

If the labor supply schedule is upward-sloping, as most textbooks draw it, the negative substitution effect outweighs the positive income effect; if the schedule is backward-sloping, the opposite response occurs. Historically, it is evident that rising wage rates have been accompanied by reduced hours of work, i.e., a substantial part of the gains from productivity growth has been directed into increased leisure. Although this does not prove that the short-run supply schedule of labor is backward-sloping (in which case taxation would raise, rather than lower, the amount of labor supplied), it should not be readily assumed that an income tax must reduce effort. While we all seem to know someone who has been discouraged by taxation and has worked less, most of us seem to respond by working more.

As noted before, much depends on the rate schedule. People will work less under a progressive than under a proportional rate schedule, if the same amount is drawn from them in both cases. Yet, work effort for taxpayers as a group need not be lower under a progressive schedule. The net effect depends on how wage earners at various points on the income scale respond. Earners at the upper end (where rates will be higher than under a proportional tax of

---

[2]See pp. 288 and 312.
[3]See p. 99.

equal yield) have more flexibility in hours worked but may also be less responsive to changes in the net wage rate, since other forms of motivation (prestige, interest in work, etc.) may dominate. Employees at the lower end of the scale have less flexibility in their work effort responses and also face lower marginal rates of income tax. The most serious problem of disincentive to work effort may well occur below the income tax range where welfare policies are such as to imply high marginal rates of tax on earned income.[4]

There is another aspect of income tax policy which may have important bearing on labor force participation. This is the tax treatment of working wives. In the absence of free child care centers and with inadequate allowance for deduction of child care expenses under the income tax, the net wage rate obtained by the working wife may be exceedingly low or negative so that there is little incentive (other than psychic income or to get out of the house) for entering the labor force. While the law now permits a substantial child care credit, the marginal rate of tax applicable to the secondary earner under joint returns is still relatively high.[5] Nevertheless, labor force participation of women has increased greatly in recent years.

Sales Taxes Effects on work effort are generated not only by the income tax but also by commodity or sales taxes which raise prices and thereby reduce the real wage rate. Such at least will be the case unless wage earners operate under a "money illusion" and consider their money wage rate only. But will not the disincentive effects be less severe than under an income tax? After all, the worker may escape the consumption tax by saving, thereby avoiding such detrimental effects on work effort as may result from an income tax. Note, however, that the comparison must be between taxes of equal yield. Since the consumption base is smaller, the rate of consumption tax must be higher, and there is no ready way of predicting which will be more favorable to work effort. The question is whether leisure is traded more readily for present or for future consumption.

Turning to selective consumption taxes, the work-leisure choice will be affected differently, depending on which types of commodities are taxed. If the tax rests on goods which are complementary to work (such as work clothing), effort will be retarded more than if the tax is on items (such as food) which are relatively neutral to the work-leisure choice. A tax on "leisure products" such as motorboats or vacation trips, on the other hand, will reduce the value of leisure, thereby reducing the opportunity cost of increased hours of work. With rising standards of living, an increasing share of income goes into the purchase of goods the consumption of which involves leisure time, so that taxation of leisure (through the taxation of leisure goods) becomes more feasible. The nature of leisure use thus becomes an important factor in tax analysis.

[4]See p. 721.
[5]See p. 382.

Expenditure Effects

Work incentives are affected not only from the tax but also from the expenditure side of the budget.

Transfer   Transfer payments may be treated as negative taxes, with the income effect now going to reduce effort. If transfers are unrelated to income, this is the entire story. But if the transfer is related positively to earnings (as in the case of a wage subsidy), this income effect will be countered by a substitution effect favorable to work effort. As in the income tax case, the net effect is again in doubt. If, on the other hand, the transfer payment declines with earnings, as is necessarily the case with most welfare schemes, the substitution effect becomes adverse to work effort.[6] Combined with the adverse income effect, this decline leaves the net effect necessarily one of reduced work effort.

Much the same holds for the "free" provision of public services. If such services were of no use to consumers, we would have to consider only the effect on work effort which results from the taxes collected to finance them. But if public goods are useful, a depressing effect on work effort will result from the expenditure side, as workers will now find it less necessary to exchange leisure for private goods.

This is shown in Figure 31-1 where leisure is measured on the vertical axis and goods are shown on the horizontal axis. The price line, in the absence of budgetary policy, is given by AB and the worker is located at E'. He or she surrenders AC of leisure (i.e., works AC hours) to obtain OD of goods. Now the government provides OM of goods which are available independent of work effort. As a result, the price line shifts parallel to the right without changing its slope. With the new price line at GF, the worker moves to E''. Since there is only an income effect, consumption of both leisure and goods will be increased. Work effort falls from AC to AJ. Free provision thus moves the individual to a higher level of welfare at E'' while reducing his or her work effort.

We now add to this provision the effects of an income tax imposed to finance it. As a result, the price line swivels from GF to GH and the new equilibrium is at E'''. Government revenue equals BF and in turn is used to provide BF free of direct charge. Compared with the prebudget position, work effort is reduced from AC to AK. Assuming that the income tax taken by itself reduces effort, E''' lies north of E''. The combined fiscal transaction then reduces work effort in two ways, the detrimental (income) effect of expenditure policy CJ being added to the detrimental net (income and substitution) effect JK of the tax measure.

Paradoxically, the work incentive effect of the entire package will be more detrimental as expenditures are better designed to correspond to what

---

[6]This will be discussed further in connection with our analysis of welfare programs. See p. 721.

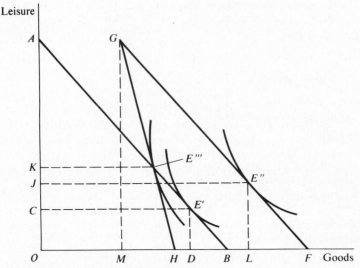

FIGURE 31-1   Effects on Work Effort.

consumers would otherwise wish to buy.[7] It is only a wasteful expenditure program which does not tend to lower work effort.

Incentives and Social Goods   This, indeed, is the dilemma of utopian communism, where persons should contribute to the community's output according to their individual ability, and compensation (the distribution of goods among individuals) should be according to need. In the absence of a self-interest–oriented economic motivation, another mechanism of work allocation and stimulus to effort would be needed. Ideally, this would be provided by the joys of cooperative effort, but whether such attitudes can be developed to deal with the problem is a different matter. Clearly, such has not been the experience in the Soviet Union, where the need for compensation in even its crudest (i.e., piecework) form was recognized at an early stage; nor can work participation or job choice in other settings, such as China or Cuba, be considered a voluntary option.

This points to an interesting implication of our earlier distinction between social and private goods. In dealing with the provision for *private goods*, society may choose between a market system and a communist system. In the market system, income is earned as wages and goods are distributed according to consumer purchases. Under pure communism, workers would be assigned to jobs (with income either not paid at all or else taxed away) and goods be distributed directly free of charge to consumers. The second case poses incentive problems which are absent in the first case. With regard to the

---

[7]The depressing effect on work effort, moreover, will be the stronger the more the public goods are complementary to leisure, e.g., ski slopes, marinas, or scenic highways. By the same token, effects will be less depressing if expenditures are work-related (commuting roads) or if taxes are imposed on leisure goods.

provision for *social goods*, this choice is not open. The goods *must* be provided free of direct charge and income must be taxed away to finance them. The incentive problem, therefore, cannot be solved entirely by a market mechanism whatever the system of social organization.[8]

Why Do Effects on Work Effort Matter?

Before leaving the timely issue of taxation effects on work effort, let us consider once more just why these effects matter. The following four reasons may be distinguished:

1. Substitution of leisure for goods in response to a progressive tax-transfer system may set an effective limit to redistribution.[9]
2. Differences in leisure responses greatly complicate the analysis of just distribution.[10]
3. Tax and expenditure policies which distort the choice between income and leisure impose an efficiency cost.[11]
4. A tax-induced reduction in work effort reduces output and GNP.

Points 1 and 2 stand by themselves, but points 3 and 4 are easily confused. To distinguish between them, we note that the substitution of a wage subsidy which raises effort and output is no less burdensome in terms of efficiency cost than is that of an income tax which lowers them. Whereas, in the tax case, a larger reduction in work effort is associated with a higher efficiency cost, the efficiency cost of the subsidy will be the larger the more work is *increased*. High work effort, therefore, cannot be identified with low efficiency cost. Concern with point 4 in particular tends to be biased by the conventional definition of output which excludes leisure. Once leisure is included and properly valued, the distinction between 3 and 4 disappears.

B. EFFECTS ON PRIVATE SECTOR SAVING

Perhaps the major impact of fiscal policy upon capacity output is through its effect on saving and on capital formation. Since labor is more productive if it is combined with a larger capital stock, capital formation raises productivity. The larger is the share of income which is saved and invested, the higher will the future level of income be. Thus, by influencing this share, fiscal policy has an important impact upon economic growth, i.e., the future level of per capita income. But economic growth has its costs. If the share of income which is currently used for capital formation is increased, that available for current consumption will be reduced. The policy problem, therefore, is one of choosing between present and future consumption. The terms on which this

---

[8]For further discussion, see Richard A. Musgrave, *Fiscal Systems*, New Haven, Conn.: Yale, 1969, chap. 1.
[9]See p. 98.
[10]See p. 101.
[11]See p. 306.

choice can be made have been the subject of much analysis during the past decade, and a brief review of the problem is given later on in this chapter. Here our concern is with the more immediate question of how saving and investment in the private sector are affected by fiscal measures.

Household Saving

Effects of tax policy upon saving in the private sector matter (1) because they bear on the division of resource use between consumption and capital formation and hence upon the growth of capacity output; and (2) because they enter into the effects of fiscal policy upon the level of aggregate demand. Our present concern is with aspect 1 only, aspect 2 having been dealt with in earlier chapters.

Private saving in 1978 totaled $320 billion, or 15 percent of GNP. As the data in Table 31-1 show, depreciation charges or capital consumption allowances are by far the most important source of saving, and corporate saving alone accounts for nearly one-half the total. The total business share in savings is even higher because personal savings, as reported by the Department of Commerce, include retained earnings of unincorporated enterprises. Purely household saving accounts for less than 20 percent of the total. Nevertheless, the division of household income into consumption and saving has received much attention by economists over the past decades. At the heart of Keynesian economics and in the genesis of modern macrotheory was the proposition that consumption is a function of disposable income (i.e., income after tax). Since then, this relationship (referred to as the "consumption function") has proven more complex than had been thought initially. Current consumption has been shown to depend not only on the level of current income but also of past and expected income. Moreover, not only is consumption a function of income, but other factors, such as the rate of interest and consumer wealth, also enter.

Household Saving as a Function of Income   Personal saving as a percentage of disposable income (i.e., personal income after personal taxes have been deducted) has ranged between 5 and 8 percent over recent decades. If all households saved at this same rate, the effect on personal saving of an income tax would be the same no matter how the tax bill was distributed among them. But in fact the fraction saved (the *average* propensity to save) rises as we move up the income scale. Thus, taxes collected from higher incomes may be expected to fall more heavily on saving than do those collected from lower incomes. The difference in the savings impact of more and of less progressive taxes, however, is less than one might think. The reason is that the difference in the consumption-savings impact of a dollar of tax paid by households at the $5,000 and the $50,000 levels of income depends on the differences in their respective *marginal*, and not their average, rates of saving; and though the average propensities to save differ sharply, the respective marginal propensities differ much less.

Line *AB* in Figure 31-2 shows a consumption function (relationship between income and consumption) with a constant marginal, though falling

TABLE 31-1
Sources of Private Sector Saving, 1978
(In Billions of Dollars)

1.	Personal saving	76.2
	Corporate saving	
2.	Undistributed profits	26.8
3.	Capital consumption allowances	132.5
4.	Noncorporate capital allowances	84.4
5.	Total private savings	319.9

Notes:
Line 1: Includes retained earnings of unincorporated enterprises.
Line 2: After inventory evaluation and capital consumption adjustment.
Line 3: After capital consumption adjustment.
Line 4: With capital consumption adjustment.
Source: U.S. Department of Commerce, Survey of Current Business, February 1979, p. 8.

average, propensity to consume.   With the marginal propensity to consume constant, all taxes would be divided in the same way between consumption and saving. But actual observation of the consumption-income relationship from cross-section data (i.e., data for a particular year, taken across households at different income levels) shows the consumption function to be slightly curved, as indicated by the dotted line AE.[13] This being the case, a more progressive distribution of tax liabilities imposes a higher burden on saving than does a less progressive one. But the departure from a linear function, and hence the difference in effects between alternative tax-burden distributions, is rather slight. Thus, replacement of the present progressive income tax rate structure with a proportional rate tax (leaving exemptions unchanged) might be estimated to raise household saving by less than 10 percent so that tax-structure changes within feasible bounds are not likely to have a major effect on the level of household saving.

Household Saving as a Function of the Rate of Return   Taxation effects on saving may result not only because the taxpayer's income is reduced, but also because an income tax reduces the net rate of return on saving, thus lowering the rate at which the household can substitute future for present consumption. As a result, one may expect the savings rate to be reduced. The

[12]Fig. 31-2 shows AB as a linear consumption function $C = a + cY$, where a is the intercept and c is the slope, generating an average propensity to consume equal to

$$\frac{C}{Y} = \frac{a + cY}{Y} = c + \frac{a}{Y}$$

which declines as Y increases.

[13]This conclusion is based on annual cross-section data. If allowance is made for the fact that consumer behavior depends on past as well as current income or that individuals base their saving decisions on expected lifetime income (also referred to as the "permanent income hypothesis"), dissaving at the lower end of the scale would be less. This is so because the influence of consumers with temporarily low income would be removed. The consumption function would tend to have a lower intercept and a steeper slope. It is not obvious, however, how the curvature (and hence the marginal propensities at various levels) would be affected.

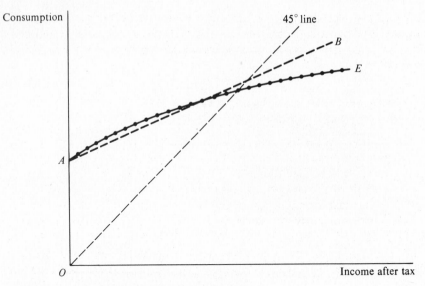

FIGURE 31-2 Income-Consumption Relationships.

magnitude of the substitution effect is difficult to assess. Since the larger part of personal saving originates in the middle- and high-income ranges where bracket rates are relatively high, the substitution effect may be substantial. Yet, as noted in our earlier analysis, economists still debate whether saving is highly elastic to the rate of interest.[14] Indeed, not all households may budget their lifetime consumption so as to save more when the rate of return rises. If their saving is geared to reaching a set level of retirement income, they may, in fact, save less when the rate of return increases.

Consumption versus Income Tax　A consumption tax tends to be more favorable to saving than an income tax, for various reasons:

1.　Consumption taxes tend to be distributed regressively, whereas an income tax tends to be progressive in its distribution.[15] With the marginal propensity to consume falling as income rises, the consumption tax (being paid more largely by lower-income households) thus has a heavier impact on consumption and a lighter impact on saving than does the income tax.
2.　A consumption tax does not reduce the rate of return on saving and therefore avoids the substitution effect of the income tax, which is adverse to saving.
3.　A temporary consumption tax, expected to be discontinued in the future, increases the rate of substitution of future for present consumption and is therefore similar in its effects to an increase in the rate of interest.

[14]See p. 318.
[15]Such at least is the case for conventional consumption taxes of the sales tax type. It need not be the case for a personalized expenditure tax. See p. 455.

For these reasons, the use of consumption taxes has been especially advocated in developing countries where a higher rate of saving is necessary to expedite economic growth, but a similar case is made for the United States economy.[16]

Business Saving

Depreciation Charges   As noted in Table 31-1, much the larger part of business saving is in the form of capital consumption allowances or depreciation charges. Since the profits tax is imposed after the deduction of depreciation, depreciation reserves are not reduced by the profits tax. But their timing may be affected. If the law permits depreciation to be taken at an accelerated pace, tax payments are moved to a later date and depreciation reserves will be accumulated more rapidly. Considering the stream of depreciation generated by a one-shot investment, this will be followed by reduced saving later on. But if a continuing stream of investment is considered, the tax, as we have noted earlier, may be postponed permanently and corporate saving may be raised on a continuing basis.

Retained Earnings   Provided that the profits tax is not shifted, after-tax profits are reduced by the tax. This reduction may in turn reduce corporate saving by lowering retained earnings, or it may be reflected in reduced dividends.

Over the last decade, dividends have been close to 25 percent of corporate cash flow (depreciation plus profits after tax), with retained earnings and depreciation picking up the remaining 75 percent. Empirical studies of dividend behavior show dividends to be a function of current cash flow and past dividend levels. They suggest that the short-run impact of the corporate tax dollar on corporate saving might be as high as 75 percent, while the long-run impact might be of the order of 50 percent. The savings impact of the corporate tax dollar is thus substantially above that of most other taxes.   A policy designed to foster growth, therefore, calls for restraint in the taxation of business profits.

The division of the corporate tax burden betwen dividends and retained earnings may be affected by differential tax treatment. "Double taxation" of dividends under present law discriminates against distribution and favors retention. A move toward an integrated system would render the system neutral with regard to retention versus distribution but, compared with the status quo, lead to reduced corporate saving. Introduction of a tax on undistributed profits would introduce a bias toward distribution. Differential rate approaches or "split rates" have been used in various countries to either retard or encourage corporate distribution.

---

[16]For similar reasoning regarding social security, see p. 735.

C. EFFECTS ON PRIVATE INVESTMENT

Saving is a necessary condition for capital formation but it is not a sufficient one. Investors must also be willing to invest, and taxes once more enter into this decision.

Nature of Investment Function

The response of investors to taxation depends on the nature of the investment function. While theory tells us how investors should behave if they seek to maximize profits, it does not follow that this describes how real-life investors do in fact behave. They may wish to maximize sales or market shares rather than profits, or they may apply rules of thumb which do not conform closely with maximizing rules. Not only is the theoretical framework controversial, but empirical testing is difficult. Statistical dependence of investment on changes in sales, for instance, may be taken to suggest that investment responds to capacity needs, or that sales serve as a proxy for profit expectations. Empirical findings support both views, but the distinction is crucial for assessing tax effects.

To assess the investment effects of taxation, a model of investment behavior must be specified. Three major approaches may be noted:

1. Investment is expressed as a function of the expected net rate of return.
2. Investment is considered a function of past changes in sales and of existing capacity in relation to sales.
3. Investment is taken to be a function of the availability of internal funds, including after-tax profits and depreciation charges.

All approaches seem reasonable on a priori grounds and actual behavior may be determined as a combination of the three. According to approach 1, which reflects the hypothesis of profit-maximizing behavior, investors will invest up to a point where the present value of the expected income stream equals cost. The profits tax here enters by reducing the expected net rate of return. According to approach 2, investment responds to the need for increased capacity generated by past increases in sales, the so-called accelerator effect. Here the major impact of taxation is through its effects on sales, including sales to consumers and to government. According to approach 3, where the willingness to invest is conditioned on the availability of internal funds, taxation enters via its effects on the flow of such funds, be it in the form of depreciation reserves or retained earnings.

Profitability Effects

Since economic analysis is typically based on approach 1, we must take a closer look at tax effects on the profitability of investment or the net (after-tax) rate of return. Given an economy where full employment is maintained automatically, the levels of investment and saving are determined by the intersection of the investment and saving schedules, with investment determined as a function of the rate of interest and saving dependent on both income and the rate of interest. The model is illustrated in Figure 31-3, where II is the investment schedule showing the available rates of return as investment proceeds at various levels (annual rates) while SS shows the supply of saving (out of full-employment income) at various rates of interest. Before tax, the two are equated at an interest rate OB and investment and saving equal OA.

Now an income tax at rate DE/DO is imposed. As a result, the investment schedule expressed in terms of net rates of return swivels downward as shown by $I'I'$. In the new equilibrium, the gross rate of interest has risen to OD, the net rate has fallen to OE and investment and saving shrink to OC. As may be seen from the figure, the decline in investment will be the larger, the more elastic are both the SS and II schedules.

In line with our earlier discussion, we note that the tax rate DE/DO is a function not simply of the statutory rate of tax, but also of the speed with which depreciation may be taken.[17] Both enter into the effective rate of tax and the resulting reduction in the net rate of return.

The same story may be told algebraically as follows. In the absence of tax, investors will carry investment to the point where

$$r_g = i + d \tag{1}$$

where r_g is the gross rate of return, i the cost of borrowing, and d the stream of depreciation needed to recover capital. The rate of return must be sufficient to match the market rate of interest plus depreciation, with the right side of the equation also referred to as the rental cost of capital. After a tax is introduced, this becomes

$$r - (tr - t\hat{d}) = i + d \tag{2}$$

where the left side now expresses the after-tax or net rate of return. The tax, shown in parentheses, includes two terms, with tr showing what the tax would be if no depreciation was allowed and $t\hat{d}$ deducting the tax saving which results because depreciation can be taken. The value of $t\hat{d}$ depends upon the rate at which depreciation is allowed as given by $\hat{d}$. Equation 2 may also be written as

$$r = \frac{i + d - t\hat{d}}{1 - t} \tag{3}$$

with the right side being the rental cost of capital in the presence of tax.[18] While it has become customary to show the tax as increasing rental cost in line with equation 3, it may also be viewed, and more simply so, as a reduction in the rate of return in line with equation 2.

[17] See p. 436.

[18] For further discussion, see Dale W. Jorgenson, "Capital Theory and Investment Behaviour," *American Economic Review*, May 1963. Also see Dale W. Jorgenson, "Econometric Studies of Investment Behavior: A Survey," *Journal of Economic Literature*, December 1971; and Gary Fromm (ed.), *Tax Incentives and Capital Spending*, Washington: Brookings, 1971.

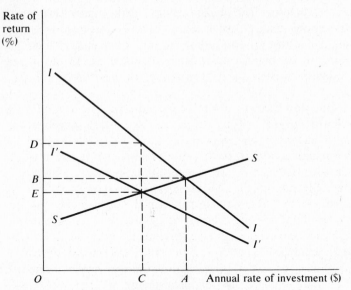

FIGURE 31-3   Tax Effects on Investment.

Loss Offset and the Return to Risk

The investment response, as given in Figure 31-3, is straightforward but oversimplifies matters. Investment is not a safe bet with a guaranteed return, but rather a risky venture which may or may not pay off. The rate of return as shown on the II schedule is thus based upon a range of probable returns and may be taken to reflect the expected value of this probability distribution.[19]

An investor in search of income who surrenders his liquidity and purchases real assets (or equity therein by buying shares) undertakes a risk. He may get his money back with a substantial return or he may lose all or

---

[19]If $q_1, q_2, \ldots, q_n$ are expected rates of return (positive and negative) and $p_1, p_2, \ldots, p_n$ the respective probabilities of their occurrence, so that $\sum_{i=1}^{n} p_i = 1$, we have

$$y = \sum_{i=1}^{n} q_i p_i$$

where y is the mathematical expectation of the percentage yield. This may be divided into a positive part and a negative part, such that

$$y = g - r$$

where g is the expected value of the positive part of the distribution and r is the absolute expected value of the negative part.

If we think of the return on investment α as a return on risk taking, we may write this as $\alpha = \dfrac{g - r}{r}$. A tax without loss offset reduces this to $\alpha = \dfrac{(1-t)(g-r)}{r}$, whereas, under a tax with loss offset, it becomes $\alpha = \dfrac{(1-t)(g-r)}{(1-t)r} = \dfrac{g-r}{r}$, thus leaving the return on risk taking unchanged.

part of it. To make an investment means to gamble, and the investor should be interested in the gamble only if the value of probable gains outweighs that of probable losses. Since the investor's marginal utility of income may be expected to decline, an even-money (fifty-fifty) bet is not acceptable. If the tax worsens the odds by reducing the expected return, investment will fall. However, it is not at all obvious that the tax really reduces the odds. A tax will reduce the investor's return if he wins but, provided that loss offset is allowed for, it will also reduce his loss if he loses. Given a proportional tax, both probable gains and probable losses will be reduced at the same rate. Depending on the circumstances of the case, the tax may induce him either to increase or to reduce his risk taking.[20]

The possibility of increased risk taking is shown in Figure 31-4 where the rate of return is measured on the vertical axis and risk is shown on the horizontal axis.[21] To simplify, suppose that the investor chooses between holding cash (which we assume to be completely safe) and a single alternative, say a corporate bond, of given risk.[22] The opportunity line OA shows the combinations of risk and return available to him by choosing different mixes of cash and bonds. With 100 percent cash holding, he will be located at O where he incurs zero risk and receives a zero return. If all his funds are invested in bonds, he will be located at B, with risk OC and return OD. Each indifference curve shows combinations of risk and return which are equally satisfactory to him, with i_2 superior to i_1 and i_3 superior to i_2.[23] Before tax, the investor places himself at E_1, the point of tangency of the opportunity line OA with the highest available indifference curve i_2. His risk equals OF and his return equals OG.

Now a 50 percent tax is imposed and we assume that full loss offset is assured. If the investor does not change his portfolio mix, he will now find himself with half the risk and half the return that he had before, i.e., in a position similar to that provided by portfolio mix H prior to tax. Since prior to tax, he would have improved his position by moving from H to tangency point E_1, he will now choose to move from E_1 to K. At K his gross risk and return have doubled but his net risk and return are what they were at E_1 before imposition of the tax. Although his private risk taking has remained unchanged, total risk taking, as seen from the point of view of the economy

---

[20]The significance of changes in the level of risk taking may be interpreted in two ways. If reduced risk taking involves the choice of less risky industries while holding total investment constant, the rate of growth may decline, since more risky investments may have a higher potential for raising productivity. If reduced risk taking means the choice of a portfolio with a larger case component, the effect may be to reduce the level of aggregate demand, thereby stepping outside the "classical" system and causing unemployment.

[21]Figure 31-4 follows James Tobin, "Liquidity Preference as Behavior toward Risk," *Review of Economic Studies*, February 1958.

[22]A convenient measure of risk is the standard deviation of probable gains and losses, but certain other measures of dispersion will do as well.

[23]The indifference curves are drawn so as to show increasing risk aversion. Successive increases in risk call for rising additions to the rate of return if the investor is to remain equally well off. This follows from the assumption that the utility of income schedule rises at a decreasing rate as income increases.

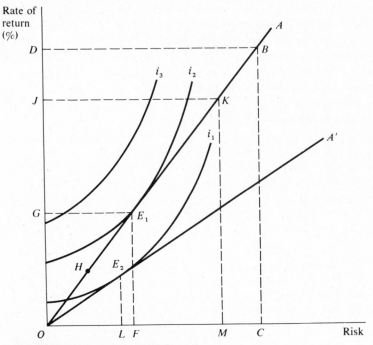

FIGURE 31-4 Taxation and Risk Taking.

as a whole, has increased. The government has become a partner, as it takes half the return and assumes half the risk. This sequence comes about because loss offset is permitted. Without loss offset, the tax would swivel the opportunity line from OA to OA' and the new equilibrium would be at a tangency point E_2, with risk taking decreased to OL.

This illustration shows that under certain conditions, a tax with loss offset will *increase* risk taking. This somewhat startling result is here obtained on the basis of rather simplifying assumptions, but it continues to hold under a more sophisticated approach. The investment choice is not simply one between cash (assumed to be riskless) and one risky asset. Inflation renders cash holdings risky, and choices among alternative risky assets must be allowed for. The outcome then depends on the precise nature of the investor's preferences or the shape of his indifference curves. The net result may be either to increase or to reduce risk taking, and no simple generalization regarding the outcome is possible.[24]

Whatever the net result of a tax with loss offset, a tax law with full loss offset will be more favorable to investment than one without. Current law comes close to doing so as it provides for the carry-over of net operating losses to the three past and seven subsequent years. Thus, a firm which has a

[24]For further discussion, see Martin S. Feldstein, "The Effects of Taxation on Risk Taking," *Journal of Political Economy*, September–October 1969, and J. E. Stiglitz, "The Effects of Income, Wealth and Capital Gains Taxation on Risk Taking," *Quarterly Journal of Economics*, May 1969.

net loss in any one year does not lose the opportunity to charge the loss against profits, provided its gains over these ten adjacent years are sufficient to absorb it. The loss carry-over is a form of averaging which protects the firm with occasional loss years but net gains over the eleven-year period. The legislation does not take care of losses in all cases, but the bulk of losses is allowed for in this fashion. Somewhat strangely, the important role of loss offset has been largely overlooked in the more recent discussion of taxation effects on investment.

Research and Development

Since the advance of productivity depends upon technological progress as well as the growth of capital stock, the tax treatment of research and development expenditure is of special importance. Such outlays may be expensed, i.e., they may be deducted in the initial year even though they are largely in the nature of investment outlays.

D. SAVING AND INVESTMENT IN THE PUBLIC SECTOR

Having considered fiscal effects on private saving and investment, we now turn to the direct role of saving and investment in the public sector.

Public Saving

For this purpose, two concepts of public saving must be distinguished. The appropriateness of one or the other depends on the nature of the economy in which the budget operates.

Saving and the Level of Employment In the preceding discussion of stabilization policy, we have viewed saving as a factor which enters into determining the actual level of income and employment. We argued that for income to be at its equilibrium level, savings must be equal to the planned level of investment. If investment falls short of what people wish to save at a full-employment level of income, then income will fall short of what is needed to maintain full employment and capacity utilization. In this context, government saving is defined as the excess of tax revenue over expenditures. Positive government saving or a budget surplus reflects the withdrawal from aggregate demand and is thus restrictive, just as negative government saving or a deficit reflects an addition to aggregate demand and hence is expansionary. The underlying assumption is that taxes reduce the level of private expenditure, whereas government borrowing does not. The state of budgetary balance, defined as tax revenue minus expenditures, thus reflects the impact of the budget upon aggregate demand and thereby upon the level of employment and, for that matter, on inflation.

Saving and the Level of Capacity Output The role of saving, public or private, differs as we consider an economy which automatically operates at full employment, i.e., where private investment always adjusts to the full-employment level of saving as previously defined. In this case, the level of budget deficit or surplus does not affect the level of employment, as income is always at full employment. It does, however, affect the way in which output is divided between consumption and capital formation. To focus on this aspect, the concept of government saving may now be redefined as its contribution to capital formation rather than to aggregate demand. This is the role of government saving in a "classical" model of income determination, as opposed to the "Keynesian" model underlying the previous paragraph.[25] While the assumption of automatic adjustment to full employment is unrealistic in the short run, this assumption is usually made when it comes to consider the longer-run effects of budget policy upon capacity output and growth.

In such a system, all government receipts—whether in the form of taxes or borrowings—must be reflected in reduced private spending, whether on consumption or investment. A dollar of tax or loan receipts alike reduces private spending by \$1.[26] Government finance, therefore, does not affect the level of aggregate demand. But it will affect the division between consumption and investment.

Suppose that taxes are paid out of income which is otherwise consumed, while loans are drawn from savings which are otherwise directed into investment. The government's contribution to the withdrawal of resources from consumption and their diversion into investment then equals the excess of tax receipts over government expenditures of the consumption type. We know that

$$E_f = C + I + G_c + G_i \tag{1}$$

where E_f is total expenditures at full employment, C and I are private consumption and investment, G_c is government expenditures for consumption, and G_i is government investment. We also know that

$$Y_f = C + S + T \tag{2}$$

where Y_f is full-employment income, S is private saving, and T is tax payments. Since $E_f = Y_f$, we have

$$(T - G_c) + S = I + G_i \tag{3}$$

On the left side we have total saving (where the term in parentheses indicates public saving), while on the right side we have private plus public investment.

---

[25]The terms "classical" and "Keynesian" are here used to describe extreme positions. In between there is the "neo-classical" model which calls for stabilization policy to intervene but assumes that aggregate demand control, by varying the mix of fiscal and monetary policy, permits compliance with both full employment and growth targets.

[26]The underlying assumption is that borrowing is from the public, so as to reduce loanable funds available to private investors. If government expenditures are financed by money creation, the argument does not hold and loan finance becomes inflationary.

The definition of public saving as $(T - G_c)$, which records the budgetary contribution to resource availability for capital formation, thus differs from our earlier definition of public saving as $T - G$, which records withdrawal from aggregate demand. The latter concept may be obtained readily from equation 3 by substituting $G = G_c + G_i$, so that

$$(T - G) + S = I + G \tag{4}$$

We may note also that government saving, as defined in equation 3, does not require a corresponding level of government investment or G_i. Rather, it may be made available to finance private investment by government lending, debt retirement, or, as discussed below, a change in the mix of stabilization policy.

Capital versus Current Budget

The two concepts of public saving in turn call for different definitions of budgetary balance. If the budget surplus is to measure public saving in the sense of reduction in aggregate demand, the surplus should be defined as the excess of tax revenue over total expenditures; but if it is designed to record availability of resources for capital formation, the surplus should be defined as excess of tax revenue over government expenditures for current consumption only. In the latter case, the budget may be divided into a current and capital budget, with the surplus in the current budget recording the government's contribution to saving and the latter balanced by definition.

An attempt is made in Table 31-2 to show how a dual budget statement would look for fiscal 1980. At the top of the table we show the comprehensive budget, including both current and capital expenditures. With total expenditures of $542 billion and tax receipts of $503 billion, the overall deficit is $39 billion. This reflects the addition to aggregate demand and expansionary stance of the budget. It also reflects the government's financing requirements, to be met by borrowing or drawing on deposit balances.[27] But though the total budget shows a deficit, the balance in the current budget shows a surplus. Estimating current expenditures at $410 billion and capital expenditures at $150 billion, we find that the current budget records a surplus of $86 billion. This surplus becomes available as revenue in the capital budget and, together with the deficit in the overall budget, serves to cover outlays in the capital budget. Even though the table shows a deficit for the budget as a whole, the surplus on current account indicates public sector saving and contribution to capital formation of $86 billion.

The construction of a capital budget seems simple enough, but some subtle issues are involved. For one thing, note that depreciation charges are carried as a cost in the current budget, thereby introducing a noncash element into the budget statement. For another, the resulting state of balance in the current budget depends greatly on how capital expenditures are

[27]More precisely, this holds for the deficit excluding depreciation as an expense.

TABLE 31-2
Federal Budget, Total, Current, and Capital
(Estimates for Fiscal 1978, in Billions of Dollars)

	TOTAL BUDGET		
Budget expenditures	531.6	Revenue	502.6
Depreciation*	10.0	Deficit	39.0
Total	541.6	Total	541.6
	CURRENT BUDGET		
Current expenditures	416.1	Revenue	502.6
Depreciation	10.0		
Surplus	76.5		
Total	502.6	Total	502.6
	CAPITAL BUDGET		
Capital expenditures†	115.5	Current surplus	76.5
		Deficit	39.0
Total	115.5	Total	115.5

*Hypothetical amount, estimated by authors, but not appearing in actual budget.
†Capital outlays or investment expenditures as defined in the budget analysis include acquisition and maintenance of physical assets, loans, and certain other items such as research, education, and foreign economic aid. The component reflecting acquisition of physical assets equals $53 billion.
Source:The Budget of the United States Government, Fiscal Year 1980, Special Analyses, Section D, O.B.M., Washington, D.C., 1979.

defined. Public acquisition of physical assets (such as an office building) should be included, *not* because the government comes to own a building but because a building is added to the capital stock of the economy. A subsidy to private investment, while adding to the capital stock of the private sector, is just as eligible. As distinct from the balance sheet of a private firm, the purpose of the public capital budget is *not* to test the financial soundness of the government by balancing assets against liabilities (public debt) but to measure the government's contribution to the economy's capital stock. Moreover, there is no good reason why capital formation should be defined in terms of brick and mortar only. Human investment may be as important to productivity growth. Thus, if students increase their skills, which is a form of capital formation, it is a matter of indifference whether the factor input is in the form of teacher's salaries or of increased classroom space. The definition of capital outlays followed in Table 31-2 takes this broad approach. If, instead, acquisition of assets only was included, capital outlays would be cut by one half and the surplus in the current budget would be reduced to $17 billion.

Though the federal budget could be presented in this form, it is not, and the President's Budget Commission recommended against the use of this form for good reason.[28] Since the nature of our economy is not such that full employment is automatically assured by the private sector, budget policy has a major effect on the level of aggregate demand. Tax and loan finance differ in this effect and the choice between them must be used as an instrument of stabilization policy. Since the responsibility for stabilization policy must rest at the federal level, presentation of a dual budget would divert attention from

[28]See *Report of the President's Commission on Budget Concepts*, Washington, 1967.

the more important focus on the aggregate demand effects as indicated by the state of balance in the total budget. Nevertheless, the contribution of the federal budget to capital formation might be brought out more strongly by giving prominent attention to the breakdown of federal expenditures between current and capital items, an aspect now dealt with only in the special analysis section of the budget. However, a good case can be made for the use of a dual-budget approach at the state-local level, where stabilization policy is less relevant and where considerations of intergeneration equity call for loan finance of investment outlays.[29]

Tax versus Loan Finance

Both these measures of budget surplus and deficit suffer from the simplifying assumption that all taxes are taken to fall on consumption, while all borrowing is taken to fall on saving. We have seen in earlier chapters that this is not the case. Some taxes, such as the payroll tax, fall more heavily on saving. It would be better, therefore, to refine the concept of surplus in the total budget (the measure of reduction in aggregate demand) as $c'T' + c'T'' - G$, where c' and c'' are the marginal propensity to consume of average taxpayers under taxes T' and T''. Similarly, it would be better to refine the measure of surplus in the current budget (the measure of provision for saving) by excluding taxes which reduce saving in the private sector. Moreover, loan finance may displace consumption as well as saving. As bonds are issued, the rate of interest is driven up and saving may increase.[30]

[29]For a discussion of this aspect see p. 706.

[30]Assuming a uniform propensity to save, this may be demonstrated as follows: With full-employment income given at Y_f, the composition of output is given by the system

$$S = a + s(Y_f - T) + bi$$
$$I = d - ei$$
$$I + G = S + T$$

where S is private saving, T is tax revenue, I is private investment, G is government purchases, and i is the interest rate. Private investment I adjusts itself to match public saving (or $T - G$) plus private saving S out of full-employment income Y_f.

For the case of tax finance, $dG = dT$ and

$$\frac{dI}{dT} = -\frac{s}{1 + b/e}$$

We find that the investment-depressing effect of tax finance is positively related to the propensity to save, s. This follows because a large s means that a large part of tax revenue comes out of saving. We also note that the investment-depressing effect is large if b is small. A small b means that the positive response of saving to an increase in the interest rate (induced in turn by the decline in investment) is weak. Finally, the resulting decline in investment will be greater if e is larger, since a large e indicates a heavy negative response of I to a rise in the interest rate.

For the case of loan finance, we have $dG = dL$, where $L = G - T$ and

$$\frac{dI}{dL} = -\frac{1}{1 + b/e}$$

Investment-depressing effects again vary directly with e and inversely with b, but s now does not enter. The investment-reducing effect of tax finance thus equals s times that of loan finance. If $b = 0$, the entire loan finance is reflected in reduced private investment.

Nevertheless, it is a reasonable first approximation to assume that taxes are drawn largely from private consumption while loan finance draws largely on saving. Tax finance (whether public expenditures are for consumption or capital items) is thus more favorable to economic growth than is loan finance. This conclusion is of considerable importance for development policy, provided again that aggregate demand is sufficient to secure the full utilization of all resources whether in the production of consumer or investment goods.

Public Investment

Having discussed the economics of public investment in Chapters 8 and 9, we will not recount it here. At this point we need only note that the role of public investment in economic growth is of obvious importance both in total magnitude and in its strategic role in the development process. The place of public capital formation in the overall picture is shown in Table 31-3.

If public investment (all levels) is defined narrowly as construction and equipment only, the total for 1977 amounted to $62 billion, or 16 percent of total government purchases. If civilian expenditures only are included, the total was $47 billion, or 15 percent of civilian government purchases. By comparison, private investment for that fiscal year amounted to $282 billion and equaled 17 percent of total private expenditures. The investment rate in the public sector was thus more or less in line with that of the private sector.

This definition, however, reflects a quite narrow concept of investment. If developmental expenditures, including investment in human resources such as health and education, are added in, the public investment rate becomes over twice this amount and exceeds the similarly adjusted private sector rate.

Technological Advance

Having noted previously the encouragement which tax policy can give to research and development in the private sector, the role of public investment is also of major importance. While publicly financed research has been largely in the context of weapons technology, there has been a substantial spillover into civilian uses. However, publicly financed civilian research — especially in health—has also been significant, and an expanded input may develop in the search for alternative energy sources.

TABLE 31-3
Gross Fixed Capital Formation, 1977
(In Billions of Dollars)

Government	
Federal	
Military	16.8
Civilian	6.5
State, local	39.2
Total	62.5
Private sector, total	282.0
All sectors	344.5

Source: U.S. Department of Commerce, Survey of Current Business, July 1978, p. 41.

E. FISCAL POLICY AND THE RATE OF GROWTH

In this section, we consider further why the rate of capital formation is important, how it can be affected by fiscal policy, and what options present themselves for public policy. Moreover, consideration is given to the interrelationship between tax incidence and growth.

Function of Saving

In an economy with perfectly flexible prices, where a full-employment level of income is maintained automatically, planned saving is always matched by a corresponding level of investment. An increase in the savings rate thus raises capital formation. An increase in capital formation in turn raises productivity and output. Thus, by increasing today's saving, tomorrow's level of income is raised. The extent of increase, and hence the importance of capital formation, will depend upon the state of technology, the existing capital stock, and the supply of other factors. But a higher rate of capital formation is not costless. It also means a lower level of current consumption. The policy issue is, therefore, how far the present generation will refrain from consumption so as to benefit the future.

The Equilibrium Rate of Growth

Before considering this question, we must draw a distinction between the effects of fiscal policy upon (1) the absolute level of income at a specified future date, and (2) the future rate of growth of income. Recent developments in growth theory have shown that fiscal policy can raise the absolute level of future income by increasing the rates of saving and investment, but that it cannot thereby affect the equilibrium rate of income growth.

Why should it be that fiscal policy cannot affect the equilibrium rate of growth? The reason is that this equilibrium rate cannot exceed, and indeed must equal, the independently given growth rate of population.[31] Suppose the economy is initially in a position of steady or equilibrium growth, where the growth rate of income, population, and capital stock all equal 2 percent. To simplify matters, the state of technology is held constant. Since population and capital stock grow at the same rate, the capital-labor ratio remains constant and so does the productivity of labor and capital. Suppose also that the savings rate, and hence the share of investment in GNP, is 20 percent. Now fiscal policy measures are taken which cause the savings rate to rise to 25 percent. As a result, the capital stock will increase faster than does the labor supply, and the ratio of capital to labor will rise. Income now grows more rapidly than before, but this increase cannot be maintained indefinitely.

---

[31]The initial statement of the basic positions of neoclassical growth theory was given by Robert M. Solow, "A Contribution to the Theory of Economic Growth," *Quarterly Journal of Economics*, February 1956. See also Solow, *Growth Theory: An Exposition*, New York: Oxford University Press, 1970. In capsule form the argument may be summarized as follows:

The crucial component of the model is the underlying production function showing the relationship between total income and factor inputs. The most commonly used version is the

The reason is that the rising capital-labor ratio also results in diminishing returns to capital. The increments to the capital stock will become less effective in raising income, and this change acts as a brake on income growth. As income rises less rapidly, the rate of increase in the capital stock also slows down. This is so because the increase in capital stock equals saving, which in turn is a fixed proportion of income.

The process continues until the rate of income growth has again fallen to that of population. At this point, the rate of growth in capital stock again comes to equal that of income and we are returned to the initial condition of equality in the rates of growth of capital stock and labor. Since there is no further change in the capital-labor ratio, diminishing returns cease to operate. We are returned to an equilibrium situation where income grows at the same rate as does population. However, the capital stock is larger than it would have been without the increase in the savings rate and the capital-labor ratio is now higher. Since the growth rate of labor has not been affected, this result means not only a higher absolute level of GNP but also a gain in the level of per capita income.

This development is illustrated in Figure 31-5, where the vertical axis measures the level of capacity output plotted on a log scale while the horizontal axis shows successive years. The straight line AY shows the equilibrium path of income with savings rate s. Given the log scale, the slope of each line indicates the growth rate, so that AY traces a constant percentage rate of income growth. Line BC shows the corresponding path of consumption, such that DJ equals consumption and DE equals savings at income JE, all measured on the log scale. Now suppose that at the beginning of year J the savings rate rises to s^*. As a result, income travels the path shown by EY^*. Initially, the growth rate is higher than it was before, but eventually

---

so-called Cobb-Douglas function, or

$$Y = AK^\alpha N^\beta \tag{1}$$

where Y is output; K is capital; N is labor; and A, α, and β are parameters. Disregarding the limiting factor of fixed natural resources and assuming constant returns to scale (i.e., a situation where doubling of K and N results in a doubling of output), we must have $\alpha + \beta = 1$ so that

$$Y = AK^\alpha N^{(1-\alpha)} \tag{2}$$

Equation 2 may, with some mathematics, be restated in terms of rates of growth such that

$$y = \alpha k + (1-\alpha)n \tag{3}$$

where y is the rate of growth of income, k is the rate of growth of capital, and n is the rate of growth of labor. Since saving and investment are a fixed proportion of Y, it may be shown further that in equilibrium, the rate of growth of capital stock k must approach that of income y. Substituting y for k in equation 3, we obtain

$$y = n \tag{4}$$

That is, the equilibrium rate of growth of income equals that of the labor force.

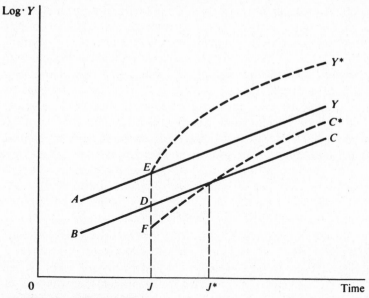

FIGURE 31-5   Growth Options.

EY* comes to parallel *AY* and the growth *rate* returns to where it was. However, the *level* of income remains higher throughout. The consumption path is now shown by *FC**, with savings at income *JE* now equal to *FE*. Consumption under the new policy is lower from year *J* to *J** but higher thereafter. Present consumption has been sacrificed for a higher level of future income and consumption.

Growth Options

In choosing between various options, two factors must be considered. The first is that successive increases in the savings rate (and hence in the resulting equilibrium capital-labor ratio) will yield decreasing gains in future consumption. Theorists have shown that there is a savings rate beyond which future consumption will decline rather than rise, as assumed in the diagram. The growth path which yields the highest future consumption is referred to as the "golden rule," a concept which has intrigued theorists with its neat property of calling for a savings rate equal to the share of capital income in national income.[32] The second consideration is that the future consumption gain must be discounted so as to compare it with the loss of present consumption forgone. It is the present value of future consumption that must be maximized, thus raising once more the problem of what discount rate to choose.[33] With a positive discount rate, the optimal rate of savings or consumption postponement will thus fall short of that indicated by the golden rule.

[32]See Edmund Phelps, "The Golden Rule of Accumulation: A Fable for Growthmen," *American Economic Review*, September 1961.
[33]See p. 184.

From a more practical point of view, the equilibrium growth rate is hardly a matter of major concern. Policy makers are not inclined to consider an infinite future, nor can they assume that a policy once set will be continued in perpetuity thereafter. Rather, their concern is with a more limited horizon, and decisions are made and revised on a continuing basis. Consequences for the absolute levels of output and consumption over the immediately ensuing years or perhaps over a decade or two are what matter, and this is still a period during which changes in the savings rate can affect not only the level, but also the growth rate, of income. Since the eventual return to the equilibrium rate of growth is a very slow one, involving a half-century or more, its significance to the policy maker is of questionable importance.

Growth and Policy Mix

With the growth rate of capacity output added as a policy concern, we now have four policy objectives: (1) provision for social goods, (2) adjustment of distribution, (3) maintaining high employment and price level stability, and (4) achieving the desired rate of growth. We may then consider what are the appropriate policy instruments by which to achieve each of these objectives, in line with the requirement of policy theory that as many instruments are needed as there are objectives.

In line with our earlier discussion, objective 1 is served by the expenditures of the "allocation branch," while 2 is served primarily by the tax-transfer system of the "distribution branch." Regarding 3 and 4, a distinction needs to be drawn between an economy which operates in line with the classical model and one that requires stabilization measures. In the former case, planned saving is always matched by private investment, and no stabilizing policies are needed. Stability is secured by permitting the money supply to grow at the rate of output. The efficient division of output between capital formation and consumption is determined by market forces, such that the return on investment is equated with the time preference of consumers. Budget policy in this case should provide for balance in the current budget so as not to affect the overall division of output between consumption and capital formation. The capital budget in turn should be loan financed so as to allocate part of saving to investment in the public sector. This is the setting where the double-budget approach is appropriate at the federal as well as the state and local levels.

The problem of fiscal-monetary policy mix becomes more complex in a system which does not assure automatic adjustment to full employment and price level stability. Suppose the situation to be such that expansionary policies are needed to secure full employment. This might be achieved by various mixes of fiscal and monetary policy. Among these, a policy which combines a relatively tight budget (small deficit or large surplus) with a relatively easy monetary policy (high rate of increase in money supply) may be more favorable to a higher rate of growth than the opposite policy mix. This is the case because the tight fiscal–easy money mix results in a lower rate of interest, and hence a higher level of private investment. Similarly, restrictive policy will be more inducive to a high rate of growth if it is implemented by tightening budget policy, so as to reduce private sector consumption, rather than by use of monetary restriction. The tight-fiscal–easy money mix is more inducive to growth than is the tight money–easy fiscal combination. Whatever the chosen mix, it will be recalled that the fiscal adjustment *can* be made so as not to interfere with the allocation and distribution functions of budget policy.[34]

Growth Effects and Tax Incidence

In discussing the incidence of various taxes, we have seen that in the longer run, the distribution of the tax burden will depend on the resulting effects on factor supplies, rates of return, and growth. Viewing this problem in terms of "comparative statics," we have shown that a tax on labor income, by depressing labor supply, may result in an increase in the gross wage rate and a decline in the return to capital, so that the net wage rate declines by less than the tax and capital shares in the burden. While this properly describes the direction of adjustment, it does not account for the truly long-run interdependence of capital and labor supply in the context of balanced growth. In recent work, the bearing of this interdependence on incidence has come under consideration.[35]

The nature of this problem is complex, but the general conclusions reached may be described by considering the substitution of a tax on capital income for an equal-yield tax on wage income (the "differential incidence" approach) and examining the results under various assumptions regarding factor supplies and savings rates.

1.   Suppose first that the supply of both labor and capital is inelastic to the rate of return and that the savings rates out of wage and capital income are the same. In this case, our tax substitution will not affect factor supplies. The rate of capital accumulation is unaffected as is the capital-to-labor ratio under equilibrium growth. Pretax rates of return to factors, therefore, are unchanged as well. The burden of the tax previously carried by labor comes now to be borne by capital.

2.   Next suppose that the supply of labor is elastic, while retaining the other assumptions. As the tax on capital income is substituted for the tax on wage income, labor supply increases. Our earlier discussion, based on a comparative-static approach, suggested that the tax substitution, by increasing the net wage rate, would result in an increase in hours worked. This in turn would reduce the gross wage rate and increase the return to capital, so that part of the burden would continue to be shared by labor. But this will not occur in the context of a

[34]See p. 17.

[35]See Martin Feldstein, "Tax Incidence in a Growing Economy with Variable Factor Supply," *Quarterly Journal of Economics*, November 1974; and Martin Feldstein, "Incidence of a Capital Income Tax in a Growing Economy with Variable Savings Rates," *Review of Economic Studies*, 1974; and Marian Krzyzaniak, "The Long-Run Burden of a General Tax on Profits in a Neo-Classical World," *Public Finance*, no. 4, 1967.

balanced-growth model, where there will again be a full transfer of the burden to capital. The increase in hours worked will not affect the long-run growth rate of labor supply, which will still be determined by population growth; and, as we have seen in the preceding summary of growth theory, it is the rate of population growth which determines the equilibrium rate of income growth. Since we assume that the propensity to save is the same for capital and labor income, there will also be no change in the growth of the capital stock. With the capital-to-labor ratio in equilibrium growth unchanged, the pretax rates of return to capital and labor will also be unaffected. With the tax on labor income replaced by a tax on capital income, the burden is thus transferred from labor to capital.

3. The situation differs, however, if the supply of capital is elastic to the rate of return. As a result, the substitution of a tax on capital income reduces capital accumulation. While the growth rate of income remains unaffected (as it is still determined by the growth of population), the equilibrium capital-to-labor ratio will now be lower. Because of this, the pretax rate of return to capital will be increased while that to labor will be reduced. Only part of the tax burden is transferred and labor shares part of the profits tax burden.

4. Finally, consider a situation where both factor supplies are inelastic to the rate of return but where the savings rate out of capital income is higher than that out of labor income. Replacement of a tax on wage income by a tax on capital income now results in a reduced rate of capital formation and similar changes as under situation 3 result. Once more, labor bears part of the burden of a tax on capital income. Putting situations 3 and 4 together, we conclude that the remaining share of the tax burden borne by labor will be the larger (a) the more elastic the supply of capital relative to that of labor and (b) the higher the savings rate out of capital income relative to that out of labor income.

Although the tax effects involved in these relationships are complex and depend on the underlying structure of the growth model, it is not unreasonable to assume that, say, one-third of the burden of a tax on capital income comes to be borne by labor. This reasoning, it must be noted, pertains to the very long-run result after the return to balanced growth has taken place. Given the very long time period involved,[36] the more limited approach of the comparative-static type of analysis may be more relevant for policy purposes. In this setting, elasticity of labor supply does matter, and the slower process of changes in capital accumulation due to different savings rates will be of less importance.

F. SUMMARY

In this chapter, various effects of fiscal measures on the level of capacity output were considered. They may operate through effects on work effort, saving, and investment. Beginning with effects on work effort, we concluded:

1. An income tax may reduce or increase work effort, depending on whether the substitution effect outweighs the income effect, or vice versa.

---

[36]See Ryuzo Sato, "Fiscal Policy in a Neo-Classical Growth Model: An Analysis of Time Required for an Equilibrium Adjustment," *Review of Economic Studies*, February 1963.

2. There is no ready way of telling whether the level of work effort will be higher under an income tax or a consumption tax.

3. Transfer payments which are related positively to income generate income and substitution effects opposite to those of an income tax, with the net outcome again in doubt.

4. Transfer payments which are related negatively to income will reduce effort.

5. The same negative result tends to hold for free provision of social goods.

6. A distinction must be drawn between resulting excess burden and resulting changes in work effort.

In considering effects on the level of saving, a distinction was drawn between household savings and savings by businesses.

7. Household saving as a percentage of income (the average propensity to save) rises with income, but the marginal propensity to save rises less. Since differences in the savings impact of more or less progressive taxes depend on differences in the marginal propensities, they are less important than one might expect.

8. Income taxes may also affect saving because they reduce the net rate of return.

9. A consumption tax tends to fall less heavily on saving than does an income tax.

10. A large part of the corporation tax tends to be reflected in reduced corporate saving.

The effects of taxation on investment may operate in a number of ways, including their impact on profitability and the availability of internal funds.

11. A profits tax tends to reduce the level of investment by reducing the net rate of return.

12. Provided that full-loss offset is assured, the tax may raise or reduce the return to risk taking.

13. Allowing for depreciation reduces the effective rate of tax, the more so the faster is the permissible depreciation rate.

14. Tax policy encourages technological progress by permitting research and development expenditures to be expensed.

Turning to the role of the public sector in determining capital formation and growth, we have examined the place of public saving and the contribution of public investment.

15. Two concepts of public saving were distinguished.

16. Assuming that taxes are drawn from consumption and that borrowing diverts funds from private investment, public saving equals the excess of tax receipts over current expenditures.

17. This is the basis for dividing the budget into a current and a capital budget with focus on the state of balance in the current budget.

18. Although taxes, in fact, tend to fall more largely on consumption than does loan finance, no sharp distinction can be drawn. Much depends on what taxes are imposed.

19. The dual-budget system is misleading at the federal level but more readily applicable at the state-local level.

20. Capital expenditures account for a substantial share of public purchases, especially if investment in human resources is allowed for. The public share then exceeds the corresponding share in private purchases. Public investment in research makes a major contribution to productivity growth.

In affecting the rates of saving and investment, fiscal policy has an important influence on the rate of economic growth:

21. The equilibrium rate of growth in the neo-classical model is determined by the rate of population growth and thus is independent of fiscal and monetary policies.

22. However, such policies will affect the level of income at any given future time as well as the rate of growth over the forseeable future.

23. Growth is favored by combining a relatively tight fiscal policy with a relatively easy monetary policy.

24. In determining the long-run incidence of various taxes, their effect on the rate of growth needs to be considered. Depending on the nature of the production function, a resulting increase or decrease in the growth rate may affect factor shares and thereby distribution.

FURTHER READINGS

Feldstein, Martin S.: "The Effects of Taxation on Risk Taking," *Journal of Political Economy*, September–October 1969.

Fromm, Gary (ed.): *Tax Incentives and Capital Spending*, Washington: Brookings, 1971.

Jorgenson, Dale W.: "Capital Theory and Investment Behaviour," *American Economic Review*, May 1963.

Chapter 32

Economics of the Public Debt*

A. Structure of the Federal Debt: *Growth of the Federal Debt; Composition of the Federal Debt.* **B. Maturity Mix and Interest Cost:** *Term Structure of Rates; Term Structure and Debt Management.* **C. Further Issues in Debt Management:** *Interest Ceiling; Debt Limitation; Inflation-Proof Bonds; Refunding; Agency Debt and Government Lending.* **D. The Market for State and Local Debt:** *Tax Exemption versus Direct Interest Subsidy; Industrial Revenue Bonds.* **E. Debt Burden and Intergeneration Equity:** *Public Debt and Fiscal Solvency; Burden Transfer through Reduced Capital Formation; Burden Transfer with Outside Debt; Burden Transfer with Generation Overlap; Borrowing by State and Local Governments; Burden Transfer in Development Finance; Justification for Burden Transfer.* **F. Summary.**

The public debt in the United States as of December 31, 1978, amounted to about $1,070 billion, $790 billion of which was federal and an estimated $280 billion state and local. We begin with federal debt and the problems of management which it poses.

*Reader's Guide to Chapter 32: The first part of this chapter examines problems of debt structure and debt management, mostly at the federal level. This continues the discussion of stabilization policy and in particular of the interaction between fiscal and monetary policy undertaken in the preceding chapters. The second part deals with problems of debt burden and intergeneration equity. These are of primary importance at the state and local levels. While the public debt has ceased to be the hot issue it was some years ago, it nevertheless continues to be of considerable importance in economic policy.

A. STRUCTURE OF THE FEDERAL DEBT

During the decades of the thirties and forties, the growth of the federal debt and the alleged dangers thereof were a prime issue in public discussion and political controversy. Since then, the debt has become recognized as a relatively minor problem, although its management—i.e., what type of securities to issue and how to conduct refunding operations—continues to be an important factor in stabilization policy. The federal debt provides its holders with more or less liquid claims which in turn affect interest rates and spending behavior. As an instrument of control over liquidity, management of the federal debt is thus closely related to monetary policy.

Growth of the Federal Debt

The growth of the federal debt between 1941 and 1978 is summarized in Table 32-1. The federal debt rose sharply in the course of financing World War II, both in absolute terms (line 1) and relative to GNP (line 5). Thereafter the absolute level of federal debt continued to rise rapidly, tripling between 1946 and 1978, but the ratio of debt to GNP fell. By the mid-sixties it had dropped to well below the pre–World War II level. In considerable part this was the result of inflation which accelerated the growth of GNP in money terms. As inflation reduced the net value of debt claims, it acted as a built-in mechanism of debt devaluation.

Since the problem of public debt management relates to privately held debt only,[1] excluding debt held by government trust funds and the Federal Reserve Banks, this segment of the debt is shown separately in line 3. The pattern follows that of the total debt. The ratio of privately held debt to GNP rose sharply during the 1941–1946 period, but by 1970 had declined to well below its pre-1941 level. Even though privately held public debt more than doubled during the 1970s, the ratio of debt to GNP rose but slightly.

A similar pattern emerges if we consider the weight of privately held federal debt in the overall liquidity structure. As shown in line 7, the ratio of debt to money supply grew sharply during World War II but since then has fallen to one-half its prewar level. The table also records the changing level of interest payments. As shown in line 4, the absolute amount of interest payments moved up through the three decades, reflecting the rising level of debt as well as of interest rates. Nevertheless, this increase lagged behind that of GNP so that interest as percentage of GNP (line 8) declined sharply from its post-World War II peak. However, the ratio turned up during the 1970s, responding to sharply rising interest rates. As we shall see later, this is the ratio which matters in considering the demands of debt service upon the tax system.

---

[1]Debt held by the Federal Reserve and the trust funds is subject to government control rather than to decisions by private investors, and therefore does not affect private spending behavior.

TABLE 32-1
Growth of Federal Debt, 1941–1974
(In Billions of Dollars)

		1941	1946	1970	1978
1.	Total gross debt (par value)	58	259	370	789
2.	Held by government agencies*	11	51	153	280
3.	Held by private investors	47	208	217	510
4.	Interest	1	5	14	45
Ratios					
5.	Line 1 as percentage of GNP	47	125	38	37
6.	Line 3 as percentage of GNP	38	100	22	24
7.	Line 3 as percentage of money supply†	63	133	32	24
8.	Line 4 as percentage of GNP	0.8	2.4	1.4	2.2

*Includes holdings by Federal Reserve Banks.
†Money supply includes demand, time and savings deposits, and currency held outside banks.
Source: *Federal Reserve Bulletin,* March 1979, and *Economic Report of the President,* January 1978. Holdings at end of year.

Composition of the Federal Debt

The composition of the federal debt by type of issue is shown in Table 32-2. The total debt is divided into marketable and nonmarketable issues, with the marketable issues accounting for two thirds of the total. Marketable issues are traded and are available to all buyers. They include bills, notes, and bonds. The main difference between them is one of maturity. Bills are issued mostly with maturities of twelve months, but the maturities can also be as short as three months. Notes run from one to ten years and bonds for longer periods. Notes and bonds pay an annual interest and are redeemable at par at the date of maturity. Bills are sold at a discount and pay no interest, with the appreciation in value to maturity representing the investor's return.

Nonmarketable issues are offered to individual holders and can be held only by the initial buyer. They are largely designed for holding by governmental agencies and are held mainly by the various trust funds of the federal government, but they are also held by state and local governments and, recently of increasing importance, by foreign governments. Less than one third of the nonmarketable issues are held by individuals in the form of savings bonds. Introduced as a major source of finance in World War II, these bonds have greatly declined in attractiveness and importance.

Distribution of the debt by types of holders is shown in Table 32-3. Of the total, 35 percent is now held by government trust funds and the Federal Reserve Banks. Most important among the former is the OASDI Trust Fund which acquired these obligations in years when current receipts from payroll taxes exceeded benefit payments. Holdings are in the form of special issues. Federal Reserve Bank holdings in turn are of the marketable type and are acquired in the process of open market purchases. Given the public nature of the Federal Reserve System (notwithstanding its formally independent

TABLE 32-2
Gross Federal Debt by Type of Issue
(Par values in Billions of Dollars, Sept. 30, Dec. 31, 1978)

Marketable	487	
Bills		162
Notes		266
Bonds		60
Nonmarketable	295	
Savings bonds and notes		81
Government account series*		158
State and local government series		24
Foreign issues†		28
Convertible bonds		2
Non-interest bearing	7	
Total	789	

*Held by United States agencies and trust funds.
†Issued to foreign governments.
Source: Federal Reserve Bulletin, December 1978.

status), such holdings are, in fact, part of the monetary base rather than part of the federal debt owed to the public.

Of the remaining debt, 73 percent is held domestically while 27 percent is foreign-held, including holdings by foreign central banks. Of domestic holdings, 18 percent is held by state and local governments and 83 percent by private investors. Of privately held debt, 30 percent is held by commercial banks, largely in the form of Treasury bills which, owing to their short-term nature, are more suited to meet the liquidity needs of such investors. Individual investors hold 37 percent, mostly in the form of savings bonds. Financial institutions, such as savings banks and insurance companies, hold 4 percent, largely in the form of longer-term issues. Viewing the picture as a whole, it

TABLE 32-3
Gross Federal Debt by Type of Holder
(Billions of Dollars, Dec. 31, 1978)

Domestic		
Public	349	
U.S. government agencies and trust funds		170
Federal Reserve Banks		110
State and local governments		69
Private	303	
Commercial banks		93
Mutual savings banks		5
Insurance companies		15
Other corporations		21
Individuals		111
Miscellaneous		58
Foreign	138	
Total	790	

Source: Federal Reserve Bulletin, March 1979, p. A32.

appears that the public debt has very largely become an investment medium for short-term funds, while longer-term funds (except for savings bonds holdings by individuals) tend to be invested in private securities or equity. This differs greatly from the pattern which prevailed in the 1930s and 1940s and reflects the upsurge of the private sector in the postwar decades. During those years, private investment outlets resumed their earlier position as preferred investment choices.

B. MATURITY MIX AND INTEREST COST

The major issue in debt management is the choice of maturities. Traditionally, it was held that the public debt should be well "funded," i.e., be in long-term maturities. Thus, the British debt during the nineteenth century was largely in the form of consols or perpetual securities which have no fixed maturity date but can be retired at the government's option provided it is willing to pay the market price. This stipulation would protect the government against the contingency that creditors would demand their money back at an inopportune time. The modern view of national debt and the position of national governments in the debt market is quite different. Debt management proceeds on the assumption that maturing issues can always be refunded. Although the overall level of the debt may be increased at some periods and reduced at others (depending on whether the needs of stabilization policy call for a deficit or a surplus), there is no expectation that accumulated past debts will ever be "paid off." As particular issues mature, they come to be "refunded" into other issues. The shorter is the average debt outstanding, the larger will be the annual volume of refunding operations, but this is of no particular concern and not decisive in determining the maturity structure.

This being the case, what basic guidelines are there to the choice of maturities which the Treasury should offer? One possible answer is that it should select the term structure of the debt so as to minimize interest cost. Since the cost of borrowing tends to differ with the maturity of the debt, those issues should be chosen which investors are willing to absorb at the lowest cost. The same principle of economy which suggests that the government should buy its pencils from the lowest-cost supplier may also suggest that it borrow from the lowest-cost lender. On closer consideration, this proves too simple a rule, but let us first see what it would imply.

Term Structure of Rates

As we look back at the history of interest rates over the course of this century, we find short rates usually have been close to or above long rates. This pattern was reversed during the depression years of the 1930s when the general level of rates declined sharply and short rates fell below long rates. Federal Reserve policy was used to maintain this low level of rates during the war years to permit financing of the war debt at low cost. This required a substantial share of the debt to be absorbed by the commercial banks and a corresponding increase in money supply. Appropriate during the war, this policy was continued until the early fifties. Defended by the Treasury, it came under attack from the Federal Reserve System. The policy proved incompatible with the application of monetary restraint since the Federal Reserve had to stand ready to purchase bonds in the open market when needed to keep their prices from falling and their yields from rising. This constraint proved untenable and the Treasury-Federal Reserve "Accord" of 1951 left the Federal Reserve free to let rates rise. Federal Reserve policy accordingly adopted a "bills only" policy under which all open market operations would be conducted in Treasury bills. After a gradual transition, the securities markets returned to the earlier pattern of higher rates, with short and long rates moving closer together and with short rates occasionally above long rates.

The development of short and long rates since 1960 is shown in Figure 32-1. It will be seen that the general rate level has been rising, with the excess of long over short rates narrowing between 1960 and 1966 and short and long rates crisscrossing each other in the later years. A similar development is recorded in Figure 32-2, where yield curves for selected years are shown.[2] We note the upward shift in the yield curve and the change from a rising to a falling term structure of rates.

Theory of Term Structure   Economists have tried to explain the term structure of rates on the basis of rate expectations.[3] In a situation where no changes in interest rates are expected, so the argument goes, there is no reason for short and long rates to differ. The yield curve is horizontal. But suppose now that an expectation of rising rates emerges. As a result, lenders (or demanders of debt) will hesitate to commit themselves for a long period as they expect to obtain more favorable terms later on. Thus, the demand for debt shifts from the long to the short market. Borrowers (or suppliers of debt), on the other hand, are eager to borrow before costs rise. Thus, the supply of debt shifts from the short to the long market. As a result, demand for debt rises relative to supply on the short end. The price of short-term debt rises and yields decline.[4] At the same time, demand for debt falls relative to supply at the long end. Consequently, the price of long-term debt falls and yields rise. Thus, the yield curve comes to slope upward. The opposite result comes about if declining rates are expected. Long rates, according to this theory, come to reflect the expected level of future short-term rates.

Others have argued that this is too narrow a view of the term-structure problem. While expectations matter, the most important influences at any one time may be generated by developments in various parts of the capital

---

[2]The yield of a bond is the internal rate of discount at which the present value of the redemption payment plus coupon payment equals the purchase price. If the Treasury issues a bond at par (i.e., its redemption value), the yield equals the coupon rate of interest.

[3]For a convenient summary of this theory, see W. L. Smith, "Debt Management in the United States," Study Paper 19, *Study of Employment, Growth, and Price Levels*, Joint Economic Committee, U.S. Congress, June 28, 1960. For the original presentation, see J. R. Hicks, *Value and Capital*, 2d ed., Oxford: Clarendon, 1946, chap. 11.

[4]See Smith, ibid.

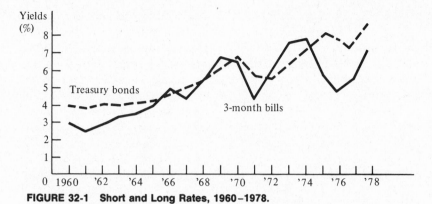

FIGURE 32-1   Short and Long Rates, 1960–1978.

(*Source: Economic Report of the President, 1974,* and *Federal Reserve Bulletin,* March 1979.)

market, resulting in structural changes in the demand for, and supply of, particular debt intruments.[5]

Effect of Inflation   Finally, how does inflation enter into the rate structure? The effect of inflation on the general level of interest rates is readily seen. Inflation does drive up rates because lenders wish to protect themselves against a loss in the real value of their claims as prices rise. Thus, if the "real" rate of interest or return in the absence of inflation is 3 percent, while the expected rate of inflation is 6 percent, the nominal rate of interest will tend to be 3 + 6, or 9 percent. The additional 6 percent is needed to maintain the purchasing power of the bond while only the 3 percent is a net gain in real terms. This inflationary adjustment accounts for a substantial part of the increase in the general level of interest rates in recent years.

The relation between inflation and the term structure of rates is less evident. As long as inflation proceeds at a *constant* rate, say 4 percent, and investors expect this rate to be maintained, the "inflation surcharge" will also stay at 4 percent, so that the term structure should not be affected. Only if the expected rate of inflation changes will the term structure be affected. Thus, an expectation that inflation will slow down will tend to make for a decline in future nominal rates and hence lead to a fall in long rates relative to short rates, and vice versa for an expected rise in the rate of inflation.

Term Structure and Debt Management

We can now reconsider the implications of the term structure of interest rates for debt management and ask whether interest cost is minimized by selling those issues which, as measured by current yields, can be placed at the lowest cost to maturity. The answer is clearly "no." Suppose the Treasury can borrow for one year at 5 percent and for twenty years at 7 percent. It does not follow that taking the one-year issue is preferable because by year's end

[5]See J. M. Culbertson, "The Term Structure of Interest Rates," *Quarterly Journal of Economics,* November 1967.

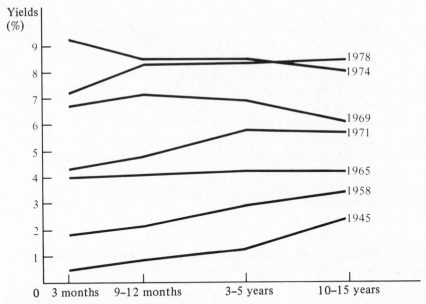

FIGURE 32-2 Yields to Maturity, 1945–1978.

Source: See Figure 32-1.

the opportunity to borrow at 7 percent may be lost if the level of rates has risen. Or, suppose that the Treasury can borrow for twenty years at 5 percent and for one year at 7 percent. The former choice is not necessarily preferable since rates may decline before the twenty years have passed.

What matters most is the *direction* in which the Treasury expects rates to change. If debt managers expect rates to rise, the proper choice is to borrow long; if they expect them to fall, the choice is to stay short. The important point is that once a commitment has been made, there is no way of escape. The interest cost contracted for must be carried for the full period even though rates may fall; and the benefits of a low rate will continue to accrue even though the rates may rise.[6] Debt management, therefore, is a fine art which requires a shrewd appraisal of market prospects for a considerable time ahead. In the hope that high inflation rates will come to pass, debt managers may be inclined to prefer short issues during an inflationary period.

[6]Suppose that the Treasury borrows $1,000 in a market in which a twenty-year bond, if selling at par, must carry a coupon rate of $6\frac{1}{2}$ percent. Having sold such a bond, suppose that after one year the market yield on a nineteen-year bond falls to $5\frac{1}{2}$ percent. As a result, the price of the old bond will rise to $1,117, i.e., the present value of $1,000 due in nineteen years plus nineteen annual coupon payments of $65 as discounted at $5\frac{1}{2}$ percent. Thus, if the Treasury were to retire the old bond (assuming that it had a call feature so that this could be done) and to reissue a new nineteen-year bond at $5\frac{1}{2}$ percent, it would have to raise $1,117 rather than $1,000 to replace the outstanding issue. This would leave its position unchanged, since the present values of the two cash flows—i.e., $1,000 in nineteen years plus nineteen annual payments of $65, or $1,117 in nineteen years plus nineteen annual coupon payments of $61.40 discounted at $5\frac{1}{2}$ percent—are the same, and each is equal to $1,117. Similar reasoning applies in a situation where interest rates rise and bond prices fall. Here, nothing would be lost by replacing the old bond with a new one. Even though the former could be retired at a lower price, the latter's coupon rate would have to be correspondingly higher.

But even if expected rate changes are allowed for, the criterion of minimum interest cost does not offer a sufficient guide. Differences in the behavior of investors who hold long and short debt must also be taken into account. After all, the central government, with its control over money creation, can regulate the level of interest rates in the market. It can always replace public debt by money, whether crudely through the printing press or more discreetly by borrowing from the central bank. Replacing debt with money would clearly be the cheapest way of handling the matter as it would involve no interest cost at all. Yet, it would not be a satisfactory solution because monetizing the debt would result in greatly increased liquidity, giving rise to an excessive level of aggregate demand and inflation.

Viewed this way, the purpose of issuing debt rather than money (or replacing maturing debt outstanding with new debt rather than monetizing it) is to purchase illiquidity. Investors must be convinced to hold debt rather than money, and the way to do this is to pay them. The question arises whether a dollar of short-term debt is as helpful in reducing liquidity as a dollar of long-term debt. If long-term debt makes the holder less liquid, it might pay the Treasury to issue such debt even if the interest cost were somewhat higher. The principle of minimizing interest costs must thus be restated as one of buying illiquidity on the cheapest terms which are compatible with the objectives of stabilization policy.

Lengthening the debt at the time of refunding will tend to be restrictive, and shortening it will tend to be expansionary.[7] Lengthening will raise long rates relative to shorts. Investors who were willing to hold a given supply of longs and shorts at a certain yield spread must now hold more longs and less shorts. To do this, they will require more favorable terms on longs and will be willing to accept less favorable terms on shorts. The restrictive effect of the resulting rise in long rates on private investment will outweigh the expansionary effect of decline in short rates, since capital expenditures are usually based on long-term financing.[8] Short-term debt being more like money, a lengthening of the debt is thus restrictive.

---

[7]A similar problem arises in open market operations of the Federal Reserve. However, such operations involve swaps between debt and money only and not between types of debt. Swaps between debt and money are given increased potency by the nature of fractional reserve banking, where (with a reserve ratio of 20 percent) substitution of $100 of debt for $100 of money may force a $500 reduction in money supply. This multiple effect does not arise with swaps between types of debts. However, even here banks may be induced to utilize excess reserves more fully or to extend their use of the discount window if their liquidity is increased by substitution of short-term for long-term debt, thus increasing the holdings of "secondary reserves."

[8]Consider an investor who is confronted with a choice among money, short debt, long debt, and real investment or equity. The individual will balance his or her portfolio among these assets so as to hold the preferred mix at given yields. For the market as a whole, the demand for, and supply of, various types of assets will result in a structure of yields at which both demanders and suppliers are satisfied. If long debt is substituted for short, the market must hold more of the former and less of the latter. Those who absorb additional long-term debt must discard some other assets, whereas those who reduce their holding of short debt must acquire other assets. It seems likely that the former will want to discard equity holdings while the latter will want to shift toward money. The reason for this is that long debt, being less liquid, is a closer substitute for equity, while short debt is a closer substitute for money. As a result, the cost at which equity funds are available will rise and investment will decline. The opposite holds true if the debt is shortened.

The same considerations which apply to refunding (or swapping of debt) also apply with regard to choosing the type of issue or addition to the debt with which a deficit is financed, or the type of issue which is to be withdrawn as the surplus is used for debt reduction.[9] In either case, debt management may be used to support the expansionary or restrictive effects of current stabilization policy. Consequently, short-run policy objectives, rather than long-run expectations of rate change and their implication for interest costs, may be the decisive factor in determining debt management policy.

Short-run adjustments aside, there remains the question of what constitutes a "sound" maturity mix insofar as the body of the outstanding debt is concerned. A long debt, as noted before, calls for a smaller volume of refunding operations, but this is hardly a decisive consideration. A debt of given size, if short, will leave the economy in a more liquid position and thus may tend to increase its volatility. As a result, the task of stabilization policy may be made more difficult. On the other hand, too long a debt may introduce rigidities into the financial structure and fall short of providing the necessary liquidity. In either case, much will depend on the size of the money stock. The effect on liquidity in the private sector of a longer debt combined with a larger money stock may be similar to the effect of a shorter debt with a smaller money supply. In the absence of better reasoning, one is left with the view that a "well-balanced" maturity structure up to, say, fifteen years is to be preferred to one which is almost entirely short or almost entirely long.

Whatever the answer, the fact is that the maturity structure of the debt was shortened greatly over the 1950s and 1960s as Table 32-4 shows. Whereas in 1950, long-term debt in excess of twenty-five years comprised 16 percent of the total and debt below one year comprised 27 percent, the corresponding ratios for 1970 showed at 4 and 49 percent. Average years to maturity fell from eight to two years. Debt management during the 1950s and 1960s thus produced a substantial shift toward increased liquidity of the debt and thereby contributed to expansionary policy. This tendency toward shortening was halted during the 1970s, but the bulk of the debt still remains heavily concentrated at the short end. As long as the current inflationary setting continues, this pattern is not likely to change. Reliance on short debt permits

---

[9]It is easy to see that shortening a given debt is expansionary and that a net addition to the debt in short form is more restrictive (or less expansionary) than a similar addition in long form. But it is more difficult to appraise the effects of a net addition of a particular type of debt considered by itself.

Consider a net addition to long-term debt. As a result, the total stock of claims and equity which investors must hold is increased. Since their preferences call for a balanced portfolio, they will not wish to absorb the entire addition in the form of a long debt. They will thus try to substitute other assets. This will increase long-term yields and may thus be expected to be restrictive. However, not only will the addition to long-term debt be reflected in an increased demand for short debt and money, but there may also be some desire to substitute equity. To the extent that this occurs, the cost at which equity funds become available is reduced and investment will rise. While less expansionary (or more restrictive) than the net addition of shorter debt, the effect of adding longer debt, taken by itself, may thus go in either direction. See James Tobin, "An Essay on Principles of Debt Management," in Commission on Money and Credit (ed.), *Fiscal and Debt Management Policies*, Englewood Cliffs, N.J.: Prentice-Hall, 1963.

TABLE 32-4
Composition of Marketable Debt by Maturity

	1950		1960		1970		1978	
	Billions of Dollars	Per-centage	Billions of Dollars	Per-centage	Billions of Dollars	Per-centage	Billions of Dollars	Per-centage
Years to maturity								
0–1	42	27	70	38	122	49	228	47
1–5	51	33	73	40	82	33	162	35
5–10	8	5	20	11	23	9	50	10
10–20	28	18	13	7	9	4	20	4
20 and over	25	16	8	4	11	5	26	5
Total	155	100	183	100	247	100	487	100
Average years to maturity	8.2		4.8		3.7		3.3	

Notes: Figures for end of year. Includes privately held issues only. Issues are classified by number of years remaining to maturity. Items may not add to totals due to rounding.
Source: Federal Reserve Bulletin, March 1979, and *Economic Report of the President,* January 8, 1974, p. 334.

the Treasury to avoid committing itself to a high-interest cost over a longer period, hoping that inflation will be checked and that nominal interest rates will fall in the future. At the same time, investors feel uncertain about the future (inflation may get worse!) and prefer to avoid a long-term commitment. Thus, it is expedient to refund maturing issues short-term, but in so doing, the liquidity of the claim structure is increased.

C. FURTHER ISSUES IN DEBT MANAGEMENT

In addition to the choice of maturities, a number of further issues in debt management will be noted, but cannot be developed in detail.

Interest Ceiling

In the later part of the 1960s the interest ceiling, as noted before, came to interfere with the sale of long-term debt. Toward the close of World War I, Congress had enacted an interest ceiling of $4\frac{1}{4}$ percent on securities in excess of five years, excluding those issued to government agencies. This ceiling remained largely ineffective until the second half of the 1960s when long-term yields in the market rose above this level. Although the ceiling could have been circumvented by selling bonds with a $4\frac{1}{4}$ percent coupon rate at a price below par, the Treasury chose not to do so, as this would have violated the congressional intention. Thus, no long-term bonds could be sold after 1965 when market yields rose above the ceiling. After repeated Treasury requests, Congress authorized a limited issue of Treasury bonds at above-ceiling yields. The limit, which now stands at $34 billion, has been extended by Congress at the request of the Treasury and has not been a factor in the trend toward reliance on short-term issues.

The story of the interest ceiling reflects the historical controversy between tight and easy money. It has been a recurrent theme in United States monetary and political history over the last century, witnessed in recent decades by the perpetual feud of the House Banking and Currency Committee (led for many years by Wright Patman) with the Federal Reserve.[10] But whatever one's view of this matter, the issue should not be resolved by a rigid ceiling. The appropriate mix of fiscal, monetary, and debt policies should be determined on its merits and in line with current policy objectives, with bond yields and refunding patterns adjusted to this policy mix. The ceiling places an undesirable constraint on the conduct of stabilization policy and its removal is thus called for.

Debt Limitation

Another congressional constraint on debt management relates to the size of the debt. Congress, usually acting several times a year, authorizes a set limit which the Treasury cannot exceed.[11] At the same time, congressional action or inaction with regard to revenue legislation and appropriations often calls for increases in government borrowing beyond the debt ceiling, thus requiring the Secretary of the Treasury periodically to appear before Congress and to beg for an increase in the ceiling. The debt ceiling, as most observers agree, is an anachronism as Congress has more direct and explicit ways by which to control the level of expenditures. This is the case especially since the Joint Budget Resolution was provided by the Congressional Budget Act of 1974.

Inflation-Proof Bonds

One proposal, advanced repeatedly over the years and again timely under current inflationary conditions, is for the issuance of a "stable purchasing-power bond."[12] The redemption value of such a bond would vary with the cost-of-living index, thus protecting small investors against the loss of purchasing power from inflation as well as depriving them of a (less likely) gain if prices should fall. The coupon rate on such a bond would be correspondingly lower, since it would carry no inflation premium. Its availability would be of great value to small investors who find it difficult to protect themselves against inflation.[13] Given these advantages, it is difficult to see

---

[10]Tight money and high interest rates are suspect because they mean higher returns for the money lender and higher costs for the borrower, who is held more deserving. This is but one aspect of the problem posed by the differential incidence (or distributional implications) of monetary, as distinct from fiscal, restriction.

[11]See Marshall A. Robinson, *The National Debt Ceiling*, Washington: Brookings, 1959.

[12]For an earlier proposal, see L. Bach and R. A. Musgrave, "A Stable Purchasing Power Bond," *American Economic Review*, December 1941.

[13]If the nominal interest rate adjusts itself to inflation (see p. 183), new investors will be protected thereby. But old investors who purchased the bonds before the inflation was expected are not helped as they do not partake in the rising yield. (Their position is the inverse of the Treasury's position noted in footnote 6, p. 698). Thus, longer-run protection can be given only by a bond whose purchasing power is maintained constant.

why such bonds have not been issued. Perhaps the explanation lies in the fact that it is difficult for the Treasury to admit uncertainties regarding the value of the dollar, or because it would generate pressure for similar escalation clauses in the rest of the economy.

Refunding

The gradual increase in the federal debt requires debt managers to decide what debt to issue, but this is only a minor part of debt management. The major problem is to expedite the refunding of maturing issues. The annual refunding volume is around $300 billion, with the payment of maturing obligations and their replacement by refunding issues a weekly operation. Whereas refunding operations have traditionally involved highly complicated procedures, requiring precise estimation of yields demanded by the market, techniques developed in more recent years have greatly simplified matters. New issues are now sold through an auction system, with closed bids received from the dealers and then met on a first-come, first-served basis. Increased reliance on short-term debt, sold at discount rather than with a coupon, has facilitated this development. In expediting the refunding process, the Federal Reserve Bank of New York, which is closest to the money market, cooperates closely with the Treasury and serves as its agent.

Agency Debt and Government Lending

In addition to the Treasury debt list in the above tables, the government is involved in the debt of federal and federally sponsored credit agencies. By the end of 1978, such debt amounted to $132 billion, with two-thirds thereof extended by housing credit agencies such as the Federal National Mortgage Association and the Federal Home Loan Bank. This type of debt has expanded substantially in recent years.

In providing for the use of these funds, government lending (as distinct from spending) enters the scene as an additional instrument of budgetary policy. Lending, like debt retirement, reduces the net debt position of the government. In a perfect capital market, extension of a $100 loan with a ten-year maturity would be equivalent to retirement of a $100 debt issue of similar maturity, assuming the same tax revenue to be used to finance either transaction. But the results of the two transactions may be quite different in an imperfect market. The recipient of the government loan might not have been able to obtain credit elsewhere. Indeed, a major rationale of government lending is to provide funds to creditors who have not been able to obtain them otherwise but who, for reasons of public policy, should be provided with funds.[14] It is thus typically used as an instrument of allocation rather than as stabilization policy, and as such, is particularly important in the context of developing countries where government-supported investment is an important feature of development policy.

---

[14]Another reason is to channel public sector savings into private investment. See p. 677.

D. THE MARKET FOR STATE AND LOCAL DEBT

The problem of debt management for state and local governments is altogether different from that at the federal level and more like that of private investors attempting to secure funds in the market. The difference holds for both the demand and the supply sides of the picture. On the demand side, the occasion for borrowing by state and local governments occurs primarily when substantial capital expenditures are to be financed. For reasons to be considered in section E, it is prudent that such outlays be loan-financed rather than tax-financed. The rationale for borrowing at the state and local level is thus quite different from that at the federal level where stabilization policy is the primary determinant. On the supply side of the market for funds, a state or local government, unlike the federal government, has no control over the money market conditions under which it must borrow. The best it can do is to obtain funds on as favorable terms as happen to be open to it; and the cost of borrowing differs widely, depending on the fiscal position of the jurisdiction and its "credit rating."

State and local debt now approaches $300 billion and has risen by an average annual amount of about $15 billion during the last decade. Its percentage rate of increase has been somewhat below that of the federal debt and of GNP. The debt is largely long-term and may take various forms, including general obligation bonds and special revenue bonds. The latter are issued by particular agencies or public enterprises, such as water or power companies operated by the state, municipality, or other subdivision, and the profits of the enterprise are pledged for the financing of debt service. The cost at which funds are available to various borrowing jurisdictions enters as an important factor into the provision of those state and local services which involve heavy capital outlays, e.g., highways and school buildings. Such outlays are important from the national as well as the state and local perspective, so that state and local borrowing enters as an additional aspect of fiscal federalism.

Tax Exemption versus Direct Interest Subsidy

As we saw earlier, federal policy gives general support to state and local borrowing by excluding interest on such securities from taxable income under the federal income tax.[15] An investor whose marginal tax rate is 50 percent will be willing (other things being equal) to substitute a municipal bond yielding 4 percent for a corporate bond yielding 8 percent. Currently, AAA-rated state and local bond may yield 6 percent, whereas corporate bonds will yield 9 percent. Taxpayers whose marginal tax rate exceeds 33 percent will thus have an inducement to hold state and local issues. This tax advantage thus diverts funds into the tax-exempt market, thereby reducing the cost at which state and local governments can borrow.

But this particular form of aid is subject to criticism on two grounds. First, it interferes with the equity of the income tax structure. High-income

[15]See p. 348.

recipients who receive tax-exempt interest pay less tax than do others with equal income from other sources. Moreover, the value of tax exemption rises with bracket rates so that vertical equity is interfered with. On these grounds alone, it would be preferable to provide such assistance as is desired in a way which does not involve tax preferences.

The second objection is that tax exemption results in a smaller gain in terms of interest savings to state and local governments than would be provided by a direct subsidy involving the same cost to the federal government. The reason, as we have noted before, is that the effective rate of subsidy for state and local governments equals the marginal tax rate of the lowest-bracket buyer for whom the incentive is effective, i.e., about 30 percent. Yet, higher-bracket taxpayers are given a benefit (with corresponding revenue losses to the Treasury) ranging from 30 to 70 percent, depending on their bracket rate. This is a further reason why a direct subsidy would be preferable to the interest exemption. Notwithstanding the opposition of state and local officials and high-bracket taxpayers, chances are that a more direct approach will be adopted before long if only because the amount of subsidy available through the exemption route will prove insufficient to attract the required amount of funds. Since at present the investor group for whom the tax benefit matters accounts for only about one-fourth of total savings flowing into the long-term debt market, a more broadly based approach will be needed.[16]

Apart from the question of how support of interest payments is best given, there is the further question of whether general support for interest payments at the state-local level is called for. With state and local borrowing used for capital expenditure, such support is equivalent to a matching grant for capital outlays. Viewed this way, the question is whether capital expenditures as a group are preferable to current expenditures and hence merit a special subsidy, be it on grounds of spillover effects or of merit-good considerations. The answer seems to be in the negative. Aside from matters of politics and constitutional history (with the earlier view that state-local instrumentalities are to be exempted from federal taxation), the very premise of general interest support seems questionable.

Support for state and local borrowing on a more selective basis, parallel to the case for categorical grants, might be more readily justified. In this connection, the creation of a financial intermediary which would itself borrow in the market and then relend to municipalities is under consideration. Such a bank might be instrumental in overcoming the element of arbitrariness now imposed by the system of credit rating, and it would reduce the cost of borrowing for smaller municipalities by spreading risks. On the other hand, it might also introduce elements of political bias into the availability of funds. In other respects, such an institution might be helpful in

[16]See G. Mitchell, "State and Local Government Borrowing," in M. E. Polakoff (ed.), *Financial Institutions and Markets*, Boston: Houghton Mifflin, 1970, p. 335; and S. S. Surrey and F. Morris, "The Case for Broadening the Financial Options Open to Government," in *Financing State and Local Governments*, Boston: Federal Reserve Bank of Boston, June 1970.

stabilizing cyclical fluctuations in borrowing costs and in modifying the
unevenly heavy impact of changes in monetary policy upon this particular
sector of the capital market.

Industrial Revenue Bonds

Finally, notice should be taken of the growth of industrial revenue bonds over
the last decade. Such bonds are issued by state and local jurisdictions, the
proceeds being used to construct industrial facilities which in turn are leased
to private firms. More recently, such practice has also been extended into
providing mortgage funds. Thus, the reduction in the cost of financing
provided through federal tax exemption is passed on to what constitutes
essentially private enterprises. From the point of view of a particular municipality, it is seen as a device to attract firms to its location. But such a policy
is not defensible from the national point of view. Congress accordingly
provided in 1969 that the tax-exemption privilege on such bonds be limited to
issues not exceeding $5 million.

E. DEBT BURDEN AND INTERGENERATION EQUITY

We now turn to quite a different aspect of the debt problem, namely, the
proposition that debt finance burdens future generations. If so, this is both a
critique of borrowing (since it may be abused by burdening future generations with the cost of services which are enjoyed currently) and an argument
for borrowing (since it may be used to secure intergeneration equity by
passing on part of the cost of capital outlays to the future). The primary
question, however, is: Does such a burden transfer in fact occur, and if so,
how?

Public Debt and Fiscal Solvency

The raging debate over debt burden in the thirties and forties was between
those who feared that the creation of debt in the course of deficit finance
(made necessary in securing high employment) would burden the future, and
others who, in defending such finance, argued that it would not do so.

More specifically, the contention advanced by the opponents of deficit
finance was that the burden of all public expenditures eventually falls on the
taxpayer, with loan finance merely delaying the tax payments to the time
when the debt will be paid off. The burden is thus postponed and future
generations are born with a chain around their necks, i.e., with the obligation
to pay off the national debt. This contention was wrong; there is no need to
pay off debt, since it becomes part of the country's claim structure and may
be refunded at maturity rather than paid off. Hence, only interest payments
create additional tax requirements.

The opposing argument was that such interest payments would impose
no burden on future generations since (assuming the debt to be held domestically) the future generation would contain both taxpayers and interest recipients. Gains and losses would therefore wash out, leaving no problem of

net burden; there would merely be a transfer from one party to another. Domestic debt imposes no burden since "we owe it to ourselves." This argument was correct in that interest payments involve no loss of resources to the group as a whole, but it overlooked the frictional effects of taxation.[17] As we saw earlier, taxation may impose an excess burden and cause deadweight losses. The severity of such effects is likely to rise with the overall level of taxation or ratio of tax revenue to GNP. As the debt–GNP ratio rises, the ratio of tax revenue (needed to service the debt) to GNP also rises. Conceivably, it becomes so large as to pose a serious tax-disincentive problem, a factor which is overlooked in the "we owe it to ourselves" proposition. Debt accumulation during wars may be so drastic as to lead to fiscal breakdown and debt repudiation in the postwar period. These events occurred in European countries after both world wars.

However, so long as the debt does not grow at a higher percentage rate than does GNP, the debt–GNP ratio does not rise and there is little reason why it should rise at a faster rate.[18] Although the finance of World War II resulted in a sharp increase in the ratio of debt to GNP, we have noted that the subsequent growth of the economy reduced the ratio (see Table 32-1, line 8) by 1970 to below its prewar level. Rising interest rates since then again raised the interest–GNP ratio to close to the 1946 level. Whereas the inflation-spurred increase in the nominal level of GNP served to contract the debt–GNP ratio, it also pushed up yields and thereby the interest–GNP ratio. But as shown in the table, this increase has been modest only. The specter of an ever-rising debt–GNP ratio which so agitated the public only a few years ago has become of more or less anthropological interest, a striking example of the demise of what once seemed a burning issue.

Burden Transfer through Reduced Capital Formation

Another and more important aspect of the burden problem focuses not on the debt itself but on the effects of loan and tax finance upon growth and the capital endowment passed on to future generations.

Once more we return to the framework of a "classical" system where investment adjusts itself to the level of saving forthcoming at a full-employ-

---

[17]Note that this problem may arise even though interest payments are included in taxable income. The tax rate t required to finance interest is given by $t = idY/(Y + idY) = id/(1 + id)$ where i is the interest rate and d is the ratio of debt to national income Y. With i equal to 5 percent and d equal to 40 percent, t equals 2 percent. If d rises to, say, 100 percent, t increases to 5 percent, and if d rises to 500 percent, t increases to 20 percent. Suppose that the level of t required for the finance of other services were 30 percent The corresponding total levels of t would then be 32, 35, and 50 percent, respectively. Thus, the need to tax-finance interest payments *could* come to absorb a substantial share of the economy's taxable capacity and thereby might displace other outlays.

[18]Suppose that, in order to maintain high employment, a deficit equal to x percent of GNP is needed. The debt then rises by x percent of GNP annually, and as GNP increases, the annual addition to the debt also grows. It may be shown, however, that the ratio of debt to GNP approaches a constant and that, given reasonable values, its level is relatively low. On this matter, see E. D. Domar, "The Burden of the Debt and the National Income," *American Economic Review*, December 1944.

ment level of income. Given such a system, we have seen that $1 of both tax and loan finance reduces private expenditures by $1, but that tax finance is more likely to fall on private consumption, whereas loan finance will tend to fall on investment.[19] For any given set of public expenditures, substitution of loan for tax finance therefore reduces the growth rate of the economy. Future generations will be left with a smaller endowment and hence will receive a lower income. It is this reduction in endowment or net worth which is the vehicle of burden transfer.

This mechanism of burden transfer operates even though the resource withdrawal from private use must occur at the very time when the public expenditure is made. In this narrower sense, the immediate cost must be borne by the generation that releases these resources. Yet, it makes a difference whether the resource withdrawal is from consumption or from capital formation. In the first case, generation 1, which finances the expenditure, assumes the burden by reducing its private consumption. In the second case, it makes no such sacrifice but reduces the future income and potential consumption of generation 2. Burden transfer, therefore, occurs whenever generation 1, in transferring funds to the government, responds by reducing its capital formation in the private sector.[20]

As noted in our earlier discussion of the capital budget, the conclusion that loan finance results in burden transfer whereas tax finance does not reflects the assumption that the former tends to fall on capital formation while the latter does not. This assumption is in the right direction, although, as we have seen earlier, the distinction may be overdrawn. Moreover, the government's ability to choose between loan and tax finance to allocate burdens between generations depends on the assumption that this financing mix does not affect aggregate demand. Under more realistic assumptions, as we noted in the preceding discussion of stabilization policy, tax finance is likely to be more deflationary, i.e., to result in a sharper reduction in private expenditures. In such a system, the combination of tax and loan finance must be set so as to secure the desired level of aggregate demand. Therefore, it cannot also be set so as to secure an allocation of private resources between consumption and investment in line with considerations of intergeneration

---

[19]See p. 680.

[20]The reader may wonder whether there is not another aspect to the matter. With loan finance, the lenders of generation 1 receive bonds in return for parting with their funds, whereas, with tax finance, the taxpayers of generation 1 do not receive any such compensation. Therefore, will not the members of generation 1 prefer loan finance, and will they not do so quite apart from their decision to respond by reducing consumption or capital formation?

The apparent conflict between this line of reasoning and that given in the text is resolved once it is noted that loan finance not only results in the handing out of bonds (receipt of which is a gain to the lenders) but also in the assumption of a future tax liability to pay interest on these bonds. Considering generation 1 as a group, these two aspects of bond issue wash out: The present value of future tax liabilities equals the value of the bond, leaving no net gain. Or, to put it differently, additional taxes equal interest receipts. Generation 2, similarly, inherits not only the bonds but also the interest obligation so that the two sides once more cancel out. Disregarding the tax friction burden, each generation does indeed owe the debt to itself. At the same time, it is not a matter of indifference to the two generations whether tax or loan finance is used, provided that the latter falls more heavily upon capital formation in generation 1, thus leaving generation 2 with a smaller capital endowment.

equity. Unless both targets can be met through appropriate adjustments in the mix of fiscal and monetary policies, the two goals may not be reconcilable. Priority may then be given to demand considerations. Such at least is the situation at the federal level. State and local finance is not subject to this constraint, so that considerations of intergeneration equity may dominate the financing choice.

Burden Transfer with Outside Debt

Having considered the role of domestic borrowing, we now turn to that of borrowing from outside sources. The mechanism of burden transfer through foreign borrowing differs in several respects. A first difference is that there is now no need for generation 1 to reduce its expenditures. Consumption and capital formation in the private sector can remain intact as the additional resources needed for the public outlay are acquired abroad. Loan finance now imposes a burden on generation 2 not by leaving it with a reduced capital endowment at home but by saddling it with an obligation to service the foreign debt. Taxes must now be paid to finance interest paid to foreigners rather than to domestic holders of the debt. Generation 2 no longer owes the debt to itself. This foreign debt burden replaces the loss of capital income which generation 2 would have suffered had there been domestic loan finance and a resulting reduction in capital formation.

Compare now our three sources of finance—(1) taxation, (2) domestic borrowing, and (3) foreign borrowing. Assuming (1) to fall on consumption and (2) on capital formation, (1) will burden the present generation while (2) and (3) will burden the future. While (2) and (3) are similar in this respect, the choice between them may not be a matter of indifference. The answer depends upon the cost of borrowing at home and abroad. If the cost is the same (if the return on domestic capital is the same as the outside rate of interest), the burden on generation 2 will be the same in each case. But if the domestic return is higher, foreign borrowing will be preferable, and vice versa if the domestic return is lower.

Burden Transfer with Generation Overlap

When we consider the problem of burden transfer between generations whose life spans do not overlap, reduced private capital formation is the only mechanism (other than foreign borrowing) by which a burden transfer to the future can occur. But this is not a necessary condition if the two generations overlap in time. Suppose that generation 1 lives from year 1 to year 50, while generation 2 lives from years 25 to 75. Also suppose that all taxes come from consumption. Now generation 1, in year 1, may be called upon to pay taxes of $200,000 to sustain the cost of a government building with a useful life of 50 years. It must do so at the cost of reducing its own consumption by this amount. But it will then be possible, in years 25 to 50, to collect taxes of $100,000 from generation 2 in order to refund generation 1, thus involving a shift in private consumption from generation 2 to generation 1. In this way generation 1, while initially assuming the entire burden, can transfer part of it to generation 2. For purposes of reassurance generation 1 may be given a promise of repayment in the form of bonds, to be redeemed later out of taxes imposed on generation 2. Such a transfer among overlapping generations can function even though there is no effect on capital formation in the private sector.

As a variant to this case, generation 1 may make a present to generation 2 and assume the entire burden without calling upon generation 2 for repayment later on. This is precisely the mechanism which applied when old-age retirement pensions were introduced and the initially aged were given benefits without having had to contribute.[21]

Borrowing by State and Local Governments

The problem of intergeneration equity arises most acutely at the state and local levels where the bulk of public investment expenditures are made and financed.

Suppose that a township is about to construct a school building,[22] the services of which will extend over thirty years. The expenditures thereon call for a sharp, once-and-for-all increase in the total outlays of the township. If it were to be tax-financed, a sharp if temporary increase in the tax rate would be needed. This would in itself be undesirable, since taxpayers find it easier to live with a more or less stable tax rate. Moreover, and more important, it would be unfair to place the entire burden on those who pay taxes in this particular year. Since the use of the facility will extend over thirty years, it is only fair to spread the burden among the successive "generations" of residents which will benefit from the service. The principle of benefit taxation is applied in allocating the burden between generations.

To accomplish this, the initial cost is covered by borrowing, typically in outside markets. In subsequent years, future generations, present and partaking of the benefits, are taxed each year in accordance with their current benefit share. In the process, the debt is amortized and repaid by the time the facility is used up. Once more, intergeneration equity is secured, with each generation paying for its own benefit share. A township which finances its school building by borrowing and amortizing the debt over the length of the asset life thus provides for an equitable pattern of burden distribution not only between age groups but also between changing groups of residents as the population of the jurisdiction changes in response to in-migration and out-migration.

Burden Transfer In Development Finance

The preceding discussion has an unhappy application to the problems of development finance and economic growth. The mechanism of burden transfer, while it may be used to spread the cost of *public* investment, cannot be used to spread the cost of a development program, broadly defined. The

[21]See p. 735.
[22]The problem does not arise if one considers a steady stream of annual investment with a constant population. Current tax finance will then match the current flow of benefits. Such at least is the case if we disregard both the position of the first generation which is discriminated against and that of the doomsday generation which will benefit.

reason is that the very objective of such a program requires that *total* capital formation (public or private) be increased. But no gain is made toward achieving this objective if public capital formation is loan-financed, where this causes an offsetting decline in the rate of private capital formation. Unfortunately, therefore, the mechanism of burden transfer through internal loan finance is inapplicable in the very situation where it would be most appropriate. This does not hold, however, with regard to foreign borrowing, the role of which will be considered further when development finance is examined.[23]

Justification for Burden Transfer

When dealing with the *feasibility* of burden transfer through loan finance, it was best to separate this problem from the expenditure issue. Analogous to the differential view of tax incidence, the problem was to see how the future generation would be affected by alternative methods of finance for a given expenditure project. When the matter of *justification* for burden transfer is considered, the expenditure side must be brought into the picture. Proceeding on the principle that public services should be financed on a benefit basis, each generation should pay for its own share in the benefits received. Applying this principle to public capital outlays the benefits of which will extend into the future, it follows that loan finance and burden transfer are called for as a matter of intergeneration equity. Assuming that tax finance falls on consumption while loan finance falls on capital formation, tax finance of current and loan finance of capital outlays is in line with intergeneration equity. Loan finance of current expenditures, on the other hand, places an undue burden on the future and tax finance of capital outlays gives it an undue benefit. This is the rationale for the use of a capital budget (especially at the level of local finance) and for the use of foreign borrowing in the case of development finance. It may also be interpreted to justify heavy reliance on loan finance to sustain the cost of war.

F. SUMMARY

Over 70 percent of the public debt is federal, with less than 30 percent state and local. Regarding the development and structure of the federal debt, we have observed that:

1. The federal debt as a percentage of GNP is less than it was prior to World War II.
2. Two-thirds of the federal debt is in marketable issues, with one-third in nonmarketable or special issues.
3. Holding of the federal debt is divided about equally between government agencies (including the Federal Reserve) and private holders.
4. The maturity structure of the public debt has become increasingly short term, with the average length to maturity now only two years.

---

[23]See p. 798.

See p. 798.

5. Interest rates have moved up sharply in recent years, especially at the short end of the rate structure.

6. The level of interest rates on long-term debt may be taken to reflect the expected level of short-term rates.

7. The nominal interest rate is increased by inflation, being equal to the sum of the real rate and the expected inflation rate. The ratio of interest on public debt to GNP has risen during the seventies and now stands close to where it was at the end of World War II.

Debt management is concerned mainly with refunding the large volume of debt which matures annually. In examining this problem, the following conclusions were drawn:

8. The policy objective is not to minimize interest cost but to purchase illiquidity at the lowest available price.

9. Short-term debt is more like money, so that shortening of the debt tends to be expansionary.

10. Further problems in connection with debt management were examined, including interest ceilings, the debt limitation, the possibility of a stable purchasing power bond, refunding techniques, and government lending.

11. Turning our attention to the market for state and local debt, we have noted that the position of state and local governments is more like that of private borrowers than that of the federal government. We have also observed the important role played by the tax exemption of interest from state and local securities under the federal income tax.

Finally, the problems of debt burden were examined beginning with the implications of servicing the debt.

12. The relationship of the public debt to the solvency of government does not depend on the absolute level of debt but on its level relative to that of GNP.

13. The public debt becomes part of the economy's claim structure and need not be paid off at maturity. The problem, rather, is one of debt service, including refunding and the finance of interest payments. While there is some merit to the contention that such interest payments are not burdensome to the economy as a whole since they involve a transfer from taxpayers to interest recipients, the efficiency costs of a high tax rate must be allowed for.

14. These costs, however, depend upon the ratio of interest payments to GNP. There is little reason to expect it to become excessive in the normal course of peacetime finance.

Turning to the relationship of debt finance to intergeneration equity, we observed the following:

15. In the absence of generation overlap, a burden transfer to the future generation has to take the form of reduced capital formation.

16. In the context of the classical model, loan finance may be expected to fall more largely on investment, whereas tax finance may be expected to fall more heavily on consumption. Loan finance may thus be a means of transferring a burden to the future generation.

   17.   This argument, however, is not readily applicable to central government in the context of an economy which requires stabilizing measures.

   18.   Foreign borrowing permits financing of public programs without placing a burden on the present generation. Applied to public investment, it is particularly important in the context of development finance.

   19.   Another mechanism of burden transfer may be applied in a situation where the present and future generations overlap.

   20.   Burden transfer is in line with intergeneration equity where the public outlay will result in future benefits.

FURTHER READINGS

Barro, Robert J.: "Are Government Bonds Net Wealth?" *Journal of Political Economy*, December 1974.

Ferguson, J. M. (ed.): *Public Debt and Future Generations*, Chapel Hill: University of North Carolina Press, 1964. Contains a selection of articles dealing with the problem of intergeneration equity.

Rolph, E. R.: "Principles of Debt Management," *American Economic Review*, June 1957.

Smith, W. L.: "Debt Management in the United States," Study Paper 19, *Study of Employment, Growth, and Price Levels*, Joint Economic Committee, U.S. Congress, June 28, 1960.

Tobin, J.: "An Essay on Principles of Debt Management," in Commission on Money and Credit (ed.), *Fiscal and Debt Management Policies*, Englewood Cliffs, N.J.: Prentice-Hall, 1963.

Part Seven

Further Policy Issues

Chapter 33

Income Maintenance Programs*

A. Overview of Income Maintenance Programs. B. Income Maintenance for the Poor: *Present Status of the Welfare System; Critique of AFDC Program; Work Incentives; Negative Income Tax.* **C. Social Insurance:** *Structure of Retirement and Disability Insurance; Issues in OASI; Health Insurance.* **D. Unemployment Insurance. E. Summary.**

The overall impact of fiscal redistribution was considered in Chapter 12, where we noted that the most important instrument of redistribution is through the transfer system. We now turn to some of the major transfer programs which contribute to the support of low-income households and retired persons.

A. OVERVIEW OF INCOME MAINTENANCE PROGRAMS

A summary of major income maintenance programs by levels of government is given in Table 33-1. In fiscal 1977, total expenditures on major income

*****Reader's Guide to Chapter 33:** Various transfer programs and techniques of fiscal redistribution are reviewed in this chapter, including the welfare system and alternatives such as the negative income tax. Next we examine social security finance. These are all issues of considerable current importance. They are examined here from a policy point of view, drawing upon our earlier discussion of the underlying principles.

TABLE 33-1
Major Income Maintenance and Welfare Programs
(Fiscal Year 1977, Billions of Dollars)

	Federal Finance	State-Local Finance	Total
Social Insurance			
1. OASI	113.2	—	113.2
2. Medicare	21.5	—	21.5
3. Unemployment	17.8	8.7	26.5
4. Workman's compensation	1.5	7.2	8.7
Total	154.0	15.9	169.9
Public Aid			
5. Public assistance (AFDC)	13.6	7.0	20.6
6. Medicaid	17.6	7.9	25.5
7. Other assistance	3.1	.7	3.8
8. Supplemental security	6.8	1.6	8.4
9. Food stamps	5.4	—	5.4
10. Other	5.9	—	5.9
Total	52.4	17.2	69.6
Selected Other Programs			
11. Hospital and medical care	4.3	5.2	9.5
12. Public housing	2.7	—	2.7
13. Vocational rehabilitation	9.5	—	9.5
14. Child welfare	3.2	.7	3.9
Total	19.7	5.9	25.6
Total	226.1	39.0	265.1

Source: *Social Security Bulletin,* June 1979. Public employee retirement pensions, Railroad Retirement, and veteran's services are omitted in this table.

maintenance programs (broadly defined) approached $300 billion, with most of the financing coming from the federal level, where such expenditures accounted for over 40 percent of total outlays. About half of the federal contribution went to finance retirement and related benefits, with various forms of welfare programs next in importance. State and local governments contributed close to $40 billion, with public assistance, unemployment insurance, workman's compensation, and Medicaid the major items.

The programs given in the table may be grouped in various ways. Items 1 to 4 are part of social insurance and account for two-thirds of the total. OASI (Old Age and Survivor Insurance) is the major item. Public aid (items 5 to 10 in the table) is given on a need basis and accounts for 26 percent. Less than half takes the form of cash programs, mainly AFDC (Aid to Families with Dependent Children), followed in importance by the Supplemental Security Income program. Though need test–based, the latter is now operated as a part of the Social Security Administration. More than half of the aid programs are not in cash form but are given in kind, with Medicaid and the food stamp program the most important items. Another way of distinguishing is between programs providing for retirement, unemployment, health, and other needs, with shares of 42, 10, 20, and 28 percent, respectively.

The three most vexing problems in the area of income maintenance policy have been (1) how to resolve the welfare issue, (2) how to deal with the future requirements of OASI, and (3) whether and how to expand health insurance. These aspects will be considered in turn.

B. INCOME MAINTENANCE FOR THE POOR

The problem of how best to provide income support for the poor has received much attention in recent years. But though there is general dissatisfaction with the status quo, only relatively minor changes have been made.

Present Status of the Welfare System

The welfare system in the United States as shown in Table 33-1 includes both cash payments and in-kind services. Among the former, Aid to Families with Dependent Children (AFDC) is much the most important. It is financed (item 5) jointly by the federal government and the states. Next in importance is the Supplemental Security Income program (item 8), which assists the indigent aged. Even though need-related it is now administered as part of social security. In addition, there is a state-financed general assistance program. Among the in-kind programs, Medicaid (item 6) is much the most important. Financed jointly by the federal government and the states, it provides medical assistance to the needy aged, offering a supplement to Medicare. Next in importance are the food stamp program and various forms of low-cost housing assistance, both of which are paid for by the federal government.

Welfare expenditures have grown rapidly in recent years. Total federal outlays for cash welfare programs increased from $3 billion in 1960 to close to over $20 billion in 1977. The lion's share of this increase was accounted for by AFDC, which rose from $1 billion to over $10 billion. This increase reflects not so much a rise in benefits or in the number of eligible recipients as in the fraction of eligible recipients claiming benefits. Since a high degree of coverage has now been reached, this rising trend should taper off. By mid-1978 some 11 million people received AFDC benefits, and over 4 million received supplemental security income benefits. Adding general assistance, over 15 million out of a total of about 17 million poor people (i.e., people with incomes below the designated poverty line) were covered by one or another program. The major groups excluded were non-aged single individuals, non-aged couples without children, and persons in families headed by a full-time worker. These exclusions are explained by the fact that AFDC ordinarily provides assistance only to families in which the father is dead, incapacitated or absent from the home. At the state's option, it can also be made available to families in which the father is unemployed.

Critique of AFDC Program

As shown in Table 33-1, the major welfare load is carried by the AFDC program. This program has been subject to severe criticism from many sides. Among the major objections which have been raised are the following:

   1. The program is too diverse, made up of fifty-four different state and territorial programs, each plan being separately administered under some broad federal guidelines. Depending on their economic conditions, the states are eligible for federal contributions of 50 to 80 percent. Because of this diversity, there are enormous variations in benefit levels and eligibility requirements. In mid-1978, the nationwide average monthly benefit for a family on AFDC was $251, but a family in New York received $375 while a similar family in Mississippi received $46, or 12 percent as much. While this differential has to be adjusted for differences in the cost of living, it nevertheless leaves a large gap in real terms which in turn encourages rural-urban migration.

2. The program is demeaning in the nature of its eligibility requirements and their enforcement. Moreover, it encourages family disintegration since payments are generally limited to families in which the male head is absent. Unemployed fathers are eligible for assistance in only twenty-three states.

3. The level of benefits is inadequate for a decent minimal standard of living.

4. Single persons and childless couples are completely excluded from the welfare system unless they are blind or disabled.

5. The working poor are not helped. Families in which the father works full time but who are still poor are excluded from the system. In fact, 40 percent of the poor live in families headed by a full-time worker.

6. The program discourages work because it involves a high marginal rate of tax on earnings. Before 1967, recipients lost $1 for every $1 earned, which amounted to a 100 percent tax on earnings. The 1967 amendments to the social security laws allow recipients to keep $30 a month and 33 cents on each $1 earned, which is equivalent to reducing the tax from 100 to 67 percent. If payroll taxes of 12 percent are added, the total rate rises to 79 percent. It may, in fact, be even higher since certain benefits are also lost as income rises.

7. Welfare payments should not be granted independent of work but should be related to a work requirement, an issue which we have encountered previously in considering the bearing of leisure on distributive justice.

8. Welfare administration would be simplified by providing all the support in cash form.

As is evident from the nature of these objections, different views are involved, with point 7 the most controversial. Nevertheless, it is undeniable that dissatisfaction with the present system is widespread. In particular, it is widely agreed that benefits should be extended to the working poor and to poor families without children, and that the disincentive provided by the present system should be modified.

In response to this dissatisfaction, a first reform proposal was made in 1969 by the Nixon administration and was renewed in more or less similar form by the Carter administration in 1977. Under the Carter proposal, the present programs (including AFDC, SSI, and food stamps) would be abolished and be replaced by a uniform system of cash grants.[1] Recipients would be divided into two tiers. Those not required to work (including persons caring for children under age seven and the aged, blind, and disabled) would receive a base annual income of $4,200 (in 1978 dollars) or 65

[1]For a description of the program, see *Congressional Quarterly, Weekly Report,* August 13, 1977.

percent of the poverty level for a family of four. Larger families would receive more. Others would be required to work and, with a family of four, receive a benefit of $2,300. The higher benefit of $4,200 would be paid if no work was available. For most of those required to work, benefits would be unaffected by earnings up to $3,800. For subsequent earnings benefits would be reduced by 50 cents per dollar of additional earning. For a family of four benefits would thus cease as earnings reach $8,400. The federal government would pay for 90 percent of the cost, with 10 percent contributed by the states. In addition, the federal government would make matching grants to states which supplement the basic benefit. The program would involve a restructuring of the present welfare system, rather than a major expansion, with the cost of cash payments estimated to increase from $17 to $22 billion (1978 levels).

The thrust of the reform would be (1) simplification, as a variety of programs would be replaced by a single cash benefit plan, (2) extension of the system to singles and childless families as well as families with children and both spouses present, thereby removing detrimental effects of the present system on family structure, and (3) extension of benefits to low-income earners, thereby reducing disincentive effects on work effort. To increase the effectiveness of the work requirement, the cash benefits would be supplemented by a jobs program aimed especially at the hard-core unemployed. Congressional action on the program is still pending, and more limited reforms have been advanced since.

Work Incentives

The central dilemma in designing a satisfactory income maintenance scheme is the resulting disincentive to work.

Given a limited amount of funds available for redistribution, the most effective way of aiding low-income families would be to distribute by filling in income deficiencies from the bottom, thereby assuring as high a minimum level as the available budget permits. But this approach implicitly imposes a high marginal rate of tax over the low-income range and thus reduces work incentives. Both income and substitution effects are adverse to work effort.[2] To dampen the latter effect, the aid has to be extended higher up the income scale, a policy which in turn reduces the amount of aid which can be given where it is most needed.

A number of alternative aid patterns and their implicit marginal rate of tax are shown in Figure 33-1. In the upper part of each panel, earnings are shown on the horizontal axis and income received (after tax and transfers) is measured on the vertical axis. The 45° line OG shows income in the absence of transfer and tax. Plan I presents the crudest of all approaches, where a fixed subsidy equal to OM is given provided earnings fall short of $OB = OM$ and where the subsidy is lost once earnings exceed OB. As shown in the upper left figure, the subsidy at various levels of earnings is given by the solid

---

[2] See also the earlier discussion of incentive effects of transfer payments, p. 320.

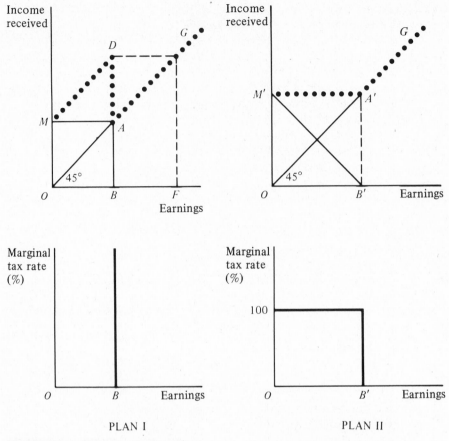

PLAN I   PLAN II

FIGURE 33-1   Alternative Welfare Plans.

line *MAB*, and total income received (or earnings plus subsidy) is given by
the dotted line *MDAG*. As shown in the lower figure, this means that the
marginal tax rate up to earnings *OB* is zero. But for the first dollar above *OB*,
an exceedingly high marginal rate ($100 \times OM$ percent) applies; then the rate
again drops to zero. A person earning *OB* would have to raise his or her
earnings by *BF* only to stay even. While such a scheme may seem absurd, it
does in fact apply where eligibility for low-income services is lost once
income exceeds a fixed limit, as, for example, in eligibility for Medicaid and,
in some state programs, for aid to families with dependent children and an
unemployed father (AFDC-UF).

Plan II, shown in the second panel of Figure 33-1, is more reasonable but
still involves a heavy disincentive. This is a plan where the subsidy equals the
difference between earnings and a set minimum level of income. If this level
is set at *OM′*, the subsidy at various levels of earnings now follows *M′B′*,
while total income (earnings plus subsidy) follows *M′A′G*. As shown in the
lower diagram, the marginal tax rate now equals 100 percent up to earnings
OB′ and becomes zero thereafter. Thus, subsidy recipients have no incentive
to work until they can extend their earnings beyond *OB′*.

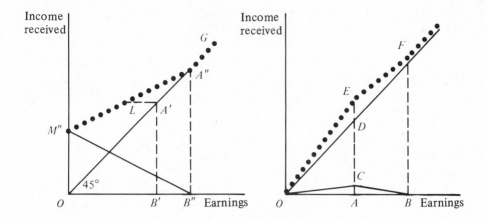

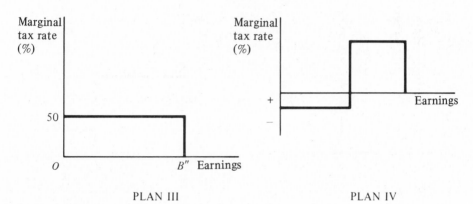

PLAN III   PLAN IV

FIGURE 33-1 (*Continued*)

Plan III, shown in the third panel, is designed to reduce the disincentive. As in plan II, the subsidy declines as earnings rise but less rapidly. Whereas, in formula II, no subsidy was given to persons whose earnings reached OB' (in turn equal to the minimum OM'), benefits in plan III are now enjoyed up to earnings OB''. The subsidy line equals $M''B''$ and the total income line follows $M''A''G$. The marginal tax rate as shown in the lower part of the figure is now less than 100 percent since the subsidy is reduced by only part of the recipient's earnings. As shown here, it equals 50 percent up to earnings OB'', where OB'' is equal to twice the minimum income level OM''. The benefit structure under AFDC is of this type. A welfare mother who earns an extra \$2 loses \$1.34 in support (over a certain range of earnings), thus paying a tax of 62 percent. The food stamp and public housing programs have similar provisions. Plan III has the advantage of imposing a lesser disincentive, since the implicit tax rate on earnings is lower than in Plan II. But it has the disadvantage of either calling for a lower basic subsidy M (as shown in the figure) or involving a higher cost.

Plan IV belongs to a quite different type of approach as the grant is not given as a lump sum amount but as a percent of earnings up to a set level and declining thereafter. The grant thus traces the pattern shown by OCB with the grant equal to AC/AD percent of earnings up to OA. The grant then decreases by AC/AD percent of earnings in excess of OC and vanishes as an income of OB is reached. OEF shows the total earnings line. The tax rate, as shown in the lower part of the diagram, is negative (i.e., a subsidy) up to earnings AB, positive from OA to OB, and zero above AB. This is the scheme followed by the earned income credit, with OA equal to $5,000, AC/AD equal to 10 percent, and OB equal to $10,000. Here the substitution effects up to OA are favorable as the wage rate is increased, with disincentive effects setting in only above that level. The disadvantage of the scheme, however, is that no grants are received in the absence of earnings and the grant rises with increasing earnings or declining need. Thus, redistribution toward the lower end is weaker.

Negative Income Tax

Plan III and variants thereof are also referred to as a negative income tax. The support given to people with no or low earnings may be viewed as a negative tax. As earnings rise, the negative tax falls and at some point reaches zero, after which a positive tax becomes due. The principle is simply that of extending the positive rate structure under the regular income tax downward, going beyond the zero-bracket range of the personal exemption into a negative range. As such, it is a logical extension of the principle of progressive taxation which is generally accepted for the positive part of the tax. Accordingly, various ways have been considered by which the negative tax may be integrated into the positive income tax structure.[3]

In understanding the negative income tax, it is helpful to think of the subsidy received by any one family as

$$s = m - te$$

where s is the subsidy, m is the minimum income, and t is the tax rate (imposed under the negative income tax plan) and applicable to earnings e until the break-even point is reached. The subsidy thus becomes zero where earnings equal m/t, which is also referred to as the break-even level b. Thus, if the tax rate is 50 percent, b will be equal to $2m$. In designing a negative income tax plan, the interesting variables are m, b, t, and the budgetary cost C. The relationship among these variables is shown in Figure 33-2. Minimum income m equals OA and the total income (earnings and subsidy) line is AGE. Break-even income b equals OD. The slope of the total income line AG or tan α equals HG/AH, or the fraction of earnings which are retained as earnings rise.[4] This fraction also equals $1 - t$ or $1 - m/b$.

---

[3]Integration involves such problems as family size, the definition of income (or absence thereof), the tying in of the tax rate on earnings below the break-even point with the regular income tax rates applicable above that level, and so forth. See J. Tobin, J. A. Pechman, and P. Mieszkowski, "Is a Negative Income Tax Practicable?" *Yale Law Journal*, November 1967.

[4]Thus, with earnings OD, total income received equals DG, or the sum of DH (the minimum income allowance) and HG, which is what is left of earnings OD after the tax.

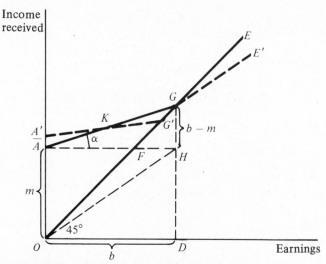

FIGURE 33-2 Structure of Negative Income Tax.

The subsidy at each earnings level equals the distance between the total income line AG and the 45° line. Assuming an equal number of earners at each level, total C cost may be taken to correspond to the area OGA.[5] It follows that for a given cost C, a higher m can be obtained only at the cost of a higher t and a lower b; or that a lower t can be had only at the cost of a lower m and a higher b. Suppose that m is to be raised to OA'. The new total income line $A'G'E$ must then intersect the 45° line at a point below G since the additional cost reflected by the area AKA' must be offset by cost reduction equal to area $KG'G$. Raising m thus raises t by lowering the slope of the total income line and lowers the breakeven point b. Since a high m and low b make for greater redistribution toward the lower end, the desire to redistribute conflicts with the desire to avoid disincentives from a high tax rate.[6]

[5] OGA is the *net* cost left after deducting tax revenue ODH (obtained by appling t to earnings up to OD) from gross cost $ODHA$. This net cost remains to be financed by increasing tax rates applicable to income in excess of OD. The resulting net income line (after allowing for the necessary increase in income tax rates above OD) is illustrated by AGE'.

[6] More generally, the system is defined by two equations:

$$t = m/b \tag{1}$$

$$C = \sum_{i=0}^{i=b} s_i = \sum_{i=0}^{i=b} n_i(m - e_i t) \tag{2}$$

In equation 2, the cost C is defined as the sum of the subsidies s applicable at each level of earnings i times the number at each level of earnings. The subsidy to a family at any one level in turn equals the flat payment m minus the product of tax rate and earnings. Given C, we have two equations with three unknowns, m, b, and t. Substituting, we may write

$$C = \sum_{i=0}^{i=b} n_i t(b - e_i) \tag{3}$$

The choice is thus an unhappy one, and much depends on the weight assigned to the various variables. Using 1975 levels of income, it has been estimated that a plan setting M at the poverty income (equal in 1975 to $5,200 for a family of four) and using a marginal tax rate of 50 percent would have increased the cost of welfare (then $40 billion) by about $30 billion.[7] Using a lower marginal tax rate of, say, 30 percent, the increase would have been above $50 billion. At 1979 levels, the additional cost might be some 20 percent higher.

In making these estimates and in choosing between alternative schemes, much depends on how severe their incentive effects will be. In recent years, various studies have been undertaken to measure these effects on an experimental basis. Sample groups of families have been given payments as would apply under various schemes, and their responses were observed. While the outcomes of such experiments must be taken with a grain of salt, indications are that the responses of primary earners are not very sensitive but that the labor supply of secondary earners is more elastic. In the above estimates, over 20 percent of the additional cost reflects induced decline in earnings and thereby increased transfer requirements.[8]

Considering the substantial increase in cost which would be involved in a generalized negative income tax scheme, it seems unlikely that the present welfare plan will undergo such a drastic overhaul. More likely, there will be a limited reform, including extension of benefits to low-income earners beyond those now provided by the earned-income credit, combined with attempts at effective work requirements as suggested by the Carter Welfare Reform Plan.

C. SOCIAL INSURANCE

The oldest and largest part of the social insurance system is the old-age and survivors insurance (OASI). Enacted in 1935, the program was extended in 1956 to provide benefits for disabled workers or disability insurance (DI). A health insurance plan (HI), giving medical benefits for persons over sixty-five and referred to as "Medicare," was passed in 1965 and has become an important part of the system.

Structure of Retirement and Disability Insurance

When OASI was enacted in 1935, the legislation specified that the program should include all workers under age sixty-five who were engaged in commerce and industry (except railroads) in the United States. Government and railroad employees already had separate schemes. A major expansion in

---

[7]See Michael C. Keeley and Philip Robins, "Work Incentives and the Negative Income Tax," *Challenge Magazine*, March-April 1979; and Michael C. Keeley, Philip Robins, Robert Spiegelman, and Richard West, "The Estimation of Labor Supply Models Using Experimental Data," *American Economic Review*, December 1978.

[8]The experiments showed reductions in hours worked (in response to a negative income tax scheme allowing for a flat payment equal to the poverty income and a tax rate of 50 percent) of 6 percent for husbands, 23 percent for wives, and 12 percent for female heads of household. See Keeley and Robins, op. cit.

coverage occurred in 1950 when regularly employed farm and domestic workers were included as well as the nonfarm self-employed (except certain professionals). By 1965 the latter entered, so that coverage of the working population (except those covered by federal civil service or railroad retirement) was virtually complete, with covered workers now comprising over 90 percent of the labor force.

Currently about 34 million people receive benefits under OASI, totaling $70 billion, and around 5 million people receive disability benefits at a cost of over $11 billion.

Financing Retirement, survivors and disability insurance (OASDI) is financed by a payroll tax, i.e., a tax on wage and salary income. Capital income is not included in the base.[9] Half the tax is paid by the employer and half by the employee.[10] The original legislation levied a combined rate of 2 percent on the first $3,000 of wages. Since then the tax rate and ceiling for covered wages has been raised many times, most recently in 1977. At present (1979–1980) the OASDI tax rate is 5.08 percent for employer and employee each. Of this, 4.33 percent goes for OASI and 0.75 percent for DI. For 1980 this rate applies to wages and salaries up to $25,900. A self-employed person pays at 150 percent of the employee rate. The 1977 legislation also provides for the combined employer and employee (OASDI) rate to rise from its present level of 10.16 percent to 10.8 percent in 1982–1984 and to 12.4 percent by 2011. The ceiling for covered wages is to be raised to $29,000 by 1981, after which it is to rise automatically with the average wage level. This sharp increase was found necessary to keep the system "solvent," a concept to be discussed below.

The level of payroll tax rates as provided under the 1977 legislation, including rates applicable in 1979–1980 and their eventual level in 2011, is as follows:

	1979–1980	2011
OASI (Old Age and Survivors Insurance)	4.33	5.10
DI (Disability Insurance)	.75	1.10
HI (Health Insurance)	1.05	1.45
Total	6.13	7.65

Applicable to employer and employee each, the total tax now equals 12.26 percent and is scheduled to rise to 15.3 percent by 2011.

Old-Age Benefits Determination of OASI benefits follows a complicated procedure. Step 1 is to derive the average monthly earnings on which contributions are paid. In computing the average, earnings since 1950 are totaled (excluding the lowest year) and divided by the number of months

---

[9]For the self-employed person, say a small-business operator, the base is defined as "earnings," which may include capital income.

[10]See p. 505.

between 1950 and retirement. In obtaining the average wage base, past monthly wages are adjusted upward or indexed to allow for the rise in the general wage level since the monthly wages were received.[11] In step 2 this figure of average indexed monthly earnings (AIME) is then used as the base to which a benefit rate schedule is applied. The rate schedule, as revised by the 1977 legislation, begins with 90 percent of the first $180 of AIME and falls to 32 percent for the next $905 and to 15 percent for the remainder. For a couple with one earning spouse only, the family benefit equals 150 percent of the single benefit. Where both spouses meet the covered-earnings requirement, they both receive their benefit claims. The law results in minimum and maximum benefits. Minimum monthly benefits equal $122 per person and are indexed to rise with the price level. Maximum benefits are computed by a special formula and for 1978 equaled $490 for a single retiree and $735 for a couple with both spouses retired. By setting a minimum benefit (which is obtained with a very small contribution only) and using a declining rate schedule, the redistributive component of the system is strengthened further. The average monthly benefit for a single worker retiring in 1978 was $278 per month or $398 for husband and wife. In annual terms, this amounted to $3,336 and $4,776, respectively, significantly above poverty-line incomes for the aged of $2,906 and $3,666, respectively.

As distinct from the income tax, the OASI system is thoroughly protected against inflation. On the contribution side, the wage ceiling up to which earnings are included is indexed beginning in 1981 to rise with the average wage level. On the benefit side, computation of AIME involves upward adjustment of past monthly wages to allow for the increase in the average wage level, thereby correcting not only for inflation but also for the average productivity gain. Moreover, the bracket limits in the benefit formula are indexed so as to rise in future years with the average wage level, and the benefit level as determined at the time of retirement is indexed so as to rise with the cost of living. The replacement rate (ratio of benefit to preretirement income) will thus remain unchanged over the years.

While the formal indexing of the system has been introduced only recently, Congress has raised benefit levels repeatedly over past years. As a result, benefits have more than doubled over the last inflationary decade, thus outrunning inflation and increasing even in real terms. While this does not prove that benefit levels are adequate, social security beneficiaries have not suffered the fate of fixed-income recipients during these years.

Disability Benefits Disability benefits are paid to persons who, prior to age sixty-five, suffer a disability. Benefits are computed in the same way as retirement benefits, and only limited earnings are permitted. The number of recipients has doubled since the mid-sixties and now totals nearly 6 million. Annual benefits amount to $12 billion (1978) and have more than quadrupled

---

[11]For this purpose a set of index numbers is provided by which to inflate the retiree's monthly wage receipts.

over the last fifteen years. This reflects both the increased number of claimants and rising benefit levels.

Issues in OASI

The design of OASI involves certain basic issues which have been debated since the introduction of the system and which are now under renewed discussion. The main issues are:

1. Should retirement insurance be compulsory and public, rather than voluntary and private?
2. Should the system be reserve-financed or on a pay-as-you-go basis?
3. Should the system be quid pro quo or redistributive?
4. Should the system be financed by payroll taxes or a general budgetary contribution?
5. What are the implications of social insurance for capital formation?

These questions though interdependent will be considered in turn.

Public versus Private Provision for Retirement   The issue here involves both the *compulsory* and the *public* nature of OASDI. In dealing with the compulsory aspect, let us suppose that society has already made such adjustments in the distribution of lifetime income as are considered desirable, so that the case of the aged cannot be viewed as part of the general redistribution problem. Why, then, should not individuals be left to decide how they wish to distribute their income over time? The answer is that while most people will provide for their old age, some will fail to do so. Assuming that society will not permit its imprudent to starve when they become aged, this will over time impose a further burden on the more prudent. To protect themselves against this contingency, they will impose compulsory insurance. Alternatively, the compulsory approach may be viewed as a paternalistic decision by society to protect the imprudent against starvation in old age.

Given that compulsory insurance is needed, why should it be *public* rather than take the form of requiring the purchase of private insurance? At first sight, there would seem little difference between requiring the purchase of policies in private insurance companies or in public insurance. The advantage of taking out a retirement insurance rather than providing on one's own is that the length of life is uncertain. By pooling the risk with others, the cost of provision is reduced. This, however, does not require public insurance. The size of private companies is such that they can exhaust the economies of scale in spreading risk. Nevertheless, public insurance can offer a better deal. Under a private system, a reserve must be accumulated that is sufficient in amount to finance the benefits for all insured and to provide the insured with a return equal to the interest that was earned. Under the public system, a pay-as-you-go approach may be used so that no such reserve is required. Each working person can be asked to support the retired population and in turn can be supported after retirement by the next generation. Viewing this arrangement as a continuing process which never ceases, it may be shown that the rate of return to the participants will be higher under the public system, provided that the combined rates of population and productivity growth (i.e., the growth of the tax base) will exceed the real rate of interest.[12] Such has been the outlook until recently, but, as noted below, the situation is changing.

A further distinction between the social and private approach is that the former permits the introduction of redistributional elements, while the latter is inherently on a quid-pro-quo basis.

Reserve versus Pay-as-You-Go Finance and the Issue of Intergeneration Equity   When the social security system was first established in the thirties, one option was to take a strict insurance view. Under this approach, the then old would go without benefits, since they had not contributed, while those working would begin to contribute so as to earn future benefits. Since contributors would become eligible only at retirement, contributions would initially exceed benefit payments. It would be necessary to build up and invest a reserve which at the later date would yield an interest income. This income, in conjunction with a constant tax rate, would pay for the benefits. In line with this principle of *actuarial solvency*, comparable to that followed by private insurance companies, a large trust fund would be accumulated and invested.[13] According to initial estimates, this fund was to grow until 1970, when the system would mature. In this way, each generation would pay for its own benefits, with the initial generation of retirees remaining out of the system.

The alternative was to treat those already retired, as well as early retirees, as if they had contributed during their working lives. This called for payroll tax rates to be set so as to keep the system on a pay-as-you-go basis, with those in the labor force contributing what was needed to pay for the benefits. Under this system, the initial generation of retirees would be given a gift by those still in the labor force. But the latter would not lose as they would be compensated later on when, at the time of their own retirement, they would be supported by the contributions of their children, who by then had moved into the labor force. This process would continue forever or, less optimistically, until doomsday, when the last generation of working age would be left with having contributed but without being able to enjoy their old age.

While there was some uncertainty at the outset as to which approach was to be followed, the system soon moved into a pay-as-you-go position. Although tax rates were set initially to provide for reserve accumulation, the trust fund grew slowly and came to be considered as a contingency reserve

---

[12]See Henry Aaron, "The Social Insurance Paradox," *Canadian Journal of Economics and Political Science*, August 1966.

[13]The mechanics of implementing this plan would involve substitution of a stabilization mix with tighter fiscal and easier monetary policy. Higher payroll tax receipts would reduce consumption while use of surplus receipts for retirement of debt would permit a higher level of private investment. Thus, debt would be shifted from the public to the social security trust fund, where the growth of interest income would permit financing of future benefits at a lower rate of payroll tax.

only. After reaching $20 billion in 1953, the fund showed little change up to the late 1960s, when it once more started to rise, reaching $39 billion in 1975. Since then, reserves in relation to current obligations have declined, with the fund now being down to below $30 billion and sufficient to sustain a few months of benefit payments only.

Nevertheless, the principle of pay-as-you-go was not to be carried to the point of setting payroll tax rates each year in line with benefit requirements. Rather, it has been considered desirable to set rates well ahead so as to cover benefit requirements for, say, a 30-year period. This concept of *pay-as-you-go solvency* has proven difficult to implement. For one thing, the long-run estimates of relevant variables such as population growth, productivity growth, retirement age, labor force participation rates and employment levels proved extremely difficult to make and went wrong repeatedly. For another, Congress repeatedly raised benefit levels beyond those assumed when setting earlier tax contribution rates. For these and other reasons, it became evident by 1977 that a substantial increase in contributions would be needed to maintain the system on a basis of pay-as-you-go basis. Thus a substantial increase in future contributions was legislated in the 1977 revision.

The necessity for this action came about because the trend toward a declining rate of population growth pointed to a rising ratio of working to retired population. Whereas 38 persons now collect benefits for 100 workers taxed, it is estimated that by the year 2030, there will be 54 supported persons per 100 workers. The average burden on the working population will be 50 percent larger, thus requiring higher contribution rates. At the same time, the outlook for productivity growth has become less favorable. The advantages of pay-as-you-go finance, which were so attractive in a period of expanding anticipations (with rapid population and productivity growth), have thus dimmed. Unless future generations prove willing to accept rising rates of payroll tax, the readers of this volume may find their participation in the scheme to yield a rather low rate of return. Nevertheless, the outlook is not all bleak. Productivity gains will continue, so higher payroll tax rates need not mean lower net incomes. Moreover, as population growth declines, the rising dependency ratio of retirees to working population will be offset in part by a declining ratio of children to adults.

Quid Pro Quo versus Redistribution: The Problem of Intrageneration Equity   Apart from the question of intergeneration equity and transfers, there is the further question of equity and transfers within each generation. If the system was conducted strictly as an insurance plan, each person would receive benefits which reflect the same rate of return on her or his contribution. The pensioner in turn would have a contractual right to such benefits. As distinct from this approach, the system from its inception has been redistributive, granting a more favorable treatment to those with lower incomes. At the same time, this has been held compatible in the context of *social* insurance, with the principle that contributions establish a contractual right to subsequent benefits.

The degree of redistribution differs depending on how one looks at the problem, i.e., whether we consider

   1. The distribution of current contributions and payments by income brackets

   2. The replacement rate or ratio of current benefits to contributions at various income levels

   3. The internal rate of return to contributors with various levels of lifetime earnings

We begin with the *distribution of benefits and contributions by income brackets*. If we assign the benefits and tax contributions (received and made in a particular year) to households arranged by income brackets, we find that low incomes show an excess of benefits over contributions while the reverse holds for high incomes. This is brought out in Table 33-2. While the estimates there given apply to 1966 data, the general pattern would be the same if repeated for the higher levels of present income. Receipts are in excess of contributions up to a point in the income scale somewhat above the median, and then fall below. Viewed in this way, OASI is highly redistributive in nature.

This way of looking at the matter, however, is misleading. The aged who receive benefits typically have low incomes, while the working part of the population who contribute typically have higher incomes. As a result, the degree of redistribution among income groups with income measured on an annual basis (as underlies the procedure of Table 33-2) will necessarily be larger than would be the case if the analysis was based on lifetime incomes.

A better picture is obtained by considering what happens to the *ratio of benefits to covered earnings* as earnings rise. For a hypothetical worker retiring in 1980, benefits as a percentage of final covered earnings are estimated to equal 55 percent for a low-income earner, 43 percent for a middle-income earner, and 27 percent for a person with maximum earnings, corresponding to 1976 earnings levels of $4,600, $9,200, and $15,300, respectively.[14] The sharp decline in this ratio, also referred to as the "replacement rate," reflects the benefit formula which gives decreasing weight to successive increments of income and which provides for minimum and maximum benefits.

This comparison, however, still remains unsatisfactory. To obtain a valid picture, we should estimate the *rates of return* which workers with various levels of contribution receive from their investment in social security claims. That is to say, we should estimate the expected benefit and cost streams and then compute the internal rate of return inherent in these two streams.[15]

In considering the various factors which enter into the rate of return, we note that ability to command a high wage rate will result in a higher lifetime

---

[14]See *Social Security Bulletin*, March 1978, p. 13. The corresponding replacement rates for a hypothetical low, middle, and high earner retiring in the year 2020 are 56, 43, and 29 percent, thus showing very little change.

[15]See p. 192 for a discussion of this concept.

TABLE 33-2
Distribution of Social Security Taxes and Benefits, 1966 Law

Items	FAMILY MONEY INCOME										
	Under $3,500	$3,500– 5,000	$5,000– 6,500	$6,500– 8,000	$8,000– 10,000	$10,000– 15,000	$15,000– 20,000	$20,000– 30,000	$30,000– 50,000	Over 50,000	All
Percentage by Brackets											
Benefits	49.7	14.7	9.6	6.6	5.0	8.6	3.6	1.6	0.3	0.3	100.0
Taxes*	4.6	5.4	8.9	13.2	16.2	29.8	13.1	6.0	2.0	0.8	100.0
As Percentage of Income											
Benefits	54.2	17.8	7.2	3.6	2.1	1.7	1.2	0.9	0.3	0.3	5.2
Taxes*	5.1	6.7	6.8	7.3	6.8	6.1	4.6	3.6	2.0	0.8	5.4
Net	49.1	11.1	0.4	-3.7	-4.7	-4.4	-3.4	-2.7	-1.7	-0.5	-0.2

*The worker is assumed to bear the entire burden of the payroll tax.
Sources: R. A. Musgrave, Karl E. Case, and Herman Leonard, "The Distribution of Fiscal Burdens and Benefits," *Public Finance Quarterly,*
July 1974; also see Table 16-1, p. 337.

income. Given the benefit formula which discriminates against successive slabs of earnings and sets a benefit ceiling, this renders the system redistributive toward lower income. There are, however, a number of factors which work in the other direction. For one thing, some low-wage earners enter the labor force at an earlier date, which lengthens the contribution period. For another, the lifetime earnings of low-wage earners tend to peak at an earlier age. As a result, their tax contributions are made sooner, which lowers the internal rate of return. Moreover, low-wage earners have a lower life expectancy and thus on the average have a shorter retirement period over which benefits are received. These latter factors dampen the redistributive pattern, but a substantial differential remains. Thus it has been estimated that for a white married couple with less than seven years of schooling (and a corresponding typical level of lifetime income) the internal rate of return is close to 6 percent, while for a white couple with over thirteen years of schooling (and a corresponding lifetime income), the rate is only 4.6 percent.[16]

Payroll Tax Finance versus Budgetary Contribution   While Congress accepted the reality of pay-as-you-go finance and recognized the redistributive nature of the system, it has held steadfastly to the idea that the system should be considered as providing for insurance, not old-age relief. This had led to insistence that benefits continue to be financed from payroll tax contributions. This position has for some time been attacked by economists who have argued that the contributory nature of the system is fictitious and that payroll taxes are an undesirable form of finance. Given that each generation of retirees has its benefits paid for by those of working age and that there is substantial intrageneration redistribution, reliance on the contributory principle is said to make little sense. Benefits, so the critics conclude, should be financed out of the general budget, making use of superior forms of taxation. Moreover, they should be viewed as part of a general income maintenance program, applicable to all low-income persons whether young or old. This is supported by the fact that a much larger portion of the aged are poor than is the case for the remainder of the population.

The argument is persuasive in some respects but pays too little attention to how retirees wish to perceive the system. Under a contributory format they are entitled to feel that benefits have been earned and are not a matter of general support. This attitude has social merit and needs to be respected in the financial design of the system. Moreover, old-age insurance, conceived as social insurance, need not be incompatible with some element of redistribution. Given these considerations, the problem is one of finding a compromise solution which respects the economic realities of the situation as well as the social attitudes which are involved.

Given the widespread support of the insurance approach, including support by labor unions, it is unlikely that a drastic revamping of social

---

[16]Based on provisions similar to those of the 1977 amendment. See Dean R. Reimer, *Projected Rates of Return to Future Social Security Retirees under Alternative Benefit Structures*, Social Security Administration, Internal Memoranda, February 1978.

security and its integration into a broader income maintenance scheme are in the cards. Nevertheless, various directions of reform may be considered.

1. Part of the OASDI system's cost may be met from sources other than payroll tax revenue, to be paid out of general budget revenue and to be transferred to the social security fund. This would protect the principle that the system should have its "own" revenue, although less use would be made of the payroll tax. It may well be that Congress might want to consider a value-added tax for this purpose.

2. Another approach would involve reform of the payroll tax itself, so as to render it less regressive. Such a change was in fact made in 1977 when the additional revenue need was met largely by raising the covered wage ceiling rather than increasing the rate of tax. Further moves in this direction could take the form of allowing an exemption, as under the income tax.

3. A third and more far-reaching reform would be to divide the system into two parts. One would be on a strictly contributory and nonredistributive basis, also referred to as a quid pro quo system, while the other would be financed out of the general budget and would be strictly redistributional in approach.[17] The latter would involve an expansion of the Supplemental Security Income payments which were made part of the social security system. However, these payments at $6 billion are small compared to OASI payments of $69 billion (1977). If the system were divided into two parts, the latter might well reach one-third of the total.

Among these various approaches, 1 and 2 are more likely to be implemented than 3, and it may well be that legislation along these lines will be adapted before another revision of this text is undertaken.

Effects on Capital Formation   Another major issue in the current discussion relates to the effects of OASI on the rate of savings. With old-age needs provided for by social security benefits, so it is argued, people will find it less necessary to set aside private savings. They save by paying payroll tax and accumulating benefit claims. This would leave total savings unaffected if their contributions were in turn saved and invested by the trust fund. But such is not the case since the system is on a pay-as-you-go basis, so that this year's contributions are used to pay this year's benefits. The hypothesis is that saving is curtailed, less capital is accumulated, and the economy grows less rapidly.

This is the basic reasoning behind the proposition that the social security system as now operated reduces saving and thereby is detrimental to growth.[18] At closer consideration, it is not so obvious, however, that people

---

[17]For such a proposal, see Munnell, *The Future of Social Security*, op. cit., chap. 5.

[18]See Martin Feldstein, "Social Security, Induced Retirement and Aggregate Capital Accumulation," *Journal of Political Economy*, September-October 1975; Alicia Munnell, *The Future of Social Security*, Washington: Brookings, 1977, chap. 6; and Alicia Munnell, *Effect of Social Security on Personal Saving*, Cambridge: Ballinger, 1974; Selig Lesnoy and John C. Hambor, "Social Security, Saving and Capital Formation," *Social Security Bulletin*, July 1975; Louis Esposito, "Effects of Social Security on Saving: Review of Studies Using US Time Series Data," *Social Security Bulletin*, May 1978.

will replace their private saving with their "social security saving." To begin with, the availability of social security benefits may cause them to retire sooner, which will increase the need to accumulate for old age. Next, the availability of a minimal retirement income may increase peoples' taste for security and raise their savings target. Finally, it may be that the availability of social security benefits to the aged will be offset by reduced support which they may expect from their children, thus leaving unaffected the incentive during working age to supplement outside support (be it from social insurance or family support) through additional own-savings.[19] Given these complications, it is not surprising that efforts to estimate the effects of social security on private saving have been controversial and inconclusive.

Moreover, even if private saving is displaced, it need not follow that the social security system results in a continuing reduction in net saving for society as a whole. As the system is introduced, and assuming pay-as-you-go finance to begin with, the initial generation of contributors may replace private saving by its payroll tax contribution, thus causing a reduction in net saving. But this is a once-and-for-all effect only. Suppose that we have a constant population with constant per capita income and an ongoing social security system. The pay-as-you-go social security system will then pay to the old in benefits what the young contribute in revenue. No net saving or dissaving will result. Much the same holds under private provision for retirement. In this case, the young will save but the old will dissave an equal amount, leaving society as a whole once more without saving. In short, while the prospect of social security benefits displaces private saving by the young, benefit payments also displace private dissaving by the old. In such a setting, there is no presumption that net saving from society as a whole will be less under the social security system.

Nevertheless, the presumption holds for a situation of increasing population or productivity. If population rises, the young who save under the private system are larger in number than the old who dissave. Similarly, if productivity increases, the young (anticipating a higher income) will save more than the old (who did their saving at a lower income level) will dissave. Under the pay-as-you-go social security system, these net savings will not result, as the young need to contribute only what the aged have accumulated in benefit claims. Stated in this qualified way, the system may be said to dampen the rate of saving, but the effect will be less than may be expected at first.

Nevertheless, concern over inadequate saving in the United States has led some observers to argue that payroll tax rates should be raised more

---

[19]The situation is more complex if family relations between parents and children are allowed for. Thus it has been argued that parents will increase their bequests to their children if (as is the case under pay-as-you-go) their children will have to support them in old age. If so, increased saving for bequests will take the place of saving for retirement, with no initial reduction in saving. (See Robert J. Barro, "Are Government Bonds Net Wealth," *Journal of Political Economy*, November-December 1974.) Alternatively, suppose that, as was the case prior to the social security system, children supported their parents in old age. Once more savings would not be affected as direct support of parents by children is replaced by payroll tax support, (See Martin Feldstein, "The Effect of Social Security on Saving," Working Paper No. 334, National Bureau of Economic Research.)

sharply than needed to maintain pay-as-you-go solvency, thus moving toward reserve finance. By making an at least partial return to reserve accumulation, social security finance may be used as a cure for undersaving. This raises issues of both intergeneration equity and economic feasibility:

1. If public sector saving is to be increased by raising taxes, such increase need not be accomplished by raising the payroll tax. It may be done also by raising other and less regressive taxes.

2. If the young are asked to contribute more, their return from social security will be reduced. Their children in turn will be left in a better position. They will have to contribute less since benefit payments to their parents will be paid for in part by the earnings of an increased Social Security Trust Fund. This spreading of the burden may be fair enough, especially in a period of aging population and declining ratio of labor force to retirees. However, increasing productivity will leave the future generation better off, so that such spreading may not be needed.

3. However this may be, the argument for reserve accumulation presumes that the reserve which is accumulated is in fact invested in capital formation, so that future incomes will be larger. For this to be possible, economic conditions must be such as to permit the budget to be operated at a lower level of deficit or higher level of surplus, without thereby interfering with the high-employment and stable-price-level goals of stabilization policy. If, instead, maintenance of high employment requires a deficit, then a surplus in the social security system may have to be offset by an increased deficit somewhere else. Finally, and quite apart from economic reasoning, it is questionable whether congressional politics would in fact put surplus payroll tax revenue to such uses.

Further Issues   A number of further issues, now under lively discussion, may be noted.

1. It has been suggested that the age of benefit eligibility be raised from its present level of sixty-five. This would relieve financing needs. However, a corresponding extension of work opportunities would be needed.

2. The earnings ceiling now applicable to persons above sixty-five might be raised further or dropped altogether so as to remove work disincentives for the aged. Indeed, incentives might be given to postpone retirement.[20]

3. At present, civil service personnel (federal, state, and local) are not required to be part of OASI but have their separate insurance systems. Broadening of mandatory membership in OASI is under consideration.

4. As with the income tax, special problems arise in the treatment of the family and second earners. A retired couple with only one eligible earner now receives 150 percent of the single benefit. Consequently, the net additional benefit obtained should the second worker become eligible is reduced. Various approaches to dealing with this problem are under consideration.

---

[20]Under present law a retired person may earn up to $5,000 ($6,000 beginning 1982) without losing benefits. For earnings beyond this amount, benefits are reduced by 50 cents per dollar of earnings. This provision does not apply to retirees above age seventy-two (age seventy beginning 1982). Unpublished manuscript.

Health Insurance

The social security system now provides health insurance (Medicare) for the aged. In addition, provision is made outside social insurance for medical assistance (Medicaid) to the indigent independent of age.

Medicare   The Medicare program has grown rapidly since its inception in 1962, reaching $7 billion by 1970 and $22 billion by 1977. The amount involved thus equals one-third of OASDI payments. Rapid further growth may be expected due to a continued rise in the cost of medical services well ahead of the average inflation rate.

The major share in the cost of Medicare goes to finance hospital insurance, based on a payroll tax contribution of 1.05 percent on employer and employee each, which rate is to rise to 1.35 percent in 1981 and 1.45 percent in 1986. The remainder of Medicare, providing for the cost of physicians' services and drugs, is financed by a contribution from the general budget.

Proposals are now under consideration to finance the entire cost of Medicare through the general budget. This would cut payroll tax finance for the system as a whole (OASDHI) by about twenty percent. Proponents argue that health hazards are not earnings-related and therefore should not be financed by payroll tax.

Beyond this, the major political controversy centers around whether health insurance should be extended to include not only the aged but the entire population, and if so, how this should be done. If coverage were extended to disaster insurance only, e.g., to major surgery, the amounts involved would be relatively limited. But if a broad coverage is applied, very large amounts equal to or exceeding those involved in OASDI may be called for. Payroll tax finance of such a program could easily add ten percentage points to present payroll tax rates. Including 12.26 percent for the present OASDHI and 4 percent for unemployment insurance, this approach could push total rates well above 25 percent, a level comparable with those found in European countries but not readily acceptable here.

Instead, a divided system might be used, calling for direct-fee finance of public health insurance in line with the cost of risks, while subsidizing fees payable by low-income contributors out of general budget revenue. The issue of health insurance finance and its claim upon payroll taxes, even more than OASDI reform, is likely to be the major factor in the future role of this tax. As noted before, broadening of health insurance and the required potential increase in the rate of payroll taxation might well offer encouragement to adoption of a value-added tax in the federal revenue system, with revenue derived therefrom used as partial replacement for the payroll tax in the finance of social insurance.

As distinct from the scope and finance of a broadened system of health insurance, there is the further question of how introduction of such a system would affect the form in which medical services are supplied, the role of private insurance carriers, the freedom to choose doctors, and so forth. As has been noted at the beginning of this volume, a distinction should be drawn between public provision and public production. Broadening of health insurance may involve varying degrees of public control over the supply of medical services, a question into which we cannot enter here.

Medicaid The Medicaid program provides health services for low-income adults and children. The program is conducted by the states, but over half the cost is provided through federal aid. Total federal outlays for the program are estimated at $12.7 billion for fiscal 1980, or about one-third of the cost of Medicare. Propelled by the rising cost of medical services, the Medicaid budget may be expected to increase sharply in future years. However, if a national system of health insurance is to be introduced, the services now rendered by Medicaid may be combined with the general insurance system, with budgetary contributions used to finance services rendered to the indigent.

D. UNEMPLOYMENT INSURANCE

Unemployment insurance is provided by a set of state systems, but tax collections and the handling of the trust funds (kept separate for each state) are managed at the federal level. Benefits in 1977 amounted to $13 billion. The average payroll tax payable by the employer is 4 percent and applies to the first $4,200 of earnings. However, tax rates vary by state and in accordance with the employment experience of particular firms. This principle of experience rating was introduced as an incentive to stabilize employment and as a way not to impose an undue burden on high-employment firms.

Congress in 1970 provided for financial support from the federal government to pay benefits for an additional thirteen weeks beyond the normal benefit period of twenty-six weeks when the unemployment rate exceeds 4.5 percent and for states which show an especially sharp rise in unemployment. Extended further in 1975, this points to a more uniform approach to unemployment insurance on a nationwide basis. However this may be, it is generally recognized that unemployment insurance can provide only a temporary solution and cannot take care of widespread unemployment. The only effective approach to unemployment consists of stabilization and manpower policies designed to maintain high-employment levels.

E. SUMMARY

Three major components of the transfer system have been distinguished, including welfare programs directed at maintaining the income of the poor, insurance programs directed at retirement and health, and unemployment insurance.

1. Among the three, the welfare program is the most controversial.

2. Among various components of the welfare program, AFDC is much the most important and has been subject to most criticism.

3. Reform proposals made in 1969 by President Nixon and repeated in quite similar form in 1978 by President Carter were not enacted. The major directions of reform would extend benefit payments to the working poor and strengthen work requirements.

4. A major problem with regard to low-income support is posed by its effect on work incentives. With aid related inversely to earnings, the recipient is in effect subject to a high marginal tax rate on his or her earnings.

5. Proposals for a negative income tax have tried to deal with this difficulty by avoiding too high a marginal rate.

Much the most important component of the social security system is the old-age, survivors, and disability insurance (OASDI) to which a limited insurance for hospital services for the aged (Medicare) was added in 1965.

6. Combined payroll tax contributions under OASDI now amount to 5.08 percent on employer and employee each, applicable to the first $25,900 of wage income.

7. Health (Medicare) is financed by a payroll tax of 1.05 percent on employer and employee each.

8. Unemployment insurance is financed by a 4 percent tax on the employer.

9. Reflecting an anticipated sharp increase in the ratio of retirees to labor force, 1977 legislation provided for substantial increases in the payroll tax in the course of the 1980s. Most of this increase takes the form of raising the ceiling for covered earnings.

10. OASDI is rendered inflation-proof by various indexing provisions.

11. While the social security system was planned originally as a system which would function on a quid pro quo basis, it has become redistributive in favor of lower-income households.

12. Originally planned on the basis of reserve finance, the system has moved steadily toward a pay-as-you-go basis.

13. Under current debate is the question of whether the finance of OASDI should be shifted in part to a general budgetary contribution, and whether the payroll tax should be amended so as to make it less regressive.

14. A major factor in the future of the payroll tax will be emerging development of a national health insurance plan.

15. Unemployment insurance continues as an important but less controversial part of the social security system.

FURTHER READINGS

Aaron, H. J.: *Why Is Welfare So Hard to Reform?* Washington: Brookings, 1973.

Brittain, J. A.: *Payroll Taxes for Social Security*, Washington: Brookings, 1972.

Green, C.: *Negative Income Taxes and the Poverty Problem*, Washington: Brookings, 1967.

Munnell, Alicia H.: *The Future of Social Security*, Washington: Brookings, 1977.

Tobin, J.: "Raising the Income of the Poor," in K. Gordon (ed.), *Agenda for the Nation*, Washington: Brookings, 1969.

Van Gorkom, J. W.: "Social Security," *Across the Board*, National Industrial Conference Board, March 1979. Offers an excellent description of the social security system.

Chapter 34

Public Pricing and
Environmental Policy*

A. Public Sale of Private Goods. B. Marginal Cost Pricing in Decreasing Cost Industries: *The Policy Dilemma; Deficit Paid from General Revenue; Deficit Paid for by User Charges: Two-Part Tariff; Deficit Covered by Price Discrimination; Public Utility Regulation; Public Pricing and Imperfect Markets; Distributional Considerations.* **C. Peak-Load Pricing:** *Given Plant; Variable Plant Size.* **D. Pricing of Social Facilities:** *Uncongested Facility; Congested Facility; New Facilities.* **E. Pricing Pollution:** *Efficiency and Equity Aspects of Pollution; Sources of Pollution and Types of Damage; The Efficient Solution; Lack of Information; Instruments of Control; Equity Aspects; Federalism Aspects; Political Aspects; Current Policies.* **F. Summary.**

Provision for social goods, as discussed in Chapter 3, typically involves situations where sale to particular consumers is either impossible (because exclusion cannot be applied) or undesirable (because consumption is nonrival).[1] In this chapter, various situations are considered where government

---

* *Reader's Guide to Chapter 34:* In this chapter, we consider two public sector activities which, though not purely budgetary in nature, involve problems very similar to those encountered in tax and expenditure policy. These are the problems of public pricing and pollution. The general reader may wish to bypass the two more technical sections dealing with peak-load pricing (pp. 748–750) and pollution abatement with variable technology (pp. 756–758). The remainder is a straightforward application of previously discussed principles to two important policy issues.
    [1]See p. 57.

supplies goods or services which *can* be sold and where direct payment may be appropriate, and yet where the pricing problem is such that it cannot be readily handled in the market. This may be due to decreasing costs, with subsidies, regulation, or public operation called for; or it may be due to the existence of external costs which are not reflected in price, in which case taxes may be used to internalize such costs and to apply the necessary correction.

A. PUBLIC SALE OF PRIVATE GOODS

The basic rule for efficient pricing is that price should be equal to marginal cost. So long as marginal cost (*MC*) falls short of price or average revenue (*AR*), society gains by producing more. This is so because marginal cost measures the resource cost to society of producing an additional unit while price measures the value of an additional unit to the consumer. The gain from increased output continues up to the point where the two are equal. Beyond this point, additional output involves a net loss to the economy since marginal cost will then lie above price or the value of the marginal unit. This is the rule of "marginal cost pricing" which is central to the discussion of this chapter.

Where private goods are provided through a competitive market, the marginal cost pricing rule is complied with. The selling firms are confronted with horizontal demand schedules since they furnish only a small part of total supply. This being the case, average revenue and marginal revenue (*MR*) are the same. The firms, by equating marginal cost with marginal revenue, also equate marginal cost with average revenue or price. In long-run equilibrium, with the industry operating under conditions of constant or increasing cost, each firm will also operate at a minimum average cost (*AC*) where $AR = AC$ and no losses or monopolistic profits are made.

In an economy such as ours, the government is generally not in the business of producing and selling private goods. This activity is typically left to private firms. However, situations may arise where government does sell such goods. Thus the sale of tobacco is run as a government enterprise in some countries; and the sale of liquor is frequently operated through state liquor stores in the United States. In these cases, the government places itself in the position of a monopolist who is confronted with the entire, and hence declining, market demand curve. Following the behavior of a private monopolist, it could equate *MR* and *MC* so as to maximize profits, leaving $AR > MC$. The efficient solution for the government is not to follow this pattern and exploit its monopoly power, but to provide the competitive industry result. While the determination of this efficient solution might be difficult without competitive markets, once achieved, it will allow for price just to cover full cost, thus permitting the cost to be charged to the consumers of the service.

If the government does not follow this rule but charges a higher price, this practice may be considered equivalent to imposing an excise tax on the product. Imposition of such a tax, as shown previously, distorts resource allocation and involves an excess burden, unless considered justified by "demerit good" considerations.[2] The latter may be the case in the pricing of tobacco and liquor products which are frequently supplied through public sales.

B. MARGINAL COST PRICING IN DECREASING COST INDUSTRIES

More typically, the government supplies goods which cannot be provided efficiently by private firms because production is subject to decreasing costs. This is the case with public utilities such as water and electricity supplies, public transport systems, and the Postal Service. These are situations—also referred to as "natural monopolies"—where a competitive market cannot function because larger firms can produce at a lower cost, and ultimately a single firm tends to supply the entire market. Without government intervention, profit maximizing behavior by the resulting monopoly would entail too little output at too high a price. Although government regulation is one alternative, the existence of decreasing costs implies that the firm would suffer losses if forced to operate where price equals marginal cost. Thus, the government may prefer to render the service itself, and a public enterprise is substituted for regulation of the private firm.

The Policy Dilemma

The situation is explained in Figure 34-1, where AC and MC are long-run average and marginal cost curves of the industry (which in this case is the same as the firm) and AR and MR are the average and marginal revenue schedules. Following the $AR = MC$ rule, the efficient price is set at P_{mc} and output equals OA. Since AC is declining, MC must lie below AC; and since $AR = MC$ at output OA, it follows that AC is larger than AR. Thus a loss is incurred. In the figure, the unit loss equals BC and the total loss equals $P_{mc}BCD$.

A private firm would avoid this problem by equating MR and MC so as to maximize profits with price P_m and output limited to OE. There is no excuse for public policy to charge P_m unless it is desired to impose what amounts to an excise tax on the product. As a further possibility, might not government avoid the loss by charging an average cost price, thus equating AR with AC? With output OF and price P_{ac}, the firm would break even, but output OF would still be below the efficient level OA. There is no getting around the fact that efficient pricing calls for price P_{mc} and output OA, but this leaves a deficit which must be covered somehow.

Deficit Paid from General Revenue

One way of covering the deficit is to tax the general public, but this poses new problems. If such a tax were imposed in the form of a lump-sum tax, no

[2]See p. 85.

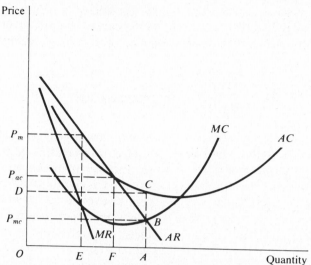

FIGURE 34-1   Marginal and Average Cost Pricing.

efficiency cost would be involved, but the solution would be unacceptable on ability-to-pay grounds. If the tax were imposed more equitably, say as an income tax, its imposition would create an efficiency cost. This efficiency cost must be weighed against that which would result if price were equated with average cost (with output reduced to OF) with no outside finance needed. The more elastic the demand for the product, the greater will be the efficiency loss due to setting price above P_{mc}; and the more elastic the labor supply, the greater will be the inefficiency caused by income tax finance. There would seem to be a presumption in most cases that the latter would involve a smaller efficiency cost than the excise tax equivalent of average cost pricing, imposed on the particular service. However, there may be exceptions, especially where demand is highly inelastic.

Deficit Paid for by User Charges: Two-Part Tariff

Moreover, general revenue finance may be held inequitable in terms of benefit taxation since the general public is charged for the financing of a specific service, rather than the users who benefit therefrom. Yet, finance by user charge so as to cover total cost would raise price above the efficient level (where $AR = MC$) and place output below it. To escape or minimize this dilemma, techniques have been developed to recover full costs from users with a smaller efficiency loss than would result from charging a unit price equal to P_{ac}.

One way of doing so is by means of a "two-part tariff." This involves supplementing a charge per unit of service with a flat charge which must be paid if any use is to be made of the service at all. Such a charge or membership fee would be in the nature of a lump-sum tax on the users of the facility. It would have a substitution effect only on the choice between total abstinence or participation; but it would not have a substitution effect on choosing the level of use once the membership fee has been paid. The assumption is that demand for general access to the service will be less elastic than that relating to the level of utilization. If the deficit with marginal cost pricing is small enough and the number of users is large, the required flat fee may be sufficiently low so that very few potential users will be kept from participation. In this case, the efficiency problem is solved without requiring general finance.[3]

Such techniques are in fact used in many instances of public utility pricing. In the case of telephone charges in many areas, local calls are not billed separately but are included in a flat user fee, with only toll calls billed on a unit basis. Electricity and water supply are also typically priced so as to include a flat charge, with additional charges related to the units of consumption. A further example, relating to highway finance, is the combined use of a basic charge and unit tolls, where tolls are reduced for cars which have paid the annual sticker fee.

Deficit Covered by Price Discrimination

Another approach would be to apply price discrimination. Here the consumer would be charged the price P_{mc} for the last unit but would be called upon to pay higher prices for the earlier units. A part of his or her consumer surplus would thus be taxed away to help cover the deficit. Since different consumers have different incomes and tastes, their demand schedules differ. An equitable solution would call for different rate schedules to be applied to the intramarginal units of various consumers. Some elements of this approach are illustrated by the granting of quantity discounts in the pricing of electric power, where intramarginal and marginal units are charged differentiated prices, and in rate differentiation among types of users, such as residential and commercial.

In a situation where the firm sells more than one product, reduction of the deficit by charging a price in excess of MC can be accomplished with a smaller efficiency cost by concentrating the excess charges on the product for which demand is less elastic to price. This stands to reason, since output will be reduced less and therefore the loss of consumer surplus will be smaller. The principle is similar to that previously encountered in considering the excess burden of product taxes which is less for goods with inelastic demand.[4]

Public Utility Regulation

Public utility regulation, in determining allowable charges, typically proceeds on the premise that total costs, including a fair return to capital, should be covered. In determining this return, the usual approach taken is that the return to capital invested in public utilities should be in line with that earned

---

[3]For a local government enterprise, the output of which is consumed by local residents, the use of a general local revenue source may be viewed as the flat-charge component of the two-part tariff, since participation in the service hinges on local residence.

[4]See W. Baumol and D. Bradford, "Optimal Departures from Marginal Cost Pricing," *American Economic Review*, June 1970.

in other industries. If the excess of revenue over necessary costs is such as to provide the utility with a competitive return, an efficient allocation of capital between public utilities and other industries is expected to result. Although this rule seems sensible, it requires determination of necessary costs. If management knows that regulation will permit a higher revenue (whether in the form of higher charges, two-part tariffs, or a larger subsidy) if costs are higher, public enterprise will be encouraged to incur unnecessary costs. The problem is similar to that posed by enterprises selling to government on a cost-plus basis. Moreover, public utility industries are encouraged to expand capital through debt finance beyond what is needed so as to be permitted larger returns.

Public Pricing and Imperfect Markets

Whenever it is argued that the price of any one product should be set in line with the efficient rule of marginal cost pricing, the assumption is made that other products are also priced efficiently. If this is not so, second-best solutions may call for offsetting departures from efficiency rules.

Thus, suppose that government sells a product, a substitute for which is sold privately at a monopoly price so that price exceeds MC. It may then be efficient for the government also to charge a price in excess of MC so as to avoid undue substitution of its product for the overpriced private product. If the competing product is complementary to that sold by government, efficiency may call for a public price below marginal cost so as to induce consumers to buy a more efficient package.

By the same token, if the competing product is underpriced, the public price should also be set at less than MC; or, if the underpriced private product is complementary to the public product, the public price should be set so as to exceed MC. An illustration of this is in the pricing of downtown parking garages. Since downtown use of cars is underpriced (because congestion costs are disregarded), a case can be made for pricing of public parking garages above marginal cost to compensate for this defect. In fact, public downtown garages generally tend to be subsidized rather than taxed, a practice that increases the distortion caused by overuse of cars.

Distributional Considerations

A further qualification to marginal cost pricing may arise where distributional considerations are allowed for in the pricing decision.[5] Since decreasing cost industries, such as public utilities, frequently provide goods which offer "essential" services like water, electricity, or subway rides, the provision of such services at subsidized prices may seem equitable and is frequently the subject of a good deal of political pressure. Nevertheless, the equity case for subsidizing such services is no better than that for subsidizing bread, milk, or

---

[5]For a view favoring more general allowance for distributional considerations in public pricing and an approach toward implementation, see M. Feldstein, "Distributional Equity and the Optimal Structure of Public Prices," *American Economic Review*, March 1972.

low-cost housing. That the services happen to be sold by public enterprise should not be the criterion for deciding whether subsidies are to be granted.

Apart from this, there is again the more basic question of whether distributional adjustments should be made by a frontal attack on the distribution of income or whether they should be implemented by a system of excise taxes and subsidies, depending on whether the products in question weigh more heavily in high-income or in low-income budgets. Our conclusion has been in support of the former approach. However, two exceptions to the rule may be noted.

1. Where a direct approach to adjustments in income distribution is not possible but differential pricing is politically feasible, the latter may be the best available solution, at least for those who accept the distributional objective.

2. The efficiency loss which results from direct measures of income redistribution may exceed that of the differential pricing approach. But even when it does, there is no reason why differential pricing should be limited to products which happen to be sold by public enterprise.

C. PEAK-LOAD PRICING

A major problem in public utility pricing results from the variability of demand for its services. Thus, the demand for power is greater during the day than at night and higher during some hours of the day than at others. How is this variation to be allowed for both in pricing the services of a given plant and in evaluating the investment decision on a new plant? How is the variation in the degree of congestion to be dealt with?

Given Plant

Suppose the capacity of a given plant is such that by charging a price equal to marginal operating cost, the demand during the peak period is greatly in excess of the maximum power supply that can be furnished, whereas in the off-peak period there is a great deal of excess capacity? It will then be necessary to allocate the limited peak-period supply to those who value it most highly. Thus, a price has to be charged to equate the limited supply with demand unless other forms of rationing are used. Consumers who do not find the use of peak-period power at this price worthwhile (or who would choose to use less) will shift their demand to the off-peak period when the service is supplied at the lower price of marginal operating cost only. Off-peak use of the facility will be increased and the consumer surplus derived from its services will be maximized.

This is illustrated in Figure 34-2 where OC is capacity use, $D_p D_p$ is peak-period demand, and $D_o D_o$ is off-peak demand. AB is the marginal operating cost schedule, here assumed constant up to capacity use, at which point the supply schedule becomes totally inelastic. Thus the peak-period

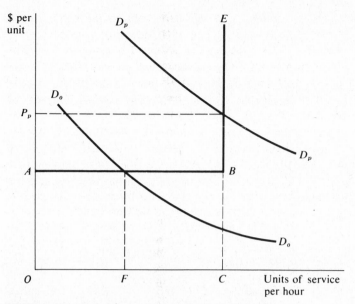

FIGURE 34-2   Peak-Load Pricing with Fixed Capacity.

price is at OP_p while the off-peak price is OA. Peak-period use is at capacity, or OC, and off-peak use is at OF.[6]

Other illustrations might be given where both the peak and off-peak demands intersect the vertical supply schedule or where there remains excess capacity in both periods but differential prices are charged because of variable operating costs. It is, however, only in the situation of constant operating cost and excess capacity in both periods that a uniform price will be appropriate.

Variable Plant Size

The solution of Figure 34-2 may be the best possible under the circumstances, but it is hardly a satisfactory situation. In the longer run, the problem is how to adjust the capacity size to the existence of variable demand. The solution to this problem proves of particular interest in the context of Chapter 3 because we may view peak and off-peak users as joint demanders for the plant's services. Or, putting it differently, we may look on the plant as a social good (of the intermediate-good type) which supplies services to peak and off-peak users who in turn can utilize these services in nonrival fashion. In appraising the profitability of providing a new investment, it is this joint demand which must be considered in applying the rule of equating long-run marginal cost with price.

---

[6]The careful reader will note that if peak and off-peak services are rather close substitutes, it is not permissible to draw the two demand schedules independent of each other. We may think of the D_oD_o schedule as it results in the end with the price for peak-time use settled at OP_p and D_pD_p as reflecting the demand schedule for peak-period use after the use of off-peak service has settled at OF.

Such a solution is illustrated in Figure 34-3.[7] The horizontal axis now measures the units of power supplied at capacity operation for various levels of capacity. D_p is the demand schedule for peak-time users and D_o is that for off-peak users, with demand in each case relating to the level of power forthcoming at capacity use. Turning to the cost side, we simplify matters by assuming that marginal operating cost is zero so that only long-run or capacity cost has to be covered. With long-run marginal capacity cost constant at OA, the long-run marginal (capacity) cost schedule is thus given as AS.[8] Since the two demands relate to different time periods (e.g., peak demand from 7 A.M. to 11 A.M. and 4 P.M. to 8 P.M. and off-peak demand from 11 A.M. to 4 P.M. and 8 P.M. to 7 A.M.) they are noncompeting in their uses of the facility. The demand curves of the two groups of users may therefore be added vertically to obtain total demand for plant capacity. The proper plant size is determined at OB where marginal capacity cost AS equals price, including OP_p to be charged to peak-period users and OP_o to be charged to off-peak users. At these prices, each group will use the plant fully during its period.[9]

While differential pricing in the case of Figure 34-3 leads to full utilization in both periods, this need not be the result. Suppose that the demand for capacity output in the off-peak period is so low that the D_o schedule falls to zero at a level below that at which D_p intersects the marginal capacity cost schedule. In this case, the efficient solution is to charge the marginal cost price in the peak period while permitting free off-peak use. Since excess capacity remains, it will be inefficient to limit its use by charging a price. This once more raises a question of equity, since peak-period users may feel that off-peak users should not be given a free ride but should contribute to the cost.

The principles underlying this type of analysis are reflected in actual pricing practices of utilities, e.g., in differential pricing of power uses in different parts of the day. In other situations, such differentiation reflects the rationing of deficient peak-period capacity output to its most urgent uses.

D. PRICING OF SOCIAL FACILITIES

Related problems arise in the pricing of social-good facilities. To separate out various issues, we distinguish among (1) the pricing of an existing and

---

[7]See P. Steiner, "Peak Loads and Efficient Pricing," *Quarterly Journal of Economics,* November 1957; and O. E. Williamson, "Peak-Load Pricing and Optimal Capacity under Indivisibility Constraints," *American Economic Review,* September 1966. The diagram given here assumes that peak and off-peak periods are of equal length and the rate of service use is uniform within each period. If differences in length or rate of service use are allowed for, D_p and D_o must be weighted accordingly in deriving the aggregate demand schedule.

[8]The marginal capacity cost shows the additional cost per unit of output which results as the capacity level of the plant is expanded, assuming each plant size to be used at optimal capacity.

[9]Since total cost is covered, note that the solution depicted in Fig. 34-3 is not the same as the decreasing cost case of Fig. 34-1, where the efficient solution leaves the firm with a loss.

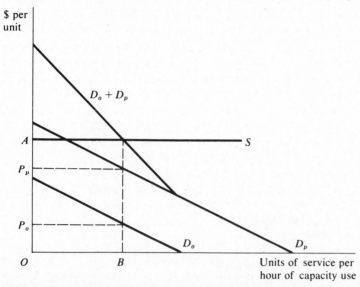

FIGURE 34-3   Peak-Load Pricing with Variable Capacity.

uncongested facility, (2) the pricing of an existing but congested facility, and (3) the pricing problem in relation to the construction of a new facility.

Uncongested Facility

Consider a facility, such as a bridge or highway, which is already built. The utilization rate is very low, so that there is no significant crowding cost. Suppose also that there is no wear or maintenance cost involved in its use. In this case, the marginal cost of additional use is zero and efficient pricing calls for free use. If there are use-related maintenance charges, a user charge covering marginal cost is called for.

Congested Facility

Next consider a situation where the existing facility has smaller capacity, so that free use results in congestion. If DD in Figure 34-4 is the demand schedule for the service while OM is the marginal congestion cost, a charge equal to OP will restrict output to the efficient level OB. If the charge is lower and the utilization rate is higher, the marginal congestion cost comes to exceed price.

Another application of the congestion problem once more involves the issue of peak-load pricing. Consider a facility, such as a subway or a tunnel, which is used heavily during parts of the day but less heavily at others. The efficient charge to account for congestion cost will be higher during the peak than the off-peak period. This will induce users who can readily substitute off-peak use to do so, thereby rationing out the more valuable peak-time space to those who value it more highly. Therefore the consumer surplus derived from the total use of the facility increases. Many of the peak-load

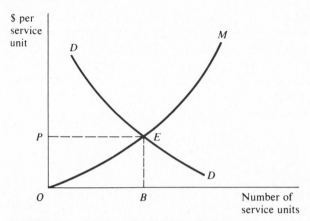

FIGURE 34-4   Pricing with Crowding Cost.

pricing practices address themselves to this problem. Thus charges for toll calls are lower at night when there is less risk of crowding out other calls.[10]

Similar problems arise in setting the prices of several facilities which offer alternative uses to the consumer. Thus, if two bridges are subject to heavy commuter traffic, the uses should be balanced so as to equalize price with marginal congestion costs for each bridge. This objective may call for differential charges in line with the respective levels of demand and congestion costs. If, instead, charges are made in line with other considerations, the outcome will be distorted. This mistake is frequently made when charges are applied only to the latest facility in order to recover its capital cost. If such cost is to be recovered, a charge should be applied to both facilities even though this approach once more raises the equity question of who should pay.

New Facilities

Finally, consider the more difficult situation where a new bridge is to be built. In this case, capital cost must be allowed for. Assuming the necessary information to be available, the problem of evaluation is simple enough. In evaluating a given bridge, for example, that is 50 feet wide, we compute the present value of the benefit stream to which it gives rise. In doing so, we assume the bridge to be used at an optimal rate such as will result if the efficient crowding charge is applied. We then compare the present value of the benefit stream with the project cost to see whether it matches or exceeds the latter. Next we apply the same analysis to the incremental costs and benefits of broadening the bridge by, say, 10 feet and proceed until no further expansion is worthwhile. For engineering reasons, it may not be possible to add to the project step by step but only in substantial and discrete amounts. Hence, the optimal size may be one for which a crowding charge is still needed.

[10]See W. Vickrey, "Responsive Pricing of Public Utility Services," *Bell Journal of Economics and Management Science*, Spring 1971.

This is simple enough conceptually, but the value of the benefit stream is not known. What is worse, imposition of a fee to test the consumer's willingness to pay results in underutilization. The government has to choose between (1) making an investment decision which is not verified, and (2) reducing the usefulness of the investment by imposing charges. Fortunately, the conflict may be eased if the government undertakes many similar projects. Then the information gained from pricing one project may be used in pricing another.

E. PRICING POLLUTION

Another set of public pricing problems arises in making corrections for the cost of pollution. Private activities, whether in production or consumption, frequently give rise to external costs which are not accounted for by the market. Where numbers are small, bargaining between those who do the damage and those who are hurt may cause such costs to be internalized; and the settlement may be left to the market.[11] But public intervention is needed to secure efficiency where numbers are large. Such intervention may involve fiscal instruments (e.g., effluent charges or subsidies to install pollution control equipment) or it may take the form of direct regulation (e.g., setting ceilings to permissible pollution). Whichever technique is used, the basic problem is one of accounting for externalities. As such, it is a problem in the provision of social goods, as discussed in sections B and C of Chapter 3.

Efficiency and Equity Aspects of Pollution

Consider the case of a chemical factory producing product X and discharging its wastes into a nearby waterway. These discharges reduce the quality of the water and its suitability for other uses, such as swimming. Since water is common property, its services (in this case the service of carrying off wastes) are not sold. The cost in terms of reducing water quality is thus overlooked by the pricing system. The price of product X is too low and inefficient resource allocation results. A similar illustration may be given for air pollution resulting from factory fumes. These external effects pose two problems.

First, failure to account for external costs leads to an oversupply of X and an undersupply of the benefits (good water and clean air) which are reduced by pollution. This is the *efficiency* problem. If the damage cost of pollution were internalized, resource use would become more efficient. The price of X would be higher, less X would be produced, pollution would be reduced, and air and water quality would be improved.

Second, the existence of pollution poses distributional or *equity* problems. They relate most directly to the relative positions of perpetrators and victims. Through the loss of environmental quality, consumers of air and

[11]The situation then resembles that of small number bargaining over external benefits (see p. 80). The proposition that the market will provide an efficient adjustment is referred to as the Coase theorem. See R. H. Coase, "The Problem of Social Cost," *Journal of Law and Economics*, 1960.

water are forced to subsidize consumers of product X much as they would if a tax were imposed on them and transferred to the latter. This raises the question of property rights to clean air and water. Are the consumers of X entitled to impose this burden on the rest of the community, or should they be made to pay compensation? Moreover, the incidence of pollution damage may fall with different weight upon low-income and high-income families, and this affects the distribution of real income. The same goes for the cost of pollution prevention and the *net* gains to be derived therefrom. In dealing with pollution policy, allowance must thus be made for equity as well as efficiency aspects of the problem.

Sources of Pollution and Types of Damage

It is wrong to think of pollution as being caused by firms and production activities only. Pollution is also caused by households and their consumption activities, where it is use of the product rather than its production that causes the problem. Thus water pollution is caused by the discharge of industrial wastes but also by discharge of domestic wastes into sewers. Air pollution arises from industrial discharges of smoke and fumes but also from consumption activities such as home use of fuel, use of automobiles, or burning of trash and garbage wastes. There are no ready estimates of the relative shares of the total pollution cost based on production and on consumption, but it would surely be wrong to overlook the pollution which results from consumption.

It is not only the perpetrators of pollution which differ, but also the media through which pollution occurs. In most cases, the quality of the natural environment is reduced by the discharge of wastes, but other forms of pollution also exist. The roar of jet engines is a form of pollution no less than engine fumes. Travel time lost by congestion is a form of pollution not dissimilar to that of automobile exhausts inhaled in the process. While deterioration in the ambience or quality of natural resources is an important form of pollution damage, it is by no means the only one. Viewed more broadly, a problem of external costs arises whenever the activities of any one individual harm someone else without being internalized and accounted for.

The Efficient Solution

The formal solution to the problem of pollution is not too difficult to determine provided that all the necessary information is available. Although one of the major obstacles to efficient pollution policy is a lack of information, it is nevertheless useful to consider what the efficient solution would be if the necessary data were known.

Fixed Technology   To begin with, suppose that the production of X involves an external cost, e.g., chemicals discharged into an adjoining river. The level of discharge increases with the output of X, as does the cost of damage. Further suppose that nothing can be done to reduce the damage done per unit of output of X. We then have the simple case of Figure 34-5,

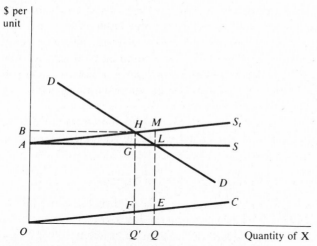

FIGURE 34-5   Pollution Control with Fixed Technology.

where AS is the firm's supply schedule in producing X, OC is the marginal damage cost (i.e., the loss of water quality, valued in dollars per additional unit of X), and AS_t is the summation of the two cost schedules.[12] With demand schedule DD, competitive output in the absence of government intervention equals OQ, since only private costs reflected in AS are allowed for. However, the efficient output would equal OQ' and make allowance for external costs as included in AS_t.

Various policy measures may be taken to achieve the efficient output OQ'. One possibility is a direct regulation requiring the firm to produce OQ'. Another possibility is to impose a tax per unit of output equal to AB, which will bring about the same result.[13] In both cases, output is reduced from OQ to OQ' and the victims of pollution are spared pollution damage equal to $Q'QEF$. As we shall see later, the distributional implications differ depending on which approach is followed. An important point to note is that the efficient solution does not call for pollution to be eliminated. Pollution damage equal to $OQ'F$ still remains. If pollution is cut back further, the gain from reduced pollution falls short of the loss from reduced consumption of X.[14]

---

[12]The slope of the marginal damage curve OC depends upon (1) the level of discharge, and (2) the cost of the damage done thereby. Assuming the rate of discharge per unit of X to be constant, the marginal damage cost may nevertheless rise as the quality of water deteriorates at an increasing rate per additional unit of discharge. This, however, need not be the result. After water has been saturated above a certain level, the additional damage may be constant or declining.

[13]Note that in order to determine the required rate of tax, the supply and demand schedules must be known. Only if the marginal damage cost is constant can the tax rate be set independently.

[14]By cutting back from Q to Q', the pollution damage avoided equals $GLMH$, which exceeds the loss of consumer surplus from reduced consumption of X or GLH. If the reduction in output is pushed beyond QQ', the loss of surplus exceeds the reduction in pollution damage at the margin.

This conclusion may not satisfy the naturalist who would like to see totally pure water or air. In the economist's language, this view would set pollution damages so high as to make the OC (marginal damage cost) schedule coincide with the vertical axis, thereby setting the efficient output at zero. As we shall see later, the evaluation of damage cost (or of the benefits of clean air and water) is a difficult matter; but damages are not to be set at an infinitely high level.

Variable Technology The fixed technology case brings out the basic issue of pollution control, but it is much too simple a view. We must now allow for the fact that technologies are not fixed and that the level of pollution can be reduced by changing methods of production. Thus, a factory may install abatement equipment to reduce the pollution content of its discharge. In this case, public policy must provide it with an incentive to do so. Moreover, the firm should be induced to carry treatment to the point where the cost of further treatment begins to exceed the benefits of reduced pollution damage.

The diagrammatics of this adjustment, which the general reader may wish to pass over, are shown in the upper half of Figure 34-6,[15] pertaining to a specified level of output. The level of discharge is recorded on the horizontal axis, and in the absence of abatement efforts, equals OA. Total damage cost TDC is shown for various levels of discharge along the curve OB. Its slope is assumed to increase with rising levels of discharge, an assumption which need not generally hold. Curve CA shows the total abatement cost TAC involved at various levels of discharge reduction. If all pollution is avoided, such cost equals OC. The slope of TAC rises with increasing abatement as it becomes increasingly difficult to reduce pollution further. Curve CFB is the total cost attributable to pollution, obtained by addition of OB and CA. It combines the cost of pollution prevention with that of the remaining pollution and is at a minimum at discharge level OE. This defines the efficient level of pollution prevention for a given level of output.

As shown in the lower part of Figure 34-6, the efficient level of abatement may also be determined by drawing the marginal damage cost curve MDC and the marginal abatement cost curve MAC. The efficient discharge level OE is now obtained by equating MAC and MDC. In order to induce a firm to carry the abatement level to the point where discharge is reduced to OE, a tax equal to OK per unit of discharge might be imposed. Over the range from A to E, the marginal abatement cost is less than the marginal tax cost so that abatement will be undertaken. Beyond this point it will be cheaper to pay the tax.

This solution (calling for a tax per unit of discharge of OK) applies to this particular level of output only. As the level of output is increased, the total damage cost without abatement will move out along the OB curve to,

[15]The diagram follows A. M. Freeman III, R. H. Haveman, and A. V. Kneese, *The Economics of Environmental Policy*, New York: Wiley, 1973, p. 85.

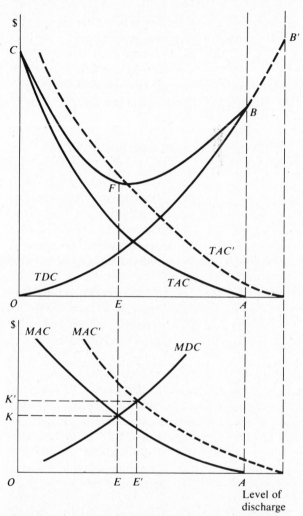

FIGURE 34-6   Pollution Control with Abatement Incentive.

say, B', and the total abatement cost curve will shift to, say, TAC'. A similar shift will occur in the marginal abatement cost from MAC to MAC'. The efficient level of abatement activity will move to E', leaving a higher damage level, while the appropriate tax per unit of abatement will rise from OK to OK'. Thus, the proper level of tax per unit of discharge varies with the level of output.[16]

The firm, confronted with a schedule of taxes per unit of discharge which varies with output, will then be induced to adjust both its abatement activity and its level of output so as to equate its marginal cost (including tax, abatement, and other costs) with market price. In equilibrium, the tax will

---

[16]The tax is invariant to the level of output only if the TDC function is linear, in which case the MDC function is horizontal.

again equal the marginal damage cost of the remaining pollution, as was the case in Figure 34-5.[17]

Lack of Information

Unfortunately, the information needed to implement so complex a procedure is rarely available. The major difficulties are as follows:

1. Measuring damage costs (the *TDC* curve in Figure 34-6) or, what is the same, the value of cleaner air or water is exceedingly difficult. In most cases, the simple solution of asking people what they would be willing to pay is not applicable. Where large numbers are involved, evaluation of preferences cannot be obtained either because exclusion (in this case from damage prevention) cannot be applied or because the benefits derived from such prevention are in the nature of social goods and nonrival in consumption, so that exclusion would be inefficient.[18]

Thus, indirect evaluation is necessary. Cleaner air results in better health, the gain from which may be estimated in terms of reduced hospital bills and increased earnings due to a longer working life. While these ways of measuring the gain are feasible and of some value, they are obviously quite inadequate. Improved health means more than just reduced hospital bills; and longer life means more than additional wages. Feeling better, living longer, and the sheer pleasure of breathing cleaner air are overlooked by such "objective" estimates. Similar problems arise with regard to clean water, the gain from which is not fully accounted for by the value of increased catches of fish or willingness to pay bathing fees. As another illustration, how can one value the gain of improved sleep due to reduced jet noise?[19] In some instances, estimates might be based on changes in the value of adjoining real estate, but this is the exception rather than the rule. In most cases, objective evaluation is incomplete or difficult and evaluation by the political process is needed. The difficulties involved in such evaluation of "social bads" are similar to those previously encountered in the valuation of social goods.

2. Although the chemical or biological content of discharges can be measured uniformly across factories, the dollar cost of the resulting pollution may differ greatly depending on the location of the polluting unit. Thus, the damage due to water pollution is greater upstream than downstream, especially if the factory is located above highly populated areas. Similarly, the air pollution cost of air transport in an urban area is greater than that caused by air travel in a rural area, jet noises are more objectionable if close to residential sites, and so forth. Obtaining physical measures of waste discharge is thus only a first step toward the more difficult problem of translating such measures into economic damage cost.

3. The cost of pollution abatement may differ greatly among firms, municipalities, and households. The cost of securing a given total of pollution reduction therefore differs markedly depending on where it is undertaken. Unfortunately, little information is available on this important problem.

---

[17]Unfortunately, this result cannot be shown in a simple two-dimensional diagram such as Fig. 34-5 because the tax rate is a function of both the level of discharge and units of output.
[18]See p. 57.
[19]See also the earlier discussion of benefit evaluation, p. 175.

4. The most efficient place to reduce pollution need not be with the party which causes the damage. There are always two parties to the pollution problem. If a factory causes air pollution which bothers nearby residents, will it be cheaper to reduce air pollution or to have residents move to less polluted areas? The choice between these two options may have important equity implications, but it must also be looked upon as an efficiency problem.

Instruments of Control

Whether for lack of information or for other reasons, governments do not attempt to implement as refined a solution as Figures 34-5 and 34-6 suggest. Rather, the usual procedure is to decide as a matter of general judgment what overall level of pollution is permitted. If this target level falls, say, 25 percent below the prevailing level, regulations will usually require firms to reduce their pollution by 25 percent on an across-the-board basis. This approach is inefficient because cutbacks should be made where the cost of abatement is lowest. Since the necessary information is hard to come by, the regulatory approach is inefficient in this respect.

This problem may be avoided if effluent charges are used. Thus, the government may impose a tax per unit of discharge and determine experimentally what rates are needed to reduce discharge by the desired degree. By letting each firm equate its marginal cost of abatement with the rate of tax, an efficient allocation of abatement effort will result without requiring information on differential abatement costs.

At the same time, the effluent charge is no cure-all because a uniform charge per unit of discharge would be appropriate only if the damage costs per unit of discharge were the same. As noted before, this is not the fact. Damage costs may differ greatly depending on where the discharge occurs, i.e., the level of the *MDC* schedule in Figure 34-6 or the *OC* curve of Figure 34-5 differs for different polluters. Therefore, the efficient solution requires differential rates of tax for different firms or at least different categories of polluters, depending on location and other characteristics of the watershed or airshed into which discharge occurs.

While the effluent charge involves the "stick approach" to incentive policy, a "carrot approach" might also be offered which would subsidize firms that undertake to reduce pollution. This approach may take the form of outright payment for pollution reduction or of subsidies for the abatement equipment. The latter has the disadvantage that it may bias the choice of prevention technology.

The effluent charge is sometimes criticized as selling the right to pollute, which is considered an immoral way of dealing with the benefits of nature. This, however, is not a well-founded objection. Once it is agreed that the efficient solution does not call for "total" elimination of pollution, some level of pollution remains permissible and the effluent charge is merely a device for allocating emissions in an efficient fashion. A regulatory approach which assigns permissible pollution quotas does essentially the same thing.

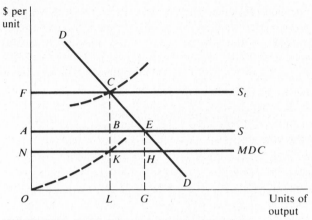

FIGURE 34-7   Equity Aspects of Polution Control.

Equity Aspects

Assuming pollution to be reduced to its efficient level, there remains the question of distributing its costs in an equitable fashion. Who should bear the costs of abatement measures; and no less important, who should bear the costs of the remaining pollution damage?

The Problem of Compensation   Consider the case of water pollution by a paper factory. To simplify matters, assume further that the marginal pollution damage is constant. We then have the situation depicted in Figure 34-7, where DD is the demand schedule and AS is the supply schedule in the absence of government intervention, with OG the corresponding level of output. MDC is the marginal damage cost curve, FS_t the supply schedule with damage costs, and OL the output if the pollution cost is included in price. We now compare three approaches to securing the efficient output OL and see how the various parties involved—including paper factory, readers, the general public, and the displaced bathers—are affected. The results are listed in the following table:

	ALTERNATIVE EFFICIENT SOLUTIONS		
	Regulatory Cutbacks (I)	Effluent Charge with Tax Cut (II)	Effluent Charge with Compensation (III)
Paper factory	+ ABCF	0	0
Readers	− AECF	− AECF	− AECF
General public	0	+ ABCF	0
Bathers	+ LGHK	+ LGHK	+ OGHN

Note: The symbol + indicates gain, and the symbol − indicates loss.

Under the first approach, the government requires the paper industry (which we assume has previously priced competitively) to form a cartel and to cut back output, leaving the resulting profits *ABCF* with the industry. The industry thus gains *ABCF* while the readers who pay more for their books and magazines suffer a loss equal to *AECF* and the bathers obtain a gain in reduced pollution equal to *LGHK*. In the second case, the government imposes a tax equal to *BC* per unit of discharge.[20] It obtains revenue of *ABCF* and uses this for tax reduction. The result for readers and bathers is the same as before, but the gain now accrues to the general public rather than to the industry. In case III the tax is used to compensate the bathers for the remaining damage. Here, the readers pay and the bathers are fully compensated.[21] In all these instances the efficient output *OL* is provided, so that solutions are equally good on efficiency grounds.[22]

At the same time, the solutions differ from an equity viewpoint. Proceeding on the premise that consumers are generally expected to pay a price equal to the marginal cost of the product which they consume, there would seem little reason to reject this principle where the costs involved are of the external type. Nor does it seem reasonable to leave the gain which results from the output correction with the industry or the general public. Rather, it seems fair to compensate the bathers who otherwise would be left with a residual damage cost. To put it differently, they are recognized as having a share in the common property right to clean water and hence are entitled to be compensated for the loss of this share if they should be deprived of it. The equity problem is basically one of entitlement and of the conditions under which society considers such entitlement to exist.[23]

Effects on Income Distribution   The problem of equity as just discussed relates to the distribution of gains and losses among polluters and pollution victims. Another aspect of the problem relates to the incidence of pollution and pollution prevention on households grouped in relation to income size. Consider, for example, the additional cost of automobiles caused by engine

[20]Assuming competitive markets, it is a matter of indifference whether the tax is imposed on the paper industry, the publishers, or the buyers of books, since the cost will be passed on to the book purchasers in either case.

[21]Matters are simplified if we assume constant marginal damage costs. Thus, revenue as measured by *ABCF* in Fig. 34-7 equals the remaining damage cost of *OLKN*. Such is not so with a variable marginal damage cost schedule. If marginal damage cost rises as shown by the dotted line *OK*, the appropriate unit tax would still be *BC*, but revenue would exceed the remaining damage cost or *OLK*. To equate revenue with remaining damage cost, the tax would now have to rise with successive units of output as measured by the dotted line *OK*.

[22]Still another possibility might be to raise general revenue and to use the proceeds to bribe the industry into reducing output to *OL* without raising price.

[23]It has been suggested that the victim should be entitled to claims if, when acquiring a property (subsequently damaged by pollution), a prudent person could not have been expected to anticipate the development of such damage. See F. I. Michelman, "Property, Utility, and Fairness: Comments on the Ethical Foundations of 'Just Competition' Law," *Harvard Law Review*, **80**:1165–1258, 1966–1967, and H. Demsetz, "Towards a Theory of Property Rights," *American Economic Review, Papers and Proceedings of the A.E.A.*, May 1967, pp. 347–379.

improvements which are required to reduce emissions. Such costs may well comprise a higher percentage of income for low-income households, so that the cost distribution of damage prevention may be regressive. Another question is how the resulting benefits of improved air quality will be distributed. Since low-income families are likely to live in central parts of the city where pollution is greater, the initial benefit distribution may be expected to be pro-poor. But the ultimate benefit distribution may not be so because real estate values (and rentals) may rise as the smog is reduced, with the benefits accruing to the landlord rather than to the residents. As can be seen from this simple illustration, the problem of benefit and cost incidence is a complex one. In other cases, such as municipal waste treatment, the cost of damage prevention is assumed by the taxpayer and thus depends on the incidence of the marginal tax dollar. The benefit in turn accrues to the consumers of recreational facilities, with incidence depending on the way in which the use of such facilities is distributed. While it is difficult to generalize about the outcome of antipollution measures of various types, there is no simple assumption that the net result will be toward a more equal distribution of real income. Environmental quality may be a luxury good.

Federalism Aspects

For various reasons, it is difficult to secure an effective solution to environmental problems without intergovernmental cooperation. The reasons are several. Territorial considerations require cooperation because waterways or airsheds frequently extend over more than one jurisdiction. The same applies to traffic problems where transportation systems, such as highways, pass through several jurisdictions. Even where there is no such overlap, cooperation may be essential because the imposition of pollution restrictions and abatement requirements are costly to the industries concerned. The effects of differential requirements on location are thus similar to the effects of differential taxation. Nor is the problem one for the industry only. If tight environmental standards and abatement requirements are imposed in one jurisdiction but not in another, industrial development will be reduced and this curtailment will impose a burden not only on investors but also on those employed in the affected industries. If the application of standards is more general, these impacts will be less severe since the compliance costs cannot be escaped by movement from one jurisdiction to another.

Political Aspects

Nevertheless, pollution controls, even if applied on a nationwide basis, will involve costs for particular industries and hence cause changes in the composition of output and employment. Like all such changes, this one will impose transition burdens on particular groups of investors and workers, groups which will be impressed but little by the proposition that the adjustment is one which will benefit the nation as a whole. The question here, as with other efficiency-increasing policies such as tariff reductions or technological change, is whether the victims of the particular adjustment should or should not be paid compensation. Obviously, failure to compensate increases political opposition to such efficiency measures.

Current Policies

As a result of the growing interest in environmental policies, important pieces of legislation have been passed in recent years to deal with pollution problems. They have resulted in a heavy involvement of the federal government in this field. Some of the more important of these measures will be noted briefly.

Air Pollution   Federal legislation in the air pollution field began with the Clean Air Act of 1963, which did not come into its own until the amendments of 1967 and especially the amendment of 1970. The latter established a federal framework for air quality improvement within which local and state governments would have to operate. The country was divided into 247 airsheds or regions, and the Environmental Protection Agency (EPA) in 1971 established air quality standards for six major pollutants: sulfur oxides, nitrogen oxides, particulate matter, photochemical oxidants, carbon monoxide, and hydrocarbons. The standards set permissible maximum pollutant concentrations, and states were required to submit plans to meet them, with target levels to be met within three years after the approval of the plan. The particular means to be used in reaching the target was left to the states, but state plans were subject to EPA approval.

The 1977 amendments to the Clean Air Act slightly modified the existing law. States must now submit revised implementation plans by 1979. These plans must provide for the attainment of the air quality standards by 1982 for most areas. Under the new law, new sources of the major pollutants will be allowed to site in areas which currently exceed the standards only if they use the "best available control technology" and attain the "lowest achievable emission rates." In addition, other sources under the same ownership already in the state must be in compliance with current emission control requirements.

The amendments specifically require the Environmental Protection Agency to prevent the significant deterioration of air quality in regions which have cleaner air than the ambient standards require. Clean air regions are divided into three classes, each allowing progressively greater deterioration. A class I designation allows very little deterioration and is required for all wilderness areas and national parks. All other areas are assigned class II unless otherwise designated by the state governor.

The amendments also strengthen the EPA's ability to enforce the air quality standards. A firm not in compliance can be fined the total cost savings achieved by being out of compliance. This may be viewed as a somewhat backhanded and not very effective move toward imposition of an effluent charge.

The 1970 legislation gave the federal government the initiative to deal with automobile pollution. The standards apply to all cars sold in the United States, with stepped-up requirements from the 1970 models to the 1975 and

1976 model years. By 1976, automobile emissions were to be reduced by 90 percent of the required 1970 level, but in response to pressure by automobile manufacturers, EPA agreed to postpone this schedule until 1978. Further postponement was provided for by the 1977 amendments. The unburned hydrocarbon standard now does not have to be met until 1980, the nitrogen oxide emission standards have been relaxed, and the nitrogen oxide and carbon monoxide standard deadlines have been extended to 1981 with the EPA having the option to delay them two years further. More important, emission controls are being threatened increasingly by the use of leaded fuel in cars designed for unleaded fuel, due to the increasing price difference between the two fuels. This practice destroys the major emission control device (catalytic converter) without hurting (some would argue actually improving) the car's performance.

Following the approach advocated by economists, the Nixon administration in 1972 proposed a tax (applicable at higher rates in low-standard areas) on emission of sulfur into the atmosphere. This proposal is of particular significance as it makes use of an economic incentive approach which will induce reduction in pollution where it can be obtained at least cost, rather than require such reduction on an across-the-board basis. Corresponding legislation was introduced by Senator William Proxmire but has remained tabled in committee. However, such a proposal is now under consideration in the state of California.

Water   Federal programs in the field of water pollution are based on the Water Pollution Control Act Amendment of 1956 and further amendments in the Water Quality Act of 1965. The federal government's function under these acts was to make grants-in-aid for the construction of municipal-based treatment plants and to assist the states in regulating water quality. The Water Pollution Control Act of 1972 greatly increased these efforts, setting the ambitious target of stopping all discharges of pollutants into navigable waterways by 1985. For this purpose, the law (which was passed over a Presidential veto) sets up tight new standards and provides for substantial federal finance. This law thus parallels in scope the Clean Air Act Amendment of 1970.

Grants involving 75 percent of project cost are to be made in support of municipal sewage treatment plants with a total of $14.3 billion granted as of August 1977. Industries are required to apply the "best practicable" control technology by 1977 and the "best available" control technology by 1983. No pollutants are to be discharged except by permission of the EPA or by state authorities, and EPA is not permitted to grant exemptions. Substantial fines are to be imposed for violations. Although the requirements are most ambitious, implementation so far has been slow and there have been increasing pressures, as a result of the energy crisis and other factors, to delay or ease requirements.

Moreover, it is questionable how effectively a program can be implemented which attempts to set specific effluent limits for each of 40,000 sources of water pollution and to determine on an industry-by-industry or even firm-by-firm basis whether adequate efforts toward improving technology have been made. An alternative approach, applying effluent charges on the various pollutants, may very well have been the better solution.

A special problem is posed by municipal sewage treatment plants. Such operations are subject to decreasing costs and, for reasons discussed in the first part of this chapter, are municipally operated. Capital requirements are met out of public funds, including federal and municipal sources. In determining the pattern of charges to finance current costs and debt service, many of the previously noted problems arise, including differentiation between home and industrial users. Further problems have arisen due to lack of funding and failure to complete or maintain plants.

Solid Waste The 94th Congress finally passed the Resource Conservation and Recovery Act (RCRA), which provides for the supervision of disposal of all hazardous wastes and assists the states with guidelines for the development of solid waste management plans. All open dumps must be closed by 1983 and new open dumping sites are prohibited. A waste disposal charge on consumer products which contribute to solid waste is also under consideration.

Conclusion It is evident that Congress, in recent legislation, has taken major steps in dealing with the pollution problem and in involving the federal government therein. This concern has been extended beyond the initial areas of air and water pollution to solid waste disposal, and a variety of steps have been taken at the municipal level to deal with jet noises at airports. All this is being accomplished at considerable cost. The Council on Environmental Quality (CEQ) estimates that the United States spent $40.6 billion for pollution control in 1977 alone. Of this, 50 percent was borne by industry, 30 percent by government, and 23 percent by consumers directly. The CEQ estimates further that $289.1 billion will be spent from 1976 to 1985 to meet current environmental legislation.[24] The choice of control technique will have major bearing on how this cost will be divided among the various parties.

Compared to only a decade ago, these programs record a sharply increased concern with environmental quality. Considerable progress has been made. It remains to be seen to what extent future emphasis on the development of new energy sources will weaken or reverse this trend.

F. SUMMARY

In the first part of this chapter, various aspects of public pricing policy were examined. The major conclusions were as follows:

1. When government engages in the sale of private goods, the efficient pricing rule calls for setting price equal to marginal cost.

[24]See President's Council on Environmental Quality, *8th Annual Report of Committee on Environmental Quality*, Washington: 1978, pp. 323–327.

2. In the case of decreasing cost industries, this approach involves a loss, and the question is how the deficit is to be covered. Various alternatives were considered, including payment from general revenue, application of a two-part tariff, and price discrimination.

3. The same principles apply to public utility regulations. The widely applied rule that price should allow for coverage of costs plus a fair return to capital is sound in principle but meets with difficulties in application.

4. A major problem in public utility pricing results from variability of demand, with differential pricing called for in peak and off-peak periods. Demand variability also makes it difficult to determine the proper level of plant capacity.

5. The efficiency rule of marginal cost pricing must be qualified if other prices are set in imperfect markets.

6. Further qualifications to marginal cost pricing are introduced if distributional adjustments are to be built into the pricing policy.

7. In pricing social facilities, no price should be charged for existing facilities unless congestion exists.

8. With regard to new social facilities, imposition of a user charge is helpful in verifying past investment decisions and in calculating the profitability of additional investments; but in the absence of crowding, user charges interfere with efficient use.

The second theme of the chapter dealt with the problem of external costs of pollution and the pricing arrangements which might be applied to internalize these costs:

9. Failure to account for pollution costs creates both inefficiencies and inequities.

10. Pollution may result from consumption as well as from production activities.

11. With fixed technology, the efficient solution is provided by a tax which will add the marginal pollution cost to the marginal private cost so that total marginal cost equals price. As a result, pollution will not be eliminated but its level will be reduced.

12. Where changes in technology can be made to reduce pollution, abatement activity should be cut back to where the marginal cost of abatement equals the marginal value of pollution avoidance.

13. Practical problems encountered in the application of pollution control include the difficulties in measuring damage costs as well as the variability of damage and abatement costs among firms and locations.

14. Among various instruments of control, effluent charges are likely to be superior to the setting of standards, but the information needed to formulate an optimal structure of charges remains difficult to obtain.

15. Various techniques will serve equally well to secure an efficient solution, but they may differ in their equity implications.

16. This involves the questions of who should pay for abatement costs and whether or not the victims of remaining pollution should be compensated.

17. Moreover, it is important that compensation be paid so as not to interfere with an efficient solution.

18. In the large-number case, determination of damage cost involves problems similar to those dealt with in the context of social goods, where preferences are not revealed but must be determined.

19. In the concluding pages, recent antipollution legislation, applicable mainly to air and water pollution, was examined.

FURTHER READINGS

Baumol, William J., and Wallace Oates: *Economics, Environmental Policy and the Quality of Life*, Englewood Cliffs, N.J.: Prentice-Hall, 1979.

Dorfman, R., and N. Dorfman (eds.): *Economics of the Environment: Selected Readings*, New York: Norton, 1972.

Economic Report of the President for 1971, "Safeguarding the Environment," pp. 114–122.

Freeman, A. M., III, R. H. Haveman, and A. V. Kneese: *The Economics of Environmental Policy*, New York: Wiley, 1973.

President's Council on Environmental Quality: *8th Annual Report of Committee on Environmental Quality*, Washington: 1978.

Turvey, R.: "On Divergences between Social Cost and Private Cost," *Economica*, August 1963.

_____ (ed.): *Public Enterprise*, Baltimore: Penguin, 1968.

Chapter 35

International Public Finance*

A. Introduction to Tax Coordination: *Interindividual Equity; Internation Equity; Efficiency.* **B. Coordination of Income and Profits Taxes:** *Taxation of Earned Income; Taxation of Capital Income; Evaluation; Corporate Tax Burden and International Competitiveness; Further Issues in United States Policy; International Division of Profits Base.* **C. Coordination of Product Taxes:** *Efficiency Aspects; Balance-of-Payments Aspects; GATT Rules; Common Market Policy; Revenue Distribution and Burden Export.* **D. Stabilization in the Open Economy:** *Multiplier Leakage; The Fiscal-Monetary Mix.* **E. Further Problems:** *Joint Provision of Public Services; International Aid and Redistribution.* **F. Summary.**

Recent years have brought increasing concern with the international aspects of public finance. Various developments have contributed to this interest. The combining of European economies into the Common Market, the increasing role of multinational corporations, the financing of joint efforts such as the United Nations and NATO, and a rising awareness of the international

---

*Reader's Guide to Chapter 35: The newest and one of the most interesting aspects of the fiscal problem relates to its role in the international setting. Many of the problems which traditionally have been dealt with only in the confines of national finance are becoming increasingly important in their application to international trade, capital flows, international organizations such as the United Nations, and the relationship between poor and rich countries. A brief survey of these new horizons is presented in this chapter.

maldistribution of income have all pointed toward the need for international fiscal coordination. In principle, these problems are similar to those previously encountered in the discussion of fiscal federalism within the confines of a single nation, but they differ in magnitude and in the international nature of the cooperative effort which is required.

A. INTRODUCTION TO TAX COORDINATION

Tax coordination has been the most discussed part of the problem, and various techniques have been developed to deal with it. Each country must decide how it chooses to tax the foreign income of its residents and the income of foreigners which originates within its borders. Similarly, it must decide how its product and sales taxes are to apply to its exports and imports. These decisions may be made in conjunction with other countries, and international tax treaties are a means of coordinating some of these matters.

As the sphere of tax policy is extended from a national to an international setting, old problems, such as the requirements of interindividual equity and effects on the efficiency of resource use, must be reconsidered, while new problems such as internation equity are added.

Interindividual Equity

If a person receives income which originates in various countries, he or she will be subject to taxation by more than one authority. Mr. A, a resident of the United States, may spend part of the year in the United Kingdom, and pay a United Kingdom tax on his earnings there. Or he may invest in the United Kingdom and derive dividend income on which a United Kingdom tax is paid. At the same time, he receives United States income and pays United States tax. Does horizontal equity require that he pay the same total of taxes (both domestic and foreign) as Ms. B, who receives the same total income but entirely from United States sources? Or should the United States simply consider taxes paid to other countries as a deduction from income and equalize tax burdens in terms of United States taxes only? In the first case equity is interpreted in an international sense, and in the second case in a national sense.

Internation Equity

A further and distinct equity problem arises in determining how the tax pie is to be divided among the treasuries of the various countries. This problem arises, though in different ways, with regard to both income and product taxes.

In regard to income and profits taxes, it is generally agreed that the country in which the income originates (also referred to as the "country of source") is entitled to tax that income, but the question is, at what rate? The United Kingdom tax imposed on the earnings of United States capital invested in the United Kingdom reduces the net return which accrues to the United States. It differs in this respect from such additional taxes as may be imposed by the U.S. Treasury. The latter do not constitute a loss to the United States but are merely a transfer between United States residents and the U.S. Treasury. The national loss suffered by the United States thus depends only on the rate at which United States capital is taxed in the United Kingdom. One reasonable view of internation equity is that the country of source should be permitted to tax income accruing to foreign investors at the same rate at which foreign countries tax the income which its own residents derive abroad. This may be referred to as the principle of reciprocity.

In the matter of product taxes, the equity issue relates to the possibility of burdening foreigners through changes in price. If country A taxes exports, the cost of exports is increased. If the country dominates the export market, export prices will rise and the foreign consumer will pay more. Thus, part of the tax burden may be shifted abroad. Similarly, if imports are taxed, foreign suppliers may find that they must sell their products at a lower net price. Once more, part of the burden is shifted to the outside. If one accepts the criterion that a country should pay its own taxes, such burden shifting may be considered as running counter to internation equity.

Efficiency

Differential profits tax rates or, as pointed out earlier, differential fiscal net benefits or burdens[1] will affect the location of economic activity and tend to draw resources from their most efficient uses. If Mr. C, an investor, finds his taxes lower if he invests in Italy rather than in the United States, he will send more of his capital to Italy than he would in the absence of the tax differential. The question, then, is how to arrange the taxation of international investment income so as not to disturb the efficiency of capital allocation on a *worldwide* basis. But international tax neutrality is not the only possible criterion. The objective may also be to implement a concept of *national* efficiency (to be explored presently), in which case a different arrangement is called for.

Differential product tax rates also cause inefficiencies but in a different way. If such taxes are imposed at the producer stage (rather than at the retail level), they affect the relative costs of producing a given product in various countries. As a result, the location of production is not determined by comparative advantage (or relative resource cost), which is the requirement for efficient trade, but is modified by differential tax costs.

B. COORDINATION OF INCOME AND PROFITS TAXES

With these general principles in mind, we now consider how they apply to the major taxes, beginning with income and profits taxes.

Taxation of Earned Income

The United States (like most other countries) reserves the right to tax the income of its residents no matter where earned. Ms. D, who spends six

[1]See p. 531.

months of the year at a job in the United Kingdom and then returns to the United States, will pay United Kingdom tax on her income earned in the United Kingdom. In determining her United States tax, she will include her United Kingdom earnings in her income, but she will credit taxes paid in the United Kingdom against her United States tax liability. Her final liability will then be the same as if the entire income had been earned in the United States. Such at least is the procedure so long as her United Kingdom tax does not exceed her United States tax on the same (United Kingdom–earned) income. If it does, no refund is given and her total tax is higher than if her income had all been earned in the United States. Special rules apply regarding the treatment of fellowship stipends, teachers' earnings, and so forth, but the general pattern is to permit income to be taxed in the country of origin with the country of primary residence extending the credit.

This is in line with a concept of internation equity which says that the country of income origin should not discriminate but may apply its own rates to the earnings of foreigners; and the granting of a credit by the country of primary residence, though involving a revenue loss to that country's treasury, is in line with the international view of interindividual equity.[2]

Due to the increased labor mobility in postwar Europe, the treatment of migrant workers under social security has become a major problem. The usual policy is to extend social security benefits without differentiation, including payment of family allowances where family members remain in the home country. Differentials in social security benefits among countries have thus become a strong factor in attracting labor to high-benefit countries, the effect having been to widen effective wage differentials.

Taxation of Capital Income

The most important and complex part of the problem concerns the tax treatment of foreign investment income. This includes the treatment of such income received by individuals and corporations, with the latter much the major item.

Present United States Practice The major rules in the treatment of foreign investment income as they now apply in the United States are as follows:

1. An individual investor residing in the United States and receiving investment income from abroad pays individual income tax thereon. The government in the country of income origin typically imposes a "withholding tax" of, say, 15 percent, which in turn is credited against United States tax. In the reverse case, a similar withholding tax is imposed in the United States, the level of withholding rates generally being agreed upon in international tax treaties.

[2]Note that United States residents will pay under the same bracket rates whether their income is received here or abroad. However, the tax applicable in the United Kingdom will relate to the rate brackets applicable to United Kingdom income only. Some might argue that the United Kingdom is entitled to tax at rates applicable to the foreigner's total income.

2. A United States corporation operating a branch abroad will find the profits of the branch subject to the foreign corporation tax in the country in which it is located. For purposes of United States tax, the profits of the parent corporation and its branch are considered as a unit. Foreign branch profits prior to foreign tax are included in the parent's taxable profits and the foreign tax is then credited against United States tax. The foreign country usually imposes no withholding taxes when the profits are repatriated. Provided only that the foreign profits tax does not exceed the United States tax, it is a matter of indifference to the United States corporation whether profits originate at home or in a foreign branch.

3. Neither of these cases compares in importance with that of the foreign incorporated subsidiary. Though owned by the parent corporation in the United States, the foreign subsidiary is incorporated abroad and is legally a separate corporate entity. Its profits are subject to foreign corporation income tax and the United States tax is "deferred" until the profits of the subsidiary are repatriated by being paid as dividends to the parent company. At that time, such profits become subject to United States corporation tax. Profits gross of foreign profits tax are included in taxable income and the foreign tax is credited against the United States tax due.[3] Provided the foreign tax is not higher, repatriated profits are thus subject to the same (United States) rate as would apply if they had been earned domestically. At the same time, profits which are retained abroad are subject only to foreign tax, with United States tax deferred until such profits are repatriated.

Evaluation

In evaluating these arrangements, we consider the merits of (1) the foreign tax credit, and (2) the deferral provision.

Credit versus Deduction of Foreign Tax   Crediting the foreign corporation tax against the United States corporation tax results in tax neutrality. Such at least is the outcome so long as the foreign tax (i.e., corporation tax plus withholding tax) is not higher than the United States tax. Since the United States rate applies whether the capital is invested at home or abroad, tax influences on investment choice are neutralized. Thus the efficient allocation of capital resources on a worldwide basis is not interfered with.

This is an important advantage, but it is not the only way of looking at the matter. While the credit device secures an efficient solution on a worldwide basis, it does not do so from a national point of view. Suppose that investment in both the United States and the United Kingdom yields a pretax return of 10 percent. Suppose further that the corporation tax rate in both countries is 50 percent, thus leaving the investor with a net return of 5

---

[3]Suppose that foreign earnings of $1 million are subject to a foreign corporation tax of 35 percent of $350,000, leaving $650,000. These earnings are to be repatriated. At the time of repatriation, an additional foreign tax (the "withholding tax") of 15 percent or $97,500 applies, reducing net profits to $552,500. In computing United States taxes, the 48 percent rate is applied to $1 million, giving a gross tax of $480,000. Foreign taxes of $350,000 plus $97,500 are then credited, leaving a net United States tax of $32,500. The investor's total tax equals $350,000 plus $97,500 plus $32,500, equaling $480,000, or 47 percent.

percent. Yet, from the national standpoint, the return on investment made in the United States is 10 percent, with 5 percent going to the investor and 5 percent going to the U.S. Treasury. The latter share is lost to the investor but not to the country as a whole. However, the return to the United States on investment made in the United Kindom is only 5 percent, the remaining 5 percent share which goes to the United Kingdom Exchequer being lost to the United States as a nation. This suggests that from the viewpoint of national efficiency, capital export should be carried to the point where the return *after* foreign tax abroad equals the before-tax return on domestic investment. This means a lower level of capital export than is appropriate under the criterion of world efficiency.

The investor will undertake foreign investment up to the point where the *net* return is the same as from domestic investment. Under the crediting approach, this will be the case where

$$(1 - t_{us})r_{us} = (1 - t_{us})r_f$$

t_{us} and t_f being the United States and foreign rates of tax, and r_{us} and r_f the United States and foreign rates of return, respectively. Thus, foreign investment is carried up to the point where

$$r_{us} = r_f$$

and the requirement of world efficiency is met. But suppose now that the foreign tax is *deducted* from taxable income rather than *credited* against the United States tax. The investor, in equating the net return from foreign and domestic investment, will undertake foreign investment to the point where

$$(1 - t_{us})r_{us} = (1 - t_{us})(1 - t_f)r_f$$

that is, where $r_{us} = (1 - t_f)r_f$. Thus, the deduction approach meets the requirement of national efficiency.

Which of the two approaches is to be preferred is an open question. From the point of view of United States investors, the credit method is the more favorable since foreign investment income after tax will be larger. In the view of others such as United States wage earners, the deduction approach might be preferred. With more capital staying at home, domestic labor will be more productive and wages will be higher. In the matter of United States foreign investment, there thus exists a common interest shared by United States investors abroad and foreign workers (both of whom benefit) and United States workers and foreign owners of capital abroad (both of whom lose).

Deferral   The deferral provision is based on the somewhat fictitious assumption that the foreign subsidiary is a truly separate entity. Thus it seems to contradict the crediting provision which implies that the subsidiary's tax is in fact the parent's tax. To be sure, deferral makes little difference to the parent corporation if the foreign tax does not fall short of what the United States tax would be, but in fact it frequently does. Western European rates are not greatly below United States levels, but those of developing countries frequently are. Consequently, it has been estimated that, on the average, a dollar of United States foreign investment pays only 70 percent of the tax payable by domestic investment in the United States.[4] Thus corporations are given an incentive not to repatriate and to divert earnings of subsidiaries into investments in low-tax (so-called tax haven) countries. In the 1960s and 1970s various steps were taken to limit such tax avoidance, but it remains a problem.

Corporate Tax Burden and International Competitiveness

Another view of the problem does not focus on tax advantages which the United States investors may obtain from investing abroad (as compared with home investment). Rather, it compares the relative position of subsidiaries of United States companies with that of other companies operating in the same country, e.g., the relative position of United States subsidiaries and British companies operating in Britain or of United States and British subsidiaries operating in France. Under the deferral rule, both will pay the same tax (that of the country in which the operation occurs) provided that profits are not repatriated.[5] But if profits are repatriated, the final taxes may differ. If they are higher in the United States, do they not reduce the ability of United States companies to compete in world markets?

What is relevant here is the comparison between taxes in the United States and those in other countries which are major sources of foreign investment funds, such as the European countries and Japan. Comparison of the levels of corporation profits taxation among these countries is difficult because allowance must be made not only for differences in tax rates but also for such provisions as depreciation rules and enforcement. Recent estimates suggest that corporate tax burdens in these countries are close to those in the United States although the average level may be somewhat lower by, say, 10 or 15 percent.[6] Because of this, it may be that the United States *share* in total (world) capital formation is less than it would be if levels of tax rates were the same; and if this were the case, the United States share of foreign investment may also be somewhat smaller. What happens will depend on whether the profits tax is shifted into higher prices, in which case exports will be retarded,[7] or whether it goes to reduce the net rate of return on capital, thereby impeding the overall level of investment.

---

[4]See P. B. Musgrave, "Tax Preferences to Foreign Investment," in *The Economics of Federal Subsidy Programs*, Part 2, Joint Economic Committee, 92d Cong., 2d Sess., June 11, 1972.

[5]A further proviso is that the guest country not discriminate against foreign capital.

[6]See the statement by the Secretary of the Treasury before the Senate Finance Committee, Oct. 7, 1971. Table 1 of that statement shows comparative data for a number of major countries.

[7]See p. 428.

Further Issues in United States Policy

Two further issues relating to United States taxation of foreign investment income may be noted. One is posed by the Domestic International Sales Corporation (DISC) provision. Introduced in 1971, the provision is designed to extend the benefit of tax deferral to part of the profits earned by domestic corporations in pursuit of their export activities. Without such an extension, so it was argued, domestic exporters would be at a disadvantage when compared to foreign affiliates. The provision has been a controversial one. Not only is it difficult to limit the benefit to production for exports, but limitation of deferral for foreign affiliates may be the better way of restoring balance. Moreover, it has been argued that the provision is in conflict with GATT rules which prohibit export subsidies.

Another controversial issue arises from the treatment of royalty payments by American oil companies to foreign governments. Such royalties, where disguised as profit taxes, are credited against United States tax. Since such payments tend to be reflected in price, it would seem appropriate to treat them as indirect taxes, thus allowing them to be treated as a deduction from income but not as a credit against tax.

International Division of Profits Base

We have argued that a country should be entitled to tax such profits as originate within its borders; but implementation of this rule renders it necessary, in the case of multinational corporations, to determine the profit shares which arise in different countries. This is not a simple matter. Suppose a United States corporation operates a subsidiary in Canada. Under the rules of internation equity, Canada is entitled to tax the profits of this subsidiary. But how can these profits be separated in a meaningful way from those of the parent company in the United States? If parent and subsidiary sell or buy from each other, profits may be easily shifted from one country to another so as to place them where taxes are lower. The difficulties are compounded where tiers of subsidiaries operating in various countries are involved.

Efforts have been made to formulate rules which will preclude profit shifting, such as the requirement that prices be determined on an "arm's-length" basis, i.e., as they would have been if the dealing had been between independent companies. Given these difficulties inherent in conducting separate profit accounting for interrelated entities, it has been suggested that an altogether different approach might be taken. The profits base of multinational corporations might be allocated among countries not by location of subsidiaries but in line with the national origin of profits earned by the business group as a whole. Such origin might be approximated by a formula including both location of value added and sales in its base. Though attractive, this approach would require an international tax administration to implement it, and it therefore remains a rather far-off alternative.[8]

[8]See P. B. Musgrave, "The Division of Tax Base and the Multinational Corporation," *Public Finance*, vol. XXVII, no. 4, 1972. See also the analogous problem posed by the allocation of corporation taxes among states, p. 424.

C. COORDINATION OF PRODUCT TAXES

The case for coordination of commodity taxes may be made on various grounds, including efficiency, balance-of-payments, and revenue considerations.

Efficiency Aspects

Whereas in the case of income taxes the concern was with effects upon capital flows, attention is now directed to effects of product taxes on product flow. The argument is most readily presented under the assumption of flexible exchange rates.

The case for a free flow of international trade is based on the proposition that all trading countries will benefit if each specializes in the production of those products in which it has a comparative advantage. Suppose that country A has a comparative advantage in producing product X while country B has an advantage in producing Y. Country A will thus export X and import Y, while country B imports X and exports Y. However, with production subject to increasing costs, A continues to produce some of its own Y and B produces some of its own X. Both A and B will be better off than they would be if there were no trade. By exporting X and importing Y, country A obtains a higher real income than if it produced all its Y at home; and vice versa for B.

Now consider how this situation may be affected by various taxes. For this purpose, we distinguish between consumption or "destination" taxes which are imposed where the product ends up and is consumed, and production or "origin" taxes which are imposed where the product originates or is produced. In deciding whether various taxes do or do not interfere with the location of production, the key question is whether the tax affects the relative prices of home-produced and imported goods. If it does, consumers will substitute one for the other and the location of production will differ from what it would be under neutral taxes.

Destination Taxes   Destination taxes do not interfere with the location of production unless there is an outright discrimination between home-produced and imported goods, i.e., unless the tax is in the form of a tariff or customs duty.

Suppose that country A imposes a general tax (e.g., a retail sales tax) on the consumption of all X and Y, including home-produced and imported goods. This will have no trade effects since consumers in A find relative prices of imported and home-produced goods unchanged.[9] Next, assume that the tax applies to Y only but again covers all Y whether imported or produced at home. As a result, consumers will increase their consumption of X and reduce their consumption of Y. This adjustment may affect the level of

---

[9]Nothing else need be said provided that the general sales tax is added to price, leaving factor costs in A unchanged. If, instead, prices stay unchanged while factor costs decline, there will be an exchange rate adjustment so as to increase the price of A's currency in terms of B's, but trade is again unaffected in real terms.

trade, but the location of production for both products (at their new levels) will still be in line with comparative advantage.[10]

The situation differs drastically if country A applies its tax to imported Y only, i.e., if it imposes a tariff. The tax now enters as a wedge between the relative prices of home-produced and imported goods, leading A's consumers to substitute home-produced Y for imports. As imports fall, the price of A's currency in terms of B's will rise. Thus, exports of X from A will also decline until a new equilibrium is established at a lower level of trade and now with a less efficient division of production of X and Y between countries A and B.

Such taxes or tariffs interfere with efficient trade, and substantial efforts have been made in recent years to reduce trade barriers, from the Kennedy Round of the 1960s to the more recent Tokyo Round.

Origin Taxes   Turning now to the question of origin taxes, we find that distortions may arise though there is no attempt to discriminate against foreign products.

Suppose first that country B imposes a *general* production tax, say a manufacturer's excise tax of 10 percent, on both X and Y. As a result, prices in B rise in line with the tax. B's consumers, finding that the prices of home-produced goods have risen relative to those of imported goods, will import more. A's consumers find themselves in the opposite position. B's exporters will add the tax to their costs, so A's consumers will find import prices increased and will import less. Under flexible exchange rates, the resulting increase in demand for A's currency and decrease in demand for B's currency will cause the price of A's currency to rise relative to that of B's. This will dampen the desire of B's consumers to import more and of A's consumers to import less. Relative prices of exports and imports are unchanged and trade is unaffected in real terms.[11]

The situation differs if B's production tax applies to only one product, say its export good Y. Consumers in A again find the cost of Y increased and will substitute domestically produced Y. As A imports less Y, the price of A's currency in terms of B's rises. B's consumers find the cost of imports increased and B therefore imports less. A new equilibrium is established at a lower level of trade and with a changed distribution in the location of production. Country A now produces more Y and B produces more X than before. Imposition of a selective product tax on Y in country B thus results in a distorting effect similar to that following the imposition of an import duty on Y in country A.

This distorting result would have been avoided if country B had granted a tax rebate on its exported Y. B's move would have forestalled a rise in the

---

[10]We do not concern ourselves here with inefficiencies which arise from the distortion of *consumption* choices between X and Y, our only concern in this context being with effects on the *location of production*.

[11]To be precise, trade will remain unchanged if government expenditures are similar to those which would have been made privately in the absence of tax; but even if the pattern of demand changes so as to affect trade, the new pattern of trade will remain efficient in responding to the new structure of demand.

price of imported Y in country A, so that there would have been no occasion for substituting home-produced Y. By granting an export rebate B's tax on Y would have been transformed from an origin tax into a destination tax. It would have been made equivalent to a retail sales tax on Y in B, a tax which, as shown before, does not distort the location of production provided only that it covers both imports and home products.

A similar story can be told if B's tax is on X. B's consumers will now substitute imported X, and a corresponding adjustment will follow. In the end, the real level of trade will be increased, but the location of production will again be distorted. More X will be produced in A and more Y will be produced in B than before. The distortion in this case might have been avoided by having B impose a compensating import duty on X. The tax once more would have been transformed into a destination tax (now a tax on all X being consumed in B) without distorting location effects.

Balance-of-Payments Aspects

Similar effects on the location of production result under conditions of fixed exchange rates. However, the equilibrating mechanims of exchange rate adjustments are then absent, and the additional problem of effects on the balance of payments arises. Taxes which worsen a country's balance of trade by raising imports or lowering exports now lead to a payments deficit.[12] Destination taxes are once more neutral, but origin taxes now worsen a country's balance of payments while tariffs improve it. The introduction of export rebates and of compensating import duties now not only forestalls production inefficiencies but also neutralizes the balance-of-payments effects of origin taxes. During the fifties and sixties when current international practices, such as the General Agreement on Tariffs and Trade (GATT) and Common Market policies, were being worked out, the setting was one of fixed exchange rates. Consequently, both efficiency and balance-of-payments considerations entered the picture, with the latter given primary emphasis. Since then exchange rates have been liberalized, so that balance-of-payment effects have declined in importance.

GATT Rules

In line with these objectives, the GATT provides that a country may grant an export rebate against product taxes which enter into the cost of production

---

[12]Two further differences between the cases of fixed and flexible exchange rates may be noted:

1. Whereas a general origin tax has no bearing on trade in the case of flexible exchanges, it *does* matter with fixed rates. If country B imposes a general origin tax, the cost of B's products in A will rise and B will export less. At the same time, domestic prices will rise relative to those of imported goods and B will import more. Thus B develops a balance-of-payments deficit, the result being the same as that of currency appreciation.

2. As B imposes a general origin tax, effects on the balance of payments can be neutralized by adding an export rebate and a compensating import duty. This, however, is based on the assumption that prices in B will rise by the amount of tax. If, as is conceivable but not likely, factor prices fall with commodity prices remaining unchanged, no rebate and duty are called for. The GATT rules are based on the premise of rising prices.

and may impose a compensating import duty on imported products.[13] Payroll taxes are not considered eligible for credit nor is the corporation tax, which is assumed to be borne by profits and not to be a component of costs.

United States practice complies with the GATT rules. Manufacturer's excises are reimbursed on exports; but this rebating of taxes is limited because United States product taxes are largely imposed at the retail level. Exports are excluded while both imported and home-produced products are subject to retail tax. In European countries, product taxes are typically imposed at an earlier stage or stages, as is the value-added tax. The volume of rebating is correspondingly larger. This has led to the complaint that exporters in European countries are given a competitive advantage because they can credit more tax; and this has been cited as supporting the case for a value-added tax in the United States. The argument overlooks the fact that higher product taxes also increase costs, so that the benefit of the larger credit is needed as an offset. Without it, European producers would be at a competitive disadvantage.

Common Market Policy

The objectives of the Common Market go beyond those of GATT. Although the rebate and compensating duty devices neutralize trade and balance-of-payments effects of origin taxes, they still call for "fiscal frontiers" in order to determine when rebates or duties are due. Yet it was hoped that, with the repeal of internal tariffs, fiscal frontiers could be discarded. To make this possible while maintaining tax neutrality, it has been decided that value-added tax rates should be made uniform across all member countries. This objective, which has not as yet been accomplished, would render export and compensating import duties unnecessary since all products, independent of origin within the market, would pay the same tax. Although this would be accomplished at the price of requiring uniformity in value-added tax rates, countries would continue to set their own rates of retail sales taxes.[14] Some observers who see coordination as a transition to a United States of Europe find the requirement of rate uniformity a desirable step, while others prefer to retain such degrees of freedom for individual countries as are compatible with the achievement of common interests.[15]

Revenue Distribution and Burden Export

In concluding this discussion of product tax coordination, the question of internation equity once more arises. The sensible rule seems to be that a country shall be permitted to tax its own consumers but not those of other

[13]See GATT, *The General Agreement on Tariffs and Trade*, Part II, Articles III and XVI.

[14]See the *Report of the Fiscal and Financial Committee on Tax Harmonization in the Common Market*. This report, prepared under the direction of F. Neumark, is reprinted in *Tax Harmonization in the Common Market*, Chicago: Commerce Clearing House, 1963.

[15]For a discussion of various approaches, see D. Dosser, "Economic Analysis of Tax Harmonization," in C. S. Shoup (ed.), *Fiscal Harmonization in Common Markets*, vol. 1, New York: Columbia, 1967, chap. 1.

countries. This approach renders destination taxes (applicable to both imports and exports) equitable, but not origin taxes. The latter, in the absence of a rebate, may serve to pass part of the burden to foreign consumers if the tax is on exports; or, in the absence of compensating import duties, foreign exporters may benefit if the tax is on import substitutes. Either result runs counter to the rule of self-finance. The rebate and compensating import duty approach is thus in line with internation equity.

An exception arises in the case of scarce and exhaustible natural resources where a rental charge on foreign users, imposed by the country of origin, may well be appropriate.[16]

D. STABILIZATION IN THE OPEN ECONOMY

In Part Six we have discussed various aspects of stabilization policy and the relation between fiscal and monetary approaches. All this was done in the context of a closed economy. Most economies are intimately linked to the rest of the world, through both product and capital flows. This linkage has important implications for the conduct of stabilization policy which must now be considered.

Multiplier Leakage

In an open economy, the effectiveness of fiscal policy is reduced substantially by the existence of trade "leakages." This is of particular importance for highly open economies such as Canada or the Netherlands and, as recent years have painfully shown, it also matters for a relatively closed system such as that of the United States. In particular, the open-economy aspect is of importance in developing countries which are highly dependent upon trade.

Expansionary measures, by raising income, lead to increased imports. These increased imports divert purchases from domestic to foreign products, thus adding another leakage from the income-spending stream to that provided by domestic saving and thereby reducing the expansionary effect. Writing E for exports, M for imports, and m for expenditures on imported consumer goods as a fraction of consumption expenditures, c is again the marginal propensity to consume. Letting consumption C include expenditures on imports as well as on domestically produced goods and services, the model underlying equations 15 to 18 in Table 27-1 may be restated as follows:[17]

$$Y = C + I + G + (E - M) \tag{1}$$

$$C = a + c(1 - t)Y \tag{2}$$

$$M = mC \tag{3}$$

$$Y = \frac{1}{1 - c(1 - t)(1 - m)} \left[a(1 - m) + I + G + E \right] \tag{4}$$

$$\Delta Y = \frac{1}{1 - c(1 - t)(1 - m)} \Delta G \tag{5}$$

---

[16]See Malcol Gillis and Meyer Bucovetsky, "Principles of Mineral Tax Design," in Gillis et al., *Taxation and Mining*, Cambridge: Ballinger, 1978.

[17]See p. 595.

Comparison of equation 5 with our earlier equation 18 shows that the multiplier has been reduced by import leakage. This renders it more difficult for a country with large trade involvement to engage in stabilization policy. Moreover, country A's expansionary policy, by raising its imports, also increases the exports of its trading partner B. As a result, demand for B's output is increased and A's expansionary policy is transmitted to B. Similarly, restrictive action by A, by reducing its imports and hence B's exports, will have a restrictive effect in B. These effects may not suit B's policy intent, leading B to take countermeasures which in turn will weaken the domestic effectiveness of A's policy. Because of this interaction, it is difficult for countries with heavy trade involvement to engage in effective stabilization policy unless cooperative measures are undertaken by countries within the same trading area.

This linkage has become of increasing importance in the context of Europe's Common Market where successive removal of economic frontiers calls for increased coordination of stabilization policies. Adoption of a common currency in particular would force unification of monetary policy and would render conduct of separate fiscal policies increasingly difficult. In the end, individual member countries would become unable to conduct their own stabilization policies, just as (and for the same reason) state or municipal governments in the United States cannot do so. The economic logic of the case will call for such policies to be undertaken by a central Common Market authority, thus providing further pressure toward political union. Whether such union will come about, of course, is a different matter.

The Fiscal-Monetary Mix

We have previously considered the problem of fiscal-monetary policy mix as it operates in a closed economy. We concluded that a given level of aggregate demand, needed to maintain full employment, may be achieved by various combinations of fiscal and monetary policy; and we also concluded that the mix may be set so as to obtain the desired rate of growth.[18] An easy money–tight fiscal combination, so we argued, is inducive to a higher rate of growth. We must now reconsider the issue of policy mix in an open economy setting.

Fixed Exchange Rates   In an economy with fixed exchange rates this poses the additional problem of securing balance in the balance of payments. Measures designed to raise the level of demand in the domestic economy, whether fiscal or monetary, will increase imports and (if prices rise) may tend to reduce exports. In a system with fixed, or only partly flexible, exchange rates, domestic expansion may thus generate a balance-of-payments deficit, and concern over this deficit may become a deterrent to the pursuit of a high-employment policy. This situation developed in the United States in the late 1950s and continued to influence policy throughout the 1960s.

[18]See p. 686.

In dealing with this problem, policy may be directed at influencing the other component of the balance of payments, i.e., capital flows. This is so because capital outflows exert a drain on the balance of payments while capital inflows strengthen it. For instance, the decision of a United States firm to buy a plant abroad means that the supply of dollars abroad is increased. The decision of a foreign investor to purchase securities in the United States means an increase in the demand for United States dollars. Since monetary policy affects the interest rate and high interest rates attract capital inflows and discourage capital outflows, monetary policy has a direct effect on capital flows and hence on the balance of payments. General fiscal measures do not have this effect. Therefore, it is argued that monetary policy should be used to secure foreign balance by acting on the capital account, while fiscal policy should be employed to secure domestic balance.

In this way, the two policy objectives of domestic balance and foreign balance may be obtained simultaneously. If domestic expansion is needed, this can be obtained by fiscal expansion, while adverse balance-of-payments effects can be forestalled by some degree of monetary restriction. To be sure, the ease with which the proper policy mix can be achieved will not be the same in all situations. Achievement of the proper mix will be easiest where trade involvement is small, the response of domestic investment to rising interest rates low, and the response of foreign capital flows large.

But even where the dual objective of domestic and foreign balance is obtained, there remains the question whether the resulting level of domestic interest rates also serves to obtain the desired rate of capital formation and growth. Quite possibly it does not. The instruments of monetary and fiscal policy are insufficient to meet the third policy objective of controlling growth. An additional policy instrument is needed. This may involve measures such as a domestic investment credit, differential interest rates on domestic and foreign funds, control over capital flows, and so forth.

Flexible Exchange Rates   During the seventies, this problem has become less serious as the United States and other countries have moved toward flexible or at least semiflexible exchange rates. With exchange rates flexible, there can be no problem with the balance of payments since balance is established automatically by adjustment in the rate of exchange. If the United States expands while its trading partners do not, United States imports will increase, and this will lead to a fall in the value of the dollar. The effect is not to create a deficit in the balance of payments, as was the case under fixed-exchange-rate regime. Rather, the effect is to change the terms of trade adversely. This will be the result whether the expansion is of the fiscal or the monetary type. However, the bearing of the fiscal-monetary mix on growth will now be less marked than in the closed-economy setting. A package involving tighter fiscal and easier monetary policy will be conducive to domestic growth by lowering the cost of borrowing, but it will also be adverse to capital inflow and even induce outflow, thereby reducing the supply of investible funds from abroad.

E. FURTHER PROBLEMS

While most of the attention in the discussion on fiscal coordination has been directed at the tax side, expenditures also enter the picture. They do so with regard to both government purchases and transfer payments.

Joint Provision of Public Services

Nations, like municipalities, may have common concerns, involving benefit or cost spillovers which lead them to engage in joint projects. The St. Lawrence Seaway, calling for cooperation between the United States and Canada; NATO, involving a joint defense effort among a score of nations; cooperation in reducing pollution in international waterways such as the Rhine; malaria prevention programs conducted by the World Health Organization; and the operation of the United Nations are cases in point.

In all such situations, a problem of cost sharing arises. Where the number of participants is small, cost shares may be bargained out in relation to the advantages which each partner hopes to obtain. For the particular case of defense, it has been suggested that cooperation proves of greater net benefit to smaller partners since even a slight strengthening in the defense posture of a large ally provides a large increase in the degree of protection obtained by the small partner.[19] Where numbers are large, the problem is similar to that of interindividual budget determination. Some tax or assessment formula has to be used, and ability-to-pay considerations similar to those applied in the domestic context may be employed. If a proportional assessment rate is to be used, each country may be asked to pay the same percentage of its GNP or national income. If progression is to be applied, the question arises whether the rate brackets should be related to the GNP of various countries (with the countries themselves considered the contributors) or whether they should be related to the per capita incomes of the residents in various countries (with individual residents considered the basic units). This problem parallels that of distributing membership votes in a legislative body (e.g., whether the Senate or the House principle of vote apportionment should be followed).

Both types of considerations are involved in determining contributions to the budget of the United Nations. While cost shares are voted upon each year and have been subject to frequent revisions, the procedure is essentially as follows:[20] The total cost is divided among member countries in line with their *contribution base* or GNP. This makes for a proportional tax in relation to GNP, independent of per capita income. This principle is then qualified by three further provisions.

---

[19]See M. Olsen, Jr., and R. Zeckhauser, "An Economic Theory of Alliances," *Review of Economics and Statistics*, August 1966; and A. Peacock, "The Public Finances of Inter-Allied Defense Provision," in *Essays in Honor of Antonio de Vito de Marco*, Bari, Italy: Cacucci Editore, 1972.

[20]See John Pincus, *Economic Aid and International Cost Sharing*, Baltimore: Johns Hopkins, 1965; and James E. Price, "The Tax Burden of International Organizations," *Public Finance*, no. 4, 1967.

The first provision is for an exemption in relation to per capita income. Countries with very low per capita income may exclude 50 percent of their GNP from the contribution base, with the exclusion percentage declining as per capita income rises and reaching zero at a per capita income of $1,000. This "vanishing exemption" makes for a progressive tax in relation to per capita income at the lower end of the per capita income scale, where the bulk of United Nations member countries are located. The second provision sets the minimum share of any one country's contribution at 0.04 percent of the total budget. This minimum reduces the significance of the exemption provision for small countries with low per capita income. The final provision relates to the upper end of the scale where, it is said, no single country shall contribute more than a certain share. This share, which limits the contribution of the United States, was until recently set at 33 percent, but has now been reduced to 25 percent. As a result, the United States share is less than it would be under the allocation-by-contribution-base approach. Moreover, it is provided that the per capita contribution of other high-income countries shall not exceed that of the United States.[21]

Other organizations have followed different patterns. Contributions to the International Monetary Fund (IMF) were rendered not on an annual basis, but as purchase of initial capital stock. The quotas were assigned on a "benefit basis," i.e., related to drawing rights which in turn were determined in line with likely needs for IMF credit. A somewhat similar procedure was followed in assigning subscriptions to the capital stock of the International Bank for Reconstruction and Development. All these contributions, it should be noted, involve relatively small amounts, so that the stakes for any particular country are not of major importance. Contributions to NATO, which did involve substantial amounts, have not been determined on a fixed formula basis but have been essentially subject to negotiation. The United States has met much the largest share of NATO costs, probably exceeding its contribution had assessment been made in relation to the levels of GNP.

International Aid and Redistribution

Those considerations, humanitarian or political, that provide the basis for concern with the domestic state of income distribution cannot be limited to the confines of one's own nation. Chances are that aspects of internation distribution will become an increasingly important element in the world politics of future decades. But, important though they may be, distribution issues at the international level are even more difficult to deal with than their domestic counterparts. Inequalities are larger and the organizational problem is more complex since there is no "central government" to deal with them and policies must be implemented by transfers among nations. Such measures may be in the form of development aid designed to raise the growth rate of low-income countries, this being the approach which has been followed on a modest scale over the last few decades. Or they might in time lead to

[21]For further discussion, see *United Nations Yearbook*, vol. 29, 1975, p. 967.

redistribution out of the existing level of world income similar in nature to a negative income tax as applied to domestic redistribution. Although this approach is not foreseeable at present, it might someday become a central concern for an international system of public finance.[22]

Magnitude of Transfer Problem   In dealing with the problem of distribution on an international basis, is the concern with differentials in average income among *countries*? Or is it with inequalities in the distribution of income among *individuals* on a worldwide basis without regard for national boundaries? To some extent the two problems overlap, since most poor people are in fact residents of the countries with low per capita income; but where they do not overlap, the basic problem is once more that of redistribution among individuals. Little would be gained if redistribution toward low-income countries were to accrue to a small group of high-income residents. The problem, it appears, is quite similar to that previously dealt with in examining the problem of equalization among jurisdictions in the context of fiscal federalism.[23]

The inequality of interindividual income distribution on a world basis is appalling.[24] Domestic inequalities are compounded with inequalities in average incomes across nations. Assuming individuals in any one country to receive an income equal to the country's average, it is estimated that the lowest 40 percent of the world's population receives around 3 percent of the world's income, whereas the top 20 percent receives 60 percent. If internal distribution within countries is allowed for, the ratios are 2 and 70 percent. This degree of inequality is much greater than that which prevails within countries, especially higher-income countries. The lower half of the world's population, including most of Asia, Africa, and the Middle East, and a good part of South America, subsists on a per capita annual income of around $300 or less, as against an average per capita income for the upper 25 percent of around $4,000 (1975 levels). Allowing for the difficulties inherent in sweeping comparisons of this sort, the degree of inequality is staggering. Moreover, there is reason to expect that per capita income in the developed countries is rising more rapidly than in low-income countries, so that the situation is worsening rather than (as tends to be occurring with domestic distribution) improving over time.[25]

If total world income could be redistributed to achieve complete equalization, a per capita income of $2,000 could be established. Although such an income would be extremely low compared with the prevailing standards of advanced countries, it would involve a vast improvement for large parts of

[22]For a general introduction to this problem, see D. Dosser, "Towards a Theory of International Public Finance," *Kyklos*, vol. 16, no. 1, 1963.

[23]See p. 530.

[24]For this and the subsequent estimates, see Richard A. Musgrave and Peter Jarrett, "International Redistribution," *Kyklos*, Summer 1979. Data for 1974 with China excluded.

[25]See G. Myrdal, *Economic Theory and Underdeveloped Regions*, London: Duckworth, 1951; and S. Andic and A. T. Peacock, "The International Distribution of Income, 1949 and 1957," *Journal of the Royal Statistical Society*, Series A, vol. 124, 1961.

the world. But obviously, such equalization would be impossible while holding total income constant. The contribution rate required from the higher-income countries to achieve large-scale equilization would be exceedingly high and substantial disincentive effects would arise.

Redistribution Patterns   Even apparently modest redistribution targets would involve substantial transfers. Such patterns are explored in Table 35-1. The results are based on a fairly comprehensive sample, including over 70 countries and covering over 2 billion people. As China is excluded, this accounts for nearly the entire remaining population.

The table shows estimates for two relatively modest redistribution targets, providing for per capita income floors of $200 and $400, respectively. Assuming the revenue to be raised by a proportional tax, rates of 2.1 and 7.3 percent, respectively, would be required. The United States would contribute around 36 percent, and the ratio of United States contribution to GDP would be 2 and 7 percent, respectively. If instead the revenue was raised through a highly progressive tax formula, providing for the slicing off of top incomes until the necessary revenue was obtained, the remaining income ceiling would be $12,585 and $8,412, respectively. The United States would contribute 17 and 43 percent of the total, with a contribution to GDP ratio of 1 and 8 percent. In comparison, United States economic aid during the 1970s has ranged from 0.7 percent of GDP during the first half of the decade to 0.4 percent in the later part. Even a modest redistribution target—leaving minimum levels vastly below those tolerated in the domestic policy of developing countries—would thus require a very substantial increase in the contribution rate of high-income countries.

TABLE 35-1
Redistribution Patterns

	$200 Floor	$400 Floor
Total transfer, billions of dollars	81	262
Proportional Tax		
Tax rate, percentage	2.1	7.3
Percentage contribution by United States	36	37
United States contribution as percentage of GDP	2	7
Percentage received by India	71	60
Progressive Tax		
Ceiling income, dollars	12,585	8,424
Percentage contributed by United States	17	43
United States contribution as percentage of GDP	1	8
Percentage received by India	71	60

Notes: Estimates for 1975 with internal distribution within each country allowed for. China is excluded. The proportional tax is applied to all individual incomes in excess of the floor. The progressive tax reflects maximum progression, i.e., income is sliced off from the top down until the necessary revenue is obtained. The estimates involve all the difficulties in international income comparison, as well as the use of sketchy data on internal income distributions. See source for further discussion.

Source: Richard A. Musgrave and Peter Jarrett, "International Redistribution," *Kyklos,* Summer 1979.

Development Aid   As has been noted before, distribution policy must not be considered only as a matter of redistributing slices in a given pie. Effects on the size of the pie, in particular the rate of economic growth, must be studied as well. If this viewpoint holds for the case of national redistribution, it holds especially at the international level where the potential scale of distributional adjustment is so much larger. Nothing would be gained if the contribution of developed countries were pushed so far as to interfere with their economic ability to render continued aid.

Indeed it is obvious that a major improvement in the condition of the world's poverty population can be achieved only by raising productivity of workers in low-income countries. An important contribution to this can be made by redirecting capital flows from high-income to low-income countries. As capital is redirected, world output will increase, since capital should be more efficient in countries where the capital-labor ratio is as yet very low. The suppliers of capital in the high-income countries stand to gain as larger returns are obtained from investment in low-income countries. There would, however, result a redistribution of income from labor in high-income countries (which would then operate with less capital) to labor in low-income countries whose productivity would be increased by the rising capital-labor ratio. An improved distribution of world income might thus be obtained at the cost of increased inequality (though over a much lesser range) in the developed countries.

A second important contribution to economic development can be rendered by opening the markets of developed countries more widely to the exports of the less developed countries. This may involve extension of preferential treatment as well as a trend away from (rather than toward) trade restrictions. In this case, labor in developed countries may suffer once more since it is less capable of moving than is the capital factor. However, labor will now gain in its role of consumer from reduced import prices.

However this may be, policies such as these hold out the hope that developing countries, after a successful takeoff, can continue their growth independently, thus avoiding the "being on welfare" syndrome, which is as disturbing in the international as in the domestic setting.

F. SUMMARY

In this chapter we have dealt with the interaction which results from the coexistence of diverse fiscal systems which are brought in touch with one another through the international flows of capital and trade.

This fact poses problems with regard to both the equity and the efficiency aspects of taxation:

> **1.** With regard to equity among taxpayers, considerations of horizontal and vertical equity may now be extended to include all taxes which a person pays to whatever jurisdiction, as distinct from taxes paid to the individual's jurisdiction of major tax allegiance only.

2. Moreover, there now appears the additional equity question of how the tax base arising from international transactions should be divided among the participating countries, or the problem of internation equity.

3. With regard to efficiency effects, a distinction is now drawn between efficiency as seen from the point of view of worldwide resource use and efficiency as seen from a nation's point of view.

In dealing with the coordination of income and profits taxes, many technical difficulties arise:

4. A United States resident earning income abroad will include such income for purposes of the United States income tax, but he or she may credit foreign tax payments against this tax. This provision applies to both wage and investment income.

5. Foreign branches of United States corporations are taxed abroad, but their income is included in the income of the parent corporation for purposes of United States corporation tax, with the foreign profits tax again credited against the United States tax.

6. Much the largest part of United States direct foreign investment is made through subsidiaries of United States corporations. Their tax treatment differs from that of branches in that the income of the subsidiary is included in the parent's income for purposes of United States tax only when this income is repatriated.

7. An important policy issue is whether foreign taxes should be credited against United States tax or deducted from taxable income. The former is in line with world efficiency, the latter with national efficiency.

8. A second important question is whether the United States tax on subsidiary income should be deferred until repatriation, a problem which also involves tax avoidance through tax-haven operations.

9. A further important policy issue relates to the way in which profits arising from international operations should be divided among the taxing authorities of the participating countries. The so-called arm's-length rule is used in this connection.

In dealing with the coordination of product taxes, our major concern was with potential distorting effects on commodity flows.

10. Destination taxes, e.g., retail sales taxes, do not interfere with commodity flows. They do so only if limited to imported goods, that is, if imposed as tariffs.

11. Origin taxes, or product taxes imposed in the country of production, do interfere with the efficient flow of trade since they affect relative costs of production, thus interfering with the flow of trade based on comparative advantage.

12. Such effects are neutralized, however, if product taxes are rebated at the point of export. GATT rules determine which taxes may be thus rebated.

13. Common Market policy in Europe aims at adoption of a uniform value-added tax, thus achieving efficiency without the need for export rebates.

Among further aspects of international fiscal coordination, the following points were noted:

14. Highly open economies cannot engage in independent stabilization policy but, instead, policy coordination is called for.

15. Nations, like states or municipalities, may engage in the joint provision of public services. Such participation poses the problem of how cost shares should be divided among them.

16. Problems of distribution policy similarly may extend across borders, as reflected in economic aid to developing countries. With rising differentials in per capita income, such extension is likely to become a major issue in the future.

FURTHER READINGS

Dosser, D.: "Economic Analysis of Tax Harmonization," in C. S. Shoup (ed.), *Fiscal Harmonization in Common Markets*, New York: Columbia, 1967, chap. 1.

Johnson, Harry G., and Mel Kraus: "Border Taxes, Border Adjustments, Comparative Advantages, and the Balance of Payments," *Canadian Journal of Economics*, vol. 3 (Nov. 1970).

Musgrave, P. B.: *United States Taxation of Foreign Investment Income: Issues and Arguments*, Cambridge, Mass.: Harvard Law School, International Tax Program, 1969.

Musgrave, R. A.: *Fiscal Systems*, New Haven, Conn.: Yale, 1969.

Chapter 36

Development Finance*

A. Ingredients of Development: *Capital Formation; Technology, Enterprise, and Efficiency; Social and Political Factors; Foreign Exchange; Balance and Bottlenecks; Role of Fiscal System.* **B. Fiscal Policy, Stability, and Growth:** *Revenue Requirements; Taxation, Saving, and the Distribution of Income; Foreign Borrowing; Aggregate Demand, Inflation, and Employment.* **C. Tax-Structure Policy:** *Taxable Capacity and Tax Effort; Tax-Structure Development; Individual Income Tax; Business Income Tax; Land Taxes; Wealth and Property Taxes; Commodity Taxes and Tariffs.* **D. Tax Incentives:** *Domestic Incentives; Capital versus Employment Incentives; Incentives to Foreign Capital; Export Incentives.* **E. Expenditure Policy. F. Summary.**

Public finances, on both the tax and expenditure sides of the budget, play a key role in the process of economic development. Many of the difficulties which obstruct the economic progress of low-income countries call for solution by the public sector; yet the institutional and social settings of such

---

* *Reader's Guide to Chapter 36:* Many of the problems discussed in the preceding chapters, especially Chapters 8, 9, and 30, apply as much to development finance as to the finance of developed countries. However, development finance poses additional problems and some of those previously considered, such as tax-structure design covered in Chapters 16 to 23, appear in a somewhat different light. For this reason, the major aspects of development finance are reviewed in this concluding chapter.

countries complicate and constrain the task of budgetary policy. For these reasons, the problems of development finance deserve special and separate consideration.

A. INGREDIENTS OF DEVELOPMENT

The requirements for economic development in low-income countries include those needed for continued economic growth in the comparatively highly developed countries, but much more besides.[1] To achieve this growth, not only are capital formation (including investment in both physical and human capital) and technological progress needed, but also certain changes are required in the social and institutional settings which have been both cause and effect of a low level of economic development. The public sector has an important part to play in all these ingredients of development.

Capital Formation

A fundamental requirement of economic development is an increased rate of capital formation relative to that of population expansion. Such capital formation should be broadly defined to include all expenditures of a productivity-increasing nature. It may take the form of investment in the public or the private sector. Particularly in the early stages of development, the former is of critical importance since, in the form of so-called infrastructure (power, communications, port facilities, etc.), it sets the framework for subsequent manufacturing investment whether public (in the socialist economies) or private (in the mixed economy case). Furthermore, capital formation includes investment in human resources in the form of education and training as well as in physical assets. Indeed, where human productivity is adversely affected by malnutrition and disease, increased food consumption and provision of sanitation and health facilities take on the aspect of investment in human capital.[2] Thus the use of resources for productivity-enhancing purposes may take a wide variety of forms, and the actual mix must be determined in the process of expenditure and resource planning. Moreover, priorities change over time, and with them, the optimum investment mix.

Leaving aside for the time being the problem of investment planning, let us focus on the sources from which these additional resources for investment can be drawn. Unless unutilized resources can be brought into use or additional resources can be procured from abroad, there has to be a reduction in current consumption to release the necessary resources for investment purposes. To a certain extent, the mobilization of unused resources may be possible. It has been argued, for example, that many low-income economies

---

[1]For broad-based discussions of development strategy, see Arnold C. Harberger, "The Fundamentals of Economic Progress in Underdeveloped Countries," *American Economic Review*, May 1959; and Hollis B. Chenery, "Growth and Structural Change," *Finance and Development*, International Monetary Fund and World Bank, November 3, 1971.

[2]See C. S. Shoup, "Production from Consumption," *Public Finance*, Chicago: Aldine, 1969, p. 173.

possess substantial amounts of underutilized labor which may be put to work on simple forms of public capital formation, such as drainage, irrigation, roads, and dams.[3] The government then enters only as organizer of this improved resource use. But this source of capital formation has its inherent limits; and putting underemployed labor to work may itself require certain supporting investments.

A further possibility is to obtain the needed investment resources from abroad in the form of official loans and grants or as private investment. Neither source, however, is likely to do the whole job, and in any case, will not be forthcoming without supportive "own" effort on the part of the host country. Private investors from abroad, like private investors at home, require the necessary infrastructure investment; and official aid will most likely be conditional upon well-formulated development plans which include provision for substantial tax-financed increases in domestic investment.

Unavoidably, then, a large part of the problem remains one of diverting the needed resources for development from their use in current consumption. In a centrally controlled economy with public enterprise predominating, this shift can be done by holding returns paid to factors of production below their marginal product earnings; but in a decentralized economy, such internal sources of capital formation must come from public or private savings. To some extent, if conditions are rendered congenial, this increased rate of saving may be generated voluntarily in the private sector. Here, the government may be helpful in securing reasonable monetary stability so that savings habits are not discouraged by continuing inflation; also, the government may play a part in facilitating, or itself creating, the appropriate financial institutions to attract household savings and direct them into productive uses. The latter is of particular importance for the small saver for whom few uses for personal savings exist beyond high-risk money lending or the collection of valuables like gold. Taxation, as will be seen, has an important role to play in providing savings incentives and/or disincentives to luxury consumption. Business saving may also be encouraged through a system of business income taxation which encourages the retention and reinvestment of earnings.

Voluntary private saving, while useful and important, cannot be expected to be sufficient in itself, particularly at an early stage of development. An economic climate conducive to private saving takes time to develop, and in the meantime, the less developed country must look to the government budget as the most promising source of finance for development purposes. We again define government savings in the "classical" sense as equal to total revenue minus government consumption expenditures.[4] Thus public sector saving may be increased by raising total tax revenue and/or reducing current expenditures. Tax revenue must be looked on as a precious and scarce

---

[3]See W. A. Lewis, "Economic Development with Unlimited Supplies of Labor," *Manchester School*, August 1954.

[4]This concept of government saving must be distinguished from the surplus in the *total* budget, i.e., total revenue minus *total* expenditures, which is relevant for the management of aggregate demand. See p. 678.

resource, hard to come by, and many a development plan has come to grief as a result of the profligate spending policies of the government, which in turn was often acting under political pressure.

Government savings generated by a surplus in the current budget may be used to finance capital formation in either the public or the private sector. In the latter case, the government savings may be channeled into private investment as debt or equity capital through the medium of government lending agencies or development banks.

Technology, Enterprise, and Efficiency

Improved technology is another important element in the development process, including manufacturing and agriculture. The massive improvements in agricultural productivity in a number of developing countries over the past decade attest to the benefits to be derived from improved technology in that sector. A principal benefit of private investment from abroad lies in the improved technologies which it brings, although it is important that these be adapted to the particular conditions and resource endowments of the less developed countries (LDCs) themselves. Tax provisions may be designed to stimulate and encourage the use of improved techniques.

Business enterprise is needed if a flourishing private sector is to develop alongside the public sector. In its absence, government enterprise must fill the gap. As with technology, the tax structure can be designed so as to encourage (or at least not to discourage) the willingness to undertake productive investment.

Needless to say, the issue of efficiency in resource use becomes of critical importance in the resource-scarce LDCs, and in the public no less than in the private sector. This factor involves proper expenditure evaluation on the part of the government as well as a development plan which avoids wasteful bottlenecks arising during the development process. Furthermore, distortions arising in the pattern of taxes and tariffs, which in turn induce an inefficient pattern of production in the private sector, should be avoided.

Social and Political Factors

Some of the most intractable problems associated with economic development include the whole range of social attitudes and organizations which have to be modified if development is to proceed. At the same time, a substantial degree of political stability is also needed to allow individual initiative to flourish, development plans to be implemented, and the necessary economic transformation to take place. It is therefore crucial that the fruits of development be bestowed broadly and that extremes of income inequality prevalent in many of the LDCs be eliminated. While certain kinds of redistribution (e.g., land reform) can be undertaken without prejudice to the level of output and indeed may be helpful in this respect, conflicts can arise between policies directed toward a more equitable distribution of income and the objective of increased saving and investment. Whereas public saving can be increased by raising the level of taxation, private incentives to invest may have to be traded off against redistributive tax policies.

Foreign Exchange

Foreign trade plays a critical role in many of the less developed economies. With limited internal markets, foreign trade involvement permits greater specialization, economies of scale, and exercise of comparative advantage. In addition, foreign exchange earnings allow the purchase of certain products (such as machinery and equipment) which are needed for the development process but for which the necessary technology is not available domestically. Yet another contribution of exports to development may be the provision of an expanding market around which "linkage" investments may be made, thereby creating an "export-led" nexus of development.

Thus, public policy must be concerned with the division of resources not only between consumption and investment but also between domestic and traded products; and among traded products there are both import-competing and exported goods. The tax structure, again, has a part to play in the general allocation process embodied in the development plan.

Balance and Bottlenecks

As economic development proceeds, various bottlenecks or limitations to the growth rate may crop up.[5] For example, it has been suggested that in the early stage, the rate of internal saving is the controlling factor. As the rate of saving, and with it the growth of the economy, increases (aided, perhaps, by capital inflow from abroad), the absorptive capacity of the economy becomes the limiting factor, i.e., all the supportive factors which are needed to render the investment productive. Finally, the development process begins to create strains in the balance of payments, outstripping the capacity of the economy to earn foreign exchange to meet imports through exports. Thus, the resources made available for development purposes may go to waste because of these bottlenecks. A sound development plan should therefore endeavor to keep the process running smoothly by a policy of balanced growth. Tax policy in particular may be employed to encourage capital inflow as well as to affect the level of imports and exports.

Role of Fiscal System

It is thus evident that the fiscal system plays a multifold role in the process of economic development:

> 1. The level of taxation affects the level of public saving and thus the volume of resources available for capital formation.
> 2. Both the level and the structure of taxation affect the level of private saving.

[5]See H. Chenery and A. Strout, "Foreign Assistance and Economic Development," *American Economic Review*, September 1966.

3. Public investment is needed to provide infrastructure types of investment.

4. A system of tax incentives and penalties may be designed to influence the efficiency of resource utilization.

5. The distribution of tax burdens (along with the distribution of expenditure benefits) plays a large part in promoting an equitable distribution of the fruits of economic development.

6. The tax treatment of investment from abroad may affect the volume of capital inflow and the rate of reinvestment of earnings therefrom.

7. The pattern of taxation of imports and exports relative to that of domestic products will affect the foreign trade balance.

B. FISCAL POLICY, STABILITY, AND GROWTH

The role of fiscal policy in securing stability and growth in the LDCs is of fundamental importance. We begin by considering certain macro aspects of this problem.

Revenue Requirements

To begin with, it is helpful to view the problem in terms of a fully employed economy and to focus on the role of fiscal policy as a means of raising the domestic savings ratio. In making a first approximation to the amount of tax revenue needed to achieve a certain target rate of growth, differences between various sources of tax revenue are disregarded. Suppose that the objective is to achieve a 2 percent annual rate of growth in income per head. With, say, a 2 percent annual growth rate of population, national income must then grow at slightly above 4 percent per year. This target rate of growth requires a certain rate of capital formation, or investment expenditures as a percentage of national income. This ratio z may be crudely estimated by the use of an incremental capital–output ratio, and is defined as follows:

$$z = \frac{\Delta K}{\Delta Y} = \frac{I}{\Delta Y}$$

K being the capital stock, I the level of annual investment ($=\Delta K$), and Y national income.[6] If g is the desired rate of growth,

$$g = \frac{\Delta Y}{Y}$$

the required investment rate I/Y may be obtained by substitution as

$$\frac{I}{Y} = \frac{\Delta K}{\Delta Y} \cdot \frac{\Delta Y}{Y} = zg$$

Thus, if $z = 3$, and $g = 4$ percent, $I/Y = 12$ percent. This investment ratio must be matched by a corresponding savings ratio to assure economic balance. Therefore, the economy must save 12 percent of national income to grow at

---

[6] In reality, macroplanning of this type would proceed on a disaggregated basis in which a weighted average of incremental capital–output ratios for different sectors of the economy is applied.

the desired rate of 4 percent. We must have

$$S_p + S_g = 0.12\,Y \tag{1}$$

where S_p is private saving and S_g is government saving. The level of private saving is given by

$$S_p = s(Y - T)$$

or

$$S_p = s(1 - t)Y \tag{2}$$

where s is the propensity to save out of disposable income, T is tax revenue, and t the tax rate. The level of government saving equals

$$S_g = tY - \alpha Y \tag{3}$$

where α is current expenditures of government as a fraction of national income.[7] Substituting equations 2 and 3 into 1, we obtain

$$t = \frac{0.12 - s + \alpha}{1 - s} \tag{4}$$

Using a typical value for s of 3 percent and for α of 10 percent, we obtain $t = 19.6$. That is to say, a tax rate of 19.6 percent is needed to obtain a growth rate of 4 percent.[8] With government current expenditures equal to 10 percent of national income, government saving equal to 9.6 percent of national income may be either used to finance public investment or loaned out to finance additional private investment. Having made this first approximation to its revenue needs, the government must then judge whether such a target is feasible and can be attained under any realistic tax reform program. This decision will depend on the institutional framework, the capabilities of tax administration, and the political will to make the necessary tax assessments stick. But two points should be noted. First, a very large effort is required to raise the revenue–income ratio by even one percentage point. Second, a development plan which is too ambitious to be implemented and requires more than the tax system can reasonably be expected to produce may be worse than no development plan at all, for it invites the waste of uncompleted projects and the danger of inflation, not to mention the social repercussions arising from unfulfilled expectations.

[7]Government saving thus defined equals the surplus in the current budget. See p. 881.
[8]Since the required savings rate equals zg, equation 4 may be rewritten as

$$t = \frac{zg - s + \alpha}{1 - s}$$

TABLE 36-1
Distribution Patterns in Less Developed Countries

	PERCENTAGE SHARES IN TOTAL		
Ranking by	*Income*	*Consumption*	*Saving*
Income	*(I)*	*(II)*	*(III)*
Top 1 percent	20	18	50
Next 9 percent	25	23	50
Next 15 percent	20	22	0
Lowest 75 percent	35	37	0
Total	100	100	100

Notes: The data in column I reflect a typical pattern among available distribution estimates for Latin American countries. Columns II and III include the authors' best guesses designed to reflect the typical situation.

Taxation, Saving, and the Distribution of Income

We must now correct the simplifying assumption of the preceding section that all tax dollars are equally useful in raising the level of domestic savings. Indeed, the central problem of tax policy in developing countries is how to obtain the necessary revenue while at the same time providing some correction for a typically high degree of inequality in the distribution of income, but without interfering unduly with private saving and investment.[9]

In Table 36-1, the setting to this problem is presented in more concrete form. The distribution of income, consumption, and saving is shown as it might apply in a typical LDC, say, a low-income Latin American country. We find that the upper 10 percent of income recipients receive some 45 percent of income and the lowest 75 percent receive 35 percent. The corresponding shares in consumption are estimated at 41 percent and 37 percent while the shares in saving are 100 and 0 percent. The degree of inequality is thus substantially greater than in developed countries such as the United States, where the corresponding income shares are 30 and 47 percent.

In addition to the highly unequal distribution of income, two other features stand out. First, a very substantial share of total income goes into "luxury" consumption. Defining luxury consumption as per capita consumption in excess of the average per capita consumption and taking total consumption to be 95 percent of total income, it appears that luxury consumption accounts for about 36 percent of income.[10] This means that luxury consumption provides a substantial potential reserve for additional taxation. Second, such private savings as there are originate largely in the very high income brackets, including corporate savings in which equity shares are

[9]See Richard M. Bird, "Income Redistribution, Economic Growth, and Tax Policy," *Proceedings*, Washington: National Tax Association, 1968.

[10]From Table 36-1, it can be calculated that the upper 25 percent of the population partake of 63 percent of consumption. Their luxury consumption (defined as that in excess of average per capita consumption) thus represents $63 - 25$, or 38 percent of total consumption. Since consumption as a whole is 95 percent of total income, this "excess" equals $.95 \times 38$, or 36 percent of total income.

owned. This means that highly progressive income taxation as well as high rates of profits tax cut heavily into private sector saving and thereby retard development.[11] Putting the two features together, we note that the key to development finance appears to lie in progressive consumption taxation.[12]

Ideally, this taxation would be applied in the form of a personal consumption tax, but few if any LDCs could do so effectively. As we have noted before, effective application of such a tax to higher incomes would require balance-sheet accounting as well as the reporting of earnings, which is difficult even for developed countries.[13] Practical policy must therefore make do with a less perfect approach, i.e., a set of excise taxes which impose higher rates on items that weigh more heavily in the outlays of higher-income households. To this may be added a progressive property tax on residences to deal with housing consumption. In this way, revenue can be obtained by drawing on the pool of luxury consumption, thereby reducing consumption inequality while stimulating rather than depressing saving.

Lest the advantages of this approach be overstated, two shortcomings need to be noted. For one thing, there still remains the problem of detrimental effects on work incentives. Such effects may be less in the case of consumption taxation than with progressive income taxation, but they are not eliminated. For another, progressive consumption taxes can reduce inequality of consumption but not inequality of income and wealth. Since the distribution of income and wealth is also significant in securing a broad sharing of development gains, progressive consumption taxes cannot entirely replace progressive income and wealth taxation. A proper balance between these forms of taxation is called for, such balance being superior to excessive reliance on the income tax approach.

Foreign Borrowing

Prior consideration was given to the role of loan finance in economic development when discussing public debt, but the problem should be noted once more in the present context.[14] The earlier conclusion was that development requires capital formation and that capital formation requires saving. Public investment which is financed by borrowing does not add to capital formation if it merely diverts funds otherwise available for private investment. This recognition also underlies the preceding model on the basis of which the required rate of taxation was determined.

The situation is different, however, if borrowing is from abroad. In this

---

[11]For emphasis on the importance of profits in the industrial sector as a source of saving, see W. A. Lewis, *The Theory of Economic Growth*, Homewood, Ill.: Irwin, chap. 5.

[12]See N. Kaldor, "The Expenditure Tax in a System of Personal Taxation," in R. M. Bird and O. Oldman (eds.), *Readings on Taxation in Developing Countries*, 2d ed., Cambridge, Mass.: Harvard Law School, International Tax Program, 1967, pp. 253–273.

[13]See p. 457. A particular difficulty in the case of LDCs is tax avoidance by shifting funds abroad, permitting tax-free spending outside the country. Tight exchange controls may therefore be necessary to close this loophole.

[14]See p. 710.

case, additional resources become available, as borrowing is accompanied by increased imports. This borrowing provides additional resources for investment and permits financing a given growth rate with a lower rate of tax and a higher rate of current consumption. While the net gain to future generations will be less than it would have been with tax finance, their surrender of consumption (to service the foreign debt) will be less burdensome than tax finance would have been to the initial generation. The reason is that other factors of production, such as labor, share in the productivity gain generated by the increased rate of capital formation. Because of this growth, the future cutback in consumption is made out of a higher level of income, and since the marginal utility of consumption declines with rising consumption levels, the resulting burden will be less severe.

It is thus the income gain to domestic factors which renders foreign borrowing such an important instrument of development policy. Other useful functions of capital import include the provision of foreign exchange and the collateral advantages gained from the introduction of advanced technology and managerial know-how.[15]

Aggregate Demand, Inflation, and Employment

In the above discussion, we have proceeded on the assumption of a fully employed economy. In this setting, the appropriate level of aggregate demand is given by the available level of output as valued at current prices. The basic rule for fiscal and monetary policy in this case is to let aggregate expenditures rise with the growth in full-employment output, neither faster nor slower. We now consider two ways in which this conclusion may be qualified.

Inflation as a Source of Saving   It has been argued at times that some degree of inflation will contribute to development because it may impose forced saving upon consumers. If credit expansion finances increased capital formation (public or private), rising prices reduce the real income of consumers, thus lowering consumption in real terms. In this way, inflation may serve to transfer real resources to capital formation.

Such indeed could be the outcome, but one hesitates to prescribe it as a policy guide. For one thing, inflationary credit creation may be used to finance consumption (especially public consumption) rather than capital formation. For another, the "inflation tax" is among the least equitable of all taxes. Moreover, the inflationary process easily becomes a habit and leads to distortion of investment decisions. Perhaps worst of all, inflationary expectations may lead to a reduction in private saving propensities. For these and other reasons, inflation cannot be recommended as a legitimate approach to development policy.

---

[15]As with all good things in life, there are also disadvantages and dangers. Foreign capital import may bring foreign control and retard the development of domestic managerial talent. For an emphasis on these aspects, see A. O. Hirschman, "How to Divest in Latin America and Why," in A. O. Hirschman (ed.), *A Bias for Hope*, New Haven, Conn.: Yale, 1971, pp. 225–253.

Underemployment and Unemployment Apart from avoiding inflation, may aggregate demand management not also be needed to assure full employment of resources? Put differently, the question is whether unemployment in LDCs is of a kind which can be remedied by an increase in aggregate demand, as is frequently possible in developed countries. This problem arises especially in the context of agriculture and migration to urban areas.

It is widely observed in LDCs that there is a surplus of agricultural labor in the sense that labor is only partially employed, except at harvesttime. Cannot such labor be drawn into industrial employment by increased demand based on a higher level of expenditures? The answer depends on the wages which such labor could obtain outside agriculture. If labor productivity is low, the gain might not suffice to offset the increased living costs which are incurred in movement from the farm. The problem may thus be one of low productivity rather than of unemployment; and if this is so, the remedy lies in capital formation and increased productivity rather than in a higher level of expenditures.

The existence of heavy urban unemployment in turn may come about as the result of out-migration, attracted by what appear to be high wages in the industrial or urban sector; but minimum wage legislation or union demands may place a floor below such wages which in turn may make it impossible to absorb the labor influx. As noted below, a remedy lies in tax provisions which counter the overpricing of labor in the market, with increased aggregate demand again an inappropriate measure.

At the same time, these difficulties do not preclude the existence of genuine "Keynesian" unemployment which can be met by more expansionary demand policy. Some observers have noted that in Latin American countries, existing capital stock is frequently underutilized, so increased employment should be possible. An expansionary fiscal policy, combined with measures to secure the necessary supportive resources, may be helpful in bringing this about.

C. TAX-STRUCTURE POLICY

We now turn to more specific issues of tax policy, beginning with a consideration of tax effort.

Taxable Capacity and Tax Effort

While it is important, in line with our earlier reasoning, to know what overall level of tax revenue is required to secure a given growth target, the feasibility of achieving that level of taxation is an important consideration which must be allowed for when the target is set. Tax policy must be considered along with other aspects of development policy, but it must not be looked at as the "dependent variable" in the system which will automatically respond to the requirements placed upon it.

How, then, can one judge what tax effort a country is capable of, and how can its tax performance be measured? We have noted in our earlier discussion of tax-structure development that the tax to GNP ratios in less developed countries are typically quite low, ranging from 8 to 18 percent. Among Latin American countries with per capita incomes below $400, the typical ratio is around 14 percent, with some countries as low as 8 percent. The ratios for African and Asian countries with similar per capita incomes tend to be somewhat (though not much) higher. This compares with developed-country ratios of 30 to 40 percent, as was shown in Figure 7-4.

Why is it that the tax effort in developing countries is so much lower, and does the lower ratio in fact signify a lower effort? The answer depends on what the term "tax effort" is taken to mean. An international lending agency may wish to make its aid contingent on the recipient country's making an adequate tax effort of its own. The lending agency may then require a country with a higher per capita income to show a higher revenue ratio in order to demonstrate the same level of tax effort.

A low-income country has less scope for the transfer of resources to public use.[16] At a very low level of per capita income, all private income is needed to meet the very necessities of life, such as food and shelter. Unless the public use of funds is to provide equally basic necessities (e.g., minimal health and sanitation programs), the diversion of funds involves an insupportably heavy current burden. This conclusion is modified where a highly unequal income distribution results in substantial luxury consumption. As noted before, this factor is frequently of considerable importance as a potential source of taxation.

Apart from the level and distribution of income, the availability of "tax handles" is related to the economic structure of the country. Thus, the administration of an income tax is much more difficult where employment is in small establishments. Profits taxation is not feasible until accounting practices attain minimal standards, and it is difficult if firms are small and unstable. Product taxes cannot be imposed at the retail level if retail establishments are small and impermanent. Effective land taxation is difficult where food is home-consumed, the agricultural sector is largely nonmonetized, and land surveys are inadequate in providing proper valuations. On the other hand, taxation is simplified in a highly open economy where imports and exports pass through major ports and thus can be readily established by tax authorities.

Finally, the feasibility of taxation depends upon how society views the need for compliance, the extent to which the courts are willing to enforce tax laws, and the availability of a competent and honest staff of tax administrators. Resort to tax farming, i.e., a system where collectors are given a percentage of their tax takes as an incentive, may be a helpful short-run device, as may be the assignment of revenue quotas to tax officials, but these are not methods on which a durable and equitable tax structure can be built.

For these and other reasons, a realistic appraisal of a country's tax effort has to allow for the tax handles which are available to it. A comparative

---

[16]See p. 156, where the relationship of "tax handles" to economic structure was discussed.

measure of tax effort may then be derived by comparing the actual ratio of revenue to GNP of a particular country with the ratio which would apply with an average response to such handles as are available. Using cross-section data from a set of LDCs, we may estimate an equation such as

$$T/Y = a + \alpha Y_p + \beta X/Y + \gamma E/Y + \delta A/Y$$

where T is revenue, Y is GNP, Y_p is per capita GNP, X is exports, E is output of extractive industries, and A is output of agriculture. We expect the α, β, and γ coefficients to be positive while δ will be negative. Having estimated the equation, we plug in the values of Y_p, X/Y, E/Y, and A/Y for a particular country to calculate its presumptive tax effort or T/Y ratio. Dividing the presumptive ratio by the actual T/Y ratio, we then obtain an index by which to compare the effort of this particular country with that of others.[17] While the results of such comparisons have to be used with care, they nevertheless offer a framework in which to appraise comparative tax efforts.

Although the setting of particular countries differs, it is usually argued that an LDC should be expected to achieve a tax to GNP ratio of at least 18 percent. Assuming one-half of this to be spent for current services and adding a private sector savings rate of 3 percent, an overall savings rate of 12 percent would be achieved. This has been postulated by W. A. Lewis as constituting the desirable minimum level.[18]

Tax-Structure Development

The problems associated with the design and administration of various taxes differ with the structure of the economy in which they are applied and with its climate of public attitudes toward taxation. However, they also differ with stages of economic development, and some general tax-structure characteristics in relation to per capita income may be observed.

Table 36-2 gives tax-structure comparisons for samples of countries at various levels of per capita income. We note the importance of taxes on external trade (mainly customs duties) and of taxes on domestic production and sales for low-income countries, as well as the low share of income taxes. As per capita income rises, the importance of income taxes increases relative to that of customs duties and taxes on domestic sales and production. Payroll taxes also rise in relative importance as per capita income increases.

In addition to changing shares under the major headings of the table, the nature of the various taxes also is subject to change. Thus, taxes classified as income taxes in low-income countries are frequently capitation taxes which

---

[17]For a recent analysis of this sort, see Alan A. Tait, Wilfred L. M. Graetz, and Barry J. Eichengreen, "International Comparison of Taxation for Selected Developing Countries, 1972–1976," *International Monetary Fund Staff Papers*, 1977.

For further discussion of such indices, see R. M. Bird, "A Note on Tax Sacrifice Comparisons," *National Tax Journal*, September 1964; H. Aaron, "Some Criticism of Tax Burden Indices," ibid., March 1965; and Bird, "Comment," ibid., September 1965.

[18]See Lewis, *The Theory of Economic Growth*, op. cit.

TABLE 36-2
Average Composition of Tax Structures for Sample of Countries at Various Levels of Per Capita Income

Per Capita Income in Dollars	Income Taxes	Taxes on Property	Taxes on International Trade	Taxes on Production and Sales	Total Excluding Payroll Taxes*	Payroll Taxes	Total
AS PERCENTAGE OF GNP							
Under 100	1.9	0.5	4.6	3.4	11.6	0.5	12.0
100–200	2.6	0.3	4.4	4.5	12.7	0.5	13.2
200–300	2.8	0.6	5.5	4.3	14.4	1.4	15.8
300–400	3.6	1.0	4.6	5.2	13.4	3.0	16.4
400–500	3.4	1.2	3.5	4.2	12.1	2.1	14.3
500–900	4.8	1.4	2.6	1.7	16.7	2.9	19.6
United States	14.8	5.7	0.3	5.3	25.0	5.7	30.8
AS PERCENTAGE OF TOTAL TAX REVENUE							
Under 100	16.3	4.1	38.5	28.0	96.7	3.3	100
100–200	19.6	2.0	33.4	33.8	96.3	3.7	100
200–300	17.5	3.9	35.2	27.3	91.3	8.7	100
300–400	22.3	5.9	27.9	30.6	81.8	18.2	100
400–500	23.4	8.4	34.7	29.2	84.9	15.1	100
500–900	24.7	7.5	13.5	8.5	85.3	14.7	100
United States	48.2	11.9	0.9	17.2	81.5	18.5	100

*Includes taxes not previously listed.
Note: Figures shown represent the unweighted averages for countries within each income category.
Sources:
For United States: See Table 15-1, p. 328. Data for 1970.
For other countries: Derived from R. J. Chelliah, "Trends in Taxation in Developing Countries," *International Monetary Fund Staff Papers*, July 1971, table 6, pp. 278–279.

bear little resemblance to the personalized individual income tax of developed countries. Similarly, the so-called business income tax is often closer to a sales tax than to a profits tax as applied in the developed countries, and so forth.[19]

Individual Income Tax

Turning now to particular taxes, we begin with the individual income tax. For various reasons, the individual income tax does not and cannot be expected to occupy the central position in the tax structure of LDCs which it typically holds in the developed countries. Nevertheless, the income tax should be established early and strengthened as development proceeds. It is elastic to growth in GNP and therefore a promising revenue source for development finance. Its contribution to total revenue in Latin American countries typically ranges around 20 percent and is thus a significant part of the revenue

[19]For further discussion of various taxes in the LDCs, see R. M. Bird and O. Oldman (eds.), *Readings on Taxation in Developing Countries*, 3d ed., Cambridge, Mass.: Harvard Law School, International Tax Program, 1975.

picture. This is true even though the feasibility of collecting a tax on wage and salary income in LDCs tends to be restricted to government, foreign corporations, and the rather limited group of large local enterprises. Employees of small establishments and the large group of self-employed, especially in agriculture, typically remain outside the orbit of the income tax. In part, this reflects exemption levels which are set high relative to average income, but it is also the result of ineffective enforcement and administration.

Difficulties in reaching capital income are even greater. The principle of self-assessment as followed in the United States is not workable. Official assessments are frequently negotiated rather than objectively based, and there is a substantial lag of final tax payment behind the income year. Use of tax withholding helps to speed up tax collections and is all to the good, but its applicability tends to be limited to the very types of wage and salary income which lend themselves to easy enforcement to begin with. This payment lag enjoyed by capital income is a substantial advantage especially where inadequate interest penalities are charged for delay and the real value of tax debts is eroded by inflation.

Although no reliable estimates are available, it may well be that the taxable income which is in fact reached usually amounts to less than one-half that which should be reached under tight enforcement. There is no magic formula by which these difficulties may be overcome. Source withholding, assignment of taxpayer numbers (especially to high-income returns), computerization and centralized handling of high-income returns, requirements for information returns on interest and dividend payments to be filed by corporations and banks, reduction in assessment lags, and higher penalities for delayed payments are all helpful. Yet they are insufficient unless the courts stand behind strict enforcement of the tax laws, a prime requirement which in the cultural and political context of developing countries is frequently difficult to meet.

Income tax administration, moreover, is bedeviled by the problem of inflation. It is not infrequent for developing countries to experience price level increases between 10 and 30 percent per year. Such, for instance, has been the case in Chile and in Brazil for many years. In adaptation to this, income tax administration may provide for an automatic annual increase in exemption levels and rate brackets as prices rise, so as to keep the relation between marginal rates and real income constant. As a result, the effect of inflation on income tax equity is neutralized, but the built-in inflation check exerted by an unadjusted progressive income tax is reduced.

The problem of capital gains, especially in relation to land and buildings, is of considerable importance in developing countries where rapid urbanization gives rise to increasing land values, much as was observed by Henry George toward the close of the nineteenth century in the United States. To meet this problem, a capital gains tax on real estate, i.e., buildings and land, is administered as a separate tax. As noted below, there is a strong economic, as well as equity, case for such a tax, especially if applied only to gains from land (as distinct from improvements).

Business Income Tax

The most difficult problems arise in the effective taxation of business income, whether under a separate corporation profits tax or as applied to partnership and proprietorship income under the individual income tax. Where business accounting has not been developed to a level sufficient to measure profits with reasonable accuracy, other methods have to be applied. Thus, many countries use a presumptive rather than a direct approach to profit determination. This may take the form of a presumptive profit margin on sales, with different margins stipulated for various industries. This method, which is widely used in Asian countries, in fact transforms the profits tax into a type of sales tax. This shift occurs since tax liability is a function of sales and the presumptive rather than actual margin.

In still other situations, the presumptive measure of profits is based on such indices as floor space and location by city blocks, a practice also to be found in the tax tradition of European countries, especially with regard to professional income. In the case of agriculture, acreage or head of cattle may be used as the presumptive base. At the same time, "stick and carrot" techniques might be used to reward the conscientious taxpayers by the use of so-called blue returns, while penalizing the laggard payers by penalty rates. Again, the process of improvement must be gradual and cannot run too far ahead of improvement in accounting methods. Tax reformers are frequently tempted to overlook the importance of improving the techniques of presumptive taxation in favor of preoccupation with technical refinements of corporation taxation which, though important in developed countries, apply to only a small part of the business sector in the LDCs.

Furthermore, the legal forms of business organization frequently differ. In Latin American countries, for example, continental European rather than common-law traditions prevail, while in Asian countries, a quite different system of property law may apply; and practices appropriate for a country such as the United States may not be applicable to LDCs, given their traditions and current state of development.[20]

Land Taxes

Since the agriculture sector in most LDCs is large, the problem of land taxation remains of major importance. One basic question is whether the tax should be imposed on the value of land, on actual income, or on the potential income which the land could yield under full utilization. In a perfectly competitive system, the three bases would be interchangeable since land values would equal the capitalized value of its income, and actual income would equal the potential. In reality, such is not the case. Land is frequently underutilized and held for speculative purposes or as a matter of social custom. Markets may be thin and current sales values not readily obtainable.

---

[20]For a discussion of business tax reform proposals, see R. Slitor, "Reform of the Business Tax Structure," in R. A. Musgrave and M. Gillis (ed.), *Fiscal Reform for Columbia*, Cambridge, Mass.: Harvard Law School, International Tax Program, 1971, pp. 463–530.

TABLE 36-3
Net Income from Land at Various Levels of Utilization and Types of Land Tax
(In Dollars)

	PERCENTAGE OF UTILIZATION				
	100	*90*	*50*	*20*	*0*
No Tax					
1. Income	100	90	50	20	0
2. Cost of underutilization to owner	0	10	50	80	100
10 Percent Tax on Actual Income					
3. Tax	10	9	5	2	0
4. Net income	90	81	45	18	0
5. Cost of underutilization to owner	0	9	45	72	90
10 Percent Tax on Potential Income					
6. Tax	10	10	10	10	10
7. Net income	90	80	40	10	−10
8. Cost of underutilization to owner	0	10	50	80	100
10 Percent Tax on Potential Income					
Plus Penalty Tax on Underutilization					
9. Tax	10	12.5	28.75	42.50	72.50
10. Net income	90	77.5	21.75	−22.50	−72.50
11. Cost of underutilization to owner	0	12.5	68.25	112.50	162.50

Thus, the three bases yield substantially different results. Moreover, the income tax is rarely applied effectively to the agricultural sector, so that land revenue frequently serves as a combined income and land tax, including not only the rent of land but also labor and improvement (capital) income in its base.

Turning now to the taxation of income from land only (excluding returns to labor and capital improvements), a strong argument can be made for basing such taxation on potential rather than on actual income.[21] This is shown in Table 36-3. Suppose that a parcel of land, at various levels of utilization and in the absence of tax, yields the income shown in line 1 of the table. The difference between actual and potential yield is given in line 2 and reflects the cost of underutilization to the owner. After a 10 percent tax on actual income is imposed, the cost of underutilization as shown in line 5 is reduced. Thus, underutilization is encouraged. This effect is avoided and the cost of underutilization is held at its pretax level if the tax is imposed on potential rather than actual income, with the result as shown in line 8. The reason is that the tax is independent of actual income so that the marginal tax rate is now zero. In line 9, we go a step further and supplement the 10 percent tax on potential income (line 6) with a penalty charge on underutilization. This charge, for purposes of illustration, rises in rate with the degree of underutilization. Thus, the first 25 percent of shortfall of actual below potential income pays a tax of 25 percent. The next 25 percent (i.e., a shortfall between 25 and 50 percent of potential income) pays at a rate of 50 percent,

[21]See J. Hicks and U. Hicks, "The Taxation of the Unimproved Value of Land," in Bird and Oldman, op. cit., pp. 431–442; and R. Bird, *Taxing Agricultural Land in Developing Countries*, Cambridge, Mass.: Harvard Law School, International Tax Program, 1973.

rising to 75 percent on a shortfall between 50 and 75 percent and to 100 percent on a shortfall between 75 and 100 percent. As shown in line 11, the cost of underutilization is now increased substantially above the pretax level, and net income at low levels of utilization becomes negative. The marginal tax rate on additional income turns negative and the tax on deficient income is in fact a tax on idle land.

Whichever approach is taken, the availability of adequate land surveys and their maintenance on an up-to-date basis are an essential requirement for an efficient system of land taxation. Frequently such surveys are not available, so that only haphazard methods of assessment can be applied.

Wealth and Property Taxes

In addition to land revenue, the taxation of urban real estate is an important part of the tax base, especially as urbanization proceeds. As noted before, a good case can be made for progressive taxation of residential property, combining multiple residences in one base so as to supplement the system of commodity taxation on luxury consumption other than housing.

Beyond this, wealth taxation of the net worth type is a frequent component of the tax structure in LDCs. Although such taxes may in the end prove to be little more than part of the system of real property taxation, with intangibles largely escaping the tax base, they are a useful supplement to income taxation as it applies (or rather fails to apply) to capital income. Real capital is visible and, once accounted for under the wealth tax, earnings therefrom may be traced to its owners under the income tax.

Commodity Taxes and Tariffs

The design of commodity taxation involves three major problems: (1) what products should be taxed and at what rates; (2) at what stages such taxes should be imposed; and (3) how taxation of domestic products should be related to import duties.

As noted previously, the twin objectives of protecting savings and of modifying a highly unequal state of distribution point to the taxation of luxury consumption as the most obvious solution. Given that implementation of a personal type of expenditure tax is hardly feasible for LDCs, the situation calls for taxation of luxury consumption. If this view is correct, the basic requirement is not for a comprehensive and flat-rate sales tax but for a system of sales taxation with differing rates.[22] The implementation of progressive consumption taxation by differentiation between products thus depends on the existence of products with sharply different income elasticities, a precondition which appears to be met in developing countries.

The stage or stages at which commodity taxes are to be imposed has to be decided on grounds of administrative feasibility and thus depends upon

---

[22]It should be noted that the distinction is not between types of products which, on nutritional or ethical grounds, may be considered as essential (e.g., bread) rather than as frills (e.g., butter) but simply between commodities which weigh more heavily in high-income and low-income budgets.

the structure of the particular economy. With a multiple-stage tax of the value-added type, failure to reach the retail stage involves only a partial revenue loss, not the total loss that would be the result under a retail sales tax. Moreover, use of the invoice method contributes to better compliance.[23] On the other hand, taxation of final products at differential rates tends to be more difficult under the value-added approach. Where products comprising an important part of the tax base originate in relatively large manufacturing establishments, manufacturer excises offer the simplest and most direct approach. In any case, there is no need to rely on one or the other approach exclusively. A combination of methods may be applied, depending on what is most expedient in any particular case.[24]

There remains the need for coordinating domestic excises with import duties. In their desire to impose heavier burdens on luxury consumption, LDCs frequently place higher import duties upon luxury products. At the same time, this measure often goes with a failure to match such duties by corresponding excises on home-produced luxury goods. Thus, luxury tariffs tend to provide protection to domestic substitutes. This is clearly poor policy. If protective tariffs are to be used to permit domestic infant industries to develop, such industries should be chosen according to their development potential and not as a side effect of luxury taxation. The best approach may well be to use largely uniform tariff rates while including luxury imports in the tax base of the domestic excise system.

Another aspect of tariff policy which requires critical review is the practice of excluding domestically used capital goods from customs duties.[25] In a situation where, for various reasons, the cost of capital tends to be undervalued relative to the cost of labor, this practice accentuates the price distortion, a matter which will be discussed later.

D. TAX INCENTIVES

We have seen that the twin objectives of economic growth and reduction of inequality can be secured best by reliance on progressive consumption taxes; but we have also seen that equity calls for this approach to be combined with the taxation of capital income under a progressive income tax. Given the potential conflict of the latter with investment incentives, it is not surprising that much attention has been given to various devices by which detrimental investment effects can be minimized. It is a matter of policy judgment, transcending considerations of tax policy only, how far a country should go in trading distributional equity for growth gains; but it is the task of tax

---

[23]See p. 462.

[24]J. Due, *Indirect Taxation in Developing Countries*, Baltimore: Johns Hopkins, 1970; and M. Gillis, "Objectives and Means of Indirect Tax Reform," R. A. Musgrave and M. Gillis (eds.), *Fiscal Reform for Columbia*, Cambridge, Mass.: Harvard Law School, International Tax Program, September 1971, pp. 559–573.

[25]Exclusion of domestically used capital goods is to be distinguished from the exclusion of raw materials or intermediate products which in turn enter into exports, this being an unobjectionable policy.

policy to make sure that additions to growth are bought at the least equity cost. Tax relief for investment which does not pay for itself in generating additional growth not only involves revenue loss without gain but, by giving the relief to high incomes, worsens the state of income distribution.

Judged on these grounds, tax incentives to investment have been generally wasteful and inequitable, so much so that many observers have been led to reject all incentive devices. But notwithstanding the rather dismal experience, total rejection is not justified. Political pressures for tax incentives will prevail no matter what the tax technician may say; and this being inevitable, they may as well be designed as efficiently as possible. Moreover, some concessions to growth may be in order provided they are made in the best way.

Domestic Incentives

In dealing with the incentive problem, it is helpful to distinguish between domestic incentives and the incentive problem as it relates to foreign capital in particular. Domestic incentives might be related to investment in general, or they might be limited to investment in selected industries or regions. Finally, incentives may be designed to stimulate exports and to strengthen the balance of payments.

General Incentives   General investment incentives may take the form of investment credits or accelerated depreciation similar to the devices used in developed countries.[26] In addition, LDCs frequently offer tax holidays during which profits from new enterprises are tax-free for an initial period of, say, five to seven years. This method relates the value of the incentive to high initial profitability, which may run counter to the need for stable and more long-run types of investment. For the case of new investment by existing firms, there is the further difficulty of distinguishing between earnings attributable to the new and old components of their capital stock. Once more this problem is avoided by an investment credit or investment grant approach. Moreover, it is a poor policy for government to make long-run commitments to tax subsidies, especially where it is hoped that there will be a declining need for such subsidies in the future.

However this may be, general investment incentives cannot be effective in raising the overall level of investment unless equal attention is given to raising the level of saving. This may be done by encouraging retention of profits as well as by giving tax credits for saving under the individual income tax. The problem, of course, is to reach savings which otherwise would not have been made and to avoid their being offset by dissaving in other parts of the taxpayer's accounts. Thus, many of the same difficulties arise as were noted previously in the context of the expenditure tax.[27]

[26]For a discussion of tax incentives in developing countries, see George E. Lent, "Tax Incentives in Developing Countires," in Bird and Oldman, op. cit.

[27]See p. 457.

Growth Industries While the effectiveness of general investment incentives is questionable, there is more reason to expect that incentives limited to particular sectors or industries will be effective in diverting capital to such industries. The big problem here lies in how to select the industries which are to be given preferential treatment.

Presumably, the industries which should be chosen are those which play a strategic role in development and which, without special favor, will remain underexpanded. Undoubtedly there exist external economies in the development process which are not allowed for in private investment decisions; and imperfect capital markets may misdirect investment even without externalities. Wise correction of such investment errors would thus be desirable, but experience has not been encouraging. Frequently the list of eligible industries is so broad as to involve little selection. In other instances, selection reflects political pressure groups, and in still others, incentives are given to sustain the market for public enterprises, such as steel mills, which should not have been constructed in the first place. Although selective use of incentives is good in principle, efficient application is hard to find.

Regional Incentives Another form of selective incentive arises in regional policy. As we have argued previously, a general case can be made for fiscal neutrality in location decisions, whether for labor or capital.[28] Yet, conditions in developing countries may call for departure from this rule. Labor may be immobile, or maintenance of the labor force in particular regions may be preferable either because excessive migration from rural to urban areas is undesirable or because national policy for noneconomic reasons calls for some degree of equalization in regional development rates. Special incentives may then be given to development in such regions.

The question is whether such incentives are given best by subsidizing investment or by subsidizing employment in the target regions. The answer depends upon the policy objective, i.e., whether the focus is on increasing production or value added in the region, or whether the purpose is to increase payrolls and to raise the standard of living of the region's population. With the latter a wage subsidy may well prove more effective, especially if there is a substantial reserve of unemployed (or underemployed) labor in agriculture which can be drawn into industrial employment if labor costs are reduced.[29] Recent evidence on an experiment with a tax credit scheme to develop the Brazilian Northeast, perhaps the most ambitious regional tax credit effort on record, points toward the inability of capital incentives to generate a high degree of labor absorption in the target area.[30]

---

[28]See p. 531.

[29]See Charles E. McLure, "The Design of Regional Tax Incentives for Columbia," in Musgrave and Gillis, op. cit., pp. 545–556. See also R. M. Bird, "Tax Subsidy Policies for Regional Development," *National Tax Journal*, June 1966.

[30]For a hopeful early appraisal, see Hirschman, *A Bias for Hope*, op. cit., pp. 124–158. For a less encouraging second look, see David E. Goodman, "Industrial Development in the Brazilian Northeast: An Interim Appraisal of the Tax Credit Scheme of Article 34/18," in R. Roett, *Brazil in the Sixties*, Nashville, Tenn.: Vanderbilt, 1972.

Capital versus Employment Incentives

The issue of capital versus wage subsidies transcends the regional issue. While incentive policy has been generally directed at increasing the profitability of capital, recent discussion has pointed toward an alternative approach which would increase the profitability of employing labor. This approach reflects dissatisfaction with an emerging pattern of development which involves increased use of capital without a corresponding increase of employment in the industrial sector. This pattern, which results from the use of highly capital-intensive and labor-saving techniques, runs counter to the objective of a broadly based development in which the gains are shared by large sectors of the population.

Use of highly capital-intensive forms of investment is encouraged by price distortions which overprice the cost of labor and underprice the cost of capital. The former tends to result from minimum wage legislation and excessive union demands, while the latter reflects preferential exchange rates, tariff exemptions, and ineffective profits taxation. In order to redress the balance, wage subsidies might be given either directly or through a "wage-bill credit" similar in principle to the investment credit. Alternatively, profits tax relief may be made contingent on the use of more labor-intensive equipment. Such measures might be appropriate in connection with regional incentives where the objective is to raise income levels in backward areas. It might also be appropriate in dealing with unemployment which results from an excessive influx of rural population into urban areas.[31] Another suggestion for inducing more labor-intensive use of capital is to provide tax incentives which reduce the labor cost for night-shift work.[32]

Incentives to Foreign Capital

Foreign capital, as noted previously, plays an important role in development policy, and tax incentives may be helpful in channeling it to the uses which are most desirable for the whole country.

From the national viewpoint, the role of tax incentives to foreign capital differs from that of incentives to domestic capital. While the latter merely involve transfers between the treasury (which loses revenue) and the investor (who gains), tax relief granted to foreign investors reduces the whole country's share in the profits earned by foreign capital. This loss must therefore be compensated for by the gains from additional capital influx if the tax incentive is to pay its way. The design of incentives may be helpful in directing foreign capital into such uses as are advantageous to the host country. The gains to be derived from foreign capital lie in the increased earnings for domestic factors of production to which the foreign capital gives rise. There is little advantage to the host country in foreign capital which

[31]See A. Harberger, "On Measuring the Social Opportunity Cost of Labor," *International Labor Review*, June 1971.

[32]See D. M. Schydlowsky, "Fiscal Policy for Full Capacity Industrial Growth in Latin America," in *Economic Development in Latin America*, Gainesville: University of Florida Press, 1975.

brings its own resources with it and uses the foreign location as a production site only.[33] Tax incentives therefore should be linked to domestic value added which the foreign capital induces. Moreover, they should be designed to encourage reinvestment and permanent operation, while discouraging quick-kill types of investments.[34]

However this may be, the LDC needs the cooperation of the investor's country of origin if effective incentives are to be granted. If the country of capital ownership taxes its foreign-earned income at its own rate while giving a foreign tax credit, lower taxation by the LDC merely results in a transfer to the other country's treasury while leaving no advantage to the investor who repatriates profits. Tax deferral, however, becomes of major importance. It not only serves to attract capital to the LDC which offers a tax incentive but also exerts a continuing incentive to reinvest earnings in the LDC. Therefore there is good reason for maintaining deferral on investment in LDCs while terminating it for investment in the developed countries.

Another device which would render incentives effective to foreign investors who intend to repatriate is the so-called tax-sparing arrangement. Under this provision, the country of capital ownership would extend a credit, upon repatriation, equal to the full tax in the LDC even though a lesser tax or no tax is paid under the incentive arrangement. This approach, however, lacks the incentive for reinvestment; and, as political pressures call for the incentive to be generalized to all domestic investment, taxation of profits in general is undermined.

A final point arises in connnection with competition among LDCs for foreign capital. To the extent that one country outbids another by offering larger incentives, LDCs as a group stand to lose. Some degree of cooperation is desirable to avoid self-defeating tax competition. This is one of the important roles of common market arrangements among groups of LDCs, such as are planned for the West Indies.

Export Incentives

Tax incentives for exports are a popular device to assist in the development of foreign markets and to strengthen the balance of payments. Such incentives, to be effective, should be related not to total foreign sales or profits therefrom, as is the typical practice, but to domestic value added. It is only the latter component of foreign sales, and not the reexport of imported material or intermediate goods, which adds to a country's foreign exchange earnings.

E. EXPENDITURE POLICY

The role of expenditure policy in economic development has been explored less extensively than that of tax policy, and comparative data are more

---

[33]"Tax haven" types of investments which result in office structures but little local employment, for example, offer little advantage to the host country.

[34]See J. Heller and K. M. Kauffman, *Tax Incentives in Less Developed Countries*, Cambridge, Mass.: Harvard Law School, International Tax Program, 1963.

TABLE 36-4
Average Expenditure Ratios for Selected Countries, 1967

	Africa	Latin America	Asia	Europe, United States, and Canada
		AS PERCENTAGE OF GNP		
Expenditures on:				
Education	3.1	3.2	3.2	4.0
Health	1.4	1.3	1.2	2.8
Defense	1.6	2.3	5.0	3.3
Transfers	3.6	4.1	3.2	16.4
Other*	13.0	11.4	7.2	10.7
Total	22.7	22.3	19.8	37.2
	AS PERCENTAGE OF TOTAL EXPENDITURES			
Expenditures on:				
Education	13.7	14.3	16.2	10.8
Health	6.2	5.8	6.1	7.5
Defense	7.0	10.3	25.3	8.9
Transfers	15.9	18.4	16.2	44.1
Other*	57.3	51.1	36.4	28.8
Total	100.0	100.0	100.0	100.0

*Equals difference between itemized expenditures and tax revenue.
Note: Items may not add to total due to rounding.
Source: Based on G. S. Sahota, *Public Expenditures and Income Distribution in Panama*, unpublished manuscript with data based on United Nations, *Statistical Yearbook, 1968*, and *Yearbook of National Accounts Statistics*, 1968. Material used with kind permission of author.

difficult to obtain.[35] However, comparisons of expenditure budgets for a sample of countries in various parts of the world are offered in Table 36-4. In comparing the patterns of African, Latin American, and Asian countries with those of European countries, some evidence regarding the role of per capita income is obtained. Low-income countries direct a higher share of expenditures to education and health services and a lower share to transfers. The higher share for education to some degree reflects the higher cost of educational services in these countries. The higher share of transfers in high-income countries reflects the more developed social security systems.

The strategic role of public investment in economic development has already been noted. This role is based in part on the undeveloped state of private capital markets and in part on local scarcity of entrepreneurial talent; it is also based on the fact that the type of investment needed at the earliest stages of development frequently includes very large outlays, such as those involved in the development of transportation systems or the opening up of undeveloped parts of the country. Moreover, infrastructure investment of this sort carries external benefits which call for public provision.

It is not surprising, therefore, that the development of public investment performs a major function in the design of development plans in LDCs. In

[35] See our earlier discussion of the relationship of expenditure growth to per capita income, p. 149.

this context, the use of cost-benefit analysis is of great importance. Developing countries can ill afford to waste scarce resources, and yet efficient project evaluation is a difficult task. In one respect, cost-benefit analysis is more readily applied in developing than in developed countries. This is because public investment is typically aimed at the provision of intermediate goods, the value of which may be measured in terms of their effects upon the prices of privately provided goods.[36] Thus the return on transportation or irrigation projects may be appraised in terms of the resulting reduction in the cost of goods as they reach the market. This is a measure which cannot be applied where public outlays go to provide final goods of the consumption type. But in other respects, the task of evaluation is more difficult.

For one thing, the direct benefits thus made available will be accompanied by indirect or external benefits which are harder to assess. For another, costs are more difficult to determine. Since market prices may not reflect the true social costs involved, shadow prices must be used in their place. If capital is undervalued while labor is overvalued, the use of market prices leads to the previously noted distortion toward excessively capital-intensive technology. Further difficulties arise in the context of dynamic development where relative prices which apply when the project is introduced may give way to a quite different set of prices applicable during the years when the services of the project are rendered. Once more, this possibility points to the importance of longer-run planning and the evaluation of individual projects in the context of an overall development plan.

Another factor of obvious importance is proper determination of the discount rate. With private capital markets not fully developed, use of a "social rate" may be more or less inevitable. Considerations suggesting the presence of external benefits indicate that the social rate should be set below the level of rates prevailing in the market, thus pointing to a higher rate of capital formation and the choice of longer-term projects. Pointing in the other direction is the fact that the cost of forgoing current consumption is very high at low levels of income; yet, in the future when the gain from postponement is realized, the marginal utility of consumption will be less since income is higher. This fact tends to be overlooked in individual savings decisions but should be allowed for by government. But here, as in other matters of discount rate determination, cruder approaches are likely to be used. In the typical development context, the government may find itself confronted with the practical necessity of determining the politically acceptable minimum path of consumption over the next five or ten years and may derive the discount rate therefrom.

Human investment, as noted before, deserves particular consideration in the development context. Education programs are important not only as a matter of growth policy but also for their important bearing on how the gains from growth will be distributed both among income groups and among various sectors of the economy. Studies have shown exceedingly high rates of

[36]See p. 176.

return on educational investment in developing countries, thus pointing to the particular importance of this form of capital formation, but it is essential that the educational inputs be designed to meet the country's need for specific labor skills.

F. SUMMARY

Fiscal policy in less developed countries differs in important respects from that in highly developed countries. This variation is due to the fact that the economic and social setting in LDCs is different:

    1. The fundamental need for capital formation and the difficulty of generating the required level of saving out of a low per capita income are dominant factors.

    2. Measures to induce technological improvement, to encourage enterprise, and to develop institutions making for more efficient use of resources are also of major importance.

    3. Pursuit of these objectives is made difficult by social and political factors as well as deficient administrative capabilities.

    4. Foreign trade is usually of prime importance, as is the need for foreign exchange adequate to secure the necessary imported capital equipment.

    5. Sectoral divisions within the economy tend to create bottlenecks and to interfere with balanced growth.

These are but some of the difficulties which arise and which must be considered in the formulation of fiscal policy:

    6. Given the target rate of growth, a certain rate of capital formation is needed. The savings rate—public and private—must be set so as to match the needed rate of capital formation.

    7. Measuring the contribution of the public sector to overall savings by the surplus in the current budget, this surplus must equal the excess of required total saving over available private saving. From this figure, the required rate of taxation may be deduced.

    8. The requirement for a tax structure which secures an adequate level of saving must be reconciled with the requirement for tax equity.

    9. While severe taxation of saving and investment by individuals and corporations may be counterproductive because it may retard growth, a substantial tax base is available in the consumption of higher-income households.

    10. While the primary concern with growth renders the fiscal policy rules applicable in LDCs more akin to those developed in Chapter 31 than to those of Chapters 27 and 28, the contingency of deficient demand with underemployment of the labor force and of inflation nevertheless arises.

    11. Indeed, inflation generated by budgetary policy is frequently found in developing countries, and it interferes with efficient resource use.

Turning to the problems of tax policy, we have dealt with the general problems of taxable capacity and the composition of the tax structure as well as with the design of particular taxes:

12. The ratio of tax to GNP of LDCs is much below that of developed countries. This fact reflects lower taxable capacity as well as lower tax effort.

13. At low levels of per capita income, tax "handles" are scarce. The tax structure tends to be dominated by production and sales taxes, especially customs duties, with a low share for profits and income taxes.

14. Effective administration of income and profits taxes is difficult owing to such factors as a high degree of self-employment, the small size of establishments, and inadequate accounting practices. In addition, taxpayer compliance and enforcement tend to be low with large-scale evasion, especially of capital income. Use of presumptive taxes has to be relied on.

15. Agricultural taxation is of major importance in most LDCs because of the relatively large scope of their agricultural sectors. However, effective taxation of land and agricultural income is unpopular and difficult to implement.

16. Wealth and property taxes may be a useful supplement to ineffective taxation of capital income.

17. Implementation of a general sales tax at the retail level is difficult because of the small scale of establishments. Typically, taxation at the manufacturer's level is more feasible and may be combined with use of value-added taxation for some products.

18. As distinct from a flat-rate consumption tax, taxation of luxury products at higher rates, with equal treatment of domestically produced and imported goods, permits a more equitable use of consumption taxes.

19. LDCs tend to make widespread use of tax incentives to investment. Frequently, these are not very effective and create tax inequities.

20. Tax incentives to foreign capital should aim at maximizing domestic value added.

21. The incentive structure should be designed to consider effects on employment as well as effects on investment.

Turning, finally, to the role of expenditure policy, we have noted these points:

22. Public investment and public lending play strategic roles in development.

23. The concept of public capital formation should be interpreted to include productivity-increasing investment in human resources.

24. Foreign borrowing increases the current supply of available resources and thus permits development with a lesser burden on the present generation.

FURTHER READINGS

Bird, R. M.: *Taxing Agricultural Land in Developing Countries*, Cambridge, Mass.: Harvard Law School, International Tax Program, 1973.

_____, and O. Oldman (eds.): *Readings on Taxation in Developing Countries*, 3d ed., Cambridge, Mass.: Harvard Law School, International Tax Program, 1975.

Chenery, Hollis B., et al.: *Redistribution with Growth*, Washington: World Bank and Oxford University Press, 1974.

Hinrichs, H.: *A General Theory of Tax Structure Change During Economic Development*, Cambridge, Mass.: Harvard Law School, International Tax Program, 1966.

Musgrave, R. A., and M. Gillis (eds.): *Fiscal Reform for Columbia*, final report and staff papers of the Columbian Commission on Tax Reform, Cambridge, Mass.: Harvard Law School, International Tax Program, September 1971.

―――: *Fiscal Systems*, part 2, New Haven, Conn.: Yale, 1969.

Prest, A. R.: *Public Finance in Under-Developed Countries*, London: Weidenfeld and Nicholson, 1962.

Appendix

Economic Recovery Tax Act of 1981

Part I

Changes in Tax Law

While the administration's initial proposal included an across-the-board cut in income tax rates and a speedup in depreciation only, the legislation as enacted included many other provisions as well. These provisions mostly arose as a matter of bargaining over the legislation. The following summary includes only the major items.

A. INDIVIDUAL INCOME TAX

The major emphasis is on individual income tax reduction, reductions which account for about 75 percent of the total revenue lost.

Rate Cuts

1. Personal exemptions and the standard deductions (or zero-bracket amounts) are unchanged (p. 336). Levels of tax-free income (p. 379, Table 17-6) are similarly unchanged.
2. The act provides for cumulative rate cuts with rates on 1981 income $1\frac{1}{4}$ percent below 1980 levels, rates on 1982 income 10 percent below 1980 levels, rates on 1983 income 19 percent below 1980 levels, and rates from 1984 on 23 percent below these levels. Table 16-1 (p. 337) is revised accordingly and shown below.

3. Corresponding reductions in withholding rates go into effect on October 1, 1981, October 1, 1982, and July 1, 1983.

4. The top-bracket rate on unearned income is reduced from 70 to 50 percent, effective January 1, 1982. With the differential between earned and unearned income eliminated, the maximum-tax provision (p. 375) drops out. Note that the top rate is then kept at 50 percent and not subject to further reductions in 1982–1984. However, the bracket limit to which it applies is raised.

5. Additional Table 16-1A has been included below to show the tax cut from 1980 to 1984. Except for the top of the scale, the cut ranges around 22 percent. At the top, the reduction is less for taxpayers with earned income and previously subject to the 50 percent maximum rate; it is more for taxpayers with unearned income and previously subject to rates from 50 to 70 percent.

6. Tax responses to inflationary changes in income are updated in a revised Table 17-9 as shown below. Our earlier comparison between 1980 and 1970 (see p. 387) had shown a reduction in effective rates (for given levels of real income) at the bottom of the scale, a substantial increase around $50,000 (1970 level), and a modest rise above it. Comparison of 1984 with 1980 shows little change in effective rates up to $110,000 (1980 level) and a sharp drop at higher levels. Comparing 1984 with 1970, there is little change up to $10,000 (1970 level), a substantial increase in the $25,000-to-$50,000 range, and some drop at the very top. The inflation-induced shift in the tax burden toward the middle-upper part of the income range continues. It may also be noted that with the exemption and standard deduction held constant, the real value of income levels at which tax liability begins is reduced.

7. Table 17-4 (p. 374) is updated to give 1983 liabilities and is shown below.

Other Provisions

8. While the provisions relating to the *earned-income tax credit* (p. 381) are unchanged, the amounts of refund go up somewhat. As shown in revised Table 17-7 included below, this reflects the lower positive tax offset due to reduced rates.

9. *Long-term capital gains* continue to be included at 40 percent (p. 350). However, with the top-bracket rate reduced from 70 to 50 percent, the rate on long-term gains falls from 28 to 20 percent. The holding period required for gains to be long-term is reduced from one year to six months.

10. The *"marriage tax"* for two-earner couples (p. 383) is reduced by permitting a deduction of 5 percent of the earnings of the lower-earning spouse, with an upper deduction limit of $1,500. In 1983 these amounts are raised to 10 percent and $3,000. Table 17-8 is adjusted accordingly and included below. Comparison of line 20 in the new and old tables shows that the marriage penalty for partners with equal earnings is reduced, especially at the lower end of the scale. Comparison of line 12

shows that for unequal earners the previous penalty is turned into a subsidy, again especially for low earners.

11. The maximum expense against which the *child care credit* can be applied is raised from $2,000 to $2,400 for each of the first two dependents. The rate of credit is raised from 20 to 30 percent for taxpayers with incomes below $10,000, dropping to 20 percent for incomes above $28,000.

12. Nonitemizers may deduct *charitable contributions* (p. 361) in addition to the standard deduction. For 1982, the deduction is limited to 25 percent of the first $100 of contribution. Thereafter the allowance rises until the entire contribution may be deducted in 1986. This provision expires after 1986.

13. The treatment of gains from *sale of first residence* is liberalized in two ways. The amount excludible by taxpayers aged fifty-five and over is raised from $100,000 to $125,000, and more time is permitted for purchase of a new residence under the rollover provision.

14. The first $75,000 of *income earned abroad* (p. 771) is made excludible, rising to $95,000 in 1986.

15. Various provisions are made to provide *savings incentives*. These include:

    a. Up to $1,000 ($2,000 for joint returns) of investment in qualified savings certificates issued by banks and thrift institutions may be excluded. The certificates must have one-year maturity, must have a yield equal to 70 percent of one-year Treasury bills, and must be issued prior to January 1, 1983.

    b. The upper limit for individual retirement account contributions is raised from $1,500 to $2,000.

    c. The maximum annual deduction for contributions to a self-employed retirement plan (Keogh or HR 10) is raised from $7,500 to $15,000.

    d. Employee stock ownership and dividend reinvestment plans are liberalized.

    e. The present interest and dividend exclusion (p. 348) of $200 ($400 for joint returns) is repealed after 1981. A $100 dividend exclusion takes its place.

Indexing

16. Starting in 1985, tax brackets, the standard deduction, and personal exemptions are to be adjusted for increases in the consumer price index (p. 386). The first adjustment will take place for returns on 1985 income.

B. CORPORATION INCOME TAX

Reductions in the corporation income tax account for approximately 20 percent of the overall revenue loss, largely reflecting a speeding up of depreciation allowances.

Rate Reduction

The 46 percent rate applicable to the bulk of corporate income (p. 397) remains unchanged. The rates applicable to small corporations are reduced as follows:

Taxable Income ($)	1980	1982	1983 on
Less than 25,000	17%	16%	15%
25,000–50,000	20	19	18
50,000–75,000	30	unchanged	unchanged
75,000–100,000	40	unchanged	unchanged
Over 100,000	46	unchanged	unchanged

Depreciation

The act replaces the present Asset Depreciation Range (ADR) system of depreciation (p. 413) with an Accelerated Cost Recovery system. Whereas ADR was intended to reflect economic asset lives and included many categories, lives provided under ACR are considerably shorter and only five classes of assets are provided for, as follows:

a. Tangible personal property (machinery and equipment) is grouped into four classes. A three-year group includes autos and trucks; a five-year group includes most equipment; utility property with ADR lives of eighteen to twenty-five years is depreciated in ten years; and longer-lived utility property is depreciated in fifteen years.
b. All real property (structures) is written off over fifteen years.
c. These shortened depreciation periods apply to new and old assets alike. In addition, the speed of depreciation within the stated periods is increased for new assets. For assets acquired in 1981–1984, 150 percent declining balance is to apply, to be raised to 200 percent declining balance for assets acquired in 1985 and after. Real property is to be depreciated using 175 percent declining balance.
d. As an aid to small business, a certain amount of property may be expensed, i.e., written off fully in the first year; $5,000 of personal property may be expensed in 1982, rising to $10,000 in 1985.

The intention of the new system is to move away from the concept of depreciation in line with length of economic life, so as to extend accelerated depreciation generally to all assets. The new system is also designed to offset the effects of inflation on the real value of the depreciation base (p. 419), but it has been criticized as not dealing correctly with this aspect such as would be accomplished by a system of replacement-cost depreciation or some variant thereof.

Investment Tax Credit

Under past law (p. 438) the investment tax credit was $3\frac{1}{3}$ percent for assets with ADR lives of three to four years, $6\frac{2}{3}$ percent for assets with lives of six years, and 10 percent for longer-lived assets. Under the new law, assets in the three-year ACR group are given a credit of 6 percent and all longer assets a credit of 10 percent. The used-property limitation is liberalized, and the carryover for unused credit is extended from seven to fifteen years.

Other Provisions

The act introduces numerous other provisions pertaining to the taxation of business income, including the following:

1. A 25 percent tax credit is given for certain *research expenditures* in excess of base-period amounts.
2. Various provisions are introduced to liberalize the tax treatment of *small business*.
3. The *windfall profits tax* is reduced in various ways:
   a. Royalty owners are given an exemption of 2 barrels a day of royalty production, to be raised to 3 barrels in 1984.
   b. Starting in 1983, stripper oil produced by independent producers is to be exempted.
   c. The tax on newly produced oil is reduced from 30 percent to 27.5 percent in 1982, with subsequent declines to 15 percent in 1985.
4. Capital gains treatment for *stock options* is liberalized.
5. The *targeted jobs tax credit* is extended but for 1982 only.

C. ESTATE AND GIFT TAX PROVISIONS

Various provisions are made to liberalize the estate and gift tax including the following:

1. The *marital deduction* previously limited to one-half of the estate (p. 497) is raised to 100 percent so that the entire estate may be left tax-free to the surviving spouse.
2. Under prior law, a *credit against tax* (combined for estate and gift taxes) of $47,000 was given equivalent to an exemption of $175,625 (p. 497, note 5). The credit is to be raised to $62,800 for 1982 with an exemption equivalent of $225,000. By 1987 the credit is to rise to $192,800 with an exemption equivalent of $600,000.
3. The *maximum rate* of 70 percent is to be reduced by 5 percent a year down to 50 percent in 1984.
4. The annual *gift tax exclusion* is increased from $3,000 to $10,000.

D. REVENUE EFFECTS

The revenue effects of the legislation as estimated for a five-year period are as follows:

	FISCAL YEARS (in $ Million)		
	1982	*1984*	*1986*
1. Individual income tax provisions	−26,929	−114,684	−196,143
2. Business tax cut provisions	−10,657	− 28,275	− 54,468
3. Energy tax provisions	− 1,320	− 2,252	− 3,619
4. Savings incentive provisions	− 247	− 4,208	− 8,375
5. Estate and gift tax provisions	− 204	− 3,218	− 5,568
6. Other provisions	+ 1,701	+ 1,674	+ 546
7. Total	−37,656	−149,963	−267,627

Source: Summary of H.R. 4242, *The Economic Recovery Tax Act of 1981*, prepared by Joint Committee on Taxation, Aug. 5, 1981, p. 57.

Note that the rising amounts of estimated revenue loss reflect both the gradual going into effect of the new provisions and the rising levels of tax base due to growth of GNP. The former factor is especially important in line (2) where the liberalized depreciation rules come to apply to an increased asset base.

TABLE 16-1, UPDATED
Tax Rate Schedule, Joint Return

Amount of Income* ($)	TAXABLE YEAR					
	1982		1983		1984 ON	
	Tax on Lower Limit ($)	Rate on Excess (%)	Tax on Lower Limit ($)	Rate on Excess (%)	Tax on Lower Limit ($)	Rate on Excess (%)
Under 3,400	—	—	—	—	—	—
3,400–5,500	—	12	—	11	—	11
5,500–7,600	252	14	231	13	231	12
7,600–11,900	546	16	504	15	483	14
11,900–16,000	1,234	19	1,149	17	1,085	16
16,000–20,200	2,013	22	1,846	19	1,741	18
20,200–24,600	2,937	25	2,644	23	2,497	22
24,600–29,900	4,037	29	3,656	26	3,465	25
29,900–35,200	5,574	33	5,034	30	4,790	28
35,200–45,800	7,323	39	6,624	35	6,274	33
45,800–60,000	11,457	44	10,334	40	9,772	38
60,000–85,600	17,705	49	16,014	44	15,168	42
85,600+	30,249	50				
85,600–109,400			27,278	48	25,920	45
109,400+			38,702	50		
109,400–162,400					36,630	49
162,400+					62,600	50

*Amount of income equals AGI minus personal exemptions and minus excess of itemized over standard deduction. The latter is reflected in the zero-rate bracket.

ADDITIONAL TABLE 16-1A
Tax Reduction 1980–1984
(Joint Return, Single Earner, without Dependents)

Amount of Income*	TAX LIABILITY				
	1980		1984	% Reduction	
$ 5,500	$ 294		$ 231	21.4	
11,900	1,404		1,085	22.7	
20,200	3,273		2,497	23.7	
35,200	8,162		6,274	23.1	
60,000	19,466		15,168	22.1	
	(a)	(b)		(a)	(b)
109,400†	44,166	47,332	36,630	17.1	22.6
215,000†	96,966	117,292	88,900	8.3	24.2

*AGI minus personal exemption and minus excess of itemized over standard deduction.
†Col. (a) assumes earned income only, while col. (b) assumes unearned income only.

TABLE 17-4, UPDATED
Effective Rates of Tax, 1983
(Joint Return, Single Earner, without Dependents)

AGI (I)	Income Subject to Tax (II)	Tax (III)	Tax as Percentage of Income Subject to Tax (III ÷ IV)	Tax as Percentage of AGI (III ÷ I)
$ 5,400	$ —	$ —	—%	—%
10,000	4,600	564	12.3	5.6
20,000	14,400	2,188	15.2	10.9
30,000	22,600	4,020	17.8	13.4
50,000	39,000	9,144	23.4	18.3
100,000	80,000	26,310	32.9	26.3
200,000	162,000	66,702	41.2	33.4

Col. II equals AGI minus personal exemptions and minus deductions. It falls short of the income shown in Table 16-1 by the amount of the standard deduction. Computation of tax in col. III assumes deductions equal to 18 percent of AGI or standard deduction, whichever is larger.

TABLE 17-7, UPDATED
Positive and Negative Taxes on Earned Income, 1983

AGI	Single (I)	Joint* (II)	Joint, Two Dependents (III)	Joint, Four Dependents (IV)
$ 2,000	$ —	$ —	$ −200	$ −200
3,000	—	—	−300	−300
4,000	77	—	−400	−400
5,000	199	—	−500	−500
6,000	341	66	−400	−400
7,000	491	176	−300	−300
8,000	641	296	−134	−200
9,000	791	426	76	−100
10,000	951	564	296	66

*One earner only.

TABLE 17-8, UPDATED
Income Tax Liabilities for Single and Joint Returns*
(1983 Levels)

	COMBINED AGI		
	$10,000	*$50,000*	*$100,000*
Single Earner			
1. Tax, single	951	11,273	31,123
2. Tax, joint	564	9,144	26,310
3. Tax effect of marriage (2−1)	−387	−2,129	−4,813
4. 3÷1	−.41	−.19	−.15
Two Earners: 3/4 to 1/4			
5. AGI of A	7,500	37,500	75,000
6. AGI of B	2,500	12,500	25,000
7. Singles tax on A	608	7,215	20,873
8. Singles tax on B	—	1,390	3,873
9. 7+8	608	8,605	24,746
10. Joint tax	527	8,707	25,210
11. Tax effect of marriage (10−9)	−81	−102	−464
12. 11÷9	−.13	−.01	−.02
Two Earners: 1/2 to 1/2			
13. AGI of A	5,000	25,000	50,000
14. AGI of B	5,000	25,000	50,000
15. Singles tax on A	199	3,873	11,273
16. Singles tax on B	199	3,873	11,273
17. 15+16	398	7,746	22,546
18. Joint tax	491	8,269	24,990
19. Tax effect of marriage (18−17)	+93	+523	+2,444
20. 19÷17	+.23	+.07	+.11

*Assumes deduction equal to 18 percent of AGI or standard deduction, whichever is larger.

TABLE 17-9, UPDATED
Change in Tax Burden with Inflation, 1970–1984
(Joint Return, One-Earner Family without Dependents)

AGI, REAL INCOME EQUIVALENTS			TAX LIABILITIES					
1970 *($)*	*1980* *($)*	*1984* *($)*	*1970 Income* *($)*	*1970 Law* *(%)*	*1980 Income* *($)*	*1980 Law* *(%)*	*1984 Income* *($)*	*1984 Law* *(%)*
5,000	11,000	14,300	489	9.8	882	8.0	1,149	8.0
10,000	22,000	28,600	1,328	13.3	2,827	12.9	3,528	12.3
25,000	55,000	71,500	3,820	15.3	11,267	20.1	15,181	21.2
50,000	110,000	143,000	10,902	21.8	29,402	26.7	41,167	28.8
100,000	220,000	286,000	30,882	30.9	86,960	39.5	99,360	34.7
500,000	1,100,000	1,430,000	227,601	45.4	557,032	50.6	568,400	39.7

Explanation:
AGI levels for 1980 equal 220% of 1970 levels, corresponding to the increase in the consumer price index of 120%. AGI level for 1984 equals 130% of 1980 level, assuming an average annual price rise of 7.5%.

1980 tax liabilities reflect capital income so that 50% limit does not apply. Deductions are assumed to equal 18% of GNP or standard deduction, whichever is larger.

Part II

Budget Outlook

In Table 30-1A (see below) we summarize the five-year budget outlook as given in OMB's *Mid-Session Review of the Budget*, July 15, 1981.

Overall Outlook

As shown in lines 1–3, receipts are estimated to rise more rapidly than outlays, leading to a balanced budget in 1984 and a surplus thereafter. The increase in receipts (line 1) allows for the revenue loss from tax reduction as proposed in the administration plan and as shown in lines 5–7. Note that the revenue loss is more than offset by built-in revenue gain due to the rising level of GNP (see line 30). The expenditure projections allow for budget cuts made this year and additional cuts (see line 19) to be made in later years.

The revenue loss under the original administration program (see line 7) may be compared with the estimated revenue loss from actual legislation (see line 8). The two are quite similar for the years up to 1984. The estimated loss from the actual legislation, however, is substantially larger for 1985 and 1986, reflecting the allowance for indexing which was not included in the original administration proposal. We have therefore added line 4 to our table showing the adjusted deficit which results if revenue loss from actual legislation is allowed for. The budget remains in deficit until 1984, and the deficit rises after that. Presumably achievement of a balanced budget would now call for larger expenditure cuts than are provided for in line 19.

Receipts

The revenue development (administration proposal) is shown in detail in lines 8 to 12. Note in particular the declining importance of the corporation income tax in the overall picture.

Outlays

Levels of outlays in current dollars and by major expenditure categories are shown in lines 14 to 20. Line 14 shows the sharp increase in national defense. Line 15 shows payments to individuals to rise in nominal terms, while line 16 shows grants to remain largely unchanged. As shown in lines 20–23, national defense expenditures increase substantially even in real terms, while other programs decline in real terms. With grants remaining constant in nominal terms, there will be a substantial decrease in real terms, placing increased burdens on state and local governments.

Lines 24–26 show the rising share of national defense and falling share of other programs in total outlays. Lines 27–29 show an increasing ratio of national defense outlays to GNP and a declining ratio for other outlays. Note that the overall ratio is estimated to fall from 23 percent in 1981 to 18.6 percent in 1986.

Economic Assumptions

These projections, especially for receipts, depend heavily on the underlying economic forecast. The administration's assumptions are given in lines 30–35. Defended as realistic by the administration, these assumptions have been criticized by others as overly optimistic, including the postulated increase in real GNP (line 32), the postulated decline in unemployment (line 34), and the sharp drop in interest rates (line 35). It also remains to be seen whether the planned cutbacks in expenditure programs will materialize and what future Congressional responses will be, especially since the program, if carried out, will call for substantial further cuts in social programs.

ADDITIONAL TABLE 30-1A
Budget Outlook, 1980–1986*
(Fiscal Years, Billion Dollars)

	Actual 1980	ESTIMATED					
		1981	*1982*	*1983*	*1984*	*1985*	*1986*
1. Receipts	520	606	662	706	759	840	923
2. Outlays	580	661	705	729	759	835	895
3. Balance	−60	−56	−43	−23	—	6	28
4. (3) Adj.[1]	...	−56	−43	−24	1	−10	−14
Revenue Loss							
5. Individual inc. tax	—	—	−28	−75	−120	−139	−160
6. Corporate inc. tax	—	−2	−10	−19	−31	−45	−66
7. Total	—	−2	−38	−94	−151	−183	−226
8. (7) Adj.[2]							
Receipts							
9. Individual inc. tax	244	286	303	317	337	386	442
10. Corporate inc. tax	65	63	67	72	76	77	75
11. Social ins. tax	161	187	214	239	263	292	323
12. Other	50	70	78	78	85	85	83
13. Total	520	606	662	706	759	840	923
Outlays							
14. National defense	136	160	188	225	254	302	341
15. Payments to individuals	237	276	296	317	337	360	383
16. Grants	92	95	88	89	89	90	92
17. Interest	53	69	76	74	68	65	64
18. Other	63	61	56	55	55	55	58
19. Additional cuts	—	—	—	−29	−44	−39	−43
20. Total	580	661	705	729	758	834	895
Outlays in 1972 $							
21. National defense	73	77	82	91	97	109	116
22. Other	222	220	209	194	185	187	188
23. Total	295	297	291	285	282	296	304
As Percentage of Total[3]							
24. National defense	23	24	27	31	33	36	42
25. Other	77	76	73	69	67	69	58
26. Total	100	100	100	100	100	100	100
As Percentage of GNP							
27. National defense	5.3	5.6	5.9	6.3	6.4	6.9	7.1
28. Other	17.3	17.4	16.1	14.0	12.6	12.1	11.5
29. Total	22.6	23.0	22.0	20.3	19.0	19.0	18.6
Economic Assumptions							
30. GNP	2,626	2,951	3,296	3,700	4,097	4,500	4,918
31. GNP in 1972 $	1,481	1,519	1,570	1,648	1,721	1,794	1,870
32. % change in (31)	−0.2	2.6	3.4	5.0	4.5	4.2	4.2
33. Inflation rate	13.5	9.9	7.0	5.7	5.2	4.6	4.2
34. Unemp. rate	7.2	7.5	7.3	6.6	6.2	5.8	5.5
35. Interest rate	11.5	13.6	10.5	7.5	6.8	6.0	5.5

*With the exception of lines 4 and 8 the table is drawn from Office of Management and Budget, *Midsession Review of the Budget*, July 15, 1981.

[1]Line 4 is obtained by raising line 3 by the difference between lines 7 and 8.

[2]Balance adjusted for the difference between (7) and (8). Whereas line 7 shows the revenue loss from the administration proposal, since the *Midsession Review* was prepared prior to the August 1981 legislation, line 8 shows the revenue loss from the actual legislation. *Source:* Summary of H.R. 4242, prepared by the staff of the Joint Committee on Taxation, Aug. 15, 1981.

[3]Based on lines 14–20.

Name Index

Name Index

Subject Index

Subject Index

843